C000179097

Early English Books Online (EEBO) Editions

Imagine holding history in your hands.

Now you can. Digitally preserved and previously accessible only through libraries as Early English Books Online, this rare material is now available in single print editions. Thousands of books written between 1475 and 1700 and ranging from religion to astronomy, medicine to music, can be delivered to your doorstep in individual volumes of high-quality historical reproductions.

We have been compiling these historic treasures for more than 70 years. Long before such a thing as "digital" even existed, ProQuest founder Eugene Power began the noble task of preserving the British Museum's collection on microfilm. He then sought out other rare and endangered titles, providing unparalleled access to these works and collaborating with the world's top academic institutions to make them widely available for the first time. This project furthers that original vision.

These texts have now made the full journey -- from their original printing-press versions available only in rare-book rooms to online library access to new single volumes made possible by the partnership between artifact preservation and modern printing technology. A portion of the proceeds from every book sold supports the libraries and institutions that made this collection possible, and that still work to preserve these invaluable treasures passed down through time.

This is history, traveling through time since the dawn of printing to your own personal library.

Initial Proquest EEBO Print Editions collections include:

Early Literature

This comprehensive collection begins with the famous Elizabethan Era that saw such literary giants as Chaucer, Shakespeare and Marlowe, as well as the introduction of the sonnet. Traveling through Jacobean and Restoration literature, the highlight of this series is the Pollard and Redgrave 1475-1640 selection of the rarest works from the English Renaissance.

Early Documents of World History

This collection combines early English perspectives on world history with documentation of Parliament records, royal decrees and military documents that reveal the delicate balance of Church and State in early English government. For social historians, almanacs and calendars offer insight into daily life of common citizens. This exhaustively complete series presents a thorough picture of history through the English Civil War.

Historical Almanacs

Historically, almanacs served a variety of purposes from the more practical, such as planting and harvesting crops and plotting nautical routes, to predicting the future through the movements of the stars. This collection provides a wide range of consecutive years of "almanacks" and calendars that depict a vast array of everyday life as it was several hundred years ago.

Early History of Astronomy & Space

Humankind has studied the skies for centuries, seeking to find our place in the universe. Some of the most important discoveries in the field of astronomy were made in these texts recorded by ancient stargazers, but almost as impactful were the perspectives of those who considered their discoveries to be heresy. Any independent astronomer will find this an invaluable collection of titles arguing the truth of the cosmic system.

Early History of Industry & Science

Acting as a kind of historical Wall Street, this collection of industry manuals and records explores the thriving industries of construction; textile, especially wool and linen; salt; livestock; and many more.

Early English Wit, Poetry & Satire

The power of literary device was never more in its prime than during this period of history, where a wide array of political and religious satire mocked the status quo and poetry called humankind to transcend the rigors of daily life through love, God or principle. This series comments on historical patterns of the human condition that are still visible today.

Early English Drama & Theatre

This collection needs no introduction, combining the works of some of the greatest canonical writers of all time, including many plays composed for royalty such as Queen Elizabeth I and King Edward VI. In addition, this series includes history and criticism of drama, as well as examinations of technique.

A treatise of the fift [sic] general councel held at Constantinople, anno 553, under Justinian the emperour, in the time of Pope Vigilius the occasion being those Tria Capitula, which for many yeares troubled the whole church (1636)

George Crakanthorpe

A treatise of the fift [sic] general councel held at Constantinople, anno 553, under Justinian the emperour, in the time of Pope Vigilius the occasion being those Tria Capitula, which for many yeares troubled the whole church

Crakanthorpe, Richard, 1567-1624.
Crakanthorpe, George, b. 1586 or 7.
Errata: p. [1] at end.
Signatures: [par.]3, A6, [symbol]2, B-Z6, 2A-2X6.
[22], 506, [9] p.
London : Printed for R.M., and part of the impression made over for the benefit of the children of Mr. Iohn Minshawe, 1636.
STC (2nd ed.) / 5984.5
English

Early History of Travel & Geography

Offering a fascinating view into the perception of the world during the sixteenth and seventeenth centuries, this collection includes accounts of Columbus's discovery of the Americas and encompasses most of the Age of Discovery, during which Europeans and their descendants intensively explored and mapped the world. This series is a wealth of information from some the most groundbreaking explorers.

Early Fables & Fairy Tales

This series includes many translations, some illustrated, of some of the most well-known mythologies of today, including Aesop's Fables and English fairy tales, as well as many Greek, Latin and even Oriental parables and criticism and interpretation on the subject.

Early Documents of Language & Linguistics

The evolution of English and foreign languages is documented in these original texts studying and recording early philology from the study of a variety of languages including Greek, Latin and Chinese, as well as multilingual volumes, to current slang and obscure words. Translations from Latin, Hebrew and Aramaic, grammar treatises and even dictionaries and guides to translation make this collection rich in cultures from around the world.

Early History of the Law

With extensive collections of land tenure and business law "forms" in Great Britain, this is a comprehensive resource for all kinds of early English legal precedents from feudal to constitutional law, Jewish and Jesuit law, laws about public finance to food supply and forestry, and even "immoral conditions." An abundance of law dictionaries, philosophy and history and criticism completes this series.

Early History of Kings, Queens and Royalty

This collection includes debates on the divine right of kings, royal statutes and proclamations, and political ballads and songs as related to a number of English kings and queens, with notable concentrations on foreign rulers King Louis IX and King Louis XIV of France, and King Philip II of Spain. Writings on ancient rulers and royal tradition focus on Scottish and Roman kings, Cleopatra and the Biblical kings Nebuchadnezzar and Solomon.

Early History of Love, Marriage & Sex

Human relationships intrigued and baffled thinkers and writers well before the postmodern age of psychology and self-help. Now readers can access the insights and intricacies of Anglo-Saxon interactions in sex and love, marriage and politics, and the truth that lies somewhere in between action and thought.

Early History of Medicine, Health & Disease

This series includes fascinating studies on the human brain from as early as the 16th century, as well as early studies on the physiological effects of tobacco use. Anatomy texts, medical treatises and wound treatment are also discussed, revealing the exponential development of medical theory and practice over more than two hundred years.

Early History of Logic, Science and Math

The "hard sciences" developed exponentially during the 16th and 17th centuries, both relying upon centuries of tradition and adding to the foundation of modern application, as is evidenced by this extensive collection. This is a rich collection of practical mathematics as applied to business, carpentry and geography as well as explorations of mathematical instruments and arithmetic; logic and logicians such as Aristotle and Socrates; and a number of scientific disciplines from natural history to physics.

Early History of Military, War and Weaponry

Any professional or amateur student of war will thrill at the untold riches in this collection of war theory and practice in the early Western World. The Age of Discovery and Enlightenment was also a time of great political and religious unrest, revealed in accounts of conflicts such as the Wars of the Roses.

Early History of Food

This collection combines the commercial aspects of food handling, preservation and supply to the more specific aspects of canning and preserving, meat carving, brewing beer and even candy-making with fruits and flowers, with a large resource of cookery and recipe books. Not to be forgotten is a "the great eater of Kent," a study in food habits.

Early History of Religion

From the beginning of recorded history we have looked to the heavens for inspiration and guidance. In these early religious documents, sermons, and pamphlets, we see the spiritual impact on the lives of both royalty and the commoner. We also get insights into a clergy that was growing ever more powerful as a political force. This is one of the world's largest collections of religious works of this type, revealing much about our interpretation of the modern church and spirituality.

Early Social Customs

Social customs, human interaction and leisure are the driving force of any culture. These unique and quirky works give us a glimpse of interesting aspects of day-to-day life as it existed in an earlier time. With books on games, sports, traditions, festivals, and hobbies it is one of the most fascinating collections in the series.

The BiblioLife Network

This project was made possible in part by the BiblioLife Network (BLN), a project aimed at addressing some of the huge challenges facing book preservationists around the world. The BLN includes libraries, library networks, archives, subject matter experts, online communities and library service providers. We believe every book ever published should be available as a high-quality print reproduction; printed on-demand anywhere in the world. This insures the ongoing accessibility of the content and helps generate sustainable revenue for the libraries and organizations that work to preserve these important materials.

The following book is in the "public domain" and represents an authentic reproduction of the text as printed by the original publisher. While we have attempted to accurately maintain the integrity of the original work, there are sometimes problems with the original work or the micro-film from which the books were digitized. This can result in minor errors in reproduction. Possible imperfections include missing and blurred pages, poor pictures, markings and other reproduction issues beyond our control. Because this work is culturally important, we have made it available as part of our commitment to protecting, preserving, and promoting the world's literature.

GUIDE TO FOLD-OUTS MAPS and OVERSIZED IMAGES

The book you are reading was digitized from microfilm captured over the past thirty to forty years. Years after the creation of the original microfilm, the book was converted to digital files and made available in an online database.

In an online database, page images do not need to conform to the size restrictions found in a printed book. When converting these images back into a printed bound book, the page sizes are standardized in ways that maintain the detail of the original. For large images, such as fold-out maps, the original page image is split into two or more pages

Guidelines used to determine how to split the page image follows:

• Some images are split vertically; large images require vertical and horizontal splits.
• For horizontal splits, the content is split left to right.
• For vertical splits, the content is split from top to bottom.
• For both vertical and horizontal splits, the image is processed from top left to bottom right.

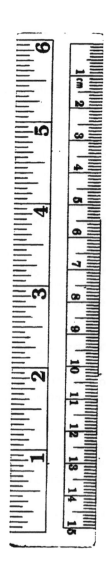

MICROFILMED — 1984

A

TREATISE

OF THE FIFT

GENERAL COVNCEL

held at Conſtantinople, *Anno* 553. under
Juſtinian the Emperour, in the time of
Pope Vigilius:

The Occaſion being thoſe *Tria Capitulà*, which for
many yeares troubled the whole Church.

WHEREIN IS PROVED THAT THE POPES

Apoſtolicall Conſtitution and definitiue ſentence in matter
of Faith, was condemned as hereticall by the Synod.

And the exceeding frauds of Cardinall *Baronius* and
Binius are clearely diſcovered.

BY

Rich: Crakanthorp Dr. in Divinitie, And
Chapleine in Ordinary to his late Majeſtie
KING IAMES.

Opus Poſthumum

PVBLISHED AND SET FORTH
BY
His Brother Geo: Crakanthorp,
Acording to a perfect Copy found written under the Authors owne hand.

LONDON,
Printed for R. M. 1636.

And part of the Impreſsion made over for the benefit of
the Children of Mr. *Iohn Minſhawe.*

Pope Vigilius.

The Occasion being those Five Capitula, which for

And part of the Impression made over for the benefit of

TO
THE RIGHT
HONOVRABLE
EDVVARD LORD NEWBVRGE
Chancellour of the Duchie of *Lancaster*,
and one of the Lords of his Majesties most
Honourable Privie Counsell.

RIGHT HONOVRABLE,

N all duty and submißion I here present unto your Lordship a Treatise concerning the fift generall Councell held at Constantinople, the cause being the Controversie of the Three Chapters which for many yeares troubled the whole Church, and was at length decided in this Councell held under Iustinian that religious Emperour. This Treatise, now printed, was long agoe penned by one well known unto your Honour; your sincere affection to the truth of God and Gods cause, gives mee good assurance of your favourable acceptance hereof. I confesse indeed, that when I call to minde the manifold affaires wherein your Honour is daily imployed, the very thought hereof had almost perswaded mee not to interrupt your more serious affaires, by drawing your Honour to the reading or view of this

¶3   *Booke;*

Booke: but when I call to minde those respects of love and duty, in which the Author hereof stood bound unto your Lordship, I was againe incouraged in his name to tender it to your Honour: And although I my selfe can challenge no interest in your Lordships favour to offer this, yet your Lordship may challenge some interest in the fruits of his labours, who was so truely (as I can truely speake) devoted unto your Honour. Among many other, hee especially acknowledged two assured bonds of love and duty by which hee was obliged unto you, and your friends; the former arose from that unfained affection which you ever bare him from your first acquaintance in the Colledge; that other, by which he was further ingaged unto you, and your friends, was, when in a loving respect had unto him in his absence, without any meanes made by him, or knowledge of his, he was called by that much honoured Knight Sir Iohn Levison his Patron, your Father in law, unto the best [a] meanes of livelihood he ever enjoyed in the Ministery, where spending himselfe in his studies, hee ended his dayes; during which time your Honour made your affection further knowne unto him by speciall expressions of extraordinary favours: In regard whereof I perswaded my selfe, that I could no where better crave Patronage for this worke, than of your Honour, that it may bee a further testimony of his love againe, who cannot now speake for himselfe. And this I intreat leave to doe, the rather, because I doubt not but hee acquainted your Lordship with his paines and intent in this, and other Tractates of the Councels; [b] for when after divers yeares study bestowed

[a] Black Notly in Essex.

[b] See his Epistle to the Reader for the defence of Justinian, printed Anno 1616.

" flowed in this argument of Councels, hee was defi-
" rous to make some use of his labours; his intent was,
" to reduce all those points into foure severall Bookes;
" 1. That the right of calling generall Councels;
" 2. That the right of highest Presidency in them;
" 3. That the right of the last and supreme Confir-
" mation of them, is onely Imperiall and not Papall.
" 4. That all the lawfull generall Councels which
" hitherto have beene held, consent with ours, and op-
" pugne the doctrines of the present Church of
" Rome. Some of these bee finished, the fourth bee
" could not so much as hope to accomplish, and there-
" fore after the examining of some particulars there-
" in, hee desisted and weaned himselfe from those stu-
" dies: And yet after some yeares discontinuance,
" being by some of his learned friends sollicited to
" communicate to others, at least some one Tract in that
" argument, consenting to their earnest desire, after
" long suspence hee resolved on this Treatise, as being
" for weighty and important matters most delightfull
" unto him. That it was not then published, let it not
" seeme strange unto your Honour, for having long
" since finished the Tract of this whole Councell, it
" was his purpose, that it should have undergone the
" publike view and judgement of the Church; but when
" he came (as I can truely testifie) unto them, whose
" art and ayde is needfull in such a businesse, and found
" an averseness in them, for that it wholly consisted of
" controversall matters, whereof they feared that this
" age had taken a satiety, he rested in this answer, as
willing to bury it. After this, being upon a speciall
command

AN
ADVERTISEMENT
TO THE CHRISTIAN REA-
der touching the Scope, Argument and manifold Vſe of this enſuing Treatiſe.

T is not ambition to live in other mens writings, but deſire, if I could, to breath ſome life into them, which hath drawn me of late rather to preface other mens works, than to perfit mine owne. It grieved me much to ſee ſuch evidences lie in the darke, which being produced to publike view, would give ſingular light to the truth : And if *Socrates*, the mirrour of modeſty in a Philoſopher, held it no diſparagement to profeſſe, that he performed the office of a *Midwife* to other mens *wits*, by helping them in the *deliverie* of thoſe conceptions wherein himſelfe had no part : why ſhould I either feare or regard any detraction from the living, for a charitable office in this kinde to the dead ? doubtleſſe if the office of a *Midwife* be at any time needfull, it is then moſt neceſſarie, when the living Child is to be take out of the dead wombe of the parent : Such was this *Poſthumus*, in whom I hope the obſervation of [a] *Plinie* concerning children thus borne will bee verified : *For the moſt part (ſaith hee) thoſe Chil-dren prove moſt lively and fortunate, of whom the Parents dye in tra-vell, never ſeeing them live, who coſt them their lives.* The in-ſtances are many & very illuſtrious, *Fabius* [b] *Caſo* thrice Con-ſul, *Scipio* ſurnamed the Africane, *Iulius Caeſar* the firſt & moſt renowned of all the Romane Emperours, and our peerleſſe K. *Edward* 6. Howbeit I confeſſe, it is an hard thing to *calculate the nativity* of a Book, and certainly foretell what hazzard the

A 2 impreſſion

[a] *Plin. Nat. Hiſt. l. 7. c. 9. Auſpicacius eneſia Parente naſcun-tur, ſicut Scipio Africanus pri-miſque Ceſarum à Ceſo matris utero dictus : ſimili modo na-tus et Manlius qui Carthaginem cum exercitu in-travit.*
[b] *Tert. lib. de reſur. carnis. Poſſumus illos recogitare qui execto matris utero vivi acrem hanſerunt, Labe-rii aliquiet Scipiones et Fa-bius Ceſo ter Conſul.*

h Bell. de Rom.
Pontif.lib.4.ca.1
in disputatione
de verbo Dei.
Iam ostendimus
iudicem contro-
versiarum non
esse scripturam,
nec seculares
Principes,&c.
ac proinde ulti-
mum iudicium
summi Pontifi-
cis esse.
i Bell.de Rom.
Pontif.lib.4.ca.5
in fine. Si Papa
erraret praecipi-
endo vitia,vel
prohibendo vir-
tutes,teneretur
Ecclesia credere
vitia esse bona,et
virtutes malas,
nisi vellet contra
conscientiam
peccare.
k Bulla Pij 4.
super forma ju-
ramenti professi-
onis fidei,anno
Dom.1564.
l Skulkę. Apolog.
pro Bell.ca.6.
Pontificia pote-
stas est vel ut
cardo,fundamę-
tū,et ut uno ver-
bo dicam,summa
fidei Christiane.
m 2 Tim.3.16.
n Bell.de ve,bo
Dei non scripto
lib.4.ca.4.
Etiamsi scriptu-
ra dicat libros
Prophetarum,et
Apostolorum esse
divinos,tamen
non certo id cre-
dam,nisi prius
crediderō,scrip-
turam quae hoc
dicit esse divi-
nam, nam etiam
in Alchorano
Mahometi pas-
sim legimus
ipsum Alcho-
ranum de Caelo
à Deo missū,&c
o Quicunq́, non
innititur do-
ctrine Romanae
Ecclesiae, ac Ro-
mani Pontificis
tanquā regulae fi-
dei infallibili,a
quā etiam sacra Scriptura robur trahit et authoritatę,hereticus est : cōtra Lutherū.

ners of the Popes transcendent power, and uncontrou-
lable *verdict* in matters of *eternall life and death.* The [h] Cardi-
dinall thus flourisheth, *In our disputations about the word of*
" *God we have already shewed, that the Scripture is not the Iudge of*
" *Controversies, nor are secular Princes, nor private persons,*
" *though learned and honest, but Ecclesiasticall Prelates; in our dis-*
" *putations of the Councels it shall bee demonstrated, that Councels*
" *generall and particular may judge of Controversies in religion, but*
" *that judgement of theirs is then of force and validity when the*
" *Pope shall confirme it, and therfore that the last judgement of all is*
" *the Popes,* to which all good Catholikes owe such absolute
" obedience, *that* [i] *if the Pope should erre by commanding vices*
" *and prohibiting vertues,the Church is bound to beleeve that vices*
" *are good,and vertues bad,unlesse she wil sinne against Conscience.*
What,sinne against Conscience in not sinning,and not sinne
against Conscience in committing sinnes knowne by the
light of nature, if the *Man of sin* command the one and forbid
the other ? *Woe bee to them,*saith the Prophet, *that call evill good,*
and good evill, put darknesse for light,and light for darknesse, bitter
*for sweet ,and sweet for bitter,*Esay.5.20. If *Bellarmines* divinity
be currant, Pope *Pius* the fourth needed not to have coyned
twelve new Articles [k] of faith, affixt to the Canons of the
Councell of *Trent :* it had beene sufficient to have added this
one, *I beleeve in the Pope his soveraigne infallibility,* for this is *pro-*
ra and *puppis,* the *Alpha* and *Omega,* the *formalis ratio* and *de-*
monstratio διʼ ἥν of a Papists beliefe. *The Popes power* (saith *Skul-*
kenius [l]) *is the hinge and foundation, and,* to speake in a word,
the summe of Christian faith : A short summe and soone cast
up. What then serves *Fathers, Councels, Church-Traditions,* and
Scripture it selfe for with them ? for little better than Ciphers,
which being added to the Popes authority in their Arithme-
tike makes something, but without it nothing. To begin
with Scriptures,they beleeve them to bee divine, but not because the Scripture saith,*that all Scripture* [m] *is given by divine in-*
spiration : For so (saith [n] *Bellarmine*) *wee read every where in the*
Alcoran of Mahomet,that the Alcoran was sent from God,yet we be-
*leeve it not;*why then doe they beleeve them to bee the word
of God ? hee answers readily, *propter traditionem Ecclesiae,*
for the Churches tradition. [o] *Silvester Pierius* outvies the Cardinall,

nall, affirming, *that the holy Scripture taketh force and authority from the Romane Church and Pope.* Vpon which promise of *Pierius Gretzer* [p] inferres this peremptory conclusion, *We doe receive and reverence that alone for the word of God which the Pope in Peters Chaire doth determine to be so.* Strange divinity to beleeve, that the Scriptures receive their authority from the Church, that is; that God receives his authority from man. May we not justly upbraid the present Romanists, as *Tertullian* [q] doth the ancient heathen, *apud vos de humano arbitratu divinitas pensitatur; nisi homini Deus placuerit, Deus non erit; Homo jam Deo propitius esse debebit; With you Deity is estimated by mans valuation, unlesse God please man; he shall not be God. now man must bee propitious to God;* for if the Pope be not propitious to the Scripture to allow it for Gods word, it shall not passe for such in Rome.

As for the Fathers; they deale with their writings as *Faustus Manicheus* did with the writings of the Apostles, in [r] which hee takes it for a good proofe, that such passages are the Apostles *true writings; because they made for him; others were spurious, because they made against him :* Fathers, saith [ſ] *Dureus, are not to bee accounted Fathers, when they teach or write any thing of their owne, which they have not received from the Church,* meaning the Romane; and *Gretzer* [t] backs this assertion with a reason drawn from the formall definition of a Father : *for,* saith he, *he is a father of the Church, who feeds and nourisheth the Church with wholesome doctrine, who being set over the Lords houshold, gives them their measure of Corne in due season;* now if in stead of wholesome food and good Corne hee give them Cockle and Tares, he becomes no father but a stepfather, no Doctor but a seducer.

To instance in some particular; *Eusebius Cæsariensis* when hee seemes to favour Popery, hee is highly extolled by *Lindane* [u], *Senensis* [x], and *Possevine* [y], hee is then *a most famous writer of the Church, most learned, worthy to bee Bishop, not of one City onely, but of the whole world;* but when the same *Eusebius* lookes awry upon Rome, then hee is branded by *Canus* [z], *Costerus* [a], and *Baronius* [b], for *a stickler for Arrius, an Arrian heretike, a ringleader of the Arrian faction, whose memory is accursed in the second Synod of Nice.* Tertullian likewise is guilded by *Lindanus* [c] and *Rehing* [d], with the glorious titles of *a very noble Author;*

---

p Gretz. defenſ. Bell. lib. 1. de verbo Dei. Id ſolum pro verbo Dei veneramur as ſuſcipimus, quod nobis Pontifices ex Cathedra Petri tradit.

q Tertul. Apol. adverſus gentes ca. 5.

r Auguſt. lib. 11. contra Fauſtum Manichæum, ca. 2. inde probo inquiebat Fauſtus, hoc iſtius eſſe, illud non eſſe, quia hoc pro me ſonat, illud contra me.

ſ Dureus adverſus Whitakerum, fol. 140. Neq; enim patres cenſentur, cum ſuum aliquid quod ab ecclesia non acceperunt, vel ſcribunt vel dicunt.

t Gretz. lib. 2. de iure & more prohibendi libros nox̄os. ca. 10. Nam Ecclesiæ pater ille dicitur, qui Ecclesiam ſalutari doctrinæ pabulo alit et paſcit, iam ergo ſi pro ſalutari doctrinæ pabulo admetiatur Lolium et Zizania non Pater eſt ſed Vitricus.

u Lindan. Panoplia lib. 1. ca. 17.

x Senenſis Bib. S. titulo Euſebius.

y Poſſevinus in apparatu ſacro.

z Canus locorum Theol. lib. 7. ca. 3.

a Coſter. in Apolog. contra Gretniū. ca. 8.

b Baron. ad annum 340.

c Lind. panoplia lib. 1. cap. 23.

d Rehing. in muris civitatis ſanctæ fund. 2. et 12.

author, the chiefe of all the Latine Fathers, the great light of Africa, a most ancient Writer and Doctour, most learned, most skilfull, most acute; where hee hath some passages which may bee detorted to give countenance to some Romish superstitions : But elsewhere when in expresse words he oppugneth some doctrines defined now for Articles of faith in the Church of Rome, he is as much besmeared with foule imputations by *Azorius* [e], *Maldonate* [f], and *Bellarmine* [g], *An hereticall author, an Arch-heretike, an enemy to the Catholike, and like to the Calvinists, a mā whose authority is not much to be set by, becauſe he was no man of the Church*: and as *Euseb.* & *Tertull.* so also *Origen* hath had contrary *testimonials* from the Church of *Rome*, where he pleaseth them hee is [h] *a famous light of the Church of Alexandria, whom S.Hier. cals another M* [t] *of the Churches after the Apostles, a* [i] *witnesse beyond all exception*; But when he fits not their humours, then *he is a Schismatike* [k], *a father of the Arrians and Eunomians, a bold* [l] *and rash man, an obstinate lover of his owne errours.*

In *Councels* the case is yet clearer; for the Cardinall sticks not in most plaine termes to hang all them upon the *Popes sleeve: The* [m] *whole strength & authority* (saith he) *of lawfull Councels is from the Pope, their* [n] *judgment then begins to be of force after the Pope shall ratifie them.* And what Councels will he ratifie ? you may bee sure not the Councell in *Trulio*, for that taxeth the Romane Church by name for inforcing single life upon the Clergy : not the Councell at [o] *Constantinople*, under *Constantine Pogonate*, for that he accurseth *Honorius* the Pope for an heretike : not the Councell held at *Frankfort* [p] in the time of Pope *Adrian*, for that condemneth their Image-worship : not the Synod of *Pisa* [q], for in that *Gregory* and *Benedict* Popes, were deposed : not the Synod [r] of *Basil*, wherein *Eugenius* was unpoped; nor the Councell of Constance [s], for in it a generall Councel is set above the Pope, and three Popes were cashiered by their Authority, (I except the later Seſſions of the same condemned Councell, which are Goſpell with them, becauſe they Anathematize the Wicliffiſts and Huſſites:) But the [t] second Synod of *Nice* shall be held for a generall Councell, becauſe it defendeth and commandeth the worship of Images; though it be full of blasphemous abſurdities and was called by an inſolent woman domineering

over

e *Azorius moral. lib.8.cap.16.*
f *Maldon. in Math.cap.16. verſ.19.p.340.*
g *Bell.de sanctorum beat. lib.1. cap.5.p.1938. Bell.de Sacram. Euchar.lib.3. cap.6.p.698.*
h *Lind. Panopl. lib.3 c.24.et 26.*
i *Dureus contra Whitac.fol.109.*
k *Canus loc.The ol. l.7.c.3.Maldon.in Ioan. cap.1.verſ.3. pag.399.*
l *Ribera in Malach.Prophet. proemium.*
m *Bell.de Rom. Pont.lib.4.ca.3 Tota firmitas legitimorum Conciliorum eſt à Pontifice Romano,et cap.1.*
n *Conciliorum iudicium tum demū firmum eſt cum acceſſerit, Rom.Pontificis confirmatio.*
o *An.Do. 681.*
p *An.Do.794.*
q *An.Do.1409.*
r *An.Do.1430.*
s *An.Do.1414.*

t *An.787.*

Irent.

over her husband, and devoted wholly to superstition. The
Councell u of Laterane, though confisting of none in a manner, but the Popes creatures, shall, in despight of the Oecumenicall Councels of *Pisa*, *Constance* and *Basil*, bee held a holy
and generall Councell, because it defines, that the Pope is a-
bove generall Councels; and for greater reason will the Pope
advance the small Conventicle of *Trent* to the honour of a
sacred Oecumenicall Councell, because it is throughly for
them in all points; though, as a learned Bishop, present at that
Councell, truely affirmes, *that matters in it came to that passe*
" *through the wickednesse of those hungry* x *Bishops, that hung upon*
" *the Popes sleeve, and were created on the sudden by the Pope for*
" *the purpose, that that Councell seemed to bee an assembly, not of Bi-*
" *shops, but of Hobgoblins, not of men, but of Images moved like the*
" *statues of* Dædalus, *by the sinewes of others.*

    Lastly, for their pretended title of Catholike Church, it
may be said of it as it was of *Pompeius* y Sirname in his decli-
ning age and fame, *Stat magni nominis umbra*, 'tis but the shadow
of a great name; for by it they meane nothing but their particular Church of *Rome*, or the Pope himselfe : Thus *Bellarmine*
glosseth upon the words of our Saviour, *Matth.*16.the Pope,
Peters successor, is bid to z *tell the Church*, that is, *to tell himselfe*
as Governour, and the Church which bee governs. Gretzer comes
off more roundly; *Thou wilt say, they interpret the Church the*
Pope : I grant it; what then? And b *Greg de Valent. By the name of*
the Church wee understand the Head of the Church, the Pope: and
Bozius c declares this mysterie more explicitely, *The Pope su-*
staineth the person of all Bishops, of all Councels, of the whole
Church.

    The learned Author then of this ensuing Tractate foyling
the Pope, consequently foyleth the whole Romane Church,
though he take onely *Vigilius* to taske, yet in overturning his
Chaire hee overthroweth, as hath beene shewed, all the Romane religion, which is *fundamentally* in the Popes Decree,
and the whole Romane Church, which is *vertually*, as they
teach, in his person. For if Pope *Vigilius*, not as a private man,
but as Pope *in Cathedra*, not sitting alone, but with his Synod, may erre, not onely in matter of fact, but in matter of
faith, judicially and doctrinally determining heresie, and

com-

u *An.Do.*1517.

x *Dudithius quinque Ecclef. Epist. ad Maxi-milianum secun-dum Cæsar.*

y *Lucan.de bello ciu.l.1.*

z *Bell de Concil. author.l.2.c.19. Dicere Ecclesiæ, id est, sibi ipsi ut præsidi, et Eccle-siæ, cui ipse pra-est.*

a *Gretz defen. Bell.lib.3. de verbo Dei : Ais tertiò interpre-tantur Ecclesiam Papam, non ab-nuo, quid tum?*

b z4. 2c. disput. 1.q.1.

c *Boz.lib.2.de signis Eccl.ca.21.* See farther in this Treatise, *cap.*13.p.174.

commanding it to bee received for Catholike truth : and if
this decision and determination of his bee reversed, condemned and accursed in a lawfully called, sacred and Oecumenicall Synod, approved by the Christian world, all which are
in the following Treatise punctually and uncontroulably
proved against all cavils of moderne Papists,

———*Ecquis posthac Paparum numen adoret ?*

Will any man hereafter, not wholly given over to be infatuated with *strong delusions*, adore the *Popes Chaire*? or *kisse his
foote* ? or pawne his salvation upon his *Cathedrall determination* ?

By all this discourse thou maist see, Christian Reader, the
maine scope of the Author; I shall not need to inlarge upon
other questions of lesser moment, though now more in
vogue, which upon the by and occasionally this learned
Writer accutely handleth both in this worke and others, especially in that imposed upon him by our late Soveraigne of
blessed memory, in defence of our Church, *Chap.* 35, 36, 37,
38, & 78.

Wherfore sith the Composer of this Treatise is most orthodoxall, the argument of great importance, the manner of
handling very exact and accurate, I doubt not but thou wilt
give it such entertainment, as that thereby others may bee incouraged to tread in his steps, and to guide thee in the right
way. What though the worke be of some bulke and waight ?
who ever found fault with gold for that it was too massie
and heavy ? When *Tully* ᵈ was asked which Oration of *De-
mosthenes* he liked best, hee answered, the longest; and questi-
onlesse in bookes of this nature, *cæteris paribus*, the largest
which meete with all possible, or at least probable objecti-
ons, and solidly refutes them, give the best satisfaction. Is it
not a shame to see in many mens studies idle Poems, *Astreas*,
Guzmans, and play-books in folio, but divinity books in *decimo sexto*, or slender paphlets, stitcht up in blew coats, without
any cognizace, glancing at Church or State, or treching upon
Controversies better buried alive, than to bee revived after
they are dead; which are cryed up by the common adversary, of purpose to foment discords betweene the professors of
the Gospell, that whilst, *Pastores odia exercent, Lupus intret Ovi-
le,*

le, the shepheards are at strife, the Wolfe may make havocke of the flocke. which I speake not for a *justitium* to any errour, or that I wish any way should bee given to those plausible tenents to corrupt reason, which one of late fitly compared to *flat bottom'd Boates sent from our neighbouring Countries to land Popery in England.* But first my desire is, that all that agree in the love of the same truth, may seeke that truth in love, and continually e *pray for the peace of Ierusalem;* next I pray, that f *our love may abound yet more and more in knowledge, and in all judgment, that wee may discerne things that differ,* and so seeke by all good and lawfull meanes to destroy the *wrigling tayle of the Adder,* whose head was smitten off 1200. yeares agoe in a Synod at *Palestine,* that yet our principall care bee to drive out the *Rómish Basiliske,* or rather the g *King of the Locusts,* against whose poyson I commend the ensuing Discourse as a soveraigne antidote.

e *Psal.* 122.
f *Phil.* 1. 9.

g *Apoc.* 9. 11

Lambeth, April 26.
Anno Dom. 1631.

Thine in the Lord Iesus

Daniel Featley.

THE
CONTENTS OF THE
SEVERALL CHAPTERS
CONTAINED IN THIS EN-
SVING TREATISE.

a   9. That

THE CONTENTS.

THE CONTENTS.

THE CONTENTS.

A

A TREATISE OF
THE FIFT GENERALL COVNCILL
held at *Constantinople* under *Justinian*, in
the time of Pope *Vigilius*: Wherein the exceeding
fraud and falshoods of Cardinall *Baronius*
are clearely discovered.

CAP. I.
That the Emperour IVSTINIAN *assembled the Fift Generall Councill, to define a doubt of Faith, about* The three Chapters.

ONCILIA *generalia mea sunt; primum, ulti-
mum, media,* saith their Romane *Thraso;*^a ^{a Camp. Rat. 4.}
Generall Councils are all ours, the first, the
last, & the middle. *Alls mine,* as said the Devill to the Collier. A vaunt too vaine, too
Thrasonicall. Divide the Councils aright,
and let each have his own due part and por-
tion, and then all the five first, and so much as they account the
sixt, that is, all which were held for 600. yeares and more; All
the golden Councils, and of the golden ages of the Church, are
ours onely, and not theirs; in many and even in the maine points
of Religion, repugnant to them and their doctrines: but in every
Decree, Canon, and Constitution of faith, so consonant to us,
that we not onely embrace, but earnestly defend them all, as
the rightfull and proper inheritance left unto us by those holy
Fathers of the ancient and Catholike Church. The middle
ranke, beginning at the second *Nicene,* unto the Councill of
Florence, which were held in those ages of the mingled and confused Church, none of them are either wholly ours or wholly
theirs, those miscellane Councils, are neither thine nor mine,
but they must all be divided. The two last, the one at *Laterane,*
the other at *Trent,* which are the very lees and dreggs of Councills, held onely by such as were the drosse of the Church quite
severed from the gold, wee willingly yeeld unto them: they and
they onely are wholly theirs, let them have, let them enjoy their
Helenaes, we envy not such refuse Councils unto them.

2. When first I set my selfe to the handling of this argument

con-

B

concerning the Councils, it was my purpose, besides those o-
ther generall questions, concerning the right of calling generall
Councils, the right of Presidencie in them, and the right of confirming them, to have made manifest those three severall points,
touching those three rankes of Councils; every one of which, is
not onely true, but even demonstrable in it selfe. And though
with a delightfull kind of toile I have made no small progresse
therein, yet alas, how unequall am I to such an *Herculean* labour?
whose time, whose strength of body, or industry of minde, is a-
ble to accomplish a worke of such amplitude, and of so vast extent, for which not *Nestors* age would suffice ? Wherefore turning my sailes, from this so long, and tedious a voyage, which
I could not so much as hope to end, & which beside many dangerous rockes, hidden Syrtes and sands, is every where beset by
many Romane enemies, specially by *Baronius* the Archpirate
of this and former ages, with whom at every turne, almost, one
shall be sure to have an hot encounter ; I thought a shorter
course far more fit, for my small and unfurnisht barke, and de-
spairing of more or longer voyages, I shall be glad if God will
enable me to make but a cut onely over some one arme of that
great Ocean, not doubting but the ice being once broken, and
the passage through these straits opened, many other will with
more facilitie, and felicitie also, performe the like in the rest, untill the whole journey through every part of these seas be at
length fully accomplished.

3. Among all the Councils I have for sundry reasons made
choice of the fift, held at *Constantinople* in the time of the Emperor *Iustinian* and Pope *Vigilius,* for authoritie equall to the former, it being, as well as they, approved by the consenting judgement of the Catholike Church ; for antiquitie venerable, being
held within 600. yeares after Christ, even in those times while
as yet the drosse had not prevailed and got the predominancie
above the gold, as in the second *Nicene* Synod and succeding a-
ges it did: for varietie of weighty and important matters, more
delightfull then any of the rest ; and, which I most respected of
them all, most apt to make manifest the truth and true Iudgement of the ancient and Catholike Church touching those Controversies of the Popes supremacy of authority and infallibility
of judgement, which are of all other most ventilated in these
dayes.

4. The occasion of this Councill were those *Tria capitula,* as
they were called, which bred exceeding much and long trouble
to the whole Church : to wit, The person and writings of *Theodorus B. of Mopsvestia* long before dead: the writings of *Theodoret B. of Cyrus* against *Cyril:* and the Epistle of *Ibas B. of Edessa* unto *Marisal* which three Chapters were mentioned in the Councill at ᵇ *Chalcedon.*

    ᵇ *Act.* 8, 9, 10.

5. The *Nestorians* (whose heresie was condemned in the third
generall Councill) when they could no longer under the name
                                      of

of *Nestorius* countenance their heresie, very subtilly indevored to ᶜ revive the same, by commending *Theodorus B. of Mopsuestia* and his writings, as also the writings of *Theodoret* against *Cyrill* and the Epistle of *Ibas* unto *Maris*. This after the Councill of *Chalcedon* they more earnestly applyed, then before, pretending ᵈ that not onely the persons of *Theodoret* and *Ibas* (who both had sometimes beene very earnest for *Nestorius* and his heresies) but that the writings also of *Theodoret* and the Epistle of *Ibas*, which is full fraught with *Nestorianisme*, and wherein *Theodorus* with his hereticall writings are greatly extolled, were received and approved in that famous Councill. And in truth the *Nestorians* little lesse then triumphed herein, and insulted over Catholikes, thinking by this meanes either to disgrace and utterly overthrow the Councill of *Chalcedon*, if their doctrine were rejected; or, if that Council were imbraced, together with it, and under the colour and authoritie of it, to renew and establish the doctrine of *Nestorius*, which (as they boasted) that councill had certainly confirmed, by their approving that Epistle of *Ibas*.

6. By occasion hereof, many who were weake in faith began to doubt of the credit and authority of that most holy councill: and those, as *Leontius* ᵉ sheweth, were called *Hæsitantes*, waverers or Doubters: Many others (who for other causes distasted that Councill) were hereby incouraged pertinaciously to reject the same, as ᶠ *Liberatus* declareth. Such were the *Agnoites*, *Gainites*, *Theodosians*, *Themistians*, and other like Sectaries, called all by the common name of *Acephali*, because they had no one head by whom to be directed. All these, though being at mortall wars one with another, yet herein conspired to oppugne the faith, and the holy Councill of *Chalcedon*, taking now advantage of that which the *Nestorians* every where boasted, and these men gladly beleeved, that in it the Epistle of *Ibas* (which maintaineth all the blasphemies of *Nestorius*) was approved. Thus the Church was by contrary enemies, on every side assailed, and so extremely disturbed, that as the Emperor ᵍ testifieth, it was in a manner rent even from East to West, yea the East ʰ was rent from the West.

7. *Iustinian* the religious Emperor, knowing ⁱ how much it was available not onely for his honor, and the tranquillitie of his empire, but for the good of the whole Church, and glory of God, to appease all those broiles: and knowing further, that the holy Councill of *Chalcedon*, though it received the persons of *Theodoret* and *Ibas*, after that they had publickly renounced the heresie of *Nestorius*, yet, did utterly condemne both that Impious Epistle of *Ibas*, as also the person and doctrines of *Theodorus* of *Mopsuestia* (both which that Epistle defendeth) together with the writings of *Theodoret* against *Cyrill*: he knowing and that ex-

Vniuersus fere orbis occidentalis ab orientali ecclesia diuisus erat. Bin. not. in 5. Conc. § Concitium. mentum nostri imperij fecimus, conjungere diuisos Sacerdotes. Epist. ad Synod. Col. 1.

actly

c *Nestorij sequaces propriam impietatē applicare volentes sanctæ Dei Ecclesiæ, & non potentes hoc per Nestoriū facere, festinaverunt eam introducere per Theodorum Mopsuestinum, necnon per impia scripta Theodoreti, & per sceleratam Epistolam quæ dicitur Ibæ ad Marin. Iust. Ep. ad Syn. 5. Col. 1. pa. 512. b. Habebat concilium ipsum in sua sententia definitiva. col. 8 pa. 584. & Lib. c. 10 d Theodori et Nestorij sequaces conantur di e e susceptam esse eam (Epistolam Ibæ) à 5. Chalcedonensi Conc. nomine ejus Theodorum & Nestorium condemnatione liberare festinantes. Iust. Edict §. Tali. Et iterum Epist. Iust. ad Synod. Col. 1. pa 519 b. Et Dicebant istam impiam Epistolam quæ laudat et defendit Theodorum et Nestorium et eorum impietatem susceptam esse à Synodo Chalc. Conc. 5. Col. 8 pa. 585. b. e Lib de sect. act. 6. f Illi (Acephali) hoc offenduntur in Syn. Chalced quod Laudes suscepit Theodori Mopsuest. Epistolam que Ibæ, quæ per omnia Nestoriana esse cognoscitur. lib. Breu ca. 24. g Sacerdotes sanctarum Dei Ecclesiarum ab Oriente usq; ad Occidentem diuisi, Iust. Epist. ad Synod. pa 519. b. h Ob tria Capitula inter se invicem tam in oriente quam in occidente fideles fuerunt scissi atq; sublimate separati. Bar. an. 547. nu. 20. i Initium et funda-*

actly all these particulars, that he might draw all the subjects of his Empire to the unitie of that most holy faith which was decreed at *Chalcedon*, set forth an [k] Imperiall Edict containing a most orthodoxall, religious and holy profession, or rather an ample Declaration of his, nay not his, but of the Catholike Faith. Among many other things, the Emperor in that Edict did particularly and expresly condemne *Theodorus* of *Mopsvestia* with his doctrines, the writings of *Theodoret* against *Cyril*, and that most impious Epistle of *Ibas*, accursing [l] all these as hereticall, and all those, who either had heretofore, or should therafter maintaine or defend them, or any one of them.

k Exlat apud Bin. tom. 2. Conc. pa. 492.

l Si quis defendit Theodorum, &c. anathema sit. Edict. pa. 496.

8. But notwithstanding all this, which the Emperor with great prudence, piety and zeale performed, very many, even some of those who bare the names of orthodoxall and Catholike Bishops, were so far from consenting to this Imperial Edict, and the Catholike truth delivered therein, that they openly oppugned his Edict, and defended the Three Chapters (by him condemned and anathematized) by words, by writings, by all meanes which they could devise, publishing libels and bitter invectives against it and the Emperor himselfe also. He seeing so generall a disturbance in his Empire, and the whole Church to be in a combustion about this cause, to end and quiet all, used that which is the best and last publick meanes which is left to the Church for deciding any doubt or controversie of faith, and of purpose to determine this so weighty a cause (whether those *Three Chapters* were to be condemned or allowed) he assembled this fifth and holy generall Councill, whereof, God assisting us, we are now to entreat.

Cap. II.

That the Fift Generall Councill, when Pope Vigilius *refused to come unto it, was held without the Popes presence therein, either by himselfe or by his Legates.*

1. Hat this Council was celebrated when Pope *Vigilius* was at *Constantinople*; that he was once, againe, often and earnestly, invited to the *Synod*, but wilfully refused to be present either personally or by his deputies, the Acts of the Councill doe abundantly witnesse. The holy Synod said [a] thus, *Sæpius petivimus. We have often entreated the most holy Pope* Vigilius; *to come together with us and make a determination of these matters.* Againe, the holy Synod said, [b] *The most glorious Iudges and certaine of us (sæpius adhortati sunt* Vigilium) *have often exhorted* Vigilius, *to come and debate and make an end of this cause touching the Three Chapters.* Neither did they onely invite, exhort, and entreat him; but in the Emperors name they commanded him to come to the Synod : *We being present*

a Coll.2.pa.524.a.

b Col.1.pa.521.b. & Coll.8.pa.584.b.

present (said the Bishops, who were sent unto him) *Liberius*, Peter, and *Patricius*, *proposuerunt Iussionem pijssimi Imperatoris sanctissimo Papæ*, proposed to the most holy Pope *Vigilius* the command of the most holy Emperor.   If all this seeme not enough, the Emperor himselfe testifieth [d] the same, *Mandavimus illi, we have commanded Vigilius, both by our Iudges, and by certaine of your selves* (he writ this to the Synod) *ut una cum omnibus conveniret, that he should come together with all the rest*, in common to debate and determine this cause touching the *Three Chapters*.

2.   What Pope *Vigilius* did, after so many invitations, entreaties, and commands, *Card. Bellarmine* doth declare, The Pope, saith he, [e] *neq. per se, neq. per legatos interfuit, was not present in the Council either by himselfe, or by his leguts.*   And more clearly in another place, The Pope, saith he, [f] *was then at Constantinople, sed noluit interesse; but he would not be present in the Councill.* Binius testifieth [g] the same.   *At the fifth Councill Vigilius was not present either by himselfe or by his deputies.* And *Baronius*, The Pope (saith he) [h] *noluit interesse, would not be present either by himselfe, or by any to supply his place.*   And this Cardinall adds [i] not without some choler, *The members assembled without the head, nulla Vigilij ægrotantis adhuc habita ratione, having no regard at all to Pope Vigilius then sick.*

3.   What? doth the Card. complaine that they had no regard of him, when himselfe a little before professeth, *noluit interesse, he himselfe was not willing to be present*? Or had they no regard of him when before ever they assembled or sate in the Synod, they writ an Epistle [k] unto him entreating his presence, and with their own request, signified [l] the Emperors command, wil, and pleasure to him, that he shold come together with the rest? when after they were assembled in the Synod, they so often, so earnestly invited, and even entreated him to come together with them? when they whom they sent to invite him were no meane, no ordinary messengers neither for their number nor dignitie, but twenty reverend Bishops, all of them *Metropolitanes*, as the *Cardinal* [m] both knew, and acknowledged, & the Synodall acts [n] doe witnesse, and of those twenty, three were Patriarks, *Eutychius*, of *Constantinople*, *Apollinarius*, of *Alexandria*, and *Domninus*, of *Antioch*? Was this a signe that they had no regard of *Vigilius*? when besides all this, in token of their most earnest desire of his presence, among divers other they proposed two most effectuall reasons to induce him to come.   The one, the promise of Presidencie among them, which so far as in them lay, they offred unto him, saying, [o] *Petimus præsidente nobis vestra beatitudine, we entreat that your holinesse being present in this Synod, the question may be debated and have an end*: The other (which should not onely in equitie, but even in common honesty have prevailed with a Pope) for that himselfe had promised and that under his owne hand-writing, that he would come to the *Synod*: we told him (said [p] the Bishop) *your holinesse knoweth,*

B 3   quod

c *Coll. 2. pa. 524. a.*

d *Epist. Iustin. ad Conc. Coll. 1. pa. 520. a.*

e *Lib. 1. de Conc. ca. 5.§ Constã.*

f *Lib. eod. 19. § Adde.*

g *Notis in Conc. gen.5. § Præsedit.*

h *Anno 553. nu. 19.*

i *Ibid. nu. 31.*

k *Epist. Eutychij ad Vigilium lecta Coll. 1. ideoq. missa ante inchoatum Synodñ. l Et primo die instantis Maij pervenimus ad Vigilium: —Diximus, Pijssimus Dominus vult te una cum alijs cõvenire : proposuerunt iussionem pijssimi Imperatoris. Coll. 2. pa. 523. b. 524. a. Concilium vero cœpit 4. die Maij. Coll. 1. m Missi sunt qui cum vocarent Episcopi numero viginti, ijdemq. Metropolitani Bar. an. 553. nu. 35. n Coll. 1. & 2. nam in utraq. missi sunt. o Coll. 1. pa. 521. a.*

p *Coll. 2 pa. 523. b.*

quod in his quæ inter nos in scriptis facta sunt, promisistis; that in those things which were done in writing betwixt us, you have promised to come together with the rest and discusse these three Chapters. And againe, we entreated his reverence (say the whole Synod) *scriptas suas promissiones adimplere; to performe that which in his writing he had promised.*

4. Had they no regard of sick Vigilius, whose infirmity being signified to the Synod at their first session, they forthwith concluded that Session, saying, *Oportet, we must defer the examination of the cause to another day?* And whereas the Pope promised to give them an answer the next day, then because his qualme was overpast, he found new excuses for his absence: one because there was but a few westerne Bishops then present with them; another because he would himself alone declare his judgement in writing, and offer it to the Emperor, for which cause he had entreated respite for certaine dayes of his highnesse. Both which were in truth nothing else but meere pretēces, as the Bishops thē sent, manifestly declared unto him. For both the Emperor, said they, *vult te in communi convenire; will have you to come together with the rest,* & therefore he ought not to have given his sentēce alone but in common and in the Synod: and for his other excuse, *Baronius* himselfe doubteth not to call that a *pretence:* for so it was indeed, seeing as the Bishops truly told him, in none of the former Councils there was any multitude of Westerne Bishops, but onely two or three, and some Clerkes, whereas at that time, there were present with the Pope at *Constantinople* many *Italian* Bishops, others out of *Africk,* others out of *Illirium,* for their number more then had beene in al the foure former Councils; whereupon they plainly and truly told the Pope to his face, *Nihil est quod prohibet vos convenire una nobiscum; there is no sufficient or allowable cause to stay you from comming to the Synod together with us:* not sicknesse, not want of Western Bishops, *Nihil est,* there is nothing else at all but an unwilling mind. So extraordinary respect had they of the Pope at this time, and so earnest were they to have him present in the Synod, of whom *Baronius* without any regard of truth shamed not to say, that they assembled having no respect at all unto sick *Vigilius.*

5. The true reason which made the Pope so unwilling to be present in the Synod, and why *Noluit interesse,* was indeed his hereticall affection and adversnes from the truth in this cause of the *Three Chapters.* He saw the Catholike Bishops, then assembled, to be bent and forward (as their durie was) for condemning those *Chapters,* which himselfe embraced and defended: he therefore thought it fit to separate himselfe from them in place, from whom in judgement and in the doctrine of faith he was so farre disjoyned and severed. This to have beene the onely true cause of his wilfull absence and of his *Noluit interesse* the sequell of this Treatise will make most evident. For this time it is sufficient, by all those honorable invitations, earnest perswasions,

ons, and Imperiall commands, to have declared that as the holy Synod for their part was most desirous of his presence, so he not onely was absent, but in meere stomacke, wilfulnesse and perversnesse, absented himselfe from the Holy Councill at this time.

CAP. III.

That Pope VIGILIVS, *during the time of the fift Council, publi-shed his* Apostolicall Constitution *in defence of the* Three Chapters.

1.
Hen Pope *Vigilius* remaining then at *Con-stantinople* where the Councill was held, by no intreaties, perswasions nor Imperiall commands could be brought to the Synod, having no other let, as before was declared, but his owne wilfulnesse, the holy *Synod* re-solved [a] without him to debate and judge the Controversie then referred unto them. And in truth what else was to be done in that case? The Emperor commanded [b] them not to delay nor protract the time, but deliver a speedy, yet withall a sound and true judgement in that cause. The necessity of the Church required this, which was now in a general [c] tumult and Schisme about those *Three Chapters*. The *Nestorians* on one side trium-phed as if the Councill of Chalcedon had approved the Epistle of *Ibas*, and thereby confirmed their heresies. The *Acephali* on another side rejected that Councill, as favoring the *Nestorians* by approving that impious Epistle. The wavering *Hesitantes* were in a maze, not knowing which way to turne themselves, whether allow the Councill of Chalcedon with the *Nestorians*, or with the *Acephali* reject it. The Catholikes against all these Sectaries, both defended the Councill of *Chalcedon*, and yet re-jected that impious Epistle and the *two other Chapters*. In such a generall rent and contention of all sides, what delay could the Church endure? which the Councill rightly considering, [d] said, That it was not just nor fit by delaying their judgement, to suffer either the Emperor or the faithful people any longer to be scan-dalized. And for the absence of *Vigilius*, they knew right well that which Card. *Cusanus* very truly observeth, [e] *that if the Pope, being invited, did not, or would not come, or send to a Synod, but wilfully refused to come, in this case the Councill without him must provide for the peace of the Church and safety of the Christian faith.* They had a very memorable example hereof, as yet but fresh before their eyes, when the Popes legats being present at *Chalcedon* were [f] in-vited and intreated to be present at the Synod there held (which was the very next before this) at the debating of the right and preeminence of the Sea of *Constantinople* but wilfully refused to
be

a *Deo juvante, fu-turo die convenien-tes, quæ oportet a-gemus.Col.2.in fine*
b *Celeriter de his quæ interrogavimus vestram manifestate voluntatem.Iust.ep. ad Synod.Col.1.pa. 520.b:*
c *Ob tria capitula fideles fuerunt scissi atque schismate se-parati.Bar.an.547. nu.29.*

d *Nec enim justum est vel Impe.atorem vel fidele populum ex dilatione scanda-lizari.Co.2.p.533.b*
e *Alioqui si expe-ctatus non mitteret, vel non veniret, vel nollet, Concilium congregatum suæ necessitati, & Eccle-siæ saluti providere debet.lib.2.de Conc. ord. Cath. cap.1.*
f *Rogavimus domi-nos Episcopos de Ro-ma, ut communica-rent ijs gestis.Conc. Chalc. act. 16. pa. 134.d.*

g *Ibid.*

be there, saying g (as *Vigilius* now did) *Non, sed alia se suscepisse mandata, No, we will not come, we have a contrary command from pope Leo,* yet that holy Councill of *Chalcedon* handled and defined that cause in their absence, and their determination, notwithstanding the Popes absence, was not onely declared h by the most glorious Iudges to be just and Synodall, but the same was both by that holy *Synod,* and all other ever since, held to be the judgement and definition of the whole generall Councill : for in their Synodal relation to the Pope, speaking of this very decree, they say, i *Confirmavimus ante, we* (to wit, this whole generall Councill) *have confirmed the sentence of the 150. Bishops for the prerogative of Constantinople.* A most cleare and undeniable demonstration, and that by the warrant of one of the most famous Councils that ever were, that the peevishnes, perversnes, or wilfull absence of one or a few Bishops, yea of the Pope himselfe, ought not, nor could not hinder a Synod to judge and determine any needful cause ; much lesse a cause of faith about which there should happen (as now there did) a general disturbance of the whole Church. Vpon these and other like reasons the holy Synod now assembled at *Constantinople,* having done as much as in them lay, yea, as k much in all points as was fit to be done for procuring the presence of *Vigilius,* and having in their first and second Sessions done nothing but waited and expected for his comming, seeing now all their invitations and intreaties to be contemned by him, and their longer expectance to be but in vaine, addresse themselves to the examining of the cause, being stird l up by the words of St. m *Peter, Be ready alwaies to give an answer to every man that asketh you a reason of your hope,* which readinesse if it must be in al Christians, much n more in Bishops: and if it must be declared towards all men, most of all towards the Emperor, who now required their speedy judgement and Synodall resolution in this cause.

h *Viri illustrissimi Iudices dixerunt: quod interlocuti sumus tota Synodus approbavit. Ibid. pa. 237.b.*

i *Ibid. pa. 140.a.*

k *Cum nos per omnia, quod decet, & servavimus & servamus, & sepius petivimus Vigilium. Col.2. pa. 524.a.*

l *Pa. eadem. b.*

m 1 Pet. 3. 15.

n *In congruum aute Sacerdotibus esse putaneis protrahere dandum à nobis responsum Christianissimo Imperatori pa. eadem.*

2. Having in their first and second Sessions declared their long and earnest, but vaine expectance of *Vigilius,* In their *third Collation* (so their Sessions are called) they set downe as a foundation to all their future acts, a most holy confession of their faith, consonant in all points to that which the holy Apostles preached, which the foure former Councils explained, and which the Holy Fathers with uniforme consent maintained.

3. In the 4. and 5. *Collations,* they at large and very exactly discusse the *first Chapter,* concerning the person and writings of *Theodorus B. of Mopsvestia,* adding so much also, as was needfull touching the *second Chapter,* which concerned the writings of *Theodoret* against *Cyril.*

o *Vigilij libellus oblatus Synodo. Bar. an. 553. nu. 47.*

p *Ibid.*

4. Now in that fifth *Collation,* as *Baronius* tells o us, the *Constitution* of Pope *Vigilius* touching the *Three Chapters* was brought unto the *Synod.* The Pope promised p that he would send his judgement thereof, *ad ipsum Imperatorem, atq, ad Synodum,* both to the Emperor, and to the Synod; which he ingenuously per-

performed; yea *q, modo opportunè præstandum putavit, he did it*   q *An. eod. nu.* 48
opportunely at this very time of the 5.*Collation:* And the *Card.* is so
resolute in this point, that he peremptorily affirmeth of the
Popes *Constitution, Cognoscitur, ͬ its knowne to pertaine to this very*   r *Ibid.*
s *Anno eod. nu.* 41.
day of their fift Collation: and it ͨ was this day offered to the Coun-
cill: for which cause he strongly imagining this *Constitution* ͭ to   t *Constitutum hoc*
ex actis 5. *Synodi*
noscitur esse subla-
be stolne out of the Synodall acts now extant, is bold to in-   *tum an. eod. nu.* 47.
sert ͧ it into the 5. *Collation;* as into his owne due and proper   v *Cum ad hunc ip-*
sum annum et diem
place, wherein it was, and now ought to be.   *Collationis* 5. *perti-*
nere cognoscitur.

5. The *Card.* is too confident about the day when it was sent   *Ibid. nu.* 48.
to the Synod, as also in his adding this *Constitution* to the Acts
of the Synod, as hereafter in due place will appeare. Thus much
is certaine and evident by the Synodall acts, that this *Constitution*
of *Vigilius* was made knowne to the Bishops of this holy Councill, before their sixt *Collation,* for in that sixt, divers things are
expressed, which have a cleare and undoubted reference to the
Popes decree, as containing a refutation of the same, and here-
in the *Card.*saith truly, The ͯ *decree* of *Vigilius* was first sent to   x *An.* 553. *nu.* 210.
y *Quæ præsenti sta-*
the Emperor, and from him to the Synod, as by the sixt *Collati-*   *tuimus Constituto.*
Vig. Const. apud Bar
on may be perceived, wherein those things which the Pope had   *an.* 553. *nu.* 208.
alledged for defence of the Epistle of *Ibas,*are refuted.   z *Statuimus et de-*
cernimus.ibid.

6. As for the dignity, credit and authority of this writing,   a *Post præsentem*
definitionem. ibid.
it is neither any ordinary nor private instruction, but as the   b *Vigilius Episco-*
Pope himselfe calleth it, a *Constitution,* ͫ a *Statute,* ᶻ a *Decree,* a   *pus huic Constituto*
nostro subscripsi. ib.
*Definition,*ᵃ or Definitive sentence : and by the name of a *Consti-*   *nu.* 209.
tution, it is subscribed unto, both by the Pope ᵇ and all ͨ the rest   c *Iohannes Marso-*
of his Assemblie; and for such it is commended by *Card.* ᵈ *Baro-*   *num huic Constitute*
subscripsi, & alij si-
nius and *Binius* ͤ. In it the Pope delivereth his *Apostolicall* sen-   *militer.ibid.*
tence & Iudgement touching the *Three Chapters,*this being ᶠ that   d *Ann.* 553. *nu.* 47.
e *Vigilij Papæ Con-*
very same answer which *Vigilius* promised to send to the Empe-   *stitutum. Bin. in*
ror, and for the advised setting downe whereof, he ᵍ requested   *Fragm.* 5. *Conc. pa.*
of the Emperor the respite of twenty dayes. During which   591.
time he did *insudare* and *laborare,* as the *Card.*saith, ͪ with much   f *Hunc ipsum esse*
scias, quem de sua
sweat and toile elaborate this large decree, (containing no   *sententia interpella-*
lesse ͥ then thirty six columes *in folio*) that it might in every re-   *tus, pollicitus est se*
spect, and for the exact handling of so weighty a cause, be cor-   *missurum ad Impe-*
respondent to the gravity and authority of his *infallible* Chaire,   *ratorem. Bar. ann.*
specially seeing he set it forth of purpose, that it might be noti-   553. *nu.* 47.
fied ᵏ not onely to the Emperor and the Synod then assembled,   g *Const. Vigil. nu.*
sed universo orbi Catholico, but to the whole Catholike Church, as   58.
a publike direction in faith for them all; in which kinde of tea-   h *Ann.* 553. *nu.* 28.
ching, *nullo casu errare potest,* saith *Card. Bellarmine,* ˡ *the Pope can*   i *Apud Bar. nu.* 553
a *nu.* 50. *ad* 210.
*by no meanes be possibly deceived.*For this cause also *Vigilius* at this   k *Bar. an.* 553. *nu.* 47
time, and in this businesse, used the help and advice of a Synod,   l *Lib.* 4. *de Pont.*
consisting of *Italian, Africane,*and *Illyrian* Bishops, then present   *Rom. ca.* 3. § *Sit.*
with him at *Constantinople,* sixteene Bishops beside himselfe, and
three *Romane* Deacons. These all consented with the Pope, and
subscribed ͫ to his *Constitution;* and in theirs was included the   m *Vide subscriptio-*
consent of the *Africane,* of the *Illyrian,* of the *Italian,* and other   *nes loc. cit. nu.* 209.

Westerne

Westerne Churches, even of the Church of *Rome* also, who all at this time agreed in judgement about the *Three Chapters* with the Pope, as *Card. Baronius* professeth [n]. So deliberate and advised was the Pope in this cause, that his resolution herein is not onely a Pontificall, but a Synodall Sentence also, yea a Decree and definitive judgement delivered by the Pope, as himselfe expresly witnesseth, [o]*Ex authoritate sedis Apostolicæ, by the authoritie of the Apostolicke sea,* an whole Synod of Bishops (the Westerne Churches consenting with them) subscribing to the same, for their number, well-neere [p] as many, as there were Bishops present in some Sessions of their Oecumenicall Councill at Trent.

7. This *Apostolicall Constitution,* which had long laid in obscuritie, about some 18. yeares since was brought to light, and first [q] of al published by *Card. Baronius* to the opē view of the world, copied by him out of an ancient [r] manuscript in their *Vaticane,* where still it is kept : and more then halfe of it, is set out by *Binius* [s], annexed as a fragment to the fifth generall Councill. But for what good purpose *Binius* clipt away the residue, being a great (no lesse then five or six columes *in folio*) and by farre the most needfull part of the Popes *Decree,* thereby not onely injuring the Popes Holines, and deluding the world, but foully maiming and disgracing his owne Tomes of the Councils, you will easily perceive hereafter.

8. The summe and effect of the Popes *Constitution* is the Defence of those *three Chapters,* which the Emperor by his most religious Edict had condemned and accursed. The Pope, saith *Baronius,* [t] during the time of the Synod, set forth *Decretum pro defensione trium Capitulorum,* his decree for defence of the Three Chapters. Againe, [u] *Vigilius* made knowne to the whole Church *pro Tribus Capitulis Constitutum à se editum,* his *Constitution* published in defence of the Three Chapters. Againe, [x] *pro ipsorum defensione laborat; Vigilius labored for defence of the Three Chapters.* But the *Constitution* it selfe maketh this most evident.

9. Concerning the *first Chapter,* whether *Theodorus* (being dead more then an hundred yeares before this Council) ought to be condemned, *Vigilius* thus decreed, *Nulli* [y] *licere noviter aliquid de mortuorum judicare personis, That it is not lawfull for any to judge ought anew of those persons who are dead,* that is, not to condemne those, who, as *Vigilius* explaining himselfe saith, [z] *minime reperiuntur in vita damnati, are not found to have beene condemned while they lived.* This for the generality of the dead: particularly for *Theodorus B. of Mopsvestia* he thus decreed [a], Seeing the holy Fathers had not, (as he saith) condemned him, *eum nostra non audemus damnare sententia, we dare not condemne him by our sentence, sed nec ab alio quopiam condemnari concedimus; neither doe we permit that any other shall condemne him.*

10. For the *second Chapter* which concernes the writings of *Theodoret* against *Cyrill, Vigilius* was so tender of the credit of *Theodoret,* that he would by no meanes permit his name to be blemished

n *Occidentales pertrahebant in sententia quâ semper fuerant pro trium defensione capitulorum. an. 547 nu. 29.*

o *Vigilij Const. apud Bar. loc. cit. nu. 209.*

p *In Sess. 1. Conc. Trid. Archiepiscopi & Episcopi non plures quam 26. ut ex actis liquet.*

q *Bar. an. 553. nu. 48.*

r *Ibidem.*

s *To. 2. pa. 591.*

t *An. 553. nu. 218.*

u *Ibid. nu. 218.*

x *Ibid. nu. 272.*

y *Vigilij Const. apud Bar. an. 553. nu. 179.*

z *Ibid. nu. 176.*

a *Ibid. nu. 175.*

blemished by condemning his writings, seeing as he faith, [b] *neither Cyril himself, nor after him the Councill of Chalcedon had condemned them.* Nay *Vigilius* further adds, [c] *that it is* valde contrarium & indubitanter inimicum; *very contrary and undoubtedly repugnant* to the judgement of the Councill at *Chalcedon,* to condemne any *Nestorian* doctrines under the name of *Theodoret.* Whereupon he definitively decreeth in this manner [d]; Statuimus atq, decernimus, *we ordaine and decree* that no injury or slaunder shall by any man be raised, or uttered against *Theodoret,* sub taxatione nominis ejus, *by taxing of his name.* So *Vigilius,* decreeing that the condemning of those writings of *Theodoret* against *Cyril,* is an injury to *Theodoret.*

11. The *third* Chapter (which indeed is the most materiall, but withall most intricate and obscure) concerns the Epistle written against *Cyril* and the holy *Ephesine Synod,* by *Ibas* B. of *Edessa* unto *Maris* a Persian and an Hereticke: the copie whereof is set downe in the 1e. Action of the Councill at *Chalcedon,* and repeated in the 6. *Collation* of this fift Councill: What the Pope decrees herein, *Baronius* doth declare, who explaining the words and meaning of *Vigilius,* saith, [e] *That the Fathers of Chalcedon,* dixerunt eam Epistolam ut Catholicam recipiendam; *said that this Epistle of Ibas was to be received as Catholike;* and further adds, [f] Ex eâ Ibam comprobatum esse Catholicum; *that by this Epistle Ibas himselfe was proved to be a Catholike,* yea that [g] he was so proved by the consenting judgement of all the Bishops at *Chalcedon.* So *Baronius.*

12. This to have beene indeed the true meaning of Pope *Vigilius,* his owne words in his *Constitution* make manifest. There he first sets downe the ground of his sentence, and that was the sayings of *Pascasinus* and *Maximus* in the Councill at *Chalcedon.* The [h] Popes legats said by *Pascasinus,* Relecta ejus epistolâ agnovimus eum orthodoxum; *By the Epistle of Ibas now read, we acknowledge him to be orthodoxall:* *Maximus* said, [i] Ex relecto rescripto epistolæ, orthodoxa est ejus declarata dictatio; *by the Epistle of Ibas now read, his Epistle or writing is declared to be orthodoxall.* *Vigilius* grounding himselfe on these two speeches, collects and sets downe two positions of his owne, concerning this third Chapter; The former, that the Councill of *Chalcedon* approved that Epistle of *Ibas* as orthodoxall, to which purpose hee saith, the [k] Fathers of the Council at *Chalcedon,* Epistolam pronunciantes orthodoxam, *pronounced this Epistle to be orthodoxall:* and yet more plainly, Orthodoxa est Ibæ à patribus pronunciata dictatio; *the Epistle or writing of Ibas was pronounced orthodoxall by the Fathers at Chalcedon;* The other, that by this Epistle they judged *Ibas* to be a Catholike; to which purpose *Vigilius* writeth thus, Iuvenalis wouldnever have said that Ibas was a Catholike, nisi ex verbis epistolæ ejus confessionem fidei orthodoxam comprobaret, *Vnles by the words of his Epistle he had proved his faith to be orthodoxall,* which words evidently shew that *Vigilius* thought in like sort all the Bishops

b *Ibid. nu. 181.*

c *Nu. 180.*

d *Nu. 182.*

e *Ann. 553. nu. 152*

f *Ibid. nu. 196.*
g *An. 448. nu. 71.*

h *Const. Vigil. loco citato nu. 187.*

i *Ibid. nu. 189.*

k *Ibid. nu. 191.*

l *Ibid nu. 193.*

Bishops at *Chalcedon* to have judged the same by the words of
that Epiftle, for it is certaine that they all embraced *Ibas* himfelfe for a Catholike.

13. Hereupon now enfueth the *Definitive* fentence of *Vigilius*
touching this Chapter, in this manner : ᵐ We following the
judgement of the holy Fathers in all things , feeing it is a moft
cleare and fhining truth, *ex verbis Epiftolæ venerabilis Ibæ*, *by the
words of the Epiftle of the reverend B. Ibas,* being taken in their
moft right and godly fenfe; and by the acts of *Photius* and *Euftathius,* and by the meaning of *Ibas* being prefent, that the Fathers at *Chalcedon* did moft juftly pronounce the faith of this
moft reverend Bifhop *Ibas* to be orthodoxall, we decree by the
authoritie of this our prefent fentence, that the Iudgement of
the Fathers at *Chalcedon* ought to remaine inviolable, both in
all other things, and in this Epiftle of *Ibas* fo often mentioned.
Thus *Vigilius* : decreeing both that this Epiftle of *Ibas* is Catholike, & that by it & by the words thereof, *Ibas* ought to be judged a Catholike; both which he decreeth upon this ground, that
the Councill of *Chalcedon* (as he fuppofeth) had judged the
fame.

14. In the end, to ratifie and confirme all that concernes
any of thefe *Three Chapters* in the Popes *Decree,* he addeth this
very remarkable conclufion; ⁿ *His igitur à nobis cum omni undiq́,
cautela atq́, diligentia difpofitis;* *Thefe things being now with all diligence, care and circumfpection difpofed, Statuimus et decernimus, we
ordaine and decree,* that it fhall be lawfull for none pertaining to
Orders and ecclefiafticall dignities, either to write, or fpeake, or
teach any thing touching thefe *three Chapters,* contrary to thefe
things which by this our prefent *Conftitution* we have taught and
decreed : *aut aliquam poft præfentem definitionem movere ulterius
quæftionē,* *neither fhall it be lawfull for any, after this our prefent definition, to move any queftion touching thefe Three Chapters.* But if
any thing concerning thefe Chapters be either done, faid, or
written, or fhall hereafter be done, faid, or written contrary to
that which we have here taught and decreed, *hoc modis omnibus
ex authoritate fedis Apoftolicæ refutamus;* *we by all meanes do reject
it by the Authority of the Apoftolike See,* whereof by Gods grace we
have now the government. *So Vigilius.*

15. Thinke ye not now, that any Papift confidering this fo
advifed, elaborate and *Apoftolicall* decree of Pope *Vigilius,* will
be of opinion that there was now a fmall end of this matter, and
that all doubt concerning thefe *Three Chapters* was for ever now
removed : feeing the *fupreme Iudge* had publifhed for a direction to the whole Church his definitive, Apoftolicall, and infallible fentence in this caufe, what needeth the Councill either to
judge, or fo much as debate this matter after this *Decree?* To define the fame was needleffe, more then to light a candle when
the Sunne fhineth in his ftrength. To define the contrary, were
Hereticall: yea after fuch an *authenticall* decifion and determination

tion, to be doubtfull ° onely what to beleeve, hath the censure of an Infidell. But thrice happy was it for the Church of God, that this doctrine of the Popes supreme authoritie and infallible Iudgement, was not then either knowne or beleeved. Had it beene, the *Nestorians* and their heresie had for ever prevailed, the Catholike faith had beene utterly extinguished, and that without all hope or possibility ever after this to have beene revived, seeing *Vigilius* by his *Apostolicall* authoritie had stopt all mens mouthes from speaking, tyed their hands from writing, yea and their very hearts from beleeving or thinking ought contrary to his *Constitution* made in defence of the *Three Chapters*, wherein he hath confirmed all the Blasphemies of *Nestorius*, and that by a Decree more irrevocable then those of the *Medes* and *Persians*. Had the holy Council, at that time assembled, beleeved or knowne that doctrine of the Popes supremacie and infallible Iudgement, they would not have proceeded one inch further in that businesse, but shaking hands with Heretickes, they and the whole Church with them, had beene led in triumph by the *Nestorians* at that time, under the conduct of Pope *Vigilius*.

16. And by this you may conjecture that *Binius* had great reason to conceale the later part of the Popes decree, for he might well thinke, as any papist will, that it were a foule incongruitie to set downe three intire Sessions of an holy and generall Council, not onely debating this controversie of faith about the *Three Chapters*, but directly also contradicting the Popes *definitive* sentence in them all, notwithstanding they knew the Pope by his *Apostolicall* authoritie to have delivered his Iudgement, and by the same authoritie to have forbidden all men either to write, or speak, or to move any doubt to the contrary, of that which he had now decreed. But let us see by a view of the particulars and of their following Sessions, how this Cathedrall sentence of the Pope was entertained by the holy generall Councill.

o Dubius in fide in fidelis est lib.5.Dec tit.7. de hereticis.

C   CAP.

CAP. 4.

*That the holy generall Councill in their Synodall Iudgement contra-
dicted the Popes Apostolicall Constitution and definitive sentence, in that cause of faith, made knowne unto them.*

1.  IN the sixt, which was the very next
Sessions after they had knowne the
Popes will and pleasure, contrary to
the *Apostolicall* authoritie and command of *Vigilius,* the Holy Synod
began to examine the Epistle of
Ibas: for the causes of *Theodorus* and
of *Theodoret* were sufficiently discussed in their former *Collations.* And
first of all, alledging a saying of the Emperour (to which themselues doe assent) they thus say, which being well obserued
giues light to the whole cause and openeth both the error of
Vigilius and the ground thereof. *Because* [a] *the most holy Emperor*

a Col.6. pa. 561.a.   *added among those things which he writ unto us, that some indeuouring
to defend the Epistle of Ibas, presume to say that it was approued by
the holy Councill of Chalcedon, using the words of one or two most religious Bishops, who were in that Councill, as spoken for that Epistle,
cum alij omnes, whereas all the rest were of another minde, we thinke it
needfull, this question being proposed, to recite the Epistle of Ibas.* Thus
said the Synod, euen at the first, calling the Popes iudgement
Presumption, and checking him both for pretending the Councill of *Chalcedon,* and for alledging the *Interlocutions* of one or
two, as the Iudgement of that Councill. For, that the whole Synod consented to that speech of the Emperor, appeareth both
by their owne words, where they shew this to be so odious an
untruth, that they all cried out against it, saying, [b] The *Decree*

b Col.6. pa.576.b.   of the Councill at *Chalcedon* condemneth this Epistle, hee
that receiueth this Epistle reiecteth the Councill at *Chal-
cedon:* and, by those speeches of *Theodorus* Bishop of *Cesarea,
Andreas* Bishop of *Ephesus,* and others, to which the whole

*c Sancta Synodus
dixit, Scimus et nos
hoc ita consequuta
esse. Col.6.p.564.a.
d Col.6. pa.563. b.*   [c] Synod assented, *Quomodo* [d] *præsumunt quidam dicere, How do any
presume to say, that this impious Epistle of Ibas was approued by the
Councill of Chalcedon?* And againe, *Miramur quomodo, we doe euen
marvell that any will defend this Epistle by the name of the Councill at
Chalcedon:* and yet more sharply reprouing *Vigilius* with others,
for using so deceitfull a proofe, they adde, *Astutia enim hæretica
utentes,* for they (who so say of the Councill at *Chalcedon*) *using
the fraud and subtilitie of heretickes,* doe produce the *Interlocutions*
of one or two, as spoken for that Epistle, whereas this is to be
set downe for a certaine rule, that in Councills, *non unius aut se-
cundi interloquutionem attendere oportet,* the speeches of one or two
must not be attended, but what is defined by all, or by the greater

ter part of the Councill. And yet further expressing their dislike
of that fallacious and sophisticall reason which *Vigilius* herein
used, the whole Councill said, The holy [e] Fathers at *Chalcedon*   e *Coll.6.p.576.a.*
did, *pro nihilo habere, quæ ab uno vel duobus pro eadem Epistola dicta
sunt,* did esteeme as nothing, or made no reckning at all of those
things which were spoken for that Epistle by one or two; And
those one or two were *Pascasinus* and *Maximus,* on whose interlocutions the Pope, as you have formerly seene, grounded his
decree, concerning this *Chapter*; and if the proofe be of so small
account by the judgement of that most holy Councill, it inevitably followeth, that the *Decree* of *Vigilius* which wholly (for
this *Chapter*) relyeth on this proofe, is no better then the ground
thereof, that is in very deed, worth nothing at all.

2. Now that all this is purposely spoken against *Vigilius* and
his *Constitution* (which before this 6 *Collation* was made knowne
unto them) beside that it is evident by the Acts themselves, seeing the Councill doth exactly mention, and refute all the principall points on which *Vigilius* doth insist, *Baronius* doth not
onely professe, but truly, upon this reason, doth prove the same:
for entreating of this 6. Session, and mentioning the contents
thereof, *This* was done, saith he, [d] *as is evident, against the Constitu-*   d *An.553.nu. 212.*
*tion of Pope Vigilius (although for reverence they doe not name him)
and partly also they excuse him, partly they reprove him, using especially
this argument, Because in Councils we must not attend what one or
two say, but what is defined by all or the most.* Thus *Baronius,* who as
he truly acknowlegeth the Council herein to have dealt against
Vigilius and his *Decree,* so in the other points, hee bewrayes too
great partialitie towards *Vigilius,* for the Councill is so far
from excusing the pope, that neither *Baronius* could, nor any of
his friends shall be ever able to shew that excuse: And for their
not naming of *Vigilius,* it proceeded not from any reverence
they bare unto him (though in every respect they gave him all
honour that was due to him, or his place) but the true reason
thereof was this, because they neither did, nor thought it fit to
name any one of those, whom they did condemne, but without
mention of their names in particular, condemned them all un-   e *Definitio Synod.*
der one generall Appellation of, *Sequaces* [e] *Nestorij et Theodori,*   *Col.8.pa.586.a.*
the followers of Nestorius and Theodorus, their Disciples, or defen-   *Defensores Nestorij
ders which titles they saw the Emperor to have used and gi-   & ejus impietatis,
ven unto them before, both in his Edict, and in his [g] Epistle   Ibid.pa.585.b.*
to the Synod, which common names to have as fitly and truly   *Theodori discipuli.
Ibid.& sæpe alibi.*
agreed to Pope *Vigilius* as to any else, the Councill knew right   f *Theodori & Ne-
well, seeing in every point concerning these *Three Chapters,* he   storij sequaces.
pa.497.a.*
wholly agreed with them all. The [h] followers of *Theodorus* and   g *Nestorij sequaces.
Nestorius* pretended, and presumed to say, that the Councill of   *pa. 519.b.*
Chalcedon approved the Epistle of *Ibas*: *Vigilius* pretended, and   h *Theodori & Ne-
presumed to say the same; The Fathers at *Chalcedon* (saith he)   storij defensores dicebant, &c. Col. 8.
pa.585. b. Et presu-*
pronounced [i] the Epistle of *Ibas* to be *Orthodoxall.* The followers   *munt dicere, Col.6.
pa.561.a.&Col.8.
pa. 586.a.*
i *Const. Vig. apud
Bar.an.553.nu.192*

C 2   of

k Col. 8. pa. 586.a.
l An.553. nu. 212.
of *Theodorus* and *Nestorius* fraudulently used the *Interlocutions* of one or two, as the l Iudgment of the whole Councill at *Chalcedon*. *Vigilius* used the very same fraud, and for this very cause, as the *Cardinall* confesseth, is reproved by the Councill. Seeing then, *Vigilius* did at this time, and in this cause, walke hand in hand, and step by step with the other followers of *Theodorus* and *Nestorius*, The holy Councill judged it most fit and sufficient (as it was indeed) to refuse and condemne both him and his *Constitution*, by that common name which agreed to all the rest, with whom in one common doctrine, both for his position and proofes thereof, he fully conspired.

3. The holy Councill hauing now fully discovered the error of the Popes *position*, and the fallacious proofe which he used to uphold the same, procedeth to refute his very *definitive* sentence, prooving that neither the Epistle of *Ibas* is to be received as Catholike, neither that by it *Ibas* was, or ought to be judged a Catholike, which were the two maine points of the Popes *Decree* touching this *Chapter*. For declaring both these, they diligently examined the whole Epistle, and found it in every part to be *hereticall* and *blasphemous*. But for the more cleare demonstration hereof, as also how untruly and unjustly *Vigilius*, and the other followers of *Nestorius* pretended, that it was received as *orthodoxall* by the Council at *Chalcedon*, they thought it not sufficient to lay open the severall impieties of that Epistle, considered by it selfe, but making a comparison or *Collation* betwixt it and the holy Council at *Chalcedon*, they set, in a direct opposition, the most holy and Catholike truths decreed at *Chalcedon*, against the blasphemous impieties and heresies contained in that Epistle of *Ibas*. The summe of which Collations, or of some of them, I will here briefly propose out of the Synodall acts, referring the Reader for the full notice of them all, to the Acts

n Col.6. pa.575. & seq.
themselves, wherein they are at large, exactly, and excellently n delivered.

4. I. The holy Councill of *Chalcedon* professeth GOD to be incarnate, and made man : The Epistle calleth them *Heretickes* and *Apollinarians*, who say that GOD was incarnate or made Man.

II. The holy *Synod* professeth the blessed *Virgin* to be the *Mother* of GOD : The Epistle denieth the *Virgin Mary* to be the *Mother* of GOD.

III. The holy Councill embraced that *forme of Faith* which was declared in the first *Ephesine Synod*, and anathematizeth *Nestorius* : The Epistle defendeth *Nestorius*, injureth, nay rejecteth,
o Primam Ephesinam Synodum reprobat hæc Epistola, Col.6. pa. 563. a.
o the holy *Ephesine* Councill, as if it had condemned *Nestorius* without due triall of his cause.

IV. The holy Councill commendeth *Cyrill* of blessed memory, and approveth his Synodall Epistles, in one of which are conteined those his 12. *Chapters* by which he condemned the

heresie

herefie of *Nestorius :* The Epistle calleth *Cyrill* an *heretike,* and his 12. *Chapters* it tearmeth impious.

V. The Holy Councill professeth their faith to be the same with *Cyrils,* and accurseth those who beleeve otherwise: The Epistle saith of *Cyrill,* & those who beleeved as he did, that they were confounded, and recanted their former doctrine.

VI. The holy Councill accurseth those, who either make, or deliver any other *Creed,* then that which was expounded at the great *Nicen Syond :* The Epistle doth extoll *Theodorus,* who besides innumerable blasphemies, made another Creed, wherein he teacheth the *Word* of God to be one person, and *Christ* another person, accursing all, who doe not embrace that his new *Creed.* This is that *Creed* of *Theodorus,* against which (being openly read before in the fourth *Collation)* the holy Councill exclamed, saying, p *the devill himselfe composed this Creed: Cursed be he* **P** Pa.536.a. *that composed this Creed: Cursed be all those that curse not the composer of this Creed.* Of this it is, that here they witnes, that the Epistle of *Ibas* praiseth and magnifieth the author and composer thereof.

VII. The holy Councill teacheth, that in Christ there are *two distinct natures,* yet but one person consisting of both : The Epistle teacheth, that as there are two natures, so also *two persons* in Christ, and that there is no personall, but onely an affectuall unitie of those two persons. Thus far hath the Synod opened, by way of comparison, the blasphemies of that Epistle, and the contrary truths decreed at *Chalcedon.*

5. Now although this *Collation* doth abundantly of it selfe manifest both the Impieties of that Epistle, of which *Vigilius* had decreed, that it ought to be received as *orthodoxall:* and how repugnant it is to the Councill of *Chalcedon,* of which *Vigilius* had decreed, that it was received as *orthodoxall,* by those holy Fathers, yet for more evidence of this truth, the holy Councill doth in plaine and expresse tearmes, expresse both these points: for after this comparison they said, q *This our Collation, doth mani-* **q** Col.6. pa.576.a *festly shew, quod contraria per omnia est Epistola definitioni; that this Epistle of Ibas is in all and every part thereof contrary to the definition of faith, which was made at Chalcedon.* And againe, *We all accurse this Epistle, who so doth not accurse this Epistle is an heretike; who so receiveth this Epistle is an heretike : who so receiveth this Epistle rejecteth the Councill of Chalcedon: who so receiveth this Epistle denieth God to be made man.* Thus said, and cryed out the whole *Synod* with one voice : accursing (as you plainly see) not onely the decree and definitive sentence of *Vigilius* as *hereticall,* but *Vigilius* himselfe as an *heretike,* as a rejecter of the Councill of *Chalcedon,* as a denier that God was incarnate, or made man.

6. Thinke ye not that the Councill was very unmannerly, daring not onely to talke and write of this *Chapter,* contrary to the Popes knowne will and pleasure, but even to condemne with one consent his sentence for *hereticall,* and himselfe for an

heretike? *Binius* was exceeding loath to have it thought, that a generall, lawfull, ancient, and approved Councill, had so directly contradicted the Popes Cathedrall judgement, and proclamed to all the world the Pope to be an heretike, yea a definer of heresie, and that by his *Apostolicall* authoritie; and therefore he not knowing any better way to save the Popes credit, thoght it most fit to suppresse and dash out that whole passage in the Popes *Constitution*, which bewrayeth this matter: *Deleatur*, let all that part of the Constitution of *Vigilius* be left out; though the omission thereof doth disgrace and maime my edition of the Councils, let the latter part of his *Apostolicall* sentence lye in obscuritie and never see the Sunne.

7. *Baronius*, who (to the eternall infamy of their Popes, of their *infallible* Chaire, and of their whole religion, which wholly relies thereon) first had the heart to publish this Hereticall decree of *Vigilius*, deviseth another medicine to salve this sore: But avoiding Sylla he falleth into Charybdis, a worse gulfe then the other, plunging himselfe, with the Pope, in a condemned heresie. There are (as he could not but confesse) *many blasphemies in that Epistle*, but *none of those*, saith he, *did either the Councill of Chalcedon or Pope Vigilius approve*. What then, I pray you, was it, which his Holinesse defended, and approved therein? Forsooth in the end of the Epistle, *Ibas* declareth that he assented to the covenants of Vnion betweene *Iohn* and *Cyrill*, *qua recepta, necesse fuit eundem probare catholicum*; which peace and union being embraced by *Ibas*, he must needes be acknowledged thereby to be a Catholike. Seeing then, this is understood, and gathered out of it, that after the Vnion, *Ibas* was a Catholike, we may see, *ob id non esse explodendam epistolam, sed ad hoc quod dixi recipiendam*, that for this cause the Epistle is not to be rejected, but to be received, for this purpose, which I said, that by the end of it *Ibas* may be proved to be a Catholike. And the *Cardinall* labours to prove this by two testimonies, the one is that of *Pascasinus*, and the other legates of *Leo*: They (saith he) "spake not amisse, when they said, *Epistola illa lecta, Ibam probatum esse Catholicum*, that by that Epistle being read, *Ibas* was proved to be a Catholike: The other is that speech of *Eunomius* B. of *Nichomedia*, of whom he thus writeth, *Hoc plane fuit*, this is cleerly that which *Eunomius* said, *ipsam Epistolam in principio apparere haereticam, in fine vero inventam esse Catholicam*; that the Epistle of *Ibas* by the beginning seemeth to be hereticall, but by the end was found to be Catholike. Thus *Baronius*, in defence of that most impious Epistle, which as he saith, by the end of it is found to be *orthodoxall* and catholike, and so to be received.

8. What is it to be an *heretike*, if this be not? Directly to contradict the judgement of an holy generall Councill, and defend that writing or part of it to be Catholike, which in every part the whole Councill hath defined to be *hereticall*? The whole
Councill

Councill y with one voice proclamed; *Tota Epistola hæretica est: Tota Epistola blasphema est, qui istam suscipit, hæreticus est: The whole Epistle is heretical, and blasphemous, who so receiveth this Epistle* (either in the whole, or in any part, as themselves expresly affirme ˣ)*he is an hereticke.*

Not so, saith the *Card.* It is not all hereticall, It is not all blasphemous: The latter part of it, is right, holy, and Catholike, by it *Ibas* was rightly judged to be a Catholike; That part, at least, is to be received and embraced, to declare *Ibas* to be a Catholike. Now though this alone were enough to refute whatsoever the *Cardinall* doth or can say in this cause, seeing it is all nothing else, but the saying, nay the cavilling of a convicted heretike, proclamed for such by the loud cryes of an ancient and holy generall Councill, yet for the full manifesting of the truth, I will doe the *Cardinall* that favour, as to examine both his assertion, and the proofes thereof. And because I shall hereafter in due place have fit occasion at large (as the obscuritie and intricacy of this cause requireth) to discusse the words and declare the true meaning of *Ibas* in that part, which the *Cardinall* doth most wilfully and heretically mistake and pervert, for this time, I will use no other proofe against him, but the cleere judgement and consenting testimony of the generall Councill, which hath professedly refuted this very cavil, which *Baronius* borrowed from the ancient heretikes of those times. And I am verily perswaded, that *Baronius* would never, for very shame of the world, have used this so untrue, so *hereticall*, and withall a rejected evasion, but that he hoped that none would compare and examine his writings by the Acts of the Councils, or if they did, that the fame and credit of Cardinall *Baronius* his name would countenance any untruth or Heresie against whatsoever opponents.

9. Is the end of the Epistle of *Ibas* Catholike? or doth that shew *Ibas* to bee a Catholike? The whole Councill expresly witnesseth the contrary. *Our* ᵃ *Collation* (say they) *doth manifestly shew that this Epistle of Ibas, contraria per omnia est Definitioni; is in every part of it contrary to the Definition of faith made at Chalcedon.* This whole Epistle is hereticall, and blasphemous. Againe, Wee have demonstrated (say they) ᵇ this Epistle, *contrariam esse per omnia; To be in every part of it contrary to those things which are contained in the Definition of faith made at Chalcedon.* Againe, ᶜ *Tota epistola impietatis plena est, the whole Epistle is full of impietie.* And more clearly to our purpose, and against this cavill of *Baronius*, they adde, *Those* ᵈ *who say that the former part of this Epistle is impious, but the latter part or end thereof is right, Calumniatores demonstrantur, such are demonstrated to be Calumniators* or Slanderers, *Posteriora enim inserta Epistolæ majori impietate plena sunt*, for those things which are set downe in the latter part or end of that Epistle, are more full of greater impietie, injuring *Cyrill*, and defending the impious heresie

Margin notes:
ʸ *Hæc omnes dicimus, &c. Col.6. pa. 576.b.*
ᶻ *Qui dicunt correctam esse vel partem eius. Col.8. pa. 587.b.*
ᵃ *Col.6.pa.576.a.*
ᵇ *Col.8.pa.5.*
ᶜ *Col.6.pa.564.a.*
ᵈ *Ibid.*

heresie of *Nestorius.* So by the judgement of the whole Councill, *Baronius* is not onely proved, but even demonstrated to be an *Heretike,* and a malicious *Caviller,* for his defending the latter part of this Epistle to be right and catholike. And this is al which he hath gained by renewing that old hereticall and rejected cavill for defence of *Vigilius.*

10. But what shall we then say to the proofes of *Baronius*? what first, to the *Interlocution* of the Popes Legates so often and with ostentation mentioned by the *Cardinall*? VVhat? Truly the very same which the holy generall Councill hath said before us, and taught, and warranted all others to say the same. The *e Col. 6. p.: 576: a.* holy Fathers at *Chalcedon* (say they) did these things, *pro e nihilo habentes ea quæ ab uno vel duobus pro eadem Epistola dicta sunt; esteeming worth nothing at all, those things which were spoken by one or two for that Epistle.* Thus testifieth the whole Synod, and themselves follow herein the judgement of the Fathers at *Chalcedon*: So by the judgement of two holy and generall Councils, that *Interlocution* of the Legates of Pope *Leo,* on which (after) *Vigilius* and *Baronius* relyeth, is worth nothing at all.

11. Yea, but *Eunomius,* as *Baronius* tells us, affirmeth, that though the beginning of the Epistle be hereticall, yet the end of it is found to be Catholike. *Baronius* indeed saith so of *Eunomius*; but what truth and honest dealing there is in *Baronius,* let the discreet Reader judge by this one saying among ten thousand the like, *Eunomius* saith not so, *Eunomius* saith the flat contrary, as in the fift Councill is clearly witnessed; where against this cavill of the old heretikes, whom *Baronius* followeth, they *f Colle. pa. 564: a.* say *f* thus, *Nullam partem epistolæ apparet Eunomium comprobasse: it's evident that Eunomius approved no part at all of this Epistle.* And *g Ibid.* againe, *Quomodo g præsumunt isti defensores calumniari interlocutionem Eunomij: how dare the defenders of this Epistle presume to slander the Interlocution of Eunomius,* as condemning one part of it, and approving another, seeing the whole epistle is full of impiety? I say yet more (which will manifest the Councils doome of *Baronius,* that he is a malicious caviller, to be most just) *Eunomius* speakes not either of the beginning or end of that Epistle in his *Interlocution,* but *Baronius,* according to his wont, foists in that clause (touching the end of the Epistle) out of his owne pate, and thereby falsifieth both the words and meaning of *Eunomius.* This in the Councill is evidently declared by reciting *h Act.10.p.116.a* the true words of *Eunomius* out of the Acts *h* at *Chalcedon*: *i Con.5. Col.6. pa.* which are these; *Ex recitatis,* *i By those things which have beene read* *564.a.* *and recited,* Ibas is shewed to be innocent : for wherein he seemed to be blame-worthy in accusing *Cyrill, in posterioribus,* or in *postremis, recte confessus, having afterwards, or at the last, made a true confession,* he hath refuted that wherein he was blamed : wherefore I also judge him worthy of his Bishoprike if, he accurse *Nestorius, Eutyches,* and their wicked heresies, and consent to the
                                                                              writings

writings of *Leo*, and this generall Councill. Thus said *Eunomius:* wherein there is neither mention nor intention of that Epistle, neither of the first, middle, nor last part thereof. But whereas in the Councill of *Chalcedon*, many other [k] things, besides that Epistle, were recited touching the cause of *Ibas*, and particularly the whole *Acts* before *Photius*, *Eustathius*, and *Vranius* B. of *Berithum*, where a Synod was held about *Ibas;* it was those Acts and judgement given by them, and performed by *Ibas*, (and not the Epistle of *Ibas*) to which *Eunomius* had respect, when he said, by the *posteriora*, or *postrema*, *Ibas* made a true confession, for so in the fifth Council it is cleerly witnessed: *It is manifest* (say they) *that* [l] *Eunomius made this speech, gesta apud Photium, et Eustathium attendens, looking at those Acts before Photius and Eustathius.* Now in those Acts, as is manifest by the diligent perusall thereof, and is further testified by the fift Councill, [m] there was a judgement pronounced by *Photius* and *Eustathius, adversus eam epistolam et quæ in ea continentur; against that Epistle, and the contents thereof: Ibas* being commanded by those venerable Iudges, both to embrace the first *Ephesine* Synod, which that impious Epistle rejecteth, and to condemne and accurse *Nestorius* and his followers, whom that Epistle commendeth : which judgement that *Ibas* then performed, the *Acts* before *Photius* and *Eustathius* doe make evident : for there it is thus said, [n] *Confessus est Ibas sic se credere? Ibas professed that he beleeved as the letters of Cyrill to Iohn did import*, and that he consented in all things to the *first* Synod at *Ephesus*, accounting their judgement as a decree inspired by the holy Ghost. Yea he did not onely in words professe this, but in [o] writing also, (at the perswasions of *Photius* and *Eustathius*) he expressed the like for the full satisfaction of such as had been before scandalized by his impious doctrine. And *Ibas* yet *further of his* [p] *owne accord promised before those Iudges, that he would in his own Church at Edessa, and that publikely accurse Nestorius as the chief leader in that impious heresie, and those also who did thinke as he did, or who did use his books or writings.* Thus much do those Acts declare.

12. This *orthodoxall confession* of *Ibas*, made before *Photius* and *Eustathius*, this accursing of *Nestorius* and his heresies, this embracing of the Ephesine Councill, is that, which *Eunomius* calleth *Posteriora*, or *Postrema*, as following by many yeares, not onely that which *Ibas* did or said before the Vnion made betweene *Iohn* and *Cyrill*, but even this *Impious Epistle* also written after that Vnion. Of this confession *Eunomius* truly said, that by it (being *posterius*, later then the Epistle) *Ibas* had refuted all for which he was formerly blamed : for by this, in effect, he refuted, condemned, and accursed this whole Epistle with all the heresies and blasphemies, both in the head and taile thereof. And for this cause, and in regard of this holy confession, the fift Councill said, that thereby *Ibas* [q] had *anathematized his owne Epistle, contrariam per omnia, being in every part of it contrary*

k Act.9.&10.

l Col.6. pa. 563.a.

m Ibid.pa.563. & seq.

n Apud Conc. Chal. act.9.pa.108.a.

o Præparavimus J. bras, quod & amplexus est, ex scripto dare quid sentit de pia fide nostra. ibid. 107.b.

p Ex abundanti an. te promisit, &c. ib.

q Ostenditur inde quod anathemati-zavit Epistolam &c Col.6. pa.564. a.

trary to the faith, both in the beginning and end thereof. And the *interlocution* of *Eusebius* B. of Ancyra, at the Council of Chalcedon, doth fully explaine the meaning of *Eunomius;* for he expresly mentioneth thofe *Acts* before *Photius* and *Euſtathius,* and the confeffion of *Ibas* then made (which *Eunomius* called

r *Act. 10. Concil. Chal. pa. 115 b.*

poſteriora) faying thus, [r] *The reading of that judgement before Photius and Euſtathius, doth teach that Ibas, in that judgement, accurſed Neſtorius and his impious doctrines, and conſented to the true faith: Wherfore I receive him for a Biſhop, if he now doe condemne Neſtorius.* The

s *Ibid.*

like faid [s] *Diogenes* B. of *Cyʒicum, Thalaſſius* Biſhop of *Ceſarea, Iohn* Biſhop *of Sebaſtia,* and they all cryed, *Omnes eadem dicimus,* wee all fay the fame. So cleare it is that upon this holy *Confeſſion* of *Ibas* made firſt before *Photius* and *Euſtathius,* and after that, before all the Councill at *Chalcedon,* and not upon this Epiſtle, nor any part, firſt or laſt thereof, *Ibas* was acknowledged and embraced for a Catholike, both by *Eunomius, Eusebius, Diogenes,* and all the whole Council of *Chalcedon.*

13. By this now appeareth not onely the error, but the extreme fraud of *Baronius,* who in excuſe of *Vigilius,* not onely affirmeth an hereticall untruth, that the latter part of the Epiſtle is *orthodoxall,* but labours to uphold and boulſter out that untruth with a malitious perverting and falfifying both of the words and meaning of *Eunomius.* And thus far proceeded the holy Councill againſt *Vigilius* in their *ſixt Seſſion,* being the very next after they had received the Popes mandatorie letters, commanding them neither to ſpeake nor write ought concerning the *Three Chapters,* otherwiſe then he by his *Apoſtolicall* conſtitution had decreed.

14. In the ſeventh *Collation,* beſides the publike reading of divers letters and writings for the manifeſtation of the truth, and of the uprightnes of their judgment in this cauſe of the *three*

t *Que jam acta ſunt, relegantur: & relecta ſunt. Col. 7. pa. 577. b.*

Chapters; all that was formerly done, was now againe [t] repeated and approved by the holy Councill. Such diligence and warineſſe they uſed in this matter, that nothing might paſſe without often recitall and ſerious ponderation by the whole Councill.

15. In the eight, which is the laſt *Collation,* the holy Councill proceeded to their *Synodall,* and *Definitive* ſentence, touching all thoſe *Three Chapters,* which *Vigilius* (as they knew) by his decree and Apoſtolicall authoritie had defended. But the Councill directly contradicting the Pope in them all, doth *Definitively* condemne and accurſe them all, and all who defend them or any of them : which ſentence of the Councill, as *Baronius* truly

v *An. 553. num. 219.*

confeſſeth [u], was pronounced *contra decreta ipſius (Vigilij) in a direct oppoſition to the Decrees of Vigilius.* Which that it may fully appeare, as you have before ſeene the words of the Popes *Decree,* ſo now conſider alſo, and compare with them, the words and *Decree* of the Councill.

16. Firſt,

16. First the holy Councill sets downe in generall their sentence concerning all the *Three Chapters*, (The defenders of which they had before ˣ, and here ʸ againe doe proclame to be heretikes) in this manner; We ᶻ accurse the *Three* forefaid *Chapters*, to wit, *Theodorus* of *Mopsvestia*, with his impious writings, The impious writings of *Theodoret* against *Cyril*, and the impious Epistle of *Ibas*, *et defensores eorum*, *et qui scripserunt, vel scribunt ad defensionem eorum*; also we accurse the *Defenders* of thofe *Chapters*, and those who have written, or who do (at any time) write for the defence of them, or who presume to say that they are right, or who have defended, *aut defendere conantur*, or who doe (at any time) indevour to defend their impietie under the name of the holy Fathers, or of the Councill at *Chalcedon*. Thus decreed the whole Synod. Now Pope *Vigilius*, as you have feene before; defended all these *Three Chapters*, he defended them by writing, yea by his *Apostolicall* authoritie, *Constitution*, and *Definitive* fentence: he defended them by the name of the holy Fathers; and of the Councill at *Chalcedon*; Pope *Vigilius* then, by the judiciall and definitive fentence of this holy generall Councill is an *Anathema*, a condemned and accursed heretike; yea a Definer of a condemned and accursed herefie. *Baronius* writeth earneftly in defence of Pope *Vigilius* and his *Constitution*, he commends him for defending thofe *Three Chapters*, faying, ᵃ *The Defenders of them were praised while they had Pope Vigilius, whom they might follow:* and *Vigilius* himfelfe he had ᵇ many and worthy reafons to make his *Constitution* in defence of thofe *Chapters*: he further prefumes to defend *Vigilius* under the name and fhew of confenting with the holy Fathers and Councill at *Chalcedon*. *Card. Baronius* then by the fame definitive fentence of this holy and generall Councill, is an *Anathema* with *Vigilius*, a condemned and accursed heretike.

17. After this generall fentence, the Councill proceedeth; in particular & feverally to condemne, each of these *Three Chapters* by it felfe. Of the firft they thus define. ᶜ *If any do defend impious Theodorus of Mopsvestia, et non anathematizat eum, and doe not accurfe him and his impious writings, let fuch an one be accurfed.* Now Pope *Vigilius* (as you have feene) would not himfelfe, neither would he permit any other to accurfe this *Theodorus*, he forbiddeth any to doe it, he made an *Apostolicall Constitution* that none fhould accurfe him: *Card. Baronius* he writeth in defence of *Vigilius* and of his *Constitution* in this point: *Thomas Stapleton* goeth further, for he is fo far from accurfing this *Theodorus*, that he exprefly calls ᵈ him a Catholike, yea a moft Catholike Bifhop: *Vigilius* then, *Baronius* and *Stapleton* are al of them accurfed by the Definitive fentence of this holy generall Councill, in this firft Chapter.

18. Of the fecond *Chapter* they ᵉ thus decree. If any defend the writings of *Theodoret* against *Cyril*, *et non anathematizat ea*,

and

ˣ *Qui hanc (Epistolam) non anathematizat, hereticus eft. Col 6. pa. 576. b.*

ʸ *Hereticorum condemnationem. Col. 8 pa. 586. b.*

ᶻ *Ibid. pa. 586. a.*

ᵃ *An. 546. nu. 40.*

ᵇ *An. 553. nu. 233.*

ᶜ *Col. 8. pa. 587. b.*

ᵈ *Conterbl. divif. 68. pa. 171.*

ᵉ *Col. 8.*

and doe not accurse them, let him be an Anathema. Vigilius would not himselfe accurse them, he would not permit any other to disgrace *Theodoret*, or injure him by accursing his writings: *Baronius* defendeth and commendeth this decree of *Vigilius*; they both then are tyed againe in this third *Anathema* of the Councill.

19. Though a threefold cord be not easily broken, yet the holy Councill addeth a fourth, which is more indissoluble then any adamantine chaine. Of the *Third Chapter* they decree in this manner; [f] If any defend that impious Epistle of *Ibas* unto *Maris*, which denieth God to be borne of the blessed Virgin, which accuseth *Cyrill* for an heretike, which condemneth the holy Councill of *Ephesus*, and defendeth *Theodorus* and *Nestorius*, with their impious doctrines and writings, if any defend this Epistle, *et non anathematizat eam, et defensores ejus, et eos qui dicunt eam rectam esse, vel partem ejus, et eos qui scripserunt et scribunt pro eâ; If any doe not accurse this Epistle, and the Defenders of it, and those who say that it, or any part of it, is right; If any do not also accurse those who have written, or who (at any time) doe write for it, and the impiety contained in it, and who presume to defend it by the name of the holy Fathers, or of the Councill at Chalcedon, such an one be accursed.* Now *Vigilius* (as was formerly declared) defendeth this Epistle, as orthodoxall, he defendeth it by his *Cathedrall* sentence and Apostolicall authoritie, he defendeth it under the name of the holy Fathers, and of the Councill at *Chalcedon*; saying, [g] *Orthodoxa est Ibæ à patribus pronũciata dictatio*; *Baronius* defendeth both *Vigilius* and this Epistle in some part thereof, he defendeth them under pretence of the Fathers and Councill at *Chalcedon*, saying, [h] *Patres dixerunt, eam Epistolam ut Catholicam recipiendam*; The Fathers at Chalcedon said, that this Epistle ought to be received as orthodoxall: Is it possible thinke you, by any shift or evasion, to free either *Vigilius* or *Baronius* from this fourth *Anathema* denounced by the judiciall and Definitive sentence of this Holy Generall Councill.

20. But what speake I of *Baronius*, as if he alone were a Defender of *Vigilius* and his *Constitution*? All who have, or who at any time doe hold, and defend, either by word or writing, that the Popes judiciall and definitive sentence, in causes of faith, is infallible (and this is held, by *Bellarmine, Gretzer, Pighius, Gregorius de Valentia*, and, as afterwards I purpose to declare at large, by all [i] and every one, who is truly a member of the present Romane Church) all these by holding and defending this one Position, doe implicitly in that, hold and defend every *Cathedrall* and definitive sentence of any of their Popes, and particularly this *Apostolicall Constitution* of Pope *Vigilius*, to be not only true, but infallible also: and so they all defend the *Three Chapters*; they defend the Defenders of them, by name Pope *Vigilius* among the rest. All these then are unavoidably included within all the

former

g *Const. loc. cit. nu. 192.*

h *An. 553. nu. 191*

i *Vt nemo Catholicus esse possit, qui illã non amplectatur Greg. de Val. in 2.2 disp. 1. par. 1. pa. 30*

former Anathemaes all denounced and proclamed to be heretikes, to be accursed and separate from God, by the judiciall
and definitive sentence of this holy generall Councill.

21. With what comfort, alacritie and confidence may the
servants of Chrift fight his battles, and defend their holy faith
and religion? or how can the servants of *Antichrift* chuse, but be
utterly difmayed and daunted herewith, feeing they cannot wag
their tongues or hands, to speake or write ought either againft
ours, or in defence of their owne doctrines, especially not of
that which is the foundation of the reft, and is virtually in them
all, but *ipfo facto,* even for that act alone, if there were no other
caufe, they are declared and pronounced by the judiciall fentence of an holy, generall, and approved Councill, to be accurfed heretikes.

22. The Councill yet adds another claufe, which juftly cha-
lengeth a fpeciall confideration. Some there are who would be
held men of fuch a milde and mercifull difpofition, that though
they diflike and condemne thofe affertions of the Popes fupremacy of authoritie, and infallibility of judgement, yet are they
fo charitably affected to the Defenders of thofe affertions, that
they dare not themfelves, nor can indure that others fhould
call them heretickes or accurfed: *Durus eft hic fermo,* this is too
harfh and hard. See here the fervour and zeale of this holy
Councill! They firft fay, Curfed be the defenders of this Epiftle
or any part thereof: As much in effect, as if they had faid, Curfed be *Vigilius, Baronius, Bellarmine,* and all who defend the
Popes judgement in caufes of faith to be infallible, that is, all
that are members of the prefent Church of Rome, Curfed be
they all. And not contenting themfelves herewith, they adde,
Curfed be he who doth not accurfe the defenders of that E-
piftle or of any part thereof : As much in effect, as if they had
faid, Curfed be every one who doth not accurfe *Vigilius, Baronius, Bellarmine,* and all that defend the Popes judgement in caufes of faith to be infallible, that is, all that are members of the
prefent Romane Church, Curfed be he who doth not accurfe
them all. The holy Councill no doubt had an eye [k] to the words
of the Prophet Ieremy, [l] *Curfed be he that doth the worke of the
Lord negligently, Curfed be he that keepeth back his fword from blood.*
To fpare when God commands, and whom he commands to
curfe or kill, is neither pitty nor piety, but meere rebellion a-
gainft the Lord, and pulls downe that judgement which God
himfelfe threatned [m] to *Ahab,* Becaufe thou haft let goe out of
thine hand, a man whom I appointed to dye, thy life fhall goe
for his life.

23. What then? is there no meanes, no hope of fuch that
they may be faved? God forbid. Far be it from my heart once
to thinke, or my tongue to utter fo hard a fentence. There is a
meanes, and that after the Scripture, the Councill exprefly and

[k] *Nos timentes ma-
ledictionem, quæ im-
minet his qui negli-
genter opera Domini
faciunt, Col.8. pa.
584.a.*
[l] Ier. 48. 10.

[m] 1 King.20.42.

often sets downe, even were they denounce all those Anathemaes, for thus they say, [n] They who defend *Theodorus*, the writings of *Theodoret* against *Cyrill*, the impious Epistle of *Ibas*, or the defenders of them, *et in his usq; ad mortem permanent, and continue in this defence, untill they dye*, let such be accursed. Renounce the defence of these *Chapters*, and of the Defenders of them, that is, forsake and renounce that position of the Popes Cathedrall infallibility in defining causes of faith: renounce the defence of all that defend it, that is, of the whole present Romane Church, *Come* [o] *out of Babylon the habitation of devils, the hold of all uncleane spirits, which hath made all nations drunke with the wine of her fornication*, which themselves [p] cannot but acknowledge to be meant of Rome: This doe, and then, *Come* [q] *unto the Lord and he will have mercy, and to our God, for he is very ready to forgive:* All your former impieties, heresies, and blasphemies shall not be mentioned unto you, but in the righteousnes and Catholike truths which ye then embrace, you shall live. If this they will not doe, we accuse them not, we accurse them not: they have one who doth both accuse and accurse them, even this holy general Council, whose just Anathemaes shal as firmely binde them before God in heaven, as they were truly denounced by the Synod here on earth, for he hath sealed theirs and all like censures with his owne signet, who [r] said, Whatsoever ye binde upon earth, shall be bound in heaven.

24. After all these just Anathemaes denounced as well in generall as in particular by the Councill against the defenders of these *Three Chapters* or any one of them; the holy Synod sets downe in the last place one other point as memorable as any of the former: And that is by what authority they decreed all these things, of which they thus say, [s] we have rightly confessed these things, *quæ tradita sunt nobis tam à divinis scripturis; which are delivered unto us both in the divine scriptures, and in the doctrines of the holy Fathers, and in the definitions of faith made by the foure former Councils.* So the holy Councill. Whence it doth evidently ensue, that to teach and affirme, that the Pope in his judiciall and cathedrall sentence of faith may erre and define heresie, and that *Vigilius* in his constitution *de facto* did so, is a truth consonant to Scriptures, fathers, and the foure first general Councils. But on the other side, to maintaine or affirme (as do all who are members of the present Romane Church) that the Popes cathedrall sentence in causes of faith is *infallible*, is an hereticall position repugnant to Scriptures, Fathers, and the 4. first Councils, and condemned by them all. So at once the Holy Councill judicially defineth both our faith to be truly ancient & Apostolical, the selfe same which the Holy Fathers, generall Councills, and the Catholike Church professed for 600 yeares; and the doctrine of the present Romane Church, even that fundamentall position, on which all the rest doe relye, to be not onely new, but

n *Col. 8. sæpe.*

o Apoc. 18. 2. 3. 4.

p *Iohannes in Apocalypsi passim Romã vocat Babylonem.* Bell. lib. 2. de po t. Rom. cap. 2. § *Præterea.* *Babylon quæ casura prædicitur, Roma quidem est* Riber. in ca. 14. in. Apoc. pa. 377. *Et, Roma qualis in fine seculi futura est.* ib. pa. 378. *Iohannes loquitur de Roma qual. sub finẽ mundi futura est.* Gretz. Def. ca. 13. lib. 3. de Rom. pont. pa. 927. *Babylon, quam esse Romam ait* lib 7 pa. 228. *sedes et civitas antichristi est.* Sand. lib. 8. de visib. Monar. ca 48.

q Isa. 55. 7.

r Matth. 18, 18.

s Col. 8. pa. 588. a.

but hereticall, such as none can maintaine, but even thereby he oppugneth and contradicteth both the Scriptures, Fathers, the foure first general Councils; and the Catholike Church for 600 yeares after Christ.

25. Further yet: because one part of their sentence is the accursing of all who defend the *Three Chapters*, either expresly, as did *Vigilius*, or *implicitè*, and by consequent, as do all who maintaine the Popes judgement in causes of faith to be infallible, that is, al who are members of the present Romane Church, and so die; it cleerely ensueth from that last clause of the Councill, that to condemne and accurse as heretikes all these, yea, all which doe not accurse these, is by the judgement of this whole generall Council, warranted by Scriptures, by Fathers, by the foure first generall Councils, and by the Caholike Church for 600 yeares after Christ: The judgement of this fifth Council being consonant to them all, and warranted by them all.

26. Neither is their *Decree* consonant onely to precedent Fathers, and Councils, but approved and confirmed by succeeding generall Councils, by Popes, and other Bishops, in the following ages of the Church. By the sixt Councill, which professeth ᵗ of it selfe that *in omnibus consonuit*; it *in all points agreeth with the fifth.* By the second *Nicene*, (which they account for the seaventh) *which reckneth* ᵘ *this fift, for one of the golden Councils, which are glorious by the words of the holy Spirit, and which all being inlightned by the same spirit, decreed those things which are profitable:* professing that themselves did condemne all whom those Councils (and among them whom this fift) did condemne. By other following Councils, in every one of which the 2 *Nicene* (and by consequent this fift) Councill is approved, as by the acts is cleare: and *Baronius* confesseth ˣ that this fift, *in alijs Oecumenicis Synodis postea celebratis cognita est atq, probata, was acknowledged and approved by the other generall Councils which were held after it.*

27. It was likewise approved by succeeding Popes and Bishops. By *Pelagius* the second, who writ an whole Epistle ʸ to perswade the Bishops of *Istria* to condemne the *Three Chapters*, telling ᶻ *them that though Pope Vigilius resisted the condemnation of them, yet others his predecessours which followed Vigilius did consent thereunto.* By Gregory, *who professing* ᵃ *to embrace & reverence the* 4 *first Councils, as the 4 Euangelists, addeth of this fift, Quintũ quoq̃, cõcilium pariter veneror;* I do in like manner reverence the fift Councill, wherin the impious Epistle of *Ibas* is rejected, & the writings of *Theodoret*, with *Theodorus* & his writings. And then of them all he saith, *Cunctas personas*, whatsoever persons the foresaid (five) *venerable Councils doe condemne, those also doe I condemne, whom they reverence I embrace: because seeing they are decreed by an universall consent, whosoever presumeth to loose, whom they bind, or bind whom they loose, se et non illa destruit, he destroyeth himselfe, but not those Councils, and whosoever thinketh otherwise, let him be accursed.* .Thus

ᵗ *Act.* 15. *pa.* 80. 2.

ᵛ *Act.* 6. *pa.* 357. *a*

ˣ *An.* 553. *nu.* 229

ʸ *Epist.* 7. *Pelag.* 2:

ᶻ *Pa.* 687.

ᵃ *Lib.* 1. *Epist.* 24:

Pope *Gregory* the great, ratifying all the former *anathemaes* of the Councill, and accursing all that labour to unty those bands. By *Agatho*[b], by *Leo*[c] the second, who both call this an holy Synod; and, not to stay in particulars, All[d] their Popes (after the time of *Gregorie*) were accustomed at their election to make profession of this fift, as of the former Councils, and that in such solemne and exact manner, after the time of *Hadrian* the second, that they professed (as their forme it selfe set downe by *Anton. Augustinus*[e] doth witnesse) to embrace the eight generall Councils, (whereof this was one) to hold them *pari honore et veneratione,* in equal honor and esteeme, to keepe them intirely *usq, ad unum apicem,* to the least iota, to follow and teach whatsoever they decreed, and whatsoever they condemned to condemne both with their mouth and heart. A like forme of profession is set downe in the Councill at *Constance*[f], where the Councill having first decreed [g] the power and authoritie of the Pope to be inferiour and subject to the Councill, and that he ought to be obedient to them both, in matters of faith and orders of reformation, by this their superior authoritie ordaineth, *That every Pope at the time of his election shall professe that, corde et ore, both in words and in his heart hee doth embrace and firmely beleeve the doctrines delivered by the holy Fathers, and by the eleven generall Councils (this fift being reckned for one) and that he will keepe, defend and teach the same faith with them, usq, ad unum apicem, even to the least syllable.* To goe no further, *Baronius* confesseth [h], that not onely *Gregory* and his predecessors (unto *Vigilius*) *sed successores omnes, but all the successors of Gregory* are knowne to have received and confirmed this fift Councill.

28. Neither onely did the Popes approve it, but all orthodoxall Bishops in the world: it being a custome, as *Baronius* sheweth[i], that they did professe to embrace the seven generall Councills, which forme of faith *Orthodoxi omnes ex more profiteri deberent, all orthodoxall Bishops by custome were bound to professe.* And this, as it seemeth, they did in those *Literæ Formatæ, or Communicatoriæ,* or *Pacifica,* (so they were called [k]) which from ancient time they used to give and receive. For by that forme of letters they testified their communion in faith, and peaceable agreemēt with the whole Catholike Church. Such an Vniforme consent there was in approving this fift Council in all succeeding Councills, Popes and Bishops, almost to these dayes.

29. From whence it evidently and unavoidably ensueth, that as this fift Synod, so all succeeding Councils, Popes and Bishops, to the time of the Councill of *Constance*[l], that is, for more then fourteene hundred yeares together after Christ, doe all with this fift Councill condemne and accurse, as *hereticall*, the judiciall and definitive sentence of Pope *Vigilius*, delivered by his *Apostolicall* authority, for instruction of the whole Church in this cause of faith: & therfore they al with an uniforme consent did in

heart

b *In Conc. 6. Act. 4. pa. 16. a.*

c *Epist. ad Constan. Imp.*

d *Bar. an. 869. nu. 58, 59.*

e *In manuscripto codice ex quo eum citat Bar. loco citato*

f *Sess. 39. pa. 1644.*

g *Sess. 4. pa. 1560.*

h *An. 553. nu. 229*

i *An. 869. nu. 58.*

k *Cum quo totus orbis commercio formatarum, concordat. Opt. lib. 2. p. 40. Quærebatur utrum epistolas communicatorias quas Formatas dicimus, possent quo vellent dare. Aug. Epist. 163. Sub probatione Epistolij, sive Pacificis, quæ dicuntur Ecclesiastica. Conc. Chalc. can. 11.*

l *Celebratum est an. 1414.*

heart beleeve, and in words professe and teach, that the Popes
Cathedrall sentence in causes of faith, may be, and *de facto* hath
been hereticall: that is, they all did beleeve and teach, that doctrine which the reformed Churches maintaine, to be truly ancient, orthodoxall and catholike, such as the whole Church of
Christ for more then 14 hundred yeares beleeved and taught:
but the doctrine (even the Fundamentall position whereon all
their doctrines doe relie, and which is vertually included in them
all) which the present Church of Rome maintaineth, to be new,
hereticall and accursed, such as the whole Church for so many
hundred yeares together with one consent beleeved and taught
to be accursed and hereticall.   It hence further ensueth, that as
this fift Councill did, so all the fore-mentioned generall Councils, Popes and Bishops, doe with it condemne and accurse for
heretikes not onely *Vigilius*, but all who either have or doe
hereafter defend him and his *Constitution*, even all, who either by
word or writing, have or shall maintaine that the Popes *Cathedrall* judgement in causes of faith is infallible, that is, all who are
members of the present Romane Church, and so continue till
their death: nay, they not onely accurse all such, but further also,
even all who doe not accurse such.   And because the decree of
this fift Councill is approved by them, to the least *iôta*, it in
the last place followeth, that the condemning and accursing for
hereticall that doctrine of the Popes infallibilitie in causes of
faith, and accursing for heretikes, all who either by word or
writing have, or doe at any time hereafter defend the same,
and so presist till they dye; nay, not onely the accursing of all
such, but of all who doe not accurse them, is warranted by Scriptures, by Fathers, by all generall Councils, by all Popes and
Bishops, that have beene for more then 14.hundred yeares after
Christ.

30. This Vniforme consent continued in the Church untill
the time of *Leo* the 10 and his *Laterane* Councill. Till then, neither was the Popes authoritie held for supreme, nor his judiciall sentence in causes of faith held for infallible: nay, to hold
these was judged and defined to be hereticall, and the maintainers of them to be heretikes. For besides that they all till that
time approved this fift Councill, wherein these truths were
decreed, the same was expresly decreed by two generall Councils, the one at *Constance*, the other at *Basil*, not long before [m] that
Laterane Synod. In both which it was defined, *that not the Popes
sentence, but the Iudgement of a generall Councill,* [n] *is, supremum in
terris; the highest judgement in earth, for rooting out of errors, and
preserving the true faith, unto which judgement every one, even the
Pope* [o] *himselfe, is subject, and ought to obey it, or if he will not, is pu-
nishable* [p] *by the same.* Consider beside many other, that one
testimony of the Councill of *Basil*, and you shall see they beleeved and professed this as a Catholike truth, which in all ages

m *Conc.Basil. fini-
tum est an. 1442. id
est, an. 74. ante con-
cil. Later.*
n *Concil. Basil. in
Decreto quinq. con-
clus. pa. 96. a.*
o *Cui quilibet eti-
amsi papali status
existat, obedire tene-
tur. Conc. Constant.
sess. 4. et Bas. sess. 2.*
p *Debitè puniatur.
Conc. Const. sess. 5. &
Basil. sess. 3.*

D 3   of

of the Church had beene, and still ought to be embraced. They having recited that Decree of the Councill at *Constance*, for the supreme authority of a Councill, to which the Pope is subject, say q thus, *Licet has esse veritates fidei catholicæ satis constet; although it is sufficiently evident, by many declarations made both at Constance, & here at Basil, that these are truths of the Catholike faith, yet for the better confirming of all Catholikes herein,* This holy Synod doth define as followeth; The *verity of the power of a generall Councill above the Pope, declared in the generall Councill at Constance, and in this at Basil, est veritas fidei Catholicæ,* is a veritie of the Catholike faith; and after a second conclusion like to this, they adjoyne a third, which concernes them both; He who pertinaciously gainsayeth these two verities, *est censendus hæreticus, is to be accounted an heretike.* Thus the Councill at *Basil;* cleerly witnessing, that till this time of the Councill, the defending of the Popes authority to be supreme, or his judgement to be infallible, was esteemed an Heresie by the Catholike Church, and the maintainers of that doctrine to be heretikes : which their decrees were not, as some falsly pretend, rejected by the Popes of those times, but ratified and confirmed, and that ʳ *Consistorialiter,* judicially and cathedrally by the indubitate Popes, that then were, for so the Councill of *Basil* witnesseth; who hearing that *Eugenius* would dissolve the Councill, say ˢ thus; *It is not likely that Eugenius will any way thinke to dissolve this sacred Council, especially seeing that it is against the decrees of the Council at Constance, per prædecessorem suum et seipsum approbata; which both his predecessor Pope Martine the fift, and himselfe also hath approved.* Besides this, that *Eugenius* confirmed the Councill at *Basil,* there are other evident proofes: His owne Bull, or embossed letters, wherein he saith ᵗ of this Councill, *purè, simpliciter, ac cum effectu, et omni devotione prosequimur;* we embrace sincerely, absolutely, and with all affection and devotion, the generall Councill at *Basil* : The Councill often mention his adhesion, ᵘhis *maximã adhæsionem* ˣ to the Council; by which Adhesion, as they teach, ʸ *Decreta corroborata sunt,* the Decrees of the Council at *Basil* made for the superiority of a Councill above the Pope, were cõfirmed: Further yet the Orators wᶜʰ Pope *Eug.* sent to the council, did not only promise, but ᶻ *corporally sweare* before *the whole Councill,* that they would defend the decrees therof, & particularly that which was made at *Constance* was, & now renewed at *Basil.* Such an Harmonie there was in beleeving and professing this doctrine, (that the Popes judgement in causes of faith, is neither supreme nor infallible) that generall Councils at this time decreed it, the indubitate Popes confirmed it, the Popes Orators solemnly sware unto it, the Vniversall ᵃ and Catholike Church untill then embraced it, and that with such constancy and uniforme consent, that, as the Council of ᵇ *Basil* saith, (and their saying is worthy to be remembred) *nunquam aliquis peritorum dubitavit, never any learned and skilfull man doubted ther-*

q *Sess.* 33.

ʳ *Per Concilia generalia, quæ summi Pontifices Consistorialiter declaraverunt esse legitima, etiam pro eo tempore, quo ejusmodi declarationes ediderunt. Conc. Basil. pa.* 144. d.
ˢ *Epist. Conc. Basil. pa.* 100. b.
ᵗ *Literæ bullatæ Eugenij lectæ sunt in Conc. Bas. Ses.* 16.

ᵛ *In sua adhæsione. sess.* 16.
ˣ *Decreto quinque Concl. pa.* 96. b.
ʸ *Sess.* 20. pa. 95. b.
ᶻ *Jurabant ejus decreta defendere, &c. Sess.* 16.

ᵃ *Hæc veritas toties et tam solenniter per universam ecclesiam declarata est. Epist. Conc. Bas. pa.* 144. a.
ᵇ *In decreto quinq; conclus. pa.* 96.

of. It may be some illiterate *Gnatho* hath soothed the Pope in his *Hildebrandicall* pride, vaunting, *Se, quasi deus sit, errare non posse*; *I sit in the temple of God, as God, I cannot erre*; but for any that was truly judicious or learned, never any such man, in all the ages of the Church untill then, as the Councill witnesseth; so much as doubted thereof, but constantly beleeved the Popes authoritie not to be supreme, and his judgement not to be infallible.

c Hildebrandum fu gloriari solitum testatur Arent. lib.5. Annal. 4.455.

31. After the Councill of *Basil*, the same truth was still embraced in the Church, though with far greater opposition then before it had : witnesse hereof, *Nich. Cusanus* a Bishop, a Cardinall, a man *scientijs pene omnibus excultus*, who lived 20 yeares after the end of the Councill at *Basil*. He earnestly maintained the decree of that Councill, resolving that a generall Councill is *omni respectu tam supra Papam quam supra sedem Apostolicam*; *is in every respect superior both to the Pope and to the Apostolike see.* Which he proveth by the Councils of *Nice*, of *Chalcedon*, of the fixt and 8 generall Councils, and he is so confident herein, that he saith, *Quis dubitare potest sanæ mentis?* what man being in his wits can doubt of this superioritie ? Witnesse *Iohn de Turrecremata*, a Cardinall also, who was famous at the same time, *He thought he was very unequall to the Councill at Basil*, in favour belike of *Eugenius* the 4. who made him *Cardinall*, yet that he thought the Popes judgement in defining causes of faith to be *fallible*, and his authority not supreme, but subject to a Councill. *Andradius* will tell you in this manner; Let us heare him (*Turrecremata*) affirming that the Definitions of a Council concerning doctrines of faith, are to be preferred *Iudicio Rom. Pontificis, to the judgement of the Pope*; and then he citeth the words of *Turrec.* that in case the Fathers of a generall Councill should make a definition of faith, which the Pope should contradict (This was the very case of the fift Councill, and Pope *Vigilius*) *dicerem, judicio meo, quod Synodo standum esset et non personæ Papæ, I would say, according to my judgement, that we must stand to the Synods, and not to the Popes sentence*: who yet further touching that the Pope hath no superior Iudge upon earth, *extra casum hæresis, unlesse it be in case of heresie*, doth plainly acknowledge, that in such a case a Councill is superior unto him. Superior, I say, not onely (as he minceth the matter) by authoritie of discretive judgement, or amplitude of learning (in which sort many meane Bishops and presbyters are far his superiors) but even by power of *Iurisdiction*, seeing in that case (as he confesseth) the Councill is a superior Iudge unto the Pope, and if he be a Iudge of him, he must have coactive authoritie, and judiciall power over him. Witnesse *Panormitane*, an Archbishop, and a Cardinall also, a man of great note in the Church, both at and after the Councill of *Basil*; He professeth that in those things, which concerne the Faith, or generall state of the Church; *Concilium est supra Papam, the Councill in those things is superior to the Pope.* He also writ a booke in defence of the

d Poss. Biblic. in Nic. Cusano.
e Obijt ann. 1464. Poss. Conc. autem finitum est an. 1442.
f Lib. 2. de Concer. Cathol. ca. 17.

g Claruit an. 1460. Tritem. de Scrip. eccl. in Ioh. de Tur.
h Poss. in Ioh. Tur.

i Lib. de author. gener. Concil. pa. 88.

k Turr. summ. de eccl. lib. 2. cap. 93.

l Tunc Synodus major est Papa, non quidem potestate jurisdictionis, sed authoritate discretivi judicij. Turrec.
m Bel. lib. 3. de ver. Dei. ca. 9. § Præterea. Et lib. 2. de cöcil. ca. 18.
n Poss. in Nich. Tudisc.
o Cap. Significasti; de Elect. extra[?].

Councill

p *Poſſ. ioco citat.*

q *Obijt an. 1467.*
& item in Ant. Roſ-
r *Monarch. p. II. 2.*
ca. 15.

s *Ibid. par. 3 c. 21*

Councill at *Baſill* ſo diſtaſtfull to the preſent Church of *Rome*, that they have forbid p *it to be read,* and reckned it in the number of Prohibited bookes in their Romane *Index.* At the ſame time lived q *Antonius Roſellus* , a man noble in birth, but more for learning, who thus writeth, r *I conclude, that the Pope may be accuſed and depoſed for no fault, niſi pro hereſi,* but for hereſie ſtrictly taken, or for ſome notorious crime ſcadalizing the whole Church: and againe, ſ *Though the Pope be not content or willing to be judged by a Councill,* yet in caſe of hereſie, the Councill may condemne and adnull *ſententiam papæ, the Iudgement or ſentence of faith pronounced by the Pope;* and he gives this reaſon thereof, becauſe in this caſe the Councill is *ſupra papam, above the Pope:* and the ſuperior Iudge may be ſought unto, to declare a nullitie in the ſentence of the inferiour Iudge. Thus he: and much more to this purpoſe. Now although by theſe (the firſt of which was a *Belgian,* the ſecond a *Spaniard,* the third a *Sicilian,* and the laſt an *Italian*) it may be perceived, that the generall judgement of the Church at that time, and the beſt learned therein, was almoſt the ſame with that of the Councill at *Baſill,* that neither the Popes authoritie is ſupreme, nor his judgement in cauſes of faith is infallible; yet ſuffer me to adde two other witneſſes, of thoſe who were after that Councill.

t *Orthuin. Gra. in*
faſc. rer. expet. p.
240.
r *Ortel. Synon.*

x *Iob. Marius lib.*
de ſchiſ. & conc. c. 2.
23.
y *Ibid.*

z *Gag. annal. Fran.*
Lib. 10.

32. The former is the Iudgement of Vniverſities, *quæ* t *fere omnes,* which all, in a manner, approved and honored that Councill of *Baſil;* The other is the Councill at *Biturice* (ſome u take it for *Burdeaux*) called by *Charles* the ſeventh, the French King, in which was made *conſenſu omnium* x *eccleſiaſticorum, et principum regni,* by the conſent of the whole clergy, and all the Peres of France, that *Pragmaticall Sanction,* which *Iohn Marius* calls y *medullam,* the pith and marrow of the decrees of the Councill at *Baſil.* One decree of that Sanction is this, z *The authoritie of the Councill at Baſil* and the conſtancie of their decrees, *perpetua eſto,* let it be perpetuall, and let none, no not the Pope himſelfe, preſume to abrogate or infringe the ſame. This *Sanction* was publiſhed with full authoritie not ſeventy yeares before the Councill at *Lateran* (as *Leo* the tenth

a *Ab ipſius Sancti-*
onis editione vix an-
nos 70 fluxiſſe. Côc.
Later. Seſſ. 11. pa.
639. b. Loquitur
autem de ſecunda e-
ius edit. nam antea
promulgata erat an.
1438. teſte Gag. &
Mario.
b *Lib. 10.*
c *In ſua Appel. à*
Leon. 10. ad Concil.
d *Io. Mar. lib. citat.*
ca. 24.
e *Homo verſutus,*
planeq, perverſus. ib.

witneſſeth a) that is, ſome foure yeares after the end of the Councill at *Baſill.* And although the Popes (whoſe avarice and ambition was reſtrained by that ſanction) did deteſt it, as *Gagninus* ſaith, b *non ſecus ac pernicioſam hereſin;* no otherwiſe then as a dangerous hereſie, yea and labored tooth & naile to admit it, yet as ſaith the univerſitie of *Paris,* c by Gods helpe, *hactenus prohibitum extitit, they have beene ever hindred untill this time of Leo the tenth.* Indeed *Pius ſecundus* indevored and labored with *Lewes* the 11. to have it abrogated, and he ſent d a ſolemne embaſſador *Card. Balveus,* a very ſubtill e fellow, to bring this to paſſe, but after much toyling both himſelfe and others, *re infecta redijt,* he returned without effecting the Popes deſire. And to goe no further, *Leo* the 10. and his *Laterane* Synod, are ample witneſſes that this

Sanction

Sanction was never repealed, before that Synod, for they [f] com-plaine that, by reason of the malignitie of those times, or else because they could not helpe it, his predecessors *toleraffe visi sunt, seemed to have tolerated that pragmaticall Sanction,* and that for all, which either they did or could doe, the same Sanction *retroactis temporibus viguisse, et adhuc vigere* ; had in former times, and did even to that very day of their eleventh Session, stand in force, and full vigor. Now seeing that *Sanction* condemneth as hereticall (as did the Council also of *Basil*) that assertion of the Popes Supremacie of authoritie, and infallibilitie of judgment in defining causes of faith, which the present Romane Church defendeth, it is now cleerly demonstrated that the same Assertion was taught, professed, and beleeved to be an heresie, and the obstinate defenders thereof to be heretikes, by the consenting judgement of Councils, Popes, Bishops, and the Catholike Church, even from the Apostles time unto that very day of their *Laterane* Session, which was the 19. of *December,* in the yeare 1516. after Christ.

33 On that day (*a day never to be forgotten by the present Romane Church, it being the birth-day thereof,*) *Leo* the tenth with his *Laterane* Councill (or as the learned Divines of *Paris* [g] account it, Conspiracie, they being not assembled in Gods name) abolished, as much as in them lay, the old and Catholike doctrine, which in all ages of the Church had beene beleeved and professed untill that day, and in stead thereof erect a new faith, yea, a new foundation of the faith ; and with it a new Church also. Hee and his Synod then reprobated [h] the Decree of *Constance* for the superioritie of a Councill above the Pope: they reprobated [i] also the Councill of *Basil,* and the same Decree renewed by them. That Councill they condemne as *Conciliabulum,* or [k] *Conventiculam, qua nullum robur habere potuerit, As a Conspiracie, and Conventicle, which could have no force at all.* They reprobated the [l] *Pragmaticall Sanction,* wherein the Decree of *Constance* and *Basil* was for ever confirmed. Now that Decree being consonant to that catholike Faith which for 1500 yeares together had beene imbraced, and beleeved by the whole catholike Church untill that day, in reprobating it, they rejected and reprobated the old and catholike Faith of the whole Church. In stead hereof they decreed the Popes authoritie to be [m] supreme, that it is, *de* [n] *neceffitate falutis; a thing neceffary to falvation,* for all *Chriftians to be fubject to the Pope;* and that not onely as they are feverally confidered, but even as they affembled together in a generall Councill: for they define *Solum* [o] *Romanum Pontificem authoritatem fuper omnia Concilia habere; The Pope alone to have authoritie above all Generall Councills.* This the Councill at *Laterane* diferte & ex profeffo docuit; taught cleerly and purpofely, as *Bellarmine* tells [p] us: nay, they did not onely teach it, but *expreffiffime definiunt* [q], they did most exprefly define it. And that their Definition

Marginal notes:
f *Conc. Later. fef. 11*
g *Leo 10. in quadam cetu, ut fcimus qualiter, tamen non in Spiritu Domini congregato. App. Univ. Parif.*
h *Que de authoritate Concilij fupra Pontificem conftituerunt, fententia Coc. Lateranenfis plane reprobata fuit, Bin. Not. in Conc. Conft. § Ex parte.*
i *Reprobarunt decretum Concilij Bafilienfis. Bel. lib. 2. de Conc. ca. 17. § Denique.*
k *Conc. Lat. fef. 11.*
l *Ibid.*
m *Hujus fanctæ fediu fuprema authoritate. Ibid. pa. 640.*
n *Ibid.*
o *Ibid. pa. 639.*
p *Lib. 2. de Concil. ca. 17. § Denique*
q *Lib. eod. ca. 13. § Deinde.*

finition is no other then a *Decree of Faith*, as the same Cardinall assures us; Decrees of faith (saith he) are immutable, neyther may ever be repealed after they are once set downe; *Tale autem est hoc de quo agimus*, and such is this Decree for the Popes supreme authoritie over all, even Generall Councils, made in their *Laterane* Synod. And what meane they (thinke you) by that supreme authoritie? Truly the same which *Bellarmine* explaineth, That because his authoritie is supreme, therefore his judgement in causes of Faith, is the *last and highest*: and because it is the last and highest, therefore it is *infallible*. So by their Decree, together with supremacie of authority, they have given *infallibilitie* of judgement to the Pope; and defined that to be a catholike truth, and doctrine of Faith, which the whole Church in all ages untill then, taught, professed, and defined to be an heresie, and all who maintaine it, to be Heretikes, and for such condemned both it and them.

34 Now, because this is not onely a doctrine of their faith, but the very *foundation*, on which all their other doctrines of faith doe relie, by decreeing this, they have quite altered not onely the faith, but the whole frame and fabricke of the church, erecting a new Romane church, consisting of them, and them onely, who maintaine the Popes *Infallibilitie* and supremacie, decreed on that memorable day in their *Laterane* Synod: a church truly new, and but of yesterday, not so old as *Luther*, a church in faith and communion severed from all former generall Councils, Popes, and Bishops, that is, from the whole catholike Church of Christ, which was from the Apostles times untill that day. And if their Popes continue (as it is to be presumed they doe) to make that profession which by the *Councils* of *Constance* and *Basil* they are bound to doe, to hold among other, this fift Councill *ad unum iota*, this certainly is but a verball, no cordiall profession; there neither is, nor can be any truth therein, it being impossible to beleeve both the Popes *Cathedrall* judgement in causes of faith, to be *hereticall*, as the fift *Councill* defined; and the Popes *Cathedrall* sentence in such causes, to be *infallible*, as their *Laterane Councill* decreed: So by that profession is demonstrated that their doctrine of faith is both contradictory to it selfe, such as none can possibly beleeve, and withall new, such as is repugnant to that faith which the *whole Catholike Church of Christ* embraced, untill that very day of their *Laterane* Session.

35 Yea and even then was not this holy truth abolished. Foure moneths did not passe after that *Laterane* Decree was made but it was condemned by the whole Vniversitie of *Paris*, as being *contra fidem Catholicam*, against the catholike Faith, and the authority of holy Councils. And even to these dayes the *French Church* doth not onely distaste that *Laterane* Decree, and hold a Generall Councill to be superiour to the Pope, but their

their Councill also of *Trent*, wherein that *Laterane* Decree is confirmed, is by them rejected. And what speake I of them? Behold, while *Leo* with his *Laterane Councill* strives to quench this catholike truth, it bursts out with farre more glorious and resplendent beauty. This stone, which was rejected by those builders of *Babylon*, was laid againe in the foundations of *Sion*, by those *Ezra's*, *Nehemiah's*, *Zorobabel's* and holy Servants of the Lord, who at the voyce of the Angell, came out of *Babylon*, and repaired the ruines of *Ierusalem*. And even as certaine rivers are said to runne ᶻunder or through the salt Sea, and yet to receive no salt or bitter taste from it, but at length to burst out, & send forth their owne sweet and delightfull waters: Right so it fell out with this and some other doctrines of Faith. This Catholike truth (that the Popes judgement and *Cathedrall* sentence in causes of faith is not infallible) borne in the first age of the Church, and springing from the Scriptures and Apostles, as from the holy mountaines of God, for the space of 600 yeares and more, passed with a most faire and spatious current, like *Tygris & Euphrates* watering on each side the Garden of the Lord; or like *Pactolus*, with golden streames inriching and beautifying the Church of God: after that time it fell into the corrupted waters of succeeding ages, brackish (I confesse) before their second *Nycene* Synod, but after it and the next unto it, extremely salt and unpleasant, more bitter then the waters of *Mara*. And although the nearer it came to the streets of *Babylon*, it was still more mingled with the slime or mud of their *Babylonish* ditches; yet, for all that dangerous and long mixture, continuing about the space of ᵃ730. yeares, this truth all that time kept her native and primitive sweetnesse, by the constant and successive professions of the whole Church throughout all those ages. Now after that long passage through all those salt waves, like *Alpheus*, or *Arethusa*, it bursts out againe; not as they did, in *Sicily*; nor neare the *Italian* shores, but (as the *Cardinall* tells ᵇus) in *Germanie*, in *England*, in *Scotland*, in *France*, in *Helvetia*, in *Polonia*, in *Bohemia*, in *Pannonia*, in *Sueveland*, in *Denmarke*, in *Norway*. in all the Reformed Churches, and being by the power and goodnesse of God, purified from all that mud and corruption wherewith it was mingled; (all which is now left in it owne proper, that is, in the *Romane*, channels;) it is now preserved in the faire current of those Orthodoxall Churches, wherein both it and other holy doctrines of Faith, are with no lesse sinceritie professed, then they were in those ancient times before they were mingled with any bitter or brackish waters.

36 You see now the whole judgement of the Fift Generall Councill, how in every point it contradicteth the *Apostolicall Constitution* of Pope *Vigilius*, condemning and accursing both it for hereticall, and all who defend it for heretikes: which their sentence, you see, is consonant to the Scriptures, and the whole
Catholike

y *Gentil. Exam. čc. Trid. Seff. 13. & Car. Bel. acc. Conc. Trid. decret. ca. 3.*

z *Alpheum fama est huc Elidis amnem, Occultas egisse vias subter mare. Virg. lib. 3. Æneid.*

a *Tot anni intersunt à Conc. Nic. 2. quod habitum est an. 787. ad annum quo Lutherus se primum opposuit indulgentijs papalibus & pontificis, qui fuit an. 1517 Cocleus una Luthero, in Brevi octavavit (Lutheri hæreses) multa regna. Bell. 3. de pontif. ca. 13. § similitudo. Et, Romana sedes amisit nostris temporibus magnam Germaniæ partem, Suetiam, Gothiam, Norvegiam, Daniam universam, bonam Angliæ, Galliæ, Helvetiæ, Poloniæ, Bohemiæ, ac Pannoniæ partem, lib. eod. ca. 21. § At postea.*

Catholike Church of all ages, excepting none but such as adhere to their new *Laterane* decree and faith. An example so ancient, so authenticall, and so pregnant to demonstrate the truth, which wee teach, and they oppugne, that it may justly cause any Papist in the world to stagger, and stand in doubt, even of the maine ground and foundation whereon all his faith relyeth. For the full clearing of which matter, being of so great importance and consequence, I have thought it needful to rip up every veine and sinew in this whole cause, concerning these *Three Chapters*, and the *Constitution* of *Vigilius* in defence of the same: and withall examine the weight of every doubt, evasion, & excuse, which eyther *Cardinall Baronius*, (who is *instar omnium*) or *Binius*, or any other, moveth or pretendeth herein; not willingly, nor with my knowledge, omitting any one reason, or circumstance, which either they urge, or which may seeme to advantage or help them, to decline the inevitable force of our former Demonstration.

CAP. V.

The first Exception of Baronius, *pretending that the cause of the* Three Chapters *was no cause of faith, refuted.*

 Here is not, as I thinke, any one cause which *Card. Baronius* in all the Volumes of his *Annalls* hath with more art or industry handled, then this concerning Pope *Vigilius*, and *the Fift Generall Councill*. In this hee hath strained all his wits, moved and removed every stone, under which hee imagined any help might be found, eyther wholly to excuse, or any way lessen the errour of *Vigilius*. All the *Cardinalls* forces may be ranked into foure severall troupes. In the first do march all his Shifts and Evasions which are drawne from the Matter of the *Three Chapters* : In the second, those which are drawne from the *Popes Constitution* : In the third, those which respect a subsequent Act of *Vigilius*: In the fourth & last, those which concerne the fift Generall Councill. After all these, wherin consisteth the whole pith of the Cause, the *Cardinall* brings forth another band of certaine subsidiary, but most disorderly souldiers, nay, not souldiers; they never tooke the Military oath, nor may they by the Law of armes, nor ever were by any worthy Generall admitted into any lawfull fight, or so much as to set footing in the field; meere theeves and robbers they are, whom the *Cardinall* hath set in an ambush, not to fight in the cause, but onely like so many *Shimei's*, that they might raile at and revile whomsoever the *Cardinall* takes a spleene at, or with whatsoever hee shall be moved in the heat of his choler: At the Emperour *Iustinian*, at

Theodora

Theodora the Empresse, at the cause it selfe of the *Three Chapters*, at the *Imperiall Edict*, at *Theodorus* Bishop of *Cæsarea*, at the *Synodal* acts, yea, at Pope *Vigilius* himselfe; we wil first encounter the just forces of the Cardinall, which onely are his lawfull warriours; and having discomfited them, we shall with ease cleare all the coasts of this cause, from all his theevish, piraticall, and disordered straglers.

2. The first and chiefest exception of *Baronius* ariseth from the matter & controversie it selfe touching these *Three Chapters*, concerning which he pretendeth, that no question of faith was handled therin, & so one dissenting from another in this cause, might not be counted or called an heretike. This was a question saith he, [a] *de personis, & non de fide;* *of persons and not of the faith.* Againe, [b] *Vigilius* knew, *Non de fide esse quæstionem, sed de personis;* *that there was no question moved herein about the faith, but about certaine persons.* And yet more clearly, In these disputations, saith he, [c] about the *Three Chapters,* as we have ofte said, *Nulla fuit quæstio de fide, ut alter ab altero aliter sentiens dici posset hæreticus;* *there was no question at all about the faith, so that one dissenting from another herein, might be called an heretike.* And this hee so confidently avoucheth, that he saith of it, *Ab omnibus absque ulla controversia consentitur;* *all men agree herein without any controversie.* Thus *Baronius,* whom *Binius* applauding, saith, [d] *Sciendum est,* bee it knowne to all men, that in these disputations and differences about the *Three Chapters, non fuisse quæstionem ullam de fide, sed tantummodo de personis;* there was no question at all concerning the faith, but only concerning the persons. So he. Whereby they would insinuate, that Pope *Vigilius* did erre onely in a personall cause, or in a matter of fact, which they not unwillingly confesse that the Pope may doe; but he erred not in a cause of faith, or in any doctrinall position of faith, wherein onely they defend him to bee infallible.

3. Truly the Card. was driven to an extreme exigent, when this poore shift must be the first and best shelter to save the *infallibility of the Apostolike Chaire.* For to say truth, the maine controversie touching these *Three Chapters,* which the Councell condemned, and *Vigilius* defended, was onely doctrinall, and directly belonging to the faith; nor did it concerne the persons any other way, but with an implication of that hereticall doctrine which they and the defenders of these Chapters under that colour did cunningly maintaine : A truth so evident that I doe even labour with abundance of proofes.

4. *Iustinian* the religious Emperour, who called this Councell about this matter, committed it unto them, as a question of faith : *We have,* saith he, [e] *commanded Vigilius to come together with you all, and debate these* Three Chapters, *that a determination may be given, rectæ fidei conveniens, consonant to the right faith.* Againe, stirring [f] them up to give a speedy resolution in this cause, hee

E   addes

a An. 547 nu. 30
& nu. 225.
b Ibid. nu. 46.

c Ibid. nu. 231.

d Not. in Conc. 5.
§. Ne quis.

e Epist. ad. Synod.
Coll. 1. pa. 520. A.

f Ibid. b.

addes this as a reason, *Quoniā qui de fide recta interrogatur: for when one is asked concerning the right faith, and puts off his answer therein, this is nothing else but a deniall of the true confession: for in questions & answers quæ de fide sunt, which are questions of faith, hee that is more prompt and ready is acceptable with God.* Thus the Emperour.

5. The Holy Councell esteemed it, as did the Emperour, to be no other than a cause or question of faith; for thus they say, *Cum* [h] *de fide ratio movetur, when a doubt or question is moved touching the faith, even he is to be condemned, who may hinder impiety, but is negligent so to doe;* and therefore, *Festinavimus bonum fidei semen conservare ab impietatis Zizanijs; We have hastened to preserve the good seed of faith pure from the tares of impietie.* So cleerly doth the whole generall Councell even in their definitive sentence call the condemning of the *Three Chapters* which themselves did, a preserving of the good seed of faith; and the defending of them, which *Vigilius* did, a sowing of hereticall weeds which corrupt the faith. Againe, [m] *We being enlightned by the holy Scriptures, and the doctrine of the holy Fathers,* have thought it needfull to set downe in certaine Chapters, (those are the particular points of their Synodall judgement) *Et prædicationem veritatis, & hæreticorum eorumque impietatis condemnationem;* both the preaching of the truth, or true faith, and the condemning of Heretikes, and their impietie. And in the end, having set downe those Chapters, and among them a particular and expresse condemning of these *Three* wth an anathema denounced to the defenders of thē, they conclude thus, [n] *We have confessed these things, being delivered unto us both by the sacred Scriptures, by the doctrine of the holy Fathers, & by those things wch are defined, de unâ eâdemq, fide, concerning one and the same faith by the foure former Councels.* Then which nothing can be more cleare to witnesse their decree touching these *Threee Chapters* most nearely to concerne the faith, unlesse some of *Baronius* his friends can make proofe, that the condemning of heretikes, and their impious heresies, and the maintaining of that doctrine which the Scriptures and Fathers taught, and the foure first Councels defined, is not a point of faith.

6. Neither onely did the Catholikes which were the condemners of these *Three Chapters,* but the heretikes also which were the defenders of them, they also consent in this truth, that the question concerning them, was a controversie or cause of faith. Pope *Vigilius* in his Constitution [o] still pretendeth his Defence of Those Chapters to be consonant to the Councell at Chalcedon, and the Definition thereof: and of the Epistle of *Ibas* hee expresly saith, *The Councel of Chalcedon pronounced it to be orthodoxall.* And none I suppose will doubt, but that the question, whether that or any other writing be orthodoxall, and agreeable to the *Definition of Chalcedon,* as *Vigilius* affirmed that Epistle to be; or be heretical and repugnant to that *Definition,* as the Holy Councell adjudged that Epistle to be, is a plaine question and controversie

h *Coll.8.pag.584.a.*

m *Ibid.pa.586.b.*

n *Ibid.pa.588.a.*

o *Apud Baran. 553-xx.106.197-208.& alibi.*

verfie of faith. *Victor* B. of *Tunen,* who fuffered imprifonment and banifhment for defence of thefe *Three Chapters,* teacheth the like, faying, P *That Epiſtle of* Ibas *was approved and judged* q *orthodox all, by the ſentence of the Councell at Chalcedon: and the condemning of theſe* Three Chapters, *is the condemning and baniſhing of that Councell. Facundus* B. of *Hermian,* who writ feven bookes of thefe *Three Chapters,* doth more than abundantly witneffe this of him. *Victor* thus writeth, r *Evidentiſſime declaravit, Facundus* hath declared moſt evidently, that thofe *Three Chapters* were condemned *in proſcriptione fidei Catholicæ & Apoſtolicæ, for the exiling and rooting out of the Catholike and Apoſtolike faith. Facundus* himfelfe doth not onely affirme this, but prove it alfo, even by the judgement of Pope *Vigilius. Vigilius,* faith he, s *eſteemed the condemning of theſe Three Chapters to be ſo hainous a crime, that hee thought it fit to be reproved by thoſe words of the Apoſtle, Avoid prophane novelties of words, and oppoſition of ſcience falſely ſo called, which ſome profeſſing have erred from the faith.* And hereupon, as if he meant purpofely to refute this Evafion of *Baronius,* which it feemeth fome did ufe in thofe dayes, he addes, *Quid adhuc quæritur utrum contra fidem factum fuerit;* why doe any as yet doubt whether the condemning of them be againſt the faith, feeing Pope *Vigilius* calleth it prophane noveltie and oppofition of fcience, whereby fome have erred from the faith? And a little after concluding, This faith he, t is not to be thought fuch a caufe as may bee tolerated for the peace of the Church, *ſed quæ merito judicatur contra ipſius fidei Catholicæ ſtatum commota;* but it muft bee judged fuch a caufe as is moved againſt the ſtate of the Catholike faith. Thus *Facundus* teftifying both his owne, and the judgement of the other defenders of thofe Chapters, and by name of Pope *Vigilius,* that they all efteemed and judged this to bee a queftion and controverfie of faith, of which *Baronius* tels us, that in it there was moved no queftion at all concerning the faith; and that Pope *Vigilius* knew that it was no queftion of faith.

7. Now whereas the whole Church at that time was divided into u two parts, the Eafterne Churches with the holy Councell condemning; the Wefterne with Pope *Vigilius* defending thofe *Three Chapters,* feeing both the one fide and the other confent in this point, that this was *a cauſe and queſtion of faith,* what truth or credit thinke you, is there in *Baronius,* who faith, that All men without any doubt agree herein, that this is no caufe or queftion of faith: whereas *all,* both the one fide and the other agree in the quite contrary. Truly the *wiſdome* of the Cardinall is well worthy obferving, He confenteth to *Vigilius* in defending the *Three Chapters,* wherein *Vigilius* was hereticall: but diffenteth from *Vigilius* in holding this to be a caufe of faith, wherein *Vigilius* was orthodoxal, as if he had made fome *vow* to follow the Pope, when the Pope forfakes the truth, but to forfake the Pope, when the Pope followeth the truth.

p *In Chron. an.* 2. *poſt Conſul. Baſilij.* q *Iudicio Synodi approbata, & orthodoxa judicata eſt. ibid.*

r *In ſuo Chron. an.* 10. *poſt Conſul Baſilij.*

s *Lib* 4. *pro defenſtrium Capit apud* B.r. *an.* 546. *nu.*57.

t *Ibid. nu.*58.

u *Vniverſus fere orbis occidentalis ab orientali Ecclesia diviſus erat. Bin. not. in* S. *Conc.*5. *Concilium.*

8. Nor onely was this truth by that age acknowledged, but by succeeding, approved. By Pope *Pelagius*, who to reclame certaine Bishops from defence of those Chapters, wherin they were earnest, and had writ an apologie for the same, useth this as one speciall reason, because all those Chapters were repugnant to the Scriptures & former Councels. *Consider*, saith he, ˟ *if the wrítings of* Theodorus, *which deny Chrift the Redeemer to bee the Lord, the writings of* Theodoret, *quæ contra fidem edita, which being publiſhed against the faith, were afterwards by himſeſe condemned; and the Epiſtle of* Ibas, *wherein* Neſtorius *the enemy of the Church is defended; if theſe bee conſonant to the Propheticall, Euangelicall, and Apoſtolicall authority.* And againe, ʸ of the Epiſtle of Ibas he addeth, *If this Epiſtle be received as true, tota ſanᶜᵗæ Epheſinæ Synodus fides diſſipatur, the whole faith of the holy Epheſine Councell is overthrowne.* Let here some of *Baronius* friends tell us how that queſtion or cauſe doth not concerne the faith, the defending whereof (which *Vigilius* did) is by the judgement of Pope *Pelagius* repugnant to the Euangelical and Apoſtolicall doctrines, and even anutter & totall overthrow of the faith. To *Pelagius* accordeth Pope *Gregory*, who approved ᶻ *this Epiſtle of Pelagius, & comended it as a direction to others in this cauſe.* And what ſpeake I of one or two, ſeeing the Decree of this fift Councell, wherein this is declared to be a cauſe of faith, is conſonant to all former, and confirmed by all ſucceeding generall Councels, Popes and Biſhops, til that time of *Leo* the 10. & his *Laterane* Synod, as before we ᵃ have ſhewed? was not this thinke you, moſt inſolent preſumption in *Baronius* to ſet himſelfe as a *Iohannes ad oppoſitum*, againſt them all, and oppoſe his owne fancy, to the conſtant and conſenting judgement of the whole Catholike Church for more than 1500 yeares together? Theſe all with one voyce profeſſe this to be a cauſe of faith: *Baronius* againſt them all maintaineth, that it is *no cauſe of faith*: and to heape up the full meaſure of his ſhame, addeth a vaſt untruth, for which no colour of excuſe can be deviſed; *Conſentitur ab omnibus*, that all men without any controverſie agree herein, that this is no queſtion nor cauſe of faith.

9. Beſides all theſe, Card. *Bellarmine* ſetteth downe divers *τεκμήρια*, and cleare tokens whereby one may certainly know when a Councell decreeth or propoſeth any doctrine *tanquam de fide*, to be received as a doctrine of the Catholike faith. This ſaith he, ᵇ *is eaſily knowne by the words of the Councell, for either they uſe to ſay, that they explicate the Catholike faith: or elſe, that they who thinke the contrary are to be accounted heretikes: or, which is moſt frequent, they anathematize thoſe who thinke the contrary.* So he. Let us now by theſe markes examine this cauſe, and it will be moſt evident, not onely by ſome one of them, which yet were ſufficient, but by them all, that the Holy Councell both held this controverſie to be of faith, and also propoſed their decree herein, as a Decree of faith.

                                                      10. For

(marginal notes:)

˟ *Epiſt.7. §. Penſate.*

ʸ *Ibid. § Sed cur.*

ᶻ *Lib.2. Ind.10. Epiſt.36.*

ᵃ *Cap.4.*

ᵇ *Lib.2. de Conc. ca.12. § Quartū.*

10. For the first, the Councell in plaine termes professeth even *c in their definitive sentence, that in their Decree they explane that same doctrine which the Scriptures, the Fathers, and the foure former Councels had delivered in their definitions of faith.* Then undoubtedly by *Bellarmines* first note, their Decree herein is a Decree of faith, seeing it is an explication of the Catholike faith.

c Coll.8.pa.588.a.

11. For the second, the Councel in like sort, in plain termes calleth the defēders of those *three Chapters*, heretikes. For thus cried al the Synod, *d He who doth not anathematize this Epistle, is an Heretike : He who receiveth it, is an Heretike : This we say all.* And in their definitive sentence they professe *e that they set down the preaching of the truth, & Hæreticorum condemnationem, and the condemning of Heretikes.* So by the second marke of *Bellarmine* it is undoubted, that the Councels Decree herein is a Decree of faith.

d Coll.6.pa. 576.b.

e Coll.8.pa.

12. The third note is more than demonstrative. For the Holy Councell denounceth, not once or twice, but more I thinke than an hundred times an *Anathema* to them that teach contrary to their sentence. *Anathema f to Theodorus; anathema to him that doth not anathematize Theodorus; we all anathematize Theodorus and his writings. Anathema g to the impious writing of Theodoret against Cyril : Anathema to all that doe not anathematize them : we h all anathematize the impious Epistle of Ibas : If i any defend this Epistle, or any part of it, if any doe not anathematize it, and the defenders of it, let him be an Anathema.*

f Coll.4.pa.537.a.
& Coll.8.pa.586.et 587.
g Coll.8.pa. 587.b.
h Coll.6.pa.576.b.
i Coll.8.pa.587.b.

13. So by all the notes of Cardinall *Bellarmine*, it is evident, not onely that this question about the *Three Chapters*, is *a question of faith*; but, which is more, that the holy generall Councell proposed their Decree herein, *tanquam de fide, as a Decree of faith.* Now because every Christian is bound to beleeve *certitudine fidei cui falsum subesse non potest, with certainty of faith which cannot be deceived*, every doctrine and position of faith, then especially when it is published and declared by a Decree of the Church to bee a doctrine of faith : Seeing by this Decree of faith which the Councell now made, not onely the Popes *Apostolicall* sentence in a cause of faith, is condemned to bee hereticall, but all they also who defend it, to be Heretikes and accursed; and seeing all defend it who maintaine the Popes cathedrall sentence to be *infallible*, that is, *all who are members of the present Church of Rome* : it hence inevitably ensueth, that every Christian is bound to beleeve *certitudine fidei cui falsum subesse non potest*, not onely the doctrine, even the *fundamentall* doctrine of the present Church of Rome to be hereticall, but all that maintaine it; that is, all that are members of that Church, to be heretikes and accursed, unlesse disclaiming that heresie they forsake all communion with that Church. *Baronius* perceiving all those *Anathemaes* to fall inevitably upon himselfe, and their whole Church, if this cause of the *Three Chapters* which *Vigilius* defended and defined by his *Apostolicall* Constitution, that they must be defended,

ded; if this I say were admitted to be a caufe of faith, that hee might fhuffle off thofe *Anathemaes*, which like the leprofie of *Gehaʒi* doth cleave unto them; thought it the fafeft, as indeed it was the fhorteft way, to deny this to be a caufe of faith, which not onely by all the precedent witneffes, but by the judgement of their owne Cardinall, and all the three notes fet downe by him, is undeniably proved to bee a caufe of faith, and that the Decree of the Holy Councell concerning it, is propo- fed as a Decree of faith.

14. I might further adde their owne *Nicholas Sanders*, who though he faw not much in matters of faith, yet he both faw and

k *Ob eafdem here- fes decrevit eos iſſe alienos à diaconatŭ honore. Lib.7.de viſib. Monarch. an.537.*

profeffed this truth, and therefore in plaine termes calleth [k] the defending of the *Three Chapters* an herefie. Now herefie it could not be, unleffe it were a caufe of faith, feeing every herefie is a deviation from the faith. But omitting him, and fome others of his ranke, I will now in the laft place adde one other witneffe, which with the favourites of *Baronius* is of more weight and worth, than all the former, and that is *Baronius* himfelfe, who, as he doth often deny, fo doth he often and plainly profeffe this to be a caufe of faith. Speaking of the Emperours Edict concerning thefe *Three Chapters*, he bitterly reproveth; yea, he reproacheth

l *An.546.nu.41.*

the Emperour for that he would [l] arrogate to himfelfe *edere fan- ctiones de fide Catholica, to make Edicts about the Catholike faith.* A-

m *An.eodē.nu.43.*

gain, the whole Catholike faith, faith he, would [m] be in jeopardy, if fuch as *Iuſtinian de fide leges fanciret, ſhould make lawes concerning the faith.* Againe, [n] *Pelagius* the Popes Legate founded an alarum

n *Ibid.nu.50.*

contra ejuſdem Imperatoris de fide ſancitŭ Edictŭ, againſt the Emperors Edict publiſhed concerning the faith. And yet againe, [o] Pope *Vigili-*

o *An.547. nu.50.*

us writ letters againſt thofe *qui edito ab Imperatore fidei decreto ſub- ſcripſiſſent, who had ſubſcribed to the Emperours Edict of faith.* So often, fo expreſly doth *Baronius* profeffe this to be a *caufe of faith*, which himfelfe, like the *Æſopicall Satyr*, had fo often, and fo ex- preſly denied to be a caufe of faith; and that alfo fo confidently, that he fhamed not to fay, *Conſentitur ab omnibus, all men agree herein*, that this is no caufe of faith; whereas *Baronius* himfelfe diffenteth herein, confeffing in plaine termes this to be a caufe of the Catholike faith.

15. The truth is, the Cardinals judgement was unfetled, and himfelfe in a manner infatuated in handling this whole caufe touching *Vigilius* and the fift generall Councell. For having once refolved to deny this one truth, that *Vigilius* by his *Apoſtolicall* fentence maintained and defined herefie, and decreed that all o- ther fhould maintaine it, (which one truth, like a *Theſean* threed would eafily and certainly have directed him in all the reft of his Treatife;) now he wandreth up and down as in a Labyrinth, toi- ling himfelfe in uncertainties and contradictions, faying, and gainfaying, whatfoever either the prefent occaſiō which he hath in hand, or the partialitie of his corrupted judgement, like a violent

lent tempeſt doth drive him unto; when the Emperour or his E-
dict (to both which he beares an implacable hatred) comes in
his way, then this queſtion about the *Three Chapters*, muſt bee a
cauſe of faith: for ſo the Cardinall may have a ſpacious field to
declame againſt the Emperour for preſuming to intermeddle
and make lawes in a cauſe of faith. But when Pope *Vigilius* or his
Conſtitution(with which the Cardinall is moſt partially blinded)
meet him, then the caſe is quite altered, the queſtion about the
Three Chapters muſt then bee no more a queſtion or cauſe of
faith; for that is an eaſie way to excuſe *Vigilius*, and the infallibilitie of his Chaire: he erred onely in ſome perſonall matters,
in ſuch the Pope may erre; he erred not in any doctrinall point,
nor in a cauſe of faith; in ſuch is hee and his Chaire infallible.

16. There remaineth one doubt, ariſing out of the words of
Gregory, by the wilfull miſtaking whereof P *Baronius* was miſſe-
led. He ſeemeth to teach the ſame with the Cardinall, where
ſpeaking of this fift Synod, hee ſaith, q *In eâ de perſonis tantummodo, non autem de fide aliquid eſt geſtum; In it was onely handled
ſomewhat concerning thoſe perſons, but nothing concerning the faith.* So
Gregory, whoſe words if they be taken without any limitation,
are not onely untrue, but repugnant to the conſenting judgement
of Councels and Fathers above mentioned, even to *Gregory* himſelfe: for ſpeaking of all the five Councels held before his time;
he ſaith, r *Whoſoever embraceth, prædictarum Synodorum fidem, the
faith explaned by thoſe five Councels, peace be unto them.* And if hee
had not in ſuch particular manner teſtified this; yet ſeeing hee
approveth (as was before ſ ſhewed) this fift Councel and the Decree thereof, & ſeeing that Decree clearly expreſſeth this to have
beene a cauſe of faith, grounded on Scriptures, and the definitions of faith ſet downe in former Councels; even thereby doth
Gregory certainly imply, that he accounted this cauſe for no o-
ther than (as the Synod it ſelfe did) for a cauſe of faith.

17. What then is *Gregory* repugnant to himſelfe herein? I
liſt not to cenſure ſo of him; rather by his owne words I deſire to
explane his meaning. There were divers in his time, as alſo in his
Predeceſſor's *Pelagius*, who condemned this fift Councell, becauſe, as they ſuppoſed, it had altered and aboliſhed the faith of
the Councell at *Chalcedon*, by condemning theſe *Three Chapters*,
and had eſtabliſhed a new doctrine of faith. *Gregorie* intreating
againſt theſe, whom he truly calleth t malignant perſons, and
troublers of the Church, denieth, and that moſt juſtly, that this
Councell had done ought in the faith; not ſimply, as if they
had done nothing at all, but nothing in ſuch a manner as thoſe
malignant perſons intended; nothing that was contrary to the
faith decreed at *Chalcedon*; nothing that was new, or uncouth in
the doctrine of faith; in this manner the Councell did nothing
in the faith. Heare the words of *Gregorie* expreſſing thus much;
Some there are (ſaith hee) u *who affirme, that in the time of* Iulian

Marginal notes:
p *An. 547. nu. 30.
& an. 553. nu.
231.*
q *Lib. 3. Epiſt. 37.*

r *Lib. 1. Epiſt. 24.*

ſ *ca. 4. nu. 27.*

t *Executes maligni
homines turbave-
runt animos veſtros.
Lib. 1. Epiſt. 10.*
u *Lib. 3. Epiſt. 3.*

there was somewhat decreed against the Councell at Chalcedon; But such men neither reading, neither beleeving those who read, remaine in their errour; for we professe, our conscience bearing witnesse unto us, de fide ejusdem Concily nihil esse motum, nihil violatum; that nothing concerning the faith of that Councell at Chalcedon, was here (in the fift Councell) moved or altered, nothing violated or hurt; but whatsoever was done in this fift Synod, it was done, that the faith of the Councell at Chalcedon should in no sort be infringed. So Gregory, who to like purpose againe saith, *In the Synod concerning the* Three Chapters *it is manifest, nihil de fide convulsum esse, nihil immutatū; that nothing concerning the faith was weakned, nothing changed therein.*

x Lib.2.Ind.10.
Epist.36.

18. Now as against their first calumnie, *Gregory* teacheth, that nothing was done contrary to the faith of the Councell at *Chalcedon*; so against their other he sheweth, that they decreed no noveltie in the faith, nor ought else but what was formerly decreed at *Chalcedon*. To which purpose he saith ᵞ of this fift Synod, that it was *in omnibus sequax, in every point an imitator & follower of the Councell at Chalcedo:* & againe ᶻ more clearly, In this fift Synod nothing else was done, *quā apud Chalcedonēsem Synodū fuerat constitutū; then was formerly decreed in the Councel at Chalcedon.* So *Gregory.* Both this fift, & that at *Chalcedon* (as also the former at *Ephesus*) decreed one and the selfe same faith, as by *Gregory* is truly witnessed : but the Councell at *Chalcedon* and *Ephesus* decreed it absolutely, without any expresse reference to those persons or writings which are condemned in the fift, though in them both was *implicitè* contained a condemnation of all these *Three Chapters*; the fift Councell decreed it with an expresse reference to these Chapters, and an explicite condemnation of them. The Decrees made at *Ephesus* and *Chalcedon* were Introductive; as first condemning those heresies of *Nestorius* and *Eutyches*. The Decree of this fift Councell was onely *Corroborative*, or *Declarative*, explaning and corroborating those former decrees, by condemning these writings of *Theodorus*, *Theodoret*, and *Ibas*, which did overthrow the same. As *Vigilius* and other followers of *Nestorius*, did not at this time broach any new heresie, but under those *Three Chapters* on which they put the visor of the Councell at *Chalcedon*, sought to revive the heresie of *Nestorius*, which before, when it came in its owne habit, was condemned : Even so the fift Councell needed not, neither did they condemne any new, but unmasked the old & condemned heresie of *Nestorius* lurking under the defence of these *Three Chapters*; they pulled off the visor of *Chalcedon* from it, under which it most subtilly now sought to insinuate it selfe, and creep into the Church. And when *Gregory* saith, that in this fift Councell they dealt *tantummodo de personis*, that *tantummodo*, in his sense doth not exclude all handling of the faith, not the explaning, not the corroborating of the faith, for both these they certainly did, and *Gregory* acknowledgeth : but it onely excludes such an handling of the faith as was used at E-
phesus.

y Lib.7.Epist.54.

z Lib.2.Ind.11.
Epist.10.

pheſus and *Chalcedon*, by making an *Introductive* decree for condemning ſome new hereſie. The fift Councell dealt onely with
perſons, without making ſuch a Decree; yet it dealt with thoſe
perſons with an intent to explane and corroborate thoſe *Introductive* decrees.

19. The words of *Gregory* next following thoſe on which *Baronius* relied, doe yet more fully explane this to have beene his
meaning. In the fift Synod nothing was done concerning the
faith, but only the perſons; and thoſe perſons, *de quibus in Chalce-
donenſi Synodo nihil continetur, concerning wᶜʰ perſons nothing is contained or ſet downe in the Councell at Chalcedon.* For as there is much
contained in that Councell concerning thoſe perſons, eſpecially
Ibas, (in whoſe cauſe, and the examining therof, two ᵃ whole A-
ctions are beſtowed) and yet in a favourable conſtruction, or ac-   ᵃ *Act. 9. & 10.*
cording to *Gregory* his meaning, he might truly ſay, that nothing
concerning them is contained there; to wit, nothing to condemne *Theodorus*, or the writings of *Theodoret* and *Ibas* in ſuch an
expreſſe and particular manner as they are condemned in the
fift Councell: Right ſo, though the fift Councell not onely
handled a cauſe of faith, but publiſhed their decree as a Decree
of faith; yet in a like favourable conſtruction, and according to
Gregories meaning he might truly ſay, that nothing was done
therein concerning the faith, to wit, nothing to make ſuch an
Introductive decree for condemning a new hereſie, as was formerly made in the Councell at *Chalcedon.*

20. By all which the true meaning of *Gregory* is now by his
owne explaning moſt evident. In the fift Councell nothing was
done contrary to the faith, (as the malignant ſlanderers of this
Councell pretended) nothing was done *de novo, to condemne any
new hereſie*; nothing was done abſolutely, or without reference
to theſe *Three Chapters*: all this *Gregory* truly intendeth, when he
ſaith, nothing was done therein concerning the faith: but ſeeing
all that was done in the Councell, was done to explane, confirme
& corroborate the faith decreed at *Chalcedon, & Epheſus*; as *Gregory* himſelfe profeſſeth, it undoubtedly followeth, that even for
this cauſe, and by *Gregories* owne teſtimonie, the queſtion here
defined was a cauſe and queſtion of faith. Vpon *Gregories* words
the Cardinall might well have collected, that *Vigilius* in defending the *Three Chapters*, erred not in any new hereſie, or new
queſtion of faith, ſuch as was not before condemned; but that he
erred not at all in a cauſe of faith, is ſo farre from the intent of
Gregory, that out of his expreſſe words the quite contrary is certainly to be collected. For how can the Pope be ſaid not at all to
erre in the faith, when by his *Apoſtolicall* Conſtitution he defendeth that cauſe of the *Three Chapters*, the defending whereof
contradicteth a former definition of faith, and utterly overthroweth the holy Councell of *Epheſus* and *Chalcedon*; yea, the
whole Catholike faith?

21. Neither

d *Cyril. epist. ad Procl. in Conc. 5. Coll. 5. pa. 550, 551.*

Cyrill doe plainly import the contrary. The Ephesine Synod, saith [d] he, *forbare in particular, and by name, to anathematize* Theorus, which they did *dispensativè, by a certaine dispensation,* indulgence, or connivence, because divers held him in great estimatiõ, or account: what needed either any such dispensation, or forbearance, had he in his life time beene publikely condemned for heresie? Againe, the Church of Mopsvestia, where hee was Bishop, for divers yeares after his death, retained his name *in* [e] *Diplicis,* that is, *in their Ecclesiasticall tables,* making a thankfull commemoration of him, as of other Catholikes in their Liturgie; which, had he beene in his life time condemned for an heretike, they would not have done. Lastly, what needed the defenders of the *Three Chapters* have beene so scrupulous, to condemne him being dead, had he in his life time beene before condemned? Or how could this have given occasion of this controversie, whether a dead man might *Noviter* be condemned, if *Theodorus* had not beene *noviter* condemned when he was dead.

e *Conc. 5. Coll. 5. pa. 552. & seq. in diff. Synod. Mopsv.*

3. Wherefore this particular being agreed upon, that *Theodorus* was not before, but after his death condemned, the whole doubt now resteth in the *Thesis, whether a dead man may* Noviter *be cõdemned.* Now that this is no personall, but meerly a dogmaticall cause, and controversie of faith, is so evident, that it might be a wonder that *Baronius,* or any other, should so much as doubt thereof, unlesse the Apostle had foretold, that *because men* [f] *doe not receive the love of the truth; therefore God doth send unto them strong delusions, that they may beleeve lyes.* Certaine it is that Pope *Vigilius,* held this for no other, but a doctrine of faith; for he sets it downe as a [g] Definition, or *Constitution* of his predecessors, decreed by the *Apostolike* See: particularly by Pope *Leo,* and *Gelasius;* and so decreed by them, as warranted, and taught by the Scriptures; for out of those words, Whatsoever ye binde, or loose upon earth, Pope *Gelasius* [h] *collecteth,* and *Vigilius* consenteth unto him, that such as are not upon earth, or among the living, *hos non humano, sed suo Deus judicio reservavit;* God hath exempted them from humane, *and reserved them to his owne judgement : nec audet Ecclesia,* nor dare the Church challenge to it selfe the judgement of such. As the Pope, so also the holy generall Councell tooke this for no other, than a question of faith; for they plainly professe, even in their Synodall resolution, that their decree concerning dead men, that they may *bee Noviter condemned;* is not onely an Ecclesiasticall [i] tradition, but an *Apostolicall* doctrine also, warranted by the texts, and testimonies of the holy Scriptures. To which purpose alledging divers places of Scripture, they adde these words; It is many wayes manifest, that they who affirme this, [that men after their death may not *Noviter* be condemned,] *nullam curam Dei judicatorum faciunt, nec Apostolicarum pronunciationum, nec paternarum traditionum;* that such have no regard either to the word of God, or the Apostles doctrine, or the tradition

f *2. Thess. 2. 10, 11.*

g *Perspeximus si quid de his predecessores nostri decreverint. Vig. Const. loc. citat. nu. 176. Hujus causa formam veneranda predecessorum nostrarum constituta, nobis apertissime tradiderunt. Ibid. Idem regula tria Apostolice sedis definiunt constituta. Ibid. nu. 179.* h *Ibid. nu. 177.*

i *Licet cognoscere-mus Ecclesiasticam de impiis traditio-nem. Coll. 8. pa. 585. a.*

dition of the Fathers. So the whole Councell judging, and decreeing Pope *Vigilius* to be guilty of all these.

4. Now when both the Pope on the one side, and the whole generall Councell on the other; that is, both the defenders, and condemners of *this Chapter* professe it to be a doctrine taught in the Scripture, and therefore undoubtedly to be a cause of faith; what insolency was it in *Baronius* to contradict them both, and, against that truth, wherein they both agree, to deny *this Chapter* to be a cause of faith? or seeing it is cleare, both by the Pope, and Councell, that the resolution of this question is set downe in Scripture, what else can bee thought of *Baronius* denying either the one, or the other part, to bee a cause, or assertion of faith, but that with him the doctrines defined, and set down in Scriptures, are no doctrines or assertions of faith, at least, not of the *Cardinals* faith?

5. Seeing now this is a cause of faith, and in this cause of faith, the Pope, and generall Councell are at variance; either of them challenge the Scripture, as consonant to his, and repugnant to the opposite assertion; what equall and unpartiall umpire may be found to judge in this matter? *Audito Ecclesiæ nomine hostis expalluit,* saith their vaine, and vaunting [k] Braggadochio; *Hast thou appealed to the Church? to the Church, and judgement thereof shalt thou goe;* at the name of which, we are so farre from being daunted, or appaled, that with great confidence, and assurance of victory, we provoke unto it.

6. But where may we heare the voyce, and judgement of the Church? out of doubt either in the writings of the Fathers, or provinciall Synods, or in generall Councels; & in which of these soever the Church speake, her sentence is for us, and our side. Her voyce is but soft & stil in the writings of single Fathers; the Church whispereth rather then speaketh in them; and yet even in them shee speaketh this truth very distinctly, and audibly. Heare Saint [l] *Austen,* who entreating of *Cæcilianus,* about an hundreth yeares after his death, saith; *If as yet they could prove him to have beene guilty of those crimes,* which were by the Donatists objected unto him, *ipsum jam mortuum anathematizaremus,* I and all Catholikes would even now accurse him though dead, though never condemned before, nor in his life time. Againe, [m] In this our communion, if there have beene any *Traditores,* or deliverers of the Bible to be burned in time of persecution, when thou shalt *demonstrate* or prove them to have beene such, *& corde & carne mortuos detestabor.* Heare Pope [n] *Pelagius,* who both himselfe fully assenteth herein to Saint *Austen,* and testifieth the assent of Pope *Leo,* in this manner; *Quis nesciat,* who knoweth not that the doctrine of *Leo* is consonant to Saint *Austen.* Heare [o] S. *Cyrill,* who speaking of heretikes, saith, *Evitandi sunt, sive in vivis, sive in mortuis;* they are to bee avoyded, whether they bee dead, or living.

F   7. The

k *Camp.Rat.* 5.

l *Epist. ad Bonif. quæ citatur Conc. 5. Coll. 5. pa. 548.b.*

m *Aug.lib. 3. Cont. Cresc. ca. 35.*

n *Pelag. 2. Epist. 7. § In his autem.*

o *Cyr.lib.cont. Thead.cit.à Conc. 5. Collat. 8. pa. 585.a.*

examine, whether part the Cardinall himfelfe will take in this quarrell; you may be fure, the choyce on either part was very hard for him : he hath here a worfe matter than a wolfe by the eares. This is *dignus vindice nodus*, a point which will trie the Cardinals art, wifdome, piety, conftancy, and faire dealing : And in very deed, he hath herein plaid *Sir Politike would be*, above the degree of commendation. The Cardinall is a man of peace, hee loves not to difpleafe either the Pope, or the Church; he knew, that to provoke either of them, would bring an armie of wafpes about his eares; and therfore very gravely, wifely, and difcreetly he takes part with them both : and though their affertions bee directly contradictory, he holds them both to be true, and takes up an hymne of *Omnia bene* to them both.

12. Firft, he fheweth that the Church faith right, in this manner : *Although* [h] *it be proved, that one dyed in the peace of the Church, and yet it doe afterwards appeare, that in his writings he defended a condemned herefie, and continuing in that herefie died therein; and but diffemblingly communicate with the Church, the holy Church ufeth to condemne fuch a man, iure, even by right.* Having faid as much as can bee wifhed, on the Churches part, the Cardinall will now teach, *that the Pope alfo faith right,* in this manner; *Pope Vigilius* [i] *had many worthy reafons for his defence of the Three Chapters, by his Conftitution; and among thofe worthy reafons this is one : for if this were once admitted, that a man who dyeth in the communion of the Church, might after his death be condemned; pateret oftium, this would open fuch a gap, that every ecclefiafticall writer, though hee dyed in the Catholike Communion, may yet after his death, out of his writings be condemned for an heretike.* Thus *Baronius*.

13. O what a *golden* and bleffed age was this, that brought forth fuch a Cardinall ! The Church decreeth, that a man after his death, *may* noviter *be condemned* for an heretike; and it decreeth aright : The Pope decreeth the quite contrary, *that no man after his death may* noviter *be condemned* for an heretike ; and hee alfo decreeth aright, and with good reafon. So both the *Church faith well,* & *the Pope faith well;* & you can fay no leffe then, *Et vitula tu dignus, & hic :* or becaufe the Cardinall faith *better* than they both; and, what *Iupiter* himfelfe could never doe, makes *two contradictory fayings* to be both true, and both faid well; heo beft deferveth, let him have all the prize, *Vitula tu dignus utráque.*

14. I told you before, and this enfuing treatife will make it as cleare as the Sunne, that *Baronius* having once loft the path, & forfaken that truth, where only fure footing was to be found, wandreth up and downe, in and out in this caufe, as in a wilderneffe, treading on nothing but thornes, wherewith feeling himfelfe prickt, he skips hither and thither for fuccour, but ftill lights on briars and brambles, which doe not onely gall, but fo intangle him, that by no meanes he can ever extricate, or unwinde himfelfe;

h *Bar.an.553. nu.185.*

i *Bar.an.553. nu. 233.*

himfelfe; for if one lifted to make fport with the Cardinall, it clearly and certainly followeth, that if the Church *fay true*, then the Pope faying the contrary, doth *fay untrue*. Againe, if the Pope *fay true*, then the Church faying the contrary, doth *fay untrue*; and then upon the Cardinals *faying that they both fay true*, it certainly followeth, that neither of them both fay true, and yet further, that both of them, fay both *true and untrue*, and yet that neither of them both faith either *truth, or untruth*.

15. But leaving the Cardinall in thefe bryars, feeing by the upright, and unpartiall judgement of the whole Catholike Church of all ages, we have proved the Popes decree herein to be erroneous, and (becaufe it is in *a caufe of faith*) heretical, let us a little examine the two reafons on which *Vigilius* groundeth this his affertion: The former is taken from thofe words of our Saviour, [k] *whatfoever ye binde on earth*, whence, as you have feene, *Vigilius*, and, as he faith, *Gelafius* alfo colleƈteth, that fuch as are not on earth or alive, cannot be judged by the Church. k *Matth* 18. 18

16. The anfwer is not hard; our Saviours words, being well confidered, are fo farre from concluding, what *Vigilius* or *Gelafius*, or both, doe thence colleƈt, that they clearly and certainly doe enforce the quite contrary; for he faid not, Whatfoever yee binde, or loofe, concerning thofe that are on earth, or living; in which fenfe *Vigilius* tooke them: but, Whatfoever concerning either the *living* or *dead*, ye my *Apoftles*, and your *fucceffors* being upon earth, or during your life time, fhall binde or loofe, the fame according to your cenfure here paffed upon earth, fhall by my authority bee ratified in heaven. The reftriƈtive termes [*upon earth*] are referred to the parties, who doe binde, or loofe; not to the parties, who are bound, or loofed. The generall terme [*whatfoever*] is referred to the parties who are bound, or loofed, whether they be dead, or alive, not to the parties who binde or loofe, who are onely alive, and upon earth. Nor doth our Saviour fay, Whatfoever yee feeme to binde or loofe here upon earth, fhall bee bound or loofed in heaven; for, (*ecclefia clave errante*) no cenfure doth, or can either binde, or loofe, either the quicke or the dead : but he faith, Whatfoever ye doe binde or loofe, if the party be once truly and really bound, or loofed, by you that are upon earth, it fhall ftand firme, and bee ratified by my felfe in heaven. So the parties who doe binde, or loofe, are the *Apoftles*, and their *fucceffors* onely while they are upon earth: the parties who are bound, or loofed, are any whofoever whether *alive* or *dead*; the partie who ratifieth their aƈt in binding and loofing, is *Chrift* himfelfe in heaven; For I fay unto you, whatfoever ye binde on earth, fhall be bound in heaven, and whatfoever yee loofe on earth, fhall be loofed in heaven.

17. This expofition is clearly warranted by the judgement of the whole catholike Church, which, as we have before declared, both beleeved, taught, and praƈtifed this authority of binding,

24. Now after the reasons of *Vigilius* fully refuted, in stead of a conclusion, I will adde one short consideration to all that hath beene said, That this position decreed by *Vigilius* is such, as doth not onely condemne the catholike church, that is, all the oppugners of it, but even *Vigilius* himselfe, and all who defend it. Say you, that a dead man may not *noviter* be condemned? In saying so you condemne the holy Councell at *Sardica*, of *Constantinople*, of *Ephesus*, of *Chalcedon*, for they all did *noviter* condemne such persons being dead, as in their lives time had not beene condemned. Now the holy Fathers of those Councels, having thus condemned the dead, dyed themselves in the Lord, and were in peace gathered to the Lord. If you say, they should not have condemned the dead, even in saying so you doe *noviter* condemne all those Fathers being now dead; and so you doe that same thing, which you say must not bee done; and even by defending your position, you overthrow your owne position; for you doe *noviter* condemne all those holy Fathers being dead; and yet you say, that no man may *noviter* condemne the dead: Nay, you condemne not them only, but even your own selfe also herein, for you condemne those, who condemne the dead, and yet your selfe condemnes all those holy Fathers, being now dead; and you condemne them for doing that, which your selfe now doe; even for condemning the dead. Such a strange discord there is in this hereticall position of *Vigilius*, that it not only fights against the truth, and the opposites unto it; but viper-like, even against it selfe, and against the favourers, and defenders of it.

Cap. VII.

That the second reason of Vigilius *touching the* first *Chapter, why*
Theodorus *of* Mopsvestia *ought not to be condemned, because he*
dyed in the peace, and communion of the Church, is erronious *and*
untrue.

a *Vigil. Const. apud*
Bar. an. 553. *nu.*
179.

b *Ibid. nu.* 184.

1. THE second reason of *Vigilius*, why *Theodorus* of *Mopsvestia* should not bee condemned, is, for that (as he supposeth) *Theodorus* dyed in the peace and communion of the Church: to this purpose he saith, *that* a *the rules of his predecessors* (which he applyeth to Theodorus) *did keepe inviolate the persons of Bishops, in pace Ecclesiastica defunctorū, who dyed in the peace of the Church.* And again, *We* b *doe especially provide by this our present Constitution, lest by occasion of perverse doctrine, any thing be derogated from the persons of them, who, as wee have said, in pace & communione universalis Ecclesiæ quieverunt; have dyed in the peace and communion of the Catholike Church; and that no contumelie be done to those Bishops, qui in pace Catholica Ecclesiæ*

siæ sunt defuncti; who have dyed in the peace of the Catholike Church. Now that *Theodorus* so dyed *Vigilius* proveth not, but takes as consequent upon the former point, which, as we have ᶜ shewed, was knowne and confessed, because ᵈ he was not in his life time condemned by the Church. Nor was *Vigilius* the first founder of this reason, he borrowed it of other Nestorians, with whom in this cause he was joyned both in hand and heart. They (to wit, the followers of *Theodorus* and *Nestorius*) flee unto another vaine excuse, saith ᵉ *Iustinian*, affirming that *Theodorus* ought not to be condemned, *eo quod in communione Ecclesiarum mortuus est;* because he dyed in the communion of the Churches.

2. I shall not need to stay long in refuting this reason of *Vigilius*: The Emperour hath done it most soundly, and that before ever *Vigilius* writ his *Constitution.Oportebat ᶠ eas scire, those men who plead thus for Theodorus, should know that they dye in the communion of the Church,* who unto their very death doe hold that common doctrine of piety which is received in the whole Church. *Iste autem usque ad mortem in sua permanens impietate, ab omni Ecclesia ejectus est;* but this Theodorus *continuing in his impiety to his death, was rejected by the whole Church.* Thus *Iustinian*. To whose true testimonie *Binius* ascribeth so much as well hee might, that whereas some reported of *Theodorus* that he recalled his heresie, this, saith he, *might ᵍ be beleeved, nisi Iustinianus,* unlesse the Emperor had testified that he dyed in his heresie.

3. The same is clearly witnessed also in the fift ʰ Councell, where, as it were of purpose, this reason of *Vigilius* is refuted in this manner; *Whereas it is said of some* (and one of those is *Vigilius*) that *Theodorus* died in the peace and communion of the Church, *mendacium est & calumnia, magis adversus Ecclesiam;* this is a lie and slander, and that especially to the Church. For he is said to die in the communion and peace of the Church, *qui usque ad mortem rectæ Ecclesiæ dogmata servavit;* who hath kept and held the true doctrines of faith, even till his death: But that *Theodorus* did not keepe those doctrines, *certum est, it is certaine* by his blasphemies: and *Gregory Nissen* witnesseth the same. And after the words of *Gregory* recited, they adde this, *quomodo conantur dicere, how doe any say,* that such an impious and blasphemous person as *Theodorus* was, dyed in the communion of the Church? Thus testifieth the Councell.

4. Can ought be wished more pregnant to manifest the foule errours of *Vigilius* in this part of his decree? *Vigilius* affirmeth that *Theodorus* dyed in the peace and communion of the Catholike Church: The Emperour and Councell not onely testifie the contrary, but for this very cause the Councell (impatient at such indignitie offered to Gods Church,) cals him in plaine termes a lyar, and a slanderer; yea, a slanderer of the whole Catholike Church in so saying. *Vigilius* from the not condemning of *Theodorus* in his life time, collecteth, that hee dyed in the peace and communion

c *Sup.ca.6.*
d *Perspeximus si quid de hîs qui defuncti sunt, & minime reperiuntur in vita damnati. Vig. loc.cit.nu.175. Quos vocat, In pace Ecclesiæ defunctos. ibid.nu.179. & 184.*
e *Iust.Edict. § Quod autem.*
f *Iust.ibid.*
g *Bin.Notis in Conc.5. verbo Theodorus.*
h *Conc.5.Coll.5. pa.552.a..*

communion of the Church: both the Emperour and Councell witnesse his doctrinall errour herein : truly teaching,
that though an heretike live all his life time; not onely uncondemned by the Church, but in all outward pompe, honour,
and applause of the Church; either himselfe cunningly cloaking,
or the Church not curiously, and warily observing his heresie
while hee liveth; yet such a man neither lives, nor dyes in the
intire peace and communion of the Church. The Church
hath such peace with none, who have not peace with God; nor
communion with any, who have not union with Christ. It condemned him not, because, as it teacheth others, so it selfe judgeth most charitably of all : It judged him to be such, as hee seemed, and professed himselfe to bee. It was not his person, but his
profession, with which the Church in his life time had communion and peace; As soone as ever it seeth him not to bee indeed
such as hee seemed to bee, it renounceth all peace and communion with him, whether dead, or alive : nay, rather it forsaketh
not her communion with him, but declareth unto all, that shee
never had communion or peace with this man, such as hee was
indeed before, though she had peace with such as he seemed to
bee. Shee now denounceth a double anathema against him,
condemning him first for beleeving or teaching heresie, and then
for covering his heresie under the visor of a Catholike, and of
the Catholike faith. So justly and fully doth the Emperour, and
Councell refute, both the personall errour of *Vigilius* in that hee
affirmeth *Theodorus* to have dyed in the peace of the Church;
and the doctrinall also, in that he affirmeth it upon this ground,
that in his life time hee was not condemned by the Church.

i Accesserunt dig-
ne cause at ratio-
nes. Bar. an. 553.
nu. 233.

5. Now whereas [i] *Baronius* saith, that *Vigilius* had just, and
worthy reasons to defend this *first Chapter* : one of which is this,
because, if this were once admitted that one dying in the communion of the Church, might after his death be condemned for
an heretike; *pateret ostium*, there would a gap be opened, that e-
very ecclesiasticall writer, *licet in communione Catholica defunctus*
esset; although hee dyed in *the communion of the Catholike Church*,
might after death be out of his writings condemned, for an heretike; truly hee feareth where no feare is at all. This gap, nay,
this gate and broad street of condemning the dead hath laine
wide open this sixteen hundred years. Can the Cardinall, or any
of his friends in all these successiōs of ages, wherin have dyed many thousand millions of Catholikes; can he name or finde but so
much as *one* who hath truly dyed in the peace and communion of
the Church, and yet hath beene after his death condemned by
the Catholike Church for an heretike ? He cannot. The Church
should condemne her owne selfe, if shee condemned any with
whom she had peace, and whom she embraceth in her holy communion, which is no other but the society with God. Such indeed may dye in some errour, yea, in an errour of faith, as *Papias*,
Irinee,

Irenee, Iustine, in that of the millenaries: as *Cyprian*, (as is likely) and other Africane Bishops in that of *Rebaptization*; but either dye heretikes, or be after their death condemned by the Catholike Church, for heretikes, they cannot.

6. But there is most just cause why the Cardinall, and all his fellowes, should feare another matter, which more neerely concernes themselves; and feare it, even upon that Catholike position, that the dead out of their writings may justly bee condemned. They should feare to have such an itching humour to write in the Popes Cause; for his supremacy of authority, or *infallibility* of his *Cathedrall* judgement: feare to stuffe their Volumes (as the Cardinall hath done his *Annals*) with heresies, and oppositions against the faith; feare to continue and persist in their hereticall doctrine: feare to die before they have attained to that which is *secunda post naufragium tabula; the second and onely boord to save them after their shipwracke*; to dye I say, before they revoked, disclamed, condemned, or beene the first men to set fire to their hereticall doctrines and writings; and at least, in words, if not, as the [k] custome was, *by oath, and handwriting, to testifie to the Church, their desire to returne unto her bosome.* These are the things indeed they ought to feare, knowing that howsoever they flatter themselves with the vaine name of the Church; yet in very truth, so long as their writings remaine; testifying that they defended the Popes *infallibility* in defyning *causes of faith*, or any other doctrine relying on that ground, whereof in their life time they have not made [i] a certaine, and knowne recantation, they neither lived nor dyed in the peace and communion of the Catholike Church, but may at any time after their death, and ought whensoever occasiō is offered, be declared by the Church to have dyed in their heresies, and therefore dyed both out of the peace of God, and of the holy Church of God. This, unlesse they seriously and sincerely performe, it is not I, nor any of our writers, (whom they imagine, but most unjustly, out of spleene and contention to speake these things) who condemne them, but it is the whole Catholike Church; Shee, by approving this fift Councell and the true decree therof, condemns this *Apostolicall & Cathedral* definition of *Vigilius*, and all that defend it; that is, all the *members* of the present Romane Church, to be hereticall; and as convicted heretikes, she declares them to die anathematized; that is, utterly separated from God, and from the peace, and most blessed communion with the Church of God; howsoever they boast themselves to be the onely children of the Church of God.

7. If any shall here reply, or thinke, that by the former examples of *Papias, Irenee, Iustine, Cyprian*, and the rest, *Baronius*, and other mēbers of the present Romane church may be excused; that these also, as the former, though dying in their error, may dye in the peace & cōmunion of the Church; this I confesse is a friendly, but no firme excuse; for although they are both alike in this,

G   that

[k] *In fine vitæ reconciliatio pœnitentibus et pænitentibus non est neganda, dum tamen, si heretici sint, recipiantur cum scriptura & juramento. Gloss in dist. 1. de pœnit. ca. Multiplex. i Satis est ut Ecclesiæ judicio constet aliquem decessisse impœnitentem, si non constet de illius pœnitentiâ, qui hereticus post mortem cōvictus est. Fran. Torrens. lib. de 6, 7, & 8. Synod. pa. 13. & ejusdem sententiæ ait Pigh. fuisse.*

that the former as well as the latter, dye in an errour of faith; yet is there extreme odds, and many cleare diffimilitudes, betwixt the state or condition of the one, and the other.

8. The firſt ariſeth from the *matter it ſelfe wherin they erre*. The former erred in that doctrine of faith, wherein the truth was not *eliquata, declarata, & ſolidata per plenarium Concilium*, as S. Auſten ᵐ ſpeaketh, not *fully ſcanned, declared, & confirmed by a plenary Councell*: Had it bin, we may well think the very ſame of all thoſe holy men, which *Auſten* ⁿ moſt charitably ſaith of S. *Cyprian, Sine dubio, univerſi orbis authoritate patefacta veritate ceſſiſſent; without doubt they would have yeelded to the truth, being manifeſted unto them, by the authority of the whole Church.* The latter erre in that, which, to uſe ſame Fathers ° words, *per univerſæ Eccleſiæ ſtatuta firmatum eſt; which hath beene ſtrengthened by the decree of the whole Church.* This fift Councell, conſonant to all precedent, and confirmed by all ſubſequent generall Councels, unto *Leo* the tenth, decreeing this cathedrall ſentence of Pope *Vigilius*, to bee hereticall: whence it doth clearly enſue, that as the former, who were ready to embrace the truth, had it beene manifeſted unto them, erred not of pertinacy, but as *Auſten* ſaith, of humane infirmitie; ſo the latter, who reject the truth being manifeſted unto them, and withſtand the knowne judgement of the whole catholike Church, even that judgement which is teſtified by all thoſe witneſſes, to be conſonant to the Scriptures, and *Apoſtolicall* doctrine, can no way be excuſed from moſt wilfull and pertinacious obſtinacy, ſeeing they adhere to that opinion, which themſelves, or their particular church hath choſen, though they ſee, and know the ſame to be repugnant to Scripture, & the conſenting judgement of all generall and holy Councels, that is, of the whole catholike Church. So the errour of the former, though it was in a point of faith, yet was but materially to be called hereſie, as being a doctrine repugnant to faith; yet being not joyned in them with pertinacie, which is eſſentially, as *Canus* ᵖ ſheweth, required in an heretike, could neither make, nor denominate them to be heretikes: The errour of the latter, is not onely an errour in a point of faith, but is formally to bee called hereſie, ſuch as being both a doctrine repugnant to faith, and being in them joyned with pertinacy, doth both make, and truly denominate them, who ſo erre, to be heretikes; and ſhew them to hold it heretically, not onely as an errour, but as a moſt proper hereſie.

9. The ſecond difference is in the *manner of their errour*. The former held their opinions as probable collections, not as undoubted doctrines of faith; and ſo long as thoſe errours were ſo held, the Church ſuſpended �q her judgement, both concerning the doctrines, and the perſons. And this was at leaſt untill the time of *Ierome*, touching the millenary opinion; for he mentioning the ſame, ſaith ʳ thus; *Hæc licet non ſequamur, tamen damnare non poſſumus, quia multi Eccleſiaſticorum virorum & martyrum iſta dixerunt:*

m *Aug. lib. 2. de bapt. ca. 4.*

n *Ibid.*

o *Aug. lib. ead. c. 1.*

p *Quod hæreſis eſſe ſine pertinacia nequeat, non eſt difficile oſtendere communi omnium Theologorum ſententia, &c. Conus lib. 12. Loc. Theol. ca. 9. § Quod.*

q *Sancta Eccleſia aliquandiu de ea re ſuperſedit, judiciumq; ſuſpendit. Bar. notus in Martyr. in Febr. 22. voce Papiæ.*

r *Hier. in cap. 19. Ieremiæ.*

dixerunt : *Thefe things* (concerning the raigne of Chrift for one thoufand yeares upon earth, in a terreftriall, but yet a golden Ierufalem) *although we doe not our felves follow, yet wee cannot condemne them, becaufe many of the Ecclefiafticall writers and Martyrs have faid the fame* : whereby it is evident, that in *Ierᵒmes* ˢ time nothing was defined herein by the Church; for then *Ierome* might, and would conftantly have condemned that errour by the warrant of the Churches authoritie, which then hee held to bee a probable, and difputable matter. In which regard alfo *Auften calleth it a tolerable* ᵗ *opinion,* and fuch as himfelfe had fometimes held, if the delights of the Saints in that time be fuppofed to be fpirituall. *Baronius* tels ᵘ us, (how rightly I will not now examine,) that when *Apollinarius* renewed this opinion, and urged it, *ut dogma Catholicum,* no longer as a matter of probabilitie, *but as a Catholike doctrine of faith;* It was then condemned by Pope *Damafus* about the time of *Ierome;* and fo being condemned by the Church, it was ever after that held for an herefie; and the defenders of it, for heretikes.

10.　Did *Baronius* and the reft of the Romane Church in like fort, as thofe *millenary* Fathers, commend their Popes *infallibility* no otherwife then as a probable, a topicall, or difputable matter, the like favourable cenfure would not be denyed unto them, but that they alfo, notwithftanding that error in faith, might die in the communion of the Church. But when Pope *Vigilius* publifhed his *Apoftolicall Conftitution,* as *a doctrine with fuch* ˣ *neceffitie to be received of all, that none either by word or writing might contradict the fame;* when the chiefe Pillers of their Church urge the Popes *Cathedrall* definitions in caufes of faith, for fuch as wherein, *nullo* ʸ *cafu errare poteft, he can by no poffibilitie bee deceived, or teach amiffe;* when they urge this, not onely as *Apollinarius* did the other, *ut dogma Catholicum, as a doctrine of faith;* but as the *foundation* of all the doctrines of faith; It was high time for the Catholike Church, as foone as they efpied this, to creepe into the hearts of men, to give fome foveraigne antidote againft fuch poyfon, and to prevent that deluge of herefies, which they knew, if this Cataraɦ were fet open, would at once rufh in, and overwhelme the Church of God. And therefore the fift generall, and holy Councell, to preferve for ever the faith of the Church againft this herefie, did not onely condemne it, decreeing the *Apoftolicall* and cathedrall fentence of Pope *Vigilius* to be hereticall; but decreed all the defenders of it to be accurfed, and feparated from God, and Gods Church; fo that whofoever after this fentence and decree of the holy Synod, approved by the whole Catholike Church, fhall defend the Popes Cathedrall judgements as *infallible,* and dye in that opinion, they are fo farre from dying as *Papias* and *Irene* did, in the peace of the Church; that by the whole catholike Church they are declared, and decreed to dye out of the peace and communion of the whole catholike Church.　　　G 2　　　11. A

Marginal notes:

ˢ *Hieronimi tempore nihil adhuc ab Ecclefia de ea re fuit definitum. Bar. notis in Martyr. loc. cit.*

ᵗ *Que opinio effet utcunq; tolerabilis, fi, &c. Aug lib. 20. de Civit. Dei. ca 7.* ᵘ *Bar. an. 118. nu. 2. et an. 373. nu. 14*

ˣ *Statuimus, nulli licere quicquam contrarium his confcribere, vel proferre. Vig. Conft. in fine* ʸ *Bel. lib. 4. de Pôt. ca. 3. et Gretz. def. ca. 2. lib. 1. de Pont. pa. 652. et alij.*

z *Cyprianus ita dixit, quid ei videretur, ut in pace unitatis esse voluerit, etiam cum eis qui de hac re diversa sentirent. Aug. lib. 2. de baptis. ca. 1 a Lib. 1. de baptis. ca. 18.*

b *Charitate presenti quaedam (veritates) venialiter non habentur. Aug. ibid.*

11. A third diſſimilitude ariſeth from the *perſons who erre*. The former, for all their errour; held [z] faſt the unity with the Church, even with thoſe who contradicted and condemned their errours; and we doubt not but that was verified of very many of them, which *Auſten* [z] affirmeth of *Cyprian*, that they kept this unitie of the Church, *humiliter, fideliter, fortiter, ad martyrij uſque coronam*; kept it *with humility, with fidelitie, with conſtancy, even to the crowne of martyrdome.* By reaſon of which their charity they were not onely faſt linked, and, as I may ſay, glued to the communion of the Church, both in their life, and death, but all their other errours, as *Auſten* [b] ſaith, *became veniall unto them:* for charity covereth a multitude of ſinnes. The latter are ſo unlike to theſe, that with their errour, and even by it, they have made an eternall breach, and ſeparation of themſelves from the Catholike Church; even from all who conſent unto, or approve this fift generall Councell: for having by their *Laterane* decree erected, and ſet up in the Romane Capitol, this pontificall ſupremacy, and *infallibilitie, they now account all but Schiſmatickes* [c] *who conſent not with them*; *they will have no peace, no communion with any, who will not adore this Romiſh Calfe of the ſupreme & infallible authoritie of their vice-god.* So the former, notwithſtading their error, died in the peace of that Church, to which, by moſt ardent affection they were conjoyned: The latter dying in this their errour, whereby they cut off, and quite diſ-joyne themſelves from the union of all, who approve the decree of the fift Councell, (and thoſe are the whole catholike Church of all ages) though they dye in the very armes, and boſome of the Queene of *Babylon*, cannot chuſe but die out of the bleſſed peace, and holy communion of the whole catholike Church, which they have wilfully, inſolently, and moſt diſdainfully rejected.

c *Nemo poteſt ſubeſſe Chriſto, & communicare cū Eccleſia qui non ſubeſt Pontifici Rom. Bell. lib. de Eccl. milit. ca. 5. Schiſma eſt quando unum membrum nō vult eſſe ſub illo capite, quare tollit unitatem eſſentialem atq; Eccleſiā ipſam. Schiſmaticus igitur non eſt de Eccleſia. Ibid. & ſimilia habent alij.*

12. The fourth and laſt difference which I now obſerve, ariſeth from the *judgement* of the Church concerning them both. The former, ſhe is ſo farre from once thinking to have dyed in hereſie, or heretikes, that ſhee moſt gladly teſtifieth her ſelfe not onely to hold them in her communion, but to eſteeme and honour them as glorious Saints of the Church. *Papias* [d] the author of that opinion, a Saint, *Irene*, [e] *Iuſtine*, and *Cyprian*, both Saints, and Martyrs. On the parties which hold the latter error, ſhe hath paſſed a contrary doome; for by decreeing the *Cathedrall* ſentence of *Vigilius* to be hereticall, and accurſing all who defend it; ſhe hath clearely judged and declared all who defend the Popes *infallibilitie* in defining cauſes of faith, to bee heretikes, & dying ſo, to die heretikes; yea, convicted heretikes, anathematized by the judgement of the catholike Church, and ſo pronounced to die out of the peace and communion of the catholike Church.

d *Natalis beati Papie. Martyr. Rom. Feb. 22.*

e *Paſſio Irenei Epiſcopi & Martyris. Mart. in martij 24 & Menol. Graec. in Aug. 23.*

13. I have ſtayed the longer in diſſolving this doubt, partly for that it is very obvious in this cauſe; and yet (as to me it ſeemed)

med not very easie; but specially that hereby I might open another errour in the *Constitution* of *Vigilius*, who from the example of those *Millenarie* Fathers (one of which, to wit *Nepos*, he expresly mentioneth) [f] would conclude, *That none at all though dying in heresie, may after their death be condemned*, seeing *Dionysius* Bishop of *Alexandria*, though he condemned the bookes and errour of *Nepos*, yet *Nepos* himselfe hee did not injure, nor condemne, *propter hoc maxime, quia jam defunctus fuerat, for this reason especially, because Nepos was dead*. But by that which now at large I have declared, it appeareth, that *Vigilius* was twice mistaken in this matter, for neither did *Nepos* die in a formall heresie, but in an errour onely at that time, to which he did not pertinaciously adhere; though *Prateolus* [g], and after him, the Cardinall, [h] upon what reason I know not, but sure none that is good, reckons *Nepos* with *Tertullian*, as one excluded from the ranke and order of catholikes : neither did *Dionysius* or the Church, for that reason at all which *Vigilius* fancieth; much lesse for that especially, forbeare to condemne *Nepos*, because he was dead: (for then they would not have condemned *Valentinus*, *Basilides*, *Cerinthus*, who also were dead [i], when the Church condemned them,) but because they judged *Nepos* as well as *Irene*, *Iustine*, and the rest, to have dyed, though in an error, yet in the unity, peace, and communion of the Church. And this the words of *Dionysius* [k], not rightly alleaged by *Vigilius*, and no better translated by *Christopherson* doe import. For *Dionysius* said not, that hee therefore reverenced *Nepos*, *quia jam defunctus fuerat*, as the one [l], nor *quia ex hac vita migravit*, as the other [m] readeth them, that is, because he was dead, (for upon that reason the holy Bishops should have reverenced also *Simon Magus*, *Cerinthus*, and other heretickes, who were then dead) but because ωϲαϲτ ϖϲιοντο which *Musculus* very rightly translateth thus; I much reverence him as one, *qui jam ad quietem præcessit*, *who is gone before mee unto rest* : that is, because hee so dyed, that his death was a passage to rest; even to that rest of which the scripture [n] saith, using the same words, *they rest from their labour* : to that rest unto which himselfe hoped to follow *Nepos* : for that *Nepos* is gone before to this rest; therefore did *Dionysius* reverence him. So both the assertion of *Vigilius* which from *Dionysius* he would prove, is untrue, that none who are dead may bee condemned, and yet the saying of *Dionysius* is true, that such as goe to rest, or dye in the peace of the Church, ought not to bee condemned.

14. After this which the Cardinall hath said in generall concerning such as dye in the peace of the Church, hee addeth one thing in particular concerning *Theodorus* of *Mopsvestia*, by way of application of that generall position unto him, saying [o] that *Vigilius* was therefore very slacke to condemne him, because hee would not condemne those, *quos sciret in catholica communione defunctos*,

G 3

defunctos,

f *Vig. Const. loc. cit. nu. 178.*

g *Prateolum Nepotem recenset inter hereticos, tum in Indice, tum in libro ipso, in suo Elench. verbo Nepos. Et ait cum fuisse authorē Epicurēe illius opinionis, in verbo Chiliastae.*

h *Mittimus Tertullianum & Nepotem extra classem hereticorum vagantes. Bar. Not. in Martyr. Feb. 22.*

i *Iustin. in Edicto § Quod autem.*

k *Apud Euseb. lib. 7. Eccl. hist. ca. 19.*

l *Vigilius.*

n *Christopher. in sua translatione.*

n *Apoc. 14. 13.*

o *Bar. an. 553. nu. 49.*

functos, whom he knew to have died in the catholike communion of the Church. So the cardinall tells us that *Vigilius* knew, and therefore that it is not onely true, but certaine, that *Theodorus* dyed in the catholike communion.

15. What thinke you doth the cardinall gaine by pleading thus for *Theodorus* a condemned heretike? Truly for his paines herein the holy Councell payes him soundly: for first in plaine termes it calls him a lyar, and a slanderer, yea a slanderer of the whole Church, and if this be not enough, it denounceth an *Anathema* unto him for so saying: Cursed bee hee that curseth not *Theodorus*; how much more cursed then is he, who acquits *Theodorus* from that curse, who makes *Theodorus* blessed? for blessed are all they that dye in the peace and holy communion of the Church, and that *Theodorus* so dyed the Cardinall for a certainty doth assure us; for *Vigilius* knew that he so dyed.

16. But what Church I pray you is that in the communion whereof the Cardinall assures us *Theodorus* to have dyed? you may bee sure it is their Romane: for in the Cardinalls idiome thats not onely *κατ᾽ ἐξοχίω* the Church, but its the *one and onely Church.* In the communion then of their Romane church, even in the communion with the Cardinall himselfe dyed *Theodorus.* Now its certaine, he died not in the communion of the Church, which was in the fift generall Councell, for they utterly disclaim him, accurse him, and call them lyars, and slanderers, that say hee dyed in their communion. Againe, its certaine that the Church of that fift Councell, was of the same communion with the whole Catholike and Apostolike Church; themselves professing to hold the same faith, and communion with all former holy generall Councells, and Catholikes, and all succeeding catholikes by approving it, professing the same faith and communion with it. Seeing then *Theodorus* dyed not in the communion of this Church, which is the true and truly catholike Church, and yet dyed as the Cardinall assures you in the communion of their Romane church, it doth clearly and certainly hence ensue, that their Romane church is neither the true catholike, neither hath full communion with the true catholike Church.

17. Lastly, seeing *Theodorus* as the Cardinall tells us, died in the peace, and communion of their Church, and *Theodorus* was most certainly an heretike, condemned by the catholike Church; declared by the same Church to bee accursed, that is, separated from God; nay to be a very Devill, as the holy Councell p proclaimed him; Their Romane church must needes bee at peace, and of the same communion with condemned heretikes, with *Arius, Nestorius, Eutiches, Eunomius,* (none of them all can bee worse then as *Theodorus* was, condemned heretikes, by the judgement of the whole Church:) of the same communion with those who are separated from God; yea it must needs be at peace, and league with the Devills communicants. Since this is the peace,

this

p *Hoc symbolum Satanas composuit, Conc. 5. ita ait de symbolo Theodori. Collat.4.pa.537.a.*

this the communion of their church (if *Theodorus* dyed, as the Cardinall assureth us he did, in the peace and communion of it) let them for ever keep to themselves, let them alone enjoy, both alive and dead, this peace, this communion, of their Church. But let dis-union, and immortall warres, be for ever betwixt us, and it; betwixt the society with God, and all communion with it.

> ———— *Nullus amor populis, nec fœdera sunto;*
> *Littora littoribus contraria, fluctibus undas,*
> *Imprecor; arma armis, pugnent cineresque, nepotesque,*
> *Et nati natorum, & qui nascentur ab ipsis.*

And let this suffice, to be opposed against the second reason of *Vigilius*, who therefore decreed that *Theodorus* ought not to be condemned, because, as he thought, nay knew, as *Baronius* saith, that *Theodorus* dyed in the peace & communion of the Church.

Chap. VIII.

That the third and last reason of Vigilius *touching the* first chapter, *why* Theodorus *of* Mopsvestia *ought not to bee condemned, because he was not condemned by former Fathers, and Councells, is erroneous and untrue.*

1. He third and last reason of Pope *Vigilius* in defence of the *first Chapter*, is drawne from the authority of the ancient *Fathers* and *Councells*; by none of which, as he pretendeth, *Theodorus* of *Mopsvestia* was condemned, and therefore ought not now by himselfe, or any other to be condemned. And *Vigilius* was so exceeding carefull to enforme both himselfe, and all others of the certainty, and truth herein, that hee saith, wee [a] added, *solicitudinis nostræ animum*, the carefull solicitude of our thoughts, and *diligentißima investigatione quærere curamus:* Wee have taken most diligent care to finde out, whether any thing was decreed, ordered, or disposed by the Fathers, *de persona, vel nomine*, either concerning the person, or the name of *Theodorus:* and againe, *Omnibus diligenter inspectis;* We have diligently viewed all things belonging to this matter. Now after all this carefull, solicitous, diligent, yea most diligent inspection, *Vigilius* saith, that, neither in the Councell of *Ephesus*[c], nor of *Chalcedon*[d], nor in *Cyril*[e], nor in *Proclus*[f], nor in other *Fathers*, could hee finde that *Theodorus* was ever condemned.

2. Truly *Vigilius* had exceeding dimme eyes in this cause: or to speake more truly, *Nestorianisme* had so blinded, and put out his eye-sight, that he could discerne almost nothing; though it were never so cleare, and obvious, unlesse it favoured the condemned heresie of *Nestorius*. Can you see neither the person,

a *Vig. Consl. nu.* 173.
b ibid. *nu.* 179.
c *Ipsam Synodum Ephesinam solicite recensentes, nihil de Theodori persona, referre cöperimus. ibid. nu.* 173.
d *Sed neq; in sanctio Chalcedonensi coacilio aliquid de Theodori nomine invenimus statutū. ibid. nu.* 175.
e *Ex quo claret beatum Cyrillum nehuisse nomen ejus* (Theodori) *mentis Synodalibus propter regulam quæ de mortuis servanda est, continueri. ibid. nu.* 173.
f *Quando scripsi oportere aut Theodorum aut alios qui pridem defuncti sunt anathemati subdi oportere. itid. ex Proclo. nu.* 174.

no_r

nor the name of *Theodorus* condemned by the Fathers? not by *Cyrill*? not by *Proclus*? not by the Councells of *Ephefus*, and *Chalcedon*? not by others? Suffer me I pray you, to helpe the Popes fight with fome better fpectacles. Of *Cyrill* and *Proclus*, the fift Councell, after a farre better view, and infpection, even in the Synodall decree, doe thus witnesse. They [g] fhew their meaning concerning *Theodorus*, *quod oportet eum anathematizari*, that he ought to be accurfed, as we have demonftrated before, out of thofe things, which *Cyrill*, and *Proclus* have written, *ad condemnationem Theodori*, for the condemning of *Theodorus*, and his impiety. In another place, [h] of them both they write againe in this manner, *Let them who pretend the names of Cyrill, and Proclus, fay if Theodorus be not by them numbred with the Iewes, Pagans, Sodomites and heretikes*; particularly of *Cyrill*, they fay [i], *Cyrill feeing that divers continued to defend the blafphemies of Theodorus, was forced to write bookes againft him and his impieties, & poft mortem ejufdem Theodori, oftendere eum & hæreticum, & impium, & fuper Paganos, & fuper Iudæos blafphemium*. And after the death of the fame *Theodorus*, to fhew him to have beene an heretike, and more blafphemous then either the *Iewes* or *Pagans*. This the Councell faw in the writings of *Cyrill*, and *Proclus*, and upon their fight and knowledge teftified the fame.

3. The words of *Cyrill*, and *Proclus* doe clearly witnesse the fame. *Cyrill* fpeaking [k] of *Theodorus*, calls him one, *whofe tongue fpeakes iniquity againft God*; *one whofe horne is exalted againft God*: *one who infulteth [l] over Chrift*, *who leffeneth the crimes of the Iewes, who pulleth him downe, ad infamiam, to infamie and difgrace*. *Proclus* alfo fpeaking [m] not only of the doctrine, but of the perfon of *Theodorus*, whom he fetteth in the fame ranke with *Arius, Eunomius, Macedonius*, and other heretikes, he calleth him as hee doth the reft, *turbulentos, & cænofos fallaciæ rivos, filthy and mirie rivers of deceit*; adding, *that the new blafphemie (which was taught by Theodorus and Neftorius) doth farre exceed, the blafphemie of the Iewes*. Thus *Proclus*. Where thinke you was the Popes eyes, when hee could not, or would not fee any of all this? Or if yet wee doubt of *Cyrills* minde herein, *Baronius* [n] himfelfe could not chufe, but obferve this out of him, you fee that *Cyrill* doth *una, eademque lance, Theodorum expendere cum Neftorio, put him in the fame fcale, and weigh him altogether alike, as he doth Neftorius*. So the Cardinall: checking the Popes fight, that would not fee him to be condemned by *Cyrill*, whom *Cyrill* efteemed every whit as wicked an heretike as *Neftorius*.

4. But this whole matter, and the unexcufable error of *Vigilius*, will be moft evident, by confidering the judgment of the *Ephefine* Councell touching *Theodorus*, and what enfued upon, or after it. That *Theodorus* of *Mopfueftia*, who dyed about fome foure [o] yeares before, was condemned in the holy Councell at *Ephefus*, *Cyrill* who was Prefident in that Councell doth declare,

a₅

g *Conc.5.coll.8.pa.585.b.*

h *Coll.5. pa.551.b.*

i *Ibid.pa.551.a.*

k *Cyrilli verba citantur in Conc.5.coll.5. pa.551.a.* l *Quoufq; infultas patienti Chrifto. ibid.* m *Epift.Procli ad Armenios, de fide, extat to.3. Bib.5. & citantur verba ejus in Conc.5.coll.5.pa.551.& 542.b. Proclus de Theodoro & ejus impietate ita dicit, &c.*

n *Bar. an. 435. nu. 11.*

o *Theodorus obijt nu.427. Bar. nu.27. Conc.Ephef. habitum nu. 431. Bar.& Bin.*

as the fift Councell witnesseth. *Cyrill* (say [p] they in the Synodall decree)writ unto *Iohn*, touching *Theodorus*, *utpote una cum Nestorio anathematizato*; as being anathematized together with *Nestorius*, in the Ephesine Synod: and this they shew out of the words of *Cyrill*, which are [q] worthy of most diligent consideration. *Peltanus*, and after him [r] *Binius*; have very unfitly translated *Cyrils* words, but in the Greeke; as also consonantly thereunto they are set downe in the fift [s] Councell, thus; *Processit adversus omnes, qui eadem sapiunt, vel sapuerunt aliquando;* τὸ ἱ ἁπλῶς ἡμᾶς καὶ τὴν ὁσιότητα ὑμῶν εἴπασιν, ὅτι ἀναθεματίζομεν: *id quod absolute, nos & vestra sanctitas dixit, Athematizamus illos, qui dicunt duos filios: That sentence of Anathema*,which we (to wit, the holy Ephesine Councell) *and your Holinesse pronounced absolutely*, (without naming any person) saying, we accuse those who say there are two Sonnes, or two Christs: that sentence proceeded against all who doe thinke so, or who have thought so. Thus *Cyrill*,and that also in one of those his Synodall Epistles,which the holy Councell of [u] *Chalcedon*,in their very definition of faith, hath approved: so that this is now not onely the judgement of *Cyrill*, but of the whole Councell at *Chalcedon*. The same is repeated againe by *Cyrill*, and more conspicuously in his Epistle [x] to *Anastasius, Alexander*, and the rest; which also hath equall authoritie by the Councell of *Chalcedon*. *Sancta Synodus Ephesi*, saith *Cyrill, The holy Ephesine Synod*, having pronounced a just sentence of condemnation against *Nestorius*, hath by the like sentence condemned the impiety of others, *qui vel postea futuri sunt, vel jam fuerunt eadem illi sapientes*; who either shall hereafter,or heretofore have thought the same; *æqualem condemnationem eis imponens*; imposing the same condemnation upon them also: for it is fit, that when one is condemned for such vaine speeches, *non contra unum tantum venire, that the sentence should not come against him alone*,but against the whole heresie, and sect. Thus S. *Cyrill* setting this downe for a golden rule to be observed, in all Synodall sentences, and judgements of faith; and being so usefull, the fift Synod doth often [y] insist upon it.

5. Seeing then *Theodorus* did not onely teach, write, and speake the same with *Nestorius*, but was indeed the Archheretike,and author of this heresie, *Nestorius* being but his [z] disciple, or the trunke to sound out or blaze abroad that hereticall doctrine,which *Theodorus* had breathed into him; it is evident by this golden rule of *Cyrill*, that though *Theodorus* was dead before the Synod at *Ephesus*, yet the *anathema* and condemnation denounced by the Synod, no lesse pertaineth to him, than to *Nestorius*, though the one was named,and not the other. And this the fift Councell out of those very words of *Cyrill*, doth collect, and warrant others to collect the same. The writings, say they, of [b] *Theodorus being in all things consonant to the vaniloquie of Nestorius, are together with his, deservedly rejected by the Councell of Ephesus, utpote anathemate quod adversus Nestorium factum*

est

p *Conc.5.Coll.8. pa. 585.a.*

q *In Epist.ad Ioh. Antioch.& Synod. cum eo.*
r *In Actis Conc. Ephes.tom.5.ca.9.*
s *Conc.5. Coll.8 pa. 585.a.*
t *Pelt.& Binius vertunt, Ita & nobis & vestra sanctitati absolute dicere liceat, anathematizamus,&c.*

u *Epistolas Cyrilli Synodicas ad Nestorium et alios per Orientem, acceptissimas habet. Sic et se ait Conc.Chal.Act.5 pa.96.*
x *Quæ extat in Act.Conc.Ephes. tom.2.Append.1. ca.6.et citantur etiam hæc Cyrilli verba in Conc.5.Coll.8. pa.585.a.*

y *Coll.5.pa.543.b. et pa.548.a.et in sententia Synodali Coll.8.pa.585.a.*

a *Theodorus doctor Nestorij.Iustin.in Epist.ad Conc.5. Coll. 1. pa.519.b.et idem ait Conc.5.in sententia Synodali Coll. 8.pa.585.b.et Nestorius Theodori verba loquutus est. Coll.5.pa.550.a.et; Nec enim Theodorus Nestorij fuit discipulus,sed iste illius Ibid.*
b *Coll.5.pa.549.b.*

est procedente etiam adversus eos, qui ante illum similia illi sapuerunt : the Anathema *which was pronounced against* Nestorius, *proceeding also against those, who before* Nestorius *thought the same which he did.*

6. This same judgement of the *Ephesine* Councell, in condemning *Theodorus,* is yet another way declared, and testified expresly by Pope *Pelagius,* Theodorum c *mortuum sancta Synodus Ephesina damnavit;* the holy *Ephesine Councell condemned* Theodorus *being dead :* which so cleare a testimony, though alone, were enough to manifest the foule errour of *Vigilius* in this point. But *Pelagius* sets downe a proofe also therof, which openeth another errour of *Vigilius.* He to excuse *Theodorus,* would perswade that d *Theodorus* was not the composer of that impious, and diabolicall creed, before mentioned. Heare now the words, and and proofe of *Pelagius,* taken from that creed: The *Ephesine* Synod, saith e he, condemned *Theodorus, nam cum ab ejus discipulis dictatum ab eo Symbolum; for when that creed, dictated and composed by* Theodorus, was brought forth before the *Ephesine* Synod, *cum authore damnatum est;* both it, and the author of it was condemned presently by the same holy Fathers. So *Pelagius* : testifying against *Vigilius,* both *Theodorus* to bee the author of that creed; and both him, and it, to have beene condemned by the *Ephesine* Councell.

7. What *Pelagius* saith was formerly delivered by the whole fift Councell, who thus say, f *Theodorus;* besides other innumerable blasphemies, *ausus est & impium exponere symbolum, was so audacious as to set out that impious creed:* & again, *hoc impium Theodori Symbolum;* this impious creed of *Theodorus* was anathematized, together with the writer of it, in the first *Ephesine* Councell: and againe, when this creed was repeated, which is by them g called, *Impium Theodori Symbolum, the impious creed of* Theodorus; the holy Synod h cryed out, *anathema* to him that composed it; (and that was *Theodorus* as themselves witnesse;) the holy *Ephesine* Councell accursed this creed, *una cum authore ejus, together with the author of it.* Thus testified the whole Councell. Before this fift Councell, *Iustinian,* in his most religious Edict, witnesseth the same. *Theodorus* (saith i hee) *who exceeds in impiety, Pagans, Iewes, and all heretikes, did not onely contemne the Nicene Creed, sed aliud symbolum exposuit, but he hath expounded another creed,* full of all impiety : and this impious creed of *Theodorus* being produced in the first *Ephesine* Synod, *cum ejus expositore, condemnatum est; was condemned, together with the author or composer of it,* by that holy Councell. So the Emperour.

8. Before all these, this is testified, and fully explained by S. *Cyrill,* who k was the chiefe Bishop in the *Ephesine* Synod: *This creed,* saith he, *composed by* Theodorus, *as they, who brought it, said, or witnessed, was rejected by the holy Councell;* and those who thought as that creed taught, being condemned (in which generall sentence *Theodorus* himselfe was especially included) *nullam*

vir

Marginal notes:

c *Pel.2.epist.7.§ In his.*

d *Symbolum quod Charisius Presbyter illic prodidit, &c. Vig.Const.loc.cit. nu.173.*
e *Pelag.loc.cit.*

f *Conc.5.Coll.6. pa. 575.b.*

g *Coll.5.pa.575.b.*

h *Coll.4.pa.537.a.*

i *Iust.Edict.§ Tuli.*

k *Cyrilli verba ex cp.ad Procl. citantur.Conc.5.Coll.5. pa.550,551.*

viri mentionem fecit dispensatione, nec ipsum nominatim anathemati subjecit propter dispensationem; the Councell by a dispensation, made no particular mention of *Theodorus,* but forbare by name to denounce an anathema against him, by a kinde of connivence, or indulgence; left some, who held him in great account, should separate themselves from the Church. So *Cyrill.* Whence two things are evident; the one that *Theodorus,* though dead before, was condemned in generall termes by the *Ephefine* Councell: The other, that they might in particular also have condemned him, as they did *Nestorius;* but they forbare that particular naming of him, onely by a dispensation, toleration, or connivence at his name: because *Theodorus* was then held by many in great account, his impieties, and blasphemies being not as yet so fully discovered to the world: Wherein the *Ephefine* Councell imitated the wisedome and lenitie of the Apostles, *who for a time by a* [1] *dispensation, and connivence, permitted the use of the Ceremoniall Law,* that so by insensible degrees the Iewes might be weaned from that, unto which they had beene so long accustomed: which examples of the Apostles, the fift Councell, even in their Synodall sentence, apply to this very cause of *Theodorus:* the Church and *Ephefine* Councell, for a time, spared by name to condemne him, even then, when by their generall sentence hee was as truly condemned, as the *Mofaicall* ceremonies were dead, (though then not deadly) to the end that the estimation which some (but very unjustly) had of him, might rather *diffui,* than *diffecari;* rather by little and little be untwined, and worne out, than by a peremptory anathema, be at once, and as it were with one violent blow, obliterated out of the hearts of such as admired him, which they saw could hardly be effected.

9. But as the Apostles, when afterwards the Gospell had been long published, and sufficient time allowed, to forget, and bury the ceremonies, then did utterly condemne all that used the same, saying, *If* [m] *ye be circumcised, Christ shall profit you nothing:* Even so did the Church in this cause of *Theodorus.* She expected that her generall sentence should have deterred all from that heresie; specially seeing the Emperours, *Theodofius,* and *Valentinian,* had strengthened that Synodall judgement, by a severe Imperiall [n] Edict, set forth some foure yeares [o] after the *Ephefine* Synod; forbidding the bookes of *Nestorius,* either to bee read, or retained: But it fell out farre otherwise; for when the *Nestorians* could no longer shrowd themselves under the name, nor countenance their herefie by the bookes and writings of *Nestorius,* they found this new device, to [p] commend their doctrine, under the name, dignity, and authority of *Theodorus* of *Mopfveftia,* whose doctrine was the very same with that of *Nestorius,* he having suckt all his hereticall poyson from *Theodorus,* and this they thought they might safely doe, *Theodorus* being not by name condemned, either in the Synodall judgement, or by the

Imperiall

[1] *Et talem dispensationem in divina scriptura est invenire. Paulus ad hoc Timotheum circumcidit, &c. Conc. 5. Coll.8.pa.585.b. et Coll.5.pa.551.b.*

m *Gal 5.2.*

n *L.66. de haret. Cod. Theod.*

o *Conc. Eph. b:bit. an.431. Baffo et Antiocho Coff. ut ex Act. liquet. Tom.2. ca.1. Ed:Actum uxto editum Theodofio.15 Coff. id est. anno 433.*

p *Confingentes enim quae Nestorij sunt, o-disse, alio iterum ea introducunt modo, quae Theodori sunt admirantes. Cyrill. cujus verba citantur in Conc.5.Coll.5. pa.550.a. et idem docet Liber.ca.10.*

p *Ibas quædam ex impijs Theodori Capitulis in Syrorum linguam transtulit, et ubique transmisit.Conc.5.Coll.6. pa.562.b.*

q Ca.10.

r Theodori scripta admirantes,et dicentes cum recta sapuisse et consonantia sanctis patribus, Athanasio,&c.Conc.5 Coll.5.pa.550.a.

s Quoniam nec susceperunt dicta illorum,et tempus quod dispensationis indigere,præterijt, jam scripserunt (patres) quæ superius dicta sunt,post mortem ejus adversus eum, et ejus scripta. Conc.5.Coll.5.pa. 551.b.

t Vt liquet ex subscriptionibus,in quibus sæpe Acatius. To.2.Act.Conc. Ephes ca.3.

u Rambulas vocatur in Conc.5.Coll.5.pa. 549.a.et apud Gratian.Cauf.24. q.2.ca.6.ex Emed. Greg.13.

x Sic à Liberato (homine Nestoriano vocatur.ca.10. et Ibas narrat Theodorum injustè à Rabula damnatum. Bar.an.448.nu.72.

y Cyrilli Epist.ad Rabulam,in Conc.5. Coll.5.pa.543 b.

z Rambulas sanctæ memoriæ Episcopus, qui in Sacerdotibus explenduit.Bexi. in Conc.5.Coll 5. pa.549.a.

a Liber.ca.10.

b Fuit nobile Concilium in Armenia celebratum,cui Acatius cum Rabula interfuit.Bar.an.435 nu.2.

c Lib.Ias transmissus est Episcopis Armeniæ Proclo,extat in Conc.5.Coll.5.pa.542.

Imperiall Edict. To which purpose they,and particularly p *Ibas,* spred abroad the bookes of *Theodorus* in every countrey, and comer, translating them, as *Liberatus* q sheweth, into the *Syrian, Armenian,*and *Persian* languages; by which meanes they deceived, and seduced many, pretending *Theodorus* r writings to bee consonant to the ancient fathers. The Catholikes seeing how little effect their connivence at *Theodorus* name had taken; and that the heretikes abused their lenitie in forbearing him, to strengthen their heresie,saw that now it was time, no longer to dispense or winke at *Theodorus*; and therefore the time s ofthat dispensation being expired, they began now in plaine termes, and by name, to condemne both his person,and his writings, as before they had in a generalitie performed them both in the Councell of *Ephesus*; and this was done by severall Bishops, in severall Countries,and by many severall wayes.

10. The first sentence wherein *Theodorus* was particularly, and by name condemned, was in a Councell at *Armenia,* where the credit of *Theodorus* had done most hurt. The chiefe Bishops in that Synod,were *Acatius* Bishop of *Melitiū* in *Armenia,* a very learned,&holy mā,who had bin one t of the chiefe also in the holy *Ephesine* Councel; and u *Rambulas,*or *Rabulas* Bishop of *Edessa,* (whose name it seemes the *Nestorians* for very spite against him, turned into x *Rabula,*that so they might with more facility revile his person)a man of such piety and high esteeme in the Church, that *Cyrill* y cals him *columnam, & fundamentum veritatis;* the *very piller and foundation of the truth*; and z *Benignus* testifieth, *that he was a faire and resplendent lampe in the Church.* These a two stirred up the Bishops of *Armenia* to reject the writings of *Theodorus, tanquam hæretici,*as one who was an heretike; yea, the author of the *Nestorian* heresie; and themselves were present in that noble Councell of b *Armenia,*wherein they not onely condemned *Theodorus as an impious person, an oppugner of Christ, and the childe of the Devill*; as by the contents of the acts of that Synod c doth appeare;but further also,they writ their Synodal letters both to *Proclus,* Bishop of *Constantinople,*& to *Cyrill* Bishop of *Alexandria,quatenus fiat unitas vestra contra Theodorum, & sacrilega dogmata ejus; that they also would joyne with them, and their Synod, in cōdemning by name,both the person and sacrilegious writings of Theodorus*;giving this as a reason thereof, because they exhort them but to doe in plaine, and expresse manner, the same thing which was done by them before,but in a generality : We write unto you,*per vos etiam antea condemnatum sine nomine, Theodorum nominatim condemnari*; that *Theodorus may now by name bee condemned by you,who hath already, though without expressing his name,beene condemned by you.* And what they exhorted *Proclus,*and *Cyrill* to doe,that *Rambulas* performed,not onely in the *Armenian* Councell, but in his owne Church at *Edessa*;for as *Ibas* in his impious

Epistle

Epistle [d] saith, *Ausus est Theodorum clarè anathematizare, hee was bold by name, and expresly, to anathematize Theodorus in his owne Church,* and, both *Benignus* and *Liberatus* witnesse the same.

11. What *Proclus* did upon receipt of those letters sent from the *Armenian* Councell unto him, is not to be learned out of *Liberatus* report of this matter, for he in the narration of this passage, is not onely untrue, and partiall, but very hereticall also, justly herein taxed by *Baronius* [g], and *Binius* [h], as borrowing his narration from some *Nestorians*; which the Reader will easily observe : but the truth herein must be taken out of *Cyrill*, and the fift Councell. *Proclus*, saith *Cyrill* [i], *sent a tome or writing to them of Armenia full of sound doctrine*, and hee adjoyned thereunto certaine chapters, *collecta è Theodori codicibus*, gathered out of the bookes of *Theodorus*, consonant to the doctrine of *Nestorius*, exhorting them, *etiam illa anathematizare*, to accurse even those doctrines of *Theodorus* also. The fift Councel explaines this more fully; *Proclus* say they [k], *writeth thus against Theodorus and his impious doctrine*. And then they cite, first those words of *Proclus* before mentioned, wherein he sets *Theodorus* in the same ranke with *Arius, Eunomius, Macedonius* [l], and other like heretikes, calling them all puddles of errours and deceit. And after this, those other words of *Proclus*, written to *Iohn* Bishop of *Antioch*, wherein he calleth the doctrines of *Theodorus*; or those chapters which were collected out of his bookes, *vaniloquie, monstriloquie, Iudaicall impietie : ad destructionem legentium evomita: doctrines vomited out by him, to the destruction of the readers and hearers:* exhorting others, to reject, to abhorre, to tread under foot, and to accurse all those chapters of *Theodorus : utpote diabolicâ insaniâ constituta, & inventiones: as being the positions and inventions of devillish madnesse*. From which words of *Proclus*, uttered both against the person, and doctrine of *Theodorus :* the Councell concludeth very justly, that *Proclus* (not onely in particular condemned *Theodorus* as the *Armenian* Councell exhorted him) but condemned him as a *Iew*, *Pagan*, and Heretike: And this was done by *Proclus* in the yeare when *Valentinian* was the 4, and *Theodosius* the [m] 15. time Consull, as the date of his letter or Tome to the *Armenians* doth declare; which declares also, that the *Armenian* Councell was held the same yeare [n] : for it followed the spreading abroad of the bookes of *Theodorus*; and that was not done till the *Nestorians* were by the Imperiall Edict forbidden to reade the bookes of *Nestorius*: Now the Imperiall Edict beares date, in the same consulship [o], which shewes evidently, that as soone as ever the *Nestorians* began to revive the honour, and name of *Theodorus* (being onely in a generality before condemned) the catholikes forthwith opposed themselves, and by name condemned him. And which is specially to be observed, *Proclus* did this against *Theodorus*, although the Easterne Bishops intreated him [p] *plurimis deprecationibus, ut ne anathematizaretur*

d *Quæ extat in Conc. Chal. Act. 10.*
e *Conc. 5. coll. 5. pa. 540. a.*
f *Liber. ca. 10.*

g *Liberatus cautè legendus, utpote qui ab aliquo Nestoriano eam videtur mutuatus historiam. Bar. an. 435. nu. 9.*
h *Historiam ca. 10. incautè nimis ab al quo Nestoriano magna ex parte mutuatos videtur. Bin. de Liberato. Notis ad Liber.*
i *Cyrilli verba citantur in Conc. 5. coll. 5. pa. 543. b.*
k *Coll. 5 pa. 551. a.*
l *In Epist. Procli quæ extat in Bibl. S. pa. 103. corruptè legitur Manichei.*

m *Corruptè legitur in editione illa epist. quæ extat to. 3. B. S. pat. Theodosio 5. pro 15. ut ex fastis Equet.*
n *Conc. Armeniæ habitum an. 435. Bar. anno illo nu. 4. is ast Coss. Theodosij 15. et Valent. 4.*
o *Coss. Theodosij 15, qui est an. 435. juxta Bar. illo an. nu. 1.*

p *Conc. 5. coll. 5. pa. 551. a.*

Theodorus, nec impia ejus conscripta, did with most earnest prayers follicite him, not to condemne the person, or doctrine of *Theodorus :* but, the truth of God which was oppugned by *Theodorus,* and the sentence of the Councell which had condemned *Theodorus,* did more prevaile then all their supplication with that holy Bishop.

12. Saint *Cyrill* did the like as *Proclus* herein, hee seeing the connivence [q], and dispensation of the Councell, not to take the intended effect, but that the Nestorians proceeded rather from worse to worse, boasting of *Theodorus* writings, that they were consonant to the ancient Fathers, and so farre applauding him, that in some Churches they would cry [r] out, *Crescat fides Theodori, sic credimus sicut Theodorus, let the faith of Theodorus increase, we beleeve as he did :* yea even stoning [s] some in the Church who spake against them, *Cyrill* seeing all this, could forbeare no longer, *Ego [t] ista non sustinui, sed fiducialiter dixi;* I could not hold my selfe to heare those things, but said with great boldnesse, and confidence, that *Theodorus was a blasphemous speaker, a blasphemous writer, that he was an [u] heretike, mentiuntur contra sanctos patres;* I said, *that they belyed the holy Fathers,* who affirmed *Theodorus* writings, to be consonant to theirs, *nec [x] cessavi increpas ea quæ scripserunt, nec cessabo : nor have I ceased, nor will I cease, to reprove those who write thus :* and which demonstrates yet further the zeale of that holy Bishop; he writ [y] the same things concerning *Theodorus,* to the Emperor *Theodosius,* exhorting him [z] *to keepe his soule unspoted from his impieties.* Thus *Cyrill* by name condemning both the person and writings of *Theodorus.*

13. The religious Emperors *Theodosius & Valentinian* moved partly by the grave admonitions of *Cyrill,* and specially by that disturbance which the Nestorians then made, by their defending and magnifying *Theodorus;* besides the former against *Nestorius,* published two other Imperiall Edicts, against *Theodorus,* declaring him by name, to have beene every way as blasphemous an heretike as *Nestorius;* and that the defenders of him, or his writings, should be lyable to the same punishments, as the defenders of *Nestorius.* Those Edicts being so pregnant, to demonstrate the errour of *Vigilius,* I have thought it needfull, to expresse some parts or clauses of them.

14. We [a] againe [b] declare that the doctrine *impiorum, & pestiferorum, of those impious and pestiferous persons* is abominable unto us: *similiter autem & omnes, and so are all who follow their error. It is just that they all have one name, and bee all clothed with confusion, lest while they be called Christians they seeme to be honoured by that title;* Wherefore we by this our Law doe inact, that whosoever in any part of the world be found, consenting to the most wicked purpose of *Nestorius,* and *Theodorus,* that from hence forward they shall bee called *Symonians,* as *Constantine* decreed, that the followers of *Arius* should be called *Porphirians.* Further let none presume either to

have

q *Quoniam ejusmodi dispensationem Cyrilli & Procli non susceperunt (Nestoriani) è contrario vero permanserunt defendentes blasphemias Theodori, videns Cyrillus crescentem impietatem coactus est libros conscribere adversus Theodorum, & post mortem ejusdem, eum hereticum, & impium, et supra Paganos et Iudæos blasphemum ostendere. Conc. 5. coll. 5. pa. 551. a.*
r *Conc. 5. coll. 5. pa. 550 a.*
s *Ibid.*
t *Ibid, citantur vero verba Cyrill. ex Epist. ad dicat.*
u *Coactus est ostendere eum esse hereticum, ibid. pa. 551. a.*
x *Ibid. pa. 551. a.*
y *Sed et ad Theodosium Imper. consonantia scribens. ibid.*
z *Rogo ut intactas, et inviolatas animas vestras conservetis ab impietatibus Theodori. ibid.*

a *Extant leges illæ Theodosij et Valent. in Conc. 5. coll. 5. pa. 544. 545.*
b *Iterum igitur doctrina Diodori, Theodori et reliquorum abominanda visa sunt. ibid.*

have, or keepe, or write their *sacrilegious bookes, especially not thofe of Theodorus, and Neftorius : but all their bookes fhall bee diligently fought, and being found, fhall be publikely burned. Neque de cætero inveniatur prædictorum hominum memoria : neither let there be found any memorie of the forefaid perfons :* Let none receive fuch as love that fect, or love their teachers, either in any city, field, fuburbs; let them not affemble in any place, either openly, or privily. And if any fhall doe contrary to this our fanction, let him be caft into perpetuall banifhment, and let all his goods be confifcate. And let your excellency (they fent this to their Lieutenant) publifh this our Law through the whole world, in every Province, and in every city. Thus did the Emperours inact, and which is fpecially alfo to be remembred, they inacted all this, *corroboran-* c *Ibid. pa. 545. a.* tes *c ea que piè decreta funt Ephefi, ftrengthning thereby that which was decreed at Ephefus.*

15. Whence two things may be obferved, the one, that *Theodorus* was not onely accounted, and by name condemned for an heretike, as by other catholiks, fo by the Emperors alfo, but that this particular condemning was confonant to the decree of the *Ephefine* Synode, this being nothing elfe but an explanation of that, which they in generall termes had fet down, and a corroboration of the fame : The other, that feeing this Imperiall decree, hath ftood ever fince the inacting thereof in force and unrepealed, by vertue of it; had it beene, or were it as yet, I fay not rigoroufly, but duly, and juftly put in execution, not any one defender of the *three Chapters*, no not Pope *Vigilius* himfelfe, nor any who defends his *Apoftolicall conftitution*, (and thofe are all the members of the prefent Romane church) not one of them, fhold either have beene heretofore, or be now tolerated, in any city, fuburbs, towne, village, or field; but befides the ecclefiafticall, cenfures and anathemaes, denounced againft thē, by the Councell and catholike church, they fhould endure, if no fharper edge of the civill fword, yet, perpetuall banifhment out of all Chriftian Common-wealths, with loffe and confifcation of all their goods.

16. After this Imperiall Law was once publifhed, the name and credit of *Theodorus* (whofe memory the Emperors had condemned and forbidden) grew into a generall contempt and hatred, whereof the church of *Mopfveftia*, where hee had beene Bifhop, gave a memorable example. They for a time efteeemed of *Theodorus*, as a catholike Bifhop, and for that caufe kept his name in their dipticks, or Ecclefiafticall tables; reciting him among the other Orthodox Bifhops of that city, in their Eucharifticall commemoration; But now feeing him detected, and condemned, both by catholike Bifhops, by Councells, and by the Imperiall Edict for an heretike, they expunged and blotted out the name of *Theodorus*, and in his roome inferted in their dipticks, the name of *Cyrill*, who though hee was not Bifhop in

that

that See, yet had by his pietie and zeale manifested and maintained the faith, & brought both the heresie & person of *Theodorus* into a just detestation, and all this is evident by the Acts of that Synode ᵈ held at *Mopsvestia*, about this very matter, of wiping out of the name of *Theodorus*.

d *Acta illa Syno-di Mopsvest. extant in Conc.5. collat.5. pa. 553. & seq.*

17. We are now come to the time of the Councell of *Chalcedon:* for, the expunging of *Theodorus* name, and inserting of *Cyrills*, followed as it seemes shortly after the death of *Cyrill*, and he dyed about seven ᵉ yeares before the Councell of *Chalcedon*. That by it *Theodorus* was also condemned, their approving ᶠ the Councell of *Ephesus*, and the Synodall Epistles of *Cyrill*, (in both which, and in the later, by name ᵍ *Theodorus* is condemned) doth manifest: and besides this the Emperour *Iustinian* expresly saith ʰ of it, that the impious Creed of *Theodorus* being recited in that Councell, both it, *cum expositore ejus, with the Author and expounder of it,* (and that was *Theodorus*) were condemned in the Councell of *Chalcedon*.

e *Cyrill.obijt an. 444. Conc.Chalced. habitum an. 451. Bar. et. Bin.*
f *Conc.Chalc.Act.5. in definit. Synai.*
g *Vt liquet ex Cyrilli Epistolis ad Iohannem Antioche, et ad Acatium, quæ citantur in Conc.5. Coll.5. pa. 549. et 550.*
h *Iustin. Edict.§. Tali.*

18. When many yeares after that holy Councell, some Nestorians began againe, contrary to the Edict of *Theodosius*, and *Valentinian*, to revive the dead, and condemned memory of *Theodorus*, *Sergius* Bishop of *Cyrus* making mention ⁱ, and commemorating him in the Collect among catholikes; the truth of this matter being examined and found, that same *Sergius* by the command of *Iustinus* the Emperour, was deposed from his Bishopricke, excluded out of the Church, and so continued even to his dying day: and this was done but six yeares before the Empire of *Iustinian*, as by the date ᵏ of *Iustinus* his letters doth appeare.

i *Vt testantur Act. Conc.5. Coll.7. pa. 578.a.et.582.a.*

k *Iustinus scripsit id edictum, Rustico Coss.Conc.5. Coll.7. pa.582. b. fuit is Coss.an. 520. ut lestatur Marcell. in Chron.et agnoscit, Bar.in illo an.nu.1 Iustinianus vero cæpit imperare an. 527. ut Marcell.et Baron.asserunt.*
l *Conc.5. Coll.5.pa. 557.a.*

19. Now if to all these particular sentences, you adde that which the fift Councell ˡ witnesseth, that *Theodorus, post mortem à catholica ecclesia ejectus est, hath beene after his death condemned, and cast out, and that even by the whole Catholike Church*, you will easily confesse, that from the time almost of his death, unto the raigne of *Iustinian* there hath beene a continuall, and never interrupted condemnation of him in the Church. But in *Iustinians* time, and perhaps before, though lesse eagerly, the Nestorians began afresh, to renew the memory and doctrine of *Theodorus*, setting now a fairer glosse and varnish on their cause, then ever they had before: for they very gladly apprehending and applauding those (to say the least) inconsiderate speeches of the Popes Legates, & *Maximus* in the Councel of *Chalcedon*, that by his dictation, or Epistle, *Ibas* was declared to be a catholike, hereupon they now boasted, that the holy Councell, by approving that Epistle of *Ibas*, had approved, both the person and doctrine of *Theodorus*, seeing they both are highly extolled, and defended in that Epistle. By this meanes was this cause brought *ab inferis* the second time, upon the stage, and that also cloaked under the name, and credit of the Councell of *Chalcedon*. And at this second

cond boute, all the defenders of the *Three Chapters*, and among them Pope *Vigilius*, as Generall to them all, undertooke the defence of *Theodorus* : and, as if there had never beene any sentence of condemnation, either in generall, or in particular denounced against him, even in his definitive, and *Apostolicall* constitution declareth, That *Theodorus* was not condemned, either by former Councels, or Fathers; and this he declareth after his solicitous, circumspective, and most diligent examination of their writings.

20. What thinke you was become of the Popes eyes at this time, that he could see none of all those condemnations of *Theodorus*, before mentioned? Not the general *anathema* of the Councels at *Ephesus*, and *Chalcedon*, in which *Theodorus* was involved : not the expresse, and particular *anathema* denounced against him by *Rambulas*, and *Acatius*, with the Councell of *Armenia*: not the condemnation of him, and his writings by Saint *Proclus*, by S. *Cyrill*, by the Church of *Mopsvestia*, by the Edict of the religious Emperours, by the whole Catholike Church. None of all these things were done in a corner; they were all matters of publike notice, and record; obvious to any that did not shut their eyes against the sun-shine of the truth. But, as I said before, and must often say, Nestorianisme, like *Naash* the Ammonite, had put out the Popes right eye, he could see nothing with that eye; all that he saw in this cause, was but a very oblique, and sinister aspect, as doth now, I hope, fully appeare, but will bee yet much more manifest, by that which in the *Constitution* of *Vigilius* wee are next to consider.

21. For, as if it were a small matter, not to see *Theodorus* condemned by the former Councels, and Fathers, (though in a man professing so exact and accurate inspection in any cause, such grosse oversights are not veniall) the Pope ventures one step further, for the credit of this condemned heretike. Hee could not finde that *Theodorus* was condemned by the former witnesses : Tush, that is nothing, he findes him acquitted by them all: hee findes by *Cyrill*, by *Proclus*, by the Councels of *Ephesus*, and *Chalcedon*, yea, by *Iustinians* owne law, that *Theodorus* ought not to be condemned. This was indeed a point worthy the Popes owne finding. But withall I must tell you, that you also shall finde one other thing, that Pope *Vigilius*, having once passed the bounds of truth, for defence of *Theodorus*, cares not now if he wade up to the eares, and drowne himselfe in untruths.

22. Let us then examine the allegations, which, for proofe of this, the Pope hath found; and begin we, as the Pope doth, with *Cyrill*. In his ᵐ Epist. to *Iohn* B. of *Antioch*, *Vigilius* found an explication, how it was said by *Cyrill*, that by a dispensation the name of *Theodorus* was not condemned; for there *Cyrill* saith, *Sed juste audient, they shall justly heare this*, though they will not: ye forget your selves, when you bend your bowes against ashes, that is,

m Eam citat Vigi. in Const. nu.173. & 174.apud Bar. an.553.

against the dead; for he who is written among them (that is, τ^{he}
dead) *nō superest, is not*; and let no man blame me for these words,
Grave est enim insultare defunctis, vel si Laici fuerint; for it is *an
hard matter, to insult over the dead, yea, though they bee but Laikes*;
how much more over those, who with their Bishopricks have
left their lives. Out of which words *Vigilius* affirmeth S. *Cyrill* to
teach it to be an injurious and hard matter, repugnant to the
Ecclesiasticall rule, to condemne any that is dead; and then certainly not a Bishop, not *Theodorus*.

23. For answer hereunto, I doe earnestly intreate the reader
to ponder seriously the Popes good dealing herein. That Epistle
which *Vigilius* commendeth unto us, under the name of ⁿ S. *Cyril*, is none of *Cyrils*, it is a base and counterfeit writing, forged
by some *Nestorians* in the name of *Cyrill*; Witnesse hereof the
whole fift generall Councell, who, of purpose, and at large, examined this matter, and refuted this cavill of *Vigilius*, before ever
he set forth his *Constitution*; for thus they ° say of it, *Some loving
the perfidiousnesse of* Nestorius, *which is all one as to say, the madnesse
of* Theodorus, *doe not refuse to faigne some things, and use certaine words, as written in an Epistle by S. Cyrill*; *Nusquam vero
talis Epistola scripta est à sanctæ memoriæ* Cyrillo; *but* Cyril *never
writ such an Epistle*, neither is it in his bookes. And then reciting
the whole Epistle, and all those words which *Vigilius* alleageth;
they adde, *Et ista quidem continet conficta Epistola*; these are the
contents of this counterfeit Epistle : and a little after, That nothing
of all, *quæ in conficta Epistola continentur*, which are contained in that
counterfeit Epistle, was writ by *Cyrill*, it is declared by that which
he writ to *Acatius* : and yet further, These things are spoken, *ad
convictionem Epistolæ, quæ à defensoribus* Theodori *falso composita
est*; to convince that Epistle to be a forgerie, which is falsely composed
by the defenders of Theodorus. The summe of this they repeate
in their Synodall sentence, saying, ᴾ *We have found, that the defenders of* Theodorus *have done the same which heretikes are wont to
doe*; for they clip away some part of the Fathers words, *quædam
vero falsa ex semetipsis componentes, & confingentes*; and devising, or
faigning other things of themselves, they seeke by them, as it were, by
the testimony of Cyrill, to free Theodorus from the Anathema. Thus
the Councell: all of them with one voyce proclaming Pope *Vigilius* for a lewd dealer, who commends, and that even in his *A-
postolicall Constitution*, a false and forged writing, for the true E-
pistle of S. *Cyrill*.

24. It is true, *Vigilius* is not the first Pope, who hath blemished their See, by such false and fraudulent dealing : *Zozimus*
and *Bonifacius* were long before this taxed, and that justly, by the
Africane �q Bishops, *for downe-facing the Nicene Canons*. *Vigilius*
was too too bold with *Cyrill*, as now you see. But if you descend
to Pope *Nicholas*, or to *Gregory* the seventh, and their successors,
they were so shamelesse and audacious in this kinde, that they
scacre

n *Beatæ recordatio-
nis Cyrillum : et be-
atus Cyrillus. Vig.
loc. cit.*

o *Conc. 5. Coll. 5.
pa. 549. a.*

p *Coll. 8. pa. 585. b.*

q *Conc. Afric. E-
post. ad Celest. ca.
105. tom. 1. conc.
pa. 645. et seq.*

scarce writ any decrees of importance, but they stuffed them with such Fathers: Even the basest, and most abject fictions, which were voyd, not onely of truth, but of braine, were fittest for the Popes, and their *Pontificall determinations*, and were they never so base, and bastardly, yet the Popes, like kind *Godfathers*, could, when they listed, christen them with the names of S. *Cyrill*, *Cyprian*, or the like, and then they must be called, or esteemed for no others, than holy and reverend Fathers.

25. *Proclus* followeth: In whose writings *Vigilius* found three testimonies, to prove, that *Theodorus* being dead, was not to be condemned: The first is out of his Epistle to ᵣ *Iohn* Bishop of *Antioch*; where these words are alleaged; When did I write to you, *oportere aut* Theodorum, *aut alios quosdam, qui pridem defuncti sunt, anathemate subdi*; that either Theodorus, *or others, being dead, ought to be anathematized?* The second is out of the same Epistle; I rejected indeed those Chapters, (annexed to my Tome) as being impious, *neque autem de* Theodoro, *neque de alio quoquam, qui jam defuncti sunt*; but *I neither writ of* Theodorus, *nor of any other who is dead*, that they should be anathematized, or rejected. The third is out of an Epistle of *Proclus* to *Maximus*; I understand, that the names of *Theodorus* of *Mopsvestia*, and of some other, is prefixed to the Chapters, *ad anathematizandum*; *to bee anathematized*, together with the Chapters, *cum illi ad Deum jam migrarunt, whereas they are now departed to God*, and it is needlesse to injure them, being now dead, *quos nec vivos aliquando culpavimus*; *whom being alive we did never reprove*. These are the Popes allegations out of S. *Proclus*; in which I confesse it is clearely taught, that neither any after their death may bee condemned; and particularly that not *Theodorus*, seeing he is gone to God, and was never in his life time once reproved.

ᵣ *Const. Vig. no. 174*

26. It is a ˢ rule in law, *semel malus, semper præsumitur esse malus*; He who is *once convicted of any crime, is presumed still to be faulty in that kinde*. *Vigilius* being lately convicted to commend forgeries for the writings of Fathers, is in reason and equitie to bee thought to alleage such a S.*Proclus*, as before hee did S.*Cyrill*: Nay, there needs no presuming in this matter; there is evident proofe, and witnesses, above exception, to manifest the same; even the whole fift generall Councell; who, out of the true, and undoubted writings of *Proclus*, testifie, that *Proclus* taught the quite contrary, both that the dead might, and particularly that *Theodorus* ought to be condemned, and that hee was by *Proclus* himselfe condemned; for in their very Synodall decree, they thus ᵗ write, *Because the disciples of* Theodorus *most evidently oppugning the truth* (thus sharply do they reprove *Vigilius*) *doe alleage certaine sayings of Cyrill, and Proclus, as written for* Theodorus; It doth appeare, that those Fathers doe not free him from the *Anathema*, but speake those things *dispensativè*, by way of dispensation, and in the very words of dispensation they declare

ˢ *De regulâ juris lib. 6. decret. reg. 8.*

ᵗ *Conc. 5. Coll. 8. pa. 585. b.*

of

of him, *quod oportet anathematizari* Theodorum, *that Theodorus ought to be anathematized*; adding, that they have demonstrated this, even out of the words of *Cyrill*, and *Proclus*, which they writ *ad condemnationē ejus, for the condemning of* Theodorus. Thus writ the Councell, unto which the whole Catholike Church hath ever since subscribed. Seeing then it is certaine that *Proclus* both taught that *Theodorus* ought to be condemned, and did himselfe write to condemne him, there can bee no doubt, but that those Epistles to *Iohn*, and *Maximus*, which *Vigilius* citeth; and wherein *Proclus* is made to avouch the quite contrary, that neither himselfe did, nor that any ought to condemne *Theodorus*, are forged in the name of *Proclus*, by such hands as had wrought the like feat in *Cyrill*: And if either those Epistles were extant, (for in that of *Proclus* to *Iohn*, recorded in the fift [u] Councell, there is no such thing at all) or, had this *Constitution* of *Vigilius* beene published, and knowne to the Councell before they had fully examined, and cleared this Chapter touching *Theodorus*; it is not to bee doubted, but the one of them, if not both would have discovered this forgery also.

[u] Coll.6.pa.562.

27. Besides all which, there are divers evident prints of a false, and hereticall hand in those Epistles. Is it injury (as that forged *Proclus* affirmeth) to condemne the dead? Nay, it is even *hereticall*, and that by the judgement of the whole Catholike Church, as before we have proved, to say, that the dead may not be condemned. Had *Proclus* writ, or said this, he had condemned the Councels of *Sardica*, of *Constantinople*, of *Ephesus*, as injurious unto the dead; nor them onely, but he had condemned himselfe, who, as we have now demonstrated, both condemned the dead, and taught, that *Theodorus*, though dead, ought to bee condemned.

28. Did *Theodorus* at his death goe (as this forged *Proclus* affirmeth) to the Lord? a *blasphemer*; an heretike; equall, by the judgement of *Proclus* himselfe, to the Iewes, and Pagans, and of the same ranke with *Arius*, *Macedonius*, *Eunomius*, and *Nestorius*; such a blaspheming heretike goe unto the Lord? why then did the *Ephesine* Councell, why did Saint *Cyrill*, why did *Proclus* himselfe adjudge him to bee anathematized, that is, separated from the Lord? Heretikes, and impious persons, as living, they goe not in the wayes of the Lord, but in their owne wayes; so dying, they goe, like *Iudas*, to their owne place; not to the Lord, not to his habitation, and place of rest; the Saints, and they onely goe that way. To them onely he faith, This day shalt thou be with me in Paradise.

29. Was *Theodorus* not so much as blamed; no, not so much as once in his life, as the forged *Proclus* faith? It seemes *Leontius* borrowed his most partiall speech, before mentioned, out of this *Proclus*, and was too credulous unto it: But the true *Proclus* living so [x] neare to the time of *Theodorus*, could not bee ignorant,

[x] *Theodorus obijt an.427. Proclus fit Episcopus an 434. Bar. in illis annis.*

nor

nor would ever have uttered so foule an untruth : for although the Church pronounced no publike censure by name against him, yet was he reproved and blamed, not onely by others complaining of his erroneous doctrine, but even by *Theophilus* B. of *Alexandria*, and *Gregory Niſſene*. This the fift Councell witneſſeth saying [y], Saint *Theophilus*, and Saint *Gregory Niſſene ſuſceptis querimonijs adverſus Theodorum adhuc viventem, Complaints being brought unto them against* Theodorus *of* Mopsveſtia, *as yet living*; and against his writings, *ſcripſerunt adverſus eum Epiſtolas, they writ Epiſtles against him :* and in thoſe Epiſtles (ſome part whereof is recorded in the Councell) they blame him as preſuming to renew the hereſie and madneſſe of *Paulus Samoſatenus*. And it is further added, *porrecta ſunt autem,* and the impious chapters collected out of the books of *Theodorus, were ſhewed and brought to* Theophilus; whence it is now evident, that thoſe Epiſtles alleaged by *Vigilius* under the name of *Proclus*, are no leſſe, by the untrue, and hereticall aſſertions contained in them, then by the cleare teſtimonies of the fift generall Councell, convicted of forgery.

30. From Fathers hee commeth to Councells, and concerning the first *Epheſine. Vigilius* noteth two points. The former that *Theodorus* was not condemned by it, to which purpoſe hee thus ſaith [z], *Solicite recenſentes, having with diligence, and ſollicitude reviewed the Epheſine Synode :* We have found that in it nothing is related touching the perſő of *Theodorus*. What, nothing? how then did Pope *Pelagius* [a] after *Cyrill,* and the fift Councell finde that in it *Theodorus* was condemned ? and if they condemned him, then certainly ſomwhat was related, & debated about him, upon knowledge whereof the Councell condemned him. But ſay indeed, is nothing found concerning *Theodorus* in that Councell? What ſay you to the impious and diabolicall Creed, which was both related [b] in the Synode, and condemned [c] together with the author of it ? Truely here *Vigilius* uſeth a ſhift, worthy to be obſerved. That Creed he found, and hee found it to be condemned : but to quite *Theodorus*, hee [d] would have it beleeved, that *Theodorus* was not the author of it ; nor that it was condemned, as being the Creed of *Theodorus*, but becauſe it was divulged by certaine Neſtorians, *Athanaſius, Photius, Antonius,* and *Iacobus.* Nor doth *Vigilius* uſe this ſhift onely about that impious Creed, but in other hereticall writings of *Theodorus. Proclus* adjoyned to his Tome certaine impious poſitions collected è *Theodori codicibus,* as *Cyrill* [e] expreſly witneſſeth. *Vigilius* likewiſe of them would have it thought, that they were none of the poſitions of *Theodorus*; and by the forged Epiſtles of *Proclus*, hee would perſwade [f] that *Proclus himſelfe did not know whoſe they were.* The Emperour *Iuſtinian* before the Synode began, ſent threeſcore ſeverall hereticall paſſages or chapters truly gathered out of the bookes and writings of *Theodorus*, hoping that

y *Conc. 5. coll. 5. pa.* 545. a.

z *Vigil. Conſt nu.* 173.

a *Theodorum mortuum ſancta Syzodus Epheſina damnavit. Pelag 2. Epiſt. 7. §. In bis.*

b *Act. Epheſ. conc. to. 2. ca.* 29, 30, 31, & 33.

c *Hoc Symbolum una cum authore Epheſina prima Synodus anathematizavit. coſư. 5. coll. 4. pa.* 537. a.

d *Sed Symbolum quod Chariſius prodidit (condemnatű) magis quia ab Athanaſio, Photio, &c. Vigil. conſt. nu.* 173. *ubi ſententia minca per dictionem (condemnatum) aut aliam ſimile ſupplendi eſt.*

e *Cyrill Epiſtola ad Acatium, quæ citat. in conc. 5. coll. 5. pa.* 543.

f *Mala quæ damnaverat, cujus eſſent, Proclus profiſſus eſt ſe ignorare. Vigil. conc. nu.* 175.

that the Pope, seeing *Theodorus* bookes so full fraught with heresies, and blasphemies, would make little doubt to condemne the writer of them. *Vigilius* turnes to his former shift, hee will not thinke, nor have others to thinke that *Theodorus* writ such heresies, though they had his name prefixed unto them: for concerning those 60. chapters (expressed both in the Popes *Constitution* [g], and in the *Synodall* [h] *acts*) he thus saith [i], *Wee decree that by those foresaid chapters, nulla injuriandi præcedentes patres præbeatur occasio : no occasion be given to injure the former Fathers and Doctors of the Church.* And again [k], *We provide by this our Constitution,* that by these or the like doctrines condemned in *Nestorius* and *Eutyches, no contumely, nor occasion of injury bee brought to those Bishops who have died in the peace of the Catholike Church :* and that *Vigilius* thought *Theodorus* so to have dyed, we have before [l] declared: yea that *Vigilius* knew it, *Baronius* assured us. Thus *Vigilius* to free *Theodorus* from condemnation, pretends those hereticall writings to be none of his.

g Conc. Vig. a nu.
60. ad nu. 173.
h Conc. 5. coll. 4.
i Vigil. in const. nu.
173.
k nu. 184.

l Sup. c. 2.7.

31. What is it that *Vigilius* will not say for defence of this blasphemous and condemned heretike ? This cavill was used, as *Baronius* [m] tells us, by the old Nestorians and defenders of *Theodorus,* denying those to bee the writings of *Theodorus, quæ diffamata, which were famously knowne through the whole East:* and which being afterwards detected, and discovered to bee truly his writings, both they, and their author with them were condemned. Now this old hereticall and rejected cavill *Vigilius* here reneweth, those writings famously knowne to be the workes of *Theodorus,* condemned as his writings, and he with them and for thē, *Vigilius* will now have thought to be none of his, nor he by them nor for them may bee now condemned. And that you may see how *Vigilius* herein doth strive against the maine streame of the truth. Saint *Cyrill* [n] who then lived, testifieth *Theodorus* to be author of those hereticall and blasphemous writings. *That wee have found certaine things in the writings of Theodorus, nimiæ plena blasphemiæ, nulli dubium est, full of blasphemie, none that thinks aright can make any doubt.* And againe [o], *I examining the bookes of Theodorus, and Diodorus, have contradicted them as much as I could, declaring that sect to be every where full of abomination.* Yea hee writ divers bookes [p] against *Theodorus,* expressing the words of *Theodorus* and his owne confutation of the same. So cleare, and undoubted was this truth in *Cyrills* dayes, who lived at the same time with *Theodorus,* that hee thought them unwise, who made any doubt of that, which *Vigilius* now calls in question. And particularly touching that impious *Creed, Cyrill* saith [q], that they who brought it to the Synode of *Ephesus,* said, *that it was composed by* Theodorus : which they said not as by way of uncertaine report, but as testifying it to be so, in so much that the whole Synode giving credit thereunto, thereupon condemned *Theodorus* [r], though by a dispensation they expressed not his name.

m Defensores Theodori, ex ipsius scripta esse negarunt. Bar. an. 435. nu. 14.

n Cyrill. Epistola ad Proclum, citata in Conc. 5. coll. 5 pa. 550. b.

o Ibid. pa. 550 a.

p Quâ Cyrilli libri citantur sæpe in Conc. 5. coll. 5 pa. 538. & seq.
q Prolata apud sanctam Synodum expositione ab eo composita, sicut dicebant, qui protulerunt, &c. Verba Cyrilli in Epist. ad Proclum citat. in Conc. 5. coll. 5. pa. 550 b.
r His condemnatis qui sic sapiunt, nullam viri (Theodori) memoriam fecerunt. Ibid.

32 The

32 The same is testified by *Rambulas*, *Acatius*, and the whole *Armenian* Councell, who after examination ſ of this cause found the true and indubitate writings of *Theodorus* to be sacrilegious : and therefore by name condemned him, exhorting both *Cyrill* and *Proclus* to doe the like. The *Imperiall* Edicts of *Theodosius* ᵗ, and *Valentinian* leave no scruple in this matter: who would never have so severely forbidden the memory of *Theodorus*, and the reading or having of his bookes, had it not by evidences undeniable beene knowne, that those were indeed his workes, and hereticall writings. If all these suffice not, when this cause about *Theodorus* was now againe brought into question, the Emperour *Iustinian*, and the fift Councell, so narrowly and so exactly examined the truth hereof, that after them to make a doubt, is to seeke a knot in a rush. They testifie those very hereticall assertions whereof *Vigilius* doubteth, to be the doctrines and words ᵘ of *Theodorus*, that impious creed also, whereof *Vigilius* is doubtfull to be composed by *Theodorus* : they are so certaine ˣ hereof, that even in their Synodall sentence ʸ, they referre the triall of what they decree herein to the true and undoubted bookes of *Theodorus*. And in their sentence is included the judgement of the whole catholike Church, ever since they decreed this which hath with one consent approved their decree.

33 After all these Pope *Pelagius*, in one of his decretall Epistles, wherein at large he handleth this cause, not onely testifieth that impious *Creed* ᶻ, and those hereticall ᵃ writings, to bee the workes of *Theodorus*, alleaging many places of them, but whereas some obstinately addicted to the defence of the *three Chapters* moved againe ᵇ this same doubt which *Vigilius* doth; and as is likely by occasion of his decree : *Pelagius* of purpose declareth those ᶜ to have beene the true writings of *Theodorus*, and consonant to his doctrine; and that hee proveth by the testimonies of the *Armenian* Bishops, of *Proclus*, of *Iohn* of *Antioch*, of *Cyrill*, of *Rambulas*, of *Honoratus* a Bishop of *Cilicia*, (and so a neighbor of *Mopsvestia* which is in the same ᵈ Province,) of *Hesychius*, of *Theodosius*, and *Valentinian* the Emperours, and of *Theodoret*, then whom not any (except perhaps *Nestorius*) was more devoted to *Theodorus* ; insomuch that he is thought to have taken from *Theodorus* the name of *Theodoret*. After which cloud of witnesses produced, *Pelagius* thus concludeth ᵉ, *blasphemias has ejus esse quis dubitat*, who may doubt but that those blasphemies are truly his, (namely of *Theodorus*,) being by so many witnesses declared to be his? Now when Pope *Vigilius* against all these Councells, Bishops, Emperors, Popes, of the same, of succeeding ages, yea against the consenting judgement of the catholike Church, shall not onely doubt, whether *Theodorus* be the author of those hereticall and blasphemous assertions and writings : but by his *Apostolicall Constitution* decree it to bee an injury to ascribe those blasphemies

ſ *Fiat unitas vestra contra Theodorum, & sacrilega capitula & dogmata ejus. Libell. Episc. Armen. ad Proclum. in Conc. 5. coll. 5. pa. 542. b.*

t *De quibus legibus supra, hoc cap. Extant vero in Conc. 5. coll. 5. pa. 544.*

u *Habemus quæ ex Theodori codicibus collegissie. Conc. 5. coll. 4. pa. 527. b. & idem docet Iustin. in suo Edict. § Si quis defendit Theodorum.*

x *Impius Theodorus aliud Symbolum exposuit. Iust. in Edicto. §. Tali, Et impium ejus (Theodori) Symbolum. coll. 4. pa. 537. a.*

y *Licet volentibus codices impii Theodori præ manibus accipere, vel quæ ex impiis codicibus ejus à nobis inserta his gestis sunt. Conc. 5. coll. 8. pa. 585. a.*

z *Ab ejus (Theodori) discipulis, dictatum ab eo symbolum in eadem Synodo Ephesina prolatum. Pelagius Epist. 7. §. In his,*

a *Ejusdem Theodori ex libris illius dicta replicemus. ibid.*

b *Hæc Theodori dicta, utrum ejus sint, fortasse dubitatur. ibid. §. Hæc.*

c *Ibidem, & seq.*

d *Secunda Cilicia, sub qua Mopsvestia constituta est. Conc. 5. coll. e. pa. 547. b.*

e *Epist. 7. §. Etsi.*

blasphemies unto him, or for them to condemne him, (as the whole Church, ever since the *Ephesine* Councell hath done) doth it not argue, nay demonstrate an hereticall, and most extreme distemper in the Popes judgment, and in his cathedrall sentence at that time.

34. The other point which *Vigilius* observeth out of the *Ephesine* Councel is worse then this, for as yet he hath onely found that *Theodorus* was not *de facto* condemned by the *Ephesine* Synode; but in the next place, he will finde by that Councell, that *Theodorus*, *de jure* ought not to bee condemned. To which purpose he saith [f], that *Cyrill* (and so the *Ephesine* Synode consenting to him as President) would not have the name of *Theodorus* contained in the Synodall Acts at *Ephesus*: *propter regulam quæ de mortuis in sacerdotio servanda est*, *for the rule which is to bee kept in such Bishops as are dead.* And that rule he explaines in the words following, to be this, that the dead should not bee condemned, nor should the living bend their bow against ashes, or insult over the dead, whereby *Vigilius* even by his *Apostolicall* decree, adjudgeth both *Cyrill*, and the whole *Ephesine* Councell consenting therein with him, to have beleeved and held a condemned heresie, as an Ecclesiasticall rule, or rule of their faith and actions; That one who is dead may not bee condemned: and so by the Popes *Constitution* both *Cyrill* and the holy *Ephesine* Synode were heretikes. Such worthy points doe the Popes finde when they use their art, and industry, to review ancient writings, with a reference to their owne determinations, and so easie was it for *Vigilius* to finde the *Ephesine* Councell, first injurious to the dead, and then hereticall in a doctrine or rule concerning the dead.

f *Vigilius in Const. stu.* 173.

35. The very like he found also in the Councell of *Chalcedon*, that *Theodorus* ought not to be condemned. His reason is this, *Iohn* [g] Bishop of *Antioch*, writ a letter to the Emperor *Theodosius* in excuse of *Theodorus* of *Mopsvestia*, *ne post mortem damnari deberet*, *that he ought not to bee condemned after his death.* Now this letter of *Iohn*, *Venerabiliter memoratur*, *is with honour*, (not onely with allowance and liking) *remembred by the Councell of Chalcedon*, in their Relation, or Synodall Epistle to the Emperour *Martianus*. Whence *Vigilius* collecteth, that seeing the Councell with reverence, embraceth that letter of *Iohn*, and that letter importeth, that *Theodorus* being dead, ought not to be condemned; therefore the Councell judgeth that none who are dead, and particularly, that *Theodorus* ought not to bee condemned: which reason of *Vigilius* was borrowed from other Nestorians, and defenders of the *three Chapters*, as appeareth by *Liberatus*, who explaineth it, and sets [h] it downe almost *totidem verbis*: *Iohn* saith he, writ three letters in the behalfe of *Theodorus* of *Mopsvestia*, praising in them *Theodorus*, and declaring his wisedome; one of those letters he sent to the Emperour *Theodosius*, another

g *Vigil. in Const. stu.* 145.

h *Liber. ca.* 10.

to

to *Cyrill*, the third to *Proclus*. Now the first, and third, containing the praises of *Theodorus*, the Councell of *Chalcedon*, in their Relation to *Martianus* the Emperour, did [i] embrace, and confirme. Thus *Liberatus* agreeing wholly herein, as you see, with *Vigilius*.

i *Duas Iohannis Epistolas laudes Theodori continentes, Chalced. Synod. suscepit, et confirmavit. Ibid.*

36. For answer of which reason of *Vigilius*, I will intreat you to spare my labour, and heare how fully, and soundly Cardinall *Baronius* doth refute it; but yet so, that hee will not seeme to taxe, or touch *Vigilius*; that had beene great insolency, and incivilitie in a Cardinall; but he payes the Deacon home to the full, who saith but the very same with the Pope: *Liberatus*, saith [k] hee, *borrowed this narration of I know not what Nestorian, & incautè nimis*; and he affirmes too indiscreetly, that the writings of *Theodorus* were praised in the letters of *Iohn*, Bishop of *Antioch*; and, which is farre worse, that those letters of *Iohn*, containing the praises of *Theodorus*, were received, and confirmed by the Councell of *Chalcedon*, in their Relation to *Martianus*; for by that meanes, *adducit in idem crimen, he makes the whole Councell of Chalcedon guilty of the same crime*; to wit, of approving the praises & doctrine of *Theodorus*. So *Baronius*. By whō it is cleare, that *Vigilius* (saying the same with *Liberatus*) makes the whole Coūcell of *Chalcedon* guilty of the same crime; that is, in plaine termes avoucheth them to be hereticall: *Videsne*, saith the [l] Cardinall, *quot, & quales lateant colubri sub uno cespite? Doe not you see how many, and how vile, and venemous snakes lye hid under this one turfe*, or tuft of untruth? And that very tuft, hath Pope *Vigilius* chosen to build up, and beautifie with it his *Apostolicall* decree. Now, if under that one turfe there lurke (as indeed there doth, and the Cardinall acknowledgeth,) so great a number of Vipers; what infinite, and innumerable heapes of most deadly, and poisonfull untruths, are compacted into the whole body of his *Apostolicall* Constitution, which containeth (if one listed narrowly to examine it) more than a thousand like turfes; nay, beyond comparison worse than this.

k *Bar. an. 435. un. 11.*

l *Ibid.*

37. But the Cardinall hath not yet done with *Liberatus*; Let us, saith [m] hee, put the Axe to the roote of the tree; and citing the very words of the Councell, and their Relation to *Martianus*, he addeth, You see that here is no mention at all of *Theodorus* of *Mopsvestia*; which reason of *Baronius*, *Binius* [n] explaneth, saying, *That which Liberatus affirmeth, that the Councell of Chalcedon received the praises of* Theodorus, *is not onely untrue, sed etiam ipsi relationi Synodicæ contraria*; but *it is plainly contrary to the Synodall Relation of the Councell at Chalcedon*, to which *Liberatus* referreth himselfe: Change but the name, and all this is everie whit as forcible against *Vigilius*, as against *Liberatus*. But the Cardinall had well learned the old lesson, *Dat veniam corvis vexat censura columbas*; the Pope offends more than any, but the poore Deacon must feele the smart, and beare all the blowes; and yet by

m *Bar. ibid. et an. 12.*

n *Bin. notis in Liberatum. § Breviarium hoc.*

I   your

your leave, through the Deacons sides the Cardinall hath cunningly given a deadly wound, and cut the very roote of the Popes *Apostolicall* decree; although he will not bee thought so unmannerly, as once to touch his Holinesse, or speake one syllable against him.

38. After Fathers, and Councels, *Vigilius* will next finde, that the Emperour *Iustinian* himselfe, who was so earnest in condemning *Theodorus*, doth yet teach, that *Theodorus* ought not to bee condemned; and how proves hee this? You, saith o *Vigilius* to the Emperour, *laudabiliter adduxistis, have with praise and approbation alleaged* that Relation of the Councell of *Chalcedon* in your law, *de sancta Trinitate*. Seeing then that Relation of the Councell approveth the letters of *Iohn*, and the letters of *Iohn*, shew, that *Theodorus* being dead, ought not to bee condemned; the Pope from hence inferreth, that by *Iustinians* own law approving that Relation, *Theodorus* ought not to be condemned. It were very easie with *Baronius* Hatchet to chop off this reason, and cut it up by the roote, seeing neither *Iohns* letters did teach that *Theodorus*, being dead, might not be condemned; nor did the Councell, in their Relation approve, either the person, or doctrine, or any praises of *Theodorus*, or so much as mention him: But I will not trouble the Cardinall in so easie a matter as this. Besides all the inconsequences in this reason, *Iustinian* is so farre from teaching, or thinking this, so much as in a dreame, that in the same title, p *de Summa Trinitate, & fide Catholica*, (which seemes to be that which *Vigilius* intended) he accurseth all heresies, and specially that of *Nestorius*; and all, *qui eadem cum ipso sentiunt, vel senserunt;* who either doe thinke, or have thought as *Nestorius did*; in which number *Theodorus* of *Mopsvestia* to be comprehended, not onely by that which we have said before, is manifest; but even by *Iustinian* himselfe, who expresly witnesseth, Theodorus q *to have thought so, and to have* r *dyed in that hereticall opinion;* and for that very cause doth he condemne, and accurse him. Now seeing that law, *de Summa Trinitate*, was published in the seventh yeare of *Iustinians* raigne, (as by the s date appeareth) and sent into twelve severall Provinces; seeing, after this, *Iustinian*, in his twentieth t yeare, set forth another Edict u concerning these *three Chapters*, wherein he particularly, and by name anathematizeth y *Theodorus*; nor him onely, but all that defend him; yea, all, who doe not anathematize him; out of which number *Vigilius* himselfe is not exempted, seeing he remained so constant in this truth, that after *Vigilius* had published his *Constitution*, both himselfe signified to the fift Councell, that he still persisted in condemning the *three Chapters*, one of which was the condemning of *Theodorus*; and the whole fift Synod testified the same, saying in their seventh Collation, *semper* z *fecit, & facit, the Emperour hath ever done, and now continueth to doe, that which preserveth the holy Church, and true faith:* Was it not a very strange thing in *Vigilius* to pretend in his *Constitution*, that by the Empe-

o *In Const. nu.* 175.

p *In Cod. Iust. leg.* 6. *iit. de summa Trin.*

q *Theodorus hereticos omnes impietate superat, &c. Iust. in edict.* § *Tali.*
r *Iste autem (Theodorus) usque ad mortem in sua permanens impietate. Ibid.*
§ *Quod autem.*
s *Datum Iustiniano Augusti. 3. Coss. Is vero est annus 7 Iustiniani, ut docet Marcell. in Chrō. et car. in eum an. nu.* 1.
t *Vt ait Bar. an.* 546 *nu.* 8.
u *Edictum hoc de quo toties mentionem fecimus. Iust. Ed. C.* § *Si quis defendit Theodorum.*
y *Iust. Ed. C.* § *Si quis defendit Theodorum.*
z *Pa.* 582 *b.*

rours owne law, *Theodorus* ought not be condemned; whereas by the Emperours Edict, not onely *Theodorus* by name; but all, who defend him, even *Vigilius* himselfe, *eo nomine*, because he defendeth him, is condemned, and anathematized.

39. And now you have seene all that *Vigilius* bringeth for defence of *Theodorus*, all that hee found after his most diligent search of the Fathers, Councels, and ancient writings; whereby I doubt not but it is evident unto all, that Nestorianisme had either quite blinded the Pope, or at least induced him to play (which he hath done very skilfully) one of the *Lamiæ* in this cause; when ought that tended to the truth, came in his way, and offered it selfe unto him, he then lockt up his eyes, and kept them fast in a basket; but when, or where ought that tended to Nestorianisme, and the defence of a condemned heretike, might in a likelihood be found; then he put his eyes in his head, and became as quick sighted, as the Serpent of *Epidaurus*. The writings of *Cyril*, and *Proclus*, condemning *Theodorus* for an heretike, worse than either Iew, or Pagan, the Councels of *Ephesus*, of *Armenia*, of *Chalcedon*, anathematizing him; the Imperiall lawes of *Theodosius*, commanding all memory of him to bee abolished, & his heretical books to be burned; the expunging his name out of the Ecclesiasticall tables, even in that Church, where hee had beene Bishop; and a number the like; none of all these could *Vigilius*, in his most diligent inquisition, finde or see : why, the *Lamia* had lockt up his eyes against all these publike, and known evidences, and records. But when the base Counterfeits, forged in the name of *Cyrill*, and *Proclus*; when the depraving, or calumniating the Councels of *Ephesus*, of *Chalcedon*, and of *Iustinian*, as being maintainers of a condemned heresie : when these, or the like might be found, oh the Pope saw these at the first; his eyes were now as cleare, as the sight of *Linceus*, he could spie these through a Milstone; nay, which is more, hee could see them, though there were no such matters at all to bee seene : And truly, if you well consider, there was good reason why hee should see the one, and not the other . For the Pope saw the Epistle of *Ibas* to bee orthodoxall, and to be approved by the Councell of *Chalcedon*; he saw in that Epistle *Theodorus* to be called a [a] Saint, a Preacher of the truth, a Doctor of the Church; Now it had beene an exceeding incongruity, to see a condemned Saint, an accursed Saint, an hereticall, or blasphemous Saint ; It was not for the Popes wisedome to see such a Saint, and therefore at all such sights, up with the eyes, locke them fast, that they see none of those ugly, and offensive sights; nothing of the condemning, of the accursing, of the heresies, and blasphemies of *Theodorus*. So bewitched was the Pope with Nestorianisme at this time, that it had the whole command of his heart, of his eyes, of his sense, of his understanding; it opened, and shut them all whensoever it listed.

a *Quorum unus est beatus Theodorus veritatis prædicator, et doctor Ecclesiæ. Epist. Ibæ in Conc. Chal. Act. 10: pa. 113. b.*

I 2   40. I

40. I have stayed too long, I feare, in examining this *first Chapter*, touching *Theodorus*; but I was very loath to let any materiall point passe, without due triall, or before I had shaken asunder every joint, and parcell of the Popes *Constitution* in this cause, and fully manifested, how erronious his *Apostolicall* decree is, as well in *doctrinall*, as *personall* matters. That *Theodorus* was dead, is *personall*; but that none after death may bee condemned for an heretike, is *doctrinall*; yea, an heresie in the doctrine of faith. That *Theodorus* dyed in the peace of the Church, is an errour *personall*; but that *Theodorus* therefore dyed in the peace of the Church, because he was not in his life time condemned by the expresse sentēce of the Church; or, that any dying in heresie, as *Theodorus* did, doe die in the peace of the Church, are errours *doctrinall*. That *Theodorus* was not by the former Fathers, and Councels condēned, is a *personall* error; but that *Theodorus* by the judgement of the Fathers, & Councels, ought not after his death to be condemned, is *doctrinall*; even a condemning of the Councels of *Ephesus*, and *Chalcedon*, as guilty of beleeving, and teaching an heresie. So many wayes is the Popes sentence, in this *first Chapter*, erronious in faith; of which *Baronius* most vainely pretendeth, that it is no cause of faith, no such cause as doth concerne the faith.

4:. There now remaineth nothing of *Vigilius* decree concerning this *first Chapter*, but his conclusion of the same: And although that must needs of it selfe fall downe, when all the reasons, on which it relyeth, and by which onely it is supported, are ruinated, or overthrowne; yet if you please, let us take a short view of it also, rather to explane, than refute the same. His conclusion hath two branches, the former, that in regard of the

b Vig.Const.n.u.179 foresaid reasons, *nostrâ* [b] *eum non audemus damnare sententia; wee dare not condemne* Theodorus *by our sentence*, wee dare not doe it, saith *Vigilius*.

42. Oh how faint-hearted, pusillanimous, and dastardly was the Pope in this cause; *Cyrill*, the [c] head of the generall Councell: *Proclus*, a most [d] holy Bishop, whose Epistle, as *Liberatus* [e] saith, the Councell of *Chalcedon* approved: *Rambulas*, the piller of the Church: the religious Emperours *Theodosius*, and *Valentinian*; the Church of *Mopsvestia*, the Councels of *Ephesus*, of *Armenia*, of *Chalcedon*, the whole Catholike Church ever since the *Ephesine* Synod, both durst, and did condemne *Theodorus*: and, besides these, *Baronius*, and *Binius*, two of the most artificiall Gnathonizing Parasites of the Pope, even they durst, and did, even in setting downe the very *Constitution* of *Vigilius*, cal [f] *Theodorus*, more than forty times, an heretike, a craftie, impious, madde, prophane, blasphemous, execrable heretike; onely Pope *Vigilius* hath not the heart, nor courage; hee onely with his sectators, dare not call him, nor cōdemne him for an heretike; we dare not condemne him by our sentence.

43. And

c Sanctissimorum Episcoporum hic coactorum caput Cyrillum, &c. Epist. Synod. Ephes. to. 4. Act. Conc. Ephes. ca.8.
d Cyrill. epist. ad A-cat. in Con.5. Coll.5. pa.543-a. Dominus meus sanctissimus Episcopus Proclus e Lib.c.10.
f Rursumq̃ hæreticus, blasph mus. &c. Bar.an.55 :.nu. 120.et seq.e: B:n. pa.595.et seq.

43. And yet when *Vigilius* saw good, hee who durst not doe this, durst doe a greater matter, he durst doe that which not any of all the former, nay which they all put together, never durst doe. *Vigilius* durst defend both an heresie, and a condemned and anathematized heretike, he durst commend forged, and hereticall writings, under the name of holy Fathers, hee durst approve that Epistle, wherein an heretike is called, and honoured for a Saint; he durst, contrary to the Imperiall and godly Edict of *Theodosius*, contrary to the judgements of the holy generall Councells, defend *Theodorus*, honor his memorie, yea honor him as a teacher of truth while he lived, as a Saint being dead; These things none of all the former ever durst doe: in these *Vigilius* is more bold and audacious then they are all.

44. Whence thinke you proceeded this contrariety of passions in *Vigilius*, that made him sometimes more bold then a Lyon, and other times more timerous then an Hare? Truely even from hence: As *Vigilius* had no eyes to see ought, but what favored Nestorianisme, so hee had not the heart to doe ought which did not uphold Nestorianisme. If a Catholike truth met him, or the sweet influence thereof hapned to breath upon him, *Vigilius* could not endure it, the Popes heart fainted at the smell thereof: but when the Nestorian heresie blew upon him, when being full with *Nestorius* he might say, *agitante calescimus illo*, not *Ajax*, not *Poliphemus* so bold nor full of courage as Pope *Vigilius*. As the Scarobee or beetle g is said to feed on dung, but to dye at the sent of a Rose: So the filth of Nestorianisme was meat, and drinke to the Pope, it was *vita vitalis* unto him; but the fragrant and most odoriferous sent of the catholike truth, was poison, it was even death to this Beetle. So truly was it fulfilled in him, which the Prophet saith h, *they bend their tongues for lyes, but they have no courage for the truth*: we dare not condemne *Theodorus* by our sentence.

g *Pier. Hierog. lib.55.*

h *Jer.9.3.*

· 45. The other branch of the Popes conclusion is, *Sed* i *nec ab alio quopiam condemnari concedimus*, neither doe wee permit that any other shall condemne Theodorus: Nay we decree k that none else shall speake, write, or teach otherwise, then we doe herein. As much in effect, as if the Pope had definitively decreed, wee permit, or suffer no man whatsoever, to teach or beleeve what *Cyrill*, what *Proclus*, what the whole generall Councells of *Ephesus* and *Chalcedon*: that is, what all Catholikes, and the whole Catholike Church hath done, taught and beleeved: we permit, nay we command, and by this our *Apostolicall Constitution*, decree, that they shall be heretikes, and defend both an heresie, (that no dead man may be condemned) and condemned heretikes, in defending *Theodorus*, yea defending him for a Saint, and teacher of truth: This we permit, command, and decree, that they shall doe; but to doe otherwise, to condemne *Theodorus*, or a dead man, that by no meanes doe we permit or suffer it to bee lawfull unto them.

i *Vig.Const.nu.179*

k *Vig.Const.nu.208*

I 3   46 And

46. And as if all this were not sufficient, the Pope addes one other clause more execrable, then all the former; for having re-cited those threescore hereticall assertions, which as we have de-clared, were all collected out of the true, and indubitate writings
l Vig. Consi. xu. 173. of *Theodorus*, he adjoynes, [l] *Anathematizamus omnem, wee accurse and anathematize every man pertaining to orders,* who shall ascribe or impute any contumely, to the Fathers, and Doctors of the Church, by those forenamed impieties: and if no Father, then not *Theodorus* for those may be condemned. See now, unto what height of impiety, the Pope is ascended, for it is as much as if hee had said, We anathematize, and accurse Saint *Cyrill,* Saint *Pro-clus,* Saint *Rambulas,* Saint *Acatius,* the Synode of *Armenia,* the generall Councells of *Ephesus,* of *Chalcedon,* of *Constantinople* in the time of *Iustinian*; yea even the whole catholike Church, which hath approved those holy Councells: all these out of those very impieties, which *Vigilius* mentioneth, have condem-ned *Theodorus,* them all for wronging, and condemning *Theodo-rus* for those impieties, we doe anathematize, and accurse, saith *Vigilius.*

47. Consider now seriously with your selves of what faith and religion they are, who hold (and so doe all the members of the present Romane Church,) this for a position or foundation of faith, that whatsoever any Pope doth judicially, and by his *Apostolike* authority define in such causes, is true, is infallible, is with certainty of faith to bee beleeved and embraced: Let all the rest be omitted, embrace but this one decree of *Vigilius,* nay but this one passage or parcell of his decree touching this *first Chapter* which concernes *Theodorus*; yet by approving this one, they demonstrate themselves, not onely to renounce, but with *Vigilius* to condemne, accurse, and anathematize both the Catholike faith, and the Catholike Church: yea to accurse all who doe not accurse them, which because none but *An-ti-Christ,* and his hereticall adherents can doe, they demon-strate againe hereby their Church to bee hereticall, cata-catholike, and Anti-Christian, such as not onely hateth, but accurseth the holy, and truly Catholike Church of Christ.
m Prov. 26.2. *But the curse [m] that is causlesse shall not come.* Nay, God doth,
n Mat. 5.11. and for ever will turne their cursings into blessings. *Blessed are [n] yee, when for my sake,* (for professing and maintaining my truth) *men revile you, and speake evill of you.* Let *Balak* hire with houf-fulls of gold: Let the Romane *Balaam* for the wages of iniquity attempt never so oft, on this hill, on that moun-taine, or wheresoever hee sets up his altars to curse the Church
o Deut. 23.5. of G O D, *the Lord [o] will turne the curse into a blessing unto them:*
p Numb. 23.23. for, *there is no sorcery [p] against Iacob, no curse, no charme, nor incantation, against Israell.* Nay their curses shall fall on their owne heads and returne into their owne bosomes, but peace, and the blessings of peace shall bee upon Israel. For
Blessed

blessed ʠ shall hee bee that blesseth thee, and cursed is hee that curseth ʠNumb.24.9.
thee.

CHAP. IX.

That Vigilius *besides divers personall, held a doctrinall errour in faith, in his defence of the* second Chapter, *which concernes the writings of* Theodoret *against* Cyrill.

1. Here was some shadow of reason to thinke, that the former Chapter was a personall matter; seeing that was indeed moved concerning the person of *Theodorus.* But in the two other, there is no pretence, or colour for *Baronius* to say,that in them the question, or cause was personall, and not wholy doctrinall; who in all the fift Councell once doubted of the persons of *Theodoret*,or *Ibas*,whether they were Catholikes, after their anathematizing of *Nestorius* in the Councell of *Chalcedon*? The onely question about them was, whether the writings of *Theodoret* against *Cyrill* were to bee condemned, which the Pope denyeth, and the holy Councell affirmeth, and whether the Epistle of *Ibas* was Orthodoxall, or he by it known to be Orthodoxal,which the Pope affirmeth,and the holy Councell denyeth. The question about them,no way concerned their persons,but onely their writings.And it might be a wonder that *Baronius* should have the face to say, that the cause in these *two Chapters* was onely personall, if it were not daily seene by experience that *necessitas cogit ad turpia,* mere necessity enforced the Cardinall to use any though never so untrue, never so unlikely excuses for *Vigilius.*

2. There are I confesse divers personall matters, and questions of facts,which concernes both these Chapters: and although they were not the controversies moved, and debated, betwixt the defenders, and the oppugners of those Chapters; yet is it needfull to say somewhat of them also; partly for more illustration of the cause of faith,& specially that we may see how foully *Vigilius* and *Baronius* have erred,not onely in doctrinall causes, which are more obscure, but even in those personall matters, which had beene easie, and obvious, if they had not shut their eyes against the truth.

3. Concerning the *second Chapter,* the Popes decree herein relyeth,and is grounded,on three personall points,or matters of fact. The first is, that *Vigilius* would perswade, that *Theodoret* was not the author of those writings against *Cyrill,* and against his twelve Chapters or Anathematizmes ᵃ, which containing a just condemnation of the twelve hereticall assertions of *Nesto-rius,* ᵃ Extant in Actis Conc.Ephes.to 1.ca 14. & tom. 5. ca. i

b *Ibid. to. 5. ca.2.*
§. *Ego vera. Et Liber.*
ca.6.
c *Act. 5. in definit.*
fidei.
d *Vigil. Constit. nu.*
180.
e *Ibid. nu. 181.*
f *Ibid.*

rius, were approved both by the Councell of *Ephesus* b, and *Chalcedon* c. To which purpose he calls them not *Theodorets*, but wrⁱtings, *quæ* d *sub Theodoreti nomine proferuntur*, which are set forth under the name of *Theodoret*. And againe, the reprofe of the 12. Chapters of *Cyrill* : *à Theodoreto* e *ut putatur ingesta*, made as is thought by *Theodoret* : adding f this as one reason, why the Councell of *Chalcedon*, did not condemne those writings, because they having those matters which were done but of late before their eyes, *Theodoretum nihil tale fecisse probaverunt*, did judge that *Theodoret* had written no such thing. Thus *Vigilius* pretending those writings against *Cyrill* not to be *Theodorets*, and that the Councell of *Chalcedon* also thought the same: whence he would inferre, (and justly upon this supposall) that *Theodorets* name ought not to bee blemished by those writings which were none of his.

4. Not his? why *Theodoret* is knowne, and testified by so many, to have beene so eager and violent in defence of *Nestorius*, and his heresie, and so spitefull both in words, and writings against *Cyrill*, and all orthodoxall professors of that time, that it were more strange if *Vigilius* was ignorant of this, then that knowing it he should deny, or make a doubt thereof. Witnesse *Binius*, *Iohn* of *Antioch*, saith he, g *perswaded* Theodoret, *that hee should with all his art and skill oppugne and refute those* 12 *Anathematizmes of Cyrill*. *Theodoret* being as much an enemy to *Cyrill*, as was *Iohn* himselfe, willingly yeelded to his petition, and by manifest sycophancy wrested every one of *Cyrills* Chapters from their true, genuine, and orthodoxall, to a false, preposterous, and hereticall sense, and *Enoptius* sent that refutation of *Theodoret* unto *Cyrill*. Againe, h *Theodoret* did once defend *Theodorus* and *Nestorius*, two most pestiferous Arch-heretikes against *Cyrill*. Yea *Binius* saith, *defendit constantissimè*, he defended them most constantly, as if to defend heresie, were with these men not pertinacie, but constancy, witnesse *Baronius*. *Theodoret* saith he i *being most addicted to Theodorus, shadowed his praise, by his friendship with Nestorius, but he utterly darkned it by his undertaking of the defence of that Arch-heretike against Cyrill*. And againe k, *Theodoret being at that time the patron of Nestorius, and an oppugner of the Catholike faith, throweth his darts against the Chapters of Cyrill, and by new writings doth oppugne them*: crying out in his letters to the Bishops of *Millaine* of *Aquileia*, and of *Ravenna*, that *Cyrill* renewed the heresie of *Apollinaris*.

5. Witnesse (men of better note then the former) *Liberatus*, who saith, l that *Iohn* of *Antioch* commanded two Bishops, *Andreas* & *Theodoret*, that they should write against the 12. Chapters of *Cyrill*, blaming him as one who renewed the heresie of Apollinaris : and that *Theodoret* consented, the event made manifest. Pope *Pelagius*, who saith m that *Theodoret, monstratur scripsisse*, is demonstrated and certainly knowne to have written against the twelve Chapters of *Cyrill*, and against the true Faith.
The

g *Ein. in argamento*
ca. 2. Append. ad to.
5. Act. Conc. Ephes.
pa. 859.

h *Bin. notis in Epist.*
Leonis. 61. to. 1.
Conc. pa. 971.

i *Bar. an. 427.*
nu. 30.

k *an. 431. nu. 182.*

l *Liber. ca. 4.*

m *Pelag. 2. Epist. 7.*
§. *Discusso.*

The Acts of the *Ephesine* Councell, wherein [n] is recorded the verie refutation of those twelve Chapters by *Theodoret*, and the answere of *Cyrill* unto it; the one still called, *Theodoreti reprehensio*; and the other, *Cyrilli adversus Theodoretum refutatio*; *Cyrill*, who, in his Epistle [o] to *Eulogius*, saith thus, *You have my refutation which I set forth against Andreas, and Theodoret, who writ against my Chapters.*

6. Witnesse *Theodoret* himselfe, who, in sundrie of his Epistles, testifieth his spleene, and spight against *Cyrill*, and the Catholike faith. In [p] one of them to *Nestorius* he professeth his most perverse, and pertinacious resolution to abide in that heresie of *Nestorius*; *I wil never*, saith he, *while I live, consent to those things which are done against you, and against the law* : (so hee taxeth, not onely the Chapters of *Cyrill*, but the decree of the holy *Ephesine* Synod) no, I will not consent unto them, though they should cut off both my hands. In another to *Iohn*, the Bishop of *Antioch*; We [q] continue still, saith he, contradicting the twelve Chapters, *ut alienis à pietate, as being contrary to pietie* : In another to *Æmerius*, *Wee [r] ought not to consent to the condemnation of the venerable, and most holy Bishop Nestorius* : in another to [ſ] *Alexander*, *I told you before, that the doctrine of my venerable, and most holy Bishop Nestorius hath beene condemned*; *nec ego, cum his qui faciunt, communicabo*; *neither will I communicate with those who condemned that doctrine* : and yet more bitterly in his Epistle to [r] *Andreas*, his fellow-oppugner of those Chapters. *Insanit iterum Ægyptus adversus Deum*; *Ægypt is againe madde against the Lord*, and makes warre with *Moses*, and *Aaron*, the servants of God : As if *Nestorius*, and his fellow-heretikes were the onely Israel; but *Cyrill*, Bishop of *Alexandria* in *Ægypt*; and the holy *Ephesine* Councell, and all Catholikes who held with them, were no other but *Pharao*, and his Ægyptian troupes, which fought against GODS people.

7. Doe we yet desire more, or more pregnant, and ample testimonies in this matter? Take this one out of the acts of *Chalcedon* : When *Theodoret*, being called, came first into the Synod, the most reverend Bishops of *Ægypt*, *Illirium*, and [u] *Palestine*, cryed out against him in this manner; The Canons exclude this man, thrust him out, *Magistrum Nestorij foras mittite*; *thrust out the master of Nestorius* : the orthodoxall Councell doth not receive *Theodoret* : *Call him not a Bishop, he is no Bishop, hee is an oppugner of God, he is a Iew, thrust him out* : *he accused, he anathematized Cyrill. If we receive him, we reject Cyrill; The Canons exclude him, God doth detest him*. Thus cryed out the Bishops against *Theodoret*, before they knew him to have renounced the heresie of *Nestorius*, which he had so long, and so eagerly defended: nor were they pacified otherwise, but that *Theodoret*, at the appointment of the Iudges, should sit onely as an accuser of *Dioscorus*, not as one having judicatorie power, or a decisive suffrage, till his owne

cause

n *Reprehensio 12. Capitulorum, diu-t Cyrilli à Theodoreto conscripta, habetur in Append. ad to. 5. Act. Conc. Eph. ca. 2. pa. 859. b*

o *Cyrill. Epist. ad Eulog. extat. to. 5. Act. Conc. Eph. c. 8.*

p *Extat in Conc. 5. Coll. 5. pa. 559. a.*

q *Extat et citat. ib.*

r *Et citatur à Pelagio, Ep. 2. 7. § Discussio.*
ſ *Citatur ibid.*

r *Extat in Conc 5. Coll. 5. pa. 558. b.*

u *Conc. Chal. Act. 8 pa. 6. a.*

cause was fully examined, and heard. Seeing now there are besides, many other which I willingly omit, so many, so evident, so
obvious, so undeniable proofes, that *Theodoret* writ against *Cyrill*, and against his twelve Chapters, in defence of *Nestorius*, and
his heresie; what can one thinke of *Vigilius*, but that he wilfully,
and wittingly resisted the truth, while he, not onely strives to
perswade, that *Theodoret* writ no such thing, and that the Councell of *Chalcedon* thought so; but takes this knowne, and palpable untruth, for one of the grounds of his *Apostolicall* decree
touching this *second Chapter.*

8. And yet there is a worse matter in this very passage of *Vigilius*, and that is, the reason whereby he proveth, that *Theodoret* writ not against *Cyrill*, or in defence of *Nestorius*; you shall
heare it in his owne words: *It is*, saith ˣ he, *undoubtedly repugnant
to the judgement of the Councell of Chalcedon, that any Nestorian doctrines should be condemned under the name of that Bishop* (Theodoret) *who, together with those holy Fathers, did accurse the doctrines of
Nestorius : Quid enim aliud est mendaces, & simulantes professionem
rectæ fidei patres in sancto Concilio Chalcedonensi residentes ostendere,
quam dicere aliquos ex ijs similia sapuisse* Nestorio : *for to say, that
any of them who were in that Councell, had thought as* Nestorius *did,
is nothing else then to shew or affirme those Fathers in the Councell of
Chalcedon to be lyers, and dissemblers in faith, as condemning that
faith which they doe allow.* Thus reasoneth *Vigilius*, who hence implyeth, that seeing *Theodoret* was one of the Bishops, and Fathers
at *Chalcedon*, if he ever writ any such things in defence of *Nestorius*, then both he, and the rest admitting him, should dissemble in their faith, and lye, professing to condemne *Nestorius*, and
yet approving him, who had writ in defence of *Nestorius.*

9. Truly I doe even admire, to consider the blindnesse of *Vigilius* in this whole cause of the *three Chapters*. Most certaine it is,
as we have shewed, that *Theodoret* did both thinke as *Nestorius*,
and write in defence of him, and his heresie, and that the Councell of *Chalcedon* knew he did so: If then to receive such an one,
as they knew *Theodoret* to have beene, be, as *Vigilius* saith, a dissembling, and lying in the faith; the whole Councell of *Chalcedon*, by the Popes judgement, and decree, were undoubtedly all
lyers, and dissemblers in the faith; a calumnie and slander so
vile, and incredible, that it alone should cause any Catholike
minde to detest this *Apostolicall Constitution* of *Vigilius* : But to say
truth, the Popes reason is without al reason. Had the holy Coūcell admitted *Theodoret* before he had renounced his heresie, or
manifested the sincerity of his faith unto them, the Pope might
have had some colour to have accused them of dissembling, as
condemning Nestorianisme, & yet receiving a known Nestorian
into their communion : but it was quite contrary. In the former
actions, till *Theodoret* had cleared himselfe of heresie, hee was, as
we have declared, no otherwise admitted, than onely as *a plain-
tiffe,*

tiſſe, *who* ⁱ *accuſed Dioſcorus for injuriouſly depoſing him, and placing another in his See.* And in the eight Action, wherein hee came to cleare himſelfe, and to be reconciled to the Church, he had no ſooner almoſt ſet his foot in the Synod, but the Biſhops cryed ᶻ out, Theodoretus *modo anathematiꝫet* Neſtorium; *let* Theodoret *forthwith anathematiꝫe* Neſtorius: let him doe it inſtantly and without any delay. And when *Theodoret* to give the Councell better ſatisfaction offered them firſt a book to reade containing the ſincere profeſſion of his faith; and when (that being ᵃ refuſed) he purpoſed at large by words ᵇ to have expreſſed the ſame; the Synod ſuſpecting the worſt, and that hee uſed thoſe delayes, as being loath to anathematize *Neſtorius,* cryed out, *He is an heretike, he is a Neſtorian, hæreticum foras mitte, out with the heretike;* and ſo they had indeed thruſt him out, but that he leaving all circuition, preſently before them all, cryed, *Anathema* to *Neſtorius; Anathema* to him, who doth not confeſſe the bleſſed Virgin to bee the Mother of God: with which profeſſion the Synod being fully ſatiſfied, the glorious Iudges ſaid, *omnis dubitatio,* now all doubt is quite taken away concerning *Theodoret;* and then the Synod both received him into their communion, as an orthodoxe, and reſtored him to his See, from which in the Epheſine latrocinie, hee was depoſed, they all crying out, *Theodoret* is worthy of his See; let his Church receive their orthodoxall Biſhop: To *Theodoret,* a Catholike Doctor, let the Church be reſtored.

10. What greater deteſtation of hereſie could the Synod poſſibly ſhew, what greater tokens of the ſinceritie of his faith, could either *Theodoret* expreſſe, or the Synod require. It was too great raſhneſſe, if not ſimplicitie in *Vigilius* to collect that the holy Councell did diſſemble in their faith, becauſe they received him who had ſometimes ſwarved in the faith; The hereticall *Theodoret,* they exclude and reject, the orthodoxall *Theodoret* they reverence and embrace. That which Saint *Auſten* ᶜ ſaith in another cauſe, *that the husband who had put away his adulterous wife, ought againe to receive her being purged by unſained repentance,* but ſo receive her, *non ut poſt viri divortium adultera revocetur, ſed ut poſt Chriſti conſortium adultera non vocetur,* that ſame may bee accommodated to any other offence, and not unfitly to this of hereſie, and the repentant hereticke; whom they before, for that cauſe had from themſelves diſioyned; but they neither call, nor count him an hereticke, whom Chriſt hath now upon his repentance unto himſelfe conjoyned. So neither is the Popes reaſon conſequent, that the Councell did diſſemble in their receiving of *Theodoret,* nor his concluſion true, which he would thence inferre, that *Theodoret* writ not againſt *Cyrill* and the Catholike faith.

11 The ſecond perſonall matter which *Vigilius* taketh for another ground of his decree is, that neither *Theodoret* himſelfe did, nor did the Councell of *Chalcedon,* require him to anathematize

y *Glorioſiſſ. Iudices dixerunt, Theodoretus in locum accuſatoris nunc ingreſſus eſt, unde pati amini ea quæ inchoata ſunt ſiniri, reſervata poſt hac omni accuſatione, et vobis, et illi. Conc Chal. act. 1. pa. 6. a.*

z *Act. 8. Conc. Chal. a N. bil ; elegi volumus, anathematiꝫet Neſtorium. lb.*

b *Ego (inquit Theoretus) quomodo crido, &c. ib. d.*

c *Aug. lib. 2. de A dulter. conjug. ca. 9*

matize his writings: *There was*, ſaith he, *divers in the Councell of
Chalcedon who ſaid, that* Theodoret *had anathematized Cyrill, and
was an heretike*; yet thoſe holy Fathers moſt diligently examining
this cauſe of *Theodoret, nihil aliud ab eo exigiſſe noſcuntur, are knowne
to have required no more of him,* than that hee ſhould anathematize
Neſtorius, and his impious doctrines; *hoc ſibi tantummodo ſufficere judicantes; judging this alone to be ſufficient for them to receive*
Theodoret. Now it is unfit, ſaith [e] he further, *nos aliquid quære-*

*re velut omiſſum à patribus, that we ſhould ſeek or require more than
did the* Councell of Chalcedon; as if they had omitted any thing
in this cauſe of *Theodoret*: ſeeing then they required no anathematizing of his writings againſt *Cyrill,* neither ought any
others to anathematize, or require of any the anathematizing
of the ſame.

12. As you ſaw *Vigilius* in the former Chapter to uſe *hareti-
ca aſtutia;* ſo may any man here eaſily diſcerne, that hee uſeth an
evident, and fallacious ſophiſtication. The Councell indeed
required not that, nor did *Theodoret* in explicite, or expreſſe
termes performe it, ſaying, I anathematize my owne writings
againſt *Cyrill;* but in implicite termes, in effect, and by an evident conſequent, both the Councell required, and *Theodoret* performed this before them all; for, hee ſubſcribed [g] *to the definition of

faith decreed at Chalcedon :* one part of that definition is the ap-
proveing g of the Synodall Epiſtles of *Cyrill* : a part of one of
thoſe Epiſtles [h] are the twelve Chapters of *Cyrill,* which *Theodoret* refuted : in every one of thoſe chapters, is an anathema denounced to the defenders of the contrarie doctrine : Then certainely, *Theodoret* by ſubſcribing to the definition, ſubſcribed to
the Epiſtles of *Cyrill,* by them to the twelve chapters, and by
doing ſo he condemned, and anathematized all who oppugned
thoſe twelve chapters, and then undoubtedly, his owne writings
which were publiſhed, as a confutation of thoſe twelve chapters. And it ſeemes ſtrange, that *Vigilius* profeſſing that *Theodoret* did *devota mente ſuſcipere, with a devout affection receive* and
approve the Epiſtles of *Cyrill,* and the doctrine of them, could
deny or be ignorant, that in doing ſo he did anathematize his
owne writings, which by the twelve chapters of *Cyrill,* are anathematized.

13. Beſides this, how often, how plainely doth the Councell
of *Chalcedon* [i] require, and urge *Theodoret* to anathematize *Neſtorius* and his doctrines? how willingly did *Theodoret* performe
this? What elſe is this, but a vertuall, and implicite anathematizing of thoſe his owne writings againſt *Cyrill,* wch defended
Neſtorius and his doctrines? None can anathematize the former, but *eo ipſo* he doth moſt certainely (though not expreſly) a-
nathematize the later; as on the contrary, none can ſay (as *Vigilius* doth, and decreeth, that all ſhall doe the like) none can ſay
that the writings of *Theodoret* againſt *Cyrill,* and his twelve chap-

ters,

ters ought not to be anathematized, but *eo ipſo,* even by ſaying ſo, he doth moſt certainly (though but *impliciſè* and by conſequent) ſay that *Neſtorius* and his hereſie, ought not to be condemned. A truth ſo cleare that Pope *Pelagius* k from his anathematizing of *Neſtorius* and his doctrine, concludeth of *Theodoret: Conſtat eundem,* it is manifeſt, that in doing this, he condemned his owne writings againſt the twelve Chapters of *Cyrill.*

k *Pelag.2. Epiſt. 7. S. Quu bic.*

14. Neither is that true which *Vigilius* fancied, that to require men to anathematize the writings of *Theodoret,* is to ſeeke, and require more then the Councell of *Chalcedon* required : It is not. It is but requiring the ſelfe ſame thing to be done in actuall and expreſſe termes, which the Councel required and *Theodoret* performed in vertuall and implicite termes. The thing required and done is the ſame : the manner onely of doing it, or requiring it to be done, is different : Even as to require of men to profeſſe Chriſt to be ὁμοούσιον, which the Councell of *Nice,* and the Church ever ſince requireth, is not to require them to profeſſe more, or ought elſe, then the Scripture teacheth, and all catholikes 1 before profeſſed, by thoſe words, *I and my Father are one :* but it is a requiring of an explicite profeſſion of that truth concerning the unity of ſubſtance of the Father, and the Sonne, which by thoſe words of Scripture they did before *impliciſè* profeſſe.

1 *Hoc teſtimonio omnes patres utun-tur contra Arianos, ut probent unam eſſe eſſentiam patris & filij. Bell.lib.1.de Chriſt.ca.6.§. Quartum.*

15. But yet at leaſt will ſome of *Vigilius* friends reply, it was unfit to require this explicite anathematizing of *Theodorets* writings, ſeeing the Councell of *Chalcedon* did not require it. No, not ſo neither. The explicite condemning of them, was not only fit, but neceſſarie at that time, in the dayes of *Iuſtinian,* and *Vigilius*; For as when the Arians denyed Chriſt to bee ὁμοούσιον, it was enough for one to cleare himſelfe of Arianiſme, to ſay, that he held this text for true, *I and the Father are one,* though therein he doe *impliciſè* profeſſe Chriſt to bee ὁμοούσιον, and though to have profeſſed that alone, before the queſtion about the unity of one ſubſtance was moved, had beene ſufficient; but now he muſt *expliciſè* profeſſe that truth which is *expliciſè* denyed and oppugned : even ſo it is in this cauſe of *Theodorets* writings, and all like it. While there was no doubt moved by heretikes, whether thoſe writings of his ought to be condemned; and whether by the Councell of *Chalcedon* they were condemed or no; ſo long it was ſufficient for one to profeſſe that he condemned *Neſtorius,* and ſubſcribed to the definition of *Chalcedon* ; both which were implicite condemning of thoſe writings of *Theodoret* : but when the Neſtorians began to boaſt, that *Theodorets* writings againſt *Cyrill,* neither were condemned, but rather with the author of them approved by the Councell of *Chalcedon,* neither ought to be condemned, the Church now was neceſſarily enforced to require of all men a profeſſion of that truth in plaine and explicite termes, which before they made onely in generall and implicite. Nor could *Vigilius,* or any other Neſtorian, who refuſed in expreſſe manner to condemne the writings of *Theodoret,* purge him-

K　　　　ſelfe

selfe of that heresie of *Nestorius* at this time, by saying they
approved the definition of *Chalcedon*, or condemned *Nestorius*;
though in both these they did *implicitè* condemne the writings
of *Theodoret*, but now they must expresly professe that which the
heretikes expresly denyed, they must in plaine termes anathematize those hereticall writings of *Theodoret*, and acknowledge
them to have bin anathematized by the Councel of *Chalcedon*, as
the heretiks in plaine termes vaûted, that neither they ought nor
were anathematized, but approved by the Councel of *Chalcedon*,
whensoever any point tending to the impeaching of faith begins
explicitè to be denyed, the holy Church may not then content
her selfe in generall and *implicitè* to condemne the same, (few
perhaps can perceive that, and many will make that generality
of termes, as *Vigilius* and other Nestorians now did, but a cloak
for their heresie) but the Church must now in most plaine, easie,
and expressed manner that can be devised, both teach, declare,
and define the same. This the Church did in this fift Councell,
as in the other two, so in this Chapter touching *Theodorets* writings. It taught but the very same which the Councell of *Chalcedon* had done before it, anathematized those his writings, which
at *Chalcedon* were anathematized before, but they did this now
in a plaine manner and *explicitè*, which by the Councell of *Chalcedon* only in an obscure manner, and *implicitè* was done before.

m *Vig. Const. nu.*
181.

16. The third personall errour which *Vigilius* [m] taketh for a
ground of his decree, is that *Cyrill* himselfe though he was so exceedingly injured by the writings of those Easterne Bishops that
tooke part with *Nestorius*, yet when he made union with them,
he required them not to anathematize their owne writings, but
overpast them in silence, as if there had never beene any such:
whence *Vigilius* inferreth, that neither ought this anathematizing of their writings (by name of *Theodorets*) bee required by
others, yea he saith, the Fathers of *Chalcedon* imitated this example of *Cyrill*, and so would not require that of *Theodoret*, which
they saw *Cyrill* not to have required of others.

17. The answer is easie by that which hath beene declared:
this saying of *Vigilius* laboureth of the same equivocall sophistication, as did the former; for both *Cyrill* required, and all who
were united unto him, and received into his, which was the communion of the Catholike Church; they all did, though not in explicite termes, which then was not needfull; yet vertually, and after a certaine, and undoubted, though implicite manner, condemne, and anathematize all their writings against *Cyrill*, and
the Catholike faith; for he received none till they had anathematized the doctrines of *Nestorius*. This doth *Cyril* himselfe most
plainly witnesse in his Epistle to [n] *Dynatus*: *I would not*, saith he,
*admit Paulus Bishop of Emisa into communion, priusquam Nestorij
dogmata a proprio chyrographo anathematizasset, untill hee had anathematized by his owne hand-writing the doctrines of Nestorius*: And
he intreated me in behalfe of the other Bishops, that I would
rest

n *Cyrill. Epist. ad
Dynat. extat in
Act. Conc. Ephes.
ta.5. ca.16.*

rest contented with that profession which they had sent, and require no more: *nulla ratione id fieri passus, I would by no meanes yeeld
unto that,* but I sent them a profession of faith; and when *Iohn* 8.
of *Antioch, cæterique, and the rest with him,* had anathematized the
doctrine of *Nestorius,* then, and not before, *communionem illis restituimus, did we receive them into our communion.* Thus *Cyrill,* who by
requiring this, did in effect require (& they performed the same)
a condemning of all their writings which were made against him,
and in defence of that heresie of *Nestorius* : And had *Cyrill* lived
to see any question made, whether those writings (by whomsoever they had beene written) ought to bee, or were by himselfe
condemned; out of all doubt that holy Father would in most
plaine, and expresse termes, have anathematized them all, as
vertually, and *implicitè* he had before, and would most strictly
have exacted the like expresse anathematizing of them, of all
those who would wash their hands of the blasphemies, and heresies of *Nestorius.*

18. Now from these three grounds (every one of which is demonstrated to be untrue) *Vigilius* collects his Conclusion, or
definitive sentence in defence of this *second Chapter,* which also is
an errour, but not as the former, personall, but doctrinall; yea, hereticall : that those writings of *Theodoret,* or going under *Theodorets* name against *Cyrill,* and his twelve Chapters, ought not to be
condemned; which is as much as if he had decreed plainly, that
the heresies of *Nestorius* ought not to be condemned; for in those
writings of *Theodoret,* they are all defended, and that with such
eagernesse, art, and acutenesse, that if all other Nestorian books
were abolished, those writings alone of *Theodoret* would suffice
as a rich storehouse to furnish the Nestorians with abundance
of all kinde of weapons, to maintaine their owne, and oppugne
the Catholike cause; nor ever can Nestorianisme bee puld
downe, or overthrowne, so long as those writings of *Theodoret*
keepe their credit, and stand uncondemned, yet shal not these be
condemned, doth *Vigilius* decree.

19. Pope *Pelagius* seeing the poison of the hereticall doctrine, which the defending of this *second Chapter* doth beare
with it, exclaimes against it in this manner °: *O my deare brethren,
who seeth not these things to bee full of all impiety ?* And againe,
who seeth not *quanta temeritate plenum sit Theodoreti scripta superi-
biendo defendere? how full of temeritie it is to defend so insolently, the
writings of Theodoret ?* The fift generall *Councell* ᴾ, *not onely accurseth those writings of Theodoret, as hereticall, but all who defend
them, yea all who doe not anathematize them.* A cleare evidence
that they not onely judged this *second Chapter* to concerne the
faith, but the *Constitution* of *Vigilius* even herein to be hereticall,
because he would not anathematize those writings of *Theodoret,*
and much more because he decreed that they should not be anathematized; and to their judgement consenteth the whole ca-

o *Pelag. 2. Epist. 7.
S. Quis hæc.*

p *Collat. 3. pa. 587*

d Vig. Conft.nu.
180.

matize his writings: *There was*, saith he, *divers in the Councell of
Chalcedon who faid, that* Theodoret *had anathematized Cyrill, and
was an heretike*; yet those holy Fathers moft diligently examining
this caufe of *Theodoret, nihil aliud ab eo exigiffe nofcuntur, are knowne
to have required no more of him*, than that hee fhould anathematize
Neftorius, and his impious doctrines; *hoc fibi tantummodo fufficere judicantes*; judging this alone to be *fufficient for them to receive*
Theodoret. Now it is unfit, faith[e] he further, *nos aliquid quaere-
re velut omiffum à patribus, that we fhould feek or require more than
did the Councell of Chalcedon*; as if they had omitted any thing
in this caufe of *Theodoret* : feeing then they required no anathematizing of his writings against *Cyrill*, neither ought any
others to anathematize, or require of any the anathematizing
of the fame.

e Ibid.nu.181.

   12. As you faw *Vigilius* in the former Chapter to ufe *hareti-
ca aftutia*; fo may any man here eafily difcerne, that hee ufeth an
evident, and fallacious fophiftication. The Councell indeed
required not that, nor did *Theodoret* in explicite, or expreffe
termes performe it, faying, I anathematize my owne writings
against *Cyrill*; but in implicite termes, in effect, and by an evident confequent, both the Councell required, and *Theodoret* performed this before them all; for, hee fubfcribed[f] to the definition of
faith decreed at Chalcedon : one part of that definition is the ap-
proveing[g] of the Synodall Epiftles of *Cyrill* : a part of one of
thofe Epiftles[h] are the twelve Chapters of *Cyrill*, which *Theodoret* refuted : in every one of thofe chapters, is an anathema denounced to the defenders of the contrarie doctrine : Then certainely, *Theodoret* by fubfcribing to the definition, fubfcribed to
the Epiftles of *Cyrill*, by them to the twelve chapters, and by
doing fo he condemned, and anathematized all who oppugned
thofe twelve chapters, and then undoubtedly, his owne writings
which were publifhed, as a confutation of thofe twelve chapters. And it feemes ftrange, that *Vigilius* profeffing that *Theodoret* did *devota mente fufcipere, with a devout affection receive* and
approve the Epiftles of *Cyrill*, and the doctrine of them, could
deny or be ignorant, that in doing fo he did anathematize his
owne writings, which by the twelve chapters of *Cyrill*, are anathematized.

f Ego autem et de-
finitioni fidei fub-
fcripfi, ait Theod.in
Conc.Chal.Act.8.
g Approbamus Sy-
nodicas Epiftolas
Cyrilli. Conc.Chal.
Act.5.in definit.
h Nam continentur
in Epift.Cyrilli et
Conc. Alexand. ad
Neftorium, que ex-
tat inter acta Con-
cily Ephef.to.1.
Act.fa.14 et repe-
titur in Conc.5.
Coll.6.pa.568.et
feq.

   13. Befides this, how often, how plainely doth the Councell
of *Chalcedon*[i] require, and urge *Theodoret* to anathematize *Neftorius* and his doctrines? how willingly did *Theodoret* performe
this? What elfe is this, but a vertuall, and implicite anathematizing of thofe his owne writings against *Cyrill*, which defended
Neftorius and his doctrines? None can anathematize the former, but *eo ipfo* he doth moft certainely (though not expreffly) a-
nathematize the later; as on the contrary, none can fay (as *Vigilius* doth, and decreeth, that all fhall doe the like) none can fay
that the writings of *Theodoret* against *Cyrill*, and his twelve chap-
                                                                    ters,

i Act.8.

ters ought not to be anathematized, but *eo ipso,* even by saying so, he doth most certainly (though but *implicitè* and by consequent) say that *Nestorius* and his heresie, ought not to be condemned. A truth so cleare that Pope *Pelagius* [k] from his anathematizing of *Nestorius* and his doctrine, concludeth of *Theodoret: Constat eundem,* it is manifest, that in doing this, he condemned his owne writings against the twelve Chapters of *Cyrill.*

k *Pelag.*2. *Epist.* 7. S. *Quu bis.*

14. Neither is that true which *Vigilius* fancied, that to require men to anathematize the writings of *Theodoret,* is to seeke, and require more then the Councell of *Chalcedon* required : It is not. It is but requiring the selfe same thing to be done in actuall and expresse termes, which the Councel required and *Theodoret* performed in vertuall and implicite termes. The thing required and done is the same : the manner onely of doing it, or requiring it to be done, is different : Even as to require of men to professe Christ to be ὁμοόσιον, which the Councell of *Nice,* and the Church ever since requireth, is not to require them to professe more, or ought else, then the Scripture teacheth, and all catholikes [l] before professed, by those words, *I and my Father are one :* but it is a requiring of an explicite profession of that truth concerning the unity of substance of the Father, and the Sonne, which by those words of Scripture they did before *implicitè* professe.

l *Hoc testimonio omnes patres utuntur contra Arianos, ut probent unam esse essentiam patris & filij. Bell. lib. 1. de Christ. ca. 6. §. Quartum.*

15. But yet at least will some of *Vigilius* friends reply, it was unfit to require this explicite anathematizing of *Theodorets* writings, seeing the Councell of *Chalcedon* did not require it. No, not so neither. The explicite condemning of them, was not onely fit, but necessarie at that time, in the dayes of *Iustinian,* and *Vigilius;* For as when the Arians denyed Christ to bee ὁμοόσιον, it was enough for one to cleare himselfe of Arianisme, to say, that he held this text for true, *I and the Father are one,* though therein he doe *implicitè* professe Christ to bee ὁμοόσιον, and though to have professed that alone, before the question about the unity of one substance was moved, had beene sufficient; but now he must *explicitè* professe that truth which is *explicitè* denyed and oppugned : even so it is in this cause of *Theodorets* writings, and all like it. While there was no doubt moved by heretikes, whether those writings of his ought to be condemned; and whether by the Councell of *Chalcedon* they were condemed or no; so long it was sufficient for one to professe that he condemned *Nestorius,* and subscribed to the definition of *Chalcedon* : both which were implicite condemning of those writings of *Theodoret* : but when the Nestorians began to boast, that *Theodorets* writings against *Cyrill,* neither were condemned, but rather with the author of them approved by the Councell of *Chalcedon,* neither ought to be condemned, the Church now was necessarily enforced to require of all men a profession of that truth in plaine and explicite termes, which before they made onely in generall and implicite. Nor could *Vigilius,* or any other Nestorian, who refused in expresse manner to condemne the writings of *Theodoret,* purge him-

selfe

selfe of that herefie of *Neftorius* at this time, by saying they approved the definition of *Chalcedon,* or condemned *Neftorius*; though in both these they did *implicitè* condemne the writings of *Theodoret,* but now they muſt expreſly profeſſe that which the heretikes expreſly denyed, they muſt in plaine termes anathe-matize thoſe hereticall writings of *Theodoret,* and acknowledge them to have bin anathematized by the Councel of *Chalcedon,* as the hereriks in plaine termes vaûted, that neither they ought nor were anathematized, but approved by the Councel of *Chalcedon,* whenſoever any point tending to the impeaching of faith begins *explicitè* to be denyed, the holy Church may not then content her ſelfe in generall and *implicitè* to condemne the ſame, (few perhaps can perceive that, and many will make that generality of termes, as *Vigilius* and other Neſtorians now did, but a cloak for their hereſie) but the Church muſt now in moſt plaine, eaſie, and expreſſed manner that can be deviſed, both teach, declare, and define the ſame. This the Church did in this fift Councell, as in the other two, ſo in this Chapter touching *Theodorets* wri-tings. It taught but the very ſame which the Councell of *Chal-cedon* had done before it, anathematized thoſe his writings, which at *Chalcedon* were anathematized before, but they did this now in a plaine manner and *explicitè,* which by the Councell of *Chal-cedon* only in an obſcure manner, and *implicitè* was done before.

m *Vig.Cmſt. nu.* 181.

16. The third perſonall errour which *Vigilius* [m] taketh for a ground of his decree, is that *Cyrill* himſelfe though he was ſo ex-ceedingly injured by the writings of thoſe Eaſterne Biſhops that tooke part with *Neſtorius,* yet when he made union with them, he required them not to anathematize their owne writings, but overpaſt them in ſilence, as if there had never beene any ſuch: whence *Vigilius* inferreth, that neither ought this anathemati-zing of their writings (by name of *Theodorets*) bee required by others, yea he ſaith, the Fathers of *Chalcedon* imitated this ex-ample of *Cyrill,* and ſo would not require that of *Theodoret,* which they ſaw *Cyrill* not to have required of others.

17. The anſwer is eaſie by that which hath beene declared: this ſaying of *Vigilius* laboureth of the ſame equivocall ſophiſti-cation, as did the former; for both *Cyrill* required, and all who were united unto him, and received into his, which was the com-munion of the Catholike Church; they all did, though not in ex-plicite termes, which then was not needfull; yet vertually, and af-ter a certaine, and undoubted, though implicite manner, con-demne, and anathematize all their writings againſt *Cyrill,* and the Catholike faith; for he received none till they had anathe-matized the doctrines of *Neſtorius.* This doth *Cyril* himſelfe moſt plainly witneſſe in his Epiſtle to [n] *Dynatus; I would not,* ſaith he, *admit Paulus Biſhop of Emiſa into communion, priuſquam Neſtorij dogmata proprio chyrographo anathematiZaſſet; untill hee had anathe-matized by his owne hand-writing the doctrines of Neſtorius:* And he intreated me in behalfe of the other Biſhops, that I would rest

n *Cyrill.Epiſt. ad Dynat. extat in Act.Conc. Epheſ. to.5.ca.16.*

rest contented with that profession which they had sent, and require no more: *nulla ratione id fieri passus, I would by no meanes yeeld unto that*, but I sent them a profession of faith; and when *Iohn 8. of Antioch, cæterique, and the rest with him*, had anathematized the doctrine of *Nestorius*, then, and not before, *communionem illis restituimus, did we receive them into our communion.* Thus *Cyrill*, who by requiring this, did in effect require (& they performed the same) a condemning of all their writings which were made against him, and in defence of that heresie of *Nestorius* : And had *Cyrill* lived to see any question made, whether those writings (by whomsoever they had beene written) ought to bee, or were by himselfe condemned; out of all doubt that holy Father would in most plaine, and expresse termes, have anathematized them all, as vertually, and *implicitè* he had before, and would most strictly have exacted the like expresse anathematizing of them, of all those who would wash their hands of the blasphemies, and heresies of *Nestorius.*

18. Now from these three grounds (every one of which is demonstrated to be untrue) *Vigilius* collects his Conclusion, or definitive sentence in defence of this *second Chapter*, which also is an errour, but not as the former, personall, but doctrinall; yea, hereticall : that those writings of *Theodoret*, or going under *Theodorets* name against *Cyrill*, and his twelve Chapters, ought not to be condemned; which is as much as if he had decreed plainly, that the heresies of *Nestorius* ought not to be condemned; for in those writings of *Theodoret*, they are all defended, and that with such eagernesse, art, and acutenesse, that if all other Nestorian books were abolished, those writings alone of *Theodoret* would suffice as a rich storehouse to furnish the Nestorians with abundance of all kinde of weapons, to maintaine their owne, and oppugne the Catholike cause; nor ever can Nestorianisme bee puld downe, or overthrowne, so long as those writings of *Theodoret* keepe their credit, and stand uncondemned, yet shal not these be condemned, doth *Vigilius* decree.

19. Pope *Pelagius* seeing the poison of the hereticall doctrine, which the defending of this *second Chapter* doth beare with it, exclaimes against it in this manner °: *O my deare brethren, who seeth not these things to bee full of all impiety ?* And againe, who seeth not *quanta temeritate plenum sit Theodoreti scripta superbiendo defendere? how full of temeritie it is to defend so insolently, the writings of Theodoret ?* The fift generall Councell P, not onely accurseth those writings of *Theodoret, as hereticall, but all who defend them, yea all who doe not anathematize them.* A cleare evidence that they not onely judged this *second Chapter* to concerne the faith, but the *Constitution* of *Vigilius* even herein to be hereticall, because he would not anathematize those writings of *Theodoret*, and much more because he decreed that they should not be anathematized; and to their judgement consenteth the whole ca-

o Pelag. 2. Epist. 7. S. Quis hæc.

p Collat. 3. pa. 587.

tholike Church, they all condemne the decree of *Vigilius* even in this point as hereticall.

q *Quacunq; scripta vel dogmata sceleratorum Nestorij & Eutychetis erroribus manifestentur consonare, anathematizamus & damnamus. Vig. Const. nu. 182.*

20. I, but *Vigilius* you will say condemneth q those very heresies of *Nestorius*, which are defended in those writings; he doth so: at least he seemes by his words to doe it: and had he not withall decreed that *Theodorets* writings should not bee condemned, he could not justly have beene reproved in this point. But in doing both, he proves not himselfe orthodoxal, by that wch he saith well, but unconstant and contrary to himselfe in overthrowing that which he saith well, for if *Theodorets* writings against *Cyrill* may not be condemned, as *Vigilius* decreth ; then may not the doctrines of *Nestorius* defended therein be condemned as *Vigilius* would seeme to doe. *Theodorets* writings and Nestorianisme are inseparable companions, either both must stand, or both fall together. Its as impossible, and repugnant to condemne the one, and deny that the other may be condemned, to condemne Euticheanisme, and yet defend the Ephesine latrocinie and decree thereof, or condemne Arianisme, and not condemne the *Arimine* Councel. Its the honor of truth, that it never is nor can be dissonant to any other truth : but heresie not onely may, but almost ever doth fight, not only against truth, but against it selfe, & overthroweth with one hand, or positiō, what it builds up by another, as in this of *Vigilius* is now apparent.

21. Now although this clearly convinceth the Popes decree to be hereticall, seeing it maintaineth two contradictory positions in a cause of faith, & the one is without all doubt an heresie ; yet is it worthy the examining, whether of these contradictories must passe for the Popes judgment & *cathedrall* resolution in this cause. Cardinall *Baronius* will certainly direct vs in this doubt: for he tells us (which of it selfe also is evident) that the Popes purpose r & intent in setting forth this *Constitution*, was to defēd the 3 Chapters: *adversus Imperatoris decretum, & sententiam Synodi*, against the Emperors Edict, and the sentence of the fift Synode. As the Emperour then and the Synode condemned, so was it the Popes maine purpóse to defend the writings of *Theodoret* against *Cyrill*, which was the *second Chapter*. This is & must stand for the judgement & cathedrall resolution of the Pope in this matter : what he speaks repugnant to this is casuall, & *præter*, nay *contra intentionem, its against his mind & purpose*; its to be thought onely by inincogitancy to have slipt from his pen. So his condemning of the Nestorian doctrine is but in shew, its onely verball, his defining that *Theodorets* writings which maintaine Nestorianisme may not be condemned, is the true purpose and intent of his mind, its cordial & real. By his verball condemning of Nestorianisme, he shuts it out in words, or as you may say at the foregate of his pallace, By his defining that *Theodorets* writings may not be condemned, he puls in Nestorianisme with all his might, & sets wide open a postren gate unto it : by condemning Nestorianisme in shew

r *Pro ipsorum defensione laborat Vigilius. Bar. an. 553. nu. 172.* f *Ibid. nu. 212.*

shew of words, he seemes to be orthodoxall, by defending Nestorianisme indeed and in truth, he demonstrates himselfe to be hereticall. Or because *Vigilius* was so very wise a Pope as hereafter out of *Baronius* you shall heare, it seemes he meant to shew one part of his wisedome, and policie, in this matter, and therefore while the heresie of *Nestorius* comes in his owne naturall habit, or in the liverie of *Nestorius*, away with it, the Popes holinesse will not admit it, hee cannot abide it: but when it comes countenanced, and graced, with the name of *Theodoret*, and in his liverie, the Pope embraceth it in both his armes, and by his *Apostolicall* authoritie commandeth all men, to give most friendly welcome and entertainement unto it.

22 You have now the judgement, and cathedrall resolution of *Vigilius*, touching this *second Chapter*, that the hereticall writings of *Theodoret* against *Cyril*, and the Catholike faith may not bee condemned. Take a view also of those two reasons, by which hee labours to strengthen, and perswade the same. The former is drawne from the Councell at *Chalcedon* : It is, saith *Vigilius*, [t] *valde contrarium, & Chalcedonensis Synodi judicio indubitabiliter inimicum, very contrarie, and without all doubt repugnant to the judgement of the Synod at Chalcedon*, that any Nestorian doctrines should now be condemned, *sub ejus sacerdotis nomine, under the name of Bishop Theodoret*. So *Vigilius*.

t *Vig.Const.xii.* 180.

23 Could he not content himselfe, to be hereticall alone, unlesse he disgraced the holy Councell of *Chalcedon* as guilty of the same heresie, as if they also had judged that none of *Theodorets* writings, not those written against the faith, ought to bee condemned? They to judge this? or is it contrary, and that *indubitabiliter*, to condemne those writings of *Theodoret*, or any writings under his name? Far was it from the thought, much more from the grave judgement of so holy a Councell. Even themselves, as before we declared, condemned and anathematized all those writings of *Theodoret*, and warranted by their judgement all others to anathematize the same. *Gregorie* [u] witnesseth of the fift Councell, that it is *sequax in omnibus, in all things a follower of the Councell at Chalcedon*. Seeing then the fift Councell, doth so often and so constantly condemne and anathematize those writings of *Theodoret*, its undoubted, that the same writings were formerly condemned by the Councell of *Chalcedon*, the fift Synod but treading in their steps and following them in that judgement, wherein they had gone before them. If to condemne those writings be repugnant to the judgment at *Chalcedon*, then is the fift Councell not a follower but a confuter and contradicter of the judgement at *Chalcedon*. Nor onely the fift Councell, but the whole catholike Church ever since the time of *Vigilius*, they all doe reject, and condemne the judgement of the Councell at *Chalcedon*, seeing they all by approving the fift Synod, and decree thereof, do anathematize

u *Lib.7.Indic.2. Epist.54.*

those

those writings of *Theodoret*, which to doe is, as *Vigilius* teacheth, *indubitanter contrarium, most certainely contrary to the judgement at Chalcedon*. If the whole catholike Church bee not hereticall (which to thinke is impietie) by contradicting and condemning the judgement of the Councell at *Chalcedon*, then undonbtedly is *Vigilius* hereticall in teaching and decreeing, that to condemne any writings of *Theodoret*, or any under his name, is repugnant to the judgement of the Councell at *Chalcedon*.

24. The other reason of *Vigilius*, is, because it were a disgrace, injury and slander, against *Theodoret*, to condemne his writings. This the Pope [x] expresseth in the very words of his sentence, in this manner; *The truth of these things*, (those are the three personall points before handled) *being weighed, we ordaine and decree, nihil in injuriam, atque obtrectationem probatissimi viri, hoc est Theodoreti sub taxatione nominis ejus, à quoquam fieri vel proferri, that nothing shall be done or spoken by any, to the injury and slander of the most approved Bishop Theodoret by taxing of his name*: and it must needs be taxed, if his writings or bookes be condemned.

x *Vigil. Const. na. 282.*

25. See here the compassionate and tender heart of *Vigilius*. Not onely *Iustinian*, and the sift generall Councell, but *Pelagius*, *Gregory*, and other succeeding Popes, and Councels, even the whole Catholike Church ever since the time of *Vigilius*, they all, by approving the decree of the sift Synod, doe not onely taxe the name of *Theodoret*, but accurse, & anathematize the writings of *Theodoret*, and that even under his name: Now, such a loving and tender affection doth the Pope carry towards the hereticall writings of *Theodoret*, that rather than they may be condemned, or his name taxed by the condemning of them; *Iustinian*, *Pelagius*, *Gregory*, and other his successors, the sift, the sixt, and other generall Councels, even the whole Catholike Church, they all must be, and are *de facto*, here declared, and by the Popes *cathedrall* sentence decreed, and defined, not onely to bee hereticall, (as the former reason imported) but injurious persons, backbiters, & slanderers, they all must be condemned, and for ever disgraced, rather then *Theodorets* name must bee taxed, or his hereticall writings condemned, or disgraced.

26. But say indeed: Is it an injurie, a slander, a disgrace to one, that his errors should either by himselfe, or by the Church be condemned? How injurious was that holy Bishop Saint *Augustine* to himselfe in writing so many retractations, and corrections of what he saw amisse? And what himselfe did, hee would not onely willingly, but gladly have permitted the holy Church to have done. Nor may we think this mind to have been onely in *Austen*, Modestie and humilitie, are the individuall concomitants of true knowledge and learning: and the more learned any man is, the more judicious is he in espying, the more ingenuous in acknowledging, the more lowly and humble, in condemning his owne errors. As it is but winde and no solid substance,

substance, which puffes up a bladder, so is it never any sound, or solid learning, but meere ventositie & emptinesse of knowledge which makes the minde to swell, to beare it selfe aloft, and either not see that truth into which his high and windie conceit will not suffer him to looke downe and dive; or seeing it, not embrace the same, though it were with a condemning, yea with a detestation of his owne error. It must never be a shame or disgrace to any man to recall and condemne his errors, till he be ashamed of being a man, that is subject to errors. Saint *Augustine* [y] more sharply saith, *That its a token not onely of a foolish, and proud selfe-love, but of a most malignant [z] minde, rather to wish others to bee poysoned with his heresies, then either himselfe to recall, or permit others, specially the Church of God, to condemne his heresies.* It was no injurie, no slander; nor disgrace to *Theodoret*, that his hereticall writings, were by the Church condemned, but it had beene a fault unexcusable and an eternall disgrace to the Church, if shee had suffered such hereticall writings to passe uncondemned.

27. Oh but *Theodoret* was, *probatißimus vir, a man most approved* by the Councell of *Chalcedon*, saith *Vigilius*; is it not an injury to condemne the writings of a man most approved? No verely, the more approved, the more eminent, learned, and orthodoxall any man is, the more carefull and ready, both himselfe, and the Church must be to condemne his former hereticall writings: When heresie commeth in his owne deformed habit, it doth but little, or no hurt at all; who will not detest it, when he reades it in the writings of *Arius, Nestorius, Eutiches,* or such like condemned heretikes? the odiousnesse of their names breeds a dislike almost of a truth in their mouthes, but certainly of an errour; But when Satan assumes the forme of an Angell of light, when heresie comes palliated, yea, countenanced with the name of a Catholike, a learned, an holy, a renowned and approved Bishop; then, and then specially is there danger of infection: The reverence, the love, the honour wee beare to such a person, causeth us unawares to swallow the poyson which hee reacheth unto us, before we take leasure to examine, or once make doubt of his doctrine.

28. It was truely said by [a] *Vincentius Lirinensis*, The errour of the Master, is the tryall of the Scholler, *& tanto major tentatio, quanto ipse doctior, qui erraret, and the more learned the teacher is, the greater still is the temptation;* which, beside other, he shewes by the example of *Origen*; he was in his age a mirrour [b] of gravity, integrity, continency, zeale [c], piety, of learning of all sorts, both divine, and humane, of so [d] happy a memory, that he had the Bible without booke, of such admirable eloquence, that not words but hony [e] seemed to drop from his lips, of so indefatigable industry, that he was called *Adamantius*, and was said by some [f] to have written six thousand bookes, by [g] *Hierome*, one thousand, besides innumerable commentaries, of such high est eeme

y *Illi quos vulgò moriones vocant, quanto magis absurdi & insulsi sunt, tanto magis nullum verbum emittunt quod revocare velint, quia dicti mali pœnitere, utique cordatorum est. Aug. Epist. 7.*

z *Nimis perversè se ipsum amat, qui & alios vult errare ut error suus lateat. ibid.*

a *Vinc. de Hæres. ca. 23.*

b *Vincent. Lir. loc. citato.*

c *Zelo dei se truncavit. Hier. Epist. ad Pamac. & excan. to. 2. pa. 194.*

d *Scripturas memoriter tenebat. ibid.*

e *Vinc. loc. cit.*

f *Hier. lib. 2. adv. Ruffin.*

g *Hier. epist. ad Pam.*

h *Trin. loc. cit.*

efteeme, and authority, that Chriftians ʰ honoured him as a Prophet; Philofophers, as a Mafter; they flocked from the utmoft parts of the world to heare his wifedome, as if a fecond *Salomon* had beene fent from heaven; yea, moft would fay, *malle fe cum Origene errare, quam cum alijs vera fentire, that they had rather erre with Origen, then thinke aright with others.* When fuch a man lapfeth into herefie, if his writings may fcape without cenfure, if it fhall be judged a contumelie, an injurie or flander, to condemne his bookes, for the honour which was given to his perfon, one fuch man as *Origen,* were able to draw almoft the third part of the ftarres of heaven after him.

i *Nobilibus parentibus nafcitur. Poffev. in Theodor.*
k *Epift. Theod. 81. ad Nonium extat apud Bar. an. 448. & nu. 12.*
l *Fuitus epifcopus fum ordinatus ibid.*
m *Erat in Syria oppidulum vehementer neglectum Cyrus nomine, a Iudeis extructum ut qualemcunque gratiam benefactori (Cyro) referret. Proc. de ædific. Iuftin. Orat. 2. in fine.*
n *Theod. Epift. ad Nonium.*

29. And if any beleeve the Epiftles going under his name, *Theodoret* was in divers refpects, not much inferiour to *Origen.* His birth noble, ⁱ *his parents being without hope of Children, vowed* ᵏ *him before his conception, like another Samuel unto God.* And accordingly even from his Cradle confecrated him to Gods fervice: *Violently* ˡ *drawne to the dignity of a Bifhop, the Citie of Cyrus in Syria, where was his epifcopall See,* he nobilitated, being before but obfcure (though worthy ᵐ of eternall memorie, as being one monument of the deliverance of Gods people, by the hand of *Cyrus,* out of the Babylonifh captivitie) So upright, blamelesse, and voide of covetoufnesse; that having beene five and twenty yeares Bifhop of that place, in all that time, *ne* ⁿ *obolum mihi in tribunali ablatum aliquis conqueftus eft, none could fay that hee had exacted, or received for caufes of judgement, fo much as one halfe pennie.* I tooke no mans goods, no mans garments, nay, which is a memorable token of integritie, none of mine houfe, faith he, hath taken the worth of an egge, or a morfell of bread: So plentifull in workes of charitie, *That he diftributed* ᵒ *his inheritance among the poore, repaired Churches,* ᵖ *builded bridges, drained Rivers, to townes where was want of water,* and fuch like, in fo much, faith he, that in all this time, I have ۹ provided nothing for my felfe, not any land, nor any houfe, no not fo much as any fepulcher; nothing, *præter laceras has veftes,* I have left nothing to my felfe, but onely this ragged attire, wherewith I am apparelled. For learning and knowledge both in divine and humane matters he was much honoured, compared to *Nilus* ʳ as watering the whole countrie, where hee abode with the ftreames of his knowledge, he converted eight townes, ˢ infected with the herefie of the *Marcionites,* to the faith, two other of the *Arians* and *Eunomians*: wherein he tooke fuch paines, and that alfo with fome expence of his blood, and hazard of his life, that in eight hundreth parifhes (within the Dioceffe of *Cyrus*) *Ne* ᵗ *unum quidem hereticorum zizanium remanfit, there remained not fo much as one hereticall weed.*

o *Quæ nobis a parentibus obvenerüt, poft eorum mortem ftatim diftribui. Theod. Epift ad Leonem. extat inter Epiftolas Leonis poft Ep. 62.*
p *Theod. Epift. 81.*
q *Epift. Theod. ad Leonem. & ad Nonium.*
r *ὡς νεῖλος ἄλλος Epig. apud Poff. in Theodor.*
ſ *Theod. Epift. ad Nonium quæ eft 81:*

t *Jbid.*

30. So learned, fo laborious, fo worthy a Bifhop was *Theodoret* : and fo defirous am I not to impaire any part of his honour, much leffe to injure, difgrace, or flander him. Whom almoft

would

would not the writings of a man so noble for birth, and parentage, so famous for learning, so eminent in vertue, move and perswade to assent unto him, if they might goe currant without taxing, without note or censure of the Church? and that much more than the bookes of *Origen*, both because *Origen* was but a *Presbyter*, but *Theodoret* a Bishop, and specially because *Origen* [u] himselfe was by the Church condemned; and so the author being disgraced, the authority of his writings must needs be very small: but the person of *Theodoret* was approved by the whole Councell of *Chalcedon*, they all proclamed [x] *him to bee a Catholike, and orthodoxall Bishop.* Here was a farre greater temptation, and greater danger when his writings are hereticall, whose person, so famous and holy a Councell commendeth for Catholike. Now, or never was the Church to shew that it honoured no mans person, writings, or name, more thā the truth of Christ. And so much the rather was the Church to doe this in *Theodoret*, because about some thirty [y] yeares, before this fift Councell, in the time of *Iustinus* the Emperour, the Nestorians (as if not onely some writings of his, but *Theodoret* himselfe had beene wholly theirs) *set up* [z] *his image in a Chariot, and with great pompe, and singing of hymnes, brought it in triumphant manner into the City of Cyrus,* where *Sergius* a Nestorian, and Bishop of that place, mentioned in a Collect *Theodorus* of Mopsvestia, *Nestorius,* and *Theodoret* as three of their principall Nestorian Saints: was it not now high time to wipe away that blemish from the name of *Theodoret,* and to condemne those writings of his which gave occasion to the Nestorians to make such boasts?

31. I appeale now unto any man, whether their condemning of *Theodorets* writings, did not much more tend to the honour, then, as *Vigilius* fancieth, to the slander, and disgrace of his person. As it is a blemish to a man to retaine a filthy spot in his garment, but the taking of it away doth grace, and make him more comely; even so the name of *Theodoret* was stained by those writings; they embold<ned the Nestorians to put him in their cursed Calender; but by the condemning of those writings was the staine and blemish wiped away from his person, his name, and honour was vindicated from the Nestorians, and brought, as it well deserved, to the holy Church of G O D; nothing of *Theodoret* left for heretikes to vaunt of, but the onely staines of *Theodoret*; nothing but those hereticall writings condemned and accursed, both by *Theodoret* himselfe, and by the whole Church of God.

32. No, no; it is Pope *Vigilius* (and such as applaud his decree for infallible) that disgraceth, and most ignominiously useth the name, person, and memory of *Theodoret*: By his decree those heretical writings of *Theodoret*, which, by the Churches sentence of condemnation are quite dulled, receive full strength, and vigour for the Nestorians against Catholikes: By him the Nestorians

have

u *Origenem, fontem Arij, Nicœni patres percussere, damnantes enim eos qui filium negant esse de substantia patris, filium (Origini) Arianimque damnaverint. Hier. Epist. ad Pammac. de error. Orig. Omnis tam orientis, quam occidentis Catholicorum Synodus, illum, hereticum denunciat. Hier. Apol. 2. adver. Ruff.*

x *Con. Chal. Act. 8.*

y *Nam Iustini rescriptum de eâ re datum est Rustico Coss. ut liquet ex Conc. 5. Coll. 7. pa. 582. Vbi rescriptum extat. Rusticus vero Consul cum Vitaliano an. 520. Marcell. in Chron. et Bar. in eum annum nu. 1.*

z *Conc. 5. Coll. 7. pa. 582. et pa. 578.6.*

have an eternall charter, and irrevocable decree, that *Theodorets* writings against *Cyrill,* and with them the heresie of *Nestorius,* ought not to be taxed, nor condemned. His *Apostolicall* Constitution is a triumphant chariot for them to set the Image of *Theodoret* in their Temples, and with Anthemes and Collects to canonize, yea adore him in their Masses, among their hereticall Saints. But for the Church of God, I constantly affirme they could not possibly have more honoured *Theodoret,* than by burning up the hay and stubble of his writings, the condemning of which the Pope decreeth to bee an injury and slander unto him.

33. May wee now in the last place consider a little what might be the intendment of *Vigilius* in pleading, and decreeing this for *Theodorets* writings? I doubt not but the love he bare to Nestorianisme might make him zealous for those writings, which are the bulwarks of the Nestorians: but *non sunt in eo omnia.* Popes are men of profound thoughts, and very long reaches; they have deepe, and mysticall projects in their decrees. *Vigilius* had, and it may be principally, an eye to this his owne, and all their *Cathedrall* Constitutions like unto it: If the hereticall writings of *Theodoret* may not be condemned, because himselfe was a Catholike, *à fortiori,* this decree of *Vigilius,* be it never so hereticall, may not bee condemned, because the Pope is the head of all Catholikes: If it bee an injury, and a slandering of *Theodoret,* to taxe him, or his name, by condemning his writings; it must much more be an injury, and slander, nay, that is nothing, even a blasphemy and sinne irremissible to taxe the Popes Holinesse, by condemning his *Apostolicall* decree: If you presume to condemne, nay, but taxe them, or their names, though their decrees shall bee as apparently hereticall, as are those writings of *Theodoret,* you are condemned for ever as injurious, as contumelious, as slandering persons. And let this suffice for the errours both personall, and doctrinall, of *Vigilius* touching this *second Chapter.*

CAP.

CAP. X.

That Vigilius *and* Baronius *erre in divers personall points, or matters of fact, concerning the* third Chapter, *or the* Epistle *of* Ibas.

1. Here remaineth now the *third* & last *Chapter*, wᶜʰ concernes the impious *Epistle* of *Ibas;* In handling whereof, being of them all most intricate and obscure, as *Vigilius* first, and then long after him his Champion *Baronius,* have here bestowed greatest paines, and used all their subtilty, judging this to bee (as indeed by reason of the manifold obscurities, it is) the fittest cloake for their heresie; so must I on the other side intreate the more serious and attentive consideration at the readers hands, while I indeavour, not onely to discover the darke and secret corners of this cause, but pull both the Pope and his Parasite out of this, being their strongest hold, and most hidden hereticall den, wherein they hoped of all other most safely and securely to have lurked; for the more perspicuous proceeding wherein, before I come to the doctrinall errours, and maine heresie which in this *third Chapter* they maintaine; I will first manifest two or three of their personall untruths, which will both open a passage to the other, and will give the reader a taste, nay, a certaine experiment what truth, fidelity, and faire-dealing he is to expect at the hands of *Vigilius* and *Baronius* in their handling of this Chapter.

2. The first, and that indeed a capitall untruth, is, that *Vigilius* avoucheth the Councell of ᵃ *Chalcedon* to have approved this *Epistle* of *Ibas* as orthodoxall. They approve that impious, and blasphemous Epistle? they rejected, they condemned, anathematized, and accursed it to the very pit of hell, witnesse the fift generall Councell, and the whole Catholike Church, which hath approved it; for thus cryed out, and proclaimed all the Bishops, *Epistolam* ᵇ *definitio sancti Chalcedonensis Concilij condemnavit, ejecit;* the definition of faith made by the holy Councell at *Chalcedon* hath condemned this *Epistle,* it hath cast out this *Epistle.* But because I have formerly ᶜ intreated hereof, I will adde no more of this which is proclaimed by the whole Church to be an untruth.

> ᵃ *Orthodoxa est lae à patribus pronunciata dictatio. Vig. Const.nu.192.*
>
> ᵇ *Conc.5.Coll.6. pa.576.b.*
>
> ᶜ *Supra ca.4.5.1. 3.13.*

3. The second untruth is like this. *Vigilius* having cited the interloquutions of *Pascasinus,* and *Maximus,* wherein they say that *Ibas* by his *Epistle* is declared to bee a Catholike, ᵈ addeth, that all the rest in the Councell of *Chalcedon* did not onely not contradict their interloquutions, *verumetiam apertissimum eis noscuntur præbuisse consensum;* but also they are knowne to have assented,

> ᵈ *Vig.Const.nu.150*

and

and that most manifestly unto those interloqutions. So *Vigilius*. It had beene enough, and too much to have said, that the Councell had assented, or had but seemed to assent: but *Vigilius* in saying that all the rest did most manifestly assent to those interloqutions, uttered a papall and supreme untruth, whereof no colourable pretence can be made, witnesse the fift generall Councell, and the whole Catholike Church, which hath approved it: They expresly ᶜ testifie, that the Councell of *Chalcedon* did *pro nullo habere, esteeme as nothing*, that which was spoken by one or two, (those were *Pascasius*, and *Maximus*) for that *Epistle*; but of this also I have spoken before.

4. Now both these vntruths, whereof *Vigilius* is so evidently, and by so ample witnesses convicted, Cardinall *Baronius* hath againe revived, telling with a face more hard than Brasse, or Adamant, *Patres* ᶠ *dixerunt eam Epistolam ut Catholicam recipiendam*; the Fathers of *Chalcedon* said, that this Epistle of *Ibas* is to be received *as orthodoxall*: and ᵍ againe, *ex ipsa Ibam fuisse probatum orthodoxum, aequè una fuit sententia omnium Episcoporum*; that *Ibas was by this Epistle approved for a Catholike, it was the consent and uniforme judgement of all the Bishops at Chalcedon*; then which, two lowder untruths, and well worthy of a golden whetstone, could hardly have beene uttered: And though he tooke them from Pope *Vigilius*, yet are they farre more inexcusable in the Cardinall, than in the Pope his Master. *Vigilius* dyed before he saw the judgement of succeeding Popes, and generall Councels; which had he knowne, wee may charitably thinke, that his Holinesse would have casseired and defaced such palpable, and condemned untruths: But Cardinall *Baronius* knew all this; hee knew that the fift ʰ generall Councell had condemned these untruths in *Vigilius*: he knew that *Pelagius*, ⁱ *Gregory*, and their successors, that the sixt, ᵏ seventh, and other generall Councels had approved the fift Councell, and so in approving it, had condemned those same untruths; and yet against the knowne consent, and judgement of all those Popes, and generall Councels, that is, against the knowne testimonie of the whole Catholike Church for a thousand yeares together; he is bold to avouch both those former sayings, for truths, which all those former witnesses with one voyce proclaime, to be condemned untruths. Such account doth the Cardinall make of Fathers, Popes, Generall Councels, and of the whole Catholike Church, when they come crosse in his way.

5. A third personall matter there is concerning this Chapter, of which not *Vigilius*, but Cardinall *Baronius* doth enforce me to intreate; and that is, whether *Ibas* was indeed the author of this *Epistle*, or no: for although it be not materiall to the intent of the fift Councell, (which, against the decree of *Vigilius*, we now defend) whether *Ibas* writ it or not, seeing neither this fift, nor the former Councell of *Chalcedon* condemned the author of this Epistle, but onely the Epistle it selfe; yet seeing the

Cardinall

Cardinall was pleafed to undertake the defence of a needleffe untruth, that this is not the Epiftle of *Ibas*. I am defirous that all fhould fee how wifely and worthily hee hath behaved himfelfe in this point.

6. *Baronius* fpeaking againft this *Epiftle*, firft makes it doubtfull whofe it is, faying [1], *author qui fertur nomine Ibæ, quifquis ille fuerit, the author of this Epiftle which paffeth under the name of Ibas, whatfoever he be;* and having thus bred a diftruft in your mindes: then as the ferpent dealt with *Eve*, hee pofitively fets downe his untruth. It is not the *Epiftle* of *Ibas*, in this manner: *Cæterum,* [m] *ut publica acta teftantur, producta in Concilium Epiftola illa, non effe Ibæ comperta,* but the publike acts döe teftifie, that when this Epiftle was produced in the Councell at Chalcedon, it was found not to be the Epiftle of Ibas : and fo it being condemned, Ibas was abfolved. Thus *Baronius,* who for proofe hereof alleageth the publike acts [n] both of the Councell of *Chalcedon,* and of the 2. Nicene Synod. And truly in the fecond *Nicene* Synod, that which the Cardinall faith, is read indeed by *Epiphanius,* a Deacon in that Synod : but it is the teftimony of the whole Councell, *Epiphanius* onely reading and propofing it in the name [o] and behalfe of the Synod. And becaufe it is a teftimony very pregnant for the Cardinalls affertion, and is cited out of a Councel which he much honoreth, & affecteth, I will do him the favour, as at large to expreffe that paffage : the rather becaufe this, as the whole anfwer read by *Epiphanius,* is not onely commended as a matter delivered [p] unto them by the holy Ghoft : *but they further requeft* [q] *all who fhall happen to light on that commentarie of theirs, that they will not read it flightly, or perfunctorily, but with fingular indagation and fearch of the fame.* And I am loth to deny thofe Nicene Fathers; fo very juft and reafonable a requeft.

7. In that place [r] there was read on the behalfe of the Iconoclafts, a teftimonie out of the ancient Father *Epiphanius* Bifhop of *Cyprus,* forbidding to fet up Images either in the Churches, or [f] in Churchyards; or in their common dwelling houfes, but every where to carie about, God in their hearts. This faying netled the Nicene Fathers not a little, who were very fuperftioufly devoted to Image-worfhip : and therefore inftead of a better anfwer, they fay that the booke whence that is alleaged, is falfly [t] afcribed to *Epiphanius,* hee was not the author of it. *Epiphanius they honor* [u] *as an holy Father and Doctor of the Catholike Church, but that booke going under his name, they reject :* which fact of theirs, they illuftrate and labour to warrant by the example of the Councell at *Chalcedon,* who received *Ibas* himfelfe, but accurfed the *Epiftle* going under the name of *Ibas, non* [x] *enim demonftrari poterat quod effet Ibæ: for it could not be proved to be the Epiftle of Ibas :* wherefore they anathematized not *Ibas,* but it : *Dicebatur enim Ibæ, cum tamen illius haudquaquam effet : for it was faid to be the Epiftle of Ibas, whereas indeed it was none of his.* Even

L   fo

[l] *Bar. an.* 432. *nu.* 71.

[m] *ibid.*

[n] *Conc. Chalc. Act.* 10. & *Conc. Nic.* 2. *Act.* 6. *citantur à Bar. ibidem.*

[o] *Epiphanius fcitam à patribus appofitam refponfionem perlegit. Bar. nu.* 787. *nu.* 34.

[p] *Quam confutationem nobis fpiritus fanctus dedit. Conc. N.* 2. *Act.* 6. *pa.* 356. *a.*

[q] *Rogamus autem, quicunq; etc. ibid. b.*

[r] *Conc. Nic.* 2. *Act.* 6. *pa.* 371. *a.*

[f] *Epiphanius Cyprius fic inquit, Ne in ecclefiam imagines inferatis, neque in cæmiterijs ftatuatis: neque in domo communi tolerentur. ibid.*

[t] *Id (ex Epiphanio lectum) nequaquam illius exiftit. ibid. a. Et, verum ut novity (libelli) et alieni falfiq; funt. ibid b.*

[u] *Commentarium illum rejicimus beatum autem patrem (Epiph.) ecclefiæ Doctorem agnofcimus. ibid. b.*

[x] *Ibid. b.*

so those false writings against venerable Images are said to bee the writings of Bishop *Epiphanius*, but they are not his. So those publike acts, and second Nicene Fathers, whose testimony concurreth and jumpeth with the Cardinall, this is not the Epistle of *Ibas*.

8. Before I come to examine those publike acts, I must observe one thing touching *Baronius*, which he will occasion and inforce me often to repeat; and this it is, that *Baronius* was meerly infatuated in his handling of this whole cause touching the *three Chapters*, and this one might almost even sweare: but any may see it as cleare as the light: besides many other, even by this one point whereof we now intreat. If a man should study and devise ten dayes together, how to confute and utterly overthrow all that Pope *Vigilius* hath decreed touching this *third Chapter*; and all which *Baronius* himselfe hath either taught or said in defence of *Vigilius* in that point, he cannot possibly doe it more clearly, more certainly, more effectually, then by denying, as the Cardinall, and his Nicene Fathers doe, that this is the Epistle of *Ibas*:
for how could either the Councell of *Chalcedon*, or the Popes Legates therein, by this Epistle, and by the dictation and contents thereof judge *Ibas* to be a Catholike (which *Vigilius* [y] decreeth, and *Baronius* [z] more then twenty times I thinke repeateth,) unlesse it were indeed the Epistle of *Ibas*; for of *Ibas* no otherwise then in the first person, or as the author and writer of it, there is no mention at all to be found or collected out of that Epistle.

y *Vigil. Conf. nu. 196.*
z *Bar. an. 553. nu. 191, 192. 193. 196. 197. &c.*

9. Now if you require testimonies, or authorities in this case, I oppose to *Baronius* the Popes Legates at *Chalcedon*, of which *Baronius* himselfe saith [a]; *This to be the Epistle of Ibas, the Popes Legates, and after them the rest of the Bishops by their subscription, confirmed,* and againe, the [b] Acts of *Chalcedon* doe teach, that this we acknowledged to be the Epistle of *Ibas*. I oppose Pope *Vigilius*, who in his *Constitution* assenteth [c] to that judgement of the Popes Legates, and those words, *relecta ejus Epistola, the Epistle of Ibas being read,* we acknowledge him to be a Catholike. I oppose the confession of *Ibas* himselfe, of which *Baronius* saith, the [d] Acts at *Chalcedon* declare *Ibam confessum esse eam esse suam, that Ibas confessed this Epistle to be his owne :* and againe [e], we have before declared *Ibam eandem Epistolam suam esse professum, that Ibas professed this same Epistle to be his owne:* and *Ibas* of all men in the world knew best, whether it was his or no. I oppose lastly *Baronius* to *Baronius*, for he [f] saith of this Epistle, *verè esse Ibæ fuisse cognitam, that it was knowne truly and indeed to be the Epistle of Ibas.* Say now in sadnesse, what you thinke of *Baronius*, and where you thinke his five wits were, when hee denyed, and that upon proofe by publike records, this to be the Epistle of *Ibas*, which the Popes Legates, with the whole Councell of *Chalcedon*, which Pope *Vigilius* whom hee defendeth, which *Ibas* his owne selfe;

a *Bar. an. 448. nu. 71.*

b *an. eod. nu. 77.*

c *Vigil. Conf. nu. 90.*

d *Bar. an. 448. nu. 77.*
e *Bar. an. 553. nu. 211.*
f *an. 448. nu. 71.*

selfe, yea which *Baronius* also acknowledgeth, confesseth, and professeth to be truly, and in very deed the Epistle of *Ibas*.

10. But what shall we then say to those publike acts, which as the Cardinall tells us, doe testifie, that this is not the Epistle of *Ibas*. What first to the acts of the Councell at Chalcedon, which he first *g* alleageth, and the tenth Action thereof? I say, and say it upon certaine grounds, that the Cardinall therein saith an untruth, for proofe whereof, I appeale to that same tenth Action of the Councell, in no part whereof it is said, nor can thence be collected, that this was not the Epistle of *Ibas*. Or if you will not beleeve my saying, yet beleeve the Cardinall himselfe, more then once testifying that which he saith to be untrue. These are his words *h*, *The Acts of the tenth Action of the Councell at Chalcedon : Eandem epistolam ut Ibæ cognitam esse à patribus docent*, doe teach, that this Epistle was knowne to be the Epistle of Ibas. And againe *i*, *Vere esse Ibæ fuisse cognitam eandem actio decima docet*, that this was knowne to have beene truly the Epistle of Ibas, the tenth action of the Councell at Chalcedon doth teach. Thinke you not that *Baronius* is more like the *Esopicall Satyr*, then a grave Cardinall of the Romane Church ? At his first blast he makes the tenth action of the Councell at *Chalcedon* to testifie that this is not the Epistle of *Ibas*; and then hee blowes a quite contrary blast, professing the tenth action of the Councell at *Chalcedon* to testifie that this is truly, and certainly the Epistle of *Ibas*.

11. O, but the second *Nicene* Councell, and the publike acts thereof, they witnesse the same which the Cardinall affirmeth, that this is not the Epistle of *Ibas*. They doe so indeed: But as it is an untruth in the Cardinalls mouth: so it is also in those his Nicene Fathers from whom hee tooke it, unlesse perhaps those men of *Nice*, knew better whose Epistle it was, then did the 600 holy Bishops of the Councell at *Chalcedon*, before whom *Ibas* stood, or better then *Ibas* himselfe who confessed it to bee his owne Epistle. The Cardinall may not be offended that we dissent from his Nicene Councell, which dissenteth from the holy Councell at *Chalcedon*, from *Ibas* his owne confession, yea from whom the Cardinall dissenteth as much as we in this point. And I cannot see, what depth of wisedome it was in his Cardinalship to alleage them for witnesses, whose testimony, himselfe in this very point for which he produceth them, doth avouch to bee untrue. But let him please himselfe in those Nice Fathers, we envie not such a Councell, nor such Fathers, nor such publike records unto them. That Nicene assembly was but a conspiracie against the truth, it was fit they should uphold untruth, by untruth. And whosoever shal be pleased to examine and rip up the Acts of that Councell, I will give him this one assured comfort, that besides their superstitious & heretical doctrins therin maintained, he shall finde them full stuft with many grosse and palpable untruths, of matters *de facto*, on which they build their doctri-

nall

g *Bar. an. 431. nu. 71.*

h *Bar. an. 448. nu. 77.*

i *Ibid. nu. 71*

nall positions, as in this concerning the Epistle of *Ibas*, it is now most manifest.

12. For this time I will not enter into so spacious a field, but yet this one thing by the way I cannot but observe; seeing those Nicene Fathers professe, that writing against Image-worship, going under the name of *Epiphanius*, to be in such sort the book of *Epiphanius*, as this Epistle going under the name of *Ibas*, is the Epistle of *Ibas* : and seeing we have now demonstrated this Epistle to be truly and indeed the Epistle of *Ibas*, it followeth even by their owne reason and comparison, that the book also against Image-worship, cited by the Councell at *Constantinople* in the name of *Epiphanius*, is in truth and in very deed the true writing of Bishop *Epiphanius*. And yet further, because those Nicene Fathers acknowledge *Epiphanius for a Catholike* [k] *Doctor of the Church*, one who held the ancient tradition [l] of the Church, and consented to the Catholikes, in and before his time : it hence againe followeth, that the doctrine of condemning Image-worship which in that booke of *Epiphanius* is delivered, & was by the generall Councell at *Constantinople* some thirty [m] yeares before this Nicene Assembly, decreed [n], that it I say is ancient, Catholike, consonant to the ancient tradition, and the doctrine of the ancient and catholike Fathers of the Church, even from the Apostles time. And this is all which *Baronius* hath gained by his alleaging those publike acts of the Nicene Fathers, to prove this not to be the Epistle of *Ibas*. And let this suffice to be spoken of the personall untruths of *Vigilius* and *Baronius* touching this Epistle of *Ibas*, which are but a *praeludium* to their doctrinall errors and heresies; wherof in the next place we are to entreat.

k *Beatum patrem (Epiphanium) catholice ecclesiae Doctorem agnoscimus. Conc. Nic.2. Act.6. pa.371.b.*
l *Illi qui antiquam ecclesiae traditionem recipiunt, beato Epiphanio non adversantur. ibid.b.*
m *Conc. Const. contra Imagines, habitum est an. 754. Bin.to.3. pa.229. Conc. Nicenum habitum. an.787. Bin. notis in id Conc.*
n *Qui imaginem ausus fuerit parare, aut adorare, aut in ecclesia, aut in privata domo constituere, aut clam habere, si Episcopus fuerit, deponitur. &c. Decretum Conc. Constant. sub Constantino Copronimo, quod extat in Niceno Conc.2. Act.6. pa.377.a.*

CHAP. XI.

That Vigilius *and* Baronius *in their former reason for defence of the Epistle of* Ibas, *drawne from the union with* Cyrill, *mentioned in the latter part of that Epistle, doe defend all the heresies of the Nestorians.*

1.  EE come now from personall matters to that which is the *Capital* point, and maine heresie contained in the defence of *this Chapter*, wherein *Vigilius*, and *Baronius* have so behaved themselves, that those former errours though they be too shamefull, are but a very sport, and play to that hereticall frenzie which here they doe expresse. For now you shall behold the Pope and his Cardinall in their lively colours, fighting under the banner of *Nestorius*, and using the most cunning stratagems that were ever devised, to cloake their hereticall doctrine, and gaine credit to that condemned

denned herefie. Those fleights are principally two. The former is gathered out of the latter part of the *Epiftle* of *Ibas*, where mention is made of the *union* betwixt *Cyrill*, and *Iohn*, which although I touched before [a], yet becaufe it is a matter of greater obfcuritie, and containeth a moft notable fraud of *Vigilius*, and *Baronius*, I purpofely referved the full handling of it unto this place, where without interruption of other matters, I might have fcope enough, to explaine the depth of this myfterie.

a *Sup. ca.4.*

2. In the time of the Ephefine Councell, there was, as all know, an exceeding breach betwixt *Cyrill*, with other Catholike Bifhops, who condemned *Neftorius*, and *Iohn* Bifhop of *Antioch*, with divers other Eaftern Bifhops, who tooke part with *Neftorius*, againft the holy Councell. And the divifion was fo great, that at the feife-fame time, in one, & the felfe-fame citie of Ephefus, they held two feverall Councels; and fet up *altare contra altare*, Councell againft Councell, Patriarcke againft Patriarcke, Bifhops againft Bifhops, and Synodall fentence againft Synodall fentence. But betwixt thofe two Councels, there was as much difference, as is betwixt light and darkeneffe, betwixt truth and herefie, betwixt the Church of God, and the Synagogue of Satan. The one confifted of holy orthodoxall and Catholike Bifhops whofe Prefident was *Cyrill*: the other of hereticall, [b] factious, and divers depofed Bifhops, whofe Prefident was *Iohn*. The former condemned *Neftorius* & his blafphemous doctrine, whereby hee denied Chrift to be God : the latter defended *Neftorius* and all his impious doctrines. The former was held in a Church, even in the Church of the Bleffed [c] *Virgin*, whofe Sonne they profeffed to bee truly God : the latter in an Inne [d], or Taverne, a fit place for them who denied Chrift to be God. The former proceeded in all refpects, orderly and Synodally, as was fit and requifite that they fhould: the latter did all things tumultuoufly [e], prefumptuoufly, and againft the Canons of the Church, fupporting themfelves onely by lies, calumnies, and flanderous reports. In a word, the former, was truly an holy, a generall, an Oecumenicall [f] Councell, wherein was the confent of the whole Catholike Church: the latter was nothing elfe, but an hereticall, fchifmaticall, and rebellious faction or confpiracie of fome thirtie [g] or fortie perfons, unworthy the name of Bifhops, infolently oppofing themfelves to the holy Councel, yea to the whole Catholike Church, in which number and faction befides others, who leffe concerne our purpofe, were

b *Coactis in unum folo nomine Epifcopis, qui una cum Neftorio defciverat: ex quibus alij erant extorres, vagi, proprijs fedibus deftituti, alij à fuis Metropolitanis depofiti, alij, Pelagij & Celeftij veneno imbuti. Epi. Synodal.fanct.Conc. Eph.ad Celeftinum, to.4.Act.Eph.c.17.*
c *Confidentibus in fanctiff.Ecclef.que appellatur Maria, to.2. act.Ephef.côc. ca.1.& fepe alibi.*
d *Iohanne in diverforio manête,facraq, illius Synodo prefente, Act.Eph.côc. to.3.ca.1.Cum vix curru diffilyffet (Iohannes) cubiculûq, ingreffus effet. Apol. Cyril.ad Imper.to.5 ca.2.pa.827.b.*

e *Iohannes cum fuis, nullam omnino vel per leges ecclefiafticas, vel per Auguftorum decretum, poteftatem obtinuit. Libel.Cyril.et Mem.oblatus f fynodo,to.4. Act.ce .   Johannes omni ecclefiaftica authoritate proculcata, omniq, ecclefiarum ordine & ritu & confuetudine contempta, &c. ibid. Que temerè vaneq, fuerant nugati, quaque praeter omnem Canonum ordinem ediderant, &c. Epift.Synod.ad Imp.to.4.ca. 8. quod contra leges et canones,amutemq, ordinem perpetrarunt. ibid.   f Omnes Orientales atq, Occidentales vel per fe,vel per legatos facerdotali huic conceffui interfunt. Act. Ephef. to.2.ca.16. Quod à nobis exijt judicium, aliud nihil effe quam communem concordemque terrarum orbis feafum atq, confenfum.Ep. Synod. Eph.Conc. ad Imp.to.2.ca.17.   g Ille(Iohannes)30.tantum numero,eufque vel hereticos vel alios illius factionis focios.Epift.Synod. 5.Conc. ad Imp.to.4.ca.2. Johannes rebellionis hujus antefignanus.ibid.ca.3.& alibi fepe.*

L 3   thefe

so those false writings against venerable Images are said to bee the writings of Bishop *Epiphanius*, but they are not his. So those publike acts, and second Nicene Fathers, whose testimony concurreth and jumpeth with the Cardinall, this is not the Epistle of *Ibas*.

8. Before I come to examine those publike acts, I must observe one thing touching *Baronius*, which he will occasion and inforce me often to repeat; and this it is, that *Baronius* was meerly infatuated in his handling of this whole cause touching the *three Chapters*, and this one might almost even sweare: but any may see it as cleare as the light: besides many other, even by this one point whereof we now intreat. If a man should study and devise ten dayes together, how to confute and utterly overthrow all that Pope *Vigilius* hath decreed touching this *third Chapter*; and all which *Baronius* himselfe hath either taught or said in defence of *Vigilius* in that point, he cannot possibly doe it more clearly, more certainly, more effectually, then by denying, as the Cardinall, and his Nicene Fathers doe, that this is the Epistle of *Ibas*: for how could either the Councell of *Chalcedon*, or the Popes Legates therein, by this Epistle, and by the dictation and contents thereof judge *Ibas* to be a Catholike (which *Vigilius* [y] decreeth, and *Baronius* [z] more then twenty times I thinke repeateth,) unlesse it were indeed the Epistle of *Ibas*; for of *Ibas* no otherwise then in the first person, or as the author and writer of it, there is no mention at all to be found or collected out of that Epistle.

9. Now if you require testimonies, or authorities in this case, I oppose to *Baronius* the Popes Legates at *Chalcedon*, of which *Baronius* himselfe saith [a]; *This to be the Epistle of Ibas, the Popes Legates, and after them the rest of the Bishops by their subscription, confirmed*, and againe, the [b] Acts of *Chalcedon* doe teach, that this we acknowledged to be the Epistle of *Ibas*. I oppose Pope *Vigilius*, who in his *Constitution* assenteth [c] to that judgement of the Popes Legates, and those words, *relecta ejus Epistola*, the Epistle of *Ibas being read*, we acknowledge him to be a Catholike. I oppose the confession of *Ibas* himselfe, of which *Baronius* saith, the [d] Acts at *Chalcedon* declare *Ibam confessum esse eam esse suam*, that *Ibas confessed this Epistle to be his owne*: and againe [e], we have before declared *Ibam eandem Epistolam suam esse professum*, that *Ibas professed this same Epistle to be his owne*: and *Ibas* of all men in the world knew best, whether it was his or no. I oppose lastly *Baronius* to *Baronius*, for he [f] saith of this Epistle, *verè esse Ibæ fuisse cognitam*, that *it was knowne truly and indeed to be the Epistle of Ibas*. Say now in sadnesse, what you thinke of *Baronius*, and where you thinke his five wits were, when hee denyed, and that upon proofe by publike records, this to be the Epistle of *Ibas*, which the Popes Legates, with the whole Councell of *Chalcedon*, which Pope *Vigilius* whom hee defendeth, which *Ibas* his owne selfe;

[marginal notes:]
y *Vigil. Const. nu. 196.*
z *Bar. an.* 553. *nu.* 191, 192, 193, 196, 197, &c.

a *B. an.* 448. *nu.* 71.

b *an. eod. nu* 77.

c *Vigil. Const. nu.* 90

d *Bar. an.* 448 *nu.* 77.
e *Bar. an.* 553. *nu.* 211.
f *an.* 448. *nu.* 71.

selfe, yea which *Baronius* also acknowledgeth, confesseth, and professeth to be truly, and in very deed the Epistle of *Ibas.*

10. But what shall we then say to those publike acts, which as the Cardinall tells us, doe testifie, that this is not the Epistle of *Ibas.* What first to the acts of the Councell at Chalcedon, which he first g alleageth, and the tenth Action thereof? I say, and say it upon certaine grounds, that the Cardinall therein saith an untruth, for proofe whereof, I appeale to that same tenth Action of the Councell, in no part whereof it is said, nor can thence be collected, that this was not the Epistle of *Ibas.* Or if you will not beleeve my saying, yet beleeve the Cardinall himselfe, more then once testifying that which he saith to be untrue.   These are his words h, *The Acts of the tenth Action of the Councell at Chalcedon: Eandem epistolam ut Ibæ cognitam esse à patribus docent,* doe teach, that this Epistle was knowne to be the Epistle of *Ibas.* And againe i, *Vere esse Ibæ fuisse cognitam eandem actio decima docet,* that this was knowne to have beene truly the Epistle of *Ibas,* the tenth action of the Councell at Chalcedon doth teach. Thinke you not that *Baronius* is more like the *Esopicall Satyr,* then a grave Cardinall of the Romane Church? At his first blast he makes the tenth action of the Councell at *Chalcedon* to testifie that this is not the Epistle of *Ibas;* and then hee blowes a quite contrary blast, professing the tenth action of the Councell at *Chalcedon* to testifie that this is truly, and certainly the Epistle of *Ibas.*

11. O, but the second *Nicene* Councell, and the publike acts thereof, they witnesse the same which the Cardinall affirmeth, that this is not the Epistle of *Ibas.* They doe so indeed: But as it is an untruth in the Cardinalls mouth: so it is also in those his Nicene Fathers from whom hee tooke it, unlesse perhaps those men of *Nice,* knew better whose Epistle it was, then did the 600 holy Bishops of the Councell at *Chalcedon,* before whom *Ibas* stood, or better then *Ibas* himselfe who confessed it to bee his owne Epistle. The Cardinall may not be offended that we dissent from his Nicene Councell, which dissenteth from the holy Councell at *Chalcedon,* from *Ibas* his owne confession, yea from whom the Cardinall dissenteth as much as we in this point. And I cannot see, what depth of wisedome it was in his Cardinalship to alleage them for witnesses, whose testimony, himselfe in this very point for which he produceth them, doth avouch to bee untrue.   But let him please himselfe in those Nice Fathers, we envie not such a Councell, nor such Fathers, nor such publike records unto them. That Nicene assembly was but a conspiracie against the truth, it was fit they should uphold untruth, by untruth. And whosoever shal be pleased to examine and rip up the Acts of that Councell, I will give him this one assured comfort, that besides their superstitious & heretical doctrins therin maintained, he shall finde them full stuft with many grosse and palpable untruths, of matters *de facto,* on which they build their doctri-

g *Bar. an.* 431. *nu.* 71.

h *Bar. an.* 448 *nu.* 77.

i *Ibid. nu.* 71

nall

nall positions, as in this concerning the Epistle of *Ibas*, it is now most manifest.

12. For this time I will not enter into so spacious a field, but yet this one thing by the way I cannot but observe; seeing those Nicene Fathers professe, that writing against Image-worship, going under the name of *Epiphanius*, to be in such sort the book of *Epiphanius*, as this Epistle going under the name of *Ibas*, is the Epistle of *Ibas*: and seeing we have now demonstrated this Epistle to be truly and indeed the Epistle of *Ibas*, it followeth even by their owne reason and comparison; that the book also against Image-worship, cited by the Councell at *Constantinople* in the name of *Epiphanius*, is in truth and in very deed the true writing of Bishop *Epiphanius*. And yet further, because those Nicene Fathers acknowledge *Epiphanius* for a Catholike [k] Doctor of the Church, one who held the ancient tradition [l] of the Church, and consented to the Catholikes, in and before his time : it hence againe followeth, that the doctrine of condemning Image-worship which in that booke of *Epiphanius* is delivered, & was by the generall Councell at *Constantinople* some thirty [m] yeares before this Nicene Assembly, decreed [n], that it I say is ancient, Catholike, consonant to the ancient tradition, and the doctrine of the ancient and catholike Fathers of the Church, even from the Apostles time. And this is all which *Baronius* hath gained by his alleaging those publike acts of the Nicene Fathers, to prove this not to be the Epistle of *Ibas*. And let this suffice to be spoken of the personall untruths of *Vigilius* and *Baronius* touching this Epistle of *Ibas*, which are but a *præludium* to their doctrinall errors and heresies; wherof in the next place we are to entreat.

k *Beatum patrem (Epiphanium) catholicæ ecclesiæ Doctorem agnoscimus. Conc. Nic.2. Act.6.pa.371.b.*

l *Hi qui antiquam ecclesiæ traditionem recipiunt, beato Epiphanio non adversantur. ibid.b.*

m *Conc. Const. contra Imagines, habitum est an. 754. Bin.to.3.pa.229. Conc. Nicænum habitum.an.787. Bin.notis in id Conc.*

n *Qui imaginem ausus fuerit parare, aut adorare, aut in ecclesia, aut in privata domo constituere, aut clam habere, si Episcopus fuerit; deponatur.&c. Decretum Conc. Constant.sub Constantino Copronimo, quod extat in Niceno Conc.2.Act.6. pa.377.a.*

CHAP. XI.

That Vigilius and Baronius in their former reason for defence of the Epistle of Ibas, drawne from the union with Cyrill, mentioned in the latter part of that Epistle, doe defend all the heresies of the Nestorians.

1.  E E come now from personall matters to that which is the *Capital* point, and maine heresie contained in the defence of *this Chapter*, wherein *Vigilius*, and *Baronius* have so behaved themselves, that those former errours though they be too shamefull, are but a very sport, and play to that hereticall frenzie which here they doe expresse. For now you shall behold the Pope and his Cardinall in their lively colours, fighting under the banner of *Nestorius*, and using the most cunning stratagems that were ever devised, to cloake their hereticall doctrine, and gaine credit to that condemned

demned heresie. Those sleights are principally two. The former is gathered out of the latter part of the *Epistle of Ibas,* where mention is made of the *union* betwixt *Cyrill,* and *Iohn,* which although I touched before [a], yet because it is a matter of greater obscuritie, and containeth a most notable fraud of *Vigilius,* and *Baronius,* I purposely reserved the full handling of it unto this place, where without interruption of other matters, I might have scope enough, to explaine the depth of this mysterie.

2. In the time of the Ephesine Councell, there was, as all know, an exceeding breach betwixt *Cyrill,* with other Catholike Bishops, who condemned *Nestorius,* and *Iohn* Bishop of *Antioch,* with divers other Eastern Bishops, who tooke part with *Nestorius,* against the holy Councell. And the division was so great, that at the selfe-same time, in one, & the selfe-same citie of Ephesus, they held two severall Councels, and set up *altare contra altare,* Councell against Councell, Patriarcke against Patriarcke, Bishops against Bishops, and Synodall sentence against Synodall sentence. But betwixt those two Councels, there was as much difference, as is betwixt light and darkenesse, betwixt truth and heresie, betwixt the Church of God, and the Synagogue of Satan. The one consisted of holy orthodoxall and Catholike Bishops whose President was *Cyrill:* the other of hereticall, [b] factious, and divers deposed Bishops, whose President was *Iohn.* The former condemned *Nestorius* & his blasphemous doctrine, whereby hee denied Christ to be God: the latter defended *Nestorius* and all his impious doctrines. The former was held in a Church, even in the Church of the Blessed [c] *Virgin,* whose Sonne they professed to bee truly God: the latter in an Inne [d], or Taverne, a fit place for them who denied Christ to be God. The former proceeded in all respects, orderly and Synodally, as was fit and requisite that they should: the latter did all things tumultuously [e], presumptuously, and against the Canons of the Church, supporting themselves onely by lies, calumnies, and slanderous reports. In a word, the former, was truly an holy, a generall, an Oecumenicall [f] Councell, wherein was the consent of the whole Catholike Church: the latter was nothing else, but an hereticall, schismaticall, and rebellious faction or conspiracie of some thirtie [g] or fortie persons, unworthy the name of Bishops, insolently opposing themselves to the holy Councel, yea to the whole Catholike Church, in which number and faction besides others, who lesse concerne our purpose, were

a Sup. ca.4.

b Coactis in unum solo nomine Episcopis, qui una cum Nestorio desciverat: ex quibus alij erant extorres, vari, proprijs sedibus destituti, alij à suis Metropolitanis depositi, alij, Pelagij & Celestij veneno imbuti. Epi. Synodal. janႿ. Conc. Eph. ad Celestinum, to.4. AⴟⴟEph.c.17. c Consistentibus in sanctiss. Ecclef. que appellatur Maria, to.2. act. Ephef. coc. ca.1. & sepe alibi. d Iohanne in diversorio manente, sacraq, illius Synᴏ praesente, Aⴟ. Ephe. coc. to. 3.ca.1. Cum vix cursu distulisset (Iohannes) cubiculuiq, ingressus esset. Apol. Cyril. ad Imper.to.5 ca.2.pa.827. b.

e *Iohannes cum suis, nullam omnino vel per leges ecclesiasticas, vel per Augustorum decretum, potestatem obtinuit. Libel. Cyril.et Mem. oblatus sⴟ synodo,to.4. Aⴟⴟ.ca.2. Iohannes omni ecclesiastica authoritate proculcata, omniq, ecclesiarum ordine & ritu & consuetudine contempta, &c. ibid. Que temere vaneq, fuerant nugati, quaque preter omnem Canonum ordinem ediderant, &c. Epist. Synod.ad Imp.to.4.ca. 8. quod contra leges et canones, amutemq, ordinem perpetrarunt, ibid. f Omnes Orientales atq, Occidentales vel per se, vel per legates sacerdotali huic concessui intersunt. Aⴟ. Ephef. to.2.ca.16. Quod à nobis exijt judicium, aliud nihil esse quam communem concordemque terrarum orbis sensum atq, consensum Ep. Synod. Eph.Conc. ad Imp.to.2.ca.17. g Ille (Iohannes) 30.tantum numero, eisque vel hereticos vel alios illius factionis socios.Epist.Synod.5.Conc.ad Imp.to.4.ca.2. Iohannes rebellionis hujus antesignanus.ibid.ca.3.& alibi sepe.*

these

h *Vt patet ex earum subscriptione. Act. Conc. Ephes.to.3.ca. 2.& tom.4.ca.7.*

i *Glic. Annal. part. 4.pa.363.*

k *Post duas dies venimus in Ephesum ait Ibasin est.sua. Conc.Chal.act.10. sequutus sum primatem meum ibid. pa.112.b.*

l *Tu Cyrille & tu Memnon, scitote vos exauctoratos, omnique episcopali honore exutos. to.3. Act.Eph.ca.2.*

m *Capita heretica à Cyrillo exposita ut que Euangelicæ & Apostolicæ doctrinæ apertè repugnant. Ibid.*

n *Act.Conc.Ephes. to.4.ca.7.*

o *At vos reliqui omnes qui Cyrilli actis consensistis, anathemati subjacete.tom. 3.Ephes. Act. ca.2.*

p *Schismaticorum conciliabulum.to.4. Act.Conc.Ephe.ca. 15.*

q *Sacra Synodus, &c. tom. 3. act. ca. 2.6.7.& alibi sæpe*

r *Confuso illarum Conciliabulo se conjunxerunt. tom. 3. act. Ephes. ca. 1. Quoddam inter se conciliabulum instituerunt.ibid.c.4.*

s *Seditiose, iniquè, contra ecclesiasticas sanctiones. regiaq; decreta consensistis. ibid.ca.2.*

t *Qui furiis quibusdam agitati, Arii, Apollinariique dogmata instaurare voluerunt. to.3. ca.18.*

v *Scitote Cyrillianos tyrannide fraudibus,&c. Append. ad to.3. act. Ephes. ca.10*

x *To.4.act.ca.15. et ca.18.*

these [h] *Iohn* Bishop of *Antioch*, the ring-leader of the rest, *Paulus* Bishop of *Emisa*, *Theodoret* of whom wee before entreated, and *Ibas*, (not then, but some three or foure yeares after Bishop of *Edessa*) whom to have beene present at that time as a Bishop, though his name bee not expressed in their subscription, both *Glicas* [i] in his Annales, and the Councell at *Chalcedon*, [k] and *Ibas* his owne words therein, doe make manifest.

3. Now though there was so great odds betwixt the holy Councell, and this factious conventicle, yet were they (as is the custome of all heretickes and schismatickes) most insolent in all their actions. As the holy Councell deposed *Nestorius* for an hereticke, so the Conventicle to cry quittance with them, deposed [l] *Cyrill* for an Arch-hereticke also, condemning [m] his twelve Chapters as hereticall, which the holy Councell had approved as orthodoxall. As the holy Councell excommunicated [n] and anathematized, *Iohn, Paulus, Theodoret, Ibas*, and all the rest of their factious adherents, and defenders of *Nestorius*, and his heresie: So did the Conventicle also excommunicate and anathematize *Cyrill*, and all [o] that tooke part with him, and defended his twelve Chapters, and so among these, even Pope *Celestine*, and the whole Catholike Church. As the holy Councell truly and justly, called themselves, the sacred and oecumenicall Councell, and tearmed *Iohn* with his adherents, a faction and hereticall [p] Conventicle of Nestorians: so did the Conventicle arrogate unto themselves, the glorious name of the holy [q] Ephesine Councell, and slandered them which held with *Cyrill* to bee a Conventicle [r], an unlawfull [s] and disorderly assembly, tearming them *Arians*, [t] *Apollinarians*, and from *Cyrill*, *Cyrillians* [v]. As the holy Councell constantly refused, to communicate with *Iohn* [x], or any of his faction, untill they did consent to the deposing of *Nestorius*, and anathematizing his heresie: so the conventicle most peevishly and pertinaciously not onely refused the communion with *Cyrill*, and other Catholikes, but bound themselves by many solemne oathes, [y] and that even in the presence of the Emperor, that they would never communicate with the *Cyrillians*, unlesse they would condemne the twelve chapters of *Cyrill*, adding that they would rather dye [z], then admit or consent unto any one of those twelve chapters. Such an unhappie and lamentable breach *Iohn* and the Eastern Bishops made in the Church at the time of that Ephesine Councell.

4. The religious Emperours *Theodosius*, and *Valentinian* whose imperiall authority, was the onely meanes to end all these strifes; had they beene personally present in the Synod, to see all these disorders, they would no doubt, either have prevented this breach, or after it had hapned, have healed and made

y *Iuravimusq; sepissime pientissimo Regi, quod impossibile sit nobis communicare his (Cyrillianis) si non exploserint capitula. Appen.to.3. act.ca.9.& 10. z Parati sumus prius mori, quam suscipere unum ex Cyrilli capitulis. ib. ca.7.*

up the same. But they residing then at *Constantinople*, were extreamely abused by the vile dealings of the Nestorians, for so much had these Nestorians prevailed, both at the Court and in the Citie of *Constantinople*, where *Nestorius* had beene Bishop, that though the holy Councell sent letters after letters, to certifie the truth of all matters to the Emperor, yet either [a] were their messengers stopt, or their letters by the malicious vigilancie of the Nestorians intercepted, so that none, no not any small notice of them came to the Emperors, whereas on the other part the frequent [b] letters of the conventicle fraught with lies & slanders, had every day accesse, yea applause in the Citie, in the Court, and before the Emperors. And which was the worst of all, Count *Candidianus*, whom the Emperours made their owne deputie, and president of the Councell, to see all good, and Synodall orders observed therein, hee failed of that trust committed unto him, and being most partiall [c] towards *Nestorius* and his heresie, by his letters also he seconded and soothed all the lies which the conventicle had writ unto the Emperors. By which meanes it came to passe, that the Emperors knowing nothing of that division amongst the Bishops, & how beside the holy Councell, there was a faction, and schismaticall conventicle held in the citie, thought all that was done, as well against *Cyrill*, and *Memnon*, in deposing them, as against *Nestorius*, in deposing him, that all this had beene in the act, judgement and sentence of one and the same Councell, upon which subreption and misinformation, the Emperors confirmed at the first the condemnation [d] of them all three; But at length a letter being brought from the holy Synod to *Constantinople* by one, who to avoid suspition put on the habit of a begger [e], and carried the letter in the trunke of his hollow staffe which for that purpose he had provided; as soone as the report of these strange disorders came to the Emperors eares, they sent for, and commanded certaine Bishops of either side, personally to come before them to *Constantinople*, that they might bee fully informed of the truth in all the proceedings : and the truth after diligent examination being found, the Emperors by their Imperiall authoritie adnulled all the Acts of the conventicle, restored *Cyrill* [f], and *Memnon*, approved [g] the judgement of the holy Councell against *Nestorius*, adding banishment also from *Constantinople*, to his deposition : But the Synodall sentence [h] of deposition against *Iohn*, and the other Bishops of his faction, that they staied, and suspended for a while, partly to prevent a greater schisme, which *Iohn* was like to procure, but specially in hope that *Iohn*, and the other Easterne Bishops might in time be

a *Arbitramur pijß. Imperatorem nihil horum dilucidè intellexiße. Ita terra mariq, obsidemur, ut nihil eorum quæ nobis hic evenerit veßre Sanctitudini significare potuerimus. Epiß. san. conc. ad Eulalium & alios. tom. 4. act. ca. 21. Qui Nestorij studiosi erant, omnia maria & publicas vias obsidentes, neminem prorsus à sacra Synodo Constantinopol. venire permittunt. to. 2. act Ephes ca. 19.*

b *Ea interim quæ inimici Christi erant, ultro citroque deferebantur. ibid.*

c *Candidianus Comes amicitiam Nestorij pietati anteponens —— ea pietati veßræ instillare studuit, quæ cum sibi tum Nestorio commoda grataq, futura intelligebat. Relatio Synod. ad Imp. to. 4. ca. 10.*

d *Et Nestorij, & Cyrilli, et Memnonis exauctorationem à Sanctitate veßra nobis insinuatam, caiculo noßro approbavimus. Sacra auße ab Auguße ad Synod. to. 3. act. Ephes. ca. 15.*

e *Epistola ex Epheso scripta, opera cujusdam mendici, qui in Scipione eam inclusam gerebat, tandem reddita est. tom. 2. act. ca. 19.*

f *Placuit plentiß. Regi ut Ægyptius et Memnon in suis locis maneant. Epist. Legatorum Conciliab. Append. tom. 3. ca. 10. pa. 791. b. et ille (Cyrillus) ad thronum suum redit, Ibid.   g Legatorum Synodi sententia publicè approbata, Orientales quidem condemnat, Nestorio vero exilium indicit. Decretum Regium, tom. 5. act. Ephes. ca. 11.   h Quæ extat tom. 4. act ca. 7.   i Imperator decrevit ut sententia Oecumenica Synodi contra Nestorium vim obtineret, quodq, in causa Iohannis constituißet, suspenderetur. Bin. not. in Conc. Ephes. § Verum. pa. 921.*

reduced

reduced and brought to vnitie with *Cyrill*, and the catholike Church, which in that height of their heat and stomacke could not have beene expected. And thus was the Councell at *Ephesus* dissolved, a farre greater rent by this means being left at the end, then had beene at the beginning thereof, and so that maladie for which it was called, not cured but encreased.

5. But the religious Emperor *Theodosius* could not bee at quiet while the Church was thus disturbed, but the very next yeare after the Ephesine Councell was ended, when time and better advise had now cooled the former heat of the Easterne Bishops, hee began to effect that vnion which before he had entended, and he so earnestly laboured therein, that himselfe professed,[k] *I am certainely and firmely resolved, not to desist in working this reconcilement, untill God shall vouchsafe to restore vnitie and peace to the Church;* To which purpose hee writ a very religious, and effectuall Epistle [l] to *Iohn* B. of *Antioch*, by many reasons perswading, and by his imperiall authoritie commanding [m] him, and with him the rest of the faction, to subscribe to the deposition of *Nestorius*, & the anathematizing of his heresie, and so to embrace the holy communion with *Cyrill*, and the catholike Church, which perswasions of the Emperor, tooke indeed the intended effect: for after some tergiversation for a while, both *Iohn* and most of the Easterne Bishops, before the end of that yeare, relented, and in a Synod held at *Antioch*, subscribed as the Emperor perswaded them, both to the deposing of *Nestorius*, and to a truly orthodoxall profession, sent vnto them by *Cyrill*, wherein they approved [n] the holy Ephesine Councell, and condemned all the heresies of *Nestorius*, and upon this their consenting to *Cyrill*, and the orthodoxall faith, were received into the peace of the Church; and so vnion and concord, was fullie concluded betwixt *Cyrill*, with the other orthodoxall Bishops, & *Iohn* with most of those Eastern Bishops, who before adhered vnto him.

6. Let us now see how *Vigilius*, and after him *Baronius* under couler of this *Vnion*, plead for *Ibas*, & his heretical Epistle. In the end of that *Epistle*, *Ibas* makes mention [o], of the vnion betwixt *Iohn* and *Cyrill*, yea mentioneth it as a great blessing of [p] God to the Church, seeing that he not onely consented, but greatly rejoyced at the same. Thus much is cleare and certaine by the Epistle. Now because the *Vnion* as we have declared, was made by consenting to the Catholike faith, it seemes that *Ibas* who consented to the *Vnion*, consented also to the Catholike faith, and so was received into the communion of *Cyrill* and the Catholike Church. Seeing then *Ibas* by this Epistle is shewed to approve and embrace the *Vnion*, and embracing of the vnion is the proofe of a Catholike, it followeth that even by this Epistle *Ibas* declares himselfe to be a very good Catholike, and an earnest embracer of the Catholike faith. This is the summe of their collection, which is, as any wil confesse, a very faire & plausible pretence, and therefore more fit for the Pope and Cardi-

k *Sacr. Imp. ad Acatium Episc. Ber. to. 5. act. Ephes. ca. 10.*

l *Sacr. Imp. missa per Aristol. ad Iohannem, tom. 5. act. Ephes. ca. 3.*

m *Iohanni mandavit ut scelerata Nestorij dogmata anathematizaret &c. Epist. Cyril. ad Dyn. to. 5. act. Ephes. ca. 16. Imperatores literas miserunt ad Acatium Bereensem et Iohannem, quibus severè praecipiunt: , ut turbas consopiamus. Epist. Pauli ad Cyril. to. 5. act. Eph. ca. 4.*

n *Cùm igitur Iohannes subscripsisse: caeterîq; qui majori authoritate apud ipsum erant, et Nestorij dogmata anathematizassent, cōmunionem illis restituimus, Epist. Cyril. ad Dynat. to. 5. ca. 16.*

o *Et communicantibus adinvicem, cōtentio de medio ablata est, et pax in Ecclesia facta. Ibae verba in sua Epist.*

p *Voluit autem Deus, quî suae semper curam gerit Ecclesiae. Ibid.*

nall to cloake their herefie under the fhew thereof. But leaft
we feeme either to wrong them, ot leave out ought which is
emphaticall in their reafon, it is needfull to heare them difpute
in their owne words.

7. It differeth much, faith q *Baronius,* to fay that the Epiftle is
Catholike, or that thofe things which are written in it are true;
and to fay that *Ibas* by this *Epiftle* was proved to be a catholike.
*Etenim nihil aliud inde acceperunt patres, nifi Ibam tunc temporis
fuiffe Catholicum,* for the fathers at *Chalcedon* tooke nothing at all
out of that Epiftle, but that *Ibas* at that time (when he writ it) was
a Catholike, feeing in it is demonftrated that *Ibas* who had fometimes erred with the Neftorians, and dealt againft *Cyrill,* after
the peace once made, did communicate with *Cyrill,* and condemne *Neftorius* with his doctrine. Againe, r the reader is here
to be admonifhed, that the fentence of the fathers at *Chalcedon*
doth not tend to this end, *ut voluerint probaffe Epiftolam Ibæ,* as if
they meant to approve the Epiftle of *Ibas,* in which there are many
blafphemies affirmed, neither did *Vigilius* meane to teach this:
*fed tantum ex ea recipiendum effe Ibam, in qua nimirum teftetur ipfe
fe jam amplecti pacem ecclefiæ, qua recepta, neceffe fuerit eundem probare Catholicum,* but both they and *Vigilius* meant onely that Ibas, *by
this Epiftle was to be efteemed and embraced as a Catholike,* feeing in
this Epiftle *Ibas* teftifieth that he embraced the peace of the
Church, which being received, it is neceffary that he be approved for a catholike. Againe, the f Fathers of *Chalcedon,* faid, that
this Epiftle was to be received as Catholike, not in regard of thofe
errors wherewith *Ibas* was once intangled, and which are recited
therein, *fed quod ex illa Ibas profitetur fe paci initæ confentire;* but
for that *Ibas* in it profeffeth himfelfe to confent to the peace or union
made betweene *Iohn* and *Cyrill:* and a little after, *Vides t non alia ex
parte,* you fee that this Epiftle was approved by the Fathers at *Chalcedon in no other part or refpect;* but for that which *Ibas* fignifieth in
the laft part of the Epiftle, that hee confented, *omnibus pactis &
conventis,* in all the conditions and covenants of the catholike
union made betweene *Iohn* and *Cyrill.* And to omit many the like
places, (for *Baronius* harps much upon this ftring) hee repeateth
this u moft plainly in this manner: *In the end of this Epiftle, Ibas
the author of it doth teftifie, that peace was made, that himfelfe confented unto it, and rejoyceth therein, feeing he gives thankes to God for the
fame.* Now feeing the peace was concluded upon this condition,
that *Neftorius* and his errours fhould be condemned, and the decrees of the *Ephefine* Councell received, it did plainely and ne-
ceffarily enfue, that *Ibas* condemned *Neftorius,* and approved the
Ephefine Councell, and fo the Popes Legates, and others at *Chalcedon* fpake not amiffe, when they faid, that *Ibas* by that Epiftle
being read, was proved to bee a catholike. Thus difputeth the
Cardinall for this impious *Epiftle,* nor did he wholly devife this
of himfelfe, but he had the ground of it out of *Vigilius* his *Apofto-
ftolicall*

q *B.r.an.448.nu. 75.*

r *B.r.an.553. nu.191.*

f *Ibid.*

t *Nu.192.*

u *An.eodem 553. nu.213.*

x *Vigil. Conſt. nu.*
192.

licall *Conſtitutiō*, where he thus ſaith, *The* x *Fathers at Chalcedon pronounced this Epiſtle of Ibas to be orthodoxall, propter illam prædicationem fidei, for that profeſſion of faith*, by which *Cyrill* and *Iohn*, and all
the Eaſterne Biſhops made concord and union by the meanes of
Paulus Biſhop of *Emiſa, quam Ibas quoque in eâdem Epiſtolâ lau-
dans libenter amplectitur; which union and profeſſion of faith Ibas
both praiſeth in this Epiſtle, and gladly embraceth.* So *Vigilius.*

8. Here firſt of all muſt be obſerved the admirable acuteneſſe
of the Pope and the Cardinall: They can ſee in the *Epiſtle* of
Ibas, more than the whole fift generall Councell, than other
ſucceeding, either Popes or generall Councels; more than the
whole Catholike Church ever did, or could; more than all the
world beſides, excepting onely the Neſtorians : They, and none
but they of all the former could ſee by the latter end of that *E-
piſtle*, or by the *union* mentioned therein, that either the *Epiſtle*
was Catholike, or *Ibas* by it to be judged a Catholike. But *Vigilius* and *Baronius*, though in ſome matters they be as blinde as a
Beetle, yet when they liſt, (*and they ever liſt when they defend hereſie*) they can ſee farre into a Milſtone : And yet, if it be well conſidered, they gaine not much by this their quicke ſight, and
quirke of the *union*, which they have ſpied in the end of that *Epiſtle*; for the whole fift Councell (approved by ſucceeding Councels, and by the whole catholike Church, as before wee have
declared) adjudgeth, not onely the beginning, and the middle,

y *Tota Epiſtola hæ-
retica eſt, tota Epi-
ſtola blaſphema eſt,
hæc omnē dicimus.
Conc. 5. Coll. 6. pa.
576. b.*
z *Poſteriora inſerta
Epiſtola majore im-
pietate plena ſunt.
Conc. 5. Coll. 6. pa.
564 a.*
a *Si quis defendit
memoratam Epiſto-
lam, & non anathe-
matizat eam, et de-
fenſores ejus, et eos
quā dicunt eam re-
ctam eſſe, vel par-
tem ejus. Conc. 5.
Coll. 8. in ſenten-
tia Synodali.
Anath. 14.*

but the end alſo, even the whole y Epiſtle, and every part, above
all, and principally, the end z thereof, to be blaſphemous, and hereticall, they anathematize a alſo as heretikes all who defend either the whole Epiſtle, or any part thereof, yea, all who doe not
anathematize every part thereof : whence it is undeniably conſequent, that both *Vigilius*, and his Procter *Baronius*, and all who
doe, or ſhall hereafter herein defend them, yea, all who doe not
anathematize them, are for this very quirke and ſubtilty of the
union found in the latter part of this Epiſtle, anathematized, and
condemned by the conſenting judgment of the whole catholike
Church. This have they gained as a juſt recompence for defending but the end onely of that *Epiſtle*, and much more for defending it by pretence of the Councell at *Chalcedon*, though they
ſhould condemne all the reſt of it.

9. But if the matter be well conſidered, it will appeare that
Vigilius by this one clauſe of the *union* makes good, not onely the
latter part, (as *Baronius* pretendeth) but even the whole Epiſtle
of *Ibas*; for had he intended to approve no more than onely the
latter part of that Epiſtle, his reaſon had beene this; The Fathers
at *Chalcedon* approved that part of the Epiſtle, wherein the
union is mentioned; therefore they approve the latter part of the
Epiſtle, which is a meere nugation, proving *idem per idem*; for
ſeeing the *union* is onely mentioned in the latter part, it is all one
as if he had ſaid, They approved the latter part, therefore they
approved

approved the latter part; and mee thinkes it founds not well, to heare such nugatory, and frivolous reasons to proceed out fo the *infallible Chaire* : Nor doth indeed *Vigilius* so conclude; but from that *union* and concord which the latter part of the Epistle testifieth *Ibas* to have approved, he inferres, that *Ibas* when hee writ this was a Catholike, and writ it as a Catholike, and so the writing, or Epistle it selfe to be Catholike; for thus stands his reason; The [b] latter end of the Epistle sheweth, that *Ibas* praised the *union* betwixt *Iohn* and *Cyrill*, and gladly embraceth it; and *propter illam fidei prædicationem orthodoxa est Ibæ à patribus pronunciata dictatio*; therefore for that confession of faith, which *Ibas* by his Epistle sheweth that he embraceth, for that did the Fathers of *Chalcedon* pronounce the writing, or Epistle (not the end onely of it) to be orthodoxall : So he takes this one part, of which hee made no doubt but it was approved at *Chalcedon*, as a *Medium* to prove that which was doubted; to wit, that the Epistle it selfe, even the whole Epistle was by the same Fathers approved; yea, and *Baronius* also, though hee in words pretends the contrary, yet seemes to be indeed of the same judgement; for he useth the very like reason as *Vigilius* doth, *quod [c] ex illa*, because *Ibas* in this Epistle professeth himselfe to consent to the *union*, therefore *Patres dixerunt eam Epistolam ut Catholicam recipiendam*; the Fathers at *Chalcedon* said, that the Epistle (loe the Epistle, saith the Cardinall, not a part onely of it) ought to bee received as Catholike.

b Vig. Conf.
nu.191.

c Bar. an. 553. nu.
191.

10. Which will be more plaine if we observe one other point out of *Vigilius* and *Baronius*, which may not well be omitted; for whereas all contained in any part of the Epistle respects things done, either before, or at, or after the *union*; in none of these, if ye will beleeve them, is this writing hereticall, or against the faith; for what was done before the *union*, though therein much be spoken against *Cyrill*, & the *Ephesine* Councell, and *Cyrill* called an heretike, yet is all that, saith [d] *Baronius*, spoken by way of an historicall narration, as declaring what was done, not as allowing that which was done; *ut ex hac parte nihil adversus Cyrillum obloquutus videatur*, that in this part there is no wrong done to *Cyrill*. At the *union*, or when it was concluded, then was *Ibas* reconciled to *Cyrill*, and received to the communion of the Church, and so would not write against the faith, so teacheth the Cardinall; *Ibas*, saith [e] he, tooke part with *Nestorius, usque ad tempus per Paulum Emissenum*; untill the time that the union was made by Paul Bishop of Emisa, *quando ipse sicut alij, communicare cum S. Cyrillo, & Ecclesia Catholica cæpit*; at which time *Ibas, as the rest*, begun to communicate with *Cyrill*, and with the Catholike Church, *Vigilius* [f] noteth the same, and out of him *Baronius* seemes to have borrowed it. By *Paulus* Bishop of *Emisa, Iohn, atque omnes orientales Episcopi, and all the Easterne Bishops*, (then *Ibas* among them) returned to concord with *Cyrill*. And *Baronius* further by the Epistle it selfe makes

d Bar. an. 448.
nu.71. Epistola historiam continet rerum gestarum inter Iohannem & Cyrillum, et quæ inter eos transacta essent, refert, &c.

e An. eodem. nu. 59.

f Vigil. Conf. nu.
192.

makes this plaine, for by it, saith g he, is declared, that *Ibas*, though before that time he had doated, *tunc temporis fuiſſe Catholicum, yet then* (to wit, when he writ this) *he was a Catholike*; and *Ibas* writ this Epistle, *eodem* h *momento pacis initæ, at the verie time and moment when the peace was made and concluded*; after which he never ſpake one undecent word againſt *Cyrill*: ſo at the time of the *union* being a Catholike, hee would not oppugne or write againſt the faith; much leſſe after the time of the *union*, for after that time *Vigilius* i teſtifieth, that *Ibas* remained ſtill a catholike, and in the catholike communion, *uſque ad exitum, even to his dying day*: And *Baronius* expreſſeth the ſame, ſaying k, that after the *union* it could not bee proved, *aliquod verbum indecens adverſus Cyrillum protuliſſe*; that *Ibas* ſpake any unſeemely word againſt *Cyrill*. Hereupon now it followeth, that the whole Epistle is to be approved, written by *Ibas* when he was a catholike, written with a catholike minde and affection; by him, who both at, and after the *union* would not write againſt the faith which himſelfe profeſſed, and what is ſpoken of matters before the *union*, that is all hiſtorically narrated, not by aſſent approved.

11. Oh how doe theſe men even labour and ſtudy to be miſerable, and to tye more faſt the knots of thoſe Anathemaes denounced againſt them by the holy Councell, which nothing but renouncing their hereticall defences of this Epistle can ever diſſolve! what will they doubt or feare to ſay, who would juſtifie that whole Epistle, as affirming nothing repugnant to the faith, (for a narration is no aſſertion of that which is related) of which the holy Conncell, and catholike Church hath pronounced, that it is wholly hereticall; and every part, head and taile, beginning and ending, an abſolute, and poſitive deniall of the faith ? what untruth will they not avouch, who deny *Ibas* after the *union* to have injured *Cyrill*, whereas the holy generall Councell witneſſeth, and that truly, as you ſhall ſtraight ſee, that even in this *union* which *Ibas* mentioneth, he wrongeth *Cyrill* and all catholikes more, than in any part of his Epiſt. yea, more thā *Neſtorius* himſelf ever did. But omitting for this time al the other untruths, which are not a few in thoſe aſſertions of *Vigilius* and *Baronius*; there are two things therein, which I may not wel paſſe over in ſilence.

12. The former is, (at the conſideration whereof I could not refraine from laughter) how curious, and even ſuperſtitious the Cardinall is in calculating the nativity of this impious Epistle, as if he had performed the office of *Iuno Lucina* unto it, and knew the very moment of time when this faire babe was firſt brought to light: It was written, ſaith hee, *eodem momento pacis initæ, in that very moment when the union was made betwixt Iohn and Cyrill.* At that very moment ? Sure the Cardinals *Ephemerides*, or the conſtellations deceived him. It was neither written in that moment, nor in that moneth, nor in that yeare, nor at the leaſt two whole yeares after the *union* was concluded: for the Epiſtle mentioneth

tioneth, not onely the praise of *Theodorus* of *Mopsvestia*, but his commendation by *Rambulas*. Now, neither did the Nestorians so much honour, nor did the catholikes by name condemne *Theodorus*, till the Emperour had by his Edict straightly forbidden the reading, writing, hearing, or having of the bookes of *Nestorius*; till then the name and writings of *Nestorius*, being a Patriarke, and of so eminent a citie as *Constantinople*, was farre more fit to credit, and countenance their doctrines, than the name of *Theodorus*, being but a Bishop, and of a very obscure and ignoble towne, or corner rather, which in likelihood had beene buried in eternall oblivion, had not he by his owne infamy made it famous, as *Herostratus* [l] did himselfe by burning the temple of *Diana* at *Ephesus* : But when both the name and bookes of *Nestorius* was now so detested by reason of the imperiall Edict, *tunc cæperunt Theodori volumina circumferre*, saith *Liberatus*, then [m] they began but to disperse the writings of *Theodorus*, w^ch *Baronius* [n] also confesseth; when the rivers, that is, *Nestorius* was stopt by the Emperors law, then the Nestorians *ipsum fontem aperuere*, opened the very fountaine, divulging the bookes of *Theodorus*, and *Diodorus*. The *Epistle* then, mentioning the expresse condemning of *Theodorus*, doth of a certaintie follow that imperiall Edict against *Nestorius* : That Edict was published, as by the date [o] appeares, in *August*, when *Theodosius* was the fifteenth time [p] Consull. The union betwixt *Iohn* and *Cyrill* was made the next yeare after the Ephesine Councell : for *Iohn* writing to *Xistus* Bishop of *Rome*, and testifying his unitie [q] and consent to *Cyrill*, saith in that Epistle, that the Ephesine Councell was held *anno proximè lapso*, *the yeare next before*. The Councell at *Ephesus* both began and ended in the yeare when *Antiochus* [r] and *Bassus* were Consuls [s]. Betwixt *Valerius* and *Ætius*, (who were next Consuls after *Antiochus* and *Bassus*, and in whose Consulship the union was fully concluded,) and the fifteenth Consulship of *Theodosius*, wherein the Edict against *Nestorius* was published, are two intire Consulships [t], as by the *Fasti*, and others is certaine. So that it is certaine, that the Epistle which mentioneth the condemning by name of *Theodorus*, was not written till more then two compleat yeares after the union ended : but how long after these two yeares it was, before *Ibas* writ it, is wholy uncertaine, in likelihood it was two or three more : for some time after the Edict must bee allowed for the Nestorians, to translate first, and then disperse the bookes of *Theodorus* : some more after that, for the condemning of him by *Rambulas* : some againe after that, before *Rambulas* dyed, to whom *Ibas* succeeded in the Bishopricke of *Edessa* : and who writ this Epistle, when hee was in possession of that See, as both the title [u] and contents [x] of the Epistle declare. By all which,

l *Herostratus, ut nomen memoria scele-ru extenderet, in medium nobilis fabri-cæ (quad inter 7. orbis miracula uni erat) manu sua struxit, sicut ipse fassus est. Sol.n. ca° 53. Strab. li. 14. & Val.Max.iu. de Cupidit. gloriæ.lib.8. ca.14.*
m *Liber.ca.10.*
n *Bar.an. 435. nu.3.*
o *Leg. ult. de hæreticis ead:Theod.*
p *It est annus Ch. 435. ut docet Marc. in Chron.& Bar. in illum annum.*
q *Placuit & nobis quoq, in sacra sancto-di sententia acqui-escere. Epist. Ioban-nis ad Xistum. Act Conc. Eph.to.5. ca. 17.*
r *Act. Conc. Ephes. to.2.ca.1. ubi habita dicitur Syno-dus post Coss.13. Theodosy.anno autem post istum Consulatum, Antio-chus & Bassus erant Consules, ut ex Marcell.in Chron: & fastis certum est. & to.3.Act. Eph. ca.17.litera Imper. ad Synodum datæ sunt Antiocho Con-sule. Cæpit autem Concilium 23. die Maÿ eo anno.to. 2. Act.ca. 1.& finitum est post quatuor (at Liber.ca.7.) vel post 3.menses ut Socra-tes ait.lib.7.ca. 33. & 37.*
s *It est an. Ch. 431. Marc.in Ch.& Bar. in eum annum.*
t *An. 433. Theodo-sius 14.et Maxi-mus Coss.an.434. Aviobinda & As-par.Coss. an.435. Theodosius 15. et Valeni.4.Coss.Fasti.*

u *Marcell. et Bar.* u *Fragmentum Epistolæ Ibæ Episcopi Edesseni.Conc.Chalc. Act.10.* x *Ex quibus unus (qui Theo-dorum condemnat) extitit (falso alicubi scribitur existit) nostræ civitatis tyrannus. Ibæ sua Epist.loc.citat.tyranni au-tem nomine significari Rambulam testatur Liber.ca.10. ubi sic ait, De quo (Rabula) successor ejus Ibas in epistola sua di-rit, hunc (Theodorum) præsumpsit, qui omnia præsumit, apertè in ecclesia sua anathematizare, etc:*

M   and

and if there were none elfe, by the laft onely, that *Ibas* writ this, being Bifhop of *Edeffa*; it is cleere, that fome good while, in likelihood three or foure yeares, were paft after the *union*, before *Ibas* writ this Epiftle, of which *Baronius* tells us fo precifely, that it was writ, *eo momento, at the very moment*, and inftant when the peace was concluded.

13. The other point, to be obferved is, what manner of a Catholike Pope *Vigilius*, and Cardinall *Baronius* have here fet forth unto us. *Ibas* when he writ this Epiftle, is with them a Catholike, a Catholike Writer, a Catholike Bifhop; in him you fhall fee the lively portrature of one of their Catholikes. Hee even in this Epiftle, written after the *Vnion* (when he was as they teach [y], a Catholike) *denyeth God to be incarnate*, and *Marie to be the Mother of God* : he condemnes the holy Ephefine Councell, and the twelve Chapters of *Cyrill*, hee commends *Theodorus* of *Mopfueftia* for a Preacher of the truth, while he lived, for a Saint being dead. Thefe are the doctrines of *Ibas*, all of them taught pofitively, and avouched, (not as the Cardinall fancieth, hiftorically related) in his Epiftle, as the words [z] thefelves do fhew, & the whole fift Councell [a] witneffeth, all taught by him, after the *Vnion*, when he was one of the Popes and Cardinalls Catholikes, yea taught confonantly to the *Vnion* which *Ibas* then embraced; yet *Ibas* teaching, writing, and maintaining all thefe blafphemies and herefies, that is, oppugning with all his art and ability the whole Catholike faith, is crowned and canonized by *Vigilius* and *Baronius* for a good Catholike. Of fuch Catholikes their Romane Church hath great ftore; nay, feeing none is now of their Church, who approves not all the Cathedrall decrees of their Popes; and therefore this of *Vigilius* among the reft, it hence enfueth, that none is now a Romane Catholike, that is, a member of their prefent Romane Church, who approves not *Ibas*, fuch as he was when he writ this Epiftle, for a Catholike, that is, who approves not the moft blafphemous heretikes, and oppugners of the whole faith, to be Catholikes, and who condemnes not the *Cyrillians*, that is, all that maintaine the Catholike faith, for heretikes.

14. But ftill as yet the doubt concerning the *Vnion* remaineth: *Ibas*, fay they, when he writ this Epiftle embraced the *union* with *Cyrill*, and none can embrace that *union* but hee fhewes himfelfe thereby to bee a Catholike: True; none can truly and fincerely embrace that *union* which *Cyrill* made with *Iohn*, the condition whereof was the fubfcribing to the holy Ephefine Synode, and condemning of *Neftorius*, with his doctrines, but hee is and muft be acknowledged to be a good Catholike. Had *Ibas* approved that *union* or confented unto it; *Ibas* had not beene *Ibas*, he had never written that impious Epiftle, which in every part, & moft of all in the end, where hee fpeakes of the *union*, is repugnant to that holy *union*. It is the *union* in Neftorianifme, the union in oppugning

y *Vig. Conft. xu. 194. & Ibam tunc temporis (cum hanc Epiftolam momento ipfo unionis fcripfit) Catholicum fuiffe. Bar.an.448.nu.75.*

z *Vide Epiftolam ipfam, & hoc clarum erit.*
a *Conc.5. coll.6.pa. 575. & 576.*

pugning and overthrowing the whole Catholike faith, which *Ibas* when he writ this Epistle embraced, and which in his Epistle he commendeth, which that it may appeare to all, wee are now to unfold the mystery of that *union* with *Cyrill*, under colour whereof *Ibas* first, then *Vigilius*, and lastly *Baronius* with all who hold the Popes judgement to bee *infallible*, doe very cunningly convey their hereticall doctrines, and contradict the Catholike faith.

15. The Nestorians being loth to forsake, or have it thought that any of them did forsake their heresies, and being withall most desperately given to lying and slandering, set forth a forme of union, forged by themselves, wherein they made *Cyrill*, and all who consented to him, that is, all Catholikes, to condemne their former Catholike doctrine decreed at the Ephesine Synod, and to assent to their heresies. And, as if this had beene the true union, and the conditions of peace agreed upon betwixt *Cyrill* and *Iohn*, they every where buzzed this into the eares of their sectaries, and spred abroad the copies thereof, triumphing in it, that now they had wonne the field, that *Cyrill* and all his partakers had now consented to Nestorianisme, and that upon this consent a generall union and peace ensued in the Church. This and no other is the union which *Ibas* in his Epistle embraceth, and by consenting whereunto Pope *Vigilius* decreeth, and *Baronius* defendeth *Ibas* to be a Catholike, to which union whosoever consenteth, or approveth others, consenting to it; they doe even by that one act, besides all the rest, infallibly demonstrate themselves, not onely to be Nestorians, and to approve all the heresies and blasphemies of *Nestorius*, but to be in the most base, abject, and low degree of all Nestorians, even such as by lyes and calumnies strive to uphold their heresies.

16. For proofe whereof, I shall produce records above exception: and first of all *Cyrills* owne testimony. *Acatius* the worthy Bishop of *Meletene* hearing by the report which the Nestorians [b] had spred abroad, that *Cyrill* in making the union had consented to the Nestorian doctrine of two natures (making *two persons*) in Christ, contrarie to his owne 12. Chapters, certified *Cyrill* of this report: *Cyrill* writ unto him at large, declaring the contrarie, and assuring him, that it was but a meere calumnie devised against him: *They reprove and accuse us, saith he* [c], *as if formerly, we had thought the quite contrarie to those things which now (at* the union) *we have written*; and I understand that they object also unto us, *quod novam fidei expositionem vel symbolū receperimus, that we have now* (at the union) *embraced a new Creed, or new exposition of the faith*, rejecting that old and venerable Creed: Thus did the Nestorians accuse *Cyrill*, as himselfe testifieth: but what answered he for himselfe? *At stultus stulta loquitur, & cor ejus vana meditatur*, he calls them in plaine termes, fooles and lyars: *the foole speaketh foolishly, and his heart meditateth lyes*. And in the end

b *Ex altera parte quidam de palatio culpaverunt Cyrillum, cur susceperit ab orientalib us E piscopis duarum confessionem naturarum, quod Nestorius dixit & docuit. hoc ipsū Valeriano, & Acatio videbatur. Liber. ca. 8.* c *Cyril. Epist. ad Acat. to. 5. Act. Conc. Eph. ca. 8. pa. 834. 835.*

he

he warneth *Acatius* not to give credit to the counterfeit Epiſtle,
or forme of union, which the Neſtorians had forged and ſpread
abroad in his name. If any Epiſtle, ſaith he [d], *be caried about as writ-*
ten by me, tanquam de ijs quæ Epheſi acta ſunt, jam dolente, & pæniten-
tiam agente, contemnat : as if I did now (ſince the union) ſorrow
and repent for thoſe things which were done and decreed at Epheſus,
let ſuch an Epiſtle he condemned : Nay the Greeke is more emphaticall, γελάσω δὲ τοῦτο *ſcorne and deride every ſuch writing.* The like
almoſt doth *Cyrill* write to *Dynatus* Biſhop of *Nicopolis,* who up-
pon the Neſtorians ſlanderous reports, ſuſpected as it ſeemeth
the very ſame of *Cyrill,* as *Acatius* did. *Cyrill* [e] having declared
the certaine truth of theſe matters unto him, ſaith in the end, *It*
is needfull that you ſhould know the cleare truth of theſe matters ; leſt
ſome men who doe vainly [f] and falſly report one thing for another, ſhould trouble any of the brethren : *Perinde ac ſi nos quæ con-*
tra Neſtorij blaſphemias ſcripſimus, retractaremus [g], as if wee had
(upon the union) recalled, revoked or denied, thoſe things which
we have written before againſt the blaſphemies of *Neſtorius.*

     17. Beſides theſe indubitate teſtimonies of *Cyrill,* the Neſto-
rians themſelves doe manifeſt this their calumnie : For although
Iohn and thoſe Eaſterne Biſhops who in their Councell at *Anti-*
och, ſubſcribed to that holy profeſſion of faith which was ſent
from *Cyrill* unto them, who were by farre the greater part, and
who therefore are counted the Eaſterne Church, though theſe I
ſay, were as they well deſerved, received into the Catholike
Cōmunion, when the *union* was concluded, yet is it moſt untrue
which *Vigilius* affirmeth, and takes it for a ground of his errour
touching *Ibas,* that *omnes* [h] *orientales Epiſcopi per Paulum Emiſe-*
num ad concordiam redierunt, that all the Eaſterne Biſhops by Paulus
Emiſenus returned to the unity and communion of the Church. They
did not all, not *Helladius,* not *Eutherius,* not *Hemerius,* not *Doro-*
theus, for whoſe reſtoring to their Sees, (for they were depoſed)
Paulus did earneſtly labour with *Cyrill,* but not being able to
prevaile for them; *manſerunt in eodem ſchiſmate, in quo etiam nunc*
perſeverant, they continued in their former ſchiſme, as rent from
the Church : and ſo they do now alſo remaine, nor was there in
the covenants of peace, any mention of them, as *Cyrill* [i] expreſly
affirmeth. But I will onely inſiſt upon two of the principall
ſticklers in the Neſtorian hereſie, and who moſt concerne our
preſent cauſe : *Theodoret* and *Ibas.*

     18. *Theodoret* beleeving the reports of his fellow *Neſtori-*
ans that the Catholikes at the time of the *Vnion* had revoked their former doctrines, and conſented to Neſtorianiſme, inſulted over them in a publike oration [k] at *Antioch,* before
Domnus, in this manner : *Vbi ſunt dicentes, quod Deus eſt qui cru-*
cifixus eſt ? where are thoſe that ſay that he was God, who was crucified ?
God was not crucified, but the man *Ieſus Chriſt,* hee who is of
the ſeed of *David,* was crucified : *Chriſt* is the Sonne of *David,*
                                           but

d *Ibid. pa. 837. a.*

e *Cyrill. Epiſt. ad*
Dynatum quæ eſt
38. & extat tom. 5.
Act. Eph. ca. 16.
f ἐψευσμένων.

g ἀ προσπεποίηνται.

h *Vig. Conſt. nu. 192*

i *Cyr. Epiſt. ad Dy-*
natum.

k *Quæ extat in*
conc. 5. Coll. 5. pa.
559.

but he is the temple of the sonne of God. *Non jam est contentio, Oriens & Ægyptus sub uno jugo est, There is now no contention, the East, and Ægypt* (that is, all who hold as *Cyrill* did) *are now both under one yoake.* Thus triumphed *Theodoret* over the Catholikes, supposing (as the Nestorians slanderously gave out) that *Cyrill* and all that held with him, that is, all Catholikes, had submitted themselues, to the yoke of their Nestorian heresie, that Christ is not God, nor that God was either borne of *Mary*, or suffered on the Crosse. And this being spoken by *Theodoret*, after the death of *Cyrill*, which was twelue [1] yeares after the *union* made, doth demonstrate the obstinate and malicious hatred of the Nestorians against the truth, who notwithstanding *Cyrill* had often by words, by writings, testified that report, to be nothing else, but a slanderous vntruth, yet in all that time, would not be perswaded, to desist from that calumny, but still let it passe for currant among them, and insulted, as if *Cyrill* and the Catholikes at the time of the union had condemned their former faith, and consented to Nestorianisme. So hard it is to reclame those who by selfe-will are wedded to any hereticall opinion.

Nam unio facta an.431. Cyril. autem obijt an. 444. Baron. in illo an.

19. The other is *Ibas*, the Popes owne Catholike doctor, whom, at that very time when hee writ this *Epistle* (which was long after the *Vnion* made betwixt *Iohn*, and *Cyrill*) to haue embraced no other then this slanderous union, or union in Nestorianisme, those very words in the later part of his *Epistle*, out of which *Vigilius*, and *Baronius* would prove him to bee a Catholike, even those words I say, doe so fully and manifestly demonstrate, that you will say, if not sweare, that nothing but the loue of Nestorianisme could so farre blind them, as to defend that part of his *Epistle*, or undertake by it to prove *Ibas* to be a Catholike. The words of *Ibas* are these [m]. *After that* Iohn *had received the Emperors letters, compelling him to make agreement with* Cyrill; *hee sent the most holy Bishop* Paulus *of* Emisa, *writing by him a true profession of faith, and denouncing vnto him, that if* Cyrill *would consent to that profession, and anathematize those who say that the Godhead did suffer* (which opinion the Nestorians slandered *Cyrill*, and all Catholike to hold) *and also those who say that there is but one nature* (that is, one natural subsistence or person) *of the divinity and humanity in Christ; then would he communicate with* Cyrill. *Now it was the will of God, who alwaies taketh care for his Church, which hee hath redeemed with his owne blood, to subdue the heart of the Ægyptian* (that is Cyrill) *that he presently consented to the faith, and embraced it, and anathematized all who beleeued otherwise. So they* (Iohn *and* Cyrill) *communicating together, the contention was taken away, peace was made in the Church, and now there is no schisme but peace, as of late there was. And that you may know what words were written, by the most holy Archbishop* Iohn, *and what answer hee received backe from* Cyrill, *I have to this my writing adjoy-*

Habentur tum in Conc. Chalc. Act. 10. tum in Con. 5. Coll. 6. pa.561.

ned

ned their very Epiftles, that your Holineffe reading them may know, and declare to all our Fathers that love peace, that the contention is now ceafed, and the partition wall is now taken away, and that they (hee meaneth Cyrill and the Catholikes) who had before feditiously enveied againft the living (Neftorius) and the dead (Theodorus) are now confounded, making fatisfaction for their faults, & contraria docentes fuæ priori doctrinæ, and now teach the contrarie to their former doctrine. For none now dare fay, that there is one nature (that is, one naturall subfiftence or perfon) of the divinity and humanity, but they confeffe and beleeve, both in the temple, and in him who dwelleth in the temple, who is one Sonne, Iefus Chrift. And this I have written to your Sanctitie, out of that great affection which I beare to you, knowing that your holineffe doth exercife it felfe, night and day, in the doctrine of God, that you might be profitable unto many. Thus farre are the words of *Ibas*, written unto *Maris* an hereticke ⁿ of *Perfia*, and

ⁿ Ad Marin Perfam, hereticum. Con 9. Coll.8. pa.587.b.

writ not as a private letter, but as an *Encyclicall Epiftle* to bee fhewed and notified to all that love peace, that is, according to their *hereticall dialect*, to all that loved Neftorianifme in *Perfia*, and in the places adjoyning, to be a comfort and encouragement to them, to perfift in their herefie, to which even *Cyrill* himfelfe, and all Catholikes had upon better advice, at the time of the union with *Iohn*, confented.

20. In which words any who hath though but halfe an eye of a Catholike, cannot chufe but clearely difcerne, the very poyfon, and malice of all the herefies, and practifes of the Neftorians, to be condenfate and compact together. Firft, here is expreffed their maine herefie, that Chrift is not God, as the houfe is not the man who dwelleth in the houfe. Secondly, is fet downe a notorious flander againft *Cyrill* and the Catholikes, that they at the union made with *Iohn*, did anathematize all who held one naturall fubfiftence, or one perfon to be in Chrift, that is, in effect did accurfe all Catholikes, and the whole Catholike Faith. Thirdly, it is a notable untruth, that *Cyril* made the union with *Iohn* upon this condition, that hee fhould anathematize all who hold Chrift to be one perfon, the condition was quite contrarie; to wit, that *Iohn*, and they on his part, fhould anathematize all who denied Chrift to be one, or who affirmed him to be two perfons. Fourthly, it is a flander, that *Cyrill* writ an Epiftle to that effect, as if he affented to that condition mentioned by *Ibas*. The Epiftle is teftified by *Cyrill* himfelfe not to bee his, but a counterfaite writing, forged by the Neftorians. Fiftly, it is a Calumnie, that *Cyrill* and the reft who condemned *Neftorius* and *Theodorus* were feditious perfons : it is as much as to fay, that the holy Ephefine Councell, was a confpiracie and feditious conventicle. Sixtly, it is an unexcufable flander and untruth, that *Cyrill* and they who held with him, that is, the Catholikes, that they were confounded, and repented of their former doctrines, or writ contrarie unto them. Thefe, befides

divers

divers the like, are the flowers wherewith the latter part of
that *Epiſtle* is deckt, even that part which Pope *Vigilius* and *Baronius* doe ſo magnifie, the one defining, the other defending,
that by it *Ibas* ought to be judged a Catholike, and his *Epiſtle*
received as Catholike: This part above all the reſt, is ſo ſtuffed
with hereſies and ſlanders, that I doe conſtantly affirme, that
none of all their Romane Alcumiſts can extract or diſtill one
dramme of Catholike doctrine, or any goodneſſe out of it. Only
Pope *Vigilius*, being, as I have often ſaid, blinded with Neſtorianiſme, and Cardinall *Baronius*, being infatuated with the admiration of their Pontificall *infallible* Chaire, they two by the new
found art of Tranſubſtantiating, wherein that ſect excelleth
Iannes and *Iambres*, and all the inchanters in the world, they by
one ſpell or charme of a few words pronounced out of that
holy chaire, can turne a ſerpent into a ſtaffe, bread into a living
bodie, darkeneſſe into light, an hereticke into a Catholike, yea
the very venome and poyſon of all Neſtorianiſme, into moſt
wholſome doctrines of the Catholike faith : ſuch, as that none
may write, ſpeake, or thinke ought to the contrarie.

21. See ye not now, as I foretold that you ſhould, both
the Pope, and the Cardinall, marching under the banner of *Neſtorius*; and like two worthy Generalls, holding up a ſtandard to
the Neſtorians, and building in the Romane Church, but very
cunningly and artificially, a Capitoll for Neſtorianiſme ? They
forſooth will not in plaine tearmes ſay that Neſtorianiſme is
the Catholike faith, that Chriſt is not God, that the Sonne of
Mary is not the Sonne of God, that *Cyrill* is an hereticke, and the
holy Epheſine Councell hereticall : Fie, theſe are too *Beoticall*,
and blunt, they could never have gotten any one to taſt of that
cup of Neſtorianiſme, had they dealt ſo plainely, or ſimply rather; *Rome* and *Italy*, are Schooles of better manners, and of
more civilitie and ſubtiltie : you muſt learne there to ſpeake
hereſie in the *Atticke Dialect*, in ſmooth, plauſible, ſweet and
ſugred tearmes; you muſt ſay the *union* which *Ibas* in his *Epiſtle*
embraceth is the Catholike union, that *Ibas* by embracing that
union was a Catholike, and ought to bee judged a Catholike;
that whoſoever embraceth not this union, which the Pope hath
defined to be the Catholike communion, cannot be a Catholike : or if you ſpeake more briefly and *Laconically*, you may
ſay, the Popes decrees and *Cathedrall* judgements in cauſes of
faith are infallible. Say but either of theſe, you ſay as much as
either *Theodorus* or *Neſtorius* did, you deny Chriſt to bee God;
You condemne the Epheſine Councell, you ſpeake true Neſtorianiſme, but you ſpeake it not after the rude and ruſticke faſhi-
on, but in that pureſt Ciceronian phraſe which is now the refined language of the Romane Church. By approving this union,
or the Popes decree in this cauſe of *Ibas*, you drinke up at once
all the blaſphemies and hereſies of *Neſtorius*, even the very dregs

of

of Neſtorianiſme; yet your comfort is,though it be ranke poiſon, you ſhall now take it as an antidote, and ſoveraigne potion, ſo cunningly tempered by Pope *Vigilius*, and with ſuch a grace and gravity commended, reached, and brought, even in the golden cup of *Babylon*, by the hands of Cardinall *Baronius* unto you, that it killeth, not onely without any ſenſe of paine, but with a ſweet delight alſo, even in a pleaſing ſlumber and dreame of life; bringing you, as on a bed of downe, unto the pit of death.

22. See here again their *Synonia* art. Oh how nice & ſcrupulous is *Baronius* in approving, or allowing *Vigilius* to approve the former part of this *Epiſtle* of *Ibas*? The *Epiſtle* ° was in no other part, but onely in the laſt concerning the union approved: Why? there is nothing at all in the former, no hereſie; or impiety ſet downe in it, which doth not certainly and unavoydably enſue upon the approving of that union in Neſtorianiſme, which *Ibas* embraceth in the latter part. Why then muſt the latter, and not the former be approved? Forſooth in the former part ᵖ the blaſphemies of the Neſtorians are in too plaine and blunt a manner expreſſed; *Cyrill* is an Apollinarian; The twelve Chapters of *Cirill, omni impietate plena ſunt*, are full of all impietie. The *Epheſine* Councell unjuſtly depoſed *Neſtorius*, and approved the twelve Chapters of *Cyrill*, which are *contraria veræ fidei*, and ſuch like. It is not for a Pope or a Cardinall to approve ſuch plaine and perſpicuous hereſies; they might as well ſay, We are heretikes, wee are Neſtorians: which kinde of *Beoticiſme* is farre from the civility of the Romane Court: But in the latter part the hereſies of *Neſtorius* and all his blaſphemies are offered in the ſhew of union with *Cyrill*, and communion with the Church; and comming under the vaunt of that union, as in the wombe of the Trojane horſe, the Pope and the Cardinall may now with honour receive them; the union (and with, or in it all Neſtorianiſme) muſt be brought into the City, the Pope and the Cardinall will themſelves put their hands to this holy worke, *pedibuſque rotarum ſub. ijciunt lapſus, & ſtupea vincula collo intendunt*, themſelves will drag and hale it with their owne ſhoulders to within the wals: nor is that enough, it muſt be placed in the very Romane Capitoll, in the holy temple, and conſecrated to God, and that the Pope himſelfe will doe by an *Apoſtolicall* and infallible conſtitution: by that immutable decree is this union ſet up as the Catholike union, *Et monſtrum infœlix ſacrata ſiſtitur arce*; this unholy and unhappy union is now embraced, by which all the gates of the City of God are ſet wide open for all hereſies to ruſh in at their pleaſure, and make havocke of the Catholike faith.

23. Now it is not unworthy our labour to conſider whether *Vigilius* and *Baronius* did in meere ignorance, or wittingly embrace this union mentioned by *Ibas*, that is in truth, all Neſtorianiſme. And for *Vigilius*, if any will be ſo favourable as to interpret

ᵒ *Bar. an.* 553. *nu.* 192.

ᵖ *Vid. Epiſt. Iba loc. cit.*

pret all this to have proceeded of ignorance, I will not greatly contend with him. It is as great a crime for their Romane *Apollo*, and as foule a disgrace to their *infallible* Chaire upon ignorance to decree an heresie, as to do it upon wilfull obstinacy; yet to cōfesse the truth, I am more than of opinion that *Vigilius* not upon ignorance, but out of a setled judgment & affection wch he bare to Nestorianisme decreed this union, and with it the doctrines of *Nestorius* to be embraced: And that which induceth mee so to judge, is the great diligence, care, and circumspection which *Vigilius* used to enforme both himselfe and others in this matter; for besides that this cause was debated, and continually discussed in the Church for the space of six yeares and more, before the Pope published this his *Apostolicall* Constitution, (all which time *Vigilius* was a chiefe party in this cause) himselfe in his decree witnesseth concerning this *third Chapter*, or *Epistle* of *Ibas*, that he examined it, *diligenti* [p] *investigatione*, *by a diligent inquisition*; yea, that he perused his bookes most [q] diligently for this point, and concludeth both of it, and the rest, that hee decreed these things, *cum* [r] *omni undique cautela atque diligentia*; *with all possible care and diligence that could be used*: And because, *plus vident oculi quam oculus*, hee added to his owne the judgement of an whole Synod of Bishops, all of them bending their eyes, wits, & industry to find out the truth in this cause. Further yet *Vigilius* speaketh in this cause of *Ibas* not doubtfully, but in words proceeding from certaine knowledge and resolute judgment, *dilucide*, [s] *aperteque reperimus*, *evidenter* [t] *advertimus*, *apertissimum* [u] *noscuntur præbuisse consensum*, *evidenter* [x] *declaratur*, *in Iba Episcopo nihil in confessione fidei fuisse reprehensum*, *illud* [y] *indubitanter patet*, *apertissima* [z] *lucet veritate ex verbis Epistolæ*, *constat* [a] *eundem Ibam communicatorem Cyrilli fuisse toto vitæ ejus tempore*, *luce clarius* [b] *demonstratur*: All which doe shew, that *Vigilius* spake out of his setled judgement and resolution, after most diligent examination of this cause. Now that the whole *Epistle*, and, of all parts, that especially where *Ibas* intreateth of the union, that this is full of Nestorianisme, is so evident, that scarce any, though but of a shallow judgement, who doth with ordinary diligence peruse and ponder the same, can otherwise chuse than observe, and see it. Wherefore I cannot thinke but that *Vigilius* both saw and knew that part of the *Epistle*, above all the rest, to containe the doctrines of *Nestorius*, and an approbation of them all, and that by approving the union there mentioned, he approved all the doctrines of the Nestorians.

p *Vig. Const. nu. 186.*
q *Gesta Concily Chalc. dili entissime perquirentes. Ibid.*
r *Ibid. nu. 208.*
s *Nu. 186.*
t *Nu. 190.*
u *ibid.*
x *Nu. 193.*
y *Nu. 195.*
z *Nu. 196.*
a *Nu. 198.*
b *Nu. 207.*

24. But for cardinall *Baronius*, that hee in defending the latter part of this *Epistle*, as doth *Vigilius* before him, that in striving so earnestly by it to prove *Ibas* to have beene a catholike, and his *Epistle* to be orthodoxall, at least in the latter part, because *Ibas* assented to the *union* mentioned therein; that he I say did herein wittingly, willingly, and obstinately labour to maintaine

taine the condemned heresie of *Nestorius* : for my owne part I cannot almost doubt, nor, as I thinke, will his best friends when they have well considered of his words : He intreating of this matter touching *Ibas* and his *Epistle*, in another place, where this *Constitution* of *Vigilius* comes not to the scanning, and so did not dimme his sight, ingenuously there confesseth, that this *Epistle* is hereticall, written by a Nestorian, written of purpose to disgrace *Cyrill*, and the catholikes, as if they at the union had recanted their former doctrines. But let us heare his owne words.

c Bar.an.432.nu. 68. absq̃ condemnatione suarum Capitulorum, cunsta arbitrio Cyrilli gesta sunt.
d An.eod.nu.69.
e Ibid.nu.70.

f Ibid.nu.71.

25. He having shewed [c] that the union was made in every point according to *Cyrils* minde, and without the condemning of his twelve Chapters, addeth this, *They* [d] *who favoured Nestorius spred abroad a rumour, that Cyrill had in all things consented unto Iohn, and condemned his former doctrines :* and a little after declaring [e] how the Nestorians did slander *Cyrill*, he saith, Besides others, who tooke part with *Nestorius*, even *Theodoret* also, *ijsdem aggressus est Cyrillum urgere calumnijs, vexed Cyrill with the same slanders,* that he had condemned his owne Chapters; and then comming to this *Epistle* of *Ibas*, he thus writeth, *Who* [f] *so desireth to see further the sleights of the Nestorians, let him reade the Epistle,* w^ch *is said to be the Epist. of Ibas unto Maris,* wherin any may see the Nestorian fellow insulting and triumphing, as if the cause had beene adjudged to him, *& jactantem Cyrillum pœnitentem, tandem recantasse palinodiam,* and vaunting that *Cyrill* repenting himselfe of his former doctrines, did now at last revoke the same, and sing a new song. And this the author of that *Epistle* writ, and sent abroad as a Circular *Epistle*, to be read throughout the Provinces, *pro solatio eorum, & ignominia Catholicorum;* for the comfort of the Nestorians, and for the disgrace of Catholikes, Thus *Baronius.* Professing as you see, that he knew this Epistle to be hereticall, and that even in the latter end, which *Vigilius* and himself defendeth as orthodoxall, yea, evē in that very point touching the *union* mentioned in that *Epistle*, to be a meere calumnie against *Cytill*, and the Catholikes, as if they, by making the *union*, had consented to Nestorianisme, and renounced the *Ephesine* Councell, and the Catholike faith.

26. Seeing now the Card. knew all this to be true, and yet afterwards for defence of *Vigilius* and his *Constitution*, teacheth and maintaineth, that by embracing the *union* mentioned in this *Epistle, Ibas* was a Catholike, and was for this cause by the Councell at *Chalcedon*, and ought by all others to be adjudged a Catholike, is it not evident that the Cardinall wittingly and willingly maintaines hereby the union with the Nestorians to bee the catholike union, and so the doctrines of the Nestorians to bee the catholike faith ? for this *union* mentioned in the *Epistle*, is, as the Cardinall professeth, an union in Nestorianisme, an union with *Cyrill*, having now renounced the *Ephesine* Councell, and the catholike faith.

27. Onely

27. Onely there is one quirke or subtilty in the Cardinals words, which may not without great wrong unto him bee omitted, where he acknowledgeth this *Epistle* to be g hereticall, & hereticall in this point of the *union*, there he will not h have it to be the *Epistle* of *Ibas*, for then by it *Ibas* should bee judged a Nestorian, which would quite overthrow the *Constitution* of *Vigilius*: when in the other i place he defends, as *Vigilius* decreeth, that *Ibas* by this *Epistle*, and by consenting to this *union* was a Catholike, and ought to bee judged a Catholike, there the *Epistle* is truly the *Epistle* of *Ibas*, but then consenting to this *union* is the note of a Catholike: So both this *Epistle* is the Epistle of *Ibas*, and it is not the *Epistle* of *Ibas*; and to consent to the union herein mentioned, is the note of a Nestorian heretike; and to consent to the same union, is the note of a good Catholike. Thus doth the Cardinall play, & sport himselfe in contradictions, and as the winde blowes and turnes him, so doth he turne his note also: If the winde blow to *Alexandria*, and turne the Cardinals face towards *Cyrill*, then the union is hereticall, lest *Cyrill* who condemned it, should bee condemned for an heretike. If the winde blow from *Africke*, and turne the Cardinals face towards *Rome* and Pope *Vigilius*, then the union is Catholike, lest *Vigilius* approving this union, should not be thought a Catholike. Or because a Cardinall so learned, so renouned as *Baronius*, may not be thought to contradict himselfe, or speake amisse in either place, let both sayings be admitted for true, and then it unavoydably followeth, that by the Cardinals divinity, and in his judgment, Nestorianisme is the Catholike faith; which aptly and easily will accord both his sayings, for so the author of this *Epistle* by approving this union shall be a perfect Nestorian, as in the one place is affirmed; and by approving this union shall be withall a perfect Catholike, as in the other place is avouched.

28. Besides this confession of *Baronius*, which is cleare enough, here is yet another meanes to demonstrate that the Cardinall by defending this latter part of the *Epistle* touching the union, did wittingly and wilfully maintaine the condemned heresie of *Nestorius*: for the fift generall Councell, approved, as wee have shewed, by the judgment of the whole Catholike Church, hath adjudged this very part k of the *Epistle*, the defence whereof *Baronius* hath undertaken, not onely to bee hereticall, but to bee more full of blasphemies than any of the rest; it hath l further judicially defined al that defend either this, or any part of that Epistle, to be heretikes, and for such it hath anathematized them, yea, all that write m either for it, or for them. Now the Cardinall had read the whole fift Councell, as appeareth by that summary collection n which he hath made of the Acts, and of every Collation thereof; nay, hee had not onely read these Acts, but tried earnestly with a jealous and carping eie, into every corner and sentence thereof, as you shall perceive hereafter; and therefore

g *Videre est Nestorianum hominem, &c. Bar. an. 432. nu. 71.*

h *Non esse Ibæ comperta. ibid.*

i *Vigilius asserere voluit ex eâ Epistolâ Ibam esse recipiendum, in qua nimirum ipse testatur se amplecti pacem ecclesiæ, qua recepta, necesse fuerit eundem probare Catholicum. Bar. an. 533. nu. 191.*

k *Posteriora enim inserta Epistolæ, majori impietate plena sunt, Cyrillum et familia ei sapientes injurantia, et omnino impiam sectam Nestorij vindicantia. Conc. 5. Coll. 6. pa. 564. a. Scimus et nos hæc ita subsequuta est, &c. ibid.*

l *Qui dicit eam rectam esse, vel partem ejus. Coll. 8. pa. 587. b.*

m *Eos qui scripserunt vel scribunt pro ea. ibid.*

n *Extat in Annal. Bar an. 553. a. nu. 33. ad 217.*

fore

fore it is doubtlesse that hee knew the judgement of this fift
Councell, concerning all that defend any part of this *Epistle*,
and specially the latter part, which concernes the *union*. Neither
onely did he know that to be the judgement of this fift Councell, but (as himselfe ○ expresly witnesseth) of all both Popes, and
generall Councels which followed it, all of them approving this
fift Councell, and the judgement thereof; whence it is cleare,
that *Baronius* knew certainly himselfe by defending this part
of the *Epistle* touching the *union*, to defend that which by the
judgment of the fift Councell, and the whole Catholike Church
ever since hath beene condemned for hereticall, and the defenders of it anathematized as heretikes : yet such was the Cardinals zeale, and ardent affection to Nestorianisme, that against
the judgement of the whole Church knowne unto him, yea,
knowne for this very cause to anathematize him, yet he defends
the *union* there mentioned, and the latter part of that *Epistle*,
wherein it is mentioned, that is in truth, all the blasphemies of
Nestorius, chosing rather, by adhering to *Vigilius* and his hereticall decree, to be condemned, and anathematized by the whole
Catholike Church for a Nestorian heretike, than by forsaking
the defence of *Vigilius*, and his decree, to condemne this latter
part of the *Epistle of Ibas*, touching the *union*, which containeth
in it the very quintessence of all Nestorianisme.

○ *At.553.nu.229.*

29. I think it is now sufficiently apparent by that which wee
have already said, that the union which *Ibas* in his *Epistle* mentioneth and embraceth, and which *Vigilius* first, and after him *Baronius* approveth, is not that true union in the Catholike faith,
which *Cyrill* made with *Iohn* and other Easterne Bishops; but
onely an union in Nestorianisme, and in denying the Catholike
faith, to which the Nestorians falsly reported and slandered *Cyrill*, with the other Catholikes, to have consented, and thereby
to have condemned and anathematized that truth, which the
yeare before they had decreed at *Ephesus*; Yet for the full satisfaction of all, and clearing of all doubts which may arise, I will
adde one thing further which will much more manifest both
the calumnie of the Nestorians, and the constancy of Saint *Cyrill*,
and that is, upon what colour or pretence the Nestorians raised
this slanderous report, which I am the more desirous to explane,
because the narration of this matter is extreamly confounded,
and entangled by *Baronius* and *Binius*, and that, as may be feared,
even of set purpose, that they might either quite discourage
others (as almost they had done my selfe) in the search of this
truth, or at least misleade them into such by-paths, that they
should not finde the truth in this matter.

30. When *Theodosius* the religious Emperour had written by
Aristolaus that earnest letter to *Iohn*, and the other Easterne Bishops, perswading, yea, commanding them to consent with *Cyrill*, and embrace the Catholike communion; they upon the Emperours

perors motion fought indeed to make an union with *Cyrill*, but they laboured to effect it by drawing *Cyrill* unto their bent, and to confent unto their herefies. This they firft attempted by a letter of *Acatius* Bifhop of *Berea*, willing [p] him to write, in all their names unto *Cyrill*, that no unity, or concord could be made, but according to thofe conditions which themfelves fhould prefcribe : and the condition prefcribed by them, was that *Cyrill* fhould [q] abolifh and condemne all that ever hee had written againft Neftorianifme, and fo both his twelve Chapters, and the Ephefine decree, and all the like. *Cyrill* anfwered [r] with great confidence : *rem eos poftulare quæ fieri plane non poffet, that they required a matter utterly impoſsible,* becaufe what hee had written touching that matter, was rightly written, and in defence of the true faith, and therefore that he could not either condemne, or deny what he had written.

31. When it fucceeded not this firft way, they next attempted to effect the *union* by *Paulus* [ſ] Bifhop of *Emiſa*, whom they fent to *Alexandria*, to negotiate for them both by words, and by a fecond letter which they fent by him. And although they were not in this fecond fo violent as in the former of *Acatius*, yet they writ [t] fome things therein alfo, not fitting, nor allowable; for they reproved the holy Ephefine Councell, as if things had been fpoken, and done therein amiffe; What did *Cyrill* anfwer? *Hujufmodi epiftolas equidem non admiſi,* truly I did not admit or allow of this their fecond Epiftle neither, feeing therein they did adde new contumelies, who fhould have asked pardon for the old. But where as *Paulus* did very earneftly excufe the matter, affirming, and that upon his oath alfo, that their purpofe was not to exafperate *Cyrill*, but to accord with him, *dilectionis gratia excufationem admiſi,* I in charity was content to admit of this excufe. And *Paulus* being very defirous to effect the *union*, confented to anathematize *Neſtorius* and his herefies; to confent alfo to the depofing of *Neſtorius*, and the electing of *Maximianus* in his place : which when *Paulus* had performed, and fubfcribed *ſuo chyrographo, with his owne hand-writing,* (which was all that either the Emperor or *Cyrill* required) *ad ſynaxim recepi,* I received him to the communion of the Church. But when *Paulus* would further have perfwaded *Cyrill*, that feeing he was fent in the name of the reft, and had fubfcribed this, *pro omnibus, & tanquam ex communi omnium orientalium perſona, for them all, and as it were in the perſon of them all :* and therefore laboured with *Cyrill*, that this his fubfcription might fatisfie for the others alfo, and that he would require no more of them, but be content with their letters which by him they had fent; *nulla ratione id fieri paſſus ſum,* faith *Cyrill*, *I could by no meanes indure that :* I told *Paulus* alfo, that his fubfcription in condemning *Neſtorius* and his herefies, *Ipſi ſoli ſufficere, could fatisfie but only for himſelfe,* but as for the reft, *Iohn* [u] and they muft perfonally, and for themfelves fubfcribe; or elfe they

N   could

p *Apud Acatium Bereenſem Epiſcopli congreſſi, ſcribi ad me curarunt, pacem concordiamq; niſi eo modo quem præſcriberent, fieri non debere, Epiſt. Cyrilli ad Acatium, quæ eſt 29. & ext. tom. 5. Act. Epheſ. ca. 7. & idem habetur in Epiſt. Cyrilli ad Dynatum tom. ead. ca. 16.*

q *Vrgebat ut omnibus quæ adverſus Neſtorium ſcripſimus abolitis & velut inutilibus rejectis, &c. Epiſt. ad Dynat. & ſimilia habentur in Epiſt Cyrill. ad Acat. locis cit.*

r *Cyrill. Epiſtola ad Dynat. & ad Acat.*

ſ *Miſerunt Alexandriam Paulum Epiſcopum Emiſenorū &c. ibid.*

t *Attulit quædam parum decore & commode propoſita, ibid.*

u *Modū omnibus opus eſſe dixi ut Habenes ſcriptam de his confeſſionem edi. ret, &c. Cyrill. Epiſt. ad Acatium.*

x Nisi chartam qua
significavi, si Iohan-
nes illi subscripserit,
tum communionem
illis reddue. Cyrill.
Epist.ad Dynat.

y Cum Iohannes
subscripsisset, cæteriq;
qui majore autho-
ritate apud ipsum
erant, Cyrill.Epist.
ad Dynat.
z Ea extat inter E-
pist.Cyrilli Epist.27.
& in Act. Conc. E-
phes.to.5.ca.5.
a Miserunt autem
eandem Epistolam,
quam ad me scripse-
runt ad Xistum &
Maximianum, Cy-
rill.Epist. ad Dynat.
b Placuit nobis Ne-
storium pro deposito
habere, pravasque
illius prophanasque
novitates anathe-
matizare. Epist. Sy-
nodalis Iohannis
Antioch. & Synodi
Antioch.to.5. Act.
Ephes.ca.5.
c Nos Dominum no-
strum Paulum ad
sanctitatem tuam
mittendum duximus
Epist.Iub. & Synod.
Antioch.loco jam ci-
tato, & ex charta,
quam Dominus meus
Paulus nunc attulit
evidenter cognosci-
mus. Continet enim
inculpatam fidei
confessionem.Cyrill.
Epist.28.quæ est ad
Iohannem Antioch.
& extat tom.5. Act.
Ephes.ca.6.
d Nempe 29. mensis
Chiath.i.Decembris.
to.6. Act.Ephes. ca.
13.in tit.
e Ibid.to.6.ca.13.
f Epist.Cyrilli 28.
quæ extat tom.5.
Act.Ephes.ca.6.

could not bee received into communion : whereupon *Cyrill* writ an orthodoxall profession x to that same effect, whereunto *Paulus* had subscribed, and sent it unto *Iohn*, requiring his personall subscription to it. This was the summe of all that was done by *Paulus* at his first comming.

32. *Paulus* returning to *Antioch*, brought this resolute answer of *Cyrill*, to *Iohn*, and the Bishops of his Synod. They seeing no other meanes to make an union, but onely by consenting to *Cyrill*; and seeing that *Paulus*, whom they put in trust as their agent, had both himselfe consented, and further undertaken that *Iohn* and they should likewise consent unto the same which hee had done, did now at length yeeld y to all the demands of *Cyrill*: and for an assurance of their sincerity therein, they writ a Synodall z and *Encyclicall* Epistle unto *Cyrill*, which they likewise sent unto Pope *Sixtus*, to *Maximianus*, and other principall Bishops, wherein they first set downe a very sound, true and orthodoxall confession of their faith, and then testifie their willing assent and subscription, to the deposing b of *Nestorius*, and the condemning of his heresies.

33. This Synodall letter they sent to *Cyrill* by *Paulus* c Bishop of *Emisa*, that he might make a finall peace, and union. At whose comming to *Alexandria* this second time, and bringing with him this undoubted testimony of the orthodoxie of *Iohn*, and the chiefe of the Easterne Bishops, and that they had now consented to all which either the Emperour, or *Cyrill* required of them, the union was fully concluded on every part, and peace made in the Church : In token whereof *Paulus* preached at *Alexandria*, in the month of December d, making there before *Cyrill*, and the whole City, so orthodoxall a profession of the faith, that the people for joy interrupting him foure or five times, exclamed e, *Bene venisti Orthodoxe, O Orthodox Paul thou art welcome to us*, *Cyrill* is orthodoxall, *Paulus* is orthodoxall : and *Cyrill* for his part writ that learned Epistle f in congratulation unto *Iohn*, and the rest which beginneth, *Let the Heavens rejoyce, and let the earth be glad*, publishing it as *an hymne of joy and thanksgiving for the union now effected in the Church*, singing *Glory unto God, and peace among men*.

34. This is the true narration of the whole proceedings betwixt *Cyrill*, and the Easterne Bishops touching this matter of the union, as they who diligently peruse the Epistles of *Cyril* to *Acatius* Bishop of *Melitene*, to *Dynatus*, and *Iohn*, and compare therewith the Epistle of *Iohn*, and the Synod of *Antioch* sent to *Cyrill* and *Xistus*, will clearly perceive, whence three things may be observed : The first is the most shamelesse dealings of the Nestorians, who slandered *Cyrill* to have at the time of the union consented in all points unto them, and to their heresie, and to have condemned his former doctrine, and the Ephesine Councell, wheras the quite contrary was true. He was most inflexible and

and constant in maintaining the true faith; more inexorable than *Æacus*, or rather, as *Moses* g would not consent to *Pharoah*, no, hot in the least hoofe, so would not *Cyrill* yeeld one heire-bredth unto them, but brought them to subscribe wholly, and in every point, to that which he desired.

35. The second is, the occasion which the Nestorians tooke for their pretended calumnie: They knew that *Iohn* and the Easterne Bishops had written to *Cyrill*, willing him to condemne his owne Chapters; yea, that they had writ so resolutely, that unlesse *Cyrill* did so, they would not consent unto any peace, or union. Thus much was true, as by the letter of *Acatius* Bishop of *Berea* to *Cyrill* is evident: Now they saw that *Cyrill* afterwards, and in that very yeare consented with *Iohn*, and made union with him, whereupon they boasted that *Cyrill* did it upon the condition required by *Iohn* at the first, which was the condemning of his former doctrine; wilfully and maliciously concealing both how *Cyrill* utterly denyed to yeeld unto them, or to that condition required by them; and how at the length *Iohn*, and so many of them as were received into communion, consented wholly unto him, and subscribed to the Catholike faith. All this they quite suppresse; and, to colour the matter, they forged h a letter under the name of *Cyrill*, as consenting to condemne his owne doctrine; which no doubt was the same letter that *Ibas* in his Epistle inclosed, and sent unto *Maris* the heretike.

36. The third is, how *Baronius* hath perverted the narration of this *union*, and strengthened the calumnie of the Nestorians by his misreporting of the same: But first we must set downe the Cardinals words; *Vpon the Emperours letters* (saith hee i) *sent unto Iohn, commanding him, and the rest, to agree with Cyrill. Iohn and the Easterne Bishops met together in a Synod at Antioch, and they agreed to* k *ratifie the condemnation of Nestorius, and his heresie, as the Emperour had required them to doe; and so to make union with the Pope, with Cyrill, and with the Catholike Church.* According to this agreement they made a Synodall decree, and Synodall l Epistle, containing the condemning of *Nestorius*, with his heresies; and an orthodoxal profession which they sent to Pope *Sixtus*, and other Catholike Bishops, to testifie their communion with them al m. This Epistle n by the way, is in effect the o same which *Paulus* Bishop of *Emisa* brought, at his second comming into *Alexandria*. The Cardinall proceeding, tels us, that this Epistle was sent as common to all, save p onely to *Cyrill*; but as for *Cyrill*, against whom they had most bitter enmity, *aliter* q *sibi agendum putarunt*; *they would take another course*, and deale after another manner with him; and marke, I pray you, how that was, they would so deale with him, *ut* r *ab eo exigerent Catholicæ fidei confessionem, quâ sua Capitula velut erronea condemnaret: so that they would exact of him a Catholike confession, wherein hee should condemne his owne twelve Chapters as erronious* : and when *Cyrill* refused so to doe,

N 2   in

g *Exod.* 10.26.

h *Si qua Epistola à quibusdam circumferatur tanquam à me, de ijs quæ Ephesi acta sunt jam delente, & pænitentiâ agente, perscripta, ea quoque consemnatur. Cyrill. Epist. ad Acat. in fine.*

i *Bar.an.* 432.nu.54

k *Consultius deliberatur, ratam habendam esse damnationè heresis Nestorianæ. Ibid.*

l *Iohannes ex Synodo tunc Antiochiæ habita, de damnatione Nestorij, et ejus hæresi, Synodalem dedit Epistolam. ib.*

m *Hactenus Epistola communis omnibus quidem Episcopis Catholicæ fidei, qui Catholicam Ecclesiarum omnium communionem nancisceretur. Bar.an. eodem na.56.*

n *Epistola illa extat to.5.Act. Conc. Eph.ca.*17.

o *Nam in utraque damnatur Nestorius, et illius hæresis, et approbatur Synodus Ephesina, vide, et confer Epistolas.*

p *Dedit Epistolam ad Sixtum.Bar.an.* 432.nu.54.*quæ erat communis omnibus Episcopis Catholicis. Ibid.nu.56*

q *Ibid.nu.57.*

r *Ibid.*

in the next place they send *Paulus* Bishop of *Emisa*, as their Legate, unto *Cyrill*, *qui si posset ab eo quod petitum antea furat, exterqueret: who should, if by any meanes hee could, wring from Cyrill that which before they required;* (to wit, the condemning of his Chapters;) but if he could not doe that, nor prevaile therein with *Cyrill, tunc de damnatione Nestorij literas ei redderet; then they willed Paulus to deliver unto Cyrill their Synodall letters, written by them, containing the condemnation of Nestorius, and his heresie.* Thus *Baronius*; and ^f *Binius* traceth him in these steps.

f *Bin. Notis in Côc. Antioch. tempore Sixti.*

37. In which narration of the Cardinall, besides many untruths wherewith it is stuffed, there are two things, above all the rest, to be observed. The former is, how wise and politike the Cardinall doth make *Iohn*, and the whole Synod of *Antioch*, to be in this matter of the union: first, they condemne the heresies of *Nestorius*, approve the Ephesine Councell, and by so doing approve the twelve Chapters of *Cyrill*; they doe this in a Synod, and publish their Synodall decree at *Rome*, at *Constantinople*, and other places, to shew and testifie themselves to bee truly orthodoxall; and when all this is done, they labour earnestly, with *Cyrill*, to make him condemne his owne twelve Chapters, which is in effect to maintaine Nestorianisme; to condemne the Ephesine Councell, (wherein his Chapters were approved) yea, to condemne their owne Synodall decree, by which themselves, at *Antioch*, had condemned *Nestorius*, and approved the Chapters of *Cyrill*. Againe, he makes *Iohn*, and his Synod to communicate with *Sixtus*, with *Maximianus*, with all other Catholikes save *Cyrill*, and them of his Patriarchship; with all the former they will communicate, though they all approved the twelve Chapters of *Cyrill*; with *Cyril* they will not communicate, unlesse he will condemne the same twelve Chapters. If they thought the twelve Chapters to be hereticall, why hold they communion with *Sixtus*, *Maximianus*; and others who approved them? nay, why did themselves approve them? If they thought them orthodoxall, why would they (being themselves orthodoxall) perswade, yea, enforce and wring out of *Cyrill* a condemnation of the orthodoxall faith? Besides, what a worthy peece of policy was this, which the Cardinall doth fasten upon *Iohn*, and all the rest? he makes them to send *Paulus*, a reverend Bishop, with a letter purposely to be delivered to *Cyrill*, which testified their Synodall, and willing consent in approving the twelve Chapters of *Cyrill*, that is, of the Catholike faith, and yet command *Paulus* to urge and wring from *Cyrill*, if he could, a condemnation of those twelve Chapters, that is, of the whole Catholike faith? What deepe dissemblers and hypocrites doth hee make *Iohn*, *Paul*, and the rest of those orthodoxall Bishops? Lastly, of what faith or religion, doe you thinke, must *Iohn*, *Paul*, and the rest be, by the Cardinals narration. By their Synodall sentence, and holy confession therein; they appove the twelve Chapters

of

of *Cyrill*, and so are perfect Catholikes; againe, by their urging of *Cyrill* to condemne his twelve Chapters, they are perfect Nestorians, for the condemning of them, is the defending of all the Nestorian heresies; so, by the Cardinals divinity, they are at the selfe same time, both perfect Nestorians, and perfect Catholikes; which can no way be effected, but by admitting the Cardinals old position, which he learned of *Vigilius*, that perfect Nestorianisme is the perfect Catholike faith.

38. Into such labyrinths doth the Cardinals foule misreporting of this matter leade, and even draw a man; whereas the truth, as, by that which formerly hath beene declared, is evident, that *Iohn*, and the rest of the Synod, when they vrged *Cyrill* to condemne his Chapters, had not made that Synodall decree for condemning of *Nestorius*; & when they had once made that decree, they never, either by word or writing, urged *Cyrill* to condemne those Chapters: Before they made that decree, and condemned *Nestorius*, they were hereticall, and held communion neither with *Cyrill*, nor *Sixtus*, nor any other Catholikes: After they had made that decree, and condemned *Nestorius* with his heresies, they were orthodoxall, & communicated no lesse with *Cyrill*, thã with *Sixtus*, or any other Catholike; nay, they cõmunicated first of all with *Cyrill*, & then with all other Catholikes.

39. The other point to bee observed out of the Cardinalls words, is, that by his narration *Cyrill* did indeed, as *Ibas* and the Nestorians slandered him, renounce & reject the Catholike faith, for the Cardinall makes *Paulus* of *Emisa* but to goe once to *Alexandria* about the union, or if any can finde in the Cardinall a second journey thither, yet by his narratiõ, the Synodall Epistle of *Iohn*, and the rest, wherein they condemne *Nestorius*, and set downe an orthodoxall profession, that Epistle was sent by *Paulus* at the first time, for he had withall in charge to urge *Cyrill* to condemne his twelve Chapters, which at his last going had beene absurd and incongruous. So then the Epistle which *Paulus*, at his first going to *Cyrill* brought with him, was the orthodoxall Epistle of *Iohn*, and the Synod. Now it is certaine by the expresse words of *Cyrill*, that the letter which *Iohn* and the rest, sent by *Paulus* at his first going, was rejected by *Cyrill*, for he saith of that Epistle, *hujusmodi epistolas non acceptavi*, I did not accept this Epistle sent by Paul: and the Cardinall [t] citing those words of *Cyrill verbatim*, and making some prettie collection out of them, could not be ignorant hereof. Seing then by the Cardinalls narration, the Epistle which *Paulus* brought at his first comming, was orthodoxall, and seeing it is certaine that *Cyrall* rejected that Epistle, which *Paulus* at his first comming brought from *Iohn*, it inevitably followeth, upon the Cardinalls narration, that *Cyrill* indeed rejected an orthodoxall and Catholike profession, containing the condemnation of *Nestorius*, and his heresies, and therefore that *Cyrill* renounced

t *Bar. an.*43 2. *nu.* 66.

his former Catholike doctrine, & consented to Nestorianisme, which is the same calumnie wherewith *Ibas* in his impious *Epistle*; slandereth *Cyrill.* And although *Baronius* doe in words deny this, as I know hee doth, yet considering the deepe projects which the Cardinall hath; it may bee feared, that he meant by this meanes, cunningly, and closely, to lay a foundation to up-hold that union, in which *Ibas* in his Epistle rejoyceth, and which *Vigilius* and the Cardinall himselfe approve for Catholike, or if the Cardinall intended not this, yet I am sure that hee hath then unwittingly devised, such a notable ground, to main-taine that slander, which *Ibas* imputeth to *Cyrill*, that at the time of the union he rejected his former doctrines, as that neither *Ibas* himselfe, nor any of the old Nestorians could possibly have forged a more faire and colourable pretence for the same.

40. My conclusion now of this their former reason, for defence of the impious *Epistle* of *Ibas*; drawne from the *union* mentioned therein, is this : Seeing that *union* mentioned and approved by *Ibas* in the later part of his *Epistle*, is no other but the *union* in Nestorianisme, unto which hee malitiously slandereth *Cyrill* to have consented : and seeing Pope *Vigilius* t, and Cardinall *Baronius* not onely approve as Catholike, the union there mentioned by *Ibas*, but prove by it and consenting to it, both *Ibas* himselfe to bee a Catholike, and his *Epistle*, in that part at least, to be orthodoxall, it hence cleerely ensueth, that *Vigilius* by his *Apostolicall* sentence defineth, and *Baronius* by name (as also all who maintaine the Popes *Cathedrall* sentence in causes of faith to bee *infallible*) *doe all defend Nestorianisme to be the Catholike union, and so Nestorianisme to bee the Catholike faith :* which whosoever affirmes; are by the judgement not o nely of the fift, but the fourth and third generall Councells, *con victed, condemned,* and *anathematized heretickes.*

CHAP. XII.

That Vigilius *and* Baronius *in their later reason for defence of the* Epistle *of* Ibas, *taken from the words of* Ibas, *wherein bee con-fesseth* two natures and one person in Christ, *doe maintaine the* *heresies of* Nestorius.

1. He other reason whereby they labour to defend this impious *Epistle*, and with no lesse fraud then they did in the former, is taken from the very confession of *Ibas*, set downe in his *Epistle*; wherein bee acknowledgeth Christ to have *two natures, and so bee one per-* *son.* His words to *Manis* the heretiche are these; neare the be-ginning of his *Epistle* a. *Cyrill* hath written twelve Chapters w hich

which I thinke your holinesse knoweth, wherein he teacheth, *quid nam est natura divinitatis & humanitatis, that there is one nature of the divinitie, and humanitie in Christ*, these things are full of all impiety; and giving a reason hereof, he addeth, for the Church, saith thus, as it hath beene taught from the beginning, and confirmed therein by the doctrine of the most blessed Fathers: *Duæ naturæ, una virtus, una persona, quod est unus filius, Dominus noster Iesus Christus, Two natures, one power, one person, which is one Sonne our Lord Iesus Christ:* Thus *Ibas*: which words seeme to be so true, so orthodoxall and Catholike, that *Vigilius* and *Baronius*, might either be themselves hereby deceived: or, which I rather thinke, judge them, as they are indeed, a most colourable pretence to deceive others, & lead them into Nestorianisme: for no Catholike can possibly in fairer tearmes, or better for shew of words, expresse against *Nestorius* the true doctrine of the Catholike faith, then to say that there are two natures in Christ, and yet but one person: This seeing *Ibas* professeth in his *Epistle*, and withall accurseth [b] those who deny two natures in Christ, sure none can thinke but this was a fit text for *Vigilius* and *Baronius*, by it to commend this impious *Epistle* as orthodoxall & Catholike, wherein so Catholike a confession seemeth to bee made. But let us see how the Pope and the Cardinall descant on these words.

2. *Baronius* saith not much, but yet hee speakes plainely of his matter; The fathers at *Chalcedon*, saith he [c], out of this *Epistle of Ibas*, gathered *Ibas* then (when he writ it) to be a Catholike, *utpote quod ex eadem epistola demonstratur ipse*, because by his very Epistle Ibas *was demonstrated*, both to have held communion with *Cyrill, execratusque esse unam naturam in Christo confitentes, confessus vero esse, naturas duas unam* [d] *[personam] efficere, Dominum nostrum Iesum Christum*, and also he was demonstrated by this Epistle, *to have accursed those who confesse one onely nature in Christ, and to have confessed the two natures, to make one person, and Lord Iesus Christ.* So *Baronius*: teaching not only that profession which *Ibas* makes in his Epistle, *of two natures, and one person*, to be Catholike; but that *Ibas* by that very confession proved, nay demonstrated to be a Catholike.

3. *Vigilius* handles this matter farre more largely, but very obscurely & mystically, as being indeed so miserably intangled in the birdlime of Nestorianisme, that hee knew not possibly how to unfold himselfe: I must first of all set downe his words, though they be many, and because they are very obscure, they will require more attentive, and serious ponderation: *Those things*, saith he [e], *which in the Epistle of Ibas, are injuriously spoken against Cyrill by a misunderstanding of Cyrills sayings, the Fathers of Chalcedon, when they pronounced the Epistle to be orthodoxall, did not receive;* for the venerable Bishop (*Ibas*) himselfe by changing, refuted those, when he had gotten better understanding of

b *Denuncians ei ut anathematizaret eos qui dicunt quia una est natura divinitatis et humanitatis. Ibas in eadem Epist.*

c *Bar. an. 448. nu. 75.*

d *Vox [personam] vitio Typographi deest apud Baron. sed ex constructione Grammatica, et ipso sensu, necessarie addendam liquet.*

e *Vig. Const. nu. 191.*

f Ibid. nu. 193.

of those Chapters which *Eunomius* in his interloquution doth most evidently declare. And [f] the interloquution of *Iuvenalis* doth signifie the same, who therefore decreed that *Ibas* should receive his Bishopricke, as holding the orthodoxall profession of faith, because he devoutly ranne, to embrace the communion with *Cyrill*, after that *Cyrill* had explaned his Chapters, and *Ibas* had understood them otherwise then before he did, though he had carped at *Cyrill*, when hee misunderstood those Chapters, for thus said *Iuvenalis*: *The holy Scripture commandeth that hee who is converted should be received, for which cause we receive such as returne from heretickes; wherefore I decree that the reverend* Ibas *should obtaine favour and receive his Bishopricke, both because he is an old man, and because he is a Catholike.* So *Iuvenalis*: By which this is understood: If wee receive such as returne from heretikes, how should we not receive *Ibas* who is a Catholike? whom it is manifest to be a Catholike, seeing hee is now converted, from that understanding of *Cyrills* Chapters, whereby hee was deceived, who while hee doubted of the understanding of those Chapters, did seem to speak against *Cyrill*: for never would *Iuvenalis* say that *Ibas* were a Catholike, unlesse he had proved by the words of this *Epistle* his confession to bee orthodoxall. And that the Interloquutions of *Iuvenalis* and *Eunomius* doe agree, the words of *Eunomius* doe shew, which are these: In what things *Ibas* seemed to blame *Cyrill*, by speaking ill, hee hath refuted all those things which he blamed, by making a right confession at the last. By which words of *Eunomius* it is evidently declared, that in the confession of faith, made by *Ibas*, nothing was reproved, seeing it is manifest, that his faith was praised; and that *Ibas* hath refuted that, which by misunderstanding *Cyrill*, hee had thought amisse of him.

g Ibid. nu. 194.

4. For [g] the same venerable *Ibas*, by the precedent Acts, (as the judgement of *Photius* and *Eustathius* doth shew) is most manifestly declared to receive and embrace all things which were done in the first Ephesine Synod, and judge them equall to the Nicene decrees, and to put no difference betwixt those and these at *Ephesus*: and *Eustathius* is shewed very much to commend the sanctity of *Ibas*, for that he was so ready and willing to cure those, who, either by suspition, or any other way did hurt the opinion of his learning: For after that *Cyrill* had explaned his twelve Chapters, and the meaning which *Cyrill* had in them was declared unto *Ibas*, after that, *Ibas* professed himselfe, with all the Easterne Bishops, to have esteemed *Cyrill* a Catholike, and to have remained, even unto his end, in the communion with him; whence it is cleare, that *Ibas*, both before he understood the twelve Chapters of *Cyrill*, and when hee suspected *one* (onely) *nature of Christ* to be taught and maintained by them, did then in an orthodoxal sense reject that which he thought to be spoken amisse in those Chapters; and also after the explanation thereof,

did

did in an orthodoxall fenfe reverently embrace thofe things which he knew to be rightly fpoken in thofe Chapters.

5. Further, [h] it doth without all doubt appeare to the minds of all the faithfull, that *Dioscorus* with *Eutiches*, did offer more wrong in the fecond Epheſine Synod, than *Ibas*, to *Cyrill* and the firſt Epheſine Councell, by underſtanding *Cyrils* Chapters in an hereticall fenfe, beleeving *Cyrill* to teach by his twelve Chapters one (onely) *nature in our Lord Iefus Chriſt*; and for this caufe did *Dioscorus* condemne fome of the Eaſterne Biſhops, who would not acknowledge *one* (only) *nature in Chriſt*; among whom he condemned as an heretike, and depofed *Ibas* from his Biſhopricke, fpecially for this very confeſſion of his faith, wherein hee moſt plainly profeſſeth *two natures, one power, one perfon, which is one Sonne, our Lord Iefus Chriſt* : and *Dioscorus* reſtored *Eutiches*, as a Catholike, for the confeſſion of *one* (onely) *nature in Chriſt*, condemning alfo *Flavianus*, of bleſſed memory, for the fame doctrine of holding *two natures* : And *Dioscorus* and *Eutiches* are found much more to indeavour to overthrow the firſt Epheſine Synod, while they defēd it under the ſhew of an execrable fenfe, (*of one nature*) and to ſlander *Cyrill* more while they praiſe him, than did *Ibas*, when, by the errour and miſconceiving of *Cyrils* meaning, he diſpraiſed him; for feeing their praiſe and diſpraiſe doe tend unto the fame thing, *Dioscorus* and *Eutiches*, who condemned *Cyrill*; are found to have commended him with an hereticall ſpirit, or in an hereticall fenfe, and therfore were they condemned in the Councell at *Chalcedon*; but *Ibas*, who at the firſt diſpraiſed *Cyrils* Chapters, thinking *one* (onely) *nature* to bee taught by them; and who, after the fenfe and meaning of them was declared unto him, did profeſſe himſelfe, with the Eaſterne Biſhops, to communicate with *Cyrill*, was judged by the fame Councell of *Chalcedon* to have continued in the right faith. Thus farre are the words of *Vigilius*, and fo much of his Conſtitution as concernes this profeſſion made by *Ibas*, of *two natures and one perſon in Chriſt*.

6. Words like the Oracles of *Apollo*, ful of thick darknes, & hiddē myſteries. Nor muſt you here expect any light at al from *Binius*; was wiſe enough to decline theſe rocks in the *Epiſt.* of *Ibas*, both that of the *union* with *Cyril*, this & of his cōfeſſing *two natures and one perſon*; at wch fearing to make ſhipwracke of faith, as *Vigilius* had done before, he thought it to be far the ſafeſt courſe at one ſtroke to wipe away and ſpunge out thoſe whole paſſages both out of the Popes *Conſtitution*, and his owne Tomes of Councels: beſt to have them ſmothered in ſilence, or buried in eternall oblivion. Add yet, to ſay truth, had *Binius* uſed all his art in this point, that alas would but have helped a little; he, poore lambe, is not able of himſelfe to wade, no not through ſhallow places, it would require an Elephant to ſwimme through ſuch a deepe : All his light is but borrowed of others, fpecially from *Baronius*, where

h Ibid. nu. 195

where *Baronius* is silent, he is more mute than a fish: yea, and when some of the Cardinals beames doe happen to collustrate his notes, yet even there they lose a great part of that vigour which they have in the Cardinals Phœbean lampe.

7. The only man in the world fit to make a full and just commentary on this text of *Vigilius*, had beene *Baronius* himselfe: He by his long acquaintance with Popes, and Court of *Rome*, by his continuall rifling of the Vaticane Manuscripts, and anatomising so many Pontificall decrees, had quicke sense of the Popes pulse, he knew every string and straine in their breasts. But so unhappily it fals out, that the Cardinall himselfe durst not touch this soare; he passeth it over, nay, rather shuffles it from him with deepe silence; wote you why? you may bee sure hee knew there was a padde in this straw, which had the Cardinall uncovered, his owne friends could not have indured the lothsome sent of the Pontificall *Constitution*, but for very shame would have swept it out of the Church of God. Now because it were great pitty that so many mysteries as lye hid in this part of the Popes decree should be unknowne to the world, and because the very explication of the Popes words, is a full conviction of his heresie, for want of a better, I will lend them my best endeavours to supply the defect of the Cardinals Commentary in this point: And although all that I can say is, *nihil ad Parmenonis suem*, nothing to that which you should have applauded, *si ipsam belluam audissetis*, if the Popes commentator had beene himselfe pleased to write hereof; yet truly, by long contemplation of the Popes workes, and industrious observing the Cardinals *artificium* in explaning the like decrees, I well hope that I shal be able *dolare*, and after a rude fashion to rough-hew a peece of a commentary at this time; onely not being trained up in their Romane Schooles, where they learne to speake silken and sugered words of their Popes, and sow the softest Pillowes under their elbowes; I must crave pardon, if according to the Macedonia rudenesse of our dialect I call a spade, a spade, a slander, a slander, and heresie, heresie, though it happen to be found even in his Holinesse himselfe, and in his Pontificall and *Cathedrall* decree: In hope of which pardon (specially since the fault is so veniall) I will now addresse my selfe to an unaccustomed taske of making a Commentary upon the Popes writings.

8. The scope and purpose of *Vigilius* in this whole passage, is, to prove not onely *Ibas* himselfe, but his faith and profession also to have beene Catholike, not onely when he writ this *Epistle*, but ever since *Cyrill* explaned his Chapters, and *Ibas* understood the same, which was before this *Epistle* was writ. And this appeares by the very words of *Vigilius*, who saith, that after *Cyrils* Chapters were explaned, and understood by *Ibas*, *in communionem ejus devote concurrerit*, he ranne, and hastened with devotion to embrace the communion with *Cyrill*; and having once embraced

it,

it, in *communione ipsius usque ad exitum permansisse; that he contin-*
ed in the same communion with Cyrill, even to the end of his life : and
as he was then a Catholike, so in this Epistle, which was writ
after *Cyrils* explanation, understood by him, hee expressed that
Catholike faith and profession, seeing [1] *Iuvenalis , ex verbis Epi-*
stolæ, ejus confessionem fidei orthodoxam comprobavit; proved the confes-
sion of Ibas to be orthodoxall by the very words of this Epistle. This is
the purpose then of my author, to shew both *Ibas* and his confession of faith, when he writ this *Epistle*, to have beene Catholike :
To prove this he useth three principal reasons; the first is drawne
from the explanation of *Cyrils* Chapters, which *Ibas* devourly
embraced; and this hee harps upon almost in every part of his
text, as you may easily see. The second is taken from his approbation of the holy *Ephesine* Councel before *Photius* and *Eustathius* ;
in these words, For the same venerable *Ibas*, &c. The third is
drawne from the very profession it selfe, and words thereof set
downe in the *Epistle* of *Ibas*, where he confesseth *two natures, and*
one person; and though there be a touch and taste of this throughout the whole text, yet is it specially and more expresly set
downe in those words, Further, it doth without all doubt appeare, &c. I must be inforced, for more perspicuities sake, to
invert the order of mine author, and begin with the exposition
of his third reason, because, if that be well understood, it will
serve for a torch to direct us in both the other.

9. In his third reason the Pope both affirmes, and by divers
meanes proves that confession of *Ibas*, which in his *Epistle* hee
makes to bee orthodoxall, and before wee handle his proofes
hereof we must diligently consider the position it selfe, or confession made by *Ibas* : *Ibas* his confession in his *Epistle* is, that
there are *two natures, and one person in Christ* : *This confession in his*
Epistle, saith *Vigilius* [m], *is orthodoxall; and for this was Ibas unjustly*
condemned by Dioscorus, but justly commended by the Councell at
Chalcedon. I must set an unpleasant, but a very true and certaine glosse upon these words, Both *Ibas*, and *Vigilius* commending him, and *Baronius* defending *Vigilius* herein, doe all Ne-
storianize; or, to speake more plainely, *Ibas* by that confession
in his *Epistle* teacheth, *Vigilius* by his *Cathedrall* decree confirmeth, *Baronius* gnatonically applaudeth, and they all three conspire in defending the condemned heresie of *Nestorius*.

10. For the full manifestation whereof it must bee observed,
that the Nestorians, the more plausibly to convey their heresie,
wherein they *denyed Christ the sonne of Mary to be God*, used the
very same words altogether which Chatholikes did. As Catholikes said that there are *two natures in Christ*, the divinity, and the
humanity, so said the Nestorians also : As Catholikes confessed *Christ to be our Lord*, so confessed the Nestorians likewise. In
words they both agreed and said the same, but in the sense and
meaning of those words they were quite contrary.

11. When

Marginal notes:

k *Ibid. nu.* 1; 4.

l *Ibid. nu.* 193.

m *Et ob hoc aliquos*
Orientales Episco-
pos, qui unius natu-
ræ prædicationem
noluerunt suscipere
Dioscorus condem-
navit, inter quotes
Ibam, propter hanc
specialiter fidei ejus
professionem, quæ
duas naturas, unam
virtutem, unam per-
sonam apertissimè
confitetur, hæreti-
cum condemnavit.
Vig. nu. 195.

11. When Catholikes said, that there are *two natures in Christ*, they meant truly & orthodoxally, that the divinity & humanity in Christ were differét in essence and substance, & yet they both made but one *hypostasis*, that is, but *one*, and not *two subsistent persons*: But when the Nestorians said, that there are *two natures in Christ*, they meant that either nature made a severall and *distinct person* by it selfe, and so they made *Christ to be two distinct persons*, each subsisting by it selfe, *two Sonnes, two Christs*, that is, in truth, *no Christ, no Saviour at all*; for a Saviour he cannot bee, unlesse the selfe same person which is man be God also.

12. Againe, when Catholikes said, that *Christ is one person*, they meant truly and orthodoxally, that both natures together make but one personall subsistence, as the humane soule and body make but one person, or one man: but when the Nestorians said, that *Christ was one person*, they meant not of that unity which is by naturall or personall subsistence, but *of unity in affection, of unity by consent and liking, of unity by cohabitation*; the person of the Sonne of God, so affecting and liking the sonne of Marie, that it inhabited and dwelt therein, as in a holy temple or house; but yet, as neither the house is the inhabitant, nor the inhabitant the house; so neither was God (by their doctrine) *the sonne of Mary, or man*; *nor yet was that man which was the sonne of Mary, God*; but onely the house or temple of God.

13. When Catholikes called Iesus Christ *our Lord*, they meant truly and orthodoxally, that the man Iesus Christ, who tooke flesh of the Virgin *Mary*, is in truth very God, the Godhead being hypostatically united unto the manhood, and both of them making but one person, who is both God and man: but the Nestoriãs in calling Iesus Christ *our Lord*, meant not that the man Christ was truly & personally God or Lord, but that he was God, and the Lord, onely by having God and the Lord inhabiting in him, and united, not personally, but onely affectually unto him; wherupon it followed, that they in adoring Christ, & giving divine honours unto him, were indeed ἀυθροπολάτραι; for they gave the honour proper onely to God, unto that person, or that mã, which, according to their doctrine, they held not to be God.

14. And, which of all may seeme most strange; whereas Catholikes not onely professed the Virgin *Mary to bee the Mother of God*, but under those very tearmes, and by that forme of words, as being most easie and perspicuous, contradicted & condemned all the heresies of *Nestorius*, which were all by consequent included in their denying *Mary* to be Θεοτόκον, the Mother of God; The Nestorians, to avoid the hatred of this speech, if they should deny it, and more plausibly to convay their heresie, said, and in words professed even this also, that *Mary was the Mother of God*; but they meant not thereby, as Catholikes did, that Christ, who tooke flesh of the Virgin *Mary*, was the same person or one personall subsistence with the Sonne of God; or, that God was

incarnate;

incarnate, and assumed the manhood to make one person with the Godhead, but all that they meant was, that the Son of God, was onely by affection, and love united unto the sonne of *Marie*, being already perfect man in the wombe of his mother, and that God was borne of her, not by assuming flesh unto him, but by inhabiting that man who tooke flesh of her. Thus in shew of words the Nestorians seemed to bee Catholikes, and to say the same with Catholikes, but their sense and meaning in those words was most hereticall; and therefore indeed and in truth themselves notwithstanding all these speeches, were heretikes.

15. For the full and ample proofe of all these, I must referre my selfe to another Treatise, if it ever happen to see the light: wherein I have at large handled this point, and proved another of their Popes somewhat more ancient then *Vigilius*, I meane *Hormisda*, to have beene as deepe in the heresie of *Nestorius*, and to have as firmly by his Cathedrall and Apostolicall sentence confirmed the same, as *Vigilius* himselfe hath done; who as I thinke, by the example and authority of his predecessor was the more emboldned to plead for Nestorianisme; it being of all heresies which ever sprung up in the Church, most full of all sophisticall subtilties, and colourable pretences of wit, was most fit of all the rest, to be commended by such as under the shew of learning, and truth, meant to defend and uphold heresie. But for this time I will now alleage onely a few evident testimonies, to declare the truth of that concurrence in words, and difference in sense, betweene Catholikes and Nestorians, which even now I mentioned.

16. *Nestorius* in his Epistle [n] to *Alexander* signifying that the two natures in Christ are also *two persons*, saith thus; *Non duas personas unam personam facimus*, we doe not make two persons, one person; but by this one name of Christ, we signifie *two natures* (to wit, making *two persons*.) And to shew how these two persons are called by them one person; *thou mayst*, saith he [o], *call him that was borne of Mary, by the name of the Sonne of God*; for the Virgin which bare Christ, *filium Dei genuit*, bare the Sonne of God, but because the Sonne according to the Natures is double, *non genuit quidem* [p] *filium Dei* she did not truly beare the Son of God (as taking flesh from her) but she bare the man or humane nature, *quà propter filium adjunctum, filij quoque appellatione afficitur*, which is called the Sonne of God, because the Sonne God is united and joyned unto him: and in another place [q], He that was framed in the wombe, and laid in the grave, is not of himselfe God: *at quia Deus in homine assumpto existit*, but because God is in the man whom hee assumes unto him; the man assumed is called God, because hee is assumed of God. So *Nestorius*; plainly calling Christ, God, and the Son of God; and *Marie*, the mother of God, and yet denying God and man to be one person; but the person of God to assume a perfect man, or the person of Man.

O   17. *Theodorus*

n Extat in Conc. Coll. 6. pa 575. b.
o Nestorij verba citata ibidem. pa. 576. a. & in Actis Conc. Ephes. to. 2. ca. 8. pa. 747 a.
p Negat Nestorius Mariam genuisse filium, ita ut ex ipsa carnem sumpserit, affirmat genuisse, ita ut ex ipsa prodierit. Hoc declarant Nestorij verba apud Cyrillum citata in Epist. ad Acatium. to. 3. Act. Ephes. ca. 7 ubi ita ait Nestorius; Deum ex Christipara virgine prodijsse ex divina scriptura edoctus sum, at vero Deum e ipsa genitum esse (eo quo dixi sensu) id nusquam edoctus sum.
q Non per se & secundum se Deus est, quod in utero formatum est, non per se & secundum se Deus est, quod spiritus sancti operâ effectum est, non per se & secundum se Deus est, quod in monumento conditum est. At quia Deus in homine assumpto extitit, assumptus assumenti coniunctus, propter assumentem Deus appellatur. verba Nestorij citata in Act. Conc. Ephes. to. 2. ca. 8. pa. 748. a.

17. *Theodorus* the master of *Nestorius* declares the same; *In ipso* [r] *plasmato Deus verbum factus est.* The Word or Sonne of God *was united to the man Christ,* being framed and formed, shewing plainly that Christ was first made a perfect man, and person, and that then the Sonne of God as another person was united unto him. And shewing that the unity of the *two natures* is not *personall*, but onely *affectuall*; hee compares the unity which is betwixt the Godhead, and the manhood in Christ, to that unitie which is betwixt man and wife, who though they bee called one, yet are they in naturall subsistence two distinct persons. Even so saith he [f] in Christ, *non nocet naturarum differentiæ unitas persona, the unity of person doth not take away the distinction of the natures.* And the two natures joyned together, *unam personam dicimus, we call one person*: which unity not to be personall no more then it is in man and wife, but affectuall, hee immediately explaneth, expresly affirming either nature in Christ, to be a perfect and distinct person, or personall subsistence by it selfe, saying, for when we discerne or teach two natures, *perfectam naturam verbi Dei dicimus & perfectam personam, perfectam autem & hominis naturam & personam similiter: we affirme both the perfect nature, and the perfect person of the Sonne of God, and also the perfect nature, and perfect person of man to be in Christ*: but when we look at the conjunction of these (natures) *unam personam tunc dicimus, then wee call them one person,* (to wit one by *affectuall,* but not by *naturall* and *personall unity,* for he said plainly before, that they were two perfect distinct persons.) Thus *Theodorus.*

18. This is to have beene the very true meaning of the Nestorians, *Iustinian* in his Edict manifestly declareth, writing thus and most divinely; *In* [t] *that the Apostle saith of the Sonne of God, that he tooke the forme of a servant, he sheweth that the Word was united to the Nature of Man: but not to any subsistence or person*: for he doth not say; he tooke him, who was in the forme of a servant, least he should imply thereby, that the Word was united unto the man being formerly formed, as impious *Theodorus* and *Nestorius* did blaspheme: *affectualem dicentes unitatem, teaching an affectuall* (and no personall) *unitie* betwixt them. The fift Councell after most exact sifting of this matter doth witnes the same, writing thus; *Theodorus* [u] *and Nestorius teaching two persons, two Christs, two sonnes, would hide their impietie by calling them two natures, and one sonne.* And a little after, *Theodorus affectualem unitatem dicens, naturas pro personis & subsistentijs accipit. Theodorus teaching an affectuall union* (onely) *to bee betwixt the two natures,* useth the word Nature for Person: and so indeed teacheth two persons; *Quomodo Nestorius duas dicit naturas: in which same sense also Nestorius teacheth two natures to be in Christ: sed pro personis tas accipit,* but hee taketh those two natures for two persons. So the generall Councell.

19. Pope *Iohn* the second, doth clearly expresse this, setting
downe

r *Theodori verba citata in Conc. 5. Coll. 4. pa. 528. a.*

f *Coll. eadem. pa. 532. a. & Coll. 6. pa. 576. a.*

t *Edict. Iustir. §. Credimus autem.*

u *Conc. 5. Coll. 6. pa. 575. b.*

downe the faith of the Romane Church. *Wee* [x] *professe Christ to be perfect in deity, and perfect in the humanity: non antea existente carne, & postea unita verbo, sed in ipso Deo verbo initium ut esset accipiens,* his flesh, (or humane nature) *not first existing; and then the Word being united unto it: but his flesh taking beginning in the very Word: nec duas personas in Christo intelligimus:* neither doe wee understand two persons to be in Christ, when wee say two natures to be in him, as madde *Nestorius* thought. Thus the Pope. But no where is this more clearly and fully explained then in the Dialogue of *Maxentius,* where the Catholike disputing with the Nestorian, saith thus: *This is* [y] *the cause of your errror, you cannot discerne the difference betwixt Person and Nature: But understanding Nature to be all one with Person,* ye confound (or use for one and the same thing) these two: *& duas omnino personas, sicut duas naturas unius filij Dei sine dubio prædicatis:* and without all doubt, you teach two persons to be in the Sonne of God, when yee professe two natures to be in him.

20. By this which I have sayd, it is now evident, that the Nestorians spake like Catholikes, but they thought contrarie to Catholikes: their words were holy and orthodoxall, but their sense, and meaning, was blasphemous, and hereticall. Neither was this any new policie of the Nestorians; The Arians, the Pelagians, almost all heretikes, have practised the like: out of them all, I will here alleage but one example. *Vitalis* [z] a Presbyter of *Antioch,* was accused unto *Damasus* to maintaine in some part the heresie of *Apollinaris,* as denying Christ to have a soule or minde; At the motion [a] of *Damasus,* he delivered in writing a confession of his faith. In that confession, *disertis verbis confessus est in Christo, sicut carnem ita & mentem* [b]: hee in plaine termes professed Christ to have as well a soule as a body. This his confession seeming at the first to be sound [c] and good, was approved for catholike, both by *Pope Damasus,* by *Gregorie Nazianzen* and other Catholikes, who suspect no hereticall fraud to lye hid under such faire and orthodoxall words, for in his confession of faith, *Scripturæ* [d] *verba sine ulla depravatione collocabat, nihil prorsus immutans, nec orationis seriem adulterans: Vitalis* had placed the very words of the Scripture; not depraved, not any way changed, neither the order, nor writing of them being corrupted. But when *Vitalis* [e] came among his owne fellowes, to whom he opened his secret meaning and his fraud, as the Manichees were wont to do among their *electi,* he then told them, *That by the soule* [f] *and mind which hee had acknowledged in Christ, he meant nothing but the very Deity it selfe,* which unto Christs body, was as the soule & mind, to animate it with life, sense, and reason, which was one part of the heresie of *Apollinaris.* As soones as Pope *Damasus,* and *Gregory Nazianzen* knew of this fraud, they not onely rejected *Vitalis* out of their communion, but condemned as hereticall, and that also with an *Anathema* denounced against it, *Fidei*

libellum,

Job.2.Epist.3. ad
Senatores.
y Iob. Maxent. Dial.
1.ca.12.

z Elias Cretens. in
Greg. Nazian. Epi-
2.ad Clidon.
a Poscente illo (Damaso) ut fidem suam exponeret, eam scriptis mandatam edidit. ibid.
b Baron. an.373. nu.3.
c Prima fronte recta & sana visa (ea professio) ideirco & Damasus & hic divinus ma ister (Gregorius) eam admiserunt, quod abditam & occultam fraudē nullo modo deprehendisserat, nec versutam malignitatem sub verbis latentem. Elias Cret. loc. cit.
d Elias Cret. ibid.
e Hi cum discipulis suis abditis & mysti, de absconditis theologicum instillant sermonē, quemadmodum & Manichei, totam eis morbum revelantes. Greg. Nazian. Epist. 2.ad Clidon.
f Animam & rationem ac mentem, (Christi) divinitatem ipsam introducunt, tanquam ipsa sola carni sit admista. Mentem, divinitatem Christi dicentes. Greg. ibid.
g Statim ac dolum sensrunt, fraudulentum hominem ab ecclesia proscribunt. Elias Cret. loc. cit.

libellum, that very same profession of faith made by *Vitalis*, which themselves before had approved; which fact *Gregorie* [h] defendeth as just and right, both for himselfe, and for *Damasus*.

21. From this, two things are specially for our present purpose to be observed. The former, that an hereticall profession may bee made in most orthodoxall termes, yea in the very words of the holy Scripture, not corrupted, not altered, not changed, for so was this hereticall confession of *Vitalis*. The other is, that the selfe same profession of faith, if wee looke onely at the words, may be allowed for orthodoxall, when the sense thereof is and appeareth to bee orthodoxall, and when there is no evidence to the contrary, but that the party who makes that profession, as he speakes orthodoxally, so also meaneth orthodoxally: and that same profession also, may justly bee condemned for hereticall, when by any overt act, or outward evidence, it doth certainly appeare, that the party who made that confession, by, and under those orthodoxall words, meant by a fraudulent, and equivocating collusion, to expresse an hereticall sense: for while there appeared no cause to mistrust *Vitalis*, Pope *Damasus* and others approved his profession, as orthodoxall: but as soone as they knew hee meant heretically, they condemned, and anathematized the very selfe same profession as hereticall. The reason of all which is, that which the same *Gregory* [i], and after him *Iustinian* [k] expresseth, *quoniam eaedem voces*, *because the very same words*, if they bee rightly expounded, and understood, are pious, but if they be taken in an hereticall sense, they are impious.

22. That which *Damasus* and *Gregorie* did in the confession of *Vitalis*, must bee done in the profession of the Nestorians: when Catholikes say there are in Christ *two natures, and one person*, their confession is orthodoxall, because they say it in an orthodoxall sense, using the words as they ought to bee in their right, naturall, and usuall signification: But when the Nestorians say the very same words, their saying is hereticall, because they say it in an hereticall sense, abusing the words, to an equivocall, unnaturall, and unusuall signification. Nay, it not onely must, but it was sayd, it was decreed in this very case of *Nestorius*, and that by the whole generall Councell at *Ephesus*, themselves being Catholikes professed in Christ, *two natures*, *and one person*, and yet they condemned [l] and accursed *Nestorius*, who in words said the very same, acknowledging in Christ *two natures, and one person*. Whose judgement herein being followed both by the Councell at *Chalcedon*, & this 5. Synod, & in a word, by the whole Catholike Church, is a warrant authenticall, that a profession being for words, one, and the selfe same, may and ought in some to be judged orthodoxal, & in others condemned as hereticall, and the saying of old *Ennius* [m] though spoken to another purpose, is verified in this, *Eadem dicta, eademque oratio aequa non aeque valet.*

23. It

h *Ne nos accusent quod Vitalis fidem prius quidem probaverimus, nunc vero repudiemus. Greg. Naz Epist. 2. ad Clidon. & similia habet in Epi. 2. ad Hell.*

i *Greg. Epist. 2. ad Clid.*
k *Iust. in Edict. §. Tali.*

l *Nestorium duas quidem naturas, et unam personam dicentem Ephesina prima Synodus condemnavit. Iust. in Edict. §. Tali.*

m *apud Gell. lib. 11. ca. 4.*

23. It is not enough then to prove either *Ibas* to be a Catholike, or his *Epiſtle* orthodoxall, becauſe in it *Ibas* profeſſeth two natures, and one perſon in Chriſt, (for *Theodorus*, and *Neſtorius* profeſſed the very ſame) but the ſenſe and meaning of his words, ſet downe in that *Epiſtle*, muſt be exactly conſidered, whether he meant not as other Neſtorians, and even as *Neſtorius* himſelfe did, two ſuch natures, as make two diſtinct perſons alſo, and whether he called them not one perſon, in ſuch a ſenſe, as meaning that they were one, not by naturall, or perſonall ſubſiſtence, but onely by affection, and cohabitation. If it may appeare that this was indeed the meaning of *Ibas* in his *Epiſtle*, then will thoſe words of his profeſſion, be ſo farre from proving either him or his *Epiſtle* to be Catholike, as *Vigilius* and *Baronius* doe thence inferre, that it will demonſtrate both *Ibas* in making that profeſſion, and *Vigilius* and *Baronius* in defending it, to approve and maintaine Neſtorianiſme as the onely Catholike Faith.

24. But can this thinke you be ſhewed indeed? It may: and that moſt clearly, and moſt certainely. The Emperour *Iuſtinian* in his religious Edict both teſtifieth and demonſtrates this. Heretickes, ſaith he [n], *omitting other blaſphemies in this Epiſtle of Ibas, alleage this onely, which the Author of that Epiſtle ſpake to beguile the ſimple thereby,* in that he profeſſeth *duas naturas, unam virtutē, unā perſonā, two natures, one power, one perſon,* which we our ſelves alſo doe confeſſe. *Sed certum eſt, quod unicuique naturæ ſuam perſonam attribuit; but it is certaine, that the Author of that Epiſtle (Ibas) doth attribute to eyther nature a ſeverall perſon,* even as doe *Theodorus* and *Neſtorius,* whom this Writer doth defend: For, they plainly teaching two natures of the Word of God, or of Chriſt, whom they eſteeme to be no more then a man, doe call them (thoſe two natures) one perſon, *per affectualem conjunctionem, by an affectuall conjunction,* and as having one dignity, and one honour. And it is cleere that the writer of this *Epiſtle,* ſaying that there is one vertue, and one power of the *two natures,* doth herein follow the foreſaid heretickes, *Theodorus* in his impious booke of the incarnation, and *Neſtorius* in many of his writings, but ſpecially in his Epiſtle to *Alexāder,* where he ſaith that there is one authoritie, one vertue, one power, one perſon, in reſpect of dignitie and honour due unto them, whereby it is declared that the author of this Epiſtle, did according to their perfidious impiety, uſe *vocabulo naturarum pro perſonis, this word Natures, for Perſons:* for one authoritie, one power, one dignity and honour, *non in diverſis naturis, ſed in diverſis perſonis dicitur, is not ſaid to bee in divers natures, but in divers perſons, of the ſame nature,* as in the Trinitie we profeſſe. Thus *Iuſtinian* both truly, and profoundly.

25. The fift generall Councell witneſſeth the ſame, and almoſt in the ſame words. *The author (ſay they* [o]*) of this Epiſtle* teacheth

teacheth two natures, one vertue, one person, one sonne. *Sed certum est quod pro personis naturas ponit, & affectualem unitatem dicit, but it is certaine that he taketh the name of natures, for persons, and understandeth an affectuall unitie,* even as doe *Theodorus,* and *Nestorius,* whom this writer doth defend and praise: Thus both the Emperour and the whole generall approved Councell, witnesse *Ibas* to meane by two natures, two persons, and by one person, one by affectuall, not by personall unitie, and they witnesse this not as a thing doubtfull, or uncertaine, but they seale it with a *Certum est, this is certaine,*

26. The *Epistle* it selfe doth so abundantly declare this truth, that none I thinke but a Nestorian, can make any doubt thereof. *Maris* to whom *Ibas* writ this was a Nestorian hereticke: The end of his writing was to confirme, both *Maris* and the rest of that sect in their heresie. Had *Ibas* writ this touching two natures, and one person, in an orthodoxall sense, he had utterly condemned that same doctrine, which he purposely commendeth, he had overthrowne Nestorianisme, which he by this *Epistle,* meant to establish. Againe, how could hee have condemned *Cyrill* or the Ephesine Councell as hereticall, had he beleeved the *two natures* to be personally united in Christ? for that is the selfe same which *Cyrill,* and the Councell defendeth. Or how could he have commended *Theodorus,* for a teacher of the truth, who denies the personall, and holds onely an affectuall unitie of those *two natures,* had *Ibas* meant that there had beene a true personall and Hypostaticall union of them? Take the words in the Nestorian sense, there is a perfect harmonie in the whole *Epistle*: take them in the orthodoxall sense, the beginning will then jarre from the middle and end, this makes a discord in the whole writing, yea, it makes the profession of *Ibas* to fight with the maine scope and purpose of *Ibas.*

27. That one place in the end of the *Epistle,* concerning the *union,* makes this most evident, *Ibas* saith that among other things *Paulus Emisenus* required, and *Cyrill* consented to anathematize those who professe, *quia una natura est divinitatis, & humanitatis, that there is one nature of the deitie and humanitie in Christ.* Had *Ibas* by one nature, meant one essence, so that both the humanitie, and deitie were one essence, why should they require *Cyrill* to anathematize that? for neither *Cyrill,* nor any Catholike ever affirmed there was onely one nature, that is, one onely essence in Christ. But by *nature, Ibas* understood Person, and so its true that *Cyrill* taught one nature, that is, one onely person in Christ, whereas *Nestorius, Ibas* and all the Nestorians affirmed *two such Natures,* that is, *two persons* to be in Christ: according to which sense *Ibas* saith, that *Paulus* dealing with *Cyrill* to yeeld to Nestorianisme, and on the behalfe of the Nestorians, required him to anathematize those who say there is but one *Nature,* that is, but *one person* in Christ: and he slanderously adds, that *Cyrill* consented

confented fo to do: that is, that he fubfcribed indeed to all Neftorianifme, and renounced the Catholike faith, the decree of
the Ephefine Councell, and his owne twelve Chapters. In which
flanderous report *Ibas* infulting faith, *Non enim quifquam audet*
dicere quia una eft natura, None dare now fay that there is one nature
of the divinitie and humanitie, one nature, that is, one effence: no
Catholike then, or ever, did fay, but none dare now fay, that there
is *one Nature,* that is, *one perfon* in Chrift, which all Catholikes
both then, and ever faid, and this the very next words doe declare; but now they doe profeffe to beleeve *in templum, & in eum*
qui in hoc habitat, in the temple, and in him who dwelleth in the tem-
ple, which was the very comparifon of *Neftorius* P, to expreffe
that the *two natures* in Chrift, are *two perfons,* as are the houfe
and inhabiters, and one not by perfonall, but onely by affectuall
unitie and cohabitation. So cleere it is that *Ibas* by his confeffing of *two natures* meant *two perfons,* and by confeffing one perfon, meant one by affection, but not by perfonall union: that
is, meant all in an hereticall, and Neftorian fenfe, and nothing in
the true Catholike, and orthodoxall meaning.

28. But what feeke I further proofe of this matter, feeing the fift Councell, approved by the whole catholike Church,
hath defined the whole q *Epiftle* to bee hereticall, accurfing e-
very one who defendeth it, or any part of it. An undeniable
proofe, not onely that the profeffion of *Ibas* made therein of
two natures and one perfon, is hereticall, but that *Vigilius* and
Baronius, for this very point are anathematized by the whole
Church, becaufe they defend that profeffion in this *Epiftle* as
Catholike and orthodoxall, which by fo many, fo evident de-
monftrations, and even by the confenting judgement of the
whole Church, is condemned for hereticall. And this I hope
may fuffice to explaine or illuftrate the Popes meaning in the
Pofition or conclufion which he undertakes to prove in his reafon, that *Ibas* was a Catholike, in making this fo orthodoxall,
and Catholike a profeffion in his *Epiftle,* of two natures and one
perfon.

29. Let us now come unto the reafons, whereby our Author
Vigilius proves this profeffion to be Catholike. Thofe are fpecially three, in which, becaufe they all depend on that which
hath beene declared in the pofition, we may be the more briefe.
The firft is, becaufe *Diofcorus* r, and the *Ephefine Latrocinie* did
judge both this profeffion of *Ibas,* and *Ibas* himfelfe for making
this profeffion, to bee hereticall, *propter hanc fidei profeffionem, for*
this profeffion of two natures and one perfon, he condemned and depofed *Ibas.* Now the judgement of *Diofcorus* to have beene unjuft, and hereticall there is no doubt, and therefore the confeffion of *Ibas* which hee condemned muft be acknowledged as orthodoxall, and Catholike; as being repugnant to the hereticall doctrine of *Diofcorus.* A very poore and filly collection for a

Pope:

P *Si quis dixerit*
Chriftum Deum ve-
rum iffe, & non po-
tius nobifcum deum,
hoc eft, inhabitaffe
naturam noftrã per
id quod unitus eft
noftræ, anathema fit,
Neftorius in anathe-
matifmo 1. cõtra Cy-
rill. anath. §.1. in
Act. Conc. Eph.2. o.
ca.5. in Appen. pa.
768.

q *Tota Epiftola he-*
retica eft, Epiftola
per omnia contraria
eft definitioni a Sy-
nodo Chalced.factæ.
Conc.5. Coll. 6. pa,
576.a.b.

r *Diofcorus Ibam*
propter hanc fpecia-
liter fidei profeffio-
nem qua duas natu-
ras, unam virtutem,
unam perfonam a-
pertiffimè confite-
tur, hereticum con-
dēnavit. Conft. Vig.
nu.595.

Pope: and I doubt not but *Vigilius* would have derided it, had not Nestorianisme at this time bereft him of all sound reason and judgement. *Dioscorus* and his Ephesine conspiracie maintained the heresie of *Eutiches*, which denieth [r] two natures at all, or any way either making one or two persons, to be in Christ after the incarnation. So whether one held the same two natures, to make but one person, as the Catholikes said, or to make two distinct persons as the Nestorians affirmed, it was all one to *Dioscorus*; The very holding of two natures to bee in Christ, either of those wayes made one an hereticke in the judgment of *Eutiches*, *Dioscorus*, and their Ephesine Synod. The heresie of *Eutiches* did equally contradict both the Catholike truth and the Nestorian heresie, because they both consented in one common truth, that there are two distinct natures, or essences abiding in Christ. If this judgement of *Dioscorus* against *Ibas*, will prove either him or his *Epistle* to be Catholike, the very like effect it must have in *Theodorus*, in *Nestorius*, in all Nestorians, and in all their writings; they all with *Ibas* professe two natures to abide in Christ, they all by the judgement of *Dioscorus* and his Synod, are hereticall. So either must *Vigilius* approve all Nestorians for Catholikes, if this reason for *Ibas* bee effectuall, or if they bee truly hereticks, whom *Dioscorus* yet hath condemned, as well as *Ibas*, then is this his reason ineffectuall to prove from the condemnation of *Dioscorus*, *Ibas* or his profession to be Catholike.

30. His second reason is drawne from the likenesse and identitie of faith in *Flavianus* and *Ibas*, *damnat* [f] *quoque propter duarum naturarum vocem*, Dioscorus *did also, or for the same cause, condemne Flavianus*, for which *Ibas* was condemned, to wit, for professing two natures in Christ. Seeing then it is knowne, that the profession of *Flavianus* was Catholike, the profession also of *Ibas* made in this *Epistle*, being like to that of *Flavianus*, must needes be Catholike; My annotation on this reason of *Vigilius* is, that it is inconsequent, sophisticall, and worth nothing at all, *Ibas* indeede in words said the like with *Flavianus*, but *Flavianus* said it in a Catholike sense, holding those two natures to make but one person or personall subsistence, and *Ibas* said it in this *Epistle* in an hereticall sense, holding those two natures to make two distinct persons, or two personall subsistences. To *Dioscorus* it was all one to say as *Flavianus* did, or as *Ibas* in this *Epistle* doth; for seeing they both jumpe in this, that two natures or essences doe remaine after the incarnation, they are both alike hereticks to *Dioscorus*, though in truth the profession of *Flavianus* made him a Martyr, and the profession of *Ibas*, set downe in this *Epistle*, being in words the same, make him an hereticke. Or if *Ibas* be a Catholike for professing in words the same which *Flavianus* did, then by this reason of our Author *Vigilius*, *Theodorus*, *Nestorius*, and all the Nestorians, are Catholikes, because

r *Eutiches dixit, confitemur ex duabus naturis fuisse dominum nostrum ante adunationé, post vero adunatione unam naturam confiteor. Dioscorus & Synodus (Ephesina 2.) dixit, consentimus huic & nos omnes. Act. Conc. Ephes. recitata in Conc. Chal. Act. 1. pa. 28. b.*

f *Vigil. Const. nu.* 195.

cause they all professe with *Flavianus*, (two natures, and one person
to be in Christ) in the same manner as *Ibas* here doth.

31. His third and last reason is drawne from the judgement
of the Councell at *Chalcedon*; they ᵗ condemned *Dioscorus* and   *t Vig. Const. nu. 195*
Eutiches, but they embraced *Ibas*: an evidence, that as they jud-
ged the profession of *Dioscorus* to be hereticall, so they esteemed
the profession of *Ibas* to be orthodoxall; yea, even this which he
maketh in this *Epistle*; for after that *Cyrill* had once explaned his
Chapters, which was before this *Epistle* was writ, after that time,
*in Catholicæ fidei rectitudine ab eâdem Chalcedonensi Synodo judicatus
est Ibas permansisse*; *Ibas was by the Synod at Chalcedon judged to
have continued in the right profession of the faith.* The only glosse fit
for this reason is, that it is fallacious, untrue, and slanderous: fallacious; for the Councell of *Chalcedon* received *Ibas* indeed, but
not for this profession made in his *Epistle*, which that holy
Councell both knew, and condemned as hereticall, but, as before
we have declared, for his consenting to the *Ephesine* Councell;
and condemning of *Nestorius* first before *Photius*, & *Eustathius*, &
then before themselves in the Councell at *Chalcedon*; upon this,
whereby *Ibas* did in truth condemne his ownprofession made in
this *Epistle*, and this whole Epistle, upon this I say; and not for
professing in this Epistle two natures and one person, was *Ibas* received by the Councell at *Chalcedon*: untrue; for neither did the
Councell of *Chalcedon* judge *Ibas* to have beene a Catholike, or
hold the *Catholike* faith, upon the declaration of *Cyrils* Chapters;
much lesse did they judge him to have continued ever after that
time, in the orthodoxie of faith: slanderous; for *Vigilius* by saying that the Councell of *Chalcedon* held *Ibas* for a Catholike, upon, or shortly after the declaration of *Cyrils* Chapters; makes
them all guilty of Nestorianisme: long after that explanation
did *Ibas* write this *Epistle*, wherein all the blasphemies of *Nestorius*, are maintained. Had they judged him, since that Explanation to be a Catholike; they must approve this *Epistle* for Catholike, and so prove themselves to be hereticall, to be Nestorians. Thus *Vigilius*, to cloake his owne heresie, would faine fasten
it upon the holy Councell of *Chalcedon*, which was so farre from
partaking with *Vigilius* herein, that by their definitive sentence,
this very ᵘ professiõ of *two natures*, and *one person*, made in this *E-*   *u Tota Epistola hæ-*
pistle; yea, every part of this Epistle, is condemned for impious,   *retica est. Conc. 5.*
and hereticall. And this I hope may serve for an explanation of   *Coll. 6. pa. 576. a. b.*
Pope *Vigilius* his third reason to prove *Ibas* a Catholike,
(drawne from this profession of faith, made in this Epistle) untill
some Annalist like *Baronius* will helpe us to a better Commentary.

32. The second reason of *Vigilius*, set downe in the words
before recited to prove *Ibas* a Catholike, is drawne from his
approving of the Ephesine Councell at the judgement before
Photius & *Eustathius*; He there, saith *Vigilius* ˣ, most plainly appro-   *x In Const. nu. 194.*
ved

ved the *Ephesine Synod,and the doctrines decreed therein,* he professed them to be equall to the *Nicene* decrees; *Photius* the Iudge, exceedingly commended *Ibas*, that hee *was so forward to professe the true faith,* and wipe away all suspition of heresie from him : how could *Ibas* then be ought else but a Catholike, who made such a Catholike confession? Truely when *Ibas* made this confession before *Photius* and *Eustathius,* there is no doubt but he was then a Catholike; but *Vigilius* his purpose is to prove him to have beene a Catholike, when he writ this *Epistle,* ever [x] since the time that *Cyrill* explained his Chapters; and *Baronius,* who is very sparing of his speech in this whole matter,yet both saw, and professeth this to be the true intent of *Vigilius;* for he [y] telling us,that wheras those words in the end of the *Epistle* of *Ibas,* [None dare now say, there is one nature, but they professe to beleeve in the Temple, and in him who dwelleth in the Temple] were wont to be taken by the Nestorians in such a sense, as if in Christ there were two persons, *ne* Ibas *putaretur ejusdem esse in verbis illis sententia cum Nestorianis;* lest Ibas *might be thought to have the same meaning with the Nestorians in those words;* *Vigilius* bringeth a declaration of those words, how they are to be brought to a right sense, and this he teacheth, by shewing how *Ibas* in the Acts (before *Photius* and *Eustathius*) embraced the Ephesine Councell. So *Baronius :* by whose helpe, besides the evidence in the text it selfe; it now appeares, that *Vigilius,* by this profession of *Ibas,* made before *Photius* and *Eustathius,* would prove *Ibas* to have beene a Catholike when hee writ this *Epistle,*and that in it *Ibas* was not *ejusdem sententia cum Nestorianis;* of the same opinion with the Nestorians.

33. A reason so void of reason, that I could not have held patience with the Popes Holinesse, had not Nestorianisme dulled his wit and judgement at this time. The judgement before *Photius* and *Eustathius,* was in the yeare when *Posthumianus* and *Zeno* were Consuls, or in the next unto it, as the Acts [x] do testifie, that is,according to *Baronius* account,*an.448.* The *union* [b] betwixt *Iohn* and *Cyrill* was made in the next yeare after the Ephesine Councell, that is, *an. 432.* The *Epistle* of *Ibas* was writ by *Baronius* Almanacke in the very moment of the *union;* but in truth, two or three yeares at the least after the *union,* as before we have proved. Now I pray you,what a consequent, or collection call you this? *Ibas* being suspected of Nestorianisme, to cleare himselfe,consented to the Ephesine Councell, and shewed himselfe to bee a Catholike, sixteene yeares after the *union;* or thirteene yeares after he writ this *Epistle :* therefore at the time of the *union,*and of the writing of this *Epistle,* he was a Catholike also,and not a Nestorian. Why, twelve or sixteen years might have a strange operatiō in *Ibas;*and there is no doubt but so it had? In so many revolutions *Ibas* saw, how both himselfe and other Nestorians were publikely cōdemned by the Church, and by the Emperour,and hated of all,who had any love to the

                 Catholike

x *His Capitulis à Cyrillo explanatis, devotè in ejus communionem concurrit.Vig Constl.nu. 193.post explanationem 12. Capitulorum Ibas professus est se habuisse Cyrillum. orthodoxum,et in communione ipsius ad exitum permansisse. Ibid. nu.194.*

y *Bar.an.553.nu. 193.*

z *Iudicium illud Photij,et Eustathij extat cum Actis in eo, in Conc. Chal. Act.9.et 10.*

a *Bar.illo an.nu.57*

b *Vt supra probatum est.Ca.11.*

Catholike faith: He saw that himselfe was personally called *corā nobis*, for maintaining that heresie: he knew, that unlesse hee cleared himselfe before those Iudges, deputed by the Emperour to heare and examine his cause; he was in danger of the like deprivation, as *Nestorius*, and some others had justly felt. The serious and often meditation of these matters wrought effectually upon *Ibas*, and therefore before *Photius* & *Eustathius* he renounced, disclamed, and condemned Nestorianisme, and so at that time proved himselfe, by his profession before them, to bee a Catholike, as he had before that time, and specially when he writ this *Epistle*, demonstrated himselfe to be, not onely an earnest, but a malicious and slanderous heretike. I cannot illustrate the Pope, my Authors reason, by a more fit similitude, than of a man once deadly sicke of the Pestilence, but afterwards fully cured and amended; for *Vigilius* his reason is, as if one should say, This man was not sicke of the Pestilence, no not when the sore was running upon him, and hee at the very point of death, because some twelve or sixteene yeares after, hee was a sound man, cleare from all suspition of the Pestilence. Nor needeth this second reason of *Vigilius* any further explanation.

34. We come now, in the last place, to that which *Vigilius* maketh his first reason in the former text; into which, because hee hath compacted the very venome of the Nestorians, wee must bee inforced to take somewhat the more paines, in our Commentary upon it. This reason (in which, it seems, the Pope puts his greatest confidence) is drawne from the explanation of *Cyrils* Chapters, of which c *Vigilius* saith, that *Ibas* at the first, & before *Cyrill* had explaned them, misconceived the meaning of *Cyrill*, and therefore seemed to speake against *Cyrill*: but so soone as *Cyrill* had explaned them, and decared his owne meaning, then *Ibas*, and all the Easterne Bishops forthwith embraced the communion with *Cyrill*; and ever after that, *Ibas* continued a Catholike. This *Epistle* then of *Ibas*, and profession of faith made therein, which certainly followed the Explanation of *Cyrils* Chapters, must needs be Catholike, & declare *Ibas*, whē he writ it, to have been a Catholike; seeing, when he made this confession of faith, and writ this *Epistle*, he held the same faith with *Cyrill*, and therefore no doubt held the Catholike faith. This is the full summe and effect of the Popes reason, taken from the Explanation of *Cyrils* Chapters, and for the excellency of it, it spreadeth it selfe into every part of the two other reasons also, as containing an explication of them, or giving strength unto them; for which cause wee are with more diligence and circumspection to examine the pith of it.

35. And that we may more clearely behold and admire the Popes *Artificium*, in handling this reason, we are to observe five severall points thereof. The first, a peece of the Popes Rhetoricke, in that he saith d that *Ibas* before the Explanation and

union,

c *Vig. Const. nu. 192 193, 194.*

d *Nu. 193.*

union, whilst hee doubted, and misconceived the meaning of *Cyrill*, *visus est ei obloqui*, he seemed to speake against Cyrill at that time. He seemed: Now *Ibas* professeth of himselfe, that hee then called ᵉ *Cyrill* an hereticke, that hee followed *Iohn* ᶠ, and the Conventicle, which held with him, and so that with them hee counted, and in plain terms, called *Cyrill* ʰ an author of schisme, a disturber of the peace of the Church, a despiser of imperiall authoritie, an upholder of open tyrannie, an Arch-hereticke, and chiefe of the conspiracie, that he condemned, accursed, anathematized him, and that with such a detestation, that though *Cyrill* ⁱ should disclaime his heresie, yet hee should never be received into their communion. These and many like intolerable calumnies, and slanders, were the usuall liveries, that *Ibas* and the rest of that Conventicle, during the time of the disunion bestowed upon *Cyrill*; so vile, and malitious, that no hyperbolicall exaggeration, can sufficiently expresse the impietie of them, and yet the Popes holinesse, by the figure called *Meiosis*, doth so artificially extenuate, and almost annihilate them, as if in al these, *Ibas* did but seeme to speake against *Cyrill*, He seemed, what, to revile? nay, he seemed but to speake against him: *Vigilius* was too sparing and diminutive in his reproofe, *Non laudo.*

36. The second part of his *Artificium* concernes Chronology; where he ᵏ saith, that when *Cyrill* had explained his Chapters, *Ibas in ejus communionem devote concurrit*; Ibas then ran, and hastened to communicate with *Cyril*. Nor did *Ibas* alone at that time accord with *Cyrill*, but he, *cum* ˡ *omnibus Orientalibus Episcopis, with all the Easterne Bishops*; they all then embraced *Cyrill* for a Catholike; and *Ibas* ever after that, ᵐ *usque ad exitum, even to his dying day*, continued in the Catholike communion with *Cyrill*. Thus *Vigilius*. I cannot flatter the Pope, nor set any glosse upon this text, but this, that is utterly untrue. All the Easterne Bishops did not, at the time of the *union* betwixt *Iohn* and *Cyrill*, much lesse at the time when *Cyrill* declared his Chapters, consent, or hold communion with *Cyrill*. Of *Theodoret* it is as evident as the Sun; for he, after the *union*, writ ⁿ to *Nestorius*, that he then held *Cyrils* Chapters hereticall, and that hee would not consent to that which was done against *Nestorius*, no, not though his hands should be cut off. The like is certaine of *Ibas*, for that hee continued a malicious and slanderous defender of Nestorianisme, after the *union*; this, his impious *Epistle*, written, at least, two whole yeares after that *union*, wherein he maintaineth all the impieties of *Nestorius*, doth demonstrate. So untrue it is which *Vigilius* affirmeth, both in generall, that all the Easterne Bishops, and particularly, that *Ibas*, upon the Explanation of *Cyrils* Chapters, which was before the *union*, consented to *Cyrill*, and communicated with him: and much more untrue it is, that *Ibas*, ever after that Explanation, even to his dying day, remained a Catholike.

37. I say yet more for the further clearing of this matter, that
neither

e *Donec seipsum interpretatus fuisset, quia Orientale Concilium eum vocabat hereticum, et ut hereticum condemnavit, hereticum eum et ego putavi. verba Ibæ, in Act. Conc. Chal. Act. 10. pa. 113. a.*
f *Quando Orientale Concilium eum, quasi hereticum anathematizavit, sequutus sum primatem meum: verba Ibæ, ibid. pa. 112. b.*
h *Ita Cyrillum vocatum à Conciliabulo Iohannis, supra ostendi ca. 11.*
i *Et juravimus quod Cyrillus, etiamsi rejecerit Capitula, à nobis suscipiendus non sit, eo quod Haresiarches factus sit. Epist. Legatorũ Conciliabuli Ephesini. to. 3. Act. ca 10. Append.*
k *Vig. Const. nu. 193.*
l *ibid. nu. 194.*
m *Ibid. et in Catholicæ fidei rectitudine judicatus est permansisse. Nu. 195.*

n *Epistola illa Theod. extat in Conc. 5. Coll. 5. pa. 558. b.*

neither all, nor so much as any one of all those Easterne Bishops, who tooke part with *Iohn*, consented to *Cyrill* upon his declaration of the twelve Chapters, for *Cyrill* set forth his explanation during the time of the Ephesine Councell, while hee was imprisoned at *Ephesus*, *Cyrill*, saith *Baronius* [o], being left at *Ephesus*, was not idle there, but knowing that his twelve Chapters were carped at by adversaries, lest by their mis-interpretations they might be infringed : *ipse illis explanationem adjecit, himselfe set out an explanation of them.*   The very title prefixed to that explanation declares the same : which is [p], *Cyrills* explanation of the twelve Chapters, *Edita Ephesi, sacra Synodo exigente, published at Ephesus, the holy Synod requiring Cyrill to doe the same.*   The Nestorians and their Conventicle witnesse this most clearly : for they who stayed at *Ephesus*, writ thus to the Legates, whom they sent to the Emperour at *Constantinople. We* [q] *have sent unto you, recens factam expositionem ab Alexandrino, hæreticorum capitulorum, the Explanation of the hereticall Chapters lately made by Cyrill of Alexandria.*   This was writ by the Ephesine Conventicle, before the dissolutiõ of the Synod, which ended about the eight day [r] of November.

38.   Now that upon this explanation published by *Cyrill*, the Easterne Bishops did not consent to *Cyrill*, nor runne to communicate with him, their owne words in the Epistle of the Conventicle last cited, doe make manifest, where they say [s] of this explanation of *Cyrill*, that he doth *evidentius per illam ostendere suam impietatem, more plainly by it shew his impiety*, then by the Chapters themselves.   So they more detested that explanation then the Chapters explaned, it was more hereticall in their judgement then the other.   And *Iohn* himselfe with the other Legates, assented to the judgement of their fellowes : *wee are ready* [t] *say they to strive unto death, and neither receive Cyrill, neque capitula ab eo exposita, neither the Chapters by him explained.*   Whence it is without all doubt, that neither all, nor any at all, not *Iohn* himselfe, who was the ringleader to the rest, did consent to *Cyrill* and hold communion with him, upon his publishing that Explanation of his Chapters, or upon their knowing thereof.

39.   But how long after this explanation, was it before their union and communion with *Cyrill* ? *Peltanus* and *Binius* say [u] that those jarres continued for three yeares after the end of the Councell.   So directly doe they controule the Popes *Constitution*, wherein *Vigilius* so often affirmeth, that upon the publishing of *Cyrills* explanation they ranne to communicate with *Cyrill* : But because the account of *Peltanus* and *Binius* is certainly false, we will not presse the Pope therewith.   Thus much is evident, that the *union* betwixt *Iohn* and *Cyrill* was not concluded till December, in the next yeare after the Councell was ended.   For *Cyrill* received neither *Iohn*, nor any of the rest (save onely *Paulus Emisenus*) till *Paulus* came the second time to *Alexandria*,

P   bringing

o *Bar. an. 431. nu.* 153.

p *Act. Conc. Ephes. to. 5. c. 1.*

q *Eorum Epist. extat in Append. ad to. 3. Act. Conc. Ephes. ca. 7. append.*

r *Kin. in Not. ad Conc. Ephes. pa. 922. a.*

s *To. 3. Act. Eph. in append. ca. 7.*

t *Epist. legatorum ad suas in Epheso. in append. to. 3. Act. ca. 10. pa. 791. b.*

u *Duravit hæc controversia duos aut tres annos post Conc. Ephesinum dissolutum. Pax quarto demum anno impetrata est. Bin. Not. ante cap. 1. to. 5. Act. Eph.*

bringing with him the orthodoxall profession of *Iohn* *, and the other Bishops with him, at which time the *union* was fully concluded, and in token thereof both *Paulus* made that his memorable Sermon at *Alexandria*, on the twenty and ninth day of the month ˣ *Chyath*, which answereth to our December; and *Cyrill* writ that ʸ Epistle, as an hymne of joy, which beginneth *lætentur cæli*, so farre were the Easterne Bishops from hastning or running as *Vigilius* saith to the communion with *Cyrill* upon his explanation made knowne unto them, that they all save *Paul*, stayed a full yeare and more after that explanation, before they made peace or consented with *Cyrill*.

40. The third part of the Popes *Artificium* is his Logicke, which in very truth is nothing else but trifling sophistication: he supposeth that *Cyrills* explanation of the twelve Chapters, was the cause and occasion of the *union* betwixt *Cyrill*, and the rest. It was not, for that was published, and knowne unto them, more then an whole yeare before the *union*: nay that explanation did more alienate their minds from *Cyrill*, they detested that, more then the Chapters themselves, as we have clearly proved; so far was it from effecting the *union*, that it increased the breach and disunion. The onely true, and certaine cause of the union, was the relenting of the Easterne Bishops, from their former stomacke, obstinacie, and heresie: their subscribing to all that *Cyrill* required of them, to wit, to the condemning of *Nestorius*, and his heresies: till they did this, *Cyrill* was unmoveable, inflexible to any *union*: as soone as ever this was done, *Cyrill* most gladly embraced them, and sung his hymne, *Let the heavens rejoyce*, for their consenting to the Catholike faith. *Vigilius* still harps on a wrong string, and fallaciously puts *non causam, pro causa*, which was not fitting for the Popes gravitie & judgment.

41. The fourth and fift which are the chiefe parts of my Authors *Artificium*, concerne his Ethicall, and Theologicall knowledge, which being confused and mingled together throughout this whole text; and manifesting the Pope to joyne to his heresie, slander, I must bee forced to handle them both together. These consist in that which the Pope so often beats upon, that *Cyrill* explaned his Chapters, and upon that explanation, *Ibas* and the other Easterne Bishops ranne to embrace him, and his communion, what thinke you is that explanation of *Cyrills* Chapters, which the Pope so eagerly urgeth, and makes the cause of the *union* with *Ibas* and the rest? Truly thats a mysterie indeed, and containes in it the pith of Nestorianisme: *Baronius* was very loath to unfold this secret of the Popes Art: but I hope to make it so perspicuous, as that none shall bemone the want of the Cardinalls Commentarie in this point.

42. The Nestorians being as *Cyrill* ᶻ saith, *tantum ad calumniandum nati, men composed of lyes and slanders*, boasted that at the time of the *union*, the Catholikes had renounced and condemned

their

their former doctrines, and in all points consented unto them.
And in particular they avouched this of *Cyrill* who was the chief
agent on the Catholikes part, and who most zealously had opposed himselfe to their heresie.   This hath beene so clearly
proved before ᶻ, both by the Epistles of *Cyrill*, by the writings of   z *Supra ca. 12.*
Theodoret, and by this very Epistle of *Ibas*, that I thinke it super-
fluous to adde ought thereunto.   Now the same Nestorians
being no lesse subtle, then malicious : when they spake or writ
of this matter to any of their owne consorts, to their *Electi*, one
of which this *Maris* was to whom *Ibas* writ,   then they said in
plaine termes, that *Cyrill* (and the other Catholikes) had recalled, condemned, or anathematized his twelve Chapters, and his
former doctrine; as in the end of this Epistle *Ibas* tells *Maris*,
and wisheth him to shew the same, *Omnibus patribus nostris pacem
amantibus*, to all their Fathers, to the whole society of *Nestorians*, and
all that loved the peace with them, that *Cyrill* did now, *contraria
docere priori doctrinæ*, teach the contrarie to his former doctrine,
that hee anathematized it and all that held it.   Loe heres plaine
dealing with *Maris*. *Cyrill* now condemneth and anathematizeth
his twelve Chapters : but when they spake to men otherwise
affected then themselves; to such as could not endure to heare
that *Cyrill* had recanted or anathematized his former doctrine,
and Chapters, then they would not use such harsh and homely
words of *Cyrill*, but they would signifie the same thing, by a
more facile, faire, and courteous phrase, saying *Cyrill* explaned
his Chapters, and they upon his explanation, received him into
their communion, and held him for a Catholike.

43. This to be that which *Ibas* and other Nestorians meant
by *Cyrills* explanation of his Chapters, the words of *Ibas* himselfe uttered in the judgement, before *Photius*, & *Eustathius*, 16
yeares after the *union*; doe make cleare ; for although *Ibas* had
then in the maine point renounced Nestorianisme : yet he still
retained a touch or smack of their Nestorian language, hee had
not as yet perfectly learned to pronounce *Shibboleth*, nor wholy
weaned himselfe; or disused his tongue from those Nestorian
phrases, which were so familiar in their mouthes. In those acts,
Maris ᵃ accuseth *Ibas* to have said of himselfe and the other   a *Extant in Conc.*
Easterne Bishops, *we would not have received Cyrill, unlesse he had*   *Chalced. Act. 10.*
anathematized his ᵇ *Chapters.* *Ibas* answered, I said, that neither I   *pa.112. b.*
nor they would have received him, *nisi seipsum interpretatus fu-*   b *Non dixisti? quia*
isset, unlesse he had explained himselfe.   And when *Maris* againe   *nisi anathemati-*
replyed, what? Did you not say, *quando flagitatum est in secreto,*   *zasset Capitula sua,*
when you were privately, and in secret demanded, did you not then   *non reciperemus*
say, I received not *Cyrill*, *donec anathematizasset sua capitula, till*   *eum. ibid.*
he had anathematized his owne Chapters ? *Ibas* to this answered :
Truly, I remember not whether I said so or no : *Si autem dixi,
verè dixi, quia orientale Concilium recepit eum sua capitula retractan-
tem, but if I said it, I said but the truth, for the Easterne Councell re-*

ceived *Cyrill when hee had recalled his Chapters*, otherwise I would have accounted him an hereticke. So answered *Ibas*: plainely calling that in the one place the anathematizing, and retracting of his Chapters, which in the other he called explaining or interpreting his Chapters; but the one was spoken in secret, the other openly, and by the one which is plaine, he sheweth what they meant by that milde phrase of explaining Chapters; and the like words are there often repeated.

c *Bar.an.* 448. *nu.* 65.

44. *Baronius* darkely saw, and closely signified this, when reciting the effect of *Ibas* answere at that judgement, he saith [c], that *Ibas* professed, that he called *Cyrill* an hereticke, before the *union* was concluded; *postquam vero declarando sua Capitula, Cyrillus ista purgavit, & ob eam causam inita est inter eos concordia,* but after that *Cyrill* by explaining his Chapters had purged them, and the *union for that cause* (of purging them) *was once made*, never after that did *Ibas* call *Cyrill* an hereticke. So *Baronius*: declaring evidently, that whē *Ibas* said that *Cyrill* expounded, or explained his Chapters, that explanation which hee meant, was in truth a purging of those Chapters. And what was there, or is, in any one of those twelve Chapters to be purged out ? They are all & wholly [d] orthodoxall, approved in ever part, both by the holy Ephesine Councell, and after that by the Councell at *Chalcedon* [e]. Seeing in them, and every part of them there is not one dramme of any drosse, seeing all of them are the pure and refined Catholike faith, if ought at all bee purged out of them, it must needs be a Catholike doctrine, a position of the Catholike faith : the purging and wiping away of any part, purgeth out the whole Catholike faith, every part of it being so connexed with golden linkes together, that no man can deny one unlesse hee renounce al; nor purge out any of that vitall blood, but in stead thereof will succeed all the blasphemous humors of the Nestorians; Since the explanation which *Ibas* meant was joyned with a purging of those Chapters, it was not, nor could it be any other but a plaine deniall, condemning and anathematizing of those Chapters, and of the whole Catholike faith.

d *Quod nulla ex parte ab Euangelica & Apostolica doctrina aberraverim, id.; postquam Epistolas quas ad Nestorium conscripseram (earum una habet illa* 12. *Capitula (ea extat. to.* 1. *act Con. Ephe. ca.* 14.) *legissent, communi omnium sententia confessi sunt omnes. Cyril. Ep. ad. Imper. to.* 5. *Act. Eph. ca.* 2. *pa.* 829. *a.* e *Conc. Chal. in defin. fidei. Act.* 5.

45. This will bee more cleare, if we consider the occasion of this phrase, and why the Nestorians called that an Explanation, which (as they meant) was a condemnation of his Chapters. S. *Cyrill*, as he was most orthodoxall in this point for his sense, so for his words he was not so strict and precise, but sometimes tooke the word *Nature* in an ample, and catachresticall signification, for *Person*, but commonly in the proper and usuall signification, for *Essence*; whensoever he tooke it in the later sense, hee never then said that there was one onely nature in Christ, which was the heresie of *Apollinarius*, and *Eutiches*, but hee still professed and maintained two natures, that is, two essences, against *Apollinarius*, to be truly in Christ. But when he said that one Nature was in Christ, he then ever meant one Person, & not

one

one Essence. And in this use of the word [Nature] hee followed *Athanasius*, whose words he alledgeth and approveth, we [f] *confesse Christ to be the Sonne of God, according to the spirit, and to be the Sonne of Man, according to the flesh, ὲ διὰ φύσεις τὸ ἓν εἶναι υἱὸν, not two natures to be one Sonne, ἀλλὰ μίαν φύσιν, but one nature of the Word incarnate*: Did *Athanasius* deny two essences, either the divinitie or humanitie in Christ? Nothing lesse: in that very sentēce he professeth him to be truly God, and truly Man: but taking the word Nature for Person, hee in that sense truly denies two, and professeth but one Nature; that is, one naturall subsistence or Person to be in him. In like sort *Cyrill* himselfe, in his Epistle [g] to *Successus*, affirmeth that there is, *una natura Dei verbi incarnati*, one Nature of the Sonne of God incarnate: that is, the Sonne of God, being now incarnate is one Nature, or naturall subsistence, or one, and not two persons, and yet one consisting of two natures, that is, two essences, the divine nature assuming flesh, and the humane nature being personally united unto the Godhead: which to bee his true meaning, besides *Iustinians* [h] testimonie, infinite places doe make evident, those especially in his booke de [i] *fide recta ad Theodosium*, where he saith [k] *the scripture sometimes ascribes all that is spoken of Christ, to the man, sometimes all, unto God, and speaketh right in both, propter utriusque naturæ in unam, eandemque personam coitionem*, by reason that both the natures doe meete in one, and the selfe same person. Nor may we thinke this diverse use of the same word, to be strange or unlawful, but as the name of Father, is given even in Scripture unto the Son [l], when it is taken essentially, or put in opposition to the creatures, but never when it is taken personally, or put in opposition to the Sonne: Even so, when the name of Nature is taken, (as in *Athanasius, Cyrill*, and others sometimes it is) without an opposition to Person, it may there signifie the same with Person, and note any naturall subsistence: but when in any speech there is expressed, or implied an opposition of Nature unto Person, there it ought onely to signifie the substances, or essences concurrant in in that person, and not the Person it selfe. Nor was it so great a fault in the Nestorians to take the word Nature for Person, but partly in drawing that which was the unproper, and abusive, into the ordinarie and usuall signification, (they seldome by Nature noting ought but Person) and specially for that they tooke Nature for Person, even in those very speeches wherein was noted and expressed an opposition of Nature unto Person, as in that profession which they made, acknowledging in Christ *two natures and one person*: where taking Nature for Person, they were enforced to take one Person, for one by affection, or cohabitation: neither of which truly making one person, they called that, one person, which in truth was not one, but divers distinct persons.

46. This profession of one Nature, that is, of one naturall subsistence

---

Marginal notes:

[f] *Athanasii verba apud Cyrillū lib. de recta fide ad Imperato 1. Act. Eph. Conc. ca. 5. §. Porro. pa. 672.a.*

[g] *Ea Epistola Cyril. citatur a Iustiniano in Edict. §. Credimus.*

[h] *Ipse pater (Cyril.) quoties unam naturam dixit verbi incarnatam, Naturæ nomine pro subsistentia usus est; Iustin. in Edict. §. Credimus, pa. 493.a.*
[i] *Extat to. 1. Act. Conc. Ephes. ca. 5.*
[k] *Ibid. §. Quin. pa. 666.a.*
[l] *Tota Trinitas est Pater noster per creationem et gubernationem; ut Esa. 63. Et nunc Domine, Pater noster es: licet persona Patris dicatur Pater Christi per naturam. Aquin. in ca.1. Epist.2. ad Cor. v.1. Et Paternitas in divinis prius importat respectum personæ ad personam, quam respectum Dei ad creaturam. Aquin. p.1. q.33. art.3.*

demned, recalled, and anathematized his Chapters.

48. We doe now clearly see, not onely that the explanation of *Cyrils* Chapters, which *Ibas*, and the other Nestorians of his time meant, is an utter condemning of them all; but upon what pretence and occasion they called his anathematizing, an Explation of his Chapters. If now it may further appeare, that *Vigilius* in his Constitution meant this Nestorian, and slanderous Explanation; I doubt not, but his text will bee sufficient, easie, and cleare in this point: And though none, who diligently peruseth the Popes words, can, as I thinke, doubt hereof; yet because it is not fit, in a just Commentary, to give naked asseverations, specially in a point of such moment, I will propose three or foure reasons to make evident the same. The first is taken from the correspondence and parity of the effect, which followed upon this Explanation, as the cause therof: It is no doubt but *Vigilius* meant such an explanation of *Cyrils* Chapters, as upon w^ch, that *union* which *Ibas* held with *Cyrill*, at the time when he writ this *Epist.* ensued; for *Vigilius* proveth *Ibas* f at that time to have bin a Catholike, because upon *Cyrils* Explanation, he forthwith embraced the *union* with *Cyrill*, and ran to communicate with him. Now it is certaine g, that *Ibas*, when he writ this *Epistle*, approved not the *orthodoxall*, and true *union*, which *Cyrill* truly made with *Iohn*; and the rest, upon their profession of the orthodoxall faith, sent unto him; but onely the union in Nestorianisme, the slanderous union, which they falsely affirmed *Cyrill* to have made; wherefore it certainly followeth, that the Explanation of *Cyrill*, which *Vigilius* intendeth, as a cause of that union, can bee no other then the slanderous explanation, wherein *Cyrill* was falsely said to have explaned his Chapters; that is, anathematized them, and the doctrine delivered in them: for the true and orthodoxal explanatiõ neither did, nor could effect that uniõ in Nestorianisme, w^ch *Ibas* embraced at the time when he writ this *Epistle*; it was the condemning of his Chapters, and in such sort to explane them, that they were anathematized; it was this, and no other explanation, which did make the union, whereof *Ibas* boasteth. Seeing then the hereticall union of *Ibas*, followed upon that explanation which *Vigilius* here meaneth, it is doubtlesse, that the explanation also which hee intendeth, is the same slanderous, & hereticall explanation, which *Ibas*, and the other Nestorians ascribed to *Cyril*, & upon which they joyned in union and communion with him. The cause was like the effect; the effect, an hereticall, and slanderous union; the cause, an hereticall and slanderous explanation.

49. The other reason is taken from the words of *Vigilius*, which, being very pregnant to this purpose, I shall desire the reader diligetly to consider the same. *Vigilius* having said h, that, upon *Cyrils* Explanation, *Ibas*, with all the Easterne Bishops, held *Cyrill* for a Catholike; addeth this collection thereupon,

Ex

f His ab eo explanatis, in communionem ejus devotè concurrit. Vig. Const. nu. 193.
g Vt ante probatum est ca. 11.

h Vig. Const. nu. 194

Ex quo apparet, By this it appeareth, *Ibas,* both before hee understood the twelve Chapters of *Cyrils,* and when he suspected one Nature to be taught thereby, *orthodoxo sensu, quod male dictum existimabat, reprobasse; then* to have reproved those Chapters in an orthodoxall sense; and also after the Explanation of them, *orthodoxo sensu, qua recte dicta cognoverat, venerabiliter suscepisse; then* to have approved them very reverently, and in an orthodoxall sense embraced that which he knew to bee rightly spoken therein. So *Vigilius:* plainly affirming the sense of *Ibas* to have been orthodoxall, both before, and after the Explanation, or *union* (made by *Iohn,* and all the i rest,) with *Cyrill:* At both those times the doctrine, sense, and meaning of *Ibas* was the same, and at both orthodoxal: and *Cyrill,* by that Explanation which *Vigilius* meaneth, declared his Chapters to have the very same meaning; and orthodoxall sense which *Ibas* had; which, when *Ibas* perceived to bee the sense of *Cyrill,* forthwith he held *Cyrill* for a Catholike; and joyned communion with him, and reverently received his doctrine, as being consonant to the sense of *Ibas,* which was still orthodoxall; so there was no alteration in the sense of *Ibas,* that both before, and after *Cyrils* Explanation, was orthodoxall, onely before the union, or Explanation *Ibas* misunderstood *Cyrils* meaning, and thought he had taught one Nature to bee in Christ, whereas *Cyrill* by his Explanation shewed, that he meant just as *Ibas* did, that there were in Christ two Natures, even in that orthodoxall sense which *Ibas* had held; as well before, as after the Explanation.

i *Cum omnibus Orientalibus Episcopis. Ibid.*

50. Oh what a Circean Cup is Heresie? specially Nestorianisme? Pope *Vigilius* doth now shew himselfe in his colours, and demonstrates that he is, as by some μεταβληκοσις, quite transformed into *Nestorius, Theodorus,* or if there be any more hereticall than they in that kinde; for what, thinke you, was that sense of *Ibas,* which the Pope commends for orthodoxall? what was it first after the Explanation and *union* made betwixt *Iohn* and *Cyrill?* I have manifested this before, and the *Epistle* of *Ibas,* written two yeares at least after that *union,* doth make it undeniably evident, that his sense was then, *that there k are two natures, making two persons in Christ,* that the temple, and the inhabiter in the temple are two distinct persons, that *Cyrils* Chapters were hereticall, in teaching one Nature, that is, one Person in Christ; in a word, his sense then was, that Nestorianisme, and nothing but Nestorianisme was Catholike, & that the decree at *Ephesus,* against *Nestorius* was hereticall doctrine. This sense of *Ibas, Vigilius,* by his Pontificall and Cathedral *Constitution,* adjudgeth, and decreeth to be orthodoxall, and Catholike. Could *Nestorius* judge otherwise, or wish any other judgement?

k *Ut liquet ex Ibx Epist.*

51. It may be the sense of *Ibas* was better before the *union,* and Explanation; what was it then? Truly it was the very selfe same: *So long,* saith *Ibas* l, *as the Eastterne Councell anathematized Cyrill;*

l *Vehu ihe in E. Ciiupud Photium in Conc.Chal. Act. 10.pa.112.b.*

Cyrill, (which was still, till the *union*) *sequutus sum Primatem meum, I followed my Primate,* that was, *Iohn* of *Antioch*; what his sense was, and the Synods with him, that was my sense. Now the sense of *Iohn,* and his Conventicle, set downe in more than twenty Synodall Epistles ^m of theirs, was, *that Cyrils twelve Chapters were hereticall, contrary to the Euangelicall and Apostolicall doctrine, that there are two Natures, making two Persons in Christ; that to teach one Nature, that is, one Person in Christ, was hereticall: that Cyrill, and all that tooke part with him, or consented to his Chapters, were heretikes; yea, condemned and anathematized heretikes; that the holy Ephesine Councell was a Conspiracie of heretikes, of seditious and factious persons.* This was the sense of *Iohn,* this the sense of *Ibas* before the *union*: and this sense the Popes Holinesse hath decreed to be a Catholike and orthodoxall sense: The sense of *Ibas,* saith hee, both before the Explanation, or union, and after it, was orthodoxall; so, by the Pope *Vigilius* his decree, it is good Catholike doctrine to teach *two Persons in Christ*; to teach, *Cyrill, Cælestine,* the whole Ephesine Councell, to be heretikes, that is, in a word, to teach Nestorianisme, and nothing but Nestorianisme to be the Catholike faith.

52. But that which I principally aimed at, out of those words of *Vigilius,* was, to observe, that *Cyrils* Explanation here mentioned, and meant by *Vigilius,* neither is, nor can be ought else but an absolute condemning, and anathematizing of his twelve Chapters; for by that explanation, which *Vigilius* intendeth, *Cyrill* shewed, that his sense was the very same with that which *Ibas* had before, and after the *union,* but that sense which *Ibas* had before, and divers yeares after the union, was, that the *two Natures* in Christ make *two distinct Persons,* and that *Cyrils* twelve Chapters, in which it is constantly taught, that there is but one Person (or, as the Nestorians spake, but one nature) in Christ, are hereticall, and to be anathematized, as being contrary to the Catholike faith; wherefore, that Explanation of *Cyrils* Chapters, which *Vigilius* intendeth, is certainly a declaring and acknowledgment, that there is not one, but two distinct Persons in Christ; and that his own twelve Chapters, for teaching but one Person, are all of them hereticall, and to be anathematized.

53. The third reason is taken from *Vigilius* his scope and purpose in this whole passage: Suppose *Vigilius* to have meant the orthodoxall Explanation ⁿ set out by *Cyrill,* seeing that is wholly repugnant to the *Epistle* of *Ibas,* which is full fraught with Nestorianisme: *Vigilius* by approving that Explanation, had condemned this *Epistle* of *Ibas,* and every part thereof. Seeing then by that Explanation which *Vigilius* intendeth, his purpose is, to confirme, and strengthen this *Epistle* of *Ibas,* and prove it to bee orthodoxall, which is onely done by approving the slanderous Explanation of *Cyrill* to be orthodoxall; the very scope, and maine purpose of *Vigilius* doth declare, that it is not, nor can be the orthodoxall,

m Vid. decretum Conciliabuli tom. 3. Act. Conc. Ephef. ca. 2. et reliquis cap.

n Quæ extat in Actis Conc. Ephef. to. 5. ca. 1.
◉ Non diceret Iuvenalis Ibam esse orthodoxum, nisi ex verbis Epistolæ, ejus confessionem fidei orthodoxam comprobaret. Vig. Constit. nu. 193.

thodoxall, but the slanderous and hereticall Explanation only of *Cyrils* Chapters, which the Pope here meant, and by which, being commended for Catholike, hee indevoureth to prove the Epistle, which shewes *Ibas* to have consented most gladly, and reverently, as the Pope saith, to it, to bee indeed Catholike.

54. The fourth and last reason is taken from the fit coherence, and congruity, which this exposition of *Vigilius* meaning, hath, with his whole text concerning this matter. Take him to speake of the true and orthodoxall explanation of *Cyrill*, his words are riddles, more obscure than *Plato's* numbers, yea, they are unreconciliable to the truth of the story: *Ibas*, saith the Pope [p], upon *Cyrils* Explanation, hastened and ran to communicate with *Cyrill*: Expound this of *Cyrils* orthodoxall Explanation, it is utterly untrue; *Ibas* detested [q] that, more than the Chapters themselves; hee neither ranne to embrace that, nor *Cyrill* for that, hee fled from it as a serpent: and the like may be said of the rest. But take *Vigilius* to speake (as indeed he doth) of this slanderous and hereticall Explanation, and then all the words of *Vigilius* are not onely coherent among themselves, but perspicuous and easie. *Ibas* by an errour [r] mis-understood the words of *Cyrill*, (as thinking him to teach *one Nature*, that is, *one Person* in Christ) and then hee spake injuriously against him, and called him an heretike; *sed intellectu [s] Capitulorum meliore recepto*; but when *Ibas* better *understood the Chapters of Cyrill*, (when hee knew that *Cyrill* professed two Natures, that is, two persons in Christ; and that *Cyrill* expounded his Chapters in such sort, that the humanitie and deitie, were each a distinct person) then *Ibas* amended all that he had said amisse of *Cyrill*, and called him no more an heretike, but embraced [t] him as a Catholike. Again, *Ibas* [u] blamed *Cyrill*, while he understood not his Chapters aright, (while he thought, that but one person had beene taught therein) but afterwards, *his ab eo explanatis & intellectis*; when *Cyrill* had explained himselfe, and *Ibas* understood his meaning, (that hee meant either nature to a severall person, and so that there were two natures in *Ibas* sense, that is, two persons in Christ) then, *devotè concurrit, Ibas ran to communicate, and shake hands with Cyrill*. Againe [x], how should we not receive *Ibas*, being a Catholike, who though hee seemed to speak against *Cyrill*, while he mis-understood his Chapters, *nunc ab eo in quo fallebatur intellectu conversus*: Now upon *Cyrils Explanation, hee is converted from that error, whereby hee was deceived*: (for now he seeth *Cyrill* to professe two Natures, in the Nestorian sense, that is, two persons, whereas he erroniously thought *Cyrill* to teach but one Person in Christ:) Againe [y], nothing is reproved of the confession of *Ibas*, (that is orthodoxall, as teaching two natures, that is, two persons in Christ) but *Ibas* hath refuted all, *quod fallente intelligentia de Cyrillo male senserat*; which hee thought amisse of *Cyrill*, by the errour of his misconceiving *Cyrils* meaning.

p *In Const. nu.* 193
q *Misimus vestre sanctitati recens factam expositionem ab Alexandrino, hereticorum Capitulorum, evidentius etiam per illam ostendete suam impietate, ait Conciliabulum Ephes. in quo Ibas in Epist. missa Iohanni, et alijs, in Appen.ad to.3.Act. Eph.Conc.ca.7. pa. 790.a. Nos ad mortem instare parati sumus, et neque Cyrillum, neque capitula ab eo exposita suscipere. Ibid. ca.10. pa. 791.b.*
r *Illa que in Iba Epistola, in injurijs beati Cyrilli per errorum intelligentie dicta sunt. Vig. Const.nu.* 192. *et quod de Cyrillo, Capitula ejus aliter intelligendo detraxerat. Nu.* 193.
[*Ibid. nu.* 192. *Postea professus quia his ab eo explanatis, et à se intellectis, in communionem ejus devote concurrerit; et de his, que prius aliter intellexerat, sit conversus. Ibid nu.* 193.
t *Post explanatione beati Cyrilli factam, et intellectum Cyrilli sibi (Iba) declaratum, Ibas, Cyrillum, ut orthodoxum habuit, et in communione ipsius permansit. Ib.nu.* 194.
u *Ibid. nu.* 193.
x *Ibid.*
y *Ex quibus evidenter declaratur in Iba Episcopo nihil de confessione fidei reprehensum, quam constat esse laudatam, sed eundem, &c. Ibid nu.* 193.

ning, (as thinking *Cyrill* to have taught but one Nature, that is, one Perfon in Chrift.) Laftly, the comparifon which u *Vigilius* fets downe, betwixt *Ibas,* and *Diofcorus,* is hereby made eafie and cleare. *Diofcorus,* though hee commended x *Cyrill,* and the Ephefine Councell, for teaching one Nature in Chrift, (to wit, one Nature in *Diofcorus* fenfe, that is, one Effence) did more wrong *Cyrill,* and the Councell, than *Ibas,* who condemned them both, teaching one Nature (to wit, one in *Ibas* his fenfe, that is, one perfon) in Chrift : For *Diofcorus* commended them in an execrable and hereticall y fenfe, (as teaching one nature (in *Diof-corus* fenfe, that is, one effence, which to affirme is hereticall) but *Ibas* z condemned them in an orthodoxall fenfe, (as thinking them to teach one nature, in *Ibas* his fenfe, that is, one perfon in Chrift) which to condemne is orthodoxall.) Againe, *Diofcorus,* though it was explaned unto him, that neither *Cyrill,* nor the E-phefine Councell taught one nature, in his fenfe; yet did hee by his hereticall fpirit perfift in commending them, as agreeing with him in that hereticall doctrine; but *Ibas* a, when it was ex-planed unto him, that *Cyrill* and the Ephefine Councell taught not one, but two natures, (in *Ibas* his fenfe) by his orthodoxall fpirit defifted prefently to condemne them, and then embraced them both, as agreeing with him in his orthodoxall doctrine, of two natures, that is, of two perfons in Chrift. Laftly, *Diofcorus,* though hee commended them, yet becaufe hee did it in an he-reticall fenfe, and with an hereticall fpirit, was juftly condemned by the Councell at *Chalcedon;* but *Ibas,* though hee condemned them, yet becaufe he did it in an orthodoxall fenfe, and with an orthodoxall fpirit, amending what by an errour, and mif-under-ftanding he had done amiffe, was approved by the Councell of *Chalcedon,* and judged by them to have continued in the right Catholike faith. Thus by our expofition, that *Vigilius* meant the flanderous, and hereticall explanation of *Cyrils* Chapters, is his whole text both coherent, and congruous to it felfe, and very perfpicuous, and eafie; which, if *Vigilius* fhould meane, or be ex-pounded to have underftood of the true and orthodoxall Expla-nation of *Cyrill,* would bee, not onely obfcure, and inextrica-ble, but even repugnant, as well to the fcope as to the words and text of *Vigilius.*

55. Thus the whole text of *Vigilius* being elucidated, it is now eafie to difcerne the two laft parts of the Popes *Artificium* which before I mentioned, for now you fee that his Divinity is meere herefie, and Neftorianifme, and that his morality is unju-ftice, falfhood, and calumnie, moft injurioufly flandering, not on-ly Saint *Cyrill,* but the holy generall Councells of *Ephefus,* and *Chalcedon* to have (like himfelfe) defended and embraced the fame herefies of *Neftorius,* which by them all, is together with this decree of *Vigilius* anathematized and condemned to the ve-ry pit of hell. There needeth not, nor will I feeke any other cen-

sure of this most shamefull dealing of *Vigilius*; then the very words of *Baronius* [a] concerning the Nestorians. *Hæc cum scive-ris, perfacile intelliges*: Seeing you have knowne these things, you may easily perceive, under whose banner and ensigne these men fight. For seeing you have seene them by calumnies, lyes, and impo-stures, publishing counterfeit Epistles, (counterfeit explanati-ons) in the names of renowned men (such as *Cyrill* was) and pat-ching lyes unto lyes, you may well know whose souldiers they are, even the ministers of Sathan, transfiguring themselves into Angels of Light. *Nescit enim pura religio imposturas*, for true Re-ligion is voyd of frauds and impostures: nor doth the truth seeke lying pretenses, nor the catholike faith support it selfe by calum-nies and slanders: sincerity geeth secure, attended, onely with simplicity; with which censure of *Baronius* (agreeing indeed to all Nestorians: but in an eminencie, and κατ᾽ ἐξοχὴν to *Vigilius* hee being the Captaine and King of them all) I end my Com-mentary on the *Constitution* of *Vigilius*; which although it be not so plausibly set downe as *Baronius* would have done, had hee thought good to have undertaken that office: yet I dare boldly affirme, it is delivered farre more truly, faithfully and agreeably to the text, then either the Cardinall himselfe, or any other of the Popes *Gnathoes* would ever have performed: for as I have not wittingly omitted any one clause, which might breed a doubt in this obscure passage; so have I not wrested the words of *Vigilius* to any other sense, then the coherence of his text: the evidence of reason, and manifold proofe out of the historical narration and circumstances thereof doe necessarily inferre, and even enforce.

56. My conclusion now of this second reason of *Vigilius* and *Baronius*, for defence of this Epistle of *Ibas*, is this: seeing the one defineth, and the other defendeth both *Ibas* himselfe, and his profession in this Epistle, in this point, and in the sense of *Ibas* to be orthodoxall, because *Ibas* professeth therein two natures, and one person to bee in Christ; and seeing as wee have certainly proved, *Ibas* meant *two such natures, as make two distinct persons*, and one person, not by a naturall, and hypostaticall union, but onely by affection, liking and cohabitation, which is the very here-sie condemned in *Nestorius*: It doth hence clearly and unavoi-dably ensue, not onely that this *third Chapter* touching the appro-ving of the Epistle of *Ibas*, doth concerne the faith, and is a *questi-on, and cause of faith*, but that *Vigilius* first, and next *Baronius*, and then all who by word or writing, doe defend either *Vigilius* or *Baronius*, or the Popes judgment in causes of faith to be *infallible*; that they all by defending this Epistle as orthodoxall; or that *Ibas* by it ought to bee judged a Catholike, doe thereby main-taine the condemned heresie of *Nestorius* to be the onely Catho-like faith.

a *Bar. an. 433. nu. 10.*

CHAP. XIII.

Two assertions of Baronius, *about the defenders of the* Three Chapters, *refuted : and two other against them, confirmed : the one,* That to dissent from the Pope in a cause of faith, makes one neither an Heretike, nor a Schismatike : *the other,* That to assent absolutely in faith to the Pope or present Church of *Rome,* makes one both an Heretike, and a Schismatike.

1. Aving now demonstratively refuted the first evasion of *Baronius,* I would proceed to the second, but that *Baronius* doth enforce me to stay a little, in the examining of two Positions', which he collects and sets downe touching this cause, the former concerning *heresie,* the later concerning *schisme.*

a An.547. nu.36.

2. His former is this, That ᵃ both the defenders, and the condemners of these *three Chapters* were Catholikes, neither of both were Heretikes. *Negatio vel assertio non constituebat quemquam hereticum;* neither the condemning of these Chapters, nor the defending of them made one an heretike, unlesse there were some other error joyned with it. Againe, in ᵇ these disputations about the *three Chapters,* the question was

b An.553. nu.23.

not such, *ut alter ab altero aliter sentiens, dici posset hareticus : that one dissenting from another herein, might be called an heretike.* So *Baronius;* who to free *Vigilius* from heresie, acquits all that deale either *pro* or *contra* in this cause, neither one side, nor the other are heretikes.

3. See how heresie makes a man to dote. That this question about the *three Chapters* is a cause of faith, wee have cleerly and unanswerably confirmed; and *Baronius* himselfe hath confessed; That the defenders of them, and condemners, were in a manifest contradiction in this cause, (the former, by an evident consequent and cunningly defending; the other condemning the heresies of *Nestorius*) is most evident, and yet both of them in the Cardinals judgement are good Catholikes: neither the one, who with the Nestorians *deny Christ to be God :* nor the other, *who affirme him to be God,* may be called heretikes. This truly is either the same heresie which the Rhetorians maintained, who as *Philastrius*

c Haeres. 43. Prateol. lib.17. Haeres.3.

faith ᶜ praised all sects and opinions, and said they all went the right way; or else it is an heresie peculiar to *Baronius,* such as none before him ever dreamed of; *That two contradictories in a cause of faith may be held, and yet neither of them be an heresie,* nor the pertinacious defenders of either of them both be heretikes. *Baronius* would be famous for a peece of new found learning, and an hereticall quirke, above all that ever went before him, such as by which he hath *ex condigno,* merited an applause of all heretiks

which

which either have beene or shall arise hereafter. For seeing in this cause of faith two contradictories may be held without herefie, the like may be in every other point of faith; and so with *Vigilius*, the Arians, Eutycheans, and all heretikes shall have their *quietus est* : say what they will in any cause of faith, none may call them heretikes. I commend the Cardinall for his wit. This makes all cocke sure, it is an unexpugnable bulwarke to defend the *Constitution* of Pope *Vigilius*.

4. Say you, neither the defenders, nor the condemners of these Chapters may for that cause bee called heretikes? For the condemners of them, trouble not your wit, they are and shall be ever acknowledged for Catholikes. But for the defenders of them, who are the onely men, that the Cardinall would gratifie by this assertion, I may boldly say with the Prophet d, *Though thou wash them with nitre and much sope, yet is their iniquity marked out* : All the water in *Tyber* and *Euphrates* cannot wash away their herefie : for as we have before fully declared, the defending of any one, much more of all these *three Chapters*, is the defending of Nestorianisme, and all the blasphemies thereof, the condemning of the holy Councels of *Ephesus* and *Chalcedon*, and of all that approve them, that is, of the whole catholike Church, and of the whole Catholike Faith. All these must be hereticall, if the defenders of those *three Chapters* be not heretikes.

5. Now against this assertion of *Baronius*, whereby he would acquit *Vigilius* and all that defend him from heresie : I will oppose another and true assertion, ensuing of that which wee have clearly proved; and this it is : That, *one or moe, either men or Churches may dissent from the Popes Cathedrall and definitive sentence in a cause of faith, made knowne unto them, and yet be no heretikes*. For to omit other instances no lesse effectuall, this one concerning *Vigilius*, doth make this most evident. The cause was a *cause of faith*, as *Baronius* himselfe often professeth. The Popes definitive and *Apostolicall* sentence in that *cause of faith*, made for defence of those *three Chapters*, was published and made knowne to the fift generall Councell, and to the whole Church : this also *Baronius* confesseth f, and yet they who contradicted the Popes *Apostolicall* sentence in this *cause of faith*, made knowne unto them, were not heretikes : this also is the confession of *Baronius*, whose assertion as you have seene is, that neither the condemners of these Chapters, nor the defenders of them were heretiks. So by the Cardinalls owne assertions : one may contradict and oppugne the Popes knowne, Cathedral, and *Apostolicall* sentēce in cause of faith, and yet bee no heretike. But what speake I of *Baronius*, the evidence and force of reason doth unresistably confirme this. For the whole fift generall Councell contradicted, yea condemned and accursed the Popes Cathedrall and definitive sentence in this cause of faith made knowne unto them. The whole Catholike Church ever since hath approved the fift

d Ier. 2. 22.

e Vid. sup. c.a. 5. nu. 14.

f An. 553. nu. 47. vid. sup. c.a. 3. nu. 6.

Councell, and the decree thereof, and therefore hath contradicted, condemned and accursed the Popes sentence as the Councell had done. And none I hope will be so impudently hereticall,
as to call not onely the fift generall and holy Councell, but the
whole Catholike Church of God, heretikes: who yet must all
be heretikes, or else the dissenting from, yea the detesting, and
accursing the Popes Cathedrall sentence in a *cause of faith*, cannot make one an heretike.

6. I say more, and adde this as a further consequent on that
which hath been declared, *That none can now assent to their Popes,
or to their Cathedrall definitions* and doctrines maintained by the
present Romane Church, but *co nomine, even for that very cause,*
they are convicted, condemned, and accursed heretikes. For the
manifesting of which *conclusion,* I will begin with that their *fundamentall* position of the Popes Cathedrall *infallibility* in defining causes of faith, whereof before I have so often made mention. And to prove the present Romane Church to bee hereticall
herein, *two things* are to be declared: the one that this is indeed
the *position* or doctrine of their Church: the other, that this doctrine is *hereticall,* and for such condemned by the Catholike
Church.

7. For the former, that the assertion of Popes *infallibility* in
defining causes of faith, is the doctrine of the present Romane
Church, I thinke none conversant in their writings will make
doubt. Give mee leave to propose some testimonies of their
owne. *The Pope* saith Bellarmine[g], *when hee teacheth the whole
Church those things which belong to faith, nullo casu errare potest, hee
can by no possible meanes then erre.* And this, as he saith, is, *certissi-
mum, a most certaine truth:* and in the end hee addeth, this is a
signe, *Ecclesiam totam sentire,* that the whole Church doth
beleeve the Pope to be in such causes infallible. So he testifying
this to be the judgement and doctrine of their whole Church.
The Iesuite *Coster,* for himselfe and their whole Church saith,
We[h] *doe constantly deny the Popes vel haeresim docere posse vel errorem
proponere, to be able either to teach an heresie, or to propose an errour to
be beleeved.* When the Pope, saith Bozius[i], *teacheth the Church,
or sets forth a decree of faith, Divinitùs illi praeclusa est omnis via,
God then stoppeth every way unto him, which might bring him into errour.* Againe[k], in making such decrees, *nunquam valuit aut vale-
bit facere contra fidem, he never was, he never shall be able to doe ought
against the faith.* We beleeve saith *Gretzer*[l], *the judgement of him
who succeeds Peter in the Chaire, non secus ac olim Petri infallibile,
to be no otherwise infallible, then the judgement of Peter was.* And
the[m] gates of hell shall never be able to drive *Peters* successours,
ut errorem quempiam ex cathedra definiant, that they shall define any
errour out of the Chaire. This is saith *Stapleton*[n], a certaine and
received truth among Catholikes, *That the Pope when he decreeth
ought out of his pontificall office, hath never yet taught any hereticall
doctrine,*

g *Lib. 4. de pont.
ca. 3. §. Sic.*

h *Ench. tit. de si. mxo
pont. §. Fatemur.*

i *Th. Boz. lib 18. de
Sig. Eccl. ca. 6. §.
Sequitur.*

k *Idem. lib. 16. ca. 8.
§. Rursus.*

l *Def. ca. 3. lib. 4. de
Rom. Pont. §. Ter-
i̅a.*

m *Idem def. ca. 28.
lib. 1. de pon. if. §.
Quocirca.*

n *Relect. Cont. 3. qu.
4. §. Circa.*

doctrine, nec tradere potest, nor can he deliver any error: yea if it bee a judgement [o] of faith, *it is not onely false but hereticall, to say that the Pope can erre therein.* They, saith *Canus* [p], *who reject the Popes judgement in a cause of faith, are heretickes.* To this accordeth *Bellarmine* [q], *It is lawfull to hold either part in a doubtfull matter, without note of heresie, before the Popes definition be given: but after the Popes sentence, he who then dissenteth from him is an hereticke.* To these may be added, as *Bellarmine* testifieth [r], *St.Thomas, Thomas Waldensis,* Cardinall *Turrecremata,* Cardinall *Cajetane,* Cardinall *Hosius, Driedo, Eccius, Iohannes a Lovanio,* and *Peter Soto,* all these teach it to be impossible, *that the Pope should define any hereticall doctrine.* And after them all, the saying of *Gregory de Valentia,* is most remarkable to this purpose: *It now appeareth,* saith he [s], *that Saint* Thomas *did truly, and orthodoxally teach, that the proposall or explication of our Creed, that is, of those things which are to be beleeved, doth belong unto the Pope:* which truth containes so clearely the summe and chiefe point of Catholike religion, *ut nemo Catholicus esse possit, qui illam non amplectatur, that none can be a Catholike, unlesse hee hold and embrace this.* So he: professing that none are to be held with them for Catholikes, but such as maintaine the Popes *infallibilitie* in proposing or defining *causes of faith.*

8. They have yet another more plausible manner of teaching the Popes *Infallibilitie* in such causes; and that is by commending the judgement of the Church, and of generall Councels to be infallible. *All Catholikes,* saith *Bellarmine* [t], *doe constantly teach that generall Councels, confirmed by the Pope, cannot possibly erre, in delivering doctrines of faith or good life:* And this he saith, is so certaine, that *fide catholica tenendum est, it is to be embraced by the Catholike faith:* and so all Catholikes are bound to beleeve it. Likewise concerning the Church, he thus writeth [u], *Nostra sententia est, it is our sentence, that the Church cannot absolutely erre, in proposing things which are to bee beleeved.* The same is taught by the rest of their present Church. Now when they have said all, and set it out with great pompe, and ostentation of words, for the infallibility of the Church, and Councell; it is all but a meere collusion, a very maske, under which they cover and convaie the Popes *Infallibilitie* into the hearts of the simple. Try them seriously who list, sound the depth of their meaning, and it will appeare, that when they say; The Church is infallible, Generall Councels are infallible, The Pope is infallible, they never meane to make three distinct infallible Iudges, in matters of faith, but one onely *infallible,* and that one is the Pope.

9. This to be their meaning, sometimes they will not let to professe: When we teach, saith *Gretzer* [x], *that the Church is the (infallible) Iudge in causes of faith, per Ecclesiam intelligimus Pontificem Romanum, we by the Church doe meane the Pope for the time being,* or him with a Councell. Againe [y]; They object unto us, that by the

o *Rel.Cont. 6. q. 3. Art. 5. §. Respondeo.*
p *Loc. Theol. lib.6. ca.7. §. Quid.*
q *Lib. 3. de verb. Dei ca.8. §. Excutimus.*

r *Lib.4. de Pont. ca.2. §. Quarto.*

s *In 2. 2. disp. 1.q. 1. punct.1 part.30.*

t *Lib 2.de Conc. ca. 2 §. Ac ut.*

u *Lib.de. Ecclef. milit.ca.14. §. Nostra.*

x *Def.ca. 10. lib.3. de verb. Dei. §. Iam. pa. 1450.*

y *Ibid. §. Ait. pa: 1451.*

Q 3   the

the Church we understand the Pope, *Non abnuo, I confesse wee meane so in deed*, This is plaine dealing: by the Church they meane the Pope. So *Gregorie de Valentia* [z], *By the name of the Church we understand the head of Church, that is, the Pope.* So *Bozius* [a], The Pope *universorum personam sustinet, sustaineth the person of all Bishops, of all Councels, of all the whole Church*, he is in stead of them all. As the whole multitude of the faithfull is the Church *formally*, and the generall Councell is the Church *representatively*, so the Pope also is the Church *vertually*, as sustaining the person of all, and having the power, vertue, and authoritie of all, both the formall and representative Church; and so the Churches or Councels judgement, is the Popes judgement; and the Churches or Councels infallibility, is in plaine speech, the Popes *infallibilitie*.

10. This will further appeare by those comparisons, which they make betwixt the Church, or Councels, and the Pope. It is the assertiō of Card. *Bellarmine* [b], as also of their best [c] writers, *that there is as much authoritie Intensive, in the Pope alone, as in the Pope with a generall Councell, or with the whole Church; though Extensive it is more in them, then in him alone* : Even as the light is *Intensive*, & for degrees of brightnes, as great in the Sun alone, as in it with all the Starres, though it is *Extensive* more in the; that is, more diffused, or spred abroad into moe, being in them, then in the Sun alone; Neither onely is all the authoritie, which either Coūcell or Church hath, in the Pope, but is in a far more eminent manner in him, then in them. In him it is Primitively, or originally, as water in the fountaine, or as light in the Sun; *Omnis authoritas est in uno*, saith *Bellarmine* [d], seeing the governmēt of the Church is Monarchicall, *all ecclesiasticall power is in one*; (he meanes the Pope) and from him it is derived unto others. In the Councell, and the rest of the Church, it is but derivatively, borrowed from the Pope, as waters in little brookes, or as light in the moone & starres. In him is *Plenitudo potestatis*, as *Innocentius* teacheth [e], *the fulnesse of Ecclesiasticall power and authoritie dwelleth in him*, in the rest whether Councels, or Church, it is onely by *Participation*, and measure, they have no more then either their narrow channels can containe, or his holinesse will permit to distill or drop downe upon their heads, from the lowest skirts of his garment. So whatsoever authoritie either Church, or generall Councell hath, the same hath the Pope, and that more eminently, and more abundantly then they either have or can have.

11. But for *Infallibilitie* in judgement thats so peculiar to him, that as they teach, neither the Pope can communicate it, unto Church or Councell, nor can they receive it, but onely by their connexion or coherence to the Pope, in whom alone it resideth. *Potestas & infallibilitas papalis, est potestas & gratia personalis*, saith *Stapleton* [f], *Papall power and infallibilitie is a personall gift*.

z In 2.2. disp. 1. q.1.
a Lib. 2. de sig. eccl. ca.21.§.His.& lib. 14.ca.16.§.His.

b Li 2. de Conc. ca. 13.§ Hec.
c Omnium qui docēt papam esse supra Concilium, ibid. quos recenset ca. 14.§. ultimo.

d Lib. 4. de Pon. Rom. ca. 24.§. Secundo.

e In n.3. ca. 1. Cum ex eo. Ex. de Penit. & cap. Proposuit et de Concess. prebend.

f Relect. Contr. 6. q 3. art. 5. opin. 5.

gift, and grace, given to the person of Peter, and his successors; and
personall gifts cannot bee transferred to others. In like sort
Pighius g, *Vni Petro, atque ejus Cathedræ, non Sacerdotali quamcun-*
que Concilio; the priviledge of never erring in faith, was obtained, by
the prayer of Christ, for Peter alone, and his Chaire; not for any
Councell, though it be never so great. To the same purpose saith
Bellarmine h, *If a generall Councell could not erre in their sentence, the*
judgement of such a Councell should be the last, and highest judgement of
the Church; but that judgement is not the last, for the Pope may either
approve, or reject their sentence. So *Bellarmine;* professing the Popes
onely judgement to be *infallible;* seeing it alone is the last, and
highest, after, and above both Church, and generall Councell.
All the infallibility which they have, is onely by reason of his
judgement to which they accord, & consent. It hence appeareth,
saith *Bellarmine* i, *totam firmitatem, that the whole strength,* and certainty of judgement, which is even in lawfull Councels, is from
the Pope, *non partim à Concilio, partim à Pontifice; it is not partlie*
from the Councell, and partly from the Pope; it is wholly; and onely
from the Pope, and in no part from the Councell. When the
Councell, and Pope consent in judgement, saith *Gretzer* k, *omnis*
infallibilitas Concilÿ derivatur à Papa; all the infallibility of the
Councell is derived from the Pope : and a little after, when the Pope
consenteth with the Councell, *ideo non errat, quia est Papa; hee*
is therfore free from erring, because he is the Pope; and not because
he consenteth with the Councell. In like sort *Melchior* l *Canus;*
The strength and firmitude, both of the whole Church, and of Councels,
is derived from the Pope : and againe m, *In generall Councels, matters*
are not to bee judged by number of suffrages, but by the waight of
them; *Pondus autem dat summi Pontificis authoritas; and it is*
the Popes gravity, and authority, which gives waight to that part
whereunto he inclineth : If he say it, one hundred Fathers with him
are sufficient; but if his assent bee wanting, a thousand, a million,
ten thousand millions; *Nulli satis sunt, no number is sufficient:* Nay,
if all the whole world be of a contrary judgement to the Pope,
yet, as the *Canonist* n tels us, the Popes sentence, *totius orbis placito*
præfertur; is of more weight and worth, than the judgement of the
whole world : So cleare it is, that all their boasting of the authority, and infallible judgement of the Church, and of generall
Councels, wherein they please themselves, more than ever the
Iews did in crying o so oft, *Templū Domini, the Temple of the Lord:*
that all this is nothing else but a Viser, to hide, or actually to
draw into mens mindes the Popes *infallibility:* they having no
meaning at all to give, or allow, either to Church, or generall
Councell, any infallibility; but onely with a reference to the
Pope, to whom alone they annex it as a *personall* gift, and peculiar
prerogative; and who, like those leane and ill favoured Kine of
Pharaoh, hath devoured, and quite swallowed up all the authority, and infallibility, both of Church, and Councels : yet thus
much

g *Lib. 6. de Eccles.*
Hier. ca. 1. § Et
quanquam.

h *Lib. 2. de Conc.*
ca. 11. § De secundo

i *Lib. 4. de Pont.*
ca. 3. §. Contra.

k *Defen. ca. 2. lib. 4.*
de Pont. § Recensent

l *Loc. Theod. lib. 6.*
ca. 7. § Quid.
m *Lib. 5. ca. 5.*
§ Non.

n *Cupers Com. in*
cap. Oportebat.
pa. 11.

o *Ier.*

much now is evident, that seeing all, who are of their present Romane Church, beleeve, and professe the Church, and generall
Councels to be infallible; & seeing their infallibility is none, but
onely by adhering, and consenting to the Pope; it necessarily ensueth, that they all, *à fortiori*, doe beleeve, and must professe the
Pope to be *infallible*; seeing on his, the infallibility of both the
other, doth wholly, and solely depend.

12. Let me adde but one other proofe hereof, taken from
Supremacy of authoritie and judgement: It is a ruled case in their
learning, *Si* [o] *errare non potest, debet esse summus judex*; He who is infallible, must be the highest, and last Iudge; and, *Vice versa*, He [P] who
is the last, and highest judge, must be infallible. *Supremacy* and *infalli-*
bility of judgement are inseparably linked: To whomsoever *Su-*
premacy is given, even for that cause *infallibility* of judgement is
granted unto him also; for seeing from the last or supreme
Iudge, there can be no appeale, it were most unjust to binde
Christians to beleeve his sentence, who might be deceived; most
unjust to binde them from appealing from a judge that were
fallible, or from an erronious judgement. Consider now to
whom *Supremacy* of judgement in *causes of faith*, belongeth: To
whom else but to the Pope? whereas some dare affirme, saith
the *Canonist* [q], that a Councell is above the Pope; *Falsissimum est,*
This is most false: The Successor of *Peter*, saith *Stapleton,* [r] *supre*
omnes est, is above all; Bishops, Church, generall Councels; above
all. *The Pope*, saith *Bellarmine* [s], *is simply and absolutely above the*
whole Church, and above a generall Councell. [t] Hee further tels us,
that this assertion, *That the Pope is above a generall Councell, is, not*
onely the judgment of all the ancient Schoole Divines, & the common sen-
tence of their Writers, (of whom he reckoneth thirteene, and, if it
were fit, three times thirtie might bee scored up with them)
but that it is the publike doctrine of their Church, decreed in their
Laterane Synod, under Leo the tenth: There the Councell, saith
he [u], *diserte & ex professo docuit, did plainly, and of set purpose teach;*
the Pope to bee above all Councels: yea, *expressissimè* [x] *eam definivit;*
that *Laterane Councell did most expresly define this*: and their definition hereof, is, *Decretum de fide, a Decree of faith*: for which
cause, in his Apology, bearing the name of *Schulkenius*, hee professeth [y], that this is, *Articulus fidei, an Article of faith*, such as
every Christian is bound to beleeve, that the Pope is, *Summus*
in terris totius Ecclesiae Iudex; the Supreme, last, and highest *Iudge*
of the whole Church, here upon earth; which he proves, besides many other authorities, by this very *Laterane* [z] decree, and by their
Trent Councell. The words themselves, of those Councels,
make the matter plaine; in that at the *Laterane* Councell they
thus decree; *Solum* [a] *Romanum Pontificem supra omnia Concilia au-*
thoritatem habere; that the Pope alone hath authority above all Coun-
cels; and this, they say, is taught, *not* [b] *onely by Fathers, and Coun-*
cels, but by the holy Scriptures; thereby shewing, that in this decree

o *Bell. lib. 3. de verb.*
Dei ca. 5. § Quintū
et lib. 4. de Pont.
ca. 1. § Denique.
et lib. 2. de Conc. ca.
11. § De tertia.
P *Affirmant ejus ja-*
dicium esse ultimū.
Hinc autem aperte
sequitur non errare.
Bell. lib 2. de Conc.
ca. 3 § Accedat.

q *Cupers com. ad*
cap. oporteb. pa. 4.
nu. 33.
r *Rel Cont. 6. q. 3.*
art. 5. opin. 10.
s *Lib. 2. de Conc. ca.*
17.
t *Lib. eod. ca. 14.*
§ Vltima.

u *Lib. eod. ca. 17.*
§ Denique.
x *Lib. eod. ca. 13.*
§ Deinde.

y *Ca. 6. § Probo.*
pa. 227.

z *Cap. eodem. § La-*
teran. pa. 249.

a *Sess. 11. pa. 639. b.*
b *Nedum ex*
Scriptura sacrae te-
stimonio, dictu san-
ctorum patrum
&c. Ibid.

cree they explicate & declare the Catholike faith, which is one of the Cardinals notes, to know when a decree is publisned by a Councell, *tanquam de fide, as a decree of faith*; and they threaten, the [c] *indignation of God, and the blessed Apostles, to the gainsayers of their decree*: A censure as heavy as any Anathema, the denouncing whereof, is another of the Cardinals notes, that they proposed this decree, as a *decree of faith*. In the other at *Trent*, the Councell teacheth [d], that *unto the Pope is given, Suprema potestas in universa Ecclesia; the Supreme power in the whole Church*. And this *Supremacy* is such, that from all Councels, all other Iudges, you may appeale to him, and hee may reverse [e], adnull, or repeale their judgement; but from him, as being the last, and highest Iudge, as having supreme power, *qua [f] nulla est major, & cui nulla est æqualis,* then which *none is greater, and to which none is equall*; *you may appeale to none, no, not* (as some [g] of them teach) *unto God himselfe*. The reason whereof is plaine; for seeing the Popes sentence in such causes, is the [h] sentence of God, uttered indeed by man; but, *assistente* [i]*, & gubernante Spiritu, Gods Spirit assisting, & guiding him therein*; if you appeale from him, or his sentence, you appeale even from God himselfe, and Gods sentence. Such soveraignty they give unto the Pope in his *Cathedrall* judgement. Now because *Infallibility* is essentially, and inseperably annexed to *supremacie* of judgement, it hence evidently ensueth, that as their *Laterane*, and *Trent* Councels (and, with them, all, who hold their doctrine; that is, all, who are members of their present Romane Church,) doe give *supremacy* of authority and judgement, unto the Pope; so with it they give also *infallibility* of judgement unto him; their best Writers professing, their generall Councels defining, and decreeing, their whole Church maintaining him, and his Cathedrall judgement in causes of faith to bee *infallible*, which was the former point that I undertooke to declare.

13. Suffer mee to goe yet one step further. This assertion of the Popes Cathedrall *infallibility* in *causes of faith*, is, not onely a *position* of their Church, (which hitherto wee have declared) but it is the very maine ground, and *fundamentall* position, on which all the faith, doctrines, and religion of the present Romane Church, and of every member thereof, doth relie. For the manifesting whereof, that must diligently be remembred, which we before have shewed; that, as when they commend the infallibility of the Church, or Councell, they meane nothing else, then the Popes *infallibility*, by consenting to whom, the Church and Councell is infallible; even so, to the point, that now I undertake to shew, it is all one to declare them to teach, that the Church, or generall Councell, is the foundation of faith, as to say, the Pope is the *foundation* thereof, seeing neither the Church, or Councell is such a foundation, but onely by their consenting with, and adhering to the Pope, who is that *foundation*.

14. This sometimes they will not let in plaine termes to professe

Marginal notes:

[c] *Ibid. pa. 340.*

[d] *Sess. 14. ca. 7.*

[e] *Pontifex ut Princeps Ecclesiæ summus; atest retractare illud judicium Concilij. Bell. lib. 1. de Conc. ca. 18. § Dico. Potest approbare vel reprobare. Idē lib. 2. ca. 11. § De tertio.*

[f] *Bell. lib. eodem 2. ca. 18. § Præterea.*

[g] *Aug. Triump. de potest. Eccl. q 6. ar 8.*

[h] *Sententia Concilij cui præest Petrus, est sententia Spiritus sancti. Bell. lib. 3 de verb. Dei. ca. 5. § Sextum. Idem asserere possunt cætera legitima Concilia. Bell. lib. 2. de conc. ca. 2. § Tertius.*

[i] *Bell. lib. 3. de verb. Dei, ca. 10. § Decimum.*

generall and approved Councell, and the consenting judgment of all that are Romane Catholikes.

17. Now all this which they have said of the Church, if you will have it in plaine termes and without circumlocution, belongs onely to the Pope, who is *vertually* both Church and Councell. As the Church or Councell is called infallible, no otherwise but by a *Synechdoche*, because the Pope, who is the head both of Church and Councell, is *infallible:* So is the Church or Councell called the foundation of faith, or last principle on which their faith must relie, by the same figure *Synechdoche*, because the Pope who is the head of them both, is the *foundation* of faith. And whosoever is a true Romane Catholike or member of their present Church, hee beleeveth all other doctrines, because the Church, that is, the Pope doth teach them; and the Pope to teach them *infallibly*, he beleeveth for it selfe, because the Pope saith hee, is in such teaching *infallible*. This *infallibility* of the Pope is the *ἀκρογωνιαῖος λίθος, the very corner stone*; the foundation stone, the rocke and fundamentall *position* of their whole faith and religion, which was the point that I purposed to declare.

18. I have hitherto declared, and I feare too abundantly, that the assertion of the Popes *Cathedrall* infallibilitie in causes of faith, is not onely a *position*, but the very *fundamentall* position of all the doctrines of the present Romane Church. In the next place we are to prove that this position is *hereticall*, and that for such it was adjudged and condemned by the Catholike Church. In the proofe whereof I shall not need to stay long. This whole treatise, and even that which hath already beene declared touching the *Constitution* of Pope *Vigilius* doth evidently confirme the same. For seeing the defending of the *Three Chapters* hath been proved f to be hereticall, the *Constitution* of *Vigilius* made in defence of those Chapters, must of necessity be confessed to be hereticall. Nay if you well consider, you shall see, that this very *position* of the Popes Cathedrall *infallibilitie*, is adjudged to bee hereticall. For the fift generall Councell knew this cause of the *Three Chapters* to bee *a cause of faith*. They knew further that Pope *Vigilius* by his *Apostolicall* decree, and Cathedrall Constitution had defined that those *Three Chapters* ought to bee defended. Now seeing they knew both these, and yet judicially defined the defence of those *Three Chapters* to be hereticall, and for such accursed it, even in doing this, they define the *Cathedrall* judgement of *Vigilius* in this *cause of Faith*, to be hereticall; and therefore most certainly and *à fortiori* define this *position* [That the Popes Cathedrall sentence in a cause of faith is infallible] to bee *hereticall*, and for such they anathematize both it, and all that defend it. And because the judgement and definitive sentence of the fift Councell is consonant to all former, and confirmed by all subsequent Councels till the *Laterane* Synod under *Leo* the tenth, it unavoydably hence ensueth, that the same *position*

f *Ca. 3. & 4.*

tion of the Popes Cathedrall *infallibility* in *causes of faith,* is by the judgement of all generall Councells untill that time, that is, by the constant, and uniforme consent of the whole Catholike Church, adjudged, condemned, and accursed for hereticall, and all who defend it for heretikes. And seeing we have cleerly proved the whole present Romane Church, and all that are members therof, to defend this *position,* yea to defend it as the maine *foundation* of their whole faith; the evidence of that assertion which I proposed g, doth now manifestly appeare: *That none can now assent to the Pope, or to the doctrines of the present Church of Rome,* but he is, *eo nomine, even for that very cause, adjudged and condemned for hereticall, and that even in the very ground and foundation of his faith.* g *Sup. hoc. cap. nu. 6.*

19. From the foundation let us proceed to the walls and roofe of their religion. Thinke you the foundation thereof is onely *hereticall,* and the doctrines which they build thereon *orthodoxall?* Nothing lesse; They are both sutable, both hereticall. That one fundamentall position is like the *Trojan* horse, in the wombe of it are hid many troopes of heresies. If *Liberius* confirme Arianisme, *Honorius* Monothelitisme, *Vigilius* Nestorianisme, these all by vertue of that one assertion must passe currant for Catholike truths. Nay, who can comprehend, I say not in words, or writing, but in his thought, and imagination all the blasphemous and hereticall doctrines, which by all their Popes have beene, or if as yet they have not, which hereafter may be by succeeding Popes defined to bee doctrines of faith? Seeing *Stapleton* h assures us, *That the Church of this, or any succeeding age may put into the Canon and number of sacred and undoubtedly Canonicall bookes, the booke of Hermas called Pastor, and the Constitutions of Clement:* the former being, as their owne notes censure it, i *hæresibus & fabulis oppletus, full of heresies and fables,* rejected by Pope *Gelasius* k with his Romane Synod; the later being stuffed also with many impious doctrines, *condemning* m *lawfull mariage as fornication, and allowing* n *fornication as lawfull;* with many the like impieties, which in *Possevine* o are to bee seene together, for which cause they are worthily rejected in the Canons p of the sixt Councell; seeing the Pope may canonize these, what blasphemies, what heresies, what lies may not with them be canonized? why may not their very *Legend* in the next Session bee declared to be Canonicall? And yet by that *fundamentall position,* they are bound (and now doe *implicitè*) beleeve whatsoever any Pope either by word or writing, either hath already, or shall at any time hereafter define to be a doctrine of faith. Because I will not stay on particulars, if any please seriously to consider this matter, hee shall perceive (that which now I intend to prove) such venome of *infidelity* to lye in that one *fundamentall position* of the Popes Cathedrall *infallibility,* that by reason of holding it, they neither doe nor can beleeve or hold with *certaintie of faith,*

h *Lib. 9. doct. prin. ca. 14. §. Manet.*

i *Nota in lib. Hermæ. 10. 5. Bibl. S. patr.*

k *Concil. Rom. primû sub Gelasio.*

m *Constt. Clem. lib. 3. ca. 2.*

n *Idem lib. 8. ca. 32.*

o *Bibl. in verbo Clemens Rom.*

p *Can. 2.*

R   any that hee ought not onely to teach with knowledge, but learne with patience; hee I doubt not would readily have demonstrated not onely how learned, but how willing to learne himselfe had beene, had this question in his life time beene debated, by such learned and holy men, as afterwards it was. I often admire that one observation, among many, which the same *Augustine* makes touching this error in *Cyprian*, of whom being so very learned, he saith, *Propterea non vidit aliquid ut per eum aliud eminentius videretur*; *He therefore saw not this one truth touching Rebaptization, that others might see in him a more eminent and excellent truth*. And what truth is that? In him we may see the truth of Humilitie, the truth of modestie, the truth of Charitie and ardent love to the peace, and unitie of the Church: but the most excellent truth that I can see, or as I thinke, can be seene in *erring Cyprian* is this, *that one may be a true Catholike, a Catholike Bishop, a pillar of Gods Church, yea even a Saint and glorious Martyr, and yet hold an error in faith*, as did that holy Catholike Bishop, and blessed Martyr Saint *Cyprian*. To him then and the other Africane Bishops, who in like sort erred as he did; may fitly be compared the state of those servants of God, who in the blindnesse and invincible ignorance of those times of Antichrist, together with many golden truths, which they most firmely beleeved, upon that solid *foundation* of the Scriptures, held either *Transubstantiation*, or the like errors, thinking them (as *Cyprian* did, of *Rebaptization*) to be taught in that *foundation* also. They erred in some doctrines of faith, as *Cyprian* did: yet notwithstanding those errors, they may be Catholikes, and blessed as *Cyprian* was, because they both firmely beleeved many Catholike truths, and their error was without pertinacie as *Cyprians* was. For none, who truly beleeves the Scripture, and holds it for the *foundation* of his faith, can with pertinacie hold any doctrine repugnant to the Scripture, seeing in his very beleeveing of the Scripture, and holding it as the *foundation*, he doth in truth, though *implicitiè*, and *in radice*, as I may say, beleeve the flat contrarie to that error, which *explicitè* he professeth. And because he doth *implicitè* beleeve the contrarie thereof, he hath, (even all the time while he so erreth) a readinesse and preparation of hart to professe the contrarie whensoever out of the Scripture it shall bee deduced and manifested unto him.

23. A second way of holding those doctrines, is of them, who together with the truths, hold the errours also of their Church, *Transubstantiation*, *Purgatorie*, or the like, thinking them to bee taught in Scriptures, as did the former, but adding obstinacie, or pertinacie to their holding of them, which the former did not. And their pertinacie is apparant hereby, if either they will not yeeld to the truth, being manifested out of the Scriptures unto them, or if before such manifestation, they be so addicted and wedded to their owne wills, and conceits,

that

that they resolve either not to heare, or if they doe heare, not to yeeld to the evidence of reason, when they are convinced by it. For it is certaine, that one may bee truly pertinacious not onely after conviction, and manifestation of the truth, but even before it also, if he have a resolution not to yeeld to the authority, and weight of convincing reasons. Of this sort were all those who ever since their second *Nicen* Synod (about which time, the Romane Church made their first publike defection from the true and ancient faith) tooke part with that faction in the Church, which maintained the *adoration* of Images, and after that, *Deposing* of Princes, then *Transubstantiation*, and other like heresies, as they crept by degrees into the Church, in severall ages. From that time untill *Leo* the tenth, the Church was like a confused lumpe, wherein both gold and drosse were mingled together : or like a great Citie infected with the plague. All as well the sicke as sound, lived together within the walls, and bounds of that Citie, but all were not infected, and of those that were, not all alike infected, with those hereticall diseases which then raigned, & more, and more prevaled in the Church. Some openly, and constantly withstood the corruptions, and heresies of their time, and being worthy Martyrs, sealed with their blood that truth which they professed. Others dissented from the same errors, but durst not with courage, and fortitude oppose themselves, such as would say to their friends in private : Thus [*] I would say in the schooles and openly, *sed maneat inter nos, diversum sentio, but keepe my counsell, I thinke the contrarie*. Many were tainted with those *Epidemicall* diseases by the very contagion of those with whom they did converse, but that strong Antidote in the foundation, which preserved *Cyprian* and the Africane Bishops, kept from their hearts, and at last overcame all the poyson wherewith they were infected. Onely that violent, and strong faction, which pertinaciously adhered to the hereticall doctrines, which then sprung up, (the head of which faction was the Pope) and who preferred their owne opinions, before the truth, out of the Scriptures manifested unto them, and by some Councels, also decreed, as namely by that at *Constantinople* in the time of *Constantinus Iconomachus*, and that at *Frankford*, these I say who wilfully and maliciously resisted, yea persecuted the truth and such as stood in defence of it, are those, who are ranked in this second order, who though they are not in proprietie of speech to bee called Papists, yet because the errors which they held are the same, which the Popish Church now maintaineth, they are truly and properly to be tearmed *Popish Heretickes*.

24. The third way of holding their doctrines, beganne with their *Lateran* decree, under *Leo* the tenth, at which time they held the same doctrines which they did before, but they held the now upon another *Foundation*. For the they cast away the old

[*] *Paralip. ad Abb Vsperg. pa. 448.*

and sure *Foundation*, and laid a new one of their owne in the
roome thereof, The Popes word, in stead of Gods, and Anti-
christs in stead of Christs. For although the Pope long before
that time, had made no small progresse in Antichristianisme,
first in usurping an universall authority over all Bishops, next
in upholding their impious doctrines of *Adoration* of Images,
and the like, and after that in exalting himselfe above all Kings
and Emperors, giving and taking away their Crownes at his
pleasure; yet the height of the Antichristian mysterie consisted
in none of these, nor did he ever attaine unto it, till by vertue
of that Laterane decree he had justled out Christ and his word,
and laid himselfe and his owne word in the stead thereof, for the
Rocke & *Foundation* of the Catholike faith. In the first, the Pope
was but Antichrist *nascent*; In the second, Antichrist *crescent*; In
the third, Antichrist *regnant*; but in this fourth, he is made Lord
of the Catholike faith, and Antichrist *triumphant*; set up as God
in the Church of God, ruling, nay tyrannizing, not onely in the
externall and temporall estates, but even in the faith, and Con-
sciences of all men; so that they may beleeve neither more, nor
lesse, nor otherwise then he prescribeth, nay that they may not
beleeve the very Scriptures themselves, and word of God, or
that there are any Scriptures at all, or that there is a God, but
for this reason, *ipse dixit*, because *he saith so*, and his saying, being a *Transcedent principle of faith*, they must beleeve for it selfe,
quia ipse dixit, *because he saith so*. In the first, and second, hee
usurped the authority and place but of Bishops; in the third,
but of Kings: but in making himselfe the Rocke and *Foundation*
of faith, he intrudes himselfe into the most proper office and
prerogative of Iesus Christ, *For other foundation can no man lay,
then that which is laid, Iesus Christ*.

25. Here was now quite a new face of the Romane Church,
yea, it was now made a new Church of it selfe, in the very essence thereof distinct from the other part of the Church, and
from that which it was before. For although most of the *Ma-
terialls*, as *Adoration* of Images, *Transubstantiation*, and the rest,
were the same, yet the *Formalitie* and foundation of their faith
and Church was quite altered. Before they beleeved the Pope
to doe rightly, in decreeing Transubstantiation, because they
beleeued the Scriptures, and word of God, to teach and warrant that doctrine: but now *vice versa* they beleeve the Scriptures, and word of God, to teach Transubstantiation, because
the Pope hath decreed and warranted the same. Till then one
might be a good Catholike, and member of their Church, such
as were the Bishops in the generall Councels of *Constance* and
Basill, and those of the fift, sixt, seventh, and succeeding Councels,
and yet hold the Popes *Cathedrall* judgement in causes of faith
to bee not onely *fallible*, but *hereticall* and accursed, as all those
Councels did: But since *Supremacie*, and with it *Infallibilitie* of
judgement,

judgement, is, by their *Laterane* decree, transferred to the Pope:
he who now gainsayeth the Popes sentence, in a cause of faith, is
none of their Church, as out of *Gregory de Valentia, he is an here-*
tike, as out of *Stapleton, Canus,* and *Bellarmine* was ᵘ declared: He   u *Sup.hoc cap.qu.7*
may as well deny all the Articles of his *Creed,* and every text in
the whole Bible, as deny this one point; for in denying it, he doth
eo ipso, by their doctrine *implicitè,* and in effect, deny them all, seeing he rejects that formall reason, for which, and that *foundation*
upon which, they are all to be beleeved; and without beleefe of
which, not one of them all can be now beleeved.

·26. These then of this third sort are truly to be counted members of their present Romane Church; these, who lay this new,
& *Laterane foundatiõ,* for the ground of their faith, whether *expli-*
citè, as do the learned, or *implicitè,* as do the simpler sort in their
Church, who wilfully blind-folding themselves, and gladly persisting in their affectate and supine ignorance, either will not use
the meanes to see, or seeing, will not embrace the truth, but con-
tent themselves with the *Colliars* ˣ *Catechisme,* and wrap up their   x *Hos.de author.sac.*
owne in the Churches faith, saying, *I beleeve as the Church belee-*   *Script.lib.3.*
veth, and the Church beleeveth what the Pope teacheth. All   § *Querit.*
these, and onely these are members of their present Church, unto whom, of all names, as that of *Catholikes,* is most unsutable,
and most unjustly arrogated by themselves; so, the name of *Pa-*
pists, or, which is equivalent, *Antichristians,* doth most fitly, truly, and in propriety of speech, belong unto them: For seeing
forma dat nomen, & esse, whence rather should they have their
essentiall appellation, then from him, who giveth life, formali-
ty, and essence to their faith, on whom, as on the Rocke,
and corner-stone, their whole faith dependeth. The saying of
Cassander to this purpose, is worthy remembring: *There are*   y *Lib.de offic.viri*
some, saith hee ʸ, *who will not permit the present state of the Church,*   *pij. § Sunt alij.*
though it be corrupted, to be changed, or reformed; and who, *Pontifi-*
cem Romanum quem Papam dicimus, tantum non deum faciunt; make
the Bishop of Rome, whom we call the Pope, almost a god; preferring his
authority, not onely above the whole Church, but above the Sacred
Scripture, holding his judgement equall to the divine Oracles, and an
infallible rule of faith: Hos non video, cur minus Pseudo-catholicos, &   z *Ecce potestas Ec-*
Papistas appellare possis; I see no reason, but that these men should be   *clesiæ supra Script.*
called Pseudo-catholikes, or Papists. Thus *Cassander,* upon whose ju-   *Enchyr.tit.de*
dicious observatiõ it followeth, that seeing their whole Church,   *Eccles.*
and all the members thereof, preferre the Popes authority a-   a *Enchyr.Ibid.*
bove the whole Church, above all generall Councels, and *quoad*   b *Tb.Boz.lib.de sig-*
nos, (which is *Cassanders* meaning) above ᶻ the Scriptures also;   *nis Eccl.16. ca.1c.*
defending them not to be ᵃ authenticall, but by the authority of   § *Illud.*
the Church; that there is, *multo* ᵇ *major authoritas, much more au-*   c *Non adeo absurde*
thoritie in the Church, than in them; that it is no ᶜ absurd, nay, it   *dictum est, &c.*
may be a pious ᵈ saying, *That the Scriptures without the authoritie*   *Gretz.Appen.2. ad*
of the Church, are no more worth than Æsops Fables : seeing they all,   *lib.1.de verb.dei*
                                                                    pa.306.
                                                      with   P *Potuit illud pio*
                                                                    sensu dici.Hos.lib.3.
                                                                    de author.Script.
                                                                    § *Fingamus.*

with one consent make the Pope the last, supreme, and *infallible* Iudge in all causes of faith; there can bee no name devised more proper and fit for them, than that of Papists; or, which is all one, Antichristians; both which expresse their essentiall dependence on the Pope, or Antichrist; as on the *foundation* of their faith; which name most essentially also differenceth them from all others, which are not of their present Church; especially from true Catholikes, or the Reformed Churches; seeing, as we make Christ and his word; so they on the contrary, make the Pope, that is to say, Antichrist, and his word, the ground and *foundation* of faith: In regard wherof, as the faith & religion of the one is from Christ truly called, Christian, and they truly, Christians; so the faith and religion of the other, is from the Pope, or Antichrist, truly, and properly called Papisme, or Antichristianisme, and the professors of it Papists, or Antichristians. And whereas Bellarmine [e] glorieth of this very name of Papists, that it doth, *attestari veritati, give testimony to that truth which they professe*; truly we envy not so apt a name unto them: Onely the Cardinal shews himself a very unskilful Herald in the blazony of this coat, & the descēt of this title unto them. He fetcheth [f] it forsooth frō Pope *Clement*, Pope *Peter*, and Pope *Christ* : Phy, it is of no such antiquity, nor of so honourable a race. Their owne *Bristow* will assure [g] him, *that this name was never heard of till the dayes of Leo the tenth*. Neither are they so called, (as the Cardinall fancieth) because they hold communion in faith with the Pope, which, for sixe hundred yeares and more, all Christians did, and yet were not Papists, nor ever so called; but because they hold the Popes judgement to be supreme, and *infallible*; and so build their faith on him, as on the *foundation* thereof, which their owne Church never did, till the time of *Leo* the tenth. It is not then the Lion of the Tribe of *Iudah*, but the Lion of that *Laterane* Synod, who is the first Godfather of that name unto them, when hee had once laid the Pope as the *foundation* of faith in stead of Christ; they who then builded their faith upon this new *foundation*, were fitly christened with this name of Papists, to distinguish them, and their present Romane Church from all others, who held the old, good, and sure *foundation*.

26. You see now the great diuersity which ariseth from the divers manner of holding the same doctrines. The errours maintained by all those three sorts, of which I have spoken, are almost the same, and materially they are Popish heresies; and yet the first sort did onely erre therein, but were not *heretikes*, because not pertinacious. The second doe not onely erre, but by adding pertinacy to errour, are truly *heretikes*, but yet not *Papists*, because they hold those Popish heresies in another manner, and on another foundation then Papists doe. The third, and last sort, which containeth all, and onely those who are members of the present Romane Church, doe both erre, and are *heretikes*; and, which

e *Lib. de. not. Eccl. cá.4.*

f *Papista deducitur à Papa, qualis fuit Petrus, & Christus ipse. ibid.*
g *Demand. 8.*

which is the worst degree of heresie, are *Papists*, that is, *Antichristian heretikes*; not onely holding, and that in the highest degree of pertinacy, those heresies which are contrary to the faith, but holding them upon that *foundation* which quite overthroweth the faith.

27. By this now doth the evidence of that truth appeare, which before [h] I proposed, that none who hold the Popes *infallibility* in causes of faith for their *foundation*, (that is, none of the present Romane Church)either doth, or can beleeve any one doctrine of faith, w[ch] they professe: For seeing the beleefe of all other points relyes upō this, so that they beleeve thē, because they first beleeve this, it followeth by that true rule of the Philosopher [i], *Propter quod unumquodq̄, illud magis*; that they doe more firmely and certainly beleeve this, which is the *foundation*, than they doe, or can beleeve any other doctrine; I say not *Transubstantiation*, or *Purgatory*, but more thā that Article of their *Creed*, *that Christ is God*, or that there is a God, or any the like, which is builded upon this *foundatiō*. And seeing we have cleerly demonstrated that *foundation* to bee, not onely untrue, but hereticall; and therefore such as cannot be apprehended by faith, it being ho true object of faith; it doth evidently hence ensue, that they *neither doe, nor can beleeve any one doctrine, position or point of faith*. Impossible it is, that the roofe should bee more firme than the *foundation* which supports the roof; or the conclusion more certaine unto us than those premisses which cause us to assent, and make us certaine of the conclusion: That one fundamentall uncertainty, & contrariety to the faith, which is vertually in all the rest, breeds the like uncertainty, and contrariety to faith, in them all; and, like a Radicall poyson, spreads it selfe into the whole body of their religion, infecting every arme, branch, and twigge of their doctrine, and faith; whatsoever errour or heresie they maintaine, (and those are not a few) those they neither doe, nor can beleeve, because they are no objects of faith, whatsoever truths they maintaine, (and no doubt they doe many) those they thinke they doe, and they might doe, but indeed they doe not beleeve, because they hold them for that reason, and upon that *foundation* which is contrary to faith, and which overthroweth the faith: For to hold or professe that Christ is God, or that there is a God, *eo nomine*, because the Devill, or Antichrist, or a fallible man testifieth it unto us, is not truly to beleeve, but to overthrow the faith.

28. This may be further cleared by returning to our example of *Vigilius*. If, because the Pope judicially defineth a doctrine of faith, they doe therefore beleeve it, then must they beleeve Nestorianisme to be the truth, and Christ not to bee God, because Pope *Vigilius*, by his judiciall and *Apostolicall* sentence, hath decreed this, in decreeing that the *three Chapters*, are to be defended: If they beleeve not this, then can they beleeve nothing at all,

h Sup. nu. 29.

i Arist. lib. 1. demo ca. 2.

eo nomine, becaufe the Pope hath defined it; and then the *foundati-on* of their faith being abolifhed, their whole faith, together with it, muft needs be abolifhed alfo. Againe, if becaufe the Pope defineth a doctrine, they doe therefore beleeve it; then feeing Pope *Cæleftine*, with the Ephefine, and Pope *Leo*, with the *Chalcedon* Councell, decreed Neftorianifme to be herefie, they, by the ftrength of their fundamental pofitiõ of the Popes *infalli-bility*, muft, at one and the fame time, beleeve, both Neftoria-nifme to be truth, as Pope *Vigilius* defined, and Neftorianifme to be herefie, as Pope *Caleftine* and *Leo* defined; and fo they muft either beleeve two contradictories to be both true, yea, to bee truths of the Catholike faith, which, to beleeve, is impoffible; or elfe they muft beleeve, that it is impoffible to beleeve, either the one or the other, *eo nomine*, becaufe the Pope hath defined it, and fo beleeve it to bee impoffible to beleeve that, which is the *foundation* of their whole faith. Neither is this true onely in o-ther points, but even in this very *foundation* it felfe: for the fift Councell, which decreed the Cathedrall and *Apoftolicall* fen-tence in the caufe of the *Three Chapters*, to be hereticall, was ap-proved by the decrees of Pope *Gregory*, *Agatho*, and the reft, unto *Leo* the tenth. If then they beleeve a doctrine to be true, becaufe the Pope hath defined it, then muft they beleeve the Popes *Ca-thedral* fentence in a caufe of faith, to bee, not onely falli-ble, but hereticall; and fo beleeve, that upon this fallible and hereticall *foundation*, they can build no doctrine of faith, nor hold thereupon any thing with certainty of faith : So, if the Pope in defining fuch caufes be *fallible*; then, for this caufe, can they have no faith, nor beleeve ought with certainty of faith, feeing all relies upon a *fallible foundation*. If the Pope, in defining fuch caufes, be *infallible*, then alfo can they have no faith, feeing, by the infallible decrees of Pope *Gregory*, *Agatho*, and the reft unto *Leo* the tenth, the Popes Cathedrall fentence in a caufe of faith, may bee hereticall, as this of Pope *Vigilius*, by their judgement, was : So, whether the Pope in fuch caufes, be *falli-ble*, or *infallible*, it infallibly followeth upon either, that none who builds his faith upon that *foundation*, that is, none who are members of their prefent Romane Church, can beleeve, or hold with certainty of faith, any doctrine whatfoever, which he pro-feffeth to beleeve.

29. Here I cannot chufe, but, to the unfpeakeable comfort of all true beleevers, obferve a wonderfull difference betwixt us, and them, arifing from that diverfitie of the *foundation*, which they and we hold; their *foundation* being not onely uncertaine, but *hereticall* and Antichriftian, poyfoneth all which they build thereon; it being vertually in them all, makes them all, like it felfe, uncertaine, hereticall, and Antichriftian; and fo thofe very doctrines, which, in themfelves, are moft certaine, and ortho-doxall, by the uncertainty of that ground, upon which, and for
which

which they are beleeved, are overthrowne, with us, and all Catholikes it fals out otherwise. Though such happen to erre in some one, or moe doctrines of faith, (say, in *Transubstantiation, Purgatory*, or, as *Cyprian* did, in *Rebaptization*) yet seeing they hold those errors, because they thinke them to be taught in the Scriptures, and Word of God, on which alone their faith relyeth, most firmely, and undoubtedly beleeving whatsoever is taught therein; (among which things are the contrary doctrines to Transubstantiatiō, Purgatory, & Rebaptization:) such, I say, even while they doe thus erre in their Explicite profession, doe truly, though *implicitè*, by consequent, and *in radice, or fundamento*, beleeve, and that most firmely, the quite contrary to those errours, which they doe outwardly professe, and think they doe, but indeed doe not beleeve. The vertue and strength of that fundamentall truth, which they indeed and truly beleeve, overcommeth all their errours, which in very deed they doe not, though they thinke they doe beleeve, whereas, in very truth, they beleeve the quite contrary. And this golden *foundation* in Christ, which such men, though erring in some points, doe constantly hold, shall more prevaile to their salvation, than the Hay and Stubble of those errours, which ignorantly, but not pertinaciously, they build thereon, can prevaile to their destruction: and therefore if such a man happen to die, without explicite notice, and repentance of those errours in particular, (as the saying of Saint *Austen* [k], that what faults Saint *Cyprian* had contracted by humane imbecillity, the same, by his glorious Martyrdome, was washed away, perswades mee that *Cyprian* did: and as of *Irene, Nepos, Iustine Martyr*, and others, who held the errour of the Chiliasts, I thinke none makes doubt :) it is not to be doubted, but the abundance of this mans faith and love unto Christ, to whom in the *foundation* hee most firmely adhereth, shall worke the like effect in him, as did the blood of martyrdome in Saint *Cypran* : For the baptisme of martyrdome washeth away sinne, not because it is a washing in blood, but because it testifieth the inward washing of his heart by faith, and by the purging Spirit of God. This inward washing in whomsoever it is found, (and found it is in all who truly beleeve, though in some point of faith they erre) it is as forcible and effectuall to save *Valentinian* [l], neither baptized with water, nor with blood; and *Nepos* [m], baptized with water, but not with blood, as to save *Cyprian*, baptized both with water, and with blood. Such a comfort and happinesse it is to hold the right and true *foundation* of faith.

30. The quite contrary is to be seene in them: Though they *explicitè* professe Christ to be God, wch is a most *orthodoxall* truth, yet because they hold this, as all other points, upon that *foundation* of the Popes *infallible* judgement in causes of faith, and in that *foundation* this is denyed, Pope *Vigilius*, by his *Cathedrall* Constitution

k *Lib. 1. de baptism. ca. 18.*

l *Ablutus ascendit, quē sua fides lavit. Amb. Orat. de obitu Valent.*
m *Qui jam ad quietem processit, ait Dionys. apud Euseb. l. 1. ca. 23.*

stitution defining Neftorianifme to be truth, and fo Chrift not to be God; it muft needs be confeffed, that even while they doe *explicitè* profeffe Chrift to bee God, they doe *implicitè, in radice,* and *in fundamento,* deny Chrift to be God: and becaufe, by the Philofophers rule; they doe more firmely beleeve that *foundation,* than they doe, or can beleeve any doctrine depending thereon; it muft needs enfue hence, that they doe, and muft by their doctrine more firmely beleeve the Negative, that Chrift is not God, which in the *foundation* is decreed, then they doe, or can beleeve the Affirmative, that Chrift is God, which upon that *foundation* is builded. The truth, which upon that *foundation* they doe *explicitè* profeffe, cannot poffibly be fo ftrong to falvation, as the errour of the *foundation,* upon which they build it, will be to deftruction: For the fundamentall errour is never amended by any truth fuperedified and laid thereon, no more than the rotten foundation of an houfe is made found by laying upon it rafters of gold or filver, but all the truths that are fuperedified, are ruinated by that fundamentall errour and uncertainty on which they all relye, even as the beames and rafters of gold are ruinated by that rottenneffe and unfoundneffe which refteth in the *foundation* : Or if they fay, that both the affertions (which are directly contradictory) are from that *foundation* deduced, *Caleftine* and *Leo* decreeing the one, that Chrift is God, as *Vigilius* decreed the other, that Chrift is not God, then doth it inevitably follow, that they can truly beleeve neither the one, nor the other, feeing, by beleeving that *foundation,* they muft equally beleeve them both, which is impoffible. Such an unhappy, and wretched thing it is, to hold that erroneous, hereticall, and Antichriftian foundation of faith.

31. My conclufion of this point is this. Seeing we have firft declared, that all who are members of the prefent Romane Church, doe hold the Popes *Cathedrall infallibility* in caufes of faith, yea, hold it as the very *foundation* on which all their other doctrines, faith and religion doth relye; and feeing wee have next demonftrated this to be a fundamentall herefie, and not onely an hereticall, but an Antichriftian *foundation,* condemned by Scriptures, by generall Councels, by ancient Fathers, and by the confenting judgement of the whole Catholike Church; that now hence followeth which I propofed to prove, *that none is, or can bee a member of their prefent Church, but the fame is convicted and condemned for an heretike,* by Scriptures, generall Councels, Fathers, and by the uniforme confent of the Catholike Church. An heretike, firft, in the very *foundation* of his faith, which being Antichriftian, is hereticall in the higheft, and worft degree that may be, razing the true foundation of faith, in regard whereof the myftery of Antichriftianifme farre furpaffeth all the herefies that ever went before, or fhall ever follow after it. An heretike, fecondly, in many particular doctrines depending

ding on that *Foundation*, among which are the heresies and blasphemies of the Nestorians, all which by the *Cathedrall* constitution of *Vigilius*, are decreed to be truths, and by all men to be defended. Lastly, an heretike vertually and *quoad radicem*, in every doctrine of faith which hee holdeth or professeth, and so hereticall therein, that the very holding of Catholike truths becomes unto him hereticall, seeing he holds them upon that *Foundation*, which is not only contrary to faith, but which overthroweth the whole faith. *Reward [o] Babylon, O ye servants of the Lord, as she hath rewarded you, give her double according to her workes, and in the cup that she hath filled to you, fill her the double.*

    32. From hence there ensueth one other conclusion, wch being worthy observing, I may not well omit. And this it is, *That in none at all, of their Church, or of the same faith with it, there neither is nor can be (so long as they remaine such) any piety or holinesse, either in their life, or in any of their actions : nor any act which is truly good* and acceptable unto God is or can be performed by any of them. For true faith is the *Foundation* and fountaine of all true pietie, and good actions, it being impossible, as the Apostle teacheth, *without [p] faith to please God :* and, *to the [q] unbeleevers all things are impure, even their mindes and consciences are defiled;* How much more their outward actions, speeches, writings, and thoughts, which all spring from the heart. To this purpose is that in the Prophet *Haggai [r]*, who demandeth of the Priests, *If a polluted person (such are all whose hearts are not purified [s] by faith) touch any of these things, either holy bread, or holy wine, or any holy thing, shall it be uncleane? And the Priests answered and said, It shall be unclean.* The pollution of him that toucheth it, pollutes all, even the most holy things that are. Then answered *Haggai,* and said, *So is this people, and so is this Nation before me, saith the Lord. So are all the workes of their hands, and that which they offer is uncleane.* The same agreeth to those of whom we intreat. The infidelity of their hearts, pollutes all their actions, seeme they never so holy : their almes-deedes and workes of charity, their righteousnesse, and workes of justice, their fastings, continency, and workes of temperance, their prayers, sacraments, sacrifices, and workes of pietie : the fountaine being poysoned with *infidelity*, and want of true faith, all the waters, every river, and little brooke derived from it, carieth the same infection in it, which it tooke at the spring. Saint *Austen* is plentifull in this point : *Where the faith,* saith he [t], *is fained or unsound, non potest ex ea bona vita existere, there can no good life be or arise from it.* In another place [u] hee sheweth, that even to keepe ones selfe chast or continent, and yet to doe this without faith, is a sinne, and that thereby, *non peccata coercentur, sed alijs peccatis alia peccata vincuntur,* sinnes are not expelled, but one sinne (of intemperancy) is overcome by another sinne, (of continency wanting faith.) To omit many the like, heare what he saith to the Manichees, boasting, as they [x] of the Romane Church doe, that they fulfilled

o *Rev.* 18.6.

p *Heb.* 11.6.
q *Tit.* 1.15.

r *Ca.* 2. 14.15.
s *Act.* 15.9.

t *Lib.* 5. *cont. Faust. ca.* 11.
u *Lib.* 1. *de Nup. & Concis. ca.* 3.
x *Potest bomo facere plus quā Deus præcipit, igitur multo magis potest implere præceptum. Bell. lib.* 4. *de Iustif. ca.* 13. S. *Accedunt, & Catholici omnes docent, legem dei justis hominibus esse absolutè possibilem, lib. eod. ca.* 16 §. *Porrò.*

S

y *Aug. lib. 5. contra Faust. ca. 5.*

fulfilled the Law. Why *doe ye boast so much of fulfilling the Law, and commandements of God?* Quid illa prodessent omnia ubi non est fides vera, etiamsi vere implerentur à vobis? *what could all the commandements profit you, who have not a true faith, though ye did truly fulfill them all?* Thus and much more Saint *Austen.* Seeing then we have proved, their faith to be not onely unsound but heretical and Antichristian, (worse then which, the faith of the Manichees could not be:) impossible it is that from such a faith, either true vertue, or any godly act should ever arise. The best that can be said of those which they call good workes, is that which *Lactantius* saith of the works of the Ethnikes, which like theirs, quoad substantiam operis, were good. *Vmbra est & imago justitiæ, quam illi justitiam putaverunt: It is but a shadow and shew of justice, which they thinke to be justice.* Omnis *doctrina & virtus eorum sine capite est,* all the knowledge and vertue which they have, wanteth the head of true knowledge and vertue: It wanteth true faith in Christ, which is the head of all knowledge, and vertue. This head whosoever wanteth, Non dubium est, quin impius sit, omnesq; virtutes ejus in illa mortifera via reperiantur, quæ est tota tenebrarum, *theres no doubt to be made, but such an one is impious, and all the vertues which hee thinkes he hath, are mortiferous and deadly.*

z *In lib. Inst. divin. ca. 6,*

a *Lib. eod. ca. 9.*

33. Where againe I cannot but observe to the comfort of all true beleevers, another exceeding difference betwixt us and them, even in these matters concerning life, and good workes: whatsoever things are either in themselves good, or being of themselves indifferent, are by the lawfull authority either of civill, or ecclesiasticall governours, commanded, we in doing any of those things, and shewing our willing obedience thereunto, performe an act not onely lawfull, but laudable and acceptable unto God. For in doing any of these, we doe *vertually* performe obedience unto Christ, who by them commandeth the doing of all such things: and in our religious performing of them, we hold firme that holy *foundation,* not onely of faith, but of good workes, which the scriptures teach. Neither onely are such workes acceptable unto God, but even those acts also which are wicked and ungodly, being committed by such as doe truly beleeve, though they be as heinous as was the crime of *David,* or the abjuration of *Peter,* even those, I say, by the strength and vertue of that *foundation,* if one doe rightly hold and beleeve it, are so covered [b], put [c] away and forgotten, that God [d] seeth none iniquity in *Iacob,* nor transgression in *Israel.* Such, so infinite is the goodnesse, and so soveraigne is the vertue which is in holding the true *foundation* of faith. The contrary of all this falleth out unto them, of the present Romane Church. For not onely their sinnes are made more sinfull unto them, there being no mantle to cover, or hide them from the eyes of God, and shield them from his vengeance, but even their best and most holy actions which they doe, or can performe, though they should

doe

b *Peccatum tectum est. Psal. 32. 1.*
c *Isa. 43. 25.*
d *Numb. 23. 21.*

doe nothing but sing hymnes with *David*, or feed Chrifts flock with *Peter*, or give their goods to the poore, and their bodies to be burned for Chrift, even thefe, I fay, are fo tainted with the venome of that *Apoftaticall foundation*, that being of themfelves holy actions, yet unto them they are turned into finne, and become pernicious and mortiferous. For whatfoever act being in it felfe either good or indifferent, any of their Church (except onely the Pope himfelfe, who is a member tranfcendent) doth performe, becaufe they doe it in obedience unto him, whofe fupreme authority they make the *foundation*, not onely of their faith, but of all good actions: in doing any fuch act, there is a *vertuall* and *implicit* obedience to Antichrift, an acknowledgement of his fupreme power to teach and command what is to be done, a receiving his marke, either in their hand or forehead: fo that every fuch act, is not onely impious, but even Antichriftian, and containeth in it a vertuall and implicit renouncing of the whole faith. In regard whereof none can ever fufficiently, I fay, not commend, but admire the zeale of *Luther* : who though he was fo earneft to have the Communion in both kinds, contrarie to the doctrine and cuftome of the Romane Church, yet withall be profeffed that, if the Pope as Pope fhould command it to be received in both kinds, hè then would receive it not in both, but in one kind onely. Bleffed *Luther*! it was never thy meaning, either to receive it onely in one, or to deny it to be neceffary for Gods Church and people to receive it in both kindes. Thou kneweft right well, that *Bibite ex hoc omnes*, was Chrifts owne ordinance, with which none might difpenfe. Thou for defence of this truth among many, was fet up as a figne of contradiction unto them, and as a marke at which they directed all their darts of malicious and malignant reproaches. Farre was it from thee to relent one hare-bredth in this truth. But whereas they *taught the ufe of the Cup to be indifferent and arbitrarie*, fuch as the Church (that is, the Pope) might either allow, or take away, as he fhould thinke fit : upon this fuppofall and no otherwife, didft thou in thine ardent zeale to Chrift, and deteftation of Antichrift, fay, that were the ufe of both or one kinde onely, a thing indeed indifferent, as they taught it to be, if the Pope as Pope fhould command the receiving in both kindes, thou wouldft not then receive it fo, left whilft thou might feeme to obey Chrift commanding that, but yet (upon their fuppofall) as a thing indifferent, thou fhouldeft certainly performe obedience to Antichrift, by his authoritie limiting, and reftraining that indifferency, unto both kindes, as now by his authority hee reftraines it unto one. The fumme is this, *To doe any act whether in it felfe good, or indifferent, but commanded to be done by the Pope as Pope, to pray, to preach, to receive the Sacraments, yea but to lift your eyes, or hold up your finger, or fay your Pater nofter, or your Ave Maria, or weare a bead, a modell, a lace, or ny garment white, or blacke, or ufe any croffing, either at Baptifme, or*

e *Kemnit. Exa. Conc. Trid. 1. Tract. de communi. fub utraq. fpecie. pa. 136.*

f *Conc. Conftant. Seff. 13. Conc. Trid. Seff. 22. in decreto fuper petit. de conceffione calicis Bell. lib. 4. de Eucbar. ca. 28.*

any

any other time, to do any one of these, or any the like, *eo nomine, because the Pope, as Pope, teacheth that they are to be done,* or commands the doing of them, is in very deed a yeelding one selfe to be a *vassall of Antichrist,* a receiving the marke of the beast, and a vertuall or implicit deniall of the faith in Christ. So extremly venemous is that poison which lyeth in the root of that fundamentall heresie which they have laid as the very rocke and *Foundation* of their faith.

34. Hitherto we have examined the former *position* of *Baronius* which concerned *Heresie.* His other concerning *Schisme,* is this: *That they who dissented from Pope Vigilius when hee decreed that the Three Chapters ought to be defended, were Schismatikes.* A most strange assertion: that the whole Catholike Church should bee schismaticall, for they all dissented from *Vigilius* in this cause; that Catholikes should all at once become Schismatikes, yea and that also for the very defence of the Catholike faith. I oppose to this, another and true assertion, *That not onely Pope Vigilius when he defended the Three Chapters, and forsooke communion with the condemners of them, was a Schismatike himselfe, and chiefe of the Schisme, but that all who as yet defend Vigilius, that is, who maintaine the Popes Cathedrall infallibility in causes of faith, and forsake communion with those that condemne it, that those all are, and that for this very cause, Schismatikes, and the Pope, the ringleader in the Schisme.*

35. For the manifesting whereof, certaine it is, that after Pope *Vigilius* had so solemnly, and judicially by his *Apostolicall* authority defined, that the *Three Chapters* ought to be defended, there was a great rent and Schisme in the Church, either part separating it selfe from the other, and forsaking communion with the other. First, the holy Councell, and they who tooke part with it, anathematized [h] the defenders of those Chapters, thereby (as themselves expound it) declaring their opposites to be separated [i] from God, and therefore from the society of the church of God. On the other side, Pope *Vigilius* & they who were on his part, were so averse from the others, that they would rather endure disgrace, yea banishment as *Baronius* [k] sheweth, then communicate with their opposites. But I shal not need to stay in proving that there was a rent and schisme at this time betweene the defenders & condemners of those chapters. *Baronius* professeth it, saying [l], *The whole Church was then schismate dilacerata, torne asunder by a schisme.* Againe [m], *After the end of the Councell there arose a greater war then was before. Catholikes (so he falsly calls both parts) being then divided among themselves, some adhering to the Councell, others holding with Vigilius and his Constitution.* Againe, *Many [n] relying upon the authority of Vigilius, did not receive the fift Synod, atq; à contraria illis sentientibus sese diviserunt, and separated or divided themselves, from those who thought the contrary:* Such were the *Italian, African, Illirian,* & other neighbour Bishops. So *Baronius:*

g *Esse schismatici convicti sunt, qui diversam à Romano Pontifice, his decernendis, sententiam sectati essent. Bar. an. 547. nu. 30.*

h *Coll. 8. talis anathema sit. seq. ibid.*
i *Nihil aliud significat anathema, nisi à Deo separationem. Coll. 5. pa. 552. b.*
k *An. 553. nu. 221.*

l *Ibid.*

m *An. eodem 553. nu. 250.*

n *An. eodem nu. 249.*

ronius: truly profeffing a fchifme to have bin then in the Church, and Pope *Vigilius* to have beene the leader of the one part.

36. But whether of thefe two parts were Schifmatickes? As the name of herefie, though it bee common to any opinion, whereof one makes choice, whether it be true or falfe, (in which fenfe *Conftantine* the great, called º the true faith, *Catholicam & fanctiſsimam harefim*) yet in the ordinarie ufe it is now applied only to the choice of fuch opinions, as are repugnāt to the faith: So the name of Schifme though it import any fciſſure or rent-ing of one from another, yet now by the vulgar ufe of Divines, it is appropriated onely to fuch a rent or divifion as is made for an unjuft caufe, and from thofe, to whom, hee or they who are feparated, ought to unite themfelves & hold communion with them. This, whofoever doe, whether they bee moe, or fewer then thofe from whom they feparate themfelves, they are truly and properly to bee termed Schifmatikes, and factious. For it is neither multitude, nor paucitie, nor the holding with, or againſt any vifible head, or governour whatfoever, nor the bare act of feparating ones felfe from others; but only the caufe, for which the feparation is made, which maketh a Schifme or faction, and truly denounceth one to be factious, or a Schifma-tike. If *Elijah* feparate himfelfe from the foure hundreth *Baalites* and the whole kingdome of *Ifrael*, becaufe they are Idolaters; and they fever themfelves from him becaufe he wil not worfhip *Baal*, as they did; If the three children for the like caufe, fepa-rate themfelves from all the Idolatrous Babylonians, in feparation they are both like, but in the caufe being moſt unlike, the *Baalites* onely, and not *Elijah*, and the Babylonians only, and not the three children, are Schifmatikes. Now becaufe every one is bound to unite himfelfe to the Catholike and *orthodoxall* Church, and hold communion with them in faith, hence it is that, as out of *Auſtine* h *Stapleton* rightly obferves i, *Tota ratio Schifmatis*, the very eſſence of a Schifme confiſts in the fepara-ting from the Church, I fay from the true & *orthodoxall* Church, for as Saint *Auguſtine* in the fame place teacheth, whofoever dif-fents from the Scriptures, and fo from the true faith, though they be fpred throughout the whole world, yet fuch are not in the (found) Church, much leſſe are they the Church. And there-fore from them, be they never fo many, never fo eminent, one may, and muſt feparate himfelfe. But if any fever himfelfe from the *orthodoxall* Church, or, to fpeake in *Stapletons* words, *fi re-nuit operari in ratione fidei ut pars eccleſia catholica, if he will not cooperate or joyne together in maintaining the faith, as a member of the Catholike or orthodoxall Church, Schifmaticus hoc ipfo eſt, hee is for this very caufe a Schifmatike.*

37. Apply now this to *Vigilius* and the fift generall Coun-cell, and the cafe will be cleare. The onely caufe of feparation on the Councels part, was, for that *Vigilius* with all his adhe-

o *Epift.ad Creſlum apud Eufeb.lib.10. ca.5.*

h *Lib.de unit.Eccl. ca.4.*
i *Lib.c.doct.princ. ca.7.§.Iſlud.*

k *Lib.10.ca.7.§. Nemie.*

rents were Heretikes, convicted, condemned; and accursed for such, by that true sentence, and judgement of the fift generall Councell, which was consonant both to Scriptures, Fathers, and the foure former generall Councels, and approved by all succeeding generall Councels, Popes, and Bishops, that is, by the judgement of the whole Catholike Church, for more then fifteene hundreth yeares together. A cause not onely most just, but commanded by the holy Apostle [1], *Shun him that is an heretick, after once or twice admonition;* much more after publike conviction and condemnation, by the upright judgement of the whole Catholike Church. On the other side, *Vigilius* and his Faction separated themselves from the Councell, and all that tooke part with it, for this onely reason, because they were Catholikes; because they embraced and constantly defended the Catholike faith; because he wold not cooperate (as *Stapleton* speaketh) with them, to maintaine the true Catholike faith, and so on their part, there was that which essentially made them Schismatickes. *Baronius* in saying that those who then dissented from *Vigilius*, were Schismatickes, speakes sutably to all his former assertions; For in saying this, he in effect saith, that Catholikes to avoid a Schisme, should have turned Heretickes; should have embraced Nestorianisme, and so have renounced and condemned the whole Catholike faith, as *Vigilius* then did. Had they so done, they should have been no Schismatikes with *Baronius*: But now for not condemning the Catholike faith with *Vigilius*, they must all be condemned by the Cardinall, for Schismatickes.

Tit.3.10.

38. For the very same reason, the whole present Romane Church are Schismatiekes at this day; and not the Reformed Churches from whom they separate themselves. For the cause of separation on their part, is the same for which *Vigilius* and his schismaticall faction separated themselves from the fift Councell, and the Catholikes of those times who all tooke part with it, even because wee refuse to embrace the Popes *Cathedrall* sentence in causes of faith, as the fift Councell refused that of *Vigilius*. The cause on our part is the same which the fift Councell then had, for that they defend the Popes hereticall *constitution*: nay not onely that of *Vigilius* (which yet were cause enough) but many other like unto that, and especially that one of *Leo* the tenth with his Laterane Councell, wherby *Supremacie* and with it *Infallibilitie* of judgement is given unto the Pope in all his decrees of faith : In which one *Cathedrall* decree (condemned for hereticall by the fift Councell, and constant judgement both of precedent and subsequent Councells, as before we have declared) not onely innumerable heresies such as none yet doth dreame of, are included, but by the venom and poyson of that one fundamentall heresie, not only all the other doctrines are corrupted, but the very *foundation* of faith is utterly overthrowne

throwne. Let them boaft of multitudes, and univerfalitie never fo much, (which at this day, is but a vaine brag) fay they were far more, even foure hundreth to one *Luther*, or the whole kingdome of *Babilon* to the two witnesses of God; yet feeing it is the caufe which makes a schifmaticke; & the caufe of separation on their part is moft unjuft, but on ours moft warrantable & holy, for that they will not cooperate with us, in upholding the ancient and Catholike faith, that especially of the fift Councell, condemning and accurfing the Cathedrall fentence of Pope *Vigilius*, as hereticall, & all that defend it, as Heretickes, it evidently followeth, that they are the only, & essentially schifmatickes, at this time, and in this great rent of the Church.

39. Whence againe doth ensue another Conclusion of no small importance. For it is a ruled cafe among them, such as *Bellarmine* [m] avoucheth to be proved both by Scriptures, by Fathers, by pontificall decrees, and found reason, *that no schifmatickes are in the Church, or of the Church*, Now because out of [n] the Church there is no falvation, it nearly concernes them, to bethinke themfelves ferioufly what hope there is or can be unto them, who being, (as wee have proved) schifmatickes, are for this caufe by their owne doctrine, utterly excluded from the Church. But I will proceed no further in this matter, wherein I have ftayed much longer then I intended, yet my hope is, that I have now abundantly cleared against *Baronius*, not onely, That one may diffent in faith, and bee disioyned in communion from the Pope, & yet neither be Heretickes nor Schifmatickes: but, That none can now confent in faith, and hold communion with the Pope, but for that very caufe he is by the judgement of the Catholike Church; both an hereticke and a schifmaticke.

[m] *Lib. de Ecclef. milit ca.5.*

[n] *Extra quam (Ecclefiam) nullus omnino falvatur. Conc. Lateran.ca.1.*

CHAP. XIIII.

The fecond Exception of Baronius, *excusing* Vigilius *from herefie; for that he often profeffeth to hold the Councell of* Chalcedon, *and the faith thereof, refuted.*

1. IS fecond excufe for *Vigilius* is taken from that profession which both other defenders of the *three Chapters*, and *Vigilius* himfelfe often maketh in his *Conftitution*, that hee holdes the faith of the Councell of *Chalcedon*, and did all for the safety of that Councell. *Both parties* faith *Baronius* [a], *as well the defenders as the condemners of thofe three Chapters did teftifie*, that they defired nothing more, *quam confultum effe catholica fidei, probata iis . Concilio Chalcedonenfi, then to provide that the Catholike faith decreed is Chalcedon might be fafe.* Againe [b] *liquet omnes*, it is manifeft that all

[a] *An.547.nu.47.*

[b] *An.546.nu.53.]*

all Catholikes (in defence of the three Chapters) at once contradicted this noveltie, (set downe in the Emperors Edict for condemning those chapters) *vindicesque se Concilij Chalcedonensis exhibuisse, and shewed themselves to bee defenders of the Councell of Chalcedon,* Of *Vigilius* in particular, hee not so little as fortie times ingeminates this : *Vigilius* c writ these things, *pro defensione & integritate Synodi Chalcedonensis, for the defence and safety of the Councell at Chalcedon.* Vigilius d *writ his constitution for no other cause* (as by it is evident) *but to the end that all things which were defined by the Councell at Chalcedon, firma consisterent, might remaine firme and by no meanes be infringed.* Againe e, *All that Vigilius or the rest did in this cause, did tend hereunto; ut consultum esset dignitati & authoritati Synodi Chalcedonensis, that the dignity and authoritie of the Councell at Chalcedon might be kept safe and sound,* Thus *Baronius*.

2. The writings of those who defended *those Chapters* declare the same. *Victor* in plaine termes affirmeth f, *the three Chapters to have been approved and judged orthodoxall by the Councell of Chalcedon, and the condemning of them, to bee the condemning of that Councell; and that for this cause, he refused to condemne them, least in so doing he should condemne the Councell of Chalcedon.* The like hee witnesseth g of *Facundus :* whose owne words set downe by *Baronius* h shew, *that hee disliked the condemners of those three Chapters, because by condemning them, Synodum improbarent, they condemned the Councell of Chalcedon.* But none shewes the like love to that Councell, and care for it as doth Pope *Vigilius* in his Constitution, we decree saith he i, *That the judgement of the Fathers at Chalcedon, shall be kept inviolable in all things, and particularly in this, touching the Epistle of Ibas : wee dare not call into question their judgement :* their judgement *in omnibus conservantes, wee keepe in all things.* Againe k, *we permit no man to innovate either by additiō, or detraction, or alteration, any thing which is ordained & set down by the Councell at Chalcedon.* Againe l, *Behold, O Emperor, it is more cleare then the light, that we have alwayes beene desirous to reverence the foure Councels, and that all things might remaine inviolable which by them are defined and judged.* This, and much more to the like purpose saith *Vigilius :* Who now reading these things in his Cōstitution, and seeing him so fervent and zealons for the Councell at *Chalcedon,* and the faith therein declared, would not thinke, nay proclaim *Vigilius* to be a most sound Catholike, an utter enemie to *Nestorianisme,* as that holy Councell at *Chalcedon* was? Or who would not applaud *Baronius* for his devise to defend and excuse *Vigilius* from heresie, because he was so earnest for the Councell of *Chalcedon* and the faith declared therein, which none can embrace, and be guiltie of *Nestorianisme*? This is his plea for *Vigilius*.

3. For answer whereunto, I am ashamed that *Baronius,* a Cardinall, and man of rare knowledge, as hee is supposed, should
shew,

c *An. 553. nu. 197.*

d *Ibid. nu. 47.*

e *Ibid. nu. 231.*

f *In Chron. an. 2. post Coss. Basill.*

g *An. 10. post Coss. Basily.*
h *An. 545. nu. 28.*

i *Apud Bar. an. 553. nu. 196.*

k *Ibid. nu. 197:*
l *Ibid. nu. 207.*

they himselfe so inconsiderate in this cause, as to seeke to excuse or defend *Vigilius*, by alledging the name, credit, or authoritie of the Councell of *Chalcedon*. For even that alone, if there were nothing else, puls upon him that just *Anathema* denounced by the fift Councell, who thus decree, *Wee* [m] *anathematize the defenders of these Three Chapters, and those who have written, or doe write for them, or who doe defend, or indeavour to defend the impiety of them, nomine sanctorum Patrum, aut sancti Chalcedonensis Concilij, by the name of the holy fathers, or of the Councell at Chalcedon.* The more then that either *Vigilius* pretends that Councell for defence of the *Three Chapters*, or, that *Baronius* pretends it for the defence of *Vigilius*, the more they are still involved in the Councels *Anathema*: and no marvell, for by alledging that Councell as a patrone of those *Three Chapters*, they slander that most holy Councell, and all that approve it, that is, the whole Catholike Church to be hereticall, and patrons of the most blasphemous, and condemned heresie of *Nestorius*.

4. Let this passe: Is this reason, thinke you, of *Baronius* of any force to excuse *Vigilius*, hee professeth to defend the Councell of *Chalcedon*, therefore he is not an heretike ? Truly of none at all; for who knoweth not that heretikes are as forward in chalenging to themselves the names and authority of ancient Councels, and in professing to defend the same faith and doctrine which they taught. Take a view but of three or foure examples; and then you will pitty *Baronius* for this so weake and silly excuse for *Vigilius*.

5. In the *Ephesine Latrocinie* there came [n] certaine *Eutychean* heretikes, to the number of 35. who being justly excommunicated by that holy Bishop *Flavianus*, desired to bee restored to the comunion of the Church: *Dioscorus* & his Synod willed them to make a profession of their faith; they did so; & their confessió was this, *Sic sapimus, sicut 318. Patres in Nicea sanxerunt, & sicut hic congregata sancta Synodus confirmarunt; wee beleeve as the Nicene Fathers decreed, and the (former) holy Synod at Ephesus confirmed, nor did we ever beleeve, or thinke otherwise than those holy Councels decreed:* wee beleeve as S. *Athanasius*, S. *Cyrill*, S. *Gregory*, *& omnes Catholici Episcopi, and as all Catholike Bishops have beleeved; and we accurse all that beleeve otherwise.* Thus professed those *Eutychean* heretikes, and upon this profession they were by *Dioscorus* and his Synod restored to the communion of the Church; yea, which is more, that same *Latrocinie* or hereticall Synod at *Ephesus*, professing [o] the former Councels to be, *tutelam nostrae Catholica fidei, the stay and prop of their Catholike faith,* (so they call their heresie) commanded the Nicene Creed, which was confirmed in the holy *Ephesine* Councell, to bee read before them, and the testimonies of many holy Fathers [p] consenting thereunto, *Peter, Athanasius, Foelix, Iulius, Cyprian,* and others; together with the decree of the Ephesine Councell, *Nulli licere proferre, vel conscribere,*

m Coll.8.pa.586.b.
& 588.a.

n Act. Concil. Eph.
recitat. in Conc.
Chal. Act.1.pa.45.

o Ibid.pa.46.

p Ibid.pa.47.

q Ibid.pa.56.

scribere, vel componere aliam fidem præter eam; that it should not be lawfull for any to utter, write, or compose any other faith, or Creed, but that which was decreed at Nice. After all these read before

x Ibid. pa. 57.

them, *Dioscorus* said, *Existimo* [x] *omnibus placere, I thinke that this faith decreed at Nice, and confirmed at Ephesus, is approved by us all, for we may not either retract, or make doubt of what they have done; and let every man say his judgement hereof*: Then said *Thalassius,* I *thinke the same, & qui contraria eis sapiunt, abominor: and I abhorre all who thinke the contrary.* *Iohn* of *Sebastia,* I detest all heresies, *& colo hanc solam fidem, and embrace this faith onely which was decreed at Nice.* Stephanus, If any beleeve otherwise than the Nicene Fathers decreed, let him be accursed, because this is the true and Catholike faith. and the whole Councell said, *Omnes sumus ejusdem fidei, we are all of the same faith, which the Nicene Fathers decreed.* Thus professed that whole *Ephesine Latrocinie* consisting of 128 Bishops, they all said, they held the Nicene faith, and none but that; accursing all that received not that: while yet at that very time when they thus professed, they were most damnable heretikes, and conspired together to abolish for ever the holy *Nicene* faith: They being *Eutycheans,* learned to make such a dissembling profession of *Eu-*

y Conciliab. Ephes. in Act. Conc. Chal. Act. 1. pa. 21.

tyches himselfe, who delivered up to that Synod [y] a confession of his faith, bemoaning, that he was persecuted, because he would not deny the Nicene faith, nor beleeve otherwise then those holy fathers had decreed, and the Ephesine Councell had confirmed; and who having repeated *verbatim* the Nicene Creed, addeth this, *Thus was I taught by my progenitors, thus have I beleeved, in this faith was I borne, in this faith was I baptized, and signed, (with the Crosse) in this faith was I consecrated, in this faith have I lived to this day, and in this faith doe I desire to dye*: And this confession doe I make, *attestante mihi tam Deo, quam vestra sanctitate, both God and this holy Councell being my witnesse hereof.* Thus *Euty-*

z Act. 6. pa. 561.

ches, of whom (notwithstanding this so holy a profession) and all his partakers, their second Nicene Councel truly saith [z], *Eutiches, Dioscorus, and the heretikes of that branne approved the Nicene faith, confirmed in the holy Councell at Ephesus, sed tamen hæretici permanserunt, yet for all that they remained heretikes.*

6. What can the Cardinall, or any of his friends oppose to this Example? If *Vigilius* be no heretike, because hee professeth to hold the faith of the Councell at *Chalcedon,* then neither *Diosco-*

u Confiteor ex duabus naturis fuisse Dominum ante adunationem, post vero adunationem unam naturam confiteor, Dixit Eutyches: sancta Synodus dixit, consentimus. Act. Conc. Ephes. in Act. Conc. Chal. Act. 1. pa. 28. b.

rus, nor the *Eutycheans,* nor *Eutyches* himselfe, is an heretike, because they all with as great earnestnesse professed to keepe inviolable the Councels at *Nice,* and *Ephesus,* & the Catholike faith explaned in them, accursing all who beleeve the contrary thereunto: If notwithstanding this so resolute and earnest profession, *Dioscorus* & the *Eutycheans,* with that *Ephesine* cospiracy, were heretikes, & *Eutyches* himselfan archheretike, as they al undoubtedly were; for even while they thus professed, they all denied [u] two natures to remaine in Christ, after the union, as the very acts of

that

that *Latrocinie* doe expresly declare; then was it a very silly reason of *Baronius*, to conclude, that *Vigilius* was no heretike, because in his decree, for defence of the *Three Chapters*, hee is so resolute to keepe inviolable the Councell of *Chalcedon*, and the faith there decreed.

7. The like may bee seene in the *Monothelites*, of whom their second Nicen Synod saith [x] thus. *Sergius Bishop of Constantinople, Cyrus Bishop of Alexandria, Honorius Bishop of Rome, and all who are called Monothelites, embraced both the Councell of Chalcedon, and the next which followed it* (which is this fift) *and the generall Councels which went before these, to wit, the Nicen, Constantinopolitane, and Ephesine: verumtamen ut hæretici a Catholica ecclesia dammati sunt, yet for all this they were condemned for heretickes, by the whole Church*; Why may not the Catholike Church give the like doome of *Vigilius* for defending the *three Chapters*, though hee professe and imbrace all the same Councels, and particularly that of *Chalcedon*, as they did?

8. Perhaps other Heretickes would dissemble in their profession, but the *Nestorians* (of which ranke *Vigilius* was) they were men of a better fashion, they would never professe to hold the decrees and faith of an holy Councell, unlesse they did so indeed. Fie, of all heretickes they were most vile in this kinde: Read the acts of their Conventicle held in an Inne at *Ephesus*, during the time of the holy *Ephesine* Councell, and you shall see, that as by lies, slanders and all base revilings they sought to disgrace *Cyrill*, and all other orthodoxall Bishops; calumniating them as heretickes, and oppugners of the *Nicen* faith, so they boasted of themselves, that they forsooth were the onely men who defended and upheld the Councell of Nice and the faith there explaned; Witnesse besides their second Nicen [x] Synod, their owne words, and writings, *Nestorius* himselfe and others of his sect, writ [y] thus to the Emperor, *we obeying your imperiall command, came to Ephesus, and our intent, and desire was, communi univeo calculo sanctorum Patrum Nicenorum fidem confirmare, to confirme with one consent the faith of the Nicen Fathers.* In those instructions, which they gave to their Legates, they subscribed in [z] this manner, *I Alexander Bishop of Hierapolis Nicenæ fidei expositioni subscripsi, have subscribed to the Nicen Faith, and if you shall doe any thing according to the faith expounded at Nice, to that I assent:* in the like sort subscribed they all. To the Emperor that Conventicle thus writ [a], *we doe earnestly desire your pietie, that you would command, that all men should subscribe to the faith expounded at Nice,* and that they may teach nothing *quod sit ab ea alienum, which is contrarie to that faith.* In another Epistle to the Emperour, *we came, say [b] they, to Ephesus without delay, manentes in sola expositione fidei Patrum qui in Nicea convenerant, abiding in that profession of faith onely, which was decreed at Nice.* In another Epistle having repeated the Nicen Creed, they add [c] this,

In

x *Act.6.pa.561.*

x *Ibid.*

y *To.3.Act.Conci Epist.ca.20.*

z *Ibid.ca.19.*

a *Ibid.ca.21.*

b *Append.1.ad tom. 3.Act.Conc. Ephes. ca.3.*

c *To.3.Conc.Ephes. ca.12.*

In hanc fidei expositionem nos omnes acquiescimus, wee all doe rest our selves in this declaration of faith made at Nice, we constantly perse- ver in it. In their ᵈEpistle to *Rufus,* we resist them, *nihil aliud spectantes, quam ut fidei Symbolum à patribus Nicenis editum, suum locum perfectè obtineat,* intending or aiming at nothing else, but that the faith of the Nicene Creed, may fully and perfectly obtaine his due place and honour. In their very Synodall sentence against *Cyrill,* and other orthodoxall Bishops, they expresse ᵉ this, *That they shall remaine excommunicate, untill they doe integrè suscipere, intirely embrace the Nicene faith, adding nothing unto it;* which they repeate againe in their Epistle to the Senate of *Constantinople,* saying: *If* ᶠ *Cyrill and the rest will repent, & forsake their hereticall doctrines, and embrace the faith of the Nicene Fathers,* they shall straight be absolved; and twentie times the like. VVho reading no more but these so manie, so earnest professions of *Nestorius* and the *Ne- storians,* to defend in every point the Nicene faith, without ad- dition or alteration, would not almost sweare that these doubt- lesse were the onely men that stood firme and constant for the *Nicene* Councell; and that *Cyrill* and they who tooke part with him (which was the whole Catholike Church) were the maine oppugners of that Councell, and the faith there decreed? And yet notwithstanding all these professions, these were blasphe- mous heretickes at that time, and most eagerly oppugned and sought to abolish that very Nicene faith, which in words they so professed and boasted of.

9. *Vigilius* and the defenders of the *Three Chapters,* as they followed the *Nestorians* in their heresie, so did they in seeking to countenance and grace their heresie, by professing to defend the Councell of *Chalcedon,* and the faith there decreed, yea to defend it so constantly as that it might not in any part or sylla- ble bee violated, pretending their opposites, who condemned those Chapters, to oppugne and condemne the Councell of *Chalcedon,* as the old *Nestorians* slandered *Cyrill,* and other Ca- tholikes of those times; to condemne the Councell of *Nice.* And yet notwithstanding all these professions, *Vigilius* and his adhe- rents were as deepe in Nestorianisme as *Nestorius* himselfe, and even while he pretends to maintaine, he doth quite over- throw the holy Councell of *Chalcedon,* and the faith therein explained.

10. But neither the old, nor later *Nestorians* are in this kind comparable to the modern *Romanists,* the last and worst sect of heretikes that ever the Church was pestered withall. Their pro- fession is not so minute, as to boast of this or that one Councell, or of some few fathers. All Scriptures make for them, All the Fathers are theirs, All generall Councels confirme what they teach. Their bookes doe swell with this ventositie. I pray you heare the words but of one of them, but such an one, as puts downe all *Nestorians, Eutycheans, Monothelites,* and al heretikes that

hat went before him; *We*, saith he g, *have All authorities, Times, and* places *for our defence : Our enemies have none at all. Our* h *doctrine* is *taught by all godly and famous professors of Divinity; All Popes, Fathers and Doctors that ever were in the Church, All Councells, particular and generall, All Vniversities, Schooles, Colledges and places of learning, since the time of Christ to* Martin Luther : *It is* i *ratified by all authority; all Scriptures, Traditions, Prophets, Apostles, Evangelists, Sibylls, Rabbins: All holy and learned Fathers, Historians, Antiquaries, and Monuments: all Synods, Councells, Lawes, Parliaments, Canons and Decrees of Popes, of Emperours, of Kings, and Rulers : All Martyrs, Confessors, and holy witnesses, by all friends and enemies, even Mahumetanes, Iewes, Pagans, Infidells; all former Heretikes, and schismatikes, by all testimonies that can bee devised, not onely in this world, but of God, of Angells and glorious soules, of Devills and damned spirits in hell.* (The fittest witnesses of all.) What, any more ? yes, the best is yet behind. *I have,* saith he k, *read and studied all the Scriptures, the old Testament in the Hebrew Text, the new in the Greeke; have studied the ancient Glosses and Scholies, Latine and Greeke. I have perused the most ancient Historians, Eusebius, Ruffinus, Socrates, Sozomene, Palladius,* Saint Ierome, Saint Bede, *and others; I have often with diligence considered the Decrees of the Popes, both of all that were before the Nine Councell and after,* (then no doubt but he diligently considered of his *Apostolicall Constitution* of Pope Vigilius.) *I have beene an auditor both of Scholasticall and Controversall questions, where all doubts and difficulties that wit or learning can devise, and invent, are handled, and most exquisitely debated; I have seene and read all the generall Councells; from the first at Nice, to the last at Trent;* (then doubt not but hee read this fift councell :) *as also all approved particular and Provinciall Councells which extant and ordinarily used; I have carefully read over all the workes and writings which be to be had of Dionysius the Areopagite,* Saint *Ignatius,* Saint *Policarp,* Saint *Clement, Martialis,* Saint *Iustine, Origen,* Saint *Basil,* Saint *Athanasius,* Saint *Gregory Nazianzen,* Saint *Gregory Nissene,* Saint *Gregory* the Great, Saint *Irene,* Saint *Cyprian, Fulgentius, Pamphilus the Martyr, Palladius, Theodoret, Ruffinus, Socrates, Sozomene, Evagrius, Cassianus, Lactantius, Vincentius Lyrinensis; all the workes of all these have I read and examined; and conferred them with* Saint *Augustine,* Saint *Ierome,* Saint *Ambrose,* Saint *Leo, Papius, Theophilact, Tertullian, Eusebius, Prudentius, and others most excellent Divines. And I take God and the whole Court of heaven to witnesse (before whom I must render an account of this protestation) that the same faith and religion which I defend, is taught and confirmed by those Hebrew and Greeke Scriptures, those Historians, Popes, Decrees, Scholies, and Expositions, Councells, Schooles and Fathers, and the profession of Protestants condemned by the same.* Thus he.

11. Did ever mortall man read or heare of such a braggadochio? for learning and languages *Ierome* is but a baby to him; more industrious and adamantine then *Origen;* then *Adamantius* himselfe. A pap, a storehouse of all knowledge; his head a Library of all Fathers, Councels, Decrees, of all writings, an Heluo, nay a very hell of books, he devoures up all. *Rabsecha, Thraso, Pyrgopolinices, Therapontigonus; all* the Magnificoes & Gloriosoes, come sit at his feet, and learne of him the

g *An Apologicall Epistle published an. 1601. pa. 118.*

h *Ibid. pa. 113.*

i *Ibid. pa. 38.*

k *Ibid. pa. 119.*

the exact forme of vaunting and reviling. What silly men were *Eutiches*, *Nestorius*, and the old heretikes? they boasted but of one or two Councells. All Councells, all Fathers, all Decrees, all bookes, writings, and records, are witnesses of his faith. They sayd it, he sweares it before God and the whole Court of Heaven, that all Scriptures, Councels, Fathers, all witnesses in heaven, earth and hell, yea the Devill and all, are his, and confirme their Romane faith, and condemne the doctrine of Protestants. Alas what shall we doe, but even hide our selves in caves of the earth, and clifts of the rocks, from the force and fury of this *Goliah*, who thus braves it out in the open field, as who with the onely breath of his mouth can blow away whole legions, *quasi ventus folia, aut pannicula tectoria*.

12. But let no mans heart faint because of this proud anonymall Philistim. Thy servant, O Lord, though the meanest in the host of *Israel*, will fight with him; nor will I desire any other weapons, but this one pible stone of the judiciall sentence of the fift generall Councell against *Vigilius*. This being taken out of *Davids* bagge, that is, derived from Scriptures, consonant to all former, and confirmed by all succeeding Catholike Councells and Fathers, directly and unavoydably hits him in the forehead, it gives a mortall and uncurable wound unto him, for it demonstrates not onely the foundation of their faith to be hereticall, and for such to bee condemned and accursed by the judgement of the whole Catholike Church, but all their doctrine, whatsoever they teach, because they all relye on this foundation of the Popes *infallibility*, are not onely unsound, and in the root hereticall, but even Antichristian also, such as utterly overthrow the whole Catholike faith. This, being one part of the Philistimes weapons, wherein he trusted and vanted, with his owne sword is his head, (the head and foundation of all their faith) cut off, so that of him and the whole body of their Church it may be truly said, *Iacet ingens littore truncus, Avulsumq; humeris caput, & sine nomine corpus*.

13. You see now how both ancient and moderne heretikes boast of Councells, and therefore, that the reason of *Baronius* is most inconsequent, that *Vigilius* was no heretike because hee professeth to hold the Councell of *Chalcedon*. Nay I say more, though one professe to hold the whole Scripture, yet if with pertinacy hee hold any one doctrine repugnant thereunto, the profession of the Scriptures themselves cannot excuse such a man from being an heretike; If it could, then not any of the old heretikes would want this pretence: or, to omit them, seeing both Protestants and Papists make profession to beleeve the Scriptures, and whatsoever is taught therein; would this profession exempt one from heresie, neither they, nor wee, should be, or be called heretikes. But seeing in truth they are, and wee in their Antichristian language are called heretikes, as *Cyrill*, and the orthodoxall beleevers in his time, were by the Nestorians, it is without question that this profession to hold the whole Scriptures, much lesse to hold one or two Councells (as *Vigilius* did) cannot free one from being an heretike.

14. You will perhaps say, can one then beleeve the whole Scripture;

ture, and be an heretike, or beleeve the faith decreed at *Nice, Ephesus,* or *Chalcedon*; and be an *Arian, Eutychean* or *Nestorian* heretike ? No verily, for as the Scripture containeth a contradiction to every heresie, seeing as Saint *Austen* truly saith[1], *all doctrines concerning faith, are set downe, and that also perspicuously therein :* so doe every one of those three Councels containe a contradiction to every one of those three heresies, and to all other which concerne the divinity or humanity of Christ. But it is one thing to professe the scriptures, or those three Councells, and say that he beleeves them, which many heretikes may doe; and another thing to beleeve them indeed, which none can doe and be an heretike, for whosoever truly beleeveth the scriptures, cannot possibly with pertinacy hold any doctrine repugnant to scriptures; but such a man upon evident declaration that this is taught in them (though before he held the contrary) presently submits his wit and will to the truth which out of them is manifested unto him. If this he do not, he manifestly declareth, that he holds his error with pertinacy, and with an obstinate resolution not to yeeld to the truth of the scriptures, and so bee is certainly an heretike, notwithstanding his profession of the scriptures, which he falsly said be beleeved, and held, when in very truth he held, and that pertinaciously the quite contrary unto them. The very like must be said of those three Councells, and them who either truly beleeve, or falsly say, that they beleeve the faith explained in them, or any one of them.

15. Whence two things are evidently consequent, the former, that all heretikes are lyars in their profession : not onely because they professe that doctrine which is untrue, and hereticall; but because in words they professe to beleeve and hold that doctrine which they doe not, but hold, and that for a point of their faith, the quite contrary: All of them will and doe professe that they beleeve the scriptures, and the doctrines therein contained : and yet every one of them lye herein, for they beleeve one, if not moe doctrines contrary to the scriptures. The *Nestorians* professed to hold the *Nicene* faith, and so they professed two natures and but one person to bee in Christ; for that in the *Nicene* faith is certainly decreed : but they lyed in making this profession, for they beleeved not one person, but pertinaciously held two persons to be in Christ. The *Eutycheans* in professing the *Ephesine* Councell, professed in effect two natures to abide in Christ after the union, for this was certainly the faith of that holy Councell, but they lyed in this profession, for they held that after the union two natures did not abide in Christ, but one onely. The Church of *Rome* and members thereof professe to hold the faith of the fift generall Councell, and so professe *implicitè* the Popes *Cathedrall* sentence in a cause of faith to be *fallible* and hereticall : but they lye in making this profession, for they beleeve not the Popes sentence in such causes to be fallible, but with the *Laterane* and *Trent* Councels, they hold it to be *infallible.* It is the practice of all heretikes to make such faire, though lying professions. For should they say in plaine termes, (that which is truth indeed) wee beleeve not the scriptures, nor the Councells of *Nice, Ephesus,* or *Chalcedon*; every man would spit at them, and

1 Lib. 2. de doct. Christ. ca. 9.

T 2   detest

deteſt them, *cane pejus & angue*, nor could they ever deceive any, or gaine one proſelyte. But when they commend their faith (that is, their hereſie) to be the ſame doctrine with the ſcriptures, which the Councells of *Nice*, *Epheſus* and *Chalcedon* taught, by theſe faire pretences, and this lying profeſſion, they inſinuate themſelves into the hearts of the ſimple, deceiving hereby both themſelves and others.

16. The other conſequent is this, That the profeſſion of all heretikes is contradictory to it ſelfe. For they profeſſe to hold the ſcriptures, and ſo to condemne every hereſie, and yet withal they profeſſe one private doctrine repugnant to ſcripture, and which is an hereſie. The like may be ſaid of the Councells. The *Neſtorians* by profeſſing to hold the faith decreed at *Nice*, profeſſe Chriſt to bee but one perſon, and yet withall by holding *Neſtorianiſme*, they profeſſe Chriſt to be two perſons. The *Eutycheans* by profeſſing to hold the Councell of *Epheſus*, profeſſe two natures to remaine in Chriſt after the union, which in that Councell is certainly decreed, and yet by profeſſing the hereſie of *Eutyches*, they profeſſe the quite contradictory, that one nature onely remaines after the union. The Church of *Rome* and members thereof, by profeſſing the faith of the fift Councell, profeſſe the Popes *Cathedrall* ſentence in a cauſe of faith to be *fallible*, and *de fide* to have beene *hereticall*; and yet they profeſſe the direct contradictory, as the Councell of *Laterane* hath defined, that the Popes ſentence in ſuch cauſes is *infallible*, and neither hath beene nor can be *hereticall*. So repugnant to it ſelfe, and incoherent is the profeſſion of all heretikes, that it fighteth both with the truth, and with it owne ſelfe alſo. The very ſame is to be ſeene in *Vigilius* and his *Conſtitution*. For in profeſſing to defend the *three Chapters*, and in decreeing that all ſhall defend them, he profeſſeth all the blaſphemies of *Neſtorius*, and decreeth that all ſhall maintaine them, and profeſſing to hold the faith decreed at *Chalcedon*, and decreeing that all ſhall hold it, hee profeſſeth that *Neſtorianiſme* is hereſie, and decreeth that all ſhall condemne it for hereſie : and ſo decreeing both theſe, he decreeth that all men in the world ſhall beleeve two contradictories, and beleeve them as Catholike Truths. Such a worthy *Apoſtolicall* decree is this of *Vigilius*, for defending whereof *Baronius* doth more then toyle himſelfe.

17. You will againe demand: Seeing *Vigilius* doth ſo earneſtly and plainely profeſſe both theſe, why ſhall not his expreſſe profeſſion to hold the Councell of *Chalcedon*, make him or ſhew him to bee a Catholike, rather then his other expreſſe profeſſion, to defend the *Three Chapters*, make or ſhew him to bee an hereticke ? Why rather ſhall his *hereticall*, then his *orthodoxall* profeſſion give denomination unto him ? I alſo demand of you, Seeing every hereticke in expreſſe words profeſſeth to beleeve the whole Scripture, which is in effect a condemning of every hereſie, why ſhall not this *orthodoxall* profeſſion make or ſhew him to be a Catholike, rather then his expreſſe profeſſion of ſome one doctrine contrarie to Scripture (ſay for example ſake, of *Arianiſme*) make or ſhew him to bee an *Arian* hereticke? The

reaſon

reason of both is one and the same. Did an *Arian* so professe to hold the Scriptures, that hee were resolved to forsake his *Arianisme,* and confesse Christ to bee ὁμόσιον, upon manifestation that the Scriptures taught this, certainely his professiō of *Arianisme,* with such a professiōto hold the Scriptures, could not make him an hereticke, no more then *Cyprians* profession of Rebaptization, or *Irenees* of the millenarie heresie, did make them heretikes: Erre hee should, as they did, but being not pertinacious in error, hereticke hee could not be, as they were not. But it falls out otherwise with all heretickes. They professe to hold the Scripture, yet so that they resolve not to forsake that private doctrine which they have chosen to maintaine: That they will hold, and they will have that to be the doctrine of the Scripture, notwithstanding all manifestation to the contrarie, even of the Scriptures themselves. They resolve of this, that whosoever, Bishops, Councells, or Church, teach the contrarie to that, or say & judge that the Scripture so teacheth, they all erre or mistake the meaning of the Scriptures. Thus did not *Cyprian,* nor *Irenee.* And this wilfull and pertinacious resolution it is, which evidently sheweth that in truth they beleeve not the Scriptures, but beleeve their own fancies, though they say a thousand times, that they beleeve and embrace whatsoever the Scriptures teach, for did they beleeve any doctrine, say *Arianisme, eò nomine,* because the Scripture teacheth it, they would presently beleeve the contrarie thereunto, when it were manifested unto them (as is was to the *Arians,* by the *Nicen* Coūcell) that the Scripture taught the contrarie to their error. Seeing this they will not doe, It is certaine that they hold their private opiniō, *eo nomine* because they will hold it, and they hold it to bee the doctrine of scripture, not because it is so, but because they will have it to bee so, say what any will or can to the contrarie. So their owne will, and not Scripture, is the reason why they beleeve it, nay why they hold it with such a stiffe opinion, for beleife it is not, it cannot be. This pertinacie to have beene in the *Nestorians,* *Eutycheans* and the rest, is evident. Had they beleeved, as they professed, the faith decreed at *Nice* and *Ephesus,* then upon manifestation of their errors out of those Councels, they would have renounced their heresies: but seeing the *Nestorians* persisted to hold two persons in Christ, notwithstanding, that the whole Councell of *Ephesus* manifested unto them that the *Nicene* Councel held but one person, and seeing the *Eutycheans* persisted to hold but one nature after the union, notwithstanding that the whole Councell at *Chalcedon* manifested unto them, that the holy *Ephesine* Synod held two natures to abide in him after the union, they did hereby make it evident unto all, that they so professed to hold those Councels, as that they resolved not to forsake their *Nestorian* and *Eutichean* heresies for any manifestation of the truth, or conviction of their error out of those Councels, and their profession of them was in effect as if they had said, we hold those Councels, and will have them to teach what wee affirme, whatsoever any man or Councell saith, or can say to the contrarie. The like must be said of Pope *Vigilius* in this cause: Had he so professed to hold the Councell of *Chalcedon,* as that upon manifestion

that

that the *Three Chapters* were condemned by it, he would have forsaken the defence of them, then certainely his defending of these 3. *Chapters* had not bin pertinacious, nor should have made him an hereticke, but his profession to hold the faith decreed at *Chalcedon*, notwithstanding his error about the 3. *Chapters*, should have made him a catholike. But seeing *Vig.* persisted to defend the 3. *Chapt.* though it was made evidēt unto him by the Synodall judgement of the fift Councell, that the definition of faith decreed at *Chalcedon* condemned them all, he by this persisting in heresie did demonstrate to all, that he professed to hold the Councell at *Chalcedon*, no otherwise then with a pertinacious resolution not to forsake the defence of those *Three hereticall Chapters*, although the whole Church of God should manifest unto him, that the Councell of *Chalcedon* condemned the same : and for this cause his defending of those *three Chapters*, with this pertinacie and wilfull resolution declareth him to bee indeed an hereticke, notwithstanding his profession to hold the Councell of *Chalcedon* and faith thereof, whereby all those Chapters are condemned, which profession being joyned with the former pertinacie, could not now either make or declare him to be a Catholike.

18. The very same must bee said of the present *Romane Church* and members thereof. Did they in such sort professe to hold the fift Councel, and faith thereof, as that upon manifestation that this Councell beleeved, taught and decreed that the Popes *Cathedrall* sentence in a cause of faith is *fallible*, and *de facto* hath beene hereticall, they would condemne that their *fundamentall* heresie of the Popes *Cathedrall infallibilitie* decreed in their *Laterane* and *Trent* assemblies, then should they much rather, for their profession of the fift Councell and faith thereof, bee *orthodoxall*, then for professing (together with this) the Popes *Cathedrall infallibilitie*, bee hereticall. But seeing they know by the very Acts and judiciall sentence of that fift Councell, by which the *Cathedrall Constitution* of *Vigilius* is condemned and accursed for hereticall in this cause of faith, touching the *Three Chapters*, that the fift Councell beleeved this, and decreed, under the censure of an *Anathema*, that all others should beleeve it, and that all who beleeve the contrary, are heretikes : seeing, I say, notwithstanding this manifestation of the faith of that Councell ; they persist to defend the Popes *Cathedrall infallibility* in those causes, yea, defend it as the very foundation of their faith; this makes it evident to all, that they do no otherwise professe to hold this fift Councell, or the other, whether precedent, or following, (for they all are consonant to this) but with this pertinacious resolution, not to forsake that their *fundamentall* heresie; and therefore their expresse profession of this fift, and other generall Councels, yea, of the Scriptures themselves, cannot be so effectuall to make them Catholikes, as the profession of the Popes *infallibility*, which is joyned with this pertinacy, is to make and demonstrate them to be heretikes.

19. There is yet a further point to be observed touching the pertinacy of *Vigilius* : For one may be, and often is pertinacious in his errour, not onely after, but even before conviction, or manifestation of

the

the truth made unto him; and this happeneth whensoever hee is not *paratus corrigi, prepared, or ready to be informed of the truth,* and corrected thereby, or when he doth not, or will not, *tanta solicitudine quærere veritatem, with care and diligence seeke to know the truth,* as after S. *Austen* [m], and out of him *Occham* [n], *Gerson* [o], *Navar* [p], *Alphonsus à Castro* [q], and many others doe truly teach.   See now, I pray you, how farre *Vigilius* was from this care of seeking, and preparation to embrace the truth ? He by his *Apostolicall* authoritie decreed [r], that none should either write, or speake, or teach ought contrary to his *Constitution,* or if they did, that his decree should stand for a condemnation and refutation of whatsoever they should either write or speake. Here was a tricke of *Papall,* that is, of the most supreme pertinancy that can bee devised : He takes order before hand, that none shall ever, I say, not convict him, but, so much as manifest the truth unto him, or open his mouth, or write a syllable for the manifestation thereof : and so, being not prepared to bee corrected, no nor informed neither, hee was pertinacious, and is justly to bee so accounted before ever either Bishop, or Councell manifested the truth unto him. Even as he is farre more wilfully and obstinately delighted in darknesse, who dammes up all the windowes, chinkes, and passages, whereby any light might enter into the house, wherein hee is, than hee, who lyeth asleepe, and is willing to be awaked, when the light shineth about him : So was it with Pope *Vigilius* at this time; his tying of al mens tongues, and hands, that they should not manifest by word, or writing, the truth unto him; his damming up of the light, that never any glimpse of the truth might shine unto him, argues a mind most damnably pertinacios in errour, and so farre from being prepared and ready to embrace the truth, that it is obdurate against the same, and will not permit it so much as to come neere unto him.

20.   The very like pertinancy is at this day in the *Romane* Church, and all the members thereof : for having once set downe this transcendent principle, the *foundation* of all which they beleeve; that the Popes judgement, in causes of faith, is *infallible,* they doe by this exclude and utterly shut out all manifestation of the truth, that can possibly bee made unto them : Oppose whatsoever you will against their errour, Scriptures, Fathers, Councels, reason and sense it selfe; it is all refuted before it be proposed, seeing the Pope, who is *infallible,* saith the contrary to that which you would prove, you, in disputing from those places, doe either mis-cite them, or mis-interpret the Scriptures, Fathers, and Councels, or your reason from them is sophisticall, and your sense of sight, of touching, of tasting, is deceived, some one defect or other there is in your opposition; but an errour in that which they hold, there is, nay, there can be none, because the Pope teacheth that, and the Pope, in his teaching is *infallible.* Here is a charme, which causeth one to heare with a deafe eare, whatsoever is opposed : the very head of *Medusa,* if you come against it, it stunnes you at the first, and turnes both your reason, your sense, and your selfe also, into a very stone. By holding this one *fundamentall* position, they are pertinacious in all their errours, and that in the highest degree of pertinancy,

which

m Epist. 162.
n Lib. 4. part. 1. ca. 2.
o Conf. 12. de pertinacia. part. 1. pa. 430.
p Ench. ca. 11. nu. 22.
q Lib. 1. de justa punit. hæret. ca. 7
r Const. Vigil. apud Bar. an. 553. nu. 208.

which the wit of man can devife; yea, and pertinacious before all conviction, and that alfo though the truth fhould never by any meanes
be manifefted unto them : For by fetting this downe, they are fo far
from being prepared to embrace the truth, though it fhould be manifefted unto them, that hereby they have made a *fundamentall* law for
themfelves, that they never will be convicted, nor ever have the truth
manifefted unto them. The onely meanes in likelihood to perfwade
them, that the doctrines which they maintaine, are herefies, were firft
to perfwade the Pope, who hath decreed them to bee *orthodoxall*, to
make a contrary decree, that they are *hereticall*. Now although this
may be morally judged, to be a matter of impoffibilitie; yet, if his Holineffe could be induced hereunto, and would fo farre ftoope to Gods
truth, as to make fuch a decree; even this alfo could not perfwade
them, fo long as they hold that *foundation*. They would fay, either the
Pope were not the true Pope, or that he defined it not as Pope, and *ex
Cathedra*; or that, by confenting to fuch an hereticall decree, hee ceafed *ipfo facto* to be Pope, or the like; fome one or other evafion they
would have ftill: but, grant the Popes fentence to be *fallible*, or hereticall, whofe *infallibility* they hold as a doctrine of faith, yea, as the
foundation of their faith, they would not. Such, and fo unconquerable
pertinacy is annexed, and that effentially, to that one *Pofition*, that fo
long as one holds it, (and whenfoever he ceafeth to hold it, hee ceafeth
to be a member of their Church,) there is no poffible meanes in the
world to convict him, or convert him to the truth.

21. You doe now clearely fee, how feeble, and inconfequent
that Collection is, which *Baronius* here ufeth in excufe of Pope *Vigilius*, for that he often profeffeth to defend the Councell of *Chalcedon*,
and the faith therein explaned : Hee did but herein that which is the
ufuall cuftome of all other heretikes, both ancient and moderne : Quit
him for this caufe, and quit them all; condemne them, and then, this
pretece can no way excufe *Vigilius* frō herefie. They all with him profeffe, with great oftentation to hold the doctrines of the Scriptures, of
Fathers, of generall Councels, but becaufe their profeffion is not onely
lying, and contradictorie to it felfe, but alwayes fuch, as that they retaine a wilfull and pertinacious refolution, not to forfake that herefie
which themfelves embrace, as *Vigilius* had, not to forfake his defence
of the *Three Chapters*: Hence it is that their verbal profeffion of Scriptures, Fathers, and Councels, cannot make any of them, nor *Vigilius*
among them, to be efteemed *orthodoxall*, or Catholike : but the reall
and cordiall profeffion of any one doctrine, which they, with fuch pertinacy hold againft the Scriptures, or holy generall Councels, as *Vigilius* did this of the *Three Chapters*, doth truly demonftrate them all,
and *Vigilius* among them, to be heretikes. And this may fuffice for
anfwer to the fecond exception, or evafion of *Baronius*.

CAP. 15.

The third exception of Baronius *in excuse of* Vigilius, *taken from his con-*
firming of the fift Councell, answered: and how Pope Vigilius, *three*
or foure times changed his judgement in this cause of faith.

I. IN the third place *Baronius* comes to excuse *Vigi-*
lius, by his act of confirming and approving the
fift Councell, and the decree thereof for condemning the *Three Chapters*, It appeareth, saith
hee [a], *that* Vigilius, *to the end he might take away*
the schisme, and unite the Easterne Churches to the
Catholike communion, quintam Synodum authori-
tate Apostolica comprobavit, did approve the fift Synod by his Apostolicall
authoritie. Againe [b], *when* Vigilius *saw, that the Easterne Church would be*
rent from the West, unlesse he consented to the fift Synod, eam probavit, he
approved it: Again [c], Pelagius *thought it fit, as* Vigilius *had thought before,*
that the fift Synod, wherein the three Chapters were condemned, should bee
approved: and again [d], Cognitum fuit, *it was publikely known, that* Vigilius
had approved the fift Synod, and condemned the *three Chapters*. The
like is affirmed by *Bellarmine* [e], Vigilius *confirmed the fift Synod, per libel-*
lum, by a booke, or writing. Binius *is so resolute herein, that hee saith* [f],
A Vigilio (quintam) Synodum confirmatam et approbatam esse nemo dubitat,
none doubteth but that *Vigilius* confirmed and approved the fift Councell.
Now if *Vigilius* approved the fift Councell, and condemned the *Three*
Chapters, it seemes that all which wee have said of his contradicting
the fift Synod, and of his defending those *Three Chapters*, is of no force,
and that by his assent to the Synod he is a good Catholike. This is the
Exception, the validity whereof we are now to examine.

2. For the clearing of which whole matter, it must bee remembred, that all, which hitherto wee have spoken of *Vigilius*, hath reference to his *Apostolicall decree*, published in defence of those *Three*
Chapters, that is, to *Vigilius*, being such as that decree doth shew, and
demonstrate him to have beene, even a pertinacious oppugner of the
faith, and a condemned heretike by the judiciall sentence of the fift
Councell : but now *Baronius* drawes us to a further examination of
the cariage of *Vigilius* in this whole businesse, and how hee behaved
himselfe from the first publishing of the Emperours Edict, which was
in the twentieth [g] yeare of *Iustinian*, unto the death of *Vigilius*, which
was, as *Baronius* accounteth [h], in the 29 of *Iustinian*, and second yeare
after the fift Councell was ended; but, as *Victor*, (who then lived) accounteth [i], in the 31 of *Iustinian*, and fourth yeare after the Synod :
and, for the more cleare view of his cariage, wee must observe foure
severall periods of time, wherein *Vigilius*, during those nine or tenne
yeares, gave divers severall judgements, and made three or foure eminent changes in this cause of faith. The first, from the promulgation
of the Emperours Edict, while he remained at *Rome*, and was absent
from the Emperor. The second, after he came to *Constantinople*, and to
the

a *An.554.nu.7.*

b *An.553.nu. 235.*

c *Ibid.nu.236.*

d *An.556.nu.1.*

e *Lib.1.de Conc. ca.5.§ Coacta.*
f *Not.in Conc.5. § Praestitit.*

g *Bar.an.546. nu.8.*

h *An.555.nu.1.*

i *In Chron.an. 17.post Coss. Basil.*

the Emperours presence, but before the fift Synod was begun. The third, in the time of the fift Synod, and about a yeare after the end and dissolution thereof. The fourth, from thence, that is, from the yeare after the Synod, unto his death.

3. At the first [k] publishing of the Edict, many of the Westerne Churches, *impugnabant Edictum*, did oppose themselves to it, and as *Baronius* saith, *insurrexere*, made an insurrection against it, and the Emperour: Pope *Vigilius*, as in place and dignity hee was more eminent, so in this Insurrection he was more forward, and a ring-leader unto them all : And because the conflict was likely to bee troublesome, *Vigilius* used all his authority and art in managing of this cause. First, he proclameth the Edict, and condemning of the *Three Chapters* to bee a prophane [l] novelty, judging [m] it to bee contrary to the holy faith, and Councell at *Chalcedon*: To this he addes writings, threats, and punishments : *Literas scripsit adversus eos*, saith *Baronius* [n], *Vigilius writ letters against all that held with the Emperor, and his Edict* : in those letters, *comminatus* [o] *est eis qui consenserunt*; he threatned those that consented to the Emperor; *edixit* [p] *& indixit correctionem*; he decreed punishment unto them, and forewarned them thereof; telling them, that unlesse they did amend their fault, hee would draw out his *Apostolike* blade against them, protesting with the Apostle [q], *I feare when I come, I shall not finde you such as I would, and that I shall be found of you such as yee would not*. Nor were his threats in vaine, as it seemeth, seeing *Baronius* [r] tells us, that for this very cause, either he or *Stephanus* his Legate, in his name did excommunicate, besides others, two Patriarkes, *Mennas* of *Constantinople*, and *Zoilus* of *Alexandria*, and with them *Theodorus* Bishop of *Cesarea*.

4. Thus he dealt with inferiour persons, but for the Emperour he took another course with him: He saw what danger it was to write against Emperors, that he would not do himself: But whē, like *Pirrhus*, *ipse sibi cavit loco*, he had provided for his owne safety; then he thrusts forward *Facundus* Bishop of *Hermian* into that busines. *Facundus* an eloquent mā indeed, as his name also imports, but a most obstinate heretike & Schismatike, seeing he persisted in defēce of the *three Chapters*, not only before, but after the judicial sentēce of the general Councel, & yet is he cōmended by *Baronius* [s] to be *prudentissimus agonistes*, a most wise champion for the Church: but the more hereticall hee is, the more like, and better liked is hee to *Baronius*. Him doth *Vigilius* [t] egge, and even command to write against the Emperour; yea, *sugillare*, (it is the Cardinals word) *to taunt and flout him*, for his Edict; nor him onely, but in him to reprove, *omnes simul Principes*, all Princes whosoever doe presume to meddle with a cause of faith, or make lawes therein, as *Iustinian* had done. *Facundus* being thus directed, incouraged, and warranted by Pope *Vigilius*, and being but his instrument in this matter, writes [u] a large volume containing twelve bookes, against the Emperor, in defence of the *three Chapters*. A worke stuffed with heresie, yet highly commended by *Possevine* [x] the Iesuite, as being a brave booke strengthned with the authorities of the Fathers. There he takes upon him to revile the Emperor in most uncivill and undutifull

---

Marginal notes:

k *Ipso exordio osseriæ ab Imperatore sententiæ. Bar. an. 546 nu. 38. et 39.*

l *Ille (Vigilius) prophanas vocum novitates sibi vendicavit arguendas. Ait Facund. apud Bar. an. 546. nu. 57.*
m *Nisi contrarium Synodo Chalcedonensi judicaret. Ibid. nu. 58.*
n *An. 547. nu. 44. et 32.*
o *Ibid.*
p *Facund. loco cit. nu. 56.*
q 2 Cor. 12. v. 22.
r *An. 546. nu. 47. et 547. nu. 45.*

s *An. 546. nu. 44*

t *Hæc Facundus jubente Vigilio. Bar. ibid.*

u *Scriptum adversus Imperatorem edidit. An. eod. nu. 39.*
x *Opus grande & elegans, et patrum authoritatibus munitum. Poss. Bibl. in Facund.*

tifull manner, as if, forfooth, *fides ¶ omnium ex ejus voluntate penderet,* the faith of all Churches did hang on the Emperours fleeve; and as if none might beleeve otherwife, *quam praeciperet imperator,* then the Emperour commanded; telling him, that it were more meet for him, *fe infra limitem fuum continere,* to keepe himfelfe within his owne bounds, as other Artificers kept their own fhops; the Weaver not medling with the Forge and Anvill, nor the Cobler with a Carpenters office. Such rude, homely, and undutifull comparifons doth the Popes Oratour ufe in this caufe: And, as if *Facundus* had not paid the Emperour halfe enough, *Baronius* helpes him with a whole Cart-load of fuch Romifh eloquence; calling the Emperour, utterly [a] unlearned, *qui [b] nec Alphabetum aliquando didiciffet; who never had learned fo much as his A,B,C, nor could [c] ever read the Title of the Bible: a Panie [d], a palliated Theologue, a facrilegious [e] perfon, a witleffe [f], furious, and frantike fellow, poffeffed with an evill fpirit, and driven by the Devill himfelfe:* Such an one to [g] prefume againft all right, to make lawes concerning matters of faith, concerning Priefts, and the punifhments of them? adding [h], that the whole Catholike faith would be in jeopardie, *fi qui ejufmodi effet; if fuch as Juftinian fhould makes lawes of faith; yea, fuch lawes, quas [i] dolofe confcripfiffent haeretici, as heretikes had craftily penned; telling [k] him, (as *Facundus* had before) that it were more fit for him to looke to the government of the Empire; and upbraiding him with that proverbiall admonition, *Ne ultra Crepidam,* Sr Cobler go not beyond your Laft & Latchet. This fcurrility doth the Cardinall ufe againft the moft religious and prudent Emperour, and his holy and orthodoxall Edict; and hee faith, that he was [l] willing to adde thefe, *ad roborandam Facundi fententiam, to fortifie the fentence of *Facundus*, whereby he, with *Vigilius*, did defend the *Three Chapters*.

5. Were one difpofed to make fport with the Cardinall, himfelfe here offereth a large field, wherein one may exfpaciate; and feeing he ufeth not others as Kings, hee might expect, *lege talionis,* not to bee ufed himfelfe as a Cardinall: But becaufe wee fhall in another place more fitly convince the Cardinall, both for his reviling the Emperor, and railing at his Edict, as penned by heretikes, for this time I will but by the way obferve two or three points touching this paffage. The firft, that *Facundus* by defending the *Three Chapters*, and *Baronius* by fortifying his defence, doe unavoydably pull upon themfelves the juft cenfure of *Anathema,* denounced by the holy Councell againft the defenders of thofe Chapters, and thofe who are abetters of them: So, the more *Baronius* doth labour to fortifie the fentence of *Facundus,* the more he entangles himfelfe in that curfe of the generall Councel. The fecond, that both *Facundus* & *Baronius* do quite miftake the matter, in carping at the Emperour, as if by his Edict, or in condemning thofe *Three Chapters*; he had taught or publifhed fome new doctrine of faith; he did not: He taught and commanded all others to embrace that true, ancient, and Apoftolicall faith, which was decreed and explaned at *Chalcedon,* as both the whole fift Councell witneffeth, which fheweth, that all thofe Chapters were *implicitè*, but yet truly, and indeed condemned in the definition of faith made at *Chalcedon;*

y *Facund. lib. 12 ejus verba citantur à Bar. an. 546. nu. 42.*

a *An. 546. nu. 41.*
b *An. 528. nu. 2. ut qui nec prima elementa calleret ut legere poffet. An. 446. nu. 42.*
c *An. 551. nu. 5*
d *Repente appofuere pulliatum Theologum. An. 551. nu. 13.*
e *An. 552. nu. 8.*
f *Ille furore percitus, ut ante admotus, correptus maligno fpiritu, agitatus à Satana. An. 551. nu. 2.*
g *Praeter juifafque praefumens. An. 528. nu. 2.*
h *An. 546. nu. 43.*
i *Ibid. nu. 41.*
k *An. 550. nu. 14.*
l *Haec addidiffe voluimus. An. 546. nu. 43.*

cedon; and Pope *Gregorie* also testifieth the same, saying of this fift Councell, that it was *in omnibus sequax*, in every point a follower of the Councell at *Chalcedon*. This the religious Emperour wisely discerning, did by his imperiall edict, and authoritie (as *Constantine*, and *Theodosius*, had done before him) ratifie that old and Catholike faith, which the *Nestorians* by defending those Chapters craftily undermined at that time. The third & speciall point which I observe, is that which *Baronius* noteth, as the cause why Pope *Vigil.* was so eager against the Emperor and his edict. And what thinke you was it? Forsooth because, *Iustinian primus* [m] *legem sancivit*, was the first who made a law, and published a Decree for condemning of those *three Chapters*. Had the Pope first done this, and *Iustinian* seconded his holinesse therein, hee had beene another *Constantine*, a second *Theodosius*, the dearest child of the Church. But for Princes to presume to teach the Pope, or make any lawes concerning the faith, before they consult with the Romane *Apollo*, or make him acquainted therewith, thats [n] *piaculum*, a capitall, an irremissible sinne, the Pope may not endure it. So then, is was neither zeale, not pietie, nor love to the truth, but meere stomacke and pride in *Vigilius* to oppose himselfe to the Emperours edict, and make an insurrection against him. A sory reason God wot for any wise man in the world, much more for the Pope, to contradict the truth and oppugne the Catholike faith. Now if *Iustinian* for doing this which was an act of prudence and pietie, tending wholy to the good and peace of the Church, if hee could not escape so undutifull usage at the Pope, & his orators in those better times, religious Kings may not thinke it strange, to finde the like or far worse entertainment at the Popes of these dayes and their instruments, men so exact and eloquent in reviling, that in all such base and uncivill usage they goe as farre beyond *Facundus*, *Tertullus*, and them of former ages, as drosse or the most abject mettle is inferiour to refined gold. This is the first Period, and first judgement of *Vigilius* touching this cause of the *three Chapters*: in defence of which, and oppugning of the Emperours edict, hee continued more then a yeare after the publishing of the Edict, even all that time while hee remained at *Rome*, and was absent from the Emperour.

6. As soone almost as *Vigilius* was come to *Constantinople*, and had saluted the Emperor, and conferred with them who stood for the Edict, he was quite another man, he changed *cum cælo animum*, the aire of the Emperors Court altered the Popes judgement, and this was about a yeare after [o] the publishing of the Edict: Now that all things might be done with more solemnitie and advise, there was a Synod [p] held shortly after his comming, at *Constantinople*, wherein *Vigilius* with thirty Bishops condemned the *Three Chapters*, and consented to the Emperors Edict. This *Facundus* expresly witnesseth, saying [q], *How shall not this bee a prejudice to the cause, if it bee demonstrated that Pope* Vigilius *with thirty Bishops or therabouts, have condemned the Epistle (of* Ibas*) approved by the Councell of Chalcedon, and anathematized that Bishop (*Theodorus *of* Mopsvestia*) with his doctrines, the praises whereof are set downe in that Councell?* Thus *Facundus.* Besides all this, *Vigilius* was now,

in An. 553. nu. 247.

[n] *Vel si regnum fuisset, recté non fieret, quia nulli Regum hinc aliquid agere, sed solis est sacerdotibus datum. Facund. & Bar. an. 547. nu. 35. Imperator est fidem coram sacerdotibus profiteri, non eosdem prascribere sacerdotibus Bar. ibid.*

[o] *Edictu editu fuit anno. 546. Bar. eo anno nu. 8. Constantinopolim ingressus est an. 547. prope die Natalis Domini. Bar. an. illo. nu. 26.*

[p] *Bar. an. eod. nu. 31. 32.*

[q] *Ibid. nu. 37.*

now so forward in this cause, that as before he had written bookes a-
gainst the Edict, in defence of the *three Chapters*; and excommunicated those who condemned those Chapters; so now on the Emperors
side, he writ bookes, and gave judgement, for the condemning of
those Chapters, and excommunicated some; by name, *Rusticus* and
Sebastianus, two Romane Deacons, because they would not condemne
them. *None can deny* saith *Baronius* [d], *that Vigilius writ a booke against
the three chapters, and sent it unto Mennas Bishop of Constantinople.* Again,
there [e] is *certaine proofe, latæ ab eo sententiæ, of the sentence (of excommunication) pronounced by* Vigilius, *against Rusticus, Sebastianus, and other
defenders of those chapters :* and this is so cleare, *ut nulla dubitatio esse
possit, that there can be no doubt at all, but that* Vigilius *approved by a Constitution the Emperors sentence, and condemned the three Chapters.* So *Baronius.* The Epistles of *Vigilius* doe testifie the same. In that [f] to *Rusticus* and *Sebastianus* he very often makes mention, *Iudicati nostri, Con-
stituti nostri, of our judgement, of our constitution* against the *three chapters,* concerning which he addeth [g], that it was ratified by his *Apostolicall authority,* saying, that no man may doe, *contra constitutum nostrum
quod ex beati Petri authoritate proferimus, against this our Constitution
which we set forth by the authority of Saint Peter.* The like hee testifieth,
in his Epistle [h] to *Valentinianus, We beleeve* saith he, *that those things may
suffice the children of the Church, which we writ to Mennas, concerning the
blasphemies of Theodorus of Mopsvestia and his person, concerning the Epistle of Ibas, and the writings of Theodoret against the right faith.* Thus *Vigilius* consenting now with the Emperor, defending his Imperiall E-
dict, and condemning the *three Chapters*; in all which, his profession
as Catholike and orthodoxall.

7. When *Vigilius* was thus turned an Imperialist, and in regard
his outward profession declared in his *Constitution,* become *orthodoxall,* (though as it seemeth he remained in heart *hereticall*) hee fell
to so great dislike of those who defended the *three Chapters,* that
they [i] did *proclamare,* proclame him to be a colluder, a prevaricator
a betrayer of the faith; one who to please the Emperour revolted
from his former judgement; yea the Africane [k] Bishops proceeded so
sore against him, that, as *Victor* Bishop of *Tunen* testifieth, *Synodaliter
eum à catholica communione recludunt; they in a Synod, and synodally excommunicated him,* or shut him from the Catholike communion. A
thing worthy observing; being done by those whom the Cardinall
professeth [l] to have beene Catholikes at that time. But let that passe:
Baronius to excuse [m] *Vigilius* from those imputations of colluder and
prevaricator, and to shew that hee was not in heart affected with the
truth, which in his Constitution he declared, tells us a rare policy of
the Pope, which for this time we omit, but hereafter will examine the
truth and validity thereof, and this it was. *Mox* [n], presently after *Vigilius* had made that *Apostolicall* decree for condemning the *three
Chapters,* he revoked the same, (touched belike with remorse for so
ruinous a crime, as to professe the Catholike faith) and he suspended
[o] and his owne judgement in that cause, till the time of a generall
Councell : decreeing [o], that untill that time all men should be whisht
and

d *An. 547.
nu. 40.*
e *Ibid.*

f *Extat in Coll.
7. Cont. 5. pa.
578.*

g *Ibid. pa. 580.*

h *Ibid.*

i *Bar. an. 547.
nu. 49.*

k *In Chron. an.
10. post Coss.
Basilij.*

l *An. 547. nu.
30. & 39.*
m *Ad hæc om-
nia excusanda,
illud satis super-
que est, Bar. ibi.
nu. 49.*
n *An. eodem
nu. 41.*
o *Rursus à Vi-
gilio promulga-
tum decretum
est, quo decer-
nebatur, ut de
controversia de
tribus Capitulis
penitus tacere-
tur, ibid.*

and filent in this caufe of faith; they muft neither fay that the *Three*
Chapters were to bee defended, nor condemned; they muft neither
fpeake one word for the truth, nor againft the truth, they muft all
(during that time) be like himfelfe, lukewarme Laodiceans, neither
hot nor cold, neither fifh nor flefh.   This was the great wifedome
and policy of the Pope, as *Baronius* at large declares, and makes no
fmall boaft thereof, adding p that the Pope remained in this mood
till the time of the general Councel. Thus you fee the fecond judgmēt
of Pope *Vigilius* in this caufe, and his cariage during the fecond period, for a fit (which perhaps lafted a weeke or a month) hee was in outward profeffion *orthodoxall*, but being weary of fuch an ague, hee prefently becomes a meere neutralift in the faith: and in this fort hee
continued till the affembling of the generall Councell, that is, for the
fpace of fix yeares and more.

8. The third period begins at the time of the fift generall Councell: Of what judgement the Pope then was, it hath before q beene
fufficiently declared. Then *Vigilius* turned to his old byas, hee condemned the Emperours Edict, and all that with it condemned the
three Chapters : he defends thofe *three hereticall chapters,* and that after
a moft authenticall manner, publifhing a Synodall, a Cathedrall and
Apoftolicall conftitution in defence of the fame.   And whereas not only others, but himfelfe alfo, had written, and fome fixe yeares before,
made a Conftitution to condemne thofe Chapters : Now after long
and diligent ponderation of the caufe, when hee had examined all
matters, *cum omni undiq; cautela, with all warineffe and circumfpection*
that could poffible be ufed : he quite cafheires, repeales, and forever
adnuls ſ that former Conftitution, and whatfoever either himfelfe
or any other, either had before written or fhould after that time,
write contrary to this prefent Decree. And this no doubt was the
reafon why *Baronius* never fo much as once endeavors to excufe *Vi-*
gilius by that former decree, or to prove him to have beene orthodoxall, by it : feeing by this later the whole force and vertue of that
former is utterly made void, fruftrate and of no effect in the world.
In this judgement *Vigilius* was fo refolute, that hee was ready to endure any difgrace and punifhment, rather then confent to the condemning of the *three Chapters* : and if wee may beleeve *Baronius* et
Binius, he did for this very caufe endure banifhment. *It is manifeſt*
faith *Binius* ſ, *that after the end of the fift Councell Iuftinian did caſt into*
banifhment both Vigilius *and other orthodoxall Bifhops,* (fo hee termeth
convicted and condemned heretikes) *becaufe they would not confent to*
the decrees of the Synod, and condemning of the three Chapters. In like fort
Baronius t, *Liquet ex Anaftafio, it is manifeſt by Anaftafius, that* Vigilius
and thofe who held with him were caried into banifhment. Againe u, *Others*
thought they had a juſt quarrell in defending the three Chapters : when they
faw Vigilius *even in banifhment to maintaine the fame,* and they thought,
fe pro facrofanctis pugnare legibus, that they fought for the holy faith; when
they faw Pope *Vigilius* himfelfe, for the fame caufe, *conſtanti animo ex-*
ilium ferre, to endure banifhment with a conſtant minde. Againe x, *Horū*
folum caufa, for this caufe onely was Vigilius *driven into banifhment,* becaufe

p *Ab hoc anno*
(547) *ad tem-*
pus Concilij in-
dictum (fuit au-
tem an. 553)
fuit inea caufa
filentium, ibid.
*nu.*43.

q *Sup.ca.3. nu.*
4. & feq.

ſ *Si quid de*
eifdem capitulis
contra hæc quæ
hic afferuimus
vel ſtatuimus—
factum, dictum
atq; confcriptum
eft, vel fuerit,—
hoc modis omni-
bus ex authori-
tate fedis Apo-
ftolica refuta-
mus. Conft.Vi-
gil. in fine.

ſ *Not. in Conc.*
5.§. Praftitit.

t *An.*553. *nu.*
222.
u *Ibid. nu.* 251.

x *An.*554.*nu.*6.

cause he would not condemne the *Three Chapters.* So *Baronius:* who often calleth this exiling of *Vigilius* and others, who defended those Chapters; persecution [y], yea, an heavy [z] and monstrous persecution, complaining that the Church under *Iustinian* and from him, endured more hard conditions, and was in worse case then under the Heathen Emperors.

9. Now this demonstrates that which before I touched, that though the Pope upon his comming to *Constantinople*, made a decree for condemning the *Three Chapters*, yet still hee was in heart an affectionate lover of *Nestorianisme*, and a defender of those Chapters, seeing for his love to them, and defence of them, he is ready not onely to bee bound, but to goe, and dye in banishment for his zeale unto them. For had he sincerely embraced the truth, (as in his former Constitution he professed,) why doth he now at the time of the fift Councell, disclame the same? Of all times this was the fittest to stand constanly to the faith, seeing now both the glory of God, the good and peace of the Church, the authority of the Emperor, the exaple of orthodoxall Bishops, and the whole Councell invited, urged, and provoked him to this holy duty. What was there or could there be to move him at this time, to defend the 3. *Chapters*, save only his ardent and inward love to *Nestorianisme*? Indeed had he continued in defence of those Chapters untill this time; and now relented or changed his judgement, it would have bin vehemetly suspected, that not the hatred of those chapters, or of *Nestorianisme*, but either the favour of the Emperor, or the importunity of the Easterne Bishops, or the feare of exile, or deprivation, or some such punishment had extorted that sentence and confession from him: But now when hee decreeth contrary to the Emperour, to the generall Councell, and to his owne former and true judgement; when by publishing this *Decree*, he was sure to gaine nothing, but the censure of an unconstant and wavering minded man, the *Anathema* of the whole generall Councell, and the heavy indignation of the Emperor; when he goes thus against the maine current & streame of the time, who can thinke, but that his onely motive to doe this, was his zeale and love to *Nestorianisme*? Love [a] (specially of heresie) is strong as death. It will cause *Vigilius*, or any like him, when it hath once got possession of their heart, with the *Baalites* and *Donatists*, to contemne launcing, whipping, and tearing of their flesh; yea to delight as much in *Phalaris* Bull, as in a bed of doune, and in the midst of all tortures to sing with him in the Orator [b], *Quam suave est hoc? Quam nihil curo?* O how glad and merry a man am I, that suffer all these for the love of my *Three Chapters?* Losse of fame, losse of goods, losse of libertie, losse of my Countrey, losse of my pontificall See, losse of communion and society of the Catholike Church, and of God himselfe: Farewell all these, and all things else, rather then the *Three Chapters*, then *Nestorianisme* shall want a defender, or a Martyr to seale it with blood.

10. You see now the third period, and the third judgement of Pope *Vigilius* in this cause. A judgement, which being delivered *ex Tripode*, and withall possible circumspection, puts downe for many

respects both the former, what hee spake the first time in defence of these *Three Chapters*, was spoken in stomacke, and in his heat and choler against the Emperor. What he spake the second time for condemning those Chapters, he did therein but temporize and curry favour with the Emperor. But what he spake now this third time, after seven yeares ventilating of the cause, when all heat and passion being abated, he was in cold blood, and in such a calme, that no perturbation did trouble his mind, or darken his judgement, that I say, proceeded from the very bottome of the heart, and from the *Apostolicall* authority of his *infallible* Chaire, which to be a true and divine judgement, he like a worthy Confessor, sealed with his banishment. And of this judgement hee continued in likelihood more, but as *Baronius* (whom I now follow) tels *c* us, about the space of a yeare after the end of the fift Councell, even till hee returned out of exile unto *Constantinople*.

c An.554. & 555.

11. The fourth and last changing of *Vigilius* was after his returne from banishment, as *Baronius* and *Binius* tell us. For while hee was there, he saw there was *urgentissima causa*, *d* a most urgent cause why he should consent to the Emperour, and approve the judgement of the holy Councell; and therefore hee was pleased once againe to make another *Apostolicall e Decree*, for adnulling his former Apostolicall judgement, and for condemning the *Three Chapters*, and confirming the fift Synod. *I thinke*, saith *Binius f*, that *Vigilius confirmed the fift Synod by his Decree and Pontificall authority, and abrogated his former Constitution made in defence of the Three Chapters in the next yeare after the Councell was ended, when he being loosed from banishment, was suffered to returne into Italy, being adorned with sundry gifts and priviledges.* Neither doth he only *opinari*, but he is certaine of it. *Dubium g non est, there is no doubt*, but *Vigilius* being delivered from exile, by the entreatie of *Narses*, did confirme the fift Synod. *We thinke*, saith *Baronius*, *that h when* Vigilius *was by the intreaty of Narses freed from exile, hee did then assent to the Emperour, and recalling his former sentence, in his Constitution declared, did approve the fift Synod.* Again *i*, *Seeing we have declared, that* Vigilius *did not approve the fift Synod, when hee was driven into banishment, for he was exiled for no other cause, but for that hee would not approve that Synod: Necesse est affirmare, it must of necessity bee said, that hee did this (approve the fift Synod;) at this time, when being loosed out of exile, he was sent home to his owne Church.* So *Baronius*. Now seeing hee returned home after hee had obtained those ample gifts and priviledges, which they so magnifie, and which are set downe in that pragmaticall sanction of *Iustinian k*, which was dated on the twelfth day of August, in the eight and twentieth yeare of his Empire : and the fift Councell was ended on the second *l* day of Iune in his seven and twentieth yeare, it is cleare, that this his last change was made about an whole yeare after the end of the fift Councell, after hee had remained a yeare or thereabouts in banishment. And in this minde, as they *m* tell us, hee returned towards *Rome*, but by the way *n*, while hee was yet but in *Sicily*, being afflicted with the stone, he dyed.

d Bar.an.553. nu.235.

e Synodum 5. eadem Apostolica authoritate comprobasse satis apparet. Bar.an. 554. nu.7. & Bini.loc.cit.§. Prestitit. f Ibid. g Ibid.§. Tunc.

h An.554.nu.4. i Ibidem.

k Extat in fine Novell.

l Conc.5.coll.8.

m Bar. & Bin. locis cit. n Bar. an. 555. nu.2.

                                         12. Here

12. Here is now the *Cataftrophe* of the Popes turnings and retum-ings,and often changing in this caufe of faith : Concerning which this is efpecially to bee remembred, that whereas all the three former judgements of *Vigilius*,the firft, when he defended thofe three Chapters, being in *Italie*, the fecond, when he condemned them upon his comming to *Conftantinople*, and the third, when he againe defended them at the time of the Councell, and after, have all of them certaine and undeniable proofes out of antiquitie, fuch as the teftimonies of *Facundus, Victor, Liberatus*, the Popes owne letters and Conftitutions, together with the witneffe of the Emperor, and the whole fift Councell; onely this laft period, and this laft change, when hee confented to the fift Councell, and condemned the *Three Chapters*, This I fay, which is the onely judgement whereby *Vigilius* is excufed from herefie, is utterly deftitute of all ancient witneffes, not any one that I can finde makes mention of this change, or of ought that can any way enforce the fame, and therefore this may and muft be called the *Baronian* change or Period,he being the firft man,that I can learne of, who ever mentioned or dreamed of this change. And although this alone were fufficient to oppofe to all that the Cardinall or any other can hence collect in excufe of *Vigilius*, reafon and equitie forbidding us to bee too credulous upon the Cardinals bare word, which even in this one caufe touching the Three Chapters, and this fift Councell, befides many the like, demonftratively to be proved untrue and falfe, I fpeake it confidently and within compaffe, in fix hundreth fayings at the leaft) yet that they may not fay wee decline the force of this fo pregnant an exception, we will for a little while admit and fuppofe it to bee true, and try, whether by this being yeelded unto them, there can accrew any advantage to their caufe, or any help to excufe either *Vigilius* himfelfe, or his *Conftitution* fet forth in defence of the *Three Chapters*, from being hereticall.

13. Say you *Vigilius* by his laft decree confirmed the fift Councell and approved the Catholike faith? Be it fo, we deny not but that *Vigilius*, or any other of their Popes may decree, and have decreed a truth, thats not the doubt betwixt us and them. The queftion is, whether any of their Popes have at any time by his *Cathedrall* authoritie, and teaching, as Popes, decreed an herefie, or untruth. That Pope *Vigilius* did fo, his *Apoftolicall Conftitution* in defence of the *Three Chapters*, is an eternall witnes againft them, a monument *ere perennius*, Had *Baronius* faid that *Vigilius* never decreed the defending of thofe Chapters,he had fully cleared him in this matter,if he could have proved what he had faid. But feeing undeniable records teftifie, and the Cardinall himfelfe with a Stentors voice proclameth, this to be the true and undoubted *Conftitution* of Pope *Vigilius*;though hee had revoked and repealed it a thoufand times, yet can not this quit his former *Apoftolicall* Decree from being *hereticall*, nor excufe their pontificall chaire from being *fallible*. It is nothing at all materiall which of the Popes Cathedrall Decrees, the firft, laft, or middle bee *hereticall* : If any one of them all bee : wee defire no more, the field is wonne.

V 3

14. Say

14. Say you *Vigilius* by an *Apostolicall decree*, confirmed the fift Councell ? Then did hee certainely decree that all writings defending the *Three Chapters*, doe defend herefie: and that all persons who defend those Chapters, for so long time as they defend them, after the judgement of that Councell, are convicted and condemned hereticks. Then the former *Constitution* of Pope *Vigilius*, set forth by his *Apostolicall* authoritie in the time of the Councell, in defence of those Chapters, is now by Popes *Vigilius* himselfe and by his *Apostolicall* authority and *infallible* Chaire declared to bee *hereticall*; and *Vigilius* himselfe for that yeare after the Councell, is now by *Vigilius* himselfe pronounced to bee an Hereticke; yea a definer of herefie, *Vigilius* now orthodoxal decreeth himselfe to have been before heretical. Nay it further followeth, that by confirming that Councell, hee confirmeth, and that by an *Apostolicall* and *infallible Decree*, that all who defend the Popes *Cathedrall* sentence in causes of faith, to bee *infallible*, are convicted and accursed heretickes, for by defending that position, they do *eo ipso* defend that Constitutio of *Vigilius* made in defence of the *Three Chapters* to bee true, *infallible*, and orthodoxall, which *Vigilius* himselfe by an infallible decree hath declared to bee erroneous, and hereticall. So far is this last and *Baronian* change from excusing *Vigilius* in this cause, that upon the admission thereof it doth inevitably ensue, both that *Vigilius* was an hereticke and a definer of herefie, and that all who defend the Popes Cathedrall *infallibitie*, in causes of faith, that is, al who are members of their present Romane Church, to bee not onely heretickes, and for such condemned and accursed, but defenders also of a condemned and accursed herefie, even by the infallible judgement and decree of Pope *Vigilius*.

15. Their whole reason whereby *Vigilius* might bee excused, being now fully dissolved; There remaineth one point, which *Baronius*, and after him *Binius*, observeth, touching this often changing of *Vigilius* : which being a point of speciall note, I should wrong both *Vigilius* and *Baronius* if I should over-passe the same. Some men when they heare of these often changings, windings, and turnings of Pope *Vigilius* in this cause of faith, and of his banishment for defending a condemned herefie, will perhaps imagine this to bee a token of some levitie, unconstancie, or folly in the Pope. O fie! It was not so, saith [o] *Baronius*; *What hee did was not onely lawfull*[p], *done by good right and reason, but it was laudable also, done with great* [q] *advise, wisedome, and consideration. Vigilius, a man of* [r] *greatest constancie; One who stood* [s] *up with courage for defence of the Church, adversus violentum ecclesia grassatorem, against* Iustinian, *a violent oppressor thereof : one* [t] *who fought for the sacred lawes, enduring exile, constanti animo, with a constant minde for the same. One who did by this meanes wisely* [u], *yea, prudentissimè, most wisely provide for the good of the Church. One who in thus doing did wisely* [x] *imitate* Saint Paul, *who condemned circumcision, and yet when hee circumcised Timothie, approved circumcision.* And though there bee a marvellous dissimilitude in their actions, the one change being in a mutable, &c, at that time, an indifferent ceremonie, the other being in an immutable doctrine of faith; Yet thus do they please themselves, and

o *Cum sepe sententiâ mutavit, haud arguendus est levitatis. an. 553. nu. 235.*

p *Cur ei nõ licuit mutato rerum statu mutare sẽtentiam? ibid.nu. 231,& jure meritoque mutavit sententiam, Bin. §. Cum igitur.*

q *Vigilius magna consideratione adhibita atque prudentiâ, diverso modo pugnabat. an. 547. nu. 50.*

r *Summa constãtie specimen edidit. ibid, nu. 49.*

s *An. 551. nu. 5.*

t *An. 553. nu. 251.*

u *An. 547. nu. 41.*

x *Prudẽs & pius pontifex hac in re prudenter est imitatus S. Paulum. Bin. in Edictum.nu 11.&2. pa.499. S. Cum, & Bar. an. 553. nu. 235.*

and applaud the Pope in these his wise and worthy changes.

16. Now in stead of a better conclusion to this Chapter, I will entreate the reader to observe with me two things touching their commending *Vigilius* in this manner. The former is, what an happie thing it is to be a Pope, or have a Cardinall for his spokesman. Let *Luther*, *Cranmer*, or a Protestant make farre lesse change then did *Vigilius*, what shall they not heare ? An Apostate, unconstant, inconsiderate, a Chamelion, a Polipus, another Proteus, even *Vertumnus* himselfe. Let the Pope say and gainesay the same doctrine of faith, and then *ex Cathedra* define both his sayings being contradictorie, to bee not onely true, but *infallible* truths of the Catholike faith : O, It is all done with rare wisdome, with great reason, and consideration, The Pope in all this deales wisely, and that in the superlative degree. If when he is absent from the Emperor, he oppugne the truth published by the Emperors edict, It is wisely done; Kings and Emperors may not make Lawes in causes of faith, no not for the faith; The Cobler must not goe beyond his latchet. If when hee is brought before the Emperor, he sing a new song, and say just as the Emperor saith, *Ait, aio : Negat, nego* : It is wisely done, *principibus placuisse viris*, for the Kings wrath is the messenger of death. If after both these hee become a meere Neutralist and Ambodexter in faith, holding communion with all sides, Catholikes, heretickes, and all, this is also an act of rare wisdome, the Pope is now become another Saint *Paul*, *factus est omnia omnibus*; with Catholikes he's a Catholike, that he may gaine Catholikes, with Heretickes, he's an Hereticke, that he may gaine heretickes, he's all with all, that hee may gaine them all. If when the Emperor, the generall Councell, the whole Church calls for his resolution in a cause of faith, if then hee step into his *infallible* Chaire, and thence by his *Apostolicall* authoritie define, that the *three Chapters*, that is, that Nestorianisme shall for ever bee held for the Catholike faith, O wisely done, he now drops oracles from heaven, *in Cathedra sedet*, the voice of God, and not of man. If, when hee is banished for his obstinacie against the truth, upon some urgent cause which then he discernes, he calls againe for his holy Trevit, and thence decrees the quite contradictorie to his former *Apostolicall* sentence, In this he's wiser then in all the rest : for by this he shews that he's more wise and powerfull then all the Prophets and Apostles ever were; They silly men could make but the one part of a contradiction to be true, but the Pope he is *tanto y potentior Prophetis, so much more wise and powerfull then all the Prophets*, that hee can make both parts of a contradiction to be *infallible* truths; and unto which of the Prophets was it ever said, *Tu es Petra* ? But the Pope is a Rocke indeed, a Rocke upon which you may build two contradictories in the doctrine of faith, and in them both say unto him, *Tu es Petra*. Such a Rocke neither the Prophets, nor Apostles, nor Christ himselfe ever was. So wise, so exceeding wise is the Pope, in all his turnings, even as wise as a wethercocke for turning with the wind and weather.

y Tanto ipse potentior est Prophetis effectus, quanto differentius præ illis nomen hæreditavit. Nam cui prophetarum aliquando dictū est, Tu es Petra? Bar. an.552. nu.9.

17. Againe, when the Pope, his instruments or Inquisitors (to whom *Phalaris, Busiris*, and all the heathen persecutors may yeeld) exercise

exercise againſt us for maintaining the truth of God, all exquiſite &
helliſh tortures (to which the old heatheniſh were but *ludus &
jocus*) all which they doe muſt be extolled as due puniſhments, and
juſt cenſures of the Holy Father of the holy Church, of the Holy
inquiſition, of the Holy houſe, all muſt bee covered with the
mantle of holineſſe. On the other ſide, when they reſiſt the moſt
religious lawes, or Ediᵭs of Kings or Emperors, when *Vigilius* or
any of them (being by an holy generall Councell declared, and
condemned for an Hereticke,) are for their obſtinate rebellion
againſt the truth juſtly puniſhed, though *Iuſtinian* yea Iuſtice it
ſelfe, ſhall uſe rather moderate then ſevere correction againſt them,
they forſooth muſt be accoumpted catholikes: Cõfeſſers, & holy Martyrs, ſuch as ſuffer for religion, for the ſacred lawes, and for the Ca-

z *Vidiſti Scelus,
& c. Bar. an. 554.
num. 2.*

tholike faith, but *Iuſtinian* the Defender of the faith, muſt be called
Iulian, Iuſtice be termed *Scelus* ᶻ, and the Church for that cauſe ſaid
to bee in farre worſe condition, then in the times of *Nero*, *Dioclefian*,
or any of the heathen Tyrants. Such an happie thing it is to bee a
Pope, or Papiſt, for then their wavering ſhall be Conſtancie, their
rebellion, Religion and fortitude : their folly, greate and rare wiſedome : their hereſie, Catholike doᵭrine : and their moſt condigne
puniſhments ſhall be crowned with Martyrdome.

18. The other thing which I obſerve, is, what a ſtrong faith, Papiſts
had need to have, who rely upon the Popes judgement, which chan-
geth out and in, in and out ſo many times : who yet are bound to beleeve al the Pope *definitive* ſentences in cauſes of faith, that is, to ſpeake
in plaine tearmes, who are bound to beleeve two contradiᵭories to
bee both true, both of them the infallible oracles of God. Or if any
of them have ſo weake a faith, that he can but beleeve the one, I
would gladly learne of ſome who is an *Oedipus* among them, In this
caſe of two Contradiᵭorie *Cathedrall* decrees, ſuch as were theſe of
Pope *Vigilius*, whether of the Popes definitive judgements, that is,
according to their language, whether of the ſayings of God is true, and
whether falſe, or what ſtrength the one hath, more then the other. If
the Apoſtolicall ſentence of *Vigilius* delivered *cum omni undique cautela*, and by his Cathedrall authoritie, in defence of the *Three Chapters*,
be repealeable by a ſecond, why may not the ſecond (which cannot
poſſibly have more authoritie) bee repealed by a third, and the third
by a fourth, and fourth by a fiſt, and ſo *in Infinitum*? If the Pope after
ſeaven yeares deliberation and ventilating of the cauſe, while bee is
all that time in peace, and libertie, may be deceived in his judiciall
and Cathedrall ſentence in a cauſe of faith, how may wee be aſſured,
that when ſome yeares after that, the tediouſneſſe of exile and deſire
of his priſtine libertie and honour perſwades him to make a contrary
deeree, he may not therein alſo bee deceived? If the Popes decrees
made in libertie, peace and proſperity be of force, why ſhall not the
decree of *Vigilius* in defence of the *Three Chapters*, be an article of
faith? If thoſe free decrees may be admitted by a ſtronger ſentence
when the Pope is in baniſhment, how may any beleeve their *Laterane*
and *Trent* decrees, as doᵭrines of faith? For why may there not once
                                                                    againſt

againe, come some other *Iustinian*, into the world, (as great pitie it is
but there should) who in these, or future times may minister that soveraigne medicine to cleare the Popes judgement, and restraine, or
close him up in some meaner estate, and farre lower place; whence,
as out of a darke and low pit, he may discerne those coelestiall truths
in the Word of God, like so many Starres in heaven, which now being invironed with the circumfused splendor of the Romane Court,
he cannot possibly behold. If those *Three Chapters* were to bee condemned, why did the Pope defend them at the time of the Councell?
If they were to be defended, why did he condemne them after his returne from exile? Nay, if the *Three Chapters* were *orthodoxall*, why
did the Pope at any time first or last by his *Apostolicall* sentence condemne them? If they were *hereticall*, why did he at any time, first or
last, by his *Cathedrall* and *Apostolicall* sentence defend them? I confesse I am here in a Labyrinth; if any of the Cardinals friends will
winde mee out, he shall for ever be *Theseus* unto me.

CAP. XVI.

That the Decree *of* Vigilius *for* Taciturnity touching the Three Chapters, *and the* Councell, *wherein it is supposed to be made, and all the* Consequents upon that Decree, *painted out by* Baronius, *are all fictitious,
and Poeticall.*

THE whole reason of *Baronius* drawne from
Vigilius his confirming of the fift Councell,
being now fully dissolved, we might without
further stay, and I gladly would, according to
my intended order in the Treatise, proceed to
his next exceptiō: but there are two points in
this last passage, touching the chāgings of *Vigilius*, which, even against my will, pull mee
backe, and call me to examine what *Baronius* sets downe, and with exceeding ostentation paints out, in his Annals, concerning them; the
due consideration whereof will cause any man to admire the Cardinals most audacious, and shamelesse dealing in Synodall affaires, and
causes of the Church: The one of them concernes the second, the o-
ther the fourth period in *Vigilius* changings. The former is this.

2. As soone as the defenders of the *Three Chapters* had notice of
that Iudiciall sentence, and *Decree* published by *Vigilius* against the
same Chapters, upon his comming to *Constantinople*, they began to
storme thereat, and condemne *Vigilius* [a] as a Prevaricator, or revolter
from the faith; whereupon *Vigilius*, as the Cardinall tels us, put in
practice a rare peece of wisedome [b], and of his Pontificall pollicy,
sententiam emissam [c] *mox suspendit, seu potius revocavit; be suspends and re-
vokes that his late judgement; & rursum ab eo promulgatum decretum, quo
decernebatur ut penitus taceretur; and he published a new Decree, wherein
he decreed, that every man should be silent,* and say never a word, either

pro,

*a Ibid, ipsum
(Vigilium) col-
luserem, preva-
ricatoremque
ab adversarijs cō-
clamatum. Bar.
an. 547 nu. 49.
b Prudenter pe-
riclitanti Eccle-
sia visum est con-
suluisse Vigilius.
Ibid. nu. 41.
c Ibid.*

d Ab hoc anno, ad illud usque tempus. Ibid. nu.43.
e Bar ibid.nu.:6 f Ibid.nu.48

g Bar.an.551. nu.2.
h Ibid.n.3.

Bar.an.547. nu.43.
k Iustinianus contra precedentis Synodi decretū,et emissam sponsionem de servando usq; ad Concilium universale siletio, appendi juffit Edictum.Bar. an. 551.nu.2.
l Bar.an.547. nu.41.
m Nam decretū editum an. 547. Bar.eo an.nu. 43. ista autem gesta an.551 Bar.eo an.nu.2. 5,6.et seq.
n Bar.an.551. nu.5.
o Sententiam excommunicationis intorquet. Ibid.Verba excōmunicationis extant.Ibid.nu.11 et 12.
p Ibid. nu.11.
q Iustinianus contra Synodi decretum publicè appendi juffit Edictum. Ibid. nu.2.
r Ibid .et confugere coactus est. An.552.nu.8.
ſ Bar.an.551. nu.2.
t Nec sacer ille locus asylum tanto Pontifici fuit.

pro, or contra,touching that question of the *Three Chapters*,till the time of the generall Councel, from d this yeare (which was the 21 e of *Iustinian*,& the same wherin *Vigilius* came to *Constantinople*)until the time of the generall Councell,*in eâ causâ ab ipso* Vigilio *indictū fuit Silentiū*. Silence was injoyned every man in that cause,by Pope Vigilius : & againe f, *Tacendū indixit*,he injoyned Silence in that cause; and very often doth the Cardinall,with no small comfort,mention this Decree of *Taciturnity*. And, for the more solemnitie of the matter,*Vigilius* decreed this in a Councell, it was not onely his; but, *decretum* g *Synodi*,the decree of a Councell, together with the Pope. Vigilius h *Synodicè statuit tacendum esse*; Vigilius decreed in,and with a *Synod*,that there should be a Silence in this cause,untill the generall Councell : To which Synodall decree, not onely *Mennas* i,and *Theodorus* Bishop of *Cesarea*, but k *Iustinian* himselfe also consented,and promised to observe the same. This was the Decree; see now the effects,and Cōsequents which ensued thereupon,declared also by *Baronius*.

3. This Decree tooke so good effect at the first,that, *res aliquandiu consopita* l *siluit*, for a space, all matters, touching the *Three Chapters*, were husht asleepe,not a word spoken of that Controversie: But some foure yeares m after the publishing thereof, when *Vigilius* saw divers contrary to his decree; to condemne the *Three Chapters*, n *erigit se, he rouzeth up himselfe for defence thereof*, and o excommunicated *Mennas* Patriarch of *Constantinople*,*Theodorus* Bishop of *Cesarea*, and many moe; and this also he did in another Councell consisting of thirteene p Bishops besides himselfe. Yea and whereas the Emperour in that yeare published,or hung out his Edict against the same Chapters contrary to his owne promise, and the Decree for *Taciturnity*, the Pope withstood him so long,and so eagerly; that *Iustinian* began to rage, to use threats,and violence against him,so that the Pope,*in* r *fuga tantum spem posuit*, was forced to flee from him out of the house where he dwelled,called (for good lucke sake) *Placidiana*, unto the Church of Saint *Peter*,where he remained a time,*in adversarios sententiam ferens;thundering out his censures against his adversaries*. But that sacred place ſ could be no Sanctuary for *Vigilius*; they buffeted u and beate him on his face; they called him an homicide, a murderer of *Sylverius*, and of the widowes sonne : whereupon hee, to avoid the fury x and violence of the sacrilegious Emperour, fled y from *Constantinople* to *Chalcedon*,and there lived in the Church of Saint *Euphemia*; taking hold of a Piller or Horne of the Altar : And even there,though in persecution,and affliction,he bated z not one Ace of his *Apostolicall* authority; but,as if he had lived in peace, and beene in the *Laterane* or *Vaticane*,he ascends into his *Apostolike* Throne a, and high Tribunall; and thence, by the fulnesse of his *Apostolicall* power, he b throwes out his darts,represseth and prostrateth his adversaries; pronounceth

An.552.nu.8. u Dedit alapam in faciem,&c.Ibid. x Ab Imperatoris furore; & ab Imperatoris sacrilegi violentia. Ibid. y Trans mare que sivit effugium,et in Basilicam S.Euphemiæ apud Chalcedonem habitare disposuit. An.552.nu. 8. z Nihil penitus remisit Apostolicæ authoritatis. Ibid.nu.9. et 10. a Idem ille locus effectus est,Pontificis; Romani præsentia,eminenti cunctisque perspicuum ad judicandum tribunal,&c. Ibid.nu. 10. b Missilia in hostes jacit, potentissimaque spiritualia spicula jacit in hostes feritque.Ibid.

sentence [c] against Bishops, yea, against a Patriarch; adnulleth the acts of the Emperour, knowing his authoritie to be greater than that Prophets was, to whom God said [d], *I have set thee above Nations and kingdomes.*

4. Now behold a miracle [e] indeed; by fleeing away, *Vigilius* overcommeth, by being persecuted hee is victorious; all humane power, even hell gates, doth, and must yeed to him: For the Emperor understanding that he was fled away, repented [f] him of that which hee had done against the Pope, and therefore sent messengers to recall him from *Chalcedon*, and those not ordinary souldiers, *sed dignam tanto Pontifice legationem; but honourable embassadours, worthy the estate of so great a Bishop*, who should assure him, even upon their oathes [g], that he should be honorably received. But, so stout, nay, magnanimous, was the Pope, and so very circumspect and wise [h], as, remembring the proverbe, *Græcorum fides*, that he would neither come out of the Church, nor beleeve [i] the messengers, though swearing unto him, unles the Emperour would presently recall and abolish his Edicts against the *Three Chapters*. The Emperour yeelded [k] to all that the Pope prescribed, yea, *constat cessisse*, it is certaine and evident, that he submitted himselfe to the Popes pleasure, and that *penitus* in every point: hee commands the Edicts, which hee had published, to be taken away, to bee removed; *& ex sententia* [l] *Vigilii, quod fecerat, abrogavit*; and according to *Vigilius* direction, he abrogated what before he had done. Nor onely did the Emperour repent, but *Theodorus* [l] also, and *Mennas*, they came and offered, *libellum supplicem* Vigilio, *a booke of supplication to intreat* Vigilius, that he would be appeased towards them, and crying, *Peccavi, suppliciter* [m] *veniam petunt;* they *beseech him in a suppliant manner to forgive their* [n] *offence.* Oh how admirable is this in our eyes! the Rocke which the builders refused, is now laid againe in the head of the Corner; and those Princes and Prelates which opposed themselves to the Pope, doe now submit, supplicate, and yeeld themselves unto him. The Pope [o], after this so ample satisfaction, was pleased to be reconciled to them all, and admitted them into his communion; & so the storme of persecution being past, the Church injoyed tranquillity, the Pope was brought againe with great joy from *Chalcedon* to *Constantinople*: For the joy [p] and solemnity whereof *Mennas* that same yeare (which was the 26 [q] of *Iustinian*, and next before the generall Councell) celebrated a feast of the *Encænia*, or dedication of the Church, of three Apostles, *Andrew, Luke*, and *Timothy*, and the holy reliques [r] of their bodies being then found, *Mennas* carried them round about the City in a Chariot of Gold, and then laid them up in the Church: After all which, *Mennas*, in the peace of the Church, and communion with *Vigilius*, in an happy manner gave up the ghost: and

[c] *Summa potestatis plenitudine adversus metropolitanos Episcopos, imò in ipsum Patriarcham Constantinopolitanum ferre sententiam, insuper et perperam facta Imperatoris rescindere magno animo aggressus est. An. 552. nu. 9.*
[d] *Ier. 1.*
[e] *Ita plane magno veluti miraculo factum est, &c. Ibid. nu. 11.*
[f] *Iustinianus facti pænitens dignam tanto Pontifice legationem ornavit, &c. Ib.*
[g] *Iuramento præstito honorifice revocaret. Ibid.*
[h] *Nuncijs licet magna pollicentibus haud putavit esse credendum, utpote (quod in proverbio est) Græcorum fides. Bar. 552. nu. 12.*
[i] *Neque juratis patricijs voluit fidem adhibere, nisi Imperator qui contra Rom. Pontificis voluntatem de tribus Capitulis cependisset Edicta protinus revocaret, atque penitus aboleret. Ibid. nu. 11.*
[k] *Constat cessisse tandem Vigilio Imperatorem, atque appensa amoveri jussisse à se prolata de tribus Capitulis Edicta. &c.*

Ibid. an. 552. nu. 15. et, Imperator appensa antea de tribus Capitulis tolli jussit Edicta. Ibid. nu. 19. l Ibid. an. 552. nu. 19. l Theodorus facti pænitens ad eum accedens humilis libellum supplicem ipsi Vigilio offert. Ibid. an. 552. nu. 19. Præstitit id ipsum etiam Mennas Ibid. nu. 20. m Ibid. nu. 19. n Quis ista considerans non miretur, atque obstupescat, &c. Ibid. nu. 20. o Tali præmissa satisfactione, Vigilius eosdem in communionem accepit, redditaque est Ecclesiæ pax. Ibid. nu. 20. p Hoc ipso anno (552) Mennas Const. Episcopus à Vigilio in communionem admissus Encænia celebravit, &c. Bar. ibid. an. 552. nu. 22. q Anno hoc 552. exordio mensis Aprilis incipit numerari Iustiniani annus 26. r Cum sacræ reliquiæ curru aureo circumvectæ ab eodem Menna reconditæ sunt. Bar. Ibid. nu. 22. [Bar. an. 552. nu. 23.

t Sic itaq; animis junctis, restitutoq; in pristinã dignitatem atq; honorem Vigilio, indicta est Synodus, &c. Bar. an. 553. nu. 14.

so the Pope *t* being reſtored to his former dignitie, *animis junctis, their mindes being joyned together*; the generall Councell, long wiſhed for by *Vigilius*, was ſummoned againſt the moneth of *May*, in the twenty ſeventh yeare of *Iuſtinian*. This is the ſumme of the narration of *Baronius*, touching the Decree of *Taciturnity*, and the manifold conſequents thereof.

5. Concerning which, none I thinke can judge otherwiſe, but that *Baronius*, as he is miſerably infatuated in this whole cauſe of the *Three Chapters*; ſo, in this paſſage, hee was growne to that extremity of dotage, that hee ſeemes utterly to have beene bereft, both of common ſenſe, and reaſon : For I doe conſtantly avouch, that in no part of all this his narration, (which, as you ſee, is very large and copious, and runneth, like a great ſtreame, through divers yeares in *Baronius* Annals) there is any truth at al. No ſuch Decree of *Taciturnity*, ever made by *Vigilius*; no Synod wherein it was decreed; no aſſent, either of *Mennas*, or *Theodorus*, or the Emperour unto it; no violating of that Decree by *Mennas*, or *Theodorus*; no excommunication of them, or other Biſhops, for doing contrary to it; no hanging up of the Emperours Edict after it; no reſiſtance made by *Vigilius* againſt the Emperour; no perſecuting of *Vigilius*, no buffeting of him, no objecting of murder unto him; no fleeing either to Saint *Peters* Church, or to *Chalcedon*; no thundring out from thence of his Pontificall Cenſures; no embaſſage ſent from the Emperour to call him thence; no ſuch magnanimitie in *Vigilius* as to refuſe to returne; no recalling, or abrogating of the Emperiall Edict by the Emperour; no ſubmiſſion of *Mennas*, or *Theodorus* to the Pope; no ſolemnizing of the *Encænia* for thoſe three Apoſtles at that time by *Mennas*; no carying of thoſe holy reliques in a triumphing manner, and in a golden Chariot; no laying them up by *Mennas*; and, in a word, in that whole paſſage of *Baronius*, there is not ſo much as one dramme, nor one ſyllable of truth. The Cardinall from an Hiſtorian is here quite metamorphozed into a Poet, into a Fabler, and in ſtead of writing Annals, matters of fact, and reall truths, he guls his readers with fictitious, anile, and more than *Æſopicall* fables.

6. For the clearing whereof I will begin with the Decree it ſelfe, which is the ground of the whole fiction, and therefore if it bee demonſtrated to bee but an idle dreame and fancie, all the reſt, which hang on it like ſo many conſequents, and appendices, will of themſelves fall to the ground. Nor doe I ſpeake to diſgrace this Decree, as if *Baronius* could gaine ought thereby, though it were admitted and granted unto him : For alas, what a poore pollicy or peece of wiſedome was this in the Pope, being a Iudge *infallible*, to command, and decree by his *Apoſtolicall* authority, that for five or ſixe, or, as it might have hapned, for forty or ſixty yeares together, no man ſhould ſpeake a word in this cauſe of faith, neither condemne the *three Chapters*, nor defend the ſame; which is in effect, that they ſhould neither ſpeake againſt, nor for Neſtorianiſme; neither dare to ſay, that Chriſt is God, nor, that he is not God, but ſuſpend their judgement in them both; that for all that time none ſhould either be Catholikes, or heretikes,

but

but be like *Vigilius*, meere Neutralists in the faith, what other wisdome is this but that of the *Laodiceans*, which Christ condemneth [u] *I would thou werst either hot or cold, but because thou art neither hot nor cold, it will come to passe that I will spue thee out of my mouth* : what other then that which *Elias* reproves [x]? *Why halt yee betweene two opinions? If the Lord be God follow him, but if Baal, or Nestorianisme, be he, goe after it.* By this Decree of Taciturnity *Vigilius* provideth that neither himselfe nor others should speake against the truth or condemne it. True; but that is not enough; He should have defended it also, and caused others by his instruction and example to doe the like.   A neutralist, *one that is not* [y] *with Christ, is against Christ* : Hee that is not with the truth is against the truth.   Silence where God commands to speake, is betraying of Gods truth.   If the Heathen wise man [z] set this, and that justly among his eternall lawes; That he who in a publike division of the Common-wealth, tooke part with neither side, should bee punished with losse of goods and banishment : how much more ought this to take place in *Vigilius*, and all such *Merij Suffetij*, who in the publike rent of the Church, and that for a cause of faith, will be of neither part, neither for God nor against him ?   Nay if we well consider, even or this very decree of silence, *Vigilius* is to bee judged an heretike, for the whole Councell of *Chalcedon* condemned *Domnus* Patriarch of *Antioch* as an Heretike, onely for this cause [a], for that hee writ that men should bee silent, and say nothing of the twelve Chapters of *Cyrill*, as both *Iustinian* and the fift Councell [b] doe testifie. Did not *Vigilius*, if the Cardinall say true, teach, nay decree the very like silence concerning the *Three Chapters*, as *Domnus* did concerning those twelve of *Cyrill* ?   These Three doe as nearly concerne the faith, as did the other twelve.   These three were certainly condemned by the Councell of *Chalcedon*, as the other twelve were approved by the Councell of *Ephesus*.   As *Domnus* by teaching silence in those of *Cyrill*, even thereby taught that men should not allow them, nor say that they might be allowed, and thereby overthrew the faith of the Ephesine Councell, which approved them, and taught all men to approve them : Even so, *Vigilius* by decreeing silence in these *Three Chapters*, decreeth that none shall condemne them, or say they are to be condemned, and so overthroweth the Catholike faith which was declared at *Chalcedon*, whereby they are all three condemned; and taught that they ought to bee condemned.   If the teaching of silence in the one can make *Domnus* an hereticke, certainly the decreeing of silence in the other, cannot chuse but make *Vigilius* an heretike.   O but this decree was to continue but for a time, *Vigilius* would expect the assembling of a generall Councell, and then he would resolve the matter to the full.   And you have seen how well he resolved it then. But what? Expect a Councell ? why is not his Holinesse able to decide a doubt in faith, without a generall Councell ?   Is he not of himselfe infallible ?   Doth his infallibilitie like an Ague goe away, and come by fits upon him ?   Is the generall Councel that Angel which must move the Poole in the Popes brest, before he can teach infallibly ?   The Pope scornes to hold his infallibility

u Apoc. 3. 15, 16.

x 1 King. 18. 21.

y Matth. 12. 30.

z Solonis lex apud A. Gellium lib. 2. ca. 12.

a Chalcedonensis S. Synodus Domnum condemnavit, quod ausus est scribere, oportere solum tacere 12. Capitula S. Cyrillij. Iust. in Ædict. S. Quod autem. b Idem asserit plane Conc. 5. Col. 6. pa. 575. b

X   *precario;*

precario, by the curtesie either of the whole Church, or of any generall Councell: He is all-sufficient in himselfe, he gives to them *infallibility*, he receives none from them; what thinke you then was become of *Vigilius* his infallibility, that for deciding a doubt in faith, hee must suspend all in silence, and stay till the generall Councel be assembled, which, for ought he knew, might bee 60. or 100. yeares after? If of himselfe he was infallible, why did he hold men in suspence in the doctrine of faith? why did he not presently, and without the Councell infallibly decide it, and so set the Church at quiet? If of himselfe he was not infallible, how could he at the time of the Councell infallibly decide it? for they make not him or his sentence infallible, but all their infallibility is borrowed from him. So little helpe is there for them in this decree of taciturnity, (if wee should admit thereof) that in very deed, it doth many wayes prejudice their cause. It is not then the preventing of any advantage which hence they might have, that causeth me to reject this decree, but the onely love of the truth perswadeth, nay enforceth me hereunto. For I professe I was not a little moved to see the Cardinalls Annalls so stuffed with untruths and figments, and see him also not onely by these to abuse, and that most vilely, his Readers, but even to vaunt and glory (as you have seene hee doth) in that which is, and will be an eternall ignominy unto him. But let us come to make evident the fiction of this Decree.

7. That *Vigilius* made no such decree of *Taciturnitie*, first the Emperor *Iustinian* in his Letters to the fift generall Councell is a witnes above exception, *When Pope* Vigilius, saith he [c], *was come to this our Princely City, we did accurately manifest unto him all things touching these three Chapters, and we demanded of him what he thought hereof: and he, not once or twise, but often in writing, without writing, did anathematize the same Chapters. Quod vero ejusdem voluntatis semper fuit de condemnatione trium Capitulorum, per plurima declaravit, and that he hath alwayes,* (ever since his comming hither) *continued in the same minde of condemning those three Chapters, he hath very many wayes declared.* And after, repeating some of those particulars, hee adds, *Et compendiose dicere, semper in eadem voluntate perseveravit, and to speake briefly, he hath ever since persevered in this minde.* So writ and testified the Emperour. In the seventh Collation the Emperour sent *Constantine* the most glorious Quæstor of his Palace, unto the Synod, to deliver unto them certaine letters of *Vigilius*, who againe testified this from the Emperour before the whole Councell: *Vigilius*, saith he [c], *hath very often manifested by writings his minde, that he condemneth the Three Chapters, which also without writing, he hath said before the Emperour in the presence of the most glorious Iudges, and of very many of your selves, who are here in the Councell: et non intermisit, semper anathematizans Theodorum, and hee hath not intermitted or ever ceased* (since his first comming almost to *Constantinople*) *to anathematize the defenders of Theodorus of Mopsvestia, and the Epistle of Ibas, and the writings of Theodoret against Cyrill:* and then delivering the letters of *Vigilius* unto them, he addeth, *Vigilius* doth by these make manifest, *quod per totum tempus, eorundem trium Capitulorum impietatem aversatur,* that for this whole time (since his first consenting to
the

c *Iustin. Epist. ad 5. Synod. Coll. 1. pa. 520. a.*

c *Coll. 7. Cont. 5. pa. 578. a.*

the Edict upon his comming to *Constantinople,* untill the assembling of the generall Councell) *hee hath detested the impiety of those Three Chapters.* Thus said and testified *Constantine* from the Emperor.

8. If I should say no more at all, even this one testimony being so pregnant, and withall so certaine, that there can bee no doubt but the Emperor both knew and testified the truth herein, this alone, I say, is sufficient to demonstrate the vanity of that fictitious Synod & decree of *Taciturnity.* For seeing it is hence certaine, that *Vigilius* persisted and persevered to condemne the *Three Chapters,* after the time of his consenting to the Emperors Edict, upon his comming to *Constantinople,* till the time of the fift Councell, it must needs be acknowledged for certaine, that in that time hee made no decree to forbid men to condemne the same; and then, not this decree of Taciturnity, which tyes all mens tongues that they shal neither defend, nor yet condemne them. And if the decree be fictitious, such as was never made, as by this testimony it is now certaine : then is the Councell fictitious wherein it was decreed, then the whole fable of *Baronius,* how the Emperor and *Mennas* violated that decree, how the Pope indured persecution for maintaining that Decree, and the other Consequents, they all are certainly fictitious, this one testimonie overthroweth the all. But I will adde a second reason drawne from the consideration of the observing and putting in execution this Synodall and pontificall Decree. For it is not to bee doubted, but if such a Decree had beene made, especially, with the consent of a Synod, and of the Emperour also; but some one or other would have observed the same; the rather, because *Baronius* [d] tels us, that upon the publishing of this Decree in the one and twentieth yeare of *Iustinian, res consopita siluit;* the controversie was for a while husht. Let us then see who those were whom this Decree made silent or tongue-tyed in this cause, and it will appeare that none at all observed it.

9. Let us begin with the Pope himselfe, who of all is most likely to have kept his owne decree; but he was so farre from observing it, that he practised the quite contrary. In the two and twentieth yeare of *Iustinian,* the very next unto that wherein this decree is supposed to be made, *Rusticus* and *Sebastianus* two Romane Deacons remaning men at *Constantinople,* and being earnest defenders of the *Three Chapters,* writ letters unto divers Bishops, and into divers Provinces against [e] Pope *Vigilius,* and the cause was, for that he condemned [f] the *Three Chapters,* and thereby as they pretended, condemned also the Councell of *Chalcedon,* and for a proofe of their accusation they dispersed [g] the copies of *Vigilius* his Constitution sent unto *Mennas* against the *Three Chapters.* A cleare proofe that as then *Vigilius* neither had made this Decree, nor revoked his judgement for condemning of those Chapters. In the 23.[h] yeare, *Vigilius* writ to *Valentinianus,* to purge himselfe of those slanders [i] and untruths, and that hee doth by referring himselfe to his judgement [k], sent to *Mennas* against the 3. Chapters, wherein he then plainly professeth, that what he had therein defined was consonant [l] to the faith of the 4. former Councels, and to the decrees of his predecessors, & he is so resolute in maintaining the

same

d *Bar. an.* 547. *nu.* 41.
e *Hi adversus Rom. Pontificē in diversas provincias literas dedere, Bar. an. 548. nu. 2. is est juxta. Bar. an. Iustin. 21.*
f *Schismatici scriptis ubiq; vulg. verant, Vigilium tria damnando Capitula impugnare Chalcedonense Concilium. Bar. an 550. nu. 1.*
g *Exemplaria (Iudicati nostri) per plurimos sacerdotes et laicos in Africana Provincia destinares ait Vig. Rustico et Sebastiano, in sua Epist. ad eos in Conc. 5. Col. 7 pa. 578. b.*
h *Epistola Vigilij ad Valentin. data est 1 5. K.al. April. anno 23. Iustiniani. extat in Conc. 5. Coll. 7. pa. 580. et seq.*
i *Etiam hoc mentiti sunt, etc. Epist. Vig. ib. pa. 581. a.*
k *Legant quæ de causa quæ hic mota est ad fratrem nostrum Mennam scribentes legimur definiuisse, ibid.*
l *Ibid.*

m Credimus e-
nim, Catholicæ
ecclesiæ filijs, ea
que tunc ad
Mēnam scripsi-
mus de blasphe-
mijs Theodori,
ejusq; persona,
deq; Epistola
Ibæ,& scriptis
Theodoreti cōtra
rectam fidem,
abunde posse
sufficere, ibid.
n Epistola Vigi-
lij ad Aurel.da-
ta est Kal.Mays
an.24.Iustiniani
Augusti, extat
in Conc. 5. Coll.
7.pa. 581.b.
o Ista hoc anno
Constantinopoli
à Vigilio ad-
versus schisma-
ticos decreta
fuerunt. Bar.
an.550.(qui est
Iustiniani 24.)
nu.36.
p Ea extat in
Conc. 5. Coll. 7.
pa.578. & seq.
& eam recita t.
Bar.an.550.nu.
16.& seq.
q Hi in sentētia
papæ & decretō
nominantur,
apud Bar.an.
eodem, nu.34.
r Immutatum te
comperimus, &
cum adversarijs
ecclesiæ qui con-
tra Iudicati
nostri seriem ni-
tebantur se,cau-
tè tractare, &c.
Vigil. in suo de-
creto contra
Rust.& Sebast.
apud Bar.an.
550.nu.21.

same judgement that he addeth of it, that it is abundant m to satisfie any man. An infallible evidence that as yet, nor till that year he had neither revoked his former sentence, nor made any decree of silence to forbid men to condemne the same Chapters. In the foure and twentieth n yeare hee writ the like Apology to Aurelianus Bishop of Arles, yea which is more, Baronius o sheweth that in that 24. yeare, he published his judiciall sentence of condemnation and deposition against p Rusticus, Sebastianus, Gerontius, q Severus, Importunus, Iohn, and Deusdedit; for that they r by defending the Three Chapters, and communicating with such as defended them, contra Iudicati nostri seriem nitebantur, dealt against the tenor of his judgement : shewing plainly that till then, and in that yeare his judgement against the Three Chapters stood so firmly in force, that by a judiciall sentence he deposed the contradictors thereof, which had himselfe revoked, and by a Decree of silence adnulled, in likelihood he wold not, certainly in justice he could not have done; and seeing hee censured them not for speaking of that controversie, but for speaking in defence of those Chapters : it is evident, that as then he had not made any Decree for silence in that cause, for then his censure should have beene, because they had done contrary to it, not because they had contradicted his judgement in condemning those Chapters.

10. Is not Baronius thinke you a very wise and worthy Annalist, who perswades you that Vigilius made this Decree of silence in the 21.yeare of Iustinian, forbidding all thereby to condemne the Three Chapters, which not to have been made either in the 22, or 23, or 24. yeares, the undoubted writing and censures of Vigilius expressed by Baronius himselfe doe make evident, and testifie that the Pope himselfe was so far from being silent therein, that both by words, by writings, by pontificall censures and judgements, himselfe condemned the 3, Chapters? who will again perswade you that the Pope suffered very heavy persecution at the Emperors hands, because he would not permit the 3.Chapters to be condemned; whereas the Pope himselfe, not onely condemned them all that time, as well as the Emperor did, but both by writings reproved, and by judiciall censures punished, condemned, and deposed such as would not condemne them, and that also eo nomine, because they would not condemne them, nor consent to his judgement whereby he had condemned them. Now that Vigilius continued of the same mind, both in the 25.& 26. yeares of Iustinian, that is, untill the time that the fift Councell was assembled, though there be no particulars to explaine, yet by the Emperours words before remembred, that per totum tempus perseveravit, and ejusdem semper voluntatis fuit, it is abundantly testified. So that it is most certain, that Vigilius at no time observed this decree of Taciturnity : and because had there beene any, he of all men was the most likely to observe it, who as Baronius fableth, was so rigorous against others, even the Emperor also, for not observing thereof, his not observing of it, is an evidence that he made no such Decree at all, but that the whole narration concerning it, and the consequents upon it, is a very fiction and fable:

11. Next

11. Next after the Pope let us see if the Emperor (who as *Baronius* saith[1], promised to observe this law, of *Taciturnity*) was silent & quiet in this cause. And truly there is a strong presumption that he neither did nor would now refuse or forbeare to condemne the 3. *Chapters*, seeing by so doing, he should have anathematized himselfe: for by his Imperiall Edict, he denoûced all those to be an *Anathema*, who do not condemne and[t] anathematize the same Chapters. The very silence in this cause, and ceasing or refusing to anathematize the Chapters, had made him guilty of his owne just *Anathema*. But to leave presumptions, Certaine it is that *Iustinian* continued the same man, constant in condemning those Chapters, and that not onely for the time after this supposed Decree, but from the first publishing of his own Edict, whereof the whole fift Councell is a most ample witnesse, who thus say[u], *omnia semper fecit, & facit, quæ sanctam Ecclesiam & recta dogmata conservant,* The most pious Emperor hath ever done (concerning this cause of the *three Chapters*,) and now doth those things which preserve the holy Church, and sound doctrine, and that to be the condemning of these Chapters, they by their Synodall sentence doe make evident, where they professe the *condemning thereof to bee the preserving of the good seed [x] of faith, the preserving of the Councell of Chalcedon, and the rooting out of hereticall tares.*

12. And if wee desire particulars of his constant dealing herein, *Victor Tunavensis* declareth the earnestnesse of *Iustinian*, in condemning these Chapters for every yeare since this Decree of Taciturnity is supposed to have beene made. The Decree, as [y] *Baronius* sheweth, was set out in the sixt yeare after the Consulship of *Basilius* (which account by Consular yeares *Victor* useth) and it answereth to the end of twenty one, and most of the 22. yeare of *Iustinian*. In the seaventh yeare after *Basilius* [z] Coss. that is, in the very next to that wherein the Decree was made, *Iustinian* writ most earnestly saith *Victor* [a] into divers provinces, *& antistites cunctos præfata tria Capitula damnare compellit,* and hee compelled all Bishops to condemne the *Three Chapters*. In the eight he sheweth that the Illyrian Bishops held a Synod, and writ unto the Emperour to disswade him from condemning those Chapters. In the ninth he shewes that *Facundus* did the like, and further in this yeare [b] the Emperor commanded the Synod at *Mopsvestia* to be held against *Theodorus*, that it might appeare how, and from how long time before then, the name of *Theodorus* had beene blotted out of the Ecclesiasticall tables, the judgement of which Synod the Emperor sent [c] to *Vigilius* to assure him of the truth thereof, that hee might with more constancie continue to côdemne the *Three Chapters*. In the tenth *Victor* declares that the Emperor sent for *Reparatus* and *Firmus* two Primates, for *Primasius*, & *Verecundus*, two Bishops to deale with them, that they would condemne the same Chapters, and that *Zoilus* Patriarch of *Alexandria*, for refusing to condemne them was deposed, which to have beene done by the Emperors command, [d] *Liberatus* sheweth. In the eleventh, which was the next before the generall Councell, *Victor* tells us, both that *Firmus* Primate of *Numidia* being wonne [e] by the Emperors gifts (so hee partially writeth) consented to

(Marginal notes:)

[1] Bar. an. 551. nu.2. cûijſſ à ſpôſione de ſervada ſilentio, &c.
t Si quis nô anathematizat Theodorû et Theodoreti ſcripta, &c. & Epiſtolâ lbc, Anathema ſit Edict. Iuſtin.
u Conc. 5. Coll. 7. in fine.
x Feſtinâtes bonû fidei ſemê purum coſervare ab impietatis Zizaniis. Conc. 5. Coll.8.pa.584.a. y Bar. an. 547. nu.1. & 41.
z Victo. Tun. in Chron. ſed vitio Typogr. ſcribitur an.8.pro 7. nam proxime præcedens ânu ſapudtû recte numeratur an. 6. poſt Coſſ. Baſ. neque ullum annum omitti ab eo certum eſt.
a Vict. loc. citat.
b Naſacra Imperatorû ad Iohâ. data eſt an. Iuſt. 24.poſt Coſ. Baſ. a.9.ext.in Côc.5 Col.6. pa.553.a.
c Facta eſt ſuggeſtio ad ſanct.papam Vigiliû ab eiſdem epiſcopis (Concil. Mopſveſteni.) Conc. 5.Coll.5.pa.557. a. Acta in Concilio Mopſveſteno ad Vigilium Iuſtiniani Concilio & opera miſſa fuere ne in futura generali Synodo Theodorus ipſe damnare aliquo modo detrectaret. Bar. anno. 550.nu.39.
d Zoilus Imperator depoſuit. Liber.ca.23.
e Firmus donis principis corruptus, damnationi 3. Capitulorum aſſenſû præbuit. Vict. an. 11.(ſcu.ſupd. ſcribitur 12.)poſt Coſ.Baſ.

to condemne the Chapters, but *Primasius*, *Verecundus*, and *Macarius* for not consenting, were all banished. So cleare and undoubted it is that the Emperor continued so constant in his condemning of these Chapters, that for every yeare since the Decree of Silence is supposed to be made, he was resolute in this cause, condemning and banishing such as consented not to the condemning of them.

13. Whence the shamelesse untruths of the Baronian narration is demonstrated. He tells you, and tells it with a *Constat*, that in the next yeare before the fift Councell, the Emperour recalled his Edict, and abrogated what he had done in this cause of the 3. *Chapters*, whereas not onely the whole generall Councell testifieth on the contrary, that hee still persisted constant in condemning of them, but *Victor* (one who had good reason to know these matters, as feeling the smart of the Emperors severity for his obstinacie in defending those Chapters) particularly witnesseth of that very yeare, that the Emperor was so eager in maintaining his Edict, and condemning the Chapters, that he both drew *Firmus*, the Primate of *Numidia* to his opinion, and banished *Macarius* Patriarch of *Ierusalem*, *Verecundus* Bishop of *Nica*, and *Primasius* another Bishop, because they would not consent to his Edict, and condemne the same Chapters. And what a brainlesse devise was this, that the Emperor in his 25. yeare should hang out his Edict, at Constantinople, so the Cardinall [f] fableth, as a matter of some great noveltie, to bee published to the Citie, whereas his Edict foure or five yeares before, was so divulged throughout the whole Church, that none may be thought to have beene ignorant thereof, seeing *universus & orbis Catholicus*, the whole Catholike Church was divided and rent into a schisme about that Edict, the one halfe defending, the other oppugning the same? Or what reason can the fabler give, why *Vigilius* should in the 25. yeare quarrell with the Emperor, rather then in the 24.23.22. in every one of which, *Iustinian* was the same man, constant in maintaining the truth published by his Edict? Did the hanging out of the Edict, more provoke the Popes zeale then the banishing, imprisoning of those who withstood the Edict? more then the Emperors enforcing, and compelling, *omnes antistites*, all the Bishops to condemne the *Three Chapters*? But enough of *Iustinian*, to manifest that he never observed this fictitious Decree of Taciturnitie.

14. After the Emperor and Pope, let us see if Catholikes, that is, those who condemned the three Chapters, did observe this Decree? They did not: but like the Emperour, they constantly continued to speake, to write against them as well after as before the time of this supposed Decree, it stopt not the mouth of any one of them, Not of *Mennas*, not of *Theodorus* [h], whom [i] for talking so much against those Chapters *Vigilius* suspended, and excommunicated, as the Baronian narration tells you, not of the other Bishops, subject to the, for *Vigilius* used the very same censure against them also, for their condemning of those Chapters, We, saith [k] *Vigilius*, *condemne thee O Mennas*, with all the Bishops pertaining to thy Diocesse, yea, we condemne also thy fellow *Eastern Bishops* though of diverse provinces, be they of grea-

[marginal notes]

[f] *Iustinianus Imp. contra tria Capitula publice (Constantinopoli) appendi jussit edictum, Bar. an. 551. (qui est 10. post Coss. Basil.) nu. 2.*

[g] *Bin. not. in Conc.5. S Concilium. & Bar. an. 547 nu. 29.*

[h] *Bar. an. 551. nu.5. Theodorus adversus tria capitula cuncta publice agere non destitit.*

[i] *Excommunicatio refertur à Bar. an. 551. nu. 11. 12.*

[k] *Idem 12.*

ter

ter or *leſſer Cities, wee condemne and excommunicate them all.* Neither
did they begin to condemne the Chapters, in that 25. yeare, wherein
this ſentence, by the accоumpt of *Baronius* was pronounced, but they
did this ever ſince the time, that the Decree of Silence is ſuppoſed to bee made; for *Vigilius* there ſaith [1] to *Theodorus*, wee have
declared *pene hoc quinquennio elapſo,* almoſt theſe five yeares laſt paſt,
our longanimitie and patience both towards you, and towards thoſe
who have beene ſeduced by you; which five yeares being reckned
backe, will fall out in the 21. yeare of *Iuſtinian*, even from that yeare
(and then was the decree of Silence ſaid to bee publiſhed) did the
Eaſtern Biſhops continue to ſpeake againſt, and condemne the *three*
Chapters. Now although this againſt *Baronius*, who applaudes that
ſentence and writing of *Vigilius*, bee ſufficient, yet becauſe it is onely
argumentum ad hominem, I will adde a more weightie teſtimonie to
cleare this matter, concerning Catholikes, & that is, of the whole fift
generall Councell, which ſaith [m], the Emperor doth manifeſt *quod*
nec quenquam latuit, that whereof no man is ignorant, that the impietie of
theſe Chapters, *ab initio aliena eſt à ſancta Dei eccleſia,* is ſtrange, and hath
beene diſliked by the holy Church, ever ſince the controverſie about them hath
beene moved. Then certainely no Catholike, none Catholikely affected
it any time forbore to condemne them, not one of them obſerved that
Decree of Silence.

15. All the Cardinalls hope is now in the Defenders of theſe Chapters; they no doubt would bee willing to obey this Pontificall and
Synodall Decree; ſeeing for the moſt part, they were *Africane, Illy-*
rian, & Weſtern Biſhops. Among them, if any where, the Pope might
hope to have his Decree obſerved. They obſerve it? They are ſilent
in this cauſe; Nay you ſhall ſee them, after the time that this Decree
is ſuppoſed to be made, to be farre more eager in defending the *Three*
Chapters, then ever they were before. For now, beſides the defending
of thoſe Chapters, they boldly and bitterly invaighed againſt *Vigilius*
himſelfe, becauſe he condemned the ſame. This [n] did *Liberatus* at
Carthage, at *Tunen Victor,* at *Conſtantinople Facundus,* the Popes owne
Orator, (who now having turnd his ſtile, whetted it as ſharpe againſt
the Pope, asbefore he had done at the Popes command againſt the
Emperor) yea the Popes owne Romane Deacons, *Ruſticus* and
Sebaſtianus, beſides others, freely, and openly declamed [o] againſt the
Pope, asone, who by condemning the 3. *Chapters,* did condemne the
Councell of *Chalcedon*: nay, they proceeded even to flout and taunt
the Pope, for his condemning of thoſe Chapters, deriding his ſentence againſt *Theodorus* of *Mopſveſtia* being dead, in this manner [p], the
Pope ſhould have condemned not onely the perſon, and writings of
Theodorus, ſed & territorium ipſum ubi poſitus eſt, but even the very
ground alſo where hee was buried, adding, that if any could finde but the
bones of *Theodorus,* (though now accurſed by the Pope) *gratanter acci-*
perent, they would very lovingly embrace them and keepe them for
holy relickes.

16. And what ſpeake I of a few particular men? In the 23. yeare
of *Iuſtinian,* that is, in the ſecond yeare after the ſuppoſed Decree, the
Illyrian

[1] *Ibid. n. 7.*

[m] *Conc. 5. Coll. 7 in fine.*

[n] *Barata. 548. n. 6. Non tantũ Ruſticus acuit ſtilum contra Vi-gilium, ſed alij plures, Libera-tus, Victor, &c. o Vtique vul-garunt ipſum Vigilium tria dictando cepi-tula impoſuere Concilium Chalc. Bar. an. 550. nu. 1. p Vigilius in ſua ſententia, ſen E-piſtola Ruſtico et Sebaſtiano in Conc. 5. Coll. 7. pa. 578. b.*

y *Vict.Tun. an.*
8.*poſt Conſ.Baſ.
ſed corrupte le-
gitur 9.*
z *Vict.Tun. an.*
9 *paſt Conſ.Baſil.*

Illyrian[y] Biſhops held a Synod, by which was both writ a booke in defence of thoſe Chapters, and ſent unto the Emperor, and *Benenatus* Biſhop of *Iuſtineanea*, was condemned by the ſame Synod, becauſe hee ſpake againſt thoſe Chapters. The next yeare [z] after that, did the Africane Biſhops hold a Synod; wherein they did *nominatim*, and ex-preſly condemne Pope *Vigilius*, excommunicate him, and ſhut him out of their communion, becauſe he was one of thoſe who con-demned the *Three Chapters*, as *Victor* Biſhop of *Tunea*, who as it ſeemes was preſent in that Synod, doth teſtifie. Now ſeeing the Cardinall

a *Bar.an.548.
nu. 6.*
b *Qui poſtea
(poſt ultimum
judicium Papæ)
ab his diſſenſere,
Schiſmatici ha-
biti ſunt. Cum
tamen interea
ante noviſſimum
Apoſtolicæ ſedis
aſſenſum, non
eſſet piaculum
pro tribus pug-
nare capitulis.
Bar. an.546.
nu. 38.*

profeſſeth [a] that theſe diviſions, and contentions were among Catho-likes, *pugnantibus inter ſe orthodoxis, orthodoxall Biſhops and Catholikes they were, who at this time fought one againſt another*, yea and by his po-ſition, Schiſmaticall they were not, becauſe [b] the Pope had not yet given his laſt ſentence. If one liſted to digreſſe, here were a fit occa-ſion to make a little ſport with his Cardinalſhip, upon whoſe aſſerti-on it clearely enſueth, that a Synod, even an Africane Synod (which with them is more) yea the whole Church of Africke, may (and *de facto* hath ſo done) judge, cenſure, excommunicate and exclude from their communion the Pope; and yet for all this, themſelves at the ſame time may be, and have *de facto* beene very good Catholikes, and nei-ther heretickes, nor ſchiſmatickes. But of that point I have before in-treated. This onely I doe now obſerve, that by the view and conſi-deration of all ſorts, and degrees of men in the Church, none at all obſerved that decree of Silence in this cauſe, not the Pope, nor the Emperor, not the Orthodoxall profeſſors, & ſuch as before condem-ned the Chapters, not the hereticall defenders of them: All theſe (and in one of theſe rankes, were comprehended all Chriſtians at that time) by their ſpeeches, by their writings, by their actions, by their Sy-nodall decrees and judgements, doe evidently witneſſe that there was no ſuch decree of Silence ever made, which without all queſtion, amongſt ſome one order and degree or other, would have been obſer-ved, and taken effect.

c *De hac Vigilij
decreto (pro Si-
lentio) et initæ cũ
Theodoro &
Menna tranſac-
tione, teſtes ſunt
acta publica.
Bar.an.547.nu.
42. Iſta Acta vo-
cat, Conſtitutum
Vigilij de Ana-
themate.an.551.
nu. 12.*
d *Extat tum a-
pud Bar.an.551
nu.6. et ſeq.tum
apud Bin.poſt.E-
piſt.16.Vigilij.*
e *Ibid.nu. 3.
pene hoc quin-
quennio.*
f *lib.nu.11.et 12*

17. To theſe I will adde one other reaſon, taken from the weak-neſſe, and unſoundneſſe of that ground whereon the Cardinall hath framed this whole narration. He tells [c] us that this Decree of Silence, the Synod wherein it was made, and divers of the conſequents (for ſome are of the Cardinalls owne invention) are teſtified by certaine publike acts or Records, to wit, thoſe which contained the ſentence and Pontificall *Conſtitution* [d] of Pope *Vigilius* againſt *Mennas, Theodo-rus*, and the reſt. In thoſe acts indeed a good part of this Baronian fable is related, how *Mennas, Dacius*, and many other both Greeke and Latine Biſhops were preſent in this Synod, at the making of this Decree: how *Theodorus*, [e] and other Eaſtern Biſhops had dealt for the ſpace of five yeares againſt that Decree : how the Pope [f] after five yeares toleration and longanimitie, called an other Synod, and ther-in pronounced a ſentence of Excommunication againſt *Theodorus, Mennas*, and the reſt, till they ſhould acknowledge their fault, and make a ſatisfaction for the ſame. Theſe and ſome other particulars are there expreſſed. Now if we can demonſtrate theſe publike Acts

of

of *Baronius* to bee no other than forgeries, I thinke none will make doubt, but that all the rest of the Baronian narration which relyes hereon, is a very fiction.

18. But can those publike Acts be convinced for such? they may, and that most evidently, besides many other meanes, by comparing the date of this sentence against *Mennas*, with the time of the death of *Mennas*. These Acts, Records, Sentence, or Constitution against *Mennas* (call them what you list) were made in the 25 yeare of *Iustinian*, for so in the date g of them is expressed; nor can it bee supposed that there is any error either in the writer or Printer, for both the Consular yeare is also added h, to wit, the tenth after the Coss. of *Basilius*, which answereth to the 25 of *Iustinian*, and the Pope accounts there almost five i yeares; since the Decree of Silence was made; which being placed by *Baronius* k in the 21, the fift current yeare after it, will directly fal to be the 25 year. So in the 25 of *Iustinian* did the Pope excomunicate *Mennas*; yea, write and send this Excommunication unto him, saying unto him in this l manner, *Teq; Mennam tamdiu à sacra communione suspendimus; we suspend thee O Mennas*, and all the other Bishops in thy Diocesse, so long untill every one of you acknowledging his errour shall make competent satisfaction for his owne fault, which satisfaction, and submission to have beene performed by *Mennas* in the next yeare; to wit, the 26 of *Iustinian*, *Baronius* m with great pompe declareth. Now *Mennas* dyed five yeares before he offered this booke of supplication, or submitted himself to *Vigilius*; & 4. before the Pope sent out this Excommunication unto him, with that admonition to submit himselfe; for it is certainly testified by the Popes Legates in the sixt generall Councell, that *Mennas* dyed in the 21 yeare of *Iustinian*. In that Councell n a sermon or speech going under the name of *Mennas*, to *Vigilius*, was produced as a part of the Acts of the fift Councell, the Legates of Pope *Agatho* cryed out before the Emperor and the whole Councell; that it was a forgery: which they proved o, and that most manifestly, because *Mennas* dyed in the 21 yeare of *Iustinian*, but the fift Synod was congregated in the 26 yeare; which ended on the first of *Aprill*, though the first Session of the Synod was not held till the *May* next after, which was in the 27 yeare of *Iustinian*. Thus testified the Popes owne Legates; and the Emperour, with the whole Synod, upon their evidence, rejected their writing for a forgerie.

19. Said I not truly unto you, that the Baronian narration was a peece of rare Poetry? might not a meane Poet make an excellent Tragedy of it? were it not a fine Pageant, to see the Pope, and so many Bishops sit in *Vtopia*, and there make a law for *Taciturnity*, the Emperour, the Senate, and people consenting unto it? would it not bee another, and farre more delightfull Act, to see the Pope and Emperour quarrelling about this law; the one beating, buffeting, and persecuting, the other fleeing both by Sea and land, from *Placidiana* to Saint *Peter*, from him to *Euphemia*, from *Constantinople* to *Chalcedon*? what a sport were it to see the Romane *Apollo* ascend into his Delphian throne, and thence, as from *Olympus*, cast his fierie darts, his thunders

g Data 19. Kal. Septemb. Imperante Domino Iustiniano an. 25. post. Cons. Basily anno decimo. Bar. an. 558. nu. 12.
h Ibid.
i Pene hoc quinquennio elapso monstravimus. Ibid. nu. 7.
k Bar. an. 547. (qui est Iustiniani. 21.) nu. 41. et 43.
l Apud Bar. an. 551. nu. 12.
m Bar. an. 552. nu. 20. Ipse Mennas libellum supplicem Vigilio obtulit.

n Conc. 6. Act. 3.

o Eo argumento manifestissimè comprobarunt, quod Mennas sex annis ante quintam Synodum sub Vigilio celebratam ex hac vita migrasset. Bin. not. in Conc. 6. in Act. 3.

ders and lightnings against that *Typhoean* generation, which durst speake when he enjoyned silence? Now the embassage which the Emperour sent to *Chalceden* to intreat his Holinesse to returne, the magnanimity of the Pope in refusing to come from the Altar, the Emperours yeelding to all that he prescribed; this of it selfe would incourage a Poet, and cause him to presume of an applause: But the most rare Pageant of all would bee, to see and heare *Mennas*, foure yeares after he was dead and rotten, to speake and dispute against the Decree of Silence (the *Silentes umbrae*, to declame against Silence) to see him a Bishop, a Patriarch, at the voyce of the Popes sentence; *Audisne haec Amphiarai sub terram abditae*; to come *ab inferis*, to come with a Bill of supplication in his hand, with a song of *Miserere* in his mouth, to the Romane *Iove*, and intreat pardon for his talking so much in the grave, and among the infernall ghosts, against the Popes Decree of Silence; & after all this to see the Pope shake hands with him, and all his Metropolitanes, and Micropolitanes ᵖ, (note the eloquence of the Pope) and so, after a most joyfull reconcilement, to see the holy Reliques caried in a golden Chariot (an excellent dumbe shew) about the City, and that by a dead man; Can you doe lesse than give the Poet *Baronius* a Plaudite for his so rare invention, or contriving of this Fable?

20. Why, but is it credible that Cardinall *Baronius*, the great Annalist of our age, hee who bestowed thirty ᵠ yeares in the study of these Ecclesiasticall affaires, that hee should so foully be overseene in a computation so easie, and so obvious, as to thinke *Mennas* to bee excommunicated, to come with a supplication to the Pope, and to ride in a triumphant Chariot, with those holy reliques, foure or five yeares after he was dead and rotten? Overseene? nothing lesse: It was no ignorance, no oversight in him; he knew all this matter *ad unguem*, hee knew that *Mennas* was dead long before that submission, and triumph: But the Cardinall was disposed, either to recreate the reader with the contemplation of this his Poeticall fiction, or else for to shew you, that, with the charme of those forgeries, and counterfeit writings, with which he hath stuffed his Annals; hee is able to metamorphoze all other men into very blocks and beetles, that they shall applaud his most absurd dotages as undoubted and historicall truths; which, that every man may perceive, it must be observed, that though in this place, where the cause betwixt *Vigilius* and the Emperor, is debated; the Cardinall is content that you should thinke *Mennas* to have been alive in the 26.ʳ year of *Iustinian*, that is, five years after he was dead; for otherwise all his narration, even the whole play had been spoiled, there had neither beene any Decree of Silence, nor any persecution by *Iustinian*, nor any flight of *Vigilius*, nor any excommunication of *Mennas* or *Theodorus*, nor any submission of them, and of the Emperour also to the Pope, the Pope had not beene knowne to bee so farre above Bishops, Patriarks, and Emperours, that they must all stoope to him, and, laying their necks at his feet, say unto him, *Calcate me salem insipidum*, punish me as you please for speaking without your Holinesse leave and licence, yea, that Kings must pull downe, abrogate, and

ᵖ *Tu cum omnibus Metropolitanis et Micropolitanis Episcopis. Vigil. sententia apud Bar. an.551.nu.12.*

ᵠ *Haec opus ante annos circiter 30 aggressus sum. Bar. in prefat. dedic. ante tom.1. Annalium.*

ʳ *Hoc anno (26. Iustiniani) fuem vivendi fecit Mennas. Bar. an.552.nu.21.*

and adnull their imperiall Edicts, if the Pope doe but becke unto them; though, for these considerations, hee is here willing that you beleeve that untruth concerning *Mennas*, for all these depend on that one sentence of *Anathema* against *Mennas*; yet, when this matter is over-past, when the Cardinall comes to a new argument, where hee hopes, this, which is said about the cause of *Vigilius*, wil be forgotten, there he confesseth the truth indeed concerning *Mennas*, and tels you a quite contrary tale : For intreating of the Acts of the sixt Councel, & particularly of that reason of the Popes Legates against the forged E-pistle in *Mennas* name, he thus ᶠsaith, *Ejusque rei certum illud attule-runt argumentum, quod Mennas diem obijt anno 21 Iustiniani Imperatoris : The Legates give a certaine proofe, that the writing was forged, because Mennas dyed in the 21 yeare of Iustinian the Emperour.* Loe, the Cardi-nall knew, and professeth it to bee, not onely true, but certaine, that *Mennas* dyed in the 21 yeare of *Iustinian*, and yet against his owne cer-taine knowledge, for maintaining this fictitious Decree of Silence, and the fables thereon depending, he perswades you to beleeve that *Men-nas* dealt against this Decree, was excommunicated by *Vigilius*, and submitted himselfe to the Pope, and rode with the relikes five yeares after he was dead.

ᶠ *Bar.an.680. nu.46.*

21. Truly this was scarse faire and honest dealing in the Cardinall, by untruths to strive to bolster out forged Acts and writing : But the Cardinals Annals are so full of such like stuffe, that, if you divide them into foure parts, I doe constantly affirme there is no more truth in three of those foure, than you have seene to bee in this fable, which from a most base forgery, knowne also to the Cardinall for such, hee hath commended for a grave and authentike history unto us : And I should grow somewhat out of patience to see the Cardinall so grosly contradict, both the truth, and his owne writings also, but that, by my long and serious tossing of his bookes, I perceive this is so fami-liar a tricke with him, that, for the usuall meeting of it, I have long since forgotten to be angry with him for such pettie faults. This I hope, which hath beene declared, will serve for a caveat unto all, to take heed how they credit any matter whatsoever upon the Cardinals relation: either it is in it selfe untrue, or it springs from some untruth, or by his purpose in relating it, it is made to serve but for a pully to draw you into some untruth, *aut aliquis latet dolus, either in the head or taile there is a sting*, beleeve him not. And I would also have added somewhat for *Binius*, who in this ᵗ, as in other fancies and fables, ap-plauds *Baronius*; but I suppose, that as hee sucketh his errours from *Baronius*, so hee will thinke, that the refuting of *Baronius* is a sufficient warning for him to purge his Edition of the Councels from such vile and shamelesse untruths. Thus much of that former point which con-cernes the second Period in *Vigilius* changings.

ᵗ *Bin.Not.in Vigilij sententi-am contra Theo-dorum, tom.2. cent.pa.504.*

[CAP.

CAP. XVII.

That Vigilius, *neither by his Pontificall* Decree, *nor so much as by a perso-*
nall profession consented to, *or confirmed the fift Councell, after the end*
thereof, or after his supposed exile.

1.  THE other point proposed concernes that fourth and last change of *Vigilius* judgement, whereby, as *Baronius* a tels us, he, by his Apostolicall Decree b confirmed the fift Councell, when, about a yeare c after the end thereof, he returned out of exile. That such a change of *Vigilius* can no way helpe *Baronius*, or his cause, though it should be granted unto him, we have before d declared; but because al which we then said was onely spoken upon a supposall and admission of this Baronian change, we will now more nearly examine the whole matter, and try whether there was indeed any such Decree ever made by *Vigilius*, and whether he did at any time after the end of the fift Councell change his judgement, in such sort, that he became a condemner of the *Three Chapters*, and an approver of the fift Synod. And truly I could wish so much good to *Vigilius*, as that there might appeare some cleare, and ancient records, to testifie his renouncing of heresie, and condemning of his owne hereticall and *Cathedrall* decree, published in the time of the Councell, for defence of the *Three Chapters* : But the truth is more precious unto me than the love of *Vigilius* or any Pope whatsoever; & because it is the truth alone which causeth me to discusse this point, I must needs confesse, that I can finde nothing at all, which can effectually induce mee to beleeve it, but there are many and pregnant reasons which inforce me to thinke, that *Vigilius* never made any such *Decree* or Change, as *Baronius* fancieth, but that this whole fourth Period and change of *Vigilius*, so gloriously painted out by *Baronius*, is nothing else but another fiction, and peece of the Cardinals owne Poetry, which, without all warrant or ground from any ancient writer, hee, like a Spider, onely out of his owne braine hath woven and devised.

2. That *Vigilius* made no such *Decree*, the reason wch *Bar.* gives in this very case, may declare: he, to prove that *Vigilius* made not this decree, either during the time of the Synod, or shortly after the end thereof, hath these words e, If *Vigilius* had then assented by his letters, *atque literæ illæ Actis fuissent intextæ; verily those letters, purchased with so great labour, would have beene inserted among the Acts of the fift Synod, and a great number of copies would have been taken thereof, spred abroad, and made knowne to all Churches, as well in the East, as West, (even as the Epistle of* Leo *was) because by those letters, validarentur quæ à Synodo sancita; those things which the fift Synod had decreed, the Pope contradicting them, and thereby they being invalid, should now be made of force, the Pope consenting to them.* Thus *Baronius.* Doth not the same reason as effectually prove,

that

that he made no such decree at al, or not a yeare after, as that he made it not within one or two moneths after the end of the Synod? with what labour, at what price would not the Bishops of the fift Synod have purchased that decree? how gladly would they have annexed it to their Acts, as the Decree of *Leo* is to the acts at *Chalcedon*? How many copies and extracts would they have taken of it, and dispersed them every where, both in the West and East, to testifie the truth of their Synodall judgement, and that the *infallible* Iudge had consented to their sentence, and confirmed the same. Or would they have done this within a month, and not a yeare after the end of the Synod? what odds to the point in hand can that small difference of time make in the cause? specially considering that the very Epistle of *Leo* [f], whereof the Cardinall speaketh, was not written till five [g] moneths after the end of the Councell at *Chalcedon*, and yet was it annexed to the acts thereof. If then the Cardinalls reason bee of force to prove that hee writ not this Decree shortly after the Synod, it is altogether as effectuall to prove he writ it not at all, nor after his returne about a yeare after out of exile.

3. The Cardinall gives yet another evidence hereof, *Pelagius*, saith e [h] *the successor of Vigilius did thinke it fit, that the fift Synod should bee approved, and the three Chapters condemned, moved especially hereunto by his reason, that the Easterne Church, ob Vigilij constitutum schismate scissa, being rent and divided from the Romane by reason of the Constitution of Vi-lius, might be united unto it.* How was the Easterne Church divided from the Romane in the time of *Pelagius*, by reason of that decree of *Vigilius* in defence of the *Three Chapters*, if *Vigilius* by another decree published after it had recalled, and adnulled it? If the Popes condemning of those Chapters, and approving of the fift Councell would unite the Churches, then the decree of *Vigilius* (had there beene any such) would have effected that union. If the *Apostolike Decree* of *Vigilius* could not effect it, in vaine it was for *Pelagius* to thinke by his approbation, which could have no more authority then *Apostolicall*, to effect that union. If the cause of the breach and disunion of those Churches was, as *Baronius* truly saith, the *Constitution of Vigilius* in defence of the *Three Chapters*, against the judgement of the fift Synod, seeing it is cleare by the Cardinalls owne confession, that the disunion continued till after the death of *Vigilius*, it certainly hence followeth, that the *Constitution* of *Vigilius*, which was the cause of that breach, was never by himselfe repealed, which even in *Pelagius* time remained in force, and was then a wall of separation of the Easterne, from the Westerne Church: Againe, if the Popes approving the fift Councell, and condemning the *three Chapters* was, as in truth it was, and as the Cardinall noteth [i] it to have beene, the cause to unite those Churches, seeing by his owne confession in *Vigilius* time they were not united (for *Pelagius* [k] after *Vigilius* his death, sought to take away that schisme) it certainly hence followeth, that *Vigilius* never by any *Decree* approved that Synod, and their Synodall condemning of those Chapters: for had he so done, the union had in his time presently beene effected.

Y

4. The

f *Ea est. Epist. Leonis 61. que incipit, Omnem fraternitatem.*
g *Conc. Chalc. desijt 28. Oct. Coss. Martiano, aut 1. Novemb. ut patet ex ult. Sess. Epistola vero Leonis scripta est 21. Martij Coss. Opilione, ut patet ex fine Epist.*
h *Bar. an. 553. nu. 236.*

i *Cujus (Vigilij) postremam sententiam (pro approbatione 5. Conc. & condemnatione triū Capitulorum) posteri omnes sequuti, universa Dei Ecclesia paucis schismaticis exceptis, eandem Synodum ut oecumenicam semper notat. Bar. an. 554. nu. 7.*
k *Bar. an. 553. nu. 236.*

4. The same may be perceived alſo by the Weſterne Church. For as that *Pontificall decree* of *Vigilius* (had there beene any ſuch) would have united the Eaſterne, ſo much more would it have drawne the Weſterne, the Italian, and ſpecially the Romane Church, to conſent to the fift Councell, and condemning of the *three Chapters* : but that they perſiſted in the defence of the *three Chapters*, and that alſo to the very end of *Vigilius* his life, may divers wayes be made evident. Whē *Pelagius* being then but a Deacon was choſen Pope after the death of *Vigilius*, and was to be conſecrated Biſhop; there could no more then two Biſhops [1] be found in the Weſterne Church that would conſecrate or ordaine him Biſhop : wherefore contrary to that Canon both of the Apoſtles [m] and Nicene Fathers [n], requiring three [o] Biſhops to the conſecration of a Biſhop (which they ſo often boaſt [p] of in their diſputes againſt us) the Pope himſelfe was faine to be ordained onely by two Biſhops, with a Presbyter of *Oſtia* in ſtead of the third. *Anaſtaſius* very ignorantly, (if not worſe) ſets downe the reaſon thereof to have beene, for that *Pelagius* was ſuſpected [q] to have beene guilty (by poiſon or ſome other way) of the death of *Vigilius*. A very idle fancie, as is the moſt in *Anaſtaſius*; for *Pelagius* was in baniſhment long before the death of *Vigilius*, and there continued till *Vigilius* [r] was dead, he had little leiſure nor oportunity to thinke of poiſoning or murdering his owne Biſhop; by whoſe death he could expect no gaine. The true cauſe why the Weſterne Biſhops diſtaſted *Pelagius*, is noted by *Victor* who then lived. Hee [ſ] *before hee came from Conſtantinople conſented to the fift Synod, and condemned the Three Chapters*. Now the Weſterne [t] Biſhops ſo deteſted the fift Synod, and thoſe who with it condemned thoſe Chapters, that among them all there could be found but two Biſhops who held with the Synod, and ſo allowed of *Pelagius* and his act in conſenting thereunto, and thoſe two with the Presbyter of *Oſtia*, were the ordainers of *Pelagius*, whom *Victor* in his corrupted language calls prevaricators. Let any man now conſider with himſelfe, whether it bee credible that in all *Italy*, and ſome Provinces adjoyning, there ſhould be but two Biſhops who would conſent to the *Apoſtolicall decree* of *Vigilius*, for approving the fift Councell, if he had indeed publiſhed ſuch a *decree*. If they knew not the Popes ſentence in this cauſe (which they held, and that rightly, for a cauſe of faith) to be *infallible*, how was not the weſterne or the Romane Church hereticall at this time, not knowing that point of faith; which is the tranſcendent principle and foundation of all doctrines of faith? If they knew it to bee *infallible*, ſeeing his judgement muſt then overſway their owne, how could there bee no more but two biſhops found among them all, who approved the Popes Cathedrall ſentence, and conſented to his *infallible* judgement? Seeing then it is certaine that the Weſterne Church did generally reject the fift Synod, after the death of *Vigilius*, and ſeeing it is not to bee thought

[1] *Dum non eſſent Epiſcopi qui eum ordinarent, inventi ſunt duo, Iohannes, & Bonus, & Andreas Presbyter de Oſtia, & ordinaverunt eum Epiſcopum, Anaſt. in vita Pelag. 1.* [m] *Can. Apoſt. 1.* [n] *Conc. Nic. Can. 4.* [o] *Certe omnino do 3 Epiſcopi debent eſſe congregati, & ita faciant ordinationem. Can. 4. Conc. Nic.* [p] *Bell. lib. de Notis Eccleſie, ca. 8. §. Ex quo. Et Bin. in Notis ad Can. 1. Apoſt. alijq;* [q] *Subduxerunt ſe à communione ejus, dicentes, quia in morte Vigilij ſe miſcuit. Anaſt. in vita Pelag. 1.* [r] *Nam Vigilius obijt anno præcedente, quam Pelagius de exilio revocatus eſt. Vict. Tun. in chron. ad an. 16. (corrupte legitur 17.) Baſilij, et ad an. ſequentem.* [ſ] *Pelagius condemnans ea (tria Capitula) quæ dudum conſtantiſsime defendebat, à prævaricatoribus ordinatus eſt. Vict. ad an. 17. (corrupte legitur 18.) poſt Conſ. Baſilij.* [t] *Adeo exhorruiſſe viſi ſunt Antiſtites occidentales ferè omnes, aliam poſt 4. admittere Oecumenicam Synodum, ut non potuerit Pelagius reperire Epiſcopos Romæ, à quibus conſecraretur. Bar. an. 556. nu. 2.*

that

that they would have perfifted in fuch a generall diflike thereof had they knowne *Vigilius* to have by his *Apoftolicall* fentence decreed, that all fhould approve the fame, of which his fentence (had there been any fuch) they could not have beene ignorant (for if by no other meanes, which were very many, *Pelagius* himfelfe would have brought and affuredly made knowne the fame unto them) this their generall rejection of the fift Synod, is an evident proofe that this Baronian decree which hee afcribeth to *Vigilius* is no better then the former of filence, both untrue, both fictitious, and of the two, this the far worfe, feeing for this the Cardinall hath not fo much as any one, no not a forged writing, on which he may ground it, it is wholy devifed by himfelfe, he the onely Poet or maker of this fable.

5. To this may be added that which is mentioned in [u] *Bede* concerning the Councell of *Aquileia* in *Italy.* That Councell was held neare about, or rather, as by [x] *Sigonius* narration it appeareth, after the death of *Vigilius*; and in it were prefent *Honoratus* Bifhop of *Millan*, *Macedonius* B. of *Aquileia*, *Maximianus* B. of *Ravenna*, befides many other Bifhops of *Liguria*, *Venice* and *Iftria*. Thefe being as *Bede* [y] faith, unskilfull of the faith, doubted to approve the fift Synod; nay, *Concilium illud* [z] *non obfervandum effe ftatuère*, they decreed that the fift Synod fhould not be allowed or received. What? would fo many Italian Bifhops in an Italian Councell decree the quite contradictory to the Popes known Iudiciall fentence in a caufe of faith? the Pope decreed (as *Baronius* faith) that the fift Councell ought to be imbraced. The Italian Synod decreeth that the fift Councell ought to be rejected. Neither onely did they thus decree, but as *Bede* [a] noteth, they continued in this opinion, *donec falutaribus beati Pelagij* [b] *monitis inftructa confenfit*, untill being inftructed by the wholfome admonitions of Pope *Pelagius*, they confented to the fift Councell, as other Churches did. Now this *Pelagius* of whom *Bede* fpeaketh, was *Pelagius* the fecond, who was not Pope till more then 20. [c] yeares after the death of *Vigilius*. He to reclame thofe Bifhops of *Iftria*, *Venice*, and *Liguria*, writ a very large and decretall Epiftle [d] (which *Binius* [e] compares to that of *Leo* to *Flavianus*) wherein he declares every one of thofe *Three Chapters*, to be repugnant to the faith and decrees of the ancient Councells. By this decretall inftruction of *Pelagius* the fecond, were thofe Italian defenders of the *Three Chapters*, after twenty yeares, and more, reduced as *Bede* noteth, to the unity of the Church, and to approve of the fift Councell. Had *Vigilius* made, as *Baronius* fancieth, the like decree, why tooke it not the like effect in thofe Wefterne Bifhops? was there more then *Apoftolicall* authority and inftruction in the decree of *Pelagius*? or was there leffe then that in the decree of *Vigilius*?

6. Nay there is another fpeciall point to bee obferved concerning that Epiftle of *Pelagius*, *Elias* Bifhop of *Aquileia*, and the reft who defended the *three Chapters*, among other reafons urged the authority of *Vigilius* [f] on their part, therby countenancing their error, in that they taught no other doctrine in defending thofe Chapters then the *Apoftolicall See* had taught by *Vigilius*; thus writ they in their Apology which they fent to *Pelagius*, ayming no doubt at that *Apoftolicall Conftitution of Vigilius*

u Be l. lib. de fex Ætatib. anno mundi, 4657. x Sigon. lib. 20. de Occid. Imper. an. 554. in fine. y Ob imperitism fidei 5. Concilium fufcipere diffidit Synodus Aquileia. Bed loc. cit.
z Sigon. loc. cit. a Bed loc. cit. b Apud Bedam legitur (beati Sergij) qui vixit annis 130. poft Vigilium, eundé errorem fequitur Platina, & alij. Sed legendum effe Pelagij non Sergij, conftat ex Ivone, cujus verbis ex decreto citat Sigonius, loco citat. & ibid. ex Beda legitur Pelagij. c Vigilius obijt, an. 556. juxta Baron. Pelagius autem 2. cœpit an. 577. juxta eundem Bar. d Ea eft 7. Pelagij 2. e Bin. Not. ad eam Epiftolam Pelagij. f Rurfus per Epiftolam veftram dicitur. A fede Apoftolica vos doctos & confirmatos ne buic rei (i. Synodo quinta & condemnationi trium Capitulorú) confentire debeatis, — Sedes Apoftolica per Vigilium reftitit. Pelag. Epift. 31. §. Rurfum.

pub-

published in the time of the Councell, whereby hee decreed that the *Three Chapters* ought by all to be defended : *for that was it as the Cardinall* g *saith, which moved, nay enforced all to follow that opinion, and to defend the Three Chapters.* What doth *Pelagius* now answer to this reason? Truly had *Vigilius* made any such later *Decree*, as the Cardinall fancieth, by which he had approved the fift Synod, and so both condemned the *three Chapters*, and repealed his owne former judgement in defence thereof; neither could *Pelagius* have beene ignorant of that decree, neither would he, being so earnestly pressed therewith, have omitted that oportunity, both to grace *Vigilius*, and most effectually confute that which was the speciall reason on which his opposites did relye. Could he have truly replyed, that *Vigilius* himselfe upon better advise had recalled his Decree made in defence of those Chapters, and by his last *Apostolicall* judgement condemned the same Chapters, this had cut insunder the very sinewes of that objection. But *Pelagius* returnes them not this answer, but knowing that to bee true which they said of *Vigilius*, bee tells them (which is a point worthy observing) that the *Apostolike See might change* h *their judgement in this cause* (and this even by *Pelagius* himselfe is a cause of faith,) *and that the ignorance of the Greeke* i *in the Westerne Bishops was the cause why they so lately consented to the fift Synod.* And so though *Vigilius* had judged that the *Three Chapters* ought to be defended, yet the successors of *Vigilius* might long after, as they did, k teach, and himselfe define, that the same Chapters ought to bee condemned, and that the fift Councell wherein they were condemned, ought to bee approved. A very strong inducement, that *Pelagius* knew not, and then that *Vigilius* made not any such *Decree* as the Cardinall commendeth unto us.

7. For any *Apostolicall Decree* then, whereby *Vigilius* after his exile recalled his former judgment, or approved the fift Councell, there was none, as besides those reasons which the Cardinall himselfe giveth, the persisting of the Westerne Churches in defence of those Chapters, not onely after the death of *Vigilius*; but till the time of *Pelagius* the second, makes evident. If *Vigilius* at all consented to the Synod after the end thereof, it was onely by some private or personall, but not by any decretall or *Pontificall* approbation. And if the reasons or pretences of *Baronius* prove ought at all, this is the most that can be collected from them. And this though wee should grant and yeeld unto them, yet can it no way helpe their cause, or excuse the Popes *Cathedrall* judgment from being *fallible*, onely it would serve, to save *Vigilius* himselfe from dying an heretike, or under the *Anathema* of the holy Councell. For as they teach, and teach it with ostentation, as a matter of great wit and subtilty, that the Pope may erre *personally*, or in his owne person hold an heresie, which onely hurts himselfe, and not the Church, but erre *doctrinally*, or judicially define an heresie he cannot, even so (to pay them with their owne coine) might it fall out at this time with *Vigilius*; bee being wearied with long exile, might perhaps for his owne person condemne the *Three Chapters*, and approve the Synod, which may be called a *personall* truth, or a personall profession in the Pope, the benefit whereof

was

g *Vigilius amplissimis scriptis contrariam sententiam (ei quæ in quinta Synodo definita est,) professus est, & ad eam sectandam universam ecclesiam catholicam impulit. Bar. an. 554. nu. 6.*

h *Cur mutatio sententiæ huic sedi in crimine objicitur. Pelag. Epist. 7. §. Debet.*

i *Latini homines & Græcitatis ignari dum linguam nesciunt, errores tarde cognoverunt. Pelag. ibid. §. Rursum.*

k *Prædecessorum nostrorum in hac causa consensus unto post maxis non fuit, ibid.* § *Debet. An illud Tanto post, referri potest ad decretum Vigilij editum anno proxime sequenti post Concilium 5? non potest.*

was onely to redound to himfelfe, either to free him from the cenfure of the Synod, or procure the Emperors favour, & goodwill, that
he might returne home to his See, but that this profeffing (fuppofing
he made it) was *doctrinall* or *Cathedrall*, delivered *ex officio* by the Pope
as Pope, fo that by it he entended to bind the whole Church to doe
the like, neither *Baronius*, nor any of all his favourers can ever prove.
Now were I fure that the Cardinall, or his friends, would be content
with this grant of a *perfonall* truth in Pope *Vigilius*, I could be willing
to let it paffe for currant without further examination. But alas, they
are no men of fuch low thoughts and lookes, their eyes are ever upon
the Supremacie and *Infallibilitie* of the Popes judgement : As *perfonall*
errors hurt them not, fo *perfonall* truths helpe them not, *Baronius* will
either have this confent of *Vigilius* to bee *Iudiciall*, *Doctrinall*, *Apofto-*
licall [1], and *Cathedrall*, or he will have none at all. And therefore to demonftrate how farre *Vigilius* was frō decreeing this, I will now enter
into a further difcuffion of this point then I firft intended, not doubting to make it evident, that none of all the Cardinalls reafons are of
force to prove fo much as a private or *perfonall* confent in *Vigilius* to
condemne the *Three Chapters*, and approve the fift Councell, after
the end of the fift Synod, or after that exile which the Cardinall fo
often mentioneth.

8. The Cardinalls reafons to prove this, are three: The firft is
taken from the teftimonie of *Evagrius* [m], who then lived. *Nicephorus*,
Cedrenus, *Zonaras*, *Photius*, and all Greeke writers, *Græci* [n] *omnes affir-*
mant, they all teftifie *Vigilius* to have affented to this fift Councell,
and that by letters, or by a booke, whence the Cardinall collects,
that feeing he confented not either during the time of the Synod, or
fhortly after, for he was fent into banifhment, becaufe he would not
confent unto it, *neceffe eft affirmare* [o] *id ab ipfo factū effe hoc tempore, cum*
ab exilio folutus eft, liberque dimiffus; It muft of neceffitie be affirmed, that he
confented at that time when he was freed from exile, and difmiffed home to
Rome. Thus *Baronius*: whom I will never beleeve to have been fo fimple
and ignorant, as that he knew not, how lame, defective, and unfound
his his neceffarie collection was. That his *Neceffe eft*, is meerly inconfequent, it is not fo good as *Contingens eft.* That *Vigilius* confented by
a booke, or letters, to the Synod, is certaine, none that I know makes
doubt of it, and that is all that *Evagrius*, or any of his other witneffes
affirme : but neither *Evagrius*, nor any one of them faith, that *Vigilius*
confented to the Synod after the end thereof, or after he was fent into banifhment : this and this onely is it which wee deny, and which
Baronius undertakes to prove : but when he comes to his proofe, hee
till, and that moft fraudulently, omitteth this which is the principall,
nay the onely verbe in the fentence. And to prove that *Vigilius* confented to the Synod in condemning the three Chapters, what needed
the Cardinall to cite all, or any one of the Greeke writers ? The very
Acts of the fift Councell doe often and expreffly teftifie this, *Vigilius*
hath oft often by writings, without writing condemned, and anathematized the *Three Chapters.* In the very Synodall fentence, [q] it is faid,
It hath happened that *Vigilius*, living in this City, hath beene prefent

[1] *Ante noviffin. ā*
fpoftolicæ fedis
affenfum. Bar.
an. 546. nu. 38.
itidemq. ejus fuc-
cefforibus licuit,
in ipfius Vigily
abire Decretum.
Bar. an. 553 nu.
231. Quintam
Synodum Apo-
ftolica authorita-
te comprobavit.
an. 554. nu. 7.
[m] *Bar. an. 553.*
nu. 223.
[n] *Bar. an. 554.*
nu. 4.

[o] *Ibid.*

[q] *Act. Conc. 5.*
Coll. 1. pa 520. c.
& Coll. 7. pa.
578. a.
[q] *Collat. 8. pa.*
584. a.

at those things which are noted concerning these Chapters, *& tam sine scriptis, quam in scriptis ea sæpius condemnasse, and to have condemned the same as well by writing as by word.* The whole purpose of the seventh Collation is no other but to shew out of *Vigilius* own writings, that he consented with the Councell in condemning the *three Chapters*, the very letters of *Vigilius*, which were read in that seventh Collation, do clearely witnesse his consent and judgement in condemning those Chapters. The Councell condemnes them, *Vigilius* condemnes them, Doth not *Vigilius* consent to, and with the Synod ? Did he not *per libellum, & literas*, expresse that assent, when his owne Epistles testifie that he condemned those Chapters, as did also the Synod : wherefore of his consent to the Synod there is no doubt. But this consent of his was before the time that the Councell made their Synodall Decree, yea before they assembled in the Synod, it was during the time of the second Period, before mentioned, shortly after his comming to *Constantinople*, untill the Councell met together, all that time he consented in judgement with the Councell, he condemned the Chapters, as the Councell did. But at the time of the Councell, when *Vigilius* should have consented also in making the Synodall *Decree* for condemning of those Chapters, then hee dissented from the Synod and published an *Apostolicall Constitution* in defence of the *Three Chapters*. So he both consented and that by letters, yea by his Decree, with the Synod, and withall he dissented, and that also by his Decree, from the Synod. His consent, which the Synodall Acts doe shew and testifie, *Evagrius* and the rest who saw and therein followed the Acts, report and that truly. His dissent, which his owne *Apostolicall Constitution* kept in their Vaticane doth shew and testifie, & which in likelyhood *Evagrius* saw not, nor knew thereof, they report not, but they deny it not. But for that Baronian consent after the end of the Synod, or after his exile, of that in *Evagrius* and the rest there is no mention, nor any small signification.

    9. It is the precedent consent of *Vigilius*, not that Baronian and subsequent consent, of which *Evagrius* and the rest intreat, which may appeare even by the very words of *Evagrius*. *Vigilius* [1] *per litteras consensit Concilio, non tamen interesse voluit*. He saith not, *Vigilius would not be present at the Councell, but after the end of it hee consented by letters, unto it,* (this is the false and corrupt glosse of *Baronius*) but *Vigilius* consented to the Councell by his letters, but would not be present. His consent by letters was the former, his deniall to come was the later. For when *Evagrius* saith, *consensit, sed noluit interesse*, he plainely sheweth that *Vigilius* might have beene present in the Councell, as well as have consented by his letters, he might, but he would not : now had his consent beene after his returne from exile, that is, an whole yeare after the end of the Councell, *Vigilius* could not possibly, though hee would never so gladly, have beene present in the Councell, nor would *Evagrius* have said, *consensit sed noluit interesse*, but hee should have said, *consensit sed non potuit interesse, hee consented indeed with the Synod, but he could not be present in it,* because when he consented, the Synod was dissolved, and ended a yeare before. The sense in *Nicephorus*

† *Evag. lib. 4. ca. 37.*

is the very same, but his words a little more cleare, *Vigilius*, saith he [f], *etsi scripto interveniente cum Eutichio conveniret, assidere tamen illi noluit*, *although he agreed with Eutichius, by a writing*, (this as it seemes was his Epistle to *Rusticus* and *Sebastianus* read in the Synod) *yet bee would not sit with him in the Councell*. Importing hereby that *Vigilius* might also have sitten with *Eutichius*, when hee consented in doctrine with him, but he would not: which is evidently to bee understood of his precedent, not of any subsequent consent after the end of the Synod. The very same is the meaning of *Photius*, Though [t] *Vigilius* was not forward to come to the sacred assembly, *communem tamen patrum fidem libello confirmavit*, yet he confirmed the same common faith, (marke, the same faith, so he accounts the cause of the *Three Chapters* to be a cause of faith, and the condemning of them to bee the confirming of the faith) by a booke, which booke is the same that *Evagrius* and *Nicephorus* meant, the booke, Epistle, or *Constitution* of *Vigilius*, made before the time of the Councell, and then read therein; but of any confirming that common faith by *Vigilius* after the end of the Synod, *Photius* hath not one syllable.

Nicep. lib. 17. ca. 27.

t Phot. lib. de 7. Synod. in Coic. 5

10. Now whereas the Cardinall [u] adds, that *Græci omnes de consensione Vigilij affirment*, *that all Greeke writers affirme Vigilius to have consented to the Councell*, it is nothing but an untrue, and vaine bragge of *Baronius* to downeface the truth, for *Zonaras* affirmes it not, nor *Cedrenus* (and yet both these are expresly named by the Cardinall to write this) nor *Glicas*, nor *Constantinus Manasses*, nor the Cardinalls owne *Theophanes*. And yet if we should admit them to say the like, or the same with *Evagrius*, *Nicephorus*, and *Photius*, that *Vigilius* did consent to the Synod by a booke or letters; yet what one of all the Greek writers, yea or Latine either, can the Cardinall produce to say that which he doth, that *Vigilius* after the end of the Synod, or after hee was sent into banishment, consented to the Synod? That by his precedent letters, and judiciall sentence he consented to the same faith, which the Synod decreed, is true; this the Cardinall doth, but should not prove; but that by a subsequent consent or writing he approved the Synod after his owne exile, t his none of the Cardinals witnesses affirme, this the Cardinall should, but neither doth nor can prove.

u Bar. an. 554. nu. 4.

11. His second reason is taken from the fact of *Iustinian* in restoreing *Vigilius*. The Emperor, saith he [x], *was most carefull for the condemning of the Three Chapters, and therefore pnnished severely such as withstood his Edict and the Decree of the Synod*: how then could hee have endured *Vigilius* to have beene freed from exile, & to returne into the West, *nisi consensisset*, unlesse he had consented to the Synod? Seeing otherwise *Vigilius* would have stird up all the Bishops in the West against the Emperors Edict, and the Synodall sentence. Now that the Emperor did free *Vigilius* from exile, and permit him to returne to the West, *Baronius* [y] proves that, by *Anastasius* [z], out of whom hee relates, that *the whole Romane Clergie entreated* Narses *that he would be a meanes to the Emperor to restore unto the Vigilius, & the rest who were banished with him*. The Emperor at the entreatie of Narses *sent presently to Gissa, Protonesus, and other places, and called them to him who were banished, and*

x Bar. an. 554. nu. 6.

y An. eodem nu. 1. et an. 553. nu. 222. liquet ex Anastasio Vigilium fuisse in exilium deportatum, &c.
z Anast. in vita Vigilij.

put

a *Vultis habere Vigilium, ut suit, Papa vester? Minusve? Hic habetis Pelagium Archidiaconum &c.* Anaft. ibid.

b *Liquet ex Anaftasio omnes ab exilio pariter revocatos.* Bar. an.553.nu.222

c *Alia nonnulla eidem petenti concessit, & ipso exigente sanctione promulgavit.* Bar. an.554. nu.6.

d *Donis, muneribus, ac privilegys ornatus in Italia redire permissus fuit,* Bin. notis in Conc.5. §. Prafixis.

e *Bar. an.554: nu.6.*

f *Quorum solùm causâ odium conflatum erat, & exilium irrogatam,* Bar. ibid.

g *Theod. hiftor. lib.2.ca.17.*

put it to their choice, whether a *they would have* Vigilius *to be their Pope*, or Pelagius *there prefent among them*: and when they defired *Vigilius, dimifit omnes cum Vigilio, he fent them all* b *home with* Vigilius. Nay the Emperor did not onely reftore him, and fend him home, but granted c divers matters (gifts, rewards, and Priviledges, as Binius d *calleth them*) and at his entreatie publifhed a pragmaticall fanction for the affaires of Italie, as the words of the fanction, Pro petitione Vigilij, doe declare. Hence now doth the Card: make his inference, that abfque e dubio, without all doubt Vigilius was very deare to the Emperor, feeing he granted fuch favours unto him, but there could have beene no friendfhip at all betwixt the, unleffe Vigilius after his returne from exile, had confented to the Synod, and condemned the Three Chapters, feeing f his not confenting thereunto, was the caufe of his banifhment, Thus Baronius : who hath very hanfomely concluded, that abfque dubio, Vigilius after his returne out of exile, confented to the fift Councell. If now wee can clear this reafon, wherein confifts the whole pith of the Cardinals caufe, I well hope that this confent of Vigilius, of which he fo much boafteth, will be acknowledged to bee nothing elfe then a Baronian dreame.

12. And firft admitting for a while the Cardinalls antecedent, the confequent fure is inconfequent. Iuftinian might upon the entreatie of Narfes, fend Vigilius home, though Vigilius had not confented to the Synod after the end thereof. Narfes was a man for his pietie, prudence, fortitude, & felicitie in warre, exceedingly beloved & honored by Iuftinian. They who are converfant in hiftories, are not ignorant that Emperors doe yeeld many times greater matters then the reftoring of Vigilius, at the entreatie of fuch as Narfes was. When the Romane Matrones g (their hufbands not daring to motion fuch a matter) entreated Conftantius to reftore Liberius to his See, from which he was then banifhed, the Emperour, though he was moft violently bent againft Liberius, and had placed an other Bifhop in his See, yet, as Theodoret writeth, fic inflectebatur, hee was fo affected with their entreatie, that he yeelded to their requeft, thinking it fitter that there fhould be two Bifhops at once in Rome, rather then he would feeme fo obdurate and unkinde, as to deny that petition in the time of his triumph. It was as great incongruitie and difproportion in the government of Conftantius an Arian, to reftore Liberius, then a Catholike, as for Iuftinian being a Catholike Emperor, to reftore Vigilius being now an hereticall Bifhop. The hatred of Conftantius to Liberius was farre greater, then Iuftinians againft Vigilius. The parties entreating are fo unequall, that Conftantius feemes to have yeelded onely for popularitie, and to get the opinion of courtifie, they having done nothing to merit fuch favour at his hands: but Narfes had by his valor and late victories, not onely won great honor to Iuftinian, and to the whole Empire, but had freed Italie from the fervitude of the Gothes, and by that meanes, befides many other, had merited the love and favour of Iuftinian, who might have feemed not onely unkind, but unjuft in denying the petition of one fo well deferving.

13. Nay, what if the intreaty of Narfes, and narration of Anaftafius

ſius doe prove the quite contrary to that which *Baronius* from them collects, that *Vigilius* had not conſented to the Synod when hee was reſtored upon that entreaty? *Narſes* did this to gratifie [h] the Romane Clergy, and the Italian Biſhops, who intreated him to bee a meanes for the reſtoring of *Vigilius* unto them. And who, I pray you, were they, or how affected in this cauſe of the *three Chapters*? Truly they were eager in defending of them, and for that cauſe rent and divided from the Eaſterne Churches, as *Baronius* [i] witneſſeth. It had beene no gratifying, but a very heart griefe and vexation to ſuch, to have *Vigilius* the condemner of thoſe Chapters, that is, in their judgement, an heretike, reſtored unto them. It was *Vigilius*, the defender of thoſe Chapters, whom they deſired, for whom *Narſes* intreated, and whom, if any, the Emperour upon his intreaty reſtored; which, by the Anaſtaſian narration, is made very evident, for he [k] ſheweth, how the Emperour upon his ſuggeſtion, *mox miſit juſſiones ſuas, preſently ſent forth his command*, to bring *Vigilius* and the reſt from exile. He ſent not to ſee if they would conſent to the Synod, and upon their conſent to releaſe them; but, without any queſtioning of that matter, hee commands that they, howſoever they ſtood affected, ſhould be free, and brought out of baniſhment: when they were returned, did the Emperour aske them one word, whether they would conſent to the Synod, or no? He did not, but al that he demanded of them was this, *vultis habere* Vigilium, will yee have *Vigilius* to continue your Pope; as hee was before, or will you have *Pelagius*, who is here among you? A demonſtration, that *Vigilius* had not then conſented to the Synod, when the Emperor ſaid this; for there was no cauſe, either to deprive *Vigilius*, or elect any other in his roome, but his perſiſting in hereſie; had he conſented to the Synod, and condemned the *Three Chapters*, the Emperor ſhould have done wrong unto him, to have ſuffered any other to have beene choſen: nay, the See being full, *Pelagius* could not, though all the baniſhed Clergy had deſired it, have beene choſen Biſhop in his ſtead. Seeing then, both the Emperours words, and the anſwer of the Clergy, as *Anaſtaſius* relateth them, doe ſhew, that if they had pleaſed they might lawfully have choſen another Pope; and ſeeing they could not by right have done that, unleſſe *Vigilius* had continued in his pertinacious defence of hereſie; even hereby it may bee perceived, that at his reſtoring he perſiſted in the ſame hereticall minde of which he was before, and that hee had not then conſented to the Synod, nor to the condemning of thoſe *Three Chapters*. So blinded was the Cardinall in this cauſe, that he could not, or rather would not ſee how his owne reaſon, drawne from the intreaty of *Narſes*, and the narration of *Anaſtaſius*, doth quite overthrow the concluſion which by them he intended to confirme.

14. And all this have I ſaid upon ſuppoſall onely of the truth of that narration touching *Narſes* his intreatie, and the Emperors yeelding thereupon, to reſtore *Vigilius* out of exile. But now I muſt adde another anſwere, which I feare will bee much more diſpleaſing to the Cardinal and his friends, and that is, that this whole narration touching the exile of *Vigilius* after the Synod, the intreaty of *Narſes*, the reſtoring

h *Tunc aduna-tus clerus roga-verunt Narſetē, ut rogaret Prin-cipem, &c.* Anaſt. in vita Vig.

i *Cum (Vigili-us) cerneret uni-verſum Orien-tem ab Eccleſia Romana divi-ſum, niſi Synodo conſentiret.* Bar. an. 553. nu. 235

k *Anaſt. in vita Vig.*

storing him from that banishment, and the rest depending thereon, is all untrue, & fictitious, such as hath no ground in the whole world, but onely the Cardinals owne Poeticall pate: For the manifesting whereof I will insist on the two principall points in the Cardinals narration, the untruth of which being declared, all the rest will easily be acknowledged to bee untrue and fabulous.

15. The former concernes the restoring of *Vigilius* out of Banishment. *Baronius*[1] following *Anastasius*, saith, that the Emperour, toge-ther with *Vigilius* restored all the rest who were banished with him, *Dimisit omnes cum* Vigilio; and by name *Pelagius* is expressed to bee one of them; of whom the Emperour then said, *Hic habetis* Pelagium, *you have here* Pelagius: *Vigilius* then with him, by name, among the rest was dismissed home. A very fiction and fable, witnesse whereof *Victor* Bishop of *Tunea*, who then lived, and who himselfe [m], after im-prisonment and whipping was banished into three severall places, for defending the *Three Chapters*; and after that was brought to *Constanti-nople* [n], where hee was an eye witnesse of the most things there hap-pening about this cause. Hee having set downe the time of *Vigilius* death, that he dyed in *Sicily*, in the 16° year after the Coss. of *Basilius*, addeth in the next yeare concerning *Pelagius*, that he, being that yeare called from banishment, which he sustained for defence of the *Three Chapters*, did then condemne them, and then was ordained Bishop of *Rome*, which demonstrateth the vanity of the Anastasian and Baronian tale: how could the Emperor say, You have *Pelagius* here, when *Pelagi-us* was then, and after that in exile? How did the Emperour dismisse them all, and particularly *Pelagius*, when *Vigilius* was sent home, see-ing *Pelagius* remained in exile till *Vigilius* was dead? But that which I principally collect is this: Seeing *Vigilius*, by the Cardinals narration, was not freed from exile, nor consented to the Synod, but at the same time when *Pelagius* was released; and seeing it is certaine, by the te-stimony of *Victor*, that *Vigilius* was not freed, nor consented unto the Synod at that time, (for *Vigilius* was dead before *Pelagius* was relea-sed) it hence certainly ensueth, that *Vigilius* neither was freed from exile, nor at all consented unto the fift Synod after his exile.

16. The other, which is indeed the speciall point, concernes the banishment of *Vigilius* after the end of the Synod, which *Baronius* so often mentioneth, and on which depends the whole fable; this banish-ment being in very deed nothing else than a Baronian fiction; the au-thor, and the onely author whom *Baronius* names for proofe of this banishment, is *Anastasius*: and because the Cardinall in good discre-tion would name the best author, and authority which hee had; him, whose antiquity and name might gaine credit to the narration: it is not to bee doubted but *Anastasius* was the best, most credible, and authentike author, which the Cardinall had for this banishment: of him then *Baronius* [p] saith thus, *Liquet ex* Anastasio Vigilium *in exilium deportatum fuisse*; It is evident by Anastasius, *that* Vigilius *and those who were with him were caried into banishment*. True; that is evident indeed by *Anastasius*: But why did the Cardinall omit the principall point to be proved? why said he not, *Vigilius* to have been caried into banish-ment

l *Bar.*554.*nu.*1.

m *Victor Tun-nensis author hujus operis, post custodias simul et plagas p[ri]mo et secundo exilio egi Mauritaniæ, tertio Alexan-drinæ, pro trium capitulorum defensione. Vict. in Chron. an.*14. *(corrupte legi-tur* 15.*) post Co-sul. Bazily.* n *Isiod. lib. de viris illust. ca.* 25. *ex Ægypto rursus Constan-tinopolin evoca-tus, &c.* d *Corrupte legi-tur* 17. *in Chron. Vict.*

p *Bar. an.* 553. *nu.*2.2.

ment after the end of the Synod, or caried for not consenting with the Synod in their condemning of the *Three Chapters?* why said he not, this is evident by *Anastasius?* Will you be pleased to know the reason herof? It is this, because, *hoc non liquet ex* Anastasio; nay, because, *contrarium liquet ex* Anastasio, *Anastasius* is so farre from saying as the Cardinall doth, that *Vigilius* was banished after the end of the Councell, or for not consenting to the Councell, that hee saith the quite contrary, and contradicteth all that the Cardinall hath said touching that banishment, both for the time, and for the cause thereof. The cause of the Anastasian banishment q of *Vigilius* was, for that hee refused to restore *Anthimus* to the See of *Constantinople,* whence hee was justly ejected by Pope *Agapetus,* and a generall Councell, more than ten r yeares before *Vigilius* came to *Constantinople,* and the time of this Anastasian banishment was two yeares after s *Vigilius* came to *Constantinople,* and while *Theodora* t was alive, which was long before the fist Synod was assembled. This, and no other banishment of *Vigilius* is to be found in *Anastasius;* from this, and no other it is, that *Anastasius* saith, he was freed by the entreaty of *Narses,* remaining an exile untill that time. Now this *ex diametro* fighteth with that exile which *Baronius* hath devised, the time of the Baronian banishment was after the end u of the fist Synod, that is, about five x yeares after the death of *Theodora;* til then *Baronius* wil acknowledge no banishment of *Vigilius.* The cause of the Baronian banishment was not *Anthimus,* nor the restoring of him, but onely y his not yeelding to the fist Synod, and refusing to condemne the *Three Chapters.* So the Cardinals owne witnesse: yea, his onely witnesse is so farre from proving what hee pretends, and affirmes, that upon his narration is demonstrated the quite contrary: For if *Vigilius* was banished in the life time of *Theodora;* as *Anastasius* declareth, and there remained till by *Narses* intreaty he was released; then most certainly was hee not cast into banishment after the end of the fist Synod, nor for refusing to consent thereunto; which is the fiction of *Baronius.*

16. And for more evidence that the same which I said is the banishment by *Anastasius,* I might alleage *Bellarmine* z, and others, but omitting them, let us heare that worthy author, to whom *Binius* a referres us concerning this matter; *Nicholas Sanders,* He o thus writeth, *That* Vigilius *was sent into banishment, because he would not restore* Anthimus: *the Romane Pontificall* (so he cals the booke of *Anastasius*) *doth testifie;* and besides it, *Aimonius, Paulus Diaconus, Marianus Scotus, Platina, Blondus, Petrus de Natalibus, Martinus Polonus, Sabellicus,* and it may be gathered out of *Nicephorus.* Thus *Sanders:* who might have added *Sigebert* c, who placeth his banishmēt divers years before the fist Councel, *Albo* d *Floriacensis,* who hath the same words with *Anastasius, Nauclerus* d, *Rhegino* e, *Hermanus* f *Cōtractus, Gotofridus* g *Viterbiensis, Otho Frisingensis* h, *Palmerius* i, their owne *Genebrard* k, *Stapleton* l, and many others: These following *Anastasius,* relate the cause of his banishmēt to have bin the not restoring of *Anthimus;* & the time, before the death of the Empresse *Theodora.* Nor can I finde so much as one, either an-

f Herm. an. 547. g Gotof. an. 527. h Otho an. 528. i Palm. in Chr. an. 557. k Genth. an. 537. l Stapl. Counterbl. ca. 19.

q *Per biennium fuere contentiones de Anthimo, sed Vigil. nullatenus voluit consentire, &c. Anast. in vit. Vig.*

r *Conc. illud sub Menna, ubi Anthimus est depositus, habitum est an. 536. Bar. illo an. nu. 72. Vigil. venit Constantinopolin an. 547. Bar. illo a. nu. 26.*

s *Per biennium, &c. Anast. loc. cit.*

t *Non fecerunt me, ut video, venire ad se Iustinian: et Theodora, sed Dioclesianus et Eleutheria. Anast. Ibid.*

u *Bar. an. 553. nu. 221. et seq.*

x *Nam Theodora obijt an. 548. Bar. eo an. nu. 24 Cōc. 5. b: bilii an. 553. Bar. eo an.*

y *Pontifex (Vigilius) non aliam ob causam in exilium actus est, nisi quod 5. Synodum minimè probare voluisset. Bar. an. 554. nu. 4.*

z *Quo circa squia voluit Anthimum restituere) ab irata Imperatrice, in exilium missus fait Vigilius, & miserè vexatus usq; ad mortem. Bell. lib. 4. de Pont. Rom. ca. 10 § Corrigit.*

a *De Vigilio et tota ejus causa vid Sanderum. Bin. not. in vit. Vigil. pa. 478. b.*

b *Sand. lib. 7. de visib. Monarch. ad an. 537.*

c *Sig. an. 540.*

d *Alb. Flor. in vita Vig.*

d *Naucl. an. 540*

e *Rheg. an. 559.*

cient or later writer, who saith, with *Baronius*, that hee was banished after the fift Councell, and for refusing to consent unto it; what a rare Poeticall conceit hath the Cardinall, who can make such a noble discourse of that fictitious banishment, and commend it as an historicall narration; for the warrant of which he had not so much as one writer, (and one is a small number) ancient or late, upon whose credit and authoritie he might report it; and for that one witnesse *Anastasius*, whom he nameth, he is so farre from testifying it; that he doth clearely testifie the quite contrary; yea, *Baronius* himselfe was not ignorant hereof, but knew right well *Anastasius* to referre [m] the beating of *Vigilius*, his flight to *Chalcedon*, the other indigne usage set downe by him, and his exile, to the time while *Theodora* lived; and therefore hee taxeth *Anastasius*, for confounding those things, and referring them to that time, whereas himselfe placeth them after the death [n] of *Theodora*: And yet for all this, though he knew *Anastasius* to teach the quite contrary, yet was not the Cardinall afraid, nor ashamed to alleage *Anastasius* for a witnesse, that *Vigilius* was cast into banishment after the fift Councell, and for refusing to consent unto it, and to say of this banishment, *Liquet ex* Anastasio, *it is clearly knowne out of* Anastasius; whereas not that, but the quite contrarie, *Liquet ex* Anastasio.

17. From hence now there issueth another consequent to bee remembred. It is agreed by all, who mention any banishment of *Vigilius*, and it is confessed also by *Baronius*, that *Vigilius* was but one banished, and from that one freed by the intreaty of *Narses*: Now that one cannot bee the Baronian banishment; for of it there is no proofe at all to bee found, no one author to witnesse it, but the Cardinall and his owne αυτος ιπα, which in matters of fact done some thousand and more yeares before the Cardinall was borne, is of no worth at all, nor can be esteemed ought but one of his owne dreames and figments. Againe, that one cannot bee the Anastasian banishment, which is said to happen before the death of *Theodora*, more than foure yeares before the fift Councell; for it is certaine by the Acts of the fift Synod [o], that *Vigilius* at that time was at *Constantinople*; yea, that untill then he lived and dwelt [p] at *Constantinople*. Seeing then *Vigilius* was neither banished before the Councell, as *Anastasius* saith, nor banished after the Councell, as *Baronius* saith, it followeth, which indeed is very truth, that *Vigilius* was not at all banished, but all which is reported of his banishment, and all that depends thereon, is fictitious and Poeticall, devised by two *Bibliothecarij* to his Holinesse; the former, and precedent to the Councell, is an Anastasian; the other, following the Councell, is a Barbarian Poeme; but both Poems both fabulous and Æsopicall narrations.

18. And truly, might wee be allowed to imitate the Cardinals Arte in disputing, this matter would easily be made plaine. There is one Topicke place of arguing *à testimonio negativè*, which is very familiar to *Baronius* in his *Annals* [q], and it is defended by *Gretzer* in his Apology [r] for *Baronius*; let us take but one example, and that also in this our present cause concerning *Vigilius*. There is in *Anastasius* [s] a narration, how *Vigilius* was violently puld away from *Rome*

by

---

m Hac plane tempore accidisse noscuntur, quæ Anastasius jungit, imo confudit cum prioribus, quæ acciderunt vivente adhuc Theodora. Bar. an. 552. nu. 8.

n Cetera quæ sequuntur (in Anastasio) post obitum Theodoræ contigerunt. Bar. an. 547. nu. 17. Inter illa cetera est Vigilij exilium.

o Conc. 5. Coll. 1. 2. 3. et 8.
p Contigit Vigilium in hac regia urbe degentem, omnibus interesse, &c. Coll. 2. pa. 584. a.
q Vid. Bar. an. 774. nu. 10 et 11.
r Respondissemus hanc argumentandi rationem (ab authoritate negativè) in eis præsertim quæ ad historiam spectant, non esse prorsus infirmam et elumbem. Gretz. Apol. pro Bar. ca.1
s Peritius.
s Anast. in vit. Vigil.

by *Anthemius Scribonius*, ſent thither for that purpoſe, by the Empreſſe; how he was apprehended in the   Church,   thruſt into the
ſhippe; how the Romanes followed reviling [t] him, curſing him, and
caſting ſtones and dung at him, praying that a miſchiefe might goe
with him. Thus it is hiſtorified by *Anaſtaſius*. The like is mentioned
by many others, who borrowed it out of *Anaſtaſius*; by *Aimonius* *, by
the *Hiſtoria Miſcella* [u], going under the name of *Paulus Diaconus*, though
it be not his; by *Marianus* [x] *Scotus*, by *Hermanus* [y] *Contractus*, by *Sige-*
bert [z], by *Luitprandus* [a] *de vitis Pontificum*, as the booke is called; by *Al-*
bo [b] *Floriacenſis*, by *Platina* [c], by *Conrade* [d], by *Nauclerus* [e], by *Marti-*
nus [f] *Polonus*, by *Blondus* [g], by *Krantzius* [h], by *Sigonius* [i], & others. Heare
now the Cardinals cenſure of this narration of *Anaſtaſius*, and the reſt
who followed him; *Aperti mendacij* [k] *redarguitur Anaſtaſius; Anaſta-*
ſius is convicted of a manifeſt lye herein; and how prove you that, my
Baronius? res adeo ignominioſa, ſo ignominious a matter as this is, could not
have beene unknowne to the Authors, who writ moſt accurately the
Acts of their times, and thoſe were *Facundus* and *Procopius*, the Cardinall names no moe: from the ſilence and omiſſion of this matter in
them two, he concludes *Anaſtaſius* to be a lyar; and his narration, ſe-
conded by many moe, to be a lye.

19. Let now but the like liberty of diſputing *à Teſtimonio negative*,
be allowed unto us, and the Baronian baniſhment (to begin with that)
muſt be rejected, baniſhed, and ſet in the ſame ranke with that lye of
Anaſtaſius; for thus wee may argue: This baniſhment of *Vigilius* after
the end of the fift Councell, and for refuſing to conſent unto it, is
neither mentioned by *Victor* Biſhop of *Tunen*, nor by *Liberatus*, nor by
Evagrius, nor by *Procopius*, who all then lived, (and in relating the affaires of the Church, were full out as exact as *Facundus* and *Procopius*)
nor by *Photius*, nor by *Zonaras*, nor by *Cedrenus*, nor by *Nicephorus*; nor
by *Glicas*, nor by *Conſtantinus Manaſſes*, nor by *Anaſtaſius*, nor by *Paulus*
Diaconus, nor by *Aimonius*, nor by *Luitprandus*, nor by *Albo Floriacen-*
ſis; nor by *Otho Friſingenſis*, nor by *Conrade* Abbat of *Vrſberge*, nor by
Hermanus Contractus, nor by *Sigebert*, nor by *Lambertus Scaſſuaburgen-*
ſis, nor by *Martinus Polonus*, nor by *Gotofridus Viterbienſis*, nor by *Al-*
bertus Stadeſis, nor by *Vernerus*, nor by *Marianus Scotus*, nor by *Rhegino*,
nor by *Bede*, nor by *Platina*, nor by *Nauclerus*, nor by *Tritemius*, nor by
Krantzius, nor by the *magnum Chronicon Belgicum*, nor by the *Chronicon*
Reicherſpergenſe, nor by *Chronico Germanicum per Monachū Herveldenſem*,
nor by *Chronica Compendioſa*, or *Compilatio Chronologica*, nor by *Blon-*
dus, nor by *Sabellicus*, nor by *Aventinus*, nor by *Huldericus Mutius*, nor
by *Sigonius*, nor by *Palmerius*, nor by *Kurauza*, nor by *Papirius Maſſoni-*
us, nor by *Genebrard*, nor by *Sanders*, nor by *Stapleton*; and I challenge
the welwillers of *Baronius*, by that love they beare unto him, & his e-
ſtimatiō; to name if they can but any one writer before *Baronius*, who
affirmeth *Vigilius* to have beene baniſhed after the Synod; for not
conſenting unto it, that therby it may be knowne, that their great Annaliſt playes the Hiſtorian, and not the Poet, in relating the Eccleſiaſticall affaires of the Church: Or if they can at any time doe this,
(which I am verily perſwaded they neither will, · nor ever can per-
formē)

Z   formē)

t *Populus cæpit*
jactare poſt eum
lapides, fuſtes, et
cacabos, et dice-
re, Fames tua
tecum, male in-
venias, ubi va-
dis, &c.
* *Aim.lib.2.de*
geſt.Franc.ca.32
u *Hiſt.miſc. lib.*
16.
x *Mar.an. 553.*
y *Her. an. 547.*
z *Sig.an.543.*
a *Luitp.in vita*
Vigil.
b *Alb.in vita*
Vig.
c *Plat.in vita*
Vig.
d *Conr.Ab.Vrſ-*
per.an.527.
e *Nauc.an.540.*
f *Mart.in vita*
Vig.
g *Blond.Dec.1.*
lib.6.
h *Krant.Met.*
lib.2.
i *Sigeb. lib.19.*
de Occ. Imp.
an.545.
k *Bar.an.546.*
nu.54.

forme) yet seeing none of all these doe mention that banishment; truly if *Baronius*, from the silence of two writers, might conclude against *Anastasius*, that he was a lyar in the former narration, I thinke none will deny; but *à fortiori*, it will follow; that seeing more than two score are silent in this matter, it may farre more justly bee said, *aperti mendacij redarguitur*, which is the Cardinals owne doome and words that hee bestoweth on *Anastasius*: and here much more fitly may the Cardinals reason take place, *res adeo ignominiosa, so ignominious a matter*; nay, so glorious a peece of martyrdome on the Popes part, as the banishment and cruell persecution of the Pope, the chiefe Bishop in the world, for such a cause, as for not assenting to the Synod, could not have bin unknowne unto those writers, who most diligently prosecute the affaires of their times, and such as concerned the Church: Nay, from the most of these wee may draw an affirmative argument also, and reason, more strongly than the Cardinall doth in his disputes. *Anastasius, Aimonius, Diaconus, Platina*, and divers moe of the forenamed authors, to the number at least of twenty, affirme, *Vigilius* was banished before the Synod, and in the life time of *Theodora*; and withall teach but one banishment of *Vigilius*, and therefore they not onely are silent of that which the Cardinal saith, but they say the quite contrary unto him; and so, both by their silence, and by their speech refute that, as an untruth, which the Cardinal so positively and historically narrateth.

20. Now, as the negative kinde of arguing disproves the *Baronian*, so doth it also the *Anastasian* banishment, and forcibly concludes, that *Vigilius* was not at all banished, either before, or after the Councel; for there is no banishmēt at all of *Vigilius* mentioned, either by *Victor*, or by *Liberatus*, or by *Evagrius*, or by *Procopius*, who all lived & writ at that time, or by *Photius*, or by *Zonaras*, or by *Cedrenus*, or by *Glicas*, or by *Constantinus Manasses*, or by *Nicephorus*, or by *Aimonius* (though *Sanders* falsely affirmed them to teach this) or by *Luitprandus*, or by *Bede*, or by *Krantzius*, or by *Mutius*, or by *Papirius Massonius*, or by *Caranza*, besides others. Adde now here againe the Cardinals words, *Res adeo ignominiosa*, surely so ignominious and shamefull a fact, as the banishing of a Pope, could not have beene unknowne to those who writ (as exactly as *Facundus* and *Procopius*) the Ecclesiasticall affaires, and occurrents in their times; and therfore seeing these so many, so exact writers, mention not that *Anastasian* banishment of *Vigilius*, it may be rightly concluded, that *Anastasius* therin *aperti mendicij redarguitur*; or if none but the Cardinall may give the lye to *Anastasius*; yet, confessing his narration to be untrue, let us leave that as a priviledge of the Cardinals, that he alone shal bestow lies, for liveries, upon *Anastasius*. Nay, seeing none of these Writers mention any banishment at all of *Vigilius*, it must further be concluded from their silence, that *Vigilius* neither first nor last, neither before, nor after the Synod was banished, but that the whole narration, touching his banishment, is a meere fiction and fable, devised, partly by *Anastasius*, and partly by *Baronius*.

21. Which may much rather be affirmed, considering that *Victor*, who

who was himselfe exiled, and brought to *Constantinople*, is not onely
carefull, but even curious; (that I say not proud) in recounting the most
eminent persons, specially Bishops, which were either deposed, or
imprisoned, or banished about this cause of the *three Chapters*, either
before or after the Synod. In this ranke he [1] nameth *Benenatus* Bishop
of *Iustinianea*, *Zoilus* Patriarch of *Alexandria*, *Reparatus* Bishop of *Carthage*, *Verecundus* Bishop of *Nica*, *Macarius* Bishop of *Ierusalem*, *Rusticus* a Romane Deacon, *Fœlix* a Monke of *Guilla*, *Frontinus* Bishop of
Salane, *Theodosius* Bishop of *Sebarsuse*, himselfe being Bishop of *Tunen*,
and *Pelagius* then a Deacon, but afterwards Bishop of *Rome*, and successor to *Vigilius*.   Had *Baronius* this negative argument *à testimonio*
in hand, how would hee insult, and even triumph in it? how easily
would he perswade the world, that certainly Bishop *Victor*, who by
name, and so particularly, recounteth meaner Bishops, yea, Deacons
and Monkes, who suffered banishment for this cause, would never
have omitted the Prince of Bishops, had hee beene exiled for it, as
they were. That one example had graced the defenders of the *Three
Chapters*, more than twenty, nay, than twenty hundred besides, seeing
by this it would have beene evident, that the Oracle of the world, the
infallible Iudge had sealed the truth of that cause with his glorious banishment, which is a kinde of Martyrdome. *Anastasius*, *Diaconus*, *O-
bo*, and all the rest, who say he was banished, should have had the lye
an hundred times at the Cardinals hands, for saying that he was banished, either before or after the Councell, rather than Bishop *Victor*, who then lived at *Constantinople*, and was fellow-partner in those
troubles and banishments, should have beene thought either ignorant or forgetfull to expresse that banishment of *Vigilius*, had there
beene truly any at all.

22. Thus from the Cardinals owne Topicks it is concluded, that
both the Anastasian, & the Baronian banishments are both fictitious:
Nor can I find what they can except against our Negative Argument,
wch will not more forcibly refute many of the Cardinals disputes, un-
esse perhaps, as *Gretzer* [m] answers in defence of *Baronius*, in another
cause, that the old Logick rule, *Ex puris negativis nihil sequi*, holds only
in Syllogismes, but not in Enthymems (for which subtilty I doubt not
but the very Sophisters in our Vniversities will soundly deride him)
so in this they will say, which, with as good warrant and reason, they
may; that an agument *à testimonio negativè*, holds onely in the Cardinals Annals, or, when somewhat is to be proved for the Pope, or his
cause; but it never holds when ought makes against the Pope, and the
Cardinall; or makes for the Protestants, and their cause.

23. But if *Anastasius*, in this narration be fabulous, what shall wee
say of *Aimonius*, and al those other Writers, who mention this banishment of *Vigilius*, as well as doth *Anastasius*? What else can bee said,
then that which *Ierome* [n] saith of divers of the ancient Writers? Before
that Southerne Devill *Arius* arose at *Alexandria*, *innocenter quædam, &
minus cautè loquuti sunt*; the ancients spake certaine things in simplicitie,
and not so warily, which cannot abide the touch, nor avoide the reprehension of perverse men: Or that which Saint *Austen* [o] observes in
himselfe,

Z 2

Marginal notes:

[1] *Vict. in Chron. an. 8. post Coss. Bas.*

[m] *Gretz. Apol. pro Baron. 1. § Respondet.*

[n] *Hier. Apol. 1. adver. Ruff. pa. 223.*

[o] *Aug. lib. 3. de doct. Christ. cap. 33.*

himselfe, and *Tyconius; Non erat expertus hanc haeresin; Tyconius* had not to deale with this heresie of the Pelagians, as I have said: It hath made us *multò vigilantiores, diligentioresque;* much more diligent, and vigilant, in scanning of this point, than *Tyconius* was, who had no enemy to stir up his diligence: Right so it fals out betwixt those Writers, and us of this age. *Aimonius, Otho, Platina,* and the rest found the banishment of *Vigilius,* and much like stuffe, as it is historied in *Anastasius:* they, in simplicitie and harmelesse innocency, tooke it upon his credit. The question about the Popes *Cathedrall Infallibility,* about *Vigilius heretical Constitution,* and such like controversies, were not moved in their dayes, and therefore they spake of these things, *innocenter, & minùs cautè,* as *Ierome* saith of the Fathers; and because they were not distrustfull of *Anastasius,* they writ not so warily of these matters, as others, whose industry, by the manifold frauds of *Baronius,* as of another *A. rius,* hath beene whetted, and they compelled to sift the truth more narrowly than they, wanting opposites and oppugners, did: It fell out to them as it did to *Ierome* himselfe. *Ruffinus* had set [p] out a book in defence of *Origen,* under the name of *Pamphilus* the Martyr: [p] *Ierome* at the first, and for divers yeares, beleeved [q] the booke to have beene indeed written by *Pamphilus,* as *Ruffinus* said it was: *Credidi* [r] *Christiano, Credidi Monacho:* I never dreamed, that such an horrible wickednesse, as to forge writings, and cal them by the name of Martyrs, could come from a Christian, from a Monke, from *Ruffinus:* but when the question about *Origen* was once set on foote, *Ierome* then sought [s] out every corner, every Copie, every Library that hee could come to, and so discovered the whole forgery. The very like hapned to *Otho, Platina,* and the rest; they found this fabulous narration of the banishment of *Vigilius,* and the consequents upon it, in the booke of *Anastasius,* the Writer of the Popes lives, of the Pontificall, the keeper of the Popes Library, a man of great name and note for learning, one in high favour with the Popes of his time; they never suspected or dreamed that such a man, a Christian, a Monke, that *Anastasius* would deale so perfidiously, and record such horrible untruths: But now, the question about *Anastasius* credit, and the cause of *Vigilius,* which was not moved in their dayes, being sifted and come to the skanning, the whole forgery and falshood of *Anastasius* is made evident to the world, both in this, and in a number the like narrations. *Anastasius* is not the man the world tooke him for; his writings are full of lyes and fictions: Not the Legendaur more fabulous than *Anastasius;* hee for a long time was the Master of the Popes Mint; by his meanes the royall stampe of many golden Fathers, yea, of some Councels also, and infinite historicall narrations, was set upon Brasse, Lead, and most base metals; and then being brought, like so many *Gibeonites* in old Coates, and mouldy coverings, *Anastasius* gave them an high place, and honourable entertainment in the Popes Librarie, and with them ever since hath the Church of God beene pestered; they past for currant among men delighted in darknesse, and errours, such as had no need to bring them to the touch; but the light hath now manifested them, and made both them and their author to be detested.

24. You

Marginal notes:

[p] *Vnus sub nomine Pamphili à te editus est, et; eadem quae sub Pamphili nomine à te ficta sunt. Hier. Apol. 2. Cont. Ruff. pa. 226.*

[q] *Inter caeteros translatores posui et hunc librum à Pamphilo editum, ita putans esse, ut à te et tuis discipulis fuerat, divulgatum. Ibid.*

[r] *Hier. Apol. 3. contra Ruff. pa. 228.*

[s] *Hier. locis citat.*

24. You see now the weaknesse, nay the nullity of the Cardinalls reason; even of his *Achilles*, drawne from the Emperours fact, in restoring or freeing him from exile; which he would never have done, unlesse he had consented to the Synod. For, seeing we have proved that *Vigilius* was not at all banished, it clearly thence ensueth, that neither *Narses* entreated to have him freed from exile, neither did the Emperour upon that entreaty free him from exile, neither did *Vigilius* consent to the Synod after his exile, and all the other consequents, which upon this foundation of *Vigilius* his exile the Cardinall builds like so many Castles in the ayre, they all of themselves doe now fall to the ground: and which I specially observe, it hence followeth, that *Vigilius* did never after the end of the fift Councell consent unto it, or to the condemning of the *Three Chapters*, either by his *Pontificall* decree, or by his *personall* profession: for the Cardinall assures us, and delivers it as a truth, which of necessity [t] must bee granted, that his consent, (whether personall or pontificall) was at no other time, but when he was loosed out of banishment.

t *Necesse est affirmare. Bar. an. 554. nu. 4.*

25. Now at that time it neither was nor could be, for there was never any such time; nor was hee at all banished, and therefore upon the Cardinals owne words we are assured that *Vigilius* after the end of the Synod never revoked his *Constitution* published in defence of the *Three Chapters*, never after that time condemned the *Three Chapters*, or consented to the Synod, either by any pontificall, or so much as by a personall profession, but that hee still persisted in his hereticall defence of the same Chapters, and subject to that censure of *Anathema*, which the fift Councell denounced against all the defenders of those Chapters.

26. Some perhaps will marvell, or demand how it should come to passe, that the Emperour, who as wee have shewed was so rigorous and severe in imprisoning, banishing, and punishing the defenders of the *Three Chapters*, and such as yeelded not to the Synod, should wink at *Vigilius* at this time, who was the chiefe and most eminent of them all: which doubt *Baronius* also [u] moveth, saying, he who published his Edict against such as contradicted him, *Num Vigilio pepercit*, may wee thinke he would spare *Vigilius*, and not banish him who set forth a Constitution against the Emperours Edict? *Minime quidem:* Truly the Emperour would never spare him, saith the Cardinall. Yes, the Emperour both would and did spare him. Belike the Cardinall measures *Iustinian* by his owne irefull and revengefull minde. Had the Cardinall beene crossed and contradicted, nothing but torture, exile, or fire from heaven to consume such rebells, would have appeased his rage. *Iustinian* was of a farre more calme, and therefore more prudent spirit: *Vigilius* deserved, and the Emperour might in justice for his pertinacious resisting the truth, have inflicted upon him either imprisonment, or banishment, or deposition, or death. It pleased him to doe none of all these, nor to deale with the Pope according to his demerits. *Iustinian* saw that *Vigilius* was but a weake and silly man, one of no constancy and resolution, a very wethercocke in his judgement concerning causes of faith: that hee had said and gainsayd the same

u *Bar. an. 553. nu. 222.*

things,

things, and then by his *Apostolicall* authority judicially defined both his
sayings being contradictory, to be true; and truths of the Catholike
faith: the Emperour was more willing to pity this imbecility of his
judgement, than punish that fit of perversenesse which then was come
upon him. Had *Vigilius* beene so stiffe and inflexible as *Victor*, as *Liberatus*, as *Facundus* were, whom no reason, nor perswasion would induce to yeeld to the truth, its not to be doubted but hee had felt the
Emperours indignation as well as any of them. But *Vigilius* like a
wise man tooke part with both, he was an *Ambodexter*, both a defender, and a condemner of the *three Chapters*, both on the Emperours
side, and against him : and because hee might bee reckoned on either
side, having given a judiciall sentence as well for condemning the *three*
Chapters, as for defending them : it pleased the Emperour to take him
at the best, and ranke him among the condemners; at least to winke at
him as being one of them, and not punish him among the defenders
of those Chapters.

27. Nor could the Emperour have any way provided better for
the peace and quiet of the Church, than by such connivence at *Vigilius*, and letting him passe as one of the condemners of those Chapters;
The banishing of him would have hardned others, and that far more
than his consent after punishment would have gained: the former, men
would have ascribed it to judgement; the latter, to passion, and wearinesse of his exile. But now accounting him as a condemner of the
Three Chapters, if any were led by his authority and judgement, the
Emperor could shew them, Loe here you have the judiciall sentence
of the Pope for condemning the *three Chapters* : if his authority were
despised by others, then his judiciall sentence in defence of the Chapters could doe no hurt : and why should the Emperor banish him if
he did no hurt to the cause ? nay it was in a manner necessary for the
Emperour to winke at him, as at a condemner of the *three Chapters* :
for he had often testified to the Councell, that *Vigilius* had condemned both by words and writings those Chapters, hee sent the Popes
owne letters to the Synod, to declare and testifie the same : those letters as well of the Emperour as of the Pope testifying this, were inserted into the Synodall Acts ˣ. Had the Emperour banished *Vigilius*
for not condemning those Chapters, his owne act in punishing *Vigilius* had seemed to crosse and contradict his owne letters, and the Synodall Acts. If *Vigilius* be a condemner of the Chapters, as you say,
and the Synodall Acts record that he is, why doe yee banish him for
not condemning those Chapters ? If *Vigilius* bee justly banished as a
defender of those Chapters, how can the Emperours letters and Synodall Acts be true, which testifie him to be one of the condemners of
those Chapters ? So much did it concerne the Emperors honour, and
credit of the Synod, that *Vigilius* should not be banished at that time.
Vigilius had sufficient punishment that he stood now a convicted, condemned, and anathematized heretike by the judgement of the whole
and holy generall Councell: but for any banishment, imprisonment,
or other corporall punishment, the Emperour in his wisedome, in his
lenity thought fit to inflict none upon him. Onely he stayed him at

Con-

x *Conc.5.Coll.1.*
& 7.

Constantinople for one, or as *Victor* saith, for moe yeares after the Synod, to the end that before he returned, the Synodall sentence and Acts of the Councell being every where divulged, and with them, nay in them the judgement of *Vigilius* in condemning those Chapters as the Synod did, might settle if it were possible, the mindes of men in the truth, or at least serve for an Antidote against that poison, which either from the contrary constitution, or his personall presence when he should returne, could proceed.

28. And by this is easily answered all that the Cardinall and *Binius* collect from those great offices, gifts, rewards, and priviledges with which the Emperor graced and decked *Vigilius*, and so sent him home: which the Cardinall thinkes the Emperour would never have done, unlesse *Vigilius* had consented to the Synod, and condemned the *three Chapters*. Truly these men can make a mountaine of a mole-hill. There is no proofe in the world that *Vigilius* was so graced at his returne: no nor that the Emperour bestowed any gifts or rewards upon him at all. That which the Emperour did was the publishing of a pragmaticall sanction, wherein are contained divers very wholesome lawes, and good orders for the government of *Italy*, and the Provinces adjoyning: The date of the sanction is in August, in the eight and twenty yeare of *Iustinian*, and thirteene after the Cons. of *Basilius*, which was the next yeare after the Councell. But that *Vigilius* at that time returned, there is no solid proofe; and *Victor* [y] who then lived, and was present at *Constantinople*, puts the death of *Vigilius* in the 31. yeare of *Iustinian*, or 16. after *Basilius*, who yet by all mens account (who write of his returne) returned from *Constantinople* either in the same, or in the next yeare before he dyed. So uncertaine, and by *Victors* account unlikely it is, that *Vigilius* at his returne home was *ornatus muneribus, donis, officiis*, and *privilegiis*, as they [z] pompously set out the matter. Now it is true that the Emperour ordered and decreed those matters upon the entreaty of *Vigilius*: for so the words *pro petitione Vigilij*, doe make evident: but that either *Vigilius* entreated, or the Emperour granted this upon any entreaty which he made, either after his return out of exile, (which certainly he did not) or after the end of the Synod, or at the time of his returne (al which are the Cardinals tales without any proofe) none of the Cardinalls friends will bee ever able to make cleare. And for my owne part, till I see some reason to the contrary, I cannot otherwise thinke, but that this petition was made by *Vigilius* some three or foure yeares before the Councell; at which time *Vigilius* consented wholly with the Emperor, was in great grace and favour with him. And I am hereunto induced by that which *Procopius* [a] expresseth: How in the 14. yeare of the Gothicke war, which is the 23. of *Iustinian*; when *Totilas* and the Gothes began to win againe divers parts of *Italy*, which *Belisarius* had before recovered, *Vigilius* and divers *Italians* and *Romanes*, who were then at *Constantinople, submissius & enixius postulabant ab Imperatore, did in very submisse and earnest manner entreat the Emperour*, that he would reduce all *Italy* into his subjection. Now it is very likely that together with this petition they signified divers matters to the Emperour, which were behoove-

full

[y] *Vict. in Chron. an. 16. (corruptè legitur 17.) post Coss. Basilij*

[z] *Bar. an. 554. nu. 6. & Bin. Not. in Conc. 5. §. Prestitit.*

[a] *Proc. lib. 3. de Bell. Goth. pa. 393.*

full for his government in the Westerne parts: and this the Emperors answer then made unto them imports; who, as *Procopius* addeth, answered them, *Italiam sibi curæ fore,* that hee would have a care of Italy: but for that time hee was busie in composing the differences about Christian doctrines. The fift Synod then being ended, and all those Ecclesiasticall affaires concluded, nor that onely, but *Totilas* and *Teias* being both vanquished, and so the whole dominion of Italy being recovered by the victorious *Narses*, the Emperour in his 28. yeare, which was next after the Synod, performed that promise which hee had made before to *Vigilius* and the other Italians, and according to their request disposed and ordered divers matters which in that sanction are set downe.

29. Now if the words of the Sanction have respect (as I verily thinke they have) to that time, then all that *Baronius* collecteth from granting that sanction, and those priviledges upon the petition of *Vigilius* after his returne from exile, or after the Synod, are meere fancies and dreames. Or if it were admitted (whereof I can find no proofe at all) that *Vigilius* made, and the Emperour granted unto him this petition after the end of the Councell, yet will it not hence follow that *Vigilius* then consented to the Synod; for as wee have before declared, the Emperour was not so eager, nor rigorous against *Vigilius*, but that upon his entreaty hee might grant to establish those Lawes, which being in themselves so commodious and behoovefull, he without any entreaty, upon the consideration of those matters, would in all likelihood have enacted. And so every joynt of the Cardinalls second reason (wherein consists the very pith of his cause) drawne from the fact of *Iustinian*, in restoring him from exile, and dismissing him home with gifts and priviledges, being now fully dissolved by that which hath beene said, it remaineth cleere, that notwithstanding all which the Cardinall hath yet brought, there appeares no proofe nor token that *Vigilius* any time after the end of the Councell, either by his publike decree, as the Cardinall boasteth, or so much as by his personall profession, consented to the Synod, and the condemning of the *Three Chapters*.

b *Bar.an.*554.
nu.5.
c *Liber.ca.*22.

30. His third [b] and last reason is drawne from those darke words of *Liberatus* [c], where he saith, *that Vigilius dyed, being afflicted by that heresie (of the Eutycheans) but he was not crowned.* Before wee examine the Cardinalls reason grounded hereon, let us first in a word observe the Cardinalls honest dealing with *Liberatus*. In that very same chapter, and in the words next before that sentence which the Cardinall alledgeth, *Liberatus* setsdowne the Epistle and profession of *Vigilius*, wherein he defendeth the *Eutychean* heresie, and anathematizeth all who hold two natures in Christ as the Councell of *Chalcedon* had defined. Of that Epistle *Liberatus* witnesseth that it is the Epistle of *Vigilius*, and was truly written by him. *Baronius* seeing that to tend to the disgrace of *Vigilius*, that the Pope should be an heretike, an Eutychean, and should accurse all that are not such, what saith he for this matter? Truly he contemnes and rejects the testimonie of *Liberatus*; *The Epistle* [d] *is not the writing of Vigilius, it is an Imposter, a forged writing,*

d *Bar.an.*538.
nu.15.

ting, a counterfeit: notwithstanding all that *Liberatus* saith: So if *Liberatus* say ought distastfull to the Cardinals palate, *Liberatus* is a witnesse of no worth, he is utterly to be contemned, to be rejected. But if in the next words *Liberatus* say ought that seemeth to favour the Cardinalls fancy, *Liberatus* then is a worthy witnesse, you may not take any exception against *Liberatus*, if he say that *Vigilius*, when hee dyed, had consented to the fift Synod, you must beleeve him. Some would thinke this to be scarce currant dealing with his own witnesse, to make him sometimes more then a thousand, sometimes lesse then a Cypher, but such are almost all the Cardinalls witnesses, they speak not so much for him in one place, as they doe against him in others, nor is he so willing to accept them in one, as he is ready to reject the in another. If *Liberatus* be to bee credited, why doth the Cardinall reject him? If he be not to be credited, why doth the Cardinall alleage him?

31. Thus one might if he listed, elude his proofe, and make a little sport with the Cardinalls Counters. But I will let the words of *Liberatus* stand in their best value; and to see the Cardinals deduction the better, wee must consider the whole sentence of *Liberatus*, which is this; *Vigilius* writing these things (to wit, that *hereticall Epistle*, in defence of *Eutycheanisme*) and that closely, to heretikes, continued fitting, (in the See of *Rome*) In whom was fulfilled that testimony of *Salomon, they shall eate the fruit of their owne way*, and they shall bee filled with their owne Counsells. *Ab ipsa haresi afflictus* Vigilius, *nec coronatus, qualem vita terminum suscepit, notum est omnibus: Vigilius being afflicted by that heresie, but not crowned, how hae ended his life, every man can tell.* Thus *Liberatus*. In which words as you see, there is no mention at all either of *Vigilius* his going into banishment, or returning out of banishment, or of his defending the *three Chapters*, or of his condemning the same Chapters, or of the Emperours either casting him into, or releasing him from exile, or of the fift Councell, or of the end thereof; and yet out of these words will *Baronius* like a very skilfull Chymick extract, both that *Vigilius* after the end of the fift Councell was banished for defending the *Three Chapters*, and after that banishment, consented to the Synod, and to condemne the *three Chapters*. And see I pray you how the Chymick distills this. If *Liberatus*, saith he [e], being one of those who fought for the *Three Chapters*, had found *Vigilius, perstantem in sententia usque ad mortem, persisting untill his death in that sentence,* which in his *Constitution* he had published for defence of the *Three Chapters*, truly he would have praised *Vigilius* for a Martyr, had he dyed in such sort. But when he saith, *Vigilius* was afflicted, and not crowned, *plane alludit ad ejus exilium, he doth plainly allude to the banishment of* Vigilius, and to his forsaking or revolt from that judgement after he came from banishment. Thus doth the Cardinall glosse upon the words of *Liberatus*.

e Bar. an. 554. m.5.

32. See the force of truth; The Cardinalls owne words doe most fully answer his owne doubt, and explane that truth which hee wittingly oppugneth: Had *Liberatus* found *Vigilius, perstantem in sententia usque ad mortem, constant, or persisting without any change or relenting*

in his defending the three Chapters, untill his dying day, then indeed *Vigilius* should have beene with *Liberatus* (an obstinate defender of that sentence) a glorious Martyr, at the least a worthy Confessor, and for that cause he should have beene condemned by *Liberatus.* But seeing he found him a changeling in his sentence, wavering and unconstant therein, turning his note as soone almost as he had looked the Emperour in the face, *Vigilius* by reason of that change, unconstancie, and revolt from his opinion, lost his Crowne, and all his commendation with *Liberatus,* not for any returning to condemne the *Three Chapters* after his exile, whereof in *Liberatus* there is no sound nor syllable. By publishing his *Apostolicall Constitution* in the time of the Councell for defence of those Chapters, and by his dying in that opinion, *Liberatus* found *Vigilius, stantem & morientem,* but not *perstantem in ea sententia usque ad mortem,* he found him standing and dying, but hee could not possibly find him persisting constantly, not persevering in that sentence which first he had embraced; for whereas he saw and knew the Synodall Acts, to testifie that for five or six yeares together, hee not onely was of a contrary judgement, but did judicially, and definitively decree the contrary, and censure also such as continued and persevered in the defence of those Chapters; this so long discontinuance, and so earnest oppugning of the defenders of those Chapters, quite interrupted his persisting and persevering in his first sentence, for this cause he lost his Crowne, and dyed *non coronatus,* in the Kalender, and account of *Liberatus.*

33. I adde further, that the words of *Liberatus* being well pondered, doe shew the quite contrary to that which the Cardinall thence collecteth. *Liberatus* as all the defenders of those Chapters, held their opposites who condemned the same Chapters, for no other then heretikes, then oppugners of the Catholike faith, and holy Councell of *Chalcedon.* And for *Vigilius,* while hee fought [f] on their side, and against the Emperour, they honoured [g] him as a Catholike, as a chiefe defender of the Catholike faith. As soone as *Vigilius* had consented to the Emperor, and upon his comming to *Constantinople* had condemned the *Three Chapters,* then they held him for no other then a betraier [h] of the faith, then an heretike, then a backslider, revolter, and lapser from the faith, and for such they adjudged, and accursed him by name in their Africane [i] Synod, at which it is most like that *Liberatus,* being a man of such note for dealing in that cause, was present; upon his returning at the time of the fift Councell to defend againe with them the *Three Chapters,* they esteemed him as one of those *penitentes,* which after their lapsing returne againe to the profession of the faith. Had *Vigilius* after this revolted, and turned againe to condemne the same Chapters, and in that opinion dyed, as out of *Liberatus,* the Cardinall would perswade; *Liberatus* and the rest of that sect would have held him for a double heretike, for a lapser, and relapser from the faith; for one dying in heresie, and dying a condemned heretike by the judgement of their Africane Synod. Now let any man judge whether *Liberatus* would have said of such an one as hee esteemed an heretike, a condemned heretike, and to dye in heresie, that hee dyed,

non

f *Complures Orthodoxi & ipse Vigilius contra eadem Capitula asserta ab Imperatore insurrexere. Bar. an. 546. nu. 38.*
g *Vigilius arguit ut probandis vocum novitates. Facundi dictum apud Bar. an. 546. nu. 57. 58.*
h *Ne Traditor videretur. Facundi dictum de Vigilio apud Bar. an. 547. nu. 37. Collusorem & Prævaricatorem conclamarunt. Bar. an. ead. nu. 49. vulgarunt ubiq; cum impugnare Concilium Chalcedonense. Bar. an. 550. nu. 1.*
i *Vigil. in Chron. an. 9. post Consf. Basil.*

non coronatus ? would he have minced and extenuated the crime of heresie, of one dying in heresie, would he not much rather have said, he dyed *Damnatus, condemned*, and accursed by the judgement of their owne Synod, and therefore utterly separated from God ? Who ever read or heard, that one dying in heresie, was called by so friendly a title as *Non coronatus* ?

43. This will most clearly appeare, if we consider that the Church and Ecclesiasticall Writers doe mention as two sorts, so also two rewards of Catholike and Orthodoxall professors. The one is of those who are couragious and constant in defending the faith, such as joyfully endure torments, imprisonment, exile, and if need be, even death it selfe rather then they will renounce and forsake the faith, and these are called *coronati*. The other is of those who being timerous, and faint-hearted, yeeld to deny the truth, rather then they will endure torments or death for confessing the same ; and yet by reason of that immortall seed which is in their hearts, they returne againe, and openly professe that truth from which they had before lapsed : and these are called, *Non coronati*, saved by repentance, and returning to the truth; but by reason of their former faintnesse, and lapsing, Not crowned. Both of these are Orthodoxall, and Catholikes, both of them placed in the blessed house of God, but not both in like blessed mansions and chambers of the house of God : *For in my Fathers* k *house are many mansions*. Both of them starres, and glorious starres in heaven, but even among those heavenly starres, *one starre* l *differeth from another in glory*. Both of them receive an infinity of glory, but in that infinitie, the weight is unequall, and the one receives but as the pennie, the other as the pound or talent of that glory. Both of them blessed in the Kingdome of God, but the former not blessed onely, but crowned with blessednesse, the later blessed, but not crowned, neither with the Aureall Crowne of Martyrs, nor with the Lawrell garland of Confessors, yet still, whether *coronati*, or *non coronati*, as they both dye in the profession of the Catholike faith, so are they both rewarded with eternall glory for profession of the Catholike faith. As for heretikes such as die in heresie, and out of the Catholike faith, they are to be sorted with neither of these, they have another and a quite different ranke; *Classis* or *Predicamens* of their owne. They may not have that honour done unto them, as to be called *non coronati*, which implies that they have a part in felicity, but not the Crowne. As the Church doth justly anathematize and accurse such, so are they to be ranked in the order of those to whom Christ shall say, m *Goe yee cursed*. The Apostle n reckoning heresies with Idolatry, witchcraft, adultery, and the like, of which he saith, *that they which doe them shall not inherite the Kingdome of God*.

35. Hence now it doth clearly appeare, that *Liberatus* in saying that *Vigilius* dyed *Non coronatus*, cannot intend as the Cardinall most ignorantly collecteth, that *Vigilius* returned from the defence of the three Chapters to condemne the same, for that being in *Liberatus* judgment a revolt from the truth, hee thereby had by *Liberatus* beene accounted an heretike, and to dye in heresie, and so had beene in the ranke

k *John* 14. 2.

l *1 Cor.* 15. 41.

m *Mat.* 25. 41.
n *Gal.* 5. 19. 20.

ranke of those who are *Damnati*; but *Liberatus*, in saying he dyed *non coronatus*, doth directly teach, that he dyed in defence of those *Three Chapters*, (which, with *Liberatus*, is the Catholike faith) from which hee had lapsed, and revolted before; but seeing at the time of the Councell, hee returned againe to that opinion, and therein dyed; hee was saved, (in *Liberatus* judgement) but not crowned: By his penitence, and returning to the defence of those Chapters, he got glory, but because he had so grievously lapsed before, hee lost the crowne of glory. And this also is the reason why *Victor*, Bishop of *Tunen* mentioneth the death of *Vigilius* in such a naked [o] manner, neither disgracing him as a Prevaricator, as hee doth *Firmus* [p], *Primasius* [q], and *Pelagius* [r]; nor honouring him as a Martyr or Confessor, as he doth *Fœlix*, *Rusticus*, and *Reparatus* [s]; intimating thereby, that *Vigilius* dyed in the confession and defence of the *Three Chapters*, and therefore hee could not condemne him; but yet because he was not constant in that profession, he would not commend him.

36. Yea, but *Liberatus* by saying he was afflicted by that heresie, [t] *plane alludit ad ejus exilium, he doth plainly allude to the banishment of* Vigilius. Plainly? Phy on such a Plain-lie out of a Cardinals mouth; he doth not so much as obscurely, not under a cloud or mist, not any way allude unto it; nor intimate or insinuate ought tending thereunto; nor could hee indeed, seeing, as we have before declared, that banishment of *Vigilius* is nothing else but a fiction, partly of *Anastasius*, partly of *Baronius*; and *Liberatus* was no Prophet, that hee could allude to their idle dreams: But if he allude not to his banishment, why then saith he that *Vigilius* was afflicted by that heresie? as if there were no afflictions in the world but banishment; what ere hee meant, he meant not that: And truly, whatsoever calamities or afflictions, either of body or minde, befell *Vigilius* after he had once consented to the Emperors Edict, & to the condemning of the *Three Chapters*, (which, in *Liberatus* account, was heresie) and because it was (as hee thought) contrary to the Councell of *Chalcedon*, even the heresie of the *Eutycheans*; all those did *Liberatus* impute to that his revolt from the faith, and to that *Eutychean* heresie which he then embraced, as *Liberatus* judged. Now there are two or three evident matters, which were great afflictions to *Vigilius*, and may well bee intended by *Liberatus*.

37. The first was the generall dislike which the Italian, Africane, and other Westerne Bishops took against him, as soone as they knew that he had consented to the Emperours Edict, they writ against him, as one who denyed the faith, and condemned the Councell of *Chalcedon*, they censured, judged, and accursed him by their Synodall sentence; they contemned him as a temporizer, as one, who, to please the Emperour, betrayed the faith: This was, no doubt, no small affliction to *Vigilius*, to bee disgraced, contemned, and accursed by his owne friends, to whom, by so many bands of duty and love, he was so nearly conjoyned; and this lay upon his stomacke for five or sixe yeares together, even from his first comming almost, to *Constantinople*, to the time of the Councell.

38. His second affliction followed upon his change in the time of

[o] *Vigilius Romanus in insula Sicilia moritur. Vict. in Chron. an. 16. post Cons. Bas.*
[p] *Firmus donis Principis corruptus, assensum prebuit, sed in navi morte turpissima periit. Vict. ibid. an. 11. post Cons. Bas.*
[q] *Primasius à Catholicis, pro prævaricatore condemnatus infœlici morte extinguitur. Ib.*
[r] *A prævaricatoribus ordinatur. Ibid. an. 17. post Cons. Bas.*
[s] *Reparatus exilio apud Euchaidam, gloriosa confessione transiit ad dominum Vict. an. 22. post Cons. Bas.*
[t] *Bar. an. 554. nu. 5.*

the Councell; for though hee then, by defending the *Three Chapters*, and publishing his *Apostolicall Constitution* for defence of them, hoped to recover the love and good opinion of the Westerne Churches; yet hee exceedingly failed of that hope. Now hee was in farre worse case than before; On one side he incurred the Emperours just indignation, and made himselfe obnoxious to deprivation; banishment, death, or whatsoever punishments may bee inflicted on pertinacious, and hereticall oppugners of the faith; which, although the Emperour in his lenity did not, nor would inflict upon him; yet what a griefe is it to have all those punishments hanging, like *Damocles* sword, over his head, and sure to fall upon him, if the Emperour at any time listed to breake or cut the haire ? What comfort could he have, who held not onely his dignitie, but his liberty, yea, his very life at the will and pleasure of another ? On another side he had incurred the heavie and just censure of the holy generall Councell, and of all Ca-holikes, being by them adjudged and accursed for an heretike. On a third side the Westerne Churches, and the defenders of the *Three Chapters*, were so farre from honouring him as he expected, that they also, for all that, held him for no other than an unconstant and wave-ing person, one that turned his faith with every winde and weather: so, whereas at the first hee was beloved and honoured of the We-sterne Churches, while hee defended the *Three Chapters*, as they did; and after that was beloved and honoured of the Emperour, and Ea-sterne Churches, while hee, with them, condemned the *Three Chap-ters*: when now againe he returned to defend them, hee was contem-ned both of the one sort and the other; they all now esteemed no bet-ter of him than a very Wethercocke. Now whether this, to see him-selfe forsaken and contemned by all, both friends and foes, both Ca-holikes and heretikes; whether this might not bee a corrasive to his heart, let any man duly consider with himselfe. Adde to these that corporeall anguish which caused his death; hee, if wee may trust *Ana-sius*,[u] *afflictus, calculi dolorem habens, mortuus est, being afflicted and vexed with paine of the stone*, or (as by *Liberatus* it may bee thought) *by some more grievous disease of his body, dyed in great affliction:* When there were so many afflictions lying at the heart of *Vigilius*, all which *Libe-ratus* imputeth to his consenting to the Emperours Edict, and con-demning of the *Three Chapters*, which he, as the rest of the defenders of them, called heresie; was not the Cardinall, thinke you, in some ex-asie of his wit, when he thought, that the affliction of *Vigilius* must needs bee his owne fictitious banishment, and that *Liberatus* doth plainly allude thereunto.

39. Thus all the reasons of *Baronius* being manie wayes, and ma-nifestly declared to bee ineffectuall, to prove that last and Baronian change in *Vigilius*, after the end of the Synod, we may now safely con-clude, that as *Vigilius*, after his *Apostolicall Constitution* in defence of the *Three Chapters* once published, made at no time after that, any publike, judiciall or Pontificall Decree to reverse and adnul the same; but that still stood in full power and strength untill the death of *Vigi-lius*; so neither did hee ever after that time declare so much as a pri-

u *Anast. in vit Vig.*

vate

vate diflike thereof, or a perfonall confent to the fift Councell, which had decreed the contrary; but 'pertinacioufly perfifting in that fentence, he both lived and dyed an hereticall defender of thofe *Three Chapters*. At the firft he was hereticall in defending them againft the Emperours Edict: at the laft he was not onely hereticall, but a condemned heretike in defending them againft the judiciall fentence of the holy generall Councell. In the middle time he had a fit of profeffing the truth, but that was only in fhew, and in appearance, that fo he might temporize with the Emperour, in heart hee was (as when the time of tryall came he demonftrated himfelfe) an oppugner of the truth, both againft the Imperiall Edict, and Synodall judgement: And therefore, as wee found him at the firft an heretike; fo, for all which *Baronius* hath faid, or could fay to the contrary, we muft leave him for a condemned heretike; even fuch a one, as not only defended, but, by his *Cathedrall* and *Apoftolicall* fentence, defined herefie to be the Catholike faith.   And thus much bee fpoken of the Cardinals third principall Exception, or troupe of evafions, marching under that Act of *Vigilius*, which, by his manifold changing in this caufe of faith, you have fully feene.

CAP. XVIII.

The fourth and laft Exception of Baronius, *in defence of* Vigilius, *pretending, that the fift Councell (wherein the decree of* Vigilius *was condemned,) was neither a generall nor a lawfull Councell, till* Vigilius *confirmed the fame, refuted.*

1. Here now remaineth onely the fourth and laft exception of *Baronius*; in which, though being the weakeft and worft of all, his whole hope now confifts: In this the Cardinall brings forth all his forces, all the Engines of his wit and malice, to batter downe the authority of the fift generall Councell. Seeing it contradicted the Pope, and *judicially* decreed his *Apoftolicall* fentence to be hereticall, it fhall bee of no authority at all; it fhall bee neither a generall, nor a lawfull Councell; it fhall bee nothing but a Confpiracy and conventicle with *Baronius* and his friends, untill *Vigilius* doe approve the fame: But heare their owne words to this purpofe.

2. The fift Councell, faith *Baronius* [a], *aliquando expers fuit omnis authoritatis*, was for a time void of all authority; yea, fo void thereof, *ut nec legitima Synodus dici meruerit*, that it deferved not to bee called fo much as a lawfull (much leffe a generall and lawfull) *Synod*; becaufe it was affembled, the Pope refifting it, & was ended, the Pope contradicting it: But when afterwards it was approved by the fentence of *Vigilius*, and other fucceeding Popes, then it got the title and authority of an Oecumenicall Synod. Againe [b], *The fift Councell at that time, when it was held,*

held, *could not have the name of an Oecumenicall Synod, seeing it was not lawfully affembled in the Holy Ghoft, becaufe the Pope,neither by himfelfe, nor by his Legates would be prefent in it.* And yet more fpightfully; Thefe things c *confidered,plane confenties,ipfam nec Oecumenica,nec privata Synodi mereri nomen; you will confent,that the fift Councell deferved not the name of an Oecumenicall,no nor fo much as of a private Synod;* it was no Synod nor Councell at all, feeing both it was affembled, *refiftente Pontifice,* the Pope refifting it,and alfo pronounced fentence, *contra ipfius Decretum,* againft *the Popes Decree.* Thus *Baronius :* in whofe fteps *Binius* treadeth, faying d, *Pope Vigilius was not prefent in this Councell,either by himfelfe, or by his deputies,Contradixit eidem, he contradicted the Synod;* the members affembled without the head, *dum ageretur non confentit,* the Pope confented not to it while it was held, nor did approve it ftraight after it was ended; yet it got the name,title, and authority of an Oecumenicall Councell, *quando ipfius Vigilii fententia,* when it was afterwards approved by the fentence of Vigilius himfelfe, and his fucceffors. So *Binius.*

c *An.eod.nu.* 259

d *Not.in Conc.* 5.§ *Prafedit.*

3 How,or where fhall I begin ? or who,though more cenforious than *Cato,* can with fufficient gravity and feverity caftigate the infolency and moft fhamelefle dealing of thefe men, who, rather than one of their Popes,even Pope *Proteus* himfelfe, fhall bee thought to erre in his *Cathedrall Decree* of faith, care not to difgrace, to vilifie, yea, to nullifie one of the ancient and facred generall Councels, approved,as before e we have fhewed,by the whole Catholike Church? For if this Councell was neither generall, nor lawfull, (as they teach) till *Vigilius* approved it by his *Apoftolicall* authority,after his returne from exile; then was it never, nor as yet is either a generall or lawfull Councell,feeing *Vigilius,* after his exile, never did,nor could approve it, as before f we have clearly proved : So this fift Councell muft for ever be cafhiered and blotted out of the ranke of Councels. And becaufe, as their fecond Nicene Synod rightly difputes g, the feventh muft follow the fixt, in the fame ranke and order,and the fixt,the fift, if there was no fift generall and holy Councell; neither can there bee any fixt,nor feventh,nor eighth,nor any other after it. So,by the affertion of thefe men, there are at once dafhed out fourteene of thofe, which themfelves h doe honour by the name of holy generall Councels.

e *Sup.ca.* 4. nu; 26.*& feq.*

f *Sup.ca.* 17.

g *Omne feptimū ordinatum in eādem numeratione quā res; praceſſerant, &c.Act.* 6.pa. 357.*a.* h *Bell.lib.* 1.*de Conc.ca.* 5.

4. I fay more, the expunging of all thofe fourteene Councels, doth certainly follow upon the Cardinals affertion, though it were granted,that *Vigilius* had confirmed this fift,as it is true, that *Pelagius* and *Gregory* did : For if it was (as he teacheth) neither a generall nor lawfull Synod, while the Councell continued, and for that whole time while it was an affembly of Bifhops; then undoubtedly it never at any time was, nor yet is either a generall or a lawfull Synod : For after the end, and diffolution thereof, it was never extant *in rerum natura* againe; it was ever after that time *Non ens :* and being neither Synod, nor yet fo much as *Ens,* it could not poffibly be either generall or lawfull. It is a Maxime, *Non entis non funt Accidentia;* If while it was extant, and while it was an affembly,it was but a conventicle; if then it was not gathered in Gods name, I pray you, when was

it

bifcum fumus, *We all doe hold communion with you, and are united unto you.*
Schifmaticall then they could not be. So the judgement of thefe men
being all Catholikes, and holding the Catholike communion, doth
evidently prove the whole Catholike Church at that time, to have
beleeved a Councell to be both generall and lawfull, though the Pope
diffented from it, and by his *Apoftolicall* authority condemned the
fame, and the decree thereof.

8. After the end of the Councell did the Church then think otherwife? Did it then judge the Councell to want authority, while it
wanted the Popes approbation, or to receive authority by his approbation? Who were they, I pray you, that thought thus? Certainly
not Catholikes, and the condemners of thefe Chapters. For they approved the Councel and *Decree* thereof during the time of the Councell, and while the Pope fo far difliked it, that for his refufall to confent unto it, he endured banifhment. Neither did the Heretikes who
defended thofe Chapters, judge thus. For they, as *Baronius* witnef-

n *An. 553. nu.*
211.

feth [n], *perfifted in the defence of them, and in a rent from the others, even
after Vigilius had confented to the Synod:* yea among them *Vigilius*

o *An. 555. nu. 2.*

[o] *redditus eft execrabilis, was even detefted and accurfed by them for approving the Synod.* Or becaufe *Vigilius* approved it not, *Pelagius* who is
knowne to have approved it, was fo generally difliked for that caufe

p *Adeo exhor-
ruiffe vifi funt
Antiftites occi-
dentales aliam
poft quartam ad-
mittere oecume-
nicam Synodum,
ut non potuerit
Pelagius reperire
Epifcopos Romæ
à quibus confe-
craretur. Bar.
an. 556. nu. 1.
q Can. 1. & Con.
Nic. can. 4.*

of the Wefterne Bifhops, *that there [p] could not be found three who would
lay hands on him at his confecration:* but in ftead of a Bifhop, they were
enforced againft that Canon [q] of the Apoftles, which they often oppofe to us, to take a Presbyter of *Oftia* at his ordination. So much did
they diflike both the fift Councell, and all (though it were the Pope)
who did approve it. Now the whole Church being at that time divided into thefe two parts, the defenders and condemners of thofe
Chapters, feeing neither the one nor the other judged the Synod to
be generall or lawfull, becaufe the Pope approved it; who poffibly
could there be at that time of the Cardinals fancie, that the fift Councell wanted all authority till the Pope approved it, and gained authority of a generall and lawfull Councell by his approving of it? *Catho-*
likes and condemners of thofe Chapters, embraced the Councell,
though the Pope rejected it: Heretikes and defenders of thofe Chapters, rejected the Councell, though the Pope approved it. Neither
of them both (and fo none at all in the whole Church) judged either
the Popes approbation to give, or his reprobation to take away authority from a generall Councell. Thus by the *Antecedentia, Conco-
mitantia,* and *Confequentia* of the Councell, it is manifeft by the judgement of the whole Church in that age, that this fift Councell was of
authority without the Popes approbation, and was not held of authority by reafon of his approbation.

9. What the judgement of the Church was, as well in the ages
preceding, as fucceeding to this Councell, is evident by that which

r *Sup. ca. 4. nu.
75. 26. & feq.*

we have already declared. For we have at large fhewed [r], that the
doctrine, faith, and judgement of this fift Councell, is confonant to
all former, and confirmed by all following generall Councells, till
that at *Lateran* under *Leo* the tenth. Whereupon it enfueth, that this
doctrine

doctrine which wee maintaine, and the Cardinall impugneth;
(that neither the Popes approbation doth give, nor his reprobation
take away authority from a Councell,) was embraced and beleeved
as a Catholike truth, by the whole Catholike Church of all ages, till
that *Lateran* Synod, that is, for more than 1500. yeares together.

10. And if there were not so ample testimonies in this point, yet
even reason would enforce to acknowledge this truth. For if this fift
Councell be of force and Synodall authority, *eo nomine*, because the
Pope, to wit *Pelagius*, approved it; then by the same reason is it of
no force or Synodall authority, *eo nomine*, because the Pope, to wit *Vigilius*, rejected it. If the Popes definitive and *Apostolicall* reprobation
cannot take away authority from it; neither can his approbation,
though *Apostolicall*, give authority unto it. Or if they say that both
are true, (as indeed they are both alike true) then seeing this fift Councell is both approved by Pope *Pelagius*, and rejected by Pope *Vigilius*,
it must now be held both to be wholly approved; and wholly rejected:
both to be lawfull, and unlawfull : both to be a generall Councell, and
no generall Councell. And the very same doome must bee given of
all the thirteene Councells which follow it : They all, because they
are approved by some one Pope, are approved and lawfull Councels:
and because they approve this fift, which is rejected by the Pope, they
are all rejected, and unlawfull Councells. Such an havocke of generall Councels doth this their assertion bring with it, and into such in-
extricable labyrinths are they driven, by teaching the authority of
Councels to depend on the Popes will and pleasure.

11. Now though this bee more than abundant to refute all that
they can alledge against this fift Councell, yet for the more clearing
of the truth, and expressing my love to this holy Councell, to which
next after that at *Chalcedon*, I beare speciall affection; I will more
strictly examine those two reasons which *Baronius* & *Binius* have used,
of purpose to disgrace this holy Synod. The former is taken from the
assembling; the later, from the decree of the Councell. It was assembled, say *Baronius* [f] and *Binius*, *Pontifice resistente & contradicente, the
Pope resisting and contradicting it*. Whence they inferre, that it was an
unlawfull assembly, not gathered in Gods name. In this their reason,
both the antecedent and consequence are unsound and untrue. Did
Pope *Vigilius* resist this Councell, and contradict the calling or assembling thereof? What testimonie doth *Baronius* or *Binius* bring of
this their so confident assertion? Truly none at all. What probabili-
ties yet, or conjectures? Even as many. Are not these men, think you,
wise & worthy disputers, who dare avouch so doubtfull matters, and
that also to the disgrace of an holy, ancient, and approved Councell;
and yet bring no testimonie, no probabilitie, no conjecture, no proofe
at all of their saying? *Ipse dixit*, is in stead of all.

12. But what will you say if *Ipse dixit* will prove the quite contrarie? If both *Baronius* and *Binius* professe, that *Vigilius* did consent
that this Councell should be held? Heare I pray you their own words,
and then admire and detest the most vile dealing of these men. *Hanc
synodum, Vigilius authoritate pontificia indixit*, saith *Binius* [t]; *Vigilius
called*

f Sup. hoc cap.
nu.2.

t Not. in 5. Conc.
5.Concilium.

u Ibid.

called and appointed this Synod by his papall authority. Againe u, *The Emperour called this fift Synod, authoritate Vigilij, by the authority of Pope Vigilius.* Baronius sings the same note: *It was very well provided,* saith

x An.553.nu.23

he x, *that this Oecumenicall Synod should be held, ex Vigilii Papæ sententia, according to the minde and sentence of Pope Vigilius,* who above all other men desired to have a Councell. Againe y, *The Emperour decreed that*

y Ibid.nu.24.

the Synod should be called, ex ipsius Vigilii sententia, according to the minde of Vigilius. And a little after; It was commendable in the Emperor, that he did labour to assemble the Synod, *ex Vigilij Papæ sententia, according to the minde and sentence of Pope Vigilius.* Neither onely did the Pope consent to have a Councell, but to have it in that very city where it was held, and where himselfe then was. Indeed at the first, the Pope was desirous z and earnest, to have it held in Sicily, or in some

z Optavimus & frequentissime supplici voce poposcimus eundē (cœtum) ad quælibet Italiæ locū, aut certe ad Siciliam, &c. Vigil.in Consst. apud Bar.an. 553.nu.56.
a Epist.Leon.24
b Quod quia fieri Serenitas vestra non annuit.Vigil.loc. cit.
c Bin. Not. in Conc.5.§.Concilium.

Westerne Citie: (even as Pope *Leo* had laboured a with *Theodosius* for the Councell which was held at *Chalcedon*:) But when *Iustinian* the Emperour would not consent b to that petition, (as neither *Theodosius* nor *Martian* would to the former of *Leo*,) *Vigilius* then, *voluntati* c *Imperatoris libens accessit, very willingly consented to the Emperours pleasure in this matter,* that the Oecumenicall Councell should be held at *Constantinople.* Say now in sadnesse, what you thinke of *Baronius* and *Binius?* Whither had they sent their wits, when they laboured to perswade this Councell to be unlawfull, because Pope *Vigilius* resisted and contradicted the assembling thereof? whereas themselves so often, so evidently, so expresly testifie, not onely that it was assembled by the consent, and according to the minde, will, pleasure, desire, authority, and sentence of the Pope; but the very chiefe act and royaltie of the summons they challenge (though falsely) to the Pope; the other, which is an act of labour and service, to be as it were the Popes Sumner or Apparitor, in bringing the Bishops together by the Popes authoritie, that, and none but that they allow to the Emperour.

13. Many other testimonies might bee produced, to declare this truth: That of *Sigonius* d: The Emperour called this Synod, *Vigilio*

d Lib.20.an. 553.
e An.544.

Pontifice permittente, Pope *Vigilius* permitting him: that of *Wernerus* e; *Vigilius iussit Concilium Constantinopoli celebrari, Vigilius commanded that* this Councell should be held at *Constantinople:* That of *Zonaras* f and *Glicas* g, who both affirme, that *Vigilius* was *Princeps Concilij, the chiefe*

f An.to.3.in Iustiniano.
g Cui Concilio præerant Eutychius, Domnus & Vigilius. Glic.annal.part. 4.pa.379.

Bishop of the Councell: not chiefe among them that sate in the Councell, for there he was not at all: nor chiefe in making the Synodall decree, for therein he contradicted the Councell: but chiefe of all who sued to the Emperour, and procured the Councell, as being desirous of the same. But omitting the rest, the whole generall Councell, yea and

h Coll.8.p.584.a

the Popes owne letters, put this out of all doubt. This say h the whole Councell, even in their Synodall sentence, *Consensit in scriptis in Concilio convenire, Vigilius under his owne hand-writing consented to come together, and be present with us in the Synod.* Againe, the Legates sent from

i Coll.2.pa.523.

the Councell to invite *Vigilius,* said i thus unto him; Your Holinesse knoweth, *quod promisistis una cum Episcopis convenire, that you have promised to come together with the other Bishops, into the Councell; and there to*

k Coll.1.p.521.b

debate this question, Vigilius himselfe writ k thus to the Bishops of the Councell:

Councell: We knowing your desire, *predictis postulationibus annui-mus, have consented to your petitions*, that in an orderly assembly being made, wee may conferre with our united brethren about the three Chapters. I doubt not but upon such faire and undoubted records, every one will now confesse, First, that if to be gathered by the Popes consent and authority, will make a Councell lawfull, (which with them is an authentike rule) then this fift Councell is without question in this respect most lawfull: Secondly, that *Baronius* and *Binius* are shamelesse both in uttering untruths, & in reviling this holy Synod, which they would perswade to be unlawful, because it was assembled, the Pope resisting it; whereas this Councell to have beene assembled, with the consent (yea as they boast with the authority also) of Pope *Vigilius*, not onely other Writers, but the Synodall Acts, the whole generall Councell, the letters of *Vigilius*, and the expresse words of *Baronius* and *Binius* themselves doe evidently declare.

14. Come now to the Consequence. Say the Pope had resisted the assembling of this Councell, was it for this cause unlawfull, was it no generall Councell? What say you then to the second Councell, which *Baronius* thus writeth [1], It was held, *repugnante Damaso, Pope Damasus resisting the holding thereof*. Will they blot that also out of the ranke of generall, and lawfull Synods? If not, why may not this it also bee a generall and lawfull Synod, though *Vigilius* had with tooth and naile resisted the same? Shall the peevishnesse or perverse-nesse of the Pope, or any Bishop hinder the assembling of a generall Councell, and so the publike peace and tranquillity of the whole Church? Open but this gappe, and there never should have been, nor ever shall be any generall Councell. The wilfulnesse of *Eusebius* Bishop of *Nicomedia*, at *Nice*, of *Iohn* Patriarch of *Antioch*, at *Ephesus*, *Dioscorus* Patriarch of *Alexandria*, at *Chalcedon*, will frustrate all those holy Councells, and make them to be neither generall nor lawfull. The saying of Cardinall *Cusanus* is worthy observing to this purpose; *I beleeve*, saith he [m], *that to be spoken not absurdly, that the Emperor himselfe, in regard of that care and custody of preserving the faith, which is committed unto him, may praeceptive indicere Synodum, by his Imperiall authority and command assemble a Synod, when the great danger of the Church requireth the same; negligente aut contradicente Romano Pontifice, the Pope either neglecting so to doe, or resisting and contradicting the doing thereof.* So *Cusanus*. This was the very state and condition of the Church at this time, when the fift Councell was assembled. The [n] whole Church had beene a long time scandalized and troubled about those *Three Chapters*; it was rent and divided from East to West. High time it was and necessary for *Iustinian* to see that flame quenched, although Pope *Vigilius* or any other Patriarch had never so eagerly resisted the remedie thereof.

15. Had the Cardinall pleaded against this Synod, that *Vigilius* had not beene called unto it, hee had spoken indeed to the purpose. For this is essentiall, and such as without which a Synod cannot bee generall and lawfull, that all Bishops be summoned to the Synod, and comming thither, have free accesse unto it, and freedome of speech and

[1] *An. 553. nu.* 2

[m] *Lib. 3. de Concor. ca. 15.*

[n] *Vid. sup. ca. 1 nu. 6.*

and judgment therein. But the Cardinall durſt not take this exception againſt this Synod, or for *Vigilius*; for none of theſe to have beene wanting in this Councell, is ſo cleare, that pertinacie it ſelfe cannot deny it. It was not the Pope (as they vainly boaſt) but the Emperor, who by his owne and Imperiall authority called this Councell, as the whole Synod even in their Synodall ſentence witneſſe : Wee are aſſembled here in this City, *juſſione piſſimi Imperatoris vocati, being called by the commandement of our moſt religious Emperor.* His calling to have beene generall, *Nicephorus* doth expreſſly declare, The Emperor ſaith he [o], aſſembled the fift generall Councell, *Epiſcopis eccleſiarum omnium evocatis, the Biſhops of all Churches being called unto it :* yea the Emperor was ſo equall in this cauſe, that *Binius* [p] teſtifieth of him, *Pari numeri Epiſcopos ex Oriente & Occidente convocavit, that he called* (in particular, and beſides his generall ſummons, by which all without exception had free acceſſe) *as many out of the Weſt, where the defenders of thoſe Chapters did abound; as he did out of the Eaſt, where the ſame Chapters were generally condemned.* And yet further, *Vigilius* himſelfe was by name, not onely invited, intreated, and by many reaſons perſwaded, but even commanded by the Emperor, and in his name, to come unto the Synod, as before [q] we ſhewed. Now what freedome hee might have had in the Councell, both that offer of the Preſidencie, doth ſhew for him in particular, and the words of the Councell ſpoken concerning all in generall doth declare; for when *Sabinianus* and others, who being then at *Conſtantinople*, were invited to the Synod, and refuſed to come, the ſynod ſayd [r], *It was meet that they being called ſhould have come to the Councell, and have been partakers of all things which are here done and debated,* eſpecially ſeeing both the moſt holy Emperour and we, *licentiam dedimus unicuiq; have granted free liberty to every one to manifeſt his minde in the Synod concerning the cauſes propoſed.* Seeing then he not onely might, but in his duty both to God, to the Emperour, and to the whole Church, hee ought to have come, and freely ſpoken his minde in this cauſe, his reſiſting the will of the Emperor, and refuſing to come, doth evidently demonſtrate his want of love to the truth, and dutifulneſſe to the Emperor, and the Church; but it can no way impaire or impeach the dignity and authority of the Councell, neither for the generality, nor for the lawfulneſſe thereof.

16. Beſides all which there is yet one thing above all the reſt to be remembred; for though Pope *Vigilius* was not preſent in the Synod either perſonally, or by his Legates, but in that ſort reſiſted to come unto it, yet he was preſent there by his letters of inſtruction, by his *Apoſtolicall* and *Cathedrall Conſtitution* which hee publiſhed as a direction what was to be judged and held in that cauſe of the *Three Chapters*, That Decree and Conſtitution he promiſed to ſend *ad Imperatorem & Synodum, both to the Emperor and to the Synod, quod & ingenuè praſtitit, which alſo he ingenuouſly performed as the Cardinall tells [s] us.* That elaborate [t] decree, to which an whole Synod, together with the Pope ſubſcribed, containing the Popes ſentence and inſtruction given in this cauſe, *Vniverſo* [u] *orbi Catholico cunctiſq; fidelibus,* not onely to the
Synod

o *Lib. 17. ca. 27.*

p *Not. in Conc. 5. §. Concilium.*

q *Sup. ca. 2. nu. 1. & 3.*

r *Collat. 2. pa. 524. b.*

s *An. 553. nu. 47.*
t *Idq; elaboravit. ibid.*
u *An. eod. nu. 48.*

Synod, teaching them what they should define, but to all Christians, teaching them what they shold beleeve, was *in conseſſu Epiſcoporum recitatum, read and recited before all the Biſhops in that Councell*, as *Binius* doth [x] aſſure us. This one kinde of preſence in the Synod, is ſuppletive of all the reſt, of more worth then 20. nay then 200. Legates, *à latere* ſent from his holineſſe. They all may deale beſides, or contrary to the Popes minde, as *Zacharias* and *Rhodoaldus* did in a Councell held about the cauſe of *Photius*; but this *Cathedrall* inſtruction is an inflexible meſſenger, no bribes, no perſwaſions, no feare, no favour can extort from it one ſyllable more then his holineſſe by the *infallible* direction of his Chaire hath delivered; yea though the Pope ſhould have beene perſonally preſent in the Synod, and face to face ſpoken his mind in his cauſe, yet could not his ſudden or leſſe premeditated ſpeech have beene for weight or authority comparable to this decree, being elaborated after ſeven yeares ponderation of the cauſe, and all things in it being diſpoſed *cum omni undiq; cautela atque diligentia, with all diligence and circumſpection*, that could poſſibly bee uſed, which the Pope though abſent in body, yet ſent as an Oracle from heaven to be a direction to the Synod, and to ſupply his own abſence. So many wayes is this former objection of *Baronius* vaine, and unſound, when he pretends this Councell to have beene unlawfull becauſe the Pope reſiſted it, and the members aſſembled without their head: for neither did *Vigilius* reſiſt their aſſembling, but freely and willingly conſented unto it; neither was hee excluded from the Synod, but moſt undutifully abſented himſelfe from it: and though the members at that time wanted the Popes head-peece, yet they had his heart, his minde, and his *Apoſtolicall* direction among them, to bee a Cynoſure unto them in that cauſe, which alone is able to ſupply both his perſonall and Legantine abſence in any Councel.

17. The other objection of *Baronius* is taken from the decree of this Synod. The ſentence, ſaith he [y], given by it, was *contra ipſius decretum, againſt the decree of Vigilius*, and therefore their aſſembly deſerved not the name of a generall, no nor ſo much as of a private Synod, : was no Councell at all. Cardinall *Bellarmine* explaines this more fully, ſaying [z], *Such Councells as define matters againſt the Popes inſtruction*; *Reprobata Concilia dici debent*, are to bee called or accounted, *Rejected Councells*; for it is all one, ſaith he, whether the Pope doe expreſly reject and reprobate a Councell, or whether the Councell deale, *contra Pontificis ſenten iam, againſt the Popes ſentence*, either of both ſuch Councells, are rejected, and ſo of no authoritie at all. So Bellarmine. What ſhall we anſwer to the perverſneſſe of theſe men? If this rule be admitted, the Church hath for ever and inevitably loſt this fift Councell, and (by their ſecond Nicen collection) the fixt, the ſeventh, and all that follow. And verily am perſwaded, that none can poſſibly excuſe either *Baronius*, or *Bellarmine* from this crime of expunging the fift Councell, and all which follow it, from the ranke and number of generall, or approved Councels. For it is as cleare as the ſunſhine at noone day, that the ſentence pronounced by the fift ſynod was contradictory to the deſinition and *Cathedrall* inſtruction ſent by Pope *Vigilius* unto them. If then

[x] *Not. in Conc. 5.§. Conſtitut.*

[y] *An.553. num. 219.*

[z] *Lib.2. de Conc.ca.11. §. Ac de.*

then to define a cause contrary to the Popes instruction be a sure note
of a Reprobate Councell, as they teach it to be; farewell for ever this
fift, and all that follow it, or approve it : they are all by the rule of
these two worthy Cardinals, Reprobated Councels, nay not so much
as Councels, but meere Conspiracies or Conventicles.

18. Besides this, see I pray you the zeale and devotion of these
men to the Catholike faith. If this Councell be for this cause a Rejected Councell, because it followed not the instructions of Pope *Vigilius* sent unto it, then it should have beene an holy, and approved
Councell, if it had followed those instructions of *Vigilius*; that is, if
it had condemned the Councells of *Nice, Ephesus* and *Chalcedon*, if it
had decreed *Nestorianisme* to be the Catholike faith, and Iesus Christ
not to be God : for *Vigilius* by decreeing that the *Three Chapters*
ought to be defended, instructed them thus to define and judge. Had
they thus done, then, because they had followed the instructions of
Vigilius, the two Cardinalls would have embraced this Councell,
with both armes, have applauded, & advanced it to the skies : seeing
it did not so, but contradicted the Popes *Apostolicall* instructions at
this time; fie on it, it is an unlawfull, a Reprobated Councell, nay it is
no Councell at all, nor of any authority. Can any with reason judge
these men to be ought else then *Nestorians*, then condemned heretikes, and obstinate oppugners of all ancient holy Councells, and of
the Catholike faith? See the strange diversity of judgement which
is in us and them. They in their hereticall dotage on the Popes Cathedrall *infallibility*, teach this fift holy Councell to bee a reprobated
synod, *eo nomine*, because it followed not the instructions of Pope *Vigilius*; we on the contrary doe constantly affirme it to bee an holy and
most approved synod, *eo nomine*, because it followed not, but rejected
and condemned those *Cathedrall* instructions of *Vigilius* : with us consent the sixt, seventh, and all succeeding generall Councells, till that
at *Laterane*, all former holy Councells also, to all which this Councell
is consonant. From them dissent all these both former and subsequent
Councells; that is, the whole Catholike Church for fifteene hundreth
yeares and more. *Vtri creditis* ? whose doctrine thinke you now is ancient, orthodoxall, and catholike ? And whether had you rather with
these two Cardinalls, account this fift synod an unlawfull assembly,
and a reprobate Councell, because it contradicted the hereticall constitution of Pope *Vigilius*, or with such an army of witnesses, honor it
for a sacred, Oecumenicall approved Councell, though it not onely
wanted the approbation, but had in plaine words the *Cathedrall* Reprobation [z] of Pope *Vigilius*.

z Si quid contra
hæc quæ statui-
mus, à quolibet
factum dictum
atq; conscriptum
est, vel fuerit;
hoc modis om-
nibus ex autho-
ritate sedis Apo-
stolicæ refuta-
mus. Const. Vig.
in fine.

19. Having now fully refuted not onely the Assertion of *Baronius*,
That this Councell was of no authority, nor an approved Councell
till Pope *Vigilius* confirmed and approved it, but also both those reasons whereby he would perswade the same: there remaineth yet one
doubt, which necessarily is to be satisfied for the finall clearing of this
point. For it will, and justly may bee demanded, what it was which
made this fift an approved Councell ? Or if it bee not the Popes confirmation and approbation, what it is in any Councell, or any decree
                                          thereof

thereof, which makes it to be, and rightly to be esteemed an approved Councell or Decree? I constantly answer, that whatsoever it be, it is no approbation, no confirmation, nor any act of the Pope; at least no more of him, than of any other Patriarke or Patriarchall Primate in the Church: An evident proofe whereof is in the second Generall Councell; for that, ever since their Synodall sentence was made against the MACEDONIANS, and ratified by the Emperour, was esteemed by the Catholike Church an Oecumenicall, and approved Councell; and that, before the Pope had consented unto it or approved the same: For that Councell being assembled in *May* [a], when *Eucherius* and *Seagrius* were Consuls, (*an.* 381.) continued till [b] about the end of *Iuly* in the same yeare. On the 30. of *Iuly Theodosius* the Emperour published his severe law against the *Macedonians*, being then condemned heretikes: Hee commanded that forthwith al Churches should be givē to those, who held the one and equall Majesty of the Father, Sonne, and Holy Ghost; and were of the same faith with *Nestorius*, *Timotheus*, and other Bishops in that Synod; but whosoever dissented in faith from them, *ut manifestos hæreticos ab Ecclesia expelli, they should all be expelled as manifest hæretikes, and never be admitted againe.* In which law seeing the *Macedonians* are called manifest heretikes, that is, such as are convicted and condemned by a generall Councell, it is doubtlesse, that at the promulgating of this law, both the Emperour and the catholike Church, held that decree of the second Councel, against the *Macedonians*, to be the judgment of an holy, lawful, & approved Oecumenical Synod, such as was the most ample convictiō of an heretike, & manifestation of a heresie. Now this Edict was published before Pope *Damasus* either approved that Councell, or so much as knew what was done therein: For the first newes what was done in the Councell, came to *Damasus*, after the Councell of *Aquileia*, as after *Sigonius* [d], *Baronius* declareth, who after the Synod at *Aquileia* described, saith [e], *Post hæc autem, After these things done at Aquileia*, when *Damasus* had received a message concerning the Councell at *Constantinople*, &c. that Councell at *Aquileia* was held [f] on the fift of *September*, when the other at *Constantinople* was ended a month before: and how long after that time it was before *Damasus* approved that Councell at *Constantinople*, whether one, two, or three yeares, will bee hard for any of the Cardinals friends truly to explane: Howsoever, seeing it is certaine, that the generall Councell was ended, and the Decrees thereof not onely approved, but put in execution by the Church, before the Pope, I say not, confirmed that Councell; but before hee knew what was done and decred therein, it is a Demonstration, that a generall Councell, or a Decree thereof, may bee, and *de facto*, hath beene judged, by the Church, both of them to bee of full and Synodall authoritie, and approved by the Church, when the Pope had confirmed or approved neither of both.

20. Nay, what if neither *Damasus* nor any of their Popes till *Gregories* time, approved that Councell? *Gregory* himselfe is a witnesse hereof: *The* [g] *Canons of the Constantinopolitane Councell condemne the Eudoxians,*

---

a *Socr. l. 5. ca. 8.*
b *Vsq; ad finem mensis Iuly producta est. Bar. an. 381. nu 80.*
c *Lib. 3. de fide Cathol. Cod. Theod.*

d *L. 8. de Occid. Imp. an. 381.*
e *An. 381. nu. 97.*

f *Bar. an. eod. nu. 81.*

g *Lib. 6. Epist. 31*

doxians; but who that *Eudoxius was, they doe not declare.* And the Romane Church, *eosdem Canones vel gesta Synodi illius, hactenus non habet, nec accipit;* neither hath, nor approveth those *Canons* or *Acts;* but herein it accepteth that *Synod* in that which was defined against the *Macedonians, by it;* and it rejecteth those heresies, which being mentioned therein, were already condemned by other Fathers. So *Gregory* : By whose words it is plaine, that the *Romane Church,* untill *Gregories* time, neither approved the Canons nor Acts of that second generall Councell: Even the condemning of *Macedonius* and his heresie, was not approved by the Romane Church, *eo nomine,* because it was decreed in that Councell, for then they should have approved the Canon against the *Eudoxians,* and all the rest of their Canons, seeing there was the selfe-same authority of the holy Councell, in decreeing them all; but the reason why they

h *Anatema in-stigimus Mace-donianis. Epist. Damas. et Sy-nod. Rom. apud Theod. lib. 5. ca. 10.*
i *Concilium il-lud Romanum habitum est tem-pore Petri Epis-copi Alexandri-ni, qui ei interfu-it. Zozom. lib. 6. ca. 23. Timotheus vero qui Petro succes-sit, sedit in Con-cilio Constan-tinopolitano, ut ex subscripti-one liquet.*
k *Lib. 2. Epist. 14*
l *Lib. 2. Epist. 10 Indict. 11.*

approved that against the *Macedonians,* was, because Pope [h] *Damasus* had, in a Romane Synod, divers yeares before [i] the second Councell condemned that heresie; and what heresies were by former Fathers condemned, those, and nothing else; did the Romane Church approve in that Councell, as *Gregory* faith. The inducement moving them was not the authority of the second Councell, but the judgement of other Fathers, for which they accepted of the second Councell therein: and this was untill the dayes or time of *Gregory;* for that is it which *Gregory* intendeth in the former words, *hactenus non habet nec accipit;* not meaning, that till the yeare, wherein he writ that Epistle, which was the fifteenth Indiction, the Romane Church received not those Canons or Acts: (for in the ninth Indiction, that is, sixe yeares before, himselfe professed [k] to embrace that second Councell, as one of the foure Euangelists, which also to have beene the judgement of their Church, he [l] witnesseth in the eleventh Indiction) but untill *Gregories* time; *hactenus,* untill this age, wherein I live, was the second Councell, the Canons or Acts thereof, not had nor approved by the Romane Church: And yet all that time, even from the end of that Councell, was both that Councell held for a generall, lawfull, and approved Synod, and their Decree against *Macedonius,* by the whole Church approved, as a Decree of a generall and lawfull Councell, such as ought to binde the whole Church.

    21. What wee have shewed concerning the Decree against the *Macedonians,* and in generall, for the second Councell, that will bee much more evident in the third Canon of that Synod, which concernes the Patriarchall dignity of the See of *Constantinople,* his precedence to the Patriarchs of *Alexandria* & *Antioch,* and his authority over the Churches in *Asia minor, Thrace,* and *Pontus,* all which was conferred on that See by that third Canon. That the Church of *Rome,* till *Gregories* time, approved not that Canon, is evident by Pope *Leo,*

m *Epist. 54-51. 61.*
n *Epist. 53.*

who in many [m] of his Epistles, specially in that to *Anatolius* [n], shewes his dislike of it; yea, rejects it, as contrary to the *Nicene* Decrees, which *Leo* there defineth (but, without doubt, erroniously) to bee immutable. The Legates of *Leo,* having instructions from him, said openly in the Councell of *Chalcedon* [o], touching the Canons of this Councell, *in Synodicis Canonibus non habentur, they are not accounted or*

o *Act. 16. pa. 736.a.*

held

held for Synodall Canons; and following the minde and precept P of the Pope, they most earnestly oppugned this third Canon. Long before *Leo* did *Damasus* reject q this Canon, *facto decreto in Synodo Romana, making a Decree against it, in a Romane Synod,* which is extant in their Vaticane, as *Turrian,* who belike saw the Decree, doth witnesse. Now seeing that Decree of *Damasus* was made, *statim post secundum Concilium, presently after the second Councell,* and was so strongly corroborated by Pope *Leo;* this may perswade, that none of their Popes before the dayes of *Gregory* would repeale the Decrees of those two Popes. Their owne *Nicholas Sanders* goes further, and saith r, *That this Canon was not allowed by the Romane Church, till the Councell at Laterane, under Innocentius the third,* which is more than sixe hundred yeares after the death of *Gregory :* and though he prove this by the testimony of *Guilielmus Tyrius,* yet I insist onely upon the time of *Gregorie,* whose words are very pregnant for this, and the other Canons of that second Councel; the *Romane Church, hactenus non habet nec accipit, did not till these dayes embrace nor approve them.*

22. Now that this same third Canon was all that time, held to be of full authority, and approved by the Church, as a Canon of an holy generall Councell, which bindeth all: notwithstanding the Popes did not approve it, nay, did even by their Synodall Decrees reject it; there are very many and cleare evidences: By warrant of that Canon did *Anatolius in the Councell of Chalcedon* s, and *Eutichius in the fift Synod* t, in the right of their See of *Constantinople take place before, and above* the *Patriarchs of Alexandria and Antioch;* none in those Councels repining thereat : nay, those Synods, and God himselfe (as is there u said) approving that precedence : And whereas this order had not beene observed in the *Ephesine Latrocinie; Flavianus* Bishop of *Constantinople* being set after the Bishops of *Antioch and Ierusalem,* the Bishops of the Councell of *Chalcedon* stormed thereat, and said x, *Why did not Flavianus sit in his proper place ?* that is, next to the Romane Bishop, or his Legates. By authority of the same Canon did *Chrysostome, when he was Bishop of Constantinople, depose* y *fifteene Bishops in Asia; ordaine others in their roomes; celebrate* z *a Councell at Ephesus, and call the Asian Bishops unto it;* none of which either could he have done, or would the other have obeyed him therein, had it not beene knowne, that they were subject to him as their Patriarke, by that Canon of the second generall Councell, to which they all must obey : And this was done about some twenty yeares after that Canon was made. So quickly was the same in force, and was acknowledged to bee of a binding authority. In the Councell of *Chalcedon,* when the truth of this Canon was most diligently examined, *Elutherius* Bishop of *Chalcedon* said, b *Sciens quia per Canones & per consuetudinem; I subscribed hereunto, knowing that the See of Constantinople hath these rights (in Asia and Pontus, as a Patriarke to governe there) both according to the Canons, and according to custome :* and the like was deposed by many Bishops of *Asia* and *Pontus.* They acknowledge, nay, they knew there was such a Canon; they knew also, that the custome and practice did *concurrere cum lege,* did *concurre with the Canon;* whereupon the glorious Iudges, after full discussing of this

cause;

p Sedes Apostolica quæ nobis præcepit. lib d. pa.137.b.
q Vehementer refutarunt hunc tertium Canone͂ Leo et Damasus. Turrian. lb de 6,7,et 8, Synodis. pa.65. Romana Ecclesia hactenus respuit hunc Canonem. Bin, not. in Conc.
2 § Approbatum r Iam primum (in Concilio Later.) Constantinopolitana sedes Romanæ Ecclesiæ assensum, publicè obtinuit, &c. Sand. lib.7. de visib. Monar. ad an. 1215.

s Act.1.et alijs ubi recensentur Episcopi.
t Coll.1.et alijs. u Ecce nos Deo volente Anatolium primum habemus. Ait Posca͂sinus in Conc. Chal. Act.1.pa. 8.b.
x Ibid.
y S.memoriæ Chrysostomus 15 Episcopos cepo suit in Asia, ex pro eis alios ordinavit. Conc. Chalc. Act.11. in fine. Zozo lib. 1.ca.6.
z Pallad. in vit. Chrys.
a Conc. habitum an.381. Chrysost. creatus Episcopus Cæsario et Attico Coss. Socr. lib. 6.ca.2. id est, circa an.398 cuius secundo anno, aut circiter, hæc evenerunt.
b Act.16.pa. 136.b.

cause, teftified [b], and fentenced, *that the Bifh. of Conftantinople had right-full authority to ordaine Metropolitane Bifhops in the Dioceffes of Thrace, Afia, and Pontus, and the whole Synod confented to them;* firft proclaiming, *Haec[c] jufta eft fententia, this is a juft fentence, this we fay all* : and then in the very Synodal Epiftle [d] to *Leo* teftifying the fame, to wit, that they had confirmed that cuftome to the Bifhop of *Conftantinople*, that he fhould ordaine *Metropolitanes* in *Thrace, Afia*, and *Pontus*; and thereby had confirmed the third Canon of the fecond Councell. This was the judgement of the whole Councell at *Chalcedon*, that is, of the whole Catholike Church in that age, to which have confented all Councels, and catholike Bifhops ever fince : All thefe doe approve, and judge to bee approved that Canon of the fecond generall *Councell*, which the Popes and Romane Church, not onely not approved, but exprefly and by Synodall decrees rejected.

23. About fome ninety yeares [e] after this, and an hundred fixty yeares [f] after that fecond Synod, did *Iuftinian* the Emperour confirme the [g] Canons, both of that fecond, and of al the former general Councels, giving unto them force of Imperiall lawes: Yea, hee further commanded thofe Canons, (this third among the reft) *Dipticis inferi, & praedicari, to be written in the Diptikes or Ecclefiafticall bookes, and publikely to be read in the Churches, in token of the publike and univerfall approbation of the fame.* This the fift Councell [h] teftifieth, as alfo *Victor*, and *Evagrius* [k], yea, the Emperour himfelfe alfo, *who both* [l] *profeffeth that he will not fuffer this cuftome to bee taken away, and fignifieth* [m] *that all Patriarkes are knowne to keepe in their Diptikes, and to recite thofe Canons in their Churches.* The Emperor doubted not but the Romane Church & Patriarke, as well as the reft, had done this, and yeelded obedience to fo holy an Edict; but the Romane Church deluded the Emperour herein: none of them, as *Bellarmine* [n] tels us, did after *Iuftinians* time, or as he accounts after the yeare 500, *reclamare*, contradict or fpeake againft that Canon, (which their filence the Emperour and others, not acquainted with the Romane Arts, did interpret to be a confent) but *Binius* [o] bewrayeth their policy; they, for peace and quietnes fake (being loth to exafperate the Emperour) did permit or connive at that honour conferred by the Canon upon the See of *Conftantinople*; yet, *nunquam à Romana Ecclefia approbatum fuit; it was never*, (thē not til *Gregories* time, which is as much as I intended to prove) *it was never*, faith hee, *approved by the Romane Church*; which hee proves by a Decretall of *Innocentius* the third; whence it is evident, feeing that Canon of the fecond generall Councell, was never, as *Binius* avoucheth, but certainly not till *Gregories* time, approved by the Pope, and yet was all that time approved by the catholike Church, even by the great and famous Councell at *Chalcedon*, & al who approve it, who are no fewer than the whole catholike Church; it is evident, I fay, that it is neither the Popes Approbation which maketh, nor his Reprobation which hindereth a Councell, or any Decree, or Canon thereof, to be an approved generall Councell, or a Synodall Canon, fuch as doth, and ought to binde all that are in the Church.

24. The Popes Approbation it is not : but what it is which makes
a generall

Marginal notes:
c Ibid.

d *Relat. ad Leo-nem poft act. 16.*

e *Conc. Chalced. habitum, an. 451*
f *Conc. Conftant. habit. an. 381.*
g *Nov. 131. ca. 3, et. 2.*

h *Coll. 2. pa. 524. a.*
i *In chron. an. 1. Iuftin.*
k *Lib. 4. ca. 11.*
l *Cod. l. 7. de fumma Trin.*
m *Nov. 115.*

n *Lib. 1. de Pont. ca. 24. § His.*

o *Not. in Conc. 2 §. Conftantinop.*

a generall Councell or Canon thereof, to be an approved Councell, or an approved Canon; and for such to bee rightly accounted, is not so easie to explane. This in an other Treatise I have at large handled, to which, if it ever see the light, I referre my selfe; yet suffer me to touch in this place so much as may serve to cleare this, and divers other doubts, which are obvious in their writings concerning this point.

25. That every Councell and Synodall decree thereof is approved or confirmed by those Bishops who are present in that Synod, who consent upon that decree, is by the Acts of the Councells most evident. For both their consenting judgement pronounced by word of mouth, and after that, their subscription to their decree, did ratifie and confirme their sentence. In that which they call the eighth generall Synod, after the sentence pronounced, the Popes Legates said P, p *Act. 10.* *Oportet ut hac manu nostra subscribendo confirmemus, it is needfull that wee confirme these things which we have decreed, by our subscribing unto them.* Of the great Nicene Councell *Eusebius* thus writeth q, *Those things q Lib.3. de vita which with one consent they had decreed,* ἐκυρώθη ἐν γραφῆς, *they were fully autho-* *Constant ca.13.* *rized, ratified, confirmed or approved,* (the Greeke word is very emphaticall) *by their subscription.* In the Councell of *Chalcedon*, when the agreement betwixt *Iuvenalis* and *Maximus* was decreed, they subscri- r *Act.6.* bed r in this forme; That which is consented upon, *confirmo, I by my sentence doe confirme;* or, *firma esse decerno*, I decree that it shall be firme: and to the like effect subscribed all the rest. Whereupon the glorious Iudges, without expecting any other confirmation either from Pope *Leo*, or any that was absent, said; This which is consented upon shall abide firme, *in omni tempore, for ever by our decree, and by the sentence of the Synod.* Of the second generall Councell, a Synod at *Hellespont* said s, s *Extat inter E-* *Hanc Synodum Timotheus una cum eis præsens firmavit, Timotheus, with the* *pist. post Concil.* *other Bishops, then present, confirmed this Synod.* The consent and subscrip- *Chal. pa.168. a.* tion of the Bishops present in the Synod, they call a *Confirmation* of the Synod. In the Synod t at *Masia*, after the sentence of the Synod t *Extat ibid. pa.* was given, they all subscribed in this forme, I M.P.D. &c. *confirmavi* 155. *& subscripsi*, have confirmed this Synodall sentence, and subscribed unto it. In the second Councell at *Carthage*, held about the time of Pope *Ce-* *lestine, Gennadius* said u, *Quæ ab omnibus sunt dicta propria debemus sub-* u *Tom.1. Conc.* *scriptione firmare*, what hath beene said and decreed by us all, wee ought by *pa.541.* our owne subscriptions to confirme: and all the Bishops answered, *Fiat, fiat, let us so doe*; and then they subscribed. So cleare it is, that whatsoever decree is made by any Councell, the same is truly and rightly said to bee confirmed by those very Bishops who make the Decree; confirmed I say, both by their joint consent in making that Decree, and by their subscribing unto it when it is made.

26. Vpon this confirmation or approbation of any Decree by the Bishops present in the Councell, doth the whole strength and authority of any Synodall decree rely; and upon no other confirmation of any Bishop whatsoever, when the Councell is generall and lawfull. For in such a Councell, lawfully called, lawfully governed, and lawfully proceeding, as well in the free discussing, as free sentencing of the cause; there is in true account the joynt consent of all Bishops and

Eccle-

Ecclefiafticall perfons in the whole world. No Bifhop can then complaine that either he is not called, or not admitted with freedome into fuch a Councell, unleffe that he be excommunicated, or fufpended, or for fome fuch like reafon juftly debarred. If all do come, they may and doe freely deliver their owne judgement; and that not onely for themfelves, but for all the Prefbyters in their whole Dioceffe. For feeing the paftorall care of every Dioceffe, even from the Apoftles time, and by them is committed to the Bifhop thereof, (all the reft being by him admitted but onely into a part of his care, and to affift him in fome parts of his Epifcopall function) he doth, at leaft (becaufe he fhould) he is fuppofed to admit none, but fuch as hee knoweth to profeffe the fame faith with himfelfe: whence it is, that in his voice is included the judgement of his whole Diocefan Church, and of all the Prefbyters therein: they all beleeving as he doth, fpeake alfo in the Councell by his mouth, the fame that he doth. If fome of the Bifhops come not perfonally, but either depute others in their roomes, or paffe their fuffrage (as often they did) in the voice of their Metropolitan, then their confent is expreffed in theirs, whom they put in truft to be their agents at that time. If any negligently abfent themfelves, neither perfonally, nor yet by delegates fignifying their minde, thefe are fuppofed to give a tacit confent unto the judgement which is given by them who are prefent; whom the others are fuppofed to thinke not onely to be able and fufficient without themfelves to define that caufe; but that they will define it in fuch fort as themfelves doe wifh and defire: for otherwife they would have afforded their prefence, or at leaft fent fome deputies to affift them in fo great and neceffary a fervice. If any out of ftomack or hatred to the truth, do wilfully refufe to come, becaufe they diffent from the others in that doctrine, yet even thefe alfo are in the eie of reafon fuppofed to give an implicit confent unto that which is decreed, yea though *explicitè* they doe diffent from it. For every one doth, and in reafon is fuppofed to confent on this generall point, that a Synodall judgement muft bee given in that doubt & controverfie, there being no better nor higher humane Court than is that of a generall Councell, by which they may bee directed. Now becaufe there never poffibly could any Synodall judgement be given, if the wilfull abfence of one or a few fhould bee a juft barre to their fentence; therefore all in reafon are thought to confent that the judgement muft be given by thofe who will come, or who do come to the Councell, and that their decree or fentence fhall ftand for the judgement of a generall Councell, notwithftanding their abfence who wilfully refufe to come.

27. If then all the Bifhops prefent in the Councell do confent upon any decree, there is in it one of thofe wayes which we have mentioned, either by perfonall declaration, or by fignification made by their delegates and agents, or by a tacit, or by an implicit confent, the confenting judgement of all the Bifhops and Prefbyters in the whole Church, that is, of al who either have judicatory power or authoritie to preach publikely; and therefore fuch a decree is as fully authorized, confirmed, and approved, as if all the Bifhops and Prefbyters in the world

world had perſonally ſubſcribed in this manner, I confirme this Decree. Hereof there is a worthy example in the third generall Councell. No Preſbyters at all were therein, nor in their owne right. Very many Biſhops were perſonally abſent, and preſent onely by their
Legates or Agents ; as almoſt all the Weſterne Biſhops; and by name
Celeſtine Patriarch of *Rome*. Some, no queſtion, upon other occaſions
neglected that buſineſſe ; as, it may be, the Biſhops of *Gangra*, and of
Heraclea in *Macedonia*, who were not at this Councell. Divers o-
thers wilfully and obſtinately refuſed to come to that holy Synod ; as
by name *Neſtorius* Patriarch of *Conſtantinople*, *Iohn* Patriarch of *Antioch*, and ſome forty Biſhops; who at the ſame time while the holy
Councell was held in the Church at *Epheſus*, held a Conventicle by
themſelves in an Inne, in the ſame Citie ; and yet notwithſtanding the
perſonall abſence of the firſt, the negligent of the ſecond, and wilfull
abſence of the laſt, the holy x generall Councell ſaith of their Synodall judgement, given by thoſe who were then preſent, that it was *nihil aliud quam communis & concors terrarum orbis ſenſus & conſenſus, nothing elſe but the common and conſenting judgment of the whole world.* How
could this be, when ſo many Biſhops, beſides three Patriarchs, were
either perſonally, or negligently, or wifully abſent ? How was there in
that decree the conſent of theſe ? Truly becauſe they all (even all the
Biſhops in the world) did either perſonally, or by their Agents, expreſſe ; or elſe in ſuch a tacit and implicit manner (as wee declared)
wrap up their judgement in the Synodall decree made by the Biſhops
preſent in the Councell.

   28. But what if many of thoſe who are preſent, doe diſſent from
that which the reſt being the greater part doe decree ? Truly, even
theſe alſo doe *implicitè*, and are in reaſon to bee judged to conſent to
that ſame decree. For every one is ſuppoſed to agree on that generall
Maxime of reaſon, that in ſuch an aſſembly of Iudges, what the greater part decreeth ſhall ſtand as the Act and Iudgement of the whole :
ſeeing otherwiſe it would be impoſſible that ſuch a multitude of Biſhops ſhould ever give any judgement in a cauſe, for ſtill ſome in per-
verſeneſſe and pertinacie would diſſent. Seeing then it is the ordinance of God that the Church ſhall judge, and ſeeing there can no
other meanes be deviſed how they ſhould judge, unleſſe the ſentence
of the greater part may ſtand for their judgement, reaſon enforceth
all to conſent upon this Maxime. Vpon this is that Imperiall Law
grounded, *Quod y major pars curiæ effecit, pro rato habetur, acſi omnes id
egerint, what the greater part of the Court ſhall do, that is ratified, or to ſtand
for the judgement of the Court, as if all had done the ſame.* And againe,
*Refertur z ad univerſos quod publicè fit per majorem partem : That is accoun-
ted the act of all, which is publikely done by the greater part.* Vpon this
ground is that truly ſaid by *Bellarmine a, That whereon the greater part
doth conſent, eſt verum decretum Concilij, is the true decree of the Councell,*
even of the whole Councell. Vpon the equitie of this rule was it ſaid
in the Councell at *Chalcedon b*, when ten Biſhops diſſented from the
reſt, *Non eſt juſtum decem audiri, It is not juſt that the ſentence of ten ſhould
prevaile againſt a thouſand and two hundred Biſhops.* Vpon the equitie of
the

x *Epiſt. Conc. E-
pheſ. ad Imper.
tom. 2. Act. Con.
Epheſ. epiſt. 17.*

y *Dig. Lib. 50.
leg. 19.*

z *Dig. Lib. 5. tit.
17. de Reg. Iuris
160.*
a *Lib. 2. de Conc.
ca. 11. §. At.*

b *Act. 4. p. 90. b.*

the fame rule did the fift generall Councell truly & conftantly judge ^c, *that the Councell of Chalcedon even in that definition of faith, which they all with one confent agreed upon, condemned the Epiftle of Ibas as hereticall; although they knew that Maximus, with Pafcafinus, and the other Legats of Pope Leo, in the Councell of Chalcedon, adjudged that Epiftle to be orthodoxall.* How was it the confenting judgement of the whole Councell of *Chalcedon*, when yet fome did expreffe their diffent therein? How, but by that implicit confent which all give to that rule of reafon, that the judgement of the greater part fhall ftand for the judgment of the whole; which the fift Councell doth plainly fignifie, faying ^d, In Councels we muft not attend the interloquutions of one or two, but what is defined in common, *ab omnibus, aut amplioribus, either by all, or by the greater part :* to that we muft attend as to the judgement of the whole Councell. But omitting all the reft, there is one example in the Councell of *Chalcedon* moft pregnant to this purpofe.

29. All ^e the Councell, fave onely the Popes Legates, confented upon that third Canon, decreed in the fecond, and now confirmed in this fourth Councell, that the See of *Conftantinople* fhould have Patriarchall dignity over *Thrace*, *Afia*, and *Pontus*, and have precedence before other Patriarches, as the next after the Bifhop of Rome. The Legates following the inftructions of *Leo*, were fo averfe in this matter, that they faid ^f not without fome choler, *Contradictio noftra his geftis inhæreat, Let our contradiction cleave to thefe Acts :* and fo it doth, to the eternall difgrace both of them and their mafter. The glorious Iudges notwithftanding this diffenting of the Legates and of Pope *Leo* him- felfe in them, faid ^g concerning that Canon, That which we have fpoken, (that the See of Conftantinople ought to be the fecond, &c.) *Tota Synodus, the whole Councell hath approved it.* Why, but the Popes Legates approved it not; they contradicted it. True, in this particular they diffented. But becaufe they as all other Bifhops, even Pope *Leo* himfelfe, confented unto that generall Maxime, That the judgement of the greater part fhall ftand for the judgement of the whole Councell, in that generall both the Legats of *Leo*, and *Leo* himfelfe, did *implicitè* and virtually confent to that very Canon, from which actually and *explicitè* they did then diffent. For which caufe the moft prudent Iudges truly faid, *Tota Synodus, the whole Councell hath approved this Canon :* either *explicitè* or *implicitè*, either expreffely or virtually approved it. Neither did onely thofe fecular Iudges fo efteeme, the whole generall Councell it felfe profeffed the fame, and that even in the Sy- nodall Relation of their Acts to Pope *Leo :* The univerfall ^h Synod faid thus, *We have condemned Diofcorus, we have confirmed the faith, wee have confirmed the Canon of the fecond Councell for the honour of the See of Conftantinople, we have condemned the herefie of Eutyches :* Thus writ the whole Councell to *Leo :* declaring evidently that act of approving that Canon to be the Act of the whole Synod, although they knew the contradiction of the Pope and his Legates to cleave unto it.

30. You fee now that in every fentence of a generall and lawfull Councell there is an affent of all Bifhops and Prefbyters, they all either *explicitè*, or *tacitè*, or *implicitè*, confenting to that decree, whether

ther they be absent or present, and whether in that particular they consent or dissent. Now because there can bee no greater humane judgement in any cause of faith or ecclesiasticall matter, than is the consenting judgement of all Bishops and Presbyters, that is, of all who have power either to teach or judge in those causes; it hence clearly ensueth, that there neither is nor can be any Episcopall or Ecclesiasticall confirmation or approbation whatsoever of any decree, greater, stronger, or of more authority, then is the judgement it selfe of such a generall Councell, and their owne confirmation or approbation of the decrees which they make; for in every such decree there is the consent of all the Bishops and Presbyters in the whole world.

31. Besides this confirmation of any synodall decree, which is by Bishops, and therefore to bee called *Episcopall*, there is also another confirmation added by Kings and Emperors, which is called *Royall* or *Imperiall*; by this later, religious Kings not onely give freedome and liberty, that those decrees of the Councell shall stand in force of Ecclesiasticall Canons within their dominions, so that the contemners of them may be with allowance of Kings, corrected by Ecclesiasticall censures, but further also, doe so strengthen, and backe the same by their sword, and civill authority, that the contradicters of those decrees, are made liable to those temporall punishments, which are set downe in *Ezra* [i], *to death, to banishment, to confiscation of goods, or to imprisonment*, as the quality of the offence shall require, and the wisedome of that Imperiall State shall think fit. Betwixt these two confirmations, *Episcopall* and *Imperiall*, there is exceeding great oddes and difference. By the former, judiciall sentence is given, and the synodall decree made or declared to be made, for which cause it may rightly be called a judiciall or definitive confirmation: by the later, neither is the synodal decree made, nor any judgment given to define that cause (for neither Princes nor any Lay men, are Iudges to decide those matters, as the Emperours *Theodosius* and *Valentinian* excellently declare in [k] their directions to *Candidianus*, in the Councell of *Ephesus*;) but the synodall decree being already made by the Bishops, and their judgement given in that cause, is strengthened by Imperiall authority; for which cause, this may fitly be called a supereminent or corroborative confirmation of the synodall judgement. The former confirmation is *Directive*, teaching what all are to beleeve or observe in the Church: the later is *Coactive*, compelling all, by civill punishment to beleeve or observe the Synodall directions. The former is *Essentiall* to the Decree; such as if it want, there is no Synodall decree made at all: the later is *Accidentall*, which though it want, yet is the Decree of the Councell, a true Synodall Decree and sentence. The former bindes all men to obedience to that Decree, but yet onely under paine of Ecclesiasticall censures: the latter bindes the subjects only of those Princes, who give the Royall Confirmation to such Decrees, and binds them under the pain only of temporal punishment. By vertue of the former, the contradicters or contemners of those Decrees are rightly to be accounted either heretikes in causes of faith, or contumacious in other matters; and such are truly subject to the censures of

the

i *Ezr.7.16.*

k *Nefas est eum qui Episcoporum catalogo adscriptus non est, Ecclesiasticis negotijs se immiscere. (nempe ut Iudice qui definiat.) Epist.Imp.ad Synod.Ephes.to. 1. Act.Ephes. Conc.ca.32.*

the Church, though, if the later be wanting, those censures cannot
bee inflicted by any, or upon any, but with danger to incurre the indignation of Princes : By vertue of the later; not onely the Church
may safely, yea, with great allowance and praise; inflict their Ecclesiasticall censures, but inferiour Magistrates also may, nay ought to proceed against such contemners of those Synodall decrees, as against notorious, convicted, and condemned heretikes; or in causes which are
not of faith, but of externall discipline and orders, as against contumacious persons. The Episcopall confirmation is the first in order,
but yet because it proceeds from those who are all subject to Imperiall authority, it is in dignitie *inferiour.* The Imperiall confirmation is
the last in order, but because it proceeds from those to whom everie
soule is subject, it is in dignity *Supreme.*

32. This Imperiall confirmation, as holy generall Councels did
with all submission intreate of Emperours, so religious Emperors did
with all willingnesse grant unto them. Of the great *Nicene* Councell
Eusebius saith [l], *Constantine sealed, ratified, and confirmed the decrees which
were made therein.* The second general Councel writ [m] thus to the Emperour *Theodosius, We beseech your clemency, that by your letters, ratum esse
jubeas confirmesque Concilij decretum, that you would ratifie and confirme the decree of this Councell :* and that the Emperour did so, his Emperiall Edict, before [n] mentioned, doth make evident. To the third
Councell the Emperor writ thus [o], *Let matters cōcerning religion and piety be diligently examined, contention being laid aside; ac tum demū à nostrae
pietate confirmationem expectate; and then expect from us our imperiall confirmation.* The holy Councell having done so, writ [p] thus to the Emperour, *We earnestly intreate your piety, ut jubeat ea omnia, that you would
cōmand, that all which is done by this holy and Oecumenical Councell against
Nestorius, may stand in force, per vestra pietatis nutum et consensum con-
firmata, being confirmed by your royall assent :* And that the Emperour
yeelded to their request, his Edict [q] against *Nestorius* doth declare. In
the fourth Councell the Emperour said [r], *We come to this Synod, not to
shew our power, sed ad confirmandam fidem, but to confirme the faith.* And
whē he had signified before all the Bishops his royall assent [s] to their
decree, the whole Councell cryed out, *Orthodoxam fidem tu confirmasti;
thou hast confirmed the Catholike faith:* often ingeminating those joyfull
acclamations. That *Iustinian* confirmed the fift Councell, his imperiall
Edict for condemning those *Three Chapters,* which after the Synodall
judgment stood in more force than before; his severity [t] in punishing
the contradicters of the Synodall sentence, partly by exile, partly by
imprisonment, are cleare witnesses. The sixt Councell said [u] thus to
the Emperour, *O our most gracious Lord grant this favour unto us, signacu-
lum tribue, seale and ratifie all that we have done; vestram inscribito imperialem ratihabitionem; adde unto them your imperiall confirmation, that by your
holy Edicts, and godly constitutions they may stand in firme force.* And the
Emperour upon their humble request, set forth his Edict, wherein he
saith [x], *We have published this our Edict, that we might, corroborare
atque confirmare ea quae definita sunt, corroborate and confirme those things
which are defined by the Councell.* To all which, that may bee added
which

l *Lib. 4. de vita
constant. ca. 27.*
m *Epist. Synod.
2. post Act.
Concil. pa. 518.*

n *Hoc. cap. nu.
19.*
o *Act. Ephes.
Conc. tom. 3.
ca. 17.*
p *Act. Conc.
Eph. to. 4. ca. 8.*

q *Imperator sen-
tentia Synodi
publicè approba-
ta, Nestorio ex-
ilium indicit.
Act. Con. Eph. ta.
5. ca. 11. et lege
ult. de heret.
Cod. Theod.*
r *Act. 6.*
s *In perpetuum
que à vobis ter-
minata sunt ser-
ventur. Ibid.*
t *Vict. in Chron.
an. post Coss. Bas.
13, 14 15, &c.*
u *Act. 18.*
x *Edict. Constāt.
Pogon. Act. 18.
Conc. 6.*

which *Basilius* the Emperour said in the eighth Synod, as they call it; *I had purposed to have subscribed after al the Bishops, as did my predecessors, Constantine the great, Theodosius, Martian, and the rest*: thereby evidently testifying, not onely the custome of imperiall confirmation to have been observed in all former Councels, but the difference also betwixt it and the Episcopall subscription; the Bishops first subscribing, and thereby making or declaring, that they had made a Synodall decree; the Emperours after them all subscribing, as ratifying by their Imperiall confirmation what the Bishops had decreed.

33. By this now it fully appeareth, what it is which maketh any Synod or any Synodal decree, to be, and justly to be accounted an approved Synod, or an approved Synodall and Oecumenicall decree. It is not the Popes assent, approbation, or confirmation, (as they, without all ground of truth doe fancy,) which at any time did, or possibly can doe this. It is onely the Vniversall and Oecumenicall consent of the whole Church, and of all the members thereof, upon any decree made by a generall Councell, which truly makes that an approved decree; which generall and Oecumenicall consent or approbation, is shewed partly by the Episcopall confirmation of that decree, made by the Bishops present therein, wherein there is ever either an expresse, or a vertuall and implicite consent of all the Bishops and Presbyters, and so of all the Clergy in the world; partly by the royall and imperiall confirmation given to that decree by Christian Kings and Emperours, in which there is an implicite consent of all Laickes in the whole Church, Kings and Princes assenting not onely for themselves, but in the name of all their Lay subjects, for whom they undertake, that either they shall willingly obey that decree, or else by severity of punishments, be compelled thereunto. If these two confirmations, or either of them be wanting, the Councell and decree which is supposed to be made therein, is neither an approved or confirmed Councell, nor decree, though the Pope send forth ten thousand Buls to approve and confirme the same: But if these two confirmations concurre in any decree of a generall and lawfull Councel, though the Pope reprobate and reject that Councell or decree never so often, yet is both that Councell an approved generall Councel, and the decree thereof an approved or confirmed Synodall and Oecumenicall decree, approved I say, and confirmed by the greatest humane authority and judgement that possibly can bee, either found, or desired, even by the whole catholike Church, and every member, whether Ecclesiasticall or Laicall, therein: And whosoever after such an ample approbation or confirmation, shall at any time contradict or contemne such a Councell or decree, he doth not, nor can he thereby impare the dignity and authority of it, but he demonstrates himselfe to be an heretike, or, at least, a contumacious person, insolently, and in the pride of his singularity despising that judgement of the Councell, which the whole Church, and every member thereof, yea, even himselfe also among them, hath approved.

34. You will yet demand of mee, why generall Councels have sought the Popes approbation and confirmation of their decrees, (as
did

Church, if hee should consent; hence it was, that if any Patriarke, Patriarchall Primate, or other eminent Bishop were absent at the time of the Councell, the Church and Councell did the more earnestly labour to have his expresse consent and confirmation to the Synodall decrees: This was the cause why both the religious Emperour *Theodosius*[y], and *Cyrill*, with other orthodoxall Bishops, were so earnest to have *Iohn* Patriarke of *Antioch*, to consent to the holy Ephesine Synod; which long before was ended; that as he had beene the ringleader to the factious conventicle, and those who defended *Nestorius* with his heresie; so his yeelding to the truth, and embracing the Ephesine Councell, which condemned *Nestorius*, might draw many others to doe the like, and so indeed it did. This was the principall reason why some of the ancient Councels, as that by name of *Chalcedon*, (for all did it not) sought the Popes confirmation to their Synodall decrees; not thinking their sentence in any cause to bee invalid, or their Councell no approved Councell, if it wanted his approbation or confirmation, (a fancy not dreamed of in the Church in those daies) but wheras the Pope was never personally present in any of those w[ch] they account the 8 general Councels, the Synod thought it fit to procure, if they could, his expresse and explicite consent to their decrees, that he being the chiefe Patriarch in the Church, might by his example move all, and by his authoritie draw his owne Patriarchall Diocesse (as usually hee did) to consent to the same decrees; whereas, if he should happen to dissent (as *Vigilius* did at the time of the fift Councell) hee was likely to cause (as *Vigilius* then did) a very grievous rent and schisme in the Church of God.

37. There was yet another use and end of those subsequent confirmations, whether by succeeding Councels, or absent Bishops: and that was, that every one should thereby either testifie his orthodoxy in the faith, or else manifest himselfe to bee an heretike: For as the approving of the six generall Councels, and their decrees of faith did witnesse one to be a Catholike in those doctrines; so the very refusing to approve or confirme any one of those Councels, or their decrees of faith, was *ipso facto*, without any further examination of the cause, an evident conviction that he was a condemned heretike; such an one, as in the pride and pertinacie of his heart rejected that holy synodall judgement, which all the whole catholike Church, and every member thereof, even himselfe also had *implicitè* before confirmed and approved. In which respect an heretike may truly bee called αὐτοκατάκριτος, being convicted and condemned not onely by the evidence of truth, and by synodall sentence, but even by that judgment which his owne selfe had given *implicitè*, in the decree of the Councell. The summe is this; The former confirmation by the *Bishops* present in the Synod, is *Iudiciall*; the later confirmation by the Bishops who are absent, is *Pacificall*. The former is *authoritative*, such as gives the whole authority to any decree: the later (whether by succeeding Councels, or absent Bishops) is *Testificative*, such as witnesseth them to be orthodoxall in that decree. The former, joyned to the Imperiall confirmation, is *Essentiall*, which essentially makes both the Councell;

y *Sacra Imper. ad Iohan. to. 5. Act. Eph. Conc. ca. 3. Cyril. Epist. 38. ad Dynatium to. eod. ca. 16.*

cell an approved Councel, & all the decrees therof, approved, synodal, and Oecumenicall decrees : the later is *accidentall*, which being granted by a Bishop, doth much grace himselfe; but little or nothing the Synod; and being denyed by any, doth no whit at all either disgrace the Synod, or impare the dignity and authority thereof, but doth extreamely disgrace the partie himselfe who denyeth it, and puls downe upon him, both the just censures of the Church, and those civill punishments which are due to heretikes or contumacious persons.

38. My conclusion now is this : Seeing this fift Councell was both for the calling generall, and for the proceeding therin lawfull, and orderly; and seeing, although it wanted the Popes consent, yet it had the concurrence of those two confirmations, before mentioned, *Episcopall* and *Imperiall*, in which is included the Oecumenicall approbation of the whole catholike Church : it hence therefore ensueth, that as from the first assembling of the Bishops it was an holy, a lawfull, and Oecumenicall Councell; so from the first pronouncing of their synodall sentence, and the Imperiall assent added thereunto, it was an approved generall Councell, approved by the whole catholike Church; and so approved, that without any expresse consent of the Pope added unto it, it was of as great worth, dignity, and authoritie, as if all the Popes since *S. Peters* time had, with their owne hands subscribed unto it. And this may suffice to satisfie the fourth and last exception which *Baronius* devised to excuse *Vigilius* from heresie.

Cap. XIX.

The true notes to know which are generall *and* lawfull, *and which either are not* generall, *or being* generall, *are no* lawfull Councels; *with divers examples of both kindes.*

HAT which hath beene said in the former Chapter is sufficient to refute that cavill of *Baronius*, against the fift Councell, whereby he pretends it to have neither been a general, nor a lawfull Synod, because the Pope resisted the assembling, and contradicted the decree and sentence thereof; but for as much as it is not victory, but truth which I seeke, and the full satisfaction of the reader in this cause, and seeing this point about the lawfulnesse of generall Councels, is frequent, and very obvious, and such as being rightly conceived, will give great light to this whole controversie about Councels; I will crave liberty to lanch somewhat further into this deepe, and explane, with what convenient brevity I can, what it is which maketh any Synod to bee, or rightly to be esteemed a generall and lawfull Councell.

2. As the name of *Synod* doth in his primary and large acception agree to every assembly, so doth the name of Councell to every assembly of consultation : The former being derived from *συνοδος*,

292   *What required to a lawfull generall Councell.*   Cap. 19.

is all one with *Cœtus*, and imports the assembly of any multitude which meeteth and commeth together: The later being derived of *Cilia* [a], (whence also *supercilium*) imports the common or joynt intending, or bending their eyes, both of body and minde, to the investigation of the truth in that matter, which is proposed in their assembly: But both of those words being now drawne from those their large and primitive significations, are by Ecclesiasticall writers, and use of speech, (*penes quem jus est, & norma loquendi*) restrained and appropriated onely to those assemblies of Bishops, and Ecclesiasticall persons; wherein they come together to consult of such matters as concernes either the faith or discipline of the Church. Of these, because some are lawfull, others unlawfull Synods, if we can finde what it is which maketh a generall and lawfull Councell, it will bee easie therby to discerne which are unlawfull Synods, seeing it is vulgarly and truly said, that, *Rectum* is *index sui & obliqui*.

3. That a Synod be generall and lawfull, there are three things necessarily, and even essentially required, the want of any one of which is a just barre and exception, why that Synod is either not generall, or not lawfull. The first, which concernes the generalitie, is, that the calling and summons to the Councell be generall and Oecumenicall; so that all Bishops be called, and when they are come, have free accesse to the same Councell, unlesse for some fault of their owne, or some just reason, they ought to bee debarred: For if the calling to any Synod bee out of some parts onely of the Church, and not out of the whole, the judgement also of such a Councell is but partiall, not generall, and the Councell is but particular, not Oecumenicall, seeing some of those who have judicatory power are either omitted, or unjustly excluded from the Synod: The want of this was a just exception taken by the Pope *Iulius*, against that Councell of *Antioch* [b], (wherein *Athanasius* was deposed by the *Arian* faction, and *Gregory* of *Cappadocia* intruded into his See) why it neither was, nor could be esteemed generall, or such as should binde the whole Church, by the decrees made by it; for said *Iulius* [c], ὅτι αὐτὸν εἰς τὴν σύνοδον ἐκ ἐκάλεσαν, *because they did not so much as call him to that Synod*; whereas the Canons of the Church forbid that any decree (which should have power to binde the whole Church) should bee made without the sentence, judgement, and consent of the Bishop of *Rome*, (either attained, or at least sought for.) The Canon which *Iulius* mentioned, might well ordaine, and if there were no such Canon, yet even reason and equity doe teach, that such decrees as concerne the whole Church, and are to binde them all, ought to be made by the helpe, judgement, and advise of them all; according to the rule, *Quod* [d] *omnes tangit, ab omnibus approbari debet*. The wilfull omission of any one Bishop, much more of the Bish. of *Rome*, who then was the chiefe Patriarch in the world, declares the Councell not to be generall, seeing unto it there was onely a partiall, and not a generall summons or calling.

4. As this first condition is required to the generality, so are the other two for the lawfulnesse and order of Synods: For if the Apostles

marginalia
a *Concilium dictum à communi intentione, eo quod in unum summes dirigant mentis obtutû: Cilia enim oculorum sunt. Isiod. Met. in suam Canon. collect.*

b *Extat tom. I. Conc. pa. 420.*

c *Apud Socr. L. I. ca. 13. et Zozom. lib. 3. ca. 9.*

d *Reg. Iurù 29.*

Hesrule, *Let c all things be done decently,and in order,* must bee kept in every private and particular Church,how much more in those venerable assemblies of Oecumenicall Councels, which are the Armies of God,& of the Angels of all the Churches of God,amõg whom doth, and ought to shine gravity, prudence, and all sacred, and fitting orders,no lesse than in the cœlestiall Hierarchy; and in the very presence of the Majesty of God. If they bee gathered in Gods name, how can they be other than lawfull and orderly Assemblies, seeing *God f is not the God of confusion g, or disorder,but of peace in all Churches.* Now the lwfulnesse and order of Synods, consists partly in their orderly assembling,and partly in their orderly government and proceedings, when they are assembled; whensoever the Bishops of any generall Councell first assemble together by lawfull authority, and then are governed by lawfull authority also; that orderly, lawfull, and due sinodall proceedings be onely used therein,as well in the free and diligent discussion of the causes proposed, as in the free sentencing thereof,the same is truly and properly to bee called ἔννομος ἐκκλησία h, *a lawfull Synod :* But if either of these conditions be wanting,it becomes unlawfull and disorderly. If the Bishops assemble together, either not being called, or if called, yet not by such as have right and authory to call them; though this in a large acception may bee called a sinod, that is; an assembly of Bishops, yet because they doe unlawfully & disorderly assemble together, it is in propriety of speech to be termed a Cóventicle,a riotous,tumultuous,& seditious assembly; such as that was of *Demetrius* i,& the other Ephesiãs,who,without calling and order;ἄτακτως, rusht k & run headlong together to uphold the honour of their great *Diana;* which both the Spirit of God condemneth, as a confused l or disorderly assembly, and the more wise among them taxed;as a riotous and seditious m tumult. If being wtfully called, yet they either want a lawfull President to governe them; or having one; yet want freedome and liberty either in discussing or giving judgement in the cause;such a Synod, though in respect their assembling it be lawfull, yet in respect of their proceedings and judgment,it is unlawfull,and disorderly, and therefore in propriety of speech to be termed a conspiracy, because those men conspire & band themselves, as did the Councell n of the Priests with *Pilate,* by unjust and unlawfull meanes to suppresse the truth; and oppresse innocency.

. But unto whõ belongs that right to call general Councels,& whẽ they are called,to see orderly & synodal proceedings observed therein? To whom? to whom else but only to those who have Imperiall & regal authority,whether they be one(as whẽ the Empire was united, the whole Christiã world subject to his authority;)or moe,as it was when the Empire was devided,and ever since that great dissolution of it in the time o of *Charles* the great : To them, and them onely, this right to belong,I have in two other bookes, the one concerning the

Cc 3

calling

Marginal notes:

c *1 Cor.14. 40.*

f *1 Cor.14.33.*
g οὐ γὰ τ ἀκαταστασίας τὴν ἀλλ᾽ εὐταξίας, κατὰ ὁπόσιι βασίας.

h *Act.19.39.*

i *Ib.v.24.et seq.*
k *Ibid.v. 19.*
l ἐκκλησία συγκεχυμένη. *v.32.*
m *Periclitamur argui seditionis. v.40.*

n *Mat.26.59. & ca. 17.2. & Act.4.27.*

o *Circa an.800.*

calling, the other concerning the Prefidencie in Councels, at large
and clearly demonftrated; & I hold them to be fo evident truths, both
by the doctrine of Scripture, and by the conftant judgement and practice of the Catholike Church, for more than eight hundred yeares
after Chrift, that if any would reade the Tomes of the Councels, hee
had need put out both his eyes, if he will not fee this.

6. To them, and them onely is the fword [p] given by God, that by
it they might maintaine the faith, and ufe it to the praife of them that
doe well, but take vengeance on them that doe evill: *They are the*
nurfing q fathers of the Church, unto whom the care is committed by
God, that all his Children, to whom they, next unto God, are fathers, *be fed with the fincere milke [r] of Gods word,* all mixture and poifon
of herefie and impiety being taken away, and fevered from it: They
are like *Iofhua* [f] and *David,* appointed by God to be πoιμένες λαων *the Pa-*
ftours [t], even fupreme Paftours of the Ifrael of God, not indeed to teach
and give the food themfelves, (which duty belongs to their inferiour
fervants) yet to performe those wch are the principall & moft [u] proper
Paftoral acts & offices, *procurare ac providere alteri cibū, ducere, reducere,*
tueri, præeffe, regere, caftigare; to provide that all the sheepe of Chrift have
wholefome and convenient food given unto them, to lead them, bring them
backe, defend, governe, and chaftife them when they will not obey their Pafto-
rall call and command. None of all which Paftorall duties were it poffible for Kings to performe, if for publike tranquillity and inftruction of Gods people they might not by their authority affemble a
generall Councell of Bifhops, and being affembled, if they might
not defend and uphold all juft and equall, but caftigate and keepe
away all violent, fraudulent, and unjuft proceedings in fuch Councels.

7. I purpofely faid *fupreme* Paftours; for none is ignorant, that
Peter [x] and all the Apoftles equally with him, as alfo all [y] who either
in their Prefbyteriall or Epifcopall authority fucceed unto them (for
in their *Apoftolicall* none of them had or have any fucceffour) that
all thefe are Paftours [z] alfo of Gods flock, but they are all fubordinate
to the Imperiall Paftours of the people of God, the sheep-hooke is
fubject to the Scepter, the Crofier to the Imperiall Crowne. Concerning Kings Saint *Peter* gives a generall precept, *Feare God [a], and*
honour the King; which honour he exprefly calleth fubjection [b] and o-
bedience in the fame Chapter; firft wee owe obedience to God, and
next God, unto Kings and Emperours. Concerning all others excepting Kings, and fuch as have Kingly authority, Saint *Paul* gives a like
generall precept, *Let [c] every foule be fubject to the higher powers,* even to
thofe, who by Gods warrant, and as his Vicegerents, doe beare [d] the
fword: to them every foule ought to be fubject; who can except thee
from this generality? This is commanded, faith *Chryfoftome [e], Not one-*
ly to fecular men, but to all, to Monkes, to Priefts and Bifhops, the Apoftle
teacheth them, *ex debito obedire, even in duty to obey Kings and Princes,*
five

p *Rom.* 13.2,3.
q *Ifa.* 49.23.
r 1 *Pet.* 2.2.
f *Numb.* 27.17.
Pfal. 78.71,72.
t Tam Hebraice
quam in 70. In-
terpr. et apud
Hier. legitur
[ad pafcendum
Iacob populum
fuum] et [pavit
eos] quod alij
vertunt, ad re-
gendum.
u Non proprie
dicitur pafcere
alium, qui cibum
quacunque rati-
one miniftrat,
fed qui procurat
et providet alteri
cibum, quod eft
terte Præpofiti, et
gubernatoris, &
Actus Paftoralis
non eft tantum
prebere cibum,
fed etiam ducere,
& c. Bell. lib. 1.
de Pont. Rom.
ca. 15. § Primū.
et § Deinde.
x *Iohn* 21. 15,
17.
y Cum ei (Petro)
dicitur, ad omnes
dicitur, Amas
me? pafce oves
meas. Aug. lib. de
agone Chrift. ca.
30.
z *Ier.* 23.1,2.
Ezech. 34. per
totum, et *Act.* 20
28. et 1 *Pet.* 5.2.
a 1 *Pet.* 2.17.
b *Ibid* v. 30.
c *Rom.* 13.1.
d *Ibid.* v. 4.
e *Chryf. in* ca.
33. *ad Rom.*

ve Apostolus sis, sive Propheta, sive Euangelista, sive quisquis tandem fu-
ris; not the Prophets, not the Apostles, not the Euangelists, not any
[r]ule is exempt from this subjection : and if not *Peter* himselfe, then
[ce]rtainly not his Vicar, as the Pope [f] cals himselfe : And this very sub-
[je]ction of the Pope, and all Bishops to the Emperours, to omit *Silve-*
[ste]r, Iulius, Leo, and *Gregorie,* Pope *Agatho* in most submissive manner
[a]cknowledgeth almost seven hundred ᵹ yeares after Christ, [h] *Omnes nos*
[con]sules, vestri imperij famuli; **All we Bishops are the servants of your im-**
[pe]riall highnesse, saith *Agatho,* and a Synod of 125 Westerne Bishops
[w]ith him; to which purpose hee cals *Italy* his servile [i] Province, and
[Ro]me his servile City; adding, that he did this at the Emperours sa-
[cr]ed command, *pro obedientia satisfactione, pro obedientia quam debuimus,*
[fo]r that obedience which hee did owe to the Emperour; nay, yet in more
[lo]wly manner, he saith not, that hee, but, *studiosa obedientia nostri fa-*
[c]ulatus implevit; the willing obedience of his owne servitude to the Empe-
[ro]ur, did performe this. Nor was this the profession onely of *Agatho,*
[an]d the Westerne Bishops, but the whole sixt Councell approved
[th]e same, *Petrus* [k] *per Agathonem loquebatur, Saint Peter spake by the*
[mo]uth of Agatho. Now because they all acknowledge the Pope to
[be] the first and chiefe Bishop in the Church, (for they all in that
[C]ouncell approve [l] the Councels of *Chalcedon,* and first *Constantinopo-*
[l]ane, in both [m] w[ch] that is decreed) seeing by the confession of *Aga-*
[th]o, by them approved, the Pope is a servant, and oweth subjection
[an]d obedience to the Emperour; much more are all other Bishops in
[th]e whole world, servants, and subjects to the Imperial command,
[an]d that by the consenting judgment of the whole catholike Church,
[rep]resented in that sixt generall Councell.

8. The same Soveraignty, and supreme Pastorall authority of
[ki]ngs, is after this againe testified in that which they call the eighth
[ge]nerall Councell, more than [n] eight hundred and sixty yeares after
[CH]RIST. Basilius the Emperour said before the Councell, in his
[let]ters [o] unto them, *The government of the Ecclesiasticall ship is by the*
[di]vine Providence committed unto us : in that ship doth saile all who are
[me]mbers of the Church, Bishops or Laicks, and the government of the whole
[shi]p is given to the Emperour; Hee, like the Pilot, rules and directs all.
[Au]derus the Iesuite, and *Binius* following him, in stead of *nobis* have
[pu]t *vobis* in the latine text; as if *Basilius* had said, that the government
[of] the Church belonged to Bishops, not to Emperours : It is a
[Ie]suiticall and fraudulent tricke, for which no colour of excuse can
[b]e made : The Greeke set on the very opposite Page [p], is ἡμῖν, *nobis :*
[in] the *Surian* Collectiō [q] of those Acts, it was rightly read *nobis;* their
[sa]me Cardinall *Cusanus* [r] out of the ancient Acts of that Synod, cites
[it] commisisset nobis : the very sense inforceth it to be *nobis,* for the Em-
[pe]rour addeth, *Therefore doe wee with all sollicitude exhort and warne*
[yo]u, that you come to the holy Oecumenicall Synod : which had beene a
[m]ost foolish collection, had he not said *nobis,* but *vobis,* for then not

to

f *Quem Prima-*
tem dioceseos
Synodus dixit,
præter Apostoli
primi Vicarium.
Nich. 1.Epist.8.
§ *Quem.*
g *Conc.6.*
habitum an.680
Bar.et Bin.
h *Conc.6.Act.4.*
pa.22. in Epist.
Agathonis et
Rom.Synodi.
i *Epist. Agath.*
Act.4.pa.12.b.

k *Sermo accla-*
matorius Conc.
generalis 6. Act.
18.pa.89.b.
l *Definit.Concil.*
6.Act.17.pa.
80.a.
m *Conc.2.Can.5*
et Conc.Chal.
Act.16.post
Can.27.

n *Conc.illud 8.*
habit.an.869.
Bar.et Bin.
o *Conc.8.Act.1.*
pa.880.b.

p *Apud Rad.pa.*
224.
q *Extat apud*
Bin.to.3.Can.
pa.858.
r *Cusan.lib.3.*
de Concor. Cath.
ca.19.

to him, but to them should have belonged the care to call the Bishops to the Synod; yet against all these evidences of truth *Raderus* and *Binius* falsifie the text, corrupt the words, and pervert the sense, by turning *nobis* into *vobis*, that so they might deprive the Emperour of that supreme authority which *Basilius* there professed to belong unto himselfe, and the Legates of the Patriarchs, in the name of the whole Synod approved the Emperours saying [f], *Recte Imperatores nostri monuere, the Emperours have said well.* To goe no further in this matter, that which was cited out of the Scripture concerning *Ioshua* and *David,* doth clear this point; for seeing all who sit in Imperial thrones, are like *Ioshua* and *David,* to feed the Israel of God; and the Israel of God containes the whole flocke and all the sheepe of Christ, *ex* [t] *hac ipsa voce Pasce, difficile non est demonstrare summam potestatem ei attribui.* It is easie even by this very word *Feed,* to demonstrate, that supreme power doth belong to Kings, seeing unto them it is said, *Feed my sheepe, feed my people :* Wherefore seeing Kings are commanded by God to rule by their Pastorall authoritie all others, and all others are commanded to obey, and bee subject unto them and their Imperiall commands, as unto their supreme Pastour here upon earth; it hence unavoydably followeth, that Bishops neither without that Imperiall command, may in a riotous manner assemble in generall Councels, nor being commanded by them, may deny to assemble, nor being assembled may refuse to bee ordered and governed by their Imperiall Presidency.

9. After these precepts of GOD, looke to the practice of the Church, and you shall see that lawfull Synods or Assemblies about Ecclesiasticall affaires, have beene gathered by no other than Imperiall authority, as well in the old as new Testament. In the time of IOSIA when the Temple was purged from those manifold Idolatries, wherewith it was polluted, who assembled Israel? the Priests? no, but *the King* [u] *sent and gathered all the Elders of Iuda, and went into the house of the LORD with the Priests and Levites:* The like had ASA done in the oath of *Association, He* [x] *gathered all Iuda:* SALOMON in the *Dedication* of the Temple, *He* [y] *assembled the Elders and the heads of the Tribes;* DAVID in bringing the Arke, and in ordering the offices of the Temple, DAVID [z] *gathered all Israel together;* Hee [x] *gathered together then all the Princes, with the Priests and Levites:* HEZECHIA in clensing the house of the Lord, [b] *Hee gathered the Priests and Levites, called* [c] *them his sonnes;* and they were gathered together, *juxta* [d] *mandatum Regis, according to the commandement of the King.* Ioshua at the renewing of the Covenant, *He* [e] *assembled all the Tribes of Israel.* And to mention no more, (for what King is there, or Iudge, or Captaine, who had all kingly authoritie, though somewhat qualified and tempered in them more than in Kings) who is not an example hereof? Consider but *Moses,* who was the first that had soveraignty in their common-wealth; how often and still with a warrant from God did he assemble the people upon urgēt occasions?

At

f Conc.8. Act. 1. pa.380.b.

t Bell.lib.1. de Pontif.Rom. ca. 35.§. At nobis.

u 2 Chr. 34.29. 30.

x 2 Chron.15. 9,10.

y 2 Chron. 5. 2.

z 1 Chron.13.5. & cap.15.4.
a 1 Chron.23.2.
b 2 Chron.29.4.
c Ibid.v.11.
d Ibid.v.15.
e Iosh.24.2.

At the first making of the covenant with God, *Moses called* [f] *the Elders*; at the publishing of the law, *Moses brought* [g] *the people out of their tents unto God*: after the bringing of the two Tables from God, *Moses assembled all* [h] *the congregation of Israel* : at the anointing and investing of *Aaron*, *Moses* [i] *assembled all the congregation*: at the repeating of the Covenant, *he* [k] *commanded all the Elders of the Tribes of Israel to come unto him*. Yea at the very first time, when God appointed him to be a Captaine and Ruler over his people, even then God gave unto him that authority (which afterwards he renewed in the tenth [l] of *Numbers*) to congregate and assemble the people of God ; *Goe*, saith God [m], *and gather the Elders of Israel together* : thereby teaching the power of assembling Gods people to be inseparably annexed unto Imperiall, regall, and soveraigne authority ; that none hath the one who hath not the other by the very warrant of God committed unto him, to the end the assemblies of Gods people might not be tumultuous and seditious, as was that of *Demetrius*, and of *Corah* [n], *Dathan*, and *Abiram*, which the Lord severely revenged, but lawfull and orderly, as God is the author not of confusion, but of order in all Churches, and in all ages of the Church.

10. Come we to the times of the Gospell. The power and rightfull authority to call Synods was ever in the Emperours and Kings, even in those three hundred years while the Church was in most grievous persecution under Heathen Emperours : The right and power was in the Heathen as well as in Christian Emperours ; in *Tiberius* as well as *Theodosius* ; in *Dioclesian*, as well as in *Constantine* or *Iustinian*. But that power which they rightly had, they did not use aright : not to call Synods to maintaine the faith, but to abolish Synods, Bishops, Christians, and utterly extirpate the Christian faith. Now because Christ had layd an absolute necessity [o] upon the Apostles, and their successors, to feed, to teach, and maintaine the doctrine of faith ; and seeing they could not doe this with the allowance, or so much as connivence of the Emperours, who in duty should have protected them so doing, yea have caused them so to doe ; this very necessity enforced them, and was a lawfull warrant unto them, both to feed the flocke, preach the Gospell, and to hold Synods in the best and most convenient manner that they then could, not onely without, but against the will and command of the Emperors, that higher command of Christ over-ruling theirs. Whereby are warranted as lawfull, to say nothing of that Acts 15. those Synods at *Antioch* against *Paulus Samosatenus* at *Rome*, against the *Novatians* in *Africke*, many in the time of *Cyprian*, and divers the like. For even the law of God, to yeeld unto necessity, the example of *David* [p], the doctrine of our Saviour, doth demonstrate ; besides those many Maximes, which are all grounded on this truth, as, that necessity [q] hath no law, nor is subject to any law, but is a law of it selfe: that many things are lawfull in case of necessity [r], which otherwise are unlawfull : that of *Leo*, *Inculpabile judicandum quod necessitas intulit* ; that is blamelesse which necessity doth warrant : and many the like, which Pope *Iohn* [t] alledgeth. This, and nothing else, doth declare those Synods to have beene lawfull, though assem-

f Exod. 19.7.

g Exod. 19.17.

b Exod. 35.1.

i Levit.8.3,4.

k Deut.5.1. & ca.31.28.

l Num.10.2. Make thee two Trumpets, that thou maist use them for the assembling of the congregation.

m Exod.3.16.

n Num.16.2. &c.

o 1 Cor.9.16. Matth.28.19.

p Matth. 12. 1,2.&c.

q *Necessitas non habet legem, sed ipsa sibi facit legem. Cauf.1.q.1 ca.39. Remissionem,*

r *Gloss. in cap. 'Discipulos de consec. distinct. 5.in marg. Citatur à Iobanne 8.in Epist. 190.§. Nos.*

t *Ibidem,*

assembled without Imperiall authority : as the times were extraordinary, so their extraordinary assembling was by those times of necessity made lawfull. But as soone as Emperours began to professe the faith, and to use their owne, and Imperiall authority, in assembling Bishops for consulting about causes of faith, the Catholike Bishops knowing that from thence that law of Necessity was now expired and out of date, attempted not then to come to Synods uncalled, nor refused to come when they were called; though sometimes they came with an assured expectance of the crowne of Martyrdome before they departed; as in the Councels of *Millane, Arimine,* and *Syrmium,* called by the Arrian Emperour *Constantius,* is most cleare.

11. Hence it is that all the ancient generall Councels, yea all that were held for the space of a thousand yeares after Christ, were all assembled by no other than this Imperiall authority. Take a short view of some, and of the chiefe of them. Of the first *Nicen, Eusebius* [l] saith, *Constantine* assembled this Oecumenicall Councell, hee called the Bishops by his letters, and his call was mandatory, for *Mandatum erat, ἐπίταγμα ad hanc rem, Constantine commanded that they should come.* The very Synod it selfe writeth thus in their Synodall letters, *We are assembled* [m] *by the grace of God, & mandato Imperatoris, and by the mandate of Constantine the Emperour:* so *Christopherson* translates συναγαγόντος ἡμᾶς Κωνσταντίνου, both in *Socrates* and *Theodoret.* Of the second, their owne Synodall Epistle to *Theodosius* witnesseth; *We came* [n] *hither, ex mandato tuæ pietatis, by the command of your Imperiall highnesse.* Of the third Councell, the Synodall acts and Epistles are cleare witnesses : *Your Highnes hath commanded* [o] *by your holy Edict, the Bishops out of the whole world to come to Ephesus.* Againe, the synod [p] being assembled ἐν δεκιμαῖς, by the Edict, decree, authority and appointment of the Emperour : and the like is repeated I think not so little as threescore times in those Acts. And as they came at the Emperors command, so would they not depart without his leave and licence. *We beseech* [q] *your piety that you will at length free us from this exile :* and the Emperour granted their request : for, *injungit* [r] *eis, he commanded & injoyned them* to returne to their owne Cities : and againe, *Regio* [s] *mandato imperatum est singulis Episcopis,* there was a mandate to all the Bishops by the Emperour to returne to their owne Provinces. Of the Councell at *Chalcedon,* the whole Synod saith in their Epistle to Pope *Leo,* This [t] holy and generall Synod was assembled by the grace of God, & *sanctione Imperatorum,* and by the sanction or decree of our most holy Emperours. Againe, this synod was gathered, *ex decreto* [u] *Imperatorum,* by the decree of the Emperours : *secundum jussionem,* according to his command. And the like is repeated almost in every action. Of the fift we shewed before that it was called *Iussione* [x] *piissimi Imperatoris,* by the command of the most holy Emperour *Iustinian.* Of the sixt it is usually said, it was assembled, *secundum* [y] *Imperialem sanctionem aut decretum,* and the like, by the Imperiall sanction or decree. And the whole Councell in their prosphoneticall oration to the Emperour, saith [z] unto him; *your mansuetude hath congregated this holy and great assembly.* Of their second Nicene it is said, that it was assembled, *per* [a] *pium Decretum, Sanctionem, Mandatum,*

l *Euseb.lib.3.de vit.Constant.c.6*

m *Citantur verba, tum à Socr. lib.2.ca.6.tum à Theodor.lib.1. ca.11.*
n *Epist.Synod. Cont.Const.1. apud Bin.to.1. Cont.pa.518.*
o εὐσεβεῖ θεσπίσματι παρεκελεύσατο. Iussit suo pio edict. Act.Conc.Ephes. to.4.ca.11.
p *Act.Conc.Ephes.to.2.ca.1.*
q *Epist.Synodi ad Imper.to.2. Act.Conc.Eph. ca.17.*
r ἐκέλευσε.to.5. Act.Conc.Eph. ca.11.
s ἐκέλευσεν ibid.
t *Epist.Syn. Chalc.post Act. 16.*
u *Conc.Chalc. Act.1.pa.1.*
x *Conc.5.Coll.8. pa.584.a.*
y *Conc.6.Act. 1.2.3.& reliqua.*
z *Conc.6.Act. 18 pa.89.a.*
a *Conc.Nic.2. Act.1.pa.297.a & act.2.pa.308*
b *& act.5.pa. 338.b.*

L   *datum,*

latum, *by the holy Decree, Sanction, and Mandate of the Emperors:* of that which they call the eighth, the synodall definition expresseth, *Quod* b *Basilio Imperatore coactum, that it was assembled by Basilius the Emperour*; and the whole Synod cryed out, We all thinke so; we all subscribe to these things. And Pope *Stephen* in his letters to *Basilius,* speaking of this Synod, saith c, Did not the Romane See send Legates to the Councell, ἐπὶ τῆς αὐτοκρατορείας σου, *te imperante, Raderus* and *Binius* translate it; but it is rather to be read, *ad imperium,* and *summam jussionem tuam,* the Pope sent Legates, not when *Basilius* was Emperour, (which was no great honour or token of duty to be done:) but at the most high command of *Basilius*; which testified his subjection and duty to the Emperour, whom the Pope in that same Epistle acknowledgeth to be the highest d person who here upon earth sustaines the person of Christ: and in the sixt Action of the same e Councell, it is said, *Imperator hanc Synodum coegit, the Emperour assembled this Synod.*

12. Thus all those Councells which are usually reckoned for generall and approved, for the space of a thousand yeares, were all called by Imperiall jussion and command; the religious Emperours exercising that right in commanding all Bishops, even the Popes to such Councels; all the Bishops, even the Popes, by their willing obedience acknowledging that authority and power to be in the Emperours, and therefore they gladly obeyed those imperiall jussions and commands. And as they were all assembled by Imperiall calling, so were they all governed by Imperiall presidency. That *Constantine* was President in the *Nicene,* Pope *Stephen* in the Epistle lately cited expresly witnesseth: *Doe you not remember,* saith he f, *what Pope Silvester said in the Nicene Synod, praesidente ibi S. Constantino, Saint Constantine being President therein.* His owne Acts in the Councell, of moderating g, and repressing the jarres of the Bishops, of burning h their bookes of accusations and quarrels, of drawing them to unity, that with one consent they should define the causes proposed, doe manifest the same: *for all these are acts of the Imperiall presidency.* That *Theodosius* was President in the second, may appeare, not onely for that he was present i therein, and present no doubt as *Constantine* had beene before, as a moderator of their actions; but that small remainder of the Acts of that Councell import also the same: for he directed, and that by his *Mandatum* k, what the Bishops should doe: and when they out of their parall affections would have preferred each his owne friend to the See of *Constantinople,* the Emperour perceiving that, corrected their partiall judgement, *Iussit* l *inscribere chartae, hee commanded them to write a roll of such men as they thought fit for the place*; himselfe nominated *Nectarius*; and though many of the Bishops at first contradicted that choice, yet he drew them all to his sentence, and so the whole Synod consented upon the ordination of *Nectarius.*

13. For the holy Ephesine Synod, all the Acts are full of this Imperiall Presidency. *The Emperours sent Candidianus* m *to keepe away tumult, and disorderly* n *persons from the Councell: to see that no* o *dissention and private quarrels might hinder their grave consultations, the free and exact discussion of the causes proposed, and to provide that every one might*

free-

b Conc.8. Act. 10.pa.897.a.

c Epist.Stephan. post Conc.8.pa. 900.

d Quamvis supremam Christi in terris personam servamq; geria. Steph. Ep. eadem.p.899.b.
e Conc.8.act.6. pa.886.a.

f Steph. Papa in Epist.ad Basil. Imper.post 8. Conc.
g Euseb.lib.3. de vit.Const. ca. 13.
h Ruff lib.1.c.2
i Ipso, praesente Theodosio. Epist. Iustin.post Conc. 5.pa.605.a.
k Insuperq; mandaret Imperator,ut diligens inquisitio fieret. Sozom.lib.7.c.6
l Sozom.lib.7. ca.7.
m Tom.1.act. Conc.Ephes.ca. 32.
n Non licet illos qui necessarij non sunt,dogmatum examen aliquo tumultu impedire. ibid.
o Vt diligenter prospiciat ne qua gravior dissentio synodi consultationum obturbet. ibid.

freely P and with leisure propose what was needfull, and have scope to refute all doubts proposed by others. The Emperours when they heard of the dissentions and disorders among the Bishops, writ unto them to take a better and more peaceable and orderly examination of the cause; saying q, *Majestas nostra ea quæ acta sunt pro ratis & legitimis habere non potest;* our Majesty cannot hold or esteeme those acts, done so disorderly, for firme and synodall; nay we decree that all things which hitherto have beene done, *pro irritis, & nullis habenda esse,* shall be accounted of no force, but utterly void and frustrate : than which no greater tokens of Imperiall Presidency can be devised. The whole and holy Synod willingly submitted themselves to this presidency. In their proceedings the Emperours letters were their direction r, and as themselves professe, the very Torch to guide all their actions. In the manifold injuries and contumelies which they endured at the hands of *Iohn*, with his Conventicle, they fled to the Emperour, beseeching s him to be Iudge of their equall proceedings, and take an exact view and examination of their doings, which upon t their request the Emperour did, and called u five Bishops of either part to *Constantinople* to declare the whole cause unto him; after which being performed, he gave judgement x for the holy Councell, and adnulled all the acts of the Conventicle, as the holy Synod had earnestly and humbly entreated him. So fully and cleerly doth that sacred and Oecumenicall Councell, wherein was the judgement and consent of the whole Catholike Church, both acknowledge this Imperiall right of Presidency in the Emperours, and submit themselves unto it.

14. For the Councell of Chalcedon, the matter is so evident, that *Bellarmine*, though strugling against the truth, could not deny it. *There were present,* saith he y, *in this Councell secular Iudges, deputed by the Emperour, who were not Iudges of controversies of faith,* (to give a decisive suffrage therein, for that belongs to no secular man whatsoever) *sed tantum an omnia fierent legitime, sive vi & fraude & tumultibus,* but they were Iudges onely of Synodall order, whether all things were done lawfully, without force, fraud and tumult. And in this doth the very Imperiall Presidency consist. And truly how religiously and worthily those glorious Iudges performed that honourable office in the synod, all the actions thereof doe make manifest : for scarce any matter was done in the synod, but the same was ordered, moderated, and guided by their prudence and authority. The Popes Legats very insolently took upon them at the beginning, willing that *Dioscorus* might bee put out of the synod, and sayd z, *Either let Dioscorus goe out, or we will depart.* The Iudges gravely reproved this stomacke in the Legates, telling them, *If you will be* a *Iudges, you must not prosequute as accusers :* nor did they suffer *Dioscorus* to goe away, but commanded him, as was fit, to sit in the place of the *Rei.* The cause of *Iuvenalis* and *Thalassius* was proposed to the synod; It could not be examined by them, till they had leave from the Emperour; *We,* said b the Iudges, *have acquainted the*

Emperour

Emperour therewith, and we expect his *Mandate* herein : and after they had received the Emperours minde, they then told the synod, *Imperator sententia veſtra permiſit de Iuvenale deliberare,* the Emperour hath upon your intreaty permitted you to diſcuſſe and judge the cauſe of *Iuvenalis, Thalaſſius,* and the reſt. In the cauſe [d] of the ten Ægyptian Biſh. the Synod had almoſt pronounced a temerarious ſentence againſt them, as hereticall, when indeed they were orthodoxall; the Biſhops cryed out, *Iſti heretici ſunt,* theſe ten are heretikes. The glorious Iudges knowing which was manifeſt, that they forbore to ſubſcribe, by reaſon of a cuſtome which they had, that they might doe nothing without their Patriarke, who was not then choſen; and not as thinking heretically in the faith, moderated the Synod in that matter, ſaying, [e] *Rationabile nobis & clemens videtur; it ſeemes to us to be reaſon, and an act of clemencie, not to have condemned them, but ſtaid till their Patriarch bee choſen :* the whole Synod conſented to this grave ſentence of the Iudges, & made a Canon [f] for that purpoſe. In making the very definition of faith, there grew a great diſſention in the Synod; ſome [g] would have it one, ſome another way ſet downe; in ſo much that the Popes Legates were ready to make a ſchiſme, and depart [h] from the Councel, and hold another Councell by themſelves. The glorious Iudges propoſed a moſt equall and fitting meanes to have the matter peaceably debated, and the whole Synod brought to unity : But when out-cryes [i] and tumult prevailed above reaſon, the Iudges complained of thoſe diſcords to the Emperour, and, *Imperator* [k] *precepit,* the Emperour commanded them to follow the direction of the Iudges, which they did, and ſo with one accord conſented on the Definition of faith. The Emperour at the earneſt entreaty of *Baſſianus,* commanded [l] the Synod to examine the whole cauſe betwixt him and *Stephanus,* to which of them in right the See of *Epheſus* belonged; The Synod would have given ſentence for *Baſſianus, Iuſtitia* [m] *Baſſianum vocat, Equity and right doth call for Baſſianus to bee the Biſhop of that place;* The glorious Iudges weighing the cauſe more circumſpectly, thought that neither of them both ſhould in right be Biſhop: The whole Synod being directed by them, altered their opinion, and ſaid [n], This is a juſt ſentence, this is the very judgment of God. When there was a difference in the Synod, about the dignity of *Conſtantinople,* the greater part [o] holding one way, and the Popes Legates the contrary [p]; the glorious Iudges judicially [q] ſentenced, which was to ſtand for the Iudgement of the Synod; and the whole Councell in their ſynodall letter conſented [r] thereunto. So many, ſo manifeſt evidences there are of the Imperiall Preſidency in that holy Councell, not any of all thoſe Catholikes once repining at, or contradicting the ſame.

15. For the fiſt, that it was ordered by the Imperiall authoritie, may appeare, in that both the Emperor was ſometimes by [ſ] himſelfe, ſometimes by his glorious [t] Iudges, preſent in the Synod; and ſpecially in that hee tooke order, that liberty [u] and ſynodall freedome ſhould be obſerved therein; yea, as the whole Synod teſtifieth, hee did [x] *omnia,* all things which preſerve the peace of the Church, and unity in the Catholike faith : The ſixt Councell is abundant with proofes of

D d　　　　　　　　　　　　　this

c Ibid.
d Act.4.Conc. Chal.92.90.Omnes clamaverut, Iſti heretici ſunt
e Act.eadem 5. pa.90 b.
f Can.30.Act.15
g Non recte habet Definitio, &c.Act.5. Côc. Chal.pa.93.b.
h Iubete nobis reſcriptum dari ut reuertamur, et ibi Synodus celebretur. Ibid.
i Suggerentur Imperatori clamores iſti &c. Act.eadem.5. pa.94.a.
k Ibid.
l Feſtinet veſtra reverentia cauſam diſcutere, &c. Litere Imper.Act.13.Côc. Chal.pa.116. b.
m Act. eadem pa.118.b.
n Ibid.
o Hec omnes dicimus.Act.16. pa.137.a.
p Contradictio noſtra a his geſtis inhereat. Ibid.
q Quod interioquuti ſumus totâ Synodus approbavit, dixerunt Iudices. Ib.
r Conſirmavimus regulam
ſ 50.patrum, &c. Relatio Synodi ad Leonem poſt Conc. Chal. pa.140.a.
t Cû Iuſtinianus Synodo intereſ ſet, Zenov. Aut. la. 8. cu Iuſtin.
t Coll.1.Conc.5. et Coll.9.
u Maximè, cum piiſſimus Imperator et nos ipſi licentiam dedimus unicuiq; ſuam voluntatem facere maniſeſtà, ſic dixit Synodus.Coll.2.pa. 524.b.
x Coll.14.982.b

this prefidency : *Macarius* faid, O our moft holy Lord, *iubeto* [y] *libros proferri, command that the bookes bee produced*; and the Emperour anfwered, *Iubemus, we command them to be brought*; wee command them to be read; and it was done. The Popes Legates fay, *Petimus* [z] *ferenitatem veftram, we entreate your highneffe* that this booke may be examined; the Emperour anfwered, *Quod poftulatum eft proveniat, let that be done which you requeft* : Againe, O moft holy Lord, we intreat [a], *that the letters of Pope Agatho may be read*; the Emperours anfwer was, what you have defired, let it be done; and they were read : *Macarius* having collected certaine teftimonies out of the Fathers, for his opinon, intreated the Emperour, *Iubeto* [b] *relegi, that he would command them to be read*; his anfwere was, let them bee read in order, and fo they were : The Popes Legates faid, *petimus*, wee intreate [c] your highneffe, that the authentike Copies may bee produced out of the Regiftrie; his anfwer was, *fiat, let it de done* : The whole Synod intreated, If it [d] pleafe your piety, let *Theodorus* and the reft, ftand in the midft, and there make anfwer for themfelves; his anfwer was, What the Synod hath moved, *fiat, let it be done*: *George* Bifh. of *Conftantinople* faid, O our Lord, crowned by God, command * that the name of Pope *Vitalianus* may bee fet in the Dipticks; his anfwer was, *quod poftulatum eft, fiat, let that be done which he hath requefted*. The Emperour commanded [e] the books of *Macarius* to be read; the whole Synod anfwered, *Quod juffum eft, what your highneffe hath commanded fhall be performed*. After the authenticall letters of *Sergius*, & Pope *Honorius* had been read in the Synod, the glorious Iudges called [f] for the like authenticall writings of *Pirrhus*, *Paulus*, *Peter*, and *Cyrus*, to bee produced and read : the whole Councell anfwered [g], that it was fuperfluous, feeing their herefie was manifeft to all : the Iudges replied, *omnino* [h] *neceffarium exiftit, this is neceffary*; that they be convicted out of their owne writings; and then their writings were produced. I omit the reft, whereof every Action of that Synod is full; and by thofe Acts the Prefidency in Councels doth fo clearly belóg to Emperors, and that alfo by the acknowledgment [i] of that whole generall Councell, that *Albertus Pighius* being unwilling to yeeld to this truth, hath purpofely writ [k] a moft railing and reviling Treatife againft this holy generall Synod, condemning both this Councell, and thefe Acts, as unlawfull, for this among other reafons, becaufe the Emperour with his Iudges, *plena* [l] *authoritate Prefidet, is Prefident with full authority in the fame*; hee doth all; he propofeth, hee queftioneth, hee commandeth, hee examineth, he judgeth, he decreeth : And yet in all thefe hee doth nothing but what belongs effentially to his Imperiall authority; nothing but what *Conftantine*, *Theodofius*, *Martian*, and *Iuftinian* had done before him, and done it with the approbation and applaufe of the whole Church, and of all the Catholike Bifhops in thofe holy generall Councels; and hee performed this with fuch uprightneffe and equality, that hee profeffed, *neceffitatem* [m] *nullatenus inferre volumus*, wee will inforce no man, but leave him at his owne freedome in fentencing the caufes propofed, and *, equalitatem* [n] *utrijufque partis confervabimus*; we will bee equall and indifferent Iudges betwixt both parties.

16. In

[y] *Conc. 6. Act. 1 pa. 8. b.*

[z] *Act. 3. Conc. 6. pa. 11. a.*

[a] *Ibid. pa. 11. b.*

[b] *Act. 5. pa. 25. b*

[c] *Act. 6. pa. 27. a*

[d] *Act. 8. pa. 30. a*

* *Ibid.*

[e] *Act. eadem 8. pa. 30. b.*

[f] *Act. 13. pa. 67. a. b.*

[g] *Sanctum Concilium dixit, Hoc fieri fuperfluum judicavimus, &c. Ibid. pa. 67. b.*

[h] *Ibid.*

[i] *Prefidente eodem pijffimo Imperatore Conftantino. Act. 1, 2, 3, 4, 5, 6, 7, 8, 9, 10 11.*

[k] *Act. Pigh. lib. de Actis 6. et 7. Synodique circumferuntur, quod parengrapha fint et minime germana. l Lib. eodem*

[s] *At Concilio illi*

[m] *Sacra Imp. Conftantini Pogon. ante 6. Conc. pa. 6. b. [n] Ibid.*

16. In the second Nicene, though by the fraud of *Anastasius* there be not many, yet are there some prints remaining of this Imperiall Presidencie; *We have received*, say the Emperours [o], *letters from Hadrian Bish. of Rome, sent by his Legates, qui et nobiscum in Concilio sedent, who also sit with us in the Synod*: Those letters, *jubemus publicè legi, we command to be publikely read according to the use in Councels*, and we command all you to marke them with decent silence: After that, you shall reade two quaternions also sent from the Bishops in the East; and the whole Synod obeyed the Imperiall commands. Pope *Hadrian* himselfe was not ignorant of this right in the Emperours, when sending his Pontificall and *Cathedrall* judgement concerning the cause of Images, hee said thus unto them, *We* [p] *offer these things to your highnesse with all humility, that they may bee diligently examined, for we have but perfunctoriè, that is, for fashiō, and not exactly gathered these testimonies, and we have delivered them to your Imperiall Highnesse to be read, intreating and beseeching your mansuetude; yea, and as if I were lying* [q] *at your feete, I pray and adjure you that you will command holy Images to bee restored.* Thus hee. When the Pope cals the Emperours his [r] Lords, and submits both his owne person to their feet, and his judiciall sentence to such tryall, as they shall thinke fit, doth not this import an higher Presidency in the Emperour, than either himselfe or his Legates had in the Synod? Nay, it is further to be remembred, which will remaine as an eternal blot of that Synod, that *Irene* the Empresse, not contenting her selfe with the Imperiall, which was her owne rightfull authority, intruded her selfe into the Episcopall also; she forsooth would be a [s] Doctrix in the Councell, she present among the Bishops to teach the whole Councell what they should define in causes of faith: *Perversas Constitutiones tradere; shee tooke upon her to give Constitutions*, and those impious also, unto them: Those Constitutions backed with her sword and authority, the Bishops of the Councell had not the hearts and courage to withstand: All which is testified in the *Libri Carolini*, which in part were written [t], and wholly set forth by *Charles* the great, being for the most part composed by the Councell at *Frankfourd* [u], and approved by them all in that great synod. A truth so cleare, that Pope *Adrian* in his reply to those Caroline bookes, denyeth not *Irene* to have done this, (which had easily and evidently refuted that objectiō, and discredited those Caroline Bookes for ever) but hee [x] defends her fact by the examples of *Helena* and *Pulcheria*, to which this of *Irene* is so unlike, that for this very cause she is by the whole Councell of *Frankford* [y], consisting of three hundred Bishops, or thereabouts, resembled to the tyrannizing and usurping *Athalia*. Lastly, when that whole Synod came to the Kingly City for the Imperiall confirmation of their Acts, seeing it is expresly testified by *Zonaras* [z], and *Paulus Diaconus* [a], that the Emperour was President in that assembly of the Bishops, why should it not by like reason be thought, that both himselfe when hee was present, and in his absence the secular Iudges, his Deputies, held the same Imperial Presidency in the Nicene Synod?

o *Conc. Nic. 2. a Act. 1. pa. 300.*
p *Epist. Hadr. Papa ad Imp. lecta in Con. Nic. 2. Act. 2. in fine Epist.*
q *Et veluti præsentes genibus advoluti, et corā vestigia pedum volutando. Ibid.*
r *Dominus piissimis Constantino et Irene Hadrianus servus servorum Dei. Inscript. Ep. Hadr.*
s *Synodus illa (Nicena) mulierem Institutricē sive Doctricem habuisse perhibetur; quod non solum divinæ legis documentis, sed ipsius naturæ lege inhibetur. Car. magni liber dict. Capitulare de non adorand. Imag. lib. 3. ca. 13. Aliud est matremfamilias domesticos erudire, aliud Antistitibus sine omni Ecclesiastico ordine, vel publicè Synodo docentem interesse. Ibid.*
t *Quod opus aggressi sumus cum cōnivētia Sacerdotum, non arrogantiæ supercilio, sed zelo Dei et veritatis studio. Carol. mag. præfatio, et Cap. ultimum illius libri fuisse Caroli agnoscit Had. in sua Epist. 3. ca. 25. pa. 281. a.*
u *Libri Carolini scripti videntur in Concilio Fracofordiensi. Bell. lib. 2. de Conc. ca. 8. § Primo quia.*
x *Hadr. Epist. 3. 3. ca. 53.*

y *Lib. Carol. lib. 3. ca. 13.* z *Commentaria in regia Præsidentibus Imperatoribus recitarunt, quæ statim obsignata sunt. Zonar. to. 3. in vita Iren. et Const.* a *Ingressi sunt omnes Episcopi in regiam, et præsidentibus Imperatoribus una cum Episcopis, lectus est tomus, et subscripsit tam Imperator, quam mater ejus. Paul. Diac. histor. misc. lib. 23. in an. 8. Const.*

i *Magnificentis-*
fimi presides
dixerunt Act. 9.
§ *Lecta.*
k *Repugnantibus*
Apost.sedis lega-
tis, utpote quod
sententia Rom.
Pontificum con-
demnati audiri
iterum non debe-
rent. Bar.an.
869.nu.27.
l *Advocensur*
cum Photio Epis-
copi quoque
Photiani, quod
nisi fiat, literam
in hac Synodo
scribemus nul-
lam. Verba Iu-
dic. sec.in Coc.8
Act.4.pa.883.b
m *Verba Baba-*
nis in Conc.8.
citata a Nich.
Cusan.lib.3.
Concor.ca.20.
n *Conc. 8.Act.6.*
verba sunt Me-
tropolite Cesa-
riensis, pa.886.b
o *Act.8.p.893.a*

17. For that which they call the eighth generall Councell, both the Emperours Deputies are called Presidents [i]; and in the sixt, seventh, eighth, and tenth actions it is expresly said, *Presidentibus Imperatoribus, the Emperours being Presidents*; yea, and both of them by their very actions declared their Presidencie. The Popes Legate [k] would not have permitted *Photius* and his Bishops to bee heard; the Emperours Deputies over-ruled [l] them, as was fit, in that matter; yea, they said to the Photian Bishops, *Imperator* [m] *jubet et vult*, the Emperours will, pleasure, and command is, that you should speake in your owne cause. Of the Emperour they intreat liberty to defend themselves, *Rogamus domine* [n] *Imperator; we beseech you, our Lord and Emperour, that without interruption we may defend our cause:* When the bookes of *Photius* were brought into the Synod, and burned in the midst thereof, this was done, κελεύσαντος Βασιλέως [o], *the Emperour commanding it*, and many the like.

18. Now these eight are all which are accounted by them in the number of generall and approved Councels, for the space of more than a thousand years after Christ: Of al which seeing it is now cleare, that they were both called by Imperiall authoritie, and governed by Imperiall Presidencie, it hence appeareth, that as by the warrant of the Scriptures, and example of the ancient Church before Christ, so also by the continued practice of the whole Catholike Church, for a thousand years together; these rights of calling and ordering generall Councels doe belong, and were acknowledged to belong onely to Kings and Emperours; they called and commanded the Bishops, the Bishops came at that call and command: they governed the assemblies in those Councels, all the Bishops (without murmuring or so much as once contradicting) willingly submitted themselves to that Imperiall government. And by this may now easily be discerned wherein the lawfulnesse or unlawfulnesse of any Synod consisteth: For wheresoever to Imperiall calling, and Imperiall Presidencie, there is added the rightfull use of that Imperiall authoritie, in seeing liberty, freedome, diligent discussion of the causes, and all due synodall order preserved in any generall Synod, the same is, and ought to bee truly called a generall lawfull Councell: But what generall Councels soever have beene heretofore, or shall bee at any time hereafter, either assembled by any other than Imperiall, and regall authority, or governed for the observing of synodall order, by any other than Imperiall Presidencie, or misgoverned by the abuse thereof, they all are, and are to bee esteemed for no other than generall unlawfull Councels.

19. Suffer mee here to propose some examples of each kinde, partly in the ancient, partly in the later times of the Church: In the order of lawfull generall Councels, principally, and by a certaine excellency above all the rest, are the five first approved Councels to bee reckned: The first at *Nice*, the second at *Constantinople*, the third at *Ephesus*, the fourth at *Chalcedon*, the fift at *Constantinople* in the time of *Iustinian*; unto these the *Sardicane*, and that at *Constantinople* under *Mennas*, are to bee added, like two Appendant Synods; the former to that at *Nice*, the later to that at *Chalcedon*: For the sixt, which was

held

held at *Constantinople* in the time of *Constantinus Pogonatus*, I am out of doubt, and doe firmely hold it to have beene both generall and lawfull: But I mention it apart by reason of that scruple touching the Canons thereof, concerning which I intend, if ever I have oportunity, to make a severall tract by it selfe. For their second *Nicene*, and the next unto it, to wit, that at *Constantinople*, in the time of *Basilius* and *Hadrian* the second; besides that there are just exceptions against their lawfulnesse, in regard of the proceedings used therin, it may be justly doubted whether either of them may be esteemed generall: specially considering that the Councell at *Frankford* utterly condemned [p] that second *Nicene*, and decreed that it should not bee called a generall Synod: and in very like manner did the Councell at *Constantinople*, held in the time of Pope *Iohn* the eighth, (or as some call him the ninth,) the next successor to *Hadrian* the second, condemne [q] that Councell which they call the eighth, held in the time of *Hadrian* the second. Now although by the judgements of these two Councels, those other which they reckon for the seventh and eighth be wholy repealed, and that most justly; yet if the authority of these Synods were omitted, there are so many and so just exceptions against the two former, that I am out of doubt perswaded, that neither of them ought to stand in the order of generall lawfull Councels: nor will any, I suppose, judge otherwise, who shall unpartially examine the Acts of them, & compare them with the histories of those times. If any at all after the sixt be to be ranked in the number of generall and lawfull Councells, I would not doubt to make it evident, if ever I should proceed so farre in this argument about Councels, that the Councell held at *Constantinople* in the time of *Constantinus Iconomachus* (whom they in contempt have with no small token of their immodesty nicknamed *Copronimus*) that this ought to bee judged the seventh; that at *Frankford* the eighth; and that at *Constantinople*, which even now I mentioned, held in the time of Pope *Iohn* the eighth, (or as some call him, the ninth) the ninth of that order. For both the generality of all these three is by the best Writers acknowledged, and all of them were called by Imperiall authority, governed by Imperiall presidency, and that in a lawfull, free, and synodall manner; as, if ever I come to handle the Councels of those times, I purpose to explaine. This rather for this time I thinke needfull to observe: that as a Councell may be generall, and yet not lawfull, so may one be both generall and lawfull, and yet erroneous in the decrees thereof: which one point rightly observed, shewes an exceeding difference betwixt those five first generall Councels, with the *Sardicane*, and that under *Mennas*, and all the rest which follow the fift Synod. The former which were all held within the six hundred yeares after Christ, in the golden ages of the Church, are wholly, and in every decree and Canon, orthodoxall, and golden Councells, no drosse, nor dramme of corrupt doctrine could prevaile in any one of them: and so they are, and ever since they were held, were esteemed not onely generall and lawfull, but in every part and parcell of their decrees, holy and orthodoxall Councels, approved by all Catholikes, and by the whole Ca-

[p] *Synodus quæ ante paucos annos sub Irene & Constantino congregata, & ab ipsis non solum septima verum etiam universalis erat appellata ut nec septima nec universalis haberetur, diceretur ve, quasi supervacua in totum ab omnibus (in Conc. Francofordensi) abdicata est.* Aim. lib. 4. ca. 85. *Similia habet* Adô Vien. in Chron. Hincm. Rhem. in lib. contra Hincm. Laud. ca. 20. Rhegino, Hermann. Strabus Fuld. Egolis. Monac. & alii quam multi.

[q] *Quartus Canon* (Concilii Constant. sub Iohan. 8.) *superiores synodos adversus Photium habitas Nicholai & Hadriani temporibus explodit, & rejicit imo ut de Synodorum numero tollantur jubet.* Fran. Turrian. lib. de 6, 7, & 8. synod. pa. 95.

 tholike

tholike Church. But in all generall Councels which follow that fift, which were held after the 600.yeare, and in those times wherein drofs and corruption began to prevaile above the gold, in them all there is some one blot or other wherewith they are blemished, and by reason whereof, although they be both generall and lawfull, yet are they not in every decree holy and orthodoxall, nor approved by the succeeding ages of the Church. Such in the sixt, is the 2. 52. and 53. Canons : in that under *Conſtantinus Iconomachus,* the 15.and 17.definitions: in that at *Frankford,* their condemning of the fact of the *Iconoclaſts,* which (untill the decree for breaking them downe was repealed by the Councell at *Frankford*) was both pious, and warranted by the example of *Hezekias* dealing with the brazen serpent : In that under *Iohn* the 8. their denying of the holy Ghost to proceed from the Son : And these examples which I have now named, are all the examples of generall and lawfull Councels, which as yet have beene held in the Church.

20. Wee come now to unlawfull Synods: wherein it is very memorable, that of such as are unlawfull by want of lawfull calling, there is no example in the ancient Church to bee found, nor more than a thousand yeares after Christ. All that time not any generall Councell assembled without lawfull warrant. The Bishops, no not they of Rome, were as yet growne to bee so insolent and headstrong as to come together without the Emperours *Mandatum.* And the very like might be said of such Synods as are unlawfull by want of Imperiall presidency. During all that time no Bishop, no not he of *Rome,* durst intrude himselfe into that Royalty and Imperiall right. As the Emperour called them all for a thousand yeares, so was he by himselfe or his deputies President in them all. But of such as were unlawfull by abuse of that Imperiall presidency, those ancient times doe yeeld abundant examples. Such among many was that at *Millane,* wherein *Conſtantius,* who should have preserved order in all others, most of all in his owne selfe used such violent and tyrannous dealing, that the only Canon [r] whereby he ruled the Synod, was his owne will : *Quod ego volo pro Canone ſit ; My will ſhall be your law :* and the onely reason whereby hee perswaded, was a most tyrannous *Dilemma, Aut ſubſcribite* [ſ]*, aut exulate ;* either *ſubſcribe to Arianiſme, or goe into baniſhment.* Such againe was that Epheſine Latrocinie ; When *Dioſcorus* could not otherwise prevaile, hee brought [t] the Proconſull guarded with clubs, with ſwords, with chaines, and by such meanes forced the Biſhops to ſubſcribe to blankes [u], and to the hereſie of *Eutiches ;* ſuch fraud, violence, and unjuſt proceedings, whereby all liberty was taken away, made that Synod, though lawfully called, and having a rightfull Preſident, to be no other than a very Latrocinie [x], as it is uſually and [y] juſtly called. Of this ſame ſort was the Councel at *Arimine,* at *Syrmium,* and divers more of the ancient Synods. But theſe are ſufficient for examples in those ancient times : the unlawfulneſſe of them all ariſing onely from the abuſe of the Imperiall and lawfull authority, not for want of lawfull authority either to aſſemble them, or governe them being aſſembled.

21. Let

z *Athan. in Epiſt. ad ſolit. vit. agent. pa. 228. b.* ſ *ibid.*
r *Introduxerunt proconſulem cũ multitudine magna, & catenis. Ath. Conc. Epheſ. in Conc. Chalc. Act. 1. pa. 39.a. Violenta facta eſt vis, cum plagis. Minabatur nobis damnatio, mine exiliy tendebantur, milites cum fuſtibus & gladiis inſtabant. ibid. Act. 1. pa. 7.b.* u *In pura charta ſubſcripſimus: ibid. pa. 7.b.* x *Vbi gladii & fuſtes, qualis ſynodus? ibid.* y *Aliud Epheſi Concilium latronum cogitur. Epiſt. Iuſtin. ad ſ. Synod. p. 605. b*

21. Let us come lower, and to later times, and then we shall have abundance of examples of all kindes of unlawfull Synods. Since the thousand yeare after Christ, there have beene ten which they honour with the specious titles of generall [z] and holy Councels. All of them held in the West, five at *Rome* in the *Laterane*; three in *France*, (two of them at *Lions*, the third at *Vienna*;)two in *Italy*, the one at *Florence*, the other, which is the last and worst of all, at [a] *Trent*. For their generality it is not unknowne what just exceptions may bee taken against them. Seeing in foure [b] of them none, in the rest but very few of the Easterne Bishops were present, they ought rather to bee called partiall, than generall; Westerne, than Oecumenicall Synods. That the Greekes held them not for generall, both that speech of theirs in the Councell of *Florence* [c], *Venio ad septimum & ultimum generale Concilium*: where they professe the second Nicene to be the last which they acknowledge for a generall Councell: and the words of *Bellarmine* do make evident; *Græci* [d] *tantum recipiunt prima septem Concilia ut notum est*; It is a thing vulgarly knowne, that the Greeke Church receiveth none but the seven first for generall Councells. And yet if wee should admit them (as we may not) for generall, what more honor were it for them that they were generall, than for the Councell at *Ariminum*, at *Syrmium*, at *Millane*, and the Ephesine Latrocine: the worst of all which is by many degrees, for sanctity and due synodall order, to bee preferred before the best of their ten. But besides this of their generality, there is another exception which can never bee removed, concerning their lawfulnesse. They all and every one of them are unlawfull Synods: and that by defect of all those conditions which are essentially required in all lawfull generall Councels.

22. Vnlawfull first they are by want of lawfull calling and authoritie to assemble them: not one of them assembled by Imperiall, all by Papall and usurped authority. *The Popes*, saith *Bellarmine* [e], *have called moe than twelve generall Councels*: Of those, these which wee have named were ten. Of the first Laterane, which is the first of the ten, *Binius* [f] saith, *It was appointed, solius Pontificis authoritate*, by the authority of the Pope alone. Of the next, which was the second Laterane, wherein were present about a thousand Bishops, *It was Innocentius* [g] *will to congregate it*. Of the third at Laterane (which is also the third in order) *It was assembled, Papæ authoritate* [h], by the authority of Pope *Alexander*. Of the fourth Laterane, (the fourth also in order) wherein among many other like matters, Transubstantiation was first of all decreed, more than twelve hundred yeares after Christ, *Authoritate* [i] *Innocentij indicta esse indicat apertissime Encyclica epistola*, the Encyclicall Epistle doth most manifestly shew that it was appointed by the Popes authority. Of the fift, which was the former at *Lions*, This Synod was appointed and congregated, *A* [k] *solo Pontifice, by the Pope alone, and by his authority*. Of the sixt, which was the second at *Lions*, Pope *Gregory Indixit* [l] *hoc Concilium*, appointed this Councell. Of the seventh, which was at *Vienna*, Pope *Clement* [m] *indixit Concilium*, appointed this Councell. Of the *Florentine*, which is the eighth, This Synod was *ab* [n] *Eugenio indicta*, ap-

z *Bin. in tomis suis Concil. & Bell. lib. 1. de Conc. ca. 5. & alij.*

a *Tridentum vò Germanicam esse, sed Italicam civitatem nemo est qui nesciat. Gravam. oppos. Conc. Trident. pa. 36.*

b *Omitto quinq; alia Concilia generalia, quia nec à Græcis recipiuntur, cum ipsi non interfuerint, — nimiù, Lugdunense sub Innocent. 4. Viennense sub Clemente 5. Constantiense, Lateranense sub Leone 10. & Tridentinum. Bell. lib. 1. de Conc. ca. 13. §. Deniq;*

c *Concil. Flor. Sess. 5. p. 421. a. Sunt autem verba Marci Ephesij, præclari Theologi, qui pro Græcis causam egit. ut liquet ex sess. 3. pa. 415 b.*

d *Bell. lib. 1. de Conc. ca. 5. §. Ex his.*

e *Bell. lib. 1. de Conc. ca. 13. §. Ad hæc.*

f *Bin. Not. in Conc. Lateran 1. §. Concilium. to. 3. pa. 1317. a.*

g *Quibus de causis Pontifex hanc Synodum congregatam voluerit, intelliges. Biz. Not. in Conc. Later. 2. pa. 1325. a.*

h *Bin. Not. in id. Conc. pa. 1350. b.*

i *Bin. Not. in Conc. Lateran. 4. pa. 1465. b.*

k *Bin. Not. in Conc. Lugd. 1. to. 3. pa. 1490 d.*

n *Bin.*

Bin. Not. in Conc. Lugdun. (ex Blond.) p. 1495. a. m *Bin. (ex Tritem.) Not. in Conc. Vien. ta. 3. Conc. pa. 1510. a.* n *Bin. Not. in Conc. Florent. to. 4. pa. 495. b.*

pointed

pointed by Eugenius, at the intreaty of the Emperour. Of the ninth, which was the fift *Laterane*, This was appointed and assembled, *Authoritate* [o] *Iulij Papa, by the authority of Pope Iulius* : nor onely was it selfe so assembled, but it [p] decreed (which was never done before) that all generall Councels ought to be so assembled. For the last (which is their faire *Helen* [q] of *Trent*) the Popes Bull, whereby hee appointed, summoned, and assembled it, is set in the forefront of it; wherein the Pope saith, *Conventum* [r] *Mantuæ indiximus, we have appointed that this Councell should bee held at Mantua*; but afterwards he removed it to *Trent*.

o Bin. Notis in Con. Later. 1. sub Leone 10. to. 4. Conc. pa. 651.
p Conc. Later. sub Leone 10. Sess. 11. p. 639. b
q Hæc est Helena, quæ nuper Tridenti obtinuit. Espenc. com. in Epist. ad Tit. pa. 41.
r Pauli 3. Bulla indict. præfixa Act. Conc. Trid.

23. Thus were all the ten assembled by Papall, not one of them by Imperiall authority. For though some Emperours and Kings consented indeed unto some of them; as to the first *Laterane, Henry* 5. to that at *Vienna, Philip* of *France*, and so in some others; yet the consent of Emperours and Kings is not sufficient for holding a Councell, the authority by which the Bishops are called and come together, must bee regall: which in all these, as *Bellarmine* [s] truly teacheth, was onely pontificial. Againe, that very consent to hold those Councels which Kings then gave, was a servile consent, not Imperiall; nor was it free and willing, but coacted and extorted. They knew certainly by the dealing of Pope *Hildebrand* with *Henry* the fourth, what they might expect, if they withstood the Popes will, or wrastled with such a Giant: no lesse than the losse of their Crownes had beene the censure for denying to consent to what the Pope would have them: their consent was no other, but that by the Popes authority the Synod should bee called and held, a consent that the Synod should be called by an unlawfull and usurped authority; even such a consent, as if a rightfull King being overcome by a Rebell, should for feare of his life consent that the Rebell should call and assemble a Parliament, and there enact what lawes himselfe listed. It is the authority by which those Councels were gathered, not by whose consent they were gathered; of which we doe now enquire. The authority whereby they were assembled was onely in the Pope, though to that authority Emperours and Kings consented: and as they are not a little brag that the Pope could doe such worthy acts by his authority; so are we so farre from denying him to have done this, that wee willingly professe the same: but withall doe affirme, which inevitably ensues thereof, that even for this very cause all those Councels are unlawfull, because they were called by Papall, and not by Imperiall authority. This demonstrates them to have assembled without lawfull authority, to have beene nothing else than so many great Routs and Riots in the Church, so many tumultuous and disorderly Conventicles, so much more odious both in the sight of God and men, as those who tumultuously and without authority convented, should have beene patternes of piety, obedience, and order unto others.

s Cur tunc non solus Pontifex concilia indixerit, ut postea factum est, rationes multæ sunt. Bell. lib. 1. de Concil. ca. 13. §. Habemus.

24. Yea and this very exception which may equally be opposed against them all, was most justly taken (to omit the rest) against their *Trent* Riot, when it was congregated by that Papall and usurped authority. The King [t] of England gave this as a reason of his refusall to send

t Innoc. Gentil. in Examin. Con. Trid. lib. 2. in initio.

ſend to it, becauſe the right to call Councels belonged to Kings and Emperours, *nullam vero eſſe poteſtatem penes Pontificem,* but the Pope had no authority to call or aſſemble a Councell. The French King writ a letter to them at *Trent,* and the ſuperſcription [u] was, *Conventui Tridentino :* The Fathers ſtormed and ſnuffed a long while at that, diſdaining that the King ſhould write *Conventui,* and not *Concilio,* and hardly were they perſwaded to read his letter : At laſt, when credence and audience was obtained for *Iames Aimiot* his Legate, he ſignified before all the *Trent* Fathers, that the King proteſted and publiſhed to al, (as alſo before he had done at *Rome*) that he accounted not that aſſembly *pro Oecumenico & legitimo Concilio, ſed pro privato Conventu; not for a generall Councell, but for a private Convent,* gathered together for the private benefit and good of ſome few; adding, *ſe ſuoſque ſubditos nullo vinculo ad parendum his quæ in eo decreta fuerint obſtrictos iri; that hee and his ſubjects would not be tyed by the decrees thereof :* exhorting further that this his proteſtation might bee recorded among the Acts of their Synod, and that all Chriſtian Kings might have notice thereof. The Electours [x] and Princes of *Germany* being aſſembled at *Nurimberge,* when *Zacharias Delphinus,* and *Franciſcus Commendonius* the Popes Legates came to warne them in the Popes name [y] to come, or ſend to the Councell of *Trent,* returned this anſwere unto them, *Mirantur illuſtriſſimi Electores & Principes,* the moſt illuſtrious Electours and Princes doe wonder, that the Pope would take upon him, *Celſitudinibus ſuis Concilij indictionem obtrudere,* to obtrude to their Celſitude his appointment of a Councell, and that he durſt call them to *Trent;* adding, wee would have both the Pope and you his Legates to know, that wee acknowledge no ſuch authority in the Pope, and we are certainly perſwaded by the undoubted teſtimonies both of Gods law and mans, *Concilij indicendi jus Pontificem Romanum non habere; that the Pope hath no authority and right to appoint, call, or aſſemble a Councell.* Thus they; whoſe anſwer is at large explaned in their *Gravamina* [z], where the firſt reaſon of their rejecting the *Trent* aſſembly is this, *quod ea illegitime, & contra manifeſtum jus indicta ſit; becauſe it was appointed and gathered unlawfully, & againſt manifeſt right,* ſeeing the Pope who called it, hath no authoritie to ſummon or call a Councel : Of the ſame judgement were other Princes. When *Hieronimus Martinengus* [a] was ſent as Legate from the Pope, to call ſome out of England to that *Trent* aſſembly in the time of the late Queene of renowned and bleſſed memory; *è Belgio in inſulam traijcere prohibuit; ſhe would not ſuffer him to ſet foote in her dominion about ſuch buſineſſe : Nec* [b] *diverſum ad Reges Daciæ & Suetiæ miſſus, reſponſum retulit;* and the Kings of *Denmarke* and *Swetia* gave the like anſwere, that the Pope had no right to call a Councell. So juſtly did they diſlike and contemne the going to that Synod, even for this cauſe, and that moſt juſtly, eſteeming it for no other than a Conventicle, or unlawfull aſſembly.

25. Said I unlawfull ? that is too ſoft and mild a word : that, and all the other nine with it, by reaſon of that Papall calling, were unlawfull in the higheſt degree, even Antichriſtian : For the authoritie whereby thoſe Synods were called, belonging in right to Emperours
and

u *Geut. in Examt. ſeſſ. 11. Côc. Trid. pa. 96. & Iob. Sleid. Comment. lib. 22. pa. 332. b. et ſeq.*

x *Epit. rerum in orbx geſt. ſub Ferd. 1. an. 1561. apud Scard. tem. 3. pa 2171. et ſeq.* y *Summus Pontifex ſacrum Concilium Tridenti celebranduſt authoritate divinitus ſibi tradita diu evit; noſq, ablegavit nuncios ſuos qui pij Pontificis nomine ſingulos conveniremus, et rogaremus ut ad Concilium hoc accederent. Ibid.* z *Gravam. oppoſita Conc. Trid. cauſa 1. pa. 21.* a *Epit. rerum in orb. geſt. ſab Fer. an. 1561. apud Scard. loc. cit.*

b *Ibid.*

and Kings, and being tyrannically usurped by the Pope, as he by intruding himselfe into the Imperiall royalties, and lifting up himselfe above all the Vicegerents of God here in earth, *that is, above* c *all that is called God,* did thereby proclame himselfe to bee that man of sinne, and display his Antichristian Banner: So on the other side, those Bishops and others, who came at his Papall call, and yeelded obedience to him, in such sort usurping, did, *eo ipso,* in that very act of theirs, receive the marke of the beast, and not onely consent, but submit themselves to his Antichristian authority, and fight under the very Ensignes and Banner of Antichrist: But of this point I have before d intreated, where I shewed, that al', even the best actions, (how much more then such tumultuous and turbulent attempts) when they are performed in obedience to the Pope, as Pope, that is, as a supreme Commander, are turned into impious and Antichristian rebellions against God.

26. This rather is needfull to bee here observed, that not onely generall, but even Provinciall or Nationall Synods are in all Christian Kingdomes to bee called onely by Imperiall, not at all by Papall or Episcopall authority; yea, and they are so called in every well ordered Church: For although there goe not forth a particular and expresse *Edict* or *mandatum* from Kings, to assemble them, yet so long as Kings or Emperours doe not expresse their will to the contrary, even that summons which is sent from Primates or other Bishops subject unto them, hath virtually and *implicitè* the Imperiall authority by wch every such Synod is assembled: The reason whereof is this: The holy Nicene Councell decreed e, that for the more peaceable government of each Church, there should be two Provinciall Synods yearly held by every Primate. Those holy Fathers meant not (as the continuall practice throughout the whole Church doth explane) so strictly to define that number of two, as that neither moe, nor fewer might be kept in one yeare: But they judging that, for those times a competent and convenient number, they set it downe, but yet as an accidentall, ceremoniall, and therefore mutable order, if the necessitie and occasions of any Church should othe.wise require. That which is substantiall and immutable in their Canon is, that Provinciall Synods shall be held by each Primate so often, and at such times as the necessity and occasions of their Church shall require: and the chiefe Iudge of that necessity and fitting occasions is no other than hee to whose sword and authority every Bishop is subject, and without whose consent first obtained, they may in no place of his Kingdome assemble together without the note of tumult and sedition. This Nicene Canon, as all the rest, when *Constantine* f, and other succeeding Emperours and Kings approved, (as who hath not approved that holy Councel?) they then gave unto it the force of an Imperiall law, according to the rule, *omnia* g *nostra facimus, quibus nostram impartimur authoritatem;* wee make that our owne *Act,* and our law which wee *ratifie by our authoritie*: And *Iustinian* more plainly expressed this, when he said: h *Sancimus vicem legum obtinere sanctas regulas; we enact, that the holy Canons of the Church set downe in the former Councels, the* Nicene, *the* Constantinopolitane,

c 2 Thess. 2.4.

d Sup. ca. 13.

e *Placuit annis singulis per unamquamq; Provinciam bis in anno Concilia celebrari. Conc. Nic. Can. 5.*

f *Quæ ab Episcopis erant editæ regulæ Constantinus sua consignabat et confirmabat authoritate. Euseb. lib. 4. de vita Const. ca. 27.*

g Lib. 1. Cod. de *Veter. jure enuc.* et lib. 2. De-cretal. tit. 23. ca. ficut noxius in Glossa.

h Novel. 131. ca. 1.

politane, Epheſine, and *Chalcedon,* ſhall have the force, and ſtand in the ſtrength of Imperiall lawes: By this Imperiall aſſent it is, that when the wiſedome of Chriſtian Emperours and Kings doth not otherwiſe diſpoſe of calling Synods in their dominions, Primates may call the ſame, two, or moe, or fewer in any yeare, as neceſſitie ſhall perſwade: but whenſoever they call any, the ſame are called, aſſembled and celebrated by the force of that Imperial authoritie, which Kings and Emperours have either given to that Nicene Canon, or which they in more explicite manner ſhall impart unto the Primates or Biſhops in their Kingdomes.

27. Now if Provinciall Councels may not, nor ever are lawfully held in Chriſtian Kingdomes without this authority, how much leſſe may generall and Oecumenicall, the occaſions of which being rare and extraordinary, the calling alſo of them is extraordinary, and both for the time & place, meerly arbitrary, at the will of thoſe who have Imperial or regal authority: To ſay nothing, how inconvenient it is even in civill government, and how dangerous unto Chriſtian States, that all the Biſh. of a Kingdome ſhould leave their own Churches naked of their guides, and Paſtours, and goe into farre and forraigne Countries, without the command of their Soveraigne Lords, eſpecially goe at the command of an uſurping Commander, and that alſo, if he require, though their owne Soveraignes ſhall forbid or withſtand the ſame, of the miſchiefe and danger whereof the example of *Becket,* among many like, may be a warning to all Kingdomes. But leaving that to the grave conſideration of others, thus much now out of that which hath beene ſaid, is evident; that ſeeing all thoſe ten forenamed Synods were called and aſſembled by no other authority than Pontificall, and ſeeing lawfully aſſemble they could not, but onely by Imperiall, it hence clearly enſueth, that for defect of lawfull calling and aſſembling, they are all of them no other than unlawfull Councels: Againe, ſeeing no Synods are congregated in Chriſts name [i], but ſuch as are aſſembled by him who hath from Chriſt authority to aſſemble them, which in Chriſtian Kingdomes none hath, as wee have ſhewed, but onely Kings and Emperours: and ſeeing none of thoſe ten were aſſembled by them, it hence further and certainly enſueth, that never one of thoſe ten were gathered in Chriſts name, and if not in Chriſts, then ſure in no other but in the name of Antichriſt, and ſo all of them, in reſpect of their calling, not only unlawfull, but even Antichriſtian Councels.

28. After their calling conſider their proceedings, for as thoſe Councels were unlawfully aſſembled, ſo were they alſo unlawfull by defect of the other eſſentiall condition; which is, due and ſynodall order: for they all not onely wanted ſynodall freedome and order, but, which is worſe, they wanted that which is the onely meanes to have ſynodall freedome and order obſerved in any generall Councell, and that is the Imperiall Preſidencie: in none of them was the Emperour, in them all [k] the Pope was Preſident: In the firſt *Laterane, Caliſtus* [l]; in the ſecond, *Innocentius* [m] the ſecond; in the third, *Alexander* [n] the third; in the fourth, *Innocentius* [o] the third; and the like might bee ſhewed

i *Congregari în nomine Chriſti nihil aliud eſt, quam ab eo congregari, qui habet à Chriſto authoritatem congregandi. Bell. lib. 1. de Conc. ca. 17. § At hoc.* k *Addamus (his 8. prima) reliqua generalia Concilia, in quibus omnibus ſine controverſia Pontifex Rom. praeſedit. Bell. lib. 1. de Conc. ca. 20 § Si ergo.* l *Papa Caliſtus 2. coram innumera multitudine cleri et populi, eidem Concilio (Viennenſem nominat Vſper. diceret Lateranenſi, ut et Bin. agnoſcit notis ſuis in illud Côc.) praeſedit. Abb. Vſper. ad an. 1119. et huic Concilio praeſedit Pontifex. Bin. notis ſuis ad id Conc. pa. 1317. b* m *Synodus maxima Romae, praeſidente ſummo Pontifice Funcêtio celebratur. Otho Friſing. lib. 7. ca. 23.* n *Omnes ſcriptores fatentur eidem Concilio Pontificem Romanum praeſidiſſe. Bin. Not. in Conc. Later. 3. § Oecumenicum io. 3. pa. 1351.* o *Ei Pontifex Rom. praeſedit. Bin. not. in Conc. Later. 4. io. 3. Con. pa. 1466 bi*

p *Bell.lib.1.de Con.ca.20.§ Si ergo.*

q *Hos ut ſe nefando jureju. rando adſtrin. gerent, adegit, putrum enim mactavit, jura-mentóq; inito ſuper ejus viſceribus, eadem ipſe cum alijs comedit. Dio Caſſ.lib.37.*

r *Catilinam luxuria primum, tũ egeſtas in neſaria Concilia oppri. mende patrie impulere, Sena-tum confodere, totam rempub. funditus tollere, et quicquid nec Hannibal vide-retur optaſſe. L.Flor.lib.4. ca.1.*

ſ *Ego Nic.ab hac hora fidelis ero S.Petro et Eccle-ſie Romane do-minóque meo Pa-pe. Papatum adjutor ero ad defendendum. Forma eſt jura-menti ſecundum quam jurant E-piſcopi et hodie omnes recipien-tes dignitatem à Papa.Extra. de jurejur.ca. Ego N.lib.2.tit. 24.ca.4.*

t *Aug.lib.2.cõt. Ep.Parm.ca.13. u Quid excogi-tare verum vel veriſi-mile poſſunt,qui-bus non vel Rex vel Caſar,non populus,non cle-rus,non genera-lis Synodus, non deniq; tota Ec-cleſia dicere po-teſt, cur ita fa-cis? Cl.Eſpen. in cap.1.ad Ti-tum.pa.76.*

x *De quo ſupra cap.Ego N.Ex-tra.de jurejur.*

ſhewed in the reſt; but that *Bellarmines* words may eaſe us of that la-bour, who ſpeaking of all thoſe ten Councels, ſaith p, *In eis omnibus fi-ne Controverſia Pontifex Rom.preſedit;* the Pope without doubt was Preſi-dent in them all.

29. Nor was this an Epiſcopall Preſidencie a preheminence only, & precedence before other Biſhops in the Synod, ſuch as any Biſh. to whõ the Emp. pleaſed to confer that dignity, might lawfully enjoy,& when he gave it to none by name, it then by his *tacit* conſent or permi-ſſion fell, as it were by devolution upon the chiefe Biſhop that was preſent in the Councell: Such a Preſidencie, though it bee not due to the Pope, ſeeing in the ancient Councels hee neither had it, nor grud-ged that other ſhould have it, yet are wee not unwilling to allow that unto him, if contenting himſelfe therewith hee would ſeeke no more: But the Preſidencie which hee now deſires,and in all thoſe ten Councels uſurped, is meerely Imperiall; the Preſidencie of governing the Synod,and ordering it by his authority and power, the very ſame which in all the generall Councels,for a thouſand yeares after Chriſt, the Emperour held, and had it as one of his Royalties and Imperiall rights, none of all the Catholike Biſhops in thoſe Councels ever ſo much as contradicting, much leſſe reſiſting the ſame: For any Bi-ſhops,moſt of all for the Pope, to take upon them ſuch a Preſidencie utterly overthrows all liberty and order in Councels; for by it all the Biſhops are to be kept in awe and order; and the Pope, who of all o-ther is moſt exorbitant,and fartheſt out of ſquare, ought by this to be curbed, & reduced into order: Even as when *Catiline* took upon him to bee the Ruler and guide to his aſſembly, and a puniſher of diſor-ders among them,though all the reſt willingly ſubmitted themſelves, and that with a ſolemne oath q, to bee ordered by him in their acti-ons; yet for all this order they were no free Romane Senate, but a Conjuration of Conſpirators, ſtriving to oppreſſe r the Romane State,liberties,and ancient lawes: Right ſo it is in theſe Synods,when the Pope,who is the Lord of miſrule,and Ring-leader of the Conſpi-rators, takes upon him this Preſidencie, to order Councels, though the reſt not onely conſent, but binde themſelves by a ſacred oath ſ, to be ſubject to his authoritie; this very uſurpation of ſuch Preſidencie doth,*eo ipſo*,exclude and baniſh al liberty & ſynodall order,& makes their aſſemblies meere Conjurations againſt the truth, and ancient faith of the Church.

30. How could it now be choſen,but that whatſoever hereſie the Pope with the faction of his Catilinarie Conſpiratours embraced, ſhould in ſuch Councels prevaile againſt the truth? The Imperiall au-thority was the onely hedge or pale to keepe the Pope within his bounds; that being once removed,he ſaid,he did, he decreed what he liſted. The rule of his Regiment was now the old Canon of *Conſtan-tius, Quod ego volo pro Canone ſit:* the proofe of all their decrees was borrowed from their predeceſſors, the old *Donatiſts: Quod* t *volumus ſanctum eſt.* Not Emperours, not Biſhops, none might controule him or ſay unto him u, *Domine, cur ita facis?* The Biſhops were tyed to him by an oath x, to defend the Papacy, (that is, his uſurped authority)

and

nd defend it, *contra omnes homines*, againſt all that ſhould wag their ongues againſt it. The Emperours and Kings ſaw how *Hildebrand* had uſed, and in moſt indigne manner miſuſed *Henry* the 4. how *Alexander* the third had inſolently trodden on the necke of *Fredericke:* what ould they, nay what durſt they doe, but either willingly ſtoop and roſtrate themſelves, or elſe be forced to lye downe at the Popes feet, nd ſay unto him, *Tread on us, O thou Lion of the Tribe of Iudah*; and ccording as it is written, Set thy foot *ſuper Aſpidem & Baſiliſcum.* Could there poſſibly be any freedome or order in ſuch Synods, where he onely meanes of preſerving freedome and order was baniſhed? ſight not the Pope in ſuch Councels doe and decree whatſoever either himſelfe, his will, or faction would ſuggeſt unto him? Say they ad neither ſwords, nor clubs, nor other like inſtruments of violence ι thoſe Synods: they needed none of them: This Papall preſidency as in ſtead of them all. It was like the club of *Hercules*, the very ſhaing of it was able, and did affright all, that none, no not Emperours rſt deale againſt it. The removing of the Imperiall preſidency made ch a calme in their Synods, that without reſiſtance, without any ed of other further violence, the Pope might overſway whatſoever deſired.

y *Alexander Imperatori juſſit ut ſe humi proſterneret, et Imperatoris collum pede comprimens ait, Scriptum eſt, Super Aſpidem et Baſiliſcum ambulabis. Nauclan.* I 177

31. And truly it may bee eaſily obſerved by ſuch as attentively ade the Eccleſiaſticall ſtories, that together with the ſtanding or fall the Empire, either the ancient faith or hereſies prevailed in the hurch. So long as the Emperour being Chriſtian, retained his digty and Imperiall authority, no hereſie could long take place, but is by the Synodall judgement of Oecumenicall Councels maturely ppreſſed: the faction of no Biſhop, no not of the Pope, being able prevaile againſt that ſoveraigne remedy. But when once *z Gregorie* e ſecond, *Zachary*, and their ſucceeding Popes to *Leo* the third, had moſt admirable and unexplicable fraud & ſubtilty, clipt the wings d cut the ſinewes of the Eaſterne Empire; themſelves firſt ſeizing on the greateſt part of *Italy*, by the meanes of *Pipin*, and then erecg a new Empire in the Weſt, the Imperiall authority being thus ringed, the Eaſterne Emperour not daring, the Weſterne in rerd of the late curteſie received from the Pope, being not willing, d neither of them both being able now to match and juſtle with the pe; this which was the great let and impediment to the Popes facon, and the diſcovering of the man of ſinne being now removed, ere was no meanes to keepe out of the Church the hereſies which e Pope affected: then the *Cataracts* of hereſies being ſet open, and edepths of the earth, nay of the infernall pit being burſt up, hereſies ſht in, and came with a ſtrong hand into the Church, and thoſe hetxicall doctrines which in ſix hundred yeares and more could never t head, paſſing as doubtfull and private opinions among a few, and lling but as a few little drops of raine, grew now unto ſuch an height d outrage, that they became the publike and decreed doctrines in ιe Weſterne Church. The Pope once having found his ſtrength in ιe cauſe of Images, (wherein the firſt triall was made thereof) no fane nor dotage was ſo abſurd for which he could not after that command,

z *Ab an.*730. *ad an.*800.

Ee   mand,

mand, when he liſted, the judgement of a generall Councell; Tranſubſtantiation, Proper Sacrifice, the Idoll of the Maſſe, (to which not
Moloch nor *Baal* is to be compared) their Purgatorian fire, their five
new-found proper Sacraments, condignity of workes, yea Supererogation, and an armie of like hereſies aſſayled and prevailed againſt
the truth. The Imperiall authority being laid in the duſt, and trampled under the ſole of the Popes foot, no meanes was left to reſtraine
his enormous deſignes, or hinder him in Councels, to doe and define
even what he liſted. And as the Imperiall authority which he ſo long
time had oppreſſed, is in any kingdome more or leſſe reſtored, and
freed from his vaſſalage; the other hereſies which aroſe from the ruine and decay thereof, are more or leſſe expurged out of that Kingdome, and the ancient truth reſtored therein: Yea and ſtill, though
but by inſenſible degrees, ſhall hee and his authority waſt [a] and conſume, till not onely all the ten [b] hornes of the Beaſt (that is, all the
Kings whoſe authority he hath uſurped, and uſed as his hornes to puſh
at Gods Saints) ſhall hate the Whore, that Romiſh *Babylon*, and
make her deſolate and naked, and burne her with fire; but till himſelfe
alſo being deſpiſed and contemned of his owne lovers, ſhall together
with his adherents be utterly aboliſhed, and caſt into that Lake of
Gods wrath.

32. You ſee now how unlawfull thoſe Synods are by reaſon of the
defect of Imperiall preſidency: you will perhaps demand whether by
the want thereof there happened any particular diſorder in them, or
ought contrary to freedome and ſynodall order: whereunto I might
in a word anſwer, that there neither was, nor could there bee ought
at all done in any of thoſe ten Synods with freedome and ſynodall order. For though otherwiſe their proceedings had beene never ſo
milde, temperate and equall, yet even for that one defect of Imperiall preſidency, and excluding the ſame, whatſoever they did was diſorderly, and they all nothing but ſynods of diſorder. But yet for further ſatisfaction of that queſtion, let us (omitting all the reſt) conſider among very many, ſome few particulars concerning their youngeſt and deareſt baby of *Trent*; Was that equall dealing in *Paul* the 3.
at the beginning of his *Trent* aſſembly, to conſpire [c] and take ſecret
counſell with the Emperour to make warre againſt the Proteſtants,
and root them out of the world? The Italian Franciſcan in his Sermon before *Ferdinand*, ſtirring up both him and others to this butchery, *Exere vires tuas*, plucke up your ſpirit and ſtrength, and root out
that peſtiferous kinde of men, *nefas enim eſt, for it is unlawfull* to ſuffer them any longer to looke upon the light: neither ſay that you will
doe it, it muſt be done even now at this preſent, and without any delay. Thus did he give the watchword, and ſound an alarme to their
intended Maſſacre: whereupon there enſued *bellum* [e] *cruentum & calamitoſum, a bloody and cruell warre againſt the Proteſtants*: concerning
which divers of the Princes of *Germanie* ſaid in their Letters to the
Emperour, Wee [f] ſhall ſo anſwer that every man may underſtand,
both that injury is done to us, and that you doe undertake this warre
Romani Antichriſti & impij Concilij Tridentini impulſu, at the inſtigation

of

a *2 Theſſ. 2. 8.*
b *Apoc. 17. 12. 16.*

c *Cum Conciliū jam haberi inciperet, Imperator et Pontifex clanculum unā, de armis ad Proteſtantes domandos ſuſcipiendis concilium inter ſe inierunt. Gen. Exam. Trident. Conc. ſeſſ. 3. nu. 5*
d *Iob. Sleid. Comment. lib. 16. an. 1545.*
e *Gent. loc. cit. nu. 6.*
f *Sleid. Comm. lib. 17. an. 1546*

of the Romane Antichrift, and the impious Councell at Trent, that the doctrine of the Gofpell, and the liberty of Germany may bee oppreffed. Was this *Concilium pacis*, or rather *Concilium fanguinis*, a confpiracie not onely againft the faith, but againft the life of Catholikes? Was it fit his Holineffe fhould play *Iudas* part, pretend love and emendation of the faith, when he entended murder, and an utter extirpation of the fervants of God? Could there be freedome for them at *Trent* in the Popes dominions, when they might not be fuffered to breathe or live at home in their owne free Cities and States? Was not this a ftratagem unknowne in the time of the Councell at *Millane* and *Arimine*, to invite Catholikes to the Synod, and promife liberty and free acceffe, but provide that they fhall have no leifure, not fo much as come to the Councell?

33. What equity or freedome could there either be, or be expected in that Councell, wherein the Pope, who is the capitall enemy of the Catholikes, took upon him to be their Iudge, yea, when himfelfe who was *reus*, guilty of herefie, befides other crimes, and who fhould have beene judged firft of all, tooke upon him to bee fupreme Iudge in his owne caufe? Let *Catiline* be held for fuch a Iudge betwixt the fenate and himfelfe; it is not to bee doubted but *Tully*, and all who ftood for the liberty of their City and Country, fhall be profcribed and condemned as rebels; and *Catiline* with his faction decreed to be the onely true Citizens, the onely men fit to rule the Empire. It was the juft exception [h] which thofe 47. Catholike Bifhops that ftood for *Athanafius*, tooke againft the Councell at *Tyre*, wherein hee was condemned, that *Eufebius* and *Theogius*, the mortall enemies of *Athanafius*, were his Iudges in that Synod; *Lex autem Dei inimicum neque teftem, neque judicem effe vult*; but the law of God prohibits a mans enemy to be a witneffe, much more to be his Iudge. The very fame exception took *Chryfoftome* againft *Theophilus* and the Synod with him. *Theophilus*, faith he, *hath called us unto judgement, before hee hath purged himfelfe of the crimes objected againft him, quod contra omnes Canones & Leges eft*, which is againft all lawes and Canons: and againe, it is not fit that *Theophilus* fhould judge us, *qui ipfe reus eft, inimicus & hoftis*, who is himfelfe guilty or accufed of crimes, and is alfo our enemy. Thus *Chryfoftome*. A matter of fuch equity, that both Pope *Nicholas* [k] the firft, and [l] *Celeftine* the third fay, *Ipfa ratio dictat*, Common reafon doth teach, that thofe who are ones enemies, ought not to be their Iudges. The Pope then being a profeffed enemie of Proteftants can be no lawfull or competent Iudge of them: and being himfelfe *reus*, called into queftion for herefies, can be no lawfull Iudge in his owne caufe, and in thofe very herefies whereof he is accufed. And truly the anfwer whereby *Bellarmine* thought to avoid this moft juft exception againft their *Trent* Councell and the reft, doth much more confirme the equity thereof: *He confeffeth that this holds* [m] *in all, fave onely in the fupreme Iudge.* He onely may be Iudge in his owne caufe, and againft his enemies alfo, all elfe muft ftand to the judgement of others. The interpretation is true, but in the application of this to the Pope, there he faileth: for hee intends the Pope to be that fupreme Iudge; than which there cannot be devifed a more

bafe

g *Tridentum liberaaut Imperij civitas non eft, fed membrum præcipuum Pontificiæ factionis. Grav.oppof.Trid Conc.pa.37.*

h *Athanaf.Apol.2.§.Non arbitramur.p.216* i *Chryf.Epift.ad Innocent. Papam tc.1. Conc. poft Epi.Inu.27.* k *Quia fufpecti et inimici, judices effe non debeant, et ipfa ratio dictat et plurimis probatur exerplis. Epift.S.Nich. 1. §.Igitur quia.* l *Ipfa ratio dictat; quia fufpecti et inimici judices effe non debeant.Extr. de Appel.ca. Secundo requiris.* m *Quod dicant, non debere eundem effe Iudicē, et paſſē,dico habere locum in privatis hominibus, non in principe fupremo.Ille e-im femper eft fummus Index etiamfi cum ipfo litigetur.Bell. lib.1 de Conc. ca.21.§.Tertia,*

n *Matth.18.17*
Hæc quod Chri-
ſtus dixit, Dic
Ecclesiæ, omnes
homines com-
prehendit, &
quod Petrus &
ejus ſucceſſores
illa authoritate
comprehendantur
oſtendit Paulus
qui in faciem re-
ſtitit Cephæ:
probat etiam hoc
authoritas uni-
verſalis Eccle-
ſiæ,&c. Reſpon-
ſio Synodalis
Concil.Baſil. pa.
105.a.
o *Conc.6.act.13*
Epiſtolas Hono-
rii omnimodo
abijiuus &
tanquam animæ
noxias extra-
mur. pa. 67.a.
&, Exclamave-
runt univerſi,
Honorio hæreti-
co Anathema.
Conc.6.act. 26.
pa.79.a.
p *Deteſtamur*
Sergium, Hono-
rium,&c. Conc.
Nic.2.Act.7.p.
386.b.
q *Quamvis Ho-*
norius poſt mor-
tem anathemate
ſit affectus, ma-
nifeſtum tamen
eſt illam de hæ-
reſi fuiſſe accu-
ſatum,qua ſola
in cauſa licet in-
ferioribus de
ſuperioribus ju-
dicare.Conc.8.
Act.7.pa.891.b
r *Poteſtati Ec-*
cleſiæ quilibet
cujuſcunq, dig-
nitatis, etiamſi
papalis exiſtat,
obedire tenetur
in his quæ perti-
nent ad fidem.
Conc.Conſtant.
ſeſſ.4.
ſ *Veritas hæc*
quod Concilium
eſt ſupra Papam
eſt veritas fidei
Catholicæ. Conc.Baſil.ſeſſ.33. t *Peccata eorum (Paparum)ſepe dicta fuerunt Eccleſiæ, et ab Eccleſiæ punita, et qui non*
audierint Eccleſiam fuerunt habiti ut Ethnici et Publicani, ut legitur de Anaſtaſio et Liberio. Reſp. Synodalis Conc. Baſ. pa.
105.a.et pa.eadem b. enumerat Ioh.12.et alios. u *Bell.lib.1.de Conc.ca.21.§.Deniq.*

baſe begging of the queſtion, and moſt ſpeciall controverſie. That he is not ſupreme, we unavoydably prove by the words of Chriſt [n], *Dic Ecclesiæ :* by the judgement of this fift Councell, which judged and condemned both the Popes *Cathedrall Conſtitution* for hereticall, and *Vigilius* himſelfe for an heretike : and in ſaying the fift Councell, it is as much as if I ſaid, by the judgement of the whole Catholike Church, all the former Councels conſenting in faith with this fift, and all that follow it approving the judgement thereof, untill their *Laterane* Synod. The ſame is further proved by the ſixt [o] generall Councell, which judged and condemned Pope *Honorius* for an Heretike; by that which they call the ſeventh, which [p] alſo condemned *Honorius* ; by the next, which they account the eighth, wherein it is decreed, that in the caſe [q] of hereſie the Pope may be judged ; (and that is the very caſe whereof the Pope is now accuſed ;) by the Councels of *Conſtance* [r], and *Baſil* [ſ], in both which it is decreed to be a doctrine of the Catholike faith, that the Pope hath a ſuperiour Iudge in the caſe both of hereſie, ſchiſme, and ſcandalous life : by the practice [t] of the Church, in judging and depoſing *Liberius*, and *Iohn* the 12. by the very words of *Bellarmine* himſelfe, *if the Biſhops*, ſaith he [u], *in a Synod can convince the Pope of hereſie, poſſunt eum judicare & deponere*, they may judge and depoſe him. And if in any cauſe he have a ſuperiour Iudge, then is he not ſupreme. Seeing then by all theſe, beſides infinite moe, it is not onely proved, but demonſtrated, that the Pope is not, nor ought to be held as ſupreme Iudge, but may in ſome cauſes be both judged, condemned, and depoſed: and ſeeing by *Bellarmines* owne confeſſion, none can be judge in his owne cauſe, or of his adverſaries towards whom he profeſſeth open enmity, but onely the ſupreme Iudge; it inevitably followeth upon the Cardinalls owne words, beſides evident reaſon, that the Pope neither was in the Councell of *Trent*, nor can be in any Councell a lawfull Iudge, either of Proteſtants, or in thoſe cauſes which he then undertooke to judge, in which himſelfe was a party and *Reus* ; ſeeing then, he ſhould be Iudge in his owne cauſe, which equity and reaſon, the law both divine and humane doe conſtantly prohibite.

34. Adde hereunto the judgement of the ancient and Catholike Church. I doe never reade, or almoſt remember the holy Councell of *Chalcedon*, but with a kinde of amazement I admire the rare piety, prudence, integrity, moderation, and gravity of thoſe moſt glorious Iudges, who ſupplying the Emperours place when he was abſent, were the Imperiall Preſidents in that Councell : Had they, or ſuch like Preſidents beene wanting at that time, it may juſtly be feared, conſidering the eagerneſſe and temerity, that I ſay not the inſolency of the Popes Legates in that Synod, that the Councell of *Chalcedon* had proved a worſe Latrociny than the ſecond *Epheſine* was. In that Councell both theſe cauſes now mentioned fell out, the one in *Dioſcorus*, the other in *Athanaſius* Biſhop of *Paros*. *Dioſcorus* came and ſate down in his place among the other Patriarks & Biſhops, as one who would be a Iudge in the cauſes propoſed; for in ancient Councels there was

a different ˣ place, and seats for the Bishops, who judged and gave sentence in the Councell, and for others who were actors, whether plaintiffs and accusers, or *Rei*, and accused. Now because *Dioscorus* himselfe was the partie who was called into question, and to be judged; and equity forbids a man to bee Iudge in his owne cause: The Councell, and by name the Popes Legates, (to whom the rest therein assented) tooke this just exception thereat, and said, ʸ *Non patimur*, we cannot indure this wrong to be done, *ut iste sedeat qui judicandus advenit*; that *Dioscorus, who is to bee judged, sit as a Iudge in his owne cause*; upon which most just and equall motion, the glorious Iudges, who were Presidents for order, commanded *Dioscorus* to remove ᶻ from the Bench, as I may say, of Iudges, and to sit in the middle of the Church, which was the place both for the Accusers and *Rei*; and *Dioscorus* accordingly sate there, as the glorious Iudges had appointed: Vpon the very same ground of equitie did the religious Emperour command in the second *Ephesine* Synod, that if ᵃ any question or cause fell out to be debated concerning *Theodoret* (whom he commanded to be present) that then, *absque illo Synodum convenire; the Synod should assemble & judge that cause without Theodoret*; he should have no judicatory power in his own cause: And the like he further commanded concerning that holy Bish. *Flavianus*: He & some others had before in the Synod at *Constantinople* beene Iudges against *Eutiches*, and condemned him. An higher, even that generall Councell at *Ephesus* (which proved a Latrociny in the end) was called to examine ᵇ that judgment of *Flavianus* and the rest, whether it was just or no. The Emperour commanded ᶜ those who had beene Iudges of late, *in loco eorum esse qui judicandi sunt*, now to bee in the place of *Rei, such as were to bee judged*. A demonstration, that if *Theodosius* or *Martian*, or such like worthy and equall Iudges as they were at *Chalcedon*, had been Presidents for order in their *Trent* assembly; the Pope, though hee had beene as just and orthodoxall as *Flavianus*, much more being in impiety and heresie farre superiour to *Dioscorus*, should not have beene permitted to sit among the Bishops of the Councell, nor have so much as one single decisive suffrage or any judicatory power in his owne cause, much lesse have had such a supremacie of judgement, that his onely voyce and sentence should over-rule, and over-sway the whole Councell besides.

35. The other example is this: *Athanasius* Bishop of *Paros* being accused ᵈ of sundry crimes, was called to triall before a Provinciall Councell at *Antioch*, held by *Domnus* Bishop of that See, unto whose Patriarchall authority *Athanasius* was subject; when hee refused to come after three citations, hee was deposed by that Synod, and *Sabinianus* by the same authority, made Bishop of *Paros* in his roome. In the Councel at *Chalcedon* *Athanasius* came, complained of wrongfull extrusion, and desired of the generall Councell, that his Bishopricke might be restored unto him, pleading for his refusall to come to trial at the Synod at *Antioch*, nothing else but this ᵉ, that *Domnus* who was the chiefe Iudge in that Synod, was his enemy; and therefore hee thought it not equall to be tryed before him, though he was

E e 3   his

x *Eusebius et Theoderitus in ordine accusantium sedent, ipsent et vos in loco accusatorum sedetis. Conc. Chal. Act.1.pa.13. a.*

y *Act.1. Conc. Chal. pa.5. a.*

z *Dioscoro secundum jussionem glor. iof. ss. Judicum, resid. te in medio. ibid.*

a *Epist. Theodos. et Valent. ad Diosc. extat in Actis Conc. Chal. Act.1.pa. 5.b.*

b *Nunc vos convenistis ut eos qui judicarunt judicetis. Elpidij dictum nomine Imper. in Conc. lib. Ephes. recitatur vero in Conc. Chal. Act. 1.pa.13.b.*

c *Ibid.*

d *Conc. Chal. Act.14 per totü*

e *Dixit Athanasius cur tert ô etiocetur à Conc. ro Antioche-no, non occurrit. Athanasius dixit, Quoniam inimicus mens erat ipse qui judicabat, et rogo hæc relegi, et veritatē probari. ib.pa. 117 b. Solum quia suus inimicus esset ipse qui judicabat, clamavit, à sancta Chal. Synodo ad causas illatas sibi examinandas reservatur. Epist. 8 Nicb.1.*

§ *Veniamus.*

his owne Patriarch. The glorious Iudges gave order that the accuſa-tions againſt *Athanaſius* ſhould within eight moneths bee examined by *Maximus* then Biſhop of *Antioch*, and a Synod with him ; and if he were found guilty of thoſe crimes, or any other worthy depoſition, he ſhould for ever want the Biſhopricke. But if either they did not with-in ſuch time examine the cauſe, or examining it, finde the accuſations untrue, that then the See of *Paros* ſhould be reſtored unto *Athanaſi-us*, as unjuſtly depoſed ; and that *Sabinianus* ſhould remaine but a ſub-ſtitute unto him, untill *Maximus* could provide him of another Bi-ſhopricke. Thus ordered the ſecular Iudges, and the whole Councell of *Chalcedon* approved this ſentence, crying out, *Nihil juſtius, nothing is more juſt*, nothing is more equall, this is a juſt ſentence, you judge ac-cording to Gods minde. O that once againe the world might bee ſo happy as to ſee one other ſuch holy Councell as was this of *Chalcedon*, and ſuch worthy Iudges to be Preſidents thereof. All the *Anathemaes* and cenſures of their Councell at *Trent*, where the Romane *Domnus* our capitall enemy was the chiefe, nay rather the onely Iudge, would even for this very cauſe be adjudged of no validity, nor of force to bind I ſay not other Churches, ſuch as theſe of *Britany*, but not thoſe very men who are otherwiſe ſubject to the Popes Patriarchall authority, as *Athanaſius* was to *Domnus*. Such an holy Councell would cauſe a *me-lius inquirendum* to be taken of all their judgements and proceedings againſt the Saints of God: and unleſſe they could juſtifie (which while the Sun and Moone endureth they can never) their ſlanderous crimes of hereſie imputed unto us, and withall purge themſelves of that An-tichriſtian apoſtaſie whereof they are moſt juſtly accuſed and convict-ed, not onely in *foro poli*, but in their owne conſciences, and by the con-ſenting judgement of the Catholike Church for ſix hundred, nay in ſome points for fifteene hundred yeares after Chriſt, they ſhould and would by ſuch a Councell bee depoſed from all thoſe Epiſcopall dignities and functions which they have ſo long time uſurped and abuſed unto all tyranny, injuſtice, and ſubverſion of the Catholike Faith.

36. As the proceedings in that Councell were all unlawfull on the Popes part, ſo were they alſo both unlawfull and ſervile in reſpect of the other Biſhops, who were aſſeſſors in that Aſſembly. Could there poſſibly be any freedome or ſafety for Proteſtants among them, being the children of that generation which had moſt perfidiouſly violated their faith and promiſe to *Iohn Hus* in the Councell of *Conſtance*, and murdered the Prophets ? Among whom that Canon authorizing tre-cherous and perfidious dealing, ſtood in force : *Quod [f] non obſtantibus, that notwithſtanding the ſafe conducts of Emperours*, Kings, or any other granted to ſuch as come to their Councels , *Quocunque vinculo ſe a-ſtrinxerint, by what bond ſoever they have tyed themſelves*, by promiſe, by their honour, by their oath, yet *non obſtante* any ſuch band they may bring them into inquiſition, and proceed to cenſure, to puniſh them as they ſhall thinke fit, and then vaunt and glory in their perfidiouſ-neſſe, ſaying, *Cæſar obſignavit* [g], *Chriſtianus orbis major Cæſare reſigna-vit* ; *The Emperour hath ſealed this with his promiſe and oath, but our Coun-*
cell

f *Conſt. Conſt. ſeſſ.19.*

g *Campian. Rat. 4.*

cell which is above the Emperour, hath repealed it ; it ſhall not ſtand in force.

37. Could there be any freedome or liberty among thoſe who were by many obligations moſt ſervilely addicted to the Pope ? The Apulian Biſhops [h] crying out, *aliorum omnium nomine, in the name of all the reſt in their Councell, Nihil aliud ſumus præterquam creaturæ & mancipia ſanctiſsimi patris : O, we are all but the Popes creatures, his very ſlaves.* The complaint [i] of the Biſhop of *Arles* might here be renewed, which he made of ſuch like Councels, at *Baſil,* that muſt bee done, and of neceſſity be done and decreed in Councells, *quod nationi placeat Italicæ, which the Italian nation ſhall affect;* which country alone [k] for multitude of Biſhops doth equall or exceed other nations : and this very Italian faction to have prevailed at *Trent,* their owne Biſhop *Eſpencæus,* who was at the Councell, doth teſtifie: *Hæc [l] illa Helena eſt, this is the Helena* which of late prevailed at *Trent* ; this Italian faction overſwayed all : whereof *Molineus* [m] gives a plaine inſtance. For when an wholeſome Canon, that the Pope might not diſpence in ſome matters, had like to have beene decreed, many in the Councell liking well thereof, the Pope procured a reſpite [n] for that buſineſſe for a month and an halfe, during which time ſome forty poore Biſhops of *Italy* and *Sicily* were ſhipped and ſent to *Trent,* like ſo many *levis armaturæ milites,* and ſo the good Canon was by their valour diſcomfited and rejected by that holy Synod. Some of the Councell alſo were the Popes penſioners, and ſtipendary Biſhops, nay rather ought than Biſhops: ſuch as among others were *Olaus Magnus* [o], the titular Archbiſhop of *Vpſala* in *Gothia,* and *Robertus Venantius* the titular [p] and blinde Biſhop of *Armach,* and yet not halfe ſo blinde in body as in minde ; Archbiſhops [q] without Archbiſhoprickes, without a Church, without a Clergy, without Dioceſſe, without any revenues, ſave a ſmall * penſion which the Pope allowed them, that they might be cyphers in the Councell, and taking his pay might doe him ſome ſervice for it, and grace his Synod with their ſubſcriptions. But all the other bonds are as nothing to that [r] oath wherewith every one of them was tyed and fettered to the Pope, ſwearing to uphold the Papall authority againſt all men, and to fight againſt all that ſhould rebell againſt him: an oath ſo execrable, that *Æneas Sylvius* is [s] mentioned to have ſaid, *Quod etiam verum dicere contra Papam ſit contra Epiſcoporum juramentum, that even to ſpeake the truth, to ſpeake for the truth, if it be contrary to the Pope, is againſt the oath of Biſhops.* By this they were ſo tyed, *ut [u] ne mutire quidem ipſis liceat adverſus Idolum Romanum,* that they might not ſo much as whiſper againſt him.

38. Verily none of thoſe Iron chaines which were uſed by *Dioſcorus* in the *Epheſine* Latrocinie are comparable to theſe : No ſubſcription unto blankes like the ſwearing to maintaine whatſoever their Romane *Dioſcorus* ſhall define. They who were not chained might have no place in the Synod ; they who were chained with ſuch bands, and ſpecially with ſuch an oath, could have no freedome in the Synod ; they muſt ſpeake, thinke, and teach nothing but what the Pope breathes into them. Had there beene ſuch wiſe and worthy Iudges
for

h *Carol. Molin. lib. de Concil. Trident. nu. 21.*

i *Cl. Eſpenc. com. in Epiſt. ad Tit. ca. 1. p. 1. q. 42.*

k *Vt quæ ſola Epiſcoporum numero nationes alias æque: aut ſuperet. ibid.*

l *Jbid.*

m *Car. Mol. loco citato.*

n *Pontifex ad ſeſquimenſem decreti concluſionem ampliari juſsit. ibid.*

o *Olaus Magnus Suevus qui Archiepiſcopi Vpſalenſis nomen et titulum retinebat, quæ quidem regio nec Pontificem unquam, nec Eccleſiam Romanam agnovit. Gent. Exam. Conc. Trid. ſeſſ. 1. nu. 3*

p *Jbid.*

q *Archiepiſcopi, ſine Archiepiſcopatu, ſine Eccleſia, ſine Clero, ſine ullo cenſu & reditu. ibid.*

* *Hos Archiepiſcopos rerum tenues & inopes Romæ ſuis ſtipendiis alebat Pontifex. ibid. Olao in ſingulos menſes 15. aureos nummos ſuppeditabat. ibid.*

r *Extr. ad Iure. jur ca. Ego N.*

l *In nova juramenti forma inſuper hoc jurant Epiſcopi, ſe hæreticos, onmeſq, rebelles Pontificii extrewe infeſtaturos, & perſequuturos. Grav. oppoſ. Conc. Trident. p. 2. cauſ. 4 pa. 52.*

t *Ibidem in Paral. ad Abbat. Vſper. pa. 418.*

u *Ibid. pa. 51.*

for Preſidents of that Councell, as there was at *Chalcedon*, could they poſſibly have endured to ſee all ſynodall freedome thus oppreſſed and baniſhed? Nay they would in their zeale to God and his truth, have broken and burſt in ſunder every linke of that chaine: And as x *Ibas* and *Theodoret* were not admitted to the Councel of *Chalcedon* as members thereof, till they had openly renounced and anathematized the hereſies which they had before embraced: So would not thoſe glorious Iudges have permitted any of thoſe *Tridentine* Biſhops to have ſit in the Councell, till they had openly renounced, anathematized, and abjured that oath, and with it their vaſſallage to the Pope, and all thoſe hereticall doctrines which by their adhering to the Pope, and following his faction, they had embraced: and thoſe are Image-worſhip, Tranſubſtantiation, proper Sacrifice, Adoration of the Hoſt, their Purgatorian fire, and the reſt of thoſe hereſies, which, ſince the Romane faction began to prevaile, (and that was about ſeven hundred yeares after Chriſt, in the dayes of *Gregory* the ſecond, who as I ſuppoſe, firſt of all by ſynodall judgement decreed the worſhip of Images,) they have maintained: For ſeeing ſince that time not truth nor equity, but faction prevailed in their Synods, and ſwayed matters in their Church, there could be no equall triall of the truth by any of their Synods held ſince that time. But when all the Biſhops were freed from thoſe chaines of their oath and ſlaviſh bondage to the Pope, ſince the faction (whereof he hath beene the leader) got the upper hand, thoſe glorious Iudges would have permitted nothing to paſſe for a free ſynodall ſentence, but that onely which could have had warrant from the Scriptures, thoſe holy Councells and conſenting judgement of thoſe Fathers who lived within the ſix hundred yeares or ſomewhat more after Chriſt, at what time partiality and faction had not corrupted and blinded their judgement, as in the ſecond *Nicene*, and ever ſince it hath.

39. But becauſe ſuch glorious Iudges and their moſt equall Preſidency was wanting, nay was baniſhed from their Aſſembly at *Trent*, ſcarce any tokens or ſhadow of freedome could take place therein. Not towards Proteſtants. *Brentius* y, and divers other learned Divines came to *Trent*, offered z themſelves and their faith to triall of diſputations, *Nulla ratione* z *impetrari potuit, this could not be obtained by any meanes*, that they ſhould come to diſpute b for the faith. c *Nullus unquam liber aditus Proteſtantibus, the Proteſtants at no time had any freedone to come to the Councell at Trent.* Not towards their owne Biſhops, if they ſpake or did ought tending to the defence of the truth. *Cornelius* Biſhop of *Bitons* ſaid d, that Chriſt offered not in his laſt ſupper his owne body and blood: this croſſed their proper ſacrifice of the maſſe, therfore *Cornelius* for that free & true ſpeech, *à Patribus univerſis exploſus eſt, was hiſſed out of their Trent Councell by all the Fathers and Divines there preſent.* *Iacobus Nachiantes* e Biſhop of *Clodia Foſſa*, ſayd, he could not approve that traditions ſhould be held in equal reverence as the Scripture, he was for this truth expulſed the Councell. *Gulielmus* f *Venetus* a Dominican Fryer, ſayd in the Councell, that the Councell was above the Pope, he was commanded to depart out of the Councell.

(marginal notes) x *Conc. chalc. act. 8. & 10.* y *Gen. Exam. Conc. Trid. ſeſſ. 15. nu. 3.* z *Obſecrant in diſputationis arenam deſcedere, & ſe certamine offerebant. ibid.* a *Ibidem.* b *Neque admiſſi fuerint ad ſuæ fidei profeſſionē proponendam & diſcutiendam, ut haud unquam admitti potuerunt ut ſuam fidei confeſſionem in ſynodi publico conventu exhiberent, ac multo minus ut dogmata quæ in ea continebantur diſputatione aſſererent. ibid Gen. in Exam. lib. 5. nu. 4. pa. 317.* c *Ibid pa. 320.* d *Melc. Can. lib. 12. loc. Theol. ca. 13. §. Extat.* e *Cypr. Valer. in Marc. 2.* f *Ibid.*

cell. Another of the Biſhops ᵍ hapning to touch, and that but lightly, the pride of the Pope in his titles, wiſhed, that ſeeing God is no where in the Scripture called *ſanctiſſimus*, but *ſanctus*, the Pope alſo would be content with the ſame title of *ſanctus*, and not take a more ample name of honour than is given in Scripture unto God. The Pope being certified hereof, ſent for him to come from *Trent* to *Rome*, and gave him to his Officers to uſe him hardly ʰ, and to bee degraded. *Petrus Vergerius* ⁱ Biſhop of *Iuſtinianople*, (he who endeavoring ᵏ to refute the Proteſtant writings, and began that booke which hee intituled, Againſt the Apoſtates of *Germany*, was himſelfe overcome by the evidence of that truth, ſpecially in the doctrine of Iuſtification, which he oppugned) came to the Councell at *Trent*: The Pope having intelligence that he was inclined to *Lutheraniſme*, writ to his Legats at *Trent*, *Ne locum ei tribuant in conſeſſu*, That they ſhould not admit him into their Councell, but command him to depart. *Ad hunc* ˡ *modum eliminatus*, by this meanes was the Biſhop excluded from their free Synod: and if *Iohannes Caſus* the Popes Legate to the Venetians, and Archbiſhop of *Beneventum*, (who writ a ᵐ booke in the praiſe of one of the moſt deteſtable and damnable ſinnes) could have prevailed to have entiſed ⁿ him to goe to *Rome*, he had not thence eſcaped ſo eaſily as he did from *Trent*. Could any of theſe or the like enormous diſorders, which utterly ſubvert all ſynodall freedome, have beene endured, had there beene equall and prudent Preſidents for Kings and Emperours in that Councell? But the Imperiall preſidency being abandoned, together with it, was all freedome and ſynodall orders excluded. So that I may truly ſay both of theſe *Tridentine*, and their other nine Synods, that as by reaſon of their want of this Imperiall preſidency, they had many diſorders, ſo by reaſon they excluded that Preſidency, they had, nay they could have nothing in them at all but diſorder.

40. You ſee now the ſeverall kinds of unlawfull Councells, as well by want of Imperiall calling, or of Imperiall Preſidency, as when neither is wanting, by the abuſe of that Imperiall authority in the Synod. And though the unlawfulneſſe of thoſe ten later Synods doth now appeare to be farre greater than of thoſe ancient Councells before mentioned; ſeeing in all the ancient there was not onely a lawfull calling, but a lawfull preſidency alſo, both which were wanting in the other tenne; beſides the unlawfull proceedings which were equally in both, or rather farre worſe in the later: yet is there one eſpeciall difference that is principally to be remembred, which iſſuing from the former diverſity of unlawfulneſſe, makes a greater oddes than at the firſt one would imagine: and this it is: When the unlawfulneſſe of any Synod ariſeth (as in their tenne Synods it doth) from the want of the firſt condition, that is, of lawfull calling and authority to aſſemble and judge, be the conſultations and proceedings of ſuch Synods otherwiſe never ſo orderly, and their reſolutions never ſo juſt and true, yet for making of any Canon or Decree, or giving any ſynodall judgement, there is an invalidity in all ſuch Synods, and a meere nullity in all their Decrees, Canons, and Iudgements. They had no authority to aſſemble in a Synod, much leſſe ᵒ have they any authority to make a Law, or

g *Car. Molin. li. de Conc. Trid. nu. 22.*

h *Satal tibus ſuis de gradu deijciendum & deriter tractandum propinavit. Ibid.*
i *Iob. Sleid. Com. lib. 21. pa. 304. & ſeq.*
k *Dum confuſidi cauſa libros adverſariorum diligenter excutit, & attente argumenta conſiderat, captus ſe victũq; ſenſit. Ibid.*
l *Ibid. & plura de eo lege apud Cypr. Valer. in Marcel. 2.*
m *Nec puduit eum ſcelus omnium longe turpiſſimum celebrare laudibus. Ioh. Sleid. loc. citat.*
n *Eum, uti Romam peteret modis omnibus hortatur Caſus; Vergerius vero qui periculum ſuum intelligeret, recuſat. ibid.*

o *Si legitima ſynodus non fuit, planum eſt nulla authoritatem potuiſſe habere: & nullius roboris ſunt illius canones. Bell. lib. 2 de Pont. ca. 18. §. Ceterum: & §. Ac deinde. & Sententia à non ſuo Iudice dicta nihil firmitatis obtinet. Greg. lib. 11. Epiſt. 56.*

or give judgement in that Synod. That which is invalid in the ſpring and originall, muſt needs in all the ſubſequent actions derived from thence, & depending thereon, retain the ſame invalidity. And ſeeing it is neither multitude, nor learning, nor wiſdome, but authority which is the fountain and foundation of all Lawes, Canons, and Iudgements, where this authority is wanting in any perſon or aſſembly, it is as impoſſible for ſuch a perſon or aſſembly to make a law, give any judgement, or pronounce any judiciall ſentence, as to erect an houſe in the ayre, or build without any foundation. And truly this toucheth at the quick all thoſe ten Councels, which wanting authority to aſſemble them, were no other but tumultuous, ſeditious, and unauthorized aſſemblies. There was no more ſtrength, validity, or vigour in any of their Decrees to binde as lawes, or ſynodall judgements, than there was in ſuch Edicts as *Spartacus* and *Catiline* in *Rome*, or *Iacke Cade* in this Kingdome ſhould have publiſhed and ſet forth: ſpecially in that which he like another Pope intended to be his fundamentall law, That all lawes ſhould proceed out of his mouth. Thoſe which they untruly call the Canons, Decrees, or Iudgements of thoſe Synods, are onely the opinions, reſolutions, and conſultations of ſo many ſeditious men which convened and conſpired together in thoſe conjurations: ſynodall Decrees, or Eccleſiaſticall Lawes and Iudgements they were not, they could not be. In the head, they are nipt and tainted with a nullity of authority, they beare this tainture and nullity throughout every part and parcell of their determinations.

41. But when the unlawfulneſſe of any Synod ariſeth (as in the ancient Councels at *Arimine*, *Millane*, and *Epheſus* it did) from the want of the other condition, that is, of orderly proceedings onely, the Biſhops being both lawfully called, and having a lawfull Preſident, the caſe is here farre different; their acts and ſentences though they bee unlawfull, yet are they truly judiciall, and have the authority of ſynodall judgements, and therefore doe binde others, though not in conſcience to accept them as true, yet with patience to ſubmit themſelves to their cenſures, till by like authority they be revoked, and repealed. Even as in civill Courts, though an unjuſt or partiall Iudge, either for feare, favour, hatred, deſire of lucre, or any other perturbation of minde, ſhall wilfully pervert juſtice and due proceedings, and pronounce an unjuſt ſentence: yet is this act judiciall, and ſtands in force of a judgement, till by the like, or higher authority it be reverſed; becauſe ſuch an one had authority and rightfull power to judge and give ſentence in that cauſe, though he abuſed his authority to injuſtice and wrong: Right ſo it is in ſynodall and Eccleſiaſticall aſſemblies, when they are lawfully called and authorized to heare and judge any matter, their want of due, orderly, and juſt proceedings makes their judgment unjuſt, and ſhewes them to be wicked and malicious conſpirators againſt the truth, but it doth not make the decree to be no judgment, or no judiciall ſentence of a Councell. The corruption is now in the branch, not in the root: the abuſe of their authority makes not a nullity in their act: It hinders not them to bee truly and rightfully Iudges, but it demonſtrates them not to bee upright, good, and juſt

Iudges,

Iudges, it shewes their sentence to be wicked and impious, but it hinders it not to be a judiciall sentence. Whereof that one (among many) in the *Ephesine* Latrociny, is a cleare example. In it p *Eusebius* Bishop of *Dorileum* was most wickedly and unjustly deposed from his See, yet this their unjust sentence stood in force, till by the like authority of another generall Councell at *Chalcedon*, it was repealed: for in it *Eusebius* sate not at the first as a Iudge, but as an accuser q of *Dioscorus*, and in the place of accusers: He entreated the holy Councell that all the Acts r and Iudgements at *Ephesus*, *viribus carere*, might be adnulled and declared to be of no force, and that hee might enjoy as before that sentence he did, *Sacerdotali dignitate, his Episcopall dignity and See.* The holy Synod consented to his just request, received him as a member s of the Councell, restored him to his See, and adnulled all the acts of the *Ephesine* Latrociny, requesting t the Emperour to ratifie and confirme that their Iudgement.

42. Such an exceeding great and most remarkable difference there is betwixt those ancient and these ten later unlawfull Synods. Though both be unlawfull, yet in the former there was a binding force for a while, till they were repealed; but in these later there never was any power to binde any, either to accept their Decrees, or to undergoe their censures, because *ab initio* there was a meere nullity in all their Acts. Againe, the inflicting of any punishment upon the judgement of the former, had the warrant, though not of divine, yet of humane authority, and was to bee presumed as just, (the sentence of every Iudge, even *eo nomine*, because he is a Iudge, being to bee presumed just, untill upon evident proofe it bee declared to bee unjust.) But what censures or punishments soever are, or at any time have beene denounced or inflicted on any, upon the warrant or Iudgement of these last ten Synods, they are all *ab initio* meerely tyrannous, and unjust, inflicted without any either divine or humane authority, (seeing those Synods had none at all) there is not so much as a presumption that they were or could be just, but for their want of authority in decreeing them, they are (though otherwise equall) presumed to be unjust.

43. And thus much I have thought good to insert concerning all sorts of Councels, as well lawfull as unlawfull: to manifest hereby not onely the injurious dealing of *Baronius* with this fift Councell, against which he declameth as an impious and unlawfull conspiracy; but their vanity also in extolling and magnifying many, and specially those last ten, for holy, lawfull, and oecumenicall Synods; of which dignity they are so farre short, that they are all most deservedly to be ranked with the *Ephesine* Latrocinie, and put in the *Classis* of those which of all other are the most base, impious, unlawfull, and disorderly Councells.

p *Flavianum et Eusebium ab omni Episcopali dignitate judicamus esse alienos. Conc. Ephes. in act. Con. Chal. act.1.pa.57. b.*
q *Et Eusebius et Theodoretus in ordine accusantium sedent, Con. Chalc. act.1. pa. 13. a.*
r *Con. Chalc. act.3. pa. 66.*
s *Nam act.6.pa. 101. b. Eusebius Dorilei subscribit definitioni sidei inter alios.*
t *Presens omne Concilium deprecatur Imperatorem quatenus pia lege sanciat, neq; Synodum istam (Ephesinam 2.) nominari, neque quidquam quod actum est in ea texeri. Conc. Chalc.act.10. p. 115. §. Anatolius. & pa.116. Omnes eadem dicimus.*

CAP.

CAP. XX.

How Cardinall Baronius *revileth the Emperour* Iustinian, *and a refutation of the same.*

1. WEE have hitherto seene and fully examined all the materiall exceptions which *Baronius* could devise to excuse Pope *Vigilius* from heresie : and in them consists the whole pith, and all the sinewes of the cause; they being the onely arguments which are to be reckoned as the lawfull warriers of the Cardinall. Now followeth that other Troupe, whereof I told you [a] before, of his piraticall and disorderly Straglers, which the Cardinall hath mustred together, not that they should dispute or reason in this cause, but to raile and revile at every thing whereat their Leader is displeased : And the Cardinall doth this with so impotent affections, in so immodest, that I say not so scurrill a manner, and with such virulency of all uncivill and most undutifull speeches, that you shall see him now, having cast away all that gravity and modesty which is fit not onely for a Divine, a Cardinall, a Disputer, but for a man of any temper, or sobriety, to act herein no other part but *Hercules Furens*, or *Ajax mastigophorus*, without all respect either of authority, or dignity, or innocency, lashing every body, and every thing that comes in his way, be it friend or foe; sparing nothing that seemes to crosse his fancy, not the Emperour *Iustinian*, not the Empresse *Theodora*, not *Theodorus* Bishop of Cesarea, not the Imperiall Edict, not the controversie and cause it selfe of the *Three Chapters*, not the Acts of the holy Generall Councell, not Pope *Vigilius* himselfe; nothing can scape the whippe of his tongue and pen. Let us begin with the Emperour, against whom *Baronius* declameth in this manner.

2. *Princes* [b] *to dare to make lawes for Priests ? who should obey the lawes made by them. Such* [c] *an one as* Iustinian *make lawes of faith ? an* [d] *abcedary Emperour : an illiterate* [e] *Theologue : utterly* [f] *unlearned : who* [g] *knew not how to reade : who* [h] *could never reade the title of the Bible : no not the very first* [i] *elements : not his* Alpha, Beta : *He on a sodaine to become a* [k] *palliated Divine ? Hee to prescribe lawes* [l] *for the Church, as subject to his ? Hee against* [m] *all right and equity to presume to make lawes of sacred matters, of Priests ? He to set downe punishments for them ? Hee who was not onely thus utterly unlearned, but withall an enemy to the Church; a* [n] *sacrilegious person : a* [o] *persecutor : a grievous, a* [p] *monstrous persecutor : one who was madde* [q], *franticke, and out of his wits, who was possessed with an evill spirit, and driven by the Devill himselfe ? Such an one* [r] *make lawes for Bishops ?*

[a] *Cap.5.nu.1.* [b] *Vides quanta iactura—— cum Principes indicere audent ipsis sacerdotibus leges, à quibus sanctitas servare ipsi debent. Bar.an.553. nu.237.* [c] *Si qui ejusmodi esset, leges sanciret de fide, an.546.nu.43.* [d] *Fuit homo penitus illiteratus, adeo ut nec Alphabetum aliquando didicisset, an.528.nu.2* [e] *Illiteratus Theologus, an.551.nu.2.* [f] *Cum esset penitus illiteratus, an.546.nu.41.* [g] *Iustiniani legere nescientia, an.538.nu.32.* [h] *Qui nunquam legere sciverit vel ipsum foris inscriptum titulum Bibliorum, an.551.nu.4.* [i] *Vt qui nec prima elementa calleret, ut legere posses, an.546 nu.43.* [k] *Fecit analphabetum Imperatorem repente palliatum apparere Theologum, an.551.nu.4.* [l] *Cui ut sibi subdita aggressus erat prascribere leges, an.551. nu.2.* [m] *Sacrarū legū cōditorem agit : de sacerdotibus leges ferre, in eosque pœnas statuere, prater jus fasq, presumens, an.528.nu.2.* [n] *Ab Imperatoris sacrilegi violentia, an.552 nu.8.* [o] *Iust.à persequutione cessavit, an.553.nu.14.* [p] *Et quod monstrosius accessit, ab Imperatore persequutio excitata fuit, et haud quidem levis, an 553.nu.221.* [q] *Ab Jmperatoris furore, an.552.nu.8. Ille furore percitus, mente dimotus, correptus maligno spiritu, agitatus à Satana, an.551.nu.2.* [r] *A quo accepturi essent leges Episcopi, an.551 nu.4.*

what

what is this else, but to confound [i] all things, to treade [t] under foote the sacred Canons, to abolish utterly the Church discipline, to [u] dissolve all divine order, and to make of the Kingdome of heaven (which the Church is) the very prison of hell, where there is nothing but confusion? Thus the Cardinall: And this is but the first pageant of his *Ajax*, and but some gleanings neither of that harvest, which is abundant in his Annals.

3. Not to seeke any exact, or methodicall refutation hereof : All that the Cardinall hath hitherto said may bee reduced to three notorious slanders, by which he laboureth to blemish the immortall fame and unspotted honour of that most religious Emperour. The first concernes *His knowledge and learning*; *Iustinian* not able to reade? not know so much as his *Alphabet*? Is there any in the world, thinke you, so very stupid, as to beleeve the Cardinall in this so shamelesse, so incredible an untruth? *Tanti ingenii, tantæque doctrina fuisse constat*, saith *Platina* [x], it is manifest, that *Iustinian* was of so great a wit, and so great learning, that it is not to bee marveiled if hee reduced the lawes, being confused before, into order : *Tritemius* [y] saith of him, *He was a man of an excellent wit, and hee is deservedly* [z] *reckoned among Ecclesiasticall Writers*; and hee expresly mentioneth three bookes which hee writ against *Eutyches*, one against the Africane Bishops : adding, that one may doubt, but that besides these, hee writ many and very excellent Epist. *Possevine* [a] the Iesuite acknowledgeth him, with *Tritemius*, for an *Ecclesiasticall Writer*; & besides the reciting of those same books which *Tritemius* mentioned, hee alleageth these words of their Pontificall, most worthy to be observed for this purpose : *Iustinian the Emperour a religious man, sent unto the Apostolike See his profession of faith, scriptam chirographo proprio, written with his own hand, testifying his great love to the Christiā Religion.* In regard of w[ch] his excellēt writings, both Pope *Agatho* [*], and the whole sixt generall Councell with him, who lived in the next age to *Iustinian*, reckoneth him in the same ranke, not onely of Ecclesiasticall Writers, but of venerable Fathers, with Saint *Cyrill*, Saint *Chrysostome* and others, whose writings doe give testimony to the truth. *Liberatus* who lived in the dayes of *Iustinian*, and who was no well-willer of the Emperour, yet could not but record, *That he* [b] *writ a Booke against the Acephali or Eutichean heretikes; in defence of the Councell of Chalcedon, and that* Theodorus *seeing him so skilled in writing against heretikes, told him, Scribendi laborem non eum de-re pati*; That he should not trouble himselfe with writing books, but maintaine the faith by publishing Edicts. *Procopius* [c], who was familiarly conversant with *Iustinian*, recites that traiterous perswasion of *Arsaces* to *Artabanus*, when he excited him to murther the Emperour; this (said hee) *you may doe easily, and without danger, for the Emperour is not mistrustfull, and he passeth the time till very late of the night in talking without any watch or guard, having none but some old and feeble Bishops about him, Christianorum scriptis miro studio revolvendis intentus,* being marvellously addicted to reade and peruse the writings of Christians. Are these, thinke you, the actions of an illiterate, of an Abcedary Emperour? And what speake I of these? The Pandects, the Code, the Authentikes, the Institutions, the whole body of the law proclame

the

(marginal notes)

[i] *Confundi omnia necesse est, an.553.nu.237.*
[t] *Canones ipse conculcat, penitusq, pessundat Ecclesiasticam œconomiam, an. 541.nu.16.*
[u] *Sicq, omnem in Ecclesia dissolveret ordinem, faceretque ex regnò cælorum ergastulum inferorum, an. 551. nu.4.*

[x] *In vita Bonifac.2.*

[y] *Lib.de script. Eccles.*
[z] *Locum inter Ecclesiasticos scriptores merito acquisivit. Ibid.*

[a] *Appar.Sac. in verbo Iustinianus.*

[*] *Conc.6.Act 4. in Epist. Agath.*

[b] *In Brevia.ca. 24.*

[c] *Lib. 3. de bell. Goth.*

the incredible wifedome, and rare knowledge of *Iustinian*, *All people*
saith he,[d] *are governed by the lawes, Tàm à nobis promulgatis quàm compos-
tis*, as well publifhed as compofed by us : and though he ufed the learning, helpe, and induftry of other worthy men, (whofe names he hath
commended to all pofterity, and never-dying fame) yet when they
offred the bookes unto him, *Et legimus & recognovimus*, faith he,[*] wee
both read them and examined them; which the gloffe explaineth,
faying, *Nos ipfi legimus*, Wee our felves have reade and perufed them.
So that I cannot fufficiently admire this moft fhamelefse untruth of
Baronius, in reviling him for an illiterate, and not fo much as an Ab-
cedarie fcholler, whofe wit, learning, and prudence hath beene, and
will for ever bee a mirrour to all ages.

4. But *Suidas* (faith the Cardinall[e]) doth affirme[f] the fame, calling
Iustinian ἀγράμματον, and void of all learning. For anfwer whereunto,
firft, I would gladly know of the Cardinal, how hee can affure us
that this is indeed the faying of *Suidas*? fpecially feeing their owne
Iefuite *Poffevine* tels[g] us for a certainty, that *Plæraque, very many things
are falfly inferted into Suidas*; and that, *à Sciolis & Schifmaticis*, by fome
fmatterers or Schifmaticks; and further, that thofe *Plæraque*, are fuch
as are *repugnant to the Euangelicall truth, and Hiftoricall finceritie*. How
may we bee affured, that this concerning *Iustinian*, is not one of thofe
Plæraque, feeing this to be contrary to Hiftoricall finceritie, doth by
thofe many and evident proofes which wee before produced, fully appeare? Againe, admitting *Suidas* for the Author thereof: is *Suidas*
thinke you of more, or equall authority and credit to their Pontificall? which witneffeth exprefly, that *Iustinian* writ the holy confeffion of his faith, *Chirographo proprio*, with his owne hand? Equall to
Tritemius and *Poffevine*, or (to winke at them) to Pope *Agatho* and
the fixt generall Councell? who all account *Iustinian* among the Writers of the Church. Who I pray you was this *Suidas*? truly an earneft defender of thofe impieties, which in their fecond Nicene Synod began to prevaile; who in reviling manner doth call[h] *Conftantine
Iconomachus, a Serpent, an Antichrift, and the difciple of the Devill*: and
all, for his not confenting to the *adoration of Images, and reliques, and to
the Invocation of Saints*. Now how this fort of men were given to lyes
and fables, the Acts of that Synod doe fully demonftrate: Or if you
rather defire to have their Iefuites judgement of *Suidas*, hee will tell
you firft, that he was hereticall, *in teaching*[i] *the Effence in the Godhead to
be generative; which their Laterane Councell hath condemned for an herefie.*
Hee will tell you further, that this booke is full of errours, fables, and
lyes, of which fort are thefe, among many. *That the world was made of
the Poëticall Chaos; that it fhal continue* 1200. *thoufand yeares: that the Sun
and Starres, are fierie fubftances, fed and perpetuated by terreftriall humours
as their nutriment : that Paradife is Hortus penfilis, a garden hanging in
the ayre farre above the earth: that* Caine *was begotten of the Devill, which
is a lye; that the Iewes adored an affes head, and every feventh yeare facri-
ficed a ftranger* : His narration (*in verbo* Nero) touching Annas *and* Caiphas, Pilate, Peter, *and* Simon Magus, *wherin multa comminifcitur, he for-
geth many things* : His narration (*in verbo* Iulianus) which hee calleth in
exprefse words, *mendacium flagiciofissimum*, a moft lewd lie: His flan-
dering

p *Inftit. Proem.*

* *Ibid.*

e *Bar.an.528.
nu.2.*
f *In verbo Iuft.*
g *In appar. ver-
bo Suidas.*

h *Suid. in verbo
Conftantinus.*

i *Poff. in verbo
Suidas.*

dering *Constantine* the great, as base of birth, and his sonne *Crispus* as
incestuous: His commending of *Acatius* and *Acesius* two heretikes:
adding, that *hee writeth many things, contra Historiæ veritatem, against
the Historicall truth*. His relation (*in verbo Apolonius*) where many things
are praised, *quæ omnia monstrosa sunt, & prorsus explodenda*; all which
are utterly to be hissed at: where also he seemeth to allow the impious
Art of Magicke, and Divinations: His approving of *Appolonius* and
Danis, two wicked Magitians, who both are *relegati ad inferos*, condemned to Hell. And to omit very many of this kinde of impieties
and fables, which abound in *Suidas* : His narration (*in verbo Iesus* :)
which not onely *Baronius* rejecteth, but Pope *Paul* the fourth, for that
cause beside some other [k] exploded the booke of *Suidas*, and placed it
in the ranke *librorum prohibitorum* : Such, even by the confession of
their owne Iesuite, is this *Suidas* : a depraver of good, a commender
of wicked men, a fabler, a lyer, a falsifier of Histories, a Magitian, an
Heretike, whose booke is by the Pope forbidden to bee read. Such a
worthy witnesse hath the Cardinall of his *Suidas*, with whom he con-
spireth in reviling *Iustinian*, as one utterly unlearned. Concerning
which untruth, I will say no more at this time than that which *Gotofrid* doth in his censure [l] of those words of *Suidas*, where calling it in
plaine termes a slander, he rejects it, as it justly deserveth, in this manner, *Valeant calumniæ, nos sinceriora sequamur*; Away with this and
such like opprobrious slanders of *Suidas* and *Baronius*; but let us follow
the truth.

5. His second reproofe of the Emperour is, for *presuming to make
lawes in causes of faith; which for Kings and Emperours to doe, brings* (as he
saith) *an hellish confusion into the Church of God :* The wit of a Cardinal!
Iustinian may not doe that which King *Hezekiah*, which *Asa*, which
Iosiah, and *Constantine* the great, the two *Theodosii*, *Martian*, and o-
ther holy Emperours before had done, and done it by the warrant of
God, to the eternall good of the Church, and their owne immortall
fame: Had hee indeed, or any of those Emperours taken upon them
by their lawes to establish some new; erronious, or hereticall doctrine, the Cardinall might in this case have justly reproved them;
but this they did not : what doctrines the Prophets delivered, the
word of God taught, and holy Synods had before decreed and explaned; those, and none else did *Iustinian*, by his Edict, and other religious Emperours, ratifie by their imperiall authority: Heare *Iustinians*
owne words, *Wee* [f] *have thought it needfull by this our Edict to manifest
that right confession of faith, quæ in sancta Dei Ecclesia prædicatur*, which
is preached in the holy Church of God. Here is no new faith; no E-
dict for any new doctrine, but for maintaining that onely faith which
the holy Catholike Church taught, and the Councell of *Chalcedon*
had decreed; wherein that *Iustinian* did nothing but worthy of eternal
praise, the whole fift Councell, and the whole Catholike Church approving it, is a witnesse aboue exception, which entreating of that
which *Iustinian* had done in this cause of the *Three Chapters*; (the chiefe
of all wch was the publishing of his most religious Edict, to condemne
the same) saith, [g] *Omnia semper fecit & facit, quæ sanctam Ecclesiam &
recta*

Ff 2

[k] *Exploserit in
Indicem lib.
prohib.*

[l] *Assertib. Instit.*

[f] *E.J.A. Iustin:
in causa trium.
Capit. Lib
princip.*

[g] *coll.7. in fine*

Had *Iuſtinian* done this to *Vigilius*, hee had beene no perſecutor: But *Vigilius* who oppugned the truth, & *Baronius* who with ſuch a virulent tongue reviles and railes at the defenders of Gods truth; they, and none but they, are perſecutors in this cauſe: They kill not the Prophets nor Apoſtles, but they kill & murther, as cruelly as they can, that truth of God which the Prophets and Apoſtles imbraced, and for defence of which they were ready to bee killed; *This ſpirituall perſecution,* as Saint *Auguſtine* teacheth, [q] *exceeds the corporall: They* [r] *murther the Prophets who contradict the doctrines of the Prophets: Mitius ageretis, It were leſſe crueltie in you to thruſt your ſwords into the bodies of the Prophets, then with your tongues to murther the doctrine and words of the Prophets.* And a thouſand like ſayings hath the ſame *Auguſtine*, by which it were eaſie to demonſtrate *Baronius* himſelfe, and not *Iuſtinian*, to bee the unjuſt, impious, ſacrilegious, and franticke perſecutor, if by that which hath beene ſaid this were not abundantly apparent.

8. Now followeth the other Pageant of this *Baronian* Tragedy in declaming againſt *Iuſtinian*. That reſpects his laſt yeares, and his death, in which part, as being the laſt, and therefore likelieſt to leave deepeſt impreſſion in the hearts of the readers, becauſe *Baronius* hath couched together the moſt vile accuſations of all the reſt, and the very venome of his poyſonfull affections, and ſplene, againſt the Emperour, I am moſt unwilling to forſake the religious Emperour in the laſt act of all, but am exceeding deſirous to teſtifie my love unto him, both for other cauſes, and for this eſpecially, that he, next unto God, was the preſerver of the Catholike faith, when in this cauſe of the Three Chapters, the Neſtorians, and eſpecially Pope *Vigilius*, laboured with might and maine for ever to aboliſh and extinguiſh the ſame: in regard of which act alone, if there were none elſe, hee deſerved to bee eternized in the bleſſed memory, and by the beſt indeavors of all that love the Catholike faith. *Baronius* [ſ] intreating of the 37. yeare of *Iuſtinian*, which was about two yeares before his death, tels us how at that time, *Iuſtinian, Vnhappy Iuſtinian ranne headlong into the hereſie of the Aphthardokites, or incorrupticolæ: who* [t] *denyed the body of C H R I S T to bee ſubject to paſſions, death, or corruption:* Theſe, as *Liberatus* ſaith [u], were alſo called *Phantaſticks*, becauſe upon their doctrine it followed, that C H R I S T had not a true and truely humane, but onely an imaginary and phantaſticall body. Into this phantaſticall hereſie, ſaith *Baronius*, did *Iuſtinian* fall, and runne headlong in his laſt age: and for proofe hereof hee alleageth [x] moſt ample witneſſes: *Authores omnes tam Græci quam Latini,* All Authors both Greeke and Latine, *they all teſtifie that hee fell into this hereſie; and they deteſt that impiety in him;* Nor did he onely fall himſelfe into it, but hee ſought to draw all others into the ſame errour: *Ita ebrius* [y] *factus eſt, ut mente motus,* Iuſtinian *was ſo drunke, that being out of his wits, hee writ an Edict* [z] *to confirme that hereſie, and bring all the Church to beleeve the ſame:* When hee prevailed not that way, then hee began [a] to uſe violence, *Exilium omnibus Epiſcopis contradicentibus comminatur,* hee threatned baniſhment to all the Biſhops who contradicted

q *Lib.* 1. *cont. liter. Petil. ca.* 27
r *Aug. lib.* 2. *cont. lit. Petil. ca.* 14.

ſ *An.* 563. *nu.* 1.
t *Evagr. lib.* 4. *ca.* 38.
Leont. lib. de ſect. Act. 10. *et Prateoll. de Hæreſ. hær.* 55. *Dicebant carnem quam ex virgine Servator aſſumpſit, ante paſſionem, incorruptibilem fuiſſe.*
u *Liberat. Brev. ca.* 19.
x *An.* 563. *nu.* 8.
y *Bar. ibid. nu.* 9
z *Illud conſtat, Imperatorem hereſin comprobaſſe eandemque ſcripto Edicto firmaſſe. An.* 564. *nu* 3.
a *An.* 563. *nu.* 12

licted that heresie, *and* [b] *so boyling in rage, raised a persecution, yea, Persecutionem* [c] *haud mediocrem, an heavy and great persecution against Catholike Bishops, casting* Eutychius *Bishop of Constantinople into banishment for this cause.* Thus *Baronius.* Who proves this concerning the Edict and persecution, partly by the *Surian Eustathius* [d], who writ the life of *Eutychius,* partly out of *Evagrius,* [e] who both mention indeed the banishment of *Eutychius,* and the Edict of *Iustinian,* written for that heresie.

9. This is the summe of that which is objected : but how *Baronius* doth amplifie, decke, and paint out the same by his Rhetorication, is not unworthy observing. He not onely taxeth this in *Iustinian* as an act of curiosity, [f] temerity, and arrogancy, for *His intermedling in sacred matters,* and of foolishnesse, for *Partaking* [g] *with the one side in the faction, as he had done with the* Prasini; for which he [h] calleth him, *Maximum jurium proculcatorem,* The greatest despiser and trampler of lawes under his feet; but he cals him also *Mente motū,* [i] a man out of his wits, a hereteike, [l] another *Ægyptian* Pharaoh, [m] *who bent all his power to oppresse the Catholike faith* ; *yea a very* Antichrist, saying thus [n] of him, *Iustinian no otherwise than* Antichrist, *setting up his Chaire and Throne in the Temple of God, and extolling himselfe above all that is worshipped, maketh sacrilegious lawes for establishing Infidelity, and writes Edicts for heresie:* And againe, [o] *any reason, but onely the Emperours authority, did erect that heresie, tanquam Idolum in Templo Dei,* As an Idoll in the Temple of God. Whereupon the Cardinall [p] in the anguish of his heart, takes up with sighes and teares the complaint of *Ieremy, O heavens be astonished at this, afraid and utterly astonished, the Emperor hath forsaken the fountaine of living waters, & he hath digged to himselfe pits that will hold no water.* After this fit of his weeping overpast, he then comes to the most base reviling & railing against the Emperor, calling [q] him *Monstrū triceps,* that Monster with three heads (like another *Cerberus,* or hell-hound) *which Ecclesiasticus* [r] *speaks of, & declares to be so odious & execrable: A poore man proud, a rich man a lyar, and an old man a foole.* Such a *Monster,* saith he, *did Iustinian now appeare,* (like three-bodied *Gerion,* in the Poets,) *seeing he joyned these three detestable faults in himselfe at this time. Hee was poore, yea most poore, Expers penitus literarum,* Vtterly voyd of learning, *not able to reade his very A.b.c. and yet hee would seeme to be more learned than all Bishops :* so he was a poore man proud. He was also a rich man, a lyar, in that he commanded all to embrace heresie, and by his power hindreth them to contradict his Edict : like him of whom it is said, [t] *The rich man spake, and all held their peace.* Lastly, when he refused the counsell of the Elders, *Planè sex cognitus est fatuus & insensatus,* He was therein plainly knowne to be an old doting foole, without wit or sense. Thus *Baronius* : concluding that Emperour to be a monster, an heretike, a hell-hound, a mad man, a lyar, a blockhead, and a very plaine foole : whom all the Christian world hath, and shall for ever, and that most justly, admire for his piety, prudence, and wisedome.

10. *Baronius,* not content with this so uncivill demeanour, tells us further what mischiefes ensued upon these detestable crimes of the Emperour. Those are of two sorts : the former is publique, concerning

ing.

b *Vbi elab. vziū ā se edictū contemni ab orthodoxis percepit, ita exæstuans, magnam perstquisitionem commovit. a. 564. nu. 1.*

c *Ibid. nu. 2.*

d *Bar. ibid. extant vero apud Sur. die 6. Apr.*

e *Lib. 4. ca. 38.*

f *An. 563. nu. 1. & 6.*

g *Prasinis eum stulte studuisse meminimus. an. 563. nu. 2.*

h *An. 558. nu. 13.*

i *an. 563. 9.*

l *an. 565. nu. 1.*

m *an. 564. nu. 21.*

n *an. 563. nu. 6.*

o *an. 564. nu. 1.*

p *an. 563. nu. 6.*

q *Ibid. nu. 7.*

r *Eccl. 25.*

t *Eccl. 13.*

ing both the Ecclefiafticall and civill State. For the Church, u *pacem profligat,* Iuftinian drove away peace and quiet from it : *be endangered, atque tandem penitus labefactat fidem,* and at laft utterly fubverted and

overthrew the faith. For the Common wealth, it did x *titubare,* reele and decline into a worfe eftate, *under this hereticall Emperour,* whom he

y accufeth, *frigefcere,* to have beene cold and carelefle *in the government of the Empire.* The other mifchiefe, which is private, concernes Iufti-nian himfelfe. For the Cardinalls hatred to Iuftinian is not fatiate with the evils of this life, he purfues him αἰδίῳ πυλέσσι, and fitting in the

z *Opinari fi cui licet, facilius eft. invenire qui Evagrij de ejus condemnatione velit fequi fentē-tiam, quam ali-otum,&c. an.565.nu.6.*
a *Lib.5.ca.1.*
b *An.565.nu.6.*
* *Apoc.4.*

chayre of *Radamanthus,* he approves z and applauds that moft rafh and undifcreet judgement of *Evagrius,* a *ad fupplicia apud inferos luenda profectus eft,* hee is gone to be tormented in hell. Yea the Cardinall proves b that he went thither in this manner; *Although it be not in mans power to bee prefent at Gods judgement, and it be utterly unlawfull to judge of the dead; yet according to that irrevocable fentence of God, which is pro-noûced of all the dead,* * *Their works follow them,* according to this fen-tence, *eadem ipfa quæ hinc abeuntem fequuta funt Iuftinianū,* thofe fame workes which followed Iuftinian when hee dyed, *doe as yet crie againft him in bookes :* and thofe are *juge bellum,* his perpetuall warre againft the Church, *which hee continually nourifhed, (having banifhed peace which he found therein) and when hee dyed left it in a flame : his unmeafurable*

c *Sa-crilegies, laying oftentimes his violent hands upon holy Bifhops, the annoin-ted of the Lord : his cruelty againft innocent Citizens : his covetoufneffe, and the reft,* which I omit. Thus *Baronius :* who plainly telling us, that thefe fo many, fo heinous crimes, and crying finnes, followed Iuftinian out of this life, (and every man knowes that thefe follow no whither but unto hell) hee moft forcibly concludeth, that Iuftinian out of all doubt, was carried hence to be tormented in thofe hellifh flames. Ne-ver could the Cardinall bee at quiet, till befides all thofe other revi-ling and difgracefull ignominies which hee hath heaped upon Iuftini-an, he had brought him into the pit and torments of hell : And yet not there alfo will the Cardinall fuffer him to be at reft, but like a Fiend or Fury, hee ftill exagitates the Emperour with his virulent tongue and ftile, worfe than any of all the infernall Ghofts; neither alive nor dead will the Cardinall ceafe to torment him.

11. Verily I know not where either to begin or make an end in this matter, nor how it is poffible for any man with fufficient gravity and feverity to caftigate the Cardinals infolent, inhumane, unchriftian demeanour againft the moft renowned and religious Emperour. Did any of thofe worthy profeffours of the civill lawes, but halfe fo much abound with leafure, as they doe with excellency of wit and learning, I doubt not but they would (as I doe heartily wifh) undertake fo ho-nourable a fervice, not onely to Iuftinian, but unto G O D and his Church, as in a juft volume to vindicate the Emperours honour from thefe fo many, fo malicious, fo bafe & immodeft calûnies of this *Rhab-fecha.* A worke not very laborious, feeing as on the Emperours part there is fuch abundant ftore and variety of all vertues and praife-wor-thy actions to fet forth his honour, as no mans ftile nor words can e-quall or come neare the fame : fo on *Baronius* part, with whom hee is

to contend, there are so many shamelesse and detestable untruths, either deuised, or applauded by him, that *Voraginensis* himselfe may seeme inferiour to him in this kinde; and I much doubt, whether so many voluminous bookes, as might equall any two Tomes of his Annals, could bee able to comprehend them all: Meane while that I seeme not to shuffle this burden from mine own to other mens shoulders, I will, with their good leaue, I hope, adde somewhat out of those bookes which concerne my own profession, and out of my shallow reading indeauour to free the Emperour from those most dishonorable imputations of the Cardinall.

12. Let us then begin with that which is the substance and ground of this whole accusation, and that is, *The Emperours supposed falling into heresie, and writing that hereticall Edict* : This if we can proue to bee a slander and untruth, all the rest, which the Cardinall builds upon this, and deriues from it, will of themselues fall to the ground. First then I doe constantly auouch that imputation of heresie to bee untrue : *Iustinian* neither held that fantasticall heresie of the *Aphthardokites*, nor made any Edict for the defence or propagating thereof, nor did hee banish or persecute any Orthodoxall Bishop for contradicting that heresie : All these are slanderous untruths which the Cardinall hath collected out of others, and maliciously uttered in disgrace of the Emperour: And truly, that very contradiction which is not onely in other writers, but in the Cardinall himselfe, in setting downe this narration, is no small presumption of the untruth thereof. [d] *Euagrius* and *Nicephorus* [e] expresly witnesse, that the Emperours Edict was not at all published. *Theophanes* [f], (as the Cardinall cals him, or *Paulus Diaconus* as others,) and after him *Sixtus Senensis* [g], expresly witnesse the contrary, that his Edict *was divulged, & ubique transmissum*, and sent to euery place. *Baronius*, not knowing whether was truer, affirmeth them both, though they be expresly contradictory : First, that he did publish the Edict, the Cardinall teacheth, [h] saying, *Iustinian when he saw his Edict, contemni ab Orthodoxis, & pro nihilo duci*; to bee contemned and set at nought by the Orthodoxall Bishops, *then hee raised his persecution*. How could that Edict be contemned, unlesse it had been published & set forth for an Edict? or how could they be banished for gainsaying that Edict, which if it was not published, had not the force of an Edict? Againe, that hee did not publish it, the [i] Cardinall likewise tels us, *Hee writ indeed, Non tamen promulgauit de heresi Edictum*, But hee did not publish that Edict. Hee did publish it: hee did not publish it : what truth in those witnesses who thus contradict themselues? If he did publish it, as the Cardinals *Theophanes*, and *Sixtus Senensis* affirme, then *Euagrius*, and *Nicephorus*, are not herein to bee credited : If hee did not publish it, how is the Cardinals *Theophanes*, or *Senensis* herein to be credited? And whether hee did publish it, or not publish it, the Cardinall who teacheth both, is certainly herein not to bee credited. This disagreement of the witnesses one with another, and of *Baronius* with his one selfe, is no good signe of truth in their Narration.

13. But that *Iustinian* neither published nor writ any such Edict, nor

d *Iustiniani Edictum minimè divulgatum est*: Lib 4.ca. 40.
e *Scriptum id, editum non est.* Lib.17.ca.30.
f *Hist. miscel. lib.16.an.38.* Iustin.
g *Iustin. praecepit hoc dogma à sacerdotibus publicè doceri, et ab omni plebe recipi.* Lib.5. Bibl. annot. 186;
h *An.*564.*nu.*t
i *An.*555.*nu.*4.

nor held any ſuch phantaſticke hereſie, a farre more faithfull witneſſe than any of the former, even *Victor* B. of Tunen, who lived in that ſame time at Conſtantinople, and who would have triumphed to have had ſo juſt an occaſion to reprove & diſgrace the Emperor, by whom he was impriſoned and baniſhed, doth make evident. Hee [k] plainly ſheweth how *Iuſtinian* continued conſtant in defence of his owne E-dict, for condemning the Three Chapters, and of the ſynodall Iudgement given therein, even to his death. In his 38. *yeare* (the very next to that wherein *Baronius* fancieth him to have fallen into hereſie,) Hee *ſent for foure Africane and two Ægyptian Biſhops*, and both perſonally by himſelfe, as alſo by ſome others, he laboured to draw them to the or-thodox faith, in condemning with him, and the fift Synod, the Three Chapters: and when he could not prevaile, *Cuſtodiæ mittuntur*, they were put into priſon. In the next yeare, he ſaith that [l] *Iuſtinian placed Iohn a condemner of the Three Chapters in the See of Conſtantinople, Euty-chius being baniſhed :* and to his very dying day, he kept *Theodorus* Bi-ſhop of Cabarſuſſus in baniſhment, *becauſe he would not condemne the Three Chapters.* So orthodoxall was *Iuſtinian*, and ſo earneſt an op-pugner of hereſies, of thoſe eſpecially which deny either the true hu-manity, or the true Godhead of Chriſt, even till his very death, by the certaine teſtimony of *Victor*, an eager enemy of *Iuſtinian*. Seeing then he continued conſtant till his death, in condemning the Three Chap-ters, and maintaining his owne Edict for the condemning of them: and ſeeing the condemning of them, or the defence of that Edict is the defence of the true faith, [m] and an oppugnation of all hereſies, which deny either the Divinity or Humanity in Chriſt, ſpecially of that of the Phantaſticks, or Aphthardokites, as the very words [n] of his Edict doe declare ; it clearly hence followeth from the certaine teſtimony of *Victor*, that *Iuſtinian* was ſo farre from embracing, or making Edicts for that hereſie, that he conſtantly oppugned the ſame, and even pu-niſhed all who beleeved or taught as the Aphthardokites did ; for in beleeving that hereſie, they contradicted the Emperours owne Edict, and the holy Councels, both at Nice, Conſtantinople, Epheſus, and Chalcedon : all [o] which the Emperour by this Edict, even untill his death conſtantly maintained.

14. VVhy, but *All Writers*, ſaith *Baronius*, [m] *both Greeke and Latine, they all doe teſtifie that Iuſtinian fell into that hereſie.* What heare I ? Doe *All*, and *All, both Greeke and Latine ?* doe they *All teſtifie this of Iuſtini-an ?* A vaſt, a ſhameleſſe, a Cardinall, a very Baronian untruth ! Of the Greekes, not *Procopius*, not *Agathias*, not *Photius*, not *Damaſcen*, though he entreat [n] of this very hereſie ; not the Cardinals owne *Suidas*, who quite contrary to the Cardinall calls *Iuſtinian* Ὀρθοδοξότατον, *a moſt Catho-lique and Orthodoxall Emperour.* Of the Latines, not *Victor*, by whom as you have ſeene, the cleane contrary is alſo teſtified : not *Liberatus*; and both theſe lived at the ſame time with *Iuſtinian* : not *Marcellinus*: not *Bede* : not *Anaſtaſius*, though ſuch was his ſplene againſt *Iuſtinian*, that he could not have concealed ſuch a diſgracefull crime : not *Aimo-nius*, of whom I pray you ſee how well his teſtimony accordeth with the Cardinall : *Iuſtinian*, ſaith [o] he, *was a man fide Catholicus, pietate in-ſignis,*

k *Vict. Tun. in Chron.*

l *An. Iuſt. 39.* m *Neceſſarium putavimus, re-Ete ſidei confeſ-ſionem quæ in ſancta Dei Ecc-leſia prædica-tur præſenti edi-cto facere mani-feſtam. Edict. Iuſt. pa. 492.* n *Ieſus Chriſtus eſt conſubſtanti-alis Patri ſecun-dum Deitatem, conſubſtantialis nobis ſecundum Humanitatem, paſſibilis carne, impaſſibilis dei-tate. ibid. & V-traq; natura in proprietate & ratione naturæ ſuæ manente, facta eſt unitas ſecundum ſub-ſtantiam. ibid.* o *Hæc cum u-niverſali Eccle-ſia conſitentes: eandem confeſ-ſionem conſerva-mus, quam 318. Patres in Nicea collecti, tradide-runt : & poſt il-los, 150. ſancti Patres, Conſtan-tinopoli expla-naverunt : &, qui in Epheſo & qui Chalce-done convenère docuerunt. ibid. pa. 495.* m *an. 563. nu. 8.* n *Lib. de hæreſ.* o *De geſt. Franc. lib. 3. ca. 8.*

signis, æquitatis cultor egregius : for his faith, Catholike; for his piety, renowned; a marvellous lover of equitie, and therefore all things did cooperate to his good:& he addeth, for the whole time of his Empire, (which was 39. yeares)*Imperium felici sorte rexit*, Hee governed the Empire in an happy manner : Not the true *Paulus Diaconus* P, who vsing the like words, faith, that *Iustinian governed the Empire in an happy* q *sort, & was Prince for his faith Catholike, in his actions upright, in judgments just : and therefore all things concurred to his good:* not *Sigebert*, not *Marianus Scotus*, not *Lambertus Scafnaburgensis*, not *Ado Viennensis*, not *Albo Floriacensis*, not *Luitprandus*, not *Conrad Abbas Vspergensis*, not *Albertus Stadensis*, not *Otho Frisingensis*, who cals r him *Christianissimum ac pijssimum Principem*, a most Christian, and most pious Prince, (vnfit epethetes for an heretike, or one condemned to the torments of hell) not *Gotofrid Vterbiensis* ſ, who likewise calls him *a most Christian Prince, one who established peace in the Church, which rejoyced under him to enjoy tranquillitie :* not *Wernerus*, whose testimonie is worthy obseruing, to see the Cardinals faith and true dealing in this cause: *Iustinian*, ſaith hee *, *was in all things most excellent, for in him did concurre three things which make a Prince glorious, to wit, power, by which hee overcame his enemies ; wisedome, by which hee governed the world with just lawes ; and a religious minde to Gods worship, by which hee glorified God, and beautified the Churches :* So farre is he from teaching him with the Cardinall, to haue beene a Tartarean *Cerberus*, or Three-headed monſter, conſiſting of three deteſtable vices, that he oppoſeth thereunto a Trinity of three moſt renowned vertues, Fortitude, Iuſtice, and Piety, of which the Emperour was compoſed : Not *Nauclerus*, not *Krantzius*, not *Tritemius*, not *Papirius Massonus*, not *Christianus Masseus*, not the *Magnum Cronicum Belgicum* : not the *Chronicon Reicherspergense*, which ſ teſtifieth, *that he did performe many things profitable to the Common-wealth, and ſo ended his life :* Not *Munster*, who t ſaith of him, that *hee was a just and upright man in finding out matters ingenious, Atque hæresum maximus hostis,* and the greateſt enemy of hereſies : not *Platina*, who u ſaith of *Iustinus*, the next Emperour vnto him, hee was *Nulla in re similis Iustiniano*, in nothing like vnto *Iustinian, For hee was covetous wicked, ravenous, a contemner both of God and men :* whence it followeth, that *Iustinian* was quite contrary, bountifull, juſt, religious, an honourer both of God and good men.

15. Now whereas all theſe (and I know not how many more, I thinke an hundred at leaſt, if one were curious in this ſearch)doe write of *Iustinian*, and not one of them, for ought that after earneſt ſearch I can finde, doe mention his fall in that fantaſticke hereſie ; nay, many of them, as you haue ſeene, doe teſtifie on the contrary, that hee was and continued a Catholike, a religious, a moſt pious, a moſt Chriſtian, a moſt orthodoxall Prince, and the greateſt oppugner of hereſies : what an audacious and ſhameleſſe vntruth was it in the Cardinall, to ſay, that, *All Authors, all both Greeke and Latine, doe witnesse and detest his impiety, and his fall into that heresie*. Beſides theſe, I muſt yet adde ſome other, and thoſe alſo farre more eminent and ample witneſſes, who doe more than demonſtrate both the honour of *Iustinian*, and
thoſe

p *Lib. 1. de Geſt. Longob. ca. 25.*

q *Felici ſorte.*

r *Lib. 5. ca. 4.*

ſ *Chron. in Iuſt.*

* *An. 504.*

ſ *An. 564.*
t *Coſmog. lib. 4. in Iuſtin.*

u *In vita Ioh. 2.*

those imputations of heresie, and the other disgraces wherewith *Baronius* hath loaded him, to bee most shamelesse calumnies and slanders.

16. The first of these is Pope *Agatho*, one of their [x] Canonized Saints: Hee in his [y] Epistle to the Emperour *Constantine Pogonatus*, to prove out of the venerable * Fathers two natures to be in Christ, tels us, that S. *Cyril*, Saint *Chrysostome*, *Iohn* Bishop of *Scithopolis*, *Eulogius* Bishop of *Alexandria*, *Ephremius* and *Anastasius* the elder, two most worthy Bishops of *Antioch*, *& præ omnibus, æmulator veræ & Apostolicæ fidei, piæ memoriæ Iustinianus Augustus*, & above all these *Iustinian* the Emperour of holy memory, a zealous defender of the true and Apostolicall faith, teacheth this, *whose integrity of faith did as much exalt the Christian Common-wealth, as by the sincerity therof it was pleasing unto God: and whose religious memory, ab omnibus gentibus veneratione digna censetur*, is esteemed by all nations worthy of veneration, *seeing the integrity of his faith, set out by his Imperiall Edicts, in toto orbe diffusa laudatur*, is spred abroad and praised in the whole world. Thus Saint *Agatho*: Whose words may justly cause all the Cardinals friends to blush and bee ashamed of his Annals. Saint *Agatho* rankes *Iustinian* among the venerable and holy Fathers of the Church: *Baronius* thrusts him among heretikes, Saint *Agatho* preferres him before Saint *Cyrill*, Saint *Chrysostome*, *Eulogius*, *Iohn* and *Ephremius*, all learned and worthy Bishops: *Baronius* debaseth him below the most rude and illiterate persons, even below any abcedary Scholler, and cals him a very blocke and a foole: Saint *Agatho* preferres him to that very *Anastasius* the elder, * surnamed *Sinaita*, because hee came from the wildernesse of *Sinai*, whom for maintaining the faith against this very heresie of the *Aphthardokites*, *Evagrius* [a], and *Baronius* [b] himselfe, cals *turrim munitissimam*, a most strong towre; and yet (as Saint *Agatho* witnesseth) a more worthy and defensed towre of faith was our *Iustinian*: *Baronius* [c] makes him and this *Anastasius* to bee contradictory in faith, and *Iustinian* to threaten banishment unto this *Anastasius* for not consenting to the heresie of the Phantasticks: S. *Agatho* commends him for his integrity & sincerity in maintaining the true and Apostolicall faith: *Baronius* condemnes him for an Antichrist, an execrable and hereticall oppugner, yea, persecutor of the Apostolicall faith: S. *Agatho* testifieth that the sincerity of his faith did both please God, and highly exalt the Church and Empire: *Baronius* revileth him, as odious to God, detestable to men, and pernicious, yea, pestiferous both to Church and Empire: S. *Agatho* witnesseth his memory to bee pious, blessed and venerable, and that in all nations: *Baronius* declames against him as accursed, and abominable to all: S. *Agatho* proclameth, that all nations, and the whole world doth consent in the praising of the faith, and veneration of the person of *Iustinian*: *Baronius* tels you, that all Authors, both Greeke and Latine, consent in condemning the faith, and detesting the heresie of *Iustinian*. *Vtri creditis?* whether doe you beleeve *Baronius* maliciously applauding an untruth, which hee found in one or two writers, of none, or little credit, or *Agatho* a Pope, a Saint, with whom consent all nations, and the whole world?

17. To

x *Martyrol. Rom. Ian. 10.* y *Agath. Epist. extat Act. 4. Concil. Gen. 6.* z *Non desunt autem et aliorū venerabilium patrum probatissima testimonia, &c. Ibid.*

* *Nam Anastasius minor Episcopatum adeptus est post mortem Iustiniani ut ex Niceph. Constanl. in Chro. liquet.* a *Lib. 4. ca. 39.* b *An. 563. 10.* c *Ibid. nu. 12.*

17. To Pope *Agatho* I adjoyne the whole Romane Synod consisting of 125. Bishops, who all together with *Agatho* give the like honorable testimony of *Iustinian*. They with *Agatho* writ a Synodall [d] letter to the same Emperour *Constantine*, wherein they exhort him to imitate the piety and vertue of *Constantine*, of *Theodosius*, of *Martian*, and of *Iustinian the great, extremi quidem, praestantissimi tamen omnium*, the last indeed (of those who had before assembled generall Councells) but the most excellent of them all, *whose piety and vertue omnia in meliorem statum restauravit*, restored all things into a better order. Thus that whole Synod: Could they more forcibly have demonstrated *Baronius* to be a slanderer? *Baronius* saith that *Iustinian* was an heretike, a persecutor, an Antichrist, one who dissipated the faith, ruinated the Empire, brought an hellish confusion into the Church; for which crimes hee placeth him among the damned in hell. Pope *Agatho* with his whole Councell, testifie, that by his piety and vertue hee restored all, both the Church and Empire into a better order: they honour him (as much, nay more than they do S. *Constantine* [*] or *Theodosius* or *Martian*,) for one of the most renowned upholders of the faith of *Christ*, for one of them, who at their death did not leave nor lose, but onely exchange their imperiall Crowne, and in stead of their earthly and corruptible, received the celestiall and immarcessible Diadem of immortality and eternall glory: among these, yea and above these Saints and glorified Emperours, as being *most excellent of them all*, is *Iustinian* placed and crowned in heaven, by the judgement of Saint *Agatho* and his whole Councell with him.

18. If yet you require more or more ample witnesses, behold, the sixt generall Councell hath approved both those Epistles of *Agatho*. Of them the whole Synod [e] said, *Petrus per Agathonem loquutus est*, Peter spake by the mouth of *Agatho*: and againe, [f] *We all consent to the dogmaticall letters of Agatho, & to the suggestion of the holy Synod which was under him, of* 125. *Bishops*. Of them *Constantine* [g] saith in the name of the whole Councell, *Omnes consonanter mente & lingua*, wee all with one heart and voyce *beleeve and professe, and admire the relation of Agatho, as the divine voyce of Saint Peter*. Of them [i] *Domitius* B. of Prusias sayd, *I receive and imbrace the suggestions of the most blessed Agatho, tanquam ex Spiritu Sancto dictatas, as being inspired by the Holy Ghost, and uttered by the mouth of Saint Peter, and written with the fingers of Agatho*. Thus doth the whole generall Councell approve those Epistles of *Agatho*: which their approbation not onely *Bellarmine* [k], but *Baronius* [l] himselfe extendeth to every part and parcell of those Epistles, saying of them, *In omnibus tum ipse Constantinus, tam sancta Synodus suscepit*, both *Constantine* & the holy Councell received these in all & every point. And againe, [m] *Epistolae Roma missae in omnibus comprobatae dicuntur*, The Epistles of *Agatho*, which were sent from Rome are said to be approved in All things set downe therein. Now seeing the whole generall Councell, by *Baronius* owne confession, doth in this sort approve the Epistles of *Agatho*, and therefore those very testimonies concerning *Iustinians* faith, piety, honour, and eternall blessednesse in Heaven: had not *Baronius*, thinke you, a face more hard than brasse or adamant,

Gg   when

d *Exta: Epist. Act.4. Conc.6. pa.21.*

[*] *Sanctum Constantinum, vocat Papa Steph. in Epist. ad Bazil. Imperat. post 8. Synod.*

e *In Sermon. prosphon. Act.18 pa.89.*
f *Ibid. & Act.15*
g *Act.18.pa.93.*

i *Act.8.pa.29.*

k *Bell.lib.4. de Pontif.ca.11. § Vbi et. Atsi.*
l *an.681.nu.24*

m *an.eod.nu.4?*

when he reviled in so immodest manner that Emperour, as an heretike, a persequutor of the faith, an Antichrist, a drunken, frantick, and
sacrilegious foole, a ruinater of the Church, and carelesse governour
of the Empire, yea as one condemned and now tormented in hell, and
who sealeth it with this saying, That his heresie is testified by *All authors*? whereas those most honourable testimonies of Pope *Agatho*,
and the Romane Synod with him, (which declare *Iustinian* to have
beene for faith orthodoxall, for vertue and piety renowned, and held
in veneration by all nations, and praised of all the world, and to have
beene equall, nay more excellent than Saint *Constantine*, *Theodosius*,
and *Martian*, and therefore to be both in his owne person, and in his
memory blessed) are approved, and that in this very point, as *Baronius*
acknowledgeth, by the sixt generall Councell to be as certaine and as
true, as if Saint *Peter*, or the Holy Ghost had uttered the same. Said I
not truly, that this cause of the Three Chapters had bereft the Cardinall, not onely of truth, but of judgement, of modesty, of civility,
yea almost of common sense, so that he cares not what he sayes, so he
speake in defence of those who defend, and in condemnation of those
who condemne the Three Chapters, though he knoweth that, which
he saith, to be testified to be a calumny and slander, not onely by historians and private writers, but by the Pope, by the Romane Synod,
by the holy general Councel, that is, by the whole Catholike Church,
by all Nations, by the whole world, by Saint *Peter*, and by the Holy
Ghost himselfe.

19. There might be added unto these, divers other pregnant testimonies, of Pope *Gregory*, who often calls [k] *Iustinian*, a man *Pia memoria*, of a pious memory; of the Legates of *Agatho*, who call [l] him, *of
divine memory*; of *Peter* B. of Nicomedia and others, who call [m] him
of *blessed remembrance*; of the Emperour *Constantinus*, who calls [n] him,
divine memoria; of the sixt generall Councell, which not so little as a
dozen times I thinke, [o] calls him of *pious, or divine memory, most holy Iustinian*, or the like; and which, to expresse that great honour which
they ascribe to the religious Emperour then present before them,
(whom they terme the driver away of heretikes,) proclame him to
be *a new Constantine, a new Theodosius, a new Martian, a new Iustinian*, crying out in his honour in divers [p] actions, *Novo Iustiniano aeterne memoria*, eternall memory bee to you our new *Iustinian*. A miserable prayse
and wish had this beene, had *Iustinian* beene an Heretike, a Persecutor, an Antichrist, a damned person in hell: for then the whole generall Councell had not onely dishonoured *Constantine* there present,
but had wished honour and immortall glory to Heretikes, to Persecutors, to Antichrist, yea to the Devill himselfe: which kinde of pray-
sing and praying, is not very sutable to the piety and faith of that generall Councell. But the former testimonies are so ample and illustrious, that they seeme to me to obscure all these and the like, and doe so
abundantly convince *Baronius* to slander and calumniate the Emperour, that I will forbeare to presse him with any more.

20. Perhaps some good friends of *Baronius* will say in his behalfe,
and for his excuse, that hee did not devise this of himselfe, nor is hee
the

*[k] Lib.2.Ind. 11
Epist.10.& lib.
3.Epist 4.
1Con.6.act.3.
m Act.10.
n Act.18.*

o Act.14.& 18

*p Act.8.& 16.
& 17. et 18.*

the firſt that accuſeth *Iuſtinian* of this Hereſie: he hath his Books, and his Authors for him. He hath ſo indeed. And ſo he hath *Neſtorius* and *Theodorus* of *Mopſueſtia* for his defending *Neſtorianiſm*. He deviſed not that neither of himſelf, he doth but ſecōd others therin. By this apology whō may not the Cardinal revile when he liſt? He may calumniate *Athanaſius* for a[1] murderer; *Celeſtine* and *Cyril* for[m] *Apolinarians*; *Conſtantine the great* for a[n] *perſecutor of the true faith*; for which crime his ſon is called *an Hereticke, a murderer, a friend of the Devill:* Saint *Paul* for a[o] *ſeditious and peſtilent fellow,* a[p] *mad man:* Chriſt himſelfe for a *glutton*[q] *and drunkard, a man poſſeſſed*[r] *by the devill,* a[s] *blaſphemer.* Thus may he revile and accuſe theſe, and al the beſt men that have ever been in the world; yea even God himſelfe, and then ſalve all with this plaiſter, VVhy, *Baronius* deviſeth not any one of theſe imputations, hee can produce his books & authors for thē all: and thoſe alſo far better than he doth for this concerning *Iuſtinian.* In one he hath the whole Councell of Tyre; in another, *Iohn* Patriarch of Antioch, *Theodoret,* & the Councel which they held at Epheſus; in a third, *Lucifer* Biſhop of Calaris, a Confeſſor, one who ſuffered whippings and tortures at the Councell of Millan, and after that, exile for the faith: in another, *Tertullus* and *Feſtus:* in the laſt, thē Iewes, the Scribes, and the High Prieſt with his Councell: would this excuſe either *Baronius,* or any that ſhould upbraid theſe crimes unto *Athanaſius, Conſtantine, Paul,* or *Chriſt,* from being revilers and ſlanderers. He who applaudeth & abetteth a ſlander, (as doth *Baronius* this of *Iuſtinian*) he is as guilty of ſlander as if himſelfe had deviſed it. The law of God doth not only ſay, Thou ſhalt not lye or deviſe a falſe tale, but[t] *Thou ſhalt not receive a falſe tale, neither ſhalt thou put thine hand w*th *the wicked* (not be a coadjutor, an acceſſary, or an abetter) *to be a falſe witneſſe.* Yea though many report an untruth, yet their multitude cannot excuſe thee: *Thou*[u] *ſhalt not follow a multitude in doing evill; neither ſhalt thou agree in a controverſie to decline after many, and overthrow the truth.* And the Apoſtles rule[x] condemnes not onely *thoſe who doe evill themſelves, but thoſe alſo* (and that much more) *who conſent unto, or who favour thoſe that doe evill:* accordingly whereunto S. *Ierome*[y] ſaith of wantonneſſe, that which is true in all other ſins, *majori procacitate defendunt libidinem quam exercent,* it is a greater impudency to defend luſt, lying, ſlandering, or any ſin, than to commit it.

21. But let us ſee who thoſe are on whoſe report the Card. frames this his ſlanderous invective againſt the Emperor. He ſaith they are *all authors.* But that, as you have ſeen, is a vaſt, and truly *Baronian* untruth. They are but ſome: and the Card. nameth three, *Evagrius, Euſtathius,* and *Nicephorus Calliſtus.* I will yeeld more unto him if he pleaſe: let him have 10. or 20. to ſay what his fore-man doth: yet the law of God is forcible againſt them, as if they were but one: *Thou ſhalt not follow a multitude to doe evill.* And alas, what are theſe, either for number, or (which is more) for gravity and authority, to thoſe which we have before produced? To ſay nothing of that cloud of Hiſtorians: what are they to S. *Agatho?* to S. *Gregory?* to the Emperour *Conſtantinus Pogonatus?* to the Romane Synod? to the ſixt generall Councel? to all nations? to the whole world? to S. *Peter?* yea to the Holy Ghoſt himſelfe?

Gg 2 VVhat

l *Conc. Tyrius apud Ath. in. Apol. 2.*
m *Conciliab. Ioannis, Epheſ. ſup. ca. 11. nu. 42*
n *Quia noluerit eſſe Arianus, idcirco Athanaſium peroſum habitum à Patre tuo, zon te fugit. Luciſ. lib. 1. prō Athan. pa. 57.*
Primò, es hereticus, deinde perſecutor, &c. et, amici tui diaboli. ait idem Conſtantino. ibid. pa. 12. et 13.
o *Tertullus, Act. 24. 5.*
p *Feſtus, Act. 25. 24.*
q *Matth. 11 19.*
r *Mark 3. 21.*
ſ *M. 11 h. 26. 65.*
t *Exod. 23. 1.*

u *Ibid v. 2.*

x *Rom. 1. 32.*

y *Lib. 2. adverſ. Iovin.*

What an army of invincible, unresistable Captaines, hath *Iustinian* to fight on his side, against two or three poore, petite, & contemptible witnesses, which the Card. hath raked together, not to be named the same day with the former ?

22. Will it please you further to take a view in particular of them? Truly of those whom the Card. would not vouchsafe once to name, I will say nothing : if they were not worthy to be named, nor to have a whistle from the Cardinall, I thinke them unworthy to bee refuted also. This onely I say of them all, they were misse-led and deceived by those whom the Card. mentioneth as his prime and principall witnesses: and those are *Evagrius, Eustathius*, and *Nicephorus*. Now for the last of these, *Possevine* shewes him to be hereticall, [a] and in Historicall narrations, erroneous: and the Card. [b] himselfe saith of him, *Fatuus judicandus est*, he is but a foole : and his reason is far worse than his censure, because he is not so virulent and spitefull in condemning the Emperour *Iustinian*, as the Card. could wish him, and as himselfe is : besides, what *Nicephorus* saith, is but borrowed from *Evagrius,* (*Possevine* [c] calls him *Asseclam*, a Page or Ape of *Evagrius*) and therefore the answer to *Evagrius* will be sufficient for him also.

23. His middle witnesse is *Eustathius*, the writer of the life of *Eutychius*, which is set forth by *Surius*. He at large indeed describeth this matter, both how *Iustinian* [d] *fell into this heresie of the Aphthardokites, how hee writ an Edict for the same, and read it to Eutychius B. of Constantinople, urging him to approve it ; how when he refused so to doe, the Emperor for this cause thrust him from* [f] *his See, and sent him into banishment ; where he lived working abundance of miracles, for the space* [g] *of 12. yeares, till Tiberius the Emperour restored him with great honour*. This is the summe of that narration of *Eustathius*; in which the Card. much pleaseth himselfe, as if all that *Eustathius* saith in this matter were an undoubted Oracle, seeing *Eustathius* (as he often boasteth [h]) *was present with Eutychius in all these occurrents, and an eye-witnesse of them*.

24. But why did the Card. mention this worthy record out of *Surius* ? could hee finde this writing of *Eustathius* in no better Author than *Surius* ? *Surius*, a man so prostitute in faith, so delighted in lyes, and forgeries of this kinde, with which he hath stuffed his *Lives of the Saints*, that at the very first naming of *Surius*, I suspected this *Eustathius* to be but a forged Author, and a fabler : the rather because neither *Photius*, nor *Sixtus Senensis*, nor *Possevine*, (who all writ *Bibliothecas*,) nor *Tritemius*, mention any such *Eustathius* to have writ the life of *Eutychius*. But after I had perused and considered the writing it selfe, I did no longer suspect, but I found (which now I do constantly affirm) that *Surian Eustathius* to be so vile & abject a fabler, and so full of lyes, that none but such as *Surius* and *Baronius*, men delighted in applauding forgeries and untruths, can give any credit at all to that *Surian Eustathius*. By one or two examples take a conjecture of all the rest.

25. That *Eustathius* describing the entrance of *Eutychius* to the See of Constantinople, tells [i] us that *after the fift generall Councell was summoned, Eutychius was sent thither by the Bishop of Amasea,* (*who then was sicke) to supplie his roome in the Councell*. *Mennas then Patri-*

a *Nicephorus Andronicum commendat quod S. Sancti à solo Patre procedere per Synodum à se coactam promulgari curaverit. Poss. in verb. Nicephorus. Et, Habet tum in dogmatibus, tum in historica veritate quæ digna sunt ut præcaveantur. Ibid.*

b *an. 563. nu. 8.*

c *In verbo Evagrius.*

d *Hic (Iustin.) cepit execrabilem opinionem probare, quæ Christi corpus incorruptum asserebat. Eust. apud Sur. 6. April.*

f *Persuaserunt Imperatori, ut eum à sede exturbaret, in eáq; alium constitueret, qui opinionibus suis consentiret: quod et factum est. Ibid.*

g *Perduravit exilium Eutychii (ut idem author affirmat) spacio 12. annorum et amplius. Bar. an. 564. nu. 29.*

h *Hæc Eustathias: Quibus omnibus præsens aderat. Bar. an. 564. nu. 20. præsens aspexit. nu. 24. et alibi.*

i *Loc. citat.*

Patriarch of Conſtantinople, exhorted Eutychius not to depart from him, and ſhewing Eutychius to the Clergie, ſaid of him by way of propheſie (for that *Euſtathius* is full of miracles, propheſies, and viſions,) unto them, *This Monke ſhall be my ſucceſſor; and then ſent him to the Emperor.* Some few dayes after this, *Mennas* dyed: and whereas many ſued for the Biſhop-ricke, the Emperour had a viſion, wherein S. *Peter* appeared unto him, ſhewing him Eutychius, and ſaying, *Fac ut hic ſit Epiſcopus, ſee that this man be the Biſhop of Conſtantinople.* The Emperour acquainted the Clergy with his viſion, and upon his oath teſtified it unto them; whereupon they all choſe Eutychius, and then he was conſecrated. Thus the *Surian Euſtathius.* A narration ſo ſottiſh and ſo abſurd, that nothing can bee more ridiculous: and ſo untrue, that there are not ſo many words as lyes therein. The fiſt Councell was not ſummoned till the 26. yeare of *Iuſtinian:* and that before then, it could not be ſummoned, *Baronius* evidently ſheweth: For the ſummons to the Councell followed, as he ſaith, [k] the reſtoring of *Vigilius,* and his reconcilement both to the Emperour, to *Mennas,* and to *Theodorus of Cæſarea:* all which he [l] placeth in the 26.yeare of *Iuſtinian.* Now it is certaine by that teſtimony of the Popes Legates, which [m] before was handled, and was uttered before the ſixt generall Councell[n], and is acknowledged for true by *Baronius* [o], that *Mennas* died in the 21.yeare of *Iuſtinian,* that is, foure whole yeares at the leaſt before the ſummons of the Councell, or before *Eutychius* came to Conſtantinople, being ſent from the Biſhop of Amaſea. What a dull and doltiſh legend now is this of *Euſtathius*? to make *Eutychius* come and converſe with *Mennas,* to be brought by him to the Clergy, to be deſigned and prophetically foretold by *Mennas* to bee his ſucceſſor, when *Mennas* was dead foure whole yeares before he did any of theſe things? what a prophane fiction is it, to make the Emperour ſee a viſion, and Saint *Peter* to command him to take care that *Eutychius* ſhould be choſen, and the Emperour to avouch all this upon his oath to be true? whereas not one ſyllable thereof is true, or ſo much as poſſible; ſeeing *Eutychius* was actually placed in that See full foure years before this viſion, or before Saint *Peter* gave that ſtrait charge unto *Iuſtinian.* They who can beleeve theſe phantaſticall dotages of that *Surian Euſtathius,* (and *Baronius* [p] applauds this with the other narrations in that *Euſtathius*) little marvell, if upon his report they upbraid that which is every way as incredible, that *Iuſtinian* fell into that hereſie of the Phantaſtickes, and baniſhed *Eutychius* for not conſenting to the ſame.

26. Of no more truth is that which the ſame *Euſtathius* ſets downe for the continuance of the baniſhment of *Eutychius,* which was the ſpace of twelve [m] whole yeares, untill Tiberius was [n] aſſociated into the Empire by *Iuſtinus,* and in the ſame yeare when Iohn [o] the ſucceſſor to *Eutychius* dyed. For *Theophanes,* as the Card. calls him, as other (though amiſſe) *Paulus Diaconus,* but the author of the *Miſcella. Hiſtoria,* expreſly witneſſeth [p] that *Iuſtinus* (who began his reigne two yeares after the baniſhment of *Eutychius*) was *crowned by Eutychius.* And *Zonaras* [q] for a certainty relates, how that (before Tiberius was aſſociated) when Iuſtinus was ſicke, be called, beſides others, Eutychius unto him, and in their preſence nomi-

Marginal notes:
k Sicq; allinᵈ junctis reſtitutq̃, Romano Põtifice in priſtinam dignitatem indicta eſt œcumenica Synodus. an.553.nu.14. l an.552.nu.19. & 20. in Sup.ca.16. nu.38. n Act.3. o an.860.nu.48

p an.553.& an.564.& alibi m Vt ex Euſtathio notat Baron.an.564.29. & an.578.nu. 3.5.6. n Ad Iuſtinum & Tiberium exclamant, ut fidei cuſtos (Eutychius) redderetur: qui id conceſſerunt. Verba Euſtath.Suriani. loc.cit. o Bar.an.578. nu.5. p Iuſtinus Imperator coronatus ab Eutychio Patriarch.lib.16 Hiſt.Miſcel. q Zonar.tu.3.in Iuſtin.

nominated *Tiberius* to be his partner in the Empire : for *Iohn*, ſaith he *being dead, Eutychius was reduced from baniſhment, & reſtored then to his See, and that Tiberius was crowned by the ſame Eutychius.* Which evidently de-monſtrates the vanity of that whole Euſtathian Narration, wherein it is ſaid, that after the Empire of *Tiberius begun, the people came to them to entreat the reſtoring of Eutychius :* that the Emperors upon their ſuppli-cation, *ſent poſt haſt to Amaſea to bring him home out of baniſhment :* that the *Angell* [t] *of God brought him miraculouſly thence :* that the people *floc-ked unto him in every place:*that they laid *their ſicke in the way, that at leaſt the ſhadow* of this ſecond *Peter* might touch them, *and according to their faith they were cured :* that he came like another Meſſias, *riding on the Colt of an Aſſe into Conſtantinople, the people cutting downe boughes, & ſprea-ding their garments for him, and ſo was with admirable joy received by the Emperors, and the whole City.* Not one word of all which is true, ſeeing *Eutychius* was long before the time of *Tiberius* reſtored from baniſh-ment, at the leaſt 11. or 12. yeares, even ever ſince the crowning of *Iu-ſtinus:* who reigned 12. [ſ] yeares alone, before he aſſumed *Tiberius* into the ſociety of the Empire. This will be further evident by thoſe words of *Nicephorus* Patriarch of Conſtantinople, on which *Baronius* relieth. *Eutychius* was recalled from baniſhment, as the Cardinall [t] teacheth, and that rightly, in the ſame yeare wherein *Iohannes Scholaſticus* (who was placed in his roome) died. *Now Iohn was Biſhop,* as *Nicephorus* [u] wit-neſſeth, *but two yeares and ſeven moneths.* Whereupon it certainly fol-loweth, that *Eutychius* was recalled within three yeares after his ba-niſhment, that is, in the very firſt yeare of *Iuſtinus,* upon whom hee ſet the Crowne, at the ſolemnity of his firſt Coronation, as was ſhewed out of the *Hiſtoria Miſcella:* and this was full twelve yeares [x] before *Tiberius* was made Emperour. Which demonſtrates, not onely the un-truth and manifold lyes of that *Surian Euſtathius,* but another hand-ſome tricke of legerdemaine in *Anaſtaſius* and *Baronius.* For *Anaſtaſius* ſeeing belike that it was needfull (for ſaving the credit of ſome ſuch like fabler as this *Euſtathius* is) that *Iohn* ſhould bee Biſhop twelve yeares, he tranſlating [y] the Greeke *Nicephorus,* in ſtead of *two yeares ſe-ven moneths,* puts in *twelve* [z] *yeares and ſeven moneths,* and gives ſo many unto *Iohn* before *Eutychius* bee reſtored : and *Baronius* finding this ac-count in the Anaſtaſian tranſlation, followeth it, [a] and ſaith, *Nicepho-rus aſcribes twelve yeares to Iohn:* whereas, not *Nicephorus,* nor his Greek edition (which hath onely two yeares and ſeven moneths) but the A-naſtaſian falſified and corrupted Latine tranſlation hath the other un-true and falſe accompt of twelve years and ſeven moneths. This, if no-thing elſe, might be ſufficient to refute the whole fiction of that *Surian Euſtathius,* the untruths whereof *Baronius* could not defend, but by ap-plauding the untrue and falſified writings of his fellow *Bibliothecarius.*

27.. Perhaps you will demand, why then did *Iuſtinian* baniſh *Euty-chius,* if not for refuſing to conſent to his opinion and hereſie of the Aphthardokites, as *Euſtathius* ſaith ? which doubt ſeemes the grea-ter, becauſe *Nicephorus* the Patriarch in his Chronology mentioneth the ſame cauſe, ſaying thus, *Eutychius was caſt out of his See by Iuſtinian, eo quod non reciperet edictum ipſius de corpore Chriſti experte omnis labe-*
factionis

t *Vere cognovi-mus Deum mi-ſiſſe Angelum ſuum & eripu-iſſe, &c.* Euſtat.
ſ *Iuſtinus per ſe ſolum ad annos 12. regnavit, & ſum Tiberio an-nos 3.* Evagr. Lib. 5. ca. 23.
t *Hoc anno, de-functo Iohanne, revocatus eſt Eutychius exul.* an. 578. nu. 5.
u *Ἐ τῷ* C Μωας ζ. Niceph. in libro.
x *Nam Iuſtinus ſolus totidem annos regnavit.* ſup.
y *Ab Anaſtaſio Bibliothecario hujus Chronolo-gia interprete. &, Chronolo-gia Nicephori converſa in La-tinum per Ana-ſtaſium. Titulo Nicephori in Biblioth. S. Pat.* to. 7.
z *Iohannes an. 12. menſ. 7.*
a *Iohannes ſedit an. 12. menſ. 7. ut habet Nice-phori Chronicon.* Bar. an. 564. nu. 29.

factionis, because *Eutychius* would not consent to his Edict, that Christs body was incorruptible. See here againe I pray you, and detest for ever the vile and shamelesse dealing of *Anastasius.* *Nicephorus* saith not so; all that hee [c] saith, is, that *Eutychius was banished because hee would not receive or consent unto the Edict of Iustinian;* but that which followeth, his Edict *de corpore Christi incorruptibili,* wherein is contained the heresie slanderously objected to *Iustinian,* of that *Nicephorus* hath not one word in his Greeke text; that is wholy pacht to him in the Latine translation by the false hand of *Anastasius,* the Arch-corrupter of all writings in his time, as I have * before more at large declared: And yet so are they delighted with lyes, & corrupted writings, this Latine translation, thus vilely falsified by *Anastasius,* is set [d] in their *Bibliotheca Sanctorum Patrum;* which much better deserves to bee called a Library of forged or corrupted Fathers, and Writers.

28. But for what other Edict, if not for this of the Aphthardokites, was *Eutychius* banished? for that he was expelled from his See, there is no doubt, that being testified not onely by the Surian *Eustathius,* *Zonaras,* *Glicas,* and others, but by *Victor* [e], who then lived, and was at *Constantinople* when these things fell out, to whom alone more credit herein is to bee given, than to five hundreth of the Surian records. Truly, whatsoever was the cause why he was banished; certaine it is, that this heresie of *Iustinian,* or any Edict made for it, was not the cause thereof: But there are two other matters, the one, or both of which may very well be thought to have incensed *Iustinian* against him: The former was this; *Eutychius* pretended a Propheticall skill whereby hee could foreshew who should succeed in the Empire; and hee began to tamper and practice this Art about *some three yeares before Iustinian dyed,* as that *Eustathius* delareth. At that time [f] hee privately called *Iustinus unto him, and told him that he should succeed in the Empire after the death of Iustinian, for so* [g] (said he) *God hath revealed unto mee.* The like good fortune hee foretold to *Tiberius, that* [h] *ere long he should have the Empire alone.* Againe, two yeares before the death of *Tiberius,* hee prophesied of *Mauritius, that* [i] *hee, and none but hee should have the Empire after Tiberius; idque juramento asseruit,* and hee confirmed this by an oath. Now this Art of Divination, and Mathematicall predictions, especially when they prognosticate of Kings their deaths, & successours, was never allowable in any wise State, nor acceptable to any prudent Emperour. It betokened no good to *Cæsar* that they foretold [k] him of those dismall Ides of *March.* *Domitian* was foretold [l], not onely of the yeare, but of the day, and the very houre when hee should dye; and when he had carefully looked to himselfe on that day, enquiring [m] the houre, his owne men of purpose told him the sixt, in stead of the fift: hee then thinking all danger to bee past, was by the Conspiratours, (who kept a better watch of the time than he did) securely murdered. What mischiefe ensued upon that prediction to *Valence,* that one whose name did begin with *Theod.* should succeed unto him, *Socrates* [n] declareth: Hee thereupon murdered most injustly all whom he could finde to be called either *Theodori,* or *Theodoti,*

Marginal notes:

c *Niceph. in Edit. Græca.*

* *Sup. cap. 17.*

d *T. 7.*

e *In Chron.*

f *Tribus circiter annis ante Imperium Iustini.* *Eust. apud Snr.*

g *Significavit mihi Deus te post avunculum tuum fore Imperatorem. Ibid.*

h *Nunc in parte reipublicæ gubernacula commisit Deus; mox autem et finem concedet. Ibid.*

i *Verè (inquit) non est alius (qui succedet) quam Mauritius. Ibid.*

k *Suet. in Iul. Cæs. cap. 81.*

l *Suet. in Domit. cap. 13.*

m *Ibid. cap. 16.*

n *Lib. 4. cap. 15.*

doti, or *Theodosij*, or *Theoduli*, or *Theodosioli*, or beginning with those letters. What hurt followed as wel in this kingdom, upon that prophesie G. should succeed unto *Edward* the fourth; as in the next, when it was foretold the Earle of Athel, that hee should bee crowned before hee dyed, who thereupon never ceased to rebell against his Soveraigne, till hee was crowned with an hot burning iron, our owne Chronicles doe declare. All kingdomes, all Stories are full of like examples. It was not without cause, that in the Code [p] both of *Theodosius* and *Iustinian*, there are so many, and so severe lawes aginst this kinde of Mathematicall diviners, their Art [q] being called *damnabilis, & omnibus interdicta*, a damnable Art, forbidden to all; the punishment denounced against them, *being* [r] *banishment, yea, death; supplicio capitis* [f] *ferietur*, hee shall bee put to death who practiseth the curiositie of divining: Now *Eutychius* taking upō him this Art of divining, cōtrary to those severe and Imperiall Edicts ratified by *Iustinian*, whether for this cause the Emperour, who by the law might have deprived him of his life, did not chuse rather to deprive him onely of his See, and liberty, I leave to the judgement of others.

p *Tit. de Maleficis, Mathematicis, et his similibus.*
q *Leg. 2. eod. tit. Cod. Iust.*
r *Non solum urbe Roma, sed etiam omnibus civitatibus pelli decernimus.* *l. ult. Tit. de malef. Cod. Theod.*
f *Leg. 5. tit. de Malef. Cod. Iust. et leg. 4. Cod. Theod.*

29. The other cause was a most impious heresie defended by *Eutychius*, whom they so much honour; which alone being duely considered, overthroweth that whole fabulous Legend of *Eustathius*. *Eutychius*, when hee had long continued in the defence of the truth, did afterwards fall both by words and writing to maintaine the Heresie of *Origen* and the Origenists, denying Christs body after the resurrection to have beene palpable, that is in effect, to bee no true humane body; and the very like hee taught of the bodies of all other men after the resurrection: This the Surian *Eustathius* quite over-passeth in silence; for it was not fit that such a Saint as *Eutychius*, so abundāt in miracles, prophesies, and visions, should be thought guilty of so foule and condemned an heresie: But Pope *Gregory* doth so fully and certainly testifie [t] it, that no doubt can remaine thereof; hee tels us, *how himselfe disputed against Eutychius, defending this heresie; how hee urged those words of our Saviour, palpate & videte; how Eutychius answered thereunto, that Christs body was then indeed palpable to cōfirme the mindes of his Disciples; but after they were once confirmed, all that was before palpable in Christs bodie, in subtilitatem est redactū*, was turned into an aërial and unpalpable subtilty; *How he further strived to prove this by those words of the Apostle, Flesh & blood cannot inherit the kingdome of heavē; how then (said hee) may this be beleeved, veraciter resurgere carnem*, that true bodies did or shall rise againe? *How he further insisted on those words, That which thou sowest is not the same body which it shall be: proving therby that which riseth againe either not to be a body, or not a palpable, that is, no true humane body. Gregory* also tels us, that *Eutychius writ* [u] *a booke in defence of this heresie, which both himselfe read, and Tiberius the Emperour after diligent ponderation of the reasons of Gregory against it, caused it publikely to bee burned, as hereticall*: adding, *that Eutychius continued in this heresie almost till the very houre of his death*. Now although *Gregory* tels not when, or at what time *Eutychius* fel into this heresie, yet it may wel be supposed, that as *Iustinian* honoured him so long as he persisted in the truth,

t *Greg. lib. 14. Moral. ca. 29. Eutychius scripsit quod corpus nostrum in illa resurrectionis gloria erit impalpabile.*
u *Libellum de Resurrectione scripsit, ostendēs quod caro vel impalpabilis, vel ipsa non erit.*

truth, ſo when once hee gave himſelfe to ſuch dotages of the Origeniſts, (which, as it ſeemes, he did about the latter end of *Iuſtinians* Empire, ſome three yeares before his death) then the Emperour, who till his end was conſtant in condemning the *Three Chapters*, as *Victor* ſheweth, (the condemning of which is, as before [t] we declared, the condemning of all the Hereſies of *Origen*, and whatſoever contradicts the verity of Chriſts deity, or humanity) as it is moſt likely, exiled him for this hereticall opinion: And this is much more probable, ſeeing *Iuſtinian* had purpoſely ſet forth, long before this, a moſt religious and orthodoxall Edict or Decree, particularly againſt *Origen*, and the Origeniſts, as *Liberatus* [u] ſheweth, and as the Edict it ſelfe, which is extant [x], doth manifeſt, condemning them in particular [y], *for denying the verity of Chriſts, and other humane bodies after the reſurrection.* Seeing then *Nicephorus* the Patriarch ſaith, that *Eutychius* was baniſhed for not conſenting to the Emperours Edict, and *Eutychius* by his defending of that hereſie of the Origeniſts, directly oppugned that his Edict; moſt like it is, that (beſides his Mathematicall Art, whereby hee was liable both to death and baniſhment, by the Emperours lawes) this Edict of *Iuſtinian* againſt *Origen*, ſhould bee that which *Nicephorus* the Patriarch meant, and for which *Eutychius* was, and that moſt juſtly, exiled. So not *Iuſtinian*, but *Eutychius*, was the heretike; nor was it any hereticall Edict of *Iuſtinian*, (as the Surian *Euſtathius*, and after him *Baronius* affirmeth) to which *Eutychius* a Catholike oppoſed himſelfe; but an orthodoxall and Catholike Edict of *Iuſtinian*, which *Eutychius*, then an heretike, and Origeniſt, oppugned, for not conſenting whereunto hee was baniſhed. Thus not onely the Emperour is clearly acquitted of that phantaſticall hereſie, whereof the Surian *Euſtathius*, and *Baronius* doe accuſe him; but *Eutychius* himſelfe, whom they honour for a Saint, a Prophet, and a Demi-god, is found guilty of that ſelfe-ſame crime, and of that very hereſie of denying the truth of Chriſts body, which they unjuſtly and ſlanderouſly impute to *Iuſtinian*. And this I thinke is abundant to ſatisfie the Cardinals ſecond witneſſe, namely that fabulous and legendary Surian *Euſtathius*.

30. All the Cardinals hope, and the whole waight of his accuſation relyes now on *Evagrius*. He, I confeſſe, ſaith well neere as much as *Baronius*, againſt *Iuſtinian*, accuſing him of *avarice, injuſtice, and hereſie*: But the credit of *Evagrius* is not ſuch, as to countenance ſuch calumnies. *Evagrius*, in ſome matters wherein hee followeth Authors of better note, is not be contemned, but in very many hee is too credulous, fabulous, and utterly to bee rejected. What credit can you give unto this Narration [a] of the Monke *Barſanuphius*, whom he reports to have lived *in his Cell, wherein he had mewed up himſelfe; and for the ſpace of fifty yeares and more, neither to have beene ſeene by any, neque quidquam alimenti cepiſſe*, nor to have received any nouriſhment, or food? What a worthy S. doth he [b] deſcribe *Simeon Moros*, that is S. Foole, to have been? How doth he commend [c] *Syneſius*, whom they perſwaded to bee baptized, and undertake the function of a Prieſt, though hee did not conſent to the doctrine of the reſurrection, *neque ita cenſere vellet*, neither would beleeve that it was poſſible? The like might

t *Hoc cap. nu.13*

u *Cap.23.*
x *Apud Bar.an. 538. nu.33. & Bin.tom.2.pa. 482.*
y (*Quæmodrem hoc quoque riſu dignum eſt*) et *Anaſt. 5.*

a *Evag.lib.4.ca. 32.*

b *Lib.eod.ca.33*
c *Lib.1.ca.15.*

by name, the Church (faith he) rejecteth; & because some ignorāt persons thought that touching *Eusebius* History not to be the words of *Gelasius*, and the Councell, *Canus* refuting those, gives this, as the reason why *Eusebius* is rejected, *because in it is set downe the Epistle of Iesus to Abgarus, quam Gelasius explodit*, which Epistle *Gelasius* doth hisse

t Bibl. sanc. li. 2.

out of the Church. This Epistle of *Iesus* to *Abgarus*, faith *Sixtus* Senensis, Pope *Gelasius inter scripturas Apochryphas rejicit*, doth reject among other Apocryphall writings *Coster* their Iesuit faith u, *Eusebius*

n Enchir. Tit. de
sac. Scrip. Palam.

relates how Christ *sent a letter to* Abgarus, *but that letter was never pro ejusmodi accepta ab Ecclesia, esteemed for such*, (that is, not for Christs) by the Church. But the words of *Gelasius*, & the whole Roman Councel with

x Concil. Rom. 1
sub Gelas.

him, are of all most remarkeable: They x having expressed and named a long Catalogue of such fabulous writings, and particularly this *Epistle of Christ to Abgarus*, (which *Evagrius* approveth) set downe this censure of them all; *These, and all like unto these, wee confesse to bee not onely refused, but also* eliminata, *cast out of the Church by the whole Romane Catholike and Apostolike Church, atque cum suis authoribus, authorumque sequacibus, sub anathematis indissolubili vinculo in æternum confitemur esse damnata*, and wee confesse as well these writings, as the Authors and the followers also of them to bee eternally condemned under the indissoluble bond of an *Anathema*. So *Gelasius* and the whole Romane Councell: whereby it is evident, that not onely this Epistle, and the Author of it, but that *the followers of the Author*, the approvers of that *Epistle*, that is, *Evagrius*, and the whole second Nicene Synod, and *Baronius* himselfe, that these also are anathematized, condemned and accursed by the judgement of the whole *Romane Catholike Church*, and that also *by an indissoluble bond of an Anathema*. Such an untrue and fabulous, yea miserable and accursed witnesse hath the Cardinall chosen of *Evagrius*, by the warrant and authority of whom hee might insult upon, and revile the Emperour: but now the Cardinall hath farre more neede to excuse *Evagrius* from lies, then by his lying reports to accuse others; and now hee may clearly see that censure of condemnation, which hee, with *Evagrius*, most rashly and unjustly objecteth to the Emperour, to fall on *Evagrius*, their second Nicene Fathers, and the Cardinals owne pate; since they all, by approving that Narration touching *Abgarus*; or being *sequaces* of the Author thereof, are pronounced to bee eternally condemned by the judgement of the whole *Romane Catholike Apostolicall Church*: It is fit such a censure should ever passe on them; who open their mouthes in reviling manner against religious and holy Emperours, the anointed of the Lord.

36. You doe now evidently see, not onely *Iustinian* to bee cleared of those odious and indigne imputations of heresie, tyranny, persecution, and other crimes, which the Cardinall in such spitefull manner upbraideth unto him, but all those witnesses whom hee hath nominated, and produced in this cause, to be so light, and of so little account, that they are utterly unworthy to bee put in the skales or counterpoized with those honourable and innumerable witnesses, which, (as wee have shewed) doe with a loud and consenting voyce proclame,

that

that Faith, Piety, Prudence, Iuſtice, Clemencie, Bounty, and all other Heroicall and Princely vertues have ſhined in *Iuſtinian*, which have beautified any of the moſt renowned and religious Emperors that the Church hath had. Let us now proceed to thoſe effects which *Baronius* obſerveth to have enſued upon the hereſie of *Iuſtinian*, and the perſecution raiſed by his maintaining of the ſame. Now indeed this whole paſſage might juſtly be omitted, for, *ſublata cauſa tollitur effectus*; ſeeing *Iuſtinian* held no ſuch hereſie as hee is ſlandered withall, there neither was, nor could there bee any effects or conſequents of a cauſe not exiſtent: Yet will I not ſo ſleightly reject the Cardinals calumnie in this point, but fully examine, firſt the publike, and then the private miſchieſes, which hee, without all truth hath fancied, and objected againſt the Emperour.

37. The publike was *partly the ſubverſion and overthrow of the faith,* and partly the *decay of the Empire in the time, and under the government of Iuſtinian. Diſertus eſſe poſſet;* Hee that would in an elaborate ſpeech refute this calumnie of *Baronius*, might have an ample ſcope to diſplay all his Art and skill in this ſo large an argument: My purpoſe is onely to point at the ſeverall heads, and not expatiate at this time. Truly, the Cardinall could hardly have deviſed any calumny more eaſie to be refuted, or more evidently witneſſing his malicious and wilfull oppugning of the truth. I will not inſiſt on thoſe private teſtimonies: of *Procopius,*[a] *Iuſtinian ſeemeth to have beene advanced by God to that Imperiall dignitie, ut totum Imperium repararet,* that he might repaire and beautifie the whole Empire: Of *Otho*[b], *Iuſtinian being a moſt valiant and moſt Chriſtiā Prince, Imperiū quaſi mortuū reſuſcitavit,* did raiſe the Empire as it were from death to life, *and exceedingly repaired the Common-wealth being decayed:* Of *Gotofrid*[c], *The whole glory of God was repaired by his vertue, and the Church rejoyced in the ſtable peace which under him it injoyed:* Of *Wernerus*[d], *Hee was in all things moſt excellent, and by his juſt lawes, and wiſedome he governed the world; by his impiety he glorified God:* Of *Aimonius*[e], *He was a Catholike, a pious, a juſt Emperour; therefore all things proſpered under his hands.* I oppoſe to that Baronian calumny, the judgment of Pope *Agatho, and of the Romane Councell with him,* wherin this is expreſly witneſſed,[f] *His integritie in faith did much pleaſe God, & exalt the Chriſtian Common-wealth:* and againe[g], *His vertue and pietie, omnia in meliorem ordinem reſtauravit,* reſtored all things into a better ſtate and condition: All, both Church and Common-wealth, both the Civill and Eccleſiaſticall ſtate: he reſtored all. I oppoſe the ſixt generall Councell, that is, the judgement of the whole Church, in wch the *ſuggeſtions of Agatho,* evē in that point, according to the Cardinals doctrine[h], *are approved as uttered by S. Peter; yea, by the holy Ghoſt himſelf.* Theſe pregnant and irrefragable teſtimonies of ſo many, ſo holy, and divine witneſſes, are able, I ſay not to confute, but utterly to confound & overwhelme *Baronius* wth his deformed & decrepit calumnie.

38. If any further pleaſe to deſcend to particulars, whether hee caſt his eyes on the Church or Common-wealth, he ſhal ſee every Region, every Province, almoſt every City & Towne proclaming the honour of *Iuſtinian*: Beſides, his *happy appeaſing of thoſe manifold broyles,*

and

Marginal notes:
a *Lib.3.de ædif. Iuſtin.pa.433.*
b *Lib.5.ca.4.*
c *In chron. part. 16. in Iuſtiniā.*
d *An.504.*
e *De geſt.Fr.lib. 2.ca.8.*
f *In Epiſt.Agat. Act.4.Conc.6. pa.18.o.*
g *Ibid. in Epiſt. Synod.pa.22.*
h *Vid.ſup.bc̄c cap.nu.18.*

and suppressing sundry heresies which infested the Church in his dayes, among which this concerning the *Three Chapters* was the chiefe: How infinite monuments did he leave of his piety and zeale to Gods glory & the good of his Church, in building new, in repairing decaied Churches, reducing both to a most magnificent beauty? The Church of *Christ* called *Sophia*, built by him at Constantinople, was the mirrour of all Ages: Of it *Procopius*, an eye-witnesse, testifieth, [i] *that the magnificence thereof amazed those who saw it, but was incredible to those that saw it not:* the [k] *height of it mounted up into the heaven, the splendor of it was such, as if it received not* [l] *light from the Sun, but had it in it selfe; the roofe deckt with Gold, the pavement beset* [m] *with Pearle; the silver of the Quire onely contained foure* * *Myriads, that is, forty thousand pounds;* in so much that it is said [n] *to have excelled the Temple of Salomon.* Further, in the honour of the blessed Virgin hee builded every where so many houses, so stately and sumptuous throughout the Roman Empire, *that if you should contemplate but onely one of them, you would thinke (saith Procopius* [o]*) his whole raigne to have beene imployed in building that alone.* At *Constantinople* he builded three [p], one in *Blacernis,* another in *Pege,* a third in *Hierio:* besides others builded in honour of *Anna,* of *Zoa,* of *Michael,* of *Peter* and *Paul,* of *Sergius* and *Baccus,* *utrumque fulgore lapillorum Solem vincit,* either of which, by the brightnesse of precious stones, excelled the Sunne; of *Andrew,* *Luke* and *Tymothy,* of *Acatius,* of *Mocius,* of *Thirsis,* of *Theodorus,* of *Tecla,* of *Theodota:* *Hæc omnia ex fundamentis erexit,* All these he raised from the very ground and foundation: *and that at Constantinople; the beauty and dignity of which cannot by words bee expressed, by viewing be perlustrated.* Nor did he this to one onely Citie, he builded like magnificent Churches, at *Antioch* [q], at *Sebastia,* at *Nicopolis,* at *Theodosia,* at *Tzani,* at *Iustinianea* [r], where hee was borne, at *Ephesus* [s], at *Helena,* at *Nice,* at *Pythia,* at *Ierusalem,* so magnificent, *ut nullum aliud æquipare possit,* that none other may compare with it; at *Iericho,* at mount *Gerazim,* at mount *Sinai,* at *Theopolis,* at *Ægila* [t], *where they sacrificed to* Iupiter Hammon *and* Alexander *the great, even to that time;* at *Boreion,* at *Tripolis,* at *Carthage,* at the *Gades,* or *Hercules* pillers, which was the uttermost border of the known world in those dayes: So that one may truly say of him, *Imperium Oceano, famam qui terminat astris;* his piety and zeale reacheth as farre as the earth, his honour as high as the heaven. And yet have I said nothing at all of the *Monasteries, Zenodochies, Nosodochies,* and other like *Hospitals,* which, out of his most pious affection to God and Gods Church, he not onely erected, but inriched *with large patrimonies and possessions,* which for number are as I suppose equall, for expences greater, than the former: all the particulars whereof I referre to be read in *Procopius,* who considering, beside other matters, al these magnificent and sumptuous buildings, did truly say of *Iustinia* [u], *Nulla honorandi Dei satietas eum cepit,* he was never wearied, never satiate with honouring of God.

40. After the Church, wil it please you to take a view of the civil state & Empire. No mans tongue or pen can equall or come neare his acts, and most deserved praise. The whole Empire at the beginning of his reigne was in a maner spoyled & defaced. In the East, the Persias held

a great

Marginal notes (left):

[i] *Proc. lib. 1. de ædif. Iustin. pa. 425.*

[k] *Assurgit in altitudinem cæli. Ibid.*

[l] *Diceres locum illum non externo sole illuminari. Ibid.*

[m] *Pavimentum ex diver si coloris unionibus perfectum. Glic. Annal. part. 4.*

* *Myriadas 4. cælati argenti habuisse fertur. Proc. loc. cit.*

[n] *Hoc ædificio Solomonem esse superatum. Glic. loc. cit.*

[o] *Lib. 1.*

[p] *Ibid.*

[q] *Pro. lib. 2.*

[r] *Lib. 4.*

[s] *Lib. 5.*

[t] *Lib. 6. pa. 453.*

[u] *Lib. 1. pa. 424.*

a great part of Aſia; in the South, the Vandals poſſeſſed Africk; in the Weſt, the Goths uſurped Italy, and Rome it ſelfe; in the North, the Franks, Almanes, and other people withdrew Germany, France, and other Northerne Countries. *Iuſtinian*, finding the Empire thus torne aſunder on every ſide, freed it from all theſe enemies; and having moſt happily ſubdued, and gloriouſly triumphed over them all; by his victorious conqueſts, hee purchaſed thoſe manifold titles, which are ſo many Trophees, Creſts, and Enſignes of his immortall honour, to bee ſurnamed *Iuſtinian the Great* [h], *happy* [i], *renowned, victorious, and Triumphant Auguſtus, Alamanicus, Gothicus, Francicus, Germanicus, Anticus, Alanicus, Vandalicus, Africanus:* So at once he purchaſed both honor to himſelfe, and peace and tranquillity to the Empire. Neither did he this only by his conqueſts, and recovery of thoſe great Nations, which the Empire had loſt; but further alſo by his prudence hee ſo fortified them, being recovered, by building and repairing their ruinated Cities, by erecting Caſtles, Forts, and ſtrong places of munition; by furniſhing them all with the commodities of waters, of wals, of promontories, of havens, of bridges, of baths, of goodly buildings, and other matters, ſerving either for the neceſſity or pleaſure of habitation, that the whole Empire by his wiſedome and government was made, as it were, one great and ſtrong City, both commodious and delightfull to his owne ſubjects, and inexpugnable to his enemies : So in Media hee fortified Doras [k]; in Perſia, Siſauration; in Meſopotamia, Baros; in Syria, Edeſſa, and Callinicum; in Commagine, Zenobia; in Armenia, Martyropolis [l]; in the other Armenia, Theodoſiopolis; in Tzani, Burgunocie; *Totam* [m] *Europā inacceſſam reddidit;* he made the whole Country of Europe unconquerable : Taureſium, where he was borne, hee exceedingly fortified, and beautified, and called it Iuſtinianea; the like hee did to Vlpiana, and called it Iuſtinianea *ſecunda:* neare to it he builded Iuſtinopolis; he repaired all Epyrus, Ætolia, Acarnania; *Vniverſam Græciam,* he fortified al Greece : the like hee did in Theſſalia, and Euboea, *Quam penitus inexpugnabilem & invictā reddidit,* which hee made inexpugnable : The like hee did in Thrace, in Miſia, and in Scythia alſo; in Libya [n], in Numidia, and at the very Gades. Time would faile me to recount the one halfe of his famous buildings in this kinde, they may bee read in *Procopius,* who thus concludeth, *Nulli* [a] *dubium eſt,* no man may doubt, *but that Iuſtinian fortified the Romane State with munitions, and ſtrong holds, from the Eaſt unto the Weſt, and to the very utmoſt borders of the Empire:* Who further in admiration of theſe workes of *Iuſtinian* not onely cals [b] him, *Orbis reparatorem,* the repairer of the whole world, but adds this memorable ſaying of him, *That there hath* [c] *not beene any in all ages, nor among all men, more provident, more carefull for the publike good, than Iuſtinian, unto whom nothing was difficult, no not to bridle and confine the Seas, to levell the Mountaines, and overcome thoſe things which ſeeme impoſſible.*

40. Even *Evagrius* himſelfe, whoſe ſpite and ſpleene was (as I conjecture by ſome welwiller of the *Three Chapters,* of which there were divers in the time of *Gregory,* when *Evagrius* writ) incenſed againſt *Iuſtinian,* could not chuſe but teſtifie this. [d] *It is reported of him, that*

h *Iuſtiniani magni.Epiſt. Agath.et Synod. Rom. Act.4. conc.6.*
i *Jn præf.ad Inſtitut. Iuſtin.*

k *Inexpugnabilē hoſtibus effecit. Proc.lib.2.de ædif.Iuſt.*
l *Ibid.lib.3.*
m *Lib.4.*

n *Lib.6.*

a *Lib.6.pa.456.*

b *Lib.4.pa.439.*
c *Quapropter nemo contenderit, per omnem ætatem fuiſſe quempiam ex omnibus hominibus Iuſtiniano magis providum, & accuratiorem.Lib.4.pd.440.*
d *Evagr.lib.4. ca.18.*

hee reſtored anew, an hundreth and fifty Cities, which were either wholly o-
verthrowne, or exceedingly decayed, and that he beautified them with ſuch &
ſo great ornaments, with houſes both private and publike, with goodly walles,
with faire and ſumptuous buildings, and Churches, *ut nihil poſſit eſſe magni-
ficentius*, that nothing can bee more magnificent : So hee. And yet all
theſe Buildings, Munitions, Caſtles and Forts, are not comparable to
thoſe moſt wholeſome *Imperiall Lawes*, whereby hee moſt wiſely ordered & governed the whole Empire : that alone was a work of ſo great
value & excellency, that I may truly ſay, that all his victories & victorious triumphs over the Perſians, the Gothes, the Vandals, and other
nations, never gained ſo much honour unto him, as did that his more
than *Herculean* labour in compoſing and digeſting the lawes, to the
unſpeakeable benefit of the whole Chriſtian world : for as by his
victories and buildings, he reſtored but the materiall Cities and wals
thereof, ſo by this he repaired the men themſelves, and their mindes,
reducing them from rude and barbarous behaviour to civility and order, ſetting them in ſuch a conſtant forme of civill government, as all
Chriſtian Kingdomes ſince have not onely with admiration extolled,
but with moſt happy ſucceſſe embraced and followed.

4 1. Iudge now, I pray you, uprightly of the Cardinals dealing, who
declames againſt this Emperor, and reviles him in moſt odious terms,
as an *unjuſt, avaricious, ſacrilegious, tyrannicall perſon*, calling him *a dolt,
a foole, a mad-man, an heretike, an Antichriſt, a perſecutor of the faith, negligent of the civill, diſturber of the Eccleſiaſticall State, under whom the
Empire and Common-wealth decayed, and declined, the Church was oppreſſed, and the faith overthrowne* : Whereas it doth now appeare by
evidences of all ſorts, that hee was a Prince, not onely Catholike, pious, prudent, magnanimous, juſt, munificent, and moſt vigilant for the
good, both of the Church and Common-wealth, but ſo adorned with
the concurrence of all thoſe heroicall vertues, which have beene ſingle
in other men of great fame, as if in him we ſhould ſee the compleate
Idea of a worthy Emperour; hee being for politicall prudence, *Solon*;
for valour and victorious conqueſts, *Alexander*; for magnificence, *Auguſtus*; for his piety, conſtant love and zeale to the faith, *Conſtantine*,
Theodoſius or *Martian*; for multiplicity of labours, undertaken for the
good of the whole Empire, more indefatigable than *Hercules*; and for
ſupporting the whole fabricke of the Church and Chriſtian faith, a
very *Atlas; Cælum qui vertice fulcit.*

f *Rom.* 1 4. 4.
g 1 *Cor.* 13. 5.
h *In ipſo Dei
Verbi Sapientiæ
templo quotannis
magnificè me-
moriam ejus
celebrari, populi
univerſi conci-
one ad rem di-
vinam coacta.
Niceph. lib.* 17.
ca. 31.
i *Idem.*

4 2. There onely remaineth now the other effect, which is private:
which as it is the laſt, ſo is it the heavieſt puniſhment that *Baronius*
could wiſh unto *Iuſtinian*, and that is, *his adjudging him to the pit and
torments of hell*. Did he not feare the Apoſtles reproofe, either againſt
raſh and temerarious judgers, *Who f art thou that judgeſt another
mans ſervant ?* or againſt uncharitable cenſures, *Charity thinketh not e-
vill g, it rejoyceth not in iniquity, but rejoyceth in the truth*. why did not the
Cardinall harken rather to the judgement of the Church of *Conſtantinople ? Wherein the memory h of Iuſtinian was yearely celebrated, and that
with great pompe and ſolemnity in the Church of* Sophia, *in the time of divine ſervice, all the people being aſſembled.* The like celebrity i of his memory
was

was observed at Ephesus in the Church of Saint Iohn, *which he had builded*: Or if the authority of these particular Churches could not sway the Cardinall, seemed it a small matter unto him to contemne the consenting judgement of Pope *Agatho*, and his Romane Councell, which ranke him among the glorious and blessed Saints in heaven, with Saint *Constantine*, *Theodosius*, and *Martian*? yea, of the whole sixt generall Councell, *wherein his memory is so often called, holy, blessed, divine, happy, and the like?* & if his memory, then much more himselfe is happy and blessed; for to the just onely doth that honor belong; *The* [k] *memoriall of the just shall be blessed, but the name of the wicked shall rot.* To which purpose that is specially to be observed which *Nicephorus* addeth in plaine termes of the sixt generall Councell, *Iustinianum* [l] *beata quiete dignatur*, It placeth *Iustinian* in blessed rest and peace: and againe, *Semper eum qui in Sanctis est Iustinianum dicunt*, That general Councell ever calleth *Iustinian* one who is a Saint, and among the Saints. Adde to all these, that seeing, by the Cardinals confession, the Epistles of *Agatho*, *In omnibus* (and therefore even in that which he saith of this holy Emperour, *That hee is a blessed Saint, venerable in all Nations*) are to be imbraced as divine Oracles; it may bee truly concluded, that *Iustinian*, not onely by the testimonies of mortall men, and of all nations, but even by the voyce of God himselfe is blessed; and hath ever since his death, and doth now rest, and raigne with God. When by the unpartiall judgement of S. *Agatho*, of the Romane Synod, of the whole sixt generall Councell, of all Nations, yea, of God himselfe, *Iustinian* is proclamed to be a venerable Saint, now resting & raigning with God in heaven: who is *Baronius*, a man of yesterday, that after a thousand years possession of that heavenly rest, he should unsaint him, dethrone him, and thrust him downe to the lowest pit and most hideous torments of hell? I'st not enough for that *Hildebrandicall* generation to devest Kings & Emperors of their earthly diadems, unless in the pride of their hearts climbing up into heaven, they thrust them out thence also, & deprive them of their crowns of immortality; & eternal glory?

43. And yet were there neither Historian nor Pope, nor Provinciall, nor Generall Councell, to testifie this felicity of *Iustinian* unto us; that very text, out of which, being maimed, the Cardinall sucked poyson, and collected *His* death & damnation, doth so forcible prove the beatitude of *Iustinian*, that it alone may bee sufficient in this cause. The Cardinall cites but one part of the text, but the whole doth manifest his fraud and malicious collection. Apoc. 14. 13: *Blessed are the dead which die in the Lord, from hence forth; even so saith the Spirit, for they rest from their labours, and opera illorum sequuntur illos*, their workes follow them: which last words the Cardinall onely alleageth, and applyeth them to *Iustinian*. Now who are Those, that are meant by, *Their works, and follow Them?* who are those *Them*, that the Spirit meaneth in that text? Out of al doubt those selfe-same of whom before he spake; *Them, that dye in the Lord, Them, that are blessed, and rest from their labours*; Of *Them*, the Spirit there saith, *Opera illorum*, Their workes follow *Them*: Seeing then the Cardinall confesseth this text to belong to *Iustinian*; and himselfe applyeth it unto him, it certainly hence followeth, that

k Pro. 10. 7.

l Loc. cit.

Hh 3 *Iustinian*

Iustinian is of their number, who dye in the Lord, and are blessed: for of *Them*, and *Them* onely doth the holy Ghost speake in that text, saying, *They rest from their labours, and* Their *workes follow* Them. So hard it is for the Cardinal to cite or say ought against *Iustinian*, which doth not redound to the Emperours honour, and the Cardinals owne ignominie.

44. But let us suppose the words to bee generall, as being uttered alone, without any reference to that text, they may bee truly affirmed both of the good & bad : There cannot be found in al Scripture more faire evidence, nor a more authentike Charter for the happy estate of any one in particular that lived since the Apostles times, then is this for *Iustinian* : For what were those *workes which did accompanie and follow Iustinian?* Truely the workes of sincere faith, of fervent zeale to GOD, of love to the Church and Children of God, the workes of piety, of prudence, of justice, of fortitude, of munificence, of many other heroicall vertues : with these, as with a garment and chaine of pure Gold, *Iustinian* being decked, was brought unto the Bridegroom; every decree made, or ratified by him for confirming the faith; every *Anathema* denounced against heresies, & heretiks, particularly those against *Vigilius*, & al that defend him, that is, against *Baronius*, and all who defend the Popes infallibility in defining causes of faith; everie Temple or Church, every Monastery and Hospitall, every City and Towne, everie Bridge, Haven and High-way, every Castle, Fort, and Munition, whether made or repaired by him, tending either immediately to the advancement of Gods service, or to the maintaining or relieving of Gods servants, or strengthning the Empire against his and Gods enemies : every booke in the Digest, Code, and Authentikes; every Title, yea, every law in any title, whereby either the Christian faith and religion, or peaceable order and tranquillity, have beene either planted, or propagated, or continued, either in the Church or Common-wealth : all these, and every one of them, and many other the like, which I cannot either remember, or recount, are like so many Rubies, Chrysolites, and Diamonds in the costly garment, or so many linkes in that golden chaine of his faith and vertues. Seeing they, *who offer but one mite into the treasury of the Lord,* or give *but one cup of cold water to a Prophet, shall not want a reward;* O! what a weight of eternity and glory shall that troope of vertues and traine of good workes obtaine at his hands, who *rewardeth indeed every man according to their workes,* but withall rewardeth them infinitely above all the dignity or condignity of their workes.

45. If *Iustinian* and those who are beautified with so many vertues and glorious works, be, as the Card. judgeth, tormented in hell, belike the Cardinall himselfe hoped by workes contrary unto these, by workes of infidelity, of impiety, of maligning the Church, of reviling the servants of GOD, of oppugning the faith, of Patronizing heresie, yea, that fundamental heresie which overthroweth the whole Catholike faith, and brings in a totall Apostasie from the faith; by these hee hoped to purchase, and in condignity to merit the felicity of the Kingdome of Heaven: This being the track and beaten path where-

in

in they walke, and by which they aspire to immortality, what *Constantine* [m] sayd once to *Acesius* the Novatian, the same may be sayd to *Baronius* and his consorts, *Erigito tibi scalam Baroni, & ad cœlum solus ascendito*, Keepe that Ladder unto your selves, and by it doe you alone climbe up into heaven. But well were it with them, and thrice happy had the Cardinall beene, if with a faithfull and upright heart towards God, he could have said of *Iustinian* the words of *Balaam*, *Let me dye the death of the righteous, and let my last end be like his.* His life being led in piety, and abounding in good workes, hee now enjoyeth the fruit thereof, felicity and eternall rest in *Abrahams* bosome: As for the Cardinall who hath so malignantly reviled him, himselfe can now best tell whether he doth not cry and pray, *Father Abraham have mercy on me, and send Iustinian that he may dip the tip of his finger in water and coole my tongue*: or sing that other note [n] unto his fellowes concerning this Emperour ; *Wee fooles thought his life to be madnesse, and his end to bee without honour, but now is he numbred among the children of God, and his lot is among the Saints : Therefore wee have erred from the way of truth, and wearied our selves in the wayes of wickednesse and destruction ; we have gone through deserts where there lay no way, but as for the way of the Lord wee have not knowne it.*

m *Socr. lib.1. ca.7.*

n *Wisd. 5.4.5.*

Cap. XXI.

How Baronius *revileth* Theodora *the Empresse, and a refutation of the same.*

1.   Ext the Emperour, let us see how dutifully the Cardinall behaveth himselfe towards the Empresse *Theodora.* A small matter it is with him in severall places to call her an [a] *impious*, an *hereticall* [b], a *sacrilegious* [c], a *furious* [d] *hereticall* woman, a *patrone* [e] *of heretikes*, and the like. Heare and consider how he stormeth but in one place [f] against her : *These so great mischiefes did that most wicked woman beginne ; sh: became to her husband another Eve obeying the serpent, a new Dalila to Samson, striving by her subtiltie to weaken his strength ; another Herodias, thirsting after the blood of most holy men; a wanton mayd of the High Priest, perswading Peter to deny Christ.* But this is not enough, *Sugillare ipsam*, with these termes to flout her, who exceedeth all women in impiety, *let her have a name taken from Hell, let her be called Alecto, or Megera, or Tisiphone, a Citizen of hell, a childe of Devills, ravished with a satanicall spirit, driven up and downe with a devillish gad-bee, an enemy of concord and peace purchased with the blood of Martyrs.* Thus the Cardinall: who tells us afterwards how when *Vigilius* came to *Constantinople*, she contended long with him for to have *Anthimus* restored, in so much that *Vigilius* was forced to smite her as from heaven, with the thunderbolt of Excommunication [g], whereupon she [h] shortly dyed. Here is the tragicall end which the Cardinall hath made of her.

a *Impiæ Theodoræ Augustæ. an. 535. nu. 59.*
b *Hereticæ fæmine impiæ Theodoræ. ibid. nu. 60.*
c *Sacrilega fæmina molita est. an. 536. nu. 123*
d *A furente hæretica fæmina excitata. an. 538 nu. 9.*
e *Ipsa hereticorum, Acephalorum, Severianorum, Eutychianorum patrona: an. 547. nu. 49.*
f *An. 535. nu. 63*
g *Sententiam excommunicationis instixit. et, Excommunicationis sententia fulminis instar cœlitus emissi prostravit. an. 547. nu. 49. & 50.*
h *Theodoram à Vigilio sanciatam dito jaculo anathematis, haud diu post ulciscente numine, est insequutus interitus. an. 548. nu. 24.*

2. Now

2. Now I would not have any think that I intend wholly to excuſe the Empreſſe; ſhe had her paſſions and errors; as who hath not? and as *Liberatus* [i] and *Evagrius* [k] ſhew, ſhe tooke part with the oppugners of the Councell of *Chalcedon*: which was for ſome time true; ſhee being, as it ſeemes, ſeduced by *Anthimus*, whom for a while ſhe laboured to have reſtored to the See of *Conſtantinople*: though afterwards, as *Victor Tununenſis* teſtifieth, ſhe being better informed, joyned with the Emperor in condemning the *Three Chapters*, and ſo in truth, in defending the Councell of *Chalcedon*, though *Victor* thought the contrarie. And of this minde in condemning the *three Chapters* ſhee was, as by *Victor* is evident, ſome yeares before *Vigilius* came to *Conſtantinople*. Her former error, ſeduction, and labour for *Anthimus*, I will not ſeeke to leſſen, or any way excuſe. But though ſhe were worthy of blame, was it fit for the Cardinall ſo baſely to revile her, and in ſuch an unſeemly and undutifull manner, to diſgorge the venome of his ſtomacke upon an Empreſſe? *tanta ne animis cæleſtibus iræ,* who would have thought ſuch rancour and poiſon to have reſted in the breſt of a Cardinall? But there was, you may be ſure, ſome great cauſe which drew from the Cardinall ſo many unſeemly ſpeeches againſt the Empreſſe; and though hee would bee thought to doe all this onely out of zeale to the truth, which *Anthimus* the heretike oppugned, yet if the depth of the Cardinalls heart were ſounded, it will appeare, that his ſpite againſt her, was for condemning the *Three Chapters*, which Pope *Vigilius* in his *Conſtitution* defendeth; *Anthimus* and his cauſe is but a pretence and colour; the *Apoſtolicall Conſtitution*, the hereſies of the Neſtorians, decreed and defined therein, that is the true marke at which the Cardinall aymeth; neither Emperour nor Empreſſe, nor Biſhop, nor Councell, nor any may open their mouth againſt that Conſtitution, which toucheth them *in capite*, but they ſhall be ſure to heare and beare away as harſh and helliſh termes from *Baronius*, as if they had condemned the *Trent* Councell it ſelfe. Had *Theodora* defended the *Three Chapters*, as *Vigilius* in his *Conſtitution* did, the Cardinall would have honoured her as a *Melpomene, Clio,* or *Vrania*; becauſe ſhe did not that, ſhe muſt be nothing but *Alecto, Megæra*; or *Tiſiphone*, and they are too good names for her.

3. If one deſired to ſet forth her praiſe, there wants not teſtimonies of her dignity, and honour. *Conſtantinus Manaſſes* [l] ſaith, that ſhe was *Iiſdem addicta cum marito ſtudiis, & iiſdem prædita moribus*: that ſhe ſo well conſorted to her huſband, *that ſhee was addicted to the ſame ſtudies, indued with the ſame manners as he was*: That *Iuſtinian* himſelfe calleth her [m], *reverendiſſimam conjugem*, his moſt reverend wife, given unto him by God: adding that he tooke her as a partner with him of his counſells in making his lawes, and after her death he [n] calleth her *Auguſtam piæ memoriæ,* Empreſſe of holy memorie, as doe alſo and very often the ſixt general [o] Councell: an unfit title to be given to an heretike, or a fury, either by a holy generall Councell, or by a Chriſtian orthodox Emperour, who was ſo earneſt with the fift Councell to condemne all that ſhould obſtinately perſiſt in the condemning of the true faith, and dye out of the communion of the holy Church. Divers the

i Liberat.ca.21, 22.
k Evagr.lib.4. ca.10.

l In annal.ſuis. pa.87.
m Participem conſilij ſumentes eam quæ à Deo eſt data nobis, reverendiſſimam conjugem. Novel.8.ca.1.
n In pragmatica ſanctione Iuſtin. ca.1.
o Ad Iuſtinianũ & Theodoram divæ memoriæ. Conc.gen.6.Act. 14.pa.73. Biſ ita ait Conciliũ. & , Ad Theodoram piæ memoriæ quondam Auguſtam.Act.3 pa.114

the like testimonies might be alledged, if one would labour to extoll that Empresse, as the Cardinall hath strained his wit and pen to vilifie and disgrace her. But because that is not my purpose at this time, I would onely observe how unjustly the Cardinall hath taxed her in respect of three severall times, and three speciall matters.

4. The first concernes the placing of *Anthimus*, an Eutychean heretike in the See of *Constantinople*, which Baronius [p] saith was done by *Iustinian*, *occultis insidiis Theodorae*, *by the cunning and trecherous meanes of Theodora*; and thereupon hee breakes [q] into many uncivill termes. Wherein the Cardinalls spite and indiscretion is utterly unexcusable: for whatsoever *Anthimus* was secretly and in his heart, he at that time when he was placed in the See, and afterwards also, outwardly shewed and professed himselfe to bee a Catholike; he was a wolfe, as the *Archimandrites* [r] and Monkes of *Constantinople*, *Ierusalem*, and other parts of the East doe witnesse, in their synodall Epistles to *Agapetus*; but he covered himselfe, and his wolvish conditions, under sheepes clothing. Againe, hee [s] and others, *religionis pietatem dissimulantes, counterfeiting the piety of religion*, thrust themselves into the Church. *Anthimus* lived not an Euangelicall (that is, sincere,) *sed fictam vitam*, *but a fained and hypocriticall life*, manifesting forth to all men the counterfeit continency of his government, and the shew of piety which by it he made. The Emperour [t] testifieth the same; *Anthimus forsooke and refused those true doctrines which hee often seemed to love, simulans sequi sanctas quatuor Synodos, faining himselfe to follow the foure holy Synods.* The whole generall Councell under [u] *Mennas* in their definitive sentence against *Anthimus* do expresly witnesse the same, *He counterfeited himselfe to embrace and receive the foure Councells*, and he kept them *in dipticis*. Againe, he used *deceptibilibus rationibus ad ejus Serenitatem, deceitfull and cozening meanes before the Emperour*, promising to doe all things which the *Apostolike* See (then Catholike) did decree, and hee writ to the most holy Patriarchs; *Se sequi per omnia Apostolicam sedem*, *that he did in all things follow the Apostolike See*: when *Anthimus* made so holy, and orthodoxall a profession, better than which no Catholike could desire; what marvell if by this faire shew, and outward orthodoxy, hee deceived both the Emperour, and the Empresse, and the whole Church? They were not; nor could they looke into his heart; it was their duty to judge him to bee such in deed, as he shewed and professed himselfe to be, a Catholike Bishop: and taking him for such, they placed him in that high Patriarchall See. Did not *Constantine* the great the like, and without any just blame or reprehension, receiving into great favour *Eusebius* of *Nicomedia*, and others, though inwardly and in heart most pestilent Arians, yet in outward profession orthodoxall, and embracers of the Nicene faith? Nay, what if *Baronius* himselfe acknowledge, that neither *Theodora* nor *Iustinian*, advanced *Anthimus* the heretike; but *Anthimus* then seeming, and being in their judgement a Catholike? Heare I pray you his owne words [x], *The Empresse favoured Anthimus, uti orthodoxo, as an orthodoxall Bishop*: and *Iustinian* sent a Constitution to him, *ut orthodoxū Antistitem, as to an orthodoxal Bishop. He did* [y] *outwardly professe the Catholike faith, but inwardly*

was

[p] *Iustinianus Augustam conjugem audiens, monstrum horrendum in sedem Pontificiam provehi. an.535. nu. 60.*

[q] *Ibid. nu. 62. & 63.*

[r] *Libell. Archimand. et Monac. ad Agapetum in Conc. Constantinop. sub Menna act. 1. pa. 426.a.*

[s] *Pa. eadem. b.*

[t] *Iustin. Constitutio contra Severum, Anthimum. &c. quae extat post Conc. sub Menna, pa. 469.a.*

[u] *Sent. Synodi contra Anthimū act. 4. pa. 438. a.*

[x] *an. 535. nu. 62.*

[y] *an. eod. nu. 59.*

enemies (that is the Gothes;) was therefore God angry for that sentence against the *Acephali*? Apply this reason to *Vigilius*, and his time, and it is not onely untrue, but unfit to the purpose of *Gregory* : for before *Vigilius* his comming to *Constantinople*, not only *Vitiges* the Goth possessed *Rome*, (from whom *Bellisarius* in the time of *Silverius* recovered it) and made great havocke in *Italy* ; but *Totilas* [n] also (before *Vitiges* came) besieged it so hard, that by reason of the famine they were driven not onely to eate mice, and dogs, but even dung also, and last of all one to eate up another: and that same yeare *Totilas* tooke *Rome*, sacked it, and had purposed utterly to have abolished it, and burnt it to ashes, but that *Bellisarius* by his most prudent and fortunate perswasions, staid him from that barbarous immanity. Now seeing not onely the siege, but captivity of *Rome* was after the comming of that Pope to *Constantinople*, and sentence against *Theodora*, of whom *Gregory* speaketh, it must needs be hee meant Pope *Agapetus*, whose sentence all the foresaid calamities follow ; and not *Vigilius*, [o] before whose comming to *Constantinople Rome* was besieged by *Totilas*, and taken also before the sentence, if it was (as by *Anastasius* is to be gathered) not denounced till the second yeare after *Vigilius* his comming thither. Neither onely had the reason of *Gregory* beene untrue, but most unfit for his purpose, had he meant *Vigilius* in this place : for hee clearly intends such a calamity as hapned before the condemning of the *three Chapters*, but after the condemning of the *Acephali*. Now it is certaine by the Acts of the fift Councell, and by the Emperours testimony, that as the Easterne Bishops, so also *Vigilius* presently after he came to *Constantinople* consented to condemne the *three Chapters*, yea condemned them by a *Pontificall* decree and judgement, and continued in that minde till the time of the fift Councell ; at which time by the general Synod they were also condemned. *Gregory* then should have spoken against himselfe, had hee meant *Vigilius*, and his comming to *Constantinople*, in saying that after the sentence of *Vigilius* against *Theodora*, the City was besieged and taken, (as it was once againe indeed taken by *Totilas* [p] in the 23. yeare of *Iustinus* :) for his adversaries to whom he writ, being defenders of the *three Chapters*, would have replyed against him, that this calamity befell them from the very same cause ; seeing both the Easterne Bishops and the Pope consented in that doctrine of condemning of the *three Chapters*. Thus it appeareth not by surmises and conjectures, but by certaine and evident proofe, that the text of *Gregory* is corrupted, or else that *Gregory* himselfe was mistaken therein, (which in a matter so neare his dayes wee may not thinke) and so that it was not *Vigilius*, but *Agapetus* whom *Gregory* intended to denounce that sentence against the *Acephali*, or *Theodora*, of which *Baronius* maketh such boast, and commends with such great ostentation, that thereby he might make the Empresse who was a condemner of the *three Chapters*, more odious, and strengthen that fiction and fabulous tale of *Anastasius*, that *Vigilius* contended with *Iustinian* and *Theodora* about *Anthimus*.

a *Totilas Romam contendit, quam statim obsedit, Proc. lib. 3. de bell. Goth. pa. 360.*

o *Vigilius venit Constantinopolin. an. 12. belli Gothic. Proc. lib. eodem. pa. 364. Romam obsedit Totilas. an. 11. ejusdem belli. lib. eodem. pa. 359. & seq.*

p *Proc. lib. eodē 3. an. 15. belli Goth. pa. 394.*

CAP.

CAP. XXII.

How Baronius *declameth against* the cause it selfe of the Three Chapters, *and a refutation thereof.*

1. *Aronius* not content to wrecke his spite upon the
Emperour and Empresse in such uncivill man-
ner as you have seene, carpes in the next place
at the very cause it selfe of the *three Chapters.*
What did Vigilius, saith hee [a], *offend, in appoin-*
ting that men should be silent and say nothing untill
the future Synod, of this cause of the three Chap-
ters ? which if it could have beene, *potius perpe-*
tuo erat silentio condemnanda, sopienda, sepelienda, atque penitus extinguen-
da ; was rather to be condemned to perpetuall silence, to be buried and utterly
extinguished. Againe [b], *I doe never feare to avouch that it had beene much*
better that the Church had remained without these controversies (about the
three Chapters) *nec unquam de his aliquis habitus esset sermo,* and that there
had never beene one word spoken of them. Thus *Baronius.*

a *Bar.an.547.*
nu.48.

b *an.553.n.239*

2. What thinke you moved the Cardinall to have such an immortall hatred to this cause; as to wish the condemning, buriall, and utter
extinguishing of those controversies ? What more hurt did this to
the Church, than the question about ὁμίον, about ϑεοτόκος, or about the
opinion of *Eutiches?* Very great calamity, saith *Baronius* [c], insued upon
this controversie; both in the East and West. True, it did so: and so
here did, and far greater and longer about the controversie of ὁμίον :
and more againe than that; upon the question whether the *Gospell* or
Paganisme should prevaile: and yet by moving those controversies
was the faith propagated, the truth of Christ spred abroad, the
blood of Martyrs was made the seed of the Gospell. No affliction,
calamity, or persecution, is a just cause either to wish that there had
never beene any such controversie, or to forsake the truth of God,
when the controversie is moved. It was an excellent saying of the
Egyptian Bishops in the Councell of *Chalcedon* [d], *Christianus neminem*
timet, a Christian feareth no mortall man ; *si homines timerentur, martyres*
non essent, if men should be feared, there would be no Martyrs. But the truth
is, it was not as *Baronius* fancieth, the controversie it selfe, nor the disputing and debating thereof, that caused so great calamities in the
East and West; that is *non causa pro causa ;* the peevishnesse and perversenesse of wicked men maintaining heresies, and oppugning the
truth, that was the true cause thereof. The controversie it selfe, if you
well marke it, was very beneficiall to the Church. *Oportet hæreses* [e] *esse,*
there must be heresies among you, that they which are approved might bee
knowne. Every heresie is a probation and tryall of mens love to God,
and his truth, whether they esteeme it more than their honours, plea-
sures, and their owne wilfull conceits ; and the greater the heresie is,
and the further it spreads, it is still a greater tryall. *Heretikes,* saith S.
Austen [f], *doe much profit the Church, though they be out of the Church, not*

c *Ibidem.*

d *Act.1.pa.8.*

e 1 *Cor.11.19.*

f *Lib.de vera*
relig.ca.8.

by teaching the truth which they doe not know, but by ftirring up thofe who are more carnall Catholikes, to feeke, and thofe who are more fpirituall, to defend and manifeft the truth. This triall and probation of men (if I miftake not) was never fo great in any controverfie or queftion, as in this of the *three Chapters*. Firft, it fifted and tryed *Vigilius* to the full, and tryed him to be a wether-cocke in faith, an heretike, and a defender of herefies even by his *Apoftolicall* authority. Next, it fifted out divers notable conclufions: as firft, that which I think was never before that tryed; that not onely the Pope, but the *Apoftolike* See alfo, to wit, the Romane Church, and with it the Wefterne Churches, all at once adhered to herefie, and forfooke the truth, and that even after it was decreed, and judged by the generall approved Councell; and fo it proved both Pope and Romane Church to be properly hereticall, the Eafterne Churches conftantly upholding the truth at that time; it fhewed that the Catholike faith was tied neither to the Chair, nor Church of *Rome*. Another conclufion then tryed, was that either perfons, or Churches, may not onely diffent from the Pope and the Romane Church, and that in a caufe of faith judicially defined by the Pope with a Synod, but may renounce communion with them, and yet remaine Catholikes, and in the unity of the Catholike Church; the Pope, the Wefterne Church, and all that adheered unto them being then by forfaking the Catholike faith, *Heretikes*, and by forfaking the unity of the Church, *Schifmatikes*.

3. Neither onely was this controverfie a triall to them in that age, a tryall of their faith, love to God, charity to the Church, obedience to the Emperour, but it is as great a triall even in thefe our dayes, and ever fince that doctrine of the Popes *infallibility* in caufes of faith hath beene defined and condemned. By this controverfie, moft happly decided by the generall Councell, all that hold the Popes definitions of faith to be *infallible*, that is, all that are Papifts, or members of the prefent Church of Rome, they are all hereby tryed to defend this *Apoftolicall Conftitution* of *Vigilius*, that is, to maintaine all the blafphemies of the Neftorians, to deny the Catholike faith, the doctrine of the Apoftles, of the primative Church, of the fift generall Councell; & fo to be not only *heretikes*, but *convicted, anathematized*, and *condemned heretikes*, by the judgement of a generall approved Councell, and fo by the confenting judgement of the Catholike Church. Further yet there is a tryall of them, whether upon that ground or foundation of the Popes *infallibility*, they will build up and maintaine any other doctrine, or *pofition* of faith, or religion; if they doe (as indeed every point of the Romifh faith and Religion relyeth upon that) they are againe hereby tryed to be hereticall, not onely in the *foundation*, but in every *pofition* and doctrine of their faith and religion, which relyes upon that *foundation*.

4. This was it which netled *Baronius*, and extorted from him thofe earneft and affectionate wifhes, that this controverfie had never beene heard of, nor mentioned in the world: he faw what a tryall was like to be made by it of men, of doctrines, of Churches, of the Pope himfelfe, and their whole Romifh Church; and feeing that tryall, he never

ver ceafed to fay, that it had beene much better that this controverfie had never beene moved, nor fpoken of; for fo they had avoided this moft notable triall. Bleffed be God, for that it pleafed him in the infinite depth of his unfpeakable wifedome to caufe this controverfie to be ventilated, and difcuffed to the utmoft; that among many other tryals, this might be one of the *Antichriftian Synagogue*, to try them even untill the very deftruction of Antichrift. It is for heretikes whofe errors and obftinacy is tryed, and difcovered to the world; it is for them, I fay, to wifh that the controverfies about Arianifme, Neftorianifme, Eutycheanifme, and the like, had never beene moved; they had fcaped the juft cenfures and anathemaes by that meanes. But Catholikes have caufe to rejoyce and triumph in fuch controverfies, by which, both the truth which they maintaine, is made more refplendent and victorious, themfelves, and their faith tryed to be like refined gold, the Church thereby is quieted, the truth propagated, herefies confounded, and the glory of Almighty God, much more magnified, and prayfed.

CAP. XXIII.

How Baronius *revileth both* the Imperiall Edict of *Iuftinian,* and Theodorus B. of Cæfarea; *and a refutation of the fame.*

 1. Eeing now, notwithftanding the wifhing of *Baronius,* this controverfie could not be buried, (it ought him and all ill-willers of it a greater fhame than that) in the next place let us fee how he declameth both againft the Emperors *Edict,* whereby thefe *three Chapters* were condemned, & *Theodorus Bifh. of Cæfarea,* who (as he faith) was the author & penner of that Edict. The Edict it felf he calleth firft, *Seminarium* [a] *diffentionū, a feed-plot of fedition,* which was never made upon a good occafion, nor had any good end. And not content herevith, he tells [b] us out of *Facundus, that it is contrary to the faith, yea even to that faith which Iuftinian himfelfe profeffed as orthodoxall:* to which effect alfo *Baronius* himfelfe faith [c] *that the Emperours Edict was fet forth contrary to the three Chapters of the moft holy Councell of Chalcedon.* But he fpecially feekes to difgrace it by the author of it, for though it was publifhed by *Iuftinian,* yet faith he [d], *it was written, and that craftily by heretikes and adverfaries to the truth;* by the [e] Origenifts, and in particular by [f] *Theodorus* Bifhop of *Cæfarea,* one gratious [g], potent, and familiar with the Emperour: and for proofe of all this the Cardinall citeth *Liberatus* [h], *Facundus,* and *Vigilius.*

2. Having thus declared *Theodorus* to be the author and writer of the *Edict;* Baronius then rageth againft *Theodorus,* as if he were to act *vetere comœdiam,* or according to the Proverbe, *ex plauftro,* to raile out of a cart againft him, calling him *factious* [i], *fraudulēt* [k], *impudēt* [l], *a moft wicked* [m], *hereticall, fchifmaticall, headftrong Origenift,* the ring-leader of

the

Marginal notes:
2 *An.534.n.21*
b *An.546.n.9.*
c *Ibid.n.8.*
d *Edere fanctiones fibi arrogat (Iuftin.) quas dolofe confcripfiffent heretici. an.546.n.41. Egerunt callide adverfarii veritatis, & c.ibid. nu.9.*
e *Ingenue profeffus eft, Origeniftarum ftudiis ea fuiffe ab Imperatore promulgata.ibid.nu.49.*
f *Illud à Theodoro confcriptū ediKum fuo nomine Iuftin. promulgavit. ibid. nu.8.*
g *an.538.nu.85*
h *an.546. nu.9. & an.524.nu. 21.& alibi.*
i *Iuftin.factioforum ftudijs fe inftruit.an.550. nu.14.*
k *Hominem vafrum. an.551. nu.4.& 564. nu.7.*
l *Ejus gratia factus impudens ibid.nu.3.*
m *Theodorum illum nequiffimum quem zirum in modum faviffe oftendimus Origenis herefibus. an.564.nu.6. & occultum hereticum, maxifeftum fchifmaticum.an.551. nu.5. Præceps Origenifta. an. eod. nu.4.*

n *Non Origenis tantum errorum affecla, fed & Eutychiane blafphemie vehementiſſimus propugnator. an. 564. nu. 7.*
o *Ita mifer (Iu-ſtinianus) cæcus cæcum (Theodo-rum) sectans, cũ ipſo pariter mer-gitur in profun-dum. an. 564. nu. 7. egit aut de hærefi Aph-thardochitarum.*
p *Inq; facrilegum (Theodarum) pfeudoepifcopum, izzio ty annum infurgit, in per-verforem legum, everforem juriũ. an. 551. nu. 5.*
q *Qui impera-tori omnium illi malorum caufa fuit. an. 551. n. 3*
s *Hic igitur ne-fandiſſimus, to-tius Ecclefie peſtis. an. 564. nu. 7.*

the Origenifts, one marvelloufly addicted to the herefie of *Origen*: nor onely a fervant to *Origens* errors, *but alfo* n *a moſt earneſt defender of the Eutychean blafphemy*; nor onely fo, *but plunged* o *in the herefie of the Aphthardokites, or Phantaſtickes,* and like a blinde guide leading the blinde Emperour into that ditch of herefie: *a facrilegious* p *perfon, a pfeudobifhop, a tyrant, a perverter of lawes, an overthrower of right, the* q *au-thor of all mifchiefe to the Empire, the very* r *plague of the whole Church:* Thus and much more doth *Baronius* utter againſt *Theodorus*, by whom being fo unworthy an author, hee would difgrace the *Edict* it felfe, which he writ, though the Emperour publiſhed it.

3. Let us firſt begin with that moſt untrue and malicious calum-ny of *Baronius*, that the Emperor publiſhed his Edict againſt the *three Chapters* of the Councell of *Chalcedon.* Truly the Cardinall ſhould and might moſt truly have faid the quite contrary, that he publiſhed his Edict for defence not onely of the *three,* but of every Chapter, of every poſition, of every decree of the Councell of *Chalcedon.* The *three Chapters* which that Imperiall Edict, and after it the fift Councell, and the whole Catholike Church condemneth, were not Chapters of the Councell of *Chalcedon,* but three impious poſitions, aſſertions, or (as they were by an equivalent word called) Chapters, which here-tikes, fpecially the Neſtorians, collected, and falfely boaſted to bee taught by the Councell of *Chalcedon*; whereas in very truth the hold-ing of any one of them (much more of them all) is the overthrow of the whole Councell at *Chalcedon,* yea of the whole Catholike faith: that Councell contradicteth and condemneth them all, no leſſe than the fift Councell, which as *Gregory* truly faith, is *in omnibus fequax,* it doth in every point follow and confent unto the Councell of *Chalce-don.* The like may be faid of that which out of *Facundus, Baronius* ob-ferveth, and citeth as a proofe of his faying, that the Emperours *Edict* is repugnant and contrary to the orthodoxall faith. *Baronius* will ſtill keepe his old wont in applauding *Vigilius* and the defenders of the *Three Chapters.* For if the *Edict* condemning them be contrary, then is the defence of them confonant to the faith, and then not the *Impe-riall Edict of Iuſtinian,* but the Pontificall *Conſtitution* of *Vigilius* muſt be approved as orthodoxall. And what is this elfe, but to condemne the judgement of the fift generall Councell, of Pope *Pelagius, Grego-ry,* and all Popes after them, of all generall Councells following it; in a word, to contradict, and utterly condemne the confenting judge-ment of the whole Church, for the fpace of 11. hundred yeares? they all approve the determination of the fift Councell, and it fo fully con-fenteth with the *Edict* in condemning the *Three Chapters,* that in their definitive fentence they differ very little in words, but in fubſtance and fenfe nothing at all from the *Emperours Edict,* which caufed *Bini-us* to fay, the Edict of the Emperour was approved by the Pope and the Councell: So Catholike and orthodoxall is it, fo advifedly and orthodoxally penned. To feeke no further proofe, *Baronius* himfelfe was fo infatuated in this caufe, that he oftentimes confuteth his owne fayings: for himfelfe gives a moſt ample and moſt obfervable teſtimo-

s an. 534. nu. 21.

ny of this *Edict,* and of the orthodoxy thereof, faying s of it, *Eſt ve-luti*

luti Catechismus, & fidei Catholicæ exacta declaratio; this Edict of *Iustini-an* is as it were a Catechisme, or an exact declaration of the Catholike faith, and an exact discussing of the *Three Chapters,* which were after-wards long controversed in the Church. So untrue is that his first ca-lumnie against the *Edict,* whereby hee would perswade, that it is contrary to certaine Chapters of the holy Councell of *Chalcedon,* or as *Facundus* plainly, but most untruely affirmeth, contrary to the Ca-tholike faith.

4. For the second calumnie, that his Edict was a seminary of sedi-tion, *Baronius* might as justly condemne the decree of *Nice,* of *Ephe-sus,* of *Chalcedon,* yea, the very Scripture it selfe, and preaching of the Gospell; Christ himselfe is set as *signum [t] contradictionis, as a butt of* t *Luk.2.34.* *contradiction,* against which they will ever bee striving, and shooting their arrowes of opposition, sedition, & contention : himselfe [u] saith, u *Luk.12.49.* *I am come to set fire on the earth, and what would I but that it should bee kindled :* and againe, *Suppose yee that I am come to give peace on the earth, I tell you nay, but rather division;* and no sooner was the Gospell preached abroad in the world, but that which our Saviour foretold them [x], came to passe; *Brother shall deliver up brother, the father the* x *Mat.10.21.* *Childe; the Children shall rise against their Parents, and cause them to bee put to death;* and ye shall be hated of all men for my names sake : what a se-minary of sedition may the Cardinal call the Gospell, that caused all these troubles, warres, seditions, murders, and burnings in the whole world ? what another Seminary was the Nicene decree against Aria-nisme, and *Constantines Edict* to ratifie the same ? after that, how sedi-tiously was *Athanasius* and the Catholikes persecuted, put to flight, to torments, by *Constantius* and the Arians ? how seditiously did the Councels of *Ariminum,* and *Syrmium* oppugne and fight against that Nicene Decree, till they had so farre prevailed, that well-neare there had needed no longer contending, the whole world almost being tur-ned Arians, and even groaning under Arianisme ? If the Cardinall, by reason of those manifold troubles and oppositions, which ensued upon this *Edict,* will condemne it for being a Seminary of sedition; let him first condemne the Nicene Decree, and Imperiall *Edict* for it, let him condemne the Gospell, and Christ himselfe; which were all such Seminaries as that *Edict* was. If notwithstanding all the oppositi-ons, seditions, & contentions raysed by heathen, heretical, & other wic-ked men, against these, they were (as most certainly they were) Semi-naries of truth; let the Card. know & acknowledge his malicious slan-der against this most religious and *orthodoxall Edict* of *Iustinian,* which was, as all the former, a sacred Sanctuary for the Catholike faith. Se-ditions, oppositions, tumults, persecutions, and the like disturbances in the Church, spring not from Christ, nor from his Word and Gos-pel, either preached by Bishops, or decreed by Councels, or confirmed by *Imperiall Edicts,* all these are of themselves causes onely of unity, concord, peace, and agreement in the Church; these onely are the proper, native, and naturall fruits, and effects that proceed from them; but contentions and seditions come from the perverse, froward, wic-ked, and malicious mindes of men, that hate the truth, and in hatred

of

dictating the *Edict* was. Admit them to bee the Dative, how knowes the Cardinall, that by [*tuis vocibus*] are ment the words of the *Edict* ? might not *Theodorus* fignifie to the Bifhops his owne great liking of the Emperours *Edict*, and perfwade them to the like, to say as he faid, to confent to his words in approving the *Imperiall Edict* ? The Card. was too fecure & negligēt in relying on thefe words[*tuis vocibus*]wᶜʰ being fo ambiguous, receive divers, & thofe alfo juft exceptions : But yet there is a farre worfe fault in this proofe; that the Epiftle, whence the Cardinall citeth thefe words, though it beare the name of *Vigilius*, yet is intruth not the Epiftle of *Vigilius*, but a very counterfeit and bafe forgery under his name, full of untruths, unworthy of any credit at all; which, befides other proofes,(hereafter to be alleaged) faineth *Mennas* to be Bifhop of *Conftantinople*, and to be excommunicated, together with *Theodorus*, by *Vigilius* foure or five yeares after hee was dead, which cenfure was to ftand in force till *Mennas* repented of his contumacie againft the Popes Decree, and fhould be reconciled to him. This lying and bafe forgery doth *Baronius* bring to prove *Theodorus*, and not *Iuftinian* to bee the author of this *Imperiall Edict*. Might not one fay here as was faid of the Affe, Like lips, like lettuce ? Such a writing is a moft fit witneffe for *Baronius*, who delighteth in untruths, and not finding true records, to give teftimony to them, it was fit hee fhould applaud the moft vile and abject forgeries, if they feeme to fpeak ought pleafing to the Cardinals pallate, or which may ferve to fupport his untruths.

9. You fee that yet it appeares not that *Theodorus* was the writer or penner of this Decree, none of *Baronius* his witneffes affirming it, and *Liberatus*, who is the beft of them all, affirming the contrary. I might now with this anfwer put off a great part of thofe reviling fpeeches which *Baronius* fo prodigally beftoweth on *Theodorus* : But I minde not fo to leave the Cardinall, nor fuffer the proud Philiftine fo infolently to revile and infult over any one of the Ifraelites; much leffe this worthy Bifhop of Cefarea, to whom hee could not have done a greater honor, than in that which he intended as an exceeding difgrace to him, to call and account him the Author and Writer of this *Edict*. It is no fmall honour, that *Iuftinian*, fo wife and religious an Emperour, fhould commit the care of fo waighty a matter to *Theodorus*; that hee fhould have him in fo high efteeme, as account his word an Oracle, to bee guided and directed by his judgement; fo to adhere unto him, as *Conftantine* did to that renowned *Hofius*, as to thinke it a *piaculum*, or great offence not to follow his advice in matters of fo great waight, confequence, and importance. Nay, this one *Edict*, (fuppofing with the Cardinall *Theodorus* to bee the Author of it)fhall not onely pleade for *Theodorus*, but utterly wipe away all thofe vile flanders of herefie, impiety, imprudency, and the like, fo often, and fo odioufly objected, and exaggerated by the Cardinall againft him; this writing and the words thereof being (as whofoever readeth them will eafily conceive, and if hee deale ingenuoufly, confeffe)the words of truth, of faith, of fobriety, of profound knowledge, evidenees of a minde full fraught with faith, with piety, with the love

of

of God, and Gods Church, and in a word full of the holy Ghoſt. As *Sophocles* [k], being accuſed to doate, recited his *Oedipus Coloneus*, and demanding whether that did ſeeme the Poeme of a doating man, was by the ſentence of all the Iudges acquitted : So none can reade this *Ediȼt*, but forthwith acknowledge it a meere calumny in *Baronius* to call the maker of it an heretike, whoſe profeſſion of faith is ſo pious, divine, and Catholike. Or rather *Theodorus* may anſwer that *Baronian* ſlander with the like words, as did S. *Paul* [l], *They neither found me making an uproare among the people, nor in the Synagogues, nor in the City, neither can they prove theſe things whereof they now accuſe mee*; but this I confeſſe, that after this way, (declared in this *Ediȼt*) which they call hereſie, ſo worſhip I the God of my fathers.

10. Now as this may ſerve for a generall Antidote at once, as it were, to expell all the whole poyſon of thoſe Baronian calumnies; ſo, if we ſhall deſcend to particulars, the innocency of *Theodorus*, as alſo the malice and malignity of *Baronius* will much more clearly appeare. The crimes objeȼted to *Theodorus* by *Baronius* are reduced to three heads; one, his threefold hereſie; another, his oppoſing himſelfe to Pope *Vigilius*, or the Decree of Taciturnity, in the cauſe of the *Three Chapters*; the third, his miſleading of *Iuſtinian* into the hereſie of the Aphthardokites, and ſo cauſing that great perſecution of the Church which thereupon enſued; all the other diſgracefull termes are but the ſuperfluity of that malice which the Cardinall beares againſt all that were oppoſite to *Vigilius*, and his *Apoſtolicall* Conſtitution. To begin then with that which is eaſieſt, the two laſt crimes are not ſo eaſily uttered as refuted, they both are nothing elſe but meere ſlanders and calumnies, without any certaine ground, or probability of truth, deviſed either by *Baronius* himſelfe, or by ſuch as he is, enemies and haters of the truth; and truly for the later, his miſleading *Iuſtinian* into the hereſie of the Apthardokites, that is not onely a manifeſt untruth, (for *Iuſtinian*, as wee have before [m] proved, did not onely at all hold that hereſie) but it is wholly forged and deviſed by *Baronius*, he hath not any one Author, no not ſo much as a forged writing to teſtifie this, no nor any probable collection out of any Author to induce him to lay this imputation upon *Theodorus*; the world is wholly and ſoly beholden to the Cardinall for this ſhameleſſe calumny; and yet ſee the wiſedome of *Baronius* herein, hee was not content barely and in a word to taxe and reprove *Theodorus*, (which had beene more than ſufficient, having no proofe nor evidence of the crime) but in this paſſage, as if hee had demonſtratively proved *Theodorus* to bee guilty hereof, hee rageth and foameth like a wilde Bore againſt him, calling him a moſt wicked man, and moſt vehement propugner of blaſphemy, the plague of the whole Church, who with a viſor affrayed the Emperour like a little Boy from the truth, and led him captive into hereſie. Doe you not thinke that the Cardinall needed to be ſent to *Anticyra*, when he writ this not onely without truth, but without braine and ordinary ſenſe?

11. The other crime, that *Theodorus* oppoſed himſelfe to *Vigilius*, and to the decree of ſilence, is like the former, ſave that this difference

rence

k *Cic. de Seneȼt.*

l *Act.* 24.12.13

m *C.1.20.*

rence is to be observed betwixt them, that the former was forged by
Baronius, but this later is grounded on a foolish and forged writing applauded by *Baronius*, fictions and forgeries they are both, but
the one was fained to the Cardinals hand, for the other hee was faine
to beate it out of his owne anvill. There was neither any such decree
for taciturnity, neither did *Theodorus*, nor needed hee to oppose himselfe to *Vigilius*, for *Vigilius*, as well as *Theodorus*, all the whole time
almost from his comming to *Constantinople* till the fift Councell was
assembled, wholly consented to condemne the *Three Chapters*, as, besides other evident proofes before alleaged, to which I remit the reader, that one testimony of the Emperour doth undeniably demonstrate; *Quod* [n] *vero ejusdem voluntatis semper fuit de condemnatione Trium*
Capitulorum per plurima declaravit; Vigilius hath by very many things
declared, that he hath been alwayes (since his comming to *Constantinople*)
of the same minde in condemning the *Three Chapters*; what thinke you
here againe of *Baronius*, who upon this occasion of contradicting *Vigilius*, & his decree of silence, reviles *Theodorus*, calling [o] him *sacrilegious*,
a *Pseudo-Bishop*, a tyrant, a *schismatike*, a perverter of *lawes*, the author of all
evils; and yet when the Cardinall hath said all this, there is no truth
nor reality in the cause and occasion for which hee thus rageth and
revileth; no opposition to *Vigilius*, no decree of silence either oppugned, or such as might bee oppugned, it was a *non ens*, a chymera
floating in the Cardinals idle fancy. Was there no *Helleborus* at
Rome or in *Italy* to purge the Cardinals braine of this extreme distemper?

12. The whole hope consists now in the Cardinals *Triary*, the three
heresies objected to *Theodorus*, that of *Origen*, of *Eutyches*, and of the
Aphthardokites. And for the two last I must say the same almost as
to the former calumnies, they are meere fictions of *Baronius*: *Theodorus*
was (saith hee [p]) an *Aphthardokite*, and an *Eutychean* heretike: what Author, what witnesse or testimony doth the Cardinall produce to
prove so hainous a crime against him? truly not one, himselfe *accusa-
tor simul & testis*, *is both the accuser and the witnesse*. But yet hee proves
it by some good consequence or reason? no nor that neither, his
proofe is no lesse foolish than his position is false. *Iustinian*, saith [q] he,
was misled into the heresie of the *Aphthardokites by some Origenists, as*
Eustathius declareth; whereupon we may easily, and without calumny affirme,
that the ring-leader of those who misled the Emperour was Theodorus Bish. of
Cæsarea, an Origenist: The ground of w[ch], (to omit that this *Eustathius*
is of no credit) being the heresie of *Iustinian*, seeing that to bee a calumnie and slander wee have before [r] confirmed, this whole collection must needs be like the foundation on which it relyeth, slanderous, and false, to say nothing how alogicall and incoherent a consequent this is from particulars. Some Origenists misled *Iustinian*,
therefore *Theodorus*; how much rather on the contrary may wee certainly conclude, that seeing *Iustinian*, who was directed in causes of
faith by *Theodorus*, continued orthodoxall, and a most worthy defender of the true faith, as before we proved, therefore doubtlesse *Theodorus* himselfe, the director of the Emperor, was, and remained orthodoxall,

n *Epist. Iustin.
ad Conc. 5. Act. 1
pa. 520. a.*

o *Locis supra ci-
tatis.*

p *Iustinianus ob-
ligatus fuit in eo
errore (Apthar-
dochitarum) ab
eis, qui ei assiste-
bant, heresis e-
jus defensoribus.
At quinam illi?
Morum Antesig-
nanus fuit Theo-
dorus ille nequis-
simus, &c. erat
is Eurycheanæ
blasphemiæ pro-
pugnator. Bar.
an. 564. nu. 6.
& 7.*
q *Ibid.*
r *Sup. ca. 20.*

doxall, and that of a certaine hee was no Eutychean nor Aphthardokite, is evident by his subscribing [1] to the decree of the fift Councell; ſColl.8.
wherein not onely the Councell, and decree of *Chalcedon* condemning
Eutyches, and in it the heresie of the Aphthardokites, is strongly confirmed, but *Eutyches* also by name, and all that hold his heresies, are
anathematized, by all the Bishops of that fift Councell; and particularly by this *Theodorus*, whom the Cardinall, without any testimony
or proofe at all, slanders to have beene an Eutychean and Apthardo-
kite, unto both which heresies he was most opposite : All which will
be more manifest by considering the first of those three heresies;
wherein *Baronius* hath the greatest colour for his saying. That *Theo-*
dorus was an Origenist, and a most earnest maintainer of that heresie, the Cardinall often, and most confidently affirmeth; where- t An. 538. nu. 36
in hee hath *Liberatus* [t] the Deacon, and Bishop *Facundus* [u] for his u An. 546.8.9.
& 49.
Authors.

13. First for *Facundus*, he doth not expresly mention *Theodorus* as
an Origenist, but yet because *Baronius* citeth him to say, that *Theodo-*
rus writ the *Edict*, and *Facundus* calleth the writers of that *Edict*, Origenists, let him be admitted for one of the Cardinals witnesses. Who
I pray you, or of what credit thinke you is this Bishop *Facundus*? Truly an enemy to *Iustinian*, an enemy to *Theodorus* of *Cæsarea*, and to all
that condemned the *Three Chapters*, a very heretike, and enemy to the
Catholike truth. Witnesse hereof that testimony which their owne
Possevine [x] giveth of him out of *Isidorus*. He writ twelve bookes in de- x Poſſ. Appar.
in verbo Facun-
dus, et verbo Se-
cundus.
fence of the *three Chapters*, whereby he proveth the condemning of
those *three Chapters* to bee the condemning or banishing of the Apostolike faith, and the Councell of *Chalcedon*. Now the defenders of
the *three Chapters*, and writers in defence of them to bee condemned,
anathematized, and accursed for heretikes by the fift Councell, and
after it the 6. 7. and in a word, by all, both generall Councels, and
Popes that follow *Gregory*, we have often before declared : So that by
the consenting judgement of all those generall approved Councels,
and Popes, *Facundus* being an earnest defender of them, and writer in
their defence, is anathematized, and condemned for an heretike. And
that he continued pertinaciously in this heresie, after the sentence and
judgement of the generall Councell, *Baronius* doth witnesse, who [y] tels y An. 553. nu.
221.
us, and that with a *Constat*, *It is certaine and manifest, that Facundus was*
sought for to be punished, because hee had written most eloquently in defence
of the three Chapters, but by lurking in some secret place he escaped. *Posse-*
vine [a] further addeth, that *Facundus* writ a booke against *Mutianus* in a In Facundo.
defence of *Theodorus* of *Mopsvestia*, and that *Theodorus* of *Mopsve-*
stia, damnatus fuit ab Ecclesia Catholica ob errores contra fidem, was con-
demned by the Catholike Church, for his heresie or errors against the faith.
Must not he needs bee an heretike, that defends a condemned heretike? yea defends those very writings and errors of him and *Ibas*, which
are condemned for hereticall ? *I confesse*, saith *Facundus* [b], *to your Holi-* b Fac. apud Bar
an. 547. nu. 38.
nesse, that I withdraw my selfe from the communion of the opposites, (those
were the condemners of the *three Chapters*, that is, to say in truth, Catholikes) *not because they condemne Theodorus of Mopsvestia, but for that*

in

in the perſon of this Theodorus they condemne the Epiſtle of Ibas as hereticall, and by that Epiſtle condemne the Councell of Chalcedon, à qua ſuſcepta eſt, by which that Epiſtle is approued. Thus *Facundus;* ſo very heretically, that *Neſtorius, Eutyches, Dioſcorus,* nor any cōdemned heretike could wiſh or ſay more than *Facundus* hath done both for their hereſies, & againſt the Councell of *Chalcedon.* For the impious Epiſtle of *Ibas* is wholly hereticall, the approuing of it is the overthrow of the whole Catholike faith: and yet *Facundus* not onely himſelfe defendeth that impious *E-piſtle* as orthodoxall, and by it defendeth the perſon and writing of *Theodorus* of *Mopſveſtia* a condemned heretike ; but avoucheth the Councell of *Chalcedon* to approve the ſame, which condemnes it and every part of it even to the loweſt pit of hell.

14. Here by the way I muſt in a word put the reader in minde of one or two points which concern *Poſſevine* and *Baronius* in this paſſage. If *Facundus* be a condemned heretike for writing in defence of the *three Chapters,* what elſe can *Poſſevine* be who prayſed thoſe bookes of a condemned heretike ? for thus he writeth [c], *Facundus* writ *opus grande atque elegans, a great and elegant worke,* containing twelve books, fortified by the authorities of the Fathers in defence of the *three Chapters.* Heretike ! Is that a brave and elegant booke that defendeth hereſie? can hereſie be fortified by the teſtimonies of the holy Fathers ? What is this elſe but to make the holy Fathers heretikes ? So hereticall and ſpitefull is *Poſſevine,* that together with himſelfe he would draw the ancient and holy Fathers into one and the ſame crime of hereſie. The other point concernes *Baronius :* hee ſayth [d] that the controverſie or contention about the *three Chapters,* was *inter Catholicos tantùm, onely among ſuch as were Catholikes :* doth not he plainly thereby ſignifie his opinion of *Facundus,* that he was a Catholike ? for *Facundus* was as hot, and earneſt a contender in that controverſie as *Vigilius* himſelfe; he writ in defence of the *three Chapters* twelve whole bookes, elegant and brave bookes, as *Poſſevine* ſaith : he bitterly inveighed againſt the Emperour, againſt all the condemners of them, againſt Pope *Vigilius* himſelfe, when hee after his comming to *Conſtantinople* conſented to the Emperor. Seeing this *Facundus* (a convicted and condemned he-hetike) is one of the Cardinals Catholikes, muſt not hereſie and Ne-ſtorianiſme bee with him Catholike doctrine ? muſt not the impious *Epiſtle* be orthodoxall, and the overthrow of the faith and decree of the Councell at *Chalcedon* bee an Article of *Baronius* faith ? even that which he accounted the Catholike faith ? But this by the way. We ſee now what manner of Biſhop *Facundus* was, an obſtinate heretike, pertinaciouſly perſiſting in hereſie. VVhat though *Facundus* call *Theo-dorus* of *Cæſarea* an Origeniſt ? Did not the old Neſtorians call *Cyrill,* and other Catholikes, Apollinarians ? of whom it ſeemes the defenders of the *three Chapters* learned to calumniate the Catholikes with the names of heretikes and Origeniſts, when they were in truth wholly oppoſite to thoſe and other hereſies. Can any expect a true teſtimony concerning *Theodorus* Biſhop of *Cæſarea,* from *Facundus,* concerning Catholikes, from heretikes, their immortall and malicious enemies, nor theirs onely, but enemies to the truth ? Such, and of ſuch

ſmall

c *Loco citato.*

d *An.547.nu.30*

finall worth is the former witnesse of *Baronius* in this cause, and against *Theodorus.*

15. His other witnesse is *Liberatus* the Deacon, who indeed sayth as plainly as *Baronius* that *Theodorus* was an Origenist; and refers the occasion of that whole controversie touching the *three Chapters* to the malice of the same *Theodorus.* For as *Liberatus* saith, *Pelagius the Popes Legate when he was at Constantinople, entreated of the Emperour that Origen, and his heresies wherewith the Easterne Churches, specially about Ierusalem, were exceedingly troubled, might be condemned; whereunto the Emperour willingly assenting, published an Imperiall Edict both against him and his errors: when Theodorus being an Origenist perceived that Origen who was long before dead was now condemned, he to be quit with Pelagius for procuring the condemnation of Origen, moved the Emperour also to condemne Theodorus Bishop of Mopsvestia, who had written much against Origen, whose writings were detested of all the Origenists: the Emperour at Theodorus his suggestion made another Edict, wherein he condemned Theodorus of Mopsvestia, and the two other Chapters touching the writings of Theodoret and Ibas, which bred so long trouble in the Church.* Thus *Liberatus.* Who as you see speaketh as much, and as eagerly against *Theodorus,* as *Baronius* could wish, and *Liberatus* lived and writ about that same time.

e In Breu.ca.24

16. *Liberatus* in many things is to be allowed, in those especially wherein by partiality his judgement was not corrupt. But in this cause of the *Three Chapters,* in the occasion and circumstances thereof, hee is a most unfit witnesse, himselfe was deeply interessed in this cause, partiality blinded him, his stile was sharpe against the adverse part, but dull in taxing any, though never so great a crime, in men of his owne faction. Of him *Binius* [f] gives this true censure, *hee was one of their ranke who defended the Three Chapters,* who also writ an Apology for *Theodorus* of Mopsvestia: againe, *Baronius* and *Bellarmine* have noted [g], that divers things are *cautè legenda* in *Liberatus*; of him *Possevine* [h] writeth, *There are many things in Liberatus which are to bee read with circumspection, those especially which hee borrowed of some Nestorians, and those are his narrations touching Theodorus of Mopsvestia, that his writings were praised both by the Emperour Theodosius his Edict, and by Cyrill, and approved also in the Councell of Chalcedon;* all which to be lies *Baronius* doth convince. Againe [i], *what Liberatus saith of the fift Councell is very warily to be read, for either they were not his own, or he was deceived by the false relation of some other, but certainly they do not agree with the writings of other Catholike fathers.* Thus *Possevine* out of *Baronius;* who might as well in plaine termes have called *Liberatus* a Nestorian heretike, for none but Nestorians, and such as slander the Councel of *Chalcedon* for hereticall, can judge the writings of *Theodorus,* w[ch] are full of all heresies, blasphemies, and impieties, to be approved in that holy Councell. Againe, *Possevine* rejecting that w[ch] *Liberatus* writeth of the fift Councell, gives a most just exception against all that he writeth either touching *Theodorus* of *Cesarea,* as being an Origenist, or of the occasiō of this cōtroversie about the 3. *Chapters,* as if it did arise from the cōdemning of *Origen,* in all this *Liberatus* by the Iesuites confession was deceived by the false relation of others, they a-

f Ja notis suis in Breu.Liber.to 2. Concz.pa.616.

g Bell.lib.1.de Conc ca. 5.
§ Ca sa.Bell et is Baronius in Liber.ti breviano, hac cautè legenda sunt donoturat. Binius loco cit.0.

h In Appar. in verbo Liberatus.
i Ibid.

Kk

gree

gree not to the truth, nor to the narrations of Catholike fathers. *Liberatus* being an earnest favourer and defender of *Theodorus Mopsvestenus*, could not chuse but hate *Theodorus* of *Cesarea*, for seeking to have him and his writings condemned: The saying of *Ierome* ought here to take place, *Professæ inimicitiæ suspitionem habent mendacij; the report of a professed enemy ought to be suspected as a lye.* The true cause why *Liberatus* is so violent against *Theodorus* of *Cesarea*, was not for that *Theodorus* was an Origenist, (as *Liberatus*, and out of him *Baronius* slandereth him) but because this *Theodorus* condemned the writings of *Theodorus* of *Mopsvestia* whom *Liberatus* defended, and the two other Chapters. Neither was the condemning of *Origen* the occasion of condemning the *three Chapters*, as *Liberatus* untruly reporteth, but as both *Iustinian* and the whole Councell witnesse; the true occasion thereof were the Nestorian heretikes, who pretending and boasting the *three Chapters* to bee allowed in the Councell of *Chalcedon*, both the Catholikes, in defence of the Councell, justly denyed the same, and the Emperour first, then the Councell to confirme the faith, condemned the *three Chapters*, which were the overthrow of the faith, as before wee have proved.

17. This were enough to oppose to all that *Facundus* and *Liberatus* say, two defenders of the *three Chapters*, and so professed enemies both to the Catholike truth defined in the fift Councell, and to *Theodorus* of *Cesarea*, who first of all suggested the condemning of them to the Emperour *Iustinian*: But now, besides this just exception against the Cardinals witnesses I will adde two cleare and authentike proofes to demonstrate both *Liberatus*, and after him *Baronius* unjustly and falsly to slander *Theodorus* of *Cesarea* for an Origenist. The former is his owne subscription to the fift Councell. In that Councell, among other heretikes, *Origen* is not only expresly & by name condemned, & that in their definitive sentence; but an Anathema also denounced against all who doe not condemne and anathematize him: these are the words of the Councell, *If any doe not anathematize Arius, Ennomius, Macedonius, Apollinarius, Nestorius, Eutyches, Origen*, with their impious writings, *talis anathema sit, such an one let him bee accursed.* To this Synodall decree did all the 165. Bishops in the Councell consent and subscribe; the eighth man was this *Theodorus* of *Cesarea*, who subscribed in this manner, *I Theodorus, decrevi quæ proposita sunt, have decreed these things which are proposed, and I confesse that the truth is as all those Chapters and doctrines above named* (of which this against *Origen* is the eleaventh) *doe containe*: when *Theodorus* himselfe confesseth *Origen* and his writings to bee condemned, accurseth them, yea, and all who doe not accurse them, is it not a vile and unexcusable calumny in *Liberatus* and in *Baronius*, to revile him as a patron of *Origen*?

18. Perhaps you will say hee was in former time an Origenist, but at the time of the fift Councell hee was become a new man. Though this were admitted, yet cannot *Baronius* bee excused, for calling him after that fift Councell an heretike, an Origenist: But hee was still the same man, both now and before orthodoxall, as by the other evidence,

dence, taken from the *Emperours Edict* in condemning *Origen*, will appeare, when the defenders of *Origen*, both for their number, and insolency, grew very troublesome in the East, specially about *Ierusalem*. *Pelagius* and *Mennas*, as *Liberatus* [o] saith, at the instigation of some religious Monks, intreated the Emperour that *Origen* and his heresies might be condemned: the Emperour thereupon published a very large and religious *Edict* against *Origen*, which he directed to *Mennas*, and the copy therof he sent also to *Vigilius*, and to other Patriarks; after many other things the Emp. thus writeth [p], *We, desiring to put away all offence from the holy Church, & to leave it without blemish, following the divine Scriptures, & holy fathers, who have cast out and justly anathematized Origen and his impious doctrine, have sent this our Epistle unto you, wherein we exhorte you, that you call an assembly or Synod of all the holy Bishops and Abbots who are now in Constantinople, and that you see that all of them doe in writing anathematize Origen, and his wicked doctrines, and all the Chapters out of him under-written; and further that you send the Copy of what you have done in this cause (to all other Bishops and Abbots within your Patriarkship) that they also may all doe the like.* Besides this, the Emperour yet commands, *that none be ordained Bishop or chosen into any Monastery, unlesse forthwith in a booke they accurse and anathematize, as Arius, Sabellus, Nestorius, Eutyches, and the rest, so also Origen and his impious doctrines.* Thus writ the Emperour, and what in this manner hee commanded *Mennas* to doe in his Patriarkship, the like was *Vigilius* to doe in the Romane, *Zoilus* in the Alexandrian, *Euphrenius* in the Antiochian. That, according as the Emperour commanded, this was done, *Liberatus* [q] is witnesse; *so that by all the Bishops in the world that then were, and by such as were after this to bee ordained, Origen with his impious doctrines was to bee condemned and accursed.* Particularly of the Synod or Bishops at *Constantinople Baronius* [r] confesseth, *The Emperour admonished Mennas to assemble a Synod, by which all these things which he had written against Origen might bee confirmed, quod & factum fuit, which was accordingly done*; and, as *Cedrenus* [s] saith, their sentence was this, *We condemne all these errours of Origen, & omnes qui ita sentiunt, & sentient, and all who do either now or herafter shall think as he doth*, condemning themselves with an anathema, if either then they did thinke so, or ever hereafter should think the like. That *Theodorus*, though he had remained at *Cesarea* subscribed to this sentence, I thinke none can doubt, the Emperours command being so strict to all Patriarks: But indeed it seemeth that *Theodorus* was not onely at *Constantinople* at this time, and there subscribed, but that hee was one of the chiefe agents with the Emperour to publish this Edict; for of him *Evagrius* [t] witnesseth, that, *cum Iustiniano assiduè versabatur, he was continually conversant with the Emperour*, hee was faithfull, and especially necessary unto him, of him *Liberatus* [u] saith, that hee was, *dilectus & familiaris Principum, deare and familiar both with the Emperour and Empresse*; of him [x] *Baronius* testifieth that he was *praepotens armiger Iustiniani, the Champion of Iustinian*, for so saith he, I may well call him that was used to sit at the Emperours Elbow, yea, of whom [y] the Emperour had conceived so great an opinion, that hee thought it the chiefe point of his duty or piety,

o *Loco citato.*

p *Edictum Iustin. contra Origenem. extat to. 2. Con. pa. 482.*

q *Dictata est in Originem damnatio, quam subscribentes, &c. Liber. ca. 23.*

r *An. 538. nu. 83*

s *Ced. in compend. Annal.*

t *Lib. 4. ca. 37.*

u *Ca. 24.*

x *An. 451. nu. 4*

y *An. 564. nu. 71*

ejus semper inhærere Vestigijs, always to tread in the footsteps of *Theodorus.*
Thus *Baronius.* Seeing *Theodorus* was so neare unto, so potent with the
Emperour, so highly esteemed by him, that hee alwayes trode in his
steps, how could *Theodorus* bee a patron of *Origen,* when the Emperor
himselfe accursed, and commanded all others to accurse him? Did
not *Theodorus* treade out this path of an anathema unto the Emperour? or had he been an Origenist, how could the Emperour, following him step by step, be an enemy to *Origen?* Or to omit many other
like consequences, seeing the Synod of *Constantinople,* (as, besides *Baronius, Liberatus* witnesseth) that is, all the Bishops there present
(among whom *Theodorus* being neare and deare unto the Emperour,
and so continually conversant with him, was doubtlesse one, and one
of the chiefe) condemned *Origen,* it is not to bee doubted but that he
was one of the first and chiefe Bishops that subscribed in that Synod
to the condemnation of him. Now this was done in the 12.[z] yeare
of *Iustinian,* that is, full fourteene yeares before the fift Councell,
so ancient, so constant was the detestation of *Theodorus* towards
Origen.

z *Hoc tempore
(12.is annus
Iustin.)Con-
stantinopoli
magnum agita-
tum est de Ori-
gene judicium.
Bar.an.538. nu.
31.et Conc.5.
habitum an. 27.
Iustin.*

19. Will any now judge otherwise of *Baronius* than a malicious
slanderer? who raileth against *Theodorus* as the most earnest Patron of
Origen, whom his owne publike and constant profession and subscription testifieth to have accursed *Origen* with all his heresies; yea, to have
accursed all that doe either defend him, or think as *Origen* did, though
outwardly and openly he doe not defend him, for that was one Article, * to which *Theodorus,* and the whole Synod under *Mennas* subscribed; á curse be to *Origen* with all his execrable doctrine, a curse
bee to every one who thinketh the same which he did, or who at any
time doth presume to defend the same.

* *Edict.Iust.cö-
tra Originem
in fine.*

20. What are the partiall, uncertaine, and malicious reports of
Facundius, of *Liberatus,* or of the Surian *Cyrill* (to adde him also among
them) to these undoubted and authentike records of Councels? when
wee reade and see the evident subscription of *Theodorus* proclaming
him to condemne and accurse *Origen,* what vanitie, malice and hatred
of truth is this in the Cardinall, to alleage two, or if you please, three
partiall testimonies against that evidence which condemneth them,
and all that they can say? So unfortunate is the Cardinall in all that
he undertakes in this cause, that hee doth not onely speake *præter,* but
contra, directly contrary to the truth, whereof, as in other passages, so
in this touching *Theodorus,* wee have seene so faire and cleare evidences.

CAP. XXIIII.

How unjustly Baronius *excepteth against the* Acts *of the* fift Councell, as being corrupted, and of no credit; *and a refutation in generall of the same.*

1. ARonius perceiving right well, that all which heretofore hath beene said either against the Emperour, or the Empresse, or the Edict, or *Theodorus* the supposed author of it, is not sufficient in any measure either to defend, or excuse *Vigilius*; in the next place he taketh a very uncouth & unusuall, but a most sure course, wherby hee may not onely weaken, but utterly overthrow all that hath or can be said against the Pope in this cause; for the *Acts* of the fift generall Councell being the most authentike records that can bee produced, to prove *Vigilius* and all that defend him, to bee heretikes; the Cardinall, and after him *Binius* will now no longer hacke at this or that person, which were agents in the cause, and but petty branches; but now hee will strike at the very roote, calling into question the Acts and evidences themselves, striving to prove them to bee of no credit; which if hee can doe; all the rest, whatsoever can bee said, will most easily bee rejected. Now because *Baronius* was willing in this passage to shew not onely the utmost subtilty of his wit, but his exact diligence in picking out every quarrell, that art or malice could suggest against the Acts of this holy Councell, I must intreate the reader not to thinke it tedious (though unto mee this was a matter almost of greatest trouble and difficultie) to heare patiently, and weigh with equity of judgement the manifold exceptions against these Acts, which he hath collected, or rather scattered upon every occasion which offered it selfe here and there, that by his inculcating, and ingeminating of the accusation he might breed some opinion of the truth thereof.

2. And before I enter into examination of the particulars, let me put the reader in minde of one or two considerations which may in generall concerne them all. The first is, that though the Cardinall, and *Binius* following him, have spared no labour to sift these Acts as diligently as Satan did Saint *Peter*, and have objected ten or twelve speciall corruptions in them, yet not any thing which they mention, or against which they except, doth any way so touch or concerne the cause of the *Three Chapters*, whereof wee have intreated, as either to shew that the Councell condemneth them not, or that *Vigilius* defendeth them not by his definitive & *Apostolicall Constitutiō*, or that the Councell by their Synodall sentence and consenting judgement did not for that cause condemne, anathematize, and accurse for heretikes all that defend them, and so Pope *Vigilius*, among the rest, and al that defend him or his *Apostolicall Constitution*. All these are matters of so certaine, evident, and undoubted truth, by the Acts, that *Baronius* or

Kk 3 *Binius*

Binius could finde nothing at all to blemish or darken them. So then, though the Acts were admitted in 100. or 1000. other points to bee corrupted, mutilated, and altered, yet the Cardinall and *Binius* are never a whit the nearer; the maine point at which they aime, is to excuse *Vigilius*, and those that defend him, but notwithstanding all that they have said, (and they have said all that industry, having borrowed serpentine eyes, could finde out) both *Vigilius* himselfe, and all who defend him, and those are all who defend the Popes *infallibility in defining causes of faith*, that is, all Papists, remaine still, as convicted, accursed, and anathematized heretikes, and that by the judgment of an holy generall Councell, approved by all succeeding, both Popes and Councels, till the time of *Luther* and *Leo* the tenth.

3. The second thing which I observe is, that corruptions which happely may bee crept into some Synodall Acts, or other writings, whether by mutilations, additions, or alterations, are no just cause to reject, as unworthy of credit, all the Acts of that Councell, or writings of the author. Admit this once, what credit can be given to the Nicene and Constantinopolitane Councels? whose Acts to bee miserably maimed, none is ignorant? yea, even the very Canons also to bee corrupted *Bellarmine* [a] and *Baronius* [b] doe professe and prove: The like corruption *Baronius* noteth in the first Ephesine Councell, wherein is set [c] downe, among other acts, *decretum Regum*, for the banishment of the Nestorians, of which *Baronius* [d] saith, *plura simul mendacia insuta habent, there are many lyes sowed up in these Acts*. In like sort in the Councell of *Chalcedon* is inserted among the Acts of the third Session [e], an Edict of the Emperor *Valentinianus* and *Martianus*, which was written a long [f] yeare after the Councell was ended, and therefore must of necessity be acknowledged to bee foisted, and unjustly inserted into the Acts. Of the sixt Councell *Bellarmine* [g] saith, that it without doubt is corrupted, and whatsoever is found there of *Honorius*, is falsly inserted. Of it *Binius* [h] after *Baronius* [i] saith, the Acts of it, are in many places depraved; and whatsoever is there reported to be said or done by *Honorius*, all that is added by the Monothelites. Of the seventh *Binius* [k] thus writeth, This fourth Action is in divers places faulty, and in the History of the Image crucified at *Beritus* it containeth divers Apocryphall narrations concerning the Image of Christ made by *Nicodemus*. Of the eighth Councell, that the Canons thereof are corrupted, and some inserted by *Anastasius*, their owne *Raderus* [l] will perswade them. Let the Baronian reason against the Acts of this fift Councell bee applyed to these: He having found among these, one Epistle of *Theodorets* which hee supposeth to bee a counterfait, concludeth upon that one example in this manner, *quam fidem rogo merentur acta hujusmodi, qua sunt his contexta commentis*; what credit, I pray you, doe such Acts as these of the fift Councell deserve, which are intangled in such fictions? May not the selfe same reason be much more justly alleaged against the Nicene and Constantinopolitane Canons; against the Acts of the Councell at *Ephesus*, at *Chalcedon*; against the sixt, seventh and eighth Synods, in every one of which, some, & in divers, more corruptions, not onely mutilations, but alterations.

a *Probatur Canones illos (Nisenos) non esse integros. Lib.2. de Pontif. Rom. ca.25. § Omissa*
b *Quod Canon 6. Con. Nic. mutilatus sit, &c. Bar.an.225.nu. 125. & Canon iste (5.Concilij Constantinopolitani) suspectus, imo plane additititius esse atque suppositus habetur, &c. Bar.an.381 nu.35.*
c *Tom.5.Conc. Ephes.ca.11.*
d *An.481.nu. 173.*
e *Pag.84.b.*
f *Concilium finitum est mense Novemb.in Cos. Martiani et Adelphij.Bar.an. 451.nu.160. Edictum vero scriptum 7.Kalen.Febr.Coss. Sporatio.*
g *Bell. lib.4.de Pontif.Rom.ca. 11. § Ad secundum depravata sunt.Bin. not. in Con.6.§ Acta.*
h *Acta Concilij multis in locis*
i *Bar.an.681. nu.13.*
k *Not.in Conc. Nicen.2.et Acti. 4.*
l *Viginti septem Canones ex Anastasii codice sumptos nullus dubitet, et bi duo Canones non nisi ex Anastasio videntur accipi. Rad.in Obser. ad Conc.8.pa. 448.*

tions, and commentitious writings are inferted by their owne confession? Let *Baronius* anfwer here his owne queftion, *Quam fidem rogo?* I pray you then, what credit may bee given to fuch Canons or Acts as are thofe of *Nice,* of *Conftantinople,* of *Ephefus,* of *Chalcedon,* of the fixt, feventh, or eighth Councell? they all muft by the Cardinals reafon be rejected, as Canons and Acts of no worth, of no credit at all: Nor they onely, but all the workes of *Auguftine,* of *Athanafius,* of *Ierome,* and almoft all the holy Fathers: none of them all by this Baronian reafon, deferve any credit, for among their writings are inferted many fuppofitious and factitious tracts, as the book *de variis Quaftionibus Scripturæ,* the Sermon of the Affumption of the bleffed Virgin, and many moe [m] in *Athanafius,* the Epiftle of *Auguftine* to *Cyrill,* and *Cyrils* to *Auften,* the author [n] of which was not onely an Impoftor, but an heretike; the booke *de Spiritu & litera,* the booke of queftions of the old and new Teftament, which is hereticall; and an heape of the like in *Auften;* the Commentaries on *Pauls* Epiftles, which favour of Pelagianifme; the Epiftle to *Demetrias* concerning virginity, and 100. like in [o] *Ierome.* *Quæ fides rogo?* what credit can bee given to thefe bookes or writings of *Auften, Athanafius, Ierome,* or the reft, in which are found fo many fictitious, & heretical treatifes, falfly afcribed unto them, mingled and inferted among their writings? Truly, I cannot devife what might move the great Card. to make fuch a collection, and reafon, as from fome corruptions crept into the bookes of fathers, or Acts of Councels, to inferre, that the whole Acts or writings are unworthy of any credit, but onely as *Iacke Cade* had a purpofe to burne all authentick records and writings of law, that, as hee boafted, all the law might proceed from his own mouth; fo the Cardinal intended to play a right *Iacke Cade* with all the ancient Councels and Fathers, that having utterly, though not abolifhed; yet difgraced, and made them all by this his reafon and collection unworthy of any credit; his owne mouth might bee an Oracle to report without controulment all hiftories of ancient matters; and what his Cardinalfhip fhould pleafe to fay in any matter, or to fet downe in his Annals, that all men fhould beleeve, as if the moft authentick Records in the world had teftified the fame: How much better and more advifedly might the Cardinall have done, to have wifhed all corruptions to bee removed? whatfoever can be certainly proved in any Acts of Councels, or writings of Fathers to be added unto them, that to be quite cut off; whatfoever might bee found wanting, that to bee added; whatfoever to be altered or perverted, that to be amended, and not in the blindneffe of his hatred, againft this one fift Councell, to fight like one of the *Andabatæ,* againft al the reft, and with one ftroke to cafhire all the Acts and Canons of Councels, all the writings of Fathers or Hiftorians, becaufe, forfooth, one or fome few corruptions have either by negligence or errour of writing, or by fraud and malice of fome malignant hand crept into them.

4. The third thing which I obferve, is, that whereas *Baronius* fo often and fo fpightfully declameth againft the Acts of this Councell, as imperfect and corrupted; this his whole accufation proceedeth of malice

m Poff. Appar. in Athan.p.127. n Poff. in Aug. pa. 147.

o Poff. in Hier. pa. 751.

lice to the Councell and thefe Acts, rather than of judgement or of truth; for I doe conftantly affirme, and who fo ever pleafeth to perufe the Councels fhall certainly finde, (and, if he deale ingenuoufly, will confeffe the fame) that as of al the general Councels which go before this fift, for integrity of the Acts, none is better, or any way comparable to this, fave that of *Chalcedon*: fo of all that follow it none at all is to bee preferred, nor any way to bee counted equall with it, unleffe that which they call the fixt Councell, that is, fo much of the Acts of that Synod as concerne the caufe of the Monothelites, leaving out the *Trullane* Canons: This, whofoever is exercifed in the Volumes of Councels cannot choofe but obferve. The Nicene & Conftantinopolitane being fo miferably maimed, that fcarce wee have fo much as a few fhreds or chips of the moft magnificent buildings of thofe Councels, which, if they could bee recovered, no treafures are fufficient to redeeme a worke of that worth and value, a worke *non gemmis, neque purpura venale, neque auro*. That of *Ephefus* is a little helped indeed by *Peltanus*, but yet it remaines fo imperfect, fo confufed, and diforderly, that as *Diogines* fought men in the moft thronged multitudes of men, fo among thofe very Acts & large Tomes of the Coücels, the reader fhall be forced to feeke the Acts of the *Ephefine* Councell. The Acts of the fecond *Nicene*, and of the next to it, which they call the eighth, are fo doubtfull, that not onely this or that part, but the whole fabrick of them both is queftionable, whether they were the Synodall Acts, or but a relation framed by *Anaftafius*, as hee thought beft. Of all the eight Councels, the Acts of *Chalcedon*, this fift, and the fixt have beene moft fafely preferved, and like the river *Arethufa* have ftrongly paffed through fo many corrupt ages and hands, and yet without tainture of the falt, deliver unto us the cleare and fweete current of antiquity and truth: And verily, when I ferioufly compare the wraek of other Councels with the entireneffe of thefe three, I cannot but admire and magnifie with all my might the gracious providence, wifdome, and love of God to his Church, for in every one of thefe there is an unrefiftable force of truth, againft that Antichriftiä authority & fupremacy which is now made the *foundation* of the Popifh faith; the fixt in the caufe of *Honorius*, the fift in this caufe of *Vigilius*, and that of *Chalcedon*, in curbing the Popes Legates, in croffing the decree, and knowne refolution of Pope *Leo*, and in being a moft lively patterne of that rightfull and ancient authority which Emperours then held above all the Bifhops in the Councell; but now the Pope ufurpes both above all Bifhops, Emperours and Councels. God would by thefe monuments of antiquity pull downe the lofty Towers, and raze from the very bottome that foundation of *Babylon*, wch can never be firme and fetled; hee would have, befides other particular witneffes, thefe unconquerable and irrefiftible forces of thefe ancient and generall Councels, againft which no juft exception can be taken: and although I will not excufe the acts of thefe, nor any of them from all defects and blemifhes whatfoever, yet I dare boldly averre, that they are fo few, fo light, and of fo fmall importance, that the maine controverfies handled in them, or relying on them, cannot be prejudicated thereby,

they

they being rather the errours of the Colle&ors, or of the writers, and exscribers of these Councels, than of the Councels themselves : And particularly for this fift Councell, against which *Baronius* doth so furiously declame : I doubt not to make it evident, that all the faults, which, after much prying, hee hath objected unto the A&s thereof, will prove so many evident testimonies of his owne most fraudulent. and corrupt dealing, and not the defe&s or corruptions in the A&s of this Councell. But let us view the particulars.

CAP. XXV.

The first alteration of the Synodall Acts pretended by Baronius, *for that the text of the Councell at* Chalcedon *is changed therein, refuted.*

T H E corruptions which *Baronius*, and out of him *Binius* obje&eth, are according to the grammaticall division reduced to three sorts of irregularity : Some by variation or alteration, others by defe& or mutilation, the rest by redundance or addition. In the first ranke hee pretendeth three examples; the first which seemeth to be of greatest moment, and carieth the greatest colour of probability is the corrupting of a certaine text of the Councell at *Chalcedon* cited by this fift Synod. Heare the accusation in *Baronius* his owne words, *We may not here omit*, saith he [a], *to note the craft of the Grecians, who, contrary to right and equitie, have corrupted the holy text of the Synodall Acts, by adding unto the Councell of Chalcedon those words, about which there was much contention in the time of Pope Hormisda, when certaine suspected of Eutycheanisme, specially some Scythian Monkes, did labour that unto the holy Councell of Chalcedon these words might bee added, Dominum nostrum Iesum Christum unum esse de sancta Trinitate; which when they could not obtaine, because the Synod was well enough without that addition, here now (in this fift Councell) where the Epistle of Ibas is compared with the profession of the Councell at Chalcedon; they recite these words of the Synod [Chalcedonensis sancta Synodus in definitione quam de fide fecit, prædicat Deum verbum incarnatum esse hominem] the holy Synod of Chalcedon in the definition which it made of faith, doth professe God the Word to have beene incarnate and made man; and they adde unto the words of the Synod, [qui est Dominus noster Iesus Christus, unus de sancta Trinitate; who is our Lord Iesus Christ, one of the holy Trinitie;]* as if the Synod of *Chalcedon* had professed that, whereas they rather would call Christ, *unam personam sanctæ Trinitatis*, than *unum de sancta Trinitate.* Thus *Baronius*: In which few words of his there are contained so many notable untruths, and hereticall frauds, that without a rare dexterity in that craft, hee could not have easily contrived and couched them in so small a roome.

[a] An. 553. nu. 214.

2. Fifſt,

2. First, that they who contended to have Christ called *unum de sancta Trinitate*, were heretikes, or Eutycheans, or unjustly suspected thereof, is not onely untrue, but bewrayes the Cardinals obstinate and obdurate affection to Nestorianisme; for as *Dionysius* [b] *Exiguus* in his Preface to the Epistle of *Proclus*, witnesseth, and most truly, the disciples of *Theodorus Mopsvestenus* began to teach an impious faith to the people, with most crafty subtilty professing the Trinity to bee in such sort of one Essence, *ut Christum Dominum nostrum unum ex Trinitate nullatenus faterentur, that they would by no meanes confesse Christ our Lord to be one of the Trinity;* and thereupon they taught a quaternity in the persons. If *Baronius* esteeme it heresie to professe Christ, *unum de sancta Trinitate*, then is hee certainly by this, besides all other evidences, convicted to be a Nestorian heretike, for it is an Article of their Nestorian, and repugnant to the Catholike faith, to deny or doubt to call Christ, *unum de sancta Trinitate*.

3. Secondly, that the Councell of *Chalcedon* made ever any doubt to professe Christ to bee *unum de sancta Trinitate*, or that they would rather call him, *unam personam Trinitatis*, is another vile Nestorian slander, and hereticall untruth of *Baronius*. The Councell of *Chalcedon*, saith *Iustinian* [c] approved the Epistle of *Proclus, wherin it is taught, that we ought to confesse our Lord Iesus Christ to be one of the holy Trinity : Proclus,* saith [d] *Dionysius Exiguus*, did marveilously resist that impiety, and hee taught our Lord Iesus Christ, *unum de Trinitate esse, to bee one of the Trinity.* When the Nestorians troubled the Church about this matter, *Iustinian* set forth a most religious *Imperiall Edict* [e], wherein hee commanded all to professe Christ to bee *unum de Trinitate;* wee anathematize, saith he, every heresie, especially *Nestorius*, and those who thinke, or have thought as he did; wee anathematize those who deny or will not confesse our Lord Iesus Christ, *unum esse ex sancta & consubstantiali Trinitate, to be one of the holy and consubstantiall Trinitie.* This Imperiall Edict the very next yeare after it was published was confirmed by Pope *Iohn*, who thus writeth [f] to the Emperour, *You for the love of the faith, and to remove heresie, have published an Edict, which, because it agreeth with the Apostolike doctrine, wee confirme by our authority :* and againe, *You have writ and published those things, which both the Apostolike doctrine, and the venerable authority of the holy Fathers hath decreed, & nos in omnibus confirmamus, and we confirme it in all points : This your faith is the true and certaine religion, this all the Fathers & Bishops of Rome, and the Apostolike See hath hitherto inviolably kept; this confession whosoever doth contradict, hee is an alien from the holy Communion, and from the Catholike Church.* Thus Pope *Iohn.* What can any man in the world now thinke else of *Baronius*, but condemne him for an accursed heretike ? Hee denyes the Councell of *Chalcedon* to embrace that profession, *unum de Trinitate*, which, as the Emperour and Pope witnesse, it earnestly embraceth; he not onely suspecteth in this place, but in plaine termes else-where [g], he calleth the *Scythian Monks Eutycheans, heretikes, and oppugners of the Councell of Chalcedon*, and that for this cause, for that both themselves professed, and required others to professe Christ to bee *unum de sancta Trinitate* ; nor content here-

b *Extat in Bib. S. pat.tom.3.*

c *Leg.7. de summa Trinit.ca.4.*

d *Loco citato.*

e *Edict. extat apud Bar. an. 533.nu.7.9.*

f *Epist. 1. Iob.2. ad Iustin.to.2. Cont.pa.404. et Bar.an 534. nu.15.et seq.*

g *Plaud compescitur eosdem ipsos (Scythie Monachos) Eutycheanos fuisse hæreticos. Bar. an.519.nu.99.*

herewith hee addeth these words, the heresie whereof with no niter can bee washt away: hee saineth, saith *Baronius* [h], that these words, *unus de Trinitate est crucifixus*, are to bee added for the strengthning and explaning of the Councell of *Chalcedon*; which sentence (*unus de Trinitate est crucifixus*) the Legates of the Apostolike Sea, *prorsus reijciendam esse putarunt*, thought to bee such as ought utterly to be rejected, as being never uted by the Fathers in their Synodall sentences; *latere enim sciebant sub melle venenum*, for they knew that poison did lye under this hony. Now seeing by *Iustinians Edict*, and the Popes confirmation thereof, all, who either refuse, or who will not professe Christ to bee *unum de sancta Trinitate*, are accursed, and excluded from the Catholike Church and communion; *Baronius* cannot possibly escape that iust censure, who condemneth that profession as hereticall, and as repugnant to the faith of *Chalcedon*. Thus while the Cardinall labours to prove by this the Acts of the fift Councell to bee corrupt, hee demonstrates himselfe to bee both untrue, hereticall, rejected out of the Church, and a slanderer of the holy Councell of *Chalcedon*, as favouring the heresie of *Nestorius*.

4. Thirdly, whereas hee saith, that the Scythian Monkes would *inferre verba ista in Synodum Chalcedonensem*, bring or thrust in those words into the Councell of *Chalcedon*, it is a slander without all colour or ground of truth: they saw divers Nestorians obstinate in denying this truth, that Christ was *unus de sancta Trinitate*, who pretended for them that these words were not expressed in the Councell of *Chalcedon*; the Monkes and Catholikes most justly replyed, that though the expresse words were not there, yet the sense of them was decreed in that Councell, that this confession was but an expression or explication of that which was truly, implicitely, and more obscurely decreed at *Chalcedon*. To falsifie the Acts of that Councell, or adde one syllable unto it, otherwise than by way of explanation or declaration, that, the Monks and Catholikes, whom *Baronius* calleth Eutyches, never sought to doe, as at large appeares by that most learned and orthodoxall booke written by *Iohannes Maxentius* about this very cause, against which booke, and the Author thereof, the more earnestly *Baronius* doth oppose himselfe, and call them hereticall, hee doth not therby one whit disgrace them (his tongue and pen is no slander, at least not to weighed) but the more he still intangles himselfe in the heresie of the Nestorians, out of which in that cause none can extricate him, as in another Treatise I purpose God willing, to demonstrate.

5. Fourthly, whereas *Baronius* saith, that the Scythian Monkes prevailed not in the dayes of *Hormisda*, *quod absque additamento Synods recte consisteret*, because the Synod of *Chalcedon* was well enough without that addition, hee shewes a notable sleight of his hereticall mind. That the Synod is well enough without adding those words, an expresse part of the Synodall decree, or as written *totidem verbis* by the Councell of *Chalcedon*, is most true, but nothing to the purpose; for neither the Scythian Monks nor any Catholikes did affirme them so to bee, or wish them so to bee added, for that had beene to

say

h *An.cod.nu 102.*

say in expreſſe words, wee will have the decree falſified, or written in other words than it was by the Councell: But that the Synod was well enough without this additament, as an explication of it, and declaration of the ſenſe of that Councell, is moſt untrue; for both *Iuſtinian* by his Edict commanded, and Pope *Iohn* by his *Apoſtolike* authoritie confirmed, that to bee the true meaning, both of that Councell, and of all the holy Fathers: And when a controverſie is once moved, and on foote, whether Chriſt ought to bee called *unus de ſancta Trinitate*, for a man then to deny this, or deny it to bee decreed in the Councell of *Chalcedon*, or to deny that it ought to be added as a true explanation of that Councell, is to deny the whole Catholike faith, and the decrees of the foure firſt Councels; and though one ſhall ſay and profeſſe in words, as did *Hormiſda* and his Legates, that they hold the whole Councell of *Chalcedon*, yet in that they expreſly deny this truth, which was certainly decreed at *Chalcedon*, their generall profeſſion ſhall not excuſe them, but their expreſſe deniall of this one particular ſhall demonſtrate them, both to bee heretikes, and expreſly to beleeve and hold an hereſie repugnant to that Councell, which in a generality they profeſſe to hold, but indeed and truth doe not. Even as the expreſſe denying of the manhood, or Godhead of Chriſt, or reſurrection of the dead ſhall convince one to bee an heretike, though hee profeſſe himſelfe in a generality to beleeve and hold all that the holy Scriptures doe teach, or the Nicene fathers decree. If *Baronius* his words, that the Councell is right without that additament, bee taken in the former ſenſe, they are idle, vaine, and ſpoken to no purpoſe, which, of the Cardinals deepe wiſedome is not to bee imagined: If they bee taken (as I ſuppoſe they are) in the later ſenſe, they undeniably demonſtrate him to bee a Cardinall Neſtorian.

6. But leaving all the reſt of the Cardinals frauds in this paſſage, let us come to that laſt clauſe which concernes the corrupting of the Councell of *Chalcedon*. This, ſaith he, which in *Hormiſdaes* dayes they could not, now in this fift Synod they obtained, now they added to the words of the Synod this clauſe, *qui eſt Dominus unus de ſancta Trinitate*: A very perilous corruption ſure, to expreſſe that clauſe which all the Biſhops of *Rome*, (*ſemper excipio Hormiſdam*) with all Catholikes, beleeved and taught, which, whoſoever denieth or wil not profeſſe, is anathematized, and excluded from the Catholike Church. Is not this thinke you a very ſore corruption of the Councell of *Chalcedon*? Is not the Cardinall a rare man of judgement that could ſpie ſuch a maine fault in theſe Acts of the fift Councell, that they profeſſe Chriſt to be *unum de ſancta Trinitate*; to which profeſſion both they and all other were bound under the cenſure of an anathema.

7. Yea, but in the Acts thoſe words are cited as the words of the Councell of *Chalcedon*, whoſe they are not. A meere fancy and calumny of the Cardinall: they are plainly ſet downe as the words of the fift Synod, whoſe indeed they are; and it relateth not preciſely the words of the Councell of *Chalcedon*, nor what it there expreſſed, *totidem verbis*, but the true ſumme and ſubſtance of what is there decreed.

creed. For thus they say[i], *The holy Synod of Chalcedon in the definition* i Coll. 6. pa. 575. a.
which it made of faith, doth professe God the Word incarnate, to be made man,
this is all they report of the Councell of *Chalcedon,* as by the opposition of *Ibas* his *Epistle* is apparent, wherein they oppose not that he denyed Christ to be one of the Trinity; but that hee called them heretikes who taught the Word incarnate to be made man. That clause which they adde [That Christ is one of the Trinity] is an addition of the fift Councell it selfe, explicating that of Christ, which the *Emperiours Edict* bound them to professe, as being the true sense and meaning of the Councell at *Chalcedon,* but not as being word for word set downe in the decree of *Chalcedon.* And even as he were more than ridiculous, who would accuse one to corrupt the Councell of *Chalcedon* for saying they professed Christ to be God and man, who was borne in *Bethleem,* and fled from *Herod* into Ægypt; so is the Cardinall as ridiculous in objecting this as a corruption of the Synod, or addition to the Councell of *Chalcedon,* that they say the Councell taught the Word of God to bee man, who is our Lord Iesus Christ, one of the holy Trinity. Both additions are true, but neither of them affirmed to be expresly, and *totidem verbis,* set downe in the Councell of *Chalcedon.* Why but looke to the Cardinals proofe; for he would not for any good affirme such a matter without proofe. What? doe yee aske for proofe of the Cardinall? I tell you, it is proofe enough that he sayth it: and truly in this poynt he produceth neither any proofe, nor any shadow of reason to prove either that those words are falsely inserted into the Acts of the fift Councell, or that the fift Councell cited them as the very expresse words of the Councell of *Chalcedon:* all the proofe is grounded on his old Topicke place *Ipse dixit,* which is a sory kind of arguing, against any that love the truth: for although against the Pope or their popish cause, any thing which he writeth is very strong evidence against them; seeing the Cardinall is very circumspect & wary to let nothing, no not a syllable fall from him which may in the least wise seem to prejudice the Popes dignity, or the cause of their Church, unlesse the maine force and undeniable evidence of truth doe wrest and wring it from his pen: yet in any matter of history, wherein he may advantage the Pope, or benefit their cause, it is not by many degrees so good to say, the *illustrissimus Cardinalis* affirmes it, which is now growne a familiar kinde of proofe among them[k], as to k *Vide Gretz. tractatus varios. & alios ejus farine.* say, *Ovid, Æsop,* or *Iacobus Voraginensis* affirme it, therefore it is certainly true. His Annals in the art of fraudulent, vile, and pernicious untruths farre excell the most base fictitious Poemes or Legends that ever as yet have seene the Sunne.

LI   CAP.

CAP. XXVI.

The second alteration *of the Synodall Acts pretended by* Baronius, for that *Ibas* is sayd therein to have denyed the Epistle written to *Maris* to be his, *refuted.*

a *Dum falsa quedam ibi (in Actis 5. Concilij) asserta reperiuntur, de impostura non mediocrem suspicionem inducunt: cum viz. ibi dictum habetur, Ibam negasse Epistolā esse suam. Baron.* 553. *nu.* 211
b *Duo aut plura mendacia de Ibe epistola teguntur. Bin. Notis in Conc.* 5. *pa.* 605.
b. *Acta Conc.* 5. *nō uno loco indicant quod Ibas Epistolam non agnoverit, verū hec sententia, &c. ibid. p.* 607. *a*
c *Ibas non est ausus eam suam dicere Epistolam Iustin. edictum pa.* 496. *b. Epistolam Ibas denegat suam. Greg. lib.* 7. *Epist.* 53.
d *Abnegans Epistolam. Coll.* 6. *pa.* 563. *b. Eo quod abnegabat Ibas illa. Coll. eadem. pa.* 564. *d. Vnde & Ibas eam abnegabat. ibid. & alibi.*
e *Loco nuper citato.*
f *Loco citato.*
g *Coll.* 6. *p.* 564. *a Johannes Sebastiæ, Seleucus Amasiæ, Constantinus, Patritius, Petrus & Atharbius, omnes Metropolitani pariter interloquuti sunt, eo quod Ibas abnegavit illa, &c.*

1.  He second thing which our *Momus* carpeth at, is for that in these Acts it is sayd that *Ibas* denyed the *Epistle* written to *Maris*, to bee his: which saith *Baronius* is untrue; for *Ibas* professed the *Epistle* to be his. And *Binius* not content to call it with the Cardinall an untruth, in plaine termes affirmes *it* to be a lye. Had not hatred to the truth corrupted or quite blinded the judgement of *Baronius* and *Binius*, they would never have quarelled with the Acts about this matter, nor for this accused them to have beene corrupt. They may as well collect the Edict of *Iustinian*, or that famous Epistle of Pope *Gregorie*, wherein he writeth of *Ibas* and the *three Chapters*, to be corrupted, and of no credit, as well as the Acts of the fift Councell: for in both c them the same is said concerning the deniall of *Ibas* which is in these Acts. If notwithstanding the avouching of that denyall, they may passe for sincere and incorrupt, it was certainly malice and not reason that moved the Cardinall and *Binius* to carpe at the Acts for this cause: which will much more appeare, if any please but to view the Acts themselves. For this is not spoken *obiter*, nor once, but the Councell insisteth upon it, repeateth it in severall d places, and divers times; and if those words were taken away, there would be an apparent *hiatus* in the text of those Acts. The words then are truly the words of the true Acts, the corruption is onely in the braine of *Baronius* and *Binius*.

2. Now whereas the Cardinall and *Binius* so confidently affirme this to be untrue, or a lye, that *Ibas* denyed his Epistle, and so accuse the whole Councell to lye in this matter, they doe but keepe their owne tongues and pens in ure with calumnies: the untruth and lye belongs neither to the Councell, nor to the Acts, but must bee returned to themselves to whom onely it is due. For the Councels truth herein, the Emperour is a most honourable witnesse, who saith e, *Demonstratur Ibas eam abnegasse, Ibas is demonstrated,* or by evident proofe knowne, *to have denyed his Epistle.* Pope *Gregory* is another witnesse above exception, who saith f, *Epistolam Ibas denegat suam, Ibas denyed the Epistle to be his*: the fift Councell also doth not onely affirme it, but prove g it by the testimony of six Metropolitan Bishops, and their interloquution in the Councell of *Chalcedon*, they all sayd they received *Ibas, eo quod negabat illa*, because he did deny *those things which were objected by his adversaries*: a great part of which was that *Epistle.* All these are witnesses for the Councell: what witnesses now doth the Cardinall or *Binius* bring to countervaile these? truly not so much as

one:

one : and one were but a poore number to be oppofed to fo many, and fo worthy men, teftifying the contrary. Now whether the teftimony of the Emperour, Pope *Gregory*, of fix Metropolitanes, and an whole generall approved Councell affirming this ; or *Baronius* without any one witneffe denying this, be more credible, let the very beft friends of *Baronius* judge : but *Baronius* loves to bee *Iohannes ad oppofitum*, to Emperours, Popes, Bifhops, and Councels : if they fay any thing that pleafeth not his palate, that is indeed, if they fay the truth.

3. But yet *Baronius* hath a proofe of his faying, which is this ; becaufe *Ibas* [h] confeffed it to be his, and hee tels us this is in the Acts of *Chalcedon*. Say he did confeffe it, as I will not deny that he did, (though I verily thinke the Cardinall fpeakes an untruth, in faying that this is in the Acts, for I finde not in thofe Acts either any fuch expreffe confeffion, or ought from whence it can be collected : and *Iuftinian* plainly faith [i], *that Ibas durft not acknowledge it to be his*, for the blafphemies contained therein,) but I admit that *Ibas* confeffed it to be his. Doth it thence follow, that he denyed it not to be his ? might he not doe both ? might he not contradict himfelfe ? doth not the Cardinall, (who neither for wit nor wifedome will yeeld one jote to *Ibas*,) doth not he as much in this very caufe of *Ibas Epiftle* : In one place he [k] fayth, the Epiftle being produced, *non effe Ibæ compertam, it was found not to be the Epiftle of Ibas*, as the Acts of *Chalcedon* doe fhew : in another [l] place he faith the quite contrary : *The true Acts of Chalcedon have it, that Ibas confeffed it to be his Epiftle*. Is not this a peece of handfome worke of the Cardinall ? The Epiftle is his, the Epiftle is not his : the Acts of *Chalcedon* fay it is his ; the Acts of *Chalcedon* fay it is not his. Could *Vertumnus* himfelfe play more cunningly faft and loofe than he doth ? Might not *Ibas* doe the like ? fometimes for his owne credit deny the Epiftle to be his, though at other times he confeffed it to be his ? Is it not more likely in it felfe, more charity in others to thinke that *Ibas* did thus, than that the Emperour, Pope *Gregory*, and a generall Councell did all confpire to tell a lye.

4. And not to difpute that (which we have now admitted) whether he confeffed it to be his or not ; that he did certainly deny it to be his Epiftle, if neither the fift generall Councell, nor *Iuftinian*, nor *Gregory* had teftified this, yet the Acts of the Councell of *Chalcedon* where *Ibas* himfelfe was perfonally prefent, have fo cleare a demonftration thereof, that I cannot fufficiently admire either the ftupidity, or the moft fhameleffe dealing of *Baronius* and *Binius*, who with their foule mouthes call it an untruth, and a lye : for that Epiftle was writ by *Ibas* not onely after the union made betwixt *Iohn* and *Cyrill*, as *Iuftinian* [m], and the fift [n] Councell truly teach ; but as wee have before clearly [o] proved, at leaft two yeares after the fame. In that Epiftle *Cyrill* is called an heretike, an Apollinarian, as both the fift Councell teftifieth, faying [p], *Epiftola Cyrillum fanctæ memoriæ hæreticum vocat* ; and the very words of the Epiftle doe make evident, wherein *Ibas* faith [q], *Cyrill is found to have falne into the doctrine of Apollinaris* : And againe, fpeaking of thefe twelve Chapters of *Cyrill*, which both the *Ephefine* and *Chalcedon* Councell confirme, he calls [r] them *plena omni*

L l 2   impietate,

h *Acta Germana habent Ibam confeffum, eam effe fuam : fed & acta Conc. thalc. eandem Epiftolam ut Ibæ cognitam effe docent. Bar. an. 448. nu. 77.*
i *Loco citat.*

k *Bar an. 432. nu. 71.*

l *Bar. 448. nu. 77*

m *Epiftola facta oftenditur poft unitatem ad orientales factâ. Edict. Iuft. loco citato.*
n *Impia epiftola poft unitatem fcripta oftenditur. Conc. 5. Coll. 6. pa. 563.*
o *Sup. ca. 10.*
p *Coll. 6. pa. 575. a.*
q *in Conc. Chalc. act. 10. pa. 113. a*
r *Jbid.*

impietate, *full of all impiety*, and contrary to the faith. Thus writ *Ibas* of *Cyrill* two yeares at least after the union was fully made. Now in the Acts before *Photius* and *Eustathius*, which are expressed in the Councell of *Chalcedon*, *Ibas* there professed before the Iudges, that after the union once made, *we all*, sayth he [f], *held communion with Cyrill*, we accounted him an orthodoxall Bishop, & *nullus eum appellat hæreticum*, *and none after that called Cyrill an heretike* : was not this a plaine denyall that he writ this Epistle ? for whosoever writ it calleth *Cyrill* an heretike, and that divers yeares after the union : now *Ibas* denyeth that ever after the union he called *Cyrill* an heretike. Could he more directly conclude that he writ not this Epistle ? unlesse one will say that to deny *Baronius* to have written or published one word after the beginning of Pope *Sixtus* the fift, be not a certaine denyall, that the Annalls which goe under his name, and were all published after the beginning of *Sixtus* [t], are the Annalls of *Baronius*. This denyall by an evident and most certaine consequent, (not any expresse denyall *totidem verbis*, as if *Ibas* had sayd, this is not my Epistle) was it which both *Iustinian* and the fift Councell meant, as their owne words doe declare : *The Epistle*, sayth *Iustinian* [u], *being full of blasphemies*, and containing many injuries against S. *Cyrill*, is shewed to be written after the union, *ex quo demonstratur Ibas eam abnegasse, whereby it is demonstrated that Ibas denyed it*, (in that he sayd, that he never called *Cyrill* an heretike after that union.) *The impious Epistle*, sayth the Councell [x], *is shewed by the contents thereof to have beene written after the union*; therefore it appeareth that *Ibas* denyed it to be his Epistle by this, in that he sayd that he spake nothing against *Cyrill* after the union: again, *Ibas* in this denyed the Epistle, *eò quod dicebat*, because he sayd [y], after the union I am not found to have sayd ought against Saint *Cyrill*. Yea this and no other, to have beene that denyall which the Councell meant, *Baronius* knew right well; for himselfe sayth [z], that it is sayd in the Councell, that *Ibas denyed the Epistle, ex eo, for this cause*, for that after the union and peace made, he denyed that he had sayd ought against *Cyrill*: yet notwithstanding all this evidence of truth, the Cardinall to disgrace the Acts of this Councell, even against his owne knowledge and conscience affirmeth it to bee an untruth, or as *Binius* calls it, (in a most spitefull manner) a lye, that *Ibas* denyed this Epistle to be his.

f *In Conc. Chalc. Act. 10. p. 113. 2*

t *Nam primum eorum Tomum dedicavit Sixto 5. an. 1589.*

u *Loco citato.*

z *Loco citato.*

y *Coll. 6. p. 564. a*

z *an. 553. n. 211*

CAP. XXVII.

The third alteration *of the Synodall Acts pretended by* Baronius, *for that the Councell of* Chalcedon *is said therein to condemne the Epistle of* Ibas, *refuted.*

HE third corruption is by a mis-report and untrue relation which *Baronius* observeth in these Acts, for that in them the Councel of *Chalcedon* is said to have condemned that *Epistle of Ibas, which he not onely saith* [a] *is untrue,* (*Binius* cals [b] also in plaine termes, a lye,) *but addeth both that the Acts of the Councell of Chalcedon doe teach the contrary, and that out of those Acts hee hath before demonstrated the same.* Call you this a corruption of the Acts ? why, it is the maine purpose of the Councell, it is their very judgement and resolution touching the *Three Chapters,* often and with acclamations repeated. The Epistle [c] is contrary to the definition, *Epistolam* [d] *definitio sancti Chalcedonensis Concilij condemnat, definitio ejecit;* in the proofe whereof they much insist. Neither onely in the sixt collation doe they at large set downe this, but in their eighth, even in their Synodall definition [e] they expresly mention, that they have not onely said, but even demonstrated before, that this Epistle is in all things contrary to the definition of the Councell at *Chalcedon;* yea, they there adde, which is more, *that the Councel of Chalcedon would in no sort otherwise* [f] *receive* Ibas; *unlesse he himselfe did condemne the impietie contained in that Epistle.* Would any in the world (save *Baronius,* a man meerly infatuated in this cause, and such as follow his idle fancies) account that to bee a corruption or depravation of the Acts, which is the maine scope, purpose, judgement, and definition of the Synod ? which they so often in their severall Sessions repeate, of which they expresly testifie in their very definitive sentence, that they before had said, proved, & demonstrated the same, without which also if it were taken away, (as the Cardinall pretends it should,) not onely the Acts should be utterly perverted, but the quite contrary to the judgement and determination of the Councell, should bee affirmed. *Baronius* might with as great truth and probability have said, that the handling of the *Three Chapters,* or judging of the *Three Chapters* had beene a depravation and corrupting of the Acts, for this assertion that *Ibas* his Epistle was condemned by the Councell of *Chalcedon,* is as necessarie and essentiall to the Acts, as the cause it selfe of the *Three Chapters,* or any sentence that is any where set downe therein.

2. But yet if it be no depravation in the Acts, yet, saith the Cardinall, [g] and *Binius,* it is untrue, It is a lye, that the Councell of *Chalcedon* condemned that Epistle: Let falshood and impudency it selfe stand here amazed and agast at these men. This definitive sentence of

a *Quod ibidem subditur, eandem Epistolam in Synodo Chalced. fuisse damnatam, ipsa acta secus docent, neutrum enim horum verum esse superius demonstravimus.* Bar. an. 553. nu. 211.
b *Duo aut plura mendacia.* Bin. not. in Conc. 5. pa. 606. b.
c *Anathematizavit Epist. contrariam per omnia, exposita definitioni à Concilio Chalc. Sancta Synodus dixit; Scimus et nos hæc ita subsequuti esse.* Coll. 6. pa. 564. a. d *Coll. eadem pa.* 576. b.
e *Quo facto demonstratum est, contrariam per omnia Epistolam esse his quæ definitione (Chalc.) continentur.* Coll. 8. pa. 584. c.
f *Juvenimus quod non aliter passi sunt Ibam suscipere, &c.* lib.

g *Loc. citat.*

this Councell, wherein it is proclamed and decreed, that the *Epistle* of *Ibas* was condemned by the Councell of *Chalcedon*, is approved by all succeeding generall Councells, by *Pelagius*, *Gregory*, and all other their successors, till *Leo* the tenth, (that is, by the consenting judgment of the whole Catholike Church, and of all Catholikes ever since that decree was made)and now *Baronius* and *Binius* stand up to give them all the lie; they all say untruths, onely *Baronius* and *Binius* are men that drop Oracles, out of whose mouths no lie nor untruth can at any time proceed.

h *Loco cit.*

3. But saith the Cardinall [h], *The Acts of the Councell of Chalcedon doe declare this, and out of them I have before demonstrated this.* Loe, the Cardinall will not onely say it, but prove it, yea, he hath even demonstrated out of the Councell of *Chalcedon* all the former Popes, and Councels, that is, all the whole Catholike Church, to lye. I feare mee, such demonstrations will not turne to the Cardinals credit: Doe the Acts of the Councell teach or demonstrate that? could none of the Popes? none of the succeeding generall Councels spie it in those Acts, till *Baronius* took thē all tardy in an untruth? What wil you say to the Cardinal and to his demonstration, if the Acts doe not teach this? nay, if they teach directly and demonstrate the quite contrary, who then, I pray you, must have the whetstone? the Catholike Church or the illustrious Cardinall? And certainly the Acts of *Chalcedon* doe demonstrate what this fift Councell, and after it the sixt, seventh, and eighth, and the rest testifie, that this *Epistle* of *Ibas* was condemned by the Councell of *Chalcedon*. First, it is cleare and certaine by those Acts that the Councell of *Chalcedon* condemned *Nestorius*, and all the impious doctrines and blasphemies of *Nestorius*, approving the *Ephesine* [i] Councell, and the Synodall Epistle of *Cyrill*, wherein they [k] are condemned and anathematized: was not this a condemning of the Epistle of *Ibas*, which defendeth *Nestorius* and his heresies, which is full fraught with all his blasphemous doctrines? Could the Councell of *Chalcedon* condemne and anathematize the doctrine of *Nestorius*, and yet not condemne that *Epistle* which defends all those doctrines? By the Acts it is cleare and certaine, that the Councell of *Chalcedon* approve [l] their owne decree of faith: now this *Epistle*, as not onely the fift Councell often [m], but after it Pope *Gregory* saith, *procul dubio definitioni Synodi probatur adversa, without doubt is contrary to the definition of the Councell of Chalcedon.* Is not the approving of their definition a rejecting and condemning of whatsoever writing is contrary to the same? By the Acts it is cleare and certaine, that the Councell even in their definition [o] forbids, and pronounceth it unlawfull for any to teach, or produce, or write, or deliver any other doctrine; which whosoever doth, if hee bee a Bishop or Clerke, hee shall bee deposed; if a Monke or Lay man, anathematized: Is not this a plaine forbidding of that Epistle to bee read, or taught, the doctrine whereof is directly contrary to their decree? when by the Councels decree it may neither be taught, written, nor read, (otherwise then with a detestation) is not this a condemning of it by the Councell? by the Acts that is cleare in the fift Councell [p], that the Councell of

Chalcedon

i *S. et magna Synodus 5. Cyrilli Synodales Epistolas amplexa est, ad arguendū Nestorianam dementiam, &c. Conc. Chalc. Act. 5. pa. 96. et Can. 1 pa. 15.*

k *Omnes Episcopi clamaverunt, Quicunque Nestoriano anathematizat, anathema sit. Omnes Nestorij Epistolas, et dogmata anathematizamus. Con. Ephes. to. 2. ca. 4. pa. 743.*

l *Huic omnes cōsentimus, omnes ita sapimus Act. 5. pa. 98.*

m *Epistolam definitio S. Chalcedonensis Concilij condemnavit. Collat. 6. pa. 576 b. et alibi.*

n *Lib. 7. Ind. 2. Epist. 54.*

o *Chal. Conc. Act. 5. pa. 38.*

p *Hoc judicium Photij et Eustathij omnes Episcopi (Chal. Cōc.) sequuti, versi exerunt ipsum (Ibam) anathematizare Nestorium et impia ejus dogmata. Con. 5. Coll. 6. pa. 563. b.*

Chalcedon approved the judgement of *Photius* and *Euſtathius*, for as *Photius* and *Euſtathius*, ſo they all at q *Chalcedon* required *Ibas* to anathematize *Neſtorius* and his doctrines, before they would receive him. Now as the fiſt Councell r truly ſaith, to approve the judgement of *Photius* and *Euſtathius*, *Nihil eſt aliud quam condemnare impiam Epiſtolam*; this is nothing elſe than to condemne the impious Epiſtle, ſeeing in it *Neſtorius* and his hereſies are defended. To be ſhort (for there are very many other evidences to declare this,) Pope *Gregory* ſ teſtifieth, that the fiſt Councell was *in omnibus ſequax, did in all things follow the Councell of Chalcedon*; if in all, then in condemning this impious *Epiſtle*, and if they followed it therein, then moſt certainly the Councell of *Chalcedon* condemned it before them. So untrue it is which the Cardinall ſaith, that the Acts doe ſhew, and that out of them he hath demonſtrated, that the Councell of *Chalcedon* did not condemne this *Epiſtle*, whereas he hath demonſtrated nothing ſo cleare, as himſelfe to bee a malicious and ſhameleſſe downfacer of moſt certaine and evident truths. Thus much of his firſt ſort of *corruptions*, namely, the *three variations* or depravations, wherewith, as you ſee, hee hath ſlandered the Acts of this fiſt Councell, to his immortall diſgrace.

q *Ibam anathematizantem Neſtorius et ejus impia dogmata, permanere in Sacerdotio volo. Euſtb. Epiſ. Accepta in Conc. hal. Act. 10 pa. 115. ſic Stephanus, Romanas, Eunomius et omnes Epiſcopi clamaverunt; omnes eadem dicimus. Ibid. pa. 116.a.*
r *Coll.&.p.563.b*
ſ *Loco citato.*

Cap. XXVIII.

The three firſt defects in the Synodall Acts, pretended by Baronius, *for that the Acts againſt the Origeniſts, the Edict of* Iuſtinian, *and his Epiſtle touching that cauſe, are wanting therein, refuted.*

1. THE ſecond kinde of the Cardinals Heteroclites, are his *defectives* a : And here he and *Binius* labour to prove the lameneſſe and defects of theſe Acts by five inſtances: The firſt of them concernes the proceeding againſt *Origen*, and the Origeniſts, which was done in the fiſt Synod, but is now wanting in the Acts thereof. Let us firſt heare what *Binius* b ſaith hereof; *The curtaling and maime of theſe Acts doe thoſe fragments declare which we have added to the end of the Synod, quodque nulla vel levis tantum mentio reperiatur de condemnatis erroribus Origenis*; and becauſe there is no mention, no not any ſmall, or light mention, found in them, touching the errours of *Origen* condemned. If one were diſpoſed to quit *Binius* with his owne uncivill words, *Binius* ſhould here be proclamed both for a moſt impudent lyar, and a ſhameleſſe belyar of theſe Synodal acts, of this holy Councell. There is expreſſe mention of condemning *Origen* in the fiſt Collation, *Origen* c *was anathematized after his death in the time of Theophilus Biſhop of Alexandria, which alſo your ſanctitie*, (hee ſpeakes to the Biſhops of this Synod) *and Vigilius Pope of Rome have now done*. Again, there is expreſſe mention of him, and his errours in the eighth collation in the very Synodall and *definitive* ſentence of the Councell, wherein

a *Intelligas quamplurima in eadem 5. Synodo deſideran. Bar. an.553 nu.243.*

b *Decurtationem et mutilationem Actorum indicant illa fragmenta quæ in fine hujus Synodi ſubjungi curavimus. Bin. not. in Conc. 5. § Conſtitutum.*

c *Coll. 5. pa. 552.*

in

in *Origen* and his impious writings are condemned; for thus it is written [c], *If any man doe not accurse Arius, Eunomius, Macedonius, Apollinarius, Nestorius, Eutyches, Origen, cum impijs eorum conscriptis, with their impious writings, and all other heretikes condemned by the Catholike Church, let that man bee accursed.* When the holy Councell not onely mentions the condemning of *Origen*, but by their judiciall sentence themselves also condemne, both him, his errors, and his impious writings; what a face of Adamant had *Binius*, against the truth, against his owne text of the Councell, against his conscience and knowledge to say, there is no mention, no not any *levis mentio*, to be found in the Acts of the errors of *Origen* condemned? or if *Binius* will not be perswaded of his untruth, for us, let him acknowledge it for his Master *Baronius* his credit, who saith [d], *In these Synodall Acts there is made onely, brevis mentio de Origine ejusque erroribus condemnatis*, a short mention in the eleventh anathematisme of *Origen, and his errours condemned*: if there bee *brevis mentio* of him and his errours, then *Binius* must cry the Acts forgivenesse, for saying there is no mention at all, no not *levis mentio*, of his errours.

2. Let us see now if *Baronius* deale any better. *Constat*, saith [e] hee; *It is manifest by the testification of many, that Origen, Didimus, and Evagrius, together with their errours were condemned in this fift Synod, and that there was written, at least recited & repeated against them those ten Anathematismes which Nicephorus setteth downe; but in the Acts there is onely a briefe mention that Origen and his errours were condemned.* Baronius adds one speciall point further out of *Cedrenus*, that in this fift Councell, first [f], they handled the cause against *Origen, and then against the Three Chapters*: So by the Cardinals profession there wants the whole first action in these Acts of this Synod, which, it may be, had many Sessions, as the other Action about the *three Chapters*: Besides this, there wants also, saith hee [g], *the letters or Edict published by Iustinian*: Thirdly, there wants [h], *the Epistle of Iustinian*, sent to the Synod about the condemning of *Origen*, which is set downe by *Cedrenus*, out of whom both *Baronius* reciteth it, and *Binius* adjoyns it at the end of the Acts among the fragments which are wanting in these Acts. These *three defects* touching the cause of *Origen* doth the Cardinall alleage.

3. But in very deed none of these three, nor ought else, which *Baronius* mentioneth, argue any defect at all in these Acts, but they evidently demonstrate in the Card. a maine defect of judgement, and an overflowing superabundance of malice against this holy Synod, and these true Acts thereof. That the cause of *Origen* was not, as hee supposeth, the first *Action*, or the first cause handled by the Synod; I might alleage the most cleare testimony of his [i] owne witnesse *Nicephorus*, who after the narration of the *three Chapters*, and the Synodall sentence touching them delivered, which he accounts for the first Session of the Synod, addeth [k], *In secunda autem Sessione*, but in the second *Sessiö*, the Libels against the impious doctrines of Origen were offred & read, and Iustinian, rursum Synodũ de eis sententiä ferre jussit, commanded againe the Synod to give sentence in that cause. So *Nicephorus*: whereby it is evident that the Cardinal and his *Cedrenus* are foully deceived in saying, that

that the cause of *Origen* was first handled by the Synod, and after that
the cause of the *three Chapters* : but I oppose to these, farre greater
and even authentike records, the *Epistle* of the Emperour [1] to the Synod, who, at the beginning and first meeting of the Bishops in the
Councell, proposed to their handling the cause of the *Three Chapters*,
and no other at all; commanding them without delay to discusse and
give their judgement in that : I oppose the *definition* and Synodall decree [m], wherein is set downe their whole proceeding, and what they
handled almost every day of their meeting, from the beginning to
the ending; so that it alone is as a Thesean thred, which wil not permit
a man to erre in this cause, unlesse he maliciously shut his eyes against
the truth, and wilfully depart out of that plaine path. They [n] came to
the Synod to decide the controversie then moved about the *Three*
Chapters, at the command of the Emperour; before they entred to
the handling thereof, they often intreated by their messengers, Pope
Vigilius to come together with them, (which was all that they did in
the first [o] & second [p] day of their meeting or Collation) when *Vigili-*
us would not come, then by the Apostles admonition, they prepared
themselves to the handling of the cause proposed, by setting downe
a confession of their faith, consonant to the foure former Councels,
and exposition of the Fathers, and promising in their next meeting to
handle the cause of the *Three Chapters*, which was the summe of the
third [q] dayes Collation : *Cumque* [r] *ita confessi sumus, initium fecimus ex-*
aminationis trium Capitulorum; and when wee had made this confession, wee
began the examination of the Three Chapters; loe, they did *initium sume-*
re, they began with this. Could they speak more plainly, that the cause
of *Origen* was not first handled? as if prophetically they meant to refute this untruth of *Baronius* and *Cedrenus*; and wee first discussed the
cause of *Theodorus Mopsvestenus* out of his owne writing there read
before us : This was all they did the fourth [s], and a great part of the
fift [t] day of their Collatiō. *His de Theodoro discussis, pauca de Theodoreto;*
next after the discussing of the Chapter touching Theodorus, wee caused a
few things to bee repeated out of the impious writings of Theodoret; for the
satisfying of the reader; and this they did in the end of the fift day or
Collation. *Tertio loco Epistola quam Ibas, &c*; *In the third place we propo-*
sed, and examined the Epistle of Ibas : and this they did at large, and it
was all they did in the sixt [u] day of their Collation. The whole cause
being thus, and, as the Councell confesseth, most diligently and sufficiently examined, the Councell (as it seemeth by their owne words
in the end of the sixt Collation) intended to proceed to sentence in
the next day of their meeting : but before ought was done therein, the
Emperour sent unto the Synod certaine letters of *Vigilius*, testifying
his condemning of those *Three Chapters*, and some other writings, the
reading of thē is all was done in the seventh [x] day of their Collation.
Now for that the cause was sufficiently examined before, and these
letters were read onely for a further evidence, but not for necessity of
the cause, and for that the Synod did nothing themselves, but onely
heard the letters, and applauded the Emperours zeale and care for
the truth, therefore it is that this seventh Collation, and what was
done

l *Extat Cont. 5. Coll. 1.*

m *Collat. 8.*

n *Pre Dei vo-luntate & justi-one piissimi Im-peratoris conve-nimus. Ibid.*

o *1. Coll. 4. die Maij.*
p *2. Coll. 8. die Maij.*

q *3. Coll. 9. die Maij.*
r *Loc. cit. Coll. 8. pa. 584.*

s *Coll. 4. 11. die Maij.*
t *Coll. 5. 14 die Maij. pridie Idus Maij. Bar. an. 553. nu. 41.*

u *6. Coll. 19. Maij.*

x *7. Coll. 26. die Maij.*

done therein is omitted in the Synodall sentence, and the Councell which on that seventh day had made ready and intended to have pronounced their sentence, by this occasion deferred it to the next, which was the eighth [y] day of their Collation, using these for the last words of their seventh dayes meeting, *De tribus capitulis altero die adjuvante Deo Synodicam sententiam proferemus* ; *God willing wee will pronounce our Synodall sentence touching this cause of the three Chapters the next day.* And so they did in that eighth, which was their last day of Collation. Thus not onely by *Nicephorus* and the Emperours *Epistle*, but by the evident testimony of the whole Synod in the synodall sentence, it is undoubtedly certaine that the cause of *Origen* was not as he fancieth the first action or cause handled in the Synod, and that he doth but play the Mome in carping at the Acts for want of the first Action.

y 8.Coll. 2.die Iunij.

4. It may bee yet that the cause of *Origen* was the second action in the fift Synod, as *Nicephorus* [z] saith, and after him *Evagrius* [*], and that is enough to prove the defects of these Acts. No, it was not the second neither ; as it was not before, so neither was it handled after the other of the *Three Chapters*, witnesse the Synodall sentence it selfe, wherein all the matters which every day they examined and discussed are set downe and repeated ; after repetition they testifie [a] also, *Repetitis igitur omnibus, quæ apud nos acta sunt, all things being repeated which were done or handled by way of discussion among us,* or in this Synod. Seeing they repeated all that was debated among them, and make no mention of this cause of *Origen,* it is undoubtedly certaine that *Origens* cause was not debated either first or last in the Synod ; it was neither the first *action,* as *Cedrenus* and *Baronius,* nor the second, as *Evagrius* and *Nicephorus* suppose; besides the very determination of the Synod, evidently declares the errours of *Nicephorus* and *Evagrius* : The books, say they [b], *against the doctrine of Origen being offered to the Synod,* the Emperour demanded of the Councell, *Quid de his statueret, What it would decree concerning those doctrines?* A matter utterly incoherent and improbable ; for in the synodall decree concerning the *three Chapters,* which they suppose to be made before this cause of *Origen* was either heard or proposed, the Councell had expresly delivered their judgement, and condemned both *Origen* and his impious writings. When they had already condemned both him and his errors, what an incongruity is it to make the Emperour demand, what they would decree of him and his errours ? Or may we thinke that the holy Synod would first condemne *Origen,* and his impious writings as they did, in the synodall sentence against the *three Chapters,* and then afterwards examin the matter, and make an enquiry whether *Origen* and his writings were to bee condemned or not ? which were to follow that disorder which the Switzers are reported to have used in judgement, (which was most justly called *Iudicium vetitum*) to execute a man, and then try and examine whether he ought to be executed or not. Farre be it from any to imagine such injustice and rashnesse to have beene in this holy generall Councell. Seeing then they condemned and accursed *Origen* and all his errours, in that which *Nicephorus* and *Evagrius* account the former Session, it is ridiculous to think that either the Emperour

z Loco citato.
* Evag.lib.4.
ca.37.

a Coll.8.p.586.a

b Niceph. et
Evag.loc.citat.

perour urged, or that they themselves would in the second Seffion goe
Switzer-like to examine the bookes and doctrines of *Origen*, whether
he & they ought to be condemned. Some doubt perhaps may arife out
of those words in the Councell [d], which the Cardinall flily [e] alledgeth,
*Origen was condemned in the time of Theophilus, Quod etiam nunc in
ipfa fecit veftra Sanctitas, which your Holineffe hath now done,* and Pope
Vigilius allo: But if the words be marked, they make nothing againft
that which I have faid: for neither hath that [*Nunc*] a relation to this
prefent Councell, (for it is certaine that in it *Vigilius* did not condemne *Origen*, feeing he was not at all prefent in the Synod,) but to
this age; he was condemned in former ages, as namely by *Theophilus*,
and now alfo, that is, in this your age; and even by your felves, and by
Vigilius: and if ought elfe were imported thereby, yet is it onely faid
that *Origen* was now condemned: which was indeed done by the Synod: but that his cause was then examined and debated there, neither
is it true, neither doe the words any way imply.

5. Nay I adde further, not onely that this Councell did not debate
this caufe of *Origen*, but it had beene both fuperfluous, and an open
wrong to themfelves, and to the whole Church, to have entred into
the examination thereof. For befide many other former judgements,
not many [e] yeares before in the time of *Mennas*, both the Emperour
in an Imperiall *Edict* [f] had condemned *Origen* and his errors; and by
the Emperours command, *Mennas* with a Synod of Bifhops then prefent at *Conftantinople*, had confirmed that condemnation; the other
Bifhops who were abfent did the like, the Emperour requiring every
Patriarke to caufe all the Bifhops fubject to his jurifdiction, to fubfcribe to the fame. The doctrines and writings of *Origen* were no
doubt at that time fully debated; all the Bifhops prefent in this fift
Councell had then fubfcribed and confented to the condemnation of
him and his errors; fo had *Vigilius* and all Catholike Bifhops in the
Weft. Seeing the judgement of the Church in condemning *Origen*
was univerfall, would the Councell, after themfelves, and all other
Catholike Bifhops, that is, after the judgement of the whole Catholike Church, now debate and examine whether *Origen* and his doctrines ought to be condemned? They might as well call into queftion
whether *Arius*, or *Macedonius*, or *Neftorius*, or *Eutyches*, and their
doctrine fhould bee condemned: the judgement of the Catholike
Church was alike paffed on them all: for this Councell [g] condemned
and accurfed *Origen* and his errors, as it did *Arius*, *Macedonius*, *Neftorius*, and *Eutyches*, but it condemned them all upon the knowne
judgement of the Catholike Church, not upon a new tryall or examination then taken of any one of them. And this verily feemes to have
deceived and led into error *Evagrius*, *Nicephorus*, and *Cedrenus*, (for
of *Baronius* I cannot for many reafons imagine it to have beene errour
or ignorance in him, but wilfull and malicious oppugning the truth,)
they knew or heard by report, (for even *Evagrius* [h], who lived in that
age, faith of that which hee writeth touching the fift Synod, *Of thefe
things fic actum accepimus, we have heard they were thus done,*) I fay, they
might heare (that which indeed was true) that *Origen* and his errours
were

d *Coll.5.p.552.a*
e *An.553.nu.42 hec acta inquit defiderantur in Synodo, &c.*

e *Anno tempe 12 Iuftiniani, & Vigilii 2. ut notat Bar.an.538. nu.29.et 31.*
f *Extat Edict. to.2.Conc. pa. 482.et feq.*

g *coll.8. pa.587*

h *Evag.loc.cit.*

were condemned in a Councell at *Conſtantinople* in the time of *Iuſtini-an* ; and they not being curious, nor carefull to ſift the diverſities of Councels, nor exact in computating times, confounded the former particular Synod under *Mennas*, wherein many of the doctrines of *O-rigen* were recited, and he with them condemned in eleven Anathe-matiſmes [i], with this fift generall Synod, held ſome fourteene years after, wherein *Origen* and his errours were alſo condemned, but nei-ther the Emperours *Edict* read, nor the cauſe of *Origen* debated, nor the particulars recited as they were in the former. Further, it is moſt likely that together with divers copies of the fift Councell were an-nexed the Acts of that former under *Mennas*, that ſo men might ſee what were the particular hereſies condemned in *Origen*, wherein ſome according to the order of time might ſet them before theſe, and others according to the order of dignity might ſet them after the acts of this fift Councell ; which might occaſion ſome with *Cedrenus* to thinke them a former, ſome with *Nicephorus* to thinke them a ſecond action of this fift Councell, whereas in truth they were the acts of a ſeverall and provinciall Councell by themſelves, and neither the firſt nor laſt, nor any acts at all of this generall Councell.

6. By this now I ſuppoſe every one doth ſee the weakneſſe of the Baronian frame, touching the anathematiſmes and proceeding againſt *Origen*. They are not extant among the acts of the fift Synod. True : nor were they ever, nor ought they to bee inſerted or ſet among the true Acts thereof : theſe anathematiſmes neither were made nor re-peated in the Councell. The Edict of *Iuſtinian* for the condemning of *Origen* is not there neither. True, neither ought it to bee ; it was ne-ver ſent to, never publiſhed in this fift Councell : but if in any, in that provinciall Synod under *Mennas*, unto which it was ſent ; and the Car-dinall to prove that *Edict* to have beene a part of theſe Acts, brings no other, nor better proofe than his owne [*putamus* k,] a proofe ſo exceeding weake, that it is not worthy a refutation. The Epiſtle of *Iuſtinian* ſent to the Synod commanding them to condemne *Origen*, which is one of the fragments that *Binius* [l] hath added, is not among the Acts. True, nor ought it to be ; for neither is it *Iuſtinians*, but an extract and briefe collection of *Cedrenus*, who out of the large Edict or Epiſtle, (as the Emperour calleth it) collected this ; neither doth it any way belong to this, but to the former Synod. The condemna-tion of *Didymus* and *Evagrius*, ſaith *Binius* [m], together with *Origen*, was made in this fift Synod, as the ſecond Nicene Councell [n] witneſ-ſeth, and that is not here among the Acts. That *Didymus* and *Evagri-us* were *nominatim* condemned in the fift Synod, the ſecond Nicene Councell ſayth it not ; no, if one would ſtraitly ſtand upon it, they do not ſay ſo much as that [o] they were at all, but that their doctrines tou-ching preexiſtence were condemned. But ſay they ſayd it ; *Didymus* and *Evagrius* were two earneſt Origeniſts [p], and defenders of *Origens* error. Now the fift Councell not onely condemneth *Origen* and his errors, *ſed eos qui ſimilia prædictis hæreticis ſapuerunt, vel ſapiunt ;* but all who teach or thinke the like that *Origen* did : in which generality *Didy-mus* and *Evagrius*, and all Origeniſts are condemned ; which generall condem-

i *Extant poſt edictum Iuſti. pa. 488.*

k *àn. 553. n. 242.* l *Poſt Conc. 5. pa. 604. et pa. 606 b. indicant illa fragmenta, &c.* m *lb. pa. 606. b.* n *Act. 1. pa. 306. a* o *Communi et generali anathe-mate vi ejecti ſunt Origenes, et Theodorus Mopſveſtenus, et quæcunq; ab Evagrio et Di-dymo dicta ſunt de præexiſtentia. Conc. Nic. 2. loco citat.* p *Didymus et Evagrius ſecta-rii Origenis. Bi. 2. loc. citat.*

condemnation is all that can be enforced out of the second Nicene Synod. Thus all the three defects which *Baronius* and *Binius* labour to prove in these Acts about this cause of *Origen*, declare a foule maime in their owne wits and judgements, but none in the Acts, and doe evidently shew, that themselves under colour of correcting these acts, doe indeed corrupt and falsifie the same.

7. And yet (which one can scarce with patience endure, or reade without scorne of their folly)they are not content to tell what is stoln or taken away touching this cause of *Origen* out of these acts, but like skilfull figure-flingers, they will name you the very thiefe, and tell particularly who maimed the Acts in this part. And who thinke you is it ? Even *Theodorus* a Bishop of *Cæsarea* ; they have an implacable hatred to him ; he is an Origenist; he the chiefe of the Origenists ; and for love of *Origen* hee corrupted the acts of this fift Synod, and stole away the proceedings against *Origen*, the Anathematismes, the *Edict*, and *Epistle* of *Iustinian*. O how blinde and besotted is a malicious minde ? that is it which put this rare skill of divination into the heart of *Baronius* and *Binius*. There is nothing stolne; as these Acts doe demonstrate, and yet they will tell you who took away the goods. They doe with *Theodorus* as the malicious Arians dealt [r] with *Athanasius*, proclamed him for a murderer, and conjurer, and little lesse than condemned him for killing *Arsenius*; and cutting off his right hand, which they brought into the open Court ; whereas *Arsenius* was both alive, and a sound man with both his hands: So this viperous Arian brood proclame *Theodorus* for cutting off one arme of these Acts, which yet hath no maime nor defect at all in that part. *Theodorus* was a Catholike Bishop, a condemner and anathematizer of *Origen* and all his errors, and yet they will enforce you to beleeve that he is an heretike, an Origenist, the chiefe patron of the Origenists. Yet these men have not very well summed up their accounts. For how did *Theodorus* take away that which was against the Origenists, whereas hee suffered to stay in the Acts an anathema to *Origen*, and to the impious writings of *Origen*, and to all that thinke as did *Origen*, yea to all that doe not anathematize *Origen*? What sillinesse was it in the Cardinall, to think that *Theodorus* or any Origenist would spoyle the Acts, and take away some discourses, and disputations against *Origen*, and leave that which is the maine matter of all, the sentence of condemnation against him, and his errors, yea against themselves, (supposing them to be such as the Cardinall slandereth them)and that also subscribed by their owne hands, as an eternall witnesse against them ? So maliciously blinded were the Cardinall and *Binius* in this cause; that so they spake against the Councell and the Catholike Bishops thereof , they regard not how untruly, how unadvisedly they slander them. But neither is it a disgrace to *Theodorus* to suffer like slander as did *Athanasius*, nor is it any honour to the Cardinall and *Binius* to slander, and doe the like as their forefathers the old Arians have done before them. And thus much of the three first defects in these Acts, which all concerne the cause of *Origen*.

CAP.

q *Quis dubitet id factū ab Origenistis cui Synodo præfuerūt, quorum patronus fuit Theodorus ralorum omniū concinnator. Bar. an. 553. nu. 244. & intelligere potes quorum arte quæ in Synodo acta sunt contra Origenem & ejus errores ex ea fuerint decurtata. ibid. Quis neget Theodorum Cæsareersem abstulisse ab actis hujus Concilij quæ suæ causæ (erat autē Origenistarum patronus) adversabantur. Bin. Notis in Conc. 5.fa.606.b.*

r *Ruff.lib.1. Eccl.hist.ca. 17. & alij.*

Cap. XXIX.

The fourth defect in the Synodall Acts pretended by Baronius, for that the Emperors Epistle to the fift Councell is wanting therein, refuted.

1. THE fourth *defect* which they finde in these Acts, is the want of that other *Epistle* of *Iustinian* directed to the Synod, set downe by *Cedrenus*, and out of him annexed by *Binius*[a] to the end of the Synod, as one of the fragments which were taken away from the Acts. Of it *Baronius*[b] thus writeth: *Cedrenus adjoyneth after this another Epistle of the Emperor sent to the Synod, containing an history of the four generall Councells, in the end whereof divers things are written against Theodorus of Mopsvestia*; the beginning of it is this, *Majores nostri fidei cultores, &c.* That this same *Epistle* sent to the Synod was inserted among the Acts thereof, *nemo jure dubitârit, none may justly doubt:* so that by this you may perceive, *Quamplurima in eadem quinta Synodo desiderari*, that very many things are wanting in the Acts of this fift Councell. Thus *Baronius*. No sure: that cannot be hence perceived: but another thing is most evident, that the Cardinall is more malicious in carping at these Acts, and correcting Magnificat, than *Momus* himselfe. May no man doubt but that this *Epistle* of *Iustinian* (as it is set downe by *Cedrenus*) was inserted in the Acts of this fift Councell? what proofe hath the Cardinall for this his confident saying? Truly none at all: nor could hee finde any sound proofe, if he had studied for one thirty yeares : for none but a carping *Momus* can, and none at all ought to doubt of the contrary, that this Epistle which is in *Cedrenus*, neither was *Iustinians* Epistle, neither was sent unto the Synod. *Iustinian* indeed sent a very large and learned *Epistle* to the Bishops of the Synod at their first assembling, containing altogether the like effect, (to wit, a history or narration of the foure former Councells, and a declaration of the impieties both of *Theodorus* of *Mopsvestia*, and of the writing of *Theodoret*, and of the impious *Epistle* of *Ibas*:) by which he commanded and authorized the Synod to examine and decide that controversie touching the *three* Chapters; and that being the true and authenticall *Epistle* of *Iustinian*, is extant in the Acts[c], and is the warrant for all that the Synod did. That which out of *Cedrenus* the Cardinall and *Binius* mention, is nothing else (as any man may easily see) but an epitome or extract which *Cedrenus* himselfe, or some other undiscreet abridger, collected out of the true *Epistle* of *Iustinian*. It is not the use of Emperours to send with their letters abridgements and briefes of the same, especially such (of which sort this is) as come farre short of the maine scope of the same. Besides, if there were nothing else, yet the untruths which the abbreviator sets down, and that quite contrary to the mind of *Iustinian*, may testifie, it was neither writ, nor sent by him to the Synod. In that Baronian Epistle *Eutyches* is sayd[d] to approve the

opinions

Margin notes:

a *Epistola 2. Justin. ad Conc. Oecumenicum. 5. Bin.pa.604.b*
b *An. 553. nu. 243.*

c *Collat.1.pa. 518. & sequ.*

d *Eutyches Nestorii opiniones probat in Fragex Cedr. apud Bin.pa.605.b.*

opinions of *Neſtorius* ; whereas the hereſie of *Eutyches* was quite contrary to that of *Neſtorius*, as *Iuſtinian* [i] truly obſerveth in his *Epiſtle* ;
for *Neſtorius taught two* [k] *natures to be in Chriſt, and to make two perſons* ;
Eutyches taught as but one perſon, ſo but one [l] *nature.* Yea the Eutycheans
utterly condemned the Neſtorians, and with them all Catholikes, as
Neſtorians, becauſe [m] they taught 2. natures after the adunation to re-
main in Chriſt. [n] *Qui dicit duas naturas, Neſtorianus eſt.* In that Baronian
Epiſtle *Eutyches* is affirmed to follow *Neſtorius*, in that [o] he ſaid that the
fleſh of Chriſt and ours are not of one nature; but *Neſtorius* taught no
ſuch thing; but the clean contrary [p], the fleſh which Chriſt took of the
bleſſed Virgin to be truly humane, and therefore the ſonne of *Mary*
to be truly, but yet onely a man ; as *Iuſtinian* alſo in his *Epiſtle* teacheth. In that Baronian Epiſtle, *Neſtorius* is ſayd [q] to have beene the
maſter or teacher of *Theodorus* ; but the quite contrary is truth; as both
the whole fift [r] Councell often, and even in their *definitive* ſentence,
and *Iuſtinian* [s] in his *Epiſtle* doe expreſly witneſſe. Are not *Baronius*
and *Binius* rare men to cure the lameneſſe of Councels, who when the
Acts are ſound and perfect, would patch unto them ſuch falſe and unworthy writings, containing ſo manifeſt untruths, repugnant to the
authenticke records of the Acts ? But woe come to all Councels, Fathers, and ancient writings, when they muſt be amended and cured
by ſuch Surgeons as *Baronius* and *Binius*. Give me the moſt lame and
impotent Councels that can be had, I had rather have them all to bee
creeples, than to come under their deadly, unfortunate, and Harpyan
hands, which defile every hiſtory or writing that they touch.

i *Neſtorio aliud
ducente Deum
verbum, et alium
chriſtum, &c.
Iuſt.epiſt.Coll.1.
pa.519.*
k *In eo te laudo
quod diſtinctio-
nem naturarum
ſecundum di-
vinitatis et huma-
nitatis rationem
prædicas. Hæc
enim vera et or-
thodoxa ſunt,
&c. Sic Neſto-
rius ſcribit Cy-
rillo, in ea E-
piſt.Neſt.que ha-
betur tom. 1.
Epheſ.Conc.ca.14*
l *Eutychei ne-
gat conſubſtanti-
alem nobis eſſe
carnem Domini.
Iuſt.in Epiſt ad
Synod. ſup.citat.
et anathem.
qui dixit duas
naturas poſt ad-
unationem, di-
cunt Eutychiani
in conciliab.
Eph.apud Conc.
Chal.Act.1.*

*Exclamaverunt, de vicina Neſtoriana hæreſi inſimantes nos; In duo ſeparate, interficite eos qui dicunt duas naturas, de
utychianis loquitur, Conc.Chalc.Act.1.pa.8.a.	n Eum qui dicit duas naturas in duo incidite, Qui dicit duas naturas,
Neſtorianus eſt. ibid.pa.12.a.	o Eutyches Neſtorii opiniones probans, dicenſq; carnem Chriſti non ejuſdem cum noſtra eſſe
natura. Epiſt.ex Cedr.pa.605.b.	p Ut liquet ex verbis Neſtorii ante citatis.	q Opera Theodori Mopſveſteni, qui
magiſtrum ſuum Neſtorium impie de rebus ſacris loquendo ſuperabat. Epiſt.ex Cedr.loc.cit.	r Et docerent non ſolum diſci-
ulum impietatis Neſtorium, ſeu etiam doctorem ejus Theodorum. Coll.5.pa.585.b.	ſ Per Theodorum Mopſveſienum,
actorem Neſtorij. Epiſt.Iuſt.Coll.1.p.519.*

CAP. XXX.

he fift defect in the Synodall Acts pretended by Baronius, *for that the*
Conſtitution of Pope Vigilius *concerning the three Chapters is wan-*
ting therein, refuted.

He fift *defect* which the Cardinall hath ſpyed in
theſe Acts, is, that the Conſtitution of Pope
Vigilius is not now extant therein. Of it the
Cardinall ſayth [a], *That it belongeth to the Acts of*
the fift Synod, is evidently declared by that which
we have ſpoken : and againe, this [b] *Conſtitution*
as alſo many other things, *Noſcitur eſſe ſubla-*
m, is knowne to be taken out of the Acts of the fift Synod. How prove you
ir, that either it belongs to it, or is taken out of theſe Synodall acts ?
Vhat ? againe ſo rude and unmannerly as aske a reaſon of the Cardinall ?

a *Aa.553.nu.48*

b *ibid.nu.*

dinall? Is it not proved sufficiently when *Baronius* hath sayd it? Truly then it is disproved sufficiently when an opposer of *Baronius* hath denyed it. For any man for truth and credit may easily oversway *Baronius.* I pray, why should the Popes *Constitution* bee part of the Acts, rather than the Emperours *Edict?* or why doth the Cardinall finde a defect in wanting the Papall, which is *hereticall,* and not of the Imperiall which is an *orthodoxall* decree?

2. *Baronius* will further tell you, out of which part of the Acts this is stolne. It c was offered to the Synod in their fift Collation, *Ad* d *hunc ipsum diem quintæ Collationis pertinere cognoscitur; It is knowne that the Popes Constitution belongs to this yeare, and to this very day of the fift Collation.* And how I pray you is that knowne? Because e the *Constitution* hath in the end of it the date of the day and yeare wherein *Vigilius* published it. A reason fit for none but a Cardinall. As if all Constitutions, Letters, and Edicts which beare date of a yeare and a day, belonged to that fift Collation, and were certainly stolne out of it. Was ever any infatuated, if not *Baronius* in this cause? But the *Constitution* beares date f on the 14. day of May, in the reigne of *Iustinian,* and the fift Collation of the Synod was on the same day. A like reason to the former: as if all Letters or Constitutions written on that day must needs be published in the Councell, or on that very day in their Collation. Admitting it was read, yet the contrary seemes much rather to follow, that it was not read on that day, but on some other after; for the *Constitution* is directed g, and was sent h to the Emperour: that could not be before the fourteenth day, on which it is dated, and in likelihood the Emperour both read and examined it with leasure before he sent it from him to the Councell: the length of the Constitution may easily perswade any, that one day was little enough for that businesse, supposing no other affaires to have distracted the Emperour. *Binius* considering this, and being better advised hereof, dissenting from the Cardinall herein, tels us that the *Constitution* was read in their sixt Collation, which was on the nineteenth k of May, foure or five dayes after the date and publishing of it. So uncertaine and unlikely is that, of which the Cardinall sayth *Cognoscitur,* it is knowne to belong to the fift Collation.

3. But indeed, as the Imperiall *Edict* was not, so neither was this Papal *Constitution* publikely read, either in the fift or sixt, or any other Collation of this Synod, much lesse was it ever any part of the Synodall Acts thereof. The Emperour, and so all the Bishops of the Synod laboured, as much as they could, to draw the whole Church to unity of faith with themselves, especially Pope *Vigilius,* whose consent might happily draw after it, if not the whole; yet a great part of the Westerne Church, which were most earnest in defence of the *Three Chapters.* They knew that in particular, and by name to condemne *Vigilius,* or his *Constitution,* might not only have exasperated, but even utterly alienated the minde of *Vigilius,* and made him (and with him his adherents) more obstinate in their heresie. They sought by silence to conceale and by charity to suppresse, as much as they could, that hereticall and disgracefull *Constitution* of his, and by their

lenity

c *Libellus Synodo oblatus pridie Idus Maij. an. 553. nu. 41. et Papæ libellus oblatus Synodo: nos hîc (in 5. Collatione) suo loco restituendū esse putamus. ibid. nu. 47.*
d *Ibid. nu. 48.*
e *Ibid.*
f *Pridie Idus Maij. Bar. an. 553. nu. 210. eo autem die habita 5. Collatio. an. eodem nu. 41.*
g *Gloriosissimo et clementissimo filio Iustiniano, Vigilius Episcopus; ita incipit Constit. Vigil. apud Bar. an. 553 nu. 50.*
h *Vigilius pollicitus fuit se missurum (decretū suum seu Constitutum) ad ipsum Imperatorem atq, ad Synodum, quod et ingenuè præstitit. Bar. an. eodem. nu. 47.*
i *Oblatum fuisse Concilio, Vigilij constitutum, &c. quibus non obscurè significatur idem Constitutum in sexto illo Patrum confessu recitatum fuisse. Bin. Not. ad Conc. 5. pa. 610. a. et Ex Actis Concilii non obscurè colligitur ipsum (Constitutum) in sexto Confessu Episcoporum recitatum fuisse. idem pa. 606. b.*
k *14. Kalendas Iunias. Coll. 6. in initio.*

lenity and faire meanes, to gaine him, and his consent to them, yea, even to the truth it selfe : for this cause, though they knew full well, that *Vigilius* had set out that decree, yea, though they confuted all the substance thereof, and condemned both it, and him in generalities, yet they forbare at all to name *Vigilius*, or in particular to mention this his decree, that had beene to proclame hostility, and have made an absolute breach betwixt them and *Vigilius* for ever.

4. Besides this, which was a very just reason, not so much as to publish (as they did not) that *Constitution* in their Synod, the Emperour had alwayes a purpose to have (as in the seventh Collation was done) the Epistles of *Vigilius* to *Rusticus* and *Sebastianus* to *Valentinianes* and o-thers, opely read & published in the Councel : In them *Vigilius* by his *Apostolicall* authority decreeth the condemning of the *three Chapters* : what a disgrace had this beene to *Vigilius* to publish first his *Apostoli-call Constitution* in defence, and shortly after, his *Apostolicall Con-stitution* for condemning the same *Three Chapters* ? How justly might this have incensed *Vigilius*, and for ever with-held him from consenting to them, who had proclamed him in their Councell, & re-corded him in their Synodall Acts to bee such a *Proteus* ? Nay, this had extenuated and vilified for ever the authority of Pope *Vigilius*, & the holy *Apostolike* See, to record two constitutions, both procee-ding *ex Tripode*, fighting *ex Diametro*, and by an unreconciliable con-tradiction opposed the one to the other. Seeing then both the Empe-rour, and the Councell meant by their so often expressing the consent of *Vigilius* to them, and by their reciting his *Apostolicall Constitution* for condemning the *Three Chapters* in the seventh Collation, seeing they meant hereby to draw others to the like consent to the truth, by the authority and credit of the Pope and his *Apostolicall* decree : it is not to bee imagined that the Emperour or Councell would at all, either publish in their Synod, or insert among their Acts the contrary *Con-stitution* of *Vigilius* in defence of the *Three Chapters*, in doing whereof they should not onely have for ever disgraced *Vigilius*, but have much impaired the reputation of their owne wisedome, and quite crossed their principall designe : Nay, what will you say if *Baronius* himselfe professe the same ? See, and wonder to see him infatuated in this point also. *The Bishops, saith he [1], of this fift Councell, that they might pretend to have the consent of Vigilius to those things which they defined, expressed in their sentence, that Vigilius had before both in writing and by word con-demned these three Chapters, tacentes omninò quid ab ipso per editum con-stitutum pendente Synodo pro defensione trium Capitulorum decretum esset, wholly concealing, or saying nothing at all of that decree, which in the time of the Synod hee made for defence of those three Chapters : Sicque nullam penitus de Vigilij Constitutione mentionem habendam esse duxerunt, so they thought fit to make no mention at all of the Constitution of Vigilius, wherein he defended the three Chapters.* So *Baronius* : whom, speaking the truth, I gladly embrace, and oppose him to himselfe speaking an untruth in malice to these Synodall Acts.

5. Now if none of these reasons, nor yet *Baronius* his owne expresse testimony can perswade, but still the Cardinall or his friends will re-

1 B.ar.an. 553. nu. 218.

ply

ply with his *cognoscitur*. It is certainly knowne, that this Papall *Constitution* did belong to this Synod, yea, to the fift Collation thereof; I would gladly intreat some of them to tell us in this, as in the former concerning *Origen*, who was the thiefe, or robber, that cut out, or pickt away *his holinesse* Constitution; a more capitall crime than the expiling of the Delphian Temple, or the house of *Iupiter Ammon*. Touch the Popes owne writings, even his *Apostolicall* decree delivered out of the holy Chaire? what *Clement*? what *Ravaillack* might be so impious, so audacious, so sacrilegious? was it some Origenist? no certainly, the *Constitution* defending, *that none after their death might be condemned*, was a shield and safe charter for *Origen* to bring him to heaven. Was it some Monothelite? nothing lesse; they knew that this *Constitution* was the overthrow of the Councell of *Chalcedon*, and all the former holy Coūcels, *Hoc Ithacus velit*, they would have wisht the *Constitution* to have stood for ever: whom may we deeme then to have stolne away that Papall decree? Truly by the old Cassian rule, *Cui bono*, none else but either some of the Popes themselves, or some of their favourites, who being ashamed to see such an *hereticall* Constitution of Pope *Vigilius* stand among the Acts, judged theft and sacriledge a lesser crime, than to have the Popes Chaire thought *fallible* and hereticall. Now because I can imagine none to have beene so presumptuous, and such is my charity and favourable opinion of those holy fathers, and their children also, that they would never commit such an hainous crime, as with sacriledge to maime the Acts of the holy Councels; I doe therefore here absolve and acquit them all of this crime, promising against any adversary, be it *Baronius* himselfe, to defend their innocency in this matter, untill some of *Baronius* his friends can either bring some further evidence against them, or else prove, which I thinke they will hardly be able, that a decree, which was never extant among the Synodall Acts, can be stolne or cut away out of the Synodall Acts.

Cap.

CAP. XXXI.

The sixt defect in the Synodall Acts pretended by Baronius, *for that the decree which advanced* Ierufalem *to patriarchall dignity is wanting therein,* refuted.

1. HE sixt and laft *defect* is of all the reft moft memorable, concerning *the advancing of* Ierufalem *to a Patriarchall See,* and annexing fome Churches unto it. That this was done in the fift Councell Baronius [a] proves by *Guil. Tyrius* [b], who writeth, *that in the fift Synod in the time of* Iuftinian, Vigilius, Eutychius, *and the reft decreed, that this Bifhopricke of* Ierufalem *fhould have the place of a Patriarke, with the reft* : And becaufe it was fituate in a manner in the limits of the Bifhop of *Alexandria* and *Antioch,* and fo there [c] was no meanes for it to have fubordinate Bifhops, unleffe fomewhat were taken from either of thofe Patriarkfhips, therefore it feemed good to the Synod to take part from either; fo they tooke from the Bifhop of *Antioch* two Provinces, *Cefarea* and *Scythopolis;* and two other from the Bifhop of *Alexandria,* Ruba *and* Beritus; befides which Metropolitane Sees, they tooke alfo from the fame Patriarks divers Bifhopricks, and erected fome other; all which (being in number twenty five) they fubjected to their new founded Patriarke of Ierufalem. Thisis the fumme of that which *Guil. Tyrius,* and out of him *Baronius* delivereth, and *Binius* [d] addeth this as a fragment or fcrap of the fift Councell, w[ch] is now not found among the Acts therof. *Baronius* [e] further gloffing on this text, tels us, that though *Iuvenalis* had attempted and obtained this before in the Councell of *Chalcedon,* when the [f] Pope Legates were abfent, yet Pope *Leo* refifting it; he prevailed not, nor was the matter put in execution; but at this [g] time the ancient order inftituted by the Nicene Councell, being inverted, *Cefarea* was now firft of all made fubject to the Church of *Ierufalem,* which now was become a Patriarchall See.

2. This whole paffage of *Baronius* (approving that teftimony of *Guil. Tyrius* which is juftly refuted by *Berterius* [h]) I cannot tell what to call, but fure I am, it confifts of divers untruths, not fo much upon ignorance (then his finne had beene leffe) as malicioufly objected againft the Acts of this holy Synod; fome of them I will explane, beginning with that which is the maine point of all. Firft then it is untrue, that this fift Synod advanced the See of *Ierufalem* to a Patriarkfhip. Not to the name and title of a Patriarke, for that it had long before, as *Bellar.* [i] and *Binius* [k] profeffe; & though it was but a fingle Bifhorick, fubject, as both *Ierome* [l] and the Nicene [m] Councell declare, to the Bi-

a *An.* 553. *nu.* 245. *Acta illa defideratari nofcuntur, quibus agebatur de adjectis Patriarchatui Hierofolymitano Ecclefiis, &c.*
b *De Bello facro, lib.* 24. *ca.* 12.
c *Non-habens unde illi urbi ordinaret fuffraganeos, nifi utrique Patriarche aliquid detraberet.*
d *Bin. inter fragmenta addit poft Cóc.* 5 *pa.*606.*a.*
e *An.* 553. *nu.* 246.
f *Poft abfentiam Legatorum. Ibid.*
g *Sic igitur inverfo antiqua ordi e à Nicæno conftituto inftituto, Cefarienfis Ecclefia, totius Paleftine Metropolis nunc primum fubjecta eft Hierofolimorum Ecclefie. Bar. Ibid.*
h *Diatr.* 2. *ca.* 2.
i *Hierofolimita- x per annos ferè quingentos habita eft quarta Pa'ria cholis; fed nomine non re, feu honore non poteftate. Bell. lib.* 1. *de Pontif. Rom. ca.* 24. *§ Porro.*
k *Binius verba Bellar. repetit, et ait id patere ex Conc. Nic. Can.* 7.
nolis in Epift. 3.

Anaclet. to. 1. Conc. pa. 105. & not. in Conc. Nicen. ca. 7. pa. 319. A. l Hec ibi (in Conc. Nic.) decernitar ut Paleftinæ Metropolis Cefarea fit, et totius Orientis Antiochia. Hier. Epift. ad Pammach. contra Johan. Epif. Hierof. m Habeat Ælia honoris confequentiam (poft Antiochiam) Metropoli propria dignitate fervata. Conc. Nic. Can. 7.

fhop

ſhop of *Antioch*, as his Patriarke, and to the Biſhop of *Ceſarea Paleſtina*, (for there is another in *Cappadocia*,) as his Metropolitane, yet for honor of our Saviors reſurrectiō in that place, it had the name of [n] Patriark, and preeminency in Councels [o] to the Biſhop of *Cæſarea*. Not to the authoritie and power of a Patriarke, for that it had, and had it juſtly, long before this fift Councell, even by the decree and judgement of the Councell of *Chalcedon*. *Iuvenalis* [p] had ſued for it in the Epheſine Councell, but the Biſh. of *Antioch*, as it ſeemeth, then being unwilling to manumit him, & as it were, free him from his ſubjection, *Cyrill* reſiſted it & writ to Pope *Leo*, praying him to do the like. But after long contention both parties being throughly agreed, the matter was brought to the Councell of *Chalcedon*, where *Maximus* and *Iuvenalis*, the Biſhops of both Sees, firſt of all, and before the whole Councell, profeſſed that they were both willing, *that* [q] *the Biſhop of Antioch ſhould hold the two Pheniciaes and Arabia*, *and the Biſhop of Ieruſalem ſhould hold the three Paleſtinaes*, and they both requeſted the whole Synod *to decree, confirme, and ratifie the ſame*. The whole Councell thereupon by their decree cōfirmed the ſame, all the moſt reverēd Biſhops cryed [r], *We all ſay the ſame, and we conſent thereunto*. After them the moſt glorious *Iudges* in the name of the Emperor, added Imperiall authority and the royall aſſent to the Synods decree, ſaying, *Firmum etiam per noſtrum decretū & ſententiam Concilij in omni tempore permanebit hoc*; *this ſhall abide firme for ever by our decree, and by the judgement of the Councell, that the Church of Antioch have under it the two Pheniciaes, and Arabia; & the Church of Ieruſalem have under it the three Paleſtines*. Thus the Iudges. The ſame Decree of this Councell at *Chalcedon* is expreſly teſtified both by *Evagrius* [s] and *Nicephorus* [t]. So untrue it is which *Guil. Tyrius*, and out of him *Baronius* avoucheth, that the Church of *Ieruſalem* was firſt made a Patriarchall See, or had the Provinces and Metropolitanes of *Cæſarea* and *Scithopolis* annexed unto it by the fift Councell, that it is undoubtedly certaine, that it had with the title and dignity, true Patriarchal authority and power over divers Provinces, together with their inferiour Biſhops conferred upon it, with a plenary conſent of the whole Church in the Councell of *Chalcedon*. And that you may ſee the moſt ſhamefull dealing both of *Bar.* and *Binius* in another place (where their choller againſt this fift Councell was not moved) they acknowledge that truth; for intreating of the Councell at *Chalcedon*: *In this ſeventh Seſſion of it*, ſaith *Baronius* [u], (and the like doth *Binius* [x]) *was the controverſie cōpoſed betwixt the Biſhops of Antioch & Ieruſalē, and the cauſe being judged, the two Phenicia and Arabia, were given to the Biſhop of Antioch, and the three Paleſtines were adjudged to the Biſhop of Hieruſalem, ex quibus jam perſpicuè apparet jus Metropolis in Hieroſolymitanam Eccleſiam eſſe tranſlatum*; *whence it doth evidently appeare, that the right of the Metropolis which before belonged to the Biſhop of Cæſarea was tranſlated to the Biſhop of Ieruſalem*. So they: who yet in hatred againſt the Acts of the fift Councell with faces of Adamant deny that truth which here they confeſſe to be cleare and conſpicuous.

3. But (ſaith the Cardinall [y]) the *decree* of *Chalcedon* was made, *poſt abſentiam Legatorum*, when the Popes Legates were now gone, and of

[n] *Hieroſolimitanus Epiſcopus ſedebat. 4. loco, ſed nulli Archiepiſcopo vel Epiſcopo præerat. Bell. loc. cit.*

[o] *Nam ſedit 4. loco in Concilio Niceno, et ſubſcribit ante Epiſcopum Cæſarienſem in Conc. Niceno, et Conſtant. ut ex ſubſciptione liquet, et in Conc. Chalc. Act. 5.*

[p] *Epiſt. 62. Leonis.*

[q] *Placuit mihi (ait Maximus) et Iuvenali propter multam contentionem ut ſedes Antiochena habeat duas Phenicias et Arabiam, ſedes autem Hieroſolymorum habeat tres Paleſtinas, et rogamus ex decreto veſtro hæc firmari. Conc. Chalc. Act. 7. pa. 105.*

[r] *Ibid.*

[s] *Evag. l. 2. ca. 18*

[t] *Nic. Calliſt. lib. 15. ca. 30.*

[u] *An. 451. nu. 124.*

[x] *Not. in Conc. Chalc. pa. 184. b.*

[y] *An. 553. nu. 246.*

so they being abfent, is to be held invalid. O the forehead of the Cardinall! Were the Popes Legats abfent? were they gone? Truly they were not onely prefent at this *decree*, and confenting unto it, but after it was propofed by *Maximus* and *Iuvenalis*, they were the very firft men that gave fentence therein, whofe fentence the whole Councell followed. For thus it is fayd [z], *Pafcafinus and Lucentius the moft reverend Bifhops, and Boniface a Presbyter, thefe holding the place of the Apoftolike See, faid by Pafcafinus; Thefe things betwixt Maximus and Iuvenalis are knowne to be done for their good and peace; & noftræ humilitatis interloquutione firmantur, and they are confirmed by the interloquution of our humility; ut nulla impofterum de hac caufa fit contentio, that never hereafter there fhould be any contention about this matter betweene thefe Churches.* Is it credible that the Cardinall could be fo audacious and impudent, as to utter fuch palpable untruths? Vnleffe he had quite put off, I fay not modefty, but reafon, fenfe, and almoft humane nature. Let this ftand for the fecond capitall untruth in this paffage.

z *Conc.Chalc. Act.7.pa.105c.*

4. Yet Pope *Leo* himfelfe, faith *Baronius* [a], withftood that *Decree* of the Councell at *Chalcedon*, becaufe it was prejudiciall to the rights of other Churches, and by reafon he confented not, it was not put in execution, as it was after this *Decree* of the fift Synod. Had the Cardinall and his friends beene well advifed, they would feare, and bee much afhamed once to mention the refiftance of Pope *Leo* to the Councell at *Chalcedon*, either in thofe Patriarks, or in the other of *Conftantinople*: for firft the refiftance of *Leo*, which was meerely ineffectuall, demonftrates, that the Popes contradiction, with all his might and power, can neither difannull nor infringe the judgement of a generall Councell; which is no fmall prejudice to his Princehood, or Princely fupremacy. Againe, it convinceth *Leo* of a very foule and unexcufable errour, feeing *Leo* judged the Nicene Canons concerning matters of order, policie, and government of the Church (fuch as thefe are about the extent of Sees, or fuperiority of one Patriarke or Bifhop above another) to be unalterable and eternall, no leffe than the decrees of faith: *The condition* (faith hee [b]) *of the Nicene Canons* (in the margent hee points at the fixt and feventh, both weh concerne the limits of Sees) *being ordained by the Spirit of God, is in no part foluble; and whatfoever is diverfe from their Conftitution, omni penitus authoritate vacuum eft, is utterly voide of all authority, by whomfoever it bee decreed,* fewer or moe. Againe [c], the Nicene fathers, after they had condemned *Arius*, made lawes of Ecclefiafticall Canons, *manfuras ufque in finem mundi, which are to ftand in force untill the end of the world;* and if ought be any where prefumed to bee done otherwife than they have decreed, *fine cunctatione caffatur, it is prefently made void.* Againe [d], the priviledges of Churches being inftituted by the Canons of the holy Fathers, and confirmed by the Nicene decrees, *nulla poffunt improbitate convelli, nulla novitate mutari;* they can bee infringed by no improbity, they can by no novelty bee altered. Againe [e], concerning *Iuvenalis* Bifhop of *Ierufalem*, who was now truly made a Patriarke, for keeping the Statutes of the holy fathers, which in the Nicene Synod are confirmed, *inviolabilibus decretis, by inviolable decrets;* I admonifh your fanctity;

a *Leo citato.*

b *Leo Epift. 53*

c *Epift. eadem.*

d *Epift. 54*

e *Epift. 61*

sanctity, that the lawes of the Churches remaine; let no mans ambition covet that which is another mans, let no man seeke by impairing another to advance himselfe, for though they thinke to strengthen their desires by Councels, *infirmum atque irritum erit quicquid à prædictorum patrum Canonibus discreparit;* whatsoever is diverse from these Nicene Canons shall bee void. Lastly f, to *Maximus* Bishop of *Antioch,* let it suffice that I pronounce this in generall, *ad omnia, for all matters,* concerning limits of Sees, and the like; that if any thing bee attempted by any man, in any Synod, against the Statutes of the Nicene Canons, *nihil præjudicij potest inviolabilibus inferre decretis,* it can bring no prejudice to these unalterable and inviolable decrees. Thus Pope *Leo* erroniously judging the order set downe in the Nicene Canons, for the bounds and preheminence of Bishops to be for ever, or by any Councell whatsoever immutable.

5. See now the wisedome of the Cardinall in alleaging Pope *Leo.* If the decree at *Chalcedon* was not of force because *Leo* contradicted it, then neither can that other decree, supposed to bee made in the fift Councell, be of force, because *Leo* contradicteth it also; for by *Leo* his judgement, at no time, by no person, by no Councell, by no authority can the order set downe at Nice bee changed. If that at *Chalcedon* was not in force, to which the Popes Legates consented, how can the Cardinall thinke this of the fift Councell to bee of force, to which neither Pope nor Legate consented, nor was so much as present in the Councell? If the judgment of *Leo* stand for good, then neither is, nor ever was either *Constantinople* or *Ierusalem* Patriarchall Sees; & then the decree of the eighth Councell g, and the h Laterane, and I know not how many Councels must bee rejected as unlawfull and impious, if the judgement of *Leo* be (as by the eighth Councell and their Laterane it is adjudged) erronious; then was *Ierusalem* a Patriarchall See, notwithstanding the contradiction of *Leo* to that decree. In a word, if *Leo* his judgement be of force, it repeales the decreee of the fift, eighth, and all other generall Councels decreeing this; if it be not of force, it neither did nor could infringe the decree of *Chalcedon.* So unadvised was the Cardinall in alleaging the resistance of *Leo* to that decree.

6. And to satisfie the Cardinall yet a little more fully, it is an untruth which hee saith i, that the *Decree* of *Chalcedon* was not put in execution before the time of this fift Synod, and this supposed decree therof, for the Councell of *Chalcedon* k decreed that their sentence in advancing *Ierusalē* to a Patriarchall See, should stand in force, *in omni tempore,* and therfore doubtlesse even then, and from that very time it was truely a Patriarchall See, the contradiction of *Leo* no more hindring it the very next or second yeare, than it did two hundred or two thousand yeares after that decree made. Againe, as it is certaine for the See of *Constantinople,* that it both before and after the *Decree* of *Chalcedon* (which was not introductory but confirmative in that point) exercised Patriarchall authority, *Iustinian* also by his Imperiall law l made some twelve m yeares before the fift Councell, confirming the same; and so it is not to bee doubted but the Church of *Ierusalem*
                                                                       did

f Epist.62.

g Hæc sancta & magna Synodus, tam in seniori & nova Roma, quam in sede Alexandriæ, Antiochiæ et Hierosolymorum priscam consuetudine decernit in omnibus conservari, ita ut eorum præsules universorum Metropolitanorum qui ab ipsis promoventur, habeant potestatem, ad convocandum eos, ad contendendum et corrigendum. Can.17 Conc.8. apud Bin. pa.850.
h Conc. Later.4. habitum sub Innoc.3.ca.5.
i Quo minus ea (quæ Chalcedone obtinuit Iuvenalis) executioni mandata essent. Leo Rom. Pont. intercessit. Nunc ergo primum (in Concilio 5.) Hierosolymorum Ecclesiæ Patriarchatu verè aucta cognoscitur. Bar.an.553.nu.246.
k Act.7.
l Novel.131.ca.1.et 2.
m Data est Novel. Basilio Coss. ut in fine ejus liquet, is verò est annus Regni Iustiniani 15. et Conc.4. habitum an.Iust.27.

did the very like in it owne Patriarchall Dioceſſe, eſpecially conſidering, that the Imperiall law of *Iuſtinian* is as forcible [n] for the one as for the other: So that for any one to have denyed or ſought then to have infringed the Patriarchall authority confirmed to *Conſtantinople*, conferred to *Ieruſalem* by the Councell of *Chalcedon*, had brought him into danger not onely of Eccleſiaſticall cenſure, but of civill puniſhments, and of the Emperours high indignation: Or if the Cardinall will not bee ſatisfied unleſſe hee ſee the practice of that Patriarchall authority, let him looke in the general Councell under *Mennas*, and there hee ſhall ſee *Iohn* Biſhop of *Ieruſalem* hold a Provinciall Councell of the Biſhops of the three *Paleſtines, qui ſub eo ſunt, who were under him*, two of which, as by their ſubſcriptions appeare, were the Metropolitane Biſhops of *Caſarea* and *Scythopolis*, with thirty moe; ſo many were then ſubject to the Patriarke of *Ieruſalem*. Againe, in another Provinciall Councell [p] held at *Ieruſalem* the tenth yeare of *Iuſtinian*, *Peter*, Patriarch of *Ieruſalem*, is Preſident [q] over all the Biſhops of the three Paleſtines there aſſembled with him, two of which were the foreſaid Metropolitanes. So untrue it is which *Baronius* to maintaine the falſe teſtimony of *Guil. Tyrius* avoucheth, that the Decree of *Chalcedon* was not put in execution before this fift Councell. Let this bee ſcored for his third capitall untruth in this ſhort paſſage.

7. A fourth untruth is that which is ſaid in the fragments, that the Councell had no other meanes to erect this Patriarchſhip of *Ieruſalem*, but by taking part from both the other of *Antioch* and *Alexandria*, for there was another meanes, as both the Decree of *Chalcedon*, and the event did ſhew, and nothing at al was taken from the See of *Alexandria*.

8. A fift untruth is, that they tooke from *Alexandria* the Metropolitane Sees and Provinces of *Ruba* and *Berithus*, for neither of theſe Sees belonged to the Patriarch of *Alexandria*, but of *Antioch*; of them both *Berterius* [r] (refuting this very fragment, which the Cardinall and *Binius* ſo gladly ſnatch at) ſaith [ſ], *certainly Ruba is placed by Ptolomé in Syria*; and it is manifeſt, that *Berithus* is the Metropolis of *Phenice*, neare *Libanus*: *Syria antem & Phenicia Orientis Provincia omnibus notæ ſunt*; but *Syria* and *Phenicia* to be Provinces of the Eaſt (and ſo belonging formerly to the See of *Antioch*) all men doe know. Thus hee; and for *Berithus* the matter is certaine, that it is not neare the bounds or limits of *Alexandria*, for that it is in the Province of *Phenicia*, not onely *Ptolome* [c] ſhewes, but the ſubſcriptions of the Biſhops, both in the Nicene [d], in the firſt Conſtantinopolitane [e], and *Chalcedon* [f] Councels, in all which the Biſhop of *Berithus* is ſet in the Province of *Phenicia*; whence againe a ſixt untruth is to bee obſerved in that fragment of *Tyrius*, for it ſaith [g], that *Berithus* was granted to the new Patriarch of *Ieruſalem*; whereas it is cleare, that it was in *Phenicia*, & that the two *Phenicia* [h], both by the agreement of *Max.* and *Iuvenalis*, and by the de-

n *Santimus dicem legum obtinere ſanctas Eccleſiaſticas regulas quæ à ſanctis 4. Concilijs expoſitæ ſunt, cut ſermalæ, Nov. eadem ca.1.*

o *Act. 5. pa. 455. et ſeq.*

p *Conc. Hieroſ. contra Severum et alios extat, to. à Conc. pa 472.*

q *Præſidente ſanctiſſimo Patriarcha Petro, aſſiſtentibus Epiſcopis trium Paleſtinarum. Ibid.*

r *Diatr. 2.66. 2.*

ſ *At certè Ruba à Ptolomæo in Syria ponitur, et Berithum Phænices Libani Metropolim eſſe conſtat, Syria autem et Phænice Orientis Provinciæ omnibus notæ ſunt. Nihil igitur ab Ægyptiaca Alexandrini Patriarchæ dioceſi accepit Hieroſolymitanus. Quod ſi ita eſt, non temere Tyrio et veteri huic ſcripto (fragmento ſci. licet. Baroniano & Biniano) ſides adhibenda. Bert. Ibid.*

c *Ptol. Geog. lib. 5. ca 15. ubi Berithum ponit ſitum in Syria.*

d *Provincia Phænices Gregorius Berithi, pag 310.b.*

e *Provincia Phænices Timotheus Beritius, pa. 513.a.*

f *Euſ. Berithi civitatis Phænices maritimæ. Act.1. pa 2.a.*

g *Subtraxerunt Alexandrino Eccleſiam Berithenſem; et quoniam iterum eundem Patriarcham (Hieroſolymitanum) oportebat habere præter ſupradictas Metropolitanos, &c. Frag. ſup. citato.* h *Concil. Chalc. Act 7. pa. 105 ut ſedes Antiochena habeat duas Phænicias, &c.*

cree of the Councell of *Chalcedon* did belong to the See and Bishop of *Antioch*, and not of *Ierusalem.*

9. Is not this now thinke you a worthy fragment which *Baronius* and *Binius* have found to be wanting, and will you, nill you, will needs fasten to the fift Councell? Are not they excellent Surgeons to cure lame Councels? who to the faire and authenticke Acts and Records of this Synod would patch such a rablement of untruths, quite repugnant to the minde of this fift Synod? For seeing as *Gregory* [i] truly saith, it was *in omnibus sequax,* in all things a follower of the Councell at *Chalcedon,* most certainly it never either decreed or approved this of taking ought from the See of *Alexandria,* or of adding *Berithus* and *Ruba* to the See of *Ierusalem*; both which are directly contrary to the *Decree* of *Chalcedon,* which this fift Councell followeth. Let the Cardinall and *Binius* themselves feed upon these and such like scraps and huskes, they are fit and dainty meat for the Cardinals tooth and palate, which relisheth little, unlesse it have a touch of falshood. But as I sayd before, so I here againe proclaime, let all Councels be a thousand times lame, rather than receive any crutches of the Cardinals and of *Binius* devising and framing. And now you have all their *defectives,* wherein I doubt not but every one seeth both the defects to rest in their corrupted judgement, and the truth of these Acts to bee much more confirmed hereby; seeing neither the craft, nor malice, nor extreme labour of *Baronius* and *Binius* was able to finde so much as any one thing which is wanting or defective in them.

i *Lib.7.Ind.2. Epist.54.*

Cap. XXXII.

The two first additions to the Synodall Acts pretended by Baronius, for that the Epistle of Mennas to Vigilius, and the two lawes of Theodosius are falsly inserted therein; refuted.

a *Iam ad postremum videamus quæ ab imposturibus fuerunt 5. Synodi nomine pervulgata. Bar. an.553.nu.247.* b *An.ead.nu. 238.* c *An.ead.nu.29.*

1.  Et us in the last place, saith *Baronius* [a], see what things Impostours have published under the name of the fift Synod; *Quæve* [b] *spuria eidem accesserunt,* and what counterfeit additions *are inserted in these Acts.* Of these in generall the Cardinall [c] tels us, *Pudenda planè in istis intexta habentur,* there are inserted very shamefull matters into these Acts, such as are altogether unworthy of an oecumenical Synod. An haynous crime indeed, if the Cardinall can justifie this. For though we might deplore the defects if ought were wanting, yet that is no prejudice to the truth of that which remaineth, no more than the extreme want and shipwracke of the Nicene Acts, doth or can discredit the truth of the Canons which are come safe to land. But if in these Acts which now are extant, and passe for the true and faithfull Acts of the fift Synod, Impostors have inserted false and counterfeit writings, that may cause one justly to misdoubt the truth of these acts which wee have: for why (will some say) may not that part, or any

one

one bee forged or foisted in, as well as this or that? Let us then see how well the Cardinal doth prove this redundant corruption in these Acts which now are extant of this fift Councell: his proofes thereof are five.

2. The first [d] is taken out of the sixt generall Councell, in which when the Monothelites alledged an Epistle of *Mennas* to *Vigilius* as out of the Acts of the fift Synod, *It was proved that those Acts were corrupted, and that the heretikes had inserted three quaternions, that is, foure and twenty leaves into the same Acts.* Againe [e], in the 7. Action or Collation it was found further, *that they added two Epistles of Vigilius, one to Iustinian, and the other to Theodora; by which you see,* saith the Cardinal [f], *that the Acts of the fift Synod have beene foully corrupted by the Monothelites.* Wee see it indeed. And wee see withall another thing no lesse remarkable and cleare, that the Cardinall is an insignious slanderer, and playes the trifling Sophister in the highest degree. Who ever doubted or denyed, but that some copies of the Acts of this Synod have beene corrupted? of this, none that read the sixt [g] Councell can make the least question in the world. For three corrupted copies were produced [h] and examined, and some other were mentioned, and the authors, both who falsified them, and who writ the inserted additions are all there recorded. Nay the three corrupted copies were not onely discovered, but *accursed* [i], *defaced* [k], and *raced* before the whole Synod, so farre as any corruption could bee found. Doth the Cardinall know any man to defend as sincere, or justifie one of those corrupted Monothelite copies? If he doe, the sixt Councell is an unresistable record against such; and we will joyne with him in consuting such audaciousnesse. Or will the Cardinall say, that the Acts of the fift Synod which are now extant, either have those additions, or were written and taken out of those corrupted and falsified copies? It is as cleare as the Sun they are not, for not one of those Monothelite additions are in these Acts now extant. These Acts, and no other are they which we defend, and which the Cardinall undertooke to disgrace, and prove to bee corrupted, and to have forgeries patched unto them. Against these Acts, the Cardinalls proofe out of the sixt Synod is so idle, and so ridiculously sophisticall, as not disputing *ad idem,* that hee had need to pray that the Sophisters in our Schooles heare not of, and applaud his rare skill in Logicke. If because some copies were corrupted by the Monothelites, those which most certainly escaped their hands must bee condemned, then no deed, nor testament, though never so truly authenticall, may be trusted, for a forgerer may exscribe it, and adde what he pleaseth in his extracted copy; or because the Romane copies of the Nicene Canons were corrupted by [l] *Zozimus, Bonifacius,* or some of their friends, therefore the authenticke records thereof (the true copies of which the Africane Bishops with much labour purchased from *Constantinople* and *Alexandria,*) must be distrusted: which yet the Africane Synod (Saint *Austen* among the rest) so much honoured, that they gave a just check to the Pope; and manifested that blot in him, which all the water in Tiber will never wash away.

Nn   3. The

d *Monoth. litarum fuit inventum ut sub tit. io 5. Synodi, epistolam Mennæ ediderint. Bar. an. 553. nu. 247.*

e *Duæ in ea (7. Actione Concil. 5.) Epistulæ inventæ sunt quæ commentias esse & suppositias manifeste probarunt ibid.*

f *Vides igitur quam fuerit 5. Synodus tum ob Origenistis, tum à Monothelitis diversis temporibus lancinata. ibid.*

g *Act.3. & Act. 14.*

h *Act. 14.*

i *Anathema libro qui dicitur Mennæ ad Vigilium. & qui eā finxerunt sive scripserunt. Anathema lib. llis qui dicuntur facti fuisse à Vigilio ad Iustinianum et Theodoram. Anathema simul eis qui falsaverunt acta sancti & universalis quinti Concilij. ibid. pa.74. b.*

k *Charta: cum volumen quod falsatum est decernimus cessari in locis, in quibus adjectiones sunt factæ: verū libros etiam eos, obelis obdaci, in locis in quibus depravati sunt, & castari, & c. ibid. pa.73.*

m *An. 554. nu. 8 Exemplaria genuina misisse noscitur Gregorius.*

n *Germana exemplaria S. Synodi vidit & cognovit S. Gregor. us. lib. 12. Epist. 7. Bin. pa. 607. a.*

o *S. Greg lib 7. Epist. 54. in depravata Synodi (quinte) exemplaria incidisse liquet, dum ait Ib. m ucgasse dictam epistolam esse suam. Bar. an. 448. nu. 76.*

p *Obyt Greg. an. 604. Con. 6. babitum. an. 681.*

q *Prefitos duos libros falsatos esse, eo quod neq; in unum è prolatu antiquis & immutilatis libris, ejusdem sancti concilij, neque in chartaceo libro qui in recenti inventus est apud bibliothecam venerabilis Patriarchij. Act. 14. pa. 73. b*

3. The Cardinall ᵐ, and after him *Binius* ⁿ, tels us a great matter and rare newes, that in Pope *Gregories* time, the Acts of this Synod were intire, and that he sent the genuine copy thereof to Queen *Theodalinda*: (An evidence by the way that the Cardinall º wittingly and wilfully slandereth the acts which *Gregory* followed to have beene corrupted; wherein *Ibas* is truly said (as the true genuine acts doe also witnesse) to have denyed the *Epistle* to be his.) But let that passe: why doe they mention the Copies of the Acts to have been sincere in *Gregories* time, as if after that time no true copies thereof could be found? In the sixt Councell more than 70. ᵖ yeares after the death of *Gregory*, divers true, ancient, and incorrupt copies �q were produced of the same: one of them were found in the very Registry at *Constantinople*, which the Monothelites of that See had not corrupted and falsified; by it and the other true and entire copies, were discovered and convinced the corruption of those three bookes which they cancelled and defaced; how will or can either the Cardinall or *Binius*, or any other, prove that these Acts now extant, are not consonant to those, or taken out, or publithed according to them? Truly I doe verily perswade my selfe, considering both that the sixt Councell was so carefull and vigilant to preserve the true Acts; and also that these which now we have, are so exact, as before I have declared, that these are no other than the copies of those selfe same ancient and incorrupted acts (save some few and light faults, which by the writers thereof have happened) which Pope *Gregory* had, and in that sixt Councell were read, and commended to all posterity. And I doubt not but the fraud of heretikes being then so fully and openly discovered, the Church ever since hath most diligently and curiously, not onely carefully, preserved the same. Which may well be thought to bee the true cause, why of all the eight Councels the Acts of these three last, that at *Chalcedon*, this fift, and the other of the sixt, are come most safe and intire unto our hands. Howsoever, certaine it is that the Cardinall and *Binius* doe most childishly sophisticate, in accusing the copies of the Acts now extant, (which onely we defend) to be corrupted, because those three or moe copies of the Acts which were produced in the sixt Synod, (which we detest and condemne much more than the Cardinall) were falsified by the Monothelites, none of those false additions being found in these.

4. The second imposture or fictitious writing which *Baronius* observeth to be inserted in these acts, are the two lawes of *Theodosius* against *Nestorius*, recited in the fift Collation. We may not omit this, r *an. 553. nu. 46.* sayth he ʳ, that those lawes of *Theodosius* against *Nestorius*, *aliter se habere in Codice Theodosiano*, are otherwise set downe both in the Code of *Theodosius*, and in the Ephesine Councell, in which there is no mention at all of *Theodoret*, as in one of these there is: and then hee concludeth, *hac de commentitiis scriptis, this may be spoken of the counterfeit writings inserted in these Acts.* Thus *Baronius*. I am somewhat ashamed that such a reason should slip from a Cardinall, specially from *Baronius*, for it bewrayes an exceeding imbecility of judgement. There is but one law s *Tit. de haeret. leg. 66. Damnato* extant in the Theodosian *Code* ˢ against *Nestorius*, and the followers of his

his sect. Now because the lawes which are recited in the Synodall Acts [t] of this fift Councell, are different from it, hereupon the Cardinall presently concludes it to be a forgery, an imposture: he might as well conclude the Gospell of S. *Luke*, or S. *Iohn* to bee forged, because they differ from the Gospels of *Matthew* and *Marke* : or the Booke of *Deuteronomy* to be forged, because some lawes in *Exodus* are different from some in *Deuteronomy*. Is it possible, or credible, that *Baronius* could be so simple, and so infatuated, as to thinke one Emperour might not make divers lawes concerning one heresie ? specially against divers persons, or divers writings; though all of them supporting one heresie ? The law in the *Code* and these in the Acts are different lawes : True, they are so : but can the Cardinall prove, or doth he once offer to prove that they are one law? and that they ought not to differ ? No : the Cardinall was wise enough not to undertake so hard a taske. For it is as evident as the Sun, that the law against *Nestorius* which is in the *Code* was one, and first published; and long after that these which are recited in the Acts. In the one of these it is said [u], *Iterum, igitur doctrina Diodori, & Theodori, & Nestorij visa est nobis abominanda*, It seemes good to us againe to detest the doctrine of *Diodorus, Theodorus*, and *Nestorius*. This *Iterum*, imports it was once done before in a former law, and now in this the Emperour would doe the same againe. As the lawes, so the occasion or them, was quite different. That in the *Code* was made indeed against the heresies of the Nestorians, but in it none of them were personally & by name condemned, but only *Nestorius*, all the rest who favoured that heresie, were in a generality, not by name condemned; because when that law was made, the Nestorians honoured, and held *Nestorius* for their chiefest patron, and urged his writings : In these two recited in the Acts, *Diodorus* of *Tarsis*, *Theodorus* of *Mopsvestia*, and their writings, are particularly, and by name condemned, as well as *Nestorius* : and in the later, the writings also of *Theodoret* against *Cyrill* : for when after that first law set downe in the *Code*, the Nestorians durst not, nor could without danger of punishment either praise *Nestorius*, or reade, write, or urge his books, which were all by that law condemned : then they began to magnifie *Theodorus* of *Mopsvestia*, and *Diodorus*, and the writing of *Theodoret*, all which were as plaine and plentifull for their heresie, as *Nestorius* himselfe : but because these were not as yet by name condemned, nor by name prohibited, they presumed more boldly to rely on them. The Catholikes, and specially they of Armenia, as is witnessed [x] in a letter from them to *Proclus*, seeing this their new device, entreated the Emperor *Theodosius* to stop that wicked course, & to condemne by name *Theodorus*, as well as hee had done *Nestorius*. Which though at the first the Emperour did not, yet seeing how insolent the Nestorians grew upon those writings, long after the former, he published these two, condemning now *explicitè* by name, and in particular, *Diodorus*, *Theodorus*, and the writing of *Theodoret*, which before were onely *implicitè*, and in a generality condemned. When the lawes, the occasion, the time of promulgation, were all different, was not the Cardinall, thinke you, bereft of judgement, who would prove these later to bee

forged

t Coll.5.pa.544. & seq.

u Pa.544.b.

x Coll.5.p2.542

forged and counterfeit, becaufe they differ from the former, with which they fhould not agree.

5. It maybe the Cardinall thought that all lawes were expreffed in the *Code*, and therefore if there had beene any fuch lawes as they, they would have beene there fet downe. A conceit I beleeve which will never enter into any mans mind, while he hath ufe of his five wits, but into the Cardinals, who hath conceits by himfelfe, and knoweth notes above *Ela*. To fay nothing of the twelve Tables, and of all the ancient Romane lawes, (no part of which are extant in the Theodofian *Code*,) the moft ancient law mentioned in the Gregorian, furpaffeth not the time of the Emperour *Antoninus* [f]; and in the Theodofian, not the time of *Conftantine*. Can the Cardinall affure us that all the Lawes of *Conftantine*, *Conftantius*, and the other Emperours till the time of *Theodofius* the younger, are expreffed in this *Code*? *Eufebius* [u], and *Zozomen* [x] mention divers of *Conftantines* lawes, *Pro liberatione exulum*, *Pro reducendis relegatis*, *Pro ijs qui ad metalla damnati erant*, *Pro confefforibus*, *Pro ingenuis*, *Quod Ecclefia fit hæres ijs quibus nemo de fanguine fuperfuerit*; *De facellis*, & *cœmiteriis*, and many the like; none of which are in the Theodofian *Code*; they were all publifhed, if the Cardinall fay [y] true, in the Confulfhip of *Licinius*, the fift time, and *Crifpus*; for which yeare the Code hath no lawes, but two [a], one *De veteranis*, and another *De parricidio*.

6. To come yet nearer to the very times of *Theodofius*: befides all thefe, he made another Edict and law againft *Neftorius* [b], commanding if any Bifhop or Clerke mention that herefie, that hee fhould forthwith be depofed; if a Laicke, bee anathematized; in which law hee particularly commandeth *Irenæus* Bifhop of *Tyrus* to be depofed from his See. This law, though it is both recorded in the Acts of the Ephefine Councell, and confeffed by the Cardinall [c] to bee truly the Emperours Law; yet is not extant in the *Code*, nor is it all one with that which is there fet downe. The Cardinall by the fame reafon might prove it a forgery, as well as thofe other two, and conclude the Acts of the Ephefine Councell to be falfified by Impoftors, and fo to be of no credit, as well as the Acts of this fift Synod. Further yet, there was another law againft *Neftorius* publifhed by the fame *Theodofius* after the Ephefine latrociny, and recorded in the Acts of the Councell [d] at *Chalcedon*; wherein the Emperour fhewes againe his deteftation of that herefie, approving the condemning and depofing of *Domnus*, of *Theodoret* and *Irenie*, Neftorian Bifhops, as alfo of *Flavianus*, and *Eufebius* of *Dorilen*, whom he thought to be Neftorians: but therein the Emperour was mif-informed, as hee had beene before, in the time of the holy Ephefine Synod, when upon like mif-information hee condemned *Cyrill* and *Memnon*, as well as *Neftorius*. That law, though acknowledged alfo by *Baronius* [e] to be true, is not extant in the Theodofian *Code*, nor doth it accord with that which is there expreffed: would not any man thinke it ridiculous hence to conclude as the Cardinall doth, that certainly it is therefore a forgery, and the Acts of Chalcedon containing fuch forgeries, are to be held of no credit? Thus while the Cardinall labours to difcredit thefe Acts, he fo foully difgraceth him

f *Nam 1. lex ibi pofita, eft imperante Antonino & Severo.* t *Vt liquet ex tit. 1. l. 1.* u *Lib. 2. de vita Conftant. ca. 30. 31. & feq.* x *Lib. 1. ca. 8.*

y *an. 318. nu. 37.* a *Vide chronol. annium Conftit. Imperat. fervata Confulum ratione. extat poft finem codicis Theod.* b *Extat illa lex tom. 5. Conc. Ephef. ca. 19.*

c *An. 448. nu. 2. & feq.*

d *Act. 3. pa. 85.*

e *an. 449. n. 130.*

himselfe, that men may justly doubt whether hee were his owne man when he writ these things; which are so voide both of truth and reason.

CAP. XXXIII.

The third addition *to the Synodall Acts pretended by* Baronius, *for that the Epistle of* Theodoret *written to* Nestorius *after the union, is falsely inserted, refuted.*

1. He third proofe which *Baronius* [a] brings to shew that these Acts are corrupted by the *additions* of some forged writings inserted among them, is an Epistle of *Theodoret* written to *Nestorius* after the union set downe in the fift Collation [b]; wherein *Theodoret* professeth to *Nestorius,* that he did not receive the letters of *Cyrill* as orthodoxall; nay, hee sheweth himselfe so averse from consenting to them, and so addicted to *Nestorius* after the union made, that hee thus writeth, *I say the truth unto you, I have often read them, and earnestly examined them, and I have found them to be free,* (that is, full) *in uttering hereticall bitternesse; nor will I ever consent to those things which are unjustly done against you, nec si ambas manus, no though both my hands should bee cut off from me.* Thus writeth *Theodoret* in that Epistle which the holy Councell first, and after them we affirme and professe to have beene the true writing of *Theodoret;* and the same to be a counterfeit, a forgery, and none of *Theodorets,* but framed by heretikes, *Baronius* confidently avoucheth.

2. Now in this cause having the Synodall Acts, and with them the judgment of the whole generall approved Councell, on our side, wee might justly reject this as a calumny of *Baronius,* but for as much as hee not onely saith it, but undertakes to prove the same, wee will examine his reasons, that so the integrity and credit of these Acts may be more conspicuous. His reasons are two. The first [c] is grounded on a testimony of *Leontius Scolasticus,* who writeth [d] thus, *It is to bee knowne, that certaine letters of Theodoret and Nestorius are caried about, in which either of them doe lovingly embrace the other, sed fictitiæ sunt, but they are counterfeit;* and devised by heretikes, thereby to oppugne the Councell at *Chalcedon;* but *Theodoret* hated *Nestorius,* &c. Thus *Leontius*: and the Card. adds [e] this, *extat ex illis Epistolis una, one of those counterfeit Epistles written to Nestorius is extant in the fift Councell,* neare the end of the fift action thereof.

3. What if wee should except against *Leontius,* (though hee [f] bee as ancient as Pope *Gregory*) as a man not of sufficient credit? Or will the Card. thinke you, defend him, and take his testimony for sound and good paiment? then farewell for ever the books of *Toby, Iudith, Wisdome;*

a Nestoriani confinxerunt mentitias quasdam Theodoreti vulgavere Epistolas, extat ex illis ad Nestorium inscripta aa finem 5. actionis 5. Synodi. an. 436. nu. 10.
b Pa. 558. b.

c Bar. loco cit.
d Leont. lib. de sect. Act. 4 extat tom 4. Bibl. S. Patrum Edit. 3.
e Bar. loco citat.
f Nam Leontius meminit Eulogij Episcopi Alexandrini, lib. de sect. Act. 5. Gregorius vero et Eulogius æquales, et extat Epist. Greg ad ipsum lib. 6. Epist. 37.

Wisdome, Maccabees, and *Ecclesiasticus;* for *Leontius* [g] reckoning the bookes of the old Testament to be twenty two, and expresly mentioning them all without these, saith, *Hi sunt libri, these are the bookes,* as well of the old, as of the new Testament, which in the Church are held for Canonical. I doubt the Card. will here say, that the case is altered; In this hee speaks against them and their *Trent* faith, not against us: Here the note of their *Index expurgatorius* [h] must bee embraced; write, saith the Index, in the margent, *diminutè Catalogum texuit Leontius, Leontius recites not fully the Catalogue of the sacred bookes:* And yet note one memorable thing by the way; God who suffered not *Laban* to speake an ill word against *Iacob,* and who turned the curses of *Balaam* into a blessing to Israell, the same God over-ruled their pen or hands, as hee did once the tongue of *Caiphas,* and in stead of *diminutè texuit,* they have uttered a Prophecy against themselves, printing even in that edition [i] which past through their Purgatorian fire of correction, *Divinitùs Catalogum librorum divinorum texuit; Leontius hath recited this Catalogue by an heavenly inspiration:* and yet for all that *divinitus texuit,* the Cardinall will not beleeve *Leontius,* whom against us he perswades all men to beleeve. But howsoever in other matters (as by name in that Catalogue *texto divinitus*) *Leontius* is to bee beleeved, of a certainty hee is no fit witnesse in this cause of the *Three Chapters;* Hee was too partiall, that I say not hereticall, in this point, too much addicted to the writings of *Theodorus* of *Mopsvestia,* and *Theodoret;* let *Baronius* himselfe say, whether his commending of *Theodorus* [k] Bishop of *Mopsvestia,* and *Diodorus* Bishop of *Tarsis,* for illustrating the whole Scripture by their Commentaries, for being such worthy men, as that no man [l] while they lived, did reprove any one saying of theirs, bee not untrue, and after, both the person of the one, and writing of both condemned by the generall Councell, impious also and hereticall. To come yet nearer to his saying concerning *Theodoret,* in the very next sentence save one before those words which *Baronius* alleageth *Leontius* saith, *Verum ne Theodoretum quidem constat unquam admisisse Nestorium, it doth not appeare that Theodoret did ever admit of Nestorius,* or hold communion with him. Had not the Cardinall skipt over (as is the wont of all heretikes) these former words of *Leontius,* hee would have beene ashamed to alleage this testimony: For not onely the Synodall acts of the Ephesine [m] Councell, but the Cardinall himselfe often teacheth and proveth it by cleare evidence, that *Theodoret* [n] admitted *Nestorius,* and that into a neare band of friendship, love, and communion. In that Epistle which *Theodoret* writ from *Chalcedon* to *Alexander,* hee calleth *Nestorius* their friend [o] *κατ' ἐχθρὸν*, and saith of him, while wee are here in this legacy to the Emperour, *non cessabimus omni virtute, ejus patris curam gerere,* wee will not cease with all our power to take care for Father *Nestorius,* knowing that wrong is done to him by wicked men. There is recorded [p] a very loving Epist. to *Nestorius* written by *Iohn* & other Eastern Bish. particularly by *Theodoret,* who all writ of themselves *tui studiosissimi,* wee are all most affectionate to *Nestorius;* of whom *Baronius* [q] saith, they who writ this to *Nestorius, eidem intima conjuncti necessitudine, being joyned*

in

g *Leont. Act.2.*

h *Magister Sac. Palat. pa.134. primi tom. Indicis Romæ editi, an.1607.*

i *Edit.3. Bibl. S. Patr. per Marg. la Bigne. Parif. an.1610.*

k *Extiterunt ijs tem;oribus duo viri, Diodorus et Theodorus Mopsveftia, qui universas litteras sacras commentariis illustrabant. Leont. Act.4.*

l *Nec ipsis vivis quisquam dicta aliquod eorum reprehendebat. Ibid.*

m *Scripsi hæc præsentibus multis Episcopis, Archelao, Apringio, Theodoreto, &c. qui omnes tui studiosissimi, una mecum te rogant, & c. sic Iohan. Antio. Neftorio. tom.I. Conc. Eph.ca.31*

n *Ex schola Theodori Mopsvesteni erant Nestorius, Theodoretus et alij, fœtus viperini dicendi. Bar.an. 4:7.nu.26.et Theodoretus ejusdem planè communionis cum Theodoro Mopsvestero,cujus adeo studiosus extitit ut crederetur eum nomê Theodoretii à Theodoro derivasse. Ibid.nu. 29.*

o *De amico autem sciat tua sanctitas. (vult autem Neftorium) Epist. Theodoret.tom.3. Ephes.Conc. Append.2.ca.9.*

p *Tom.1.Eph. Conc.ca.31.*

q *An.431.nu.*

in a most neare band of familiarity, stood afterwards for him in the Councell, *Maximè vero eidem addictus Theodoretus; but of them all Theodoret was most addicted unto him.* And againe [r], having cited some words of *Theodoret*, he addeth, Seeing *Theodoret* saith thus, *Iam non solùm cum Nestorio unanimem fuisse vides, sed dixerim etiam concorporeum: you see that he was not only a loving friend, and of one minde, but if I may so say, one incorporated, and concorporated to Nestorius.* Thus *Baronius*, when himselfe so expresly contradicts his owne witnesse *Leontius*, and in this very cause touching *Theodoret* and *Nestorius*, yea, in that which is the ground of *Leontius* errour touching this Epistle; should hee require us to beleeve that which is but a collection from the former, which is his fundamentall errour? may *Baronius* reject him in the former clause, must we embrace him in the next, which is but a dependant on the other? *Leontius* because hee thought, and thought erroniously, that *Theodoret* never embraced the friendship and communion with *Nestorius*, thought also erroniously this Epistle (which testifieth *Theodorets* love and communion with *Nestorius*) to bee a counterfeit; the Cardinall, who knoweth and professeth against *Leontius*, that *Theodoret* was most inward, and even almost incorporated to *Nestorius*, ought likewise to hold against *Leontius*, that this Epistle which testifieth such ardent affection to *Nestorius*, is the genuine and true *Epistle* of *Theodoret*.

4. And that every man may see the force of truth, and with what a seared conscience the Cardinall dealt in this cause, behold himselfe within few years after, against this testimony of *Leontius*, acknowledgeth, professeth, and sets downe this very *Epistle* as the true and certaine Epistle of *Theodoret* to *Nestorius*, which here no doubt, against his owne judgement and conscience hee denyeth, and proves out of *Leontius* not to bee the Epistle of *Theodoret*, but a counterfeit, and a forgery, for thus he writeth [r], *Theodoret indeed received the forme of faith sent from Cyrill, (at the time of the union) and subscribed unto it, but he could not so quickly forsake the friendship of Nestorius, whom hee had so long affected, for at this time (to wit after the union was made) hee writ an Epistle to Nestorius, which was read in the fift generall Synod;* and then repeating every word of the Inscription and Epistle, hee adds at the end, *hactenus ad Nestorium Theodoretus, thus writ Theodoret to Nestorius:* and againe, *Theodoret obstinately professed in his letters lately recited, that hee would never assent to the sentence against Nestorius.* Thus *Baronius;* who hereby demonstrates himselfe to be a meere calumniator, who to disgrace the Synodal Acts of the fift Councell, affirmes, and would seem by *Leontius* to prove that Epistle of *Theodorets* to bee none of his, but a forgery, which to bee no forgery but the true writing of *Theodoret,* himselfe knew, testifieth and professeth. Thus much of his former proofe out of *Leontius.*

5. His other proofe is taken [t] out of divers Epistles of *Theodoret,* specially out of that to *Dioscorus* Bishop of *Alexandria*, to Pope *Leo,* and divers others; and because it might bee replyed, that these were written long after the time of the *union,* whereas, onely at that time, and somewhat after, *Theodoret* might bee said to have been hereticall, and

[r] *Anced.nu.169*

[r] *An.432.nu.80 81.et seq.*

[t] *Bar.an.436; nu.11.*

and a favourer of *Nestorius*, as by this Epistle is signified: to wipe away this suspition, he addes these words, *post initam quidem pacem, truly after the peace and union once made with Cyrill*, that ever after that time *Theodoret* was addicted to *Nestorius*, *Nulla prorsus est mentio, there is no mention at all*; but there are many monuments, that (since then) *strenuè atque impigrè laboravit, that he laboured stoutly and diligently for the Catholike faith.* To which purpose he againe saith ⁿ, *Post restitutam Ecclesiæ pacem, after the peace and unity of the Church, Theodoret* by all Catholikes was knowne to bee orthodoxall, and to communicate with those that were orthodoxall. Which orthodoxy of faith, saith hee ˣ, those Epistles of his doe so abundantly testifie, that by them *plus satis absterfit, he hath too much wiped away*, purged and abolished all the blots and blemishes which he had contracted by his acquaintance with *Nestorius*. Thus *Baronius*, denying *Theodoret* at any time after the union made, to have beene hereticall, or a favourer of *Nestorius*; and then undoubtedly this Epistle, which both is hereticall, and wherein such entire love and affection is expressed to *Nestorius*, and which is recorded to have beene written after the time of the union, can be none of *Theodorets*, but must be rejected for an imposture, a forgery.

6. Doe you not verily beleeve the Cardinall had sent his wit out of the Country, when hee writ that whole part of his Annals, which concernes these *three Chapters*? A little before he professeth ʸ this to be truly the Epistle of *Theodoret*, and now hee will prove that it was not, that it could not possible be the Epistle of *Theodoret*. Yea which is no lesse worthy of observing, hee before not onely allowed this Epistle, (with the inscription, wherein it was sayd that it was writ to *Nestorius* after the union) to be *Theodorets*; but he further sayth ᶻ, that *Theodoret* seemes to have beene of this minde, (which is noted in this Epistle) *etiam post concordiam*, even after the agreement, union, and concord made with *Cyrill*, seeing *Theodoret* so obstinately professeth in his letters, that hee would never assent to the sentence against *Nestorius*, *Sicque certum est aliquandiu perseverasse, and so it is certaine that Theodoret continued some while* (after the union) *with an angry minde against Cyrill*. But now hee will prove the quite contrary, that *Theodoret* for a certainty writ no such things, nor had any fellowship with *Nestorius* after the union. So both it is certaine that *Theodoret* writ this, and yet it is certaine he writ it not; certaine that hee writ it after the union, and yet certaine that he writ it not after the union. That is, to speake plainly, it is certaine the Cardinall demonstrates himselfe and his Annals to be false, untrue, and ridiculous, repugnant both to the truth, and to his owne writings.

7. This might suffice to oppose against whatsoever *Baronius* can produce. If he prove by any testimony this Epistle not to be *Theodorets*, I on the contrary will prove it to bee *Theodorets*, by the Cardinals owne testimony: If he prove by any reason *Theodoret* after the union not to have favoured *Nestorius* and his heresie; I on the contrary will prove that after the union hee favoured *Nestorius*, by a stronger reason, even by the Cardinals owne confession. If hee bring *Theodoret*, I bring *Baronius*, and so I might *Par pari referre; quod male*

male mordeat hominem. But beſides this confeſſion of *Baronius*, (which diſproves whatſoever he can prove againſt us in this matter) I will adde ſomewhat concerning thoſe Epiſtles of *Theodoret*, on which hee much relyeth. Thoſe Epiſtles comming out of the [a] Vaticane (the very *Mint-houſe* of forgery) are in truth nothing elſe but counterfeits, as hereafter I purpoſe more fully to demonſtrate; for this time I will onely mention that which moſt concernes this preſent cauſe, out of thoſe Epiſtles which the Cardinall moſt urgeth, and thoſe are his Epiſtles to *Dioſcorus*, & to Pope *Leo*, ſpecially ſeeing that to *Dioſcorus* (as the Cardinall [b] tels us) declareth the faith of *Theodoret* to bee ſuch and ſo orthodoxal, that it is enough, *ad abſtergendum ſuſpitionem, to wipe away all ſuſpition of hereſie,* wherewith, by reaſon of ſome counterfeit writings in the Synod, (I thinke he meanes the fift Councell) bee was blamed: And indeed in thoſe Epiſtles there is a plain condemning of the hereſies of *Neſtorius*; but firſt thoſe Epiſt. were writ long after [c] the *union,* and ſo cannot helpe the Cardinall at all in this point: and if they had beene writ preſently upon that *union,* yet thoſe not to bee truely *Theodorets,* divers circumſtances doe make evident. In the Epiſtle to *Dioſcorus* [*] *Theodoret* is made to relate how long before that time hee had beene a Biſhop, and where hee had preached. The yeares of his Biſhopricke he reckons [d] to bee twenty ſix, all which time he continued a Preacher at *Antioch.* Whence *Baronius* [e] obſerveth, *Theodoretum Epiſcopum publicum ſemper egiſſe Catechiſtam Antiochiæ, that Theodoret being a Biſhop, was continually the publike Catechiſt at Antioch,* during that time of three Patriarchs, *Theodatus, Iohn,* and *Domnus:* And at leaſt it might bee ſuppoſed that hee was a Preacher, or (as the Cardinall cals him) a Catechiſer in that City, before hee was Biſhop; another of thoſe Epiſtles (that *ad Nonium* [f]) wil aſſure us the contrary, for there *Theodoret* ſaith of himſelfe, I ſtayed in a Monaſtery, *quouſque Epiſcopus factus, till I was made a Biſhop;* And *Baronius* [g] further explanes this, ſaying, *creatus Epiſcopus,* after *Theodoret* was made and ordained Biſhop, he was held at *Antioch* to be the preacher there, firſt by *Theodatus,* then by *Iohn* his ſucceſſor: *Theodoret* goes on to ſet forth his owne orthodoxy and praiſe, ſaying [h], *that though hee ſo long continued a preacher at Antioch, yet in all thoſe yeares, neither* [i] *any of the Biſhops, nor any of the Clergy did reprove his doctrine or ſayings*; which hee explanes in that other Epiſtle [k] to Pope *Leo,* ſaying thus, *Whereas I have beene a Biſhop theſe ſixe and twenty yeares,* yet in all this time, *non ſubij quantumvis levem reprehenſionem, I have not beene ſo much as lightly reproved for my doctrine, but by the favor of God I have delivered more than* 1000 (or as *Baronius* [l] corrects it, more than ten thouſand) *ſoules from Marcioniſme, Arianiſme, Eunomianiſme, ſo that in eight hundred Pariſhes (ſo many are in my Dioceſſe of Cyrus) there hath not remained no not one weede, but my flocke is free from all hereticall errour.* Thus hee in that Epiſtle. Which his orthodoxy hee yet more fully declares in another Epiſtle [m], *Looke on my writings both before and ſince the holy Epheſine Councell, in ſingulis quæ edidimus operibus, Eccleſiæ ſanus ſenſus & mens mihi conſpicitur; in all and every one of my writings, the doctrine of the Church, and my ſound*

in Epiſt. Theodoreti [*] 1. *ad Euſebium Ancyræ Epiſcopum apud* Bar. an. 443. nu. 12.
opinion

a *Epiſtolas Theodoreti (157. numero) Græcè ſcriptas continet codex Vaticanus, &c. Bar. an. 430. nu. 48.*
b *An. 444. nu. 20.*
c *Epiſtola ad Leonem ſcripta erat poſt Epheſinum Latrocinium illud habitum an. 449. altera ad Dioſcoru. ſcripta eſt an. 444. ut cit. Bar. illo an. nu. 18. at unio facta eſt an. 432. Bar. illo an. nu. 72.*
[*] *Extat apud Bar. an. 444. nu. 21.*
d *Sex annos ibi ego docens tempore Theodoſi alios tredecim annos tempore Iohannis, frater hac jam ſeptimus agitur annus quo Domnus ſedet. E, iſt. Theod. apud Bar. an. 444. nu. 23.*
e *Ibidem.*
f *Extat apud Bar. an. 443. nu. 12. et ſeq.*
g *An. 423. nu. 10.*
h *Epiſt. ad Dioſcorum apud Bar an. 444. nu.*
i *Et uſque hodiè cum tantum tempus præterierit nullus neq; Dei dilectorum Epiſcoporum, neque pijſſimotū Clericorum, ea quæ à me dicta ſunt, reprehendit aliquando. Ibid.*
k *Epiſt. Theod. 113. extat apud Bar. an. 449. nu. 115.*
l *An. 424. nu. 39.*

n *Theodor.Epiſt.*
31.apud Bar.an.
448.nu.14.
o *An.444.nu.*
18.Defuncto Cy-
rillo,ſuffectus eſt
hoc anno in locu
ipſius Dioſcorus.
p *Hoc eodem an-*
no Theodoretus
Cyri creatus eſt
Epiſcopus ; id
plaſe colliges ex
&c. Bar. an.
423.nu.10.
q *Nam in ea E-*
piſt. (que eſt
Theod.113.)
narrat ſe iaiuſte
in eo Concilio
Epheſino depo-
ſitum. apud
Bar.an.444.nu.
118.
r *Non hoc an.*
(448.) ſed ſe-
quenti Epheſi
famoſam habi-
tam eſſe Synodu,
certum eſt. Bar.
an.448.nu.58.
ſ *In Notis ſuis*
ad conciliab. E-
pheſ.pa.1017.b.
t *Viginti ſex an-*
nis Eccleſiam
rexi. Epiſt. The-
od. ad Leonem
apud Bar. an.
44..nu. 119.
quos ab an. 423.
inchoandos eſſe
neceſſario ſtatuit
pro certo. Bar.
an. 423.nu.10.
u *an.444.nu.23*

x *Cum Theodo-*
retus teſtatur ſe
anno 440.habere
in ſede Epiſco-
pali annos 26.
utique in hunc
annum (423.)
neceſſe eſt revo-
ces ſedis ejus
primordia. Bar.
an.423.nu.10.

opinion is conſpicuous : And againe in that to *Nomus* [n] ſpeaking of the ſame his integrity of faith, in all theſe five and twenty yeares,ſaith he, *Nec à quoquam accuſatus, nec quenquam accuſavi, Neither have I beene ac-cuſed of any man, neither have I accuſed any.* Thus is *Theodoret* made to write in thoſe Epiſtles.

8. Let us omit the vanity and folly of the forgerer, who reports this as an honour to *Theodoret,* that hee even when hee was a Biſhop, was a Catechiſer for ſix and twenty yeares together, and that out of his owne Dioceſſe: that withall hee makes *Theodoret* boaſt of a moſt unlikely matter, that by his care and diligence (even during that his abſence) he had ſo rooted all weeds of hereſie out of his owne Dio-ceſſe, that *ne unum zizanium, not ſo much as one weed remained,* in all thoſe eight hundred Pariſhes whereof he was Paſtor.Doe but obſerve here two moſt palpable and ridiculous untruths of the forgerer. The former, that he makes *Theodoret* to write in the firſt yeare of *Dioſco-rus,* that is, as *Baronius* o aſſures us, *an.* 444. that hee had then beene a Biſhop ſix and twenty yeares. Now hee was created Biſhop, as the Cardinall p demonſtrates, and ſets downe for a certainty, *An.*423.to which if you adde 26. I doubt not but any Arithmetician will eaſily ſhew it to be impoſſible that at the yeare 444. he ſhall be 26.yeares a Biſhop. Nay ſee and deride the folly of this impoſtor. In the Epiſtle to *Leo* written after q the Epheſine Latrociny, which the Cardinall r, *Binius* ſ, and all confeſſe to have beene *An.* 449. he makes *Theodoret,* account the whole time of his Biſhopricke, to bee but twenty t ſixe yeares, which was ſo much when hee writ to *Dioſcorus,* five yeares before that.

9. And here withall note by the way the rare wiſedome of Car-dinall *Baronius.* He upon that Epiſtle u to *Dioſcorus* ſets downe this Memorandum, *Obſerva lector,* Note here gentle reader, that all theſe twenty ſix yeares Biſhop *Theodoret* was a Catechiſt ; and withall note how long each of thoſe three Patriarches ſate (to wit, ſix and twenty yeares) from the time that *Theodoret* was made Biſhop, till this yeare 444. *Obſerva lector,*Note againe good reader,the dotage of the Car-dinall. *Theodoret* was made Biſhop *An.* 423. and by adding 26.the Cardinall cannot finde above 444. Truly it was fit he ſhould be be-ſotted, who undertakes to defend Impoſtours, and moſt ſottiſh un-truths. But in the meane ſpace doe you not thinke *Baronius* a very fit man to write Annals of 1200. yeares, that is ſo exact in calculating ſo ſmall a ſumme, as to account 23. and 26. to make juſt 44. though at another time, when by ſuch a falſe accompt he had no purpoſe to diſ-grace or refute the Acts of this Synod, he x could then ſumme thoſe particulars to make 49.

10.The other untruth which I mentioned is common to both theſe Epiſtles, and demonſtrates them both to be counterfeits, or *Theodoret* if he writ them to be a moſt ſhameleſſe lyer, and in theſe his writings of no credit at all. In all thoſe 25. or 26. yeares,ſaith he, I was not ac-cuſed, nor reproved : no not lightly reproved for my doctrine by any man. Not accuſed ? not reproved ? no not lightly reproved ? Fye, both he and his doctrines were condemned and accurſed for hereti-call,

call, and before hee writ this to *Leo,* himſelfe was depoſed alſo from
his Biſhoprick in a generall Councell. Of all which there are undoubted evidences as cleare as the Sun. His impious and hereticall writings againſt *Cyrill,* and his twelve Chapters, ſo often recorded both
in the fift Councell, in the Imperiall Edict of *Iuſtinian,* in Pope *Grego-*
ry and *Pelagius,* acknowledged by *Baronius* for impious and heretical,
theſe being writ in the time of the holy Epheſine Councell directly in
defence of Neſtorianiſme, and againſt the Catholike faith, did the
doctrine of the Church ſhine in them ? were not they reproved ? not
ſo much as lightly reproved ? when the holy Epheſine Councell expreſly condemned and accurſed all the doctrines of *Neſtorius,* and all
who defend them: was this thinke you no reproofe of *Theodoret* his
writings ? There is extant among the acts of the Epheſine Councell,
the decree which *Iohn* [a] Biſhop of Antioch made with the reſt that
tooke part with *Neſtorius,* and which falſely called themſelves the holy Synod of *Epheſus,* whereas they were nothing elſe but a meere con-
ſpiracy of deteſtable heretikes. In that decree they depoſe *Cyrill* and
Memnon as being Apollinarians, heretikes, contemners of the holy
Fathers and their doctrine, turbulent, ſeditions, and the like: they
accurſe all the reſt of the Biſhops who conſented to *Cyrill,* that is, all
who were of the holy Epheſine Councell; and they binde them with
an *Anathema* ſo long, till they did accurſe the twelve chapters of *Cyrill,*
(that is, till they did renounce and accuſe the Catholike faith, and
maintaine Neſtorianiſme.) To this hereticall, falſe, ſlanderous, and
diabolicall decree of the Neſtorians, *Theodoret* ſubſcribed by name a-
mong the reſt. What thinke you now ? Did *Theodoret* all this time
accuſe none ? or was this decree to which he ſubſcribed not accuſed ?
was it not reproved, not lightly reproved of any ? Reade but the ſeventh Chapter of the fourth Tome of thoſe acts [b], and there you ſhall
ſee that this their whole conventicle, and among the reſt *Theodoret* is
particularly condemned, and anathematized by the holy Oecumenicall Synod of *Epheſus,* for this their hereticall dealing : and I ſuppoſe
this was ſome reproofe of *Theodoret,* to bee, and that moſt juſtly, condemned and excommunicated for an heretike by the conſenting judgment of an holy Oecumenicall Synod; that is in truth by the whole
Catholike Church. Thoſe Acts of the Epheſine Councell containe
1000. like demonſtrations of that untruth, uttered in thoſe Epiſtles.
Among them all conſider but that Sermon [c] which *Theodoret* made to
the Neſtorians at *Chalcedon,* during the time of that Epheſine Councell, of which *Peltanus* ſayth, *Theodoret* is caryed, *inſano impitu,* with a
furious rage againſt *Cyrill,* and the other Orthodoxall Biſhops of the
holy Councell, comparing them to Serpents, Baſiliskes, murderers,
and the like. Neither doth he onely vomit out his choler againſt them,
but he plainly girded at the Emperour alſo.(Did he accuſe none when
he uttered all this ?) Nay he [d] affirmes Catholikes which hold Chriſt
God and man to be one perſon, and ſo to be paſſible, to be worſe than
Heathens. The Heathens, ſayth he, taught, the Heaven, the Sun, and
the Starres to be impaſſible, and ſhall wee beleeve the onely begotten
Son of God to be paſſible, and ſuch as may dye ? *Abſit Salvator, ne ſic*
ſimus

y *Sancta Syno-*
dus, pari ſenten-
tia condemnavit
aliorum vanilo-
quentium, quot-
quot vel poſt
Neſtorium, vel
certe iiſum fuere
q i eadem ſape-
rent. Append. 1.
ad tom. 2. Act.
Epheſ.Conc.ca.6
pa.679.
a Tom.3. Act.
Eph.Conc.ca. 2.
pa.775.

b Pa.797.

c Append. 5. ca.
3.nd tom. 6. Act.
Conc.Eph.p.907

d Theod.loc. cit.

*simus Apostatæ; farre be this from us, O Saviour, let us not be such Apo-
states,* as to teach this, let us not suspect that our Saviour could suffer.
Let any man now judge whether it be not a shamelesse untruth which
those Epistles avouch that *Theodoret* was not reproved for this doctrine, no not lightly reproved in all those 26. yeares; whereas both
then and ever since, the whole Catholike Church hath accursed his
impiety and heresie, which he so insolently then preached? And omitting infinite like proofes of the falshood of that Epistle, the next yeare

after the Ephesine Councell, there was a Synod e held at Antioch,
where *Iohn* and divers other Bishops concluded the full *union* with
Cyrill, wherein they all condemne & anathematize the heresies of *Nestorius,* which their profession of faith, and this condemning of the
Nestorian heresie, *Iohn* sent, both to *Cyrill,* to Pope *Sixtus,* and to *Maximianus* Bishop of *Constantinople.* Now seeing *Theodoret* not onely in
former time had beene so violent and furious in defence of that doctrine, but then and long after continued in the same minde, was not
his doctrine reproved, nay was it not accursed and anathematized by
Iohn Patriarch of *Antioch,* and many other Bishops subject to his Patriarchship? What a most vile and shamelesse untruth then is it, which
the Impostor makes *Theodoret* to utter, that in the whole space of 25.
or 26. yeares he neither accused any, nor was accused nor reproved,
no not lightly reproved either by *Iohn* or any other, but that all and
every one of his writings, contained the true doctrine of the Church?
But enough of those Epistles, which to be forged and false this which
is already sayd may for this time suffice.

    11. Having now declared how untrue that is which *Baronius* affir-
meth, that *Theodoret* after the *union* did never embrace the heresies
of *Nestorius,* and withall seene how weake and unsound his proofe is
in this point, I will yet adde one consideration which will further manifest, and even demonstrate the same. That is taken from the history
of *Theodoret.* Certaine it is, that when *Theodoret* writ that history,
he was earnestly addicted to Nestorianisme, whereof in the very last

Chapter f he gives an eminent proofe, commending *Theodorus* Bishop
of *Mopsvestia* for a worthy teacher of the whole Church, and for an
oppugner of all heresies: adding, that whereas he was a Bishop thirty
six yeares, he never ceased, *optimam herbam sanctis Christi ovibus suppe-
ditare, to feed the flocke of Christ with the best herbes.* None can doubt
but hee who so much extolleth so detestable an heretike, and approveth those most damnable heresies which from him *Nestorius* suckt, for
the best herbes or doctrines, but he must needs be confessed to bee as
deepe in Nestorianisme as *Nestorius* himselfe. If now it may appeare
that this history was writ by him after the union, there can no doubt
remaine but that after the union *Theodoret* favoured *Nestorius* and all
his heresies.

    12. *Baronius* knowing this inevitably to follow, to decline the

whole force of this, tels g us that *Theodoret writ his history not onely before the union, but before the jarre also; yea before the time of the holy Councell at Ephesus;* whereof having given so sleight conjectures, in the end hee
concludes, *Dicendum est, It must be sayd that Theodoret writ this history in*

the

the space of those three yeares which were next-precedent to the holy Ephesine *Councell*. So he. Shall I say the Cardinall was deceived and overseene herein? No, I will not suspect that such an evident error could creepe into the minde of so exact an Annalist. I rather thinke his intent was, wilfully and wittingly to deceive others, and that therefore hee sayd this to smother that truth touching *Theodorets* continuance in Nestorianisme, which he elsewhere so often denieth. *Theodoret* [h] mentioneth in that his history the translation of the body or reliques of *Chrysostome*, and bringing them to *Constantinople*. The Cardinall was so far from being ignorant hereof, that himselfe citeth [i] *Theodoret* with a *memorandum*, He, *ante omnes*, above them all mentioneth this translation, but in few words. That translation, as *Socrates* [k] and *Marcellinus* [l] witnesse, was when *Theodosius* was the sixteenth time Consull, that is, as the Cardinall also accounteth, in the yeare 438. Now seeing the union betweene *Iohn* and *Cyrill* was made in the yeare 432. it unavoydably followeth, that either *Theodoret* writ not his History till seven yeares at least after the union, and how much more I know not, whether 8. 10. or 16. after it, (for it is uncertaine:) or if hee writ it, as the Cardinall divineth, before the Ephesine Synod, that he writ it prophetically, writing those Acts which happened not till eight or nine yeares after his history was written. The truth is, an orderly and historicall continuation of things done, he doth not write, but onely to the death of *Theodorus* Bishop of *Mopsvestia*, where his history (for any such continuation of succeeding matters) doth end: but to shew and testifie that he writ his history after the yeare 438. hee purposely mentioneth some of those acts which fell out in that yeare: and hereof further there may be a presumption, because *Theodoret*, as *Baronius* tels [m] us, followed *Sozomen* in his commending of *Theodorus* of *Mopsvestia*; now *Sozomens* history was continued unto the 17. Consulship of *Theodosius*, as himselfe witnesseth: So that if *Theodoret*, as the Cardinall tels us, tooke it out of *Sozomen*, and his booke was not published till the yeare 439. sure the Cardinall of all men had reason to thinke that *Theodoret* could not before that time (otherwise than prophetically in this point) write his history. It remaineth now, seeing *Theodoret* was an earnest defender of *Nestorius* at the time when he writ this history, and it was written after the yeare 438. that out of all doubt till then hee remained hereticall; and devoted to all the blasphemies and heresies of *Nestorius* and *Theodorus*, which in that history he commends for most wholsome food, and Catholike doctrine.

11. But not to stay longer in a matter very cleare, my conclusion of this former point is this; Seeing the Cardinall tels us that from the time of the union *Theodoret* was not onely a Catholike and orthodoxall Bishop; but that he did manfully fight for the Catholike faith, it evidently followeth, that in the Cardinals judgment, Nestorianism and those herbes, nay most poysonfull weeds of *Theodorus* are Catholike doctrines, seeing as now we have proved for many (but of a certainty for seven yeares at least) after the *union*, that doctrine which *Theodoret* embraced, and so earnestly defended, was no other than the

h *Lib.5.hist. Eccl.ca.36.*

i *Bar.an.438. na.6.*

k *Lib.7.sa.44.* l *Insuo Chron.*

m *Eequid mirum, si quod dixerat Sozomenus, à Theodoreto repetitum inveniatur. Bar. in Martyr.Rom. Decemb.13.*

blasphemous hereſies of *Neſtorius* and *Theodorus.* And let this ſuffice for the third *addition*, which he unjuſtly objecteth to the Acts of this fift Councell.

Cap. XXXIV.

The fourth addition *to the Synodall Acts, pretended by* Baronius, *for that the Epiſtle of* Theodoret, *intitled to* Iohn *Biſhop of Antioch, is falſ- ly inſerted therein; refuted.*

1. Is fourth inſtance concernes an Epiſtle of *Theo-doret,* inſcribed to *Iohn* Biſhop of *Antioch*, ſet downe neare the laſt end of the fift Collati-on; wherein *Theodoret* exceedingly rejoyceth for the death of *Cyrill.* In handling whereof, *Baronius* and *Binius* doe more than triumph, as if the field were certainly wonne. That E-piſtle; ſayth *Binius* [a], *nequiſſimi & ſceleſtiſſimi alicujus nebulonis Eutychiani commentum eſt, is the forgery of ſome moſt naughty and nefarious Eutychian varlet,* and by fraud and ſurreption is thruſt into the Acts of this Synod. We have before diſcovered, ſaith *Baronius* [b], the impoſture of that Epiſtle, but we are not grieved to re-peat the ſame things here againe, that it may be ſhewed that they are not the true Acts of the Synod, *ſed nebulonis cujuſdam ex cogitatione commentum, but a forgery deviſed by ſome knave:* and therfore we ſay, that Epiſtle which is recited under the name of *Theodoret* to *Iohn* c. Anti-och, *Omni ex parte convinci, is every way convinced not to bee Theodorets.* Againe [c], *There is an Epiſtle ſet downe in the fift Synod, under the name of Theodoret, written unto Iohn, rejoycing in the death of Cyrill, and babbling very many things againſt him, which you may more truly call a Satyre, or in-famous libell, than an Epiſtle. And we take it very indignely that it ſhould goe under the name of Theodoret, which is rather the figment of ſome Neſto-rian:* and againe [d], it is *figmentum impudentiſſimi cujuſdam nebulonis,* a fiction of ſome moſt ſhameles varlet. Thus & much more *Baronius.* The like doth *Binius* with no leſſe confidence and virulency againſt theſe Acts affirme. The maine ground on which they both relye, is, for that *Iohn* Biſhop of *Antioch* to whom this Epiſtle is inſcribed, was dead before *Cyrill.* How could *Theodoret,* ſaith *Baronius* [e], write to *Iohn* touching the death of *Cyrill,* ſeeing *Iohn* was dead ſeven yeares before *Cyrill:* which, ſaith he, *exploratum habetur,* is ſure and certaine, both by *Nicephorus* and others who writ the ſucceſſion of Biſhops, as alſo by an Epiſtle which *Cyrill* writ to *Domnus* the ſucceſſour of *Iohn,* both which proofes *Binius* [f] alſo alledgeth.

2. My firſt anſwer hereunto is, that if this bee a demonſtration of forgery, becauſe an Epiſtle is written to one that is dead, themſelves, and not we, ſhall be the greateſt loſers hereby. There is a decretall Epiſtle [g] written by Pope *Clement* to *Iames* Biſhop of *Ieruſalem,* and

bro-

brother of our Lord: in that Epiſtle the Pope tels *Iames*, how *Peter* being now ready to bée martyred, tooke *Clement*, ordained him Biſhop, gave him the keyes, ſet him in his owne chayre, and when hée was ſet therein, ſayd unto him, *Deprecor te O Clemens, O Clement I beſeech thee* before all that are here preſent, that thou write unto *Iames* the brother of our Lord, how thou haſt beene a companion with me of my journyes, and of my actions, *ab initio uſque ad finem, from the beginning to the end*; and write alſo what thou haſt heard mee preach in every City, what order of words, of actions, I have uſed in my preaching, and alſo what an end I make of my life in this City. Neither feare that he will be ſory for my death, ſeeing he will not doubt but I dye for pieties ſake; yea it will be a great comfort unto him, to heare that I doe not leave my charge to one that is ignorant or unlearned. According to this requeſt and command of *Peter, Clement* writ an Epiſtle to *Iames*, exhorting him, that he command all that which *Peter* taught, to be diligently obſerved. This and much more writ *Clement* to *Iames* after the death, and of the life and death of *Peter*. Now *Iames* unto whom hee writ was dead ſixe or ſeven yeares before *Peter*: For *Iames* was ſlaine in the ſeventh, and *Peter* in the thirteenth yeare of *Nero*, as out of S. *Ierome* [h], *Euſebius* [i], *Ioſephus* [k], and others, is evident; and as *Baronius* [l], and after him *Binius* [m], not onely profeſſe but clearly and rightly prove: and becauſe this is a decretall [n] Epiſtle, an *Apoſtolicall* [o] writing, ſent from *Clement* being Pope, which was not till the tenth [p] yeare of *Domitian*, and that is thirty yeares after the [q] death of *Iames*, it hence enſueth that it was writ to *Iames* thirty yeares after he was dead. What ſhall now become of this decretall and *Apoſtolicall* Epiſtle? Will they be content that by the Cardinals demonſtration it bee rejected as the forgery of ſome lewd varlet? Fye! By no meanes. *Binius* [r] cals it the Epiſtle of Pope *Clement*; *Baronius* [s] tels us that it is not only Pope *Clements*, but that this and the other written to the ſame *Iames* the dead Biſhop of *Ieruſalem*, are *integræ & illibatæ, intire and incorrupted writings of Clement*. In their Canon law [t], and that corrected by the Pope, it is ſtiled the epiſtle of Pope *Clement* to *Iames*: and that which is there related muſt ſtand for the words and doctrine of S. *Peter* [u]; yea the authority of it, as other decretall Epiſtles, *Conciliorū* [x] *Canonibus pari jure exæquatur*, is every way equall to the Canons of *Nice*, of *Chalcedon*, of other holy Councels. If that bee too little, what Saint *Auſten* [y] ſayth of the very ſacred Canonicall Scriptures, indited by the Spirit of God himſelfe, that doth *Gratian* (wretchedly abuſing Saint *Auſtens* words) apply to this and the reſt of the Popes decretall Epiſtles, ſaying of them [z], *Inter Canonicas Scripturas, decretales Epiſtolæ connumerantur; the decretall Epiſtles are to be reckoned among the Canonicall Scriptures*. *Bellarmine* [a] not onely in generall defends this ſaying of *Gratian*, telling us that the decretals may well be called Canonicall, that is, either ſuch as are a rule, and have force to binde; or Canonicall in that ſenſe as the ſeventh Synod calleth the Decrees of Councels, *Conſtitutions* inſpired from God; but particularly alſo

Marginal notes:

[h] *Hic Iacobus 30. annū rexit Eccleſiam, uſq; ad ſeptimum Neronis annum, Hier. in Catal. ſcrip. in Iacobo, Petrus ad ultimum annum Neronis, id eſt, 14. Eccleſiam rexit, idem in Petro.*

[i] *Euſeb. an. 7. Neronis ait Iacobum occiſum. an. Chriſt. 63. Petrus an. 14. Neronis, idem an. 70.*

[k] *Ioſeph. Iacobū lapidatū ait an. poſt chriſtum natum 63. Antiqu. lib. 20. c. 8.*

[l] *Anno 7. Neronis, Iacobi necem accidiſſe omnes conſentiunt. Bar. an. 63. nu. 2. Petrum autem anno 13. Neronis occiſum probat. Bar. an. 69. nu. 2.*

[m] *Annot. in Epiſt. 1. Clem.*

[n] *Inter Decretales epiſtolas Pontificum numerat eam Turrian. lib. 2. ca. 13. & hoc probat. p. 109 ō Apoſtolicorum Pontificum. Tur. lib. 2. in præf. pa. 150. et ſui authoribus, id eſt Apoſtolicū, digniſſimus. ibid. pa. 152.*

[p] *Clementem ingreſſum in Papatum an. Chr. 93. is eſt Domitiani an. 10. probat Baron. an. 93. nu. 2.*

[q] *Nam ū obijt (ut probatum eſt) an. chr. 63.*

[r] *Epiſtola 1. Clement. Pape. [An. 101. nu. 6.*

[t] *Clemens Papa,*

ad Iacobum Epiſt. 1. Diſtinct. 80. ca. 2. ſic iterum Cauſ. 6. q. 1. ca. 5.   [u] *Petrus in ordinatione Clementis: cauſ. 11. q. 3. ca.*
[x] 2. *attendite ſermoni iſtius, qui nobis per B. Clementē recitatur. Nich. 1. Epiſt. 49. et beatus Petrus prohibebat. Cauſ. 6. q. 1. ca. 5.*
[x] *Diſt. 20. ca. Decretales.*   [y] *Lib. 2. de doct. Chriſt. ca. 8.*   [z] *Diſt. 19. ca. 6.*   [a] *Lib. 2. Conc. ca. 12.*

he defends [b] by the authority of *Ruffinus* this to be the true Epistle of Pope *Clement* unto *Iames* : and to omit others, their Iesuite *Turrian*, to whom *Baronius* [c], *Binius* [d], *Gretzer* [e], and others, refer us for the credit of these Epistles, hath writ a whole booke in defence of them; wherein he cals them (and particularly he mentioneth and defendeth this of *Clement* to *Iames*) *sanctissimas* [f], *verissimas, &c. most holy, most true Epistles,* most worthy of their authors; that is, men Apostolike, consecrated by the reverence of the whole world, full [g] of all gravity, learning and sanctity, confirmed by the testimony and use of all ages: and which is most worthy remembring for our present purpose, the Iesuite writes in defence of them thus [h], *What if in these Epistles sometimes there meet us some such matters as are not easie to all? must wee therefore doubt of their authority? by no meanes.* Therefore if any man doe not understand how the Epistle of *Clement* could bee written to *Iames* the brother of our Lord, who was dead more than eight yeares before, such an one, if he be a learned, modest, and temperate man, he will ask of others, and in the meane space containe himselfe within his owne bounds; that is, as himselfe explaineth, handling this Epistle [i], he must so firmly hold it to be written by Pope *Clement, ut dubitare nefas existimet, that he esteeme it a great sinne to doubt thereof.* Besides all this, the Iesuite hath a large Chapter [k] purposely to defend and shew this Epistle to be truly *Clements,* though it was written to *Iames* long after he was dead. Some there were (whom *Baronius* [l], *Possevine* and *Binius* follow) who thought it was written indeed by *Clement,* but not unto *Iames,* who was then dead, but unto his successor *Simeon.* Against these their owne *Turrian* holds resolutely [p] that it was writ not to *Simeon,* nor to any but to *Iames;* and whereas some would think it a folly [q] and madnesse to write to such an one as was dead, and which was knowne to be dead to the author who writ it, (for who should be the carier of this letter unto him?) especially to write unto him as a governour in the Church militant, & to instruct and exhort [r] him what he should carefully observe, *Turrian* tels [f] you that there were divers great and waighty reasons why Saint *Peter* commanded *Clement,* and why *Clement* did write this to a dead man, whom they both knew to be dead: and having given divers very wise and worthy reasons hereof, one taken from transfiguration [u], another [x] from imitation, a third from avoyding [y] hatred, if he had writ to any that had beene alive; a fourth [z], for to be a testimony of the Resurrection, (belike because that Saint *Iames* shall then reade this holy Apostolicall Epistle, and see what

Marginal notes:

b *Ruffinus meminus epistolae Clementis ad Iacobum, et eam se vertisse dicit ex Greco. Bell. lib. 2. de Pont. Rom. ca. 14. §. Ad hec.*

c *Tu consule Turrianum. Bar. an. 102. nu. 6.*

d *Cuius fidei sint hae Clementis epistolae, Vide Turrianum. Bin. notis in Epist. 1. Clem. pa. 31.*

e *Defens. ca. 14 lib. 2. de Pont. Rom. §. Altera.*

f *Turr. pro epist. Pontificum. lib. 2. praef. pa. 152.*

g *Omni gravitate, doctrina et sanctitate refertas, ibid.*

h *Praef. eadem. pa. 150. 151.*

i *Lib. eodem. 2. ca. 13. pa. 215.*

k *Ca. 13. lib. 2.*

l *Si Clementis germanam epistolam bene esse dixerimus (ut Bar. ipse ait. an. 102. nu. 6.) falso inscripta est, & ad Simeonem potius tunc Hierosolymorum Episcopum, quam ad Iacobum longe antea defunctu, scripta fuit. Bar. an. 69. nu. 43. m Poss. in Clemente, in suo apparatu.*

m *Hac epistola potius ad Simeonem qui etiam*

frater Domini dicitur, scripta est: & in titulum epistole mendose, vox (Iacobum) irrepsit. Bin. notis in epist. 1. Clem. p *Ne si ad Simeonem Iacobi successorem, aut Marcum Alexandrie Episcopum, aut alium ullum scribere iussisset, &c. Tur. ca. illo 13. pa. 211.* q *Quid coegit eum et imprudentie delabi, ut ad eum scribere Clementem mandaret Petrus, quem ipse sciebat iam mortuum. ibid. pa. 208.* r *Hec tibi frater Iacobe ab ore sancti Petri accepi, tibiq insinuare studui, ut servari omnia immaculate precipiam. Epist. Clem. in fine.* f *Causa gravissima scribendi ad Iacobum iam mortuum iussu Petri, de doctrina ad omnes Episcopos pertinente. Tur. loc. cit. pa. 211.* t *Ita certe est ut isti dicunt, non potuisse ignorare Petrum fuisse iam ante annos: 8. Iacobum mortuum. ibid. pa. 208.* u *Causa gravissima scribendi per transfigurationem. pa. 211.* x *Simile exemplum in aliis eiusdem Clementis libris cernitur. Jn utroque est quedam fictio seu inductio persone quod genus totum ad imitationem personarum pertinet. ibid. pa. 212. Vtrobique est imitatio personarum. pa. 213.* y *Si ad ullum aliquem vivorum scripsisset, videretur magis eum diligere aut honorare, & emulationis, vel invidie materiam prebuisset: Anne parvi momenti hec cautio? Quis tam obtusus sit, ut sic sentiat? ibid. pa. 211.* z *Cum Petrum mandat Clementi ut ad Iacobum mortuum scribat clarissimum testimonium resurrectionis prebet. ibid. pa. 212.*

godly

godly exhortation and advice for government of the Church *Clement* gives unto him :) and such like ; in the end he concludes [p], that such as are Catholikes must not doubt [q] of the truth of this Epistle, though they know not the reason why it was written to a dead man: and withall, that with men who have reason and judgement, *certum esse debet*, such must assure themselves that both S. *Peter* and *Clement* had and knew reasons why the one commanded to write, and the other did write unto a dead man. Whereas now the Cardinals worthy demonstration ? Had hee and *Binius* beene men of reason and judgement, and considered (as no doubt but they read) that tract of *Turrian*, (seeing unto it they referre us) they might have scene therein divers reasons why *Theodoret* might write to *Iohn*, though he were dead; for every one of *Turrians* reasons is as forcible to defend this Epistle of *Theodoret*, as they are to excuse *Clement*, for writing to *Iames*, who was dead long before : But the case is now altered, the Cardinals demonstration holds onely in those writings that distaste him; or make for us, and against their cause. But *si in rem sint*, if any such writing bring (as all the decretals doe) either honour to the Romane See, or gaine to the Romane Court, though they were writ to one that was dead, I say not seven, but seven times seven yeares before, they shall bee honoured as the true and undoubted writings of the authors.

3. Let mee adde but one other example; but that is such an one as doth cut all the sinewes, yea, the very heart-strings of the Cardinals demonstration. The translation of *Chrysostomes* body or reliques by *Theodosius* the younger, more than thirty yeares after his death, from *Comana*, where hee dyed in banishment, to *Constantinople*, is a matter so testified by *Socrates* [r], *Theodoret* [s], *Marcellinus* [t], the great Menology [u], their Romane Martyrology [x], and others, that we doe not doubt of the truth therof. But since it is [y] retranslated, as they say, from *Constantinople* to *Rome*, the onely shop indeed to utter all such ware, and make the people goe a whoring after them : That those his supposed reliques may be had in reverence, it is worthy the considering, how miraculously they have made the manner of his Translation. *Nicephorus* [z] relates the summe of it, but, as by *Baronius* [a] it seemes, he borrowed it out of the luculent Oration of one *Cosmas Vestiarius*, whether one of the Vaticane [b], or a Baronian author I know not, but so ignoble, and so unworthy an author, that *Possevine* judged him not worthy to bee named in his Bibliotheca, or reckoned among his *testes veritatis*. Out of this Tailors Oration hath the Cardinall [c] stitcht a very pretty Anile, the summe whereof is this : *Proclus* on a time making a panegyricall Oration in the praise of *Chrysostome*, the people were so flamed with the love and longing desire after him, that they interrupted the Bishop, and would not suffer him to make an end of his Sermon, crying out with many loud vociferations, they would have *Chrysostome*, *Chrysostome* and his reliques they would have: *Proclus* moved herewith, intreates the Emperour; the Emperour, at this their earnest sute sent divers Senators (some [d] say an army together, with Clerks and Monkes) to bring with all pompe the body of *Chrysostome* from *Comana*; thither they goe, and come to the place where *Chryso-*

stomes

Marginal notes:

[p] *Catholici vero si qui sint, &c. pa.215.*

[q] *Etiamsi unde, aut quomodo ad nos profecta sint nesciamus, tam é propter antiquorum authoritatem ita teremás, ut de eis dubitare nefas esse existimemus. Ibid.*

[r] *Lib.7.ca.44.*
[s] *Lib.5.ca.36.*
[t] *in suo Chron. an.438.*
[u] *Die 27. Ianu.*
[x] *Die 27. Ian.*
[y] *Inde postea Romam translatum est. Martyr. Rom. Ibid.*
[z] *Lib.14.ca.43.*
[a] *Recitat idem Cosmas literas, à quibus puto Nicephorum exscripsisse. Bar. an 438.nn.8.*
[b] *Habemus cum (Cosmæ sermonem) in nostrá Bibliotheca descriptú. Bar. annot. in Martyr. Ro. Jan.27. et an.438.nu 7.*
[c] *An.438.*
[d] *Misit exercitum militum urá cum clericis. Georg. Patriar. Alex. in vita Chrysostomi, fol.77.*

b *In theca argentea, sacra Iohannis pignora asservabantur, inde ea auferre et deferre conantibus, nemine resistente minimè concessum fuit, yes sæpe frustra tentata. Bar. an. 438 nu. 8*

c *Sacro corpore instar silicis, loco inhærescente et immobili permanente. Ibid.*

d *Imperatoris sententia ab omnibus æque probata atque laudata suit. Ibid.*

e *Iohanni, aureoris Patriarchiæ. Nic. lo. cit. et, At tu pater patrum, &c. lb.*

stomes body was kept in a silver Coffin: Once, againe [b], and very often they assay, yea, labor & strive with all their strength, wth all their skill, to lift up the Coffin, all was in vaine, the sacred body [c] was more immovable than a rock; they certifie this news to the Emperor, who called *Proclus*, & other holy men to advise further about that matter; in the end the resolution of them all [d] was, that the Emperour *Theodosius* should write a Letter to *Chrysostome, Supplicis instar libelli*, in forme of a supplication, asking him forgivenesse for the sinnes which *Arcadius* his father had committed against him, & *humilibus precibus*, to beseech him with most lowly prayers that hee would returne to *Constantinople*, and take his old See againe, praying him that hee would no longer by his absence afflict them, being so desirous of his body, yea, of his ashes, yea, of his shadow. The Emperour did so, the forme of whose letter of supplication out of the *Tailor Cosmas*, first *Nicephorus*, and then *Baronius* expresse, though the Cardinall for good cause was loath to give *Chrysostome* the title of a Patriarke, and *Pater Patrum*, which *Nicephorus* [e] sets downe; those either the Tailor or the Cardinall concealeth or altereth. The Emperours letters were sent and brought to the dead corps, and with great reverence laid upon the brest and heart of *Chrysostome*, and the next day the Priests with great ease took up the body, and brought it to *Constantinople* into the Church of the holy Apostles. There first (as out of *Nicephorus* the Cardinal relateth) the Emperour with the people, *supplex communem precationem pro Parentibus fecit, made an humble prayer for his Parents*, and more specially entreated for his Mother, that her grave [f], which had shaken and been sicke of a palsie, and made a noise and ratling for thirty five yeares together might now at length cease; & the holy man heard the request, granted it; the graves palsie was cured, so that it shaked no more. Then *Proclus* the Bishop placed dead *Chrysostome in eundem Thronum*, in the very same See and Episcopall seat with himselfe, all the people applauding and crying, O Father *Chrysostome* receive thy See; and then by a miracle beyond the degree of admiration, the lips [g] of *Chrysostome* (five and thirty yeares after hee was laid in his grave) opened and blessed all the people, saying, *Peace be to you*; and this both the Patriarke *Proclus*, and the people standing by, testified [h] that they heard. Thus farre the Cardinals narration out of his Tailor *Cosmas* and *Nicephorus*.

f *Precatus est, ut tumuli ejus motus atq; strepitus consisteret, 35. enim annis jam is quatiebatur. Bar. ibid. nu. 12.*

g *Ipse Chrysostomus labÿs rursum apertis, ad populum dixisse fertur, Pax vobis. cosmas apud Bar. loco citat. et Niceph.*

h *Id circumstantes homines et Patriarcha Proclus, se audisse, testati sunt. Cos. et Niceph. loc. cit.*

i *Ad optimum quemq; lectorum πραςιναν Carthusians post vitam Chrysost. apud Geor. pat. Alex.*

4. Say now in earnest, is not this a story able to put downe *Heliodore, Orlando*, and all the fictions of all the Poets? their wits are barren, their conceits dull, they are all but very botchers to the Cardinals Taylor. It is not my purpose to stand now to refute such a lying legend: The Cardinals friends may see the censure which their Carthusian Monke [i] *Tilmannus* gives of it and of *Nicephorus*, the onely author that he knew, till *Baronius* pull'd this blinde Tailor out of a corner; Though I beleeve (saith hee) God to bee omnipotent, yet I beleeve not all which is here written of *Chrysostome, sed fides penes lectorē esto, let the reader choose whether hee will beleeve it or not*, for the writers of mens lives, who lived before *Nicephorus*, (and hee writ about the yeare 1328.) would not have concealed or smothered in silence, *rem tanti*

tanti momenti, a matter of so great moment. Thus the Carthusian, whose judgement may justly be thought to bee the more weighty, because of all the ancient Fathers there is none (I speake it confidently) who hapned to have more fabulous writers than are *Palladius* (as he is called) *Leo* and *George* the writers, or rather the devisers of *Chrysostomes* acts, his life and death. Any one of them doting after such miraculous reports, would have painted out this miracle of miracles, with all the wit and words which they had: That which I onely observe is the strange, and if you please, miraculous lewd dealing of *Baronius.* This Epistle of *Theodosius*, though it was written to *Chrysostome* more than thirty yeares after his death, the Cardinall approves, applaudes, and for a rare monument hee commends [k] it, and all that appendant fable to all posterity. Why? it is an excellent story indeed to perswade the adoration of reliques, invocation of Saints, prayers for the dead, and such like. Had this Epistle of *Theodorets* contained such stuffe, it should have had every way the like applause from his Cardinalship; because it wants such matters, and crosseth in very many things the Cardinals Annals, Oh it is nothing but a fiction, and a very forgery of some lewd naughty varlet. It is demonstrated to be such, because it was written to *Iohn* Bishop of *Antioch*, who was dead but 7. yeares before, whereas more than foure times seven yeares, cannot hinder the Epistle of *Theodosius* written to the Bishop of *Constantinople* after hee was dead, to be an authentike and undoubted record. This may serve the Cardinall for the first answere, who is now bound in all equity, either to confesse his owne demonstration to be fallacious, or to proclame the Epistle of Pope *Clement*, and the other of *Theodosius* with that whole narration, to be fictitious, and his owne Annals a fabulous legend.

5. My second answer is, that though *Iohn*, to whom this Epistle is directed, was dead, yet that proves onely the title or inscription to be amisse, or that *Theodoret* writ not this Epistle to *Iohn*; it cannot prove (which the Cardinall undertooke to doe) that the Epistle is forged, and not written by *Theodoret*: For the Epistle it selfe to bee truly *Theodorets*, his owne Sermon publikely preached at *Antioch* before *Domnus* after the death of *Cyrill*, and mentioned in the Synodall Acts [l] next after this Epistle, doth clearly manifest; for the scope and purpose of that sermon is the same which is expressed in the Epistle. In the Epistle *Theodoret* declareth his eagernesse in defending the doctrine of *Nestorius*, and withall rejoyceth and insulteth over *Cyrill* being dead, who was then the chiefe oppugner of the heresies of *Nestorius.* The very same eagernesse for Nestorianisme, and love to his heresies, as also the like joy for *Cyrils* death doth his sermon expresse more fully, saying, *Nemo neminem jam cogit blasphemare, none doth now* (seeing *Cyrill* is dead) *compell any man to blaspheme,* (so hee cals the Catholike faith.) Where are those (to wit *Cyrill*) who teach that God was crucified? It was the man Christ, and not God who was crucified: It was the man I E S V S that dyed, and it was G O D the Word who raised him from the dead. *Non jam est contentio, Now* (seeing *Cyrill* is dead) *there is no contention; Oriens & Egyptus sub uno jugo est,* the East & Egypt

(that

k *Concionem illam rati, tibi fore chariorem. Baron 438. nu. 2. Cosmas vestiarius luculenta oratione de eadem translatione habita quæ gesta fuerunt exactè recenset. Ibid. nu.7. et alia similia habes.*

l *Conc. Coll. 5. 5. pa. 559. b.*

(that is, as well those who are under the Patriarke of *Alexandria*, as they who are under the Patriarke of *Antioch*) are all under one yoke; that is, all submit themselves to one faith, that is, to Nestorianisme. *Mortua est invidia, & cum eo mortua est contentio;* Envy (hee meaneth *Cyrill,* who so much hated and oppugned the doctrine of *Nestorius*) is *now dead, and all contention is dead and buried with him.* Let now the *Theopaschites,* (hee meanes Catholikes, who taught God to have suffered and dyed) let them now bee at quiet. Thus preached *Theodoret* after the death of *Cyrill,* insulting over him being dead, triumphing that now (seeing *Cyrill* was dead) Nestorianisme did and would prevaile. Who can imagine, but that the Epistle, maintaining the same heresie insulting in the same triumphing manner at the death of *Cyrill,* was written by *Theodoret,* when he publikely in his sermon before a Patriarke, uttered the same matter. Would *Theodoret* feare or forbeare to write that in a letter, which hee neither did feare, nor could forbeare to professe openly in a sermon, and that in so solemne a place and assembly? or was *Theodoret* orthodoxall, and a lover of *Cyrill* in his writings before the death of *Cyrill,* who was hereticall, and so full with the dregs of Nestorianisme after the death of *Cyrill,* that he must vent them, and with them disgorge his malice and spite against *Cyrill* in an open Pulpit, and in the hearing of a Patriarke, and all the people of *Antioch?* It is not the inscription or title of the Epistle, but the Epistle it selfe which the fift Councell and wee after it doe stand upon. Had not they knowne the Epistle to bee *Theodorets* they needed not by it to have proved that *Theodoret,* after the *union,* yea, after the death of *Cyrill* was eager, violent, yea, virulent also in defence of the heresies of *Nestorius;* that his publike sermon by them cited and preached after *Cyrils* death, and against *Cyrill,* had beene a sufficient proofe and demonstration of that; but because they were sure this was the true Epistle of *Theodoret,* they thought good to testifie that he was in writing the selfe same man as hee was in preaching, that is in both a spitefull maligner of *Cyrill,* in both a malicious and malignant Nestorian, and that long after the *union* made betwixt *Iohn* and *Cyrill,* yea, that even after the death of *Cyrill* he continued both to write and to speake the same.

6. Observe now by the way the fraudulent dealing of *Baronius* and *Binius* in this cause. This passage taken out of a sermon publikely preached at *Antioch* against *Cyrill,* and in an insulting manner for his death, this they doe not, nor durst they carpe at it. It is testified by all the Bishops of the fift Councell to have beene a part of *Theodorets* sermon: the Epistle which likewise is testified by them all to bee *Theodorets,* containing the same matter with his sermon, that they raile at, and revile both it and the writer of it, because in the inscription thereof they have espyed an errour. It had beene honest dealing in the Cardinall and *Binius,* seeing these are fethers of one wing, either to have acknowledged both, or denyed both to bee the brood of *Theodoret.*

7. Againe, the Cardinall undertooke to prove, that still after the *union* betwixt *Iohn* and *Cyrill, Theodoret* was a Catholike, and defen-

der

der of the Catholike faith, and becauſe the Epiſtle demonſtrates the
contrary, he will not allow it to bee *Theodorets*, but a forgery written
in his name. Admit it were, yet that part of *Theodorets* ſermon is truly his, nor doth eyther *Baronius* or *Binius* deny it to bee his. Now by
this ſermon is *Theodoret* as effectually proved and demonſtrated, as by
the Epiſtle to have beene an eager oppugner of the Catholike faith,
and an obſtinate defender of all the hereſies of *Neſtorius* after the
death of *Cyrill*, which was twelve [m] yeares after the *union*: So that
although the Epiſtle were not *Theodorets*, or had never beene extant,
yet the Cardinals poſition for *Theodorets* Orthodoxy is clearly and
certainly refuted by the ſermon of *Theodoret* made twelve yeares after the *union*.

m *Vnio facta an. 432. Bar. ille an. nu.77. Cyrillus autem obijt an.444. Bar. illo an. nu.9.*

8. Further yet the Cardinall to defend the Orthodoxy of *Theodoret* urgeth ſtrongly, and relyeth upon the Epiſtles, which in their Vaticane or Mint-houſe are ſtamped with the name of *Theodoret*; whereas if there were no other proofes, this one ſermon of *Theodorets* is an
undoubted evidence that they can bee none of *Theodorets*, but are forged in his name; for the whole ſcope, at which thoſe Epiſtles [n] ayme,
is to magnifie *Theodoret* both for his integrity of life, uprightneſſe in
judgement, laborioufneſſe in preaching, and ſpecially for his ſound-
neſſe in the Catholike faith, that he was never reproved nor accuſed
by any, no not in ſixe and twenty yeares, for his doctrine; that he never accuſed any, and ſpecially for *Cyrill*, that *Theodoret* loved and honoured him for a learned and pious man, *& mirificè coluit ejus memoriam*, when *Cyrill* was dead, *hee wonderfully honoured his memory*, calling
him a man of bleſſed memory; all which and a hundred ſuch like matters contained in thoſe Epiſtles are undeniably convicted to bee untrue by this ſermon of his, wherein he vomiteth out in a moſt ſolemne
aſſembly, together with the blaſphemies of *Neſtorius*, moſt ſlanderous
revilings not onely againſt *Cyrill*, at whoſe death hee inſulteth, but a-
gainſt all Catholikes, whom he, according to the Neſtorian language,
cals *Theopaſchites* and heretikes: with ſuch falſe, fained, and lying writings doth the Cardinall fight againſt the fift Synod and the Acts
thereof.

n *Vt clarum eſt ex Epiſt. Theod. ad Dioſcorum, ad Leonem, ad Nomum, de qui-bus diximus ſu-pra, ca.33.*

9. Yea, but ſtill the Cardinall will reply, the Inſcription unto *Iohn*,
who before was dead, ſhewes the Epiſtle to *Iohn* to bee forged, and to
be none of *Theodorets*: It doth not; for the inſcription or title of an
Epiſtle or other writing, may bee erronious, and the Epiſtle truly his
whoſe name it beares, which the Cardinal may ſee, if need were, in a
hundred examples.

10. In the Epiſtle of Pope *Clement* unto *Iames*, whereof before wee
ſpake, the Cardinall [o] and *Binius* [p] both confeſſe the inſcription to be
falſe, and yet they both hold the Epiſtle to bee Pope *Clements*, yea,
they can excuſe that, and ſay it was but an errour in writing *Iames* [q] in
ſtead of *Simeon* in the title, were they not too too partiall and malicious againſt this holy Synod, they would as eaſily have uſed the ſame
excuſe for *Theodorets* Epiſtle, and have ſaid, the Epiſtle is truly his, but
in the inſcription in the Acts, the name of *Iohn* is, by the writers miſtaking, ſet in ſtead of *Domnus*.

o *An.69.til.43* p *Notis in 1. E-piſtolam Clemen-tis.* q *In titulum E-piſtole, mendoſè vox [Iacobum] irrepſit. Bin. loc.cit.*

11. *Theodoret*

r *Lib.5. ca.10.
et secundum
Chryst. ca.11.*

11. *Theodoret* in his history [r] sets down an Epistle of Pope *Damasus*, against *Eunomius* and other heretikes, the title in him is thus, The confession of faith which Pope *Damasus* sent to *Paulinus* Bishop of *Thessalonica*; and with this inscription it is also published in the *Venice* edition of the Councels by *Nicholinus*. Did *Damasus* write or send this to *Paulinus* Bishop of *Thessalonica*? No, he did not; there was no *Paulinus* then, nor long after that Bishop of *Thessalonica*, as [f] *Baronius* and [t] *Binius* at large prove and professe. What then? may we here conclude by the Cardinals demonstration; certainly this Epistle was none of Pope *Damasus* writings, it is a forgery and a counterfeit, seeing it is written to *Paulinus*, whereas there was no such man at all? No, the demonstration holds not in Pope *Damasus*; nor in his writings; for notwithstanding this errour in the title, *Baronius* and *Binius* [u] hold it both to be the true, undoubted, and Synodall Epistle of Pope *Damasus*, and truely sent from him; but sent to *Paulinus* Bishop of *Antioch*, not to any *Paulinus* Bishop of *Thessalonica*. Applie now this to the Epistle of *Theodoret*, may not it likewise be true, and truly written by *Theodoret*, though the title be either false or unpossible? If any demand how that errour in *Theodores*, touching the title of the Epistle, might happen, *Baronius* and *Binius* impute [x] it to the malice and wilfull fraud of *Theodoret*; but I much rather ascribe it to the writer, who finding in *Theodoret* the name of *Paulinus*, without any addition, either ignorantly or wickedly, inserted the false addition of *Thessalonica*. Would the Cardinall have dealt favourably with the other inscription of *Iohn*, and in stead of it have put *Domnus*, who was then Bishop of *Antioch*, he might have spared his labour in this point.

[ʃ] *Vides Lector,
ne fingi quidem
posse ut Pauli-
nus, quem iactat
Theodoretus, fu-
erit Episcopus
Thessalonicensis.
Bar.an.378. nu.
43.*
t *Bin. not. in
Conc. Rom. 3.
sub Damaso
post professionem
fidei Apollina-
rii, &c. pa. 508.
u Scripta fuit
Synodalis Epi-
stola à Damaso
ex Concilio Ro-
mano ad Pauli-
num Antioche-
num. Bar.an.
378.nu.41.
Itidem Binius
loco citat.
x Locis citatis.*

12: In the sixteenth Novell of *Iustinian* the inscription is to *Anthimus* Bishop of *Constantinople*, now the date of that Edict is on the thirteenth day of *August* in the yeare after the Consulship of *Bellisarius*, at which time it is certaine that not *Anthimus*, but *Mennas* was Bishop; for *Mennas* sate in the generall Councell held that yeare at *Constantinople*, which began on the second of *May*; yea, the Emperour himselfe on the sixt of *August* in the same yeare and Consulship, dates another Edict unto *Mennas*. So that undoubtedly there is an errour in the inscription, and yet notwithstanding this errour, the Edict it selfe is without all doubt *Iustinians*, nor will the Cardinals demonstration hold in this.

y *Extat tom. 2.
Conc. pa. 390.
a Hac chronolo-
gia mendosa est,
nam hoc mense
Bonifacius jam
Pontifex creatus
erat, ut patet su-
pra. Bin. not. in
eam Epist. et
Bar.an. 530.
nu.1.
b Facile accidis-
se potuit, ut loco
Bonifacij, Felicii
nomen fuerit ap-
positum. Bar.
loco citat.
c Epist.1.Sylv.
extat tom. 2.
Conc. pa.476.*

13: The Epistle of *Fælix* the fourth [y] to *Sabina*, was written and dated on the twefth of the Kalends of *November*, at which time [a] *Fælix* was dead. What, may it by the Cardinals demonstration be rejected for a counterfeit? No, the Cardinall [b] will tell you, it was indeed the Popes Epistle but of *Boniface* the successor of *Fælix*, and not as the inscription tels, of Pope *Fælix*, *& facile accidisse potuit, it might easily happen*, that the name of *Fælix* might bee put in stead of *Boniface* his next successor. Might not the very same: and as easily happen in this Epistle of *Theodoret*, that the name of *Iohn* might be put in the inscription in stead of *Domnus* his next successor?

14. There is an Epistle of Pope *Silverius* [c], wherein he writ an excommunication against *Vigilius* usurping his See, it is dated in some

Copies in the yeare of *Basilius*, in others of *Bellisarius*, being Consuls. Now in all the time ᵈ *Silverius* was Pope, neither was *Basilius* nor *Bellisarius* Consuls. What then? shall the Popes Epistle be rejected as a a forgery, a counterfeit? No, by no meanes. The Cardinall ᵉ often mentioneth it, honours it for a rare monument; and to helpe that errour, he tels us the date is added more than should be. Might not the like happen to the inscription of *Theodorets* letter in the Synodall acts? Might it not happen that the inscription was onely to the Archbishop of *Antioch*, & that the name of *Iohn* was added more than should be? *Epiphanius* in his Book of heresies sayth ᶠ that *Iustine Martyr* dyed when *Adrian* was Emperour; a manifest untruth, for *Iustine Martyr* writ an Apology for the Christian faith unto *Antoninus* ᵍ the successor of *Adrian*, and he was put to death under *Mar. Aurelius*, and *Verus*, 24. yeares ʰ after the death of *Adrian*. Will the Cardinall have his demonstration to hold here in *Epiphanius*? so that his booke against heresies must be condemned for a counterfeit, and none of *Epiphanius* writing? No, *error irrepsit, there slipt an error into Epiphanius*; for *Adrian* is written in stead of *Antoninus*, as the Cardinall tels you: but it rather seemes in stead of *Aurelius*, (under whom *Iustine* dyed.) Had the Cardinall beene any way as indifferent to *Theodorets* letters, hee would likewise have said, *error irrepsit, an error is slipt into the inscription*, by writing *Iohn* in stead of his successor *Domnus*, rather than have condemned the writing for a forgery.

14. In the twenty third Cause, *Question* 4. *Cap.* 30. in the ancient title it was cited ᶠ as a text of *Sylvester*, a manifest errour of *Sylvester* in stead of *Sylverius*. Did the Gregorian Correctors, for this false title or name of *Sylvester* inserted, condemne that Canon or Epistle as a counterfeit? no, but approving the text as true they amended the title, and restored it to *Sylverius*. In the very same Chapter it is said, that *Guillisarius* caused *Sylverius* to bee deposed, there was no *Guillisarius* that ever did that, but it was *Bellisarius*, yet for that error of the name, which yet remaines ʰ uncorrected, is not the Canon or Epistle rejected?

15. In that fragment of this Synod which *Binius* ⁱ out of *Tyrius* commendeth, it is sayd that the fift Synod which decreed the Patriarchall dignity to the Bishop of *Ierusalem*, was held in the time of *Vigilius* of *Rome*, *Eutychius* of *Constantinople*, and *Paule* of *Antioch*. Now that by the Cardinals demonstration was never; for it is certaine that there was no *Paul* Bishop of *Antioch* in Pope *Vigilius* his dayes. Before this Synod, was *Ephreem* ᵏ, who sate eighteene yeares, in whose fourteenth, or fifteenth yeare began *Vigilius* ˡ to be Pope, to him succeeded *Domnus* ᵐ, hee sate 18. yeares, in whose ⁿ seventh or eighth yeare this fift Councell was held, and himselfe personally subscribed unto ᵒ it, and about his tenth yeare dyed *Vigilius* ᵖ. So this decree, by the Cardinals owne reason, is but a forgery (as in very truth it is.) Now if he to save the credit of that worthlesse fragment, will admit an error of the writing, *Paulus* being put for *Domnus*, why should it be so hard hearted against the other writing of *Theodoret*, as not to thinke a like errour of the pen in it, and *Iohannes* to be put for *Domnus*?

16. That

ᵈ *Temporibus Sylverii nullus converit Bellisrij consulatus, neq; Basilii. Bar. an. 539. 3. & idem cit. Biz. Not. in margin. ad eam epistolã. c An. 539. nu. 1. & 4.*

ᶠ *Epiph. hær. 46.* ᵍ *Iust. Mart. ad Antoninum pium defensio.* ʰ *Nam Hadrianus obiit an. 140. Bar. illo an. nu. 1. Iustinus vero an. 165. Bar. illo an. nu. 1* ⁱ *Loc. citat. & Notis in Martyr. Rom. Apr. 13* ˣ *Guillisarius, quia est initium capitis non est mutatum. Not. Greg. in illud cap.* ˣ *Post 5. Concil. pa. 606. a.* ᵏ *Ephreem sedere cœpit. an. 526. Bar. ea an. nu. 55 sedet autem an. 18. Niceph. in Chron.* ˡ *Vigilius cœpit. an. 440. Bar. eo. an. nu. 9 ii est Ephraimi an. 15. Niceph. in Chron. & Bar. an. 446. nu. 68* ⁿ *Nam 8. Domni est an. 553. quo habitum est concilium hoc.* ᵒ *Collat. 8. pa. 588. a.* ᵖ *Domnus cœpit an. 446. qua re ejus an. 10. erit 555. quo anno obiisse Vigilium, ait Bar. an. 555. nu. 1.*

16. That *Edict* of *Iustinian* which wee have so often mentioned in the ancient editiõs of Councels before *Binius* had this title; The *Edict* of *Iustinian* sent unto Pope *Iohn* the second. *Contius* the learned Lawyer, defends that inscription. *Baronius* himselfe somewhat forget-full of what elsewhere hee writeth, cals this *Edict, Constitutio data ad Iohan. a Constitution sent to Pope Iohn*, & again, *Iustinian expresly witnes-seth this in his Edict to P. Iohn*, a false title & inscriptiõ without al doubt, *Iohn* being dead ten yeares before this *Edict* was either published, or writ, as *Baronius* himselfe both declares and proves; professing that Inscription to be false. Had the Cardinall remembred his demonstra-tion drawne from the title and Inscription, oh how happily, how ea-sily had he avoided all his trouble of defending *Vigilius* for writing a-gainst, and contradicting that Edict: Hee might have said; Why, that Edict was none of *Iustinians*, nor ever published by him; for the Inscrip-tion is to Pope *Iohn* who was dead long before. And because the fift Councell was assembled for discussing that truth which the Emperor in his Edict had delivered, and *Vigilius* with the other Nestorians did oppugne, the Cardinal againe might have denyed that ever there had beene any such fift Councell, or any Synodall Acts at all of it; for if there was no Edict there could bee no Councel, which was assembled and gathered for that onely cause, to define the truth delivered by the Edict. This had beene a short cut indeed, and the Cardinall, like ano-ther *Alexander*, by this one stroke had dispatched all the doubts and difficultes which neither hee nor all his friends can ever untwine or loose in this Gordian knot. But the Cardinals demonstations were not in force as then, nor ever, I thinke, till the acts of this fift Synod, and in them the Epistle of *Theodoret*, came to his tryal: for notwithstan-ding the falshood of that inscription & title, the Card. very honestly acknowledgeth that to bee no counterfeit, but a true imperiall Edict, truely published by *Iustinian*, contradicted by *Vigilius*, confirmed as touching the doctrine of the *Three Chapters*, by the fift Councel. Here he can say that addition to *Iohn* is added, & put amisse in by the title some later hand, by some who knew not accurately to distinguish the times: may not the same as truly excuse this writing of *Theodoret*? the name of *Iohn* is added in the title by some who knew not accurately to distinguish the times, but yet the Epistle it selfe it is truely *Theodorets*. It had beene honest and faire dealing in the Cardinal, any one of these waies to have excused this errour in the title *Theodorets* of Epistle, rather than by reason of such an errour, as happeneth in many Epistles and writings, to declame, not onely against the Epistle as a base forge-ry, and none of *Theodorets*; but even against all the Acts of this holy generall Councell, as unworthy of credit, because among them an E-pistle with an erronious Inscription is found extant.

17. None, I thinke, doe nor ever will defend the Acts of this or any other Conncel, or any humane writings to be so absolutely intire, and without all corruption, as that no fault of the writer or exscriber hath crept into them; such faults are frequent in the Acts almost of all Councels. To omit the rest; in those of *Chalcedon*, the Ephesine La-trociny is said to have beene held when *Zeno* and *Posthumianus* were

Consuls,

s It appeuded ad Cod. Iustin. f Bar. an. 451. nu. 129.
t An 530. nu. 4.

u Iohannes 2. obijt an. 9. Iusti-niani. Bar. an. 535. nu. 26. & Edictum editum an. 10. Iustiniani Bar. an. 546. nu. 8.
x Iohannis Papa tempore editum, mendaci inscrip-tione notatur Bar. an. 546. nu. 10. liquido con-stat, quum ante prasens tempus (an. vid. 20. Iu-stin.) potuisse es-se cunscriptum libellum illum. Bar. ibid. & constat Edictum Vigilij tempore conscriptum, an. 534. nu. 21.

y Imperator pro-mulgavit Edi-ctum, Bar. an. 546. nu. 8. Ha-betur Iustiniani Edictum, ibid. nu. 37. ut sapis-sime simile.
z Scias parperam additum, ipsum missum ad Io-hannem. Bar. an. 534. nu. 31. & an. 546. nu. 10. a At quam fidem togo, merentur Acta huiusmo-di, qua sunt his contexta com-mentis? Bar. an. 553. nu. 46.

b Act. 1. pa. 8 n.

Confuls, in the third Indiction. An undoubted errour; For that E-phefine Conventicle was held when [c] *Protogenes* and *Aſterius* were Confuls, not when *Zeno* and *Poſthumianus*; neither were *Zeno* and *Poſthumianus* Confuls in the third, but in the firſt [d] Indiction: neither was the Councell held either in the firſt or in the third, but in the [e] ſecond Indiction; and therefore both *Baronius* [f], and *Binius* [g] ſay, theſe words [*tempore Zenonis & Poſthumiani venerabilium Conſulum indictione tertia*] are falſe, and by ſurreption crept into the Acts. Againe, the ſixteenth Action or Seſſion is ſayd to have beene on the twenty eight [h] of Octo-ber. A manifeſt errour; ſeeing their thirteenth Action [i] or Seſſion was on the nine and twentieth, and their fourteenth [k] Seſſion on the thirtieth of October. Yea there are in thoſe Acts farre greater faults than theſe. For in the third Action [l] is ſet downe the Imperiall Edict of *Valentinian* and *Martian*, for condemning of *Eutyches*: and yet that Edict was not publiſhed untill the 26. of Ianuary, when [m] *Sporarius* was Conſull: whereas the Councell of *Chalcedon* and all the Acts ther-of was ended on the firſt day of November [n] the yeare before: that is, more than two moneths before that Edict was made. In the ſeventh Seſſion alſo there is inſerted by *Binius* [o] and *Baronius* [p] an whole Acti-on concerning *Domnus*, who was depoſed in the Epheſine Latrociny, where the Councel decreed that *Maximius* ſhould allow *Domnus* ſome charges to ſerve him *pro victu & veſtitu*. A forged Action, and that in the higheſt degree; as not onely the time when it was held; to wit, on the twenty ſeventh [q] of October; whereas the Seſſion [r] which follow-ed it was held on the five and twentieth, or ſix and twentieth day of the ſame moneth, doth declare; but becauſe this *Domnus* was dead be-fore the Councell of *Chalcedon*, as both the Imperiall Edict of *Iustini-an* [t], and the fift Councell, doe certainly witneſſe. Could the Cardi-nall have found ſuch additions or forgeries inſerted into the Acts of this fift Councell; *quos ludos daret*, how would hee have triumphed in the diſgrace of theſe Acts, to have writings in them, and as parts of them and their Synodall Acts, which were not made long after the end of the Councell? to have an whole Action or conſultation, what allowance ſhould be made to a dead man for proviſion of his food and rayment? Here had beene a field indeed for the Cardinall to have in-ſulted over theſe Acts. And yet, notwithſtanding theſe errors in the two firſt, and undoubted additions of the Emperours Edict in the third, and that whole ridiculous action, nay fiction, in the fourth, pat-ched unto the Acts of *Chalcedon*, the Cardinall will not ſo diſgrace thoſe Acts, as to uſe his demonſtration againſt the credit of them, or that Councell: And yet ſee his unequall and unhoneſt dealing in theſe matters, becauſe but one name is inſerted into the inſcription, or by an error put in ſtead of another: the Cardinals choler breakes out in this manner againſt the Acts of this fift Synod, *Quam fidem* [u], *rogo*, I pray you what credit is to be given to ſuch Acts?

[c] *Marcell. in chron. & hinc certo liquet, quia Conciliabulum Epheſinum ſequutum eſt illud Conſtantinople habitum, in quo condemnatus eſt Eutyches à Flaviano, at hoc Conſtantinopoli habitum eſt, Protogene et Aſterio. Coſſ. ut patet in Concil. Chalc. Act. 1. pa. 30.*

[d] *Ut liquet ex Marcell. in Chron.*

[e] *Ut liquet ex eodem Marc.*

[f] *Ba. an. 448. n. 58.*

[g] *Hæc verba [tempore Zenonis et Poſthumiani Ind. A. one 3.] mendoſa ſunt & ſurreptitia. Bin. Not. in Concili-ab. Eph. to. 1. Conc. pa. 1017. b.*

[h] *Quinto Ka-lendas Novem-bris. Act. 16. Conc. Chal.*

[i] *3. Kalend. No-vemb. Conc. Chal. Act. 13.*

[k] *Pridie Kalend Nov. Conc. Chal Act. 14.*

[l] *Pa. 84. b.*

[m] *Datum 7. Ka-lend. Febr. Spa-rario Coſſ. in fine Edicti.*

[n] *Nam ultima Seſſio habita eſt Kalendis No-vemb. dicitur enim ibi, heſternâ die, poſtquam po-teſtas veſtra ſur-rexit, &c. quare ultima Seſſio fuit proxima die poſt Seſſionem in qua Actio 14. & 15. continen-tur, at actio 14. habita eſt pridie Kalend. Novem.*

[o] *Act. 7. pa. 105 b.*   [p] *Bar. an. 551. nu. 128.*   [q] *Actio de Domno habita eſt 6. Kalend. Nov. Bar. an. 451. nu. 129. & Bin. Not. ad Conc. Chalc. pa. 18.*   [r] *Nam actio ſequens quæ etiam alia Seſſio eſt, in qua Theodoreti cauſa tractatur, habita eſt ſub octav. Kalend. Nov.*   [t] *Chalcedonenſis Synodus Domnum poſt mortem condemnavit. Edict. Iuſt. to. 2. Concil. pa. 498. & idem repetit Conc. 5. Coll. 6. pa. 575 b.*   [u] *An. 553. nu. 46.*

18. Some three or foure errors of the pen, besides this of the inscription, I confesse are also in the Acts of this fift Synod. The fift Collation is sayd to have beene on the eight [m], (it should bee on the thirteenth or fourteenth) of May, seeing the fourth Collation was held on the twelfth [n] of that moneth. In the same fift Collation [o] *Cyrill* is alledged to say, *Non jam quidem sancta Synodus*, the holy Synod did not now pronounce a sentence against *Nestorius*: the negation (*non*) is by negligence either of *Binius*, or the Printer, crept in, and is certainly to be blotted out, which otherwise not onely makes Saint *Cyrill* to speake untruly, but even to contradict himselfe. In the same Action [p], there is recited an Epistle to *Andreas* Bishop of Samosat, in the inscription whereof *Theodorus* is written in stead of *Theodoretus*, seeing of the next Epistle being *Theodorets*, it is sayd, *ejusdem ad Nestorium*. It may be some few moe such errors may be found in these Acts of the fift Councell; but for the honour of them, I professe, they are so incorrupt and intire, that moe than these I doe not remember my selfe to have for a certainty observed in them. Neither doe such errours creep only into humane writings, their owne learned *Iansenius* [q] (after *Beza* [r]) will tell them, that the very sacred Scriptures are subject to the same: for whereas *Matth.* 27. 9. the Euangelist sayth it is written in the Prophet *Ieremy*; seeing the text there cited is not found in *Ieremie*, but in *Zachary*; although some thinke it to be a slip [s] in memory in Saint *Matthew*; others, that it is in some apochryphall [t] writing of *Ieremy*; others, that *Zachary* had two names (as many other Iewes) and so might be called either *Ieremie* or *Zacharie*; yet *Iansenius* not liking any of these conjectures, rests on this answer as most neare the truth, that either the name of *Zacharie* is *Scribæ culpâ commutatum in Ieremiam*, *by the errour and fault of the writer turned into Ieremy*; or else, that whereas the Euangelist sayd no more, but that this is written in the Prophet (in which sort without any addition or mention of name, some copies to have read that place, Saint *Austen* [u] is witnesse, and not onely *Rupertus*, but the *Syriack* translator read it in the same manner) some more audacious hand expressed the name of *Ieremy*. Do you thinke the Cardinall would or durst use his demonstration in this text? that seeing a wrong name is inserted (not in the title or inscription (as in this Epistle it is) but in the very text,) he would account the Gospell a forgery, and unworthy of credit? It is true, they are too too bold even with the Scriptures also: whereof they gave a notable proofe; first when (as it was credibly reported [x] to the relator) some of the Iesuites, even in their solemne Sermons in *Italy*, censured Saint *Paul* for an hot-headed person, who was transported with his pangs of zeale and eagernesse, beyond all compasse in his disputes, and that there was no great reckoning to bee made of his assertions; yea that he was dangerous to reade, as savouring of heresie in some places, and better perhaps he had never written: and againe, when (as some Catholikes [y] told it in the hearing of the relator) they held a consultation among them, to have censured by some meanes, and reformed the Epistle of Saint *Paul*. Though such be their audaciousnesse, yet I hope the Cardinall will not bee so censorious with the holy Gospell.

What

m *Octavo Idus Maias.* Coll. 5. pa. 537. b.

n *Collatio 4. die 4. Idus Maias.*

o Pa. 548. a.

p Pa. 558. b.

q Cap. 140. Concord. Euang.

r *Bez. in cap. 27 Matth. v. 9.*

s *Videtur huc inclinare Aug. lib. 3. de cons. Euan. ca. 7.*

t *Sic Orig. sensit Homil. 35. in Matth.*

u *Loco citato.*

x A Relation of the state of Religion in the West parts. fol. L4.

y *Ibid.*

what hard hap then hath *Theodoret*, that hee alone among all writers, divine and humane, may not have the benefit of his book at the Cardinalls hand; but for one such fault, not onely his writing must be rejected as a forgery, but the Synodall Acts, among which it stands, must be condemned as worthy of no credit?

19. If none of these can mollifie the Cardinals heart, let it yet further be considered, that in his owne Annals [a] it is sayd of the consent of *Vigilius* to the Edict, the fift Synod doth often give witnesse, *quin etiam sexta Synodus Actione septima continet monumenta*, Further also the sixt Synod in the seventh Action containes the writings of Pope *Vigilius* against the three Chapters. A saying so voyd of truth, that those monuments of *Vigilius*, yea almost any one of them, is able to eat up all that whole seventh Action, it is such a pittance to those large writings of *Vigilius*. Besides, in that seventh action of the sixt Councell, there is neither monuments of *Vigilius*, nor so much as any mention of *Vigilius* at all, nor of the *three Chapters*. Let him againe consider how hee saith [b]; that *Cælestine* called the Ephesine Councell by the Emperour *Theodorus*; that is to say, never, if the Cardinall be not relieved with an error or scape of the writer. That elsewhere in the same Annalls he [*] sayth, that by the Catholike Church the Romane Church is signified, as appeares *ex Epistola Hormisdæ Papæ ad Iustinum Imperatorem*, *by the Epistle* (he quoteth the 22.) of Pope *Hormisda* to *Iustinus*. An evident error. For neither is that 22. Epistle written to *Iustinus*, but to *Dorotheus* a Bishop; neither is that which the Cardinall alledgeth, either in that 22. or in any other of all the epistles (they are five) which *Hormisda* writ to *Iustinus*. But the Card. by a pretty mistaking, first turnes *Iustinian* into *Iustinus*, and then pretends that to be written Epist. 22. and by *Hormisda*, and to *Iustinus*; which is written by *Iustinian*, and to *Hormisda*, and which followeth the 56. Epistle. Further yet let him remember, how in the same Annals [c] it is said, that before the Edict of *Iustinian* was written, those controversies happened betwixt *Theodorus* (Bishop of *Cæsarea*) and *Pascalis* the Deacon. The Card. might as wel have said, that the *Edict* was never written nor published; for there was never any contention nor controversie betwixt *Pascalis* the Deacon, and *Theodorus*; and I doubt, or rather am out of doubt, that there was never any such contention as the Cardinal dreameth of (the best author for it being *Liberatus*, one heretically affected in this cause, and maliciously bent against *Theodorus*) but if there was any such controversie, it was not betwixt *Theodorus* and *Pascalis*, but betwixt *Theodorus* and *Pelagius*. *Pelagius* & not *Pascalis* was the Popes Agent at *Constantinople* at that time, as not onely *Liberatus* [d]; but *Procopius* [e], a man of better note testifieth. Now these foule errours (whereupon is consequent that almost all which the Cardinall hath historified for some 10. or 11. yeares is utterly untrue) being extant and recorded in his Annals, though there be violent presumption, to thinke that the Cardinall judged some of them to be indeed no errors, neither of his own memory, nor of the writers pen, seeing when he reviewed or retracted his Tomes, and corrected therein small slips, and very motes to such beames as these, as the mistaking of a few months or dayes, or miswri-

ting

a *an.547.nu.40*

b *Bar.an.536. nu.32.*

* *Bar.an.534.*

c *Bar.an.546. nu.10.*

d *Pelagius annitus existens Theodoro, volens cinocere. Liber. Brev.ca.23.24. & Pelagius Apocrisiarius Agapeti, Silverij & Vigilij. Bar. an.5;6.nu 116. e Lib.3. de Bell. Goth.pa.365. Pelagius diu Constantinopoli commoratus.*

ting a word or syllable, and the like; yet hee not once mentioneth any correction in these places, yet am I content to allow these to bee but slips of the writer or Printer, as writing *Theodorus* in stead of *Theodosius*, *Pascalis* for *Pelagius*; from *Hormisda*, for, to *Hormisda*; to *Iustine*, for, from *Iustinian*; and *sexta* for *quinta*, or *eadem quinta*; upon condition that the Cardinall and his friends will in like sort consent, that by an error of some writer of these Synodall acts, the name of *Iohn* is either inserted when there was no name, or written in stead of *Domnus* in that inscription. But if they be obstinate and refuse such a reasonable profer, the Card. and all his friends must be patient to heare, how justly and forcibly his owne demonstration may in his owne words be retorted upon himselfe, & these errors of his. Certainly these are patent and manifest lyes and frauds, devised by some hereticall knave or varlet, they are such as every man may perceive to be written by him who was not in any measure a lover of Christian piety : *Sed impudentissimi cujuspiam Nestorij figmentum*, but they are the fiction of a most impudent Nestorian forgerer. *Et quam fidem rogo, merentur?* and what credit in the world can bee given to those writings or Annals, which have such untruths and fictions inserted in them, and are *contexta*, composed and woven together with such untruths? This being abundantly sufficient to satisfie any indifferent man in this matter, yet would I a little further let the Reader see, how childishly and corruptly *Baronius* dealeth in this cause. It is true, I confesse, that *Iohn* dyed before *Cyrill* : for this is cleare and certaine, by many undoubted testimonies in the Councell of *Chalcedon* f, not one of all which the Cardinall had the grace to alledge. But all the Cardinals reasons are so weake and withall so full of fraud and untruth, that it is worthy your considering to see his blindnesse and perversenesse even in proving that which is true.

f *Act.14. Vbi extat germana Cyrilli Episcopi Alexandrini Epistola ad Domnum Antiochenum.pa. 122. & sæpius fit mentio Cyrilli mortui tùm Domnus ille sedebat Antiochiæ.*
g *Bar.an.444. nu.16.*

20. His first reason is this; *I have shewed* g *this apertissimè, that Iohn dyed seven yeares before Cyrill by the Epistle which Theodoret writ to Domnus foure yeares since*, (that is, foure before the yeare 444.) *in the behalfe of one Felicianus, whose estate Theodoret recommends to Domnus.* Truly the Cardinall hath shewed himselfe an egregious trifler hereby: For neither in the 440. nor in any foure yeares either before or after that, doth hee set downe any Epistle of *Theodorets* to *Domnus*, in the behalfe of *Felicianus*. The Epistle which the Cardinall dreameth of, is in behalfe of *Celestianus*, and that is indeed expressed *An.*
h *To.6.an.440. nu.9.*
440 h. where note I pray you, that the Cardinall by a slip either of his owne penne or memory, (as I verily suppose) or of his Scribe, names *Felicianus* in stead of *Celestianus*: God even by this, demonstrating how unjustly he carpes at the Synodall Acts, for that very errour or slippe of a penne, which the Cardinall himselfe falls into, even while hee, for the like slippe, declameth against those holy Synodall Acts. And yet there is a worse fault in this reason. For it is no more shewed that *Iohn* dyed before *Cyrill* by that Epistle, than by *Tullies ad Atticum*. That Epistle having neither date, nor any circumstance to induce that, may as well bee written *Anno 448.* as *Anno 440.*

21. His

21. His second reason is this : *There are letters*, saith hee [i], *extant of Theodoret to Domnus the yeare following*,(to wit, *an.* 437.) *and that Epistle of Theodoret I will set downe in his due place, anno sequenti, the next yeare.* Now in that next yeare, *viz. an.* 437. there is no Epistle of *Theodoret* set downe by the Cardinall, nor is either *Domnus* or *Theodoret* so much as named in all his discourse of that yeare. Is not this now shewed *apertissimè* ? you may bee sure the Cardinall would not have feared to performe his promise; but that there was somewhat in that Epist. wch would have bewrayed his lewd dealing in this cause.

22. His third reason is drawne from the testimony of *Nicephorus* Bishop of *Constantinople*. This, saith hee [k], *exploratum habetur, is sure and certaine by Nicephorus.* No, it is sure and certaine by *Nicephorus* that *Baronius* is erronious in this matter; for *Nicephorus* [l] accounteth *Iohn* to have beene Bishop of *Antioch* eighteene yeares, and the Cardinall [m] will allow him no more but thirteene, now the first yeare of *Iohn* cannot possibly be before the yeare 427. for in that year *Theodotus*, the next predecessor of *Iohn*, dyed, as *Baronius* [n] himselfe proveth. Add now unto these seventeene moe, and then the death of *Iohn* by *Nicephorus* will bee *an.* 444. which is the selfe same yeare wherein *Cyrill* dyed. Is not this a worthy proofe to shew *Iohn* to have dyed seven years before *Cyrill*, as the *Cardinall* avoucheth that he did ? Or do not you think the Cardinal was in some extasy, to produce *Nicephorus* as a witnesse for him, whereas *Nicephorus* (as the Cardinall himselfe also confesseth) gives to *Iohn* 18. yeares, and the Cardinall allowes him but thirteene ; and whereas the Cardinall of set purpose refuteth the account of *Nicephorus* ?

23. But will you bee pleased to see how the Cardinall refuteth him ? *Domnus*, saith hee [o], *was Bishop of Antioch an.* 437. *as is proved by an Epistle of Theodorets written to Domnus in that yeare, which Epistle I will set downe in his due place, to wit, an.* 437. Lo, all his proofe is from that Epistle, which the Cardinall, contrary to his own promise, doth not, and, as I thinke, durst not set downe.

24. But see further how the Cardinall is infatuated in this cause : *Iohn*, saith he [p], *dyed an.* 436. *having beene Bishop* 13. *yeares. Iohn succeeded to* [q] *Theodotus, who dyed an.* 427. Say now in truth, is not the Cardinall a worthy Arithmetitian, that of 427. and 13. can make no more than 436 ? And is not this a worthy reason to refute *Nicephorus* ? But this is not all, for *Baronius* [r] glossing upon *Theodorets* letter to *Dioscorus*, which, as hee [s] saith, was written, *an.* 444. there observes with a *memorandum*, that by this passage of *Theodoret* you may see how long *Theodotus* [t], *Iohn*, and *Domnus* had sitten in the See of *Antioch*, to wit, 26. yeares in all, from the time that *Theodoret* was made Bishop unto that 444. yeare, *viz. Theodotus* 6. *Iohn* 13. and *Domnus* 7. untill that yeare *Theodoret*, as *Baronius* [u] will assure you, was made Bishop, *an.* 423. Add now unto these six of *Theodotus*, thirteene of *Iohn*, and 7. of *Domnus*, and tell me whither you thinke the Cardinall had sent his wits, when hee could summe these to bee just 444 ?

25. Or will you see the very quintessence of the Cardinals wisedome ? *I will*, saith he [x], *set downe the next yeare* (that is, *an.* 437.) *the very*

[k] *Bar. an.* 553. *nu.* 44.

[l] *Ἰωάννης ἔτη* ιη'. *Niceph. in Chrō.*

[m] *Johannes obiit cum sedisset annos* 13. *licet Nicephorus in Chronico tribuat ei* 18. *Bar. an.* 436. *nu.* 12.

[n] *Post hæc Theodotus ex hac vita migravit, qui ad hunc usque annum pervenisse proditur, &c. Bar. an.* 427. *nu.* 25.

[o] *Bar. an.* 436. *nu.* 12.

[p] *Bar. ibid.*

[q] *Bar. an.* 427. *nu.* 26. *Defuncto Theodoto, subrogatus est in ejus locum Iohannes.*

[r] *Bar. an.* 444. *nu.* 23.

[s] *Theodoreti ad Dioscorum data hoc anno Epistola sic se habet. An. illo nu.* 18.

[t] *Hinc discas annos cujusque ipsorum Episcopatus. Bar. an.* 444 *nu.* 23.

[u] *Bar. an.* 423. *nu.* 10. *Hoc anno Theodoretus creatus est Episcopus.*

[x] *Bar. an.* 437. *nu.* 12.

very Epistle of Theodoret to Domnus, which was then written unto him; & eam quâ monstratur, & I wil also set downe in his due place (to wit, *an.* 444.) *that Epistle of Theodoret to Dioscorus, whereby is shewed, that Iohn was Bishop of Antioch just thirteene yeare.* Thus *Baronius*; who by these two Epistles of *Theodoret* will prove both these. As much in effect as if hee had said, I have already [y] proved, that *Iohn* began to bee Bishop of *Antioch an.* 427. and this being set downe for a certainty: I will now prove by *Theodorets* Epistle to *Domnus*, that *Iohn* dyed *an* 436. that is, in his ninth yeare; and then I will prove againe by *Theodorets* Epistle to *Dioscorus*, that hee dyed in his thirteenth yeare, and so dyed not till the yeare 440. Or, as if hee had thus said, I will first prove, that mine owne Annals are untrue, wherin it is said [z], that *Iohn* dyed in the yeare 436. which is but the ninth yeare of *Iohn*; because he dyed not, as *Theodoret* in one Epistle [a] witnesseth, untill his thirteenth yeare, which is *an* 440. And then I will prove unto you, that mine own Annals are againe untrue, wherein it is said [b], that *Iohn* was Bishop thirteene yeare, and so dyed not till *an.* 440. (beginning the first, *an.* 427) because *Theodoret*, in another Epistle [c], witnesseth, that *Iohn* dyed *an.* 436. Or thus, I will first prove, that *Iohn* was dead *an.* 436. though he was alive *an.* 440. and thē I will prove unto you, that *Iohn* was alive *an.* 440. though he was dead *an.* 436.

26. Is not this brave dealing in the Cardinall? is hee not worthy of a cap and a fether too, that can prove all these? and prove them by *Theodorets* Epistles? or doe you not think those to be worthy Epistles of *Theodoret*, by which such absurdities, such impossibilities may bee proved? Nay, doth not this alone, if there were no other evidence, demonstrate those Epistles of *Theodorets* to bee counterfeits? If that to *Domnus* be truly his, as *Baronius* assures [d] you, wherby *Iohn* is shewed to have dyed *an.* 436. then certainly the other to *Dioscorus* must needs bee a forgery, whereby *Iohn* is shewed to live *an.* 440. Againe, if that to *Dioscous* be truly his, as *Baronius* [e] assures you, wherin *Iohn* is said to live *an.* 440. then certainely the other to *Domnus* must of necessity bee a forgery, wherein *Iohn* is said to be dead *an.* 436. And as either of these two Epistles demonstrates the untruth and forgery of the other, so they both demonstrate the great vanity of *Baronius*, who applauds them both, & who wil make good what they both do affirm; that is, the same man to bee both dead and alive, a Bishop and no Bishop; at the selfe same time, and by these worthy reasons doth the Cardinall refute his owne witnesse *Nicephorus*, who by giving eighteene yeares to *Iohn*, shewes plainly that *Iohn* and *Cyrill* dyed within one yeare, which account perhaps gave occasion to the exscriber of the Synodall Acts to thrust in the name of *Iohn*, whom, upon *Nicephorus* account hee thought to live after *Cyrill*, whereas in very deed hee dyed somewhile before *Cyrill*.

27. His fourth and last reason is drawn from a Canonicall Epist. of *Cyrils* to *Domnus*, which is set done in the adjections to *Theodorus Balsamon*, whence it is out of all doubt, saith the Cardinall [f] that *Iohn dyed* before *Cyrill*, seeing *Cyrill* writ unto his successor *Domnus*. But howsoever the Cardinall vaunteth, that this reason will leave no doubt, yet, if you
observe

y *An.* 427. *nu.* 26

z *An.* 436. *nu.* 12. *Hoc anno Iohannes diem obijt extremum.* a *Theodor. Epist. ad Diosc. opud Bar. an.* 444. *nu.* 23. *Alias* 13. *tēpore Iohannis.* b *Bar. an.* 436. *nu.* 12. *Iohannes sedit annos* 13. c *Anno sequenti* (*vid. an.* 437.) *extant literæ Theodoreti ad ejus successorem Domnum. Bar. an.* 436. *nu.* 12.

d *Extant literæ Theodoreti ad Domnum Bar. an.* 436. *nu.* 12. e *Hactenus Theodoreti ad Diosc. Epistola Bar. an.* 440. *nu.* 29.

f *Bar. an.* 553. *nu.* 44.

obferve it, there are two great doubts therein: The former is, whether that Epiftle be truly *Cyrils*: And befides other reafons, that one point which the Cardinall himfelfe mentioneth, may juftly caufe any to thinke it none of his; for as the Cardinall g faith, the Author of that Epiftle afcribes fuch authority to *Domnus*, that he might *ad libitum, at his pleafure put out Bifhops, and at his pleafure reftore them.* Now there is none that knowes the learning, moderation, and wifedome of *Cyrill*, that can thinke *Cyrill* ever to have written in fuch manner either to any Metropolitane, or to any Patriarke, fpecially feeing *Cyrill* was not ignorant of that Canon of the Councell at *Antioch* h, let not a Metropolitane doe any thing in fuch caufes, without the advife and confent of the other Bifhops in the Province.

28. The other doubt is, whether that *Domnus*, to whom this Epiftle is written, bee the fame *Domnus* that was Bifhop of *Antioch*, and fucceffor to *Iohn*. The Cardinall is much troubled in removing this doubt, and hee windes himfelfe divers wayes. Sure it is, faith *Baronius* i, *that hee who had fuch authoritie muft needs bee fome eminent Bifhop, and not one of an inferior See.* True, but hee might bee a Metropolitane and fo have inferiour Bifhops under him, and yet bee no Patriarke. Againe, faith hee k, *There is no Domnus elfe but this Domnus Bifhop of Antioch, mentioned either in the Councell of Ephefus or Chalcedon, who had fuch authority, as to depofe and reftore Bifhops, ad libitum.* As if *Domnus* of *Antioch* might doe it *ad libitum*: But in fuch lawfull manner as *Domnus* of *Antioch* might doe it, there were others called by the name of *Domnus*, and thofe mentioned in thofe very Councels, who might upon juft caufe, and by due and Canonical proceeding depofe and reftore their inferiour Bifhops: looke but into thofe Councels, and you will admire both the fupine negligence of the Cardinall in this point, and his moft audacious down-facing of the truth; for, to omit others, both in the Conventicle of *Ephefus*, and the Councell of *Chalcedon*, there is often mention of *Domnus* Bifhop of *Apamea*, a Metropolitane Bifhop, as the words of *Miletius* l doe witneffe, *I Miletius Bifhop of Lariffa, fpeaking for Domnus the Metropolitane Bifhop of Apamea*, and for this *Domnus* hee fubfcribed m. And that you may fee how fraudulently the Cardinall dealt in this very point, he neither would fet downe that Epiftle, nor acquaint you with that which in *Balfamon* n is expresfly noted; that *Peter* the Bifh. whom that *Domnus* unto whom *Cyrill* writeth, had depofed, was *Alexandrinus Sacerdos, a Bifhop of the patriarchall dioceffe of Alexandria*, what had *Domnus* of *Antioch* to doe with the Alexandrian Bifhops. So cleare it is by *Balfamon*, that this *Domnus*, unto whom *Cyrill* writ, was not *Domnus* of *Antioch*, as the Card. I feare againft his knowledge, avoucheth.

29. Thus you fee all and every reafon which the Cardinall bringeth *Iohn* to bee dead feven yeares before *Cyrill*, not only to be weake and unable to enforce that Conclufion, but withall to bee full fraught with frauds and untruths: So that if I had not found more found and certaine reafons to perfwade this, I could never by the Cardinals proofes have beene induced to thinke that an errour in the Infcription of *Theodorets* Epiftle. But feeing upon the undoubted teftimonies

in

---

g *Nullus alius nomine Domnus infcriptus legitur, qui tanta polleret authoritate ut ad libitum (quod dictã eft) deponere atq; reftituere Epifcopos poffet. Bar. an. 553. nu. 44.*
h *Conc. Antioch. fub Iulio 1. can. 9.*

i *Vnde apparet, non inferioris fedis aliquem effe potuiffe ejus nominis Epifcopum. an. 553. nu. 44.*
k *Certè quidem in ferie Epifcoporum Orientalium, qui Concilio Ephefino, et Chalcedonenfi interfuerunt, nullus alius ejus nominis Domnus infcriptus reperitur. &c. Ibid.*

l *Act. 3. Conc. Chal. pa. 75. b.*

m *Act. eâdem pa. 81. et Act. 6. pa. 101. a.*
n *Sic enim in margine iftius Epiftole notat ur, videtur tempore Cyrilli, emiffa effe Romam, hujus Alexandrini Sacerdotis Appellatio.*

and a great number of Biſhops to aske pardon of the Pope for that wherein they profeſſe themſelves no way to bee guilty? *I have [e] done no injuries to your Holineſſe,* yet for the peace of the Church, *veluti ſi eas feciſſem veniam poſtulo,* *I pray you forgive mee that which I never did, as if I had done it.* Can any man thinke this the ſubmiſſion of wiſe men, of ſuch ſtout and conſtant mindes as *Mennas* and *Theodorus;* beſides the reſt, had? or what could bee deviſed more repugnant to that which *Vigilius* is made to ſay in his excommunication [f] of *Theodorus; Thou ſcandaliȝing the whole Church, and being warned, entreated, threatned by me, haſt refuſed to amend:* & *nunquàm à pravâ intentione ceſſaſti,* and never haſt thou ceaſed from thy wicked deſigne, nor to write and preach novel-ties, (ſo he cals the condemning of the *Three Chapters*) yea, after the Conſtitution for ſilence, to which thou hadſt ſworne, thou haſt openly read in the Pallace a booke against the *Three Chapters;* thou haſt beene the fire-brand and the beginner of the whole ſcandall, thou haſt deſpiſed the authority of the *Apoſtolike See.* Thus ſaith the Excommunication. Was *Vigilius* well adviſed, thinke you, to accept, as a ſatisfaction and ſubmiſſion for ſo many and ſo hainous crimes of inſolency, contempt, perjury, ſacriledge, and the like, this confeſſion at the hands of *Theodorus,* wherein he doth in effect give the Pope the lie, ſaying and avouching, I have written no bookes at all contrarie to that Decree of Silence made by your Holineſſe, and for the injuries which have beene done to your holineſſe, and to your See, *eas quidem non feci,* truely I have done none at all. Is not this a worthy ſubmiſſion? the Pope ſaith, he hath done innumerable and very hainous injuries to him, ſuch as deſerved the cenſure of excommunication: No, ſaith *Theodorus,* I have done none at all unto him: and this the Pope, like a wiſe man, takes for a good ſatisfaction [g], or an humble ſubmiſſion upon which hee is pre-ſently reconciled, and ſhakes hands with that capitall offender. Or where was the Cardinals judgment when he ſaith [h] of this confeſſion, that in it *Theodorus* did *ſuppliciter,* humbly intreat pardon of *Vigilius, de irrogatis in ipſum probris* & *contumelijs,* for the ſcoffes and contumelies which hee had uſed against the Pope. If this confeſſion was true and reall, then certainly the Excommunication of *Vigilius* is not only moſt un-juſt, but a very fooliſh fiction: If the Excommunication was true and reall, then muſt needs this ſubmiſſion bee fained and fictitious. True they cannot bee both, but that both ſhould be falſe and counterfaits, is not onely poſſible, but certaine.

    5. If nothing elſe, the time when this Confeſſion was made by *Theodorus* and *Mennas* demonſtrates this. It was made after the De-cree [i] of *Taciturnity,* and the Synod wherein that was concluded, and that was indeed never: that decree and Synod are meerely *Chymeri-call,* this Confeſſion then made after them, and mentioning that de-cree, cannot poſſibly be reall: It was made, as the Cardinall [k] aſſures us, after that *Vigilius,* fleeing the perſecution of *Iuſtinian,* had fled, firſt, to Saint *Peters* in *Conſtantinople,* then to the Church of *Enthennia* at *Chalcedon;* yea, after that the Emperour had revoked and abrogated his Edict against the *Three Chapters,* and *Vigilius,* at the earneſt intrea-ty of the Emperour, was now returned from *Chalcedon* to *Conſtantino-ple;*

[e] *De injurijs be-atitudini veſtra factis, ego quidē nullam feci,* &c. *Ibid.*

[f] *Extat inter E-piſt. Vigilij poſt Epiſtolam 16.*

[g] *Tali præmiſſâ ſatisfactione Vi-gilius eoſdem in communio-nem accepit. Bar. an. 552. nu. 20.* [h] *An. eodem nu. 19.*

[i] *Bar. an. 551.nu. 4. et 552.nu.19.*

[k] *Bar. an. 552. nu. 8 et ſeq.*

ple : and this was at Nevermaſſe : neither did *Iuſtinian* perſecute *Vigilius*, neither did *Vigilius* for feare of his perſecution flee either to S. *Peters*, or to *Chalcedon*, neither did *Iuſtinian* intreat him to returne from thence, whither hee fled not at all, nor ever did the Emperour adnull or revoke his *Edict* againſt the *three Chapters :* then certainly the confeſſion wᶜʰ by the Cardinalls own profeſſion & acknowledgement followed all theſe, muſt needs be like them, a fiction and meere forgery, never really & truly made by *Mennas, Theodorus*, and the reſt of thoſe Biſhops. Laſtly, it was made the next yeare before the fift Councell was held, that is, *anno* 552. which is the twenty ſixt of *Iuſtinian*, as the Cardinall witneſſeth [1]; before which time it cannot bee imagined to have beene made; for the excommunication of *Theodorus* was publiſhed but in that yeare in which *Vigilius* came to *Chalcedon*, as *Baronius* [m] confeſſeth. Now it is a riddle which *Oedipus* cannot diſſolve, how *Mennas*, who, as wee have certainly proved by the Acts of the ſixt Councell, dyed in the 21. yeare of *Iuſtinian*, ſhould come now in his 26. yeare, that is, foure or five yeares after his death, to offer up a ſupplication to *Vigilius*, and aske pardon of him for doing no offence againſt him. Me thinkes either the Pope ſhould be afrighted with ſuch a gaſtly ſight, or *Baronius* aſhamed to applaud ſuch ſottiſh fictions, as is that excommunication of *Mennas* made by *Vigilius :* and the *Encyclycall* Epiſtle of *Vigilius*, which mentions and approves that excommunication, and this forged confeſſion; none of which will ſuffer the ghoſt of *Mennas* to reſt, but bring a dead man out of his grave, to heare the Popes ſentence thundred out againſt him, and then come with a bill of ſupplication to beg forgiveneſſe of his Holineſſe, who had more reaſon to have prayed pardon of *Mennas* for diſquieting and waking him out of that long and ſound ſleepe.

6. So both the occaſion, the contents, and the time, beſides other circumſtances, doe evidently convince that ſubmiſſion to bee a counterfeit. But how comes it then into the Popes *Conſtitution*? You muſt enquire this of *Baronius;* or of thoſe who have acceſſe to the Vaticane whence this *Conſtitution* was taken : might one have the ſight of the Vaticane copy, I doubt not but either there are ſome evident prints of error, in inſerting this confeſſion into it; or which I exceedingly miſtruſt, *Baronius* hath uſed a little of the Vaticane art in this matter. Howſoever, certaine it is that this confeſſion hath neither fit coherence, nor any dependence at all of ought in the Conſtitution, but it is both complete and much more orderly, this being wholly expunged, than if ſo idle a fiction be annexed unto it. But let the Cardinall and his friends looke to this matter by what meanes or whoſe fraud this was inſerted, I thought needfull to admoniſh thē of the fault, nor for the love and affection I beare to that Conſtitution of *Vigilius*, could I with ſilence ſee and ſuffer it to be blemiſhed therewith.

7. The ſecond is *Euſtathius*, of whom I would have ſpoken more in this place, but that his fained and fabulous narrations are ſo clearly diſcovered before, that I thinke it needleſſe to adde ought concerning him, or them.

8. The third writing is a book in very great requeſt with *Baronius*, and

1 Anno illo 552. nu. 19.

m Hæc de ſententiā in Theodorum ac Mennam lata Vigilius, quæ ipſe ſcripſit anno ſequenti in Baſilica S. Euphemiæ Chalcedone. Bar. an. 551. nu. 18.

and that is, those Epistles which beare the name of *Theodoret*, of which though much hath beene sayd before, yet will I here adde somewhat to manifest them further to bee counterfeit and most false. Among them, two are most eminent; that to *Dioscorus*, and the other to Pope *Leo*. That the former is forged, the other doth demonstrate. For by that to *Dioscorus* which was writ *anno* 444; *Theodoret* is made to say, that he had then beene Bishop 26. yeares [n], whereas by the later written *anno* 449. it is cleare that in that yeare he had beene Bishop, no more [o] than 26. yeares. So *vice versa*, that the later is forged is demonstrated by the former; for by that to *Leo* written *an.* 449. *Theodoret* is made to say that he had then beene Bishop just 26. whereas by the other to *Dioscorus* written *anno* 444. it is witnessed that hee had beene Bishop 26. [p] yeares, five yeares before he writ to *Leo*. And they are both demonstrated to be meere fictitious, in that *Theodoret* is made in them both to testifie that for that whole time of 26. yeares he had beene orthodoxall in faith, and for proofe thereof he appeales [q] to his owne writings, written 12. 15. and 20. yeares before that; whereas it is as cleare as the Sunne that hee was a most earnest defender and writer in defence of *Nestorius* and his heresies, and for this cause was justly condemned by the holy Councell of *Ephesus*, yea and his writings yet extant [r] doe undenyably convince the same. Besides in that to *Dioscorus*, hee professeth [s] his ardent affection and love to *Cyrill*, whereas after *Cyrils* death, in an open assembly at *Antioch* he most bitterly [t], unjustly, and spitefully declamed against him. Further, in that to *Dioscorus*, it is said that he was orthodoxall [u] *anno* 444. when that Epistle was written; whereas in his Epistle written *anno* 448. [x] or after, unto *Irene* a Nestorian Bishop of *Tyre*, justly deposed [y] by the Emperour, he bemones both the publike cause and the case of *Irene*, comparing his to the cause [z] of *Susanna*, and lamenting that either [a] they must offend God, and hurt their owne conscience, (if they forsake Nestorianisme,) or else fall into unjust decrees and punishments of men, (if they continued in that doctrine;) and who further calls this deposed and hereticall Bishop, *Dilectissimum* [b], *& piissimum Irenæum, The most beloved, and most holy Irene.* The like forgery might be shewed in his Epistle to *Nomus*, written also *anno* 448. [c] wherein hee exclameth against the Emperor *Theodosius*, as if he had given toleration [d] & free liberty of Religion to Arians, Eunomians, Manichees, Marcionites, Valentinians, & Montanists, & yet restrained yea excluded him *ab omni civitate, from every City in his Empire*; which to bee a most vile and unjust slander, the piety and zeale of *Theodosius*, highly renowned both by *Sozomen* [e], and Pope *Leo* [f] doth demonstrate; and whose [g] Edicts against heretikes do also manifest the same, seeing therein out of his hatred to heresie, and specially to Nestorianisme, he forbids any [h] such to

Marginal notes:

n *Apud Bar. an. 444. nu. 23.*
o *Cum 26. annis Ecclesiam rexerim. Theod. apud Bar. an. 449. nu. 119.*
p *Apud Bar. an. 444. nu. 23.*
q *In Epist. ad Leonem. apud Bar. an. 449. nu. 120. A me enim scripta sunt alia quidem ante annos viginti, &c.*
r *Extant tom. 5. act. Conc. Ephes. pa. 859. et seqq. sub hoc titulo. Reprehensio 12. Capitulorum Cyrilli, à Theodoreto Episcopo Cyri.*
s *Hominem summus admirati, et scripsimus ad Cyrillum beatæ memoriæ, &c. Theod. apud Bar. an. 444. nu. 28.*
t *Theodoreti alloquutio, apud Conc. 5. Coll. 5. p. 559. b.*
u *Ego multas habeo myriadas hominum quæ doctrinæ veritatem et rectitudinem mihi testantur. Theod. apud Bar. an. 444. nu. 22.*
x *Literæ quæ à Theodoreto ad Irenæum tunc (id est, ut i? se explicat, hoc anno 448.) redditæ sunt. Bar. an. 440. nu. 7 8.*
y *Statuimus ut Irenæus à sancta Tyriorum Ecclesiâ statim expellatur. Edict.*

Theodos. quod extat to. 5. Conc. Ephes. c. 19.   z *Beatissimæ Susannæ sum recordatus, &c. Theod. epist. ad Iren. apud. Bar. an. 448. nu. 9.* a *Et nunc Domine duo nobis proponuntur, vel Deum offendere et conscientiam ladere, vel incidere in injusta hominum decreta, &c. Theod. ibid.* b *Epistola eâdem.* c *Illa Theodoreti Epistola scripta ad Nomum hoc ipso anno. Bar. an. 448 nu. 11.* d *Alijs quidem omnibus aperta est civitas, non solum Arij et Eunomij sectatoribus, sed et Manicheis, et Marcionistis, &c. Theod. epist. ad Nomum apud Bar. an. 448. nu. 12.* e *Nullum non virtutis genus sedulo excoluisti, &c. sic Theodosium juniorem alloquitur Sozom. in præfat. ad suam histor.* f *Piissimam solicitudinem Christianæ religionis habetis, ne in populo Dei aut schismata, aut hereses, aut ulla scandala convalescant. Leo. epist. 7. quæ est ad Theodosium.* g *Leg. 66. de hær. cod. Theod. et id quod extat in Conc. Chal. act. 3. pa. 84.* h *Definivimus eos cæterìs debere ultionibus subjacere, &c. Edict. Theod. in Conc. Chal. loc. cit.*

enjoy their Sees, or to scape unpunished; and being misinformed that *Flavianus* and *Eusebius* of *Dorileum* were Nestorians, hee upon that misinformation, unjustly and rashly subjected [i] them to that censure: but being truly enformed of *Domnus* and *Theodoret*, that they embraced Nestorianisme, he justly confirmed their deposition, forbidding any either to reade or have the bookes or *Theodoret* [k], or of *Nestorius*, *Theodorets* being every whit as bad as the bookes of *Nestorius*. It were easie to shew the like prints of forgery in all those Epistles going under the name of *Theodoret*, which the Cardinall so much magnifieth: but I am loth to stay too long in them, the falshood of which hath beene so often before demonstrated.

9. A fourth is that Action concerning *Domnus*, inserted by *Baronius* and *Binius* into the Acts of the Councell [q] at Chalcedon. This to be undoubtedly a forgery and fiction, was before proved, because *Domnus* was dead before the Councell at *Chalcedon*; for so both the Emperour *Iustinian* [r] in his *Edict*, and the fift Councell [s] expresly witnesse, saying, the holy Councell at *Chalcedon* condemned *Domnus post mortem, after he was dead*; for that he durst write that the twelve chapters of *Cyrill* should not be spoken of. Now that whole Action containing nothing else but a consultation and decree for the maintenance of *Domnus*, by some annuall allowance out of the revenewes of the See of Antioch, none I thinke will once imagine that so grave, so wise and worthy an assembly of 603. Bishops, would either consult or make a decree for the allowance of a stipend or maintenance to be given to a dead man: specially not to *Domnus*, whose deposition in the Ephesine latrociny the whole Councell of *Chalcedon* approved: and it is very unlikely they would judge him worthy to have maintenance out of that Bishopricke, of which by reason of his heresie they judged him most justly to bee deprived. But if there were no other reasons to manifest this, the place whence it comes might justly cause one to distrust the same: for is it thinke you in the Greeke and originall copies of that Councell? No certainly, it is not: as both the Cardinall [t] and *Binius* will assure you; *Desideratur in Græco, it is wanting in the Greeke or originall*: nor onely is it now wanting there, but *certum est eadem caruisse Græca exemplaria tempore Iustiniani*; It is certaine the Greeke copies had not this Action in the time of Iustinian the Emperour. Is it mentioned in *Liberatus*? or in *Evagrius*? or in *Nicephorus*? all which set downe the summe of the Actions in that Councell? No, it is not in any of them. Whence then comes this worthy action that so carefully provides victuals for a dead man? Truly out of their old Minthouse the Vaticane: *Hæc Actio scripta in Latino veteri codice Vaticano*: There is in the *Vaticane* an old manuscript Latine copie, which is sayd to have beene the copy of *Albinus* and *Proculus*, and in that old written booke, this Action is found, saith *Baronius* [u]. A very *Gibeonite* you may be sure. It came with old moulded bread, (such as was fittest to feed a dead man) with old mouldy shooes and torne clothes, and so deceived the Cardinall: No, it deceived him not, but by it hee would deceive others, and not onely most shamefully deprave and corrupt the Acts of the holy Councell of *Chalcedon*, as hee and *Binius* have

[i] *Excludi ab Episcopatu (volebamus) Flavianum & Eusebium, Domnum quoque & Theodoretum. ibid.*

[k] *Sed nec habeat quis, vel legat, proferatve, Nestory codices; neque Theodoreti scripta. ibid.*

[q] *Conc. Chalc. Act. 7.*

[r] *Iust. Edict. to. 2. Conc. pa. 498. [s] col. 6 5.575. b.*

[t] *Hæc actio desideratur in Græco codice. Bar. an.451.nu.129. & Bin. not. in Conc. Chal. p.185*

[u] *an.451.n.136*

done

done herein, but make a way, and shew an occasion to carpe at the Synodall Acts of the fift Councell: and had not the Cardinall beene conscious of this fault in this Action, you may be well assured that he would not have omitted so foule an errour in the fift Synod, and the Acts thereof, as to avouch *Domnus* to have beene dead before the Councell of *Chalcedon*, when hee scraped and raked together all that he could finde (and they are all but motes to this beame) whereby he might disgrace those Acts.

x *an. 451. n. 130*

10. But the Cardinall will not for all this yeeld in this matter, nay he will defend this Action also: For objecting [x] *to himselfe how any such Action could be held concerning Domnus, seeing Iustinian testifieth hee was dead before the Councell of Chalcedon, hee answereth, Iustinian was ignorant of this Action, and he had some other Action of the Councell of Chalcedon touching Domnus, Quam nusquam legimus, Which we no where finde.* So *Baronius:* Who hereby would have it thought, that *Iustinian* and the fift Councell had not the true Copies of the Councell at *Chalcedon*, but that these which the Cardinall frameth, they are the onely perfect and entire Acts thereof. Certainly *Iustinian* was ignorant of this Action, and so was the fift Councell. And no marvell, when the Councell of *Chalcedon* it selfe was ignorant thereof. And whether the Emperour and the whole fift generall Councell, wherein were present foure Patriarkes, and the Bishop of *Chalcedon* also, whether these living about an hundred yeares after that Councell, bee not like to have had more true Copies of the Councell at *Chalcedon*, than *Baronius*, living eleven hundred yeares after it, it is not hard to judge.

y *Ex quibus apparet Iustinianum alicujus alterius actionis, quam nusquam legimus, cognitionem habuisse. Bar. loc. cit.*

11. Now for that which the Cardinall would perswade, that whereas *Iustinian* and the fift Synod sayd, that the Councell of *Chalcedon* condemned *Domnus* after he was dead, they sayd this, as he supposeth, out of some other Action [y] of *Chalcedon*, which is not now extant, and thereby would blemish the Acts of the Councell of *Chalcedon* as being defective, and wanting that Action: Truly his Cardinalship is foully mistaken herein. Neither *Iustinian*, nor the fift Councell, had any such Action, as he vainly and idlely dreameth of. It was these very Acts which now wee have, out of which they affirme that. For they say not that the Councell did that in any action particularly concerning *Domnus*, nor yet that in expresse termes they condemned *Domnus*: But they say, the Councell condemned him, and so they did, in that they approved both his condemnation and deposition decreed in the Ephesine Latrociny. That this they did the acts now extant doe declare; whereas [a] the most holy Bishops of *Rome* accounted all that was done in the second Ephesine Synod to be void, it is manifest that the judgement concerning the Bishop of *Antioch* is excepted; so sayd the Popes *Legates*, and *Stephen* [b], *I also judge those things to be voyd which were done at Ephesus, absque his quæ gesta sunt adversus Domnum, excepting those things which were done against Domnus:* and to the like effect sayd they all. *Domnus* then being dead, at the time of the Councell at *Chalcedon*, and having beene in the Ephesine Latrociny, both condemned and deposed, seeing the Councell of *Chalcedon* approved both his condemnation and deposition, and the

a *Act. 10. pa. 115.*

b *Ibid.*

sub-

substitution of *Maximus*, (which were all done in that Ephesine Latrociny,) as just and lawfull: hence it is that the fift Councell sayth, and that out of these very Acts and no other, as themselves explaine, that c the Fathers at *Chalcedon* condemned *Domnus* being dead, whose condemnation they approved, when at that time of their approving it hee was dead. So neither are the Acts of the fourth Councell imperfect, nor these of the fift untrue, in affirming this of *Domnus*; but that Vaticane and Gibeonitish Action, inserted into the Acts of *Chalcedon*, and approved by *Baronius* and *Binius*, is both false, ridiculous, and impossible.

12. The last whom I will now mention, is *Anastasius*, the writer of the lives of their Popes. An author whom *Baronius* much followeth, and relyeth upon, almost in all parts of his Annals: whom I doe not mention in this place, as doubting whether those lives are truly his, but as doubting, nay rather without doubt assuring both my selfe and others, that such credit is not to bee given to him and to his reports, as the Cardinall and *Binius* doe give. This I doubt not to demonstrate, if ever I come to handle the second Nicene Synod, and that which they call the eighth, wherein *Anastasius* was a stickler, yea and the penner of the one, and corrector of the other: For this present, I will onely examine the life of *Vigilius* written by him; wherein I doe constantly affirme, that there are not so many lines as lyes set downe by *Anastasius*. Which that it may appeare that I doe not speake in any spleene against *Anastasius*, but out of the evidence of truth, give me leave to take a view of some particulars therein, those especially which most concerne this our present cause.

13. First, *Anastasius* d describing the entrance of *Vigilius* to have beene *eodem tempore*, at that time when *Bellisarius* made warre against *Vitiges* the King of the *Gothes*, sayth that *Vitiges fled away by night, but Iohn surnamed the bloody, pursued after him, and brought him to Bellisarius and Vigilius at Rome, and there Bellisarius tooke the Sacrament to bring him safe to Iustinian*. All untrue. First, it is untrue that *Vitiges* fled away by night; or secondly, that hee fled at all; or thirdly, that *Iohn* did pursue him in flight; or fourthly, that *Iohn* tooke him; or fiftly, that *Iohn* brought him to *Bellisarius*; or sixtly, that hee brought him to *Vigilius*; or seventhly, that he brought him to Rome; or eightly, that *Bellisarius* tooke any such oath; or ninthly, any Sacrament; or tenthly, tooke it in the Church of *Iulius*; or eleventhly, tooke it to assure them that hee would bring *Vitiges* to *Iustinian*: all these are the fictions of *Anastasius*: For as *Procopius* who was Counsellor e to *Bellisarius*, and present with him in all his warres, testifieth, *Vitiges* and the Gothes willingly yeelded f themselves and Ravenna unto *Bellisarius*; yea *Vitiges* perswaded and even entreated him to accept the kingdome: and *Bellisarius* tooke *Vitiges* g himselfe, and kept him in custody: yea he sent away *Iohn* h and *Narses* before either he entred in *Ravenna*, or tooke *Vitiges*, and being taken, he cari-

c *Chalcedonensis Synodus Domnum condemnavit, cum confirmasset condemnationem ejus, & suscepisset Maximi ordinationem. Conc.5.Coll.6. pa.575.*

d *Anast.in vita Vigil. Nam Anastasius continuavit historiam Damasi, ab obitu Damasi usque ad Adrianum secundum. Possev.in App.* e *Bellisario Consiliarus adfuit Procopius, & rebus omnibus dum agerentur interfuit.Procop. lib.1. de bello Persico.* f *Gothorum Optimates Bellisarium Hesperiæ Regem appellare constituunt, ad eumque mittunt qui obsecrarent ut imperium susciperet. Vitiges*

quoque formidine percitus Bellisarium et ipse ad suscipiendum imperium hortatur. Proc. lib. 2. Bell. Goth. pa. 340. qui paulo post quomodo se turpiter dediderunt Vitiges et Gothi declarat: idem docet Leon. Aret. lib. 1 .de bello Ital. pa. 669. g *Bellisarius Ravenna potitus Vitigem imprimis honorifice custoditum servabat.ibid. pa 341.* h *Bellisarius Iohannem & Narsetem diversim abire cum suis copijs jussit. His abeuntibus Ravennam contendit, ib. p. 340.idem et Leon. Aret. loco citato.*

i *Bellis. iter aggreditur, Byzantiumq; rectà contendit.ibid. pa. 343. et cum Vitige Gothorumq; optimatibus Bizantium venit. Idem lib.3. pa. 343. Bellisarius cum Vitige Bizintium navigavit.Leo. Aret. loc. cit.*

k *Bellisario ad se celerius vocato. Proc.lib.2. pa. 341. et Leonar. Aret.pa. 670. Iustinianus Bellisarium ex Italia confess:m revocavit.*

l *Nam Silveriū à Bellisario e. jectum narrat. Proc.lib. 1. pa. 287. eiq; tum suffectus Vigilius.ibid. Id sactum an.3.belli Goth. vel ante, liquet ex lib.2. pa.313.ubi sic ait, Iam tertius bello huic annus exibat.*

m *Nam Silverius obijt an.14. Iustiniani,Bar. an.540.n.2. at Vitigem capit et Constantinopol. adduxit Bellisarius an. 15. Iustiniani,Bar. an. 541.nu.3.*

n *Liber.in Brev. cc.22.*

o *Hoc anno(14. Iustiniani) similac de legitima Vigilii electione nuncium Constantinopol. perlatum est,Imperator protinus Epistolam ad eū dat. Bar. an. 540.nu.11.*

q *Epist.Vigilii extat apud. Bar. an.540.nu. 20. & sequ.*

r *Nam litere ad Mennam date*

ed him not to *Rome*, but the straight way by Sea to i *Constantinople*, whither himselfe was then k called by the Emperour, and commanded to come without any delay. So in the very entrance of his narration, *Anastasius* hath in few words couched together at the least ten or eleven evident untruths.

14. Next, *Anastasius relates, how the Emperour and his wife demanded of Bellisarius when he came to Constantinople, how he had placed Vigilius in stead of Silverius, and thanked him for it.* Truly *Anastasius* had small wit to thinke that the Emperour had leasure to confer with *Bellisarius* concerning a matter done about three l yeares before : and specially which with the death of *Silverius* m was now dead and buried. Yet say he did. Againe, what an idle discourse was this about the placing of *Vigilius* in the roome of *Silverius*, seeing the Emperour knew the whole matter long before, how *Silverius* was banished, upon an accusation of a Letter written to the Gothish King, to come and take possession of Rome, and himselfe had taken order that the cause of *Silverius* should be againe examined, and if that letter was truly writ by *Silverius*, that he should be banished ; if it were found a calumny, that he should bee restored, as *Liberatus* n sheweth. Hee knew o also that *Silverius* was dead, and that *Vigilius* was peaceably and with his consent placed in the Romane See before *Bellisarius* came, for hee had written p unto him as the onely lawfull Pope, and both the Emperour and *Mennas* had received Letters q from him the yeare r before. But *Anastasius* thought the Emperours discourses to bee as idle as his owne. Besides, whereas he addes that the Emperour thanked him for placing of *Vigilius* in the roome of *Silverius*; *Binius* is bould therein to tell *Anastasius* of his untruth, seeing all that, as he saith b, was done without the knowledge of *Iustinian*, by the plotting of *Theodora*. I will account these for no more than two untruths.

15. After this, *Anastasius tels us that Iustinian then sent Bellisarius againe into Africke, who comming thither killed by trechery Gontharis King of the Vandalls, and then comming to Rome offered some of the spoiles of the Vandalls to Saint Peter by the hands of Pope Vigilius, to wit, a Crosse of gold beset with precious stones, being a hundred pound in waight, wherin were writ his victories, two great silver tables guilded, which unto this day stand, saith hee, before the body of Saint Peter: also hee gave many other gifts, and many almes to the poore, and built an hospitall in the broad way, and a Monastery of Saint Iuvenalis at the City of Orta, where hee gave possessions, and many gifts.* Thus *Anastasius*; whose narration as it must needs testifie in what great honour the Romane Church was in those ancient times, and how bountifull they were then unto it, so may it serve for an incentive to inflame the zeale of Emperours, and great persons to doe the like after their victories and conquests; and no doubt but by such lyes and fables as this is their Church had gained the best part of her treasures and possessions; for all this not one syllable is true or probable. *Bellisarius* when hee came to *Constantinople*

sunt 15.Kalend.Oct. Iustino Consule,id est,an.14. Iustiniani.Bar. an.450.nu. 25. Bellisarius autem Constantinopol. redit Consul.Basilio,id est,an.15.Iustin. Bar.an.541.n.3. ¶Patet quod ipse Imperator Bellisario hac de causa gratias non egit.Bin.Not. in vitam Vigil.§. Gratias.

with

with *Vitiges* was not then sent into the Welt, but into *Persia* [t] against *Cosroes*, as *Procopius*, who was present with him, testifieth, and in those warres hee continued full three [u] yeares: When hee was sent Westward hee was not sent into *Africk*, for thither *Ariobindus* [x] was sent, with whom was sent *Artabanus* : Neither did *Bellisarius* either by villany or victory kill *Gontharis*, but *Artabanus* killed [y] him treacherously when they sat together at a feast in *Gontharis* Chamber: nor came *Bellisarius* from *Africk* to *Rome*, (for after his second comming (which was from *Constantinople*) into *Italy*, he stayed there till his returne to *Bizantium* five [z] yeares after, and returned backe no more [a])nor brought hee thence with him any of the spoyles of the Vandales; nor offered hee them to Saint *Peter*; nor offered he, by the hand of *Vigilius* either that golden Crosse of an hundred pound waight (which is a golden lye, consisting of an hundred latchets)nor the silver table, nor those many other gifts, nor built he an Hospitall; nor gave hee either possessions or donations. All these, if they be well summed, will make at least twelve grand capitall mother lyes, which have many moe in their wombs; such an art of devising untruths hath *Anastasius*. Or if this oblation bee referred, as *Binius* [b] saith perhaps it ought, to the time when *Bellisarius* wanne *Rome* from *Vitiges*, which was, as *Procopius* [c] sheweth in the third yeare of the warres against the *Gothes*, and 12.of *Iustinian*, yet this can excuse no one of all the untruths of *Anastasius*; for neither then was *Vigilius* but *Sylverius* [d] the Pope, neither did *Bellisarius* then come out of *Africk*, or bring the spoyles of the Vandals with him, of which this oblation was made by the hands of Pope *Vigilius*:

16. Next to this, *Anastasius* saith, *eodem tempore Theodora scripsit, at that same time Theodora the Empresse writ to Vigilius to come to Constantinople, and restore Anthimus to his See; but Vigilius refused, saying, I spake foolishly before when I promised that, but now I can no way consent to restore an heretike:* Whence *Baronius* [e] observes a rare miracle, that *Vigilius* was now turned to a new man, & now *Saul* was one of the Prophets, of a blasphemer chaged to a true Preacher, of a *Saul* into a *Paul*; all weh change proceeded from his very sitting in the Popes Chaire, *momento temporis novam formam accepit, at that very moment* when he became the true Pope, *hee had a new forme, a new speech*, and then prophesied consonantly to the fathers: and the like miracle doth *Binius* [f] note, *statim ut sanctam sedem ascendit, as soone as ever Vigilius had stept into the holy Chaire*, hee was wholly changed into a new man, and then condemned the heresies, which before hee approved. A right *Neanthes* indeed, of whom it is written, that before being ἄνος ωεῖς λέγει, having

t *Bellisarius Vitigem captivum eo tempore Bizantium duxit quando Iustinianus Cosroem adivit bellum movisse. Proc. lib. 2. Bell. Pers. pa. 156. Imperator res Orientis in duos divexit duces, circa flavium Euphratem omnia Bellisario tradidit regenda. Ibid. pa. 158.*

u *Totilus cum exercitus parte ad loca Romae vicina tetendit, eius profectione cognit, Imperator, eius adhuc fortissime e sito tutissime Pc sit, mittere rursum in Italiam Bellisarium cogitur. Itaq, novus huius belli annus exibat. Proc. lib. 3. de bell. Goth. pa. 356. redierat autem ex Italia constantinopolim anno 6. belli Gothici, ut liquet ex Proc. lib. 2. in fine, et lib. 3. in initio.*

x *Imperator Ariobindum ducem in Africam misit, & Artabanum, sed inutile futans duorum ducum Imperio res administrari, Ariobindi totius Africae curam delegavit. Proc. de bell. Vand. lib. 2. pa. 239.*

y *Convivium Artabanus Gontharidi latus dextrum capulo tenus confodit, ex quo ille statim moribundus cecidit.*

erat in conclavi, ubi tres mensae paratae, ipse in prima accubuit, cui Athanasium & Artobanum adhibuit. Gontharidem adcessit, quasi clam ei aliquid dicturus, Gontharidi saucio exilire conanti Artabanus ensem educens, quum per quinquennium ex Italia nusquam abcessisset. Pro. lib. 3. de bell. Goth. pa. 302. sicque 14 annus huius belli exibat. Ibid. pa. 394.   a Bizantium cum pervenisset, ibi diutius commoratus, ex otio vivere, et in delitiis affluentibus ovibus agere, rebus ante hac foeliciter gestis, contentus. Proc. ibid pa. 393.   b Bin. not. in vitam Vigily. § De spolijs.   c Vrbs Roma recuperata à Gothis per Bellisarium post annum sexagesimum quo eam tenuerunt Gothi, et post Iustiniani annum undecimum. Proc. lib. 1. de bell. Goth. pa. 171. et post hec ait, Iamque tertius huic bello annus exibat. Lib. 2. pa. 313.   d Duodecimus annus Iustiniani respondet anno 2. Sylverij. Bar. an. 538. nu. 1. Sylverius autem sedit annos 3. Bar. an. 540. nu. 1, & An. 540. nu. 13.   f Bin. not. in vit. Vig. pa. 478.

now got the harpe of *Orpheus*,hee thought he was alſo able to worke wonders therwith, as well as *Orpheus* had done; he would needs then, *Saxa movere ſono teſtudinis*, but all in vaine: Even ſo *Peters* Chaire made *Vigilius* as infallible as *Peter* himſelfe, being once ſet there hee could doe nothing elſe but drop Oracles, and his fidling on *Orpheus* harpe made an heavenly harmony, but how hee failed in his skill, and proved no better than *Neanthes*, his Conſtitution touching the *Three Chapters* is an eternall record,and yet all that time hee ſat in the Chaire and propheſied,for as the common ſaying is, *Vbi Papa, ibi Roma*; ſo it is as true,*Vbi Papa, ibi Cathedra*,it is more eaſie for the Pope to take the Chaire with him, than, like an Elephant, to carry the whole City of *Rome* upon his backe to *Conſtantinople*,and goe up and downe the world with it.

17. But is this narration, thinke you, of *Anaſtaſius* true? verily not one word therein; neither did the Empreſſe write, nor *Vigilius* anſwer any ſuch thing,for both theſe were done, as *Anaſtaſius* ſaith, *eodem tempore, at,or after that ſame time*,when *Belliſarius*, having killed *Gontharis*, came out of *Africk*,and offered thoſe ſpoiles of the Vandales,and ſeeing,that, as wee have proved, was never; this writing of *Theodora* and anſwer of *Vigilius* was at the ſame tide of Nevermas. Againe, this anſwer of *Vigilius* was given, *ſtatim ac ſanctam ſedem aſcendit,at his very firſt placing in the Sèe*,as *Binius* ſheweth,and that was in the fourteenth g yeare of *Iuſtinian*; for then *Sylverius* dyed: now ſeeing *Theodora* writ not this till *Gontharis* was overcome, and that was,as *Procopius* h ſheweth,in the nineteenth yeare of *Iuſtinian*; it was a fine deviſe of *Anaſtaſius*,to tell how this new Saint anſwered a letter (by way of propheſie)three or foure yeares before the letter was written. Further,*Vigilius*, as *Liberatus* ſaith i,*implens promiſſum ſuum,quod Auguſtæ fecerat*,*performing his promiſe to the Empreſs*,writ a letter in this manner, hee performed it as much as hee could, he laboured a while to doe it, and this was both before and a little after the death of *Sylverius*; but when hee could not effect it, and after that the Emperor had writ unto him to confirme the depoſition of *Anthimus* : *Vigilius* ſeeing his labour to be loſt therein, left off that care untill hee could have a better oportunity to overthrow the Councell of *Chalcedon*, which, ſo long as it ſtood in force,was a barre unto *Anthimus*.If *Vigilius* could have prevailed to have had the fift Councel and the Church approve his *Conſtitution* publiſhed in defence of the *Three Chapters*, by which the Councell of *Chalcedon* had beene quite overthrowne, then in likelihood he would have ſet up *Anthimus*,& all who with *Anthimus* had oppugned the Councell of *Chalcedon*, but till that were done,till the Councell were repealed,*Vigilius* ſaw it was in vaine to ſtrive for *Anthimus*;and therefore waiting for another oportunity for that,hee in two ſeverall Epiſtles, the one to *Iuſtinian*, the other to *Mennas*,confirmed,as the Emperour required him to doe, the depoſition of *Anthimus*;and this hee did the yeare before *Belliſarius* returned to *Conſtantinople* with *Vitiges*, namely in the fourteenth yeare of k *Iuſtinian*,and five yeares before the death of *Gontharis*. Would the Empreſſe then write to him to come and doe that which he knew

not

g Bar.an.54-nu.2.

h Hoc modo(cade nummum Göthridis et aliorum) Artabanes Carthaginem Iuſtiniano reſtituit anno ipſius decimo nono. Procl-lib.2.de Bell.Vandal. pa.244.

i Liberat.ca.22.

k Vt ante probatum eſt hoc cap.

not onely the Emperour moſt conſtantly withſtood, but *Vigilius* alſo, to have five yeares before publikely teſtified to the Emperour, that hee would not doe? ſpecially ſeeing, as *Baronius* [1] ſaith, *Vigilius* by that his letter to the Emperour, *Omnem prorſus, ſive Theodoræ, ſive alijs ſpem ademiſſet, would put both Theodora, and all elſe out of all hope*, that he ſhould ever performe his promiſe in reſtoring *Anthimus.* So although thoſe words, *eodem tempore*, were not (as they ought to be) referred to the time after the killing of *Gontharis*, but to the time when *Belliſarius* came with *Vitiges* to *Conſtantinople*, which was the yeare [m] after *Vigilius* his letter ſent to the Emperour; yet the *Anaſtaſian* narration isnot onely untrue, but wholly improbable, that *Theodora* ſhould then ſend to him to come and reſtore *Anthimus*, who had the yeare before confirmed the depoſing of *Anthimus*, and profeſſed both to the Emperour and *Mennas*, that hee would not reſtore him, and that he ought not to bee reſtored. Laſtly, at this time when *Anaſtaſius* faineth *Theodora* to write to *Vigilius* to come and reſtore *Anthimus*, (which following the death of *Gontharis*, muſt needs bee in the nineteenth or twentieth yeare of *Iuſtinian*) the cauſe of *Anthimus* was quite forgotten and laid aſide, and the *Three Chapters* were then in every mans mouth, and every where debated: The Emperor having in that nineteenth yeare, as by *Victor* [n], who then lived, is evident, if not before, publiſhed his Edict, and called *Vigilius* about that matter to *Conſtantinople*. *Anaſtaſius* dreamed of ſomewhat, and hearing of ſome writing, or ſending to *Vigilius* about that time, he not knowing, or, which I rather thinke, willing to corrupt and falſifie the true narration, for his great love to the Pope, conceales the true and onely cauſe about which the meſſage was ſent to *Vigilius*, and deviſeth a falſe and fained matter about *Anthimus*, and indeavors to draw al men by the noiſe of that from harkning after the cauſe of the *Three Chapters*, which he ſaw would prove no ſmall blemiſh to the Romane See. Iuſt as *Alcibiades* [o] to avoyd a greater infamy, cut off the taile of his beautifull dog, which coſt him 70. *minas Atticas*, (that is of our coyne [p] 218. pound and 15. ſhillings) and filled the mouthes of the people with that trifle, that there might bee no noiſe of his other diſgrace. The true cauſe of ſending to *Vigilius*, as *Victor* ſheweth [q], was about the *Three Chapters*, this of *Anthimus*, which *Anaſtaſius* harpes upon, is in truth no other but the dogs taile, and the din of it hath a long time poſſeſſed the eares of men; but now the true cauſe being come to the open view, fils the world with that ſhamefull hereſie of *Vigilius*, which *Anaſtaſius* would have concealed and covered with his dogs taile. But enough of this paſſage, wherein there are not ſo few as twenty lyes.

18. The next paſſage in *Anaſtaſius* containes the ſending for *Vigilius*, and the manner how hee was taken from *Rome* and brought to *Conſtantinople*: He tels us that the people of *Rome* taking that oportunity of the diſpleaſure of *Theodora* againſt him for his former conſenting to reſtore *Anthimus*, ſuggeſted divers accuſations againſt him, as that by his Counſell *Sylverius* was depoſed, and that hee was a murderer, and had killed his Nephew *Aſterius*, whereupon the Empreſſe ſent *Anthimus Scribo to take him*

Marginal notes:

[1] Bar. an. 540. nu. 22.

[m] Nam literæ Vigilij miſſæ Iuſtiniano ſunt an. 14. Iuſtiniani. Bar. an. 540. nu. 14. Belliſarius autem rediit Conſtantinopolim cum Vitige an. Iuſtiniani 15. Bar. an. 541. nu. 3.

[n] Iuſtinianus Vigilium compelit ut ad urbê regiam properaret. an. 4. poſt Conſulatum Baſily. Vict. in Chr. in eum an. is autem eſt an. 19. Iuſtiniani ſecundum Bar. an. 545. nu. 1.

[o] Plut. in Alcib.

[p] Nam mina Attica valet noſtri nummi 3. l. 2. ſ. 6. d. ut teſtatur Edovardus Breirwooddus in lib. ſuo de Pond. ca. 4. quem librû accurate admodum hac tractare, non eſt cur doſti dubitent.

[q] Imperator Vigilium ad regiam urbem compellit venire, ut tria Capitula condenaret. Vict. in Chron. an. 4. poſt Coſſ. Baſilij.

r Trium Capitu-
lorum causâ
tantum vocatus
est.Bin.not.in
vita Vigily.
§ Tuas Romani.
Non alia causâ
profectionis Vigi-
lij Constantino-
polim cognosci-
tur.Bar.an.546.
nu.55.
ſ Bar.an.eodem
546.nu.54.
t Putavit Vigili-
um, quibus pos-
set fieri,blandi-
tijs concilian-
dum.Bin.loc.cit.
Eum sibi quibus
valuit,studuit
conciliare blan-
ditys.Bar.an.
546.nu.55.
u Ba.an eo.n.54
x Bar.an eod.
546.nu.60.
y Interea Vigili-
us ab Impera-
re ex Siciliâ e-
vocatus,Bizanti-
um venit.Nam
ut cò contende-
rent,diutinam
in eâ insult
traxerunt morâ.
Proc.lib.3.de
bell.Goth.p.364
Evocatus autem
fuit circa fiaem
an.11.bell.Goth.
ut ſquet,expre-
ced'étibus verbis;
unde:imus hujus
bellise verterat
annus.Interea
Vigilius,&c.
Iam 11.illius
belli est Iustinia-
ni 20.nam bellu
capit anno ejus
nono prope fini-
to,ut testatur.
Proc.lib.1. Bell.
Goth.pa.252.
Imperatur se ad
bellum parat,
annus novenos
patitus Imperio.
z Victor loc. cit.
etiam et Marcel-
linus anno priori
evocatum ab
Imperatore,sed
sequenti Constan.
venisse expressè
docet.In Chron.
an.546.et
547.

him wheresoever hee were,except onely in the Church of Saint Peter. Scribo came and tooke him in the end of November,and after many indignities both in words and actions, as that the people cast stones,and clubs, and dung after him,wishing all evill to goe with him; hee in this violent manner was brought to Sicilie, in December, and on Christmas eve to Constantinople,whom the Emperour then meeting, they kissed and wept one over the other for joy,and then they led him to the Church of Saint Sophie,the people singing an hymne, behold the Lord commeth. Thus *Anastasius*. Which whole narration to bee a very lying and dunghill legend, were easie to demonstrate, if *Baronius* and *Binius* had not much eased us in this part, for they not onely condemne this as untrue, but prove it by divers arguments to be such. The first, for that *Vigilius* was called to *Constantinople* onely r for the cause of the *Three Chapters*; and therefore *Anastasius* putting downe other causes thereof,*aperti mendacij* ſ *arguitur,is convin-*ced of an evident untruth. The second,because seeing, as they say,*Men-nas* and the chiefe Easterne Bishops would not subscribe to the Edict of the Emperour untill the Pope had consented, *Iustinian* would con-ciliate t the Pope unto him by all faire meanes, and intreate him no otherwise but favourably,least if the Pope were displeased, he should not yeeld his consent,and then the whole purpose of the Emperour should bee made frustrate. Their third reason is an argument *à testimonio negativè*, because neither u *Procopius* nor *Facundus* mention any such violence or abuse offered to the Pope,of which rea-son I have spoken before.A fourth is taken from the time;whereas he saith,that *Vigilius* came to *Constant.*on Christmas eve,*mendacij* x *redar-*guitur, hee is proved to lye, by that which *Procopius* saith. Many o-ther reasons might bee added, but these of *Baronius* and *Binius* are suf-ficient to convince *Anastasius* of lying,and open lying in this passage, which is, as now you see, nothing but a fardell of lyes;for neither did the people take that oportunity to accuse *Vigilius*, nor did they ac-cuse him of those crimes,nor did the Empresse for that cause send for *Vigilius*,neither did shee, but *Iustinian* call him to *Constantinople*, neither did shee send *Anthimus Scribo* to pull him away by violence, neither commanded shee him not to forbeare *Vigilius* in any place,but only in Saint *Peters* Church(this was but the kind affection of *Anasta-*sius to the honour of *Peters* See) neither did shee sweare to excom-municate *Scribo* if hee brought not *Vigilius*, neither did *Scribo* appre-hend him in the Temple of Saint *Cicile*, neither did *Vigilius* distribute a largesse at that time when he was apprehended, neither did they violently carry him to *Tiber* and there ship him, neither did the peo-ple follow him, and desire him to pray for them; neither when the ship was gone, did they revile him,nor cast stones,nor clubs,nor dung after him, nor imprecate and curse him, neither was hee at that time brought,but as by *Procopius* y appeareth, long before hee voluntarily went to *Sicilie*, and made so long stay there, that the Emperour ha-ving called him the yeare before, as by *Victor* z is cleare, by reason of his long abode in *Sicilie*, he called him the yeare after againe out of Sicily, as *Procopius* sheweth. Neither came he to Constantinople on Christmas Eeve, but either on the five and twentieth of Ianuary, as

Mar-

Marcellinus [a] saith, or as by *Procopius*, who is farre more worthy of credit, may bee gathered [b], about the middle of *April* next ensuing; neither did the Emperour when they met, kisse him, nor did they weepe for joy, the one of the other, nor did they sing the hymne of *Ecce advenit Dominus Dominator, behold the Lord the Ruler is come.* It was a very pretty allusion of *Anastasius*, and very apt for the season, in honour of the Pope to take part of the text expressing the joy for Christs Advent in the flesh, and turne it to an *Anthem* to congratulate the Popes Advent on Christmas eve to *Constantinople*; but I feare it will hardly be beleeved; that men in those dayes did use such base, nay, blasphemous flattery to the Pope; this hymne would have better befitted the time of *Leo* the tenth, when in the open Councell they durst say [c], to Pope *Leo*, Weepe not O daughter Syon, *Ecce venit Leo de Tribu Iuda, behold the Lion of the Tribe of Iuda commeth,* the roote of *Iesse*; behold GOD hath raised up to thee a Saviour, who shall save thee from the hands of the destroying Turks; and deliver thee from the hand of the Persecutors; O most blessed *Leo*, wee have looked for thee, we have hoped that thou shouldest come and be our deliverer. The former *Anthem* had beene sutable to such a time; the art of their blasphemous *Gnatonisme* to the Popes, was not halfe learned in *Iustinians* dayes, and most incredible it is, that *Iustinian* would use, or could endure in his presence, such entertainment of *Vigilius*, knowing that hee was an earnest and violent oppugner of his Imperiall Edict; in which he had expresly anathematized and accursed all that did defend the *Three Chapters.* This proclaming of an *Anathema* against *Vigilius*, and the hymne of *Ecce advenit Dominus Dominator*, with kissing & weeping for joy, make no good concord nor harmony together. Let this be accounted for no moe than twenty Anastasian lyes, and those are the fewest which are bound up in this fardle.

19. After that *Anastasius* hath, as you have seene, safely landed the Pope at *Constantinople*, then hee tels you, *That for two yeares space there was continuall strife about Anthimus, the Emperour and Empresse laboured to have Vigilius restore him, urged him with his promise and handwriting, but Vigilius would no way consent; and when he found them so heavy towards him, he said, I perceive now it was not Iustinian and Theodora, but Dioclesian and Eleutheria that called mee hither, doe with me what you will: thereupon they buffeted him, and called him homicide, and killer of Sylverius; then hee fled to the Church of Euphemia, and held himselfe by a Piller of the Altar, but they puld him thence, cast him out of the Church, put a rope about his necke, dragged him through all the City till evening, and then put him in prison, feeding him with a little bread and water, and after this they banished him also with the rest of the Romane Clergy.* And these, like the rest, are meerely the fond and sottish dreames of *Anastasius*, or, as *Baronius* useth to call them, lyes. *Baronius* will assure you, that it was not *Anthimus* or his restoring, but the *Three Chapters* about which *Vigilius* was sent for. The cause of *Anthimus*, who was deposed tenne [d] yeares before, was quite forgotten: and to see the sottishnesse of *Anastasius*, *Iustinian* had long before [e] written to *Vigilius*, requiring him to confirme the deposition of *Anthimus*, *Vigilius* [f] had done this upon the Emperours

a *Vigilius Constantinopolim ingressus est 8. Calend. Febr.*

b *Nam adventus Vigilij Constantinopolim ponitur à Procopio, in initio 12. anni belli Gothici, lib. 3. pa. 364. jam 12. an. illius belli inchoatur in fine anni 10. Iustiniani; is autem imperare cœpit 1. die Aprilis, ut docet Marcell. in Chr. an. 527.*

c *Conc. Later. sub Leone 10. sess. 6. in Orat. Simeonis Begnij.*

d *Anthimus depositus in Conc. Constant. sub Menna, Act. 4. an post Cons. Basilij, qui est primus belli Gothici, Vigilius autem venit Bizantium an. 12. ejusdem belli.*

e *Anno nimirū 540. Bar. in illum an. nu. 12.*

f *Bar. an. eod. nu. 18.*

gapetus called him *Dioclesian*; that *Agapetus* disputed with *Anthimus*, and overcame him before the Emperour; that the Emperour thereupon humbled himselfe to the Pope, and adored [x] the most blessed *Agapetus*; that then hee banished *Anthimus*, and entreated *Agapetus* to consecrate *Mennas* in his roome. Now *Anastasius* perceiving these his fictions concerning *Iustinian* and *Agapetus*, wherein hee had some ground of truth, to be plausible, and his end being this, *Papæ ut placerēs, quas fecisset fabulas*, hee brings in *Iustinian* and *Vigilius* to act the very same pageant againe, and that without any ground of truth, they for sooth, tenne yeares after *Anthimus* was deposed, and for ought appeareth was dead at that time, must come in quarrelling againe about *Anthimus*, as fresh as ever the Emperour and *Agapetus* had done before: nay they must contend two other whole yeares after the former tenne: about this *Helena*, *Iustinian* and his Empresse must for want of variety of phrases be termed *Dioclesian* and *Eleutheria*, *Vigilius* must be buffeted and beaten, haled, dragged, imprisoned, and banished. Truly *Anastasius* had some ground for the act under *Agapetus*, for this of *Vigilius* he is beholding to none but his own poeticall pate; & lest any little scene or shadow of resemblance might be wanting, *Baronius* [y] supplying one defect in *Anastasius*, tels us how *Vigilius* for the same cause of *Anthimus*, excommunicated *Theodora* at his comming to *Constantinople*, even as *Agapetus* had done before. Who sees not all this to be nothing else but a *mimesis* of the acts of *Agapetus*, and a meere fiction of *Anastasius*? in which there are not so few as thirty lyes.

22. You have seene the tragicall part of this Anastasian fable, now followeth the *Catastrophe* or sudden change of all this hard fortune: *Tunc Gothi fecerunt*, then (saith he) *the Gothes made Totilas their King*, who comming to Rome besieged it so sore, that the City was pressed with a great famine, so that they did eate their owne children. Totilas entred the Citie at the gate of Saint Paul, in the 13. Indiction, and for a whole night caused a Trumpet to be sounded, till all the Romane people were fled away, or hid in Churches. And Totilas dwelled with the Romanes, quasi pater cum filijs, even as a father with his children. Thus *Anastasius*. Who would not think by this narration that *Totilas* were made King after the beating, dragging, and imprisonment of *Vigilius*, and banishment of him & his fellows, upō which *Anastasius* presently adjoyneth, *Tunc Gothi fecerunt*, then the Gothes made *Totilas* King; and yet *Totilas* was King [a] not onely before all that tragicall act, but foure or five yeares also before *Vigilius* came to *Constantinople*, or before the Emperour sent for him, and in like sort *Totilas* his besieging of *Rome* by *Anastasius* narration follows all the former: whereas by *Procopius* [b] it is evident that *Totilas* besieged *Rome* while *Vigilius* stayed in *Sicilie*, before he set forward to *Constantinople*. The like errour is in the note of the Indiction; for *Totilas* tooke the City, not as *Anastasius* saith in the 13. but as [c] *Marcellinus* witnesseth, and that aright, in the 10. Indiction: neither did he enter at the gate of Saint *Paul*, but as *Procopius* [d] expresly declareth, at that which was called *Asinaria*: neither did *Totilas* sound any such Trumpet, to give them warning or space to flee, but entring the City in the night, and that by trechery of the watch, he stayed [e] his army together

[Marginal notes:]

x *Augustus adoravit beatissimū Agapetum Papam. Anast. ibid.*

y *Bar. an. 547. nu. 49.*
a *Totilas creatur Rex Gothorum anno 7. belli Gothici. Proc. lib. 3. pa. 346. Is est annus Iust. 16. ut ait Bar. an. 542. nu. 1. Vigilius Bizantium venit anno 12. belli Gothici. Proc. lib. 3. pa. 364. is est Iustiniani 31. & isto anno Constantinopolim venisse Vigilium, ait Bar. an. 547. nu. 26.*
b *Totilas Romam contendit quam statim obsedit. Procop. lib. 3. pa. 360. Per id tempus (obsidionē) cum Vigilius in Sicilia esset, &c. lib. eod. pa. 364.*
c *Indictione 10. & 6. post Cons. Basilij anno, Totilas Romam ingreditur. Marc. in Chron. Is est juxta eundem Marc. an. 547. cui consentit Bar. an. 547. nu. 12.*
d *Vniverso exercitu instructo ad portam Asinariam duxit, &c. Proc. lib. 3. p. 372.*
e *Vnum in locum copias omnes cœgit hostium insidias veritus. Proc. ibid.*

ther

ther till morning, for feare that some danger might befall himselfe or his army in the darke, by the lying in wait of the enemies. And when after this, *Bellisarius* having recovered the City, *Totilas* againe wan it from the Romanes, which was three yeares after this, to wit, in the 15. yeare of the Gothicke warre, as *Procopius* [f] sheweth, which was the 24. of *Iustinian*, whereas his first taking it was in the 21. of *Iustinian*; then indeed *Totilas*, as *Procopius* [g] declareth, caused divers Trumpets to sound an alarum on the river of Tyber in the night time, as if hee would on that side assault the City, while hee had his army in readinesse on the contrary side, and entred there by trechery also of the Watch; the Romanes giving little regard to that part. These Trumpets gave the occasion to *Anastasius* his fiction, which is so blockish, that what *Totilas* used as a warlike stratagem to deceive, and more easily to overthrow and kill the Romanes, that *Anastasius* in his simplicity takes and relates as done in favour of the Romanes, that they might escape and not be killed. And yet the taking of the City, whereof *Anastasius* speaketh, cannot be this second, wherein the Trumpets were sounded, but the former, (at which time *Totilas* used no such policie) as appeares by the famine which *Anastasius* [h] mentioneth, which happened in this former [i], and not at this second taking of *Rome* by *Totilas*. So very incoherent and false is all that *Anastasius* writeth of this matter. But whereas *Anastasius* addes of King *Totilas* that hee dwelt among the Romanes as a father among his children, I know not how to checke so great a folly. The barbarous Gothes, after that long and miserable siege of the Romanes, having by trechery in the night entred the City, the very next [k] morning when they saw there was no danger of the enemy, *Quos obvios habent, obtruncant; killed all that they met*; and had made no end of slaughter, if *Pelagius* [l] comming in most submissive manner had not stayed their Gothish fury. The Romane people [m], so many as could by flight, sought their safety: there remained of their innumerable Romane troups, but to the number of five hundred, the Noblemen [n] and better sort who remained among them, led a life more ignominious and miserable than death, being spoyled of all, *domos circumeundo, foresq, appulsando cibum dari sibi suppliciter precabantur; from doore to doore in most abject and beggerly manner praying for some reliefe of the proud and insolent victor*: nor was *Totilas* content herewith, but he was resolved [o] to ruinate and utterly deface the whole city of *Rome*, which also he had then done, had not the most prudent perswasions [p] of *Bellisarius* never sufficiently even for this onely cause to bee commended, hindred so barbarous a designe. And which is noted as one of the most miserable spectacles of all other, in Rome which was the most frequent, populous, and eminent City in the whole world, *Totilas* when he went away left not so much as one man [q], woman, or childe to remaine or inhabit therein; would any but *Anastasius* call or account this fatherly usage? what is then, or can

f *Annus 14. exibat hujus belli, Totilas deinde copias Romanas duxtavit, &c. Proc.l.3.pa.394.*

g *Praecepit ut quanta vi posset buccina clangorem eliderent, &c. Proc. ibid. pa.394.*

h *Et facta est fames in civitate talis, &c. Anast. in vita Vigilij.*

i *Vt testatur Proc.l.3.p.367.*

k *Vbi primum illuxit Gothi, &c Proc.pa.373.*

l *Pelagius Totilae supplex factus, non prius precari hunc desiit, quam ille clementiorem fore in Romanos pollicitus esset. Proc. lib.3.pa.374.*

m *Pars maxima fugam capessunt, pauci in templo perfugium habuere, constat è plebe ad quingentos in urbe residi. Proc. ibid.pa.372.*

n *Inter hos erat Rusticiana filia Symmachi, et uxor Boethij Senatoris. Proc.ib.*

o *Totilas Romã ad solum prosternere decernit. Proc.pa.375.*

p *E duobus (sic ad eum scripsit Bellisarius) alterum necesse est ut aut bello victus succumbas, aut ut nos vincas. Si viceris, et Romam demoliaris, non alterius urbem sed tuam delebis, quã servata,*

longe opulentior fies. Si victus sis, Romã incolumi reservata, gratia tibi nec mediocris apud victorem conciliabitur, qua deleta nullus tibi ad clementiam locus relinquetur. His (inter similes alias) persuasionibus usus est Bellisarius apud Totilam, ut refert Proc.lib 3.pa.375. q *Nullo hominum in urbe relicto, quam penitus destitutam demiscrat. Proc.lib.eod.p.376. Roma fuit ita desolata ut nemo ibi hominum, nisi bestiae morarentur. Marcell. in Chron.an. 547.*

truely even on the helpe of *Mary* the Mother of God, who being invocated by our prayers may riſe againſt the enemy, for of her the Church ſingeth,*Terribilis ut Caſtrorum acies,thou art terrible as an army well ordered.* Thus the Cardinall,wreſting and abuſing the Scripture, to draw mens confidence from the Lord of Hoſts to the bleſſed Virgin,making her,contrary to her ſexe,to be another *Mars*,and a chiefe warrier in all the greateſt battels of the Chriſtians. But for the truth of the matter, what *Narſes* did,*Procopius* doth declare, who thus writeth [e] of him;When *Totilas* was overcome,*Narſes* being exceeding joyfull,*id omne Deo acceptū ut erat in vero indeſinenter reſerre,did continually attribute all that victorie to God,to whom in truth it was to be aſcribed.* *Evagrius* the Cardinals own witneſſe,teſtifieth the ſame,even in that place which the Cardinall alledgeth, his words are theſe [f], φασὶ τὰνη, they who were with *Narſes* report, that, *dum precibus divinum numen placeret,while he appeaſed or pleaſed God by his prayer,& other offices of pi-ety,and gave due honour vnto him,the Virgin,Mother of God, appeared vnto him,and plainly ſet downe the time when he ſhould fight with the enemies,nor fight wᵗʰ thē til he received a ſign from above.* Thus *Evag.* in whoſe words three things are to be obſerved:Firſt,that *Narſes* uſed no invocatiō or prayers to the bleſſed Virgin,or any other,but only to God,it was *Divinū numen,the very Godhead,*which hee did in his prayers, & offices of piety adore. Secondly, that *Evag.* mentioneth not either invocation, or adoration,uſed by *Narſes* to the Virgin, or any confidence that hee repoſed in her,or that ſhe at al helped him in the battle,but only that ſhe appeared unto him as a meſſenger,to ſignifie what time he ſhould fight. Now as the Angel *Gabriel* was no helper to the Virgin *Mary*,either in the cōception of Chriſt, or in his birth,though,as a meſſenger from God, hee ſignifieth them both unto *Ioſeph*,(*Ioſeph* neither invocating him nor relying on him,but on God,whoſe meſſenger he was) even ſo, admitting the truth of this apparition, the Vigin *Mary* did ſignifie from God the time when *Narſes* ſhould fight,but neither did *Narſes* invocate or adore her, nor did ſhee her ſelfe more helpe in the battle than the Angell in the birth of Chriſt; nor did the confidence of *Narſes* relie on her,but on God,whoſe meſſenger he then beleeved her to be. Let the Cardinall,or *Binius*,or any of them prove forcibly (which they can never doe) out of *Evagrius* any other invocation or adoration uſed by *Narſes* to the bleſſed Virgin,and I will conſent unto them in that whole point. Thirdly, all that *Evagrius* ſaith of that apparition of the bleſſed Virgin,is but a rumour and report of ſome who were with *Narſes* : φασὶ τὰνω, ſome ſay, *Evagrius* himſelfe doth not ſay it was ſo,or that *Narſes* either ſaid or beleeved it to be ſo,but reported it was by ſome of the ſouldiers of *Narſes*, whether true or falſe,that muſt relie on the credit of the reporters.Now for the Cardinall to avouch a doctrine of faith out of a rumour or report of how credible men themſelves knew not, from ſuch an uncertainty to collect, that Generals ought to relie on the aide of the bleſſed Virgin in their battels,and that ſhee,*interpellata precibus, being invocated by their prayers,*riſeth up,and becomes a warrier on their ſide; this,by none that are indifferent can be judged leſſe than exceeding temeri-ty, ty, and by thoſe that are religious will bee condemned as plaine ſuperſtition and impiety. But let us returne now to *Anaſtaſius*, whoſe narration, as it is untrue in it ſelfe, if the comming of *Narſes* into *Italy*, and victory over the *Gothes*, bee referred to that time, when *Totilas* had before wonne *Rome*, ſo it is much more untrue, if it bee referred, as by *Binius* gloſſe it is, either to the yeare wherein the Emperour recalled his Edict, (which was never) or to the tenth yeare of *Totilas*, which was wholly ended before the comming of *Narſes* into *Italie*, and before the fift Councell, and the Baronian baniſhment of *Vigilius*.

25. After the victory of *Narſes* it followeth in *Anaſtaſius, tunc adunatus Clerus*, then the Romane Clergy joyned together, beſought *Narſes* that hee would intreat the Emperour, that if as yet Pope *Vigilius*, with the Preſbiters and Deacons that were carried into baniſhment with him, were alive, they might returne home.   In that they ſpeake of this exile, as long before begun, even ſo long that they doubted whether *Vigilius* were then alive or no, it ſeemeth evidently, that *Anaſtaſius* ſtill hath an eye to that baniſhment for the cauſe of *Anthimus*, after he had beene two yeares in *Conſtantinople*; that falling five whole yeares before the victory of *Narſes*, they had reaſon to adde, *ſi adhuc*, if *Vigilius* doe live as yet, that is, after ſo long time of baniſhment, remaine alive. Now ſeeing it is certaine, that *Vigilius* was not at that time (to wit, not within two yeares after his comming to *Conſtantinople*) baniſhed, as by the fift generall Councell is h evident, it hence followeth, that as this Anaſtaſian exile, ſo all the conſequents depending thereon are nothing elſe but a meere fiction of *Anaſtaſius*, without all truth or probability : for ſeeing *Vigilius* was not then baniſhed, neither did the Romanes intreat *Narſes*, nor *Narſes* the Emperour for his delivery, nor the Emperour upon that ſend to recall him or them from exile, nor uſe any ſuch words about *Pelagius*, nor thanke them if they would accept *Vigilius*, nor did they promiſe after the death of *Vigilius* to chuſe *Pelagius*, nor did the Emperour diſmiſſe them all (for of *Pelagius* that hee three yeares after the end of the Councell remained in baniſhment, is certainly teſtified by *Victor* i) nor did they returne from exile into *Sicilie*, all this is a meere fiction. So in this Cataſtrophe, beginning at the time when *Anaſtaſius* ſaith *Totilas* was King of the Gothes, there are contained at leaſt forty capitall untruths, to let paſſe the reſt, as being of leſſer note and moment. Let any now caſt up the whole ſumme, I doubt not but hee ſhall finde, not onely, as I have ſaid, ſo many untruths as there are lines, but (if one would ſtrictly examine the matter) as there are words in the Anaſtaſian deſcription of the life of *Vigilius*; & I am verily perſwaded, that few Popes lives ſcape better at his hands than this : But I have ſtayed long enough in declaring the falſhood of *Anaſtaſius*, on whom *Baronius* ſo much relyeth, and who is a very fit author for ſuch an Annaliſt as *Baronius*.

g *Nam Vigilius venit Conſtantinopolim anno 12 belli Gothici. Proc.lib.3.pa. 364. Narſes autem Totilam vicit, et Romam recepit an.18. ejuſdem belli. Proc.lib 3.pa. 408.et ſeq.* h *Nam ex eo E. quet, Vigilium a primo ejus adventu Conſtantinopolim, illic manſiſſe ad finē Concilij, dicitur enim illic à Iuſtiniano, quod Vigilius ſemper ejuſdem voluntatis fuit de condemnatione Trium Capitulorum.Conc.5. Coll.1.pa.520.d Semper, viz. à primo ejus advētu et conſenſu ad tempus 5. Concilij.* i *Nam Victor ait Pelagium rediſſe ab exilio anno 12.poſt coſſ.Baſilij. Vict.Tun in Chron.et Concilium habitum ait ille an.13. poſt ejuſdem Conſulatum.*

CAP.

Cap. XXXVI.

That Baronius *reproveth Pope* Vigilius *for his comming to* Constantinople, *and a refutation thereof; with* a description of the life of the same
Vigilius.

1. AFter all which the Cardinall could devise to
disgrace either the Emperor or the Empresse,
or *Theodorus* Bishop of *Cesarea,* or the cause it
selfe of the *Three Chapters,* or the Synodall
Acts; in the last place let us consider what he
saith against Pope *Vigilius;* for, this cause so
netled him, that whatsoever or whosoever
came in his way, though it were his Holinesse
himselfe, hee would not spare them, if he thought thereby to gaine never so little for the support of their infallible Chaire: And what think
you is it that he carps at, and for which hee so unmannerly quarrels
Pope *Vigilius?* was it for oppugning the truth published by the Emp.
Edict, or was it for making his hereticall *Constitution,* and defining it
ex Cathedrâ, in defence of the *Three Chapters ?* or was it for his pevish-
nesse in refusing to come to the generall Councell, even then when he
was present in the City where it was held, and had promised under
his owne hand that hee would come unto it ? or was it his pertinacious obstinacy in heresie, that he would rather undergoe both the just
sentence of an *anathema* denounced by the generall Councell, and also
the calamity and wearinesse of exile inflicted by the Emperor (as *Baronius* saith) upon him, then yeelding to the truth and true judgement
of the Synod in condemning the *Three Chapters ?* Are these (which
are all of them hainous crimes, and notorious in *Vigilius*) the matters
that offend the Cardinall ? No, none of these, hee is not used to finde
such faults in their Popes, these all hee commends as rare vertues, as
demonstrations of constancy, of prudence, of fortitude in *Vigilius ?*
what then is it that his Cardinalship dislikes ? Truely, among many
great and eminent vices in *Vigilius,* which are obvious, and runne into
every mans sight, it hapned that once in his life he did one thing worthy of commendations, and that was his obedience in going to *Constantinople,* when the Emperour [a] called and requested [b] him to come
thither, and the Cardinall winking at all the other, reproves his Holinesse for this one thing, which both in equity and duty hee ought to
have done: This forsooth is it which hee notes as a very [c] dangerous
and hurtfull matter, and a speciall point of great indiscretion in Pope
Vigilius, that leaving *Rome,* that holy City, hee would goe to *Constantinople,* and to the Emperours Court, which his predecessors, *Leo* and
others, in very great wisdome would never do, nor goe into the East,
nor suffer themselves to bee pulled away from their See fixed at
Rome.

2. Truely, I never knew before that there was such vertue in the
Romane, or such venome in the Constantinopolitane soile, or in the
Easterne

a Vigilius ab Imperatore evo-catus, Bizantium venit Proc.lib.3 pa.364.
b Ipsum summâ celeritate venire rogans. Bar.an. 546. nu.54.
c Ceterum Vigilij profectionem Constantinopo-lim, magnum in-tulisse Catholica Ecclesia damnu eventa declara-runt, que et sig-ficarunt quam prudentissime egerunt illius pradecessores, S. Leo, et alij, qui vocati sepe ab orthodoxis li-cet Imperatori-bus nunquam passi sunt se ab ipsâ fixâ Româ sede divelli,&c. Bar.an.546. nu.55.

Easterne ayre, specially seeing the holy Land and the holy City, and the holy Temple were all in the East: All the Westerne nations are beholding to the Cardinall for this conceit; *Shall there not bee given* [2 King.5.17.] *to thy servant two Mules load of this Romish earth?* But let us a little more fully see why the Pope, and particularly *Vigilius* might not goe to *Constantinople.* Oh, saith the Cardinall [d], it is found by experience, [d Bar.loc.cit.] that the Popes going from *Rome* to the Court, *obfuisse haud modicum,* hath done great hurt to the Church; for then partly by the threats, and partly by the favours and faire intreaties of Emperours, as it were with two contrary windes, the ship of *Peter* is exposed to great hazzard. *Modica fidei,* phy, a Cardinall to feare or distrust any wracke of Saint *Peters* ship, though never so dangerous a tempest happen, though, *Vna Eurusque, Notusque ruant, creberque procellis Africus.* S. *Peter* hath left such a Pilot in his *Rome,* that a thousand times sooner might he himselfe, than his ship sinke; *Pasce oves, tu es Petra, & oravi pro te Petre,* will uphold it against all winde and weather: And truly I would gladly know of his Cardinalship for my learning, how any of their Popes can forsake their See or *Rome.* They have heretofore held it for a maxime, [e] *ubi Papa, ibi Roma,* let the Pope goe to Peru; yea, *ultra Garamantas & Indos,* he hath a priviledge above all creatures but the Snaile; hee carrieth not onely their infallible Chaire, but the whole City of *Rome* on his backe, whithersoever hee goes. If not so, or if the Chaire bee fixt to *Rome,* where sate all their Popes for those seventy yeares [f], when they were at *Avinion?* or how shall they sit in the Chaire, when their Babylonish Rome for her Idolatries shal be burnt with unquencheable fire, and sinke like a Milstone into the bottome of the Sea? which being foretold by Saint *Iohn,* of the Romane City; which yet remaineth, as their owne Iesuite *Ribera* [g] doth truely and undeniably demonstrate, is a most certaine Article of the Catholike faith, though they seldome thinke of it, and will hardly put it into their Creed. When their Pope (goe whither hee will) carieth still with him his infallible Chaire; was it not infidelity in the Cardinall to dreame or doubt lest that ship should any where miscarry, more at the Court or Kings Pallace than in a Country Cottage; more in the Trullane than in the Laterane Temple?

3. Yea, but, *usu rerum reperitur* [h], experience teacheth, that their going to the Emperour hath done exceeding hurt, and particularly for *Vigilius,* that his going to *Constantinople* hath brought [i], *magnum damnum,* great harme to the Catholike Church, *declararunt eventa,* the events have shewed. Events and experience are the most woesull arguments in Divinitie, that can possibly be devised. Measure the Gospell by temporall calamities which ensued upon it, the bloody murdering of the Apostles, of the Saints of God, almost for three hundred yeares together, and hee may as well conclude, that the Gospell and truth of Christ is found by woesull experience to have brought exceeding great hurt to the Church. The Cardinall was driven to a narrow strait, and an exceeding penury of reasons, when he was forced to put, *Argumentum ab eventu,* for one of his *Topicall* places.

[e Sententia illa omnium ore versata, Vbi Papa, ibi Roma.Bar. an.552.nu.10.]

[f Clemens 5. propter seditiones Italicas sedé Pontificiam ab urbe Roma, Avionem Galliæ urbem, ubi successores mansere annos 70. transtulit. Geneb.in Chron. in an.1305.]

[g Iohannes in omnibus quæ de Babylone loquitur, adversus urbem Romanam vaticinatur, &c. Rib.Com.in ca. 14. Apoc.nu.57. et Vicarius Christi ubicunq; sit, erit Episcopus Romæ, etiamsi illa penitus excisa sit.Ibid.nu. 48.]

[h Obfuisse haud modicum usu rerum reperitur, Pontificam ab urbe profectio ad comitatum.Bar. an.546. nu.55.]

[i Ibid.]

4. But

4. But say, what hurt can he tell us that ever any Emperours presence with the Pope, brought unto the Church? If both were Catholike, or both hereticall, they agreed well enough together. As not Satans, so much lesse is Gods Kingdome devided against it selfe; if the Emperour Catholike, and the Pope hereticall, the worst the Emperour ever did, was but to inflict just punishment on an heretike, the worst the Pope sustained was but a just recompence of his heresie and hatred of truth: The execution of Iustice never did, nor ever can hurt the Catholike Church. If the Emperor were hereticall and the Pope orthodoxal, there was trial of the Popes art & skil in converting such a man to the truth; triall of his constancy and love unto Gods truth, whether by feare or favour he would forsake it: triall of his patience and fortitude in induring all torments, even death it selfe, for his love to Christ. All the hurt which such an Emperour did, or could doe, was to crowne him a glorious Martyr, and in stead of the white garment of innocency, to send him in scarlet robes unto heaven; and woe be to that Church which shall thinke Martyrdome an hurt unto it, which was, and ever will bee the glory of the Catholike Church. *Non decet sub spinoso capite membrum esse delicatum*, when Christ, his Apostles, and glorious Saints, and Martyrs, have gone before upon thornes and briars, wee must not looke to have a silken way, strewed with Roses and Lillies, unto the Kingdome of God. This, which is yet the

Reu. 14. 13.

very worst that can befall any Catholike, is no harme to him who hath learned that lesson, *Blessed are they which die in the Lord*; so whether Pope and Emperour be both of one, or of a different religion, his presence with the Emperour may happen to doe good, but it is certaine it can never possibly doe hurt unto the Church. The greatest hurt that was ever done to the Church by this meanes, was when *Constantine* after his baptisme by Pope *Silvester*, in lieu of his paines, and in

k *Donationis exemplar extat Dist. 96. ca. Constancinus.*

token of a thankful minde, sealed unto him that donation [k] of the Romane and Westerne *Provinces*: That one fable I must particularly except, for by it hath beene lift up the man of sinne, Christian Empires have beene robbed, the ignorant seduced, the whole Church abused: *Nero* did not the thousand part so much hurt by martyring *Peter* and *Paul* when they were present with him, as the most falsly supposed donation hath done to the Catholike Church.

5. Will you yet see the great vanity of the Cardinall in this reason drawne from the event, and the Emperours presence. Some [l] ten yeares before this, Pope *Agapetus*, being sent by *Theodotus* King of the

l *Agapetus Barbarico coactus Imperio, &c. Bar. an. 536. nu. 10. qui Agapeti profectionem eo anno contigisse probat.*

Gothes, came to *Constantinople*, and to the same Emperour: It so fell out, that at that time *Anthimus* an heretike and an intruder, held the Sea of *Constantinople*: *Agapetus* deposed him, that is, hee declared and denounced (which was true indeed) that hee was never lawfully Bishop of that See, and that himselfe did not, nor ought others to hold him for the lawfull Bishop thereof; whereupon *Mennas* was chosen and consecrated Bishop by *Agapetus* in *Anthimus* his roome. *Vigilius* was called by the Emperour, *Agapetus* sent by a Gothish usurper; *Vigilius* called by a religious and most orthodoxall Professor, *Agapetus* sent by an heretike and Arian King; *Vigilius* called purpose-

ly

ly about causes of faith, *Agapetus* sent only about civill, and but casually intermedling wth Ecclesiasticall causes. You would now even blesse your selfe to see how the Card. here turns this argument *ab eventu*, & by it proves the Popes presence at the same Court with the same Emperor, to have brought such an infinite & unspeakeable good unto the Church, as could scarce bee wished. *Agapetus* ^m no longer sent from *Theodotus* a barbarous Goth, but even from God himselfe, and by him commanded to goe thither with an errant from heaven; hee seemed to bee sent to intreat of peace, but hee was commanded by God to goe, *ut imperaret imperantibus, that he should shew himselfe to be an Emperour above the Emperour*: He, like Saint *Peter* ^n, had not gold nor silver being faine to pawne the holy Vessels for to furnish him with money in the journey, but he was rich in the power and heavenly treasures of working miracles. Now was demonstrated ^o the highest power of the Pope, that without any Councell called about the matter, as the custome is, hee could depose a Patriarke, (at other times hee may not have that title) and a Patriark of so high a See as *Constantinople*, and so highly favoured by the Emp. & Empresse. Now was demonstrated ^p, that, *Pontifex supra omnes Canones eminet, that the Popes power is above all Canōs*, for herby was shewed, that he by his omnipotēt authority may do matters wth the Canōs, without the Canons, against all Canons; & seeing his judgement was without a Synod, (wch in a Patriarks cause is required) *fuit secundum supremam Apostolicæ sedis authoritatem, it was according to his supreme authority*, which is transcēdent above all Canōs; or to use *Bellarmines* ^q phrase, hee did shew himselfe to bee, *Princeps Ecclesiæ*, one that may doe against the whole Church. Nay, if you well consider ^r, *admirari non desines, you will never cease to wonder*, to see that *Agapetus* a poore man, as soone as hee came to *Constantinople* should *imperare Imperatoribus, eorū facta rescindere, jura dare, omnibusq, jubere, to command Emperours, to adnull their Acts, to depose a Patriarke and thrust him from his throne, to set another there, to set downe lawes, and command all men*, and to do all this without any Synod: & such a Pope ^s was *Agapetus*, that I know not, *an similis alius inveniri possit*, whether such another can bee found among them all. Thus declameth *Baronius*. Where thinke you, all time was the Cardinals argument *ab adventu*? Experience teacheth, that when Popes leave their See, and goe to the Court or Emperours presence, the ship of S. *Peter* is then in great hazzard: If *Agapetus* his comming to *Constantinople* or to the Emperour did not hazzard or endanger the Church, how came it to bee perillous a few yeares after in *Vigilius*? and where were now the most wise examples of Pope *Leo* and the other, who in great wisedome could never be drawne to the East, and from their owne See? how was the holy Church now fixed to *Rome*, when *Agapetus* had it in the greatest majesty and honour at *Constantinople*? perceive you not how these arguments lie asleepe in the cause of *Agapetus*, which the Cardinall rouseth up when *Vigilius* goes to *Constantinople*? This, *ab adventu*, as all the Cardinals Topicke places, is drawne from the art and authority of Esops Satyr: If they make for the Pope, as the event did in *Agapetus*, then the Cardinall with his Satyrs blast will puffe them up and make them

m *Agapetus sicet à Rege visus sit missus ad Imperatorem, à Deo tamen proficisci; missus apparuit, ut imperaret imperantibus, &c. Bar. an. 536. nu. 12.*

n *Illud ipsum ferme contigit Aga:tto, quod olim Petro, &c. Ibid. nu. 13.*

o *In his omnibus peragendis summa potestas Apostolicæ sedis Antistitis demonstrata est, &c. Ibid. nu. 22.*

p *Ibid. nu. 23.*

q *Bell. lib. 1. de Conc. ca. 18. Pontifex et Princeps Ecclesiæ sumus, potest retractare judicium Concilij, et non sequi majorem partem.*

r *Bar. an. 536. nu. 31.*

s *Ibid. nn. 70.*

Emperour *Iustinian*; and specially becaufe *Vigilius* being the fubject, (in a manner) of this whole Treatife, it feemes to mee needfull to ex-preffe the moft materiall circumftances, touching the entrance, the actions, the end of him, who hath occafioned us to undertake this fo long, and as I truly profeffe, both laborious and irkfome labour.

9. I confeffe I have no good faculty in writing their Popes lives, *Nec fonte labra prolui Caballino, nec in bicipiti fomniaffe Parnaffo memini*; I have not tafted of their ftreames of *Tiber*, more holy than *Helicon*, nor ever had I dreame or vifion in their facred *Parnaffus*; yet with their leave will I adventure to fet downe fome parts of the life of *Vigilius*, which doe afford as much variety of matter, and are as needfull to be knowne and remembred, as any other of that whole ranke from S. *Peter* to *Paul* the fift.

10. That many of their Popes have unjuftly climbed up to S. *Peters* Chaire, I thinke none fo unskilfull as not to know, none fo malitious as to deny: But whether any of them all, I except none, not the boy-Pope u *Iohn* the 12. not the Fox x *Boniface*, not *Silvefter* the fecond, who had it y by a compact with the Devill, of whom hee purchafed it with the gift of his foule; not *Iohn* the 23. called a Devill incarnate z, not any elfe; whether any of them all, I fay, obtained the See with more impiety, or greater villany than *Vigilius*, may be juftly doub-ted. He, intending to be a good cammock, beganne (according to the Proverb,) to hooke and crooke betimes, and gape after that emi-nent Throne. His firft attempt a was in the time of *Boniface* the fe-cond, with whom he prevailed fo far, that when *Boniface* b in a Roman Synod had made a Conftitution that he fhould nominate his fuccef-for, before them all he named and conftituted *Vigilius* to fucceed to himfelfe: for the performance of which, both he and all the reft of the Synod did binde themfelves, both by fubfcription, and by a folemne oath. *Vigilius* feemed for a while to be cocke-fure of the See: but it fell out contrary to his expectation at this time: the Senate of Rome juftly withftood (as Pope *Silverius* c witneffeth) that nomination. It may be they knew the crooked difpofition of *Vigilius*, how unfit hee was to make a Bifhop: nor the Senate onely, but the Ecclefiafticall Canons refifted it: Thou endeavouredft this *contra jura canonica*, faith Pope *Silverius* d, *againft the Canonicall right*. The Italian lawes alfo refi-fted it at that time; *Theoderick* e, and after him *Odoacer* f, having en-acted, and that as they affirme by the advice of Pope *Simplicius*, *electio-nem Romani Pontificis ad Regem fpectare, that the election of the Pope fhould belong to the King*; and that no election fhould be made without the confent of the King of *Italy*, as by the fourth Romane Councell under *Symmachus* doth appeare: For which caufe *Boniface* called a fecond Sy-nod to *Rome*, wherein he recalled g his nomination of *Vigilius*, and

u *De quo Otho Imperator di-xit poftquam fe-diffet 8 annos, Puer eft: erat enim cum invi-fit fedem non nifi annorum 18. Bar.an.955.nu. 1.& 2. Cujus electioni lex nul-la fuffragata eft, fed vis & metus omnia impleve-runt. ibid.n.3.*

x *De quo dicitur, Intravit ut vul-pes, regnavit ut leo, mortu9 eft ut canis. Geneb. in fuo Chron.ad an. 1303.*

y *Pontificatum adjuvante dia-bolo confecu-tus eft, hac ta-men lege, ut poft mortem totus illius effet. Plat. in Silv.2.*

z *Johannes in-ter Chrifti fide-les, vitam & mores ejus cog-nofcentes, vul-gariter dicitur Diabolus incar-natus. Conc. Conftan.Seff.11. pa.1579.*

a *Contra jura canonica, tem-poribus Bonifa-tij Papæ, ipfo vi-vente, fucceffor ejus defignari conaberis. Epift. 1. Silverij quæ eft ad Vigilium.*

b *Bonifacius 2. congregavit Sy-nodum, & fecit Conftitutum ut fibi fuccefforem nominaret, quo Conftituto, cum*

chirographis Sacerdotum, et jurejurando, Diaconum Vigilium conftituit. Anaft. in vita Bonif.2.   c *Ampliffimi Senatus tibi obviavit juftitia. Silv. Epift. 1.*   d *Ibid.*   e *Electionem Rom. Pontificis ad Regem fpectare Theodericus ftatuerat. Bar.an 531.nu 2.*   f *Bafilius vices agens Odoacris dixit, Admonitione beatiffimi Papæ Simplicij, hoc nobis fub obteftatione meminiftis fuiffe mandatum, ut non fine noftra confultatione, hujufmodi (Pontificis) celebretur electio. Conc. 4. fub Symmacho. Et, lex una Odoacris erat, ne abfque confultatione & confenfu Regis Italiæ, electio fummi Pontificis fieret. Bin. Notis in illud Conc.4.*   g *Bonifacius facta iterum Synodo reum fe Majeftatis confeffus eft quod Diaconum Vigilium conftituiffet, ac ip-fum conftitutum incendio confumpfit. Anaft. in vit. Bonif.2.*

burned

burned his former Constitution, acknowledging himselfe (and by consequence all the rest of the former Synod) to bee *reus Majestatis, guilty of high treason*, for presuming to name *Vigilius*. This was the first onset of *Vigilius*, seeking the Papacy both by violation of the Canons, and treason against the King, and perjury of the Pope, and of the whole Synod, whom he had cunningly drawne to that snare, either by making him Pope to incurre treason, or by defeating him of it to incurre perjury.

11. *Hâc non successit*, he could not by such petty offences, as treason, perjury, and contempt of the Canons prevaile: about he will againe, and try another course, and that is by treason against Christ himselfe, and abnegation of the Catholike faith. For after the death, first of his old friend *Boniface*, then of *Iohn* the second, then of *Agapetus*, who died at *Constantinople*; *Vigilius*, that he might effect his purpose, tampered and consulted with the Empresse *Theodora*, who though of her selfe at that time she was too earnestly affected to *Anthimus*, and being by him seduced, sought for his cause to overthrow the Councell of *Chalcedon*; yet *Instigabat* [h] *ardentem Vigilius*; *Vigilius* incited her by his ambitious desires. She and *Vigilius* the Deacon having advised about the matter, and covenanted, it was concluded betwixt them, as *Liberatus* [i] sheweth, that the Empresse for her part should procure *Vigilius* to be Pope, and give him 700. peeces [k] of gold; and that *Vigilius* for his part, and in recompence of so ample wages, and so great a reward, should when he were Pope, abolish [l] and adnull for ever the Councell of *Chalcedon*, and restore *Anthimus, Theodosius*, and *Severus*, three Eutychean Bishops to their Sees. The words of *Liberatus* are very worthy observing: *Libenter suscepit Vigilius promissum ejus, amore episcopatus, & auri*; *Vigilius* gladly tooke the offer, for his desire both of the Popedome, and of the pounds of gold. O ambition, *& auri sacra fames*, what will not it effect in such a *Balaam*, such a *Iudas* as *Vigilius* was? It was a very bitter scoffe, and some touch also to the credit of Pope *Damasus*, that *Pratextatus* [m] an heathen man said in derision of him, *Facite me Romanæ urbis Episcopum, & ero protinus Christianus*, make me Pope, and I will be a Christian: But see the difference betwixt this heathen man and *Vigilius*; *Pratextatus* would renounce paganisme, and become a Christian, so hee might gaine the Popedome thereby; *Vigilius* will renounce Christ and Christianity, and turne quite Pagan, to obtaine the same honour. What thinke you would *Vigilius* have sayd to him that made the offer, *All these will I give thee and fall downe and worship me*, when he was so glad for the offer of 700. peeces of gold, and the triple Crowne, that for them onely he undertakes, and bindes himselfe in an obligation under his owne hand to renounce Christ, and abandon out of the world the whole Catholike faith? Which is every whit as bad, if not all one with falling downe to adore the Devill. *Vigilius* having now the Empresse warrant, seemed sure and secure of the Papacy, and in this confidence hee [n] posts from *Constantinople* to *Rome*: but it fell out so unhappily, that when he came, he found [o] *Silverius* placed by *Theodotus*, & holding quiet and peaceable possession of the See. This had beene enough to have

S f   discou-

h *Blond. Decad. 1. lib. 5. in initio.*
i *Lib. in Brev. ca. 22.*
k *Promittens dare centenaria septem, (iuta auri, nam duo ex his centenariis auri Vigilius Bellisario promisit.) Lib. loc. cit. Videntur autem fuisse aurei illi qui à Valentiniano cusi Sextala nicebantur, quod essent sexta pars unciæ. Aureus autem quisque talis valebat de nostro nummo 10. s. ut observat doctissm. vir Edw. Breirwood. lib. suo de antiquis nummis. ca. 15. Ita summa Vigilio promissa fuit 350. li.*
l *Augusta vocans Vigilium propteri sibi secreto ab eo stzigitavit, ut si Papa fieret, tolleret Synodū, & fidem firmaret Anthimo, &c Liber. loc. cit.*
m *Hier. Epist. ad Pammach. adversus err. Iohannis Hicros.*
Math 4. 9.
n *Vigilius facta professione (Theodoræ) Romam profectus est. Liber. loc. cit.*
o *Invenit Silverium, Papam ordinatum. Lib.*

p 1 Reg. 15. 5.
q Liber. loc. cit. & misit Augusta iussiones suas ad Bellisarium per Vigilium Anast. in vita Silver.
r Liber. loc. cit
s Intentabat Silverio calumniā quasi Gothis scripsisset ut Romam introirent. Liber. loc. cit. & Exierunt quidam falsi testes qui dixerunt, Invenimus Silverium, &c. Anast. in vita Silv.
t Marc. in Chron. an. 547. Silverium faventem Vitigi, Bellisarius submovit.
u Oborta suspicione Silverium defectu-rum ad Gothos transmisit in Greciam Bellisarius, & Vigilium suffecit. Proc. lib. 1 de bell. Goth pa. 286 Bellisarius mandavit eis ut alium Papam eligerent, & favore Bellisarij ordinatus est Vigilius. Liber loc. cit.
x Hoc anno (548) expulsus est Vigilius. Bar an. 547. m. 21. obijt autem Silverius a. 540. Bar. an. 540. m. 2.
y Vigilius qua Pontificij muneris erant, exequi minimè pratermisit. Bar. an. 538. nu. 21
z Hac eadem scriptissimus ad beat iss. Papam sensoris Roma Vigilium. sic ait Iustin. in suis literis ad Menn. qua extant apud Bar. an. 538. nu. 24 & 77. Illam autem epistolam missam tam Mennam quā ad Vigilium, isto anno 547. ex hoc liquet, quod ba litera Concilium illud Constantinopolitanum precedit, in quo Origenis damnatus est, nam Mennam admovet Imp. ut Synodum de hac re habeat. Epist. apud Bar. n. 77. Concilium autē illud habitum est isto anno. testatur Bar. an 538. nu. 31 & nu. 83.
a Bar an. 538. nu. 21. & 25. Legitimorum Pontificij vestigijs insistit.
b Epist. 2. Vigilij, apud Bin pa. 482.

discouraged a faint heart : but *Vigilius* was of a better courage: though he found it not, he will make the See vacant. He comes to *Bellisarius*; *Sinite me praeterire,* how gladly would I passe by this fact and fault of *Bellisarius,* one for warlike prowes, wisedome, and successe, inferiour to no Generall that *Rome* ever had, by whom the Persians were subdued, the Vandals expelled *Africke,* the Gothes out of *Italy,* the Empire restored with an overplus also to his pristine beauty and dignity! But it so fals out that all men, even the most praise-worthy, yea the most holy, *Abraham, Lot, Sampson, Peter,* and the rest, they all have some blemish or other, like a moale or wart in a faire body, they must all be commended as God himselfe praised p *David,* with an exception of that one matter of *Vriah : Peter* a most holy Apostle, save onely in the matter of denying Christ. *Bellisarius,* a most worthy and renowned man, save this one matter of *Silverius.* To this renowned *Bellisarius* comes *Vigilius,* and delivered unto him q *praeceptum Augusta,* the Empresse mandatory letters to make him Pope ; and to perswade him more easily, knowing what strong operation gold had in himselfe, *Duo* r *ei auri centenaria promisit ;* he promised to part stakes with him, and give him two hundred pieces of gold. I wish any but *Bellisarius* had beene the instrument of so vile an action. But so it was, either the command of the Empresse, or the importunity of *Vigilius,* or both, caused him to condemne s Pope *Silverius* as guilty of treason, for practising to betray the Imperiall City of *Rome* to the Gothes, under pretence of which false accusation, (for I cannot assent to *Marcellinus* t, who thinks *Silverius* guilty thereof) *Silverius* was expelled u and thrust away, and then *Vigilius* by the same meanes of *Bellisarius* intruded himselfe, and stept into the *Apostolicall* See, usurping it about two yeares x during the life time of *Silverius:* all which time he caried himselfe y for the onely lawfull Pope ; as Pope he received z Letters from *Iustinian,* as Pope he gave answer a and judgement to *Etherius,* to *Casarius* b, as true and Catholike, you may be sure, as if S. *Peter* had given them : the Chaire would not permit him to speake amisse.

12. Now though it was too bad for any Pope, to enter into the holy throne of S. *Peter,* by open injustice, by slander, and false accusations, by a sacrilegious extrusion of the lawfull Bishop, by Symonie, by undertaking to restore condemned heretikes, and to abolish the holy Councell of *Chalcedon,* which is in effect utterly to abandon the whole Catholike faith; yet the sequell of his actions bewrayes further the most devillish minde of *Vigilius.* Who would have thought but that *Vigilius* would have kept touch, and performed his sacrilegious and symoniacall contract with the Empresse and *Bellisarius? Liberatus* c notes of him that he would doe neither, not restore *Anthimus, timore Romanorum,* it was not out of conscience, he feared the people, he feared his owne life : Not pay the 200. *Centenaria* to *Bellisarius, avaritia patrocinante,* better lose all his credit, faith, and honesty, than two hundred peeces of gold; better break his promise, than hurt his purse: But all this is nothing to his usage of Pope *Silverius:* Was it not e-

c Vigilius post ordinationem suam compellabatur a Bellisario ut impleret promissionem suam Augusta, & sibi redderet duo auri centenaria promissa. Vigilius autem timore Romanorum, & avaritia patrocinante nolebat sponsiones suas implere. Liber. loc. cit.

nough to usurpe and violently thrust himselfe into his See, to set up
altare contra altare, Pope against Pope, S. *Peters* Chaire against S. *Peters* Chaire, but hee must adde indignities also to the holy Bishop?
Had he permitted him to live in his owne Country, in some quiet,
though meane estate, it had beene some contentment to innocent *Silverius* : But *Vigilius* could not endure that, away with him, out of
Rome, out of *Italy*, out of *Europe*. So by *Vigilius* meanes is *Silverius*
sent to *Patara*, a City in *Licia* [e], once famous for the Temple and O-
racle of *Apollo* [f] : there hee is fed with the bread of tribulation, and
with the water of affliction. But the rage of *Vigilius* was further incensed by two occasions, the former on *Silverius* part. He, though in
exile, yet as then being the onely true and lawfull Pope, in a Councell
held * at *Patara*, by the authority of S. *Peter*, and the fulnesse of his
Apostolicall power, thundred out from *Patara* a sentence of excommunication, of deposition, of damnation against the usurper and invader
of his See, *Vigilius*. Which being an authenticke and undenyable record of the good conditions of *Vigilius*, and how fit a man he was to
make a Pope, I will relate here some parts thereof. Pope [g] *Silverius*
having told *Vigilius* how he sought against law to obtaine the Papall
dignity in the time of *Boniface* the second, addes this, At that [h] time
the pastorall and pontificall authority should have cut away, *execran-
da tua auspicia, thy execrable beginnings*, but by neglect a little wound
insanabile accrevit apostema, is become an incurable imposture, which being senslesse of other medicines, is to be cut off with a sword. *For thou
art led* [i] *with the audaciousnesse of the most wicked fiend, thou art franticke
with ambition, thou labourest to bring the crime of error or heresie into the
Apostolike See ; thou followest the steps of Simon Magus, whose disciple thou
shewest thy selfe to be, by thy workes, by giving money, by thrusting out me,
and invading my See : Receive thou therefore this sentence of damnation, sub-
latumq; tibi nomen, & ministerium sacerdotalis dignitatis agnosce; and know
that thou art deprived of the name, and all function of priestly ministery,
being damned by the judgement of the holy Ghost, and by the Apostolike authority in us :* for it is fit, *ut quod habuit amittat*, that hee should lose that
which he hath received, who usurpes that which he hath not received. Thus
Silverius : who being then the onely true Pope, pronounced this sentence of deprivation, of degradation, and damnation out of the highest authority of their *Apostolike* Chaire : which alone is so authenticall
a testimony, of the most execrable conditions of *Vigilius*, that if I said
no more, few Logicians I thinke would complaine that the description of *Vigilius* were imperfect, being so fully, so plainly, and so infallibly expressed, both by his *Genus*, a damnable and damned intruder,
and by his foure *differences*, or at least properties, *hereticall, schismaticall, symoniacall, Satanicall*.

13. This no doubt moved the choler of *Vigilius* not a little, to heare
such a thundring from *Patara*, as if *Apollo* were there set againe on his
sacred trevet. But the other accident was farre worse than this. For
perhaps *Vigilius* had learned that maxime which *Lewis* [k] the French
King sometime uttered, That hee who feared the Popes curse should
never sleepe a quiet night. Many other Catholikes, and among them
the Bishop of *Patara* grieved much to see the injury and ignominy of

e *Pomp. Mel. in Lib. 1. in Licia.*
f *Unde Patareus Apollo dictus. Vad. in Pom. Mel. loc. cit.*

* *Silverius habito istic Concilio Episcoporum in Vigilium sententiam damnationis intorquet. Bar. an. 538. nu. 18. & Vigilio veniente Pataram venerabilis Episcopus, &c. Liber. loco cit.*
g *Silverij Epist. 1 que est ad Vigilium pseudopapam.*
h *Viz. tempore Bonifacij.*
i *Nequissimi spiritus audacia, ambitionis phrenesin concipiens. Silv. ibid.*

k *Contin. of the History of France, collect. by Thomas Dannet, in Lewes 11 in fine.*

l *Venerabilis Patare Episcopus venit ad Imperatorem, & judicium Dei contestatus est, de tante sedis expulsione, &c. Liber.loc.cit.*
m *Imperator revocari Romam Silverium jussit, & de literis illis (à Silverio ut aiebant ad Gothos scriptis) judicium fieri, ut si probaretur &c.Liber.loc.cit.*
n *Prævalente Imperatoris jussione Silverius ad Italiam reductus est.Liber. ibid.*
o *Cujus adventu territus Vigilius ne sede pelleretur, Bellisario mandavit,Trade mihi Vigilium, alioquin non possum facere, quod à me exigis.Liber.ibid.*
p *Dictum Theodoti de Pompeio, apud Plut. in vita Pomp.*
q *Ita Silverius traditus est duobus Vigilii servis, qui in Palmariam insulam adductus, sub eorum custodia defecit inedia. Liber. loc. cit.*
r *Ferro sævior est fames.Veget. f Lament.4.9. Melius est mori gladio, quam fame.*
t *Bin.Not. in vitam Vigilÿ.*
u *Bar.an.540. nu.4.*

the innocent and miserably afflicted Bishop *Silverius*, went [l] to the Emperour to plead on his behalfe; declaring both his innocency and extreme oppression. The Emperour whose delight it was to doe justice to all, and relieve the innocent, especially sacred persons, and most of all the Pope, was so affected therewith, that he commanded that [m] *Silverius* should be brought againe from exile to *Rome*, and that there should be taken a *melius inquirendum* of the whole cause, and if he were found guilty of the treason objected, then hee should be for ever exiled; if innocent, he should be restored to his See, which *Vigilius* then usurped. *Silverius* [n] was hereupon brought backe with speed, and being come as neare as *Italy*, *Vigilius* was then netled indeed, and fearing [o] to be dethroned, he bestirres himselfe, and stirres every stone. Then he comes againe in very earnest manner to *Bellisarius*, and tels him he will now performe all his covenants, if he would deliver *Silverius* to his custody. By which sollicitation *Silverius* the lambe was committed to the wolfe, who (intending now to make as sure worke with him, as he who sayd [p], *mortui non mordent*,)by two of [q] his servants convayed him out of *Italy* to the Iland *Palmaria*, where after all other injuries, indignities, and calamities, hee spared not the innocent life and soule of that holy Bishop,but murdered him by a kinde of languishing death, namely by famine, which [r] *Vegetius* and the Prophet [f] also judged worse than the sword.

14. And now that which onely hindred *Vigilius*, being by a strong writ *de ejectione mundi* quite removed, there was none to make opposition against him, or hinder his exaltation to the *Zenith* of Pontificall dignity, but onely God, and the sting of his owne most guilty conscience, both which (though you may be sure he lightly regarded, yet) for abundant caution he by a fine sleight and policy will pacifie and appease: for as hitherto he had played the Wolfe and Tiger, so now you shall see him act the Foxe: and that in so lively and native manner, that hee meaneth to cozen not onely all men, but his owne conscience, and Almighty GOD himselfe. As hee had murdered the true & lawfull Pope *Silverius*,so in token of remorse he will needs die & kill himselfe also,being the usurping Pope:but his death is no other than they fancy of Antichrist the beast in the Apocalyps;he dyeth,but within few dayes he revives againe.He considered he had entred violétly & injuriously into the See;that he was as yet nothing but a mere intruder and usurper of it;the holy & conscionable man will not hold his dignity by so bad a title:and therefore [t] *abdicat se pontificatu,he puts off his Popedome*;& considering [u] how he was blemished with Symony, heresie, murder, and other crimes, that he was also excommunicated and accursed,*à sede male occupata descendit*,he forsakes & comes downe from the papall chaire,and resignes the keies into the hands of S.*Peter* or Christ,and makes the See void,that there might be a new election of a lawfull Pope. They shall chuse freely whom they will,as for himself,either they shall bring him by a lawfull election in at the doore,or he (so côscionable is the Fox now become)wil for ever stand without: climbe in at the window he will no more; either Christ himselfe shall reach the keyes unto him, that he may be his lawfull Vicar, or open and shut who will for *Vigilius*. Thus by the death of *Silverius*,   the

the true and lawful Pope, and by the abdication or resignation (which is a death in law) of the usurping Pope *Vigilius*, the See is wholly vacant, and that was, as *Anastasius* [x] witnesseth, for the space of sixe dayes.

15. In this vacancy of the See *Baronius* not onely tels you, that there was (w[ch] is not unlike) very great deliberatiō about the election of a new Pope, but, as if hee had beene present in the very conclave at that time, or as if by some Pythagoricall *metempseuchosis* the soules of some of those Electors, comming from one beast to another, had at last entred into the Cardinals breast, declares their whole debatement of the matter, *pro & con*, what was said for *Vigilius*, what against *Vigilius*; which kinde of poetry, if any be pleased with, they may have abundance of it in his Annals; for my selfe, I told you before I never dreamed as yet in their Romane *Parnassus*, that I dare presume to vent such fictions & fancies: in that one he sounded the depth indeed both of *Vigilius* counsels, and of the consultations of the Electors; Of *Vigilius* hee saith [y], *that hee gave over the Popedome, not with any purpose to leave it, but, as it were, to act a part in a comedy, and seeme to doe that which he never meant*, & that he did it, [z] *fretus potentia Bellisarij, quod esset eum mox iterum conscensurus*; because he knew, that by the meanes of *Bellisarius* hee should shortly after bee elected and placed in it againe; or, to use the Cardinals own comparison, he did not play [a] at mum chance, but knowing how the election would goe after hee had given over, *haud dubiam jecit aleam*, hee knew what his cast would be, and what side of the Die would fall upward, hee knew his cast would bee better than *jactus venereus*, it would be the cast of the triple Crowne; As for the Electors [b] he tels us, *that they chose him not for any worth, piety, vertue, or such like Pontificall qualifications*, (of which they saw none in him) *but to avoid* [c] *a schisme in the Church*, because they knew if they should choose another, the Empresse and *Bellisarius* would maintaine the right of *Vigilius*, and as they had thrust him in, so they would uphold and maintaine him in the See, and for this cause, at the instance of *Bellisarius*, they all with one consent chose their old friend *Vigilius*, and now make him the true and lawfull Pope, the undoubted Vicar of Christ, which was a fine cast indeed at the Dies.

16. Now though this may seeme unto others, to demonstrate great basenesse and pusilanimitie in the Electors at that time, who fearing a little storme of anger or persecution, would place so unworthy a man in the Papall throne, and though it testifie the present Romane policy to be such, that if *Simon Magus*, nay, the devill himself can once but be intruded into their Chaire, & put in possession thereof, he shall be sure to hold it, with the Electors consent, if hee can but storme and threaten in a Pilates voyce to incense the Emperour, or some potent King to revenge his wrong, if they ever choose any other; yet the Cardinal who was privy to the mysteries of their Conclave, commends [d] this for *salubre consilium*, a very wholesome advice; & wisely was it done to chuse *Vigilius*, nay, as if that were too little, he adds, it was, *Divinitus inspiratum consilium*, God himself inspired this divine counsell from heaven into their hearts, rather to choose an ambitious,

SsS3   ous,

Marginal notes:

x *Cessavit Episcopatus dies sex. Anast. in vit. Silv. Ex quibus intelligas Vigilium qui sedem usurpasset ad hoc tempus, minimè diutius sedere perseverasse. Ba. an. 540. nu. 4*

y *Bar. an. 540. nu. 5. quod Vigilius id fecerit tanquam repræsentans in scena comædiam, non ex animo, facile mihi persuadeo.*

z *Bar. ibid. nu. 4 Et, vaser homo, hujusmodi sibi viam aperientiâ curavit, ut ob perpetrata delicta ejici inde nunquam posset, securus de Bellisarij voluntate, &c. Bar. an. eod. 540. nu. 5.*

a *Haud dubiam jecit aleam, cum sciret eandem quam vellet, faciē redituram. Bar. ib. nu. 5.*

b *Clerus longè abhorret, ut hominem tot criminibus implicatum in sedem eveheret Pontificiam, id præsertim sacris Ecclesiæ legibus prohibentibus, et omnes, ut ab execrando facinore, ab ejus electione, longè longius abhorreret. Bar. an. 540. nu. 7.*

c *Contra, accuratius rem expendere manifestè cernebant si alium eligerent, scindendam mox fore Ecclesiam, dito schismate, ideo divinitus inspirato consilio evehunt ipsum in Pont. thronū, &c Bar. an. 540. nu. 7. & 8.*

d *Bar. ibid. nu. 8.*

ous, an hypocriticall, a Symoniacall, a schismaticall, an hereticall, a perfidious, a perjured, a murderous, a degraded, an accursed, a diabolicall person to be their Pope, rather than hazzard to sustain a snuffe of *Bellisarius*, or a frowne of *Theodoraes* countenance. Howsoever, chosen now *Vigilius* was by common consent, and *solennibus* [c] *ritibus*, made the true and lawfull Pope from thence forward, and with all solemnity of their rites placed in the Papall throne, and put, not onely in the lawfull, but quiet and peaceable possession thereof, the whole Romane Church approving and applauding the same. Thus *Vigilius* at last got what in his ambitious desires hee so long gaped and thirsted after: At the first onset hee sought the Papacy, but got it not; at the second turne hee got it, but by usurpation and intrusion onely; but now at this third and last boute hee hit the marke indeed, hee got the rightfull possession of it, and is now become what hee would bee, the true Bishop of *Rome*, and Vicar of S. *Peter*.

16. I have stayed somewhat long in the entrance of *Vigilius*, and yet because I have set downe no more but a very σκίασμα, a naked & undecked narration, or as it were, onely rough hewed; I must pray the reader that hee will permit mee to set downe some few exornations and polishments of it out of Cardinall *Baronius*, for though all men knew him to bee one, whose words concerning their Popes are as smooth as oyle, and who will bee sure to say no more ill of any of them, than meere necessity and evidence of truth inforceth him, yet so unfit am I to write their Popes lives, that for want of fit termes I am inforced to borrow from him the whole garnish and varnish of this Description of *Vigilius*; heare then no longer mee, but the great Cardinall, the deare friend of *Vigilius*, telling you what a worthy man the Electors at this time chose for their Pope: heare him defining *Vigilius* in this manner; Hee was an ambitious [f] Deacon, who by a madde [g] desire, burned with pride, whom thirst [h] of vaine glory drove into madnesse, and into the hellish gulfe, by meanes whereof he makes shipwracke in the very haven, becomes a Rocke of offence, and seemes an infidell in faith; a bondslave [i] to impious and hereticall *Theodora*, that is, to *Megera* [k], to *Alecto* and the hellish furies, who, with *Lucifer*, desired to ascend [l] into heaven, and exalt his throne above the Starres, but being loaden with the weight of his heinous crimes, fals downe into the depth, which crimes with *Cain* [m] he having so inclosed in his breast, must needs wander up and down like a Vagabond: Vnsavory salt [n], worthy by all to bee trodden under foote, and cast into the dunghill of heresies, who had got unto him the stench [o] of heretical pravity, who bound himselfe [p] by an obligation under his owne hand, yea by his oath also, to patronize heretikes, who promised [q] to abolish the faith and Councell of *Chalcedon*. It was the just iudgement [r] of God that hee should fall from the faith, who became a Vassall to vaine glory, a schismatike [s], a Symoniacke [t], a murderer [u], whose sacriledges [x] cried

c *Bar. ibid.*
f *Ab ambitioso Diacono procurata. Bar. an. 538. nu. 9.*
g *Insana cupiditate flagrans ambitione Vigilius. Ibid. nu. 5.*
h *Eum in quod baratbrum infelice hominem conjecit ambitio, in quantam insaniam, & infamiam adegit eu vanæ gloriæ cupido, cujus cau̅sa cogatur in ipso portu pati naufragium, & in Petra Petræ scandalum esse, et in fide infidelem haberi. Ibid. nu. 17.*
i *Se Theodoræ Augustæ instar mancipij turpissimè vendidit. Bar. an. 540. nu. 8.*
k *Accipiat (Theodora) nomen potius ab inferis, Alecto, vel Megera, vel Tisiphone nu̅cupanda. Bar. an. 535. nu. 63.*
l *Du̅m sursum ascendere meditatur, deorsum demergitur. An. 538. nu. 18.*
m *Vagetur necesse est cum Caine qui intus clausum habet, quod eum agit in adversa, peccatum. Ibid.*
n *Quid reliquu̅ esse potuit salis infatuati, nisi ut conculcetur et proijciatur in sterquilinium heresum. An. 538. nu. 17.*
o *Putorem contraxit heretica pravitatis. Ibid.*
p *Pactis conventis conscripta jurataque hereticorum defensio. An. 540. nu. 4.* profiteri flagitavit, ut tolleret Synodum, lubenter suscepit Vigilius promissum ejus. Hæc cum ipsa sacrilega fœmina molita est. An. 536. nu. 123.
q *Augusta Vigilium sibi*
r *Ita planè sententia̅ Domini judicatur à fide excidere qui gloriæ mancipium se constituit. An. 538. nu. 17.*
s *Vigilij schismatica, an. 538. nu. 20.*
t *Athenæ sedis emptor. Ibid. et Symoniaca labes eum deturpavit. An. 540. nu. 4.*
u *Sil. very necis cooperatia eum reda̅rgua̅t. Ibid.*
x *Clamantibus undique sacrilegis, an. 538. nu. 19.*

unto heaven, an usurper [y], a violent invader, an intruder of the *Apostolike* See, a bastard [z] and unlawfull Pope, whom the true and lawfull Pope hath bound [a] with eternall chaines, against whom hee hath shot the dart [b] of damnation, and shewed to the whole world that he ascended into the throne, *ut lapsu graviore ruat,* that hee might have a greater and more shamefull fall, that hee did not represent [c], nor was the successor of *Simon Peter,* but of *Simon Magus,* and that hee is the Vicar, not of Christ, but of Antichrist, an Idol [d], even the abomination of desolation standing in the holy place, and set up in the temple of God; one rightly [e] to bee called by no other name than a Wolfe, a Thiefe, a Robber, a Pseudobishop, and even Antichrist: and, which after all the rest is especially to bee remembred as the cloze of the Cardinals Description, all this time *Vigilius* [f] both was, and was known to the Electors, to be a very sound and true Catholike. A true Catholike? Such Catholikes indeed doth the Cardinall describe and commend unto the world; a Catholike Schismatike, a Catholike heretike, a Catholike Antichrist, a Catholike Devill: If such were their Romane Catholikes and Catholike Popes in those ancient times, O gracious God, what manner of Catholike Popes are they in these ages? Then, and untill the yeare 606, was the golden age of the Church, their Romane Bishops were then like the head of *Nebuchadnezzers* Image to the late and moderne Popes, *Vigilius* a golden Bishop indeed to the brazen, iron, and clayish Popes of these later ages, the basenesse of which no tongue or pen can expresse; when the gold is so full of drosse, when the heads, which give life, motion, and beeing to all the rest, are so full of abomination, what manner of Catholikes thinke you are the armes, the legs, the feet and tailes of that their Babylonish Image, which all must bee proportionable? But let us returne to *Vigilius,* whom, I hope, you will now confesse to be exactly and graphically described by the pensill of their owne Apelles.

17. After his instalment, wee are to come to his Acts and gests; those, I confesse, are very few in number, they are but two. *Anastasius* a man slavishly addicted to the Papall See; was the chiefe compiler of his life, which had a man of integrity and indifferency writ, it is not unlike but many other matters had bin recorded of *Vigilius,* yet those two are very memorable, and such as most nearely touch the Pontifical office. The former concerns the performance of that promise which *Vigilius* made to *Theodora;* that when he were Pope he would abolish the Councell of *Chalcedon,* and restore *Anthimus, Severus,* and other *Eutychean* deposed Bishops: of it *Liberatus* [g] writes, that *Vigilius, implens promissionem suam quam Augusta fecerat, talem scripsit Epist. fulfilling his promise* w[ch] he had made to the *Empresse,* writ this *Epistle. Victor B.* of *Tune,* sheweth [h] also, that *Vigilius* by the means of *Antonia* the wife of *Bellisarius,* writ unto *Theodosius* of *Alexandria, Anthimus* of *Constantinople,* and *Severus* of *Antioch,* a good while since condemned by the Apostolike See, *tanquam Catholicis, as unto Catholikes,* & signified, that himselfe was of the same opinion concerning the faith with them. The summe then of the Epistle of Pope *Vigilius* was to signifie to these hereticall and deposed Bishops, that himselfe was an Eutychean, as they were;

[Marginal notes:]

y *Situ: y vixentis sedem ajurpasse, & malis artibus nactam esse, imo & vixisse eum intelligit, an. 540. nu. 4. violentus intrusor, an. 538. nu. 11.*

z *Agit Rom. Pontificem, quamvis spurius, et penitus illegitimus, an. 538. nu. 21.*

a *Sciens cunctos sibi subjectos, quos vel absolvat, vel eternis vinculis obliget, authoritate, &c. an. 539. nu. 4.*

b *Adversus Romanæ Ecclesiæ invasorem, spuriúsque intrusum Pontificem, valide telum damnationis intorquet, an. 539. nu. 4.*

c *Silverius ostendit universo orbi, Vigilium non referre Simonem Petrum, sed Magum, neque Vicarium Christi, sed Antichristum. ibid.*

d *Cernebant quod rursus Idolum collocandum esset in Templo, constituendáque abominationem desolationis stante in loco sancta, an. 540. nu. 7.*

e *Quonam alio nomine quam lupus, fur et latro, Pseudoepiscopus, ac denique Antichristus jure potuit appellari? an 538. nu. 20.*

t *Cum Vigilij personam satis perspectam haberent, cum semper esse hominem vevera Catholicum, an. 540. nu. 8.*

g *Lib. ca. 22.*

h *Vict . in Chron.*

were,the Epiftle it felfe, fet downe both in *Liberatus* and in *Victor*, clearly teftifieth the fame,for therein *Vigilius* writeth thus, *eam fidem quam tenetis,Deo adjuvante, & tenuiffe me,& tenere fignifico,I fignifie un-to you,that,by Gods helpe,I have held,and doe now hold the fame faith which you doe*: but the Pope adds one claufe further for fecrefie,wel worthy obferving;*Oportet ut hæc quæ fcribo nullus agnofcat,it is needfull,that none know of thefe things which I write unto you*, but rather your wifedome muft have me in fufpition, more than any other, that fo I may more eafily effect,and bring to paffe thofe things which I have begun. See you not here, as in a glaffe,the deep hypocrifie and herefie of *Vigilius* ? with what fubtilty and clofeneffe he labours to undermine the Coun-cell of *Chalcedon*,and the whole Catholike faith, even then when hee would feeme to favour it, and therefore wifheth the Eutycheans to fpeake of him as one who they fufpected moft of all to bee againft them. *Liberatus* adds,that *Vigilius* under his Epiftle writ a confeffion of his faith alfo,*in quá duas in Chrifto damnavit naturas, wherein hee con-demned the teaching of two natures* in Chrift: and diffolving the Tome of Pope *Leo*,hee faid,*non duas Chrifti naturas confitemur, we doe not acknow-ledge two natures in Chrift*,but one Sonne, one Chrift, one Lord com-pofed of two natures,(to wit, two before the adunation) and againe, *qui dicit in Chrifto duas formas, whofoever faith that there are two formes or natures in Chrift*, either working according to his owne property, and doth not confeffe one perfon, one effence, *anathema fit, let fuch a man be accurfed*.Could *Arius, Eutyches*,or any heretike in the world more plainly condemne and accurfe the Councell of *Nice*,of *Ephefus*, of *Chalcedon*,yea, the whole Catholike Church,and Catholike faith ? It is here a fine fport to fee how the two Cardinals,*Baronius* and *Bel-larmine*, how other pettifoggers,fuch as *Gretzer* and *Binius*,doe here beftirre themfelves to quit *Vigilius* of this blemifh,and of the herefie and impiety taught in this Epiftle. Firft, *Vigilius* writ not this Epiftle, it is but a counterfeit and forgery : Next, if hee did write it, yet he did it while he was an ufurper,not when hee was the true and lawfull Pope. Laftly, hee did not hereby embrace herefie *ex animo*,nor define it as Pope,but onely by an exteriour act hee condemned the faith. Thus they toile themfelves to wafh the Ethiopian,and turne a Black-amore into a mike white Swanne.

18. Truely, I am exceeding loath now at the fhutting up of this Treatife,and after founding of the retreat, to enter into a new & frefh conflict,and prove *Vigilius* to have taught Eutycheanifme,as before I have fhewed, that hee taught the quite contrarie herefie of Neftoria-nifme, might I not fay, *Spectatum fatis & donatum jam rude, tandem, Quæritis hoc iterum antiquo me includere ludo?* I have not now the like vi-gor of minde at the putting off of the armour,as at the firft comming into the field; and, to fay truth, what courage can I or any have to fight againft a foiled enemy,which is but to cut off a dead mans head, by proving him to bee an heretike, who is not onely proved, but by moft ample judgment and fentence of the whole Catholike Church, already condemned for an heretike ? yet becaufe I have a defire to handle this whole argument concerning *Vigilius*, if the reader bee not
as

as much tyred as my selfe, after conquest of the generall, I will, as *Abner* did, play a little with these stragling Asaels in this point also; or if you please to suffer me to give aime a while, I will onely *παρακύπτειν*, commit the two Cardinals into the pit to fight it out, and day the matter betwixt themselves.

19. *Commentitium est, it is a forged Epistle,* saith Cardinall [k] *Baronius,* it is none of *Vigilius* writing. I here one say so, saith Cardinall *Bellarmine* [l], but I say, *Vigilium scripsisse illam Epistolam, & damnasse Catholicam fidem,* that *Vigilius* did write that Epistle, and condemne the Catholike faith, *Epistolam quidem scripsit nefariam,* truely he writ [m] that nefarious Epistle, unworthy of any Christian. Here is worke indeed, saying against saying, Cardinall against Cardinall, and whether Cardinall is the stronger let the spectators consider: But the best sport is, that whereas Cardinall *Baronius* [n] tels us, that this Epistle was written by some unskilfull Eutychean heretike, and Cardinall [o] *Bellarmine* tels us, that it was writ by *Vigilius,* it followeth upon the two Cardinals sayings joyned together, that *Vigilius* was both an heretike, and an unskilfull Eutychean heretike.

20. From their words let us come to their strokes and sad blowes, *Causa cum causa, ratio cum ratione pugnet.* Cardinall *Bellarmine* hath but one reason, but that is indeed a very sound one, like the Cat in the fable, which hath but one shift against the hounds; his reason [p] is the testimony of Saint [q] *Liberatus* who then lived, who not onely testifieth *Vigilius* to have writ this, but sets downe the very Epistle it selfe of *Vigilius*; and whereas some pretended both that *Liberatus* was corrupted by heretikes, and that his narration was contrary to their Pontificall; the Card. tels us for a certainty, that there [r] is neither any footstep nor print of corruption in *Liberatus,* neither doth he [s] herein dissent from the Pontificall. Cardinall *Baronius* boasteth [t] of his reason, as the Fox did in the same fable, that he had a number of sleights and shifts to deceive the dogs; but the hounds comming suddenly upon them both, the Cat skipt into a tree, which was her onely pollicy, and there shee saw the Fox with all his hundreth wiles torne in pieces: even such are Cardinall *Baronius* his sleights in this cause; hee hath many, but never a one that is worth a Rush, none that would save from tearing if the hounds should happen to come upon him. His first is, because the [u] Acts of the sixt generall Councell doe shew, that heretikes had counterfaited some Epistles in the name of *Vigilius,* and particularly those bookes, which are said to be writ from *Vigilius* to *Iustinian* and *Theodora* of blessed memory. Thus say the Acts; To which the Card. assumes, *sane quidem inscriptio recitata Epistolæ; Truly the inscription of the Epist. recited in the name of Vigilius, ad Dominos, to my Lords,* doth demonstrate that it was written to *Iust.* and *Theodora.* Alas that this must be one of the Cardinals shifts, and that it must bee for the worth of it stiled [x] a demonstration: Why, there needs here, neither mastive nor hound, any beagle or brache will rent this reason into 20. pieces. First, what meant the Cardinal to expresse the words of the sixt Councell, where *Theodora* is called an Empresse of blessed memory? had he forgot what in another place [y] hee said, *that she died miserably,*

k *Bar.dn.538. nu.15.*

l *Bell.lib.4.de Pont.ca.10.*

m *Bell.ca.eod.*

n *Nomine Vigily ab aliquo Eutychiano esse suppositam, eoque imperito, ex plaribus colligi potest.Bar.an.538 nu.19.*

o *Bell.loc.cit.*

p *Bell.loc.cit.*

q *Breviarium collectum à sancto Liberato, sic inscribitur apud Binium.to.2.pa.610.*

r *Vestigium nullum apparet corruptionis in libro Liberati. Bell.*

s *Revera non pugnat narratio Liberati, cum narratione Pontificalis. Ibid.*

t *Plura sunt quæ persuadent. Bar. an.538.nu.15. et ex pluribus colligi potest. An. eod.nu.19.*

u *Bar. an. 538. nu.19.*

x *Inscriptio ad Dominos, demonstrat hanc Epistolam scriptam esse ad Just.et Theodoram. Bar.ibid.*

y *Bar.an.545. nu.24.*

miferably, being blafted by the Popes thunder-clap? Againe what a demonftration is this; fome Epiftles were forged in the name of *Vigilius, ergo,* this is forged. *A pari,* fome bookes are forged, the Cardinals Annals are fome bookes,*ergo,* they are all forged; or fome man is as wife as *Chorebus,ergo,* fo is the Cardinall. Take heed, I pray you, the hounds fent not thefe confequences of the Cardinall, grounded on that old maxime, *A particulari non eft Syllogifari.* Further yet, what a reafon call you this; fome bookes fent in *Vigilius* name to *Iuftinian* and *Theodora,* were forged,*ergo,* this Epift. is forged. It is a demonftration,*à baculo ad Angulum,* for this Epiftle was writ neither to *Iuftinian,* nor to *Theodora,* but to *Anthimus,Theodofius* and *Severus;* The Cardinall may know this clearly by *Victor,* who teftifieth the fame in expreffe words; he might have perceived it by *Liberatus,* who faith, that *Vigilius* writ this Epiftle to heretikes; whereas not Pope *Leo* himfelfe was more orthodoxall in this point than *Iuftinian,* as befides infinite other proofes, is evident both by his Epiftle [z] to *Mennas,* confirming the depofition of *Anthimus,* and by that his Epiftle [a] written to *Epiphanius* Bifhop of *Conftantincple,* foure [b] years before *Silverius* was expelled, wherein hee profeffeth to embrace all the foure Councels, and hee anathematizeth all that are anathematized by any of them, declaring that he will not permit within his Empire any that oppugned thofe Councels. But for all this the Card. will prove by the Infcription [c] of this Epiftle, that it written to *Iuftinian* and *Theodora.* What if it were? can hee prove withall that no other Epiftle or booke was writ to them in the name of *Vigilius?* No, hee never offers to prove that, and till that bee proved his reafon at the beft is but *à particulari,* fome Epiftle writ in the name of *Vigilius* to *Iuftinian* and *Theodora* was forged, *ergo,* this; fome man deferves a whetftone,*ergo,* fo doth the Cardinall. Befides this inconfequence, the Antecedent is fo falfe that I am afhamed to take the renowned Cardinall fo tripping in his demonftration: The Infcription, faith hee, demonftrates that it was writ to *Iuftinian* and *Theodora.* Truly the Infcription demonftrates the Cardinall to be of no truth or credit at al. The Infcription in *Liberatus* (and him the [d] Cardinal followeth) is *Dominis & Chriftis* [e] *Vigilius,Vigilius tó my Lords and Chrifts.* An Infcription indeed with a witneffe, and a leffon for the Cardinall; *Iuftinian* Chrift, *Theodora* Chrift, and yet the Cardinall rankes the one Chrift among the Furies of hell, the other Chrift hee condemnes to the pit and torments of hell; what a Cardinall to bee fo malitious and fpightfull againft Chrift, and Chrifts?

21 The Infcription, faith the Cardinall, points [f] at *Iuftinian* and *Theodora:* I rejoyce to fee the Cardinall once fo charitably affected, as to thinke *Iuftinian* to be Chrift, *Theodora* Chrift, let all applaud the Cardinall in this faying; feldome fhall you take him, nor will hee long perfift in fo good a mood or minde. The Infcription of the Epiftle is to Chrifts, the Infcription demonftrates and points at them, as the Cardinall tels us; Chrifts then they were, Chrifts they are againft the fpite of all flandering tongues, Chrifts let them bee, and with Chrift let them reft forever. But will you now fee a fine fleight indeed

[z] *Conftitutio Iuftiniani vocatur. Extat autem poft finem Conc. Conftantinopolitani fub Menna. 10.2.pa.469.*
[a] *Epiftola illa ad Epiphanium extat.Leg.7.Cod. de fumma Triz.*
[b] *Data eft ea Epift. Iuft. 3. Conful. Is eft an. 533.*
[c] *Sane quidem Infcriptio demonftrat.Bar. an.538.nu.19.*

[d] *Bar.an.538. nu.13.*
[e] *Sic habetur in Lib.c.22. apud Bin.pa.624.b.*

[f] *Demonftrat.*

deed of the Cardinall, such as put downe the Fox, and Cat, and all. Truely, saith hee, the Inscription, *ad Dominos*, demonstrates, that this Epistle was writ to *Iustinian* and *Theodora* : why, what meanes this Inscription, *ad Dominos* ? why doth the Cardinal clip away the one halfe of the Inscription? The Inscription in *Liberatus* is, *Dominis & Christis*; the Cardinall belike misdoubted by *Christis* could not bee demonstrated *Iustinian* and *Theodora*, *Christus* is the Popes prerogative, it demonstrates him, and therefore lest the Pope should frowne upon the Cardinall for saying this Inscription, *Dominis ac Christis*, doe demonstrate *Iustinian* and *Theodora*, hee corrupts the Text, and maimes the Inscription, and makes it to bee but *ad Dominos*, and so the Inscription, *ad Dominos*, may well point at the Emperour and Empresse.

22. Yet take the Cardinals maimed Inscription as it is, doth this title, *ad Dominos*, demonstrate the Emperour ? may not one write *Domino*, or *ad Dominum*, but onely to the Emperour ? how many thousand millions of Emperors will the Cardinall coine unto us ? every servant, every prentise may write, *Domino*, or *Dominis*, unto their Master, and then by the Cardinals demonstration you shall have Coblers, and Tailors, and Weavers, and all Artificers in the world turned into Emp. and their wifes into Empresses, for, *sanè quidem*, verily this Inscriptiō, *ad Dominos*, demonstrates that the Epist. is writ to the Emperour and Empresse. Doe you think, I say not, that Philosophers and Logicians, but any elementary boy that hath learned to decline *Dominus* can hold himselfe at the hearing of such demonstrations? But to put the matter out of all doubt, and demonstrate the other demonstration to bee as idle a fancie as can be devised, the Inscription which is but in briefe set downe by *Liberatus*, is fully and at large expressed by *Victor*, who lived and writ also at that time : *The tenour (saith hee* [g] *)of Vigilius Epistle is proved to bee thus, Bishop Vigilius, Dominis ac fratribus, to Theodosius, Anthimus and Severus Bishops, my Lords and brethren, joyned to us in the love of Christ our Saviour :* What is now become of the Demonstration, *ad Dominos* ? how doth the Inscription, *ad Dominos*, *sanè quidem*, truly and verily demonstrate *Iustinian* and *Theodora*, when, together with *Dominus*, is expresly set downe and named who those *Domini* were, to whom *Vigilius* writ, even three deposed hereticall Bishops ?

[g] *Vict.Tur. in Chron. sub an. 2. post conf. Basilij.*

23. The Cardinall, and *Binius* [h] following him, will not yet let goe this demonstration, but much please themselves in a new device; The Epistle; saith hee [i], is inscribed also *ad Patres*, now it is unusuall for Popes to call Emperours their Fathers, and therefore sure it is but a counterfeit Epistle in *Vigilius* name : Why, but if Popes doe not use that terme, it is their owne fault, thy might justly so call Emperours; Emperours are the fathers of their whole Empire, and that in a more eminent manner than any other father, Imperiall Fathers, commanding and compelling fathers, fathers superiour to all other fathers, even to all Pontificall fathers; but where, I pray you, is that Inscription *Dominis ac Patribus* ? Not in *Victor*, not in *Liberatus*, at least not in the best Edition of him, not in that which *Binius* hath set forth, there the Inscription is faire, and cleare, *Dominis ac Christis*; and yet so ridicu-

[h] *Bin. in not. ad Liberatum.*
[§] *In historia.*
[i] *Bar. an. 528. nu. 19. Abhorret à consueto scribendi more, &c. et, quodnam unquam extitit praedecessorum exemplum, ut Imperatores Romanus Pontifex Patres nominaret.*

lous

lous was *Binius*, and so foolishly addicted to *Baronius*, that he proves
this Epistle to bee forged, because the Inscription is, *Dominis ac Patri-*
bus, whereas himselfe in the leafe before had set downe the Inscription to bee *Dominis ac Christis*, let it bee *Patribus* : the Cardinall and *Bi-*
nius surely doated when they concluded, that the Epistle was writ to
the Emperour, for as out of *Liberatus*, but most clearely out of *Victors*
words is demonstrated, it was writ to father *Anthimus*, father *Theodo-*
sius, and father *Severus* : *Vigilius* might well call them *Patres*, when in
the Inscription he called them Bishops [k].

k *Dominis*
Theodosio, An-
thimo et Severo
Episcopis. Apud
Victorem loc.
cit.
l *Bar.loc.cit.*

24. And certainly *Baronius* was conscious to himselfe, that this E-
pistle was writ to Bishops, not to the Emperour and Empresse; for as
misdoubting that this would, and justly might bee replied to his demonstration, hee adds [l], *Si dicas scriptum ad Episcopos*, *if you say the Epi-*
stle was written to Bishops, and not to the Emperour, yet even so it is a
forgery also, and why? for, *Qui novus iste mos est*, *what a novelty is it*,
and utterly unusuall, that the Pope should call his fellow Bishops,
Patres & Dominos? or if you say that it should be read *fratribus*, and
not *Patribus*, yet certainly that *procul abhorret*, *is very abhorrent*, that he
should call the same both brethren and Lords. What is the demonstration come now to relye upon this, It is new, It is unusuall; as if
nothing that is new or unusuall were done or writ :   It was new and
unusual to thrust out and murther the true Pope, yet *Vigilius* did it for
all the novelty thereof. Could *Vigilius* act a matter so horrible being
new and unusuall, and might not hee write a phrase, or give a title being new and unusuall? It is unusuall, I trow, for Popes to call hereticall Bishops, deposed by generall Councels, their brethren beloved
in Christ; he that would honour deposed heretikes with such loving
termes, would hee doubt to call them by an unusuall title, *Dominos ac*
Patres, or, *Dominos ac Fratres?* and yet neither of both is so unusuall as
the Cardinall would have it thought. In the Councell at *Barre* [m], when

m *Guil. Malf-*
bur.lib.1.de gest.
Pontif. Angl.pa.
127.

the Greekes disputed against Pope *Vrbane* so eagerly against the pro-
cession of the holy Ghost, that the Pope was at a *non plus*, and unable
to answer,   being driven to that exigent, and remembring that Anselme Archbishop of *Canterbury* was in the Councell, *exclamat he cri-*
ed aloud before the whole Councell, *Pater et Magister Anselme ubi es?*
Oh my father and Master Anselme where are you? come now and defend
your mother the Church.   And when after much crying and
shouting, they brought him in presence among them, Pope *Vr-*
bane said, *includamus hunc in orbe nostro quasi alterius orbis Papam; let us*
inclose him in our circle, as the Pope of the other world. Might not *Vigilius*
do that to three Patriarks, which *Vrbane* did to an Archbishop? might
not *Vigilius* call them fathers, as well as *Vrbane* called *Anselme* father
and Master? Might not that bee done secretly, and in a private letter
which the Pope did openly in the audience of the whole Councell?
Is it more incongruity for the Pope to call the Patriarcke of *Alex-*
andria, or of *Antioch*, his father or Lord, than to call the Patriarke of
England, father, master, yea, Pope in his owne Patriarchal Diocesse in
England?

25. But the Cardinall still harps on a wrong string; *Vigilius* neither

ther in the Inscription, subscription, nor body of the Epistle, called them fathers, but brethren: That title is given them indeed three or foure times, both in *Liberatus* and in *Victor*, *fraternitati vestra*, *fraternitatem vestram, & orate pro nobis mihi fratres in Christo conjuncti: pray for us my brethren in the Lord.* Which evidently shewes, that *Baronius* and *Binius* either themselves corrupted, and followed some corrupt Edition of that Epistle, when they so craftily persist on the Inscription, *Dominis ac Patribus*; for had hee stiled them in the title fathers, hee would not in the Epistle have so often called them brethren, and never once fathers. Now to say as the Cardinall [n] doth, that it is abhorrent either from reason or practice to call the same parties both *Dominos* and *fratres*, argues, either extreme and supine negligence, or obstinate perversinesse in the Cardinall and *Binius*, scarce any thing in antiquity being more frequent. Pope *Damasus* [o] writ a Synodall letter to *Prosper* Bishop of *Numidia*, and others, he inscribes it thus, *Dominis venerabilibus & fratribus Prospero, Leoni, Reparato, Damasus Episcopus: Bishop Damasus to my reverend Lords and Brethren Prosper, &c.* So the Councell of *Carthage* [p] in two letters, written the one to Pope *Boniface*, the other to Pope *Celestine*, writes in both in this manner, *To our Lord and honourable brother*: So *Cyrill* [q] Patriarke of *Alexandria* writ to *Arelius Valentinus*, and the other Africane Bishop, *Dominis honorabilibus, to the honourable Lords*, and holy brethren. In like sort *Atticus* [r] Patriarke of *Constantinople* to the same Africane Bishops, *Dominis sanctis, to the holy Lords*, & our most blessed brethren, fellow Bish. Why might not *Vigilius* call other Patriarks Lords and brethren, when *Atticus, Cyrill*, the Councell of *Carthage*, yea, Pope *Damasus* himselfe called other Bishops, *Dominos ac fratres*. Nay, seeing the Pope is used to inscribe his letters to the Emp. *Dominis ac* [s] *filiis*, or, *Domino ac filio*, as doth P. *Hadria* to *Constant*. and *Irene*, & to *Charles* [t], why may not he as well call his brother as his son, Lord ? is the title of son more compatible with *Dominis*, than the title of brother ? or whether title, thinke you, Lord or brother, may not the Pope give to his fellow Bishops ? the name of brother is almost every where seene in his letters, the Cardinall envies not that unto them; it is the name of *Dominus* that seeme somewhat harsh. The Cardinall would not have the Pope call or account other Bishops his Lords; and yet how can they, even the meanest of them, but bee his Lord, when hee gladly stiles himselfe their servant, yea, servant [u] to every servant of the Lord? So that if the Popes Secretary were well catechized, and knew good manners, his Holines should write thus to his own servants, To my Lord Groome of my stable, to my Lord the Scull of my Kitchen, I am indeed your servant, I am *servus servorum Dei*: But let the title of the Epistle bee howsoever yee will, whether, *Dominis ac Christis*, as it is in *Liberatus*; or, *Dominis & fratribus*, as it is in *Victor*; or, *Dominis & Patribus*, as the Cardinall (without any authority that I can finde) would have it, certaine it is, that the parties to whom *Vigilius* writ it, were the three deposed Bishops to whom *Vigilius* was like to give any of all those titles, and not to the Emperour and Empresse, as the Cardinall without all shadow of truth, affirmeth, and saith that he hath demonstrated

Tt   the

Marginal notes:

n *Vel si fratres legas, certè procul abhorret, ut eisdem dicat. & Dominos. Bar. an. 538. nu. 19.*

o *Epist. S. Damasi apud. Bin. to. 1. Conc. pa. 501.*

p *Habentur in Concil. Africano sub Calest. et Bonif. ca. 101. et 105.*

to. 1. Conc. pa. 644. & 645.

q *In eodem Conc. Afric. ca. 102.*

r *In eodem Conc. ca. 103.*

s *Sic Adrianus scribit ad. Constantinum et Irenem. Tom. 3. Conc. pa. 254.*

t *Adrianus Papa to. cod. pa. 263.*

u *Servus servorum Dei, sic se scribit Gregor. 7. qui priùs Hildebrandus dictus est. Epist. 13, 14. et reliquis plus centies.*

the same, but it is with such a demonstration as was never found in any but in *Chorebus* his Analyticks.

26. Another of the Cardinals reasons to prove this Epistle to be a forgery, is taken from a repugnance and contrariety of the words in the Subscription, wherein *Vigilius* [x] first professeth to hold but one nature in Christ, and then anathematizeth *Dioscorus*, who held the same. The Cardinall should have proved, that *Vigilius* could not, or did not write contrarieties. As the Cardinall, though he hath beene so often taken tardy in contradictions, yet will not deny the Annals for that cause to bee his owne faire birth; so hee might thinke of this writing, though it bee repugnant to it selfe, yet it might proceed from such an unstayed and unstable minde, as *Vigilius* had: But I doe acquit *Vigilius* from this contradiction, it is not his, hee condemned not *Dioscorus* in his Subscription. In his Epistle he professeth to hold the same doctrine of one onely nature in Christ with *Eutyches* and *Dioscorus*; there is little reason then to thinke, that hee did in his Subscription adjoyned, condemne the professors of that doctrine, of which *Dioscorus* was one of the chiefe, as deepe in that heresie as *Eutyches* himselfe: What shall wee say then to *Liberatus*, in whom *Dioscorus* is named? Truely had not malice and spight shut the eyes of *Baronius* and *Binius*, they could not but have seene, that the name of *Dioscorus* is by the oversight or negligence of the writer, inserted in stead of *Nestorius*: It was *Nestorius* and not *Dioscorus* whom *Vigilius* there accursed, the very conclusion and coherence, not onely with the Epistle, but with the next precedent words in the Subscription, doe evidently demonstrate thus much; for having professed in his Epistle [y] to hold, as did *Dioscorus*, but one nature in Christ, having againe in his Subscription and next words before, anathematized [z] all who admit two, or deny but one nature in Christ, hee in particular declares who those are, that hee therein anathematized, saying, *Anathematizamus ergo*, therefore we accurse (by this our condemnation of those who deny but one nature) *Paulus Samosatenus, Nestorius, Theodorus*, and *Theodoret*, and all who have or doe embrace their doctrine. Now it was *Nestorius*, not *Dioscorus*, who embraced the same doctrine with *Paulus Samosatenus*, with *Theodorus* of *Mopsvestia*, and *Theodoret*, all these concurred in that one and selfe-same heresie of denying one nature in Christ, they all consented in teaching two natures, making two persons in Christ, which *Dioscorus* and *Eutyches* condemned. Of *Theodorus* and *Theodoret* it is cleare by the Councels, both of *Ephesus* and *Chalcedon*, and the fift Synod. Of *Paulus Samosatenus*, the writing or contestation of the Catholike Clergy of *Constantinople*, set downe in the Acts of *Ephesus* [a], doe certainly witnesse and declare the same; the title of which is to shew, partly, *Nestoriū ejusdem esse sententia cum Paulo Samosateno*, that *Nestorius is of the same opinion with Paulus Samosatenus*; and in the contestation it selfe it is said thus, *I adjure all to publish this our writing for the evident reproofe of Nestorius the heretike, as one who is convinced to teach and openly maintain, eadem prorsus qua Paulus Samosatenus*, the same doctrines altogether which *Paulus Samosatenus* did; and then they expresse seven heretical assertions taught alike by them both.

x *Quo pacto, rogo, potuit Vigilius anathematizare Dioscorum, si cum Dioscoro Eutychianam haeresin praedicat? Haec enim sibi invicem adversantur, ut utraque vera esse non possint. Bar. an. 538. nu. 16. et idem habet Bin. not. in Lib. pa: 626. a.*

y *Eam fidem quam tenetis, & tenere me, et tenuisse significo. Epist. Vigilij in apud Liber. ca. 22. et Vict. Tan. in Chron. an. post Cons. Basilij 2. z Qui dicit in Christo duas formas, et non confitetur unam personam, unam essentiam, Anathema sit. Ibid. apud Liber.*

a To. 1. act. Conc. Ephes. ca. 1.

both. Seeing then *Vigilius* accursed him who taught the same with *Paulus*, *Theodorus*, and *Theodoret*, and that was *Nestorius*, not *Dioscorus* : it is undoubtedly certaine, that not *Dioscorus*, but *Nestorius* was the party written and named by *Vigilius* in his subscription : and that *Dioscorus* was not by *Vigilius*, but by the oversight and negligence of the exscriber of *Liberatus*, wrongfully inserted in stead of *Nestorius*. And truly the like mistakings are not unusuall in *Liberatus*. In this very Chapter it is sayd that *Vigilius* a little after the death of *Agapetus*, and election of *Silverius*, when he came from *Constantinople* to *Rome* with the Empresse her letters for placing him in the Romane See, he found [b] *Bellisarius* at *Ravenna* ; a manifest mistaking of *Ravenna* for *Naples* ; for there, and not at *Ravenna* was *Bellisarius* at that time, as by *Procopius* [c] is evident : and because this is no way prejudiciall to their cause, *Baronius* and *Binius* can there willingly admit [d] an error or slip of memory in *Liberatus*, and not so hastily conclude as here they doe, that because *Bellisarius* was not then at *Ravenna*, as in *Liberatus* is falsly affirmed, therefore that Chapter of *Liberatus* is forged, and not truly written by him. Would his Cardinalship have beene as favourable to *Liberatus* in naming *Dioscorus* for *Nestorius*, which the like evidence of truth and all the circumstances doe necessarily enforce, the Epistle might as well passe for the true writing of *Vigilius*, as that Chapter for the writing of *Liberatus*. In this very Epistle of *Vigilius*, it is said in *Liberatus* [e], I know, *quia ad Sanctitatē vestrā fidei mea crudelitas pervenit, that the cruelty of my faith is before this come to your eares*; and the very same word of *crudelitas fidei* is in *Victor* also, w[ch] argues the fault to be very ancient. It is true that the faith of *Vigilius* was indeed cruell; for he by it cruelly condemned, abolished, and as it were murdered the Councell of *Chalcedon*, that is in truth, the whole Catholike faith: and so this happened to be not onely a true, but a fit and significant error. Yet the Cardinall was so friendly and charitable here, as to thinke that it was but a slip of the penne, or negligence of the writer, in saying *crudelitas*, for *credulitas*, as the Cardinall readeth [f] it; might not by the like negligence, and with lesse disgrace to *Vigilius*, *Dioscorus* slip into the text in stead of *Nestorius* ? In the inscription of the Epistle *Liberatus* reades it, *Dominis ac Christis* ; *Victor*, *Dominis ac fratribus* ; the Cardinall corrects both, and makes it worst of all, *Dominis ac patribus*. May he play the Criticke, and turne *Christis*, or *fratribus*, into *patribus*, and that without, nay against reason, and may not others in the subscription restore *Nestorius* for *Dioscorus*, when the truth and necessary circumstances enforce that correction? It was *Nestorius* then not *Dioscorus* whom *Vigilius* accursed ; it is but the errour or corrupt writing of *Vigilius* Epistle in *Liberatus*, (which wee also condemne) and not the Epistle of *Vigilius* at which the Cardinall unjustly quarrelleth.

27. His third and last shift is worst of all. If *Vigilius* had indeed writ this Epistle, *why then* (saith he [g]) *was it not upbraided unto him at Constantinople, neither by the Empresse Theodora, when shee contended with him, about the restoring of Anthimus, nor by Theodorus Bishop of Cæsarea, and Mennas, when Vigilius excommunicated them both, and they*

b *Quin & Ravenna refert Bellisarium. Liber.ca. 22.*
c *Nam Silverii ait ejectum à Bellisario.p. 287 id fuit anno 3. belli Gothici, ut liquet ex pa.313 ubi ait, Tertius belli hujus annus exibat, at Bellisarius non cepit Ravennam ante finem anni 5. ejus belli, ut ait Proc.340. & 343. ubi ait, Iam annus 5. exibat.*
d *Hic puto Liberatum memoria lapsum, Ravennam pro Neapoli posuisse.Bar.an. 538.nu.7. & idem Bin.Not. in Liber.*
e *Apud Bin. to. 2.pa.514.*
f *Bar.an 538. nu.14.*
g *Bar.an.538.] nu.15.*

vexed him so long ; nor by the Emperour *Iustinian*, when he was furiously in-
raged against him ; nor by the fift *Synod*, which was offended with him for
refusing to come to the Councell ; nor yet by *Facundus*, when he writ angerly
against him ? these were publikely debated, *nec tamen de dicta epistola,
vel usquam mentio* ; yet is there not any mention, or light signification of any
such *Epistle*. Thus the Cardinall. Of whom I againe demand where
he learned to dispute *ab authoritate humana negative* ; the old and good
rule was, *Neque ex negativis recte concludere si vis* ; but the Cardinall
hath new Analytickes, and new-found rules of Art, *Ex negativis po-
teris concludere si vis*. Himselfe witnesseth [h] and proclameth *Vigilius*
to have beene a Synoniack, and to have compacted with *Bellisarius* for
200.peeces of gold, to have beene excommunicated, deposed, degraded, by Pope *Silverius* prououncing out that sentence of his *Apostolike*
authority, and from the mouth of God : why was not this Symony,
why was not this censure of *Silverius* upbraided, neither by *Theodora*,
nor *Theodorus*, nor *Iustinian*, nor the fift Councell, nor *Facundus* ? that
being a publike and knowne censure, had beene a matter of farre gre-
ter disgrace to *Vigilius*, farre more justifiable than the epistle writ privately and secretly to *Anthimus*, and commanded by *Vigilius* to bee
kept close that none might know it. See you not how vaine this shift
of the Cardinall is ? How it crosseth him in his Annals, to slander *Vigilius* as symoniacall, as censured by *Silverius*, both which seeing they
are not upbrayded to him by the forenamed persons, but set downe
in the Cardinals Analytickes, sure they are impostures, and forgeries.
What though none of them upbrayded this Epistle unto him ? Is it
not enough that it is assuredly testified and recorded by S. *Liberatus*,
by Bishop *Victor*, two who lived and writ at that same time ? what if
most of them knew not of this Epistle, which was sent secretly by
Vigilius, and by his advice kept closely by *Anthimus* and *Severus* ?
what if they all knew it, and yet having other crimes enough to object,
thought it needlesse to mention that, as it seemes they did the Symony of *Vigilius*, and censure of *Silverius* ? what if they were not so spitefull as the Cardinall is, and therefore would not say the worst they
could against his Holinesse ?

28. But see the strange dealing of the Cardinall! How or why
should *Theodora* upbrayd this to *Vigilius* for the not restoring of *Anthimus* ? that quarrell for the restoring of *Anthimus* (as I have often
sayd, and clearly proved) was a meere devise and fiction of *Anastasius*,
it was nothing but *Alcibiades* dogs tayle. Or how should *Iustinian* upbraid it, when he was so enraged against *Vigilius*, and persecuted him
for not restoring *Anthimus* ? Seeing neither *Iustinian* persecuted *Vigilius*, nor was enraged against him, but for the space of five of six yeares
they both sang one note, they fully consorted together?or how should
Mennas and *Theodorus* upbraid it, when they were excommunicated by
Vigilius ? Seeing that excommunication, & all the circumstances of it
are merely fictitious, as by the death of *Mennas*, (which was long before that forged excommunication of him) was demonstrated ? Are
not these worthy reasons to disprove this Epistle to bee writ by *Vigilius*, which all relie on fictions, and most untrue and idle fancies ? And
                                                                whether

whether *Facundus* upbraided it or no, may bee questioned, nor will it bee clearly knowne, untill they will suffer *Facundus* to come out of their *Vaticane*, where hee lyeth yet imprisoned. But as for the sift Councell, it was great sillinesse in the Cardinall, once to thinke that they should or would upbraid this Epistle to him, they used the Pope in the most honourable and respectfull manner that could be wished, they uttered no one harsh or hard word against him, but what was rightly said or done by him, as his condemning of *Origen*, his condemning the *Three Chapters* before the time of the Councell, that they often mention and approve it also. They sought by lenity to win the Popes heart to consent unto the truth, which they defended: seeing they could not prevaile with him; yet they would have the whole world to testifie, together with the Popes peevishnesse, their owne lenity, equity and moderation used towards him, and that it was not hatred or contempt of his person, nor any precedent occasion, but onely the truth and equity of that present cause, which enforced them to involve him (remaining obdurate in his heresie) in that *Anathema* which they in generall denounced against all the pertinacious defenders of the *Three Chapters*, of which *Vigilius* was the chiefe, and standard-bearer to the rest. Did the Cardinall thinke with such poore sleights to quit *Vigilius* of this Epistle? If nothing else, truely the very imbecillity and dulnesse of the Cardinals reasons and demonstrations in this point may perswade, that *Vigilius* and none but he was the author of it. *Baronius* was too unadvised without better weapons to enter into the sand, with old Cardinall *Bellarmine* in this cause, who is knowne to bee, *plurimarum palmarum vetus ac nobilis gladiator*, and in this combate with *Baronius* hee hath played the right *Eutellus* indeed. Come, let us give to him in token of his conquest, *corollam & palmam*, and let *Baronius* in remembrance of his foile, leave this Epistle to *Vigilius*, with this Impresse,

Vigilio scriptum hoc, Eutello palma feratur.

29. *Vigilius* now, by just Duell, is proved to bee the true author of this Epistle: Be it so, say they [k], yet that is no prejudice at all to the *Apostolike* See, because he writ it in the time of *Sylverius*, while as yet *Vigilius* was not the lawfull Pope, but an intruder and usurper, and Pseudopope, and herein they all joyne hand in hand, *Bellarmine* with *Baronius*, *Gretzer* and *Binius* with them both. But feare not the tailes of these smoaking firebrands, nor the wrath of *Rhesin, Aram*, and *Remalias* sonne; because they have taken wicked counsell against the truth. Nor needed there here any long contention about this matter, for how doe they prove this saying of theirs, that *Vigilius* writ it whē *Sylverius* lived, and not afterwards. Truly by no other but the Colliers argument, It is so, because it is so, proofe they have none at all, they were so destitute of reasons in this point, that laying this for their foundation to excuse the Pope for teaching heresie, they begge this, or rather take it without begging or asking, by vertue of that place called, *Petitio Principij*. Let us pardon *Binius* and *Gretzer*, who gathered up onely the scraps under the Cardinals tables, but for a Cardinal so basely and beggarly to behave himselfe, as to dispute from such so-

k *Etiamsi ista verè scripsissit Vigilius, nullum tamen ob id infertur prajudicium Apostolicæ sedi, cujus tunc ipse erat invasor, Silverius autem germanus Pontifex. Bar. an. 538. nu. 15. Fecit id cum adhuc viveret Silverius, quo tempore Vigilius non erat Papa, sed Pseudopapa. Bell. lib. 4. de Pont. ca. 10. Non mirum si Pseudoepiscopus et quasi Antichristus ad schisma, hæresin addidisset. Bin. not. in. Lib. pa 626. a. ita etiam Gretz. in Defens. ca. 19. lib. 4. Bell.*

Tt 3　　　　　　　phisticall

phistical topicks, is too foule a shame and blemish to his wit and learning. And why may not wee take upon us the like Magisteriall authority, and to their, I say it is so, oppose, I say it is not so? Doe
they thinke by their bigge lookes, and *sesquipedalia verba,* to down-
face the truth?

30. But because I have no fancy to this Pythagoricall kinde of learning, there are one or two reasons which declare, that *Vigilius* writ
this Epistle after the death of *Silverius,* when he was the onely and
true lawfull Pope; for the former is the narration of *Liberatus,* who in
a continued story of these matters, after the death of *Silverius* relates
how *Vigilius* writ this; *Silverius,* saith he [1], *dyed with famine;* *Vigilius*
autem implens promissum, And *Vigilius* to fulfill his promise, writ this
Epistle. Oh, saith *Gretzer* [m], *Liberatus* useth here an anticipation, and
sets downe that before which fell out after. Prove that *Gretzer;* Prove
it? why, his proofe is like his Masters, It is so; because it is so: Other
proofe you shall have none of *Gretzer:* He thought, belike, his words
should passe for currant pay, as well as a Cardinals, but it was too
foolish presumption in him to take upon him to dispute so *Cardinali-*
ter; that is, without reason; why should it not be thought, seeing we
find nothing to the contrary, that *Liber.* in his narration followed the
order and sequell of things and times, as the law of an historian re-
quires, rather than beleeve *Gretzers* bare saying, that it is disorderly
and contrary to the order of the times and event of things?

31. This will further appeare by the other reason drawne from
the time when this Epistle was written: *Baronius* referres it to the
yeare 538. wherein *Silverius* was expelled, and saith [n], that though
Vigilius had truly writ it, yet it is no prejudice to the *Apostolike* See,
cujus tunc ipse invasor, of which hee was an invader and intruder at that
time when it was written. But the Cardinal is mistaken in this point,
for it is cleare and certaine by the testimony of *Liberatus* [o], that *Vigili-*
us had not writ this Epistle when *Silverius* returned out of exile from
Patara into *Italy;* for *Vigilius* hearing of the returne of *Silverius,* and
being in great feare of losing the Popedome, hee hastened then to
Bellisarius, and intreated him to deliver *Silverius* into his custody, o-
therwise, said hee, *non possum facere quod à me exigis, I cannot doe that*
which you require me.Bellisarius required of him two things, as the same
Liberat. witnesseth, the one to performe his promise to the Empresse,
& that was [p] the overthrowing of the Councel at *Chalcedon:* the other,
to pay him the two hundred pieces of Gold, which hee promised to
himselfe; whereby it is most evident, that at *Silverius* returning into
Italy,Vigilius had done neither of these, and so not writ this Epistle.
Now it is most likely, that *Silverius* returned into *Italy, an.*540. for
seeing he dyed [q] in the month of *Iune* that yeare, and being presently
upon [r] his returne sent away into the Iland of *Palmaria* by *Vigilius,* a
little time, you may be sure, would serve to famish an old & disheart-
tened man. But *Gretzer* easeth us in this point, and plainly professeth [s],
that this Epistle was writ in that same yeare 440. wherein *Silverius*
dyed. If now you doe consider how little time there was betwixt the
death of *Silverius,* and his delivery to *Vigilius,* and how in that short
time

l *Liber.ca.22.*

m *Gret.loc.cit.*

n *Bar.an 538.*
nu.14.& 15.
o *Lib.loc.cit.*
p *Augusta Vigi-*
lium profiteri
flagitavit ut si
Papa fieret tolle-
ret Synodum,
&c.Lubenter
suscepit Vigilius
promissum.Liber.
loc.cit.
q *Silverius hoc*
anno obijt,12.
Kalend.Iulij.
Ba.an.540.nu.2
r *Ita Silverius*
traditus duobus
Vigilij servis,
qui in Palma-
riam abductus
sub eorum custo-
dia defecit ine-
dia.Lib.loc.cit.
s *Mors Silverij*
fuit an.540.et
hoc ipso iridem
anno Vigilius ad
Theodoram
scripsit,promissa
exolvere volens.
Gretz.def.ca.10
lib.4.de Pont.

time also *Vigilius* had a greater worke, and of more importance to
looke unto, than the writing of letters to deposed Bishops, to wit, to
provide that *Silverius* should not live, that himselfe should not bee
expelled his owne See, and how upon *Silverius* death himselfe might
be againe lawfully chosen Pope; none I thinke will suppose that *Vig.*
writ this before *Silverius* death in that yeare; but after it, and after all
his troubles ended; when hee having quiet possession of the See, had
leisure to thinke on such matters. But why stay I in the proofe hereof,
this being clearly testified by *Nauclerus*, who thus writeth [t], *Silverius
being dead, Vigilius was created Pope, quod postquam comperit Theodora,*
which when *Theodora* understood, she writ unto him to performe his promise
about *Anthimus*, but *Vigilius* answered, farre be this from me, I spake unadvisedly before, and I am sorry for it. So *Nauclerus*; who therein no doubt
followed *Anastasius*, for hee [u] having set downe both the same motion
made by *Theodora*, and the answer given by *Vigilius*, *Binius* [x] observes,
that this was done when *Vigilius* was now the rightfull and true
Pope: wherefore seeing *Theodora* writ to Pope *Vigilius*, and that after
the death of *Silverius*, to performe his promise, it is certaine, that before then he had not done it, and so that untill hee was the onely true
and lawfull Pope hee did not write this Epistle, which would have
given full content to *Theodora*; and seeing againe we have clearly proved that hee did write it, it remaineth that hee writ it after the death
of *Silverius*, when himselfe was the onely lawfull and true Bishop of
Rome. One doubt in this matter remaineth, which *Binius* [y] sleightly
mentioneth, for that *Vigilius* after he was true Pope, did not onely a-
nathematize *Anthimus*, and confirme his deposition, but professe himselfe also to defend the Councell of *Chalcedon*, as appeares both by his
Epistle to *Iustinian* and *Mennas*, dated foure months [z] after hee was
the true Pope; and by that answer, which, as *Anastasius* and *Nauclerus*
say, hee sent (in [a] writing) to *Theodora*, that hee would not now restore
Anthimus, being an heretike: Whence it may bee collected, that after
he was once the true and lawfull Pope, *nihil horum dixerit, scripserit vel
egerit, that hee neither said, writ, nor did any such thing*, as it is expressed
in this Epistle, for confirming the heresie of *Eutyches*; for how is it credible, that he should write both these; being directly contrary the one
to the other?

32. I answer, that had *Vigilius* bin an honest man, or a man of credit,
of constancy, and resolution, he would never have thought or dreamed
to write both those. But *Vigilius* was *perpaucorum hominum*, you may
goe through the whole Catalogue of the Romane Popes, (and there
is the best choise of wicked men in all formes and fashions of impiety
to bee found) and not picke out such a *Polipus*, a turncoate, a weather-
cocke, as Pope *Vigilius*: *Baronius* compares him to King *Saul*, and
saith [b], that as soone as hee was made the true Pope, hee was then
Saul inter Prophetas. It is true in many things, hee was like King *Saul*,
but in that act of prophesying, wherein the Cardinal compares them,
there is a marvellous dissimilitude betwixt them; *Saul* was moved by
Gods Spirit, *Vigilius* by his owne will; *Saul* was acted and driven to
utter those prophesies, which God put into his mouth, *Vigilius* himselfe

t *Naucl.Gener.* 18.

u *Anast.in vit. Vigilij.*
x *Ecce ut Vigil. statim ac san- ctam sedem as- cendit, &c. Bin. not.in vit.Vig.*

y *Bin.not.in vit. Vig.* § *Ex Actis*

z *Epist.Vigilij ad Mennam* 15 *Calend.Octob. data est.Ea ex- tat apud Bar.an.* 540.nu.25. *et eodem tempo- re missa est etiam illa ad Iustinia- num, apud Bar. an.*540. *nu.* 15. *et* 22.
a *Ad hec re- scripsit Vigilius. Anast. in vit. Vig.*

b *Bar.an.*540. *nu.*13.

33. Wee have now proved, firſt, that *Vigilius* writ this hereticall Epiſtle againſt their firſt evaſion, next that hee writ it when hee was the onely true and lawfull Pope, againſt their ſecond evaſion; there remains as yet two other Pretences of *Bellarmine*; but ſuch, as *Baronius* was aſhamed to uſe ſo poore and petty excuſes for their Pope. The third evaſion then is this, that *Vigilius* in heart embraced the true faith, and onely fained himſelfe in this Epiſtle to be a favourer of the Eutychean hereſie. *Vigilius*, ſaith the Cardinall [d], was here in a great ſtraite, for if hee openly profeſſed hereſie; hee feared the Romanes, who would never indure an heretike to ſit in *Peters* Chaire; if hee ſhould on the other ſide profeſſe himſelfe a Catholike, he feared *Theodora* the hereticall Empreſſe, that ſhe would not indure him; *Itaque rationem illam excogitavit, therfore he deviſed this policy*, (and I pray you note it well) that [e] at *Rome* (or openly) hee would play the Catholike; but (ſecretly) in his private letters to the Empreſſe, and to *Anthimus*, he would faine himſelfe an heretike. Thus *Bellarmine*, who fully expreſſeth the nature and diſpoſition of Pope *Vigilius*, as if hee had not onely felt his pulſe, but beene in his boſome : Hee was indeed another *Catiline, Simulare, ac diſſimulare, hee could ſemble and diſſemble*, conceale what indeed hee was, ſeeme to bee what hee was not : At *Rome*, and in ſhew of the world a Catholike; at *Conſtantinople*, and in his ſecret and cloſe actions an heretike. Thus farre the Cardinall ſaith well; but hee is extremely miſtaken in one circumſtance, in that hee ſaith, that his open or Catholike profeſſion was mentall, and *ex animo*, and his private and ſecret deteſtation of the Catholike faith, was verball and fained. It was quite contrary, his heart and Intrals were all hereticall, nothing but his face and outward ſhew was Catholike : for proofe whereof I will not urge, that the Pope in this Epiſtle accurſeth and [f] anathematizeth all who hold the Catholike faith, or who beleeve otherwiſe than *Eutyches* did, for ſo hee doth alſo in his other Epiſtle to the Emperour and *Mennas*, condemne Eutycheaniſme; and yet it is no commendation for his Holineſſe, either to curſe the Catholike faith, or to curſe that faith which in his heart hee beleeveth. But this I would have conſidered, that *Vigilius* promiſed [g] under his hand-writing, yea, hee ſwore [h] alſo that he would aboliſh the Councell of *Chalcedon*, and reſtore *Anthimus*; for performance whereof hee writ[i] that private Epiſtle, which was all that as yet hee could doe. Let *Bellarmine* now ſay, if their Popes doe uſe to promiſe, and that under their hands, yea, to ſweare alſo to doe that, which they meane not to doe. Who may bee beleeved upon their words, upon their oathes, if not the Popes Holineſſe ? if hee, not onely in words and writing, but in his ſolemne oathes equivocate, whoſe oath, among all that generation, can bee thought ſimple and without fraud ?

34. Againe, to what end ſhould Pope *Vigilius* diſſemble ſecretly and among his intire friends, ſuch as were *Anthimus, Theodoſius*, and *Severus* ? where or to whom ſhould he truly open himſelfe and his inward heart, if not to ſuch ? The firſt leſſon that men of *Vigilius* metall learne, is that of *Lucilius* [k], *Homini amico ac familiari non eſt mentiri*
                                                                meum;

d *Bell.lib.4.de Pontiſ.ca.10. § Sciendum.*

e *Vt Roma Catholicum ageret, et interim per literas apud Imperatricem, hareticum ſimularet-Bell. ibid.*

f *Qui dicit in Chriſto duas formas (i. naturas) et non confitetur unam perſonam unam eſſentiam anathema ſit. Vigil. in Epiſt. apud Liber. loc. cit.*
g *Adimple nobis quæ pronâ voluntate promiſiſti. Anaſt. in vita Vigil.*
h *Conſcriptaque jurataque hereticorum defenſio. Bar. an. §40. nu.4.*
i *Vigilius impleus promiſſionê ſuam quam Auguſtæ fecerat, tale ſcripſit Epiſtolam. Liber.ca.22*
k *Ex quo citat Lactant.lib.6. divin. Inſt. ca.18.*

meum. The *Priscilians*, who as S. *Austen* [l] shewes, were the very teachers of lying and dissembling, and who perswaded their fellow heretikes unto that base art and trade; yet even they taught that Lucilian lesson, (and most impiously pretended [m] to collect it out of the words of the Apostle) Speake the truth every man to his neighbour, for we are members one of another. To his neighbour and fellow member, sayd they, we must speake the truth: but to such as are not joyned [n] to us in the neighbourhood or fellowship of the same Religion, and who are not of the same body with us, to them *loqui licet oportetq, mendacium,* to them you may lye, nay you must not speake the truth to such. *Anthimus, Severus,* and *Theodosius,* they were the next neighbours to *Vigilius,* all conjoyned [o] and concorporated into *Eutycheanisme.* Had he dissembled with them, he had beene worse than the *Priscilianists,* nay worse than the devils themselves, for they though they lye to all others, yet speake truth among themselves, and to *Beelzebub,* otherwise his kingdome could not endure. It was *Iustinian* and the Catholikes, who were of a contrary religion to *Vigilius,* there was little or no neighbourhood at all betwixt them: they were not concorporall, not members of one body with him, to them not being his neighbors, *& commembres* with him by the rules of that blacke Art, he might, he ought to lye: but to *Anthimus* and *Severus,* being of one body with him, he must speake the truth.

35. Further yet, looke to that old Cassian rule, *Cui bono?* where, and with whom was Pope *Vigilius* to gaine more by his cogging and counterfeiting? He had now rightfull possession of the See of *Rome,* which was the onely marke he aymed at. What hurt could three deposed Bishops, or the Empresse her selfe doe now unto him, being backt by the Emperor, by all Catholikes, and which is best, by a good cause? what needed he for pleasing them to faine himselfe an heretike? Could they thrust *Vigilius* from his See, who could not hold their owne? or could the Empresse deprive *Vigilius,* who could not restore *Anthimus?* There was nothing that could move *Vigilius* to faine himselfe an heretike, or to write that hereticall Epistle, if he had been in heart a Catholike. But being in heart hereticall, there was many most urgent and necessary inducements, why he should faine himselfe a Catholike. Had hee shewed his inside unto the Emperour, and the Church, had he opened to them the heresie lurking in his brest, had he made it knowne that he would abolish the Councell of *Chalcedon,* and the Catholike faith, hee had instantly incensed all against him; both the Emperour and the Romanes, as *Bellarmine* [p] sayth, yea the whole Catholike Church would have joyned in the expulsing and deposing of such a wolfe and wretched heretike out of the See. S.*Peters* Chaire had beene too hot for him. *Vigilius* wisely considered that it was no lesse art to keepe, than to get the See; he knowing that without deepe dissimulation, and without faining himselfe a Catholike, he could not possibly hold it, much lesse could he effect that which he purposed, and had both promised and sworne to performe, and therefore by his private letter assuring *Anthimus, Severius, Theodosius,* and *Theodora,* of his hearty and serious intent to joyne with them, and

when

when time served to worke his feat, by his other publike and orthodoxall letters to *Iustinian, Theodora* and *Mennas,* hee did but cast a
mist before their eyes, that they should not spy his heresie; and under
that visor of a Catholike, he did labour to undermine the whole Catholike faith. And thus much in his private letter he signifieth to *An-*
thimus and the rest, warning them first q of secresie, lest if his powder-
plot should be discovered (as indeed most happily it was) the sudden
blow should not hit the Councell of *Chalcedon :* and next, that besides
their secresie they should dissemble also no lesse than hee did, they
should still seeme r to suspect and bee jealous of him as of their onely
enemy, that their feare might make Catholikes secure of him, and
of that sudden blow which in a moment by the publishing of his Apostolike Edict for the adnulling of the Councell of *Chalcedon* he meant
to give.

36. But *Bellarmine* s for all this will prove by two reasons that *Vigi-*
lius was not in heart t an heretike, nor did *ex animo* write this Epistle.
The former is, because, *non palàm in ea condemnavit Catholicam fidem, sed*
occultè ; he did not openly and publikely, but onely *in secret and closely con-*
demne the Catholike faith : for hee writes therein, *Vt sint omnia occulta*
usque ad tempus ; that they should keepe all private untill a fitter time. Condemne then he did the Catholike faith, but not *ex animo,* because hee
did secretly condemne it. *Ex studio occultandi,* saith *Gretzer* u, *by his*
desire of concealing it. Bellarmine collecteth this, that *Vigilius* did not
seriously and from his heart, but dissemblingly write that impious E-
pistle. As if one may not doe the same thing *ex animo,* and seriously,
and yet doe it secretly. What thinkes he of *Iudas ?* his plotting to betray Christ was close and secret, his owne fellow Apostles knew not
of it, but sayd, Master, is it I ? his friendly conversing with Christ, sitting at table, and kissing, was open and publike, yet his outward cour-
tesie, even his kisse was dissembled, and trecherous; his malice, treason, and murderous affection which were secret and covered under
those outward shewes of love, were true and serious. The Powder-
plotters dealt closely and secretly, all underboord : their pretended
subjection was open, and yet the treason was serious, their obedience
but fained. *Bellarmine* was but a meere novice in the Romane Court
when hee writ this, and imagined that Popes doe not seriously that
which they doe secretly.

37. His other reason x to prove that *Vigilius* was not in heart hereticall, when he writ this Epistle, is, because he writ it not with an hereticall minde, *sed propter cupiditatem presidendi,* but in an ambitious
desire of presidency. What I pray you, Is an hereticall and ambitious
minde incompatible ? doth ambition exclude heresie ? or in ambition
for one to teach heresie, doth that hinder him from being in heart an
heretike ? Scarce was there any Heresiarch, whom ambition hath not
inflamed, and who in ambition layd not the foundation of his heresie.
Valentinus, sayth *Tertullian* y, hoped for but missed a Bishopricke, in revenge thereof he kindled his heresie, and set fire in that Church, wherein himselfe could not be governour. When *Marcion,* (sayth *Epiphanius* z) got
not the presidency, he invented his heresie, and puft up with pride, sayd,
Ego

q *Oportet ut hec*
quæ scribo nullus
agnoscat. Epist.
Vig. apud Lib.

r *Sed magis su-*
spectum me ante
alios, habeat sa-
pientia vestra ut
facilius possim
quæ cæpi, opera-
ri perficere. Ib.
s *Bell. lib. 4. de*
Pont. ca. 10.
§ *Sciendum.*
t *Non fuit ani-*
mo hæreticus.
Ibid.

u *Gret. loc. cit.*

x *Bell. ubi supra.*

y *Tert. cont. Va-*
lent. ca. 4.
z *Epiph. hær. 42*

Ego findam Ecclesiam, Ile rend asunder your Church. VVhen *Aerius* b mif- b Epiph. har. 75.
fed the Bifhopricke which *Euftathius* obtained, in his ambitious pride
he deviſed his hereſie, *that a Presbyter was all one with a Biſhop.* Heare
Cardinall *Bellarmines* c owne words: *All Arch-heretickes have one com-* c Bell. lib. de
mon vice, and that is pride, they ſpring up in divers places, but pride is the not. Eccl. ca. 13.
mother of them all. If *Vigilius* was no heretike in heart, becauſe he was
ambitious, neither was *Neſtorius*, nor *Arius*, nor *Aerius*, nor *Mon-*
tanus, nor *Valentinus*, by *Bellarmines* divinity heretikes, becauſe they
were all ambitious. if they notwithſtanding their ambition were (as
certainly they were) Arch-heretikes, and taught their hereſies with
hereticall minds, then not onely the Cardinals reaſon is inconſequent
and ridiculous, but *Vigilius* for all his ambition may not onely write
that Epiſtle with an hereticall minde, but be even an Hereſiarch, or
rather a Pope heretike.

38. Againe, did he not write this with an hereticall minde? why
did not the Cardinall expreſſe what that hereticall minde is, which
was now wanting in *Vigilius*? An hereticall minde is no other but a
minde pertinaciouſly and obſtinately addicted to hereſie. It was hereſie doubtleſſe which he writ, in teaching with *Eutyches* but one nature to be in Chriſt. That he writ this obſtinately, is cleare, ſeeing he
writ it againſt the knowne judgement of the holy Councell of *Chalce-*
don, that is, of the Catholike Church; which none can doe but even
thereby he ſhewes an obſtinate and pertinacious minde, rebellious a-
gainſt the Church. If this be not, no hereticke in the world ever had
an hereticall minde. If *Arius*, *Neſtorius*, and *Eutyches*, when they writ
or taught their doctrines with this minde, were hereticall and heretikes, then moſt certainly *Vigilius* who writ this Epiſtle with the like
obſtinate and pertinacious minde, muſt needs bee judged to be rebellious againſt the Church, and as heretically affected in minde, as *Ari-*
us or *Eutyches* himſelfe. Pride and inſolency is ſo farre from excluding
an hereticall minde, as *Bellarmine* would here perſwade, that it is even
an individuall companion, yea eſſentiall unto it. None can poſſibly
have an hereticall, but *eo nomine* he hath an ambitious heart; the pride
whereof cauſeth him to condemne the juſt ſentence of the Catholike
Church, and prefer before it his owne fancy and opinion.

39. You ſee now how inconſequent both theſe reaſons of the Cardinals are, ſeeing *Vigilius* might bee hereticall in heart, though both
his writings were ſecret, and his minde ambitious. Let us yet a little
further debate this matter with the Cardinall. Say you that *Vigilius*
did not write this hereticall Epiſtle *ex animo*, or from his heart? I pray
you when looked your Cardinalſhip into the heart of *Vigilius*? how
know you that he was not an heretike in heart, when he was ſo hereticall in profeſſion? or how know you of S. *Hildebrand*, of *Boniface* 8.
or of any of all the Popes that lived ſince their times, that they were
not heretikes and plaine Infidels in heart, when their words were Catholike? I would gladly for my learning be informed how *Bellarmine*,
or the moſt acute *Lynceus* of them all do or can know, otherwiſe than
by their outward profeſſions, what any of all the Popes beleeved and
thought in their heart. What *Innocent* the third, when he decreed the

V v   doctrine

doctrine of Transubstantiation: what *Leo* the tenth, when he condemned *Luther* : or what *Paul, Iulius,* and *Pius* the fourth, when they confirmed their *Trent* Councell? How know you that in their hearts they beleeved those doctrines? or that they did not dissemble and faine, as you say *Vigilius* did? What can you say for *Pius* the fourth, which may not be sayd for *Vigilius* also? Doth *Pius* say, he did before, and now doth thinke as the *Trent* masters doe? Pope *Vigilius* sayth the like, and most plainly, *Eam fidem quam tenetis,* that faith which you (*Anthimus, Severus,* and *Theodosius*) doe hold, I signifie unto you, that I have held, and that I doe now hold the same. Doth *Pius* call the *Trent* Fathers his beloved brethren in Christ? so doth *Vigilius* call those hereticall Bishops his beloved brethren in Christ: nay in *Liberatus* he calls them even Christs. Doth Pope *Pius* professe an unity betwixt himselfe and them, all making one body of the Church? Pope *Vigilius* doth the like, and he doth it more significantly: We, sayth he, preach this same doctrine that you doe, *Vt & anima una sit & cor unum in Deo ;* so that there is in you and mee but one soule, and one heart in *God.* How can any speech be cordiall, if this testifying himselfe to be one soule and one heart with them, doe not come *à fibris,* but onely *à labris?* Doth Pope *Pius* approve the doctrine of the *Trent* conspirators? So doth Pope *Vigilius* the doctrine of those *Eutychean* heretikes? Doth *Pius* condemne and anathematize *Lutherans, Calvinists,* and all who thinke or teach otherwise than himselfe and his *Trent* Conventicle taught or beleeved? so doth Pope *Vigilius* condemne and anathematize all who deny two natures in Christ, all who beleeve otherwise than himselfe and his *Eutychean* fellow heretikes did. In all these there is as much to be sayd for Pope *Vigilius,* as for Pope *Pius* : and if you please to adde that one other agreement also, as of *Vigilius* it is sayd, that they knew *crudelitatem fidei ;* so may it in like manner bee truly sayd of Pope *Pius,* that this did manifest unto all men, *crudelitatem fidei, the cruelty of his and his Trent Councels faith.* If by these outward acts the Cardinall can know *Pius* the fourth to have *ex animo* condemned their *Trent* heresies, why can he not by the like outward acts know *Vigilius* to have *ex animo* condemned the Catholike faith? If *Vigilius* for all these outward acts, and so many testimonies and evidences of a willing minde did dissemble, and thinke in his heart otherwise than he writ, how will or can the Cardinall prove unto us that *Pius* the 4. and the whole Councell of *Trent* did not dissemble, and both write and speake otherwise than they thought in heart? Hath the Cardinall some windowes to pry into the secrets of the heart of *Pius* the fourth and the *Trent* Councell, which are dammed up that he cannot see into the brest of *Vigilius?* If Pope *Pius* upon his word and writing be to be credited, much more is Pope *Vigilius,* seeing he did not only by words and writing teach this hereticall doctrine, but (which *Pius* did not) he bound himselfe by a sacred oath that hee would teach the same. And which is yet a farre greater evidence, *Vigilius* after this did teach the like hereticall doctrine, to overthrow the same Councell of *Chalcedon,* in the cause of the *Three Chapters,* which hee did so unfainedly and so cordially, that for teaching the same he incurred the just indignation

nation of the Emperour, the curse of the holy generall Councell, the publike hatred of all Catholikes, and, if wee may beleeve *Baronius*, even exile and persecution also. Why might not the same *Vigilius* from his heart teach *Eutycheanisme*, as well as *Nestorianisme*? The faces of those two heresies looke contrary wayes indeed, but their tayles, like *Sampsons* Foxes, are joyned together to undermine the Catholike faith, and the holy Councell of *Chalcedon*: Hee who once is proved to be treacherous in this sort, and to doe this once from his heart, *semper præsumitur*, is always to bee presumed treacherous in the same kinde: Hee who did this in the *Three Chapters*, would have done it in *Eutycheanisme*, his heart, his desire, his purpose at both times was the same; the odds was accidental in the oportunity which served better in the one, than in the other; what need they excuse his teaching *Eutycheanisme* to have been only labiall, when it is cleare his teaching of *Nestorianisme* was cordiall? If they cannot excuse Pope *Vigilius* for teaching *Nestorianisme* from his heart, which cannot possibly be done, what need they be so nice in denying his teaching of *Eutycheanisme* to have come from the same heart? his fault in them both being alike, one answer will alike serve for them both.

44. But what, thinke you, meant the Cardinall so to busie himselfe, and bee so curious about the heart and secret minde of *Vigilius*? what though hee did not in heart, yet, *exteriori professione*, by his hereticall writing, by his outward confession, by that *Vigilius* condemned the Catholike faith, as the Cardinall [d] acknowledgeth, & it is the Popes outward profession, not his inward cogitation, by which wee prove his Chayre to bee *fallible*; what have wee, nay what hath the Cardinall or any of them all to doe with *Vigilius* intent or inward thoughts? leave those to his Tribunall, who onely [e] knoweth and seeth the hearts of all the sonnes of men, let men, who cannot see the heart, looke to his words, to his writings, to that profession, by which hee teacheth others. If that be hereticall, what boots it them though his heart bee orthodoxall? *Confirma fratres, & pasce oves*, are outward acts, they looke abroad and outwardly, not to the inward and hidden man in the Popes breast. If he think as *Simon Peter*, and teach as *Simo Magus*, as *Arius*, *Nestorius*, or *Eutyches* did, is he not an hereticall teacher, an hereticall Pope, a confirmer of his brethrē in heresie, a feeder, nay, a very prisoner of the sheepe, with worse weeds than the Socraticall *Cicuta*? If the Pope onely thinke and beleeve heresie, why, thought is free, (to wit, from mans eye, much more from his censure) his thought is for himselfe; that errour is personall, it hurts none but the Pope himselfe. If either by word or writing hee teach heresie, that is Pontificall, it is the fault of his office, of his Chayre, which should have beene infallible, this hurts his sheepe and his brethren: Nor skilleth it at all in what manner, whether by word or writing, by what occasion or motive hee teacheth heresie, but whether at all, or upon any occasion hee wittingly and willingly teach it; that is the onely point which is questioned. *Vigilius* condemned the Catholike faith, saith Cardinall *Bellarmine* [f], but hee did it for ambition, and desire of presidency. Bee it so: If the Pope for ambition

d Dico Vigilium scripsisse illam Epistolam, et damnasse Catholicam fidem, saltem exteriori professione. Bell. lib.4. de Pont. ca.10.§.Respondeo, multi. e Reg.8.39.

f Bell. loco cit.

may condemne the Catholike faith; why may hee not doe so, for feare of exile, of disgrace, of losing the Emperours, or the King of *Spaine*; or the French Kings favour? If for feare, why not for favour to purchase the good will of those, or any of them? If for favour, why not for hatred, hatred of *Henrie* the fourth, the Emperour; of *Henry* the eighth, for pulling away the best feather out of the Popes Plume; of *Luther* for being so busie in medling with his Indulgences, and the triple Crowne? If for hatred or favour, why not for desire of lucre, and to keepe the gaine of their crafts-men and Image workers, who continually sing that note in the Popes eare, Great is *Diana* of the E-phesians, great is the Church and S. *Peters* Chayre? Why not for any like passion of the minde may the Pope condemne the Catholike faith? On what a ticklish and slippery ground doth their whole faith stand, when either the Popes ambition, or feare, or favour, or love, or hatred, or anger, or desire, or a fit of any other perturbation, which disturbeth his minde, may procure, as at this time it did in *Vi-gilius*, an anathema to the Catholike faith? Best it were for them to renew the Stoicall sect and doctrine, and receive it in the Church, that out of those sober and unmoved mindes, as out of an happy Nursery of Popes, the Cardinals might in the Conclave still elect a Pope voyde of all passions and perturbations, and transplant him out of the Stoicall to their *Apostolicall Chaire*. But sure, so long as they goe no further than the Conclave, they shall never finde any but of the same metall with *Vigilius*, one that may bee tossed every way with ambition, with envy, with love, with hatred, with feare, and every passion of his minde, as a powder-plot to blow up the whole Catholike faith; and when he hath done that by his words, by his writing, by his preaching and teaching, by any of his outward acts whatsoever, Cardinall *Bellarmine* can excuse it, and wipe away all the disgrace of it, as here hee doth in *Vigilius*; hee did it not with an hereticall minde, for hee did it for ambition, hee did it for feare, hee did it for hatred; hee did it for some other passion, hee did it onely by an exteriour act, and not *ex animo*: But in the meane time whether hee did it *ex ani-mo*, or otherwise by his exteriour act, the Catholike faith is blowne up from the foundation thereof, as much by the Popes act, as by the act of *Arius*, of *Nestorius*, of *Eutyches*, or any other heretike; and the Church hath a goodly amends indeed, that the Pope forsooth did not (which is impossible for him or all heretikes in the world to doe) blow it up with an imagination or inward thought, but with an exteriour act of his teaching by word or writing.

41. Oh but, sayth *Bellarmine* f *non damnavit fidem palam, sed occultè, Vigilius did not openly but closely condemne the Catholike faith*: Closely, so he did indeed; it was his purpose and intent so to doe. He came not now as *Nero*, or *Dioclesian*, with open force to batter; but as *Simon Ma-gus*, *Arius*, *Nestorius*, *Eutyches*, and other heretikes, with *Synomian* arts, to undermine the Church; all his worke was under the vault. The Anathema denounced in this Epistle against all who hold two natures in Christ, was the powder that should have blowne up the holy Synod, and Senate, the House of God, and whole City of God: The

thepowder, the perſon and all was ready, onely, which the Cardinall obſerves g, the time for the open publiſhing of that Anathema, and ſetting fire to the traine was not yet come. The gracious Providence of God, which watcheth over Iſraell, the admirable zeale, piety, pru-dence, and *vigilancy*, which God put into the heart of *Iuſtinian*, the conſtancy of faith in the Greeke Church, which at that time moſt happily fell out to bee greater than at any time before or ſince; by theſe was the fatall blow intended by *Vigilius*, moſt happily preven-ted. This cloſe and ſecret working proves Pope *Vigilius* to have beene both ſubtill and malicious in condemning the faith; it doth excuſe him neither *à toto*, nor *tanto*, from his condemning the faith or from being an hereticall Pope, labouring by his hereticall doctrine to ſub-vert the faith.

g *Vt ſint omnia occulta, uſque ad tempus. Bell. loc. cit.*

42. The fourth and laſt Evaſion or excuſe for *Vigilius* fact in wri-ting this Epiſtle, is *Bellarmines* alſo; *Vigilius*, ſaith hee h, did not at that time define any thing againſt the faith, *tanquam Pontifex*, as hee was Pope. What ſhuffling and ſhifting is this in the Cardinall? hee did not define any thing againſt the faith, as Pope: Hee did then define that which was againſt the faith, but hee defined it not as Pope, for otherwiſe it had beene fooliſh to ſay, he defined it not as Pope, when hee defined it, neither as Pope, nor as no Pope, when hee defined it not at all. Againe, what a worthy ſaying is this of a Cardinall? *Vigi-lius* did not at that time define it as hee was Pope; at that time, to wit, while *Silverius* lived and was the onely Pope, at which time, as himſelfe in expreſſe words ſaith, *Vigilius Papa non erat, Vigilius was not then the Pope.* What needed the Cardinall ſay hee defined it not at that time as hee was Pope, when at that time he was not Pope? This reduplication, *quatenus Papa*, implies hee was Pope, and that be-ing Pope hee defined it, but hee defined it not as hee was Pope, but as hee was a private man, or ſome other way: Would not the Cardinall laugh, if *Gretzer* or any ſuch good friend of his ſhould ſay, *Bellarmine* at that time while hee was at *Ingolſtad* writ not his Controverſies as he was Pope; or, hee writ them not as he was a Turke, a Iew, or Mahume-tane? But leaving theſe ſhifts, which demonſtrate plainly, that *Bellar-mine* had a deſire to ſay ſomewhat in excuſe of *Vigilius*, but knew not what, and therefore ſnatched at this or that, or any thing, though it were never ſo croſſe unto himſelfe, and ſuch alſo as he could not hold. Let us conſider the Exception it ſelfe; *Vigilius* writ this Epiſtle, that is confeſſed; hee writ it when hee was the onely true and lawfull Pope, that wee have proved; hee defined hereſie in it, and that which is againſt the faith, that *Bellarmine* implyeth; hee condemned in it the Catholike faith, that *Bellarmine* in plaine words expreſſeth. Thus far the cauſe is cleare. Now whether Pope *Vigilius* in it defined here-ſie, and condemned the Catholike faith, as he was Pope, or no, that is the point here to be debated.

h *Bell. 4. de Pot. ca. 10. § Sciendū*

43. Some may thinke, that *Bellarmine* by thoſe two reaſons drawne from ſecreſie and an ambitious minde, by which he laboured before, to prove, that *Vigilius* did not condemne the faith *ex animo*, meant alſo that he condemned it not as Pope, for it followeth in the

next sentence, *siquidem Epistolam scripsit,* as giving a reason of his saying. If any like to take *Bellar.* words in that sort, then his reasons are before hand refuted; for as *Vigilius* might, *ex animo,* write heretically, both privately and out of ambition, so also might hee, *tanquam Pontifex,* condemne the faith, notwithstanding both his secrecy and ambitious mind; secrecy and an ambitious mind are no more repugnant to the one, than to the other, they are compatible with them both; the Pope may use his *Apostolicall* authority in teaching, as wel privately as publikely, as well with *Iudas* in ambition, as with *Iohn* or *Peter* in sincerity of heart. But the Cardinals Apologist, who it may be consulted with the Cardinall about his intent herein, doth ease us of those reasons, for hee [i] tels us plainly, that from *Vigilius* his desire of secrecie, *nil aliud colligit, Bellarmine collects or proves nothing else,* but this, that *Vigilius* did not write his letter from his heart or *serio,* that hee did it not in earnest. It is but a sport with *Gretzer,* or with the Pope, to condemne the Catholike faith; they doe it, but they doe it not in earnest, they doe it *jocularitèr* not *serio.* Have ye indeed such May-games & sports at *Rome,* as to condemne the faith, and then say, I was in jest, and in sport? Are not these men new Philistines, Call in *Sampson,* Condemne the Catholike faith, to make us pastime? But let us leave them to their sports, till the fall of their Babylonish house make a catastrophe and dolefull end both of their actors & spectators: That which I now note, is, that *Bellarmine* doth not in those words, *Siquidem Epistolam scripsit, &c.* from the privatenesse or secrecy prove any thing else, but that *Vigilius* writ it not *serio,* in earnest and from his heart; that hee writ it not, *tanquam Pontifex,* this those words prove not, *Bellarmine* in those words collects not: So we have now nothing but the bare saying of *Bellarmine,* without any proofe, without any reasons, and I must needs confesse, I hold it a most sufficient encounter for any man to *Bellarmines ipse dixit,* to oppose, *ipse dico,* yet because I desire rather to satisfie such as seeke the truth, then contend with those who seeke to smother and betray the truth, I will a little further enlarge this point, and see if it may be cleared by evidence of reason, that Pope *Vigilius* did not onely condemne the Catholike faith at that time, but that he did it even as hee was Pope, and, *tanquam Pontifex,* condemne the Catholike faith.

44. What it is for a Pope to teach an errour as Pope, may be perceived by other Arts and Sciences, in the practice or exercise whereof, together with knowledge, judgement, and skill, fidelity also is required; were *Baronius* or some Romane *Facundus* to examine this point, they would quickly sute the Pope to some Cobler, Pedler, or suchlike companion: I love not to deale so rudely with his Holinesse, yet if I should happen at any time to let slip a word that way, you know how the Cardinall quitted the religious Emperour with, *Ne ultra crepidam.* If a Physitian, or Lawyer, or Iudge in any discourse should speake barbarously or incongruously, they erre therein but as Grammarians, not as Iudges, Lawyers or Physitians; But if a Iudge for any sinister respect should pronounce that sentence as just, which is against the law; or if a Lawyer should after his diligent sifting of
the

i Gretz. loc. cit.

the caufe, affirme that title to bee found, which were clearely voide in
law; or if a Phyfitian fhould prefcribe to his patient Coloquintida for
an wholefome diet, each of them now erred & offended in his owne
profeffion, & in that proper duty wch belongeth to them; the Iudge as
a Iudge, the Counfellor as a Counfellor, the Phyfitian as a Phyfitian,
becaufe they failed either in skill or in fidelity in thofe faculties wherin they profeffe both to know themfelves, and to make knowne unto
others what is right and good : If in other matters they tranfgreffe, it
is not, *quatenus tales*; if any of them bee prophane, covetous, or intem-
perate, they offend now, *quatenus homines*, as they are mortall men in
thofe duties of morality, which are common to them with all men :
If they bee feditious, rebellious, and confpire in treafonable practice,
they offend, *quatenus Cives*, as they are parts of the Common-wealth,
in thofe duties which are common to them with all fubjects; but when
they offend in Phyfick, law, or judgment, thofe are their own peculiar
Arts and Sciences, they then offend, neither *quatenus homines*, nor *quatenus Cives*, nor in any other refpect, but *quatenus tales*, as they are fuch
profeffors : for now they tranfgreffe againft thofe proper duties,
which, as they are Iudges, Counfellors, or Phyfitians, are required of
them. The like of all Artificers, of Gramarians, Logicians, Poets, Philofophers, of Presbyters, of Bifhops, of the Profeffors of Theology,
which is *fcientia fcientiarum*, is to bee faid. If a Divine fhall fpeake
rudely, incongruoufly, *ad populum Antiochenum*, he offends as a Grammarian, not as a Divine, unleffe perhaps it bee no fault when it doth
fo happen for edification, that hee ought fo to fpeake, as Saint *Auften* [k] did ufe divers barbarifmes, and fay, *offum* for *os*, *floriet* for *flo-
rebit*, *dolus* for *dolor*; *Malo me populus*, I had rather edifie with rude-
neffe of words than fpeake nothing but pure Ciceronian without edi-
fying them, without honouring God; But if a Bifhop or any Divine,
in ftead of truth teach herefie, either becaufe hee knowes not the
truth, or knowing it, oppugnes the truth, hee is now in his owne ele-
ment, he offends no longer as a Rhetorician, or Grammarian, but, *quatenus talis*, as hee is a Bifhop, as hee is a Divine, as hee is one who both
fhould know, and bring others to the knowledge of the truth. And
this, befide that by reafon it is evident, is grounded on that faying
of *Auften* [l], *Aliter fervit Rex qua homo, aliter qua Rex*, for as a King fer-
veth God, *qua Rex*, in doing that which none but a King can doe; fo a
King, or a Bifhop, or any other offendeth God, as a King, or Bifhop, in
doing againft that duty which none but they are to doe.

k *Auft.lib. 4. de doct.Chrift.ca. 16.et Tract.7. in Joban.*

l *Aug.Epift. 50.*

45. Now, what is faid of all Sciences, Arts and myfteries, that is
in due proportion to be applyed to that greateft myfterie of myfteries, and Craft above all Crafts, to their Pope-craft, or myfterie of Iniquity : He is the fheepheard to feed all; the Phyfitian to cure all, the
Counfellor to advife all, the Iudge to decide al, the Monarke to command all, hee is all in all, nay, above all; hard it is to define him or his
duties, hee is indefinite, infinite, tranfcendent above all limits, above
all definitions, above all rule, yea, above all reafon alfo : But as the
Nymphs not able to meafure the vaftnes of the Gyants whole body,
meafured onely the compaffe of his thumbe with a thred, and by it

knew

shop to erre as Bishop, they must not thinke much if wee exempt not the Pope as Pope: For, to speake that which is the very truth of them all, and exactly to measure every thing by his owne line, a Iudge simply as Iudge, doth pronounce a judiciall sentence, as a skilfull and faithfull Iudge, an upright judiciall sentence; as an unskilful or unfaithfull Iudge, an erronious or unjust sentence. A Bishop or Presbyter simply as Bishop or Presbyter, doth teach with publike authority in the Church; as a skilfull and faithfull Bishop or Presbyter he teacheth the truth of God; as an ignorant and unfaithful Bishop he teacheth errours and heresies in the Church, the one without, the other with judicall power to censure the gainsayers. The like in all Arts, Sciences, and faculties is to be sayd, even in the Pope himselfe. A Pope simply as he is Pope and defined by them, teacheth both with authority to teach, with power to censure the gainsayers, and with a supremacy of judgement binding all to embrace his doctrine without appeale, without doubt, as an *infallible* Oracle: as a skilfull or faithfull Pope he teacheth the truth in that sort, as an unskilfull or unfaithfull Pope he teacheth errour or heresie with the like authority, power, and supremacy, binding others to receive and swallow up his heresies for Catholike truth, and that with a most blind obedience, without once doubting of the same.

48. Apply this to *Vigilius* & his hereticall Epistle: In a vulgar sense; *Vig.* erred as Pope, because he erred in those very Pontifical duties of feeding & confirming, wch are proper to his office. In a strickt sense; though hee did not therein erre simply as Pope, but *quatenus talis* taught onely with a supreme binding authority, yet hee erred as an unfaithfull Pope, binding others by that his Pontificall and supreme authority to receive *Eutycheanisme* as Catholike truth, without once moving any doubt or making scruple of the same. What may wee thinke will they oppose to this; If they say *Vigilius* doth not expresse in this Epistle, that hee writ it by his *Apostolicall* authority. Hee doth not indeed. Nor doth Pope *Leo* in that Epistle to *Flavianus*, against the heresie of *Eutyches*, which to have beene writ by his *Apostolicall* authority, and as he was Pope none of them doe or will deny, that Epistle being approved by the whole Councell ¹ of *Chalcedon*. Pope *Leo* by his Papall authority condemneth *Eutycheanisme*, Pope *Vigilius* by his Papall authority confirme *Eutycheanisme*: both of them confirmed their doctrine by their Papall authority; both writ as Popes, the one as *orthodoxall*, the other as a perfidious and *hereticall* Pope; neither of both expresse that their *Apostolicall* authority by which they both writ. The like in many other Epistles of *Leo*, and of other Popes might easily bee observed. Not the tenth part of their decretal Epistles; such as they writ as Popes, have this clause of doing it by their *Apostolicall* authority expressed in them. It is sufficient that this is vertually in them all, and vertually it is in this of Pope *Vigilius*: Yea, but hee taught this onely in a private letter to a few, to *Anthimus, Severus* and *Theodosius*, not in a publike, generall, and encyclicall Epistle, written for instruction of the whole Church. What, is the Pope fallible in teaching of a few, in confirming three of his brethren? why

why not in foure, in eight, in twenty ? and if in twenty, why not in an hundred? if so, why not in a thousand? if in one, why not in two, foure, or ten thousand ? *Caude<g>, pilos at equinæ paulatim vellam* ; where, or at what number shall we stay, as being the least which with infallibility he can teach ? Certainly, *confirma fratres, & in cathedra sede, & pasce oves*, respects two as well as two millions. If in confirming or feeding three, the Chaire may bee erroneous, how can wee know to what number God hath tyed the infallibility of it ? But the sixt generall Councell may teach them a better lesson. Pope *Honorius* writ an he-reticall Epistle [f] but onely to *Sergius* Bishop of *Constantinople*, *Vigilius* writ this to three, all of patriarchall dignity as *Sergius* was. *Honorius* writ it privately, as *Vigilius* did, which was the cause, as it seemes, that the Romane Church tooke so little notice thereof: yet though it was private, and but to one, it is condemned by the sixt Councell, for [t] a domaticall writing of Pope *Honorius*, for a writing wherein hee con-firmes others in heresie: and Pope *Leo* [u] the second judged it to bee such as was a blemish to the *Apostolike* See, such as by which *Honorius* did labour to subvert the Catholike faith. The like and more danger was in this, to these three deposed patriarchs. It confirmed them in heresie ; it confirmed the Empresse ; it confirmed all that tooke part with them; it was the meanes whereby the faith was in hazard to have beene utterly subverted. For plurality or paucity it is not materiall, be they few, be they moe: if the Pope as Pope, or as an hereticall pope may confirme three, or but one, that one is abundant to prove his Chaire and judiciall sentence not to be *infallible*.

49. But he taught this alone, not in a Councell, not with advice of his Cardinalls, and Consistory : why, he did it not as a member of a Councell, but as [x] *Princeps Ecclesiæ*. He did this as did *Agapetus* [y] in deposing *Anthimus*, above and besides the Canons. The whole po-wer of his *Apostolike* authority much shined in this decision, more than in any other, where either his Cardinals or a Councell hath ought to doe : much more was this done by him as Pope, than any of them. And yet had he listed to follow the judgement of others, or of a Sy-nod herein, what better direction, advice, or counsell, could his Car-dinalls, or any Synod in the world give unto him, than the decree of the whole Councell of *Chalcedon* ? That *Vigilius* had before his eyes at this time, that was in stead of a thousand Cardinals unto him, seeing he as *Ecclesiæ Princeps*, defined *Eutycheanisme*, notwithstanding that most holy and generall Synod, yea against that Synod, what could the advice of another, or of a few Cardinals have avayled at this time ?

50. Thus all the evasions which they use, being refuted, it may now be clearly concluded, not onely that *Vigilius* writ this impious and he-reticall Epistle, and writ it when he was the true and lawfull Pope ; but that he writ it also *ex animo*, even out of an hereticall heart, and writ it as he was Pope, that is, in such sort as that by his Pontificall and supreme authority hee confirmed that heresie which hee taught therein. And this is the former of his Acts, which as I told you is ve-ry remarkable, his purpose and intent therein being the overthrow of the Councell at *Chalcedon*, and of the whole Catholike faith.

51. The

[f] *Quæ recitatur Conc.6.Act.12. p.2.64.*

[t] *Vocantur istæ et aliæ Epistolæ, dogmatica scrip-ta. In eodem Conc. Act. 12. p.65.a. et retra-ctantes dogmati-cas Epistolas, à Sergio, et ab Ho-norio ad Sergi-um. Act.13. p. 67.a. et, Hono-rius impia dog-mata confirma-vit. Ibid.*

[u] *Anathemati-zamus quoque Honorium, qui hanc Apostoli-cam Ecclesiam, et immaculatam fidem prophana proditione sub-vertere conatus est. Leo 2. Epist.1*

[x] *Pontifex non ut præses Conci-lij, sed ut Prin-ceps Ecclesiæ summus potest iudicium Conci-lij retractare, &c. Bell.lib.1: de Conc. ca.18.*

[§] *Dico secundo.*

[y] *Agapeti Papæ contra Anthimi iudicium absq; Synodo fuit, se-cundum supre-mam Apostolicæ sedis authorita-tem, qua supra omnes Canones Pontifex eminet. Extat.an.536. n.23.*

Eccius, of the *Laterane, Florentine,* and *Trent* conspirators, of all who have whet their tongues against other truth, and specially to uphold that fundamentall heresie of the Popes *infallibility.* Their writings for heresie are evident, that they ever reclamed those writings, it is inevident: and if ever they and their cause come to bee tryed, in such a free, lawfull, and oecumenicall Councell as was this fift under *Iustinian,* they may justly feare, and certainly expect from the Church, (unlesse the disclaming of their writings may by certaine proofe be made knowne) the very like sentence, though a hundred yeares after theirs, as passed upon *Theodorus* of *Mopsvestia* an hundred yeares after his death. And because the houre-glasse for repentance is runne out to the former, all that we can doe, is (which I seriously now doe from my heart) to cry amaine unto others, to admonish, exhort, yea even pray and entreat them by the mercies of God, and by the love of their owne soules, first that they keepe their tongues and pennes from once uttering any heresie; or (if they have not done that) with the same hands to give the medicine, wherewith they gave the wound, and as openly, nay much more openly to disclame than they have ever proclamed their impious and hereticall doctrines.

53. You have now some view both of the life and death of *Vigilius.* The exact pourtraiture of the Popes lives, *Baronius* had beene able to set forth if he had listed; but he addeth such *fucos,* and so many sophisticall colours, that indeed scarce you shall see any one of them in his Annals set out in his native and naturall habit. If ought be amisse in this our description, and not set forth according to the lively lineaments of *Vigilius* and his impieties, the equall reader will not too rigorously censure the same. I acknowledge that I can but *dolare* in this kinde; to polish and set forth the lively image of their Popes, I have not learned: That is an Art which may not bee too vulgar, lest their Romane policies be too farre divulged. But by this it is easie to perceive what a silly excuse it is which *Baronius* useth in this cause, blaming *Vigilius* for coming to *Constantinople,* as if not the Popes owne hereticall minde, but the ayre of *Constantinople* had wrought such effects, as to produce that hereticall, and yet as they count it, *Apostolicall Constitution* in defence of the *Three Chapters.*

FINIS.

Laus Deo sine fine.

Errata hæc corrigat benevolus Lector.

In Textu.

Pag.48.lin.2.read *Theodorus.* ibid.lin.9.*diptiss.* p.509.l.14.*tex.* p.99.l.3.*John* B. p.125.l.38.Catholikes. p.141 l.35.*Bism*,he was. p.145.l.39.Son of God. p.163.*prope finem,* substances. p.164.l.5.explanation. p.172.l.20.of the Pope. p.182.l.45.their presence. p.199.*prope finem, Catholice.* p.216.l.17. it. p.224.l.25. Popes. p.227.l.5.yeeld. p.289.l.33.the. p.350.l.30. *æquiparare.* p.435.l.8. where is. ibid.l.27.Commana. ibid.*Marcellinus.* l.42. inflamed. p.442.*in fine, Euphemia.* p.462.l.11. quarrels with Pope. p.465.l.35.all this time. p.478.l.23. it was written. p.495. l.37.poysoner of. p.500.l.35.righthand.

In Margine.

Pa.9.lit.(c). lege, *Marsorum.* p.67.lit. (e).*Antiochenum.* p.233.lit.(f).*emissam.* ibid.lit.(e). *corruptè.* p.409.lit. (e). *commentitias & suppofititias.* p.410.lit.(q). *Confilij* 5. p.437.lit.(l). *Concil.*5.*Coll.*5.

AN ALPHABETICALL
TABLE OF THE CHIEFE
THINGS CONTAINED IN
THIS TREATISE.

persons, pa.145. sect. 16. so *Theodorus* the Master of *Nestorius*, sect. 17. to affirme this, is plaine Nestorianisme, proved by *Iustinian*, pa.146.sect.18. by Pope *Iohn* the second.

The *Nestorians* in words orthodoxall, in sense and meaning hereticall, pa. 147 .sect. 20. and p.448. sect.22,23. witnessed by *Iustinian*, p.449.sect.24. by the fift Councell, sect.25. by the epistle it selfe, sect.26,27.

The *Nestorians* by Nature understand Person, p.162.sect.46,47.

The *Nestorians* slander *Cyrill* to teach two persons, p.163.sect.47.

Narses for his piety and prudence beloved of *Iustinian*, p.248.sect.12.

Narses intreated not for *Vigilius*, pa. 249. sect.14.

Narses overcame not *Totilas*, if *Binius* his glosse be true, p.458.sect.23.

Narses overcame not the Gothes by the intercession of *Mary*, p.459.sect.24.

O.

THe *occasion* of the fift Councell was those *tria capitula*, p.2.sect.3.

Origen commended for his gifts and learning, p.103.sect.28.

Origen condemned by the Acts of the fift Synod, p.392.sect.1,2.

Origens cause not the cause of the first action in the fift Synod, p.393.sect.3. nor the cause of the second action in the Synod, sect.4.

The *order* of lawfull generall Councels, pa. 304.sect.19.

P.

PApists are truly such as ground upon the Popes infallibility, p.187.sect.26.

Pope *Vigilius* excommunicated in an African Synod, p.236.sect.16.

The *Pope* refuseth to come to the Synod, p. 4.sect.2,3,4. and the true reason why, pag.6. sect.5.

The *Popes* presence not needfull in a generall Councell, p.273.sect.14,15.

The *Pope* present in the fift Councell by his letters of instruction, p.274.sect.16.

The *Popes* consent makes not a Councell to be approved, p.275.sect.27. *vid.lit.C.*

In the *Pope intensive* there is as much authority, as in the Pope with a generall Councell, *Bellarmines* assertion, p.174.sect.10.

The *Pope* vertually both Church and Councell, p.178.sect.15. p.180.sect.17.

The name *Papist* not heard of till *Leo* the 10. p.188.sect.25. to be a *Pope* an happy thing, for all is held for truth that they define, pag.223. sect.16.

Papist had need of a strong faith, relying on the Popes judgement, p.224.sect.18.

Paulus Bishop of Emisa subscribed to the anathematizing of *Nestorius*, to perswade an union betweene *Iohn* and *Cyrill*, p.133.sect.31 his Sermon at *Alexandria*, containing an orthodoxall profession of the faith, p.134.sec.33.

Pelagius Pope after *Vigilius*, consecrated by two Bishops onely an a Presbyter of Ostia, pa. 242.sect.4.

A *Pope* may erre personally, they say, but doctrinally he cannot, p.244. sect.7.

The *Pope* no competent Iudge of Protestants, being an enemy unto them, pag. 315. sect.33.

Pope *Clements* epistle to *Iames* a forgery, pa. 422.sect.2.

Paul censured by some for an hot-headed person, 434. sect.18.*in fine.*

R.

THe Church of *Rome* holdeth no doctrine by certainty of faith, p.181. *in fine.*and pa. 282.sect.20. and p.189.sect.27,28.

The *Romish* doctrines may bee held three wayes, p.183.sect.21 *in fine.*First, of them who hold the Scriptures for the foundation, p.183. sect. 22. such were our forefathers. Second way, by grounding upon Scripture, but with pertinacy, p.184.sect.23. A third way of holding them, is on the Popes word, p.185.sec.24

They of the *Romane* Church are heretikes, p.192.sect.31.

In their *Romane* Church no true holinesse, p.193.sect.32.

They of the *Romish* Church are schismatikes p.196.sect.34.

Rome miserably besieged by *Totilas*, p.456. sect.22.

Ruba not taken from Alexandria, pag.407. sect.8.

S.

THe *Synod* resolves to judge the controversie about the three Chapt. the Pope being absent, p.7.sect.1.

Sergius Bishop of Cyrus deposed from his Bishopricke, p.706.sect.18.

Scripture being the ground of a mans faith is a comfort unto him, though in some things

9 781171 278603

FINIS.

persons, pa. 145. sect. 16. so *Theodorus* the Master of *Nestorius*, sect. 17. to affirme this, is plaine Nestorianisme, proved by *Iustinian*, pa. 146. sect. 18. by Pope *Iohn* the second.

The *Nestorians* in words orthodoxall, in sense and meaning hereticall, pa. 147. sect. 20. and p. 448. sect. 22, 23. witnessed by *Iustinian*, p. 449. sect. 24. by the fift Councell, sect. 25. by the epistle it selfe, sect. 26, 27.

The *Nestorians* by Nature understand Person, p. 162. sect. 46, 47.

The *Nestorians* slander *Cyrill* to teach two persons, p. 163. sect. 47.

Narses for his piety and prudence beloved of *Iustinian*, p. 248. sect. 12.

Narses intreated not for *Vigilius*, pa. 249. sect. 14.

Narses overcame not *Totilas*, if *Binius* his glosse be true, p. 458. sect. 23.

Narses overcame not the Gothes by the intercession of *Mary*, p. 459. sect. 24.

O.

THe *occasion* of the fift Councell was those *tria capitula*, p. 2. sect. 3.

Origen commended for his gifts and learning, p. 103. sect. 28.

Origen condemned by the Acts of the fift Synod, p. 392. sect. 1, 2.

Origens cause not the cause of the first action in the fift Synod, p. 393. sect. 3. nor the cause of the second action in the Synod, sect. 4.

The *order* of lawfull generall Councels, pa. 304. sect. 19.

P.

PApists are truly such as ground upon the Popes infallibility, p. 187. sect. 26.

Pope *Vigilius* excommunicated in an African Synod, p. 236. sect. 16.

The *Pope* refuseth to come to the Synod, p. 4. sect. 2, 3, 4. and the true reason why, pag. 6. sect. 5.

The *Popes* presence not needfull in a generall Councell, p. 273. sect. 14, 15.

The *Pope* present in the fift Councell by his letters of instruction, p. 274. sect. 16.

The *Popes* consent makes not a Councell to be approved, p. 275. sect. 27. *vid. lit. C.*

In the *Pope intensive* there is as much authority, as in the Pope with a generall Councell, *Bellarmines* assertion, p. 174. sect. 10.

The *Pope* vertually both Church and Councell, p. 178. sect. 15. p. 180. sect. 17.

The name *Papist* not heard of till *Leo* the 10. p. 188. sect. 25. to be a Pope an happy thing, for all is held for truth that they define, pag. 223. sect. 16.

Papist had need of a strong faith, relying on the Popes judgement, p. 224. sect. 18.

Paulus Bishop of Emisa subscribed to the anathematizing of *Nestorius*, to perswade an union betweene *Iohn* and *Cyrill*, p. 133. sect. 31 his Sermon at *Alexandria*, containing an orthodoxall profession of the faith, p. 134. sec. 33.

Pelagius Pope after *Vigilius*, consecrated by two Bishops onely an a Presbyter of Ostia, pa. 242. sect. 4.

A *Pope* may erre personally, they say, but doctrinally he cannot, p. 244. sect. 7.

The *Pope* no competent Iudge of Protestants, being an enemy unto them, pag. 315. sect. 33.

Pope Clements epistle to *Iames* a forgery, pa. 422. sect. 2.

Paul censured by some for an hot-headed person, 434. sect. 18. *in fine.*

R.

THe Church of *Rome* holdeth no doctrine by certainty of faith, p. 181. *in fine.* and pa. 282. sect. 20. and p. 189. sect. 27, 28.

The *Romish* doctrines may bee held three wayes, p. 183. sect. 21 *in fine.* First, of them who hold the Scriptures for the foundation, p. 183. sect. 22. such were our forefathers. Second way, by grounding upon Scripture, but with pertinacy, p. 184. sect. 23. A third way of holding them, is on the Popes word, p. 185. sec. 24

They of the *Romane* Church are hereticks, p. 192. sect. 31.

In their *Romane* Church no true holinesse, p. 193. sect. 32.

They of the *Romish* Church are schismatikes p. 196. sect. 34.

Rome miserably besieged by *Totilas*, p. 456. sect. 22.

Ruba not taken from *Alexandria*, pag. 407. sect. 8.

S.

THe *Synod* resolves to judge the controversie about the three Chapt. the Pope being absent, p. 7. sect. 1.

Sergius Bishop of Cyrus deposed from his Bishopricke, p. 706. sect. 18.

Scripture being the ground of a mans faith is a comfort unto him, though in some things he

F I N I S.